BOOKS SHOULD BE RETURNED ON OR BEFORE THE LAST DATE
SHOWN BELOW. BOOKS NOT ALREADY REQUESTED BY OTHER
READERS MAY BE RENEWED BY PERSONAL APPLICATION, BY
WRITING, OR BY TELEPHONE. TO RENEW, GIVE THE DATE DUE AND THE
NUMBER ON THE BARCODE LABEL

FINES CHARGED FOR OVERDUE BOOKS WILL INCLUDE POSTAGE
INCURRED IN RECOVERY. DAMAGE TO, OR LOSS OF, BOOKS WILL BE
CHARGED TO THE BORROWER. *last copy*

Leabharlanna Poiblí Bardas Átha Cliath
Dublin Corporation Public Libraries

DATE DUE	DATE DUE	DATE DUE
22. DEC 04.		
15. MAR 10		
2 8 NOV 2017		

The Dictionary of Global Culture

The Dictionary
of
Global Culture

Edited by

Kwame Anthony Appiah

and

Henry Louis Gates, Jr.

Michael Colin Vazquez, *Associate Editor*

PENGUIN BOOKS

PENGUIN BOOKS

Published by the Penguin Group
Penguin Books Ltd, 27 Wrights Lane, London w8 5TZ, England
Penguin Putnam Inc., 375 Hudson Street, New York, New York 10014, USA
Penguin Books Australia Ltd, Ringwood, Victoria, Australia
Penguin Books Canada Ltd, 10 Alcorn Avenue, Toronto, Ontario, Canada M4V 3B2
Penguin Books (NZ) Ltd, 182–190 Wairau Road, Auckland 10, New Zealand

Penguin Books Ltd, Registered Offices: Harmondsworth, Middlesex, England

Published in the United States by Alfred A. Knopf, Inc., New York 1996
Published in Great Britain by Penguin Books 1998
1 3 5 7 9 10 8 6 4 2

Set in Electra
Printed in Great Britain by Clays Ltd, St Ives plc

A CIP catalogue record for this book is available from the British Library

ISBN 0–670-85774-2

for Barbara Johnson and Marjorie Garber

Acknowledgments

Behind the finished manuscript of *The Dictionary of Global Culture* lie years of research, writing, and editing. The project, conceived of in 1989, set up office in February 1990 at Duke University, with the immediate task of compiling a table of contents. Because the breadth of knowledge necessary for this project exhausted the areas of expertise the editors could supply, we relied on colleagues for topic suggestions. Hundreds of letters were sent to academics in various disciplines worldwide, and the response was delightful. We received many lists of suggested topics, far more than could be included in a single volume. With the assistance of our advisers, we culled from these lists a working table of contents and set about the task of researching and writing the entries. Each section of the manuscript was then edited by outside readers—experts in the field—and as a result of their comments, entries were changed, omitted, or added.

The Dictionary of Global Culture owes its existence to the enthusiasm and expertise of many people, both scholars and students, whom we would like to thank. Without their support and guidance, this project could not have been completed. We would especially like to thank the following individuals for their assistance in writing and editing entries (asterisks denote those who wrote the first versions of some of the entries): Marion Aguiar,* Alp Aker,* Hamid Algar,* Abbass Amanat,* Virginia Askan,* Debbie Aukett,* Martin Bernal, Agehananda Bharati,* Stephen Burt,* David Chandler, Jennifer Chertow,* Eric Columbus, Ted Davidson, Elizabeth Dore,* Jamal Elias,* Halina Filipowicz, Sander Gilman, Andrew Gordon, Thomas Hudak, Steven James,* Ahmet Karamustafa,* David Kurnick,* Thomas Lahusen, George Lang,* Linda Locklear, Sarah Manguso,* Moumié Maoulidi,* K. Kyriel Muhammad,* Alex Patterson,* Dwight Reynolds,* Abdulaziz Sachedina,* Eddie Sahakian,* Jack Sasson, Ernest Scatton, Jana Sequoya,* Maria Soliz,* Shawkat Toorawa,* Philippe Wamba,* and John Weeks.*

We would also like to thank those scholars who assisted in compiling the list of contents: Carlos Alonso, Guitty Azarpay, Sandra Barnes, Anthony Barthelemy, Charles Berry, Agehananda Bharati, A. D. H. Bivar, Ross Brann, Richard Broome, Robert Buswell, Jr., Clark Cahow, Jules Chametzy, David Chandler, Bob Cherry, King-Kok Cheung, Miriam Cooke, Ted Davidson, Elizabeth Dore, Ariel Dorfman, Fedwa Malti Douglas, Jamal Elias, Fred Ellison, Jeannette Faurot, Halina Filipowicz, Ken Finney, Richard Fox, Gerald Friesen, Sander Gilman, Victor Golla, Anibel González, Andrew Gordon, Kenneth Hall, J. León Helguera, Thomas Hudak, Cornelius Jaenen, Satti Khanna, Ali Kincaid, Kenneth Kiple, David Kurnick, Richard Lariviere, Bruce Lawrence, Peter Li, Françoise Lionnet, Carol Meyers, Eric

Meyers, Chris Miller, James Morita, Mildred Mortimer, Don Nakanishi, Robert Nelson, Ambeth Ocampo Rulan Chao Pian, Vincente Rafael, A. K. Ramanujan, Esperanza Ramirez-Christensen, Barbara Ramusack, Anthony Reid, Stefan Reif, Frank Reynolds, Renato Rosaldo, A. LaVonne Brown Ruoff, Greg Sarris, Annemarie Schimmel, Jim Scott, Jana Sequoya, Prayag Raj Sharma, Derek Smith, Charles Stansifer, Brian Stross, Diana Taylor, John Thompson, Nicanor Tiongson, Shawkat Toorawa, Andrew Topefield, Conrad Totman, Vineeta Vijayaraghavan, Philippe Wamba, Timothy Wong, Ma Xiao Hong, and Marc Zimmerman.

Other scholars who also assisted the project include Ben Anderson, Sarah Moment Atis, Diane Bell, Anita Desai, K. M. de Silva, Doreen Fernandez, Amy Ling, and Frank Silbajoris.

We owe a special debt to a group of young scholars of the Islamic world, R.A.A.L., who undertook not only to suggest items but to write the pieces.

None of the entries is signed. Even where an outside author penned the piece, we have felt free to edit and to alter it. Responsibility for the results—including any errors we may have introduced—remains with us.

We would also like to thank our research assistants at Duke University: Michael Alexander, Glen Brewster, Deborah Chay, Vitaly Chernetsky, Dan Daily, Cynthia Davis, Elizabeth Eckhart, Marcus Embry, Kelly Kobor, Jimmy Lu, Michael Maiwald, Andrew Miller, Alexandria Nabatoff, Emily Owens, Chris Pavsek, Joanna Riseman, Michael Roy, Silvia Tandeciarz, Susan Trukawinski, Maurice Wallace, Kent Wicker, and Joselyn Zivin. And at Harvard University: Marion Aguiar, Thom Freedman, Helina Hanson, Ali Kincaid, David Kurnick, Peter Silver, Woden Teachout, Vineeta Vijayaraghavan, Philippe Wamba, and Katonja Webb.

We thank also our fact checkers: Peggy Ackerburg, Felipe Agredano, Avril Alba, Jon Alterman, Anurima Bhargava, Adam Biggs, Matt Christianson, Andrés Colapinto, Karen Dalton, Ellen Elias-Bursac, Melinda Gray, Bill Grimes, John Henriksen, Nina Jiang, Amelia Kantanski, Jennifer Kirer, Anne-Marie Lescowitz, Bei Ling, Anne Malcolm, Sarah Manguso, Richard Newman, Karen Peña, Nathan Rein, Alex Ross, Seth Saunders, Engin Sezer, Michael Soto, Michael Train, Katherine Trainor, Yolanda Tsuda, Nick Weiss, and Pai Yang.

We consulted with so many people along the way that we are sure we have not acknowledged all those we should have. If your name is not here and it should be, we apologize.

A final, special acknowledgment is due to the two people who ran the office for us: Lisa Gates, at Duke; and Mike Vazquez, at Harvard. Lisa coordinated the vast bulk of the research—and the researchers—and handled most of the enormous correspondence. Without her there would have been no book. And Mike did yeoman work supervising the checking of the manuscript and working to eradicate inconsistencies, to check facts, and, generally, to improve the final version. Without him this would have been a much less good book.

In a collective project one can accept responsibility for the result, but one cannot claim it. What virtues the result has are the products of the labors of all of us; the vices are the responsibility of the editors. We accept this responsibility gladly. And when errors—of omission or commission—are detected, we shall accept responsibility for them, too; and we shall hope, in the next edition, to put them right.

Global Culture: A Dictionary

Every newspaper we read, every edition of the evening news on every television channel, takes it for granted that we know the date. And so we all know that we are living in the last decade of the second millennium—in the 1990s—approaching a third millennium, whose beginning many of us will mark as a significant event. And "us" here means "us human beings," because this system of dating is in use these days (sometimes alongside others) on every continent around the earth.

Most Europeans and Americans take for granted that our dating system refers back to the birth of Christ. But it is worth stopping for a while to consider the significance of this fact: that the only dating system now officially in use all over the world takes as its starting point the beginning of *Christian* history. Roughly two thousand years ago was the birth of a certain Jesus, son of Mary and Joseph, an event that Christians celebrate each Christmas as the incarnation of God in human history, that Muslims recognize as the nativity of a great prophet, that Jews traditionally regard as the birth of a false messiah. These three great religions developed in a single geographical region, and all acknowledge that what Christians call the Old Testament is a holy book. In each of these religions there is the same tradition of awaiting a messiah whose arrival will end secular history. Orthodox Jews believe that the messiah has not yet come; Orthodox Christians and Muslims hold that the rebirth of Christ will usher in the end of human history.

In the great civilizations of Asia, in India and China and Japan, there are many Muslims, some Christians, a few Jews. But for the vast majority of Asians—for Hindus, Buddhists, and Jains, Confucians, Taoists, and Shintoists—the incarnation of Christ has no religious significance: it is someone else's story.

All the more extraordinary, then, that this story should have become the basis of the one dating system that most cultures use. And the way it happened is part of the story of how the military, economic, and cultural expansion of the cultures of Christian Europe over the last five hundred years or so has led us into the first period of a truly global human history. Whatever their intentions, Europeans and their descendants in North America, a civilization we now call "the West," began a process that brought the human species into a single political, economic, and cultural system whose details are, of course, the work of people from all around the globe.

It is also a fact that five-hundred-odd years ago a certain Christopher Columbus, an Italian sea captain (whose first name, appropriately enough, means "the Christ-bearer"), an adventurer in the service of an Iberian monarch, set off to look for a new route to India and bumped into the Americas on his way. For the cultures of Christian Europe this represented the discovery of a "New World." Perhaps Scandinavian seacraft had brought Norsemen to "Vinland" much earlier; perhaps Africans had sailed to the Americas before Columbus. Certainly for the peoples then living in the New World—the Caribs in the "West Indies" and the people who came to be called "Indians" in honor of Columbus's confusion—the arrival of Columbus was not the discovery of a new world but the beginning of the end of an old one.

Columbus's journey was one of many in this age of European exploration. Through colonization and conquest in the Americas, Australasia, and parts of Africa, and through conquest without colonization in many other parts of the world, the cultures of Western Europe gradually assumed dominance of the globe in the four hundred years after Columbus's discovery. By 1882, India was officially within the British Empire, with Victoria as queen-empress. Africa was divided at the Congress of Berlin in 1884 among Britain, France, Germany, Spain, and Portugal; Australia and New Zealand were governed by peoples of European descent; and the Americas were dominated in their northern half by people of British origin and in their southern part by people from the Iberian peninsula. In the north of Europe the Christian emperor of Russia ruled a vast empire that would become the world's first Communist state in less than three decades. The Chinese Empire was already feeling the impact of European cultural and political incursions; and Japan, which had been forced by American naval pressure to open to the West in the 1860s, was engaged in flexing its own imperialist muscles in the Korean peninsula. And on Europe's borders the old Islamic empire of the Turks was soon to be ended by Arabs with European allies, in a complex process that produced the modern political geography of what we now call the Middle East.

And yet at the very height of the European empires, on the eve of the First World War, the end of the formal political domination of the earth by Europe and her colonial offspring was not far off. By 1950, halfway through our century, India was independent; the only remaining European colonies in China were Hong Kong and Macao; Japan (like Germany) was under occupation as the result of the Second World War, but had never been colonized and was recognized, even under occupation, as an independent state. In the Middle East, Egypt, Iraq, Israel, Jordan, Lebanon, Saudi Arabia, Syria—all the major states of the region—were already in place. In the 1960s most of Africa was decolonized.

Also in the 1960s, in a process initiated in 1954 by the constitutional outlawing of segregation in education, the United States began its gradual recognition of the full civil rights of Americans of non-European origin, including the descendants of the African slaves on whose labor the U.S. economy had been built, and the "Indians," the Americans whose ancestors had lived on the continent before Columbus. In recent years similar movements have arisen to recognize the rights of the descendants of slaves and of aboriginal Indians in Latin America and of the Indians in Canada (along with the French-speaking peoples of Quebec). As these changes are carried to their natural conclusion, the world we will enter at the beginning of the third millennium of the Christian era will be another New World, a world that has moved out of the half-millennium of domination by Europe and people of European descent.

But we doubt that anyone will insist on changing the dating system, even to one beginning, say, from the founding of the United Nations after the Second World War. And we believe that in a world that is increasingly free of domination by "the

West," we will be able both to acknowledge more frankly the evils that were done in the course of Europe's expansion and to celebrate the very real achievements of those Western cultures—and at the same time to take pleasure in the benefits of the creation of a global culture under the steam of the economic, technological, religious, and cultural ideas of Europe and her heirs.

In coming to this recognition, however, we shall also come increasingly to see that, largely because of Europe's involvement in half a millennium of trade and of empire, her economy, technology, religion, and culture are not the products only of "white" people, of Europeans and their descendants outside Europe. Take two entirely different, but representative, examples: that the rebirth of European philosophy in the European Renaissance owed a great deal to the Arab scholars who had kept alive Greek classical learning during the European "Dark Ages"; and that the idea of democracy in the United States was refashioned in part out of the contributions of African Americans whose understanding of freedom was deepened by their understanding of the Old Testament and by their experience of racial slavery. In the vast process of the development of the modern global system, cultures and traditions have mixed and melded to produce in many places—but perhaps above all in the old centers of power, in the United States and Western Europe—new kinds of culture that draw on traditions from all over the planet. It may be true that in some parts of Africa and Asia contemporary cultures are still local traditions with only a thin veneer from the West; but in the United States, at least, both "high" culture—literature, music and dance, painting and sculpture, film and television— and the everyday life of "ordinary" culture—of cuisine, of language, of games and sports—draw on contributions that are an inextricable mixture of elements from Europe, Africa, America, and Asia, and draw also on an endless stream of new ideas in the creative glory of humankind. And so, when the culture of the United States circulates in music and movies and television throughout the world, it is not always a simple matter of something foreign corrupting a "native" culture; sometimes, as when some of Paul Simon's music comes to South Africa, we see cultures returning home.

What we are suggesting, in effect, is that we all participate, albeit from different cultural positions, in a global system of culture. That culture is increasingly less dominated by the West, less Eurocentric, if you like. And so there must be more and more people in the West, like ourselves, who are both aware of their ignorance of many of the "other" traditions and want to know more. Our idea in making this book was a simple one: to give those people (to give ourselves) a sampler of cultural contributions from around the globe. In doing so, we have placed some of the achievements of Western culture alongside those of many other cultures and traditions. We have done this in part because those juxtapositions enrich our understanding and appreciation of the achievements of "our" culture; in part because we think that in preparing the new generations for a culture that is more global, it is essential for them to learn about William Shakespeare as they learn about Wole Soyinka from Nigeria, Murasaki Shikibu from Japan, Rabindranath Tagore from India. As we in the West develop a more global culture, we do so in the context of Western traditions: we do so because an understanding of other cultures enriches, without displacing, our own.

This project began when we asked our colleague Jiaxing Wang, a professor of English at the Beijing Foreign Studies University (and an expert in African-American literature), to give us a list of a few products of Chinese civilization that, in her opinion, all educated people should know. To our surprise, she suggested the following entries:

1. Confucius and Confucianism
2. Forbidden City
3. *Xi You Ji* (*Journey to the West*)
4. Beijing opera
5. Silk Road
6. Spring Festival
7. Tiananmen Square
8. Great Wall
9. terra-cotta warriors

We had expected, of course, to find the Great Wall and Confucius. But we knew nothing of the Spring Festival; and things we had imagined might be on even a short list—gunpowder, Mao Zedong, noodles—were nowhere to be found. We were fascinated with the results of this small experiment; and we decided that the only way to avoid our own biases, inherited from our Western education, would be to ask scholars *from* other cultures—along with Western scholars *of* other cultures—to tell us what, in their opinions, were the signal elements of those civilizations essential to a beginning understanding of them. To escape our own prejudices, we replicated that first experiment with Jiaxing Wang dozens of times, now with scholars and creative artists from China to Chile. *The Dictionary of Global Culture* is the result.

Our procedure, then, in constructing this book was simple: we asked academic experts in universities in many countries to suggest around fifty of the most important cultural contributions from the region in which they were expert. We collated their suggestions, producing for each region a master list of the top fifty or so topics mentioned more than once. Some of what the experts included—and omitted—surprised us, as Jiaxing Wang's list had surprised us. But their advice is what made this book possible.

Then we set to work with a team of researchers, scouring the sources available in American university libraries to discover what we could about each of the topics on these lists. The written results were received and modified in turn by scholars in the field. We had the good fortune also to come across scholars, based in five continents, who volunteered not only to help make our lists but to write entries for us. We are extremely grateful to them, as we are to all the scholars listed in our acknowledgments. It is one of the great joys of working in the academy that we can learn from—and share our learning with—others.

We hope to persuade you that—starting with this book—it is worthwhile to look deeper into cultures about which you do not yet know very much; and so we have tried to find examples of the great cultural achievements, figures, and events of many cultures, and then to say enough about them to make them interesting and engaging. As you browse through the book, we hope you will share our sense that there is something for us human beings to be proud of not just in the traditions that we think of as our own but in all the traditions of our species.

It is obvious that a single book cannot hope to be exhaustive: American culture is not exhausted by all the books in the Library of Congress, nor is British culture captured in the British Museum Library, nor French culture in the Bibliothèque Nationale. But it cannot claim to be representative either, for how can you *represent* millennia of recorded Chinese cultural achievement, or the treasures of the Italian Renaissance, or the cultures that flourish in the thousand or so languages of Africa?

Both these problems—of exhaustiveness and of representativeness—have been with us in Western cultures since the process of developing encyclopedias and dictionaries took off in the Enlightenment (the best-known English-language encyclopedia, the *Encyclopaedia Britannica*, first appeared in 1768). Diderot's famous encyclopedia, the first modern one (produced between 1751 and 1772), was called the "encyclopedia or rational dictionary of the sciences, of the arts, and of occupations." Like our dictionary of global culture, it was organized alphabetically. But it did not, it could not, literally contain all the organized theoretical, aesthetic, and practical knowledge of European scholarship of its day, and it could not explain the meaning of every term, even of every *important* term, in geography and physics, literature and medicine, art and politics. And that is as true of the latest *Encyclopaedia Britannica* or the current *Oxford English Dictionary* (which first appeared in 1884) as it was of Diderot's *Encyclopédie* or Samuel Johnson's famous *Dictionary of the English Language*, produced in 1786. New words are being introduced into the language every day, just as new ideas, new works of art, new scientific discoveries, new cultural practices are constantly in the making. Yet a dictionary like Dr. Johnson's can be enormously important in recording and systematizing usage, and in making it possible for readers both to begin to understand words they did not know and to deepen their understanding of words they knew already. We hope that our dictionary will be an invitation for readers to begin the process of understanding those cultures that most of us educated in the West barely know.

But even the most complete dictionary, even one daily updated with new words, is not all you need to understand a language: you need also to know the grammar—how the words defined in the dictionary can be put together to make statements, ask questions, give orders, and even make sense of and produce poems. Similarly, understanding a culture is never a matter of simply learning a list of its elements: knowing how objects and ideas fit together into the lives of the people whose ideas and objects they are is as important as knowing something about their meaning in isolation. A dictionary can never represent the whole range of culture, just because a culture is a whole as well as a collection of parts. The final reason we have called our work a dictionary is to remind you that it cannot do the job of explaining to you the whole world of any culture, let alone cover the cultures of the whole world. "Had we but world enough and time," we could no doubt cover everything. But just as a dictionary of Swahili would be a good start in preparing for a visit to Mombasa, and a dictionary of Tamil might help in a trip to South India, a dictionary that introduces you, however haphazardly, to a few of the central ideas and objects in many of the world's civilizations is, we believe, a good beginning for our lifelong travel through the range of human cultures.

There are many ways, of course, in which cultures are not like written languages, so that the idea of literacy—of mastering the skills of writing and reading a language—is not a perfect analogue to understanding cultures. Someone who understands a culture, after all, has to know a language and more; and cultural understanding is something that is never completed, that deepens even for those in the culture throughout their lives. But no analogy is ever *perfect* (that is what makes it an analogy, after all!), and the major implication of the image of global literacy—the idea that we ought to prepare ourselves for the beginning of a global civilization, just as our local literacy in a written language prepares us for life in our local culture—is one we find both essential and enticing. We are *not* saying that the emerging shared culture of our kind consists simply of the sum of the thousands of traditions of the local cultures of the past (any more than a world language is the sum of the languages of the world). But we *are* convinced that an essential starting point for a more open and equal participation by Westerners in that emerging global civilization is an appreciation of some of the central cultural ideas and accomplishments of others, whose traditions we in the West are only beginning to learn . . . and to learn to respect.

When we started we knew this process would expand our own knowledge and our own visions. But the pleasures and the benefits of this experience have far exceeded our expectations. And we hope that as you delve into this miscellany of human achievement you will be as surprised and delighted and enlightened as we have been in making it for you.

Kwame Anthony Appiah
Henry Louis Gates, Jr.
Harvard University

The Dictionary of Global Culture

A

Abakwa, Sociedad

Secret society of African extraction based in Cuba. Like the better-known Santería, the Abakwa blend religious ideas derived from West African (Efik and Iboso) sources with elements of Catholicism. The members of the society, exclusively male, are called Nañigos, and include large numbers of Castilian Cubans as well as Afro-Cubans. In ritual masquerades, the Nañigos assume fearsome masks and perform dances to commemorate and reexperience the feats of cultic ancestors, accompanied by drums and song; modern Cuban dance theater makes use of some Abakwa folk elements. The syncretic forms of the Abakwa Society represent one of the important New World reinterpretations of African religious traditions.

abangan

Indonesian term. *Abangan* refers to the large Javanese peasant community in Indonesia which is considered to be only nominally Muslim by the Indonesian majority. The centuries-old term, propagated by strictly observant Muslims (the *santrí*) means "brown ones" or "red ones," a reference not to skin color or ethnic background but to relaxed religious devotion: the *abangan* are regarded as "unclean" or profane, irreligious, and therefore "of the earth." Many of their cultural, artistic, and religious practices are elaborations of Hindu and pre-Hindu beliefs from before the eras of Christian (Dutch) and Islamic colonization. In the twentieth century, the distinction acquired a political significance in the 1950s and 1960s, when Indonesian nationalists courted *abangan* votes and sympathies in a bid to weaken Islamic political hegemony. The Indonesian Communist Party made a similar appeal, reenvisioning Marxism-Leninism as a sort of primitive utopian egalitarianism indebted to *abangan* religious mythology.

'Abbâsid

The second major dynasty of Islamic rulers, or caliphs. The 'Abbâsids ruled the Islamic world, however fitfully, from 750 until 1258 C.E., when Baghdad, their capital city, fell to the Mongols and the thirty-seventh 'Abbâsid caliph was slain. They take their name from the first 'Abbâsid caliph, Abū al-'Abbās as-Saffāh (d. 653), the paternal uncle of the Prophet Muhammad.

The 'Abbâsids, under the leadership of Abū Muslim, overthrew their predecessors, the Ummayyads, in the Battle of Great Zab River in 750, through a carefully organized underground movement that capitalized on the dissatisfaction of non-Arab Muslims who felt persecuted by the ruling Arab Muslims. The "coup" culminated in the massacre of the entire reigning Ummayyad family, save one young man who escaped to Spain and established an Ummayyad kingdom there.

Founded in 762, shortly after the 'Abbâsid accession to power, Baghdad, the round "City of Peace," was an architectural wonder; it served not only as administrative headquarters to a vast government machinery but also as home to a great number of commercial, educational, and literary communities. Baghdad under the 'Abbâsids was at the vanguard of global culture: here reigned Hârûn al-Rashîd, the fifth caliph of the 'Abbâsid dynasty (786–809), who sent Charlemagne an elephant on the occasion of his coronation; his reputation as a just ruler and munificent patron of the arts and sciences led to his commemoration in numerous folk tales and as a character in the fourteenth-century Synlah manuscript *Alf laylah wa-laylah* (*The Thousand and One Nights*). At the colleges of law in Baghdad the greatest legal minds of Islam gathered, taught, disputed, and forged the guild system of Islamic legal practice. Numerous academies, observatories, medical schools, and hospitals were built, and some of the finest literary figures of the day flourished here.

'Abbâsid power began to decline as early as the late ninth century. Although the caliph retained his symbolic importance, his independence was undermined by the consolidation of an administrative bureaucracy made up of "secretaries" or ministers and the military elite. As the caliphs' power became increasingly abstracted, consumed in the habitual exercise of luxury, the royal family's grip on the empire weakened. Moreover, the allegiance of the outlying provinces, like Egypt and North Africa, was constantly in question, contested by ambitious regional governors.

In the eleventh and twelfth centuries, political and military power devolved almost entirely upon regional and local dynasties. The 'Abbâsids were unable to unite the Islamic community in the face of the invading European Crusades. When the caliph unconditionally surrendered Baghdad in response to the approach of the assembled Mongol armies in 1258, the 'Abbâsid dynasty came to an end.

'Abd al-Nâsir, Gamâl (1918–1970)

(Nasser) Egyptian political leader. The first ethnically Egyptian leader since the time of the pharaohs, Nasser led a military coup in 1952 to overthrow the Egyptian monarchy. He immediately proceeded to nationalize aristocratic landholdings and guaranteed free education and full employment, though it was not until 1956 that he assumed the presidency of Egypt. The most controversial of his actions was the nationalization of the Suez Canal Company (owned largely by British and French interests), which had a concession to run the Suez Canal. Incensed by Nasser's action, the British responded with military action, arranging an Israeli attack on Egypt as a pretext for British and French intervention. But when the United Nations intervened and supported the Egyptian claim to the canal, Nasser's move became a major victory for Egypt as well as other Third World nations.

Nasser also founded the Non-Alignment Movement with leaders from other Third World countries, in an effort to keep these nations independent of both the Western and then-Communist powers. To many Arabs, Nasser's name is synonymous with Arab nationalism, for he supported independence movements and sent Egyptian teachers and technicians throughout the Arab world. He attempted to put the ideal of Arab unity into practice by amalgamating Egypt and Syria as the United Arab Republic (UAR) in 1958; the UAR lasted only three years.

In the process of building the Egyptian state, Nasser faced internal opposition from Communists and the Muslim Brotherhood; he responded with brutal repression. Nasser's Egypt was overseen by an elaborate intelligence network of secret police, responsible for imprisoning thousands; intellectuals, often the brunt of the repression, were alienated from the new Egypt.

The 1967 Arab-Israeli war—in which the Israelis, blockaded by Syria and Egypt, launched an offensive that routed the Egyptian army in six short days—broke the political will of Nasser, a long-time foe of Israel. Though his resignation was refused by Egyptians in a massive demonstration of support, the country was demoralized, and the aura of his authority began to fade. Nonetheless, at his death in 1970, the entire Arab world mourned the loss of one of its greatest twentieth-century heroes.

Achebe, Chinua (1930–)

Nigerian essayist and novelist. The first major African novelist to publish in English, Achebe was born in eastern Nigeria and raised by a Christian Igbo family. His novels are daring fictional explorations of the transformations of an African culture from precolonial times to the era of national independence. *Things Fall Apart* (1958), Achebe's first novel, is about the breakup of the traditional Igbo society during the colonial period, and has become a standard text in secondary education in English-speaking Africa and around the world. (Only Camara Laye, who writes in French, has had a comparably wide influence.) In addition to *Things Fall Apart*, Achebe wrote *No Longer at Ease* (1960), in which he describes the downfall of an idealistic young Nigerian who returns home to Lagos, the Nigerian capital, after studying in England, and *Arrow of God* (1964), which vividly describes the corrosive encounter between traditional village society and colonial modernity. A fourth book, *A Man of the People* (1966), sounded a warning about the potential for despotism in the newly independent African nation-states. Along with his novels, Achebe arranged for the publication of a great number of essays on the representation of Africa in fiction by Africans and other writers. Some of this work grows out of his experience as a teacher of literature at universities in the United States and Nigeria. The Nigerian Civil War (1967–70) was a traumatic experience for Achebe, a partisan for the stillborn Biafran republic; the poet Christopher Okigbo, a friend and literary collaborator, was killed early in the conflict. Disillusioned, Achebe abandoned the novel form, confining his literary output to essays, short stories, and poetry until 1987, when he returned to the novel with the publication of *Anthills of the Savannah*. He continues to live and teach in the United States.

adab

Arabic term meaning "manners" and "literature." To a tenth-century Arab or Persian, having *adab* meant being well versed in the poetry, proverbs, and history of the Bedouin Arabs; having a fluent and accurate command of the Arabic language; being acquainted with the wise sayings of the Persian kings and the Greek philosophers; and even being able to swim and play polo. In this sense, *adab* was "refinement," a concept that in the medieval Islamic world implied the possession of knowledge, skills, and techniques necessary to certain professions and social functions: books were written, for example, on the *adab* of bureaucrats ("keep your memos as short as your signatures") and even of dinner-party guests. Those with *adab* were well bred, and their breeding was expressed in their accomplishments, one of the most important of which was literature. Hence, *adab* carried a sense of "erudition" as well as "good manners." In the classical period it also came to denote a specific literary genre, and in contemporary modern Arabic it is used to signify "literature" as a whole.

The employment of *adab* to mean

"literature" is derived from the use of books as a source of diversion and secular instruction, a process which began in the Arabic-speaking world in the eighth century C.E. The key figures in this development were the *kâtibs*—scribe-like bureaucrats employed by the central government. Their duties required them to come up with a clear, concise Arabic prose style, and their predominantly Persian background included a knowledge of literary sources unknown to the Arabs. The *kâtib* Ibn al-Muqaffa' (d. 757) translated a number of works from Persian into Arabic, including the internationally popular *Kalîlah wa-Dimnah* (fables from the Indian *Panchatantra*, also known as *The Fables of Bidpaï*).

The greatest practitioner of medieval Arabic *adab*-literature was al-Jâhiz (d. 869). The grandson of a black slave, al-Jâhiz began his career writing pamphlets in support of the 'Abbâsid regime in Baghdad and in defense of rationalist philosophy. His later works are masterpieces of scholarship and wit, addressing themselves to the varied interests of his audience, and characterized by sharp attention to human character and material culture. Of his own work, al-Jâhiz says: "The only way I can hope to win your attention is to present my book to you in the most attractive form possible," promising to include religious and philosophical disputes, proverbs, and poetry. His *Book of Animals* contains a wealth of zoological information, mostly recounted in the form of dialogues and anecdotes, although its real purpose is the psychological dissection of human beings—the animals al-Jâhiz finds most fascinating of all.

Works by other authors also reflect the omnivorous curiosity and wide-ranging imagination characteristic of medieval *adab*. The genre includes collections of stories about people rescued from horrible predicaments by unexpected strokes of luck, and even an account of an imaginary journey to heaven and hell containing interviews with prominent personalities of the past. Also in the category of *adab*-literature are the picaresque *magâmât*—adventurous tales of rogues and con men wandering in disguise—written in an erudite rhymed prose style filled with unusual vocabulary and ingenious wordplay.

adat

Arabic term for the system of customs and legal arrangements indigenous to large parts of Islamic Southeast Asia (including Malaysia, Indonesia, south Thailand, and the southern Philippines). Distinct from, and sometimes hostile to, the Sharî'ah, or Islamic law, *adat*, which today means simply "law," originated in pre-Islamic (and pre-Hindu) village society. Governed by shamans, *adat* invested every practice and detail of daily life with spiritual meaning. Over the course of the various Indonesian invasions, *adat* came to stand for the enduring rule of customary usages and local tradition. The term became formalized in the nineteenth century under the influence of Dutch and British colonial governors, anxious to find a suitable and workable legal framework distinct from Dutch and British, as well as Muslim, strictures. Today the customary or common law of the *adat* is codified in the national and state law of Malaysia and Indonesia, inflected with the prescriptions of the Sharî'ah and modified to suit local usage.

Adé, King Sunny (1946–)

Nigerian musician. Internationally renowned for his heroic brand of dance-pop Yoruba juju music, Adé was born a prince in the royal Odon family in Nigeria. Scorning his parents' wishes, Adé became a musician, learning to play guitar at the age of fifteen. Still in his teens, he formed his first band and soon began playing juju music almost exclusively.

Distinct from other forms of African

music like Afro-Beat or African reggae, Adé's juju stretches back to the 1920s, when performers combined guitars and the balanced complexity of Yoruba rhythms with folk tales and religious stories. Interested in producing his own unique form of juju music, Adé claims that he does not incorporate the influence of American artists into his music; however, he confesses to listening to it all, from jazz great Louis Armstrong to country-western singer Jim Reeves to funk great James Brown. Adé's music preserves popular Nigerian mythologies, filtering them through a layman's pop sensibility.

His success has been tremendous: his first hit, sung in tribute to the 1967 winner of soccer's World Cup, won Adé instant fame, selling over 500,000 copies in Nigeria. Having released over forty albums in Nigeria alone, Adé sells nearly 1 million records annually. The upswing of interest in world music during the Afropop renaissance of the 1980s has propelled Adé to the forefront of the international music scene.

adobe

Building material. Adobe is a heavy clay soil used to make sun-dried bricks; it also denotes bricks made from the clay, and buildings (especially huts) made with adobe bricks. The word "adobe" is Spanish in origin, but the material has been used for thousands of years in arid or semiarid climates. In the Western Hemisphere, it has been found in numerous pre-Columbian sites, from what is now the southwestern United States down to Peru. Dwellings made from adobe are ubiquitous in desert climes, where wood is scarce, as adobe bricks are easily made and provide excellent insulation from extremes of cold and heat. It's also fashionable: southwestern motifs (including adobe bricks and terra-cotta roofs) now appear across the United States, lending commercial establishments the mud-baked look of authenticity.

Aeschylus (525–456 B.C.E.)

Greek playwright. Born at Eleusis, Aeschylus began his career as a dramatist during the 490s B.C.E. He was one of the most popular tragedians of his period, winning thirteen victories in the Athenian competitions. As was customary for the day, Aeschylus played the lead in many of his own plays. He is credited with expanding the dramatic capacities of tragedy by introducing multiple characters and reducing the role of the chorus.

Although Aeschylus is believed to have written about ninety plays, only seven bearing his name survive, comprising the oldest corpus of Greek drama still extant. Six plays have been authenticated: *The Persians* (472 B.C.E.), *Seven Against Thebes* (467), and *The Suppliant Women* (466–459); and *Agamemnon*, *The Libation-Bearers*, and *Eumenides*, a trilogy of works that together form the *Oresteia* (458). (*Prometheus Bound*, once ascribed to Aeschylus, is now thought to belong to a later era.) Scholars maintain that most, if not all, of his plays fit into larger play cycles, most of which have been lost.

Human history as a progression of guilt and vengeance, honor, pride, and criminality is the great theme of Aeschylus' work. He dramatizes the precarious situation of mankind, battered by the often petty demands and punishments of the gods, driven to crime and despondency by the passions of the immortals. Some critics, however, contend that Aeschylus believed that the cycle of moral corruption and decay could be broken, and that the future of Athenian democracy might offer an escape from tragedy.

Afghan, *see* Pushtun

African Methodist Episcopal Zion Church

Protestant denomination. Founded in 1796 by black members of the John Street Methodist Church on Manhattan

Island, the African Methodist Church was the product of racial discrimination. The congregation built a church in 1800, and was serviced by white ministers from the Methodist Episcopal Church for many years. In 1821 a group of six black congregations held a conference to select a black bishop; at that time the church was officially organized. In 1848 it adopted its current name, the African Methodist Episcopal Zion Church, and by the late nineteenth century it had missions in the United States, Africa, South America, and in the West Indies. The church maintains Livingstone College in Salisbury, North Carolina, and its membership is about 1.2 million people, making it one of the largest African Methodist bodies.

Agnon, Shmuel Yosef (1888–1970)

Israeli novelist and short-story writer. Born Samuel Josef Czaczkes to a Polish Jewish family of merchants, rabbis, and scholars, Agnon began writing in both Hebrew and Yiddish at the age of nine. In 1907 he immigrated to Palestine, only to return to Europe some five years later. After more than a decade living and writing in Germany he went back to Palestine in 1924, this time for good. His first published work, Agunot (1908; Forsaken Wives), was a commercial and literary success that made it possible for him to make a living as a writer thereafter. Agnon, his pen name, was derived from the title of his first book and has two radically different meanings, "anchored" and "forsaken." Such contradictory double meanings became a trademark of his fiction, as they captured the state of flux in which modern Judaism found itself. Caught between the Old World (Europe) and the New (Israel and the United States), tradition and change, Agnon's generation suffered a disorienting loss of identity as it plunged into the process of developing new individual and collective affinities. Like Agnon, other twentieth-century

writers have expressed a similar ambivalence toward the modern age, notably Franz Kafka, Thomas Mann, and James Joyce. Agnon's peculiar genius, however, was to infuse European literary modernism with traditional Jewish folklore and mysticism, drawing on the biblical and rabbinical texts he had studied in his youth. His characters are victims of a universal fate: they struggle on long, arduous treks in quest of some precious object, only to discover that the "treasure" is a fraud and their suffering bears no reward. Yet their predicaments are distinctively Jewish; their pain is meted out in mindless persecutions and brutalities, which in turn provoke hapless and sometimes cruel responses on the part of other Jews. Agnon's compassion for his characters, damaged by history, is profound; but his resigned confidence in the blind and punishing inevitability of fate lends his vision a pessimistic irony. His novels include Ore'ah nata lalun (1939; A Guest for the Night) and 'Tmol shilshom (1945; The Day Before Yesterday). One of the most popular and acclaimed writers of the new state of Israel, Agnon twice received the Israel Prize (in 1954 and again in 1958) and in 1966 became the first author writing in Hebrew to win the Nobel Prize in Literature.

Agüeybana el Bravo (c. 1500)

Arawak Indian resistance leader. Chief Agüeybana el Bravo was one of Puerto Rico's several rulers when the Spanish conquest and colonization of the island began in 1493, with the arrival of Christopher Columbus. Mistreated by the conquistador Cristóbal de Sotomayor, Agüeybana coordinated a mass uprising of all the island's various Indian tribes against the Spanish invaders. Sotomayor was killed in the first attack; soon afterward, Agüeybana organized another attack in the region of Yagüeca; however, his fighting force was surprised by troops led by the Spanish explorer Juan Ponce de León, and Agüeybana was slain in the battle. Agüeybana el Bravo has been lionized as the first leader of the anti-colonial resistance movement and as an abiding symbol of the struggle for Puerto Rican national self-determination.

Aguinaldo, Emilio (1869–1964)

Philippine independence leader and president. A member of the clandestine Katupunan revolutionary society, Agui-naldo took command of the 1896 insur-rection against Spain and won several decisive battles, most notably the Battle of Binakayan. Briefly exiled to Hong Kong under the terms of the 1896 peace treaty with Spain, Aguinaldo eventually returned to the Philippines in 1898, at the outbreak of the Spanish-American War. Partly in gratitude for the help Aguinaldo had lent the winning Ameri-can side in the war, the Philippines were declared independent on June 12, 1898, and Aguinaldo was made president of the provisional government in early 1899.

However, as a stipulation of the Treaty of Paris, the Philippines were conceded by Spain to the United States, and Aguinaldo's government faced a new op-ponent. Relations between the young nation and the United States deterio-rated, and in less than a year a struggle for independence from the United States began. The Filipinos were out-numbered and in 1901 the rebel Agui-naldo was captured at his secret head-quarters. After swearing allegiance to the United States, he retired from public life. Aguinaldo eventually returned to politics, in the first-ever Philippine pres-idential election in 1935, but was de-feated by Manuel Quezon. During the Second World War, the occupying Jap-anese army used Aguinaldo as a mouth-piece for anti-American propaganda; the ploy was unsuccessful, though he was briefly imprisoned by American forces for his complicity with the Japanese. Ap-pointed to the Council of State in 1850,

he spent the last part of his life working toward the promotion of democracy and nationalism in the Philippines.

Agustini, Delmira (1886–1914)

Uruguayan poet. Born in Montevideo, Uruguay, Delmira Agustini was an im-portant voice in Latin American poetry and an important modernist precursor. One of the first women to write boldly about themes of sensuality and passion, she also documents in her poetry the struggle of a woman artist to forge an individual voice in the oppressive world of Latin patriarchy.

She was educated at home by her mother, and was privately tutored in French, piano, and painting. Agustini received tremendous support from her parents; her mother would keep the household quiet in the mornings so her child could rest easily after a night of writing. When Agustini would emerge from her bedroom, her mother was known to exclaim, "At last! The sun has come out!" Her father was of great as-sistance in collecting and transcribing her poems, and in getting them pub-lished. Her first volume of poetry, *El li-bro blanco* (*The White Book*), appeared in 1907 and was received favorably. It was followed by *Cantos de la mañana* (1910; *Songs of the Morning*) and her most ambitious work, *Los cálices vacíos* (1913; *Empty Chalices*).

Agustini's public persona verged on the bizarre. She was presented to the Uruguayan public as a little girl, "La Nena," an innocent and virginal muse prone to trance-like fits of poetic inspi-ration, even as she aged from sixteen to twenty-seven. She was herself complicit in her mythologization: her letters to Enrique Job Reyes, her longtime suitor, are written in a sort of "baby-talk." The popular image of "La Nena," however, was scandalized by the erotically explicit verse in *Empty Chalices*, a volume en-ergized by a powerful and daring sen-suality, an unconventional sensibility that earned her a place in the vanguard of Latin American literature.

Agustini's marriage to Reyes in 1913 lasted a mere twenty-one days; her upbringing had not prepared her for what she considered the unremitting vulgarity of married life. As their divorce proceeded, the couple continued to correspond and meet secretly. One month after the divorce was finalized, Reyes shot and killed Agustini in a bed they had shared, then took his own life.

Some contend that Agustini's dramatic relationship with Reyes concealed a more compelling, if unconsummated, love for Manuel Ugarte, an Argentine poet whom she met in 1912 with Rubén Darío. (The correspondence between Ugarte and Agustini suggests that many of her decisions—including her marriage and divorce—were undertaken at Ugarte's urgings.) The year 1924 saw the posthumous publication of another volume of poems, *El rosario de Eros* (*The Rosary of Eros*), as well as an edition of her *Obras completas* (*Complete Works*).

Ahl al-Kitâb

(Arabic for "People of the Book.") Islamic legal categorization. Under Islamic law, Ahl al-Kitâb are those named in the Qur'ân as "those who profess Judaism, and the Christians, and the Sabians." The Jews, Christians, and Zoroastrians were given special dispensation to practice their religions, since they were grounded in a Holy Book and the legitimate revelations of Allâh, the One True God, through his prophets (including Abraham, Noah, Moses, David, and Jesus). Each of those religions was considered to be a precursor of Islam itself.

Also known as Ahl al-Dhimmi (the Protected People), those in this category were granted a number of privileges not granted to pagans, including freedom of worship and freedom from religious persecution. However, it was incumbent upon them to pay a special tax (*jizya*) for their exemption from military service

in Muslim armies. After the death of the Prophet Muhammad, who was adamant about respecting the rights of Ahl al-Kitâb, the caliphs and their many generals and vice-regents were instructed to continue his practices.

Muslim men were permitted to marry women from Ahl al-Kitâb even if the women chose not to convert, though any children produced by such a union would be raised as Muslims; but a man of Ahl al-Kitâb who desired to marry a Muslim woman was required to convert to Islam.

Today the legal systems in most officially Islamic countries do not recognize a separate legal status for the Ahl al-Kitâb.

Airlangga (1000–1049)

Celebrated Javanese monarch. Lionized for his quiet heroism, Airlangga was given the Mataram crown at the age of nineteen. (Mataram was the capital city of the Sailendra kingdom of central Java, established in 929.) During his reign, Airlangga reunified central and eastern Java, beginning the process of wresting power away from entrenched regional elites, and he revitalized the Javanese economy by revolutionizing water-control techniques in the Brantas River Delta, an ambitious project that created new peasant communities, a deepwater harbor, and miles of new riceland. Following the stunning defeat of the Sumatran maritime empire by Rajendra Chola of South India, Airlangga moved quickly to put an end to the historic enmity between Sumatra and Java, marrying a princess from the Sumatran ruling family of Srivijaya. In a cunning maneuver, Airlangga recognized both Hinduism and Buddhism, and then appropriated the extensive estates of both religions, weakening the power of religious authority altogether. His reign also saw the promotion of indigenous Javanese culture, in contrast to the Indocentric policies of previous rulers. He did, however, prove less reliable as a progenitor, having left no direct heir. Therefore, fearing a violent struggle for power, Airlangga divided his kingdom between two illegitimate children, creating separate and eventually rival states. Despite this ultimate failure to create lasting Javanese unity, the extraordinary accomplishments achieved by Airlangga became the model for Javanese rulers in later centuries.

Ajanta caves

Site of famous Buddhist temples. Located outside the Ajanta village in north-central Maharashtra state, India, these stone-hewn cave temples and monasteries are internationally famous for their wall paintings. The caves have been hollowed out of the granite cliffs on the inner side of a seventy-foot ravine and were once the dwelling places of Hinayana Buddhist monks. There are approximately twenty-nine caves in the valley, *caityas* (the temples proper) and *viharas* (monasteries), all excavated and decorated sometime between the second century B.C.E. and the seventh century C.E. Although the lavish architecture of these temples, especially the richly ornamented *caitya* pillars and the sculptures that adorn them, is widely acclaimed, the frescoes on the interior walls, ceilings, and columns of the caves merit the greatest attention. Painted in shockingly vibrant colors and with a fluid grace rare in Indian art, these unframed scenes merge into one another, creating a panoramic effect, and depict legends and divinities of the Buddhist faith. Some of the paintings have been damaged by time and weather, but the caves at Ajanta still represent one of the incomparable achievements of Indian art.

Akhenaten (died c. 1354 B.C.E.)

Ancient Egyptian pharaoh. Akhenaten was an Egyptian king of the eighteenth dynasty (reigned c. 1372–1354 B.C.E.) who founded the monotheistic religion of Aten.

Before Akhenaten, the Egyptians worshiped an elaborate hierarchy of gods, each one requiring certain duties and obligations. The Egyptian political establishment was similarly well ordered; the eighteenth dynasty had ruled for two hundred years (1539–1292 B.C.E.), and the holdings of the Egyptian empire included Phoenicia, Nubia, and Palestine. The pharaoh was the interpreter of the gods; in practice, this meant that the king served as a figurehead for the establishment in return for his title, wealth, and leisure.

On ascending the throne c. 1372 B.C.E., Akhenaten retained his family name, Amenhotep, and continued to worship the old gods. Shortly thereafter, however, he turned to the worship of a new god, Aten, the One True God whose emblem was the sun. This affront to religious orthodoxy was accompanied by an assault on the political establishment as well: Akhenaten moved the capital city from Thebes to Amarna, which he renamed Akhetaten ("Horizon of Aten"). He also reintroduced the tradition of divine kingship.

The religion of Aten apparently existed without an ethical code or sanction, another dramatic departure from the punishing system of the old religion: worshipers were simply enjoined to be grateful for life.

Akhenaten's rule was marked by corruption and rebellion at home and in the provinces. After his death, his successors, including Smenkhkare and Tutankhamen, aggressively restored the old religious and political traditions.

Akhmatova, Anna [Andreevna] (1889–1966)

Russian poet. Akhmatova's work is associated with the Acmeist movement, which rejected Symbolism and instead emphasized "beautiful clarity"; it included such poets as Nikolai Gumilyov (her first husband) and Osip Mandelshtam.

Born Anna Gorenko, the daughter of a maritime engineer and his aristocratic wife, Akhmatova began writing poems at the age of eleven and was first published in 1907. That same year she began law studies in Kiev, later transferring to St. Petersburg to study literature, but left school in 1910 to marry Gumilyov, a union that lasted eight years. (Gumilyov was executed in 1921, charged in an anti-Soviet conspiracy.) Between 1912 and 1922 Akhmatova published five volumes of poetry, but her independent spirit and highly personal (read "bourgeois") themes made it impossible for her to publish from 1922 to 1940. She was allowed to publish for a brief time in the 1940s, but was again attacked and in 1946 was expelled from the Soviet Writers' Union. (Her Soviet critics, including Andrei Zhodanov, director of Stalin's cultural restriction program, labeled her "half nun, half harlot.") Even a few forced poems about the "glorious" Soviet struggle failed to improve her standing or help her son, who had been exiled to Siberia. Although her fortunes improved after Stalin's death, the vast majority of her work remained obscure or unpublished during her lifetime. Her masterworks include *Rekviem* (*Requiem*), written between 1935 and 1940, a moving chronicle of a mother's anguish over her son's arrest and imprisonment, and *Poema bez geroya* (*Poem Without a Hero*), completed in 1962, a meditation on time and life and the contingency of art. Both poems were first published in Russia long after her death, the former only in 1987. Today she is a cultural hero, one of the most important Russian poets of this century.

Aleichem, Shalom (1859–1916)

Yiddish author and humorist. Born Solomon Yakov Rabinovitz in Ukraine to a middle-class Jewish family, Aleichem attended the traditional Jewish *heder* and the Russian *gymnasium*. He worked as both a tutor and a rabbi before turning to writing after his marriage in 1883 to the daughter of a wealthy Jewish landowner. Though he was fluent in Rus-

sian, Hebrew, and Yiddish, Aleichem elected to write in Yiddish, the vernacular common to Jews throughout Europe and Russia, but with only a recent tradition as a literary language. He chose the pen name Shalom Aleichem (a traditional greeting meaning "Peace be with you") because he did not wish to offend his father, a devotee of Hebrew literature.

Admired for his warm and generous portraits of folk culture and his sometimes cutting satire of the Jewish bourgeoisie, Aleichem wrote stories recalling life in the Jewish village, or *shtetl*, and introduced a host of archetypical characters, full of humor and pathos. His stories of Tevye the milkman became the basis of the American musical *Fiddler on the Roof*. Several of his works have been translated and collected in *Stories and Satires* (1959) and *The Collected Stories of Shalom Aleichem* (1979).

After a vicious pogrom in his home city of Kiev during the 1905 Revolution, Aleichem immigrated to America in search of a peaceful and profitable new home. Life in New York proved unpleasant, however, and he returned to Europe within two years. Plagued by financial problems, to support himself Aleichem was forced to undertake a punishing schedule of reading tours, a schedule that cost him his health. Finally, in 1909, a committee of sympathetic authors purchased the publishing rights to Shalom Aleichem's writings and remitted them to the author, thereby guaranteeing him an annual income for the remainder of his life. He died during a second, equally abysmal tour of the United States in 1916, a European exile from the First World War.

As a writer, Aleichem faithfully recorded the traditions, folklore, and spirit of Eastern European Jewry just as that distinctive culture was disappearing. He is celebrated not only for his embrace of a rich vernacular language but for his rendering of a distinct cultural moment in Jewish life, now long since past.

Alf Laylah Wa-Laylah

Medieval Arabian tale. Though most commonly known as *The Thousand and One Nights* or as *The Arabian Nights*, the famous narrative in which Scheherezade postpones her own execution by recounting fantastic tales to King Shahriyar each night is not Arabic at all. It was translated into Arabic from a Pahlavi Persian collection of tales that may have been Indian in origin. Scribes added Arabic literary tales of folk inspiration during the Middle Ages to expand the translated Persian collection. Then, beginning in the early eighteenth century, Arabic manuscripts of the *Nights* were translated into European languages. The collection of tales so well known in the West, however, owes much of its modern content and form to its European translators and editors who freely inserted stories from other sources and expunged erotic materials from the Arabic texts.

Many of the tales that have become most popular in the West (including "Aladdin" and "Ali Baba") are not from the Arabic manuscripts at all, but only became part of the collection in the early eighteenth century when recounted at dinner parties in Paris by a visiting Syrian Christian. Antoine Galland, the first European translator of the *Nights*, jotted these stories down in his diary and months later completely reworked them in order to publish them as sequel volumes to his rapidly expanding version of the *Nights*.

Previous to Galland's translation (published 1704–17), the *Nights* were neither well known in the Middle East nor considered by literary Arabs to be great literature. Ironically, the *Nights* achieved such sustained acclaim in Europe that printed editions incorporating the spurious European materials were eventually created in Middle Eastern languages. When Sir Richard Burton worked on his "translation" of the non-Arabic tales, he chose to retranslate a Hindu translation of Galland's French text so as to retain its "Oriental flavor."

Although European scholars and editors well knew that over half of the *Nights* had been subsequently added, many still touted the work as the best available guidebook for understanding "the Orient." Though many of the stories in the *Nights* bear some resemblance to oral folk tales of the Arab world, the hundreds of versions and editions of the *Nights* created over the past three centuries remain a monument to Western fantasies about the Middle East, not true examples of Middle Eastern folk literature.

algebra

A branch of mathematics developed by medieval Islamic scholars. The English word "algebra" comes from the Arabic *al-jabr*, a term that first appears in *Jabr wa-al-Muqâbalah* (*The Book of al-Jabr and al-Muqâbalah*), written in Arabic by the Persian mathematician al-Khwârizmî (from whose name the word "algorithm" was taken) about 825 C.E. *Al-Jabr* means the removal of negative terms in an equation, and *al-Muqâbalah* means the combination of similar terms, both functions central to algebra.

Because Arabic numerals were not yet in use, the "Book of Algebra" is a huge collection of word problems that also contains many diagrams, as the author solves many of his equations geometrically.

Al-Khwârizmî wrote his book for the 'Abbâsid caliph al-Ma'mûn (d. 833), a patron of the sciences and the founder of the Bayt al-Hikmah ("House of Wisdom"), the library and translation academy of Baghdad. The intercultural contacts that took place in this period led to two important developments in the history of mathematics. First was the adoption by the Arabs of the Indian numerical system, which includes zero (in Arabic, *sifr*, hence the English words "cipher" and "zero"), making it possible to write out long numbers using zero as a placeholder. (The so-called Arabic numerals used in the West are actually the North African versions of the figures that the Arabs learned from the Indians.)

The second important development was the translation of Greek works on mathematics, geometry, and astronomy into Arabic. Drawing on the geometrical techniques of Archimedes, Euclid, and Apollonius enabled Islamic mathematicians in the nineteenth century to discover non-Euclidean geometry.

Just as Islamic scholars mastered and expanded the Greek legacy, Western Europeans in turn built upon the work of their Middle Eastern predecessors. Parts of al-Khwârizmî's "Book of Algebra" were translated into Latin, first by Robert of Chester in 1145, then by Gerard of Cremona (d. 1187). Given the enormous practical utility of algebra, as well as its fundamental importance in the history of mathematics, its development by medieval Islamic scholars is a great and lasting contribution to scientific knowledge.

'Alī (c. 600–661)

Founder of the Shi'ite sect of Islam. The cousin and son-in-law of the Prophet Muhammad, 'Alī is regarded as the fourth caliph by Sunnî Muslims while Shi'ite Muslims identify him as the Prophet's successor. After leaving the home of his destitute father, Abu Talib, 'Alī moved to the home of Muhammad. A child of ten, he converted to Islam and remained Muhammad's disciple for the rest of his life. Legend recounts that 'Alī's devotion to the Prophet reached the degree that he impersonated his beloved teacher by sleeping in his bed on the night of Hegira in 622, when Muhammad fled from Mecca to Medina under the threat of assassination. Upon later reaching Medina himself, 'Alī married Muhammad's daughter, Fātima. They bore Hasan and Husayn, who would prove to be important figures in Islamic history. During the Prophet's lifetime, 'Alī participated in most of the battles between the Muslim community in Medina and its opponents in Mecca; his bravery during these battles was said to have been legendary.

After Muhammad's death in 632, a dispute arose between 'Alī and other associates of the Prophet concerning succession; this dispute split the Muslim community. Those sympathetic to 'Alī's claim were known as the Shi'a or Shi'ites (partisans) of 'Alī and regard him as the first imâm (leader) of Muslims; however, those who accepted Abū Bakr as next in line for succession became known as Sunnî Muslims. Eventually choosing to relinquish his claim, 'Alī retired quietly into a life of religious studies. Only after the assassination of the third caliph, 'Uthman, in 656, did the Muslim community ask 'Alī to assume the position of caliph, a position he occupied from 656 to 661.

In the year 661, a member of the Kharijite sect, which had seceded from 'Alī's partisans, struck 'Alī with a sword in the mosque of Kufa in Iraq. He died two days later at the age of sixty-three and was buried at Najaf; his mausoleum at Najaf is an important site for Shi'ite pilgrimage and a center of learning for Shi'ite scholarship.

'Alī's reputation within Islam varies among Muslim sects. His stature as a distinguished judge, pious believer, and ardent warrior of Islam is recognized by almost all Muslim biographers, historians, and jurists, but the belief that, along with God and the Prophet, 'Alī is an anchor for religious belief, is rejected by Sunnî Muslims. In the Shi'ite and Sufi pious literature, where 'Alī's profoundly religious spirit is emphasized, he is called "friend of God," the saint in whom divine light resides.

Ali, Muhammad (1942–)

American professional boxer. Well known for his phrase "I am the greatest!" Ali was the most popular professional fighter in the age of televised fights, and the only boxer to hold the heavyweight title three separate times.

Born Cassius Clay in Louisville, Kentucky, to parents of very modest means, Clay was introduced to boxing as a boy by a local policeman. Becoming an avid amateur fighter, he won the Golden Gloves title of Kentucky six times and the National Golden Gloves title in 1960. That same year, he fought in the Olympics in Rome, winning the gold medal in the light-heavyweight division.

During the early years of his professional career, Clay acquired a reputation as a smug, playful, energetic fighter and performer who would intimidate his opponents by denigrating their ability or by making (mostly accurate) predictions of how the fight would progress and in which round and how he would win. Often these predictions were contained in poems he would recite to the delight of the crowds. Muhammad Ali's media-ready provocations and fighting prowess helped inflate boxing revenues from $4 million in 1950 to $18.1 million in 1964. In 1963 he joined the Nation of Islam and changed his name from Cassius Clay to Muhammad Ali.

On February 25, 1964, in Miami Beach Ali beat Sonny Liston for the world heavyweight championship. After defeating World Boxing Association heavyweight titleholder Ernie Terrell, he became the undisputed champion. Drafted by the army in 1967, Ali claimed exemption as a conscientious objector on religious grounds. He was subsequently convicted of violating the Selective Service Act (later reversed in 1971 by the Supreme Court), was barred from boxing in the United States, and was stripped of his title. When he resumed fighting in 1970, Ali suffered his first professional defeat at the hands of Joe Frazier, only to emerge victorious in a rematch four years later. In 1974 Ali fought George Foreman and became the undisputed heavyweight champion for the second time. Seven months after losing a split decision to Leon Spinks in 1978, Ali won a unanimous decision over Spinks and regained the title for the third and final time. He retired as champion in 1979. By the 1980s Ali's public appearances were limited as a result of his struggle with Parkinson's disease, an ailment that developed during his years in the ring.

Allende Gossens, Salvador (1908–1973)

Chilean political leader. A physician by training, Salvador Allende spent his life committed to both medicine and politics. He helped found Chile's Socialist Party (1933) and later served in the senate and as a minister of health in Chile's coalition governments. Despite the seriousness of his political engagements, Allende continued his public service as a doctor: taking a leading part in medical congresses, working with a number of Chilean medical institutions, editing medical journals, and publishing a book called *La realidad médico-social chilena* (1940; *Chilean Medico-Social Reality*), which received a literary prize. Allende was first nominated by the Socialist Party for the presidency in 1952; although he came in last, the election solidified his reputation as Chile's leading Socialist. He was instrumental in the creation of the Frente de Acción Popular (FRAP) and in the reunification of the Socialist factions in 1957. In 1958 he again ran for the presidency, losing by a narrow margin. Allende lost again in 1964, when, in the wake of the Cuban Missile Crisis, public sentiment turned against Marxism.

Allende was finally successful in his 1970 campaign as the candidate of the Popular Unity ticket, propelled by a bloc of Socialists, Communists, Radicals, and some dissident Christian Democrats. Inaugurated in 1970 as the first Marxist head of state in the world to win power democratically, Allende began restructuring Chilean society along socialist lines. He retained a democratic form of government, respecting civil liberties and due process of law, and embarked on a program of state control, nationalizing mineral resources, foreign banks, and monopolistic enterprises. His expropriation of U.S.-owned copper companies in Chile without compensation served to antagonize the U.S. government and to weaken foreign investors' confidence in his regime. Allende also took over large agricultural estates for use by peasant cooperatives, and in an attempt to redistribute incomes, he authorized large wage increases and a price ceiling. By 1972 Chile was suffering from a serious economic crisis that precipitated widespread strikes, rising inflation, food shortages, and domestic unrest. International lines of credit had been exhausted; an increasing radicalization of the public sphere, complicated by Allende's inability to control the more extreme elements among his supporters, made for simmering hostility among the middle classes. In 1973 his government was overthrown by a military coup, engineered with the support of the U.S. Central Intelligence Agency. Allende was killed in the attack on the presidential palace, and a conservative military junta led by Augusto Pinochet took over.

Allende, Isabel (1942–)

Chilean writer. Best known for her internationally acclaimed novel *La casa de los espíritus* (1982; *The House of the Spirits*), Allende spent her early life with her mother in the home of her grandparents in Santiago; it was this house that served as the backdrop for the novel. When her mother remarried, Allende left Chile to live in Europe, the Middle East, and Bolivia, returning to Santiago at the age of fifteen. A year later, Allende left school and took up journalism, but her life changed dramatically after the 1973 military coup in Chile that deposed the socialist government of Salvador Allende Gossens. As Allende has stated, this moment split her life in half and she left Chile with her husband and children for Venezuela. Seven years later, Allende's grandfather stopped eating and resolved to die. In response to his belief that people did not die but were only forgotten, Allende began writing a long letter to him recounting the events in her memory that would keep him alive for her. It is this letter that eventually became *The House of the Spirits*. Inspired by Gabriel García Márquez's *Cien años de soledad* (1967; *One Hundred Years of Solitude*), it is a family chronicle tracing the life of the Truebas, up to and including the coup of 1973. Because it is written from a woman's perspective, Allende has referred to it as a critical examination of the role of *machismo* in the perpetuation of a traditional pattern of economic injustice, heterosexual and generational tensions, and oligarchic political control in Latin American societies. Based on the critical and commercial success of this work, Allende became the first woman to be included in the ranks of the elite Latin American writers. Allende's other works include *De amor y de sombra* (1984; *Of Love and Shadows*), which focuses on the reign of terror under Augusto Pinochet following the 1973 coup; *Cuentos de Eva Luna* (1987; *Stories of Eva Luna*); and *Plan infinito* (1993; *Infinite Plan*).

Amado, Jorge (1912–)

Brazilian novelist. His youthful experiences growing up on a cocoa plantation are reflected in most of his writing. Having graduated from Federal University in Rio de Janeiro, he completed his first novel as a twenty-year-old. The many novels he composed throughout his life were translated into thirty languages. His earliest work, such as *Terras do sem fim* (1943; *The Violent Land*), explores the injustices of Brazilian society, focusing on the exploitation of the cocoa plantations. His later novels, including *Gabriela, cravo e canela* (1958; *Gabriela, Clove and Cinnamon*) and *Dona Flor e seus dois maridos* (1966; *Dona Flor and Her Two Husbands*), feature young heroines who rise above their impoverished circumstances to become self-sufficient adults.

In addition to his prolific literary career, Amado has also been an active political participant. Imprisoned in 1935, serving as a federal deputy for the Communist Party in the Brazilian parliament in 1946, he was often exiled for his radical beliefs, and his books have periodically been banned in Portugal and Brazil. He was the 1951 recipient of the Stalin Peace Prize and was awarded the Gulbenkian Prize in 1971, as well as the Italian–Latin American Institute Prize in 1976. *O sumiço da santa* (1989; *War of the Saints*) is his most recent novel.

Amarna, Tell el

Site of ruins and tombs of Akhetaten, one of the few Egyptian cities to be excavated. Meaning "Horizon of Aten," Akhetaten was completed by 1348 B.C.E. under the reign of the pharaoh Amenhotep IV, who eventually took the name Akhenaten (reigned c. 1372–1354 B.C.E.). Built as the result of Akhenaten's departure from the worship of Aten, the city Akhetaten was declared the new capital of Akhenaten's kingdom, dedicated to the worship of the sun god, Aten.

The most significant finds at Tell el Amarna were the portrait busts of Nefertiti, wife of Akhenaten, and 382 cuneiform tablets, known as the Amarna Letters, which were part of the royal archives of the pharaoh Amenhotep III (reigned c. 1411–1372 B.C.E.) and his son, Akhenaten. These tablets have proven to be one of the most important sources of information about pre-Israelite Pales-

tine. Most of the letters were written to the Egyptian court by Canaanite scribes and concern military, economic, and political affairs in the Levant. Many of them contain the petitions of one Rib-Addi, the governor of Byblos, for assistance against Habiru and Hittite marauders. Rib-Addi's increasingly desperate pleas were ignored by Akhenaten, whose domestic reforms left few resources for foreign policy. (The only reply he seems to have received from the throne involved a request for Byblosian cedarwood to make chests and trunks; Rib-Addi was eventually forced to flee after his subjects revolted.) In addition to providing valuable information about the political intrigues of the day, the texts reveal much about the culture and language of the Canaanites.

The city was viable only for the duration of the reign of Pharaoh Akhenaten. Four years after his death, the city was abandoned and the new court reestablished the kingdom's capital in Thebes.

Amaterasu Ōmikami

Sun goddess of Shintō mythology. All Japanese emperors (the Sun Kings) trace their ancestries to Amaterasu, the powerful patroness of Japan, the "Land of the Rising Sun." As the daughter of the primal god Izanagi, born of the tears that washed his left eye when he saw the ragged, decaying body of his mate Izanami in the underworld, Amaterasu was given Takamagahara, the "High Celestial Plain" and home of all the spirits, to rule and keep. (The spirits of Takamagahara are called *kami*, and range from gods like Amaterasu, through clan gods and spirits of place, to divinized heroes and ancestors.) Her brother, Susanoo no Mikoto, the storm god, born from Izanagi's nose, was sent to the sea. Before parting, he and Amaterasu pledged filial loyalty, sealing their bond by producing children in magical fashion—she chewed up the sword he gave her and spit out living pieces; he did the same with her fine jewels. Soon after, Susanoo betrayed their alliance by insulting Amaterasu, trampling her rice fields and defiling her halls. Bitterly offended, the goddess of the sun buried herself away in a deep cave, abandoning all creation to the cold outer darkness of chaos. The other deities plotted to draw her out; they hung a bait of jewels on a tree, with a mirror beside it and a cock perched before it. They broke into loud revelry, laughter and dancing. This intrigued the hidden goddess. When she wondered how they could celebrate so in darkness, they told her they had found a goddess even more shining than herself. Peeking out jealously, she saw her own dazzling reflection in the mirror and was flushed from the cave by the rooster's crow of delight. The *kami* then roped off her cave with a cord of sacred rice straw to keep her out in the world.

Amaterasu's fabled mirror, along with her sword and jewels, became the imperial regalia. According to legend, she gave them to her grandson Ninigi no Mikoto when she sent him to rule the Japanese islands; his great-grandson Jimmu became the first emperor when he took them and set up a shrine to his ancestress. The mirror, which is believed to represent the *kami*-body of Amaterasu, resides still in the Ise Shrine, the central shrine of Shintō. Amaterasu, goddess of the sun, is a remarkable character in world mythology, which almost always casts the sun as a male deity and the moon as female.

Ambedkar, Bhimrao Ramji (1893–1956)

Political leader of the Harijans, the Hindu "untouchable" caste. Ambedkar was the fourteenth child born to an "untouchable" family in western India, and as a boy he experienced firsthand the scorn of the higher castes. With scholarship assistance, Ambedkar studied law in London and received his doctorate from Columbia University in New York City and the London School of Economics. Upon his return to India, frustrated by the ill treatment he endured because of his caste status, Ambedkar became an outspoken advocate for the rights of the Harijan caste. He launched several Harijan journals and in 1924 started the Bahishkrit Hitkarnini Sabha (the Depressed Classes Institute) in order to study and improve the moral and material progress of untouchables. On behalf of his caste, Ambedkar led several important *satyagrahas* (nonviolent protests). In addition, Ambedkar directed the drafting committee of the Indian constitution. He led the conversion of more than 3 million untouchables to Buddhism and organized the ultimately unsuccessful efforts to create a separate political body for them.

Ambedkar founded the Independent Labour Party, which captured all the seats allotted to the Harijans in the 1936 general elections. In 1942 he organized the All-India Scheduled Castes Federation as a political party. And in a triumphant moment for the Harijan caste, Ambedkar was appointed India's law minister in 1947, the pivotal year in which India declared its independence from the British Crown. His expertise in constitutional law led to his playing an important part in framing the Indian constitution and in outlining the Hindu Code. This outlawed discrimination against untouchables, who were to be known henceforth as "Manus," after Manu, the celebrated Hindu lawgiver.

Although Ambedkar was able to pilot the Hindu Code successfully through the assembly, in ensuing years he became convinced that his caste status seriously impeded his influence in the new government. Increasingly bitter, he resigned from his position as law minister in 1951. His despair over ever changing Hindu doctrine on untouchability is illustrated by his decision, in the final year of his life, to convert from

Hinduism to Buddhism in a mass ceremony with 200,000 fellow Harijans.

American Indian Movement

Militant American Indian civil rights group. Organized in Minneapolis, Minnesota, in 1968 by Dennis Banks, Clyde Bellecourt, and George Miller of the Ojibwa tribe and others, the American Indian Movement, or AIM, was sparked by discriminatory arrests of American Indians made by police in Minneapolis and St. Paul. AIM soon came to the defense of American Indians across North America who had been displaced from reservations to urban ghettos by the federal government. Eventually, AIM broadened its position to include the economic, legal, cultural, and territorial interests of American Indians. More specifically, AIM demanded the reorganization of the U.S. Bureau of Indian Affairs (BIA) and compliance with American Indian–U.S. government treaties. In dramatic protest of government policies that concerned American Indians, five hundred AIM members occupied the BIA building in Washington, D.C., for one week in November 1972. Then, three months later, AIM members gained worldwide attention during the ten-week-long occupation of Wounded Knee, the historic Oglala Sioux village on the Pine Ridge reservation in South Dakota that was the site of the bloody 1890 massacre. AIM members were also involved in the takeover of Alcatraz Island (1969–71).

By 1978 much of the AIM leadership had been imprisoned and local organizations were struggling. But the movement survived these volatile years, expanding beyond its mission of political and social activism to become a spiritual movement advocating native religion. AIM membership is contingent upon a potential member's participation in the Sun Dance ritual on the Pine Ridge reservation. In the late 1980s, AIM had an estimated membership of 5,000.

American Revolution (1775–83)

Also called the War of American Independence. Though initially a small-scale war in which thirteen of Great Britain's North American colonies attempted to establish their independence, the insurrection became an international affair, with Britain's army supported by German mercenaries, and American forces being aided by France, Spain, and the Netherlands.

After successfully defeating France in the French-Indian War of 1763, the government of Britain spent the next twelve years in a campaign to reap more money from its North American colonies through a series of new taxation and trade policies, including the Stamp Act and Townshend Acts of 1767. Colonists' resentment grew as Britain established these new regulations without allowing for American representation in the British Parliament. Britain's lack of response to colonists' complaints led to dissatisfaction that erupted in protest on a number of occasions; for example, in the Boston Massacre of 1770, over fifty colonists clashed with British forces in the streets of Boston, and in the Boston Tea Party of 1773, rebellious colonists threw British goods into the ocean to protest the new taxes. The unrest eventually culminated in a bid for independence by the colonists.

In 1775 open fighting broke out between the forces of the British general Thomas Gage and the American "minutemen" in Lexington and Concord, Massachusetts. The minutemen seized and held Boston until the American general Henry Knox arrived and forced the British, under General William Howe (Gage's replacement), to leave. That fall, American forces also laid siege to Montreal until they were forced by British forces to retreat to Fort Ticonderoga in the spring. An unsuccessful American campaign against the city of Quebec was also launched at this time, resulting in the death of the American general Richard Montgomery.

In 1776, after the colonists declared their independence, Britain attempted to forge a peace treaty, saying they would pardon the colonists if they laid down their arms. When this offer was rejected, General Howe landed on Long Island to defeat American forces under the leadership of their commander in chief, George Washington. Forced to retreat to Manhattan, Washington was then drawn north, where his army was defeated near White Plains on October 25. Washington's garrisons at Manhattan and Fort Lee were both destroyed, but Washington launched an attack on the British leader Lord Charles Cornwallis's troops in Trenton. Crossing the Delaware River to Trenton on Christmas night, Washington succeeded in taking 1,000 prisoners. This and his later victory in Princeton sent a feeling of optimism throughout the colonies.

Although the balance of power did not significantly shift in 1777, the year saw many victories and defeats on both sides. The British general John Burgoyne was thwarted by American forces in the summer and fall while attempting to march on Albany, New York. Howe proved more successful, however, when he defeated Washington on September 11 at Brandywine Creek and took hold of Philadelphia (then the American capital) on September 25.

The year 1778 saw the definitive beginnings of American victory. The primary cause is most likely France's decision to openly declare war on Great Britain in June, although France had been covertly aiding the rebels since 1776. French forces were particularly vital in the south, where they participated in the sieges of Savannah and Yorktown. In addition, Washington's troops received military training at Valley Forge under the direction of Baron Friedrich Wilhelm von Steuben, which greatly contributed to the Americans' success at Monmouth, New Jersey, on June 28, 1778. Cornwallis's southern losses led to the eventual surrender of his 7,000-man army at Yorktown on October 19, 1781.

The war ended with the signing of the Treaty of Paris on September 3, 1783, when Great Britain recognized American independence.

amoraim

Authors of the Talmud. Taken from the Hebrew and Aramaic, meaning "interpreter," *amoraim* refers to the group of Jewish religious scholars who completed the Talmud, the principal corpus of Jewish law that covers nearly every aspect of daily life. From the third to the sixth century C.E., *amoraim* in various centers of Jewish learning analyzed and expounded upon the Mishna (Jewish oral law) in the same way that Mishnaic scholars, known as the *tannaim*, had studied and written about the Bible: by strict (though by no means uninspired) interpretation of the text. The Palestinian and Babylonian Jewish communities each produced their own version of the Talmud, to reflect the differences in the legal codes of their non-Jewish neighbors. Because the Babylonian Talmud was longer and more complete than the Palestinian version, it came to be favored as the definitive text, a pride of place it still enjoys today.

ancestor worship

Rituals of ancestor veneration. Considered an element of religious expression, and practiced in various ways throughout the world (including Africa, Asia, and the Pacific), ancestor worship is a form of respect shown to the deceased. For those who participate in these rites, the deceased have as much (if not more) influence in the world of the living as they did when they were alive. In fact, some worshipers believe that through death, deceased ancestors acquire special powers that can be used for the benefit or the detriment of the community.

Therefore, relatives of the deceased have a variety of reasons for their worship: the need to alleviate grief and perhaps guilt, the desire for potential blessings from the deceased, and the fear of angering an ancestor who may now be endowed with these powers.

Although the reasons and rituals of this practice vary according to the culture of which they are a part, the fundamental element of the worship is the same: to revere and honor the dead. In many places in tropical Africa and the Pacific, ancestor worship is believed to connect the world of the living with that of the dead. Through ritual ceremonies, dances, and songs the living evoke the spirits of the past. However, some African groups dislike the term ancestor "worship," and instead insist that the practice be referred to as ancestor "veneration," claiming that they are not worshiping these ancestors as gods, but merely paying homage to their memory.

Likewise, in Asia, especially China, emphasis is placed on the unity of family and the veneration of ancestors. Beginning in prehistoric times, ancestor worship was eventually adopted officially into Confucianism, the main religion of China. To Confucianist Chinese, these rituals involve prayer, the burning of incense, and the offering of food, performed on wooden tablets upon which the names of deceased ancestors are recorded. These ancestors remain central to a culture which ranks filial piety among its highest virtues.

In addition to the religious function of ancestor worship, there is perhaps an equally important social function: to unite or bond a community. Those who participate in these rituals are connected to and defined as a member of the "group," reinforcing not only filial piety but societal piety as well.

al-Andalus

Ancient Muslim empire on the Iberian Peninsula. Muslims (or "Moors") first landed in Iberia in 711 under the command of the Berber general Târiq ibn Ziyād, for whom Jabal Tariq (Gibraltar) is named. Muslim armies quickly swept through the entire peninsula, reaching as far as the French city of Poitiers in 732, where they were repelled by Frankish ruler (and grandfather of Charlemagne) Charles Martel (719–741).

The Iberian peninsula became the intellectual and cultural capital of Europe under Muslim rule. Arab and Arabic-speaking philosophers like Ibn Rushd (Averroës), Ibn Bâjja (Avempace), and Mûsâ ibn Maymûn (Moses Maimonides) flourished and became known all over Europe through Latin translations of their works. These translations were carried out in Toledo, where many Christian scholars came to study the Arabic language and the burgeoning corpus of philosophical and scientific works written in Arabic. Distinctive Hispano-Arab art and architectural forms developed, preserved today in monuments like the Great Mosque of Cordova and the Alhambra palace in Granada. The development of widely admired strophic and vernacular poetry may have served to transmit traditionally Arab themes of courtly love to medieval European literature. The cosmopolitan, synthetic culture of urbanity in al-Andalus was the nexus of Islamic and Christian cultures, a civilization that had a decisive impact on the formation of the European Middle Ages.

However, Muslim rule was punctuated by periods of massive unrest; internal political rivalries contributed nearly as much to the state of affairs as did the long frontier with Christian Europe. The Reconquista (the reconquest of Spain by Christendom, active between the eleventh and thirteenth centuries), which Pope Gregory VII (1073–1085) promoted, certainly benefited from this political disintegration. Toledo was retaken by Christians in 1085, Cordova in 1236, and Seville in 1248. In 1492 the combined kingdoms of Aragon and Castile in northern Spain defeated the last enclave of Muslim rule in Granada, and when all Muslims were officially expelled from Spain in 1609 by Philip III, refugees formed communities in North Africa. Traces of their distinctive culture may still be found there today.

Andersen, Hans Christian (1805–1875)

Danish author. Though Andersen wrote in many literary genres—plays, novels, travel literature, poems—he is best known for the fairy tales, 168 altogether, that he composed between 1835 and 1872. These tales are of multifarious origins: some are Danish folk tales, others draw on the folklore of other countries, but most are the products of his own invention. Stories such as "The Princess and the Pea," "The Emperor's Clothes," and "The Ugly Duckling" are known all over the globe and have been translated into hundreds of languages.

Andersen's beginnings, however, were less than auspicious. Born in a slum, the child of semiliterate parents, he traveled to Copenhagen at the age of fourteen, hoping to become famous as an actor or singer; failing in that endeavor, Andersen did succeed in finding a kind benefactor, one of the directors of the Royal Theater in Copenhagen. The director raised the necessary money to send Andersen to grammar school and later to the University of Copenhagen. He then began his life as a writer, publishing his first important work in 1829, a fantastic tale in the style of E. T. A. Hoffmann, the German Romantic. Later, he tried his hand at playwriting, with moderate success, but found true fame with his collections of tales for adults and children. Andersen's stories represented a break with the literary tradition of his day, as he wrote in the idioms and construction of the spoken language. Andersen also traveled widely, throughout Africa, Asia Minor, and Europe, and recorded his journeys in several travel books.

Andrić, Ivo (1892–1975)

Bosnian writer. Ivo Andrić, a prominent Serbo-Croatian novelist and short-story writer, was born in Dolac, Bosnia, on October 10, 1892. He was educated in Zagreb, Kraków, Vienna, and Graz. Involvement in anti-imperial activities during World War I led to his arrest and detention by Austro-Hungarian authorities, a period in which Andrić wrote his first major work, Ex Ponto (1918), a prose poem. This work solidified his reputation as a writer and paved the way for publication of collections of his short stories after 1920. After World War I, Andrić joined the diplomatic service of the newly formed Yugoslavia and worked in Bucharest, Madrid, Rome, Berlin, and Geneva, but he remained thematically rooted in Bosnia in his writing, which generally sought to capture the psychology and character of the people of his native province. He completed three novels during World War II, two of which, Travnička hronika (1945; Bosnian Story) and Na Drini ćuprija (1945; Bridge on the River Drina), dealt closely with Bosnian history. Andrić was awarded the Nobel Prize in Literature in 1961. He died on March 13, 1975, in Belgrade, Yugoslavia.

Angel Island

Former detention center for Chinese immigrants to the United States. Now a state park, Angel Island is an island off the San Francisco shore that served as a prison-like detention center for would-be Chinese immigrants from 1910 to 1940. Although the racially discriminatory legislation that began with the Chinese Exclusion policy of the 1880s severely restricted Chinese immigration, many still entered the U.S. based upon inclusion in one of the exempt classes (government officials, students, merchants) or claims of citizenship by birth or relation. But documentation of these claims was often difficult to find, and in many cases immigration officials relied on detailed questioning and cross-examinations of the applicant and the witness to determine the authenticity of the claim. As a result, "coaching" books containing detailed information, either factual or fictional, about the applicant's village, home life, and family were often brought on the long voyage to America, and then thrown overboard when the ship reached port. Although immigration officials attempted to isolate immigrants during their hearings, information was often smuggled to them. The Zizhihui (Angel Island Liberty Association), a group of male detainees who formed an orientation and welcoming organization for new male immigrants, became one of the most important of these informational networks. Through bribes paid to the Chinese kitchen help on the island who took periodic trips to the mainland, this organization was able to create a link between the immigrants on the island and the Chinese community in San Francisco. If the testimonies of the applicant and his witness were similar, the applicant was granted entry into the country. If not, the applicant was held on the island until he or she was deported. Many committed suicide rather than return to the political and economic chaos from which they had escaped. Individual tales of suffering and sorrow are recorded in poems written on the barracks walls on Angel Island.

Angkor era

Golden Age of the Khmer empire. For nearly five hundred years, from the ninth to the fifteenth century, the Khmer empire flourished in the area now known as Cambodia. Influenced by the Hindu cult of *devaraja*, in which both divine and religious power was united in a god-king, or *devaraja*, Jayavarman II (802–850) formed the Khmer empire early in the ninth century. All of Khmer civilization quite literally centered on this king at Angkor, and made possible a new era of government consolidation and accumulation of re-

sources. With a stable and unified empire, successive kings turned their attention to larger projects, such as the construction of elaborate religious temples and irrigation networks. The system of reservoirs and canals, initiated by the king Indravarman I (r. 877–889), was vital to the development of the Angkor empire, as it increased the production of rice from a subsistence level of one crop per year to a surplus level of two to three crops each year. This surplus, in turn, further encouraged the concentration of population in the royal urban centers. It was this urban population, working in service to both god and king, that developed what has come to be known as Angkor civilization, famous for both the delicacy of its artistry and the scope of its vision. Greatly influenced by Indian culture, the Angkor empire may have left behind more ancient Sanskrit inscriptions and monuments than stand today in India itself. Almost every Angkor king, for example, built both a temple honoring his parents and an even larger temple-mountain for his own tomb, intended to duplicate the divine Mt. Meru of Hindu mythology. Each of these structures required the work of thousands of citizens, and was centered within vast systems of urban boulevards, canals, walls, reservoirs, and fortresses that interconnected with other such monuments. They are themselves evidence of an increasingly advanced technology and artistry, sporting delicately carved figures and ornaments, possessing an overall beauty almost classical in its sense of proportion and perspective. Most of what we know about Angkor culture is gleaned from the ruins of these structures, as well as from the many Sanskrit inscriptions scattered across Cambodia.

The advanced Angkor civilization began to decline in the twelfth century and finally succumbed to invasion by the Thai Ayutthaya kingdom in 1444. The kingdom was divided into smaller Khmer states and its monuments left to decay and disappear, only to be "discovered" and restored by French archaeologists in the late nineteenth century.

Anti-Rightist movement

Communist political movement in China. In May 1957 the Chinese Communist Party decided to carry out the so-called Double Hundred Policy, a policy that Chinese Communist leader Mao Zedong (1949–76) explained by saying, "Let one hundred flowers bloom, let one hundred schools of thought contend." The slogan was supposed to encourage a new openness and healthy diversity of speech and thought in Chinese society. Party leaders urged people to debate a variety of issues, including the conduct of the Communist Party itself.

Both the policy and the slogan echoed the Chinese schools of philosophy, known as the Hundred Schools, that flourished during the late period of the Zhou dynasty (1027–256 B.C.E.). These schools enjoyed great freedom in voicing different ideas, a freedom rare in Chinese intellectual life, and especially surprising under the leadership of Mao. However, one month after the "flowers bloomed," when many, especially intellectuals, had expressed their candid opinions about local officials and the Communist Party as a whole, Mao realized the extent of popular opposition to the Communist regime and abruptly changed course. As a result, the Communist Party, under the direction of Mao, launched the Anti-Rightist Campaign in 1957, an attempt to "reeducate" critics of the regime. Those who had spoken out critically were identified as "rightist" and fined or even imprisoned; others were sent to the countryside. Mao and his supporters attempted to systematically suppress all other schools of thought, even within the party, in order to enforce a massive cultural and political unanimity. Millions of people suffered under this sudden political attack, and many remained labeled as "rightists" for more than twenty years, until the Great Proletarian Cultural Revolution (1966–76) officially ended and the party admitted that the Anti-Rightist movement was a "gross mistake."

Antonioni, Michelangelo (1912–)

Italian film director. Born into a bourgeois family in northern Italy, the young Antonioni had a passion for architecture and painting; his traditional early education eventually led him to the University of Bologna, where he studied classics, economics, and commerce. It was not until he began writing film criticism for a Padua newspaper that he declared his desire to be a filmmaker.

After spending a few months studying at a film school in Rome, Antonioni gained his first work experience with Italian filmmaker Roberto Rossellini, on Rossellini's feature film *Un Pilota ritorna* (1942; *A Returned Pilot*); he also worked with the French director Marcel Carné, on *Les Visiteurs du soir* (1942; *The Devil's Envoys*). In 1943 Antonioni began working independently: the filming of *Gente del Po* (1947; *The People of the Po*), a documentary, was interrupted by Italy's participation and defeat in the Second World War. Although *Gente del Po* would be released in 1947, it was not until the 1950s appearance of *Cronaca di un amore* (1950s; *Story of a Love Affair*), his first feature film, that Antonioni began to establish his reputation.

Antonioni's films defy comparison with other cinematic works. They are noted for their complexity and a lack of convention, displaying a discontinuous and often erratic narrative style. They often border on the absurd, and exhibit what might be considered a marked absence of dramatic reality. Unlike Hollywood cinema, where the viewer is encouraged to identify with what is being viewed, Antonioni's cinema emphasizes viewer alienation and displacement. Yet, despite his difficult style, he has gained international attention and critical acclaim, most notably for *L'Avventura* (1959; *The Adventure*), his first international success; *Blow-up* (1966), his first full-length film in English; and his first American film, *Zabriskie Point* (1970).

Although his later films did not elicit the same critical acclaim, Antonioni is remembered for his contributions to the cinema and his influence on the sensibility of twentieth-century viewers. In 1995 the American Academy of Motion Pictures honored him with a lifetime achievement award.

apartheid

South African racial policy. Apartheid (from the Afrikaans word for "apartness") was a social and political policy of racial segregation and discrimination enforced by white minority governments in South Africa from 1948 to 1994. The term was coined in the 1930s and used as a political slogan of the National Party in the early 1940s, but the policy itself extends back to the beginning of white settlement in South Africa in 1652. After the primarily Afrikaaner Nationalists came to power in 1948, the social custom of apartheid was systematized under law.

The implementation of the policy, later referred to as "separate development," was made possible by the Population Registration Act of 1950, which put all South Africans into three racial categories: Bantu (black Africans), white, or Colored (of mixed race). A fourth category, Asian (Indians and Pakistanis), was added later.

The system of apartheid was enforced by a series of laws passed in the 1950s: the Group Areas Act of 1950 assigned races to different residential and business sections in urban areas, while the Land Acts of 1954 and 1955 restricted nonwhite residence to specific areas. These laws reserved over 80 percent of South African land for the white minor-

ity and attempted to limit contact between the races as much as possible, a division ensured by the enforcement of "pass" laws that required nonwhites to carry documents authorizing their presence in restricted white areas. In addition, other laws prohibited most social contacts between the races, enforced the segregation of public facilities and the separation of educational standards, created race-specific job categories, restricted the powers of nonwhite unions, and curbed nonwhite participation in government.

The Bantu Authorities Act of 1951 and the Promotion of Bantu Self-Government Act of 1959 furthered these divisions between the races by creating ten African "homelands" administered by reestablished African tribal organizations, pseudo-states within South Africa with varying degrees of independence. The Bantu Homelands Citizenship Act of 1970 made every black South African a citizen of one of the homelands, effectively excluding blacks from South African politics. Most of the homelands, lacking natural resources, were not economically viable and, being both small and fragmented, lacked the autonomy of independent states.

Though the implementation and enforcement of apartheid was accompanied by tremendous suppression of opposition, there was consistent resistance to apartheid within South Africa. A number of black political groups, often supported by sympathetic whites, opposed apartheid using a variety of tactics, including violence, strikes, demonstrations, and sabotage—strategies that often met with severe reprisals by the government. Apartheid was also denounced by the international community; in 1961 South Africa was forced to withdraw from the Commonwealth by member states who were critical of the apartheid system, and in 1985 the governments of the United States and the United Kingdom imposed selective economic sanctions on South Africa in protest of its racial policy.

As antiapartheid pressure mounted within South Africa and externally, the South African government, led by President F. W. de Klerk, began to dismantle the apartheid system in the early 1990s. The year 1990 brought a National Party government dedicated to reform, and saw the legalization of formerly banned black congresses and the release of imprisoned black leaders. In 1994 the country's constitution was rewritten and free general elections were held for the first time in the nation's history, and with Nelson Mandela's election as South Africa's first black president, the last vestiges of the apartheid system were finally eliminated.

Aqhat, Poem of

Canaanite epic poem. During an excavation of the ancient city of Ugarit (now Ras Shamra) in present-day Syria in the early 1930s, the *Poem of Aqhat* was discovered. Written on clay tablets that are believed to date from the fourteenth century B.C.E., this poem is less closely related to religious ritual than its counterpart, the *Poem of Baal*, which was also uncovered at Ugarit.

Part of the larger myth concerning Aqhat's father, Danel, a royal figure of legendary wisdom and righteousness, the *Poem of Aqhat* opens with a seven-day incubation ritual that Danel hopes will help him produce a son. On the seventh day, the Canaanite god of fertility, Baal, Danel's patron, addresses the assembly of gods on Danel's behalf. In response, El, the Creator of All, blesses Danel and lists the various benefits that a son will provide. (The list had more than ritualistic significance; it was a book of rights and manners, detailing a son's responsibility to his father, and the proper conduct of kings and of all humans in their relationships with one another and with the gods.)

Following the birth of Aqhat, Danel receives a beautifully crafted bow-and-arrows set for his son. When Anat, Baal's sister, offers Aqhat immortality in exchange for the weapon, he refuses her and scoffs at her claim that she could deliver such a gift. Scorned and furious at his suggestion, Anat sends her henchman, in the form of a vulture, to kill Aqhat. He is slain and drought strikes the land. As Danel and his daughter, Pughat, survey the scorched ground, a messenger appears with the news of Aqhat's death. Danel decides to rend the innards of all the world's vultures in search of Aqhat's remains. When he finds them, he gives them a proper burial and returns to his palace to mourn for the next seven years. At the end of the mourning period, Pughat asks for Danel's blessing as she sets out to avenge her brother's death.

The *Poem of Aqhat* is difficult to interpret because of significant gaps in the text and its abrupt ending. There are, however, striking parallels between Aqhat and the tales of Gilgamesh and Osiris, which suggests that the *Poem of Aqhat* is yet another example of an ancient culture's attempt to explain the annual cycle of life and death in relation to the seasons.

Aquin, Hubert (1929–1977)

Canadian activist and novelist. Considered by many to be French Canada's premier novelist, Aquin earned a degree in philosophy at the Université de Montréal in 1952, studied political science in Paris for the next three years, and returned to Canada to work as a journalist. A founding editor of the magazine *Liberté*, he subsequently wrote radio and television plays and was a producer for Radio Canada and the National Film Board of Canada. During the early 1960s he was an executive member of the French-Canadian nationalist party Rassemblement pour l'Indépendance Nationale. An outspoken advocate of Quebec separatism, he was arrested on

suspicion of terrorism in 1964, incarcer-
ated in a mental hospital after pleading
temporary insanity, and ultimately acquitted. During this time he wrote his
first novel, *Prochain épisode* (1965), a
"spy novel" about a revolutionary who is
recruited by the separatist cause to murder a counterspy but who fails and ends
up in prison, where he reviews his career; the story reflects Aquin's own imprisonment and serves as a metaphor for
the plight of French Canadians. Aquin
attempted to move to Switzerland in
1966 but was deported quickly, at what
he thought was the request of the Canadian government. His second novel,
Trou de mémoire (1968; *Blackout*), was
widely hailed as a French-Canadian
contribution to the *nouveau roman*: self-
reflexively absorbed in its own production, suffused with eroticism, violence,
and death, the narrative intentionally
obscure, the narrators many. *L'Anti-
phonaire* (1969; *The Antiphonary*) repro-
duces these concerns, adding epilepsy
(from which Aquin suffered) as a central
metaphor for existential indeterminacy.
Aquin taught literature at the Université
du Québec in 1969, that same year refusing a Governor-General's Award because of his commitment to Quebec
separatism. His last novel, *Neige noire*
(1974; *Hamlet's Twin*), ostensibly a
movie script about a television play of
Hamlet, plays havoc with the boundaries between "real" and "fictional" narratives, and is considered by many a
masterpiece of neomodernism. Aquin
worked briefly as an editor for Editions
de la Presse in 1976, though he left after
publicly excoriating his superiors for
"colonizing" Quebec culture. He committed suicide in 1977.

Aquino, Corazon [Conjuangco] (1933–)
President of the Republic of the Philippines from 1986 to 1992. A reluctant candidate for president, Aquino rose to
prominence as the leader of the so-
called people-power movement against

the waste and corruption of Ferdinand
Marcos's regime. Her administration restored democratic procedures to her
country's government and made efforts
to improve conditions for the poor of the
Philippines, but was hindered by a host
of problems: disloyal generals, a weak
economy, an entrenched oligarchy, a
civil war with Maoist guerrillas in the
south, and her own political inexpe-
rience.

Born into a wealthy and politically influential family and educated in the
United States, Aquino returned to Manila to study law, but her legal career
was cut short by her 1954 marriage to
Benigno "Ninoy" Aquino, a young journalist and politician. For the next
twenty-nine years Corazon Aquino remained almost completely out of public life while her husband rose through
the political ranks, eventually occupying
a seat in the Philippine senate. He was
ousted in 1972 during Marcos's crackdown on political rivals and opponents,
and remained imprisoned until 1980,
when he was allowed to go to the United
States.

Corazon Aquino's rise to power began
after the 1983 assassination of her husband at the Manila airport. Because the
assassination occurred shortly before the
anticipated 1984 parliamentary elections,
it effectively solidified public outrage
against Marcos. Aquino quickly took up
the mantle of her husband's opposition
to the Marcos government; she assumed
leadership of the Philippines after Marcos failed to steal the election and then
fled the country. Though Aquino's presidency was troubled, she will be remembered for leading the bloodless coup that
restored civilian government to her
homeland and that brought the Philippines steps closer to a just and democratic social and political order.

'Arabiyya
'Arabiyya, or "Arabic," the language of
the Qur'ân and, since the triumph of Is-

lam, of educated discourse in the Arab world. In pre-Islamic Arabia, Arabic varied from tribe to tribe; 'Arabiyya may have developed out of the dialect of Quraysh, Muhammad's tribe in Mecca, but the language is inflected with many other tribal dialects, a heterogeneous but coherent pan-Arab lingua franca. Many non-Semitic languages bear traces of 'Arabiyya, a language suffused with religious and cultural authority; it has lent its script to Persian, Ottoman Turkish, and Urdu.

'Arabiyya is the most prized cultural possession of the Arabs, the language of a rich literary, religious, and intellectual tradition more than 1,400 years old. Since the beginning of its written history, Arabic has swollen with meanings, developing new terminology to express new concepts. At the same time, it retains virtually all of the vocabulary and grammar that it ever possessed; while some words and expressions may not be commonly used, they are never considered obsolete. Above all, the Qur'ân occupies a unique position in Islamic society not only as a religious text but also as a literary masterpiece whose style has always represented the ideal of the language.

The science of grammar was the basis of an Islamic education and a prerequisite for inquiry in any other field. Scholars use different terms to refer to varieties of Arabic: classical Arabic, modern standard Arabic, and colloquial Arabic are the most common terms. The term "classical Arabic" refers to the formal register of intellectual and religious activity, which is characterized by grammatical features absent from other varieties. "Modern standard," a simplified form of classical, is used in most written discourse today, and "colloquial Arabic" refers to regional vernacular dialects, used in daily communication. Although they are commonly referred to by country—for example, Egyptian Arabic or Moroccan Arabic—these "national" lines do not accurately reflect the contours of any linguistic map that could be drawn.

In addition to its literary, religious, and cultural importance, 'Arabiyya has come to have profound political significance for its speakers. This language is the one secure tie that binds together 200 million people in twenty-two countries, providing a means of communication that cuts across ethnic and religious differences and Western-imposed political boundaries. It is at the very core of one's identification as Arab.

Arany, János (1817–1882)

Hungarian epic poet. Born in Nagyszalonta, Hungary, to a poor Calvinist farming family, Arany began his schooling in Debrecen but quit his studies to join a group of traveling actors.

Arany's first major work was *Toldi* (1847), the first part of an epic trilogy, published in 1847 to widespread acclaim. Set in the fourteenth century, the epic chronicles the adventures of Toldi, a youth of incredible physical strength (a character taken from a sixteenth-century verse by Péter Ilosvai Selymes), as he travels to the royal court, and was written in an accessible language and style that became popular among Hungarians eager for a national literature. *Toldi* even gained the attention of Sándor Petőfi, a prominent Hungarian poet, who began a friendship with Arany after writing a poem in his praise.

In 1848 Arany participated in the Hungarian revolution, holding a government position editing a newspaper for peasants and turning to teaching when the revolution was eventually crushed. The same year also saw the completion of the second part of the epic trilogy, *Toldi szerelme* (1848–79; *Toldi's Love*). In 1854 he finished the trilogy with *Toldi estéje* (1854; *Toldi's Evening*), concluding the epic with the tale of Toldi's conflicts with the king and his eventual death.

From 1851 to 1860 Arany was the classical and Hungarian master at Nagykorös, and in 1858 he was elected to the Hungarian Academy and began to edit a literary periodical, the *Szépirodalmi Figyelö* (later known as the *Koszorú*). He was later elected first secretary of the Academy, and in 1870 he became the organization's general secretary.

Though the Toldi trilogy is Arany's major work, he did produce other significant writings; *Bolond Istók* (1850; *Stephen the Fool*) is a bitterly introspective yet humorous epic poem, while *Buda halála* (1864; *The Death of King Buda*) is the first part of an unfinished trilogy that deals with Hungarian prehistory. In addition to being a master of the ballad, Arany was also a translator of the highest merit, producing editions of Shakespeare, Goethe, and the complete works of Aristophanes. Often melancholy, Arany's creative work is preoccupied with moral conflict as well as the author's own fate and that of his nation, perhaps best exemplified by the *Öszikék*, a series of poems written just before his death.

Arcand, Denys (1941–)

Canadian film director. Born in Quebec and raised in the Roman Catholic Church, Arcand attended parochial school, and later the Université de Montréal, where he received a master's degree in history. He directed several feature films and television dramas, but is known largely for the success of two recent films: *The Decline of the American Empire* (1986), a sex comedy that earned Arcand an Oscar nomination in 1986, and *Jesus of Montreal* (1989), a tongue-in-cheek revision of the Passion Play, which was nominated for an Oscar for Best Foreign Film in 1990. Reevaluating traditional conceptions of alienation, martyrdom, and redemption, this latter film, much to its artistic credit, strikes a precarious balance between the sacred and the sacrilegious.

Arendt, Hannah (1906–1975)

Political theorist. Born in Germany, Arendt studied at the universities of Marburg and Freiberg before receiving her Ph.D. from Heidelberg in 1928 under the attentive tutelage of Martin Heidegger. After the Nazi seizure of power in 1933, Arendt, like many other German Jews, fled Germany—first to Paris and then to the United States, where she became a U.S. citizen in 1951. Arendt worked in publishing for several years before the success of her own books made her a much sought after lecturer and academic. From 1963 to 1967 she was on the faculty at the University of Chicago; thereafter she taught at the New School for Social Research in New York City.

Arendt's seminal work, *Origins of Totalitarianism*, written in 1951, immediately established her as an important political thinker. In it she argued that the rise of totalitarianism and the disintegration of the traditional nation-state in this century were continuations of trends begun in the nineteenth century, particularly imperialism and anti-Semitism. Ever greater concentrations of economic and political power had rendered the old international system obsolete; the obsessive pursuit of power in the modern age made the totalitarian state almost inevitable. Although *Origins of Totalitarianism* is considered to be her masterpiece, most of Arendt's other works were also well received. They included *The Human Condition* (1958), *Between Past and Future* (1961), *On Revolution* (1963), *Men in Dark Times* (1968), *On Violence* (1970), and *Crises of the Republic* (1972). *Eichmann in Jerusalem* (1963), a meditation spurred by the trial in Israel of Adolf Eichmann, might be her most powerful and rewarding book, a controversial exploration of the complicity of the European nations in the destruction of the Jews and of what Arendt termed the "eerie banality of the Nazi evil."

Arguedas, José María (1911–1969)

Peruvian novelist. As a writer, Arguedas championed the language and literature of the Quechua Indians. The son of a white father and a Quechua Indian mother, Arguedas was born in Peru and learned Quechua before Spanish. After his mother's death, Arguedas spent most of his childhood with his stepmother and her sons. His father was often away on business, and Arguedas was treated cruelly by his new mother and brothers. He found refuge with the Indians of the community, and through his contact with the native Quechua he was introduced to their communal values, music, and culture, which had a profound and lasting effect on him. The sense of desertion that dominated his childhood was compensated by feelings of love and compassion among the Indians, an experience that shaped his vision of Peruvian culture and society. All of Arguedas's work reflects the tensions of Peruvian society, in which the Indians, a majority of the population, have been marginalized by a dominant Spanish culture.

Arguedas published his first collection of stories, *Agua* (*Water*), in 1935; in them he juxtaposes the violence and injustice he observed in the white world with the peaceful and orderly existence he found in the oppressed but passive Indians. *Yawar fiesta* (*Bloody Feast*) appeared in 1941, and the autobiographical *Los ríos profundos* (*Deep Rivers*), often considered his masterpiece, in 1958. Other works by Arguedas include *El sexto* (1961; *The Sixth One*), based on his imprisonment during Oscar Benavides's dictatorship; *Todas las sangres* (1964; *All the Races*); and an unfinished semiautobiographical novel, *El zorro de arriba y el zorro de abajo* (1971; *The Fox from Above and the Fox from Below*). This last work describes the agony of a man completely shattered and disillusioned by life. It includes journal entries in which Arguedas methodically and passionately notes the events leading to his suicide in 1969 in a deserted classroom in Lima.

Aristophanes (427–388 B.C.E.)

Greek playwright and poet. One of Athens's most celebrated poets, Aristophanes produced brilliant comedies during the fifth century B.C.E. (the only surviving texts are those preserved in medieval manuscripts). Aristophanes' work is typical of the comedy of his time—possessed of a wild and unrestrained exuberance. His plays often contain implausible, outrageous plots that quickly give way to a succession of slapstick routines. His humor is broad, irreverent, and dark, applied with equal vigor to such topics as sex, excrement, rape, torture, blindness, starvation, and violence. More reputable qualities, such as honesty and decency, are usually absent, and the "comic hero" is characteristically possessed of a shrewd cunning.

Although Aristophanes clearly wrote to entertain, his works are the vehicle for a loose and jocular criticism of politicians and intellectuals, most notably Socrates and Euripides. The authorities were not consistently amused by his satire, however; Aristophanes was in fact prosecuted for slandering government officials. Scholars credit Aristophanes with some forty plays, of which eleven survive, including *Banqueters, Babylonians, Acharnians, Lysistrata, The Clouds* (which satirizes Socrates), *The Birds*, and *The Frogs*. A precocious youth, his first three plays (*Banqueters, Babylonians*, and *Acharnians*) were produced by another, older man; he is also believed to have given some of his later plays to his son, two of which were probably produced after his death.

Aristotle (384–322 B.C.E.)

Ancient Greek philosopher and scientist. Aristotle, one of the most influential Greek philosophers, was born in Stagira, a Macedonian village, in 384 B.C.E. His father, Nicomachus, was the court physician to the king of Macedonia, and Aristotle was exposed to the study of medicine and biology early in life.

Nicomachus died when Aristotle was still a boy, and Aristotle was sent to the Athenian Academy of Plato, where he studied under the famous philosopher for twenty years. After Plato's death in 348, Aristotle traveled Greece for twelve years, founding academies in Assus and Mytilene before moving to Pella, the capital of Macedonia. Aristotle's habit of teaching while walking earned his students the name Peripatetics. In Pella, Aristotle tutored the young man who would become known as Alexander the Great before returning to his family's property in Stagira. In 335 Aristotle went to Athens and founded the Lyceum, an institution of higher learning where research was conducted in all of the fields of knowledge, most notably in biology and history. When Alexander the Great died in 323, anti-Macedonian rioting broke out in Athens and forced Aristotle to flee to Chalcis, a town north of Athens. He died there in 322.

It is believed that Aristotle's early works were written in adherence to the Platonic dialogue, but that as Aristotle's own thought matured, he depended less on Plato's guidance. The *Physics* (*Physike*) and *Metaphysics* (*Ta meta ta physika*) are among Aristotle's most important works of theoretical philosophy; in the *Metaphysics* he defines reality as consisting not of transcendental ideas like Plato's Forms but of observable phenomena. Motion is a crucial concept in the rejection of Plato's thought, since it is this motion that changes matter from one form to another. Aristotle's moral philosophy, as delineated in *Nicomachean Ethics* (*Ethika Nikomacheia*) and *Eudemian Ethics* (*Ethika Eudemeia*), depends on the concept of the ethical mean, within which each virtue occupies a position between two extremes. His political philosophy declares constitutional democracy to be the best government, since it aims for the greatest good for all its citizens. Aristotle also developed a considerable body of literary criticism; among these works are his *Rhetoric* (*Techne rhetorike*) and *Poetics* (*Peri poietikes*). Prominent in these works is Aristotle's concept of mimesis, or imitation, by which art seeks not only to supplement nature but to represent it imitatively.

Most of Aristotle's surviving works, which were organized and catalogued by Andronicus of Rhodes, the last of the Lyceum's leaders, nearly three hundred years after Aristotle's death, are the texts of lectures that Aristotle gave at the Lyceum, a concentrated survey of various categories of human knowledge that have had a profound impact on Western and Eastern thought.

Armah, Ayi Kwei (1939–)

Ghanian novelist and journalist. Born in the western region of Ghana, Armah's career has taken him to three continents. Attending local schools and receiving his secondary education at Achimota College near Accra, Armah came to the United States in 1959, receiving a degree in sociology from Harvard University. Shortly after, he moved to Algiers and began working for the weekly *Révolution Africaine* as a translator. Later returning to Ghana, Armah taught English and wrote for Ghana Television, eventually enrolling in 1967 in the Graduate Writing Program at Columbia University. He subsequently joined the staff of *Jeune Afrique* (Young Africa), but soon left Paris in 1968, accepting professorships first in the U.S. and then in Tanzania. He has spent much of his later life in Senegal.

Known for his novels, short stories, and poems, Armah is famed for his venomous attacks on the leaders of Ghana, particularly of Prime Minister (1953–60), and later first president (1960–66), Kwame Nkrumah, for perpetuating what Armah saw as the corrupt and abusive practices of the colonial governments.

He is also known for the force and sweep of his prose, a sturdy complement to the power of his polemic. Best known for his three novels, *The Beautyful [sic] Ones Are Not Yet Born* (1968), *Fragments* (1970), and *Why Are We So Blest?* (1971), Armah critically examines the political and social elements of Ghanian society as the result of colonization, leaving readers with little optimism for future change. Armah's later novels, *Two Thousand Seasons* (1973) and *The Healers* (1978), become much more allegorical and less dependent on realistic detail, a noticeable shift from his earlier work.

Armstrong, Louis (1901–1971)

African-American jazz trumpeter, singer, bandleader, and entertainer. Known by various nicknames, including "Satchmo," "Satchel Mouth," "Dippermouth," and "Pops," Louis Armstrong was a jazz pioneer, renowned for his gravelly singing voice and expressive trumpet playing. He was also among the most imitated jazz musicians of his day, and has had a powerful influence on jazz instrumentalists and singers.

Armstrong grew up poverty-stricken in Storyville, the brothel district of New Orleans, where he was first exposed to music in local saloons, dance halls, and churches. After his release from the Colored Waifs' Home for Boys, where he played in a brass band and studied with Peter Davis, Armstrong was given a cornet and informal lessons by his idol, Joseph "King" Oliver. Becoming Oliver's protégé, Armstrong moved to Chicago to join Oliver's band in 1922, but soon left to join Fletcher Henderson and his band in 1924. Armstrong played and recorded with various groups throughout the 1920s, including his own Hot Five and Hot Seven recording groups (1925–28), and his wife Lillian "Lil" Hardin Armstrong's Dreamland Syncopators (1925–26). His innovations of that period were captured on such recordings as

"Potato Head Blues" (1927) and "Struttin' with Some Barbecue" (1927). The cornet was Armstrong's principal instrument until 1928, when he switched permanently to the trumpet.

The success of these recordings made Armstrong a celebrity; he toured extensively, traveling to Europe for the first time in 1932, where his nickname "Satchmo" was coined by an editor of *The Melody Maker*. By the 1940s Armstrong was internationally famous, appearing in films such as Bing Crosby's *Pennies from Heaven* (1936) and in Broadway musicals like *Hot Chocolates* (1929) and *Swingin' the Dream* (1939). By the time of his death, Armstrong was a musical legend, known to an international audience through his film appearances and his numerous musical tours through Africa, Asia, Australia, and South America with his New Orleans sextet, the All-Stars.

Arnold, Matthew (1822–1888)

English poet and critic. The son of Thomas Arnold, a well-known educational reformer, Matthew Arnold also took up the issue of societal reform in his writings. Though his poetry is lesser known than, and somewhat eclipsed by, that of his contemporaries Alfred, Lord Tennyson and Robert Browning, it is considered one of the finest embodiments of the Victorian predicament. In the famous poem "Dover Beach" (1867), Arnold uses the metaphor of the sea to recount modern society's crisis of faith. In "The Scholar Gypsy" (1853), he critiques the modern world in his retelling of the legend of an impoverished Oxford scholar who leaves the university to join a band of Gypsies.

Unlike the scholar of his poem, Arnold secured a position as an inspector of schools following his graduation from Balliol College, Oxford (1844), a position he held until shortly before his death. He wrote poetry through much of his early life and published several volumes. Shortly after his appointment to the professorship of poetry at Oxford in 1857, Arnold abandoned verse for prose. His critical work more thoroughly explored the themes introduced in his poems and became the most influential body of work in English and American criticism through the time of American poet T. S. Eliot (1888–1965). Arnold believed literature to be a powerful cultural force, the centerpiece of a democratic education. Accordingly, in his highly influential critical essay *Culture and Anarchy* (1869), he called for a revision of literary canons and for a shift in the class-specific participation that characterized Victorian England. He felt that the upper class had become too materialistic and argued for the conversion of the middle-class "Philistines" from what he termed "Hebraism," which had led them to narrow puritanical tastes, to "Hellenism," which he felt would revitalize high culture. Of his critical texts, other influential essays have been *On Translating Homer* (1861) and *Essays in Criticism* (1st series, 1865; 2nd series, 1888).

Artha-sastra

Indian treatise on political organization. From the Sanskrit, meaning "Science of Material Gain," the *Artha-sastra* is divided into 15 *adhikaranas* (sections) and 180 *prakaranas* (subjects), each of which are subsequently divided into 150 *adhyayas* (chapters). Focusing on the governing of a small kingdom through centralized control, the *Artha-sastra* outlines the proper role of the king, establishes criteria for the selection of ministers, provides guidelines for the waging of war, and suggests the use of an aggressive system of surveillance to maintain order.

Although most scholars agree that Kautilya (also known as Visnugupta or Chanakya), the chief minister to King Chandragupta, is the primary author of the text, questions have arisen about the full extent of his authority, and it appears unlikely that he himself was the direct author of each of the 150 chapters. Regardless, the *Artha-sastra* has greatly influenced the development of Indian statecraft, and is often compared with similar manuals written by Western philosophers, such as Plato's *Republic* or Machiavelli's *The Prince*.

In his play *Mudrakshasa* (*Minister Raksasa and His Signet Ring*), playwright Vasakadhatta (c. fifth century C.E.) dramatizes the relationship between Kautilya and his king. The drama contends that Kautilya was instrumental in the defeat and death of the Nanda king, ensuring the installation of King Chandragupta (322 B.C.E.), founder of the Maurya dynasty.

Arthurian legend

Collection of medieval stories and romances. Centered on the mythical medieval king Arthur, these stories became popular before the eleventh century in Wales. Little is known of the real Arthur, thought to have been a sixth-century Celtic chieftain who lived in Wales, save that he was fatally wounded in 537 in the Battle of Camlan and died in Glastonbury, England. There may have also been an archaic Celtic deity named Arthur from whom these legends arose.

While various stories exist surrounding the birth of Arthur, the adventures of his knights, and the relationship between his wife, Guinevere, and his most valiant knight, Sir Lancelot, it was the publication of Sir Thomas Malory's *Le Morte D'Arthur* (1485; *The Death of Arthur*) that established Arthur as king-hero in Britain. Renowned for his bravery, Arthur, in Malory's version, proves his right to the English throne by pulling the sword Excalibur from a block of stone. Equally famous for their brave and daring acts are a group of knights who sit at Arthur's Round Table and help him triumph over twelve princes led by Lot, the king of Norway.

The act of treason perpetrated against Arthur, the unraveling of his court, and the circumstances of his death vary. However, in the important fourteenth-century Arthurian poem *Sir Gawain and the Green Knight*, it is not Arthur's death but that of Sir Gawain (a knight of the Round Table) which marks the high point of the poem. In many versions of the legend, it is Guinevere and Modred, Arthur's nephew and most hated enemy, who cause Arthur's demise. Regardless of how it is resolved, the Arthurian myth remains a powerful theme in English literature and has been treated by many authors, including Alfred, Lord Tennyson in *Idylls of the King* (1867), T. H. White in his collected novels *The Once and Future King* (1958), and Mark Twain in *A Connecticut Yankee in King Arthur's Court* (1889).

Aryan

(Sanskrit for "noble people.") Ancient tribal group. The Aryans were a semi-nomadic pastoral people who settled in Iran and northern India around the second millennium B.C.E. Living in tribal societies and village communities, the Aryans were led by a rajah, or warrior chief. Indo-European languages of South Asia descend from the Aryan language, and in the nineteenth-century vernacular, Aryan became the synonym for both "Indo-European" and Indo-Iranian languages. Although properly a linguistic term popularized by the nineteenth-century philologist Max Müller, Indo-Aryan is often used to designate the early Indo-European-speaking people who entered the Indian subcontinent from Central Asia.

In a book published in 1854, the French writer Count Joseph Arthur, comte de Gobineau (1816–1882), developed the meaning of an Aryan "race." His best-known work, *Essai sur l'inéga-lité des races humaines* (1853–55; *The Inequality of Human Races*), defines the Aryan "race" as fair-skinned people who

speak Indo-European languages; Gobineau claimed that Aryans were responsible for all the progress mankind had ever achieved and were morally superior to the "Semites," "yellows," and "blacks." He identified Teutons as the purest modern representatives of the Aryans. Along with the political philosopher Houston Stewart Chamberlain (1855–1927), an English-born Germanophile, Gobineau popularized his racist theory; it aroused significant interest in Germany, where it was espoused by the composer Richard Wagner, among others. In the twentieth century, particularly through Chamberlain's *Die Grundlagen des neunzehnten Jahrhunderts* (1910; *The Foundations of the Nineteenth Century*), Gobineau's ideas became an integral part of Nazi racial theory. Chamberlain's book developed the political implications of Gobineau's thesis beyond sociological determinism, creating a discourse of race that influenced the Nazi movement of German dictator Adolf Hitler (1889–1945), who equated the Aryans with the Nordic race and used the theory to justify his persecution of Jews.

In India the concept of a separate Aryan "race" effectively disappeared with the advent of the Vedic age (1500 B.C.E.–C.E. 650) and the consolidation of the Hindu caste system. The original caste system was based on *varna* ("color") and distinguished between the fair-skinned Aryans and the darker-skinned Dasas. The Aryan tribes were divided into three caste positions: the Brahmans, or priests; the Kshatriyas, or warriors and rulers; and the Vaishyas, or businessmen. The lowest caste position included the Dasas. The process of Aryanization or Sanskritization refers to the assimilation of non-Aryan and Aryan peoples, with the general precept that non-Aryans emulated the "superior" Aryans more than the reverse.

Asante golden stool

A sacred relic of the Asante (also spelled Ashanti) people, who live in present-day Ghana. According to legend, during a violent thunderstorm, under the direction of Okomfo Anokye, the chief priest of the new kingdom, the heavens opened and a golden stool, *sika gwa*, was given to Osai Tutu, the unifier of the Asante nation in the eighteenth century. The stool, like much of Asante art, is made of wood and covered with gold leaf and various charms and ornaments. Believed to contain the spirit of the Asante nation, the king is lifted over the stool during his installation, or "enstoolment." Treated with the same respect shown to the king, the stool has its own palace and servants, and on the rare occasions when it is on public display, it travels like a chief, in its own palanquin.

Asante gold weights

Weights used in measurement. These weights, also called "brassweights," were used by the Asante (also spelled Ashanti) people in Ghana to weigh and measure gold dust. Created by a process known as lost-wax (more commonly known by the French term *cire perdu*), the weight is molded in wax, then encased in clay or earth. After the encasement dries, a hole or several holes are drilled into the top, forming canals through which the melted metal is poured. This process creates weights which were not only functional but also representational. Taking the symbolic form of animals, plants, and human figures (as well as abstract forms), brassweights were created for a commercial purpose, but became a way in which the Asante expressed and illustrated their culture through art.

Asé

A metaphysical concept central to the Yoruba religion as practiced in Nigeria, Benin, Brazil, Cuba, and Haiti. Asé (pronounced Ah-shay) literally means "Amen" or "So be it," although a more appropriate translation into a Western idiom might be logos, or "the breath of god." The concept exists in a variety of languages, including Spanish (*Aché*) and Portuguese (*Axé*).

Asé means "the power to bring things into existence," a concept fundamental to the Yoruba. Considered neither positive nor negative, Asé in its most simple terms means *power* and the ability to speak and make things happen—in essence, the "power of the word."

Ashkenazim

Jews of German origin. Taken from the medieval rabbinic Hebrew word for "Germany" (itself derived from "Ashkenaz," the name of Noah's eldest grandson, on the theory that some Jews migrated to Germany after the Flood), the Ashkenazim and the Sephardim (from the Hebrew word for "Spain") are the two branches of European Jewry. Although they concur on the major theological tenets of Judaism, each developed its own distinctive language, culture, and liturgical practices in the centuries of their geographic separation. Throughout the Middle Ages, the Sephardic Jews, largely due to the tolerance of the Islamic empire in its Golden Age, dominated European Judaism. By the seventeenth century, however, the fortunes of the two groups had reversed, and the Ashkenazim became far more influential in shaping modern Jewish culture. They spread out from Germany to France to Eastern Europe, adapting many of the characteristics of the surrounding society but maintaining their own language—Yiddish—and customs.

A new wave of persecutions in the closing decades of the nineteenth century forced massive numbers of Ashkenazic Jews to flee Eastern Europe. Many of them crowded into the Jewish quarters of Western European cities while millions immigrated to the United States, establishing New York as a major

Jewish cultural center. After the Second World War and the genocidal Nazi regime in Central Europe, many Ashkenazic Jews emigrated to Palestine and were instrumental in founding the Zionist state of Israel in 1948. Although their ranks had been decimated by the European atrocities, the Ashkenazim still outnumbered Sephardim in numbers of immigrants to Israel. Relations between the two groups have often been strained by their enormous cultural differences, and their religious traditions are both represented in the separate chief rabbinates in Jerusalem.

Ashoka (died c. 232 B.C.E.)

Indian emperor of the Maurya dynasty. Ashoka was the last major emperor in the Maurya dynasty of India, and his Rock and Pillar edicts provide most of the information known about him today. He reigned from 269 to 232 B.C.E. During his reign, Ashoka vigorously promoted Buddhism throughout India; he embraced Buddhism primarily due to his feelings of guilt after his violent conquest of the Kalinga country in the eighth year of his reign.

After conquering Kalinga, Ashoka renounced arms and embraced the *dharma* (principles of right life) in his daily life and as state policy, preaching it to all peoples. Ashoka maintained a general policy of respect toward all religions, speaking of Buddhism only to fellow practitioners. His belief in nonviolence, honesty, and benevolence led him to encourage people to live up to their own ideals without being adversely critical of others.

Ashoka attempted to bring about the practical application of *dharma* in his rule, seeking to strike compromises with his subjects rather than commanding them. His *dharma* ministers, whose duties were to relieve the suffering of the rural poor and the otherwise needy, were public servants in the truest sense. Ashoka himself toured the country, ordering that all public welfare concerns be addressed directly to him.

Until his death (and the subsequent disintegration of the Maurya empire), Ashoka's humanitarian services and tributes to Buddhism were at the core of his existence. Within the confines of the religion itself, Ashoka suppressed feuds and provided a course of scriptural studies for followers. In addition to the building of monasteries and *stupas* (burial mounds), tradition holds that Ashoka sent his own children to Ceylon as Buddhist missionaries. Ashoka's social utility programs included the construction of rest areas, watering sheds, and hospitals for people and animals. Although many of Ashoka's policies were later discontinued, the memory of his personal standards of benevolence survives to this day.

Asian heroism

Twentieth-century trend in Chinese-American literature. In an ongoing effort to debunk racist perceptions of the meek and effeminate Chinese-American male, several Chinese-American authors — led by Frank Chin and Jeffery Paul Chan — have identified and celebrated an Asian heroic tradition rooted in classic Chinese and Japanese works of literature such as *Sun-tzu ping fa* (sixth century; *The Art of War*); *San kuo chih yeni* (fourteenth century; *Romance of the Three Kingdoms*); and *Hsi-yuchi* (sixteenth century; *Journey to the West*). They promote characters who embody traditional Chinese male qualities like loyalty, revenge, and individual honor, situating them within a militant cultural tradition. According to writers like Chin and Chan, these heroic figures help dispel racist cultural myths that plague Chinese-American males, stereotypes that they are all timid, subservient, effeminate, and underendowed. These writers contend that Asian males in U.S. society were robbed of their masculinity by racist laws that prevented Chinese laborers from bringing their wives into the U.S. or marrying white women. They conceived the book *Aiiieeeee! An Anthology of Asian American Writers* (1974) as a project dedicated to recovering lost Chinese masculinity.

The new Asian heroism has received criticism from many Chinese-American women for its antagonistic relationship to Chinese-American feminism. Feminist critics agree that the Chinese-American male has suffered extensively because of racial discrimination and stereotypes, but point out that a reassertion of Chinese patriarchy simply replaces one oppressive structure with another. Maxine Hong Kingston's *China Men* (1980), while sympathetic to the plight of the Chinese-American male, scrutinizes the violence directed at women as a result of traditional "heroic" conventions of masculine behavior.

Assyria

Near Eastern culture in antiquity. The Assyrians were the inhabitants of the kingdom of northern Mesopotamia, the northernmost part of present-day Iraq, and established one of the greatest empires of the ancient Near East. Gaining its independence from Babylon in the fourteenth century B.C.E., Assyria soon became a major power in Mesopotamia, Armenia, and northern Syria. Although Assyrian power temporarily declined after the death of Assyrian ruler Tukulti-Ninurta I (c. 1208 B.C.E.), during the ninth century B.C.E. a period of expansion was begun by the Assyrian kings. For the next two hundred years, under the leadership of several strong Assyrian leaders, including Tiglathpileser III (c. 744–727 B.C.E.), Sargon II (c. 721–705), Sennacherib (c. 704–681), and Esarhaddon (c. 681–669), the mid eighth to the late seventh century B.C.E. marked a period in which much of the Middle East, from Egypt to the Persian Gulf, was united by the Assyrians.

Assyrian literature was taken primarily from Babylon or, at the very least, written in the Babylonian dialect. Only administrative and scholarly documents were written in Assyrian. An emphasis on art and architecture emerged under the rule of Ashurnasirpal II (c. 883–859 B.C.E.). A prominent form, the carving or painting of war and hunting scenes (typically accompanied by explanatory inscriptions), was borrowed from Anatolia. With the growing sophistication of Assyrian art came the increased use of enameled tiles in architecture. Most impressive was Kalakh, the royal palace, which would eventually become the cultural center of the empire. Decorated in elaborate murals, the palace walls displayed mythological scenes, fertility rites, and war pictures. Ashurbanipal, the last great Assyrian king, died in 627 B.C.E., and the Assyrian state was finally destroyed by a coalition of Medes and Chaldean tribes c. 614–609 B.C.E.

Asturias, Miguel Angel (1899–1974)

Guatemalan novelist and diplomat. The first Latin American writer to receive the Nobel Prize in Literature, Asturias was born in Guatemala City during the dictatorship of Manuel Estrada Cabrera. For political reasons, his family relocated to the small town of Salemá, where Asturias came into contact with marginalized descendants of the once powerful Maya Indians. In 1907 the Asturias family returned to Guatemala City, although Estrada Cabrera remained in power until 1920. Asturias's childhood among the rural peasantry and his adolescence in the capital, in an atmosphere of pervasive fear, provided the fund of materials from which nearly all his novels are drawn.

At the Universidad de Guatemala, Asturias joined the student movement against Cabrera's dictatorship, and shortly after receiving his law degree he left for London. Later studying the culture of the Mayan Quichés at the Sorbonne in Paris, Asturias became a disciple of the Surrealist movement fronted by André Breton. In Paris Asturias completed the critically acclaimed *Leyendas de Guatemala* (1930; *Legends of Guatemala*), a series of eight narratives and one allegorical play about the life and culture of the Mayas before the Spanish conquest.

After returning to Guatemala in 1933, Asturias began his diplomatic career in 1946, filling posts in Central and South America. In that year, he also published his most famous work, *El señor presidente* (1946; *Mr. President*), which he had begun in 1922. Most often read as a bold denunciation of the Estrada Cabrera dictatorship, the unnamed dictator in the novel is also persistently likened to an idol of the type worshiped by the Mayas. *Hombres de maíz* (1949; *Men of Maize*), which narrates the crisis in Indian culture precipitated by its contact with modern, "progressive" technology, followed in 1949. Next came the "banana cycle" novels: *Viento fuerte* (1950; *The Cyclone*), *El Papa verde* (1954; *The Green Pope*), and *Los ojos de los enterrados* (1960; *The Eyes of the Interred*), three books that document the exploitation of the Guatemalan fruit industry by American firms.

In 1966 the new government of President Julio Méndez Montenegro named Asturias ambassador to France and he was awarded the Soviet Union's Lenin Peace Prize; one year later he received the Nobel Prize in Literature. Asturias not only contributed to Latin American literature a workable style of mythological narrative, a device that would later be adopted by authors like Carlos Fuentes, but he also introduced Surrealism. *Mr. President* is considered to be a prototype of the "new" Latin American novel and the "magical realism" of writers like Gabriel García Márquez and José Donoso.

Atahualpa (c. 1502–1533)

Incan emperor. The last of the Incan emperors, Atahualpa's capture and execution by Spanish *conquistador* Francisco Pizarro secured Incan lands for the Spanish monarchy.

Son of Emperor Huayna Capac, Atahualpa was the last of the family of Incas to rule the united empire, its territory extending from present-day southern Colombia through Ecuador, Peru, Bolivia, and into northwestern Argentina and northern Chile. Although not the legitimate heir, Atahualpa seems to have been his father's favorite son, receiving the northern half of the empire at his father's death in 1528. Atahualpa's brother, Huáscar, received the southern half of the kingdom. This division eventually led to a civil war that ravaged the empire and culminated in 1532 with the defeat of Huáscar; that year also marked Francisco Pizarro's arrival in Peru with a force of approximately 180 men.

Pizarro reached Atahualpa's base at Cajamarca in 1532. Planning the emperor's capture, Pizarro invited the Incan ruler to the town's main square, where he had prepared an ambush. When Atahualpa refused to swear obedience to the king of Spain and to acknowledge Christianity as the "true" religion, Pizarro's men attacked, firing cannons and guns and charging with horses. Atahualpa's men were overwhelmed and he was taken prisoner. In an attempt to purchase his freedom, Atahualpa offered to fill his cell with objects made of silver and gold—twenty-four tons in all. The Spanish accepted the offering, but refused to release the Incan leader from their "protective custody" because Pizarro was outnumbered by Incan troops and feared for his safety. Atahualpa was later tried and convicted of conspiring against the Spanish and of causing the death of Huáscar. He was to be burned to death, but his sentence was commuted to execution by strangulation when, on the scaffold, Atahualpa agreed to accept Christianity and be baptized. After Atahualpa's execution, the two halves of the Incan empire were left without leadership, supremely vulnerable to the European invaders.

Atatürk (1881–1938)

Turkish soldier and statesman. The founder and first president of the Turkish Republic, Mustafa Kemal was given the name Atatürk (Father of the Turks) by the Turkish parliament in 1935. Born in Salonika (Thessalonika), then an Ottoman city, Atatürk entered military school in 1893 and continued his studies in Istanbul, where he graduated from the war academy in 1905. After a brief incarceration for his opposition to the Ottoman sultan Abdulhamid II (r. 1876–1909), Atatürk received a military assignment in Damascus, where he founded a revolutionary group among his fellow officers called "Fatherland and Freedom." Despite his radical credentials, Atatürk played only a minor role in the Committee of Union and Progress, the group that eventually overthrew Abdulhamid II in 1908.

Commissioned as a military attaché in Bulgaria during World War I, Atatürk distinguished himself as a soldier, particularly at the Battle of Gallipoli in 1915, one of the few Ottoman victories of the war, and became a national hero. When the armistice was signed in 1918, Atatürk, now a general, was incensed at the severity of the terms imposed on the Ottomans by the Allies. In opposition to both the Allied forces and his own sultan, Atatürk moved to northeastern Anatolia to begin his revolution in May 1919. By July he had convened a congress of Anatolian notables and mobilized a new army for the salvation of the country. In April 1920 he oranized the Grand National Assembly of Turkey, which elected him the speaker. This new parliament-in-exile rejected the Treaty of Sèvres signed by the sultan's government. As the commander in chief of the Turkish forces, Atatürk, in a struggle that lasted three years, rid the country of Allied troops, especially the Greek forces that had occupied İzmir (Smyrna) and western Anatolia. As head of the Grand National Assembly, he negotiated the Lausanne Treaty of 1923 that established Turkey's present borders. In October 1923 Turkey became a republic, with Atatürk as its first president.

Beginning an intense modernization campaign, Atatürk abolished the Ottoman sultanate and state religion, expelled the last caliph (the titular head of the Islamic community) in 1924, and introduced parliamentary government, albeit with a single-party system. He also established a new alphabet, state schools, and European-style civil, criminal, and commercial codes. The reforms even extended to clothing when Atatürk banned the veil and the fez, two symbols of the Ottoman past. In 1934 women were given the right to vote, and in the 1935 election seventeen women were elected to Parliament.

Atatürk's single-minded devotion and strength of purpose made him something of a despot. He was often ruthless in supressing opposition through special tribunal courts, as in the trial and punishment of the conspirators in an abortive plot on his life in 1926. By his death in 1938, however, Atatürk had succeeded in removing almost all of the social and administrative vestiges of the Ottoman empire and had established a secular republic.

Atrahasis, Epic of

Ancient Mesopotamian epic. Composed during the Old Babylonian period (1800–1600 B.C.E.), this tale closely parallels the Old Testament story of the Flood in Genesis, chapters 6–9. According to the text, when the seven great gods seized power, the remaining gods were forced to provide food for them. After a time, the lesser gods grew restless and rebelled. To quell the rebellion, Enki, the wisest of the seven gods, developed a plan to create human beings to do the gods' work for them. Humans multiplied and spread across the face of the earth, but in time the noise they made became so loud that the gods could not stand it. They sent plagues of famine and salt, to starve the humans and make the soil barren, in hopes of reducing their numbers. But humanity, with Enki's help, survived and continued to make noise. So the gods sent the Flood, the ultimate destruction, in order to wipe out the human race in a torrential storm. Enki ordered one man, Altrahasis, to build an ark for himself and his family. And with no more humans to gather food, the gods grew hungry and thirsty. They reluctantly decided to renew human life, but with new restrictions: barren women were created, along with a demon to cause stillbirths and infant mortality.

Atwood, Margaret [Eleanor] (1939–)

Canadian novelist and poet. One of Canada's most celebrated literary figures, Atwood was born in Ottawa, Ontario, into a proud Nova Scotian family. Atwood's creative versatility is evidenced by her ten volumes of verse, six novels, two children's books, and numerous short stories. A talented dramatist, cartoonist, and illustrator, Atwood has received her share of controversy as well as acclaim. While she unabashedly addresses such issues as cultural nationalism, feminism, and human rights in her writing, Atwood's works have demonstrated that she is, above all else, a talented stylist. In her first important collection of poetry, *The Circle Game* (1966), which received the Governor-General's Award, Atwood juxtaposes the pulsing, ceaseless flux of nature and the static, encrusted character of humankind's unnatural creations. In *Surfacing* (1972), her second novel, Atwood writes a book of self-discovery. With the Canadian wilderness as the novel's backdrop, *Surfacing*'s heroine must reconcile herself to her mythic past as she journeys into nature searching for her missing father. Perhaps the most controversial of Atwood's works is *Survival: A Thematic Guide to Canadian Literature* (1972). In this highly personal assessment, Atwood identifies victimization as a common theme in Canadian literature. Common fictional victims, according to Atwood, include women, families, artists, and animals. Her breakthrough novel, *The Handmaid's Tale* (1985), is an indictment of modern threats to freedom, including freedom of choice. Atwood's most recent novel, *The Robber Bride*, was published in 1993.

Augustine, St. (354–430)

Christian philosopher. Augustine (Latin name: Aurelius Augustinus) was born in North Africa, the son of a Christian mother and pagan father. Educated in Latin literature, he spent his early years teaching rhetoric in Rome and Carthage, and later Manichean philosophy in Milan. Through his association with St. Ambrose, bishop of Milan, Augustine became interested in Neo-Platonism and ultimately Christianity. He was baptized by Ambrose on Easter in 387 and returned to North Africa, where he led a monastic life devoted to theological studies. In 391 he was ordained, and became the bishop of Hippo four years later. Though he rarely left his diocese, his influence was widespread in the Christian world through the circulation of his letters, of which about 250 still survive. In them, as in his dialogues, St. Augustine championed Christianity over the Manichean, Pelagian, and Donatist sects of his day and developed theories of predestination and grace that were important to the later teachings of Roman Catholicism, as well as to the tenets of John Calvin, Martin Luther, and the Jansenists. Augustine is also well known for his autobiographical *Confessions*, in which he describes his conversion to Christianity and his regrets about his earlier non-Christian life, such as his lustful dealings with concubines. The most famous of his writings is the remarkable *De civitate Dei* (*City of God*), which describes how Christianity could provide a model for a new social order. *Retractions*, a later work, modifies some of his earlier views. St. Augustine was killed in 430, when Vandals sacked the city of Hippo. He remains an important figure in the theological development of the Christian Church.

Austen, Jane (1775–1817)

English novelist. One of the Western world's great novelists, Jane Austen created complex comedic and satirical portraits of everyday English middle-class life.

Born the seventh of eight children to a country pastor, Austen, as was common for eighteenth-century "ladies," spent her early life largely within her family circle. This web of family and friends in the small community of country clergy and minor landed gentry provided Austen with material for her novels. Although she was interested in entertaining her readers, her goal was not pleasure alone; as a moral writer, she was also concerned with proper conduct and judgment in relationships. Her sophisticated comedy is considered by some to be unsurpassed in the English novel.

Though the theme of marriage is central to Austen's work, she herself never married; there are numerous stories regarding her romantic associations, but most are unverified. (Her family censored or destroyed many of her personal letters after her death.) Nevertheless, Austen's large family and numerous nieces and nephews provided her with both company and a rapt audience for her novels-in-progress. Four novels were published anonymously in her lifetime and were well reviewed in English literary circles.

Austen's novel *Sense and Sensibility* (1811) was her first publication, although the novel she wrote first was "First Impressions" (which would become *Pride and Prejudice*). Finished in 1797 yet rejected by London publisher Thomas Cadell, *Pride and Prejudice* was published only in 1813. *Northanger Abbey* (written in 1797–98), a novel Austen said displayed the "opposite of the playfulness" of *Pride and Prejudice*, was published posthumously, along with *Persuasion*, in 1818. It was with the publication of these two works, after Austen's death, that her authorship was finally revealed in a biographical note by her brother, Henry Austen. Two other of her well-known novels are *Mansfield Park* (1814) and *Emma* (1815). Austen died from what is now known as Addison's disease.

Australian Aborigine

A member of the indigenous Australoid geographic race inhabiting Australia and Tasmania. Australian Aborigines (the word "aborigine" literally means "first inhabitant") were estimated to number between 300,000 and 1 million and encompassed five hundred or so language groups when white settlers arrived in the late eighteenth century and made Australia a British penal colony. Contact with European settlers has had a major impact on the Aboriginal way of life.

Archaeological finds indicate that Australia has been occupied for at least 60,000 years. Aborigines are believed to have migrated from Asia either by sea or by the now submerged Sahul Shelf, but it is uncertain whether they arrived in one wave or many.

Due to the dry climate and lack of animals suitable for herding, the Aborigines became hunter-gatherers whose main preoccupation was securing sources of fresh water. As numbers increased, subgroups detached themselves from the primary group to search for other waters. Ties between the original settlement and other descendant subgroups in the language-named group remained, however, with the main focus of the expanding "tribe" continuing to be the original watering place settled by the groups' ancestors. The preservation of this link between the founding group and its numerous descendants developed into a codified system of assumed kinship between groups within a large "tribe."

The principally nomadic Aborigines considered shortages in food and water to be the results of disturbances in the moral and social order of their lives. Totems of natural species were therefore integrated into Aboriginal rituals to incorporate them into the social system. The men of the clan were divided into lodges bearing the name of one or more of the adopted species in order to oversee the ritual interactions between man, animal, and ancestral heroes. However, only the old men were considered authorities on the Dreaming, or Dreamtime. This referred to an important creation myth that was reenacted through ritual to assure the continuation of human and animal existence.

Subjection to a bloody "pacification by force" in the nineteenth century, a difficult assimilation into urban life, dispossession, disease, and poverty have afflicted the Aborigines since the arrival of the European settlers. In 1986 Aborigines made up under 2 percent of the total Australian population, numbering fewer than 228,000. Their unemployment rate is more than six times the national average, while their average wage is half the national rate. Articulate Aboriginal groups in the south have emerged since World War II, urging integration with the European population while still attempting to retain their cultural identity.

avatara

Human or animal incarnation of Hindu divinities. According to the famous Hindu poem the Bhagavadgita (c. 200 B.C.E.), the *avatara* appears whenever *dharma* (virtue) is on the decline and *adharma* (sin) prospers. The literal translation from the Sanskrit, "descent," im-

plies both the descent of the god to earth and the decline in status inherent in the shift from godly to human or animal form.

According to Hindu scripture, the Hindu god Vishnu the preserver, part of the tripartite pantheon (with Brahman the creator and Shiva the destroyer), has already appeared in nine forms, or *avataras*, in order to restore cosmic order and worldly stability; it is believed Vishnu will appear in a tenth *avatara* sometime in the future. Each of Vishnu's appearances has an accompanying legend: for instance, it is said that Vishnu first appeared as a fish in order to save Manu Vaivasvata, the founder of the human race, from certain drowning. As Kalki, the final *avatara*, Vishnu will appear in human form astride a white horse, bringing an end to this age, punishing the corrupt and rewarding the virtuous.

The number and description of Vishnu's *avataras* vary according to regional preference; they include Matsya (fish), Kurma (tortoise), Varaha (boar), Narsimha (half man, half lion), Vamana (dwarf), Parasurama (Rama, the axwielder), Rama (hero of the *Ramayana* epic), Krishna (the divine cowherd), Buddha, and Kalki (the future incarnation).

In addition to its religious meaning, *avatara* has also developed a secular meaning. Avatar has come to mean the personification and embodiment in human form of abstract principles or intangible qualities.

Averroës, *see* Ibn Rushd

Avicenna, *see* Ibn Sînâ

Awolowo, Obafemi (1909–1987)

Nigerian statesman. The Yoruba chief Obafemi Awolowo, or "Awo," was an important leader in the tribal and political factions that formed the independent nation of Nigeria.

The son of a farmer, Awolowo was educated at great cost to his family. He studied at local mission schools, training to be a teacher after his father's death. But Awolowo soon became involved in Nigerian commerce, founding the Nigerian Produce Traders Association and assuming, in the late 1930s, the position of secretary of the Nigerian Motor Transport Traders Association. In 1943 Awolowo organized the Trades Union Congress of Nigeria, and the following year traveled to London to study law. There he established a Yoruba cultural and political group, the Egbe Omo Oduduwa, and published *Path to Nigerian Freedom* (1947), in which he argued for a federated government.

Law degree in hand, Awolowo returned to Nigeria in 1947, and was appointed general secretary of Egbe Omo Oduduwa in 1948. Awolowo helped found the Action Group, a political party identified with the Yoruba people, and led the government of the western region in the period leading up to independence in 1960. In the next few years the Action Group, originally moderate and pro-Western, turned hard left under the influence of younger, more radical party members. Late in 1962, in the wake of an embittered party split, Awolowo and several associates were charged with treason. He received a fifteen-year sentence and wrote *Thoughts on the Nigerian Constitution* (1967) while in Calabar prison. Freed by the new military government in 1966, Awolowo reentered the political scene as leader of the Yoruba-dominated western region of Nigeria. In 1967 he was appointed minister of finance, a post he held until 1971. His publications include *Awo: The Autobiography of Chief Obafemi Awolowo* (1960; republished in 1968 as *My Early Life*), *The People's Republic* (1968), and *The Strategy and Tactics of the People's Republic of Nigeria* (1970).

Ayers Rock

Aboriginal mythological and religious site in southwestern Northern Territory,

Australia. Referred to as "Uluru" by the regional Aborigines, the Yankuntjatjara and the Pitjantjatjara, this monolith, rising 1,100 feet above the ground, is considered the world's largest. In the shallow caves near its base are ancient rock carvings and paintings, which the Aborigines hold sacred. Oval in shape, the monolith is composed of arkosic sandstone and changes colors according to the position of the sun. It can be climbed via only one route.

The first European to see the monolith was Ernest Giles in 1872; the rock was named for Sir Henry Ayers, former South Australian premier. Official ownership of the rock was given to the Aborigines in 1985, though they have since leased both the rock and the area known as the Uluru National Park to the Australian government for the next ninety-nine years. The rock remains Australia's biggest single tourist attraction.

Aymará

South American Indian culture. Aymará denotes an Indian culture and language centered in the Bolivian and Peruvian highlands; it refers broadly to several different South American Indian groups who speak variations of Aymaran languages. The independent Aymará states, such as the Colla and the Lupaca, were subsumed into the Incan empire by the southern conquests of the emperor Viracocha around 1430. With the arrival of the Spanish *conquistadores*, the destruction of Aymará culture was essentially complete. The colonial agrarian economy was based on the systematic exploitation of the Aymará—they worked in the mines, as household servants, and on the coca plantations, hundreds of thousands dying in the colonial mines of Potosí and Carabaya. As a result, the Aymará participated in a rebellion against the Spanish that began in 1780 and continued until Peruvian independence in 1821. Transformed by their contact with the Incas, the Spanish, and modern capitalism, the Aymará today maintain a rich syncretic religion, supporting a class of magicians, diviners, medicine men, and witches, and melding native beliefs in the world of spirits with a Christian vision of the world hereafter.

Ayutthaya

Powerful Thai state. Ayutthaya (also spelled Ayudhya or Ayuthia) was founded by Ramathibodi I around 1350 in the rich rice plains of the Chao Phraya Basin, succeeding the Sukhothai empire in 1378. One of the most powerful kingdoms in Southeast Asia, the Ayutthaya regime was especially absorptive of the cultural and political traditions of its neighbors; Khmer, Mon, Burmese, and Chinese influences were profound. Khmer influence was particularly strong at the upper levels of society. In government, for example, the Sukhothai image of the "father-king" was replaced with the Khmer model of the "god-king." Accordingly, the kingship and social structure became more formal, ornate, and ceremonial. The king served as a divine intermediary, at the apex of a system of patronage in which every person fulfilled material and social obligations to someone above him, receiving in return his patron's protection. One could improve one's status by gaining the special favor of an important patron. This system of formal patronage was accompanied by the codification of principles of government and law, based on the Hindu and Khmer systems.

Militarily, Ayutthaya was united and strong, capable of resisting moves by the Khmer, Angkor, and Burma, although it borrowed heavily from all of those states. China, a trading partner, provided luxury goods and a definition of affluence. Theravāda Buddhism, introduced through Sri Lanka, was the chief religion in Ayutthaya society—Buddhism was as central to Ayutthaya as it had been to Sukhothai. The Buddhist monasteries were educational centers, home to philosophy, literature, and the fine arts. It was in this religious sphere that the influence of Khmer and Indian cultures on Ayutthaya was most apparent. The state of Ayutthaya came to an end in 1767 with the Burmese invasion of the Myanmar, in which much of the prized art, architecture, and literature of the kingdom was destroyed.

Azad, Maulana Abul Kalam (1887–1958)

Leader in the Indian independence movement. The son of a Muslim refugee and an Arab woman, Azad was born in Mecca and raised and educated privately in Calcutta. At age twelve, he commenced what would prove to be a long career in journalism with the publication of his first article. In 1912, having served in various editorial capacities at several papers, Azad founded his own weekly Urdu paper, the *Al-Hilal*. A bold thinker, he was a critic of cooperation with the British as well as the separation of Muslims and Hindus in the struggle; in the pages of *Al-Hilal* he called upon Indian Muslims to join in the fight for Indian independence. His radical views led to the suppression of the journal by the British authorities in 1914, when he received the first of many prison terms. While in prison, Azad prepared the first draft of a translation and commentary upon the Qur'ân.

In 1923 Azad was elected president of the Indian National Congress, the youngest person ever to hold the office. Elected again in 1940, he continued to serve until June 1946. During his second term as president he undertook negotiations with the British to secure Indian independence. After the achievement of an independent India in 1947, Azad worked as education minister in Nehru's cabinet, championing educational reform. His book, *India Wins Freedom*, was published posthumously in 1959.

al-Azhar

Cairo's first congregational mosque and one of the world's oldest functioning universities. The mosque of al-Azhar lies at the heart of the old section of Cairo, the Egyptian city founded in 969 C.E. by the Fatimid caliph al-Mu'izz.

Shi'ite Fatimids, who claimed descent from the Prophet Muhammad through his daughter Fātima, came to conquer Egypt from Tunisia in North Africa. Having already established relations with the West, they waged war against Byzantium, and occupied Sicily. Forsaking the old Arab-Islamic capital, al-Fustât, they founded a new royal city, al-Qâhira (Cairo), meaning "The Victorious," to rival the capital of the Islamic 'Abbâsid dynasty at Baghdad.

The cultural efflorescence brought to Egypt by the Fatimids is evident in the artistic works of the era, many of which are now housed in Western treasuries like the Cathedral of St. Mark in Venice. Most of the great works of Fatimid architecture no longer stand. Al-Azhar itself has been massively altered, expanded, and restored over the centuries; only a few original details, including some decorative stucco work and window grilles, have survived. The mosque at al-Azhar, however, has always been more than a cultural treasure. By 989 C.E. it had become a major center of theological learning, training many of the missionaries responsible for spreading Fatimid beliefs. It was, therefore, a natural target for the ambitious Syrian commander and eventual vizier in Egypt, Saladin, who in 1171 C.E. defeated the Fatimid caliphate, razed much of Cairo, and abolished Friday prayers and teaching from al-Azhar.

The ensuing century marks the only period in which al-Azhar was not put to use as a religious and teaching establishment. When prayers and lessons were resumed in 1287, they followed the Sunnî system reinstated by Saladin.

Since then, al-Azhar has remained the preeminent Sunnî institution in the world for the teaching of the Islamic religious sciences (as well as a modernized curriculum in the natural and social sciences), and has served as the custodian of Arabic language and literature. To be a *shaykh*, or teacher, at al-Azhar is to become a sort of cultural and spiritual elder, articulate and persuasive but mindful of precedence and submissive to *ijmâ'*, the consensus of the leaders of the community. To this day the al-Azhar plays an important role in shaping Islamic law and suggesting answers to the new and complex problems faced by Muslims on the cusp of the twenty-first century.

Azikiwe, [Benjamin] Nnamdi (1904–1996)

Nigerian president. An Igbo from western Nigeria, Azikiwe was educated at mission schools in Lagos. He clerked briefly for the treasury in Lagos, then left Nigeria in 1925, a stowaway on a ship bound for the United States. In the States he studied history and political science while supporting himself as a coal miner, casual laborer, dishwasher—even as a boxer. While a graduate student at the University of Pennsylvania, he became familiar with Marcus Garvey and the "Back-to-Africa" movement.

Azikiwe published *Liberia in World Affairs* in 1934, when he moved to Ghana and became editor of the *Africa Morning Post*. He returned to Nigeria in 1937, joined the Nigerian Youth Movement's executive committee, and started a chain of newspapers, including the *West African Pilot* and four other journals. Azikiwe was appointed secretary-general of the Nigerian National Council in 1944, and later appointed president. As the nationalist political movement gained strength, Azikiwe figured prominently. He was unanimously elected the first president when Nigeria became a republic in 1963. In 1966 he was removed from office by a military coup but he returned to Nigeria after the fall of the Biafran state to serve as chancellor of the University of Lagos. Azikiwe's other publications include *Renascent Africa* (1937).

Aztecs

Meso-American Indian people. Much is known of the pre-encounter Aztec culture, due to the detailed accounts of their history and culture compiled by Bernardino de Sahagun, a Franciscan priest who arrived in Mexico in 1520 and learned the native language, Náhuatl. For thirty years, between 1547 and 1577, Sahagun listened as Aztec nobles and priests told countless stories, revealing the religious, scientific, political, domestic, and economic life of the Aztec people. Sahagun's reconstruction of their stories, written in both Spanish and Nahuatl, is known as the *Historia general de los cosas de Nueva España* (1547–77; *History of Ancient Mexico*).

From their origins in Aztlán (the White Land), the Aztecs came to conquer the Toltec civilization of central Mexico. Betraying their nomadic forefathers, the Chichimec group of tribes, the Aztecs became farmers. They experimented boldly in agriculture and irrigation, transforming what remained of the Toltec cities into vast urban centers. At its apex, the Aztec empire extended over a territory stretching from central Mexico to the Yucatán, a kingdom to rival the Incas in Peru.

Aztec society was highly stratified and comprised three major castes: the *pipiltin* (nobility), *macehual* (commoner class), and *mayeques* (serfs, pawns, and slaves). Serfs were attached to private or state-owned estates and were distinct from pawns, who sold themselves or members of their family for a set period of time, like indentured servants. Slaves were employed as workers, but were often treated as expendable wealth and sacrificed in religious ceremonies. Noble elders, responsible for education,

taught poetry and songs to the young, and priests served as intermediaries between the gods and man, performing all ceremonies and sacrifices. Aztec society valued conformity and severely punished those who deviated from its norms. Adultery, theft, and murder were all punishable by death, as was disobedience on the battlefield. Gender roles, too, were clearly defined: men worked hard in the fields and women cared for the home and family. Women could own property, take cases to court, and participate in business contracts, but had significantly fewer rights than men. Aztecs married within their social class and lineage groups, and polygamy was common practice among the nobility. When Spanish conquistador Hernán Cortés (1485–1547) took the Aztec capital, Tenochtitlán, in 1521, effectively ending the Aztec civilization, his victory was aided by those who had long been oppressed by the strictures of Aztec society.

Considering themselves the chosen people of the war god Huitzilopochtli, the Aztecs called themselves "People of the Sun." According to their creation myth, Four Suns existed before the present world of the Fifth Sun, a world that would end in cataclysm. In order that this sun would not disappear, Aztecs were to nourish the sun with blood and hearts, spilled in human sacrifice. Slaves, usually captured in war, were sacrificed on the steps of the great Aztec temples. Cannibalism also played a part in Aztec religious practice.

The Tonalpohualli, the divinatory calendar stone derived from the Mayan calendar, was believed to entirely determine Aztec destiny. The solar year was made up of eighteen months, each comprising twenty days and five additional "unlucky" days. Time was further divided into fifty-two-year cycles. The cycles were associated with the Aztec and Mayan belief in the periodic destruction and genesis of the universe; at the end of a cycle, household utensils and idols were replaced, temples were renovated, and great sacrifices were made to the sun. The calendar also predicted the precise date of the great cataclysm, the giant earthquake the Aztecs expected would bring an end to the world of the Fifth Sun.

Azuela, Mariano (1873–1952)

Mexican writer. Like many of his contemporaries, Azuela was heavily influenced by the Mexican revolution of 1910, helping to create what has become known as the genre of the "novel of the Mexican revolution." Spending his earlier years studying at a seminary, Azuela eventually left the seminary in 1889 and entered medical school at the University of Guadalajara. It was while practicing medicine that Azuela began to first publish under the pseudonym "Beleno." As an escape from his medical practice, Azuela continued to write, producing his first novel, Los fracasados (1908; The Failures). Although the novel did not receive wide attention, Azuela was encouraged by other writers to continue.

His writing soon became more political. After the government's collapse in 1913, Azuela joined the unsuccessful revolutionary forces of Julian Medina, and was forced to immigrate to Texas. There he published his best-known work, Los de abajo (1915; The Underdogs), consid-ered to be perhaps the greatest novel of the Mexican revolution. Ostensibly written by the campfire during forced marches, the novel describes the horrors of the revolution. It was first published as a newspaper serial, and its literary merit went unacknowledged until its rediscovery a decade later; it remains an influential novel of social protest.

In 1916 Azuela returned to Mexico City. Registering his discontent with revolutionary politics, he wrote several novels, including Las tribulaciones de una familia decente (1918; The Trials of a Respectable Family), in which he criticized the new regime and empathized with the lower classes. In later works, Azuela experimented with stylistic devices that were later adopted by the "new novel." These include La malhora (1923; The Evil Hour), El desquite (1925; Revenge), and La luciérnaga (1932; The Firefly).

After retiring from medicine in 1943, Azuela began a career as a lecturer on Mexican, French, and Spanish novelists. He was named a member of the Colegio National in 1943 by Mexican president Manuel Ávila Camacho; in 1949 he was awarded the Mexican National Prize for literature, and was considered by many to be the foremost Mexican novelist until his death in 1952.

B

Baal

Canaanite god of weather and fertility. "Baal" is the generic Semitic word for "lord" or "possessor" and was often used as a prefix to denote lordship or divinity. The Canaanite Baal is perhaps most widely symbolized as the golden calf outlawed by the Israelites in the Old Testament of the Hebrew Scriptures. Moses and Elijah, bitter foes of the graven image, made Baal synonymous with "false god." In fact, the Old Testament prophets seem to have misread the significance of the golden calf. The calf was a sacred animal upon which the gods, including Baal, stood, but the calves were not actual objects of veneration.

Recently unearthed at Ugarit (in present-day Syria) was the Canaanite *Poem of Baal*, which probably dates to well before the fourteenth century B.C.E. The poem describes Baal's successful quest to become king of the gods, his struggle against his rivals Yam (the god of the sea) and Mot (the god of death and the underworld). After defeating Yam in a fierce battle, Baal reigns over both weather and agriculture. He builds a great palace on earth, set with enormous windows: when Baal opens them, the rains fall from heaven, irrigating the earth. Secure in his rule, Baal sends a message to Mot, refusing tribute to the dark god. The cunning Mot invites Baal to the underworld for a banquet. Baal agrees to attend, though he undertakes elaborate ritual precautions: he smears his body with red ocher to ward off demons and copulates with a heifer eighty-eight times, in order to gain strength. Still, Baal and his henchmen disappear into the gullet of Mot, literally the belly of the underworld, and the earth is threatened by a great dryness. Anat, Baal's sister and consort, counterattacks, slicing Mot into pieces and sowing his sundered limbs in the fields. The freed Baal summons the rains and restores fertility to the land, the enmity between Baal and Mot providing a mythical explanation for the seasons, the annual cycle of fecundity and want.

In addition, the *Poem of Baal* also elucidates some of the more obscure passages in the Old Testament. Parts of Joel and Zephaniah, for example, satirize Canaanite myth and ritual, and in Isaiah, Yahweh (Hebrew for "God") is credited with slaying the dragon of the oceans, a feat suspiciously similar to that of Baal. There are also obvious parallels with Greek mythology. The triumvirate of Air, Water, and Earth—Baal, Yam, and Mot—align closely with Zeus, Poseidon, and Hades.

Baal Shem Tov (c. 1700–1760)

Principal founder of Hasidism. Literally translated from the Hebrew as "Master of the Good Name," Baal Shem Tov led the Hasidic movement, a popular Jewish spiritualist movement opposed to secularization and Jewish rationalism. Born Israel Ben Eleizer, Baal Shem Tov was a popular healer and noted holy man who founded a spiritual community following a series of messianic revelations and visions in the 1730s. Scorning the strict asceticism of many other Jewish leaders, Baal Shem Tov took his message to the common people, dressing simply and preaching in the marketplace. He defended his unorthodox lifestyle to his critics as a "descent for the sake of ascent."

He spent years as an itinerant preacher, spreading his message throughout Poland and Lithuania. After his death, his disciples, including his grandson, Rabbi Baruch of Medzhibozh, continued to disseminate Hasidism. Another pupil, Rabbi Jacob Joseph of Polonnoye, recorded many of Baal Shem Tov's teachings, which were extremely popular among eighteenth-century Jews. They stressed the holiness of everyday life and the conviction that mortification of the body and extreme self-denial were not necessary aspects of a devout life.

Although Hasidism began as a dynamic spiritual movement, by the late nineteenth century it had become increasingly institutionalized. Whereas Baal Shem Tov's vision was criticized as unorthodox, twentieth-century Hasidism has become an essentially conservative orthodoxy.

Babel, Isaac [Emmanuilovich] (1894–1941)

Russian short-story writer and playwright. Lauded for his portrayal of the Jewish gangster world of Odessa in *Odesskie rasskazy* (1931; *The Odessa Tales*) and of his experiences in the Russian Civil War in *Konarmiia* (1926; *Red Cavalry*), Babel enjoyed enormous fame in the early 1930s until both he and his work fell victim to the purges of Soviet Communist leader Josef Stalin.

Babel was born into a Jewish family in Odessa. Inspired by the favorite writings of his youth, those by French writers Flaubert and Maupassant, he published his first stories, some of which were later included in *The Odessa Tales*, in a St. Petersburg journal edited by Maxim Gorky. Though the czarist censors labeled Babel's stories obscene, Gorky was impressed by the young writer's talent and encouraged him to seek out new experiences. Babel followed Gorky's advice, joining the Red Army in the Russian Civil War that followed the Bolshevik Revolution of 1917. Babel's experiences as a soldier and correspondent on the Polish front in 1920–21 led to the stories contained in *Red Cavalry*, a collection of impressions and images of startling intensity, akin to Ambrose Bierce's depiction of the American Civil War. The often humorous stories contained in *The Odessa Tales*, collected in 1931, provide a touching and somewhat romanticized picture of the Jewish underworld in Odessa. A meticulous and demanding craftsman, Babel revised his stories obsessively; some of them exist in more than twenty versions. He also wrote plays, including *Zakat* (1928; *The Sunset*), a gloomier portrayal of Jewish life in Odessa, featuring many of the same characters of *The Odessa Tales*. Babel's popularity waned in the mid-1930s, as Stalinist cultural policies were codified and the incessant triumphalism of Socialist Realism became the order of the day. His last published work, a tribute to his patron Gorky, appeared in 1938. He was arrested in 1939 and died shortly thereafter, though it is unclear whether he was executed or died of "natural" causes, like so many others languishing in Soviet labor camps. After Stalin's death, Babel was "rehabilitated" and his works were free to circulate once again.

Babi Yar

Site of a massacre during Second World War. At Babi Yar (also spelled Baby Yar), a large ravine on the northwest edge of the city of Kiev, more than 150,000 people were killed by Nazi SS squads between 1941 and 1943 during the occupation of Ukraine; the victims were primarily Jews, but also included Soviet prisoners of war, Ukrainian nationalists, and Gypsies. One of the first actions taken by the Nazis after the fall of Kiev was to round up Soviet Jews and mark them for death. The first mass execution took place over a thirty-six-hour period on September 29–30, 1941, when nearly 34,000 Jews were forcibly marched to Babi Yar, stripped, and gunned down into the ravine, which was immediately covered; many of the victims were buried alive. Babi Yar was then encircled with barbed wire and declared a restricted zone, though it continued to operate as a sort of mass internment center. As the German armies retreated from the Soviet Union, the Nazis attempted to destroy evidence of the slaughter; the bodies were exhumed by labor-camp inmates and burned in great pyres. After the war, Babi Yar acquired an expressly political significance, especially in the context of officially sanctioned anti-Semitism in the U.S.S.R. The tragedy of Babi Yar was brought to world attention by the 1961 publication of Yevgeny Yevtushenko's powerful *Babi Yar*, a poem that was eventually set to music by Dmitri Shostakovich as part of a choral symphony first performed in Moscow in 1962. Both artists were subsequently criticized by the Soviet government, which refused to acknowledge the specifically Jewish significance of Babi Yar, insisting instead that the event was a tragic instance of fascist violence against heroic Communist resisters; the Babi Yar memorial, unveiled in 1976, made no reference to the Jewish annihilation. In 1991, the year of Babi Yar's fiftieth anniversary, Soviet president Mikhail Gorbachev made a major speech commemorating the Jewish tragedy and attacking the state-sponsored anti-Semitism that had suppressed knowledge about Babi Yar and the Holocaust.

Babylonia

Ancient civilization of Mesopotamia. Babylonia was the region in southeastern Mesopotamia between the Tigris and the Euphrates rivers (present-day southern Iraq), comprising the kingdoms of Sumer and Akkad. It was bounded in ancient times by Elam in the east, the Persian Gulf in the southeast, the Arabian Desert in the south and west, and Assyria in the north. Before gaining the name "Babylonia," the region was called Sumer and Akkad, and under the Kassites, Karduniash. The el-Obeid and Warka periods (c. 3600–3000 B.C.E.) represent the beginning of settled culture in Babylonia proper. Around 2000 B.C.E., the Amorites, a group of Semitic tribes, came to power, establishing Babylon as a political, cultural, and commercial center of the Near East. Under the reign of Hammurabi (c. 1792–1750 B.C.E.), the empire grew to encompass all of southern Mesopotamia and part of Assyria. Hammurabi's Code, adumbrated during this period, is the most famous ancient Near Eastern set of laws.

After Hammurabi's death, the Amorite empire endured until 1595 B.C.E., when Kassite invaders established a new dynasty. Religion and literature flourished under the Kassites; the *Enuma elish*, the Babylonian creation epic, was probably written during this time. The Assyrians succeeded in establishing their independence from Babylonia at this time as well; attacks from the Elamite empire would later occasion the fall of the Kassite dynasty (c. 1157 B.C.E.).

In the twelfth century B.C.E., a new line of Babylonian kings emerged, establishing the second dynasty of the City of Isin. Among the rulers of this dynasty, Nebuchadnezzar I (reigned c. 1124–1103 B.C.E.) is particularly well known; he defeated the Elamites, another rival empire, and held the Assyrians at bay for many years.

Following Nebuchadnezzar's death came a period of decline, marked by alternating skirmishes and alliances with Assyria. After the death of Nabu-Nasir

(r. 747–734 B.C.E.), an uprising of Babylonian Chaldeans prompted Tiglathpileser III (r. 744–727 B.C.E.) to seize Babylon. After a century of Assyrian rule, the Chaldeans took control of the area under the rule of Nabopolassar (r. 625–605 B.C.E.). His son, Nebuchadnezzar II (reigned c. 605–562 B.C.E.), led the empire to its last great period by rebuilding the capital city and the Temple of Marduk. Nebuchadnezzar is probably best known for his destruction of Judah and Jerusalem in 587 B.C.E. and the ensuing Babylonian Captivity of the Jews, and his construction of the Hanging Gardens, one of the Seven Wonders of the World.

Babylonia fell without a struggle to the Persians c. 539 B.C.E. and, with the destruction of Babylon's walls in 514 B.C.E., it ceased to exist as an independent entity. In the year 331 Alexander the Great arrived, attempting to make Babylon the capital of his empire. He failed, and his death, in the palace of Nebuchadnezzar, was the epitaph to Babylonia's importance in world history.

Bach, Johann Sebastian (1685–1750)

German composer. Born into a family of musicians, Bach took his first lessons on the violin from his father, Johann Ambrosius. Orphaned at the age of ten, he left his birthplace of Eisenach, moving to Ohrdruf to live and study keyboard playing with his eldest brother, Johann Christoph. Bach began his professional career as an organist at churches in Arnstadt and Mühlhausen from 1703 to 1708. During this period he wrote prolifically for the organ, the complexity and heavy ornamentation of his chorale preludes, sonatas, toccatas, and preludes bringing him into conflict with pietistic congregations in both towns.

Called to Weimar in 1708 to serve as court organist to Duke Wilhelm Ernst, Bach developed a mastery of international styles and genres. After nine years—and a brief internment by the duke, who was reluctant to lose him—

he went to Cöthen as Prince Leopold's musical director. There, largely free of church duties, he concentrated on composing for the extraordinary court orchestra (of which the prince himself was a member). Over the next five years Bach wrote his greatest instrumental and orchestral works, including his solo violin partitas and sonatas, the six *Brandenburg Concertos* (1711–20), and the first part of the *Das Wohltemperierte Clavier* (c. 1722; *The Well-Tempered Clavier*), a magisterial set of keyboard preludes and fugues for beginners. While at the court, his wife (and cousin), Maria Barbara Bach, died suddenly, and within a year he took a second wife, Anna Magdalena Wilcken. From these two marriages came twenty children, many of whom went on to become musicians in their own right.

After 1721, Prince Leopold's new wife (and cousin), a princess of Anhalt-Bernberg, was able to discourage her husband from devoting so much time and money to music-making. Disgruntled, Bach resigned from the court in 1723 and assumed the prestigious position of cantor and musical director at St. Thomas's Church, Leipzig, where his children could be educated in a more conventionally Lutheran environment. Responsible for the production of a weekly cantata and many occasional and holiday pieces, Bach redirected his efforts to church music. Most of his nearly three hundred church cantatas date from his first five years in Leipzig. This period included the composition of four large sacred masterpieces: the *St. John Passion* (1724), the *St. Matthew Passion* (1727), the *Mass in B Minor* (1747–49), and the *Christmas Oratorio* (1734–35). In his last years, Bach concentrated on abstract and technically grueling pieces, such as the *Goldberg Variations* (1742) and the *Musical Offering* (1747).

Thoughout the 1740s, Bach suffered from tremendous eye trouble and ultimately became blind. Although he underwent numerous eye operations, by 1749 he was unable to work any longer. During his lifetime, Bach's primary fame was as an organist, his work as a composer often overlooked. Though his works were appreciated by a handful of successors, including Austrian composer Mozart, it was not until the revival of the awe-inspiring *St. Matthew Passion* by German composer Felix Mendelssohn (1809–1847) in the nineteenth century that Bach's vast achievement as a composer came to the fore.

Bada'uni, 'Abd al-Qadir (1540–c. 1615)
Persian historian. An orthodox Sunnî Muslim, Bada'uni was appointed to a religious post at the court of the Mughal emperor Akbar in 1574. Under Akbar's commission, Bada'uni wrote many works, including the *Kitâb al-Hadîth*, the sayings of the Prophet Muhammad; a section of the *Tārīkh-e alfī* (*History of the Millennium*); and a translation of the historian Rashid ad-Din's *Jāmi'āt-tawārīkh* (*Universal History*). Bada'uni is perhaps most famous for his *Muntakhab ut Tavarikh* (*Selection from History*), a history of the Mughal empire in Muslim India and its prominent figures. Also known as *Tārīkh-e Badā'ūnī* (*Bada'uni's History*), this work contains a bold attack on Akbar and certain of his nonorthodox religious practices, including harsh criticism for Bada'uni's forced translation by Akbar of Hindu texts such as the *Ramayana* and the *Mahabharata* from Sanskrit into Persian. *Bada'uni's History* is often read as a corrective to the *Akbarnama*, a cheerleading tribute to the emperor written by Emperor Akbar's official court historian and brother, Abu'l Fazl.

Baeck, Leo (1873–1956)
Jewish religious leader. Baeck is best known as a reformist rabbi and theologian, a liberal Jewish philosopher, and the spiritual leader of German Jewry during the Nazi persecution. Even as a

newly ordained rabbi, Baeck exhibited a stubborn independence. When a Protestant theologian claimed that Christianity had no historical links with Judaism, Baeck refuted him in a sharp and controversial treatise of his own, *Das Wesendes Judentums* (1905; *The Essence of Judaism*). Baeck insisted on the dynamic, evolutionary character of religious development. The text was a tour de force, and established Baeck's reputation as a leading liberal Jewish thinker.

Baeck had many critics among both traditional Jews and Christians for his assertion that Jesus Christ was a profoundly Jewish figure. They also resisted his call in *Das Evangelium als Urkunde der judischen Glaubensgeschichte* (1938; *The Gospel as a Document of Jewish Religious History*) to place the Gospels on a level with classic rabbinical texts. Baeck's final philosophical works were indelibly marked by his years spent in the Theresienstadt concentration camp. *Dieses Volk; Jüdische Existenz* (1955; *This People Israel: The Meaning of Jewish Existence*), mostly written at Theresienstadt, ties his earlier philosophical ideas to the ongoing experiences of the Jewish people. Remarkably hopeful, Baeck displays his faith in humanity.

As well as a great teacher and thinker, Baeck was an active and committed leader, attempting always to live according to his own principles regardless of the risks. Together with Otto Hirsch (1885–1941), the jurist and community leader killed in the concentration camp of Mauthausen, Baeck led the National Agency of Jews in Germany, an umbrella organization established in 1933 to counter the growing Nazi threat to German Jewry. They dispensed millions of dollars each year to encourage emigration and ease the lot of those who chose to stay in Europe. The group was severely criticized after the war; some critics, including Hannah Arendt, claimed that Baeck and his followers willfully misled Jews into believing that the concentration camps were simply detention centers, rather than slaughterhouses. They charge that countless Jews would have resisted, fought, or run away had they known what awaited them. Baeck defended himself weakly, arguing that he did not wish to deny hope to the victims, false though it was.

Nevertheless, Baeck's judgment, not his integrity, should be questioned. Throughout the 1930s his negotiations with the Nazis made it possible for many German Jews to escape. In 1939 he led a group of Jewish children to safety in England and immediately returned to Germany. Arrested five times before finally being thrown into the Theresienstadt concentration camp, Baeck managed to surmount the horrors of life in the camp, lecturing his fellow prisoners on the philosophies of such thinkers as Kant and Plato. Baeck was spared execution by the Russian liberation of Theresienstadt in 1945, and his first act as a free man was to prevent the murders of his former jailers.

baggataway

Modern sport, developed by American Indians before the arrival of Europeans. Originally called *baggataway* (and now known as lacrosse), the game was played by the Six Nations of the Iroquois, with two teams carrying crosses, long-handled racket-like implements made of hickory and bent on the end, forming a hook with net strung in between, to carry and throw a ball. The game was considered to be a form of training for combat, and was preceded by dances and sacred rituals.

The original game was much more violent than the present version, the sides composed of sometimes hundreds of players, the goals miles apart, and the games sometimes lasting for three days. The players' first responsibilities were to disable as many of the opposing players as possible, then to concentrate on car-

rying the ball and scoring a goal. The Cherokee called their version "little brother of war," because of the endurance and fortitude it developed in the players. When the French saw the sticks, they thought their shape similar to a bishop's crozier and named the game *la crosse*.

Europeans in Canada first learned the game in 1840, and for many years the best competition was from the Indians. The game was standardized by George Beers of Montreal, and declared the national game of Canada in 1867. Lacrosse was included in the Olympic Games in 1904 and 1908, but there was insufficient worldwide interest to maintain it as an Olympic sport. Beginning in the mid-1950s, lacrosse grew popular in the United States and Canada from elementary school through college and even club competition. In 1970 the NCAA (National Collegiate Athletic Association) began sponsoring intercollegiate competition and championships.

Bahá'í

Persian-derived universalist religion. Bahá'í was founded in the nineteenth century by the Persian mirza Hoseyn Ali Nuri (1817–1892), known as "Bahá' U'lláh" (Arabic for "Glory of God"). Bahá' U'lláh was an adherent of Babism, a nineteenth-century Persian religious sect that offered an alternative path to discovering Islamic truth. In the mid-1860s he proclaimed himself the *avatara* (reincarnated spirit) of God on earth predicted by Báb (1819–1850), the founder of Babism, who had been executed in 1850 and whose sect officially broke with Islam in 1848. The followers of the Bahá'í faith believe that Bahá' U'lláh was the latest of the divine manifestations that included the prophets Jesus, Muhammad, Zoroaster, and the Buddha. The eldest son of Bahá' U'lláh (1844–1921), 'Abd al-Bahá (Servant of the Glory), became his father's doctrinal interpreter.

Bahá' U'lláh left more than one hundred works, which he said were God's revelation. Central to his doctrine are the unity of religion and the unity of humankind, the goal of world peace through education, and the equality of men and women. The Bahá'í have no clergy, no sacraments, and no initiation ceremony; services consist of readings from sacred texts of all religions and are open to all faiths. Daily prayer is urged, as is attendance at the gathering for the Nineteen-Day Feast on the first day of the nineteen-month calendar established by Bāb. Other strictures include fasting for nineteen days a year, abstaining from drugs and alcohol, and practicing monogamy. The church also advocates an international government and language. In practice, local spiritual assemblies elect national spiritual assemblies, which in turn elect the supreme governing body, the Universal House of Justice. The desire to abolish competition among religions and discrimination based upon race, gender, or class has proven particularly attractive to some followers and has contributed to its worldwide growth in the twentieth century, especially in parts of Africa. It has also provoked severe repression from fundamentalist religious authorities, particularly in Iran after the Iranian revolution of 1978. Today the Bahá'í world headquarters is in Israel.

Bai-lian Jiao

Chinese sect. Although it can be indirectly traced to the fourth century, Bai-lian Jiao, or the White Lotus society, originated as a heterodox Buddhist sect dedicated to overthrowing the Mongols of the Yuan dynasty in the fourteenth century. The sect had roots in Amidist pietism, but developed into a movement that abandoned requirements of celibacy for priests, encouraged vegetarianism among its followers, simplified many of the important rituals and texts, and eventually adopted various cult practices such as talismanic magic, prognostication, and exorcism. During the Yuan dynasty (1260–1368), the White Lotus doctrine included the belief in the imminent appearance of the Maitreya, or the Buddha of the future. It was also during this period that the White Lotus society took on a more violent character, due to members' eschatological beliefs in their imminent victory over their enemies. During the Ming dynasty (1368–1644), the society reached its mature form, as the sect adopted the worship of the Wusheng Laomu, or Eternal Mother, as well as belief in deliverance by the Maitreya.

Although the White Lotus was one of the secret societies that hastened the fall of the Yuan dynasty, it is perhaps best known for widespread rebellion during the Qing dynasty (1644–1911). This rebellion (1796–1805) to overthrow the Manchus who had conquered China and established the Qing dynasty was prompted in part by the hardship caused by widespread bureaucratic corruption. The sect drew upon the millenarian visions of rebellion leaders, and predicted imminent catastrophe. Reacting against the presence of imperial troops in the province of Hubei who had been called in to end another rebellion, White Lotus members in that province attacked and captured small cities that they were not able to hold for long. Driven into the mountains, members of the society waged guerrilla warfare with considerable success.

It was only in 1799, when the Jiaqing emperor took power after his aging father died, that the corrupt ministers under Heshen were removed, and the campaign against the White Lotus society began to be carried out through the use of freshly trained local militias. Pledges of amnesty to the rank-and-file members, and large bounties on the White Lotus leadership, eventually helped end the rebellion.

Ba Jin (1905–)

Chinese novelist and short-story writer. Born Li Fei-gan, the Chinese anarchist adopted the name Ba Jin by combining parts of the names of the great Russian anarchists Bakunin and Kropotkin. Ba Jin has published more than twenty novels and novellas, hundreds of short stories, and numerous essays and travelogues since 1927. His first novel, *Miewang* (*Extinction*), was published in 1929; however, he is best known for his autobiographical trilogy, *Ji-liu: Jia, Chun, Qiu* (*Torrent Trilogy: The Family, Spring, Autumn*), finished in 1940. *Jia* (1933; *The Family*), the first volume of his *Torrent Trilogy* and his most successful work, was made into a film in 1953; the novel describes the tensions between Confucian convention and modern ideas. Like most of his works, it attacks the traditional Chinese family and thematizes the contradictions of Chinese life caught between past and future.

Most of Ba Jin's work was produced between 1927 and 1947. In late 1946, after completing *Han-ye* (*Bitter Cold Nights*), Ba quit the novel to devote himself to editorial and translation work. His translations include Turgenev's *Ottsy i deti* (1862; *Fathers and Sons*) and Oscar Wilde's *The Happy Prince* (1916), as well as works by German and Polish writers. He served as chief editor of various magazines and publications. Despite being an early opponent of Communism, Ba Jin's leftist sympathies earned him the respect of the Maoists; after the formation of the People's Republic of China in 1949, Ba assumed important posts in national cultural and literary organizations. During the Great Proletarian Cultural Revolution, Ba was labeled a "bourgeois man of letters" and his work ignored until after Mao's death and the arrest of the Gang of Four. He was elected a deputy to the National People's Congress and a member of its Standing Committee in 1978. Since then, he has been vice chairman of the Federation of Literary and Art Circles and acting chairman of the Chinese Writers' Association.

Baker, George (1880–1965)

African-American religious leader and social activist, also known as Father Divine. Father Divine's Peace Mission was one of the most successful religious communal movements of the twentieth century. The Great Depression of the 1930s left the black working class desperate for employment and with a deepening need for social justice. Many clergymen of the period recognized the imperative for social reform and led the fight for civil rights as well as spiritual well-being. One of these men, George Baker, started his evangelical career in the South in the late nineteenth century. The major tenets of his faith were derived from his early years as a preacher, when he fought against the rise of Jim Crow laws (discriminatory social and legal laws against African Americans established during the last two decades of the nineteenth century) while affirming the sanctity of the Christian Scriptures. He took the biblical statement that "the spirit of God dwelleth in you" literally and became known to his followers as "God" the divine father. Peace, brotherhood, and honesty were the ideals of his congregation, coupled with a fierce passion for equality and an enthusiasm for integration.

After spending a few years in Baltimore, he moved to Brooklyn in 1915. By 1919 the commune had the funds to purchase a house in the all-white neighborhood of Sayville, Long Island. In the 1920s his flock grew in number, and busloads of worshipers (both black and white) were carried to Sayville from New York to hear him preach. The weekly gatherings became more and more enthusiastic; his neighbors had Divine charged with disturbing the peace in November 1931. As a result, he was given the maximum sentence in May 1932. During his sentencing, Divine warned the judge of retribution. The judge, who had been a healthy man, died a few days later, and Divine convinced his followers that this was an act of "divine" retribution. When informed by his jailers of the judge's death, Divine reportedly said, "I hated to do it!"

During his jail term, Divine's popularity soared, and on the date of his release, June 25, 1932, he was greeted by 7,000 followers and a "Monster Rally to Our Lord" celebration. The Peace Mission moved to Harlem in 1933, and with the death of another religious leader, George Wilson Becton, Divine became even more powerful. The Peace Mission movement spread and diversified. In 1934 a group of disciples in Los Angeles started to publish a religious journal, *The Spoken Word*, while *New Day* was founded in New York City. Through these journals, Divine spread his spiritual teachings and political views throughout the country and the world. Divine died in September 1965, and his Peace Mission was taken over by his second wife, Edna Rose Ritchings, known to the congregation as "Sweet Angel." However, never as popular as it was during his life, after Divine's death the Peace Mission movement eventually declined.

Baker, Josephine (1906–1975)

American singer and dancer. Born into poverty in Kansas City, Missouri, Baker left home at the age of thirteen, looking to break into show business. She worked as a dresser for a traveling show, occasionally dancing in the chorus and playing small comic parts. In 1921 she auditioned for the theater production of *Shuffle Along*; rejected, she followed the show to New York City, where she got a job working in costumes for the second touring company. She was fortunate to substitute for one of the chorus girls, and her antics thrilled audiences and critics, enabling her to move to the premier touring company in Boston. Noting her talent and popularity, Noble Sissle and Eubie Blake wrote her into their next theater production, *Chocolate Dandies*, which opened in New York in 1924. Known as "that comedy chorus girl," Baker was a fantastic success; her genius at playing the role of hapless pixie won widespread acclaim.

Baker established her name in Paris in 1925, appearing in Caroline Dudley's *La Revue Nègre* (*Black Review*). Soon she was starring at the Folies Bergère and headlining at European clubs showcasing American "Negro" jazz music. In 1936 she went back to the United States to join the cast of the *Ziegfeld's Follies*, but discovered that American audiences were less receptive to her talents. Eventually returning to France, she became a member of the Resistance, working with Free French forces in North Africa during World War II, for which she earned several honors, including the Medallion of the City of Paris. After the war, Baker returned to a lavish estate in the French Dordogne Valley, equipped with a castle, a heart-shaped pool, and its own post office. She populated her new home with twelve children adopted from all over the world in a personal effort to promote world peace. Though busy with her growing family, Baker continued to perform and made a triumphant return to the United States in 1973, appearing in a series of concerts in Harlem and at Carnegie Hall. She died in 1975, two days after premiering a review in Paris to celebrate her golden anniversary in show business.

Bakong

Ancient Khmer temple. Built by the Khmer king Indravarman I in 881 B.C.E., the Bakong is one of the extant step-pyramid structures designed to serve as the king's mausoleum and was the first such temple to be made from stone instead of brick, and in a precisely pyramidal shape. These tombs were intended to replicate the mythical Mt. Meru, which was believed to lie north of the Himalayas, at the center of the universe. Like Mt. Meru, the temples were homes for the gods, as well as for the kings and other worthy souls who had passed on to heaven. The Bakong still stands at Roluos (formerly the ancient city Hariharalaya), though the bas-reliefs that decorated the walls have long since disappeared.

al-Bakri, *see* Ghana

Balassi, Bálint (1554–1594)

Hungarian poet. Born in Zólyom, Hungary, in 1554 to a rich Protestant family, Bálint Balassi (also spelled Balassa) was the leading Hungarian lyric poet of his time and maintained a strong literary influence on Hungarian poetry for nearly two centuries.

A romantic figure, Balassi grew up fighting against the Turks and bickering with relatives who sought to cheat him of his inheritance. Much of his poetry glorifies the valor of war, while other work dwells on the physical beauty of pastoral landscapes. Though he first wrote conventional lyric poems, Balassi soon developed an original style, inventing a verse structure that was widely imitated by later poets. Late in his life, Balassi converted to Roman Catholicism, and the influence of his religious conversion is evident in his poetry of this period, which is highly religious in nature and preoccupied with spiritual questions. An active soldier to the end, Balassi died from wounds sustained during the siege of Esztergom.

Baldwin, James (1924–1987)

American novelist, essayist, and playwright. Baldwin's impassioned commentary on black life in the United States made him the single most read and quoted American on the subject of race relations in the late fifties and early sixties.

James Baldwin was born and grew up in Harlem, and spent his youth helping to raise his eight younger siblings. As a child, he was intimidated by the prevalence of drugs, prostitution, and violence in his neighborhood; he would later write that young people in Harlem at the time could belong either to a pimp or to God. Baldwin chose the church, becoming an ardent believer and a preacher in a revivalist church.

Baldwin's faith lasted only a few years, however. As he became disillusioned with religion in the years following high school, he also suffered anxiety over his homosexuality and his country's deeply embedded racism. He would write about both after moving to Europe in 1948. In Paris, he completed his first novel, *Go Tell It on the Mountain* (1953), an autobiographical story of a Harlem family, and wrote his landmark essay "Notes of a Native Son," a meditation on the Harlem riots of 1945 that widens into a critique of American racism. In this work, Baldwin insisted on the centrality of the issue of race to American life; what had previously been known as the "Negro problem" became, in Baldwin's essays, the central dilemma of the nation.

Although he spent most of his time in France, Baldwin was an important figure in the agitation for American civil rights, participating in marches and protests and writing some of the central texts of the movement. In the two decades after his departure from the U.S., he would produce most of his important works of nonfiction, including *Nobody Knows My Name* (1961) and *The Fire Next Time* (1963). These years also saw the publication of several novels exploring racial, national, and sexual identity, including *Giovanni's Room* (1956) and *Another Country* (1962). His powerful writing style combined the biblical cadences of the black church with the subtle psychological shadings of Henry James. Like James (one of his favorite authors), Baldwin was obsessed in all his writing with the American character, especially the dangers inherent in its famous "innocence" and willingness to forget the past.

His prominence as a supposed spokesperson for black America eventually made him a target of critics from all sides. Frequently assailed by whites as "too bitter" for his uncompromisingly bleak diagnosis of American society, Baldwin also angered a younger generation of radicals with his disdain for black nationalism. Although he continued writing until his death, none of his work from the seventies and eighties received the attention of his earlier writing.

Other works include the novels *If Beale Street Could Talk* (1974), *Tell Me How Long the Train's Been Gone* (1968) and *Just Above My Head* (1979), the plays *Blues for Mister Charlie* and *The Amen Corner* (1964), and the nonfiction *The Devil Finds Work* (1976) and *The Evidence of Things Not Seen* (1985).

Baluchi

Largely Muslim ethnic group in Pakistan. The Baluchi peoples, numbering some 4 million, make up the largest province of Pakistan—Baluchistan—and also occupy neighboring areas of Iran, Afghanistan, Bahrain, and India. Traditionally nomadic, the majority of Baluchi have now settled into an agrarian existence.

The Baluchi did not enter the region of present-day Baluchistan until the fourteenth century C.E. A tumultuous history of invasions and annexations followed. In 1595 the region was conquered by Mughal emperor Akbar (who reigned from 1556 to 1605) and became a part of the Mughal empire. Late in the eighteenth century, it became a dependency of Afghanistan. In 1839 the British Indian army marched through it on their way to an invasion of Afghanistan. As a result, Baluchistan came under control of the British Indian empire by 1843, with its capital city, Quetta, formally annexed in 1847. During the nineteenth century, Persia conquered the western part of Baluchistan, fixing its boundary in 1872.

Since becoming a part of Pakistan after the 1947 Partition of India, Baluchistan has endured several periods of unrest, including organized opposition to the government of Zulfikar Ali Bhutto (Pakistani president from 1971 to 1973, and prime minister from 1973 to 1977) in the 1970s and disturbances in the region in 1979 in the wake of the Iranian revolution. The most rural and sparsely populated of Pakistan's provinces, Baluchistan remains one of the poorest areas of the country, despite government-assisted economic development. In the 1980s massive numbers of Afghan refugees fleeing the Soviet takeover of Afghanistan created makeshift mud-hut villages throughout Baluchistan.

Balzac, Honoré de (1799–1850)

French writer. Considered one of the founders of literary realism, Balzac's work also exhibits the balance of the romantic and realistic that characterizes the work of Stendhal and Flaubert.

Balzac's passion for literature developed at a young age, as a means of escape from taunting schoolmates and boring teachers. He read voraciously, and following a brief study of jurisprudence at the University of Paris decided to become an author. The young Balzac was fired by dreams of fame, fortune, and love; his family, however, was horrified. Therefore, in compromise, Balzac agreed to write for two years, and if unsuccessful, seek a more secure profession. At the end of this period, Balzac had produced only one, yet unsuccessful, play, *Cromwell* (1819), and in a desperate attempt to pay his bills, he turned to writing sensational novels under a pseudonym. He then tried his hand at a variety of business ventures—printing, publishing, and a type foundry—all with disastrous results.

His first commercial success as a

writer came with the publication of *Les Chouans* (*The Chouans*) and *La Physiologie du mariage* (The Physiology of Marriage) in 1829, and *Scènes de la vie privée* (*Scenes from Private Life*) in 1830. The following year, Balzac added "de" to his name and acquired a larger apartment in Paris and a valet. He continued his frenzied writing pace, often sitting at his desk for fourteen or fifteen hours at a time, drinking countless cups of coffee. In 1832 he met Évalyne Hanska, a Polish countess who was married to an elderly Ukrainian landowner. They became lovers the following year and decided to marry after the death of Hanska's husband. Their courtship is recorded in Balzac's *Lettres à l'étrangère* (1832–44; *Letters to a Foreign Lady*).

Though his courtship with Hanska would last another eighteen years, Balzac began a prolific period of writing, in an attempt to clear his debts before his marriage. In a three-year period (1832–35), he produced over twenty works, including *Le médecin de campagne* (1833; *The Country Doctor*) and *Le Père Goriot* (1835; *Old Man Goriot*), considered one of his masterpieces. His tour de force was a sixteen-volume work, *Comédie humaine* (1842–46; *The Human Comedy*). Under this title, Balzac collected some of his finest novels and stories, written over a twenty-year period. Taken as a whole, the work is Balzac's ambitious attempt to represent the social history of France; though stylistically unremarkable, this masterpiece reveals Balzac as a supreme observer and chronicler of French society.

Balzac died in 1850, just a few months after his marriage to Hanska. The body of work he left behind established Balzac as a leading practitioner of the classical novel, and is of major importance in the development of realism in fiction.

Bambara

African ethnolinguistic group. The million or so Bambara (sometimes called Bamana), who speak languages of the Manding group, live primarily in Mali beside the Niger River. They are descendants of the people of ancient Mali, who founded both the Segu and Kaarta kingdoms.

Bambara means "unbeliever" or "infidel," a name the group acquired in the course of resisting Islam after it was introduced in 1854 by the Tukulor conqueror el-Hajj Umar. Religion and agriculture for the Bambara are intertwined: for example, the high god of the Bambara is represented as a grain from which the whole of creation is born. The Bambara recognize one god, Bemba or Ngala, as the creator of all things, a being who cannot be perceived by humans through the usual senses, but whose existence is manifested as an immaterial force, often as a whirlwind or a thought. Many of their religious beliefs are symbolized in their famous masks and carvings, which often feature the antelope, who they believe taught men to grow crops. Although many present-day Bambara are Muslim, they still make masks, mostly to sell to tourists.

The traditional social organization of the Bambara is the large united clan, a group of families descended from a common ancestor. Family heads are obligated to obey the village chief, who not only organizes the village for religious activities but also acts as mediator for the chief of the earth spirits. Although the Bambara are linked by clan, there is a great deal of intermingling among tribes, and for this reason there is no strong centralized organization.

Traditionally agriculturalist—growing millet and guinea corn—the Bambara have also begun to grow such crops as peanuts, rice, and cotton, and many now travel south to work on the cocoa and coffee plantations of Ghana and the Ivory Coast.

Bantu

African language family. Bantu includes most of those African languages spoken south of a line from Duala, Cameroon, in the west, to the Great Lakes of East Africa. The word *bantu*, or something similar to *bantu*, means "people," referring not only to the language itself, but to the group of people who speak Bantu. The similarities among the many Bantu languages suggest a recent and vast population migration, though scholars continue to disagree as to the location of the Bantu linguistic center or how the language spread.

Some scholars believe that Proto-Bantu, the "ancestor language" from which Bantu evolved, was first spoken in the Cameroon-Nigeria border area, which would help explain similarities between Bantu and other West African languages. According to this theory, Bantu speakers migrated east and south from this Cameroon-Nigeria border area, possibly because of population pressures, eventually dominating the region where it is presently found. As a result of this migration, Bantu displaced many of the older Khoisan languages, and much of the "click" language of the San hunters of southern Africa.

Bao Dai (1913–)

Vietnamese ruler. Born Nguyen Vinh Thuy, Bao Dai was the last emperor (1926–45) of the Nguyen dynasty in Vietnam. Educated in France, he returned to Vietnam in 1932 to assume the role of emperor. Initially he hoped to reinvigorate the empire by making Vietnam a French protectorate with limited autonomy; however, during the August Revolution in 1945 various Vietnamese groups, including Vietnamese political leader Ho Chi Minh and his political party, the Viet Minh, gained significant political leverage. The rise of Ho Chi Minh forced Bao Dai to abdicate his throne, and while, in a propagandistic gesture of deference to Vietnam's history, the Ho Chi Minh government appointed Bao Dai an adviser, Bao Dai left immediately for Paris.

The French succeeded in suppressing the Viet Minh by 1947, and Bao Dai returned to Vietnam in 1949, to serve as president of a hand-selected Council of Ministers. Many historians suggest he served merely as a French puppet, in what was publicized as the "Bao Dai solution," another failed attempt by the French government to legitimate their colonial rule. After the French were finally expelled by Ho Chi Minh's revolutionaries in 1954, Bao Dai was stripped of his office as chief of state and exiled to France.

Baraka, Amiri (1934–)

American playwright and poet. The major voice of the Black Arts Movement of the 1960s, Baraka transformed the national theater with his angry, confrontational plays. Although he has faded in prominence since the sixties, Baraka continues to write, augmenting a body of work that has moved through Beat aesthetics, black nationalism, and Marxism.

Amiri Baraka was born Everett LeRoi Jones in Newark, New Jersey. Although in his youth he considered becoming a minister, his interests had turned more toward the arts by the time he began studies in English and philosophy at the all-black Howard University in Washington, D.C. He spent three years in the U.S. Air Force before moving to New York and joining the bohemian artistic scene flourishing there.

With his first wife, a Jewish-American woman named Hettie Roberta Cohen, Jones edited a literary magazine called *Yugen* from 1958 to 1962. They published such celebrated New York avant-garde writers as Allen Ginsberg, Gregory Corso, Diane DiPrima, and Peter Orlovsky. Jones's first group of published poems, *Preface to a Twenty Volume Suicide Note . . .* (1961), reflects the influence of these Beat writers. Over the next several years racial concerns would become increasingly central to Baraka's work. *Blues People* (1963) is a history of African-American music, and the poetry collection *The Dead Lecturer* (1964) addresses the need for black artists to disassociate themselves from an oppressive Western aesthetic tradition.

Baraka's most acclaimed theatrical work was produced in 1964. *The Toilet, The Slave*, and *Dutchman*, all of which display the influence of absurdism, are confrontational one-acts meant to shock audiences into a recognition of the fallacies of racial integration. In *Dutchman*, the most famous, a white bohemian woman flirts with, taunts, and eventually murders a middle-class black intellectual man on a subway train. *Dutchman* represents Baraka's most successful integration of an avant-garde aesthetic with a black nationalist political message.

In 1965 Baraka founded the Black Arts Repertory Theater and School in Harlem to serve as a center for his brand of politicized theater. As a reflection of his commitment to black nationalism, he changed his name in 1968 to Imamu Amiri Baraka and married a black woman named Sylvia Robinson (later Amina Baraka). In the early 1970s he disavowed his earlier nationalism in favor of an internationalist Marxist creed. Baraka's other works include the plays *J-E-L-L-O* (1965), *Junkies Are Full of (SHH . . .)* (1970), *Sidnee Poet Heroical* (1975), and *The System of Dante's Hell* (1965), an autobiographical novel.

Bartók, Béla (1881–1945)

Hungarian composer. Born in what is now part of Romania, Béla Bartók moved with his pianist mother around Eastern Europe after his father's death in 1889. Bartók excelled as a pianist from an early age, performing his own work publicly at the age of eleven. In 1893 he and his mother settled in the large town of Pozsony, where he received solid grounding in musical fundamentals. In 1899 he entered the Budapest Academy

of Music, leaving in 1903 to produce *Kossuth*, a symphonic poem honoring the leader of Hungary's revolution in 1848. In the early years of the century, Bartók embarked on exhausting European concert tours, playing work that displayed the strong influences of German composer Richard Strauss, the Hungarian giant Franz Liszt, and the more conservative Brahms; he was slow to find an individual voice.

A crucial step forward for Bartók was his deep engagement with Hungarian folk music. With a friend, Zoltan Kodály, he published a collection of Magyar folk songs that aimed to rescue native music from the distortion of popular arrangements. From 1906 on, Bartók spent a great deal of time traveling in order to record, transcribe, and write about Hungarian folk music as well as the folk traditions of the Balkans, Turkey, and North Africa. Listening closely to these sources, Bartók discovered radical harmonic and rhythmic devices for his own concert style.

Appointed professor of the piano at the Budapest Academy of Music in 1907, Bartók held the position until 1934. In 1911 he and Kodály formed the New Hungarian Musical Society, and throughout the decade he continued to collect and study ethnic folk tunes—well over 9,000, according to his biography. As a composer, he devoted himself to an ambitious sequence of stage works: the short opera *Bluebeard's Castle* (1911), the ballet *The Wooden Prince* (1914–17), and the pantomime *The Miraculous Mandarin* (1918–19). This last work saw the sudden emergence of Bartók's mature "middle" style, marked by savage dissonances, convulsive rhythms, and unadorned folk motifs. He extended this style into a major sequence of instrumental works, including the two violin sonatas, the *Third* and *Fourth String Quartets*, the *First Piano Concerto*, and several other pieces for the piano.

In the 1930s Bartók began to write in

a more expansive, lyrical style, looking back to his Romantic roots. Although the advent of fascism forced a painful and disruptive immigration to the United States in 1940, he produced an unbroken succession of masterpieces until his death in 1945. The *Fifth* and *Sixth Quartets* (1934 and 1939) capped one of the greatest twentieth-century quartet cycles; the *Music for Strings, Percussion, and Celesta* (1936) and the *Concerto for Orchestra* (1943) unified radical techniques and conventional symphonic narratives; and the *Third Piano Concerto* (1945) ended his career on a note of luminous repose.

Bashō, *see* Matsuo Bashō

Baudelaire, Charles [Pierre] (1821–1867)

French poet. Though he published only a single volume of poetry, *Les fleurs du mal* (1857; *Flowers of Evil*), Baudelaire's poetic style and use of symbolism have exerted an enormous influence on the development of modern Western poetry. Baudelaire was a rebellious youth, and this rebellion was to mark both his adult life and work. He lost both parents at a young age, and was left in the care of a stepfather. By the age of eighteen, he had been expelled from school and contracted the venereal disease that would later contribute to his death, and was already fully committed to a bohemian, decadent lifestyle. As a disciplinary measure, his stepfather dispatched him on a sea voyage around the Cape of Good Hope, but upon his return, Baudelaire received his father's inheritance and plunged into the Parisian art scene. His work as an art critic, though quite important, did not pay his expenses, and much to his chagrin, his inheritance was placed in a trust by his family. Frustrated by his financial circumstances, his estranged relationship with his family, and what he felt was inadequate literary achievement, Baudelaire attempted suicide in 1845. His first major literary success followed soon after, with his translations of the works of American poet and author Edgar Allan Poe. These translations were enormously popular, and have since become classics in France. Finally, in 1857, Baudelaire published *Flowers of Evil*, the work of many years. The concise, almost understated use of symbolism in these poems stands in direct contrast to the more effusive prose of the Romantics. Stylistically, his poems are classical, but his subject matter—the beauty of decay and complex emotional states—foreshadows the preoccupations of modern poetry. This, of course, was not the opinion of the work at the time; Baudelaire's verse shocked the puritan aesthetic sense of the day, and legal proceedings were instigated against him. His book was declared obscene, and though Baudelaire was quite disheartened, he continued to write and publish his poems and prose, including an augmented edition of *Flowers of Evil* (1861). Toward the end of his life he grew increasingly ill, and he died in Paris in 1867.

Bauhaus

German school of design. The Bauhaus (or Staatliches Bauhaus), which merged the Grand Ducal Saxon Academy of Arts and the Grand Ducal Saxon School of Arts and Crafts, was founded by the architect Walter Gropius, who wanted to combine timeless artistic principles with twentieth-century technology. By focusing on artifacts both functional and aesthetically pleasing, the Bauhaus made a concerted effort to bring consistent craftsmanship into the twentieth century while simultaneously focusing on mass production. The Bauhaus, or "house of building," was originally located in Weimar until 1925, moved to Dessau until 1932, and then spent its last months in Berlin.

A six-month introductory course (alternately taught by Johannes Itten, Josef Albers, and László Moholy-Nagy) was compulsory for all students who wished to take workshops at the Bauhaus. The workshops themselves were generally taught by two people (a craftsman and an artist) and covered such diverse fields as stained glass, painting, pottery, and carpentry. Students were also expected to take courses in sociology and accounting (in keeping with the school's ideal of successful, mass-produced art). A journeyman's diploma was granted to students after completion of workshop instruction (generally three years).

One of the school's primary aims was the unification of all the creative arts in architecture. The Bauhaus's cornerstone, the department of architecture, was not actually founded until 1927. Prior to this, members' work could most notably be seen in the Dessau school itself—especially in the educational, residential, and administrative buildings designed by Gropius. His buildings were minimalist yet functional, employed bold and simple lines, and included such space-saving designs as removable sliding walls. Hannes Meyer, who was chairman of the school of architecture, became director of the school in 1928, until politics forced his resignation in 1930. Meyer was succeeded by Ludwig Mies van der Rohe, who directed the school until it was closed by the Nazis in 1933. Most members of the Bauhaus faculty then moved to the United States.

The wide influence of the Bauhaus is due to the faculty and students who disseminated Bauhaus methods throughout the world. Prominent admirers of the Bauhaus, such as Albert Einstein and Le Corbusier, also worked to spread the school's ideology. Moholy-Nagy founded the New Bauhaus (later renamed the Institute of Design) in Chicago in 1937. Later that year, Gropius was appointed chairman of the Harvard School of Architecture. In 1938 Mies van der Rohe moved to Chicago to form the Department of Architecture at the Illinois Institute of Technology. Cur-

rently, most art schools include courses on the fundamentals of design based on the Bauhaus model.

Baule

African group occupying the Ivory Coast between the Komoé and Bandama rivers. The Baule descended from a group of the Asante (also spelled Ashanti) people of western Africa, who, after a dispute over royal succession, immigrated to their new location along the Ivory Coast in the mid eighteenth century under the leadership of Queen Awura Pokou. The rise of palm oil commerce along the Alladian coast contributed to economic and political conflicts within the southern Baule interior during the mid nineteenth century. But when France conquered the area at the turn of the twentieth century, the Baule were forced to abandon that trade and accept a new role as peasant farmers. Until the Republic of Côte d'Ivoire achieved autonomy in 1958, resistance to and collaboration with French imperial rule was the overwhelming issue confronting the Baule people.

At present, Baule culture is reemerging and the Baule have recovered both cultural and economic autonomy. Now primarily agriculturalists, they tend cocoa and coffee crops. However, the most symbolically important crop of the Baule is the yam, essential to the Baule religion and the focus of their annual harvest festival.

Baule society recognizes matrilineal lineage, and like the Asante people of Ghana, the Baule have "stools" (or seats) that they believe contain the spirits of their ancestors. In addition to these "stools," Baule artisans produce a variety of wooden sculptures and religious masks that are grouped into "families," corresponding to the different deities in the Baule religion. Examples of Baule masks are that of Guli, the spirit of the dead, represented in the *kple-kple* mask, which is made of a simple bright red or black disk, with pieces of mirror for eyes and topped with bull horns, as well as Gu, the god of wind, represented by a mask of shiny black wood. Formerly connected to ancestor worship, these masks are now generally made for tourists.

Baxter, James Kier (1926–1972)

New Zealand poet. Born in Dunedin, New Zealand, on June 29, 1926, James Kier Baxter became one of New Zealand's leading poets after World War II. After studying writing in New Zealand and England, Baxter's first publication was *Beyond the Palisade* (1944), a collection that hinted at the talent that was to make him a central figure in New Zealand literature. In 1948 he published *Blow, Wind of Fruitfulness*, a less well-received but more mature collection. Branching into literary criticism, Baxter wrote a critical work that discussed his own work and that of his New Zealand colleagues, *Recent Trends in New Zealand Poetry* (1951). This was followed by another critical work in 1968, *Aspects of Poetry in New Zealand*, but Baxter was primarily recognized as a poet, publishing a number of important poetry collections before his death in Auckland in 1972, including *The Fallen House* (1953); *Iron Breadboard* (1957); and *Pig Island Letters* (1968). Throughout his career, his work was noted for its startling imagery and Baxter's masterful versification style.

Beauvoir, Simone de (1908–1986)

French feminist, philosopher, and writer. Simone de Beauvoir was famous for her lifelong companionship with French philosopher and novelist Jean-Paul Sartre, whom she met in 1929, and her association with the existentialist school of thought. Completing her *agrégation* in philosophy at the Sorbonne, in Paris, de Beauvoir taught before becoming a writer. In addition to her personal relationship with Sartre, de Beauvoir also developed a professional relationship with him when, in 1945, they began editing the monthly review *Les Temps Modernes* (*Modern Times*).

De Beauvoir wrote a number of novels preoccupied with existential themes; the best-known of these is *Les Mandarins* (1954; *The Mandarins*), which recounts the postwar politicization of the intellectual elite. The author of several autobiographical works, de Beauvoir rendered passionate and thoughtful portraits of herself and of a generation of French intellectuals. She is most famous for *Le Deuxième Sexe* (1949; *The Second Sex*), a historic analysis of the varieties of women's oppression; many consider it to be a founding text of modern Western feminism. De Beauvoir's less-known writings on aging and the elderly, *Une Mort très douce* (1964; *A Very Easy Death*), written after the death of her mother, and *La Vieillesse* (1970; *The Coming of Age*) broach a topic largely ignored by other leftist thinkers. Her last publication was an account of the last years of Sartre's life, *La Cérémonie des adieux* (1981; *Adieux: A Farewell to Sartre*).

Beckett, Samuel [Barclay] (1906–1989)

Irish novelist, poet, and playwright. Winner of the Nobel Prize in Literature in 1969, Beckett was an innovator in language and stagecraft whose experimental works have influenced an entire generation of avant-garde writers. His bleak landscapes, debilitated and confused characters, and pessimistic outlook are exemplary depictions of the absurd and anguished aimlessness representative of Western culture after World War II.

Born in Dublin to a well-to-do Protestant family, Beckett received bachelor's and master's degrees in modern languages from Trinity College in Dublin. In 1928 he moved to Paris, where he spent the rest of his life. In Paris he met another Irish writer, James Joyce, the greatest influence on his own writing, who was then at work on his final novel, *Finnegans Wake*. Though it is not true, as is often claimed, that he served as Joyce's paid secretary, Beckett provided Joyce with enthusiastic and diligent company, performing many literary tasks for him. Beckett soon began writing in earnest, contributing his first essay to a collection celebrating Joyce's work, *Our Examination Round His Factification for Incamination of Work in Progress* (1929), and publishing a book of poetry, *Whoroscope* (1930). *Proust*, a short book of criticism, came in 1931, followed by a short-story collection, *More Pricks than Kicks*, in 1934. Rejected by over forty publishers, *Murphy*, his first novel, finally appeared in the United States in 1938, though it went virtually unnoticed. During these difficult years Beckett suffered from a variety of illnesses, some of which may have been psychosomatic, as they usually worsened on his infrequent visits to Ireland on family business. After 1939, Beckett wrote most of his works in French, translating them into English himself.

During World War II, Beckett worked in intelligence for the French Resistance and later received the Croix de Guerre. Between 1947 and 1957 he created the works for which he is best known, the trilogy of novels *Molloy* (1948), *Malone Dies* (1948), and *The Unnamable* (1950), and the plays *Waiting for Godot* (1949) and *Endgame* (1956). Debuting in Paris in 1953, *Waiting for Godot* was a social and intellectual event that made Beckett famous overnight. The play broke with dramatic and literary convention, and its innovative staging and ultimate ambiguity came to define what would be termed the "Theater of the Absurd" and heralded the aggressive experimentalism of Beckett's later work. In these austere, brief plays, Beckett placed decreasing emphasis on the body of the performer, finally eliminating it altogether; performances employed disembodied voices, or no voice at all, as in

Breath (1971), a thirty-second piece in which a faint cry is the only sound heard. In *Play*, the second half of the play repeats the first half verbatim, and the "dramaticule" *Come and Go* consists of ten minutes of repeated action.

Beckett was awarded the Nobel Prize in 1969; sixteen volumes of his *Collected Works* were published the following year. His last years were spent traveling and supervising productions of his plays. Beckett died of respiratory failure at the age of eighty-three.

Beethoven, Ludwig von (1770–1827)

German composer. Beethoven displayed tremendous musical gifts at an early age. Though his father tried to exploit his talents for commercial gain, he was never as successful as Austrian composer and child prodigy Wolfgang Amadeus Mozart (1756–1791), whom Beethoven met in 1787 in Vienna. However, his hopes to study with Mozart were cut short by his mother's death; when he finally did move to Vienna in 1792, Mozart had died, so Beethoven studied instead with Austrian composer Franz Joseph Haydn (1732–1809).

Beethoven first gained attention as a brilliant, unorthodox pianist, capable of delivering wild improvisations and thundering sonorities. Nonetheless, he became a versatile composer who contributed masterpieces to every known genre. His Achilles' heel might have been opera; he struggled long and hard with his one attempt, *Fidelio* (1814), and was never entirely happy with the result. His thirty-two piano sonatas required a transformation of the instrument for which they were written; his nine symphonies led to the modern concert orchestra; his sixteen string quartets were not fully understood until a century later. Beethoven was an irascible, impossible, but deeply moral man who believed in the promise of human freedom. His *Ninth Symphony*, with its exultant choral setting of Friedrich von

Schiller's *Ode to Joy*, showed once again its power to lift the spirit when it was played near the ruins of the Berlin Wall in 1989.

Though he began losing his hearing in 1801 and was almost completely deaf by 1817, his later work was, if anything, characterized by greater depth and complexity. The first composer able to live independently of a musical post, with the financial support of wealthy Austrian friends, Beethoven stayed in Vienna for the remainder of his life and dedicated himself to music.

A milestone in the history of classical music, Beethoven's oeuvre also serves as the transition between the classical and Romantic periods in Western music. His works are the crowning glory of the classical period, developing classical forms like the sonata to their highest degree of sophistication, but the force and passion of his compositions herald the era of musical Romanticism.

Beijing opera

Traditional Chinese opera. Beijing opera is one of dozens of major traditional operas performed in China, and one of the most famous of China's art forms. It originated in the Beijing area, but quickly developed during its two hundred years of history into a national theatrical form after assimilating the best of other operas.

The arias and makeup are highly stylized in Beijing opera. There are five major character groups the audience can easily tell apart by the patterns of their facial makeups. These are *sheng* (males), *dan* (females), *jing* (rough and bold males), *mo* (lesser males), and *chou* (clowns). Each group is subdivided into *wen* (scholars), *wu* (warriors), *lao* (old), and *xiao* (young). Hence, a *xiaosheng* is a young male while a *laodan* is an old woman. (Until recently, however, all the parts were played only by male actors.) The opera combines singing, dancing, recitation, and acrobatics, with highly stylized, exaggerated, and symbolic body movements, distinct rhythms, and very colorful and elaborate costumes. A good Beijing opera performance is meant to bring all of these elements into perfect unity.

The plots of the majority of the plays are based on historical novels, romances, and fairy tales, but reflect political and military struggles and social problems. The plays based on *Xi-you ji* (*Story of the Monkey*), *Shui-hu zhuang* (*The Water Margin*), and *San guo yan yi* (*The History of the Three Kingdoms*) are most popular. Since 1949, plays on contemporary themes have been produced, which have brought about innovations in acting, singing, music, makeup, and stage decoration—not, however, always very successfully. During the Cultural Revolution (1966–76), only eight "model" Beijing opera plays, all depicting the Communist revolution, were allowed to appear onstage. Traditional themes have dominated the stage in recent years.

Bello, Andrés (1781–1865)

Venezuelan poet, essayist, and scholar. Bello was born in Caracas, where he received a classical education, studying philosophy, law, medicine, and the classics. After meeting the German naturalist Alexander von Humboldt (1799), he developed an interest in geography. In 1810 he traveled to London with his friend and fellow student Simón Bolívar; their (ultimately unsuccessful) mission was to secure British recognition of Venezuelan independence and economic assistance for the new nation. Bello elected to remain in London, serving as secretary to the legations of Chile and Colombia and continuing his studies of languages and literature. While in London, Bello wrote *Odas americanas* (1826–27; *American Odes*), two poems celebrating the majestic landscape of South America, which were to become part of an unfinished epic poem called

America. The second poem, *La agricultura de la zona torrida* (1826; *Ode to the Agriculture of the Torrid Zone*), glorifies country over city life, emphasizes the wealth and fertility of the New World, and underscores the theme of patriotism; it remains one of the best-known Spanish-American poems of the nineteenth century. After spending nineteen years in London, Bello accepted a post in the Chilean Ministry of Foreign Affairs and moved to Santiago, where he remained until his death. He was made a senator of his adopted country and later founded the University of Chile (1843), where he served as rector for the remainder of his life. An expert in law, Bello wrote the *Principios de derecho internacional* (1832; *Principles of International Law*) and is largely responsible for the Chilean Civil Code (1855), which was adopted by Colombia and Ecuador. Among his prose works, the most important are those dealing with language, particularly his *Gramática de la lengua castellana* (1847; *Grammar of the Spanish Language*), which continues to be an authoritative text in South American linguistics.

Benedetti, Mario (1920–)

Uruguayan poet and writer. Mario Benedetti was raised in Uruguay's capital city, Montevideo, which provides the very urban setting for much of his literary work. Benedetti's early work (in various genres) highlights the everyday life of middle-class Uruguayans in the city. Later regretting the publication of his first book of poems, he did not include any of the poems from that book when selecting his "collected" poems in the 1963 volume *Inventario* (*Inventory*). In addition to his own writing, Benedetti also became involved with several literary magazines in these early years, editing *Marginalia* (1948), *Número* (1943–55; 1966), and the literary section of the journal *Marcha* (1954; 1960). In 1948 Benedetti published a book of essays

called *Incident and Novel*, which won the Premio del Ministerio de Instrucción Pública; several works followed, including two collections of short stories, *Esta mañana* (1949; *This Morning*) and *El ultimo viaje y otros cuentos* (1951; *The Last Trip and Other Stories*), and a volume of poetry, *Only in the Meanwhile* (1950). Although none of these works is explicitly political, Benedetti's portrayal of his characters' weaknesses does portend an impending crisis in Uruguayan society. His next book of verse, *Poemas de la oficina* (1956; *Office Poems*), was an instant success, due in part to the novelty of the subject matter. In these poems, Benedetti succeeded in capturing the poetry of the bureaucracy, the contorted rhythms of life of the middle classes in urban Uruguayan society. With the success of *Montevideanos* (1959), the novel *Tregua* (1960; *The Truce*), and the essay collection *País de la cola de paja* (1960; *The Country with the Straw Tail*), Benedetti acquired national and international fame, becoming the most widely read Uruguayan writer.

The year 1959 marked a significant change in Benedetti's politics. He traveled to the United States, recording his experiences in several poems and short stories, as well as in *Gracias por el fuego* (1965; *Thank You for the Fire*), his third novel and a document of revolutionary enthusiasm. He also became interested in the Cuban revolution, and spent two years working on the island during the 1960s. The revolution was a major influence on him, as evidenced by works like *Cuaderno cubano* (1969; *Cuban Notebook*) and the autobiographical novella *El cumpleaños de Juan Angel* (1971; *The Birthday of Juan Angel*).

In the 1970s Benedetti turned his attention to the political unrest in his native Uruguay. Becoming the leader of the "Movement of the Independents of 26 March," a coalition of left-leaning parties, he continued to write speeches and publish articles criticizing governmental repression and commenting on Uruguayan life. Among many intellectuals who went into exile, Benedetti continued to publish, drawing global attention to the situation in Uruguay, and, indeed, in all of Latin America. Much of this material is compiled in *Des exilio y otras conjecturas* (1984; *The Refusal of Exile and Other Conjectures*). In addition, Benedetti transformed historical, personal, and collective events into literary works, such as the play *Pedro y el capitán* (1979; *Pedro and the Captain*), which deals directly with the horror of the Uruguayan military regime.

Benin bronzes

African bronze art. The bronze sculptures of the Benin empire are among the most prized examples of African art. The bronzes—full-scale heads or portraits, statues of people and animals, small devotional objects, and bas-relief plaques—date back hundreds of years, some as far back as the thirteenth century, when startlingly advanced processes of metalworking and casting were introduced into Benin from elsewhere in Nigeria. (The Benin bronzes imitated the great sculptural works of the Ifé African peoples, who pioneered a kind of figural realism centuries before the Europeans.) Benin, today the principal city of the Edo people of southern Nigeria, was the capital of the kingdom of Benin, which flourished from the thirteenth to the seventeenth century. At the height of its power in the fifteenth century, it was the greatest empire in the Gulf of Guinea. In 1897, after a long period of decline, the city was torched by the British, who ransacked its cultural treasures and took back with them numerous works of bronze and ivory. The appearance of the Benin bronzes surprised and amazed the Europeans; some were incredulous as to the age and the style of the pieces, as well as the advanced metalworking techniques employed in their production. The appearance of the Benin bronze castings heralded the full-scale importation of African art into European culture in the twentieth century.

Benin, kingdom of

Benin City, the ancient capital of the Bendel state in contemporary Nigeria. Once the heart of the great Benin empire, the kingdom of Benin gained prominence in the fifteenth century under the rule of the *oba*, or king of Benin, Eware "the Great" (reigned c. 1440–80). Oba Eware established the empire's political organization and consolidated its territory by conquering Yoruba lands to the west and Igbo lands to the east. Despite the arrival of Portuguese merchants in the late fifteenth century, the kingdom maintained independence from European control, and under Oba Eware, as well as the next two *obas*, relationships between the people of Benin and the Portuguese were largely peaceful and cooperative.

In the sixteenth century, under the rule of Oba Esigie, the son of Oba Ozoula "the Conqueror" (c. 1481 – c. 1504), and the grandson of Oba Eware, the empire continued to grow. Like many of the great African empires, Benin was intimately involved in the slave trade; various border conflicts and civil disturbances were exploited to send large numbers of non-Benin Africans to the Americas. The empire's power waned throughout the eighteenth and nineteenth centuries as neighboring Yoruba states, especially the Oyo empire, gained prominence. In 1897 the city of Benin was taken by the British, forcing Oba Ovonramwen (d. 1914), the last of the independent kings of Benin, into exile and effectively ending the independence of Benin; in 1900 Benin was incorporated into British colonial administration within the protectorate of Southern Nigeria.

Although the position of *oba* is not obsolete, the present-day Benin *oba* has only an advisory role in the government. The story of the defeat of the Benin empire is told in *Ovonranwem Nogbaisi* (1973), a tragic drama written by the Nigerian playwright and director Olawale Rotimi.

Benjamin, Walter (1892–1940)

German aesthetician and literary critic. Benjamin was born into an upper-middle-class Jewish family. He studied philosophy in Berlin, Freiburg im Breisgau, Munich, and Bern before settling in Berlin in 1920 to work as a translator and literary critic while finishing his doctoral dissertation. Though later published and hailed as a brilliantly original analysis, his unorthodox thesis, *Ursprung des deutschen Trauerspiels* (1928; *The Origin of German Tragic Drama*), which exemplified the metaphysical bent of his early critical physical thought, was rejected by the University of Frankfurt, ending his academic career.

Benjamin continued to live in Berlin until 1933, when the rise of Nazism prompted him to move to Paris. In Paris he wrote essays and reviews for literary journals, developing a dense yet poetic style and establishing some of his important philosophical ideas about literature. His writing of this period has clear Marxist leanings and a trademark sense of historical nostalgia and pessimism. In the 1920s and 1930s, Benjamin was peripherally associated with the Frankfurt School (or Institut für Sozialforschung), a school of thought that attempted to situate aesthetic texts in a wider, sociohistorical context.

When Germany invaded France in 1940, Benjamin fled south, hoping to escape to the United States through Spain. In the town of Port-Bou on the Franco-Spanish border, a police chief told him that he would be turned over to the Germans, and Benjamin committed suicide.

Much of Benjamin's substantial body of work has been published posthu-mously to widespread acclaim. He made a posthumous reputation as a literary critic, as an essayist, and as a critic of mass culture who explored the disappearance of traditional aesthetics in a world of mechanical reproduction. A short time before his death, he had finished his influential *Über den Begriff der Geschichte* (*Theses on the Philosophy of History*). Benjamin's forcible intellect is perhaps best expressed in the extended essay "Goethe's *Wahlverwandtschaften*" (1924–25; "Goethe's *Elective Affinities*") and in the collection of essays *Illuminationen* (1961; *Illuminations*).

Bentham, Jeremy (1748–1832)

English philosopher and legal critic. Jeremy Bentham is best known as the founder of utilitarianism. Discussed in the 1789 publication of his book *An Introduction to the Principles of Morals and Legislation*, utilitarianism maintains that the principle of the "greatest happiness of the greatest number" should be the chief aim of moral choice and social policy. A child prodigy, Bentham was said to have read Latin at the age of four; he received his degree from Queen's College, Oxford, at the age of fifteen. He then studied law, devoting himself to untangling the principles underlying philosophical ideas about right and duty, punishment and reward. Bentham understood himself to be engaged in a scientific critique of law and morality, a critique that would abolish fallacious notions of natural rights, natural law, or social "contracts" in favor of calculable principles of efficiency. He maintained that utilitarian principles should be applied to all judicial decisions; though he was often thwarted in his efforts to effect legal reforms, Bentham's work had an enormous influence on the great nineteenth-century reforms undertaken in England on criminal law, judicial organization, suffrage, and parliamentary organization. Bentham was also a central influence on British philosopher and economist John Stuart Mill; Bentham, John Stuart Mill, and James Mill (John Stuart Mill's father) all belonged to a group called the Philosophical Radicals, partisans of utilitarian principles, and in 1824 Bentham founded the *Westminster Review*, an influential journal. Upon his death, and according to his own instructions, in the presence of his friends, Bentham's body was carefully dissected. The skeleton, removed, was then reassembled, a wax head replacing the original. Reconstituted, the figure was dressed in Bentham's clothes and preserved in a glass case at University College in London, where it can still be seen. In recent years, scholarly interest has turned to Bentham as a theorist of penal reform as well as a theorist of ethics and of parliamentary democracy, in such work as A *Catechism of Parliamentary Reform* (1817).

Berber

Indigenous non-Arabic people of North Africa, and their language. The term "Berber" derives from Greek (*barbaros*, "the stammering unwashed," or *barbarians*) and was first employed by the Roman conquerors of North Africa. It currently refers to descendants of the North African peoples conquered by Bedouin Arabs in the twelfth century C.E. The Berbers do not form a single ethnic or religious group, although their languages are closely related to members of the Hamitic language family. Their ethnoreligious profiles vary: some tribes were Jewish and some Christian, although most converted to Islam. While the majority mixed with the Arabs who settled in North Africa, some Berbers maintained distinct linguistic and cultural communities; these peoples now live mainly in mountainous or desert areas in Morocco and Algeria, where they make up a sizable part of the population. Smaller numbers live in Tunisia, Mauritania, Mali, Senegal, Niger, Libya, and western Egypt.

While outsiders still use the term "Berber," the Berber refer to themselves according to regional, dialectal, or tribal affiliations: the Shluh, for example, speak the Shilha dialect and live in the Atlas Mountains; the Rifi tribes speak Rifiyya and live in the Rif Mountains; and so on. Berber cultures have been influential in North Africa, in regional forms of architecture, music, dance, textiles, and painting. Written forms of Berber languages use the Arabic or Latin alphabets, although unique Berber characters, called *tifinagh* (tifinar in English) do exist. Though the language is not taught in North African schools, increasing numbers of written works—a literature of poetry and prose—have been produced in the last few decades.

In addition, Berber dynasties like the Almoravids (eleventh and twelfth centuries) and Almohads (1130–1269) played central roles in the Islamic history of North Africa. For example, the Berber general Tariq ibn Ziyād, for whom Jabal Tariq, "Gibraltar," is named, led the Islamic conquest of Spain.

During French colonial rule in North Africa, the colonists attempted to drive a wedge between Arab and Berber to splinter opposition to French occupation. In Morocco and Algeria, Berbers were granted special privileges in the hope that they would identify with the colonial power rather than their countrymen. France's attempt to annex Algeria failed: after a bloody eight-year war, from 1954 to 1962, a united Algerian people won independence in the famous "Revolution of a Million Martyrs." Today there are calls for greater recognition of Berber culture, especially in the context of revived Muslim fundamentalism in Algeria. Some groups promote a form of Berber nationalism, keen on gaining a dominant role in society; others emphasize the need for cultural pluralism in a peaceful and cooperative coexistence.

Bergman, Ingmar (1918–)

Swedish filmmaker. One of the most popular and critically acclaimed filmmakers of all time, Bergman was born in Uppsala, Sweden, the son of a Lutheran minister. The influence of his religious upbringing, and the religious art with which he was surrounded from an early age, is evident in his work, which is highly visually wrought and often concerned with the conflict between good and evil.

Bergman attended the University of Stockholm, where he studied art, history, and literature, and became an active member of the student theatrical group. His interest and apparent talent in the field led him to a job as an apprentice director at the Master Olofsgården and Sagas theaters. In 1942 he was appointed to the Swedish Royal Opera, and later attained his first full-time directing job in 1944, at the Hälsingborg municipal theater. That same year he met Carl-Anders Dymling, the head of the Svensk Filmindustri, who was so impressed with Bergman's work that he commissioned a screenplay. The resulting script, Hets (1944; Frenzy, or Torment), was directed by Sweden's leading director at that time, Alf Sjöberg, and was so successful in Sweden and abroad that Bergman was offered the chance to write and direct his own film. This project became Kris (1945; Crisis), the story of an unhappy love affair that ends in suicide.

Several films followed in close succession throughout the 1940s, most of which dealt with contemporary social issues (love, military service, youth), and solidified his reputation as a director. Films such as Fängelse (1949; Prison, or The Devil's Wanton), which chronicled the misadventures of a young director obsessed with the role of evil in the world, were a testament to Bergman's emerging style and his imaginative approach to the medium.

After a short hiatus in 1951 during a Swedish economic crisis, Bergman directed two films in 1952, Kvinnors väntan (Waiting Women, or Secrets of Women) and Sommaren med Monika (Summer with Monika, or Monika), and was appointed the director of the municipal theater in Malmö. In this period he also began to assemble a company of actors who became regulars in his films. Though by now firmly established in the Swedish film industry, Bergman did not have an international hit until 1955's Sommarnattens leende (Smiles of a Summer Night), a romantic comedy. He followed this triumph with two others, Det sjunde inseglet (1957; The Seventh Seal), a medieval morality play about a knight who challenges Death to a game of chess, and Smultronstället (1957; Wild Strawberries), a lyrical study of the abyss between youth and old age, often classified as Chekhovian. These films established Bergman as an international celebrity and as one of the most important figures in film.

The early 1960s saw the production of what many consider Bergman's finest work, a trilogy of films, Såsom i en spegel (1961; Through a Glass Darkly), Nattsvardsgästerna (1963; Winter Light), and Tystnaden (1963; The Silence), which explored the topic of familial violence, the emptiness following the loss of faith, and the fear of verbal inadequacy. It was this trilogy that most profoundly examined the anguish arising from personal isolation and the problem of God's absence, ideas crucial to Bergman's increasingly complex worldview.

The windswept island of Fårö, where Bergman had purchased a house, became the setting for a cycle of films from the late 1960s and early 1970s, including Persona (1966), Vargtimmen (1968; Hour of the Wolf), Skammen (1968; Shame), and Beröringen (1971; The Touch). Persona, which tells the story of a woman who has lapsed into catatonic silence and the loquacious nurse who cares for her, has been hailed as one of Bergman's most sophisticated works.

Bergman continued to direct during the 1970s, and in 1978 the Swedish Film Institute created an award for excellence in filmmaking in his name. In 1983 he released *Fanny and Alexander*, an acclaimed account of a boy's growing up in early twentieth-century Sweden.

Berlin Wall

Concrete and wire barrier that separated East from West Berlin from 1961 to 1990. At the end of World War II, Berlin was divided by the United States, Great Britain, France, and the Soviet Union at the Potsdam Conference in 1945. The Berlin Wall was erected by Soviet leader Nikita Khrushchev and the East German government overnight in August 1961 to stem the massive migration from the East to the West. It became an emblem of the Cold War, the focal point and abiding symbol of the contest between the Eastern bloc—the Communist Eastern European countries, as well as the Soviet Union—and the capitalist West, led by NATO and the United States. Originally a ramshackle fence fashioned from barbed wire, it was built up into a ten-foot concrete wall surrounded by a network of barriers, electric fences, guarded checkpoints, and observation towers extending twenty-eight miles through Berlin and seventy-five miles around West Berlin, cutting it off from East Germany. Though the exact number is unknown, as many as 191 people were killed attempting to defect, shot by border guards. Popular sentiment, amplified by President Mikhail Gorbachev's *perestroika* in the Soviet Union, provoked massive demonstrations that led to the opening of the Wall late in 1989. The Wall itself was torn down in 1990, resulting in another flood of emigration from East Germany; the fall of the Wall was catalyzed by the liberalization of emigration policies in neighboring Hungary, which created an opening for the free passage of German refugees on East Germany's northeastern border. (It also made possible a lucrative market in Berlin Wall fragments that boomed briefly in the early 1990s.) Unified Berlin was the necessary first step in the reunification of East and West Germany that became a reality later in 1990.

Berlioz, [Louis-] Hector (1803–1869)

French Romantic composer. Berlioz is considered an orchestral radical; both in practice, as in his symphonies, overtures, and operas, and in theory, as in his *Traité d'instrumentation et d'orchestration modernes* (1844; *Treatise on Modern Instrumentation and Orchestration*), he celebrated the brilliance and wildness of pure sound. His *Symphonie fantastique* (1830) is a dream-like musical canvas in which the whole orchestra glows in fierce, and sometimes grotesque, new colors.

As a youth, Berlioz had little formal musical training; at his father's behest he went to Paris to study medicine. Realizing that his true love was music, he studied at the Paris Conservatory for eight years, much to the chagrin of his parents. Inspired by Beethoven's revolutionary symphonies, Berlioz sought unheard-of combinations of instruments—flute with trombone, for example—shocking the staid audiences of Paris. Not surprisingly, his career was marked by great failure as well as success. While certain works—his *Symphonie fantastique, Harold en Italie* (1834; *Harold in Italy*), and *Roméo et Juliette* (1839; *Romeo and Juliet*)—were well received by the public, Berlioz's opera debut, an adaptation of Benvenuto Cellini's autobiography, was disastrous. Despite this fiasco, he devoted further energies to opera, working for many years on *Les Troyens* (1856–63; *The Trojans*), a large-scale production of Vergil's love story of Dido and Aeneas. Berlioz was far ahead of his time and had little patience with petty musical politics. He was forced to make a living for much of his career as a music critic; his wit and eloquence as a writer paradoxically distracted attention from his music. Only after his death did his full achievement become clear. Other important works include the vast *Requiem* (1837), the *Damnation of Faust* (1845–46), *L'Enfance du Christ* (1850–54; *The Childhood of Christ*), and *Béatrice et Bénédict* (1860–62), a surprisingly light, lyrical operatic adaptation of William Shakespeare's play *Much Ado About Nothing*.

Beti, Mongo (1932–)

Cameroonian writer and teacher. One of the best-known Francophone writers of Africa, Mongo Beti is famous primarily for a sequence of four popular novels, briskly produced in the 1950s.

Born Alexandre Biyidi in Cameroon, Beti was educated in local Catholic schools until his expulsion at the age of fourteen, for rebelliousness. He took the French B.A. (Honors) in 1951 and moved to France, where he studied at Aix-en-Provence and the Sorbonne universities, taking the honors "license." Beti published his first novel, *Ville cruelle* (1954; *Cruel Town*), under the pseudonym Eza Boto, but later repudiated both the work and the pseudonym. His second novel, *Le Pauvre Christ de Bomba* (1956; *The Poor Christ of Bomba*), is set in the Cameroon of his youth and satirizes the Church and French colonialism. *Mission terminée* (1954; translated as *Mission to Kala* in 1958) won the Sainte-Beuve Prize for 1958. Beti's last novel of this period was *Le Roi Miraculé* (1958), which was translated in 1961 as *King Lazarus*; it chronicles the effects of Christianity and European values on an African culture.

To support his family, Beti took an additional degree from the University of Paris in 1966 and became a teacher of Greek, Latin, and French literature. A staunch Marxist, Beti has written several articles criticizing the regime in his native Cameroon. In 1972 he wrote a political essay, *Main basse sur le Cameroun* (*The Plundering of Cameroon*), which denounced the neocolonial practices of the Cameroon regime, independent since 1960. In 1978 he founded a journal, *Peuples Noirs, Peuples Africains*, to explore new African possibilities. In his later novels *Perpetua* (1974), *Remember Ruben* (1974; title in pidgin English), and *La Ruine presque cocasse d'un polichinelle* (1979; *The Almost Laughable Downfall of a Buffoon*), he chronicles the cycles of oppression and resistance in his homeland.

Bhagavadgita

Sanskrit religious poem. Believed to have been written in the first or second century C.E., the Bhagavadgita is part of Book VI of the *Mahabharata* (*Great Epic of the Bharata Dynasty*). The poem's seven hundred verses are divided into eighteen chapters, and it is one of the most widely read and beloved works in the literature of the world's religions.

Sanskrit for "Song of God," the Bhagavadgita is the dialogue between the warrior Prince Arjuna and Krishna, the earthly incarnation of the Hindu god Vishnu, who is acting as Arjuna's charioteer and friend. Their conversation takes place on a battlefield moments before the start of a great war. Prince Arjuna, espying many of his friends and relatives among the enemy ranks, expresses his doubts to Krishna about the ethics of fighting, killing, or being killed in this war. Krishna in turn reminds Arjuna of his *dharma* (duty) as a warrior, and of the Hindu belief that the highest path, the way to demonstrate one's perfect faith in God and to attain *moksha* (liberation from the cycle of rebirth), requires the dispassionate and nonselfish discharge of one's duty without concern for one's private motives, gain, or loss.

What begins as military advice thus

becomes religious counsel and spiritual instruction, as Krishna goes on to elaborate upon the more metaphysical questions of the nature of God and man's relationship with and knowledge of God. In the process of answering these questions, Krishna provides a summary of the history of Indian religious thought and practice.

Teaching that human beings have both a provisional material or natural existence and a spiritual and immortal existence, the Bhagavadgita considers the latter the higher nature of the two. The ultimate goal of human life, according to the poem, is the recognition that the *atman*, or self, is at one with the divine reality of the "Highest Spirit" and that liberation can come only when the individual grounds his *karma*, or actions, in the divine will. In order to achieve liberation, or *moksha*, however, the reader is instructed to practice and combine the three main forms of Yoga, or systems of spiritual discipline: *jnana* (knowledge) in the form of *jnanayoga*; *bhakti* (devotion) in the form of *bhaktiyoga*; and *karma* (action) in the form of *karmayoga*.

Bhanu Bhakta Acharya (1871–1926)

Nepali poet. Considered the founder of Nepali literature, Acharya wrote exclusively in Nepali. Acharya's writings, and his promotion of a standard Nepali language, were powerful tools in the struggle against the dispiriting dominion of the British colonials.

Acharya's preferred mode of writing was a simple, lyric narrative, the *sloka*, a form he employed to write about the moral dilemmas of the common people. A deeply religious man, Acharya is said to have been inspired to translate the *Adhyatma Ramayana* into Nepali after a conversation with an old grass cutter, though this story may be apocryphal. Acharya used the story of Ramayana of Ayodhya, who spent his life in exile, as an allegory of Nepali life, patient and

hopeful of deliverance from the scourge of British occupation. The image of exile recurs in the *Ramayana* and particularly in the four cantos that were translated during the months Acharya spent in debtors' prison in Kumari-Chawk.

Acharya's major works, including "Bhaktamala" ("Garland of Devotion"), "Badhu Shikshya" ("Advice to the Daughter-in-law"), and "Ramgeeta" ("Song of Rama"), often use moments of everyday life to create poems of traditionalist moral instruction. Acharya's "Badhu Shikshya," for example, was inspired by a visit to a friend's home, during which Acharya overheard an argument between his friend's wife and mother-in-law. It contains, among other things, advice to daughters-in-law regarding their proper conduct and duties in their husband's family. His final work, "Ramgeeta" (1924), composed of twenty-two *slokas*, contains philosophical discourses and was composed during the final years of his illness.

bharata-natyam

Indian classical dance. Originally called *dasi-attam* (dance of the *devadasi*, or female temple dancers), this classical dance form was renamed in the late 1940s, soon after it was brought to the stage for public performance. Of the five classical dance styles of India, which include the *kathak, kathakali, manipuri,* and *orissi, bharata-natyam* is the principal one. It is an ancient form, indigenous to the Tamil Nadu region around Madras, and has been attributed to Ulupi, the wife of Arjuna. In its traditional form, *bharata-natyam* was performed exclusively by *devadasi* and served as an expression of Hindu religious themes and devotions, first mentioned in the *Natya-sastra*, the ancient treatises of the Brahmin sage and priest Bharata.

After the eleventh century its popularity diminished, but it was still performed by the *devadasi* and by the court dancers of the Marāthā kings of Tanjore. In the latter half of the nineteenth century, four brothers tried to renovate and modernize the dance form; however, despite these efforts, it was not until the 1940s, when girls from respectable families took the dance to the stage, that *bharata-natyam* once more became popular.

In stage performances of *bharata-natyam*, one dancer, usually female, performs for two hours without interruption and without changing costume. She is accompanied by an orchestra of drums, drone, and singer, all located at the back of the stage. The dancer squats, her feet beating out complicated counter-rhythms to the orchestra, her arms, neck, and shoulders moving throughout. Pantomime is an important part of the dance, during which the dancer's hands gesture the story while her face conveys the mood. In its pure form, the dancer's hands are restricted to eleven poses.

In the Cola temples of Tanjore and in temples and shrines in Vijayanagara and throughout southern India, sculpture and frieze-work dating from the fourteenth to the seventeenth century depict the series of movements in the *bharata-natyam*. These artistic renditions not only are impressive works of art but also served as cue cards: if aspiring dancers forgot the required movement or pose, they could look to the art to find their next move.

Bible

Sacred text of the Jewish and Christian religions. Considered by many to be the word of God, the Bible is the most widely read and distributed book in the world; the ideas and moral codes contained within it are extremely pervasive, and serve as one of the keystones for much Western thought, as well as, increasingly, that of Africa, Asia, and Latin America.

The Bible is divided into two parts, the Hebrew Scriptures and the New Testament. The Hebrew Scriptures are the sacred text of the Jewish faith; the first five books (Genesis, Exodus, Leviticus, Numbers, and Deuteronomy) are called the Pentateuch, the five books of Moses, or the Torah. These writings contain the laws that God gave Moses for the Jews. Along with the book of Joshua, the Pentateuch relates the creation of the universe, the world, humanity, and the historical development of the Jews as God's chosen people and their founding of the nation of Israel. The Prophets (Nevi'im), including Joshua, Judges, Samuel, Kings, Isaiah, Jeremiah, Ezekiel, and the twelve minor prophets, continue the history of Israel with a description of the development of the social hierarchy and the monarchy. The remaining books of the Hebrew Scriptures are called the Writings (Ketuvim) of Hagiographa, and are more philosophical (Job and Ecclesiastes) or poetical (Psalms, Song of Solomon). The authors of these books are anonymous, but scholars have grouped various writings by the styles and the different references to God: some books use the name Yahweh; some use the name Elohim. Despite these investigations, there is no certainty about the number of authors, or the dates when the books were written. The Hebrew Scriptures were principally written in Hebrew, though there are thought to be a few short elements first written in Aramaic. When the Persians controlled the Mediterranean basin, the Jews translated the original Hebrew into the new lingua franca. And when Greek was the ruling language in the mid third century B.C.E., the Hebrew Scriptures were rendered into a Greek translation called the Septuagint. After Christianity combined the New Testament with the Hebrew Scriptures and converted many populations to Christianity, the translations proliferated.

In the Hebrew Scriptures and the New Testament, fourteen books are regarded by most Protestants as of dubious origin (which is to say, not divinely inspired), but eleven of these are recognized by the Roman Catholic Church. Together these books are called the Apocrypha. The books of the Apocrypha are usually presented, at the end of the Hebrew Scriptures, in bibles for Roman Catholic use, and include Tobias, Judith, the Book of Wisdom, Baruch, and Maccabees. The Apocrypha is also often published on its own. In effect, these writings continue the history of Israel into the second century B.C.E.

The New Testament is much shorter than the Hebrew Scriptures, and tells the story of one man, Jesus Christ, seen as the son of God, and the hundred or so years after his death—the time of the founding of the Christian Church. The first four books are the Gospels, which narrate the birth, life, death, and resurrection of Christ. The Book of Acts (the Acts of the Apostles) details the spread of Christianity until the death of Paul, and the Epistles contain various correspondences between early leaders of the Church, especially Paul, as they built the foundations of the organized religion. The last book, Revelations, is the only apocalyptic book, containing a vision given to St. John the Divine of the last days of the world and the return of Christ to lead those who have followed him.

The remarkable similarity between the New Testament's depiction of Jesus and the prophecies of the Hebrew Scriptures is no coincidence: those prophecies were believed to prefigure Jesus' life and teachings. Indeed, the New Testament is often most fascinating when compared with the Hebrew Scriptures, particularly in the light of the eventual, widespread acceptance of Christianity. Where the Hebrew Scriptures present a fearsome god of revenge and jealousy, constantly sending the Jews into slavery as punishment for their disobedience, the New Testament reveals a god with a message of forgiveness and salvation. This broad appeal of Christianity contributed to its success in the waning days of the Roman empire, as significant portions of the population became restless with corrupt governments and pagan religions. Early Christians debated whether the message of Christ was applicable to all people or only to the Jews; this debate appears throughout the Epistles.

In 313 the emperor Constantine I declared toleration of the Christian religion within the Roman empire in the Edict of Milan; by then the writings of both the Old and New Testaments had been translated into Coptic, Ethiopian, Gothic, Latin, and other languages. In 405 St. Jerome consolidated the various sources into a Latin version that became the Vulgate translation and served as the official Bible for more than a thousand years. Although there were arguments and controversies in the production of that edition, the Vulgate was considered holy. Translations of the Vulgate into English and German were crucial to the rise of Protestantism. The invention of the printing press and the publication of Bibles in the vernacular also helped standardize and codify languages like English and German, which had previously existed in multiple and sometimes conflicting dialects and regionalisms. Today, because of the extensive work of missionaries around the world, the Bible has been translated into nearly every language.

Biko, Stephen (1946–1977)

South African political and cultural leader. Biko, a medical student, became interested in politics in the 1960s, eventually founding the Black Consciousness movement. In 1968 he cofounded and served as the first president of the all-black South African Students' Organization (SASO), whose agenda involved the development of "black consciousness," including political self-reliance and the unification of black university students. However, the popularity of SASO reached not only students but other black people throughout South Africa, and a coalition of over seventy black organizations elected Biko to serve as honorary president of the newly established Black People's Convention in 1972.

Prior to completing his degree in medicine, Biko was expelled from the University of Natal in 1972 because of his political activities. He then served as a full-time organizer for the Black Community Programs in Durban, until the organization was officially banned in 1973 by the South African government. The organization was proscribed for "threatening national security," and Biko's movements were closely watched by the Security Police. He was restricted to the King William's Town magisterial district, where he was prohibited from speaking to more than one person at a time, writing publicly, or speaking to the media.

Despite the ban, Biko continued to organize on behalf of the Black Community Programs, though in 1975 the ban was tightened to restrict him from doing so. Biko was detained by the Security Police several times on various criminal charges, although he obtained his release in every case; however, in 1977 Biko was arrested by the Security Police for his alleged involvement in inciting riots and disorder in Port Elizabeth. Eighteen days later, Biko went into a coma after twenty-two hours of interrogations, torture, and beating; during his detention Biko was allegedly bound in chains and prevented from exercising or having fresh air. Despite the obvious seriousness of his physical condition, medical examinations completed by the Security Police failed to detect any critical health problems, and five days later Biko, who had been denied food and water, was taken to Pretoria, some six hundred miles away. He was transported naked and restrained in manacles, and eventually died of a brain hemorrhage as a result of head injuries sustained while in custody. An autopsy revealed that Biko had also suffered numerous other injuries, including multiple bruises and abrasions. His death refocused world attention on the continuing injustices of white minority rule in South Africa.

al-Biruni, Abu ar-Rayhan (c. 973–1048)

Arab scholar and philosopher. Born in Khwārizm, south of the Aral Sea, al-Biruni is considered one of the most learned men of his time. Writing in Arabic but fluent in Turkish, Persian, Sanskrit, Hebrew, and Syriac, al-Biruni wrote treatises on astronomy, including *al-Qanun al Mas'udi* (*The Mas'udi Canon*), mathematics, medicine, mineralogy, physics, and history, most notably *Arthar al-baqiyah* (*Chronology of Ancient Nations*) and *Tā'rīkh al-Hind* (*A History of India*). His accomplishments won him patronage in the courts of Khwārizm, Jurjan, and Ghaznavid, and his renown stretched from the Aral Sea to eastern Iran and northern India.

Traveling widely, al-Biruni wrote an encyclopedic description of life in ancient India and corresponded with the Islamic philosopher and physician Ibn Sînâ (980–1037), known in the West as Avicenna. Al-Biruni's signal works of Islamic scholarship are powerful documents from this period of tremendous Muslim cultural achievement.

Bishop, Elizabeth (1911–1979)

American poet. Despite her relatively slight poetic output—her *Collected Poems* includes only around a hundred original works—Bishop has become known since her death as one of the greatest American poets of this century. Her work is characterized by technical mastery and a quiet, sometimes detached tone.

Born in Worcester, Massachusetts, in

1911, she spent much of her childhood in Canada's Nova Scotia with her maternal grandparents; she would later memorialize the area in such landscape poems as "At the Fishhouses." She attended Vassar College, where she met and began a forty-year friendship with Marianne Moore, an older poet whose polite, witty poems would influence Bishop's. Bishop spent much of her life outside her native country, traveling in Europe and North Africa before settling in Ouro Preto, Brazil, where she lived for nearly fifteen years with her lover Lota de Macedo Soares. After Soares's suicide in 1969, Bishop returned to the States. Some of her better-known poems ("Arrival at Santos," "Questions of Travel") explore the traveler's appetite for new experience and delve into the ironies of tourism and modern displacement.

Although frequently described as "discreet" and "unassuming," Bishop's work explores complex issues of poverty, cultural displacement, and sexuality, and some assessments have obscured the engaged, occasionally bitter aspect of some of her work. This slant has partly been due to Bishop's own retiring demeanor and her disdain for labels such as "woman writer" or "lesbian poet."

An accomplished translator and prose writer, Bishop translated poems by Mexican writer Octavio Paz and the Brazilian Carlos Drummond de Andrade. She also composed short stories and nonfiction travel accounts. Her books of poetry include *North and South* (1946), *Questions of Travel* (1965), and *Geography III* (1976). A portion of her voluminous correspondence (with such friends as Moore and the poets Robert Lowell and James Merrill) was published in *One Art* (1994).

Black Arts Movement

African-American literary movement. The Black Arts Movement was a loosely defined grouping of African-American poets and authors in the 1960s, whose work explored the possibilities of black nationalism and radical black politics. As noted by black writer Larry Neal in "The Black Arts Movement," a defining essay of 1968, "Black Arts is the aesthetic and spiritual sister of the Black Power concept. . . . One is concerned with the relationship between art and politics; the other with the art of politics."

The Black Arts Movement, involving poets like Imamu Amiri Baraka (born LeRoi Jones), Sonia Sanchez, Nikki Giovanni, and Haki Madhubuti (born Don L. Lee), articulated an angry and often violent black political voice that denounced white racism and championed the cause of black racial solidarity and self-determination. Though the movement did not espouse a specific political platform, its poetry adopted a characteristic aggressive approach and sought to capture a black linguistic style and rhythm to forge what many of its proponents called a "black aesthetic." Baraka's "Black Art" (1971), one of the movement's quintessential works, is a call encouraging black poets to produce politically radical black nationalist poems, and it demonstrates some of the hallmarks of Black Arts style and political ideas. In it Baraka calls for "poems that wrestle cops into alleys / and take their weapons leaving them dead / with tongues pulled out and sent to Ireland . . . Airplane poems . . . / Setting fire and death to whitey's ass."

Black Arts poems generated controversy among black and white writers and critics alike, who often labeled such work hate-filled and racist, but the movement influenced later black writers like Ishmael Reed, who applied some of the Black Arts ideas in novels like *Mumbo Jumbo* (1972).

Blake, William (1757–1827)

English poet, artist, and mystic. At the age of fourteen, Blake was apprenticed to an engraver. Receiving his only education in art, he eventually attended the Royal Academy of Art in London. A short time later, he met and married Catherine Boucher, whom he taught to read and who assisted him with his engravings.

Central to Blake's poetry and painting are his visionary experiences, which began in childhood. He believed that through these visions he experienced God directly, without the mediation of religion, and received his own personal mythology as well as direction for his artistic work. In 1787 Blake became engrossed in a new method of printing his own poems, which was supposedly revealed to him in a vision by his deceased brother, Robert. Blake wrote his poems and then illustrated them with watercolors. The first of his books to be printed in this way was *Songs of Innocence* (1789), which together with his later and more cynical publication *Songs of Experience* (1794) form one of the most original bodies of work in Western art and literature. He is best known for the "prophetic" books, produced with the aid of his wife, which include his principal prose work, *The Marriage of Heaven and Hell* (1793).

Unfortunately, none of these publications were especially popular or commercially successful during his lifetime, and Blake was forced to make his living by illustrating texts for various patrons. Among these are the magnificent illustrations he produced for an edition of Italian poet Dante's *Divina commedia* (1310–14; *Divine Comedy*), which Blake worked on until his death. A generous patron, John Linnell, introduced Blake to a group of admiring younger artists who formed a group known as "The Ancients," providing Blake with a measure of recognition for his unique and visionary work. Though in his own day he was ignored by the public and lived on the verge of poverty, Blake is now hailed by some as the earliest and greatest of the English Romantics.

blaxploitation

American film genre. Developed in the early 1970s in an effort to attract a larger number of African-Americans to the movie theaters, blaxploitation was also a commercial response to the growing self-awareness of black Americans.

These films were predominantly directed, produced, and distributed by whites; little effort was made to recruit blacks to write scripts or direct. Wildly popular with black audiences, the films were nevertheless attacked by critics for encouraging gross stereotypes and one-dimensional characters. When the movies were set in urban northern ghettos, the characters tended to be pimps, prostitutes, hustlers, drug dealers, hit men, and the like. Titles include *Superfly* (1973), *Shaft* (1971), *Coffy* (1974), and *Jones* (1974). In southern settings, the films—like *Slaves* (1969), *The Quadroon* (1971), *Mandingo* (1975), *Drum* (1976), and *Passion Plantation* (1978)—promoted stereotypical characterizations and sensationalized sex and violence, often dwelling on issues of miscegenation. Criticism of these films focused on the employment of stereotypical images of black characters, their romanticization of violence, degrading portraits of women, and depictions of violent sex.

The Coalition Against Blaxploitation, formed in Hollywood by more than four hundred black members of the film industry, along with national black organizations, including the NAACP (National Association for the Advancement of Colored People), the SCLC (Southern Christian Leadership Conference), and the Urban League, stridently opposed the image of black people in these films. The blaxploitation genre died out by the late 1970s, partly from changing audience tastes, and also through the extensive media coverage these groups garnered for their cause. In the 1990s a guarded reevaluation of the genre was propounded by critics who noted that the blaxploitation explosion of the early seventies opened the movie industry to black actors and, eventually, black directors, producers, and writers.

blues

Secular African-American folk music. As a musical genre, blues has had one of the most abiding influences on Western popular music, and its history closely parallels that of jazz. The vocal style associated with the blues probably came out of the solo calls of work songs sung by nineteenth-century black farmworkers in the American South. Early blues instrumental style, which centered on string instruments like the banjo, imitated the sounds of traditional African string instruments like the *bania* or *khalam*; these instruments also assumed prominence because of the ban on drumming on slave plantations.

The blues first emerged as a musical form in the 1890s, born of the ballads of the Reconstruction era following the American Civil War, and was popularized by traveling singers during the early twentieth century. Blues styles fall into three broad categories: country, classic, and urban. Country blues, which originated in the Mississippi delta and east Texas, feature a male singer and acoustic guitar and highly flexible singing style and guitar accompaniment. Wide dissemination of country blues began with Blind Lemon Jefferson's recordings in 1926; other famous country blues singer-guitarists include Charley Patton, Blind Blake, and Robert Johnson. Classic blues features a pianist or jazz band accompanying a female singer, and is best known through the work of Mamie Smith, Ma Rainey, and Bessie Smith. Urban blues developed after World War II and was heavily influenced by gospel music and the electric guitar. Big Bill Broonzy, John Lee "Sonny Boy" Williamson, and B. B. King were among those who experimented with and developed this postwar-era sound.

Blyden, Edward Wilmot (1832–1912)

Liberian educator and clergyman, foremost nineteenth-century advocate of Pan-Africanism. Edward Wilmot Blyden is best known for his ideas about race relations, as set forth in his collection of essays, *Christianity, Islam and the Negro Race* (1887), which foreshadowed the "Back-to-Africa" movement of Marcus Garvey and the concept of Négritude developed by Aimé Césaire and Léopold Senghor.

Blyden was born in the West Indies, the son of free, literate blacks, who claimed descent from the Igbo tribe of Nigeria. A precocious student, Blyden traveled to the United States to study theology, but he immigrated to Liberia (which had been colonized by American blacks in 1822) after being openly discriminated against. There he became active in politics but was nearly lynched in 1871 because of his close association with Liberia's president, Edward Roye. Roye was Liberia's first dark-skinned president, and was later deposed and murdered by lighter-skinned mulatto factions. Blyden escaped to Sierra Leone, where he held several political and educational appointments.

Of greater importance are Blyden's intellectual contributions. Like Jamaican "Back-to-Africa" movement leader Marcus Garvey, Blyden believed that only in Africa could blacks attain their true potential. Despite his training as a Christian minister, he was largely dismissive of Christianity because of its association with European racism. He advocated Islam as a unifying religion for the continent. Blyden's vision of a greater West African nation led him to embrace European imperialism in Africa as a tactical means to achieve the end of a secure and unified governmental entity. As a result, Blyden was a supporter of the failed British coup of 1909; because of his age, his punishment was lenient. He died in Sierra Leone, penniless. Blyden's phrase

"Africa for the Africans" became the watchword of many in the African independence movements following World War II.

Bogomils

Balkan religious sect. Born of various doctrines imported from Paulician sects of Armenia and Asia Minor, as well as local Slavonic attempts to reform the Orthodox Church, Bogomilism flourished between the tenth and fifteenth centuries. (Paulicians, whose earliest communities were in Armenia in the seventh century C.E., held to a Manichean belief in two Gods, one good and one evil.) The Bogomils were an intensely nationalistic as well as religious movement.

Named for a priest, the Bogomils believed that the material world was created by the devil, Christ's older brother: they therefore rejected everything that brought man into contact with matter, including marriage, procreation, manual labor, meat eating, and wine drinking. The organizational structure of the Orthodox Church was rejected, along with its ritual trappings. There was no church and no set form of worship.

The movement spread throughout Europe and into Asian parts of the Byzantine empire, remaining powerful in Bulgaria through the fourteenth century—until the Ottoman conquest, when many Bogomils were converted to Islam. Good information on the Bogomils is hard to come by; the only texts that make reference to them come to us from their orthodox Christian enemies.

Bohra

Indian Muslim community. The name Bohra comes from a corruption of *vahaurau*, a Gujarati word meaning "to trade." Originally designating a caste or group position, for the middle or merchant classes Bohra came to refer to Hindu converts to Islam, especially Shi'ite Muslims of the Must'li sect. To-

day there are over 200,000 Shi'ite Bohra, although the sect does include a small minority of Sunnî Muslims as well.

Founded in Egypt, the Must'li sect established its religious center in Yemen and spread throughout the South Asian subcontinent in the eleventh century, propelled by missionary zeal. After 1539 and the rise of the Bohra community in Gujarat and elsewhere throughout India, its base was transferred from Yemen to Sidhpur in India.

Bohra religious authority had been entrusted to one *da'i*, or leader, from the time of the first *da'i*, Dhu'aib ibn Musa, to the rule of the twenty-sixth *da'i*, Dawud ibn 'Adjab Shah. However, after the death of Dawud, around 1590, the Bohra sect was divided between two rival leaders, the Indian Dawud ibn Qutb Shah and the Yemeni Sulayman. Both factions still exist, and both make their home in Bombay. A more telling, and recent, division in Shi'ite Bohra occurred in the twentieth century, with the formation of conservative and progressive ("modernizing") factions among the Dawudis. Where the conservative faction stands for maintaining traditional practices and supports the Mulla-dji, or high priest, the progressives, the "anti-Mulla-dji," aim to align religious doctrines and practices with modern ideas about education and the quality of life. The progressives seem to have strong popular support.

boleadoras

South American Indian weapon. The boleadoras, or bola, comes from the Spanish word for "balls." Boleadoras consist of two or three balls made of stone or some other heavy material wrapped in leather and attached to long ropes, also usually made of leather and sometimes of rhea tendons. Originally used by the Indians to capture rheas, guanacos, and other animals, they were quickly adopted by the gauchos (South American "cowboys") and then by soldiers who fought in the wars of independence. The boleadoras are whirled in the air like a sling and then thrown toward the ground to entwine around the prey's legs. During the wars of independence, they were used, quite effectively, to immobilize and bring down an opponent's horse.

Bolívar, Simón (1783–1830)

Latin American general and statesman. Known as "the Liberator," Simón Bolívar led a series of revolutions against Spanish rule, bringing political independence to what would become Colombia, Venezuela, Ecuador, Peru, and Bolivia. Born in Venezuela to an aristocratic family of Spanish descent, and orphaned as a child, Bolívar was sent to Madrid to complete his education. Returning to Europe in 1804, at the height of Napoleon's career, Bolívar was inspired by the French general and vowed to liberate the Americas from foreign powers.

In 1810, after the Spanish captain general in Caracas was overthrown, Bolívar, in London, persuaded the exiled revolutionary Francisco de Miranda to return with him and take command of the independence movement. In 1811 Venezuela proclaimed its independence, only to succumb to Spanish forces once again.

Fleeing to Cartagena, Bolívar published the first of his political statements, *El manifesto de Cartagena* (1812; *The Cartagena Manifesto*). He also organized a new army, routed the Spanish, and in 1813 entered Caracas victorious, again proclaiming the liberation of Venezuela. He was named "the Liberator" and made dictator, but his triumph—and the second Venezuelan republic—lasted only a year.

Once more in exile, this time in Jamaica, Bolívar again tried unsuccessfully to enlist British support, drafting the greatest document of his career, *La carta de Jamaica* (*The Letter from Jamaica*). In it he outlined his project for liberation, which consisted of establishing constitutional republics throughout Latin America modeled on the government of Great Britain; his goal was to bring about political union in all Spanish America through a triple federation made up of Mexico/Central America, the northern nations, and the southern nations.

In the spring of 1819, he launched an attack on New Granada, invading Santa Fé de Bogotá, in what is considered one of the most daring ventures in military history. His soldiers marched through lands the Spanish thought impassable to take the Spanish forces by surprise; in the Battle of Boyacá, the bulk of royalist forces surrendered to Bolívar. Although Spanish dominion did not completely end until the Battle of Carabobo in 1821, this victory at Boyacá was the turning point in the history of northern South America.

Bolívar was made president and military dictator of the republic of Gran Colombia in December 1819, even though Venezuela and Quito (Ecuador) were controlled by royalist troops. After a six-month armistice, Bolívar waged the battle of Carabobo, securing Venezuelan independence. In the fall of the same year, a congress convened to draft a constitution for Colombia; Bolívar found its provisions too liberal to guarantee the survival of his federation; disappointed, he left the administration of Colombia to Francisco de Paula Santander. He continued his military campaign in Ecuador, which, with the help of Antonio José de Sucre—one of his most brilliant officers and the first constitutional president of Bolivia—by year's end was also liberated. There Bolívar also met the great love of his life, Manuela Sáenz, an ardent revolutionary who accompanied him from the battlefields to the presidential palace.

Only Peru remained to be liberated. Here Bolívar joined José de San Martín, another visionary, who had liberated Argentina and Chile. San Martín had already entered Lima and proclaimed Peru's independence when Bolívar arrived, but he had been unable to fully eradicate the Spanish forces. The two military leaders met in Ecuador to discuss possible strategies, but they were unable to reach an agreement concerning the problem of territorial boundaries or the political design of Latin America. San Martín withdrew his troops and resigned his office in Lima, granting Bolívar center stage. The military campaign was successful, and the Spanish surrendered in 1824.

By 1825 Bolívar was president of Gran Colombia, Peru, and Bolivia, though his authoritarian constitutions later failed. In 1826 a league of Hispanic-American states was created, proving an important example for future hemispheric solidarity and organization in Latin America. At the time of his death, strife and political disintegration were becoming commonplace. Abandoning his post in Lima to become dictator of Gran Colombia, Bolívar narrowly escaped an assassination attempt, seeking refuge at a hacienda in Colombia, where he eventually died of tuberculosis.

Böll, Heinrich (1917–1985)
German novelist, short-story writer. Böll remains Germany's most popular modern writer; with Günter Grass, he has dominated postwar literature in that country. Often hailed in his lifetime as "the conscience of West Germany," Böll wrote of the necessity to remember the national past and condemned the materialism of modern culture.

Heinrich Böll was born into a liberal Catholic family in Cologne during World War I. He served briefly in the German army during World War II, and after being wounded was taken prisoner by American troops. After the war, he returned to Cologne with his young wife and family, working odd jobs and writing industriously. His early stories, collected in *Wanderer, kommst du nach Spa . . .* (1950; *Traveler, If You Come to Spa . . .*) reflect a disillusionment with notions of wartime bravery. He wrote several novels before his breakthrough work, *Und sagte kein einziges Wort* (1953; *Acquainted with the Night*), finally brought him financial security. The book criticized corruption in the Catholic Church and the coldness of modern German society.

Böll's success was followed by difficulties with government and church officials in West Germany. Böll made public his opposition to the national rearmament campaign and published a story satirizing the commercialization of Christmas that angered the Church. He traveled to Ireland to avoid criticism for these positions. His experiences there are published in *Irisches Tagebuch* (1957; *Irish Journals*).

In the late 1950s Böll became increasingly interested in socialism, and in 1962 traveled to the Soviet Union as part of a cultural exchange. A new, more straightforward approach characterizes his fiction of this era, notably *Ansichten eines Clowns* (1963; *The Clown*), which tells the story of an aimless young man discouraged by a meaningless modern society.

Other important works include *Gruppenbild mit Dame* (1971; *Group Portrait with Lady*) and *Die verlorene Ehre der Katharina Blum* (1974; *The Lost Honor of Katharina Blum*). The latter, which remains one of his best-selling novels, is a parable of journalistic distortion. Böll was awarded the Nobel Prize in 1972.

Bombal, María Luisa (1910–1980)
Chilean novelist and short-story writer. With two short novellas, *La última niebla* (1934; *The Final Mist*) and *La amortajada* (1938; *The Shrouded Woman*), Bombal revolutionized Chilean writing, cementing the achievements of genera-

tions of Chilean women authors. Born to an upper-middle-class family, she was twelve when her father died and she moved with her mother to Paris. There she studied philosophy and literature at the Sorbonne and witnessed the development of the Latin American literary avant-garde through the work of writers like Vicente Huidobro, Alejo Carpentier, and Miguel Angel Asturias, and painters like Diego Rivera and Roberto Matta, who were then in Paris.

In 1931 Bombal returned to her family estate in Chile. Two years later, political unrest forced her to leave for Argentina, where the political climate was calm and the arts were undergoing a renaissance. She lived in the house of Chilean consul Pablo Neruda, who introduced her to major literary figures, among them Federico García Lorca. According to her accounts, Bombal and Neruda spent hours working together at the kitchen table, sharing and commenting on their work. By 1934, the year she married Argentine painter Jorge Larcos, Bombal had finished the manuscript of *The Final Mist*. It was published the same year in a little-known edition along with three short stories: "El árbol" ("The Tree"), "Islas nuevas" ("New Islands"), and "Lo secreto" ("The Unknown"). The 1935 first official edition of the novel established Bombal as one of the most innovative stylists of Latin America. *The Shrouded Woman* appeared three years later and is considered a masterpiece of Hispanic fiction. Bombal stunned her audience with the mysterious and poetic aura of her prose, her concise descriptions, and the self-conscious ambiguity of her language, qualities that have elicited comparisons to Virginia Woolf. Her work is considered a form of social protest and, on a deeper level, an expression of the rupture between a woman and the reality in which she is meant to discover the meaning of her life.

Bonifacio, Andrés (1863–1897)

Philippine nationalist leader. Succeeding José Rizal as the leader of the reformist society La Liga Filipina, Bonifacio subsequently became one of the founding members of the secret society Katipunan, an abbreviation of a Philippine phrase meaning "The Highest and Most Respectable Society of the Sons of the People." The Katipunan, organized along Masonic lines, was established in 1892 to spearhead the national liberation struggle against Spain, which had controlled the islands since 1594. In the nineteenth century, the opening of the port city of Manila to foreign trade and the opening of the Suez Canal greatly expanded economic, political, and intellectual commerce for the Filipino people—an expansion that directly contributed to the rise of Philippine nationalism in the latter part of the nineteenth century. Bonifacio was a student of the French Revolution, and as a leader of the Katipunan, adopted and promoted many of its ideals, such as political autonomy and popular rule. But where Rizal was a European-educated intellectual who spoke through La Liga Filipina to the concerns of the growing Philippine middle class, Bonifacio was a laborer, and the composition of the Katipunan was considerably working class and peasant.

In March 1896 the Katipunan formally broke its public silence by issuing the first edition of the journal *Kalayaan* (Liberty), which boosted membership in the Katipunan to around 30,000. Yet while Bonifacio and the Katipunan were widely recognized as being in the vanguard of the Philippine revolutionary movement of the 1890s, other nationalist factions under different leaderships developed simultaneously throughout the islands. While the combined efforts of these military and political organizations succeeded in driving the Spanish from some of their provincial seats, internecine struggles for power among the revolutionary leaders resulted in the downfall of Bonifacio, and the deterioration of the Katipunan itself. Defeated in the society's presidential elections in the spring of 1897, Bonifacio contested the outcome, solidifying a schism that had developed within the ranks. Successful presidential candidate (and fellow Katipuneur) General Emilio Aguinaldo put down the Katipunan's internal rebellion and ordered rival opposition leader Bonifacio executed. Under Aguinaldo's leadership, the Katipunan entered into the Spanish-American War in 1898, assisting American naval forces commanded by Admiral Dewey in ousting the Spanish from the Philippines. Later years saw the Katipunan decline in significance as its provisional alliance with the Americans resulted in more colonial victimization, the Philippines again yoked to a colonial power. By the end of World War II, when the Philippines were granted the right to political self-determination by the United States, the Katipunan had devolved into an idiosyncratic and quasi-religious sectarian society.

Bonnard, Pierre (1867–1947)

French painter, lithographer, and illustrator. Considered to be one of the great colorists of modern art, Bonnard is renowned primarily for his small, intimate domestic scenes, such as *Coupe de fruits* (c. 1933; *Bowl of Fruit*) and *Salle à manger à la campagne* (1913; *The Dining Room*).

After studying the classics, Bonnard attended law school at the encouragement of his father, and in 1888 began working in a government office. He also began to study at the École des Beaux-Arts, eventually transferring to the Académie Julian. Befriending several French artists of the new generation, namely Maurice Denis and Édouard Vuillard, Bonnard and his contemporaries joined a theatrical producer, collab-

orating on productions for the Théâtre de l'Oeuvre in Paris.

In the 1890s Bonnard became a leading artist in a group called the Nabis, who specialized in the painting of small domestic scenes. By 1908 he began what was known as his Intimist period, concentrating instead on landscapes and larger-scale canvases and experimenting with grander modulations of color. His *Nu à contre-jour* (1908; *Nude Against the Light*) is a notable example of his work in this period. During the 1920s, worried that he had sacrificed too much in his pursuit of colorful theatrics, Bonnard embarked on a series of famous nudes painted with grace and an ease of form, using his longtime companion and wife, Marie Boursin, as a model. These later paintings—nudes, self-portraits, and landscapes—retain the powerful colors of his middle period.

Pierre Bonnard became a member of the English Royal Academy in 1940, and since his death has become more widely recognized for his contributions to "pure" painting.

Bonner, Neville Thomas (1922–)

Aboriginal political leader. Neville Thomas Bonner was the first Aboriginal Australian to be elected to the country's parliament. Bonner was born in Tweed Heads in New South Wales, Australia. After being educated at a state school in the southeastern region of Queensland, he worked as a carpenter and became active in the Liberal Party, holding several branch offices. Eventually, he gained a seat in the party's State Executive, and in 1971 he was elected a senator, representing Queensland. Serving in Parliament until 1983, Bonner then chose to resign in protest against the Liberal Party's decision to place him third on the list of Liberal Senate candidates in the 1983 election. Bonner later became the director of the Australian Broadcasting Corporation. Although less radical than many other of

Australia's Aboriginal leaders, Bonner continues to be an active spokesman for Aboriginal rights and social welfare and reform.

Book of the Dead

Ancient Egyptian religious text. The texts that compose the Egyptian Book of the Dead were consolidated by the German Egyptologist Richard Lepsius, who published them in 1842. Also known as the Book of Going Forth by Day, this collection of small texts or chapters contains magical formulas, spells, hymns, and prayers, all intended to assist the dead in navigating the obstacles and trials they would face in the afterworld.

The Book of the Dead expands on another, smaller-scale compilation of Egyptian spells. Originally consisting of short, discrete chapters, the various texts of the book were copied by scribes onto rolls of papyrus, painted on tomb walls, or carved into the coffins themselves. The magic spells were supposed to safeguard and instruct the dead, detailing ways of surviving the encounter with the god of the underworld, Osiris: when the mummy faced judgment, it was believed that a cunning spell, well said, could hide unpleasant facts from the mind of the judge.

The Book of the Dead contains materials dating back four millennia, and provides profound insight into ancient Egyptian religious beliefs and practices.

boomerang

Hunting weapon of the Australian Aborigines, and a toy. "Boomerang" is the name given to the curved throwing sticks initially used by a tribe living in New South Wales, Australia, near the Georges River. Similar weapons have been discovered in other indigenous societies; however, the boomerang is believed to be a strictly Australian creation. Hunting boomerangs do not return to the thrower. Instead, these boomerangs, which tend to be longer and heavier than the returning model, are used as a type of club and are thrown at prey. In addition, boomerangs were originally used as digging sticks and clapping sticks in local ceremonies.

Today boomerangs are best known for the unique design that makes them spin in the air while in flight and return to their thrower. In fact, returning boomerangs are used and recognized more for sport and recreational activity than for hunting, so much so that in 1978 the Confederation of Australian Sport established the Boomerang Association of Australia. This association holds boomerang competitions and annual national championships.

Borges, Jorge Luis (1899–1986)

Argentinean poet, essayist, and short-story writer. As a child in Buenos Aires, Borges learned English before Spanish, and read, in English, American writer Mark Twain's *The Adventures of Huckleberry Finn* and the works of H. G. Wells and Edgar Allan Poe. In 1914 he moved with his family to Geneva, where he learned French and German and later received his B.A. from the Collège de Genève. He left with his family in 1919, spending a year in Majorca and in Spain before returning to Buenos Aires. While in Spain, Borges met the young writers of the Ultraist movement, a group that denounced and rebelled against the "decadence" of established authors of the Generation of '98. Influenced by the French Symbolists and Parnassians, Ultraist poetry was characterized by free verse, complicated metrical innovations, and daring imagery and symbolism. Although Borges later denied it, he is credited with bringing modernism to Latin America through Ultraism.

Borges published his first book, a collection of poems called *Fervor de Buenos Aires* (1923; *Fervor of Buenos Aires*), two years after his return from Europe. During this period he also established three literary journals, wrote several volumes of essays and poems, and published his first book of fiction, *Historia universal de la infamia* (1935; *A Universal History of Infamy*). In 1938 he accepted an important post at a Buenos Aires library, which he held for nine years. That same year, Borges suffered a severe head wound and blood poisoning, an injury that nearly killed him. The experience seems to have unleashed his deepest creative imagination. Inventing a hybrid of the story form and the essay, in the following eight years he produced his best fantastic stories, later collected in *Ficciones* (1944; *Fictions*) and in the volume *El Aleph* (1949; augmented in 1952; *The Aleph and Other Stories, 1933–69*). He also collaborated with Adolfo Bioy Casares on detective stories that appeared in 1942 as *Seis problemas para Don Isidro Parodi* (*Six Problems for Don Isidro Parodi*) under the pseudonym of H. Bustos Domecq. In 1944 Borges received the Gran Premio de Honor from the Sociedad Argentina de Escritores (the Society of Argentine Writers), of which he was elected president in 1950.

With Argentinian leader Juan Perón's rise to power in 1946, Borges was dismissed from his library position and was forced to rely on friends to help him find places to lecture, edit, and write. In 1952 he published what some consider his best analytical essays: *Otras inquisiciones, 1937–1952* (*Other Inquisitions, 1937–1952*). Eventually, with Perón's downfall, Borges was appointed director of the national library, an honorific position, and professor of English and American literature at the University of Buenos Aires. By this time Borges was blind and dictated his texts to his mother, secretaries, or friends. Works from this period include *El hacedor* (1960; *Dreamtigers*), *El libro de los seros imaginarios* (1967; *The Book of Imaginary Beings*), *El informe de Brodie* (1970; *Dr. Brodie's Report*), and *El libro de*

arena (1975; *The Book of Sand*). He has received numerous national and international prizes in literature, and Latin American writers such as Gabriel García Márquez, Ernesto Sabato, Carlos Fuentes, Mario Vargas Llosa, and Julio Cortázar have acknowledged their debt to Borges for his tremendous contribution to Spanish literary language.

Borobudur

Javanese Buddhist monument. Constructed in 778–824 C.E. under the patronage of the Sailendra monarchs ruling Java during the eighth and ninth centuries, Borobudur was probably intended to serve as a mausoleum for the Sailendra king Indra (782–812), during whose reign the majority of construction was done, though no remains were ever actually placed there. The Borobudur is Indo-Javanese; the style is imported from Gupta India, but was executed by Javanese artists who incorporated indigenous elements into the many reliefs decorating Borobudur. The monument looks like an enormous *stupa* (Buddhist monument) from afar, but is really composed of nine terraces cut from a single hill.

These nine terraces represent the nine lives of Siddhartha Gautama (563–483), before he became Buddha. The temple itself is also designed in such a way that the pilgrim undergoes nine "rebirths," reminiscent of the spiritual journey to nirvana. The *stupa* is shaped like a *mandala*, a mythical model of the universe that combines the symbols of the circle (heaven), the square (earth), and the Buddha. The pilgrim must walk around the *stupa* nine times before reaching the top, and at each level is "swallowed" by a *kala* (monster) and then "reborn" into the next level. The first terraces are richly decorated with reliefs, Buddhas, and other ornaments, but later give way to simple, unadorned terraces—symbolic of the pilgrim's progression from an attachment to the material world to the spiritual liberation of nirvana and release from *samsara*, the cycle of reincarnation. With more than 2,000 pictorial panels and 400 statues of the Buddha, the Borobudur provides a complete textbook of the Nalanda school of Buddhism.

Borowski, Tadeusz (1922–1951)

Polish poet and short-story writer. Borowski, the author of a startlingly original group of stories based on his concentration camp experiences, was born in Ukraine. His father, a Polish worker, moved the family from the Soviet Union to Warsaw. As a result of the 1939 Nazi invasion, Borowski found himself compelled to complete his high school studies in a school set up by the Polish underground. He went on to study literature at the University of Warsaw, which was also operating clandestinely. Yet Borowski did not participate actively in the Resistance, choosing instead to devote his energies to poetry.

In his first book of poetry, *Gdziekolwiek ziemia* (1942; *Wherever the Earth*), which was illegally distributed in mimeographed form, Borowski depicted the catastrophe brought on by the occupation in stark and despairing terms. Shortly thereafter, the catastrophe enveloped him. In 1943 Borowski, looking for his girlfriend, wandered into an apartment that was under surveillance by the Gestapo. Mistaken for a member of the Resistance, he was initially sent to Auschwitz, where his girlfriend had also been sent, but was transferred to Dachau.

He survived, as did she. After his release in 1945, Borowski wrote a series of stories based on what he had experienced at Auschwitz. These stories first appeared in a volume that was published under the names of Borowski and two other camp survivors, but were later collected in Borowski's *Pożegnanie z Marią* (1948; *Farewell to Maria*). His camp stories were markedly different from his earlier, Romantically inflected works: the morally ambiguous life of survivors in the death camps discomfited many of his contemporaries. In his second collection, *Kamienny świat* (1948; *World of Stone*), Borowski denounced the effort to reestablish "normal" conditions in Germany in the wake of the horror of the concentration camps as hypocritical. As West German de-Nazification was abandoned in favor of normalization, Borowski's contempt for the West grew, and his political sympathies turned leftward.

Borowski took up the cause of Marxism-Leninism, writing for the Polish Communist Party. He worked mostly as a journalist, and became an ardent proponent of Socialist Realism. Disappointed in love and politics, he took his own life in 1951 at the age of twenty-nine.

Bosch, Hieronymous (1450–1516)

Flemish painter. Bosch produced paintings that had an enormous influence on the paintings of Pieter Breughel the Elder. Their grotesque, macabre figures are often cited as forerunners of Surrealism. An orthodox Catholic and member of a religious brotherhood, Bosch often painted religious pictures, allegories of sin and evil, using a personal symbolism that critics speculate is culled from popular superstitions, religion, and astrology. Indeed, Bosch's strange and unique style in painting remains an enigma even today, as so little of his life is known. It seems certain, though, that Bosch was both geographically and artistically isolated from centers of art activity, such as Haarlem and Antwerp. He remained in Hertogenbosch, the town from which he took his name, for his entire life, and the town itself became his artistic center. *Hooiwagen* (1480–85; *The Haywain*) and *Tuin der lusten* (c. 1510; *Garden of Earthly Delights*) are perhaps his best-known works. Bosch was quite famous in his own day, solicited by many prominent Catholics, including Philip II of Spain, who brought his work to Spain.

bossa nova

Brazilian musical style. Bossa nova became an international sensation in the 1950s and 1960s, initially through the efforts of Brazilian musicians such as Antonio Carlos "Tom" Jobim, João Gilberto, and Astrud Gilberto, as well as American jazz musicians such as Stan Getz.

The term "bossa nova" referred to the "new" way of playing the samba, or *bossa*, already popular in Rio de Janeiro in the 1950s, emphasizing lyrics and melody over samba rhythm (and hence guitar and piano over drums). Bossa nova first appeared in the beach neighborhood of Ipanema, and quickly became standard fare in elegant Copacabana nightclubs. Bossa nova was, and continues to be, associated with Brazil's middle and upper classes, as opposed to the more regional forms of samba and folk music, although like samba it owes a musical debt to choro, the original music of Rio's carnival.

Antonio Carlos Jobim was a classically trained musician who frequented and performed in the clubs. In 1957 the singer João Gilberto released *Desafinado* (*Out of Tune*), featuring songs by Jobim, which brought bossa nova to a broader audience. Bossa nova became a musical fixture in Brazil, showcasing the talents of Gilberto, Jobim, and Vinícius de Morães, Jobim's frequent collaborator. In 1959 bossa nova gained a worldwide audience through the film *Orfeo Negro* (*Black Orpheus*), which won an Academy Award and Cannes Film Festival prizes, and featured a soundtrack with music by many of the Brazilian artists. In 1963, with the release of "Girl from Ipanema," bossa nova became an international phenomenon. The song, written by Jobim, featured vocals by João and Astrud Gilberto and a solo by Stan Getz; it went on to win four Grammy awards.

Ironically, it was bossa nova's rapid success that paved the way for its dissipation as a Brazilian style of music. Imitations and reproductions of bossa nova tunes began to flood the international market. These "Americanized" versions, with faster tempos and elaborate orchestrations, were immensely popular, and soon superseded the simpler arrangements of Jobim and de Morães. At the same time, the military coup in Brazil in 1964 impeded expressions of indigenous Brazilian creativity; many of the bossa nova innovators fled to Europe and North America, while those who remained were branded as subversives by the new military government. Brazilian record companies released only a handful of new bossa nova records. Indeed, it was not until 1983 that Jobim was able to perform again in Brazil.

In the United States, artists like Stan Getz, Chet Baker, and other West Coast jazz musicians took to bossa nova as a departure from the stringent musical athleticism of bebop. Getz, "Cannonball" Adderly, Herbie Mann, and Paul Winter made new recordings of older bossa nova tracks, including "Black Orpheus," "Blue Bossa," "Desafinado," and "The Wave," which in turn became jazz standards.

The 1990s has seen a revival of interest in bossa nova, in Brazil and across the world. Brazilian artists such as Djavan, Eliane Elias, Gilberto Gil, João Bosco, Dorival Caymi, Luis Bonfa, Ivan Lins, Pedro Caetano, Chico Buarque, João Gilberto, and Vinícius de Morães continue to write songs in the style. Jobim died in New York City in 1995.

Botev, Khristo (1849–1876)

Bulgarian poet and revolutionary leader. One of the three great national heroes of the Bulgarian revolutionary movement against Ottoman rule in the 1870s, Botev was born on January 6, 1849, in Kalofer, Rumelia, a Bulgarian province governed by the Ottoman empire. In 1863 he traveled to Russia to further his education, where he was greatly influenced by socialism. When he returned to Bulgaria in 1867, convinced that national liberation would come only through the efforts of the Bulgarians, he joined the revolutionary movement against the Turks. Soon after, he fled to Romania to work in support of the Bulgarian liberation movement through writing and organizing. In 1876 the Bulgarian dissidents launched a disastrous insurrection. That May, with the revolt already shattered, Botev led a band of more than two hundred rebels into Bulgaria and was killed by Turkish soldiers, along with most of his followers. His numerous publications include *Pesni u stihove* (*Songs and Verses*), a collection of patriotic poems published in 1875.

Botticelli, Sandro (1445–1510)

Italian Renaissance painter. Born Alessandro di Mariano Filipepi, Botticelli is best known for his masterpieces *Primavera* (c. 1477; *Spring*) and *La nascita di Venere* (c. 1485; *The Birth of Venus*). Sponsored in his endeavors by the powerful Italian Medici family, of whom he made several portraits, he also did some illustrations for Italian poet Dante's *Divine Comedy*. In Rome, he was commissioned to work with other artists on the frescoes of the Sistine Chapel, his contribution being the *Mosè punisce i ribelli alla sua legge* (1481; *Punishment of Korah, Dathan, and Abiram*). Little is known about the life of Botticelli. His artistic training began with an apprenticeship to a goldsmith, then with the painter Fra Filippo Lippi, whose influence is particularly strong in Botticelli's earlier works. Though Botticelli enjoyed a very successful career and his artistic achievements were duly recognized and financially supported, his artistic contribution was overshadowed by the fathers of the High Renaissance style. Since the nineteenth century, his work has been reexamined and championed by critics.

Boxer Rebellion

Chinese political uprising. This nineteenth-century revolt in northern China takes its name from the group who began the uprising, the Yihequan, or "the Righteous and Harmonious Fists." Known to the West as the Boxers, the Yihequan practiced a form of martial arts similar to shadowboxing, which was supposed to serve as protection from bullets. Originally an antidynastic and antiforeign movement, the Boxers changed both their slogan and their program when the Qing dynasty (1644–1911) agreed to help them drive foreigners out of China.

The rebellion grew from two major tensions: the brisk antiforeign sentiment generated by territorial concessions, namely the Treaty of Nanking (now written Nanjing) in 1842, in which Hong Kong was ceded to Great Britain, and the Treaty of Shimonoseki in 1895, in which Japan took control of Taiwan, and a series of natural disasters in northern China. While the loss of territories led to fears that China would be completely divided up among foreign powers, the drought and flooding were taken as a sign of disturbance within the natural order and an omen of change or disaster for the nation. Incited by a decline in domestic commerce and increased unemployment, both of which were blamed on foreign commercial domination, the Boxers led the uprising against foreigners in 1898. They were particularly resentful of missionaries and Chinese Christians, killing thousands. In 1900 an international armed force was sent in to protect Western interests in China. The force of 2,000 soldiers set out for Peking (now written Beijing) but were forced back by the Boxers, who then entered Peking and slaughtered many Christians, also laying siege to the foreign embassies, where foreigners and Chinese Christians had fled to escape the Boxers. Although the Dowager Empress had declared war on the foreign powers, many of the Chinese regional governors-general ignored the order, thereby limiting the potential scope of the rebellion. A larger international force of 20,000 troops entered Peking in August and successfully lifted the siege of the foreign legations, forcing the Dowager Empress to flee to Xi'an. The following year, 1901, China was forced to sign the Boxer Protocol, which demanded a monetary payment to foreign powers and punished Chinese government officials who had colluded with the Boxers.

Bradstreet, Anne [Dudley] (1612–1672)
English-born American poet. Generally recognized as one of the first poets to develop in the English-speaking New World, Bradstreet was also recognized as a poet in Britain before she left for New England.

A precocious child, Bradstreet was educated by private tutors and had ready access to her father's library. She immigrated to Massachusetts in 1630 at the age of eighteen with her husband (Simon, later governor of Massachusetts) and parents. Her current literary reputation rests chiefly on the mid-nineteenth-century publication of "Contemplations," a series of religious poems that explore romantic views of nature.

Previously, Bradstreet had been known best for work published in 1678, six years after her death, under the title *Several Poems*. While her first volume of poetry, *The Tenth Muse Lately Sprung Up in America* (1650), published in England without her knowledge, is often considered tedious and difficult, Bradstreet attempted to imitate those poets she most admired, including English poets Edmund Spenser (1552–1599) and Sir Philip Sidney (1554–1586). The year 1678 saw the first expanded and revised American publication of *The Tenth Muse*, under the title *Several Poems Compiled with Great Variety of Wit and Learning*.

In later works, Bradstreet reflects on the rigors of life in the wilderness of Massachusetts, and these works are considered more original and revealing of her poetic talents. Bradstreet's writings also explore the mystery of nature, Puritan piety, and marital and parental love. The poem *Homage to Mistress Bradstreet*, published in 1956, was written by John Berryman as tribute to her writing.

Brahma
Hindu god. The word "brahma" is the nominative form of *brahman*, meaning "hierophant." Brahma is one of the major gods of the late Vedic period of India. The creative deity of the classical Hindu trinity, he is the supreme being, but curiously has always lacked the numerous cults of the other two members of the triad, Vishnu (the Preserver) and Shiva (the Destroyer). In Hindu myths, Brahma, creator of the earth and all of its creatures, is linked to Prajapati (the Vedic creator god) and eventually subsumes his identity. According to early Hindu mythology, Brahma was born from a golden egg, but later variants claim that he emerged from a lotus that grew from Vishnu's navel as he reclined. Brahma (a masculine god) should not be confused with Brahman, a force that constitutes the ultimate power of the universe.

Trimurti doctrine reconciles these different traditions and aligns Brahma, Shiva, and Vishnu as aspects of the supreme being. The Smartas' worship of five deities in the seventh century, however, ignored Brahma. And though all temples dedicated to Vishnu or Shiva possess an image of Brahma, no sect is devoted exclusively to him. Still, in Hindu temples, the central spot is consecrated to Brahma, aligned to correspond symbolically with the cosmos. He is represented as having four faces and arms that point in the cardinal directions. This fourfold orientation symbolizes the four social classes (*varnas*), the four ages (*yugas*), and the four earliest

Indian sacred scriptures (*Vedas*). Accompanied by his consorts, Savitri and Sarasvati, Brahma is often portrayed riding on a swan or seated upon a lotus throne wearing white garments and holding a book, sacrificial instruments, and prayer beads.

Brahmanas

Hindu religious commentaries. These prose commentaries accompany the Vedas, the most ancient texts of Hindu sacred literature. The *Brahmanas* (Disquisitions about the Ritual) date from 900 to 700 B.C.E., when *Samhitas* (collections) of the sacred verse hymns became prevalent; they use myth and legend to illustrate Brahman teachings and to explicate the ritual and the hidden meanings of the *Samhitas*. The *Brahmanas* are principally concerned with rituals of sacrifice, which they often relate by telling stories. Some of the more popular ones include that of Shunahshepa in the *Aitareya-brahmana* and King Pururavas and the nymph Urvashi in the *Shatapatha-brahmana*. Although the *Brahmanas* are not considered "literature," their influence upon subsequent prose styles and expositions has been extensive.

The more philosophical *Aranyakas*—chapters appended to the *Brahmanas*—are referred to as "forest texts," because they stipulate that the material in these chapters should only be taught in the forest, away from the village. The *Aranyakas* serve as a link between the *Brahmanas* and the later, more mystical Upanishads, which were composed after a philosophical shift of emphasis from sacrifice to mystical and esoteric knowledge, especially concerning the relationship between the *atman* (self) and the *brahman* (godhead).

Brahms, Johannes (1833–1897)

German composer. Born in Hamburg, the son of a poorly paid double-bass player, Brahms was steered toward music from birth. He began studying piano at the age of seven and gave his first concert at the age of ten. Forced to make his own way in his teens, he played the piano in local saloons frequented by sailors and gave lessons. His career suddenly advanced when he met the Hungarian violinist Eduard Reményi and, through him, the great virtuoso Joseph Joachim.

Finally, in 1853, Brahms was discovered and proclaimed a genius by the German composer and critic Robert Schumann. Schumann died in the grip of mental illness three years later, but Brahms maintained contact with the composer's musically gifted wife, Clara. Many have speculated that Brahms and Clara were in love; if so, the relationship was never consummated. (They remained close friends until Clara's death in 1896.) From 1857 to 1859, Brahms worked at his first major orchestral piece, the turbulent *Piano Concerto in D Minor*. Denied a post in his native Hamburg, he moved to Vienna as conductor of the Singakademie in 1863. He cemented his reputation with the *German Requiem* (1857–68) and the long-gestating *First Symphony* (1855–78).

By the time of his death in 1897, Brahms was a giant in Vienna, the clear successor to Beethoven and Schubert. In awe of Beethoven, Brahms hesitated many years before setting down his powerfully argued sequence of four symphonies. He made distinctive and atypical contributions to the virtuoso concerto repertory with two works, the *Violin Concerto in D* (1878) and the *Double Concerto* (1887). But he may have left his most significant legacy in his chamber and piano music: bold, dramatic statements in his early years, reflective and deeply melancholy gestures toward the end. His *Clarinet Sonatas* (1894) and *Clarinet Quintet* (1891) recall Mozart's lyricism, but the harmonies are often otherworldly and strange, looking into the next century.

Brancusi, Constantin (1876–1957)

Romanian sculptor. Brancusi is renowned for his radically simplified, abstract sculpture, executed in wood, steel, stone, or bronze and finished to meticulous smoothness. His most famous sculptures, *Le Baiser* (1908; *The Kiss*), *Mademoiselle Pogany* (1913), and *L'Oiseau dans l'espace* (*Bird in Space*), display his love of elemental, almost archetypal forms and his penchant for phallic designs. Brancusi was first apprenticed to a carpenter and cabinetmaker before entering the Bucharest Academy of Fine Arts. In 1904 he moved to Paris, where his work attracted the attention of Rodin and an invitation to work with him, which Brancusi declined. His early adult years were spent in poverty, and he worked as a Russian Orthodox cantor to finance his art. Gradually, his reputation as a pioneer in modern sculpture grew, assisted by numerous controversies. Brancusi's *Buste de la princesse X* (1916; *Princess X*) was rejected by Parisian authorities, and declared obscene; in 1933 U.S. Customs officials attempted to assess *Bird in Space* for duty as raw metal rather than a work of art. (Brancusi later won his lawsuit against the government.) Massively supported by art critics, galleries, and art collectors, Brancusi is recognized as one of the finest sculptors of the twentieth century.

Braque, Georges (1882–1963)

French painter. Together with Spanish painter Pablo Picasso (1881–1973), Braque is the founder of the art movement called Cubism. Though the harsh, analytical angularity of Cubism characterizes Braque's early work, he is better known for his later paintings of more representational nudes and still-lifes. His series *Les Oiseaux* (1952–63; *Birds*), for example, is renowned for its elegant use of color. Braque also introduced the technique of *papier collé*, which inaugurated the creative use of collage in his own work and that of other artists. Braque first came to Paris in 1900, joining a group of painters called the Fauves, who worked with pure pigments and bright colors. His work with Picasso flourished in the ensuing years but was interrupted by his service with the French infantry in World War I. Suffering a serious head wound in battle, he was released from the army. After this, his work began to depart from the austere geometry of Cubism and move toward softer forms and freer, looser brush strokes. By 1919 Braque was an established modern master, well connected in the circles of upper-class French society, a position he enjoyed throughout his career. Toward the end of his life, he was honored with numerous retrospective exhibitions, including one at the Louvre in Paris (1961), making him the first artist to be so honored while still alive.

Brecht, Bertolt (1898–1956)

German poet, dramatist, and theorist. Brecht was an avowed Marxist, and his work was highly acclaimed on both sides of the party line. Born Eugen Berthold Brecht, Brecht began his writing career early in life. His first staged play, *Trommeln in der Nacht* (*Drums in the Night*), was produced in 1922 and received the Kleist Prize. Other successful plays include *Mann ist Mann* (1926; *A Man's a Man*), *Mutter Courage und ihre Kinder* (1939; *Mother Courage and Her Children*), and his best-known work, *Die Dreigroschenoper* (1928; *The Three-Penny Opera*), written in collaboration with Kurt Weill. Brecht's plays—all highly satirical and critical of modern society—are technically and politically complex documents. The kind of theater Brecht would later call "epic" avoided both bourgeois illusionism and Soviet realism; a sort of Soviet modernism, Brecht's work called for a radical and disruptive staging, for performances that would estrange and provoke audiences into a questioning and politicized consciousness. *The Three-Penny Opera*, based loosely on English poet and dramatist John Gay's *Beggar's Opera* (1728), is among the best moments of the epic theater.

Unlike his writing career, Brecht's personal life was turbulent. He moved to Berlin in 1925 to find more sympathetic audiences for his work, but was forced to flee after the Nazi takeover in 1933 because of his ties to the German Communist Party. One day after the symbolic burning of the Reichstag in Berlin, Brecht and his second wife, actress Helene Weigel, fled to Prague and began a fourteen-year exile in Denmark, Sweden, and the United States. Writing prolifically during this period, Brecht produced a number of plays, stories, and poems. Called before the U.S. House Committee on Un-American Activities in 1947 for his Communist affiliations, Brecht eventually left for Switzerland, finally settling in East Berlin in 1949. Though somewhat restricted by the East German government, in the same year Brecht founded the state-supported Berliner Ensemble and there produced several plays until his death. In 1951 Brecht was awarded the East German National Prize, and he was awarded the International Stalin Peace Prize in 1954.

Breton, André (1896–1966)

French poet and essayist. Born in Tinchebray, France, Breton was one of the chief founders and promoters of Surrealism, an artistic movement of the 1920s and 1930s.

As a medical student, Breton was fascinated with mental illness and the work of Viennese psychoanalyst Sigmund Freud. In 1915, while in the middle of his course of study, Breton was drafted into the army. After the First World War, he joined the Dadaists, an avant-garde artistic group experimenting with literature and theater. With Louis Ara-

gon and Philippe Soupault, both of whom he had met while in the army, he founded *Littérature*, a literary review. Seeking a way to introduce the concept of the unconscious into the production of art, Breton and Soupault published "Les Champs magnétiques" (1920; "Magnetic Fields"), the first example of "automatic writing," a form of composition based on free association.

By 1924 Breton had organized a group dedicated to Surrealism and had issued his *Manifeste du surréalisme* (1924; *Manifesto of Surrealism*), the declarative statement of the movement, defining it as "the dictation of thought, free from any control by the reason and of any aesthetic or moral preoccupation." This spirit of creative exploration and freedom is evident in much of Breton's work; the novel *Nadja* (1928), for example, questioned the division between madness and sanity, while *L'Imaculée Conception* (1930; *The Immaculate Conception*) (cowritten with Paul Éluard) attempted to capture the essence of insanity in words. Similarly, *Les Vases communicants* (1932; *The Communicating Vessels*) and *L'Amour fou* (1937; *Mad Love*) blurred reality in extensive exploration of dreams. *L'Amour fou* illustrates the importance of love, one of the basic articles of Surrealist faith.

In addition, Breton wrote theoretical and critical essays, including two other Surrealist manifestos in 1930 and 1942 respectively, and "Les Pas perdus" (1924; "The Lost Steps"), "Légitime Défense" (1926; "Legitimate Defense"), *Le Surréalisme et la peinture* (1928; *Surrealism and Painting*), *Qu'est-ce que surréalisme?* (1934; *What Is Surrealism?*), and *La Clé des champs* (1953; *The Key to the Fields*).

In the 1930s many members of the Surrealist movement became involved with politics. Breton and several others joined the Communist Party. He left the party in 1935 because of the incompatibility between the total personal freedom that Surrealism advocated and the individual submission to the collective that Marxism required. Nevertheless, Breton continued his involvement in leftist politics by forming the Fédération de l'Art Révolutionnaire Indépendant (Federation of Independent Revolutionary Art) in Mexico with Leon Trotsky in 1938. When Germany invaded France during World War II, Breton fled to the United States, continuing to promote the Surrealist movement through his writings and an exposition at Yale University in 1942. He returned to France in 1946 only to find existentialist thought ascendant, but he tried to keep Surrealism alive, organizing one last exhibition in 1947 and publishing a final collection of poems in 1948 (*Poèmes*) before his death in Paris in 1966. A posthumous collection, *Selected Poems*, was published in London in 1969.

Brontë, Anne (1820–1849), Brontë, Charlotte (1816–1855), AND Brontë, Emily (1818–1848)

English novelists. Children of a curate, the Brontë sisters were born in Thornton, England, but soon after their mother's death they were packed off to boarding school. Unfortunately, conditions at the school were dreadful, aggravated by the administration's belief that physical discomfort led to spiritual growth. (The Lowood school in Charlotte's *Jane Eyre* is modeled on that place.) The two elder sisters, Maria and Elizabeth, developed tuberculosis and died; the other girls returned to their father's parsonage. Back at home, the sisters, joined by their brother, Branwell, romped and roamed the Yorkshire moors, spending hours constructing imaginary kingdoms. Charlotte and Branwell invented the kingdom of Angria, a vast African empire, and kept accounts of the adventures of its inhabitants. Emily and Anne created the kingdom of Gondal, keeping a journal about its affairs and writing several poems. These

were eventually published, together with some of Charlotte's work, as *Poems by Currer, Ellis and Acton Bell* (1846). The book was financed with a small inheritance, but was a complete commercial failure: Charlotte reported two copies sold. The sisters set to work on novels. Charlotte's *The Professor* (1857) made the rounds at many a publisher's office, but was accepted by none. After months of rejection, Emily's *Wuthering Heights* (1847) and Anne's *Agnes Grey* (1847) were accepted. *Jane Eyre* (1847), Charlotte's second effort, was an instant success upon publication. The sisters, still writing under the pseudonym Bell, and their publishers hoped to capitalize on *Jane Eyre*'s appeal by encouraging the story that the three Bells were actually the same person.

In the interim, Branwell Brontë withdrew so completely from family life that he knew nothing of his sisters' literary ventures. He suffered from tuberculosis, compounded by his abuse of alcohol and opium, and he died in 1848. A few months later, Emily, too, succumbed to the disease. Anne died in 1849. After her sisters' deaths, Charlotte returned to the parsonage in Haworth with her father and continued to write, publishing *Shirley* (1849) and *Villette* (1853). In 1854 she married her father's curate but died nine months after her marriage.

Of the three sisters, Emily is considered the most talented. Her poems and her one novel attest to a profound mysticism, an intense poetic imagination. Though it was no great success in its day, *Wuthering Heights* is generally regarded as one of the finest novels written in the English language. It was rumored after her death that her brother Branwell was the actual author, or part author, and that Emily, as a woman, could not have written a novel containing such brutality; yet this charge seems to be unsubstantiated. Though Charlotte's novels were a commercial success, she is often faulted for attempting to force straight autobiography into her texts. *The Professor* (1857), for example, is of mainly biographical interest, a thinly disguised account of Charlotte's love for a former teacher, M. Héger. Anne's novels are less noteworthy; indeed, if it were not for her famous sisters, her work most likely would have been forgotten.

Brooke, Frances (1724–1789)

British-Canadian novelist. Brooke's *The History of Emily Montague* (1769) is usually considered the first Canadian novel. Born Frances Moore in Claypole, England, she was orphaned at age thirteen and went to live with her aunt and her minister uncle. In the 1750s she lived in London, writing poetry and plays, and made the acquaintance of a number of literary figures, including English literary great Samuel Johnson. Under the pseudonym Mary Singleton, she published *The Old Maid*, a weekly review of society, politics, and the arts, from November 1755 to July 1756. In 1756 she married the Reverend John Brooke but remained in London when he sailed to Canada to be a military chaplain the following year. She gave birth to their only child, John Moore Brooke, soon after. Unsuccessful at getting her early plays produced, she translated a French sentimental novel by Marie Jeanne Riccobini as *Letters from Juliet, Lady Catesby* (1760). Its immediate success was followed by that of her first novel, *A History of Lady Julia Mandeville* (1763), conventional in its epistolary form and thwarted romantic plot but unconventional in its examination of women's social roles. Her husband was named the British garrison chaplain in Quebec in 1760, and when it officially became British territory in 1763, Brooke joined him. Her next work, the first published novel with a Canadian setting, *The History of Emily Montague* (1769), is again a tale of courtship among the upper classes told in a series of letters primarily from Canada to England. The letters are from a variety of perspectives and provide a great deal of information about the new British colony and give voice to further protofeminist concerns in a new social setting. In 1768 the Brookes returned to London, where Frances resumed translating and undertook the management of an opera house. *All's Right at Last; or, The History of Miss West*, a novel set in London, Quebec, and Montreal, and published anonymously in 1774, is usually attributed to her. Brooke was increasingly successful as a dramatist, with the mildly acclaimed *The Siege of Sinope* (1781) and *Rosina* (1782), the most popular comic opera of the time. A second comic opera, *Marian*, was produced in 1788, and a utopian sequel to her first novel, *The History of Charles Mandeville*, was published posthumously in 1790, one year after her death.

Brooks, Gwendolyn (1917–)

American poet. Brooks's often stark poetry is an exploration of urban black experience. In 1950 she became the first black poet to win the Pulitzer Prize.

Gwendolyn Brooks was born in Topeka, Kansas, and spent her childhood in Chicago. Dark-skinned and poor, she learned in elementary school about the class and color snobbery that existed even among her black classmates. She would fictionalize these childhood experiences in *Maud Martha* (1953), her only published novel.

Brooks began writing poetry at age seven. Her adolescent work is mostly traditional poetry examining the changing of the seasons and praising domestic comforts. But in these early years she mastered standard poetic metrical patterns, which she would later transform. Early encounters with the African-American writers James Weldon Johnson and Langston Hughes encouraged her in her writing, and she contributed frequently to the Chicago *Defender*, a black newspaper.

After two years at a junior college she

married in 1939. Her writing was now becoming tighter and more realistic. Her first collection, *A Street in Bronzeville* (1945), was named after the black section of Chicago's South Side. The book was followed by *Annie Allen* in 1949 and *The Bean Eaters* in 1960. *In the Mecca* (1968) is a cycle of poems about black life in a Chicago apartment building. Brooks's work is often characterized by abrupt beginnings and unusual, sometimes jolting rhythmic patterns. The spare realism of her lines is punctuated with striking imagery.

Her later work has been influenced by the militant stance of many younger black authors. In 1971 she left her publishers of twenty-five years, Harper and Row, to publish with Broadside Press, a small black publishing house in Detroit. Her later works include *Beckonings* (1975); *Winnie* (1988), a cycle of poems inspired by Winnie Mandela; and an autobiography entitled *Report from Part One* (1972).

Browning, Elizabeth Barrett (1806–1861)

English poet. Elizabeth Barrett's early poems became well known in England during the 1840s, and while living in her father's house, she was permitted to receive many literary visitors, with one of whom, Robert Browning, she fell in love. Robert and Elizabeth eloped to Italy in 1846 against her father's wishes, and they remained there until her death in 1861. Barrett Browning's popular sequence of poems *Sonnets from the Portuguese* (1850) describes their love and features the famous lines "How do I love thee? Let me count the ways. . . ."

In Italy she became involved in the Italian nationalist movement and bore one son. Her book-length poem *Aurora Leigh* (1857), modeled in part on Romantic English poet William Wordsworth's *The Prelude*, describes the life and thoughts of a woman poet; it may be the first long work by a woman in English to have a female writer for its protagonist. Several often-anthologized short poems also address the problem of what it means to be a "woman writer" or artist. Barrett Browning's lack of interest in technical innovation caused her reputation to drop sharply during the early twentieth century; contemporary interest in questions of gender and authorship, and Barrett Browning's forthrightness in raising such questions, have caused a revival of interest in her work.

Browning, Robert (1812–1889)

English poet. Born in 1812 to middle-class parents in Camberwell, a London suburb, Browning was thoroughly and eclectically educated at home, learning French and Italian from tutors. His first published poem, *Pauline* (1833), a book-length, soul-searching narrative modeled on Shelley, was fiercely panned by the English philosopher John Stuart Mill. Browning's verse drama *Paracelsus* (1837) met a better reception. Browning then spent ten years as a playwright; by 1846 six of his plays had premiered in London, but none had succeeded.

In writing speeches for imagined characters, however, Browning found his true talent. Many of his earliest poems explore the psychology of vanity and evil. In "My Last Duchess" (1842) an imaginary duke shows off a portrait of his late wife to a visitor whose daughter he seeks to marry; in the course of the fifty-five-line poem, the Duke explains why he arranged to have his wife killed and inadvertently reveals much of his own sinister character. With this poem Browning invented the dramatic monologue: a poem spoken by an imaginary or historical character in a defined scene to a defined listener, and which shows more of the speaker's inner life than the speaker had expected.

In 1846 Browning eloped with the older, more successful poet Elizabeth Barrett; they moved to Italy, where they resided happily and raised a son. There Browning completed *Men and Women*

(1855), whose vigorously spoken monologues explore the basis of art and the nature of romantic love; many are set in Renaissance Italy, others in the era of Christ. In "Andrea del Sarto," the gifted painter reveals that he has sacrificed his chance at greatness to placate his materialistic wife, who cannot return his love.

When Elizabeth died in 1861, Browning returned to England, where he remained, publishing voluminously to broad acclaim until his death in 1889. His major long poem, *The Ring and the Book*, comprises twelve monologues spoken by the parties in a scandalous Renaissance murder case; telling a single story from several perspectives, the poem anticipates later narrative techniques like those of the American writer William Faulkner and Japanese filmmaker Akira Kurosawa. Browning's later long poems, often devoted to arguments in philosophy or theology, were well received in their day but are now nearly unread; these works inspired many Browning Societies, which looked on the poet as a teacher and thinker.

Browning's dramatic monologues exerted much influence over twentieth-century poets: T. S. Eliot and Ezra Pound modeled many of their early poems on Browning's, and Robert Lowell and Randall Jarrell also used Browning's form for important poems. With Tennyson, Hopkins, and Arnold, Browning is generally held to be one of the great English poets of his era.

Bruegel, Pieter, the elder (1525/30–1569)
Flemish painter. Influenced by the works of Flemish painter Hieronymous Bosch (1450–1516), Pieter Bruegel, like Bosch, is best known for his brightly colored, realistic paintings of landscapes and peasant life, as well as fantastic representations of biblical subjects, most notably his painting *The Tower of Babel* (1563), which has not survived.

Relatively little is known of Bruegel's early life, save that he was first apprenticed to a sculptor in Antwerp, whose daughter he later married. Living in Antwerp, Bruegel was commissioned as a drawer by an engraver, Hieronymous Cock, in whose employ he would remain until his death. Though his early fame rests on these prints, Bruegel later fell under the spell of Bosch. However, unlike the horde of cheap Bosch imitators, Bruegel took the Boschian idiom and fashioned his own distinctive style. In 1563 Bruegel moved to Brussels with his wife and there produced some of his greatest paintings. Falling into three categories, Bruegel's work is generally classified as fantasy, genre scenes, and biblical subjects, although these divisions usually overlap. *The Massacre of the Innocents* (c. 1565–67), *The Sermon of Saint John the Baptist* (1566), and *The Parable of the Blind* (1568) are some of his best-known works.

Buber, Martin (1878–1965)
Jewish philosopher, scholar, and Zionist. Born to assimilated Viennese Jews, Buber attended some of the finest German-language universities of his day. He completed his doctoral dissertation in philosophy at the University of Vienna, and was greatly influenced by the work of the German philosopher Friedrich Nietzsche (1844–1900).

Becoming editor of the weekly Zionist publication *Die Welt* (The World), at the prompting of Zionist leader Theodor Herzl, Buber eventually resigned over his contrasting views with Herzl regarding a Jewish state. Whereas Herzl hoped to establish the legitimacy of a Jewish homeland, Buber was far more interested in the spiritual aspect of Zionism and advocated an immediate agricultural settlement. These spiritual concerns were powerfully reflected in his seminal work *Ich und Du* (1923; *I and Thou*), in which Buber elaborates on the spiritual crisis in modern society. Buber began studying Hasidism soon after his marriage to a non-Jewish, pro-Zionist author, Paula Winckler, in 1901. (She converted to Judaism.) He believed that in many ways, early Hasidism successfully confronted and cured what he saw to be the deterioration of Judaism, and felt that Zionism should take heed of the Hasidic example.

Buber tried to live his life in strict accordance with his principles. When anti-Semitic Nazi policies closed off educational venues for German Jews, he became the director of the Freies Judisches Lehrhaus in Frankfurt am Main, an organization dedicated to adult education. His outspoken criticisms of Hitler's racist ideology resulted in a ban on his speaking or publishing in Germany. Finally, at the age of sixty, Buber immigrated to Palestine and established himself as an academic at Hebrew University. He worked tirelessly to keep the peace between Arabs and Jews. When he died in 1965, at a point of great tension within the Middle East, his efforts were acknowledged with a wreath from the Arab Students' Organization. Buber tried to bridge the gap between Jews and Christians as well, and his humanistic philosophy has been influential in non-Jewish as well as Jewish circles.

Buddha

Founder of Buddhism. From the Sanskrit, meaning "the enlightened one," the title of Buddha is given to Siddhartha Gautama (563–483 B.C.E.). According to legend, Gautama was born to a royal family, the eldest son of a chief of the Sākya clan at the castle Kapilavastu, in what is now Nepal. At his birth, Hindu priests interpreting a dream of Gautama's mother predicted he would become a great teacher or leader. His father, King Suddhodana, raised his son in great luxury, but at the age of twenty-nine Gautama experienced a major spiritual crisis. Disturbed by the inevitability of age, disease, and death, he renounced his material possessions and left his wife and child to become a wandering as-

cetic. After six years of itinerant wandering, fasting, and prayer, Gautama received spiritual enlightenment while meditating under a Bo, or Bodhi, tree at Bodh Gāyā. Here he withstood the attacks and temptations of the evil Mara, and finally took possession of the eternal truths he had been seeking. From this point, he became the Buddha, "one who has awakened to the truth." His first sermon, which he delivered to his five companion ascetics, outlined the Four Noble Truths and the Noble Eightfold Path, which together became the basic tenets of Buddhism. During the remaining forty-five years of his life, Buddha continued to teach his doctrines, traveling throughout central India and forming a *sangha*, or order of monks, that included both men and women, who propagated his teachings. He died at Kuśinagara at the age of eighty and was cremated.

Buddhism

World religion based on the teachings of Buddha. The teachings of Buddha can best be understood from the perspective of his renunciation of his identity when he left home to become an ascetic. Rather than exist as an individual in luxury, he sought to understand universal human suffering. His enlightenment led to his doctrine, or *dharma*, explained in the Four Noble Truths, which say: (1) life is full of suffering; (2) suffering is the result of craving or desire; (3) suffering can end when desire ends; and (4) the way to end desire is to follow the Noble Eightfold Path (*ariya atthangika magga*). The eight "stages" of this path are often summarized as right views, right aspiration (regarding one's mind-set), right speech, right conduct, right livelihood (regarding one's ethics), right effort, right mindfulness, and right contemplation (regarding one's knowledge).

Many have seen the rise of Buddhism as contemporaneous with other important changes occurring in the Ganges River Basin and eastern India in the sixth century B.C.E. During this time, cities became population and cultural centers, which in turn grew to become small nations. These changes were concomitant with the shift from monarchies based on barter to confederated governments and monetary economies. Within this context, there were pressures to repudiate the extremely rigid caste system that had previously structured society. Not only did Buddhism accept both men and women; it did not accept caste distinctions, especially since the Buddha himself was not from the Brahmin caste, the highest level of the caste system.

These changes in social hierarchies sparked many "metaphysical" debates about the dualities of death and life, finitude and infinity, and body and soul. Buddhism stressed the Middle Way in these dualities, arguing that there is no "self" (*atman*) and no difference between the subjective and the objective world. Importantly, Buddhism does not posit the existence of an almighty God or a "first principle"; instead it maintains the unity of everything, and posits the existence of the path of enlightenment, which rejects the Hindu doctrine of reincarnation.

Buddhist monasteries served as religious sanctuaries, schools, hotels, hospitals, old-age homes, libraries, and museums. This versatility was a major asset as Buddhism spread throughout Asia, reaching most areas of Asia between the seventh and ninth centuries C.E. India, however, its land of origin, was conquered by Muslims in the twelfth century, and by the fourteenth century Buddhism had all but disappeared there.

Contemporary Buddhism has evolved into three main schools: the Theravāda, (Doctrine of the Elders), found in Sri Lanka, Myanmar, and Southeast Asia; the Mahāyāna (Great Vehicle), found in China, Korea, and Japan; and the Vaj-rayāna (Diamond Vehicle), found in and around Tibet.

Introduced to China in the first century C.E., Buddhism was integrated with Taoism's (mystical Chinese philosophy) concern with immortality. Originally in Sanskrit, Buddha's teachings were slowly translated into Chinese, and as Buddhist missionaries penetrated farther and farther into the country, the translations proliferated into all dialects and attracted the intellectual elite, who appreciated the peace of the monasteries in a country rent by constant wars of succession. Gradually, Buddhism merged with Chinese values and concentrated more on temporal relationships between individuals and their families.

Spreading from China to Korea in the fourth century and Japan in the sixth century, Buddhism predictably was accepted by some rulers, and considered insulting to native gods by others. Those who opposed Buddhism were defeated in battle, and Buddhism spread freely through Japanese society, mutating into a staggering number of specific schools and sects, all differentiated by particular concentrations, concerns, and rituals. Japanese Buddhism is usually described as nonrationalistic in character, more intuitive and emotionally appealing. This is evidently a result of Buddhism's successful merging with the native Japanese religion of Shinto. Today, six-sevenths of Japan's population are Buddhist.

The Buddhism that missionaries carried to southern Asia in the third century B.C.E. is called "Southern Buddhism," or the Doctrine of the Elders. It adheres more closely than all other forms of the religion to the original teachings in the Pali vernacular of the oldest Buddhist texts, and is considered the best contemporary representation of early Buddhism.

In the eighth century, Buddhism was introduced to Tibet, and its fusion there with folk beliefs gave rise to a form of Buddhism involving the worship of lamas ("superior ones") as incarnations of their predecessors; their highest authority is called the Dalai Lama. This form of Buddhism eventually spread through Mongolia and northeastern China.

Today Buddhism remains the predominant religion of Asia, although Christianity has made some inroads. Its greatest challenge has come from political ideology, however, as the conflicts between governments and "communist" (and other) revolutions have usually resulted in attempts to destroy or repress all worldly religion.

Bulgakov, Mikhail [Afanasievich] (1891–1940)

Russian writer. Trained as a physician at Kiev University, Bulgakov practiced medicine until 1919, serving as a field doctor with the White Russian Volunteer Army. Resigning from his military position in 1919, he began a literary career, eventually moving to Moscow in 1921 and remaining there until the end of his life.

Bulgakov is considered by many to be one of the most important Russian writers in the twentieth century. *Belaia gvardiia* (1924; *The White Guard*), his first novel, chronicled the fate of Russian intellectuals and officers of the czarist army caught up in revolution and civil war. Appearing in the literary journal *Rossiya*, *The White Guard* forced the journal to cease publication altogether. This first experience foreshadowed Bulgakov's literary career, as most of his lifetime was spent writing works that were constantly banned by the Russian government. At the request of the Moscow Art Theater, Bulgakov later wrote *Dni Turbinykh* (*The Day of the Turbans*), a play based on *The White Guard*, which premiered in 1926. Despite fierce criticism from the Communist Party, which would eventually ban the play from 1929 to 1932, it enjoyed enormous success and continued to be produced until 1941. His two satirical plays on contemporary themes, *Zoikina kvartira* (1926; *Zoya's Apartment*) and *Bagrovyi ostrov* (1928; *The Crimson Island*), were staged with great success, though they also provoked hostile attacks in the Soviet press. His second civil war play, *Beg* (1929; *Flight*), was banned while still in rehearsals.

In 1929–30, after all of his plays had been banned and his prose works were no longer in print, Bulgakov started writing letters to Stalin and influential litterateurs like Russian writer Maxim Gorky, requesting that he be allowed to emigrate or at least to earn money working in the theater. Stalin personally responded by telephone in 1930, and Bulgakov was allowed to work at the Moscow Art Theater as an assistant producer, a job he held until 1936. Nevertheless, this concession did not protect him from the watchful eye of the Soviet government; his play *Kabala svyatosh* (1930; *Molière*, also known as *Cabal of Hypocrites*), based on the life of the French dramatist Molière (1622–1673), was banned after only seven performances, as was the biography of Molière that Bulgakov was commissioned to write in conjunction with the play. His final attempt to return to theater failed; *Batum* (1939), written at the request of the Art Theater in honor of Stalin's sixtieth birthday, was abandoned before rehearsals because Stalin felt it was "unnecessary."

Bulgakov's masterpiece, the novel *Master i Margarita* (*The Master and Margarita*), was begun in 1928, and he continued to edit it even on his deathbed. It is an immensely complex tour de force with three interwoven strands of narration. Manuscripts of Bulgakov's works were saved by his widow, Elena Sergeevna, and were published in the late fifties and early sixties, culminating with the 1966–67 publication of *The Master and Margarita*. At the end of the twentieth century, Bulgakov has emerged as one of Russia's literary greats, his fame growing continuously.

Bulosan, Carlos (1913–1956)

Asian-American writer. Best known for his three novels, *The Voice of Bataan* (1943), *The Laughter of My Father* (1944), and *America Is in the Heart* (1946), Bulosan wrote about his own and other Filipinos' experiences as economic refugees, and the emotional and cultural process by which they came to feel themselves "Americans." By situating the Filipino immigrant experience within popular conceptions of the European immigrant experience, as children of the "melting pot," Bulosan found a sympathetic and interested audience in his adopted country. With anti-Asian racism at a new peak at the close of the war with Japan, Bulosan's depiction of Filipino immigrants as a hardworking, assimilationist-oriented people was promoted as an example of how "foreigners"—particularly Asians—ought to behave in the "land of opportunity." Bulosan was applauded for what appeared to be his humble acceptance of the difficult and often brutal conditions of migrant labor—virtually the only form of work available to Filipino immigrants at the time—as well as the remarkable achievements of his own life, working his way up from a cannery worker in Alaska to a respected author.

Bulosan was also, however, a labor activist; he did political work for various unions, writing frequently for union publications. Toward the end of his life, Bulosan became bitterly disillusioned by the America of his earlier dreams. While his novels had been well received, he was shocked and disgusted that painfully recounted moments—often thinly disguised autobiography—were perceived and reviewed as "comic" rather than ironic commentary. At the time of his death, Bulosan was employed as the editor of the United Cannery and Packing House Workers of America (UCAPHWA) yearbook and was writing a biography of Filipino writer and patriot José Rizal.

Bunraku

Japanese puppet theater. Named for its founder, Uemura Bunrakuken, this traditional theater features large puppets manipulated by skillful master puppeteers; the play's text is performed by a chanter, accompanied by the music of the three-stringed samisen. The puppets are two-thirds to three-quarters life-size, and each requires as many as three men to manipulate. One controls the right hand and the head, making expressive gestures with the eyes, lips, and hand, while the others work the puppet's left hand and feet. The main operator has high status; he appears in elaborate dress, unmasked, behind the puppet, while his assistants wear black robes and hoods that effectively conceal them from the audience. The heads of the puppets themselves are modeled on five standard characters: Musume, the beautiful young maiden; Bunshichi, the noble grieving hero; Fukeoyama, the wise matron; Danshichi, the violent warrior; and Chari, the lovable buffoon.

Although puppetry has existed in Japan since the eleventh century, Bunraku as a distinct art form matured in the eighteenth century with the work of Chikamatsu Monzaemon, whose tragedies often treated the plight of lovers caught between social duty and their own passions. The popularity of Bunraku faded with the rise of Kabuki, another form of Japanese theater, which overtly derived many of its stylistic conventions, and indeed many of its stories, from the Bunraku stage.

Buñuel, Luis (1900–1983)

Spanish film director. Despite Buñuel's image as the quintessential "Spanish filmmaker," his wildly diverse and ambitious works defy simple classification. Buñuel is also closely identified with the cinematic traditions of both France and Mexico.

His work is largely divisible into four periods, the first beginning in 1925, when Buñuel moved from his native Spain to Paris at the invitation of film-maker Jean Epstein. He eventually became a member of the Surrealist group, and his films of this period, including *Un Chien andalou* (1928; *An Andalusian Dog*, which he made with Salvador Dalí) and *Las Hurdes—Tierra sin pan* (1932; *Land Without Bread*), were pioneering works of disturbing oneiric cinema. He utilized the cinema as it had never been utilized before, to define and explore surrealistic perspectives.

During the second period, 1939–42, Buñuel was employed at the Museum of Modern Art in New York, preparing documentaries for distribution to Latin American countries. In this capacity, he became a virtually anonymous cinematic functionary, and was eventually dismissed from this position in 1942, suspected of Communist activities.

The years 1944–46 mark the third period of Buñuel's career. During this time, he returned to Hollywood to produce Spanish versions of Warner Brothers films, which merited him only occasional attention outside the Latin American commercial markets, therefore keeping him in Hollywood only a short time.

When he settled in Mexico in 1947, the final period began. There he made *Los Olvidados* (1950; *The Young and the Damned*) and *Nazarin* (1958). After 1960, he directed films in Italy and France, although he continued to reside in Mexico. At the invitation of the Spanish government, in 1961 he returned to Spain, where he made *Viridiana* (1961), which, despite the critical acclaim it received, was banned because it was considered too controversial. Two of his films from the 1970s, *Cet obscur objet du désir* (1977; *That Obscure Object of Desire*) and *Le Charme discrèt de la bour-* *geoisie* (1972; *The Discreet Charm of the Bourgeoisie*), were critical successes that continue to earn Buñuel fervent cult audiences.

Bunyan, John (1628–1688)

English writer and preacher. Most famous for his religious work *Pilgrim's Progress*, Bunyan's life and writings were dedicated to the cause of religious freedom. The son of a traveling tinker, a trade to which he was apprenticed as a youth, Bunyan was steeped in the popular literature of the Puritanical countryside. In 1646, during the English Civil War, he served with the parliamentary army, and after his discharge he married a poor woman, who carried in her dowry two devotional books, *The Plain Man's Path-Way to Heaven* (1664), by Arthur Dent, and Lewis Bayly's *The Practice of Piety* (1665). Inspired by these texts, Bunyan underwent a gradual spiritual conversion and became a lay preacher at a Baptist church. He refused to obey edicts banning nonconformist teaching and was imprisoned from 1660 to 1672 for his preaching. During his twelve years in prison, Bunyan devoted himself to a study of the Bible and Foxe's *Book of Martyrs* (1610) and wrote many of his books, including the autobiographical *Grace Abounding to the Chief of Sinners* (1666).

Upon his release, he accepted a ministry at a nonconformist church, a position he held until his death. He was imprisoned again in 1675, and during these months completed his most celebrated work, *The Pilgrim's Progress from This World, to That Which Is to Come* (1678; second part, 1684), an allegorical account of religious conversion. Bunyan continued to write and preach throughout his life, and his *Pilgrim's Progress* was soon found alongside the Bible in every English home. His work was embraced by the Romantic movement as a work of genius, a judgment that many would still accept today.

Burgos, Julia de (1914–1953)

Puerto Rican novelist. Born into extreme poverty, Julia de Burgos saw six of her thirteen siblings die from malnutrition and disease. By borrowing money and obtaining scholarships for her education, at the age of nineteen de Burgos received her degree in teaching. Between 1935 and 1939 she wrote and published—using her own funds—two books of poetry; the first, *Poema en veinte surcos* (1938; *Poem in Twenty Furrows*), she tried to sell herself, while the second, *Canción de la verdad sencilla* (1939; *Song of the Simple Truth*), received a prize from the Institute of Puerto Rican Literature that same year. An impassioned feminist, she used her poetry to protest the poverty and oppression that made difficult her own self-realization as a woman.

In almost every poem of her first collection, de Burgos contrasts the social pressure to conform and become a passive woman with her own desire to grow and forge her own identity. Although the second collection abandons the more explicit sociopolitical themes, consisting more of a hymn to love, it, too, uncovers the contradictions, inequalities, and prejudice that shatter the notion of love as a form of salvation. De Burgos lived to see only these two collections in printed form; in 1941 she completed her third, *El mar y tú* (*The Sea and You*), but it was not published until after her death. In 1961, the Puerto Rican Institute of Culture published her *Obra Poetica* (*Poetic Works*), but the collection is incomplete and her entire works have still not been gathered for publication. From 1939 to 1942 she was involved with Juan Isidro Jiménez Grullón, a politician from the Dominican Republic. They lived together in Puerto Rico, New York, and Cuba, and when the couple broke up, Julia de Burgos returned to New York, where she spent the last eleven years of her life.

Burns, Robert (1759–1796)

Scottish poet. Burns, Scotland's national poet, is famous for his use of conversational rhythms in the Scottish dialect in his songs and lyrics. Burns was equally noted for his satire of the orthodox Calvinist theology and morality. The craftsmanship and poetic genius of Burns's verse are especially resplendent in those satires of his that simultaneously uplift the common man and rail against institutional religion.

The self-educated son of a struggling farm laborer, Burns, a tenant farmer himself, was highly affected by his father's unsuccessful attempts to forge a better life. Rebelling against the existing social order, Burns was deemed a dangerous radical by the Calvinist powers he mocked. So pervasive was his reputation that his initial offer of marriage to Jean Armour, with whom he later had twins out of wedlock, was rejected.

The publication of *Poems, Chiefly in the Scottish Dialect* (1786) led to Burns's immediate social and literary success among all classes. Among the poems included in this volume are "The Holy Fair" (addressed to a clergyman against whom he had a grudge), "To a Mouse," "To a Louse," "A Red, Red Rose," and "A Man's a Man for a' That," which reflect the author's democratic sensibilities.

Arriving in Edinburgh after the success of this work, Burns became editor for James Johnson's *The Scots Musical Museum* (1787–1803) and George Thompson's *Select Collection of Original Scottish Airs for the Voice* (1793–1818), which contain the majority of Burns's songs. Burns always sought to find exact phrases to compliment old Scottish tunes, and the well-known folk classic "Auld Lang Syne" is often attributed to him, even though Burns did not take credit for it. Burns saw himself as a spokesman for and servant of the Scottish people and freely intermingled with the various classes.

Burton, Sir Richard [Francis] (1821–1890)

English scholar and explorer. The first European to visit Lake Tanganyika in Africa and several previously forbidden Muslim sites, including Mecca, Burton published forty-three volumes on his explorations and thirty volumes of translations, including an unparalleled translation of *The Arabian Nights* (1885–88). His sensitive and highly detailed accounts of the various cultures· with which he came into contact were classic ethnographic studies.

Endowed with an amazing gift for languages (he mastered twenty-five, including various dialects, which raises the number to forty), Burton began his career as a favored intelligence officer with the British army in India. There he developed a keen ability to assume the identity of a member of the native community. This ability allowed him to travel in disguise as a Muslim merchant to the bazaars to gather information. Following his military service, Burton again demonstrated these talents by disguising himself as an Afghani Muslim and traveling to Cairo, Suez, Medina, and finally to Mecca, where he was able to measure and sketch the sacred mosque and holy Muslim shrine, the Ka'bah.

In 1855 Burton set off on what was perhaps his best-known expedition, a quest to discover the source of the Nile River. In this venture, he was accompanied by a British East India officer named John Hanning Speke. Though this expedition was forced to turn back after being attacked by indigenous groups, the effort was resumed in 1857–58. This second mission was also beset by countless hardships, including Burton's own bout with malaria. When he wished to return to England to prepare for a new expedition, Speke insisted on continuing to Lake Victoria, which he believed was the Nile's source. Burton refused to accept this claim without further exploration, and thus began a very public feud between the two that lasted until Speke's death in a hunting accident in 1864. Burton maintained that Speke had committed suicide.

In 1861 Burton joined the British foreign office and for the next several years held posts in West Africa, Brazil, Syria, and finally Trieste. His many vivid accounts of the cultures with which he came into contact frequently earned the scorn of his superiors in Victorian London. In 1886, four years before his death, Burton was finally recognized for his accomplishments when Queen Victoria made him Knight Commander of St. Michael and St. George. A brilliant and iconoclastic mind, Burton possessed a highly refined erotic sense; at his death, his wife destroyed the majority of his papers, including a number of important translations of Eastern erotica, in an attempt to create an image of Burton as a good Victorian, proper and upright in attitude.

Byōdōin

Japanese temple. This celebrated temple, founded in the eleventh century in Uji, originally served as a villa where the powerful minister Fujiwara no Michinaga practiced Buddhist meditation at the turn of the century. His son, Fujiwara no Yorimichi, consecrated the site in 1053 as a temple, and completed a hall and dedicated a statue to the Amitābha (Amida in Japanese) Buddha, leader of the cult of Amitābha, which came from China and flourished in Japan in the twelfth and thirteenth centuries.

As an architectural monument, the Byōdōin is best known for the Hōōdō, or "Phoenix Hall," named for the sprawl of its ground plan, like a giant bird spreading its wings: from a central hall, two corridors stretch to either side, with a third at the back. On the roof, small bronze statues of birds continue the phoenix theme. The hall of the temple contains some of the most refined art and architecture of the late Heian period (897–1185). The temple was modeled after Amida's celestial palace, following depictions in religious paintings of the East Asian tradition. Yorimichi spared no expense in honoring his father with this project. He oversaw the completion of a "lotus hall" and an elaborately jeweled pagoda containing a representation of the Five Wisdom Buddhas in gold. He also built and dedicated another hall to the Five Wisdom Kings, whose bell has since been declared a National Treasure. The central statue of Amida is also a National Treasure, focusing the whole shrine's sense of removal from the mundane, a sacred place purified from worldly concerns.

Byron, George Gordon [Noel] (1788–1824) English Romantic poet. (Known as Lord Byron.) A description of the "Byronic hero," the melancholy, brooding man created by Byron in so many of his works, could also apply to the poet himself. Though he did not match the physical description of his heroes—indeed, Byron was short, stout, and club-footed— the tales of his debauchery and wildness certainly rival any of those he ascribed to his characters.

Byron's father died when he was quite young, and he was raised by his tempestuous mother in Scotland. At the age of ten, he inherited the family title and estate at Newstead Abbey, where he moved with his mother. He was educated at Harrow and Trinity College, Cambridge, from which he received his M.A. in 1808. In 1809 he assumed the family seat in the House of Lords. His first published work, *Hours of Idleness* (1807), received terrible reviews, and Byron submitted his anonymous satire,

English Bards and Scotch Reviewers (1809), in retaliation. Soon after, he left England for a tour of the Mediterranean, which inflamed Byron's romantic sensibilities and provided him with much material for later poems. His second book of poems, *Childe Harold's Pilgrimage* (1812), was published upon his return and made Byron a minor celebrity. The passionate poet, already notorious for his liaisons with both men and women, continued to have affairs, including a rumored relationship with his half-sister, Augusta Leigh. In 1814 he married Anne Isabella Milbanke, and they had a daughter, Augusta Ada. Due to Byron's philandering, he and Lady Byron eventually separated, provoking an embittered Byron to leave England for good. Staying with the poet Percy Shelley and his wife, Mary, on Lake Geneva, Byron later journeyed to Italy and finally settled into a somewhat stable relationship with the married, nineteen-year-old countess Theresa Guiccioli. It was during this time that Byron began work on his poem *Don Juan* (1819–24), the masterpiece for which he is largely noted today. Through Guiccioli's father and brother, Byron became an active supporter of the Greek war for independence. He outfitted a ship and sailed to Greece, but his battle plans were cut short by a serious illness en route. Byron died soon after and was mourned by the Greek people as a hero. His body was refused burial at Westminster Abbey and was buried in the vault of his ancestors in Newstead. One hundred forty-five years after his death, a plaque in his honor was placed on the floor of Westminster Abbey.

Considered to be among the best of his works are his satires *Beppo* (1818) and *The Vision of Judgement* (1822), and *Don Juan*, which he began in 1819 and was still unfinished at his death.

C

Cabral, Amílcar (1921–1973)

Guinean agronomist and politician. A leading African independence movement leader and nationalist politician of the 1960s, Amílcar Cabral was born in Bafata in Portuguese Guinea in 1921. Cabral was educated in Lisbon, where in 1948 he cofounded the Centro de Estudos Africanos, an organization devoted to African Studies. Returning to Guinea in the 1950s, Cabral organized and led an open military war against the Portuguese colonialists, founding the Partido Africano da Independência da Guiné e Cabo Verde (PAIGC; African Party for the Independence of Guinea and Cape Verde) in 1956 and leading it as general secretary. He also cofounded a liberation movement in Portuguese-controlled Angola with Angolan independence leader Agostinho Neto in the hopes of ending Portuguese colonial rule continent-wide. By the late 1960s, though the Portuguese army had not been entirely expelled from the country, Cabral's army had gained control of much of Guinea, and he ruled those areas as de facto leader. He formed the Guinean People's National Assembly in 1972 as an independent provisional government, headquartered in Conakry, that administered Guinean territory captured by the PAIGC. On January 20, 1973, Cabral was assassinated outside his home in Conakry, Guinea. His essays on the role of culture in nationalist consciousness have proved increasingly influential in Africa since his death.

Cabral, Pedro Álvares (c. 1467–1520)

Portuguese explorer. Cabral is believed to be the first European to have had contact with the indigenous people of what is now Brazil.

The son of Fernão Cabral and Isabel de Gouveia, Pedro Cabral descended from a Portuguese noble family with a long tradition of service to the throne; while still in his twenties, he received the personal favor of King Manuel I of Portugal, an honor that included the habit of the military Order of Christ, a personal allowance, and the title of Counsellor to His Highness. In 1450 Cabral was placed in command of Portugal's second major expedition to India, having been instructed to follow the route earlier scouted by Vasco da Gama. As admiral, Cabral commanded thirteen ships and was ordered to extend his predecessor's conquests and to protect Portugal's commercial investments.

On March 9, 1500, Cabral set out, as instructed by da Gama, on a southwesterly path, so as to bypass the becalmed waters of the Gulf of Guinea. This path offered the added advantage of providing a course along territory that the Portuguese had claimed under the Treaty of Tordesillas of 1494. The course eventually became known as the "circle around Brazil." On April 22, Cabral landed on what he thought was an island. Claiming the territory for Portugal, he named it Island of the True Cross. It was later renamed Holy Cross by King

Manuel, but eventually took its modern name, Brazil, from the *pau-brasil* dyewood that is found there. After this significant addition to the Portuguese empire, maps of the time showed the new area as a vast expanse of land serving as a port of call between Europe and the Cape of Good Hope.

Cabral began an ill-fated journey to India after staying in Brazil for only ten days. Four ships were lost in storms as the fleet rounded the Cape of Good Hope on May 29; among the dead was Bartolomeu Dias, the Portuguese explorer who had discovered the cape in 1488. Further problems arose when Cabral arrived at present-day Calcutta, India, on September 13. Although Cabral and his crew were initially welcomed by the Muslim ruler, trade disputes arose and a large force assailed the Portuguese trading post on December 17. Many Portuguese perished in the surprise attack, and Cabral retaliated by executing the crews of ten Muslim vessels. He then sailed for the Indian port of Cochin, where he traded for rare spices. After further trading at the ports of Carangolos and Cananor, Cabral began his return voyage on January 16, 1501. On the way, two ships foundered, and Cabral returned on June 23, 1501, with a fleet of only four ships.

Although King Manuel was reportedly pleased with the outcome of the voyage, the disasters of Cabral's expedition caused him to be replaced by da Gama, who was appointed head of a new and more extensive expedition. Stripped of his position of authority at the Portuguese court, Cabral returned to his estate in the Beira Baixa province of Portugal, where he spent the rest of his life.

Cabrera Infante, Guillermo (1929–)

Cuban short-story writer and novelist. As a young child, Cabrera Infante was introduced to radical politics by his parents, whose involvement with the Communist Party resulted in their imprisonment by Cuban president Fulgencio Batista's regime in 1936. Cabrera Infante's father was blacklisted, and the family moved to Havana to find work. The family spent many years there in dire poverty, an experience that would provide the material for his second novel, *La habana para un infante difunto* (1979; *Infante's Inferno*).

Cabrera Infante began his literary career as a scriptwriter, dramatizing the lives of the saints for a Catholic association and later as magazine editor, including the popular Cuban magazine *Bohemia*. In 1948 he published his first short story, "Aguas de recuercio" ("Waters of Memory") in *Bohemia*, written in a realistic mode and inspired by Guatemalan novelist Miguel Angel Asturias's *Señor Presidente* (1946; *The President*). Other stories from this period are collected in *Así en la paz como en la guerra* (1960; *As in Peace, So in War*), Cabrera Infante's first major publication, although he later rejected these expressly political works, calling their socialist-naturalist style "aesthetically hideous."

Though jailed and fined for his political work, Cabrera Infante was undeterred. He turned to film, writing critiques under the pseudonym G. Caín, continuing his activity in the resistance to the Batista regime.

In 1956 he tried to turn the Cuban Film Society, which he had helped found in 1951, into an anti-Batista organization, but Batista's forces took it over. With the defeat of Batista's regime by Communist leader Fidel Castro, however, Cabrera Infante assumed a prominent position in Cuban intellectual and political life. He was appointed editor of the now aboveground journal *Revolución*, and chairman of the National Cultural Council and of the new film institute. After the Bay of Pigs, however, he became disenchanted with Castro's rule and several confrontations ensued; when his brother's film about Havana nightlife was declared decadent by the film institute and confiscated in 1961, Cabrera Infante protested and was dismissed from his various positions. It was at this time that he began *Tres tristes tigres* (*Three Trapped Tigers*), the novel generally considered to be his masterpiece.

Totally disillusioned with Castro's government, Cabrera Infante moved with his family first to Spain, and then to London. There he scraped by as a screenwriter and published a completely revised version of *Three Trapped Tigers* in 1967. While in London, he publicly denounced the Castro regime and was declared not only a traitor, but also persona non grata in Cuba. Cabrera Infante's international reputation was launched when he received the Biblioteca Breve Prize in 1964. In addition, he was awarded a Guggenheim Fellowship in 1970.

Cahan, Abraham (1860–1951)

Journalist, editor, novelist, and socialist leader. Born near Vilna, then part of the Russian empire, Cahan attended the government teachers' seminary, where he was introduced to non-Jewish Western culture and ideas. He was soon swept up in the socialist revolutionary ferment then prevalent among younger, educated Russians. After narrowly escaping arrest, Cahan sailed for New York City, a popular destination for Eastern European Jews fleeing czarist persecution. With his writing talent, language skills, and remarkable energy level, Cahan soon found his way onto the pages of Joseph Pulitzer's *World*. Still, Cahan quickly discovered that Russian-Jewish immigrants were hungry for Yiddish journalism and lectures. In 1897 he helped found the Yiddish newspaper *Vorwärts!*, also known as the *Jewish Daily Forward*, a newspaper he would edit for the next fifty years, and which was hailed as the most influential Yiddish newspaper in turn-of-the-century

America. Used as a forum for Cahan's socialist agenda, *Vorwärts!* advocated trade unionism and greater economic opportunity for newly arrived workers. In addition, Cahan continued to publish stories in other journals and newspapers in an effort to reach beyond the Yiddish-speaking immigrant audience, writing several well-received novels about the Jewish immigrant experience: *Imported Bridegroom* (1898), *The White Terror and the Red* (1905), and *The Rise of David Levinsky* (1917).

Constantly reevaluating his own beliefs, Cahan avoided resorting to dogmatism. Originally opposed to Zionism, he softened his attitude toward the settlement of Palestine after a visit there in 1925. His unflagging faith in socialism did not blind him to the brutality of the Stalinist regime, and he was one of the first American leftists to speak out against the Soviet Union, nearly being expelled from the Socialist Party after publicly hailing Franklin D. Roosevelt for his innovative Depression-era policies.

caliph

Religious leader and figurehead of Islam. "People! Whosoever served Muhammad, Muhammad has died. But whosoever served God, He is alive and never shall He die!" With these words, Abū Bakr became the first of the four "Rightly Guided Caliphs." Caliph (in Arabic, successor or delegate) was the title of the political and religious leader and figurehead of the Muslim community from the Prophet Muhammad's death until abolition of the institution early in the twentieth century.

Caliph originally signified a delegate left behind in the Prophet Muhammad's absence to take his place as imâm (leader of ritual prayers). At Muhammad's death in 632, however, the fledgling Muslim community was left without a procedure for choosing a successor. According to Sunnî Muslims, the

Prophet, on his deathbed, appointed Abū Bakr (r. 632–34) to lead the community in ritual prayers, despite the misgivings of some and the reluctance of Abū Bakr himself. Shi'ite Muslims, on the other hand, cast the appointment of Abū Bakr and his next two successors as an unjust usurpation from 'Alī ibn Abī Tâlib (r. 656–61), who eventually became the fourth Rightly Guided Caliph, after Abū Bakr, 'Umar, and 'Uthman.

The appointment of Abū Bakr established the political and religious authority of Sunnî caliphs; in contrast, the failure to appoint 'Alī began a parallel line of Shi'ite imâms—anticaliphs in a sense—who also commanded spiritual authority among their adherents, but never enjoyed the political power of caliph and thereafter remained a troubling source of political and doctrinal opposition for the Sunnîs. For Sunnî Islam, the rule of the Rightly Guided Caliphs remains an idealized period, revered as the highest example of the now lost unity of the Muslim community. It was, however, also a period of two civil wars, the assassination of three of the four caliphs ('Umar in 634; 'Uthman in 656, and 'Ali in 660), and the events which prefaced the division of Islam into Sunnîs and Shi'ites.

'Alī eventually became the fourth caliph in 656, after the assassination of the third caliph, 'Uthman. However, after a civil war, 'Alī's victorious rivals, the Umayyads (r. 661–750), reigned from Damascus and transformed the caliphate into a dynastic institution. Under their rule, a more or less unified Islamic empire extended from the Pyrenees in the West to Bukhara in the East. After a second civil war, a group descended from the Prophet Muhammad's uncle 'Abbâs, the 'Abbâsids (r. 750–1258), capitalized on dissatisfaction with Umayyad rule and founded a similar dynasty of caliphs who ruled from Baghdad.

During the 'Abbâsid period, the empire fragmented into numerous principalities that paid only lip service to the Baghdad caliphate. When the Mongols ravaged the Islamic world in 1258, they put an end to the caliphate, savagely murdering the thirty-seventh 'Abbâsid caliph and sacking Baghdad. The weakening of central authority from the ninth century on had allowed rival caliphates to emerge in Spain, Egypt, and later in Ottoman Turkey and the Indian subcontinent. Political theorists attempted to account for the weakening of caliphal authority by acknowledging the de facto separation of power from religious legitimacy. The abolition of the caliphate on March 3, 1924, some months after the proclamation of the Turkish republic, doubtless represented a powerful event for Muslims as the abdication of an important symbol of Sunnî Muslim unity. Subsequent conferences in Cairo, Mecca, and Jerusalem were unable to revive the institution and, unlike the Sharî'ah, the Islamic legal code, it appears to be a dead issue in the politics of the Muslim Middle East today.

calumet pipe

Indian ceremonial pipe. Commonly referred to as the "peace pipe" or the "sacred pipe" in American Indian culture, the name "calumet" was given to this ceremonial object by French missionaries. This tobacco pipe consists of two parts: an elaborately carved stem of reed or wood, and a bowl made from catlinite stone or clay. Smoked in private devotions and public ceremonies between tribes, the calumet pipe gained an important symbolic status. In public gatherings, the pipe was used as an expression of friendship, to make peace, to declare an alliance, and occasionally to signify a declaration of war. If the pipe was decorated with white feathers, it signified a peaceful intention; if decorated with red paint and feathers, the calumet signaled a hostile event, usually war.

Also used for purposes of communicating with the spiritual world in personal prayer rituals, the smoke of the calumet pipe was thought to convey the feelings and sentiments of the smoker and carry them to the appropriate spirits during an invocation.

Calvin, John (1509–1564)

French Protestant theologian. John Calvin (the anglicization of Jean Cauvin) is the founder of Calvinism, an influential religious movement during the Protestant Reformation of the sixteenth century. Calvinist tenets differ markedly from those of the Roman Catholic Church, especially in their belief in predestination and in salvation by faith alone, as well as in their rejection of papal authority. Sociologists have connected the emergence of the so-called Protestant work ethic, seen as a harbinger of capitalism, to Calvinist doctrine, with its stress on hard work, devotion to community, and self-sacrificing renunciation.

Studying theology and law before experiencing a sudden conversion in 1533, Calvin turned his attention to the Reformation. Because of the radical Protestant views he espoused in a public speech to have been given at an inaugural ceremony at the University of Paris, he was forced to flee the city, and later the country, to escape persecution. He moved to Geneva in 1535 and while there composed his theological treatise, the *Institutio Christianae Religionis* (1536; *Institutes of the Christian Religion*), but was banished in 1538. Eventually welcomed back to Geneva in 1541, he continued his theological work.

Calvin's theology exerted enormous influence, particularly in the Puritan sects of Scotland, England, and the United States. Unlike Lutheran or Anglican sects, Calvinism recognized the Bible as the sole source of knowledge and religious authority, and its rather gloomy outlook held that man was a totally depraved being—the result of Adam's fall—whose only chance of salvation was God's grace, which was bestowed on the Elect only. Because people did not know if they were predestined to receive God's grace, all had to lead pious and holy lives. Pleasure and frivolity were frowned upon. Despite these rather bleak doctrines, John Calvin's teachings were enormously popular, making him one of the most influential theologians of the Western world.

Calvino, Italo (1923–1985)

Cuban-born Italian novelist and short-story writer. After World War II, Italo Calvino settled in Turin, pursuing a degree in literature while working for the Communist paper *L'Unita*. He completed his first novel, *Il sentiero del nidi di ragno* (1947; *The Path to the Nest of Spiders*) at the age of twenty-four. Though the novel is based upon his experiences in the Italian Resistance during the Second World War, Calvino's propensity for fantasy is already detectable. A collection of stories, *Ultimo viene il corvo* (1949; *Adam, One Afternoon, and Other Stories*), also draws on his wartime experiences.

Preoccupied with the act of storytelling, Calvino spins wonderfully fantastic and humorous tales. In the 1950s his signature blending of fantasy and reality was realized in a masterful "historical" trilogy, *Il visconte dimezzato* (1952; *The Cloven Viscount*), *Il barone rampante* (1957; *The Baron in the Trees*), and *Il cavaliere inesistente* (1959; *The Nonexistent Knight*). During the same period he was working on the trilogy, Calvino was also collecting Italian folk tales, which he published in 1956 under the title *Fiabe italiane* (*Italian Folktales*).

In many of his later works, including the acclaimed *Se una notte d'inverno un viaggiatore* (1979; *If on a Winter's Night a Traveler*), Calvino explores the issues of chance and possibility, change and momentum. Calvino is widely considered to be one of the most important

Italian fiction writers of the twentieth century.

Cambodian art and architecture

The classical era of Khmer art and architecture roughly corresponds to the most vigorous period of the Angkor empire, from the ninth through the thirteenth century. Jayavarman II (d. 850), founder of the empire and creator of the notion of the Khmer state as being ruled by a *devaraja* ("god-king"), was succeeded by numerous kings equally interested in creating a great empire, in which was included art and architecture. Cambodian architecture was a syncretic discipline, blending Indian themes, forms, and techniques with local artistic traditions and interests. Its most remarkable achievement may be the application of Indian architectural ideas to wood.

Khmer kings built extravagantly, commissioning reservoirs, canals, roads, and other public works, sometimes constructing temples and temple mountains to showcase their wealth and power. Temples built in the classical Angkor style were enclosed by a series of concentric moats and walls, making them more impressive in size and appearance than previous shrines. According to the dictates of Indravarman (r. 877–889), the temple Bakong was built in 881. An immense variation on the typical Khmer temple-pyramid, this temple consisted of five stone terraces, sixty meters square and fifteen meters high, topped by a light structure and surrounded by eight brick towers, and was intended to serve as his sarcophagus after his death. The Banteay Srei, or "Citadel of Women," completed in 968, the first year of the rule of King Jayavarman V (968–1001), was a small Shivit temple, sculpted from red sandstone, featuring three towers nine meters high and three meters at the base built on a common platform, with a rectangular room filled with beautifully carved friezes.

Perhaps the most famous work of Angkor architecture is the large sandstone temple of Angkor Wat, built under the rule of Suryavarman II and completed around 1150, the year of his death. Located just south of the present site of the ruins of Angkor Thom, this structure is surrounded by a lake-like moat almost 2.5 miles in length and 650 feet wide, and is directly accessible only by a great, sculptured causeway. Neglected and covered with forest growth, it was "discovered" by French explorers around 1860 and is considered a masterpiece of Angkor (and world) civilization. The structure at Angkor Wat is a sublime example of the Angkor temple-mountain, an enormous structure lurching out of the Cambodian flatlands in imitation of the divine Mt. Meru of Hindu mythology. Each detail, architectural and decorative, is of cosmological significance.

In all Cambodian art, the detail is almost perversely rich. At Angkor Wat and Banteay Srei, sandstone is made to resemble wooden architecture. Walls are seldom left blank: in typical classical Khmer style, they are filled with carvings of floral motifs and lace-like abstract patterns. The walls of the outer gallery are decorated with over a mile of striking bas-reliefs more than two meters high, depicting scenes of Hindu myth and Khmer history.

The temple-center of the capital city Angkor Thom was over two miles square, and surrounded by a wall more than twenty feet high and a moat 330 feet wide. Over the moat cross five massive decorated causeways, supported by giant sculptures depicting scenes from Hindu mythology. Each of these causeways leads to a monumental gateway topped by a gigantic, four-faced head of the city's patron deity, the bodhisattva Lokesvara, gazing in each of the four directions. Boulevards from each gateway lead into the city, where the Royal Palace, the Terrace of the Elephants, and the Terrace of the Leper King are located. At the very center of Angkor Thom stood the famous Mahāyāna Buddhist temple of the Bayon, now much in ruins. The shrine, built in the late twelfth century under the rule of Jayavarman VII (r. 1181–1215), contains a sculpture of the Buddha sheltered under the hood of a naga snake. A 150-foot-tall tower crowned with the four-faced head of Lokesvara was built in the center. Clustered around the chapels of the central tower are some fifty smaller towers, each also adorned with four serene, inscrutable faces. Most impressive, however, are the beautiful galleries decorated with bas-reliefs, which depict the everyday life of the common people: besides musicians and acrobats, we see people at the market, at wrestling matches, fishing, engaged in farm work, and attending cock fights.

Camões, Luis Vaz de (c. 1524–1580)

Portuguese lyric poet. Best known for his epic poem, *Os Lusíadas* (1572; *The Lusiads*), Camões (also known as Luis Vaz de Camõens) wrote many sonnets and plays and is considered one of Portugal's greatest lyrical poets. Little is known of his life, save that written by his earliest biographer in the seventeenth century, much of which is open to debate. However, it is speculated that in 1552, while a youth living in Lisbon, he was involved in a street brawl in which a royal officer was wounded; the result was incarceration, from which he was later pardoned in 1553 by the Portuguese king, John III. It has been suggested that Camões's later decision to join the Portuguese army was perhaps a condition of his pardon. Nevertheless, he set sail for India in the king's service, where he remained for seventeen years.

In India, he was briefly imprisoned for allegedly embezzling government funds, and nearly died in a shipwreck while being transported to Goa. Legend maintains that Camões, one of the few survivors, swam to shore, holding the manuscript copy of *The Lusiads* over his head, out of the water.

For several years after his release, he lived in extreme poverty, finally returning to Lisbon in 1569 with the assistance of friends. There he sought royal permission to publish his epic, and managed to secure a royal pension as a poet in 1572. In his later years, he wrote very little, perhaps exhausted by his journeys. He died of the plague in 1580, and was buried in an unmarked common grave with other plague victims in Lisbon.

Camus, Albert (1913–1960)

French writer. Camus, best known for his novels of the absurd, was born in Algiers to a poor family. Educated at the University of Algiers, he studied philosophy, paying his own way through school. Before the outbreak of World War II, Camus worked as a journalist in Algiers and Paris. During these years (1937–41), he completed the works that established his literary reputation: the novel *L'Étranger* (1942; *The Stranger*), the essay *Le Mythe de Sisyphe* (1942; *The Myth of Sisyphus*), and the play *Caligula* (1944).

Camus was a founder and the chief editor of the underground paper *Combat*; he became one of the leading intellectuals of the French Resistance in Paris. Closely associated with the French philosopher and writer Jean-Paul Sartre and the existentialist school, Camus finally parted ideological ways with Sartre over Sartre's increasingly vocal Communism. The break was finalized when Sartre published a scathing attack on Camus in his journal, *Les Temps Modernes* (Modern Times).

Despite his belief in the absurdity of human existence, Camus maintained a stubborn humanist streak, expressed in his characters' seemingly endless will to resist even the most hopeless circumstances. In *La Peste* (1947; *The Plague*), for example, Camus narrates the struggle of men to survive in the midst of disaster. His philosophical positions are also more clearly articulated in a book of political philosophy, *L'Homme révolté* (1951; *The Rebel*), which discusses the question of human freedom.

During the 1950s Camus began to work actively in the theater, writing and directing adaptations of works by the American novelist William Faulkner and the Russian novelist Fyodor Dostoevsky. In 1957 he was awarded the Nobel Prize in Literature and was killed shortly after, in 1960, in an automobile accident. The incomplete manuscript of a novel Camus was carrying with him at the time has been published as *Le Premier Homme* (1994; *The First Man*).

Canaanites

Ancient tribe of the Levant. The Canaanites were inhabitants of the Levant (modern-day Syria, Jordan, and Israel) from the third millennium B.C.E. until the start of the Hellenistic period in the fourth century B.C.E. Though authorities dispute the date of their arrival in this region, some believe that the Canaanites were Semitic migrants from Arabia and the Persian Gulf. Many authorities equate the first northward wave of this migration with the rise of Akkadian ascendancy in Mesopotamia about 2350 B.C.E. (Akkadian was the ancient Semitic language of Mesopotamia, as well as the term used to refer to the inhabitants of Mesopotamia before the year 2000 B.C.E.) While this dating is not beyond question, the discovery of the Amarna Letters and other surviving records make it clear that the region and people were referred to in Akkadian as "Kinahu" or "Kinanu" by the fourteenth century B.C.E.

Prior to the nineteenth century, the Bible was one of the few sources of information about the Canaanites. However, it is now generally acknowledged that the Hebrew descriptions of the Canaanites in the Old Testament are polemical and therefore unreliable as the sole source of information. More complete and reliable evidence of Canaanite culture has come from ancient texts discovered over the past century: the royal archives at Mari, most notably a collection of what is believed to be prophetic texts; the Amarna Letters, diplomatic correspondence between the Egyptian pharaohs Amenophis III (r. 1390–53 B.C.E.) and IV (r. 1353–36 B.C.E.), which were discovered at Tell el Amarna (south of present-day Cairo, Egypt); and remains found at Ras Shamra (ancient Ugarit) and Ras Ibn Hani (both in present-day Syria). Of these three sources, the finds at Ugarit are considered to be the most significant, because they show that the ancient city had contact with a wide range of other peoples in Egypt, the Aegean, and Mesopotamia.

Because of the attention they receive in the Old Testament, the Canaanites are perhaps best known for their religion, especially their supposedly sensual rituals and their worship of the deity Baal. More important, however, the Canaanites were responsible for one of the most significant developments in human history: a written alphabet. The Canaanite alphabet developed in the mid second millennium B.C.E. is the parent of the Phoenician script that later influenced the Greek and Latin alphabets.

Canción de Protesta (Protest Song)

Latin American music tradition. In 1966, in Santiago de Cuba, a new musical habitat called *La Casa de la Trova* (The House of the Trova) was created. It was a place where the old *trovadores* would gather to sing, and although these older musicians did not take steps to record their music and obtain publicity, the move was significant in that it kept the tradition of the *trova* alive. A meeting known as the *Primer Encuentro de la Canción de Protesta* (First Encounter of the Song of Protest) took place in 1967; musicians from all over Latin America who had been working independently gathered for the first time, and out of this encounter the Movimiento de la Nueva Trova (MNT; Movement of the New Trova) was born. These singers discovered they had a similar style, instruments, approach, and musical creativity, and collectively put their energies in the service of Marxist ideology. The Protest Song was thus born out of an artistic attitude, along with a faith and loyalty to certain principles. The MNT in Cuba was influenced by protest singers in the United States, such as Joan Baez; a second influence originated in the southern part of Latin America, especially in Chile, with the songs of Yupanqui, Viglietti, and Violeta Parra. From Europe, in turn, came the voices of Juan Manuel Serrat and Raimon.

The two central figures of the MNT are Silvio Rodriguez and Pablo Milanés, who are famous both for their combative songs and for their more lyrical pieces. Pablo Milanés, for example, wrote a song to Chilean political leader Salvador Allende Gossens called "A Salvador Allende en su combate por la vida" ("To Salvador Allende in His Fight for Life"), and Silvio Rodriguez similarly sings about loss and pain in a turbulent land in "La era esta pariendo un corazon" ("The Era Is Giving Birth to a Heart"). Some of the more famous names from the southern part of Latin America include Mercedes Sosa, Piero, and Charly García from Argentina; and, from Chile, Violeta Parra, Eduardo Gatti, Los Prisioneros (The Prisoners), Inti Illimani, and especially Victor Jarra, who was killed by the Chilean military shortly after the coup of 1973, when the Allende government was overthrown. His name has become synonymous with "Canción de Protesta."

Cantar de Mío Cid

Twelfth-century Spanish epic. The *Cantar de Mío Cid* (*Song of My Cid*) is a landmark of Spanish literature. Though the original manuscript is thought to have been written in 1140 by an unknown author, the earliest existing copy, known as the *Poema del Cid*, dates from 1307. The poem is written in a rough-hewn style and contains a considerable amount of dialogue; it greatly popularized the conception of a Spanish national character. Though the verse is characterized by assonance and lines of varying length, fourteen-syllable lines predominate. The poem chronicles the disgrace and eventual exoneration of "the Cid," Rodrigo Díaz de Vivar (1043–1099), an eleventh-century Castilian nobleman and military leader who became Spain's national hero.

As a symbol of the Spanish national character, the Cid is portrayed as loyal, generous, humane, sober, democratic, brave, religious, and devoted to his family. The poem couples a realistic tone and detailed treatment of the historical setting and landscape with the poetic artistry and flair that helped to promote its tremendous popularity. *Cantar de Mío Cid* has inspired plays, ballads, and other epic poems and prose chronicles, and has been widely copied and adapted by writers in Spain and elsewhere, perhaps most notably by the French dramatist Pierre Corneille, whose *Le Cid* (1637) is one of the outstanding examples of French Neoclassical drama.

Cao Dai

Vietnamese religious sect. Cao Dai (full name Dai Dao Tam Ky Pho Do) was established in the early twentieth century by Ngo Van Chieu, a Vietnamese civil servant, as a cult of divine force. Believing that the Cao Dai, the supreme power in the universe, had communicated with him (as well as with a host of saints, ranging from Buddha to Jesus Christ to Joan of Arc), Chieu spread his revelations to a group of converts. The syncretism of the sect, combining ancient concerns, Buddhism, Taoism, and Confucianism with Western spiritualism and Christianity, responded to the complex hybrid colonial identities of Vietnamese society.

Centered in the town and province of Tay Ninh, Cao Dai grew rapidly in the Mekong Delta. Its anti-French cast appealed to many Vietnamese nationalists, who, as elsewhere in colonial Asia, were also often participants in the colonial sector. For this reason, Cao Dai also appealed to peasants, who found that through the religion they could establish good relations with state representatives active in the movement. By 1938 Cao Dai had over 300,000 members and had established an army of 50,000 to protect their interests; in many ways, the Cao Dai area existed as a strong and stable mini-state. The government of President Ngo Dinh Diem found the areas formidable opponents in his 1954 attempt to consolidate the South Vietnamese state; one year later the Cao Dai submitted to military pressure from the Diem government. Most Cao Dai leaders were incorporated into the South Vietnamese bureaucracy and military. An estimated 1.5 million South Vietnamese still identify themselves as part of the Cao Dai.

Čapek, Karel (1890–1938)

Czech dramatist, novelist, and journalist. Suffering from a spinal disease his entire life, Karel Čapek still managed to emerge as the most popular writer of the original Czech Republic. After studying philosophy in Prague, Berlin, and Paris, Čapek eventually settled in Prague, beginning his literary career.

Čapek's early work was often written in collaboration with his brother, Josef, a prominent avant-garde painter and writer, who helped Karel compose and often illustrated his books as well; most notable among these is Ze zivota hmyzu (1921; The Insect Play). These early stories are concerned with man's ill-fated attempt to alter his destiny. However, he is perhaps best known for his works of science fiction, set in bleak utopias, which further examine this theme. His

play R.U.R. (1921; Rossum's Universal Robots) received international acclaim and also introduced the word "robot" into the world's lexicon. In Čapek's play, man invents the robot, which performs far better than man himself and soon dominates the earth, threatening the extinction of mankind.

Čapek's democratic and humanist ideals become evident in his biography of the Czech founder in his book Hovory s T. G. Masarykem (1928; President Masaryk). These ideals, and the dangers which haunt them, figure prominently in many of his works, though they often assume varied forms. Although he is most famous for his science fiction, some of Čapek's best writing can be found in his trilogy of novels: Hordubal (1933), Povětroň (1934; Meteor), and Obyčejný život (1934; An Ordinary Life). Considered his most mature work, these novels are psychological explorations of the human self, the motivations for human actions, and humans' relationship to the world.

Capra, Frank (1897–1991)

Italian-born American film director. Capra is best remembered as a populist filmmaker whose work enjoyed tremendous success among the moviegoing public, especially during the Depression era of the 1930s. Capra's films characteristically portrayed the common man as honorable and decent, a little man of heroic proportions struggling against a harsh and corrupt world, who overcomes adversity through the support of family and friends.

Capra's family left Italy for California when he was six. After a series of menial jobs in the filmmaking industry Capra eventually moved to Columbia Studios, where he directed some of his more successful movies, and transformed Columbia into a blockbuster company. While at Columbia, Capra worked with several future stars, including Jean Harlow (Platinum Blonde, 1931) and Barbara Stanwyck (The Miracle Woman, 1931, and *The Bitter Tea of General Yen*, 1933).

Capra's next film, *It Happened One Night* (1934), starring Clark Gable and Claudette Colbert, received nationwide attention—and five Oscars—and is generally recognized as the film that launched Capra's filmmaking career and popularity. Two of his most successful films, *Mr. Deeds Goes to Town* (Gary Cooper, Jean Arthur, 1936) and *Mr. Smith Goes to Washington* (James Stewart, Jean Arthur, 1939), portrayed the hero as a naïve idealist who is nearly defeated by corrupt lawyers, politicians, and businessmen. Abiding by honesty and decency, Capra's heroes successfully overcome their adversaries, and wind up in the arms of the heroine. Capra was able to overcome the overwrought and implicit sentimentality of these stories through the injection of lighthearted comedy.

Capra's next films, including *You Can't Take It with You* (1938), which received an Oscar for Best Picture, and *Meet John Doe* (1941), were less popular, and despite the great success of *It's a Wonderful Life* (1946), many criticized his increasingly heavy-handed sentimentality. With the changing times came different public sensibilities; as cynicism and sarcasm became more prevalent cinematic themes, Capra's films ceased to appeal to the moviegoing public. *Pocketful of Miracles* (1961), an unsuccessful remake of his original *Lady for a Day*, was Capra's last film, after which he retired.

Cardenal, Ernesto (1925–)

Nicaraguan poet. Considered the greatest Nicaraguan poet after Rubén Darío, Cardenal was educated at Jesuit schools in Nicaragua and Mexico, and at Columbia University in the United States. In 1957, following a religious conversion, he entered the Trappist monastery in Kentucky. In 1965 he completed his theological studies and was ordained a priest in Nicaragua. Known for his protest poetry, in his early poems collected in *Epigramas* (1961) Cardenal denounces the violence of the Somoza regime in Nicaragua. *Zero Hour and Other Documentary Poems* (1960), in turn, describes the effects of domestic tyranny and American imperialism in Central American history, and is considered a masterpiece of protest poetry. In later works Cardenal began using commercial slogans and empty phrases to signal an alienating world. The poetry in *Salmos* (1964; *Psalms of Struggle and Liberation*) expresses the tension between Cardenal's revolutionary political fervor and his religious faith. Based on the biblical psalms of David, they condemn modern-day evils and culminate with an apocalyptic vision of the world.

In 1965 Cardenal published *Oración por Marilyn Monroe y otros poemas* (*Prayer for Marilyn Monroe and Other Poems*), a collection in which he applies his earlier prophetic tone to contemporary events, presenting the death of American actress Marilyn Monroe as symbolic of what he views as the dehumanizing corruption of the capitalist system. He uses clichés, slogans, newspaper clippings, and advertisements in these poems as symbols of noncommunication. Among his prose works are a book of philosophical essays entitled *Vida en el amor* (1970; *To Live Is to Love*), and *En Cuba* (1972; *In Cuba*), a book of recollections of his visit to Cuba in 1970. Cardenal participated in the Sandinistan revolution that ousted Anastasio Somoza in 1979, and went on to serve as minister of culture for the next decade, until the Sandinistas were defeated in the elections of 1990. In this post he sponsored popular workshops in poetry and theater and helped spread Sandinistan political ideals. In recent years he has published *Los ounis de oro* (1988; *Golden UFOs: the Indian Poems*) and *Cantico cosmico* (1989; *Music of the Spheres*).

carnival

Roman Catholic festival. Carnival, a period of feasting and merrymaking that traditionally occurs in the week immediately preceding Lent in the traditional Christian calendar, is thought to have originated in pre-Christian times from spring celebrations that took place in ancient Babylonia, Greece, Egypt, and Rome. The ancient Roman festival of Saturnalia was held in honor of Saturn, the god of crops and harvests. During the celebration, social class, status, and rank were temporarily forgotten as slaves dined with their masters and gifts were exchanged in an atmosphere of hedonistic excess. This festival resembled many other ancient carnivals, and elements of these traditions can be found in the carnivals of today.

Though carnival is still celebrated in European countries like Italy, Spain, Portugal, and France, the festival has especially flourished in South America and the Caribbean, where the mixing of European and African peoples and cultures has made for especially lively and elaborate carnival celebrations. In these areas, European carnivals fused with festival traditions brought by slaves from Africa in the sixteenth century; on many Caribbean islands and in many South American societies, these annual celebrations were the only opportunities many slaves had for entertainment and carefree enjoyment. Trinidadian carnival is now one of the largest and most famous carnivals in the world and is characterized by calypso steel bands, colorful floats, and grotesque masks and costumes. The Trinidadian festival has spawned smaller carnivals for West Indians abroad in cities such as London, New York, and Toronto. Brazil's carnival in Rio de Janeiro is similarly renowned as a well-planned and highly celebrated event in which people from all levels of society become passionately involved. An equally strong carnival tradition has long existed in New Orleans, Louisiana, where French, Creole, and African traditions have mixed to yield culinary, musical, and cultural hybrids.

Many sociologists see carnival as a cathartic "safety valve" that allows often poor and powerless celebrants to momentarily release the pent-up frustrations of their daily lives. Others point to the festival as a vehicle for promoting national and cultural unity.

Carpentier, Alejo (1904–1980)

Cuban novelist and short-story writer. Born to a family of French and Russian immigrants, Carpentier had a mixed cultural experience that shaped his later literary ventures considerably. Educated in Paris and Havana, exposed to French and Russian intellectuals at home and to Hispanic and African elements in his environment, Carpentier attempted to harmonize in his work the diverse elements he found in his own Cuban and Latin American world. During the 1920s he worked as a journalist in Cuba and took part in intellectual movements, spiritually identifying himself with the avant-garde and Afro-Cuban cultural movements of that period.

In 1927 Carpentier was accused of being a Communist and was imprisoned.

After his short time in jail, Carpentier went to Paris, where he became involved in the Surrealist movement and frequently contributed to French Surrealist poet André Breton's journal *Révolution surrealiste*. Later, he rejected orthodox Surrealism in favor of his own, less heavily Freudian vision, which Gabriel García Márquez in turn popularized in the magical realism of *Cien años de soledad* (1967; *One Hundred Years of Solitude*).

Carpentier returned to Cuba in 1939 and began work as director of a radio station, editor of the newspaper *Tiempo Nuevo* (New Times), and professor of musicology at the National Conservatory. He traveled extensively during the 1940s and 1950s, and following a 1943 visit to Haiti, he wrote *El reino de este mundo* (1949; *The Kingdom of This World*), an imaginative re-creation of

Haitian history, which emphasizes the haunting spell of legend rather than historical fact. With a mixture of fantastic events grounded in historical reality, Carpentier retold Haiti's violent past during the turbulent reign of nineteenth-century tyrant Henri Christophe. His third novel, *Los pasos perdidos* (1953; *The Lost Steps*), is loosely based on a trip he took to the interior of Venezuela in 1941. Usually considered his masterpiece, it attempts to define the essence of Latin American reality as a product of the coexistence between primeval myths and European civilization. Its narrator journeys through the Orinoco jungle back to the origins of art, music, and thought, to the beginnings of human civilization and time itself; its apocalyptic vision criticizes the modernized and cosmopolitan world as rootless, meaningless, and decadent.

His other major works include the novels *Guerra del tiempo* (1958; *War of Time*), *El siglo de las luces* (1962; *Explosion in the Cathedral*), and *El recurso del método* (1974; *Reasons of State*), as well as a study of Cuban music, *La música en Cuba* (1946; *Music in Cuba*).

With the triumph of Communist leader Fidel Castro's revolution in 1959, Carpentier returned to Cuba and served in various official posts. Carpentier has been translated into more than twenty languages, and in 1978 he was awarded the Miguel de Cervantes Saavedra Prize for literature.

castes

Hindu system of social stratification. The caste system appears to have developed during the Vedic age. Each caste, or *jati*, is distinguished by its own *dharma*, or set of obligatory rules for moral righteousness.

While the highest Brahman and lowest "untouchable" caste positions are relatively rigidly defined and maintained, the distinctions in between are more fluid. The Hindu Brahmans, who created the traditional caste ideology, claim that rank order is ultimately based on ritual purity. In the Vedic age (1500 B.C.E. to 600 C.E.), society was divided into three *varnas* (literally, "colors"): these were the priests, or Brahmans; the warriors, or Kshatriyas; and the agriculturalists and merchants, or Vaishyas. A fourth caste category soon emerged, the Shudras, or servants, as the need arose to accommodate the numerous non-Aryan peoples in Vedic society. *Jati* provided a convenient measure used to distinguish between ethnic and occupational groups and to encourage hereditary specialized occupations. This did not mean, however, that there was an automatic correspondence between caste and economic status.

The influence of the Hindu caste system was felt as well within the ostensibly egalitarian Muslim religion. The Islamic caste system was derived from Hindu converts who persisted in their social conventions even after their conversion to Islam. The primary division in the Islamic caste system is between the *ashraf* (Arabic plural of *sharif*, or nobleman), which represents Muslim Arabs, and the non-*ashraf*, primarily Hindu converts.

The caste system remains even today the cornerstone of Hindu society. Birth decides membership in a given caste: even if a Hindu loses a caste identity by being thrown out of a caste for a severe offense, the offender does not then become a member of another (lower) caste. In turn, acquiring wealth does not entitle a caste member to climb up the caste ladder. It is possible, however, for low castes that are not considered "polluting" ("untouchable") to improve their position by collectively adopting such higher "clean" caste practices as vegetarianism, dowry, and the following of rituals practiced by the Brahman caste: this process of improvement is generally known as "Sanskritization." In order to ensure the purity of the caste, endogamy—marriage within a defined group—is strictly practiced, as the prominence of caste membership in the personal ads in Indian newspapers would attest.

Although caste originally had its origins in ritual and status, in modern times this definition has been weakened and downplayed as a conception of caste as a kind of ethnicity has strengthened. As a result, though caste status is no longer legally recognized as a barrier to education or employment, caste remains an important basis of social organization, and many political movements are caste-based. Discrimination within the caste system continues to be a problem for Indian society.

Castro, Fidel (1926–)

Cuban revolutionary and political leader. President of Cuba since 1959, Castro was a symbol of Communist possibility in Latin America and the Third World. Educated by Jesuits, Castro studied law at the University of Havana, where he was active in Latin American revolutionary politics. Castro became a practicing attorney in 1950, specializing in public-interest law. He was a candidate for Congress with the Partido Ortodoxo in 1952, though the elections scheduled for that year were canceled after Fulgencio Batista's coup d'état deposed President Carlos Prío Socarrás.

Outraged, Castro became an outspoken opponent of the Batista regime and began secretly organizing against him. An attempt to take over a military barracks in Santiago on July 26, 1953, failed, with Castro narrowly escaping death. He spent several months in prison and defended himself at his trial, where he delivered a famous five-hour speech defending the historical right to rebel against tyranny and outlining his radical reform program. Freed on a general amnesty, Castro left Cuba for Mexico in July 1955, founding the July 26 Revolutionary Movement with the intention of deposing Bastista.

In Mexico, he met South American guerrilla leader Ernesto "Ché" Guevara (1928–1967). Ché, Castro, and eighty-one armed men launched an assault on Oriente Province in November 1956. Due to a timing blunder, Cuban air and land forces awaited them, killing most of the party. Castro, Ché, and Castro's younger brother, Raúl, escaped to the Sierra Maestra mountains and immediately began to wage guerrilla war. By 1959 President Batista's unpopularity and an activist peasantry gave Castro a revolutionary opening, which he exploited. Though Castro's forces numbered less than 1,000 men, Batista's forces proved ineffectual. Castro entered Havana in January 1959, after Batista had fled the country.

The first, relatively liberal, governing coalition under Castro soon dissolved; Castro became prime minister, and his followers took control of the schools, civic and professional groups, and mass organizations. Elections were canceled, and repressive measures were taken against prominent anti-Communists. In 1961 Castro merged his movement with the Cuban Communist Party, formalizing the anticapitalist, anti-American tendencies of the new Cuban government and making possible large-scale aid from the Soviet Union.

Castro's policies in Cuba were often very popular: vastly expanded educational opportunities and institutions, redistribution of economic wealth, income, and health facilities, and guaranteed employment secured him the support of large sectors of the population. Chronic shortages, exacerbated by a U.S.-led trade embargo, did somewhat undermine his authority on economic matters. His regime curtailed civil liberties and nationalized most industries, prompting hundreds of thousands of Cubans to seek political asylum in the United States. The government still controls all mass media, and national elections were not held until 1976, and even then democratic procedures applied only to local governments.

Cuba assumed center stage in the Cold War struggle between the United States and the U.S.S.R. in 1962, when the Soviet Union installed ballistic missiles in Cuba and brought the world to the brink of nuclear war. Despite persistent attempts by the United States Central Intelligence Agency to assassinate him, Castro has survived to underwrite leftist guerrilla movements in Latin America and Africa. Increasingly isolated since the fall of Communism in Eastern Europe and the former Soviet Union, Castro remains a charismatic personality, dedicated to the maintenance of the Cuban revolution and the cause of revolutionary communism.

Cather, Willa [Sibert] (1873–1947)

American novelist. Cather spent most of her formative years in Red Cloud, Nebraska, where she and her family lived among immigrant European families. For the rest of her life she would write about pioneer traits and themes: courage, sensitivity to the land, the debilitating tediousness of small-town life on the prairie, the quest for a historical past. She attended the University of Nebraska and discovered a talent for writing.

Most of her employment after graduating involved some form of journalistic work, though she did publish some of her writing. *April Twilights*, a book of poems, appeared in 1903, and *The Troll Garden*, her first collection of short stories, was published two years later. In 1906 Cather accepted an editorship at *McClure's Magazine* in New York. But in 1912, following the advice of her late mentor Sarah Orne Jewett (1849–1909), Cather decided to give up journalism in order to focus on fiction.

Cather's first novel was *Alexander's Bridge* (1912), an account of modern life in an urban environment. For her second and third novels, however, Cather turned to more familiar material and wrote about the strength and spirit of frontier life in Nebraska. *O Pioneers!* (1913) and *My Ántonia* (1918) are generally heralded as her best works. *Song of the Lark* (1915), *Youth and the Bright Medusa* (1920), and the late novel *Lucy Gayheart* (1935) reflect on the struggle of gifted people who feel smothered and stunted by the constraints of country life.

Cather won the Pulitzer Prize for *One of Ours* (1922), a novel similar in content to *A Lost Lady* (1923). Both novels portray the sadness Cather felt concerning the eventual evaporation of the pioneer spirit with which she had grown up. Among Cather's later novels are *The Professor's House* (1925), *Death Comes for the Archbishop* (1927), *Shadows on the Rock* (1931), *Obscure Destinies* (1932), *Not Under Forty* (1936), and *Sapphira and the Slave Girl* (1940).

Catherine the Great (1729–1796)

Russian empress. Catherine II ruled the Russian empire from 1762 until 1796. Initially a great reformer and enthusiast of the Enlightenment, her correspondents included French writers Voltaire and Diderot, whom, with French philosopher Montesquieu, she read voraciously. Catherine's rule turned oppressive after the peasant uprising of 1773 and the French Revolution of 1789. The daughter of German nobility, she was born Sophie Augusta Friedericka, Prinzessin von Anhalt-Zerbst. Receiving a poor education and living in relative obscurity, in 1744 she was invited by Empress Elizabeth of Russia to visit St. Petersburg. Catherine, a woman with poor social prospects, was chosen to marry her cousin, the future Peter III of Russia. Their marriage was unhappy, however, and Catherine freely sought sexual satisfaction outside of the marriage.

After Peter's ascension to the throne in 1762, Catherine staged a bloodless coup with the aid of army officers angry at Peter's peace with Prussia and intended campaign against Denmark.

(Her powerless husband was later murdered, as were several rivals for the throne.) She proceeded to negotiate a favorable alliance with Prussia. She also kept Russia neutral during the turmoil in Europe brought on by the American Revolution (1775–83). During her rule, Russia expanded its possessions, gaining the northern coast of the Black Sea and adjoining lands from Turkey, as well as a significant portion of Poland. She embarked on a program of reform, as outlined in her book *Nakaz* (1766; *Instruction*), in an attempt to systematize bureaucratic institutions and modernize Russia's socioeconomic base. The rights of professional serfs were addressed, and she made a grand attempt to invent an urban middle class to offset the traditional peasant and aristocratic classes. Though that effort proved largely unsuccessful, she did compose a series of charters for the towns and the nobility, creating a well-ordered state built on estates with specific rights and privileges.

The French Revolution of 1789 rejected the aristocratic model of society as an amalgam of estates in favor of the citizen and representative body, a direct repudiation of Catherine's thinking about the state. She responded to the riot of revolutionary activity at the end of the century by hardening her policies and cracking down on cynics and dissidents. Satirical journals that she had previously supported were banned. Critics of her rule or of Russian society were imprisoned. She bloodily suppressed a Cossack uprising led by Emelian Pugachev in 1774. Although she was opposed to the new republicanism brewing in France, she remained a Eurocentric admirer of the Enlightenment, and her policies modernized Russia considerably. Although it is a popular myth and often repeated as fact, Catherine the Great did not die bearing the brunt of a horse during a sexual maneuver, but instead died of a stroke in her lavatory.

caudillos

Military or political dictators of Latin America. *Caudillos* are military men who assume dictatorial powers, ruling by charismatic authority and are backed by military or police forces. Emerging after the Wars of Independence as military leaders vied for power and leading armies of *gauchos* or *llaneros*, *caudillos* have been fundamental to the development of Latin American political systems since the early nineteenth century. The latter part of the nineteenth century, a chaotic period wracked by intermittent civil wars, is referred to as the "age of *caudillos*" for this reason, and Latin American general and statesman Simón Bolívar (1783–1830) is considered by many to be the first great *caudillo*. Other notable *caudillos* of the nineteenth century include Antonio Gúzman Blanco in Venezuela (1870–88), Juan Manuel de Rosas in Argentina (1829–52), and Antonio López de Santa Anna in Mexico (1829–55).

Although many of the Latin American countries have achieved constitutional forms of government, the presence of *caudillos* remains a salient aspect of contemporary Latin American politics. Notable *caudillos* of the twentieth century include Fulgencio Batista in Cuba; Anastasio Somoza and his son, Anastasio Somoza Debayle, in Nicaragua; and François Duvalier in Haiti. More recently, Getúlio Vargas in Brazil (1930–45), Juan Perón in Argentina (1945–55), and even Fidel Castro in Cuba (since 1959) have participated in this political tradition, using charisma and force to erect a strong political base and adopting a number of social and economic reforms. The *caudillo* tradition prefigures the recurring presence of the modern "dictator" in Latin America. Some observers have argued that *caudillismo* is desirable since it provides a strong centralized authority capable of "saving" the nation from social and political anarchy and economic chaos. Most critics, however, condemn this system as a variety of fascism, characterized by despotism, brutality, and antidemocratic tendencies.

Cellini, Benvenuto (1500–1571)

Florentine sculptor, metalsmith, and author. Cellini's *Autobiography* (1728) is one of the greatest works of the sixteenth century, a brilliant evocation of life during the Italian Renaissance. He began writing the autobiography in 1558, dictating to an apprentice. The book was translated into English, German, and French, and has influenced artists as diverse as Goethe and Berlioz.

Cellini's fame as an artist is derived primarily from his wonderfully ornate metalworks and his statues, such as *Perseo* (1545–54; *Perseus*). Although he received numerous commissions from Pope Clement VII, only two medals survive; and of his goldsmithing work, only a salt cellar, completed for the king of France, still exists. This piece is considered to be the supreme example of Renaissance goldsmithing.

Cervantes [Saavedra], Miguel de (1547–1616)

Spanish novelist, dramatist, and poet. Miguel de Cervantes's reputation as a writer rests primarily on his famous novel, *El ingenioso hidalgo Don Quijote de La Mancha* (Part I, 1605; Part II, 1615; *The Ingenious Gentleman Don Quixote*), recognized as a Western classic. An adventurer, he traveled to Italy in 1569 and fought in the naval battle of Lepanto, permanently losing the use of his left hand. During his return trip to Spain in 1575, his ship was captured by Barbary pirates, and Cervantes and his brother were brought to Algiers as slaves. His attempts at escape were futile, and Cervantes remained in captivity for five years, until the Trinitarian friars finally paid five hundred ducats in ransom. After his return to Spain, Cervantes married, fathered an illegitimate child, and secured a position with the navy. Cervantes was twice imprisoned for debt, and court records document the impoverished conditions under which he and his family lived.

His financial situation improved markedly with the publication in 1605 of *Don Quixote*, which was an instant success. Written to satirize the romantic literature that idealized medieval life and chivalry, the story's two main characters are Quixote, an aging knight who has lost his sanity after reading too many chivalric romances and ventures out on his horse Rocinante to fight against injustice, and Sancho Panza, a simple servant who views the world realistically and takes care of his master. The comical element of the novel is complemented by Cervantes's skillful portrayal of the human situation. Life is seen to be a sequence of events where tragedy and humor, the real and the ideal, coexist uneasily. In the second part, Cervantes poses a series of questions about the reality of texts and their role in constructing or deforming reality. The profits from this book enabled Cervantes to move to Madrid and devote his remaining years to writing.

Cervantes wrote between twenty and thirty plays, one of which, *Los banos de Argel* (1784; *The Baths of Algiers*), details the lives of Christian slaves in Algiers. Of all his plays, only one, *Pedro de Urdemalas* (1615; *Pedro the Schemer*), has met with critical favor. His final work, *Los trabajos de Persiles y Sigismunda* (1617; *The Tasks of Persiles and Sigismunda*), is a romance, published posthumously, which Cervantes believed would be either his best or his worst contribution to Spanish prose. In its prologue, signed just four days before his death, Cervantes quoted an old Spanish ballad that described someone with "one foot already in the stirrup," gracefully announcing his own death.

Césaire, Aimé (1913–)

West Indian poet. Césaire is best known for his invention of the neologism "Négritude" (meaning blackness) in the 1930s to describe a particular mode of black experience in a given culture. Together with Senegalese poet and eventual president of Senegal Léopold Senghor, and Guianean writer L. G. Damas, Césaire placed Négritude at the center of his work. The Négritude movement held to the view that black Africans and their descendants, by virtue of race as well as acculturation, feel, sense, and value differently from other peoples. Césaire was a proponent of this idea of an experiential blackness, and became widely recognized as an intellectual leader of African liberation. French philosopher and writer Jean-Paul Sartre proclaimed him a "Black Orpheus."

Born in Martinique, Césaire studied in Paris, where he was profoundly influenced by Marxism and Surrealism. He helped start the journal *L'Étudiant Noir* (The Black Student), a forum devoted to the exploration and proud reclamation of the African experience. He wrote his best-known work, *Cahier d'un retour au pays natal* (1947; *Return to my Native Land*), a collection of poems, while preparing to return to Martinique. In Martinique Césaire continued to write and to teach literature. His works include the combined French and English text *Aimé Césaire: The Collected Poetry* (1983), the plays *La Tragédie du roi Christophe* (1963; *The Tragedy of King Christopher*), and *Une saison au Congo* (1966; *A Season in the Congo*), and many essays, such as his *Discours sur le colonialisme* (1950; *Discourse on Colonialism*).

In 1945 Césaire was elected mayor of Fort-de-France and deputy to the French Assembly from central Martinique in the French legislature, as a member of the French Communist Party. He left the party in 1956, though not due to any ideological conflicts, emerging as the head of the Martinican Progressive Party (PPM) in 1958. He has remained a representative of Martinique ever since, though he is best known, in North America, in Europe, and in Africa, as a great Francophone poet and as the theorist of Négritude.

Cézanne, Paul (1839–1906)

French painter. Cézanne is considered by some to be the greatest Post-Impressionist painter; his work was enormously influential in the development of several modern art movements, most notably Cubism. Paradoxically, Cézanne spent much of his life painting in relative isolation and only in the later years of his life did his reputation as an artist extend beyond a small circle of Impressionist painters.

Born to a well-to-do bourgeois family, Cézanne received a classical education at the Collège Bourbon in Aix-en-Provence. His first attempt to study painting in Paris lasted only five months and would have been of an even shorter duration were it not for the encouragement of his friend, French novelist Émile Zola (1840–1902). Cézanne returned to Aix, but, unable to content himself with work in his father's bank, he soon returned to Paris with greater determination. He became associated with a circle of French Impressionist artists that included Édouard Manet (1832–1883), Camille Pissarro (1830–1903), Claude Monet (1840–1926), Pierre-Auguste Renoir (1841–1919), and Edgar Degas (1834–1917). Inspired by Eugène Delacroix's (1798–1863) use of color, Cézanne began to develop an artistic style almost opposite to that of his mature works, characterized by extremes of light and shadows and loose composition.

In 1870 Cézanne left Paris for Provence, partly to avoid being drafted into the army. Here he worked extensively with landscapes, and developed a style that was indebted to Impressionism's color schemes but figurally distinct. *La Maison du pendu* (1872–73; *The Suicide's House*) is considered the best example of his work from this period.

This period also marked the time in which Cézanne began to experiment with cubic masses and architectonic lines, setting the stage for the move to partial abstraction in Cubism. During the 1880s and 1890s, Cézanne moved toward his mature style, producing some of his most brilliant paintings, including many portraits like *Madame Cézanne au fauteuil jaune* (*Madame Cézanne in a Yellow Armchair*) and *La Femme à la cafetière* (*Woman with Coffee Pot*), both produced between 1890 and 1894, and *Les Joueurs de cartes* (1890–92; *The Card Players*), of which there are five versions.

By the time Cézanne reached the final years of his career, he was obsessed with his work. Although his fame spread, Cézanne became somewhat of a recluse, and after the death of his mother he began to pull away from his family and friends. The year after his death in 1906, a highly acclaimed retrospective exhibition of his works was held in Paris.

Chaco Canyon

Ancient Anasazi ceremonial site. A national monument in northwest New Mexico since 1907, Chaco Canyon is the site of thirteen pre-Columbian Anasazi ruins, the largest of which is the massive five-storied communal dwelling called Pueblo Bonito. Extending over two acres, Pueblo Bonito contains more than eight hundred rooms and thirty-two *kivas*, or ceremonial chambers.

Chaco Canyon has provided evidence of the sophisticated culture of its inhabitants—adept in farming, toolmaking, weaving, and pottery, and skilled in the development of irrigation systems, roads, and trails. At the height of the region's activity, Chaco Canyon may have supported as many as 6,000 people. It is believed that Chaco Canyon was more a ceremonial and religious center than a residential one.

Controversies about the creators of the site raged until the mid twentieth century. Some speculated that "foreign visitors" had been responsible for the buildings, while others considered the Aztecs or the Toltecs the likely architects. Carbon dating and other modern techniques proved, however, that the ruins of Chaco Canyon predate even the Aztecs.

The astronomical and religious purposes of the buildings have become clearer in recent years. The *kivas* were shaped in circular formation to reflect the sky. The *kiva*'s main door, like the entrance to the circular formation of the Stonehenge monument in England, faces the north star, around which all other celestial bodies revolve. A window to the right of the north door provided entry for rays of sunlight to strike the northwest *kiva* wall, where the journey of the sun could be marked to indicate the summer solstice. This, too, is similar to the Stonehenge monument, where the axis of symmetry is likewise oriented toward the sunrise of the summer solstice. At the winter solstice, pillars or towers in the canyon behind which the sun rose served as calendar markers during that season.

The Anasazi studied the heavens carefully, but for religious, not scientific, purposes. The movements of the sun and moon especially were believed to chart the journeys of the gods. This knowledge would in turn reveal the proper times for planting and harvesting, as well as for rituals and important ceremonies.

Chagall, Marc (1889–1985)

Russian-born painter and forerunner of Surrealism. Born into a Russian-Jewish family in the Byelorussian town of Vitebsk, Chagall studied painting in St. Petersburg in 1907 with Léon Bakst (1886–1925), one of the leading members of the influential World of Art group. After his arrival in Paris in 1910, Chagall was introduced to Cubism, and incorporated Cubist principles into his highly imaginative works. World War I left him stranded in his hometown, where he stayed during the Russian Revolution of 1917. An enthusiastic partisan, he became the local commissar for art, and launched ambitious projects for a local academy and museum. But after two and a half years of intense activity, marked by increasingly bitter aesthetic and political quarrels, he gave up and went to Moscow. There he worked primarily on stage designs, but in 1922 decided to leave Russia for good. He spent time in Berlin before eventually settling in Paris in 1923.

He produced his famous book illustrations for Russian writer Nikolai Gogol's *Mertvye dushi* (*Dead Souls*) in 1948 and for French writer Jean de La Fontaine's *Fables choisies* (*Fables*) in 1952. His later paintings, which include crucifixion scenes and twelve stained-glass panels, *Les Douze Tribus d'Israël* (1960–61; *The Twelve Tribes of Israel*), for the synagogue of Jerusalem's Hadassa Medical Center, reflect a heightened sense of religious and social awareness, probably gathered through Chagall's experience of two world wars and the Russian Revolution. In 1941 Chagall and his family took refuge in the United States, producing sets and costumes for the New York productions of ballets by Russian composers Pyotr Ilich Tchaikovsky and Igor Stravinsky.

In 1948 he returned to France, settling on the Riviera. His other famous late works are a ceiling he painted for the Paris Opéra (1964) and an enormous mural at Lincoln Center in New York City (1966). Much of Chagall's work is preserved at his museum in Nice, France. The story of Chagall's early life is contained in his autobiography, *Ma vie* (1931; *My Life*).

Chang'e

Chinese moon goddess. According to Chinese mythology, Chang'e, a beautiful lady, swallowed an elixir stolen from her husband that enabled her to fly to the moon and become immortal. In antiquity, China's poets and novelists seem to have loved Chang'e as much as the moon itself. While her beauty and loveliness are often celebrated in poems and novels, the Chinese people show their affection for her with the famous Zhongqou Jie, or Mid-Autumn Festival. On the fifteenth day of the eighth lunar month according to the Chinese calendar, people eat sweet mooncakes and look up at the shining full moon to enjoy the goddess's beauty. They also take the opportunity to express remembrance and concern for their family and friends far away.

Changing Woman

Navajo god. Also referred to as Earth Woman, Changing Woman, the daughter of First Boy (thought) and First Girl (speech) is the most revered and benevolent of the Navajo gods. She symbolizes regeneration, renewal, and rejuvenation. Believed to be the mother of all Navajo, Changing Woman is credited with the creation of the heads of the four original clans. Considered the protector of the Navajo people, Changing Woman protects the Navajo from disease and provides for their food and shelter. According to Navajo beliefs, she is the original life-giver, whose spirit inhabits the heart of the living earth.

Chanson de Roland (c. 1100)

French epic poem. *La Chanson de Roland* is an epic poem of twelfth-century France, commonly known as a *chanson de geste* (song of deed), and known in English as *The Song of Roland*. The poem is believed to have been written by a Norman poet named Turold in England c. 1100, and tells the story of

Charlemagne's defeat at the Battle of Roncesvalles. Though the battle was not truly significant, the monumental, mythical tone of the poem reflects the artistic production encouraged by Charlemagne (king of the Franks, 768–814 C.E.), who saw himself as a god among men, a Christian warrior battling against the Arabs. The events of the poem, however, are more legend than fact.

At the beginning of the story, Charlemagne sends the knight Ganelon to negotiate peace with the Saracen king, Marsile, over the Saragossa territory. In a fit of rage, Ganelon vows to seek revenge on his stepson, who had recommended Ganelon for the task, and plots with the Saracens to ambush the rear guard of Charlemagne's army, led by Roland. Roland's close ally, Oliver, tries to save the troops and Roland by sounding a horn to alert Charlemagne to the disaster, but the horn is heard too late. Roland's intended, Oliver's sister, falls dead upon hearing of her lover's death. Charlemagne later tries Ganelon, who is eventually executed. The poem ends with a visit to Charlemagne from the angel Gabriel.

The poem's stoic style of writing reinforces the harsh realities that arise from human conflict. *The Song of Roland* is both a religious document and an examination of feudal loyalties in the service of Christianity.

Chaplin, Charlie (1889–1977)

British film director and actor. Chaplin is widely recognized as the premier star of the American silent film, as well as a pioneer in the artistic development of the cinema. His trademark persona, the "Tramp" with cane, derby, floppy shoes, tight jacket, and baggy pants, was popular throughout the world, and made him one of the most recognizable figures of the silver screen.

Chaplin began his theatrical career in 1898 as a music-hall performer and in 1907 was employed by the English-based Fred Karno Pantomime Troupe, an internationally recognized music-hall group. During a tour of the United States, Chaplin was spotted by a representative of Keystone Films, and in 1913 began working for them. The "Tramp" first appeared in Chaplin's second film for Keystone, *Kid Auto Races at Venice* (1914), and continued to evolve both personally and within the context of increasingly complex and ironic social situations. Although generally portrayed as an underdog figure in a world of lechery, deceit, police corruption, and greed (*Easy Street, The Adventurer*), the Tramp possessed his own more malicious side as demonstrated in *The Masquerader* and *Dough and Dynamite*.

After several studio changes, Chaplin eventually moved to First National, a film studio where he worked as a director, writer, and actor, completing close to seventy films. In 1919 Chaplin, along with D. W. Griffith, Mary Pickford, and Douglas Fairbanks, founded United Artists and completed eight films, producing four features between 1925 and 1936: *The Gold Rush* (1925), *The Circus* (1928), *City Lights* (1931), and *Modern Times* (1936). *Modern Times*, a satirical look at the dehumanization of man in the industrial age, remains one of Chaplin's most popular and critically acclaimed films. In these films, referred to as his "marriage group," the Tramp searches for sexual and romantic companionship.

Chaplin utilized sound in his final three American films: *The Great Dictator* (1940), a burlesque treatment of Hitler and the Nazis; *Monsieur Verdoux* (1947), with Chaplin as a dapper mass-murderer; and *Limelight* (1952), costarring fellow American silent screen star Buster Keaton, a farewell to the silent-screen era. In 1940 Hearst publications publicly criticized Chaplin for *The Great Dictator*, and in 1947 he was attacked both by the press and by politicians as a Communist sympathizer.

The years before his death were filled

with personal and political hardships, including troubles with the U.S. Internal Revenue Service for nonpayment of taxes, his steadfast support of liberal political causes, and the continued boycotting and picketing of his films by the political right because of his suspected Communist affiliations.

In 1952 Chaplin left the United States to visit Europe, at which time the State Department summarily revoked his reentry permit. Chaplin did not return to the United States for twenty years and refused to allow any of his films to be distributed there. In 1957 he made *A King in New York*, a disappointing satirical commentary on U.S. democracy. In 1972, recognizing the enormous contributions Chaplin had made in the development of the cinema as an art form, the Motion Picture Academy awarded him a special Academy Award. He was knighted by Queen Elizabeth II in 1975.

Charlemagne (c. 742–814 C.E.)

Emperor of the Holy Roman Empire. Charlemagne (also known as Carolus Magnus and Charles the Great) was king of the Franks from 768 to 800, and the first emperor of the revived empire in the West, from 800 to 814. As the founder of the Holy Roman Empire, Charlemagne played a pivotal role in the extension of the Catholic Church throughout much of Western Europe.

Charlemagne fought numerous campaigns on behalf of the Church. One of the earliest of these, against the Lombard kingdom in 773–74, was conducted at the request of Pope Hadrian I. The Lombards, a Germanic people who had settled in Hungary, had been a continual source of irritation to the papacy. Charlemagne's defeat of the Lombards expanded the territory of his own kingdom while fulfilling the wishes of the Vatican. He led a similarly successful campaign against the Saxons of the northern German plain, between 770 and 784. After each of these victories, Charlemagne granted parts of each territory to the papacy, a move that earned him the continuing support of church officials. He conquered northern Slavs, Asiatic Avars, and other cultures on the European fringe, opening new regions to Christian missionaries. Although his campaign against Muslim Spain was stopped in 778, subordinate commanders were able eventually to expand Frankish authority as far south as the Ebro River.

Devoted to the full conversion of peoples in conquered territories, Charlemagne instituted the death penalty for those who resisted the Church's missionary efforts, including those who refused baptism, destroyed church property, or celebrated pagan rituals. Other forms of Christianity were likewise forbidden. He also had a profound interest in learning, employing some of the most eminent Italian and British scholars at the Palace School. It is believed that he spoke Latin, understood Greek, and had some familiarity with Hebrew. Charlemagne saw monasteries and other church institutions as ideal conduits for the enlightenment of the general public. At some point around 780, he asked these institutions to begin forwarding copies of books in their possession for inclusion in his newly established court library. By 790 this library included an extensive collection of early Christian as well as pre-Christian writings.

After his intervention on behalf of Pope Leo III (pope 795–816) in 800, Charlemagne's ties with Rome were further strengthened. Responding to a request by the beleaguered pope, Charlemagne went to Rome to establish Leo's innocence of charges that had been lodged against him. On Christmas Day, after taking a vow of innocence, a thankful Pope Leo III agreed to crown Charlemagne as Augustus, Emperor of the Romans.

Charlemagne regarded the coronation as a recognition of his rightful place to sit among the succession of Caesars who had preceded him, and a further affirmation of the pope's willingness to establish what Charlemagne envisioned as a worldwide empire that the Roman Church would dominate. His coronation was viewed quite differently by rulers of the Eastern Empire, however, who saw it as a direct threat to their sovereignty. Charlemagne's coronation in 800 served to heighten tensions between the Eastern and Western empires.

Chaucer, Geoffrey (c. 1343–1400)

English poet. Considered the most important writer of Middle English and one of the greatest writers in Western literature, Chaucer is famous primarily for his unfinished masterpiece, *The Canterbury Tales*.

Details of Chaucer's early life are sketchy. By the year 1357 he had joined the royal service, as was the tradition in his family, participating in the English army's invasion of France. However, he was captured and was later ransomed by King Edward III (r. 1327–77). About 1366 he married Philippa, one of the queen's attendants and the sister of Katherine Swynford, who later became the wife of John of Gaunt, one of Chaucer's most important patrons. The following year, Chaucer was given a life pension by the king and thereafter remained in royal service, traveling abroad on several diplomatic missions. This travel proved quite important to his writing, as it was through these trips that he discovered Italian writers Dante, Petrarch, and Boccaccio, whose works greatly influenced his own. After the death of his wife in 1387, Chaucer fell into temporary royal disfavor and dire financial straits. He later received another life pension from Richard II (r. 1377–99) and attended to Richard and his successor, Henry IV (r. 1399–1413), the son of Chaucer's patron, John of Gaunt.

Chaucer's writings can be roughly divided into three periods. His first works are heavily influenced by the French tradition of love poetry. Chaucer's major work of this period is the allegorical *Book of the Duchess* (1370), written as an elegy for John of Gaunt's first wife. With his travels to Italy and his introduction to the works of Dante, Petrarch, and Boccaccio, Chaucer entered his second period of writing, producing the unfinished *The Legend of the Good Woman* (1387), which introduced the rhymed heroic couplet; *Parliament of Fowls* (1382); and *The Loves of Troilus and Criseyde* (1382), based on a work by Boccaccio and considered one of the great love poems of the English language. Chaucer's mature writing began about 1387, when he was writing *The Canterbury Tales*; upon his death, *The Canterbury Tales* (c. 1343–1400) consisted of 17,000 lines. It narrates the journey of a group of pilgrims traveling to the shrine of St. Thomas à Becket in Canterbury. Along the way, members of the group tell stories that vividly depict medieval attitudes toward love, marriage, and religion. Though Chaucer's storytelling was overlooked for centuries, his works were rediscovered in the eighteenth century and restored to their proper place as some of the greatest poems of English literature.

Chavchavadze, Ilya Grigorievich (1837–1907)

Georgian writer and nationalist leader. A central figure in Georgian political and literary life in the second half of the nineteenth century, Chavchavadze was born to one of Georgia's most distinguished princely houses. Educated at home until the age of ten, Chavchavadze later enrolled in a private school in Tiflis (Tbilisi) and attended St. Petersburg University as a law student. In 1861 he was expelled for participating in student demonstrations. Upon his return to Tiflis in 1863, he edited the liberal newspaper *Sakartuelos Moambe* (The Georgian Herald) while serving in state and civic institutions and writing.

For many years Chavchavadze was chairman of the Society for the Dissemination of Literacy Among Georgians. In

1877 he founded the newspaper *Iveriia*, which he edited until 1902. An outspoken opponent of Russian colonialism in Georgia, Chavchavadze became the principal leader of the Georgian nationalist movement. He was placed under police surveillance, and many of his literary works were censored. After the Revolution of 1905, however, he became a member of the upper house of the newly created Russian Parliament and an advocate for liberal reform.

Chavchavadze believed that reality was best understood through literature, and he insisted that the experiences of life were the foundation for artistic creativity. Art for art's sake was an oxymoron for Chavchavadze, who believed that art has a purpose: to give form to ideological beliefs in an attempt to promote social progress. For Chavchavadze, that meant writing about Georgian life. His works include narrative poems such as "The Vision" (1859), centering on the denunciation of serfdom, and "The Hermit" (1883), inspired by his belief in public service and social reform. In addition to these poems, he also wrote the novellas *Otaraant Kurivi* (1888; *Otar's Widow*), which was eventually made into a film, and the novel *K'atsia-adamiana* (1859–63; *Is He a Human Being?*), in which Chavchavadze depicts the everyday life of the landowning class—a work for which he was heavily criticized by the Georgian gentry. Chavchavadze also wrote dramas, critical essays, and translations of major Russian, German, and English authors, as well as works on history, economics, and social issues.

He became a member of the Russian Parliament in 1905, and on returning to Georgia in 1907, he was murdered under mysterious circumstances.

chbap

Khmer literary form. Literally meaning "rules," *chbap* consists of short didactic poems featuring puns and a moral ending. Composed by Buddhist monks from the fourteenth to the seventeenth centuries, until fairly recently these rules were memorized by Cambodian schoolchildren. Many stress the importance of behavior and language appropriate to one's place in society, especially in dealing with authority figures such as parents or teachers. The best-known are the *Rules on Behavior* and the *Rules for Men*. The popular *Chbap Ker-Kal* is a small treatise on domestic economy, which contains most of the Cambodian proverbs, in the guise of the advice that a father gives to his son in order to "make a life."

Chekhov, Anton [Pavlovich] (1860–1904)

Russian short-story writer and dramatist. One of Russia's great literary figures, Chekhov was a trained physician who took to literature and achieved world renown for his stories and plays. The third of six children born to a grocer in southern Russia, he studied medicine at Moscow University, writing on the side as a means of making money. Chekhov submitted sketches, humorous stories, and jokes to local papers and journals, using pen names such as "My Brother's Brother" or "The Doctor Without Patients." His early collections secured him a position with a leading St. Petersburg paper, which permitted him to concentrate on the quality of his stories. Along with the brilliant humorous tales, Chekhov also wrote more scathingly satirical and poetic stories as well. By the late 1880s he had found his mature style. He had already written many of his greatest works by this time, including "Step" (1888; "The Steppe") and "Skuchnaia istoria" (1889; "A Dreary Story").

Chekhov had contracted tuberculosis at the university and was eventually forced to give up medicine because of his health. In 1892 he bought a small estate outside Moscow for his family and there wrote some of his best-known works, including the short novel *Ward*

No. 6 (1892) and his plays *Chaika* (1896; *The Seagull*) and *Diadia Vania* (1897; *Uncle Vanya*). The first production of *The Seagull* in St. Petersburg in 1896 was a failure, and Chekhov almost abandoned playwriting. However, two years later, it was resurrected at the Moscow Art Theater and was so successful that the theater chose the gull as the emblem of the company.

In 1898 Chekhov moved to the resort town of Yalta in the Crimea because of his deteriorating health. Here he met often with the Russian writers Maksim Gorky and Leo Tolstoy and concentrated his writing efforts primarily on plays, producing *Tri Sestry* (1901; *The Three Sisters*) and *Vishnevyi sad* (1903; *The Cherry Orchard*) for the Moscow Art Theater. His politics turned increasingly liberal, and when in 1902 the government annulled the election of Gorky to the Russian Academy, Chekhov joined another writer, Vladimir Korolenko, in resigning his membership in protest.

Chekhov is a master of the short-story form and often recounts the sadness of human existence, the inability of human beings to relate to one another. His plays concentrate on the dying of the landed gentry and their inadequate response to the historical changes of the period. These are simple plots, but they give Chekhov room to explore the inner landscape of his characters.

In 1901 he married the actress Olga Knipper of the Moscow Art Theater, but they lived apart for much of their short marriage due to Chekhov's health. The letters he wrote to his wife rival his fiction in their brilliance. He died in a spa in Badenweiler, Germany.

Chiang Kai-shek (1887–1975)

Chinese military leader. Also written Jiang Jie-shi. Born to a merchant family in Zhejiang province, Chiang was inspired to pursue a career in the military by the writings of the ancient strategist Sunzi. Although he attended the Baoding Military Academy in North China in 1906, it was not until his stay in Japan (1907–11) that his fervor against the Qing dynasty (1644–1911) found a suitable outlet. While attending a Japanese military academy, Chiang met Sun Yatsen (or Sun Zhong-shan), another revolutionary who became a key figure in Chiang's early rise. Chiang returned to China just as revolution broke out, a large-scale rebellion against Manchu (or Man-zhou-guo) imperial rule. He fought in Shanghai under Chen Qimei in 1911 and 1913, but when Chen was assassinated in 1916, Chiang briefly retired from public life. He resurfaced to join Sun Yat-sen's revolutionary group, the Guomindang, or GMD. Although Chiang began as an officer, he soon moved up the GMD ranks, particularly when his suggestion that their military forces be reorganized along Red Army lines was adopted. Chiang went to Russia to study military organization in 1923, and in 1924 he became the head of the Huang-pu Military Academy, the training institution for many future Chinese military leaders.

After Sun's death in 1925, Chiang became involved in a protracted power struggle within the GMD. Although Chiang was able to prevail over the left-wing faction of the GMD and to gain initial advantages over the rival Communists, his inability to eradicate the Communists from Chinese military and political life would eventually haunt him. Nevertheless, Chiang achieved the unification of all of China south of the Great Wall through a series of military campaigns culminating in the capture of Peking (now written Beijing) and in 1928 became the chairman of a new national government. Yet Chiang's insistence on viewing Chinese Communists, rather than the imperialist-minded Japanese, as his main threat, resulted in many costly purges that sapped China's strength. In the 1936 Xi'an Incident,

Chiang's own troops captured and held him for a week, releasing him only after he promised to form the United Front with the Communists to fight Japan. (War with Japan followed in 1937.) By 1939 Japan controlled almost half of China's population and territory.

During World War II, the Allies established the China Theater of Operations, of which Chiang was named the supreme commander in 1942. Theoretically, Chiang was supposed to engage the Japanese army and divert it from any other activities. But his fear of the Communists and his belief in the inevitability of a Chinese civil war following Japan's defeat led him to save many of his best troops for the struggle that he knew would come. The strategy backfired. Since the Communists did much of the fighting against the Japanese, they grew in popularity with the majority of Chinese while Chiang fell in stature. When civil war did break out, the Communists won and established the People's Republic of China in 1949. Though Chiang fled to Taiwan that same year and resumed his rule there, he was unable to oust the Communists from the mainland.

Chichén Itzá

Pre-Columbian Mayan city. Meaning "Mouth of the Wells" (chi means mouths and chén means wells), Chichén Itzá was founded in the sixth century in south-central Yucatán state, Mexico, and chosen as the site for the city because of the two wells found in the midst of the arid land. Many historians believe that the tenth century marked the demise of many of the southern Mayan cities, and that Chichén was overtaken by the Itzá tribe, who were heavily influenced or led by the Toltecs of central Mexico. Other historians believe that the Itzá arrived two to three hundred years after the collapse of the Mayan city, and perhaps after the Toltecs themselves used the city as their capital; nevertheless, it is from the invasion of the Itzá tribe that the official name, Chichén Itzá, is derived.

While occupying Chichén Itzá, the Itzá tribe briefly joined the tribes of the Uxmal and Mayapán, forming what was known as the League of the Mayapán, a confederacy that survived until 1450. With the rise of the city of Mayapán, Chichén Itzá seems to have lost much of its dominance; nevertheless, the brilliance of the Itzá architects and mathematicians made Chichén Itzá undeniably remarkable. The Itzá were responsible for constructing many of the great structures discovered in the city, such as the Castillo (the great pyramid), the ball court (where the game tlachtli was played), the grave of the high priests, the Colonnade, and the Temple of the Warriors.

A Mayan-Toltec architectural hybrid, Chichén Itzá was heavily influenced by religious beliefs, most dramatically illustrated in the structure of the Castillo. The height and steepness of the ascent made it virtually unsafe to climb the steps in any way other than to take a snake-like zigzag route, a deliberate architectural feature that exemplified the Itzá's worship of the snake. To the Itzá, the snake—especially the rattlesnake—was associated with fertility and rain. At the equinox, precisely timed by the Itzá, there is a moment when the pattern of shadows cast on the pyramid steps appears as the body of a large snake. Another dramatic example of serpent iconography is the enormous twin serpents that form the entrance to the Temple of the Warriors, one of the most important structures at Chichén. Their heads form the base of the columnar support, while their tails support the lintel of the doorway. The reclining figure of Chac-Mool, the Mayan fertility and rain god, is located in the front doorway of the temple.

When the Spanish arrived in the sixteenth century, the Mayans had already abandoned their cities and moved to small towns. Chichén Itzá was overtaken by jungle until rediscovered by explorers in 1904, first under the direction of American archaeologist Edward Herbert Thompson (1856–1935). Archaeologists found that the Spanish had done much damage to Chichén Itzá and other ruins by destroying much of the serpent imagery and statuary, which they reviled as pagan and phallic.

Chikamatsu Monzaemon (1653–1724)

Japanese playwright. Often called Japan's greatest dramatist, Chikamatsu, also known as Sugimori Nobumori, is especially famous for his Bunraku, or puppet theater, pieces. Born to a samurai family, the young Chikamatsu served various members of the court in several capacities, where he learned the literary and dramatic conventions of the court culture. Writing his first puppet drama, *Yotsugi Soga (The Soga Heir)*, in 1683, and in 1684 his first Kabuki, another form of Japanese theater developed after Bunraku in the seventeenth century, he was mainly affiliated with the Takemotoza Theater in Osaka, where he moved in 1705.

In the small puppet theaters where most of Chikamatsu's work was performed, a single speaker chanted the text of the play, while small puppets manipulated from below acted the scenes on a simple stage. A player of the stringed samisen provided background music. Performances were often given in the homes of samurai and other aristocrats. Chikamatsu's works were remarkable in the puppet and Kabuki theaters because they aspired to dramatic merit in themselves, rather than serving simply as vehicles for the virtuoso demonstrations of puppeteers and actors. Before Chikamatsu, Bunraku plays had been mostly in the unrealistic style of fantasy, myth, and fairy tale. He attempted to correct this without falling into the simplistic, pedestrian realism that was becoming popular among his contemporaries.

"Art," he said, "is something that lies in the slender margin between the real and the unreal." Chikamatsu's artistic project was to finesse this line in the highly stylized Bunraku and Kabuki conventions.

In early plays, such as *The Soga Heir*, Chikamatsu followed the style of war chronicles. He soon developed Bunraku in the style of historical romances. He created fictional scenarios, as in *Shusse Kagekiyo* (1686; *Kagekiyo Victorious*), which chronicled the betrayal and suicide of a noble courtesan, but also adapted true incidents for the stage. *Sonezaki shinjū* (1703; *The Love Suicides at Sonezaki*), for example, was written three weeks after a shop clerk and a prostitute committed suicide together; and perhaps his most renowned work is the historical drama *Kokusen'ya kassen* (1715; *The Battles of Coxinga*). Chikamatsu wrote over twenty such dramas, which offer a compelling picture of the brothel system, a system of sexual slavery. Chikamatsu's plays made such strong public impressions at the time that such suicides became disturbingly frequent; laws were subsequently enacted that made the survivor guilty of murder, and the corpses were exposed like those of common criminals.

Distinct from such historical romances are Chikamatsu's "domestic tragedies," the dramas of common lives. Their moving realism in presenting common people caught between duty and affection set the thematic standard for the puppet theater.

Chilam Balam

Collection of Mayan historical records. The *Chilam Balam* are made up of many books that take the name of their town of origin. Created by many authors, in many styles and epochs, their accounts date back to the fifth century. Referred to as the *Books of Chilam Balam*, these books contain summarized hieroglyphic records of Mayan civilization as kept by Mayan priests, and were transcribed by learned Indians after the Spanish conquest in the seventeenth and eighteenth centuries. They are called *Chilam*, a sacerdotal title, in honor of the individual who interpreted the books and the will of the gods, and *Balam* because it refers to the jaguar or sorcerer.

Filled with ancient songs and poetry that were transmitted orally, the *Chilam Balam* are considered to be part of the indigenous Latin American literary tradition. Historical chronicles for the most part, they are composed of myth, divination, prophecy, medical texts, astronomical almanacs, and interpretations of events. It consists of four autonomous parts that are linked chronologically: the first two parts refer to the migration of two principal factions; the third to the League of Mayapán; and the fourth to the epoch of the encounter and conquest. The *Chilam Balam* constitute one of the best primary sources concerning Mayan history.

Chinese dynasties

Succession of ruling Chinese monarchical families. Spanning some three thousand years, the exact dates of the major dynasties are sometimes difficult to determine; nevertheless, the first legendary Chinese dynasty was the Xia dynasty, beginning around the year 2200 B.C.E. and the last was the Qing, which ended in 1911 C.E.

The Xia dynasty is believed to have begun around the year 2200 B.C.E., lasting roughly until the end of the eighteenth century B.C.E. (c. 1766 B.C.E.). This loosely defined period was marked by cultural expansion and some of the earliest instances of attempts by farmers to settle permanently. While it is considered the first of the dynastic periods, it was not until the creation of the Shang (or Yin) dynasty (c. 1766–1122 B.C.E.) that the foundation of organized Chinese civilization was established. Begin-

ning as an amalgam of groups in the eastern Henan province, the first Chinese dynasty worthy of the name saw the emergence of cities, the invention of the first Chinese calendar, the development of a written language, and advances in bronze metallurgy.

The Shang were conquered by marauders from western China, the Zhou, who founded their own dynasty in 1027 B.C.E. Under pressure from barbarian attacks and internal dissent, the Zhou moved their capital eastward in 771 B.C.E., inaugurating the Eastern Zhou period, which lasted until 256 B.C.E. Zhou authority diminished throughout this period, which coincided with the Warring States era (403–221 B.C.E.). In this time of constant infighting between feudal states, models of authority and competence based on merit came to supplant models based on divine or natural right. The civil-religious systems of Taoism and Confucianism grew in popularity and definition during this time.

From the confusion of the Warring States period emerged the ultra-legalist Qin dynasty, a brief (221–206 B.C.E.) but bold and ultimately successful attempt to transform China and the dynastic system. The Qin centralized the state, unified the writing system, established a universal system of weights and measures, undertook the construction of the Great Wall, and succeeded in beating back barbarian armies in the north and south, creating the first real Chinese empire. They were swiftly overthrown, but the Han dynasty that followed (202 B.C.E.–220 C.E.) built on the Qin organizational structure, though its rulers took greater care not to alienate the peasantry. Confucianism was officially promoted, as evidenced by the creation of the examination system.

Factionalism and poor economic performance led to the dissolution of the Han dynasty, which was followed by the Period of Disunion, a three-hundred-year riot of warring states and competing interests. (During this time Buddhism became a powerful force in Chinese society.) The Sui (581–618 C.E.) attempted to restore the glory of the Chinese empire, rebuilding the Great Wall, fashioning the Grand Canal, and reestablishing a central government. Burdensome taxes and military failures led to their almost immediate overthrow, but the Tang dynasty (618–906 C.E.) built on Sui foundations to forge a powerful empire, stretching from Korea to Persia. The capital city of Xi'an was home to a million people, and the arts, lyric poetry, and Confucianism all prospered. Military adventurism led to the Tang's demise, and China was a power vacuum until the Song took power in 960. The Song dynasty (960–1279) saw the emergence of cultural patterns that would hold for nearly a millennium, as urban areas expanded and trade became increasingly important, an educated middle class assumed responsibility for the bureaucratic administration of culture and society, and a state orthodoxy (Neo-Confucianism) combined aspects of Buddhism and Confucianism. The Song dynasty gave way to Mongol (or Meng-gu) rule after the successful campaigns of the barbarian Genghis Khan. His grandson Kublai Khan established the Yuan dynasty (1260–1368). Although native Chinese were discriminated against by the Yuan, their rule saw a massive expansion of trade within and outside China. Diverse religions and ethnicities were tolerated, even patronized, by the Yuan, and numerous Europeans traveled throughout China, including Marco Polo. Nonclassical vernacular literatures also flourished, thanks to official repression of classic forms. Chinese resentment was never ameliorated, however, and a massive peasant rebellion ended Mongol rule.

The Ming dynasty (1368–1644), a powerful despotic era, moved the capital to Beijing and oversaw the rapid expansion of Chinese agriculture, literature, and population. Porcelain and the Chinese novel achieved their greatest development, while massive scholarly projects attempted to gather and systematize the accumulated learning on medical, technological, and historical subjects.

The final Chinese dynasty, the Qing, was the product of another foreign invasion, this time by the Manchu (or Man-zhou-guo). They ruled from 1644 until 1911, managing a largely sedentary society. They extended the reach of the empire and governed with great success for over a hundred years, although by the nineteenth century widespread corruption and expensive military campaigns had drained the regime of its vitality. The encounter with the West, begun in earnest as British imperialism jockeyed for shares of the opium trade, proved embarrassing for the Chinese, who lost several wars with foreign powers and ceded Hong Kong to the British in 1842. Reform movements at the turn of the nineteenth century attempted to revitalize the dynastic system, but they were unsuccessful, as underlined by China's humiliating defeat in the Sino-Japanese War of 1894–95. Radical reforms in the early 1900s precipitated the crisis that resulted in a revolutionary situation. On February 12, 1912, the last emperor of the dynastic system abdicated in favor of the provisional republic headed by Sun Yat-sen, ending over three thousand years of dynastic rule.

Chinese examination system
System of entry into Chinese civil service. Initiated in the first century C.E. as an entrance requirement for the newly created civil service, the Chinese examination system flowered under the Ming (1368–1644) and Qing (1644–1911) dynasties. Because of the length and expense of the exams, it was usually only wealthy families who could support candidates through the often decades-long preparation period. Even with as-

siduous preparation, success was rare—during the rule of the Han dynasty (202 B.C.E.–220 C.E.), when the exams were invented, only 1 percent of the candidates passed. The material covered by the exam was broadened under the Tang dynasty (618–906) to include not only the Confucian classics but administrative problems as well. Despite the elaborate exam process, which gave the impression of strict meritocracy, most of the offices were bought by wealthy individuals seeking prestige and status.

During the Song dynasty (960–1279), the development of printing facilitated the education of a much greater percentage of the population, enabling a wider social base to compete for civil service positions. The Song introduced a three-part division of the exams, rationalizing the system by creating distinct prefectural, departmental, and palace-level examinations. Completion of the first two stages exempted the candidate from labor service and corporal punishment. The final stage of the exam was held only once every three years in the various regional capitals in China.

Despite widespread corruption within the system and the selling of lower degrees by the government, the examination system retained its function as a meritocratic ideal and as a means of introducing new talent into the system. When the Jesuits came to China in the seventeenth century, they were impressed by the examination system; it was eventually imported throughout Europe and the United States in the nineteenth century, becoming the model for civil service exams. In the twentieth century, additional attempts to modernize and reform the exams failed; the exams were given for the last time in 1904, and were abolished by imperial edict in 1906.

Chinese exclusion

United States immigration policy. During the Gold Rush of 1849 and the construction of the Central Pacific Railroad, large numbers of Chinese immigrants, mostly males from Kwantung province, provided cheap labor along the West Coast in both the United States and Canada. The Burlingame Treaty (1868) codified this influx of Chinese into the United States, but it was not long before racial prejudice and economic conditions led to restrictions on Chinese immigration. The depression of the 1870s dampened the demand for cheap labor, and soon native whites were competing with Chinese immigrants for available work. Anti-Chinese sentiment, which became an important factor in California politics in the 1860s and 1870s through the agitation of Denis Kearney's Workingmen's Party, exploded into the violence of the San Francisco riots of 1877. The trade union movement around San Francisco sprang up partly as an anti-Chinese phenomenon; the ubiquitous union labels on products furthered racial discrimination by allowing consumers to differentiate between items made by whites and by nonwhites.

In 1879, a Senate committee altered the Burlingame Treaty, passing the Fifteen Passenger Act in Congress. President Rutherford B. Hayes vetoed the act, but a new treaty, which allowed for restrictions on Chinese immigration, was drafted to supplant the liberal Burlingame Treaty. The new treaty, which exempted teachers, students, travelers, and merchants, led to a series of increasingly severe legislative acts, beginning with the Chinese Exclusion Act of 1882, which prohibited immigration of Chinese workers. The ban on Chinese immigration lasted until 1943, when China became a U.S. military ally, and even then a race-based quota system admitted only a token 105 Chinese immigrants. This system remained in place until 1965, when an amendment eliminated ethnic discrimination in immigration policies.

Chinese inventions

Gunpowder, compass, paper, printing. All four of these inventions, which would change the face of Europe after their eventual transmission, were developed in China centuries earlier, and attest to the tremendously advanced civilization in China stretching back to before the Christian era.

Gunpowder was discovered by Chinese alchemists in the eighth century, when they developed the ability to separate the salts of alkaline metals. When they were able to isolate saltpeter (potassium nitrate) and combine it with charcoal and sulfur, these alchemists stumbled upon gunpowder. The first military use of gunpowder in China occurred during the tenth century. By the eleventh century, it was used in mines and in hand grenades and other projectiles. Gunpowder did not reach Islamic nations, via the Mongols, until the thirteenth century, and was not adopted until the fourteenth century in Europe, where military technology was soon to surpass what had been developed in China.

The compass was adapted from the lodestone-carved "south pointing spoon" in the divining boards of the second century B.C.E. The first crude compass was constructed in the seventh or eighth century out of a magnetic pivoted needle floating in water. A major refinement of this tool occurred in the eighth or ninth century, when magnetic declination was discovered. Since the needle did not point in an exact north-south direction, the compass readings needed to be adjusted. The Chinese used a compass to navigate a ship as early as 1111, a full century before the compass was used on European vessels.

Perhaps the greatest Chinese inventions were paper and printing. Paper was invented in western China in the first century. This first paper was made of mulberry bark, hemp, and other fibers. By the fourth century, the production of paper had been refined, and materials such as bamboo slips and silk cloth were used. It was not until the Tang dynasty (618–906), however, that papermaking

became both a fine art and a mass-production process. The precise date of printing is harder to determine, since rubbings were made from stone onto thin paper as early as the Han dynasty (202 B.C.E.–220 C.E.). By the eighth century, wood blocks with texts carved into them were used to print books in the form of a pasted-together scroll. Because of the often poor quality of this type of printing, the majority of books were still copied out by hand in manuscript form. It was not until 1040 that Bi Sheng invented a movable-type printing press in which characters made out of ceramic were used. Later presses used wood, copper, and lead, as well as ceramic for the characters. Because the process was expensive and difficult, owing to the Chinese language's use of thousands of characters instead of a few dozen letters, block printing predominated in China until the nineteenth century. Nevertheless, the Chinese possessed a movable-type machine four hundred years before it came into use in Europe.

Chinese painting

One of the most prestigious aspects of Chinese culture, Chinese painting dates back to the tomb paintings of the fourth century B.C.E. Chinese painting utilized wall, silk, and paper as surfaces, and worked with a brush made of animal hair and an inkstone. When silk and paper paintings became the most popular forms, scroll painting became the most convenient medium for the art, superseding the more fragile screen painting and the immovable wall painting. From its earliest inception, Chinese painting concerned itself with religious and mythological themes as well as human life. Despite this emphasis on humanistic and religious themes, Chinese painting found its idiom with the development of landscape painting during the first half of the Song dynasty (960–1279). Advances in brushwork techniques and the rendering of space were matched by an attempt to associate individual aspects of nature with philosophic connotations. Later Chinese painting was dominated by the scholar-artist, who viewed painting as an outlet for personal expression, in league with Confucianism. Beginning with the Ming dynasty (1368–1644) and with the advent of the Qing dynasty (1644–1911), however, the traditional style in Chinese painting gave way to a multiplicity of styles and a riot of forms, reflecting a creative resurgence among Chinese painters.

Chinese rites

Confucian ritual of ancestor worship. During the sixteenth century, under Matteo Ricci (known in Chinese as Lu Madou), one of the Jesuit pioneers in China, the Jesuits established a strategy of cultural "accommodation" in an attempt to convert the Chinese to Roman Catholicism. Unlike other Roman Catholic orders, the Jesuits, also known as the Society of Jesus, were sensitive to the native culture of the countries to which they traveled. Having studied the workings of the dynastic court, the Jesuits insisted that Confucianism, the religion of the upper classes, was not incompatible with Christianity. They proceeded, therefore, to incorporate native beliefs and practices into Christianity. The various ceremonies and traditions of ancestor worship were taken to be civil and social observances, and thus were incorporated into a new, syncretic Catholicism. By allowing Chinese converts to keep their Confucian rituals, the Jesuits hoped to broaden Christianity's appeal, rather than reject all Chinese traditions as pagan. Instead, the Jesuits argued that Confucianism was devoid of any spiritual or religious content, and the moralistic tenets of Confucianism were viewed as a complement to the spiritual aspect of Roman Catholicism.

The Jesuits felt that it was both necessary and important to accommodate the culture in which they found themselves, and this system of "accommoda-tion" included Jesuits learning the native language, taking on new names, wearing indigenous clothing, and working to convert the powerful and well-educated classes. This strategy of accommodation was encouraged by the eclectic spirit of the late Ming dynasty (1368–1644), in which the three traditional teachings of Confucianism, Buddhism, and Taoism were viewed as essentially one teaching, with a much more liberal spirit of Confucian orthodoxy.

The Jesuits managed to convert 150,000 Chinese by 1651. Highly trained scientists and technicians as well, the Jesuits assumed positions of power within Chinese institutions. After the Manchu invasion and the establishment of the Qing dynasty (1644–1911), there was a return to a much stricter sense of religious orthodoxy in China, and hostility toward Christianity became pronounced. Nevertheless, the Jesuits continued to enjoy prestige and influence in the Qing court.

Ironically, it was from within the Catholic Church that the Jesuits encountered the greatest hostility. Non-Jesuit Catholic orders, the Dominican and Franciscan orders, believed that ancestor worship and other Confucian practices were pagan heresies, setting off what would become the Chinese Rites Controversy. Although the Jesuits, with the backing of the Chinese Imperial Court, insisted that their brand of Confucianized Catholicism was not heretical, in 1704 the Vatican sided with those opposed. Continuing to serve as court mathematicians and astronomers, the Jesuit order was eventually abolished by the pope in 1773, and the inroads that Christianity had made in China were abandoned. (The Jesuit order was restored after the defeat of Napoleon in 1814.)

chōka

Japanese literary form. The *chōka* is a form of long poem, or *nagauta*, distinguished in classical Japanese verse from the thirty-one-syllable *tanka* (short poem) by its pattern of alternating five- and seven-syllable lines, or by the later form of *haiku*. There can be any number of these lines—traditional representatives of the form vary from seven lines to 149—but they are always closed with an extra seven-syllable line. One or more "envoys" may follow the main *chōka*; these brief *tankas* restate or expand the theme of the long poem.

Most popular in the late seventh and early eighth centuries, the *chōka*'s renowned practitioners were Kakinomoto no Hitomaro (689–700) and Yamanoe no Okura (660–773), whose works are collected in the oldest volume of Japanese poetry, the *Man'yōshū*, which dates to 759. The Heian period (794–1185) marked the end of the form, in favor of the more condensed and popular form of *haiku*.

Chopin, Fryderyk [Franciszek] (1810–1849)

Polish composer. Considered the most important European composer ever to have written primarily for the piano, Chopin was born in Warsaw. His parents placed him under the tutelage of Wojciech (Adalbert) Zywny, a talented musician and teacher, who assisted the young Chopin greatly. At the age of seven, Chopin published his first composition, *Polonaise in G Minor* (1817), and had his first public recital at the age of eight.

In his teens, Chopin studied music theory with Józef Elsner, the director of the Warsaw Conservatory of Music. With Elsner's help, Chopin's reputation as a composer and performer flourished; by 1829 he had become a *cause célèbre* in Vienna as well as in Warsaw. Within a year, however, the jaded denizens of the Vienna scene began to tire of Chopin, and in attempts to avoid fighting in the mounting conflict between Russia and his native Poland, Chopin left for Paris, where his musical talents and delicate looks soon placed him in great de-

mand as a salon pianist and a private piano teacher. He extended his great sequences of poetically charged miniatures: études, preludes, nocturnes, mazurkas, polonaises, and waltzes.

Chopin stayed in Paris, where he achieved fame as a composer and as a lover of women. His most famous affair was with Aurore Dudevant, better known as the novelist George Sand, whom he met in 1836. Shortly thereafter, Chopin's health began to deteriorate. Escaping to the relaxed atmosphere of Nohnat, the country house belonging to Sand, Chopin produced some final major works, including the Sonata in B Minor (1844) and the *Polonaise fantaisie* (1845–46).

The rampant emotionalism that became a trademark of Chopin's personal life also characterized his compositions. Yet Chopin was also a careful craftsman, conscious of theory, who experimented with harmony and counterpoint, especially near the end of his life. Although his works are often noted for their simple melodies, his textural elaborations are exhilaratingly complex, and had a profound influence on subsequent nineteenth-century artists, including the Hungarian Franz Liszt (1811–1886) and the German Robert Schumann (1810–1856).

Chopin, Kate (1851–1904)

American novelist and short-story writer. Attacked in her own day for her feminist concerns and skeptical attitude toward many societal conventions, Chopin has become celebrated today for precisely the same qualities. Her greatest work, the novel *The Awakening* (1899), is today seen as an eloquent and daring protest against the constraints society imposes upon women's personal, artistic, and sexual aspirations.

Chopin was born in St. Louis, but after her marriage to Louisiana native Oscar Chopin the couple moved to New Orleans, and later to Cloutierville. Her husband died after fourteen years of marriage, and Chopin returned to St. Louis and began writing. She took as her subject the Louisiana she had witnessed during her marriage, and published more than a hundred short stories, many of which were well received. Her work was characterized by polished and lyrical prose, and the use of symbolism and carefully crafted plot structures.

These qualities found their best expression in *The Awakening*. It is the story of Edna Pontellier, a Kentucky woman on vacation in Louisiana. In the Europeanized and vigorous culture of New Orleans she sees the possibility of an escape from her loveless but secure marriage, and the realization of her artistic ambitions and sensual yearnings. As Edna begins to ignore familial and social duties and to take steps to fulfill her desire, her own personal limitations and naïveté are revealed to the reader. Eventually, having renounced her marriage but also having failed in achieving her liberated ideal, she commits suicide.

The Awakening met with much critical opprobrium because of its frank treatment of sex, and reviewers faulted Chopin's sympathetic treatment of Edna. In doing so, however, they overlooked the novel's greatest sources of power: Chopin's intelligent and balanced depiction of the forces that constrain women in society, and the skillful construction of plot and language that made the tragic ending seem inevitable. It is this insightful and nonpolemical treatment of feminist issues that is largely responsible for the recent resurgence of interest in Chopin's works.

Chopin's first novel was *At Fault* (1890); her stories are collected in *Bayou Folk* (1894) and *A Night in Acadie* (1897).

chowgan

Equestrian sport. *Chowgan*, now known as polo, has been played in Iran since at least the sixth century B.C.E. From there it was exported to Central Asia, northern India, and Tibet. The game spread to China and Japan, where it was modified considerably. The British learned the sport in India and exported it to the Western world as polo. Polo continues to be popular among the Turkic peoples of Central Asia, and in Afghanistan and northern Pakistan. This is a different version of the game, having fewer rules and being quite violent. The sport was originally played with the skull of an animal (or possibly that of a prisoner).

A related sport, called *buzkashi*, is played in Central Asia. A member of one team picks up the headless carcass of an animal and carries it on horseback toward a goal while the opposing team attempts to stop him by any means at its disposal. A third equestrian sport popular in this region is tent-pegging. This entails spearing a wooden peg stuck in the ground at a full gallop. The original purpose of the game was a cavalry exercise to practice uprooting tent pegs in surprise raids, causing the tents to collapse on an unsuspecting enemy.

Christianity

World religion. Christianity originated in Palestine, founded by the followers of Jesus Christ. A system of faith that has affected innumerable cultures across the globe, it embodies the belief that Jesus of Nazareth is the Son of God, the second person of the Trinity of God: the Father, the Son, and the Holy Ghost. The central Christian tenet holds that his mission in life and accomplishment in death were to prove God's love for mankind and to redeem humanity's sins by his death. The religion promises eternal salvation for those who believe and practice the doctrine, or gospel, preached by Jesus Christ.

While the story and lessons of Christ are contained in the New Testament of the Holy Bible, much of the ethical background is deeply rooted in Old Testament writings, particularly the Ten Commandments. Christianity is also characterized by the performance of rites called Sacraments, rituals that celebrate one's progression through life and within the faith. Most services are conducted in an official church by a trained clergyman, but in its 2,000 years Christianity has been practiced in countless unorthodox ways, as interpretations of right worship and the proper scope of church life have been contested and modified. In addition to heterodox interpretations, the three major streams of Christianity prevalent today are Roman Catholic, Orthodox Eastern, and Protestant. This last subsumes a large number of divergent denominations.

Christianity is essentially an offshoot of Judaism in that Jesus Christ, a Jew himself, was considered to be the long-awaited messiah foretold in the Old Testament. His evangelism emulated Jewish practices of the day, and helped consolidate Christianity as a missionary, expansionist religion. The new faith spread quickly through Asia Minor to Alexandria and to Greece and Rome, because of the devotion and genius of its early missionaries, most notably St. Paul. Such missions continue today on a reasonably large scale and remain a major element of Christianity. They were an integral part of Western colonization schemes in the nineteenth and twentieth centuries, although missionaries, especially the Jesuits, had initiated independent missions long before the heyday of European colonialism.

There is some evidence that a monarchical hierarchy, with bishops governing parishes, may have existed as early as the second century C.E. This governing hierarchy came to be institutionalized in the Roman Catholic Church, with the bishop of Rome (the pope) as the head of all bishops. The need for a strong central authority to discipline and regulate Christian religious practice was great, as Christianity proved to be a powerful syn-

cretic force from the beginning. Worshipers combined new Christian beliefs with older pagan beliefs and practices, showing a theoretical openness at one time exemplified by St. Paul in his mission to the Corinthians. Within a few centuries the promotion of an official interpretation of the life and teachings of Jesus was institutionalized in the Roman Catholic Church and the New Testament of the Bible, especially the Four Gospels, which were selected and canonized in the third century C.E.

Christianity's first 250 years were marked by its relentless persecution by Roman emperors (most famously Nero), who banned Christian practice and envisioned themselves as gods. With the Edict of Milan in 313 under Constantine I and Licinius, tolerance of Christianity was made official. In the West, the Bishop of Rome remained independent of the Imperial power. In the East, where centralized religious authority was lacking, church doctrine came under the Emperor's control. This practice, called *caesaro-papism*, was initiated by Constantine and later made law by Justinian.

The three hundred years following the decriminalization of Christianity were plagued with doctrinal controversies regarding the nature of Jesus Christ, his relationship to God, and the question of the Holy Spirit. These questions were addressed at a series of general councils of bishops, which resulted in the development of the Nicene Creed, an outline of the official orthodox position. Many influential Christian thinkers wrote during these centuries, including St. Basil the Great, who introduced the first well-organized elements of monasticism to Christianity, and Origen and St. Jerome, who played a large role in determining the content and organization of the Bible.

In the seventh and eighth centuries, Islam gained a preponderance of influence in the East. The struggle over iconoclasm further exacerbated the alienation of the East from the West, and by the ninth century the two Christendoms had few cultural ties between them. Even the practice of their common Christian faith was distinct. The schism became official in 1054, when ecclesiastical animosity between Rome and Constantinople attained a sort of legal permanence, formalizing the break between the Roman Catholic and Eastern Orthodox churches. In the sixteenth century, increasing discontent with the rituals and practices of the Catholic Church, as well as its extensive involvement in temporal affairs, led to the outbreak of the Protestant Reformation. Refusing to acknowledge the bishop of Rome, the pope, as the infallible arbiter of God's will on earth, the partisans of the Reformation founded splinter sects that rejected many of the hierarchical organizational features of the Roman Catholic Church, preferring more spartan and personal forms of devotion to the lavish, ritualized worship of the Catholics.

While Christianity's influence on European politics and society has diminished somewhat over the last several hundred years, it remains a powerful and growing force in the margins of the industrialized world. In the twentieth century, particularly in Latin America and Africa, Christianity has made great inroads. In the Eastern European countries emerging in the 1990s from decades of Communist rule, various forms of Christianity, particularly Roman Catholicism and Eastern Orthodoxy, are formidable political and social forces.

Christmas

Christian holiday. Christmas is a popular Christian festival usually celebrated on December 25. The word "Christmas" is derived from the old English "Cristes maesse" (Christ's mass), a religious celebration commemorating the birth of Jesus Christ. The earliest mention of Christmas can be found in Roman records dating from the fourth century C.E.

Some Eastern Orthodox churches celebrate Christmas on January 6, the feast of the Epiphany, but most other churches have adopted December 25. It is unclear why the twenty-fifth was so popular with early Christians, but it may have been an attempt to conjoin Christmas with a pagan Roman festival commemorating the birth of the sun.

Many of the traditions associated with Christmas are derived from non-Christian roots; pre-Christian Romans exchanged gifts on December 17 (Saturnalia) and celebrated the New Year (January 1) by decorating their houses with plants and candles. When the Germanic and Celtic tribes penetrated the Roman empire, their traditions of food, camaraderie, the Yule log, fir trees, and the exchange of gifts were added to these holidays.

Christmas is now an important secular festival in some parts of the world. It has become associated with a celebration of the family, with particular emphasis on children, whose patron saint Nicholas (Santa Claus) is considered the mythical bearer of gifts for all.

Chulalongkorn (1858–1910)

Thai ruler from 1868 to 1910. Also known as Phrachunlachomklao and Rama V, Chulalongkorn was the son of Mongkut, another great leader of the Thai nation. As the result of colonial politics, Chulalongkorn attempted to institute wide-ranging reforms throughout Thailand, looking to imitate the successes of the West.

In the latter half of the nineteenth century, Thailand (then known as Siam), with its weak military, was forced to concede territory to the French and English. Chulalongkorn hoped to fend off the colonial powers by demonstrating that Thailand was a world-class civilization and a powerful modern nation. With the help of farsighted administrators, he launched a massive modernization campaign: he established a centralized bureaucracy, increased government revenues, brought vassals and far-flung dependents into an organized provincial administration, abolished forms of slavery and indentured servitude, instituted public education and other state services, and introduced technological advances such as telegraph and railway lines. In each of these measures Chulalongkorn hoped to displace the arbitrary administration based on patronage that had hitherto dominated Thai society, replacing affect and nepotism with a system of impersonal law.

Even as he brought Thailand into the modern world politically and economically, Chulalongkorn strove to maintain traditional Thai cultural identity. For instance, *The Royal Ceremonies of the Twelve Months*, a long work attributed to him, describes the rituals for manipulating cosmic forces to promote the success of the state, thus proving and preserving the influence of Buddhism on Thai culture.

Despite such gestures, Chulalongkorn's reforms encountered stiff resistance from conservatives, or "ancients," in the court. They accused Chulalongkorn, whom they called "Young Siam," of selling out to the West. Still, his reforms were largely successful, succeeding in the dual task of forestalling Western military adventurism and shunting aside old-guard criticisms.

Chung Yüan

Buddhist and Taoist holiday. Chung Yüan is celebrated in Vietnam and the People's Republic of China on Moon 7, Day 15 of the lunar calendar (which falls sometime in July or August on Western calendars). The event is known as the Feast of the Hungry Ghosts, when the souls from purgatory wander the earth.

In China, where it is known as Chieh Tsu (the Receiving Ancestor's Festival),

families prepare elaborate feasts and gifts of gold, silver, green, and red paper money for the ghosts of the dead. Paper clothing is hung on the walls in preparation for their visit, and at sundown the heads of the family place these gifts on the street near the door. Incense is burned; in prerevolutionary China, the traditional obeisance of three kowtows (bows) were performed. During the three days of ancestral presence, men congregate in teahouses and women gather in sewing circles; families often visit the final resting places of their forebears. On the festival's final evening, the paper clothes and the rest of the money are burned, with a prayer that the ancestors find their way home and leave quickly. Paper lanterns are lit and set afloat on rivers and lakes to conclude the event.

In Taiwan, the day is called "the opening of Hell's gate." Prayers, banquets, and incense are thought to release the souls from their suffering. Hell's gates are said to remain open until the thirtieth day of the seventh month, the birthday of the Buddhist saint Te-chông ông, who presides over hell and purgatory and tries to ease the suffering of its denizens. Images of the gods of other temples are paraded around the city during the festival in order to control the "hungry ghosts" as they go on their journey. Images of the generals Fan and Hsieh, traditionally seen as the guardians of the gates of hell, are placed throughout the city as additional measures of security. This is done because the ghosts of those who have no family to make offerings, or who had died unnatural deaths, are thought to wander the earth unless led to the relief of the Western heavens or the torment of the infernal regions.

In Vietnam, Trung Ngyuen (Wandering Souls' Day) is second in importance as a holiday only to Tet. As in other Buddhist and Taoist countries, the sacrifices and prayers are believed to comfort the ghosts who have been cast from hell or purgatory unclothed and unfed, and are a way to absolve the spirits of their sins.

Churchill, Sir Winston [Leonard Spencer]
(1874–1965)

British prime minister, statesman, and author. Born to an American mother and a British father, Lord Randolph Churchill, Winston Churchill was perhaps the most charismatic and prominent leader of World War II. Ironically, however, he was a poor student and failed the entrance examinations for military college three times before finally passing. Churchill began his military career in 1895, traveling to Cuba, Spain, India, and South Africa as a journalist and soldier. It was also during this period that Churchill launched his writing career with the publication of *The Story of the Malakand Field Force* (1898), *The River Way* (1899), and a novel, *Savrola* (1900), all based on his military experiences.

Resigning his commission in 1899, Churchill devoted himself to writing and to politics. Though he lost his first bid for office as a Conservative candidate, in 1900 he won a seat in the House of Commons. After a dispute with the Conservative Party over the issue of tariffs, he switched to the Liberal Party in 1904, coming under the influence of Liberal British politicians John Morley and David Lloyd George. While serving as undersecretary of state (1906) for the colonies and then as president of the Board of Trade (1908), Churchill agitated for social reform, calling for an eight-hour day for miners, a minimum wage, and state labor exchanges to combat unemployment. When the House of Lords rejected the budget of 1909 because it included higher taxes to finance these reforms, Churchill led an attack against the Lords, helping to establish the Parliament Act of 1911, which limited the power of the House of Lords. This action earned him popular support,

acclaim, and the post of home secretary.

Later transferred to the Admiralty in 1911, Churchill pressed for a naval military buildup to counter the growing threat from Germany, and worked during World War I as a military officer (1915–16) and as minister of munitions (1917–18). After the war, he became secretary of war (1919–21), his major concern being the Allied anti-Bolshevik campaign in Russia.

The next few years of Churchill's political career marked a shift in his views. His time spent as secretary of war, combined with the time he served as the head of the Colonial Office (1921–22), where he pressed equally for the creation of new Arab states in the Middle East as well as a Jewish homeland in Palestine, led him to a more politically conservative stance. This shift was fully emphasized in the 1924 general election, when he won a seat as a Conservative and was named Chancellor of the Exchequer by the Conservative government, a position he held from 1924 to 1929. Nevertheless, the following years did not prove easy for Churchill; the politics of the Conservative government caused massive unemployment, a miners' strike, and the General Strike of 1926. By 1931 Churchill was mistrusted by every political party and found himself out of office. He returned to his writing, publishing a number of books (mostly biographies) and articles calling for a "Grand Alliance" to resist the rearmament of Germany by Hitler.

When Britain declared war on Germany on September 3, 1939, Churchill was renamed to his old post in the Admiralty, and after Prime Minister Neville Chamberlain's forced resignation in 1940, with great popular support, Churchill became prime minister and minister of defense, both offices in which he served for the duration of the war. Churchill forged his "Grand Alliance" with the Free French, as well as with the U.S. president Franklin D. Roosevelt, and when Hitler invaded the

Soviet Union, Churchill welcomed Russia as an ally as well. Yet, in the final stages of the war, Churchill and Roosevelt came to disagree over the threat of Russian Communism to the new Europe, Churchill fearing the rise of the Soviet Union as a world power. After the war, to the surprise of many, Churchill and the Conservatives were turned out in the general elections. Churchill once more returned to writing, producing his six-volume book, *The Second World War* (1948–1953), for which he won the Nobel Prize in Literature in 1953.

In 1951, at the age of seventy-seven, Churchill was again elected prime minister, as well as minister of defense; he was also named Knight of the Garter in 1953, and in 1963 was declared an honorary U.S. citizen by an act of Congress, an unprecedented gesture. His death in London at ninety years of age was followed by a state funeral attended by many world leaders.

Chūshingura

Japanese theater piece. Also known as *The Loyal Forty-seven Rōnin, Chūshingura* was originally written in 1748 by Takedo Izumo and his collaborators for the Bunraku, or puppet theater. However, like many elements of the enormously popular puppet theater, *Chūshingura* was adapted by Kabuki, another form of Japanese theater, and has become the most popular of Kabuki pieces. The plot is based on a series of historical events that took place between 1701 and 1703 in what is now Tokyo. The play tells the story of forty-seven *rōnin*, or masterless samurai, who avenge the death of their master, Lord Asano Naganori, when he is tricked by his enemy Lord Kira into drawing his sword in the shogun's palace. Since this is an offense punishable by death, Lord Enya Hangan commits ritual suicide, or *seppuku*, but not before his senior retainer, Ōishi Yoshio, accepts the responsibility of avenging his death. The play follows the lives of the various *rōnin* who, years later, act upon their duty and kill Lord Kira. Because of the ten-hour length of the play, it is almost never performed in its entirety.

Ciurlionis, Mikalojus [Konstantinas] (1875–1911)

Lithuanian painter and composer. The son of an organist, Ciurlionis studied music at Warsaw and Leipzig conservatories, and although he briefly attended the Warsaw Academy of Art, for the most part he taught himself painting. He began to work with pastels in 1902 but did not take painting seriously until 1905, an outgrowth of an interest in mysticism and mystical expression too great for music. A proponent of Symbolism, Ciurlionis based his aesthetics on the "national romance" of Lithuanian folklore, and his works reflect his conception of music and the visual arts as analogous. He designed his paintings as musical abstracts in which the forms expressed cosmic forces, and gave them the titles of fugues and sonatas: *Pavasario sonata* (1907; *Spring Sonata*), *Jūros sonata* (1908; *Sea Sonata*), *Saulės sonata* (1907; *Sun Sonata*). In this obsession with the common ground beneath painting and music he is joined by Kandinsky and Captain Beefheart.

After exhibitions in St. Petersburg and Vilnius, where his originality was noted by distinguished critics, Ciurlionis was invited to join the avant-garde artists' group the "World of Art," and he took part in the exhibitions and concerts arranged by the group. Despite the acclaim of critics and peers, he remained quite poor, often unable even to buy paints. In 1909, overworked, he suffered a mental breakdown and was taken to a sanatorium near Warsaw; he was already showing signs of improvement when he died unexpectedly. Ciurlionis's musical works include symphonic poems (such as *The Sea*, 1907), chamber works, adaptations of folk songs, and numerous piano compositions.

civil disobedience

Nonviolent resistance. Also known as passive resistance, civil disobedience entails a refusal to obey the commands or demands of a government or occupying power and a refusal to resort to violence of any means in this resistance. Civil disobedience is a movement that works within a system to bring about changes within that system without bloodshed. Practitioners see themselves as motivated by a higher law than those of the governing structure they oppose. Yet the fact that civil disobedience is nonetheless a crime under that government's laws makes it a form of protest. By submitting to the punishment the government metes out, the disobedient hopes to set a moral example that will ultimately motivate the government to change its policies.

Though the movement is most closely associated with Mohandas Gandhi (1869–1948) and the nationalist movement in India, the philosophical origins of the concept can be traced as far back as to Roman statesman Marcus Tullius Cicero (106–43 B.C.E.) and subsequently to Italian philosopher and eventual saint Thomas Aquinas (1224/25–1274), English philosopher John Locke (1632–1704), U.S. president Thomas Jefferson (1743–1826), and American writer Henry David Thoreau (1817–1862). Civil disobedience has been adopted as a form of political praxis around the globe, in the civil rights movement led by Dr. Martin Luther King, Jr. (1929–1968) in the United States, in nationalist movements in India and in Africa, and by labor, antiwar, and antiabortion demonstrators in many countries.

Ci Xi (1835–1908)

Dowager Empress of China. Initially one of the low-ranking consorts of Emperor Xian Feng, with cunning and ability Ci Xi managed to become the de facto ruler of China for many years.

Tong Zhi, the child of Ci Xi and the only son to be born to the emperor, became the new emperor in 1856 after the death of Xian Feng. With the accession of Ci Xi's son to the throne, a regency council was created to rule for the young emperor until he reached legal age; however, the power of the regency was transferred to Ci Xi, who, with the help of Dowager Empress Ci An and the brother of Xian Feng, began to rule the country *chuilian tingzheng*, or "behind the screen." Although the regency ended in 1873, when Tong Zhi came of age, Ci Xi's control continued untouched. It has even been suggested by some historians that Ci Xi was responsible for the death of her son two years later.

Next Ci Xi named her three-year-old adopted nephew to the throne. He died suddenly in 1889, and after the death of Ci An, Ci Xi was left the sole ruler of China, a position she eventually relinquished, choosing instead to retire to her summer palace in Beijing. However, after the Sino-Japanese War (1894–95), when Emperor Guang Xu proved sympathetic to the cause of radical reformers, the empress, with the support of conservatives, took immediate action to stop him. Fully supported by the imperial army, Ci Xi placed Emperor Guang Xi under house arrest, forcing him to sign his own dethronement, and she ordered the immediate execution of six of the leaders of the reformers.

Back in power, Ci Xi continued supporting the Boxer rebels, who were against foreigners in China. By 1900 the Boxer Rebellion was at its height, but after the city of Beijing was captured by foreign troops, Ci Xi was forced to flee. She returned in 1902 and, ironically, began to implement many of the reforms she had previously opposed. Although Ci Xi is generally judged harshly for her reactionary politics, which some suggest helped to seal the fate of the dynastic system, she is often remembered, nonetheless, as the most powerful woman in China's history.

Cleopatra (69–30 B.C.E.)

Queen of Egypt. Upon her father's death in 51 B.C.E., Cleopatra, aged seventeen, married her brother Ptolemy XIII, aged ten; in accordance with pharaonic tradition, they jointly ascended the throne. When her father's ministers, intent on making young Ptolemy their puppet, ousted her, Cleopatra fled to Syria, where she assembled an army. Julius Caesar, representative of Egypt's Roman governors, then arrived to arbitrate the conflict.

Cleopatra was persuasive in arguing her case: Caesar restored her to the throne. When young Ptolemy was killed in battle, Caesar suggested that Cleopatra marry her next-youngest brother, Ptolemy XIII (aged eleven), and thereby remain queen. Caesar stayed in Egypt and became Cleopatra's lover; they had a son named Caesarion. Some have argued that Caesar's assassination was motivated partly by Roman resentment of his adulterous relations with Cleopatra, as well as the fear that he would make Cleopatra queen of Rome.

In 43 B.C.E., Cleopatra's husband died by poison, which many attribute to Cleopatra. She proceeded to make her son coruler, keeping Egypt from becoming a Roman province even under the new dictator, Marc Antony. She traveled by barge to Tarsus to petition him, dressed as the goddess Venus. Cleopatra won Antony's support for her government, as well as his favors: Antony and Cleopatra became lovers, and proceeded to have three children.

Cleopatra aided Antony in his military exploits, and he in turn gave Egypt the eastern provinces of Rome. The Roman Octavius denounced their alliance and declared war, defeating them soundly in 31 B.C.E. Antony committed suicide after the loss. Cleopatra made one last effort to negotiate with Octavius to save Egypt's freedom, but when told that Egypt was to be made a province and that she would be sent to Rome as a captive, she committed suicide by exposing herself to a poisonous snake.

coca

Tropical plant found largely in the Andean regions above two hundred meters altitude. Coca leaves are used to produce cocaine; their medicinal, therapeutic, and stimulating effects were noted before the consolidation of the Inca empire, when coca was cultivated on a small scale by secular workers. During the Inca empire, its use was restricted to the nobility, and sometimes was offered as a favor to soldiers and individuals who had performed exceptional services. It was also offered in sacrifices to obtain protection from ancestors and to ensure safe journeys. After the Spanish conquest around 1532, the opinion of the Spanish with regard to coca was divided. Despite the reservations of some Spanish, it was often given to Indian workers to increase their labor capacity. The custom of chewing and sucking on coca leaves, called *coquear*, is still practiced today to alleviate hunger and fatigue, especially in the Puna de Atacama. It is also used during religious and magical rituals, and by Andean Indians to foretell the future. Most Indians who use the coca leaf limit their use to stable quantities, and rarely is the substance abused.

Cocteau, Jean (1889–1963)

French film director. Cocteau's cinematic contribution is extremely eclectic, drawing on multiple genres of artistic expression, including plays, poetry, novels, ballet, and sculpture. Considered to be one of the most important influences on the New Wave of French filmmaking of the 1960s, he had an approach to the cinema that was highly individualistic, motivated by a keen personal vision, and largely indifferent to more conventional models of French filmmaking of his period.

Cocteau began his career as an actor in Paris, and in 1917 he worked with Picasso on the play *Parade*, which so scandalized audiences that the authors received threats. During the 1920s Cocteau wrote poetry, *The Angel Shock-Kiss*; the play *Orphée* (*Orpheus*); a libretto for Russian composer Igor Stravinsky's opera *Oedipus Rex*; and a novel, *Les Enfants terribles*. He remained in Paris during the German occupation of World War II, during which time his play *Les Parents terribles* was forbidden by the authorities.

Cocteau's most noted and critically acclaimed work was a series of three films exploring the personal myth of the poet as Orpheus: *Le Sang d'un poète* (1930; *The Blood of a Poet*), *Orphée* (1950; *Orpheus*), and *Le Testament d'Orphée* (*Ne me demandez pas pourquoi*) (1960; *The Testament of Orpheus*). Although they were made over a period of thirty years, these three films embody a singularity of inspiration and draw heavily on Cocteau's fascination with poetry as a creative process and with the many diverse ways in which an audience could be fascinated, including the use of stars and trickery, sheer fantasy, and found material.

codex

Collection of stitched-together pages. The earliest type of manuscript in book form, codices replaced the earlier rolls of papyrus and wax tablets, and were found to be more beneficial because it was possible to write on both sides of the leaf. In Latin America, codices were made by the Aztecs of Mexico as early as 1000 C.E. These books contained pictographs and ideograms rather than written script and were used to make astrological predictions, record royal history, and serve administrative purposes such as noting the collection of tribute. The most important Aztec codices include the Vienna Codex, the Codex Colombino, and the Codex Fejérváry-Mayer.

Cohen, Hermann (1842–1918)

German-Jewish philosopher. Originally intending to become a rabbi, Cohen became intrigued by philosophy. He studied at the universities of Berlin and later Halle, where he received his doctorate in 1865. Accepting an invitation to lecture at the University of Marburg, where he taught until 1912, Cohen developed his neo-Kantian philosophy, for which he is best known.

According to Cohen, philosophy can be divided into three parts, each of which governs a particular mode of consciousness. Logic corresponds to thought, ethics regulate the human will, and aesthetics are associated with emotions and the senses. His early works critiqued the idealism in the works of Plato and Kant, and these interpretations expressed in his early works became the basis for the Marburg School of Neo-Kantianism. His later works, *Logik der reinen Erkenntnis* (1902; *The Logic of Pure Intelligence*), *Die Ethik des reinen Willens* (1904; *The Ethics of Pure Will*), and *Ästhetic des reinen Gefühls* (1912; *The Aesthetics of Pure Feeling*), emphasize his approach. Like Kant, Cohen was a rationalist who considered philosophy to be closely linked with science and mathematics; in fact, the philosopher's role was to explain the logical underpinnings of scientific knowledge. Cohen, however, also believed that perception is a construct of thought, a theory he called the "principle of origin."

Although Cohen appears to have been spared much anti-Semitism, he was called upon several times in his career to defend German Jewry from charges of disloyalty and criminality. In response to Treitschke's attack on the Jews in *Ein Wort über unser Judentum* (1879), Cohen published *Ein Bekenntnis zur Judenfrage* (1880), in which he asserted that German Jews could be both patriotic and true to their religion. A few years later, in an 1888 trial, Cohen again responded to anti-Semitic charges that the Talmud instructed Jews to be scrupulously honest with fellow Jews but exonerated duplicity in dealing with Gentiles. Cohen testified that, on the contrary, Judaism preached the brotherhood of all mankind.

Toward the end of his life, Cohen devoted more of his time to reconciling his theories of ethics with Judaism. In 1912 he left the University of Marburg for a teaching position at the School of Jewish Studies at Berlin, where he remained until his death.

Colette, [Sidonie-Gabrielle] (1873–1954)
French dramatist, journalist, and novelist. Colette's extensive body of work includes some seventy titles. Her work often defies definition, and her talent for using accepted literary signs to create ambivalent or ambiguous texts challenged many established theories of literature. Colette was particularly adept at crossing and mixing genres, genders, classes, and cultures.

Born in Saint-Sauveur-en-Puisaye, a village in Burgundy, Colette moved to Paris in 1893 after marrying Henry Gauthier-Villars, or "Willy." She was nineteen at the time. Willy, fifteen years her senior, was a character in Paris literary circles well known for his mildly risqué novels, many of which were ghostwritten by young writers whom he paid extremely poorly. Colette's first novel, *Claudine à l'école* (*Claudine at School*), was published under Willy's name in 1900. It was rumored that Willy treated Colette as yet another ghostwriter, locking her in the closet for four hours a day, with instructions to write a titillating account of her girlhood. This first novel, and the other three novels that became the enormously popular *Claudine* series, were based upon her schoolgirl experiences in Burgundy and made Willy a considerable sum of money. In 1904 Colette began signing her works "Colette Willy," although by 1923 she signed them simply "Colette." The true source of "Colette" is uncertain, as it is both her father's surname and a French girl's first name.

From 1905 to 1913 Colette studied mime, touring and acting in mimodramas, and appearing in the music-hall theater circuit, the so-called demimonde of Belle Époque lesbian Paris. Colette and Willy had separated in 1906, a move that left her with no money of her own, despite the fact that her novels had been extremely successful.

Following her divorce from Willy in 1910, she married Henri de Jouvenel, editor-in-chief of *Le Matin*. During World War I, Colette worked as a journalist, reporting from the front. She wrote *Chéri* (1920), often considered her most important work, and *Le Blé en herbe* (1923; *The Ripening Seed*), books that focused on relationships between older women and younger men. These works were to mark the beginning of Colette's independent literary career, and to establish her as one of France's most popular authors. She did not shy away from controversy, either; the semi-autobiographical nature of her writing often led her to pen frank and questioning accounts of sexuality and issues of sexual orientation, most notably in *Pur et l'impur* (1941; *The Pure and the Impure*).

Colette was divorced from de Jouvenel in 1925, the same year she met and began her lifelong relationship with Maurice Goudeket, sixteen years her junior; Colette and Goudeket were married in 1935. She traveled throughout the world, and was made a member of the Belgian Royal Academy (1935) and the first woman member of France's Goncourt Academy (1945), and named Grand Officer of the Legion of Honor (1953). At her death in 1954, she was granted a secular state funeral.

colono
Latin American term referring to various land workers. *Colono* are *mestizo* or Indian people who, lacking their own property, work for a large landowner in

exchange for the right to live on and cultivate a piece of land. The *colono* receives food and coca in exchange for his labor, which may consist of growing the hacienda's crops, caring for the landowner's cattle, or performing special tasks for the owner. This feudal system of work in exchange for shelter and a piece of land is called *colonato*, and is still present in some Latin American countries. The term is applied to such farmers and rural workers in Peru, Bolivia, Guatemala, and El Salvador. *Colonos* in Colombia are squatters, and in the Río de la Plata region, inhabitants of rural immigrant colonies.

Coltrane, John (1926–1967)

Jazz musician. A saxophone virtuoso, Coltrane was a leader in the avant-garde jazz movement of the 1960s. He is renowned for his innovative solos—his "sheets of sound"—that combine an inborn melodic and rhythmic adventurousness with influences drawn from the music of India, Africa, and the Middle East.

Coltrane was born in North Carolina to a musical and religious family. His mother was a church pianist and member of the church choir, his father sang and played violin, and both of his grandfathers were ministers in the A.M.E. Zion Church. Studying music in local public schools, Coltrane later attended the Ornstein School of Music in Philadelphia, Pennsylvania. He began playing the clarinet when he was twelve, and took up the alto saxophone a year later.

Enlisting in the navy in 1945, he played in a navy band, and after the war began what would eventually become an illustrious career. Touring with Eddie Vinson's rhythm and blues band led Coltrane to Dizzy Gillespie, with whom he began working in 1949. He later joined Earl Bostic's band (1952) and Johnny Hodges's (1953) band. The year 1955, the same year he joined Miles Davis's band, marked the beginning of his solo career. After playing for a short period with Thelonious Monk, Coltrane formed his own group in 1960 with Elvin Jones, with whom he developed his mature style.

With Albert Ayler, Coltrane was a seminal figure in the "free jazz" movement. By the time of his death, he played in his quartet with a highly personal style, in which drums and saxophone conducted a dialogue over the piano and bass. His late recordings, *My Favorite Things* (1961) and *A Love Supreme* (1964), exemplify this style.

Columbus, Christopher (1451–1506)

Italian explorer. Columbus is historically significant as the first known European to have had contact with the indigenous people of the Americas, whom he mistakenly called "Indians" in the erroneous belief that he had been successful in his mission to reach eastern Asia by sailing west.

Columbus's expeditions were financed by King Ferdinand and Queen Isabella of Spain in 1492, and he was granted three ships to complete his mission, the Niña, the Pinta, and the Santa María. Columbus's first expedition set sail on August 3 from Palos and sighted land in what is now known as the Caribbean on October 12. His second voyage (1493–96) proved more strenuous, although it was during this trek that Isabella, the first European city in the New World, was founded. Although he reached the South American mainland on his third journey (1498–1500), his poor administrative skills resulted in his forced resignation as viceroy of the Indies. In spite of this, Columbus completed a final mission from 1502 to 1504. Never fully recovering from illness contracted on this last trip, Columbus died two years later and was buried in Seville, Spain. His remains were exhumed in 1542 and placed in the cathedral of Santo Domingo in Hispaniola.

Though long celebrated as the "discoverer of America," Columbus has become a controversial figure in recent years, denounced by American Indian groups and revisionist historians as the herald of European colonialism in America and as a pioneer of European exploitation and decimation of Indian peoples.

Comte, Auguste (1798–1857)

French philosopher. Comte is generally recognized as the father of sociology and Positivism—a system of thought designed to provide a political framework for the organization of a modern industrial society.

Comte was born in Montpellier, France, near the Spanish border. Both his father, Louis Comte (a tax official), and his mother, Rosalie Boyer, were devout Roman Catholics and resolutely royalist in their beliefs. Comte decisively rejected these loyalties at an early age and aligned himself with the skeptical republicanism that proliferated in France during his lifetime.

At the age of nine, Comte was sent as a boarder to the local secondary school, where his unhappiness at being separated from his parents and his precocious disposition led him into conflict with the administration. His dislike for officials did not interfere with his academic success, however; he excelled in several areas and, at fifteen, attained an extremely high grade in the entrance examinations for the École Polytechnique—a Parisian school for advanced sciences. Conflicts between Comte's rebellious nature and the École's strict code of discipline cut his studies short, and a dispute with a tutor led to a police escort back to Montpellier in 1816.

Comte soon returned to Paris and began his independent exploration of philosophy and history; he was greatly influenced by the writings of the philosophers Montesquieu, Condorcet, Immanuel Kant, and, in particular, Henri de Saint-Simon. In fact, Comte contributed some of his first articles to Saint-Simon's publications. In May 1821 Comte met a young prostitute named Caroline Massin whom he married later that year, but who eventually left him in 1842.

Comte spent several years developing his "system of positive philosophy," which analyzed the nature of political organization, and began a tour of lectures to private audiences of intellectuals in 1824. Interrupted by a mental breakdown, a brief stay in an asylum, and a suicide attempt in 1827, Comte resumed the lecture series in 1829 with the presentation of his "law of the three stages." This defined the historical course of human development as having passed first through a theological era wherein gods and spirits were used to explain the world, a metaphysical era in which the world was viewed in terms of essences and vague abstractions, and a final, positive stage characterized by an acknowledgment of the limits of human knowledge. Comte argued that traditional quests for absolute truth should be discarded in favor of investigation of the laws governing interactions between phenomena, and further contended that these individual searches for positive knowledge were unified by the new, overarching science of sociology. These theories were published between 1830 and 1842 in his *Cours de philosophie positive* (*The Positive Philosophy of Auguste Comte*) and were presented as a basis for a polity designed to fit the needs of an industrialized society.

Comte's next major work, *Système de politique positif* (*System of Positive Polity*), was produced between 1846 and 1854 and included his complete formulation of the new science of sociology. It earmarked moral progression as the central concern of a modern society and outlined the political structure necessary to promote such a sociological development.

Confucianism

System of Chinese beliefs. Confucianism is the way of life espoused by Confucius (551–479 B.C.E.) and has had a fundamental impact in China for more than 2,000 years. Alternately styled by Western scholars as both a religion and a philosophy, Confucianism dictates social mores and is considered the repository of Chinese thought.

The teacher Confucius lived during a time of great unrest in China and devoted himself to developing regulatory codes of thought and action aimed at restabilizing society. He advocated following the ways of ancient kings, seeing himself as only a messenger of their teachings. Confucius believed that all human beings carried with them an innate possibility of perfection that was all too easily subverted by actual existence. The notion of *ren* (human virtue) was an integral part of Confucianism. The concept is so essential that its preservation was considered by Confucians to be more important than the preservation of one's life. Fully realized, *ren* involved perfect attention to one's own nature (*zhong*), to reciprocity or the famous "Golden Rule" (*shu*), to propriety (*yi*), to filial piety (*xiao*), and to social ritual (*li*). An individual of such character was an ideal, superior man (*jun-zi*), qualified to be a ruler.

Confucius's thought was compiled by his disciples in the *Lun Yü* (commonly translated as *Analects*). Among the most famous of the aphorisms attributed to Confucius is his definition of knowledge: "When you know a thing, say that you know it; when you do not know a thing, admit that you do not know it. That is knowledge." Also included was Confucius's discourse on government, which stems from a political ideal (commonly called government by virtue) in which ministers are selected for their virtue and talent rather than for their social rank. Although Confucius discussed religion, he did not portray himself as a messenger of God. He spoke of the concept of heaven but did not associate his beliefs with any organized religion.

Confucius's teachings were only one of the major schools of thought at this time; it was not until the Han dynasty (206 B.C.E.–220 C.E.) that Confucianism was adopted by the state, proclaimed an orthodox doctrine by emperor Han Wu-ti, and augmented by legalistic concepts. Confucianism became so entrenched that detailed knowledge of it became the core of the civil service examination system in use until the fall of the Qing dynasty at the beginning of the twentieth century.

Mencius (c. 371–289 B.C.E.), referred to as the "Second Sage" of Confucianism, elaborated on Confucius's principles. He held that, in addition to their perfectibility, humans were endowed by heaven (*t'ien*) with innate goodness; and that the ultimate examples of that goodness were Confucianist saints who protected the "royal path" (*wang-tao*) from ignorance and immorality. He also distinguished between governments based on the concept of *ren* and those based on tyranny; he defended the people's right to rebel against the latter. Mencius reasoned that if human nature was intrinsically good, evil was anathema to the self and its "child-like heart." Mencius's beliefs were contradicted by Xun-zi (c. 298–230 B.C.E.), who believed that humans had to be taught goodness.

Traditional Confucianism retained its ideological hold on Chinese culture through the fall of the Han dynasty (220 C.E.) and the founding of the Song dynasty (960 C.E.). Between the third and eighth centuries C.E., however, Buddhism and Taoism grew in popularity. Mystical traditions such as the *I-ching* were introduced or revived, and philosophical thought turned to ideas of a primordial principle like the *Tao*, justifying traditional ethics with metaphysical considerations. "Neo-Confucianism" attempted to restore the dominance of Confucian thought, though it was influenced by the contributions of Taoism and Buddhism despite its proclaimed opposition to them.

In the modern period, China's increasing contact with the West inevitably led to a reevaluation of traditional Chinese ways of life and thought. In 1905 the official state examinations were abolished, and with the beginning of the Republican era in 1911, Confucianism lost the institutional support it had enjoyed since the Han dynasty. The government of the People's Republic of China has denounced Confucian values, and though these values are still deeply rooted in Chinese society (and East Asian society in general), as a formal school the philosophy has disappeared.

Confucius (551–479 B.C.E.)

Thinker and educator. Born in what is now Shandong province, Confucius lived during the end of the so-called Spring and Autumn period, an era of great political violence. Deeply troubled by the constant warfare raging among rival states, Confucius developed his own political philosophy, which he taught to as many as 3,000 students and 72 disciples. He was not, however, well known during his lifetime; it was only through the efforts of his disciples, especially Mencius, that his philosophy took root.

In his philosophy, Confucius was much concerned by the disintegration of established standards of social behavior. He stressed the concept of *jen*—meaning love, humaneness, and virtue—which he regarded as the supreme moral achievement in a man. Such a man was called a *junzi* (a virtuous gentleman), who acted in accordance with *li* (proper ritual norms) and remained loyal to his true nature (*zhong*), which he received from heaven; he should guide those who were less favored intellectually by heaven, and observe his filial duty (*xiao*). Confucius believed that if a ruler abided by the above principles, his moral example would inspire the subjects to lead virtuous lives in a manner far more effective than systems of law

and punishment. Reform, he believed, must start from the rulers.

His teachings were passed down mainly through *Lun Yu*, or *Analects*, compiled by his disciples. Apart from *Lun Yu*, major classics in the Confucian tradition are *Chunqiu* (*Spring and Autumn*), *Daxue* (*Great Learning*), *Zhongyong* (*Doctrine of the Mean*), *Liji* (*Collections of Rituals*), and *Yijing* (*Book of Changes*).

conquistador

Title of leaders of the Spanish conquest in South America and the Caribbean. From the Spanish for "conqueror," the *conquistadores* were authorized by the Spanish crown to subdue the Indians, Christianize them, establish new settlements, and at times govern them. For the most part, however, these men were more interested in the search for gold and the conquest of civilizations than in governing, and they were quickly supplanted by Spanish administrators and settlers. The conquest of the larger Indian settlements in the New World was achieved over a period of fifty years: the Aztecs were defeated by Hernán Cortés in 1521, the Mayas by Diego de Almagro in 1525, the Incas by Francisco Pizarro in 1535, and the Chibchas by Gonzalo Jiménez de Quesada in 1538.

The *conquistadores* were noted for their courage, resourcefulness, ambition, greed, and ruthlessness. Their military achievements remain unmatched by any other conquerors: Cortés set out to take the Aztec capital with only 1,300 soldiers; Pizarro started with 168 men, although when he finally succeeded he had 1,200 Spaniards; Quesada set out to conquer the Chibchas with 166 Spanish soldiers; and Almagro had only 420. The reasons for the *conquistadores'* great success varied, but included are the assistance of other Indian tribes; superior military technology; the use of the horse, which frightened Indian fighters; and their ability to turn Indian myths and internal strife to their advantage. Cortés, for example, was mistaken for the fair-haired god who had promised to return from the sea, and Pizarro took advantage of the civil war that had weakened the Inca empire. The *conquistadores* succeeded in capturing over 20 million Indians and opened up vast lands, which the Spanish settled and exploited for the next three hundred years. As a result of overwork, disease, killing, lack of food, and dislocations, the native Indian population, estimated to be around 20 to 25 million in 1500, was halved by 1600.

Conrad, Joseph (1857–1924)

Polish-born English novelist. Born Teodor Jósef Konrad Nalecz Korzeniowski in Poland, Conrad wrote only in English, a language in which he proved to be a remarkable stylist. Though he was primarily renowned for his seafaring adventure stories during his lifetime, he has since become known for the moral complexity of his novels, which chronicle human malevolence and the inner battles between good and evil. Conrad is considered by many to be one of the greatest writers in the English language, a proto-existential writer of penetrating insight into the human condition.

Conrad's journey from Poland to England was a long and arduous one. He was born to an ardently nationalist Polish family, and at the age of four traveled with his parents to northern Russia, where they were exiled for Conrad's father's participation in a Polish insurrection. His mother soon died of tuberculosis, and Conrad lived alone with his father, learning English by reading Shakespeare in translation. In 1869, Conrad senior succumbed to tuberculosis, and Joseph was left in the care of his uncle in Kraków. Conrad, however, yearned to go to sea, and in 1874 left for Marseilles to sail with French merchant ships. Though this period of his life was somewhat unhappy—he was often heavily in debt and once attempted sui-

cide—these sea journeys enabled Conrad to see much of South America and the Far East and provided him with much material for his novels and stories. He joined the British merchant navy in 1878 and, despite speaking very little English, gradually worked his way to the rank of captain. In 1889 he realized a childhood dream and led an expedition down the Congo River in Africa. Conrad spent four months in the Congo altogether, a deeply debilitating journey that he recorded in his famous novel *Heart of Darkness* (1902). On this voyage Conrad also contracted a recurrent fever and gout, which plagued him for the rest of his life.

He ended his sea journeys a few years after his trip to the Congo, and in 1895 he published his first novel, *Almayer's Folly*, under the name of Joseph Conrad, settled in England, and married Jessie George, with whom he had two sons. Though his greatest novels and stories, such as *Lord Jim* (1900), *Heart of Darkness* (1902), *Nostromo* (1904), *The Secret Agent* (1907), and *Under Western Eyes* (1911), were quite popular, he lived in near poverty for much of his life. It was not until he received a Civil List pension in 1910, and American collector John Quinn began buying his work, that Conrad gained financial security. In addition to his many novels, Conrad also wrote two autobiographies, *The Mirror of the Sea* (1906) and *Some Reminiscences* (1912; retitled *A Personal Record*). He declined an offer of knighthood from British statesman Ramsay MacDonald in 1924 and died soon thereafter.

Constable, John (1776–1837)

English landscape painter. Though he received relatively little attention in his native England, Constable's series of landscape paintings were enormously influential in France, most notably on the works of Delacroix and the Barbizon School, a group of nineteenth-century French landscape painters. Constable was a self-taught painter and often painted the same landscape again and again, as in his series of paintings of Salisbury Cathedral. The English countryside figures prominently in Constable's canvases; his careful observations reflect his early life in a country village. Constable's work is characterized by the bold use of color and looser, flowing brush strokes, designed to convey changes in light and the movement of clouds on the landscape. Some of his well-known paintings include *View on the Stour* (1819) and *The Hay Wain* (1821). Constable is considered by many to be the greatest of English landscape painters.

Copernicus, Nicolaus (1473–1543)

Polish astronomer. Copernicus, the first modern astronomer to develop a theory that placed the sun at the center of the solar system, was born in the town of Turun in central Poland. After studying at the University of Kraków, he proceeded to Italy, where he specialized in medicine and canon law. In 1497, the year he left for Italy, Copernicus was selected as a canon to the cathedral at Frauenburg in Warmia, a diocese in northern Poland; when he returned from Italy in 1503, he took up this appointment.

Copernicus came to Frauenberg with a passion for astronomy, and by 1510 he had developed a model of the solar system that accounted for planetary orbits on the basis of the position of the sun rather than that of the earth. This was in direct conflict with the generally accepted model, established in the second century C.E. by the Greek astronomer Ptolemy, who accounted for planetary motions without sacrificing the earth's centrality. Copernicus, probably out of prudence, made little attempt to publicize his anti-Ptolemaic views. Between 1510 and 1514 he circulated in manuscript form among his friends the *Commentariolus*, which provided a synopsis of the earliest version of his theory, but

it was not until 1540 that he allowed even a preliminary account of the fully developed theory to be published, and it was only on the day of his death that a complete account at last appeared in the treatise subsequently known as *De Revolutionibus Orbium Coelestium* (*On the Revolutions of the Celestial Spheres*). Copernicus spent much of his life working studiously to buttress his argument with reams of planetary data. He ultimately passed on an opportunity to become a bishop because it would have affected his research. Still, despite the emphasis he placed on this empirical aspect of his work, Copernicus was careful to present his theory in such a way that it could be interpreted as simply an elegant hypothetical model for the motions of the planets. Only after Galileo's discoveries would the extent of Copernicus's prescience, and intellectual daring, become truly apparent.

Complanter, *see* Kaiiontwa'ko

Cortázar, Julio (1914–1984)

Argentinian novelist and short-story writer. Cortázar was raised by his mother and aunt in a suburb of Buenos Aires. He earned his degree as a primary and secondary school teacher in 1935 and taught at various secondary schools until 1944. In 1946 he began law studies and worked at the Argentine Publishing Association. From 1948 to 1951 he worked as a public translator, then received a scholarship to study in Paris, where he spent the rest of his life, obtaining French citizenship in 1981.

Bestiario (1951; *Bestiary*), his first collection of short stories, was published the month he left for Paris; his decision to remain there seems prompted by his dissatisfaction with the government of Argentinian leader Juan Perón and the dead-end consciousness of the Argentine middle class. Heavily influenced by the Surrealists, Cortázar's stories focused on what he saw as the other side of "reality," venturing from the most normal and conventional setting into the fantastic, the repressed, the hidden, the taboo, and the oneiric. Like the Surrealists, he did not consider the repressed aspects of humans to be pathological or abnormal; instead, he saw them as keys and necessary bridges to a dimension of existence that would allow one to live in full contact with the entire world. Thus he focused on rites of passage and games that could open doors to hidden, authentic realities; he took up the theme of otherness and tried to tap into some form of real communication; exposing what lay beyond surface reality, Cortázar suggested different ways of seeing, and he resisted convention and traditional forms that he found curtailed individual freedom of expression. His second collection of short stories, *Final del juego* (1956; *End of the Game*), displayed a growing concern with individual character as well as an exploration of eroticism. His later stories, collected in *Alguien que anda por ahí* (1977; *A Change of Light and Other Stories*), focus more explicitly on political themes.

Perhaps best known for his novels *Los premios* (1960; *The Winners*) and *Rayuela* (1963; *Hopscotch*), divided into three sections, Cortázar established his international reputation as one of the most important Latin American writers of the twentieth century. The story line focuses essentially on the character Horacio Oliveira's quest to live a more authentic existence; as a product of Western civilization, he is constantly rationalizing his experience and drowning in a well of dialectic possibilities that leave him incapable of feeling.

In 1953 he married Argentine translator Aurora Bernárdez, although he spent the latter part of his life with longtime companion Carol Dunlop; his last work, *Les autonautas de la cosmopista* (1983; *The Space Vehicles of the Cosmic Freeway*), was written in collaboration with her and published the year she died.

Cortés, Hernán (1485–1547)

Spanish *conquistador*. With Francisco Pizarro, Cortés is considered the greatest of the Spanish *conquistadores*. In 1511, on an expedition to conquer Cuba, he sailed with Diego Velázquez, who would eventually become governor of Cuba. While there, Cortés met Catalina Juárez, and although he courted Catalina, he then refused to marry her, which aggravated the animosity already developing between him and Velázquez, who was courting her sister. Imprisoned by Velázquez, Cortés escaped and fled, but returned to marry Catalina, for which he obtained from Velázquez the post of mayor of Santiago in 1518. Despite these disputes, Velázquez named him head of an expedition to establish a colony on the mainland. Later regretting this appointment, Velázquez apparently tried to sabotage Cortés's expedition; Cortés, however, defied Velázquez and actively recruited forces, managing to gather six ships and three hundred men within a month's time.

When he finally sailed in 1519, he had eleven ships, 508 soldiers, approximately 100 sailors, and 16 horses. It is said that when he arrived in Mexico, he burned all his ships, committing himself and his entire force to survival through conquest. Cortés's success in Mexico was the result of a series of accidents. He encountered a captured Indian princess, whom the Spaniards had dubbed Doña Marina. Known as La Malinche, she served as his interpreter and adviser and also became his mistress. Montezuma, ruler of the Aztecs, saw Cortés's soldiers with their white skin, yellow hair, horses, and their thunder-like cannons, and assumed that this was the party of the god Quetzalcóatl returning to settle accounts with the people, a misapprehension that Cortés exploited, manipulating tense relations between the Mexicans loyal to Montezuma and the Tlaxcaltecas.

In 1521 Cortés conquered Mexico-

Tenochtitlán (which was then five times larger than Madrid) after Montezuma's death. Having defeated the Aztec empire with a mere four hundred soldiers, in 1524 he embarked on an expedition to Honduras that proved disastrous to his health and his political position. Velázquez and other enemies once again worked to discredit him, questioning his loyalty to the Spanish crown. Three judges arrived one after the other to try him (the first two having died suspiciously soon after their arrival). The third judge exiled Cortés from the capital, and in 1528 he sailed for Spain to plead his case with the emperor. Charles V confirmed him as captain general and named him Marqués del Valle, but he did not restore his government. Accused of treason, disobedience, and of murdering his wife, Catalina Juárez, Cortés returned to his estate in the New World with his new wife and mother in 1530. He died in Spain in 1547.

Cossack

Member of a people dwelling in the northern hinterlands of the Black and Caspian seas. The name "Cossack" is derived from Turkic *kazak* (free man), meaning anyone who could not find his appropriate place in society and went into the steppes, where he acknowledged no authority. The term first appears in European sources in the mid thirteenth century. By the end of the fifteenth century, the name was applied to Ukrainian and Russian peasants who had fled from serfdom in Poland, Lithuania, and Muscovy to the Dnieper and Don regions, where they established free, self-governing military communities.

Polish kings in the early sixteenth century began to organize Zaporozhian (Ukrainian) Cossacks into military colonies to protect Poland's borders. Throughout the sixteenth and the first half of the seventeenth centuries, these Cossacks retained political autonomy, briefly forming a semi-independent state under Bohdan Khmelnitsky. But threatened by Polish domination, they signed a treaty in 1654 in which they recognized Russian authority under the condition that their autonomy be respected. The Russians likewise used the Cossacks first as defenders of the Russian frontier and later as advance guards for the territorial expansion of the Russian empire in Siberia and the Far East. Though they initially had greater freedom under Russia than they had under Poland, Russia soon came to dominate the Cossacks.

When their privileges were threatened in the seventeenth and eighteenth centuries, the Cossacks revolted, led by famous rebel leaders such as Stenka Razin, Kondratii Bulavin, and Emelian Pugachev. Their success, however, was mixed; the Zaporozhian Cossacks lost their autonomous status completely by the late eighteenth century, while the other hosts retained very limited independence. In the nineteenth and early twentieth centuries, the Cossacks were used extensively by the Russian government to suppress revolutionary activities. During the Russian Civil War of 1918–20, the Cossacks were divided and many of them went abroad. Under Soviet rule, especially after the forced collectivization of 1929, Cossack communities ceased to function as administrative units. Though Cossacks today lead lives scarcely distinguishable from the other Soviet farmers and workers, they still treasure their heritage, customs, and cultural identity.

creole/criollo

Originally a term used to denote white people born of Spanish parents in Latin America, as opposed to American residents born in Spain. These terms, *creole* in Spanish and *criollo* in French, were first used in the sixteenth to eighteenth century. Although legally Spaniards and Creoles were considered to be equal in colonial Spanish America, Creoles were regularly excluded from high offices in both church and state, positions that Spanish subjects were awarded as honorific posts. Their commercial practices also were restricted. The Creoles are responsible for the revolutions that achieved the expulsion of Spanish monarchic control in Latin America in the early nineteenth century; both Simón Bolívar and José de San Martín belonged to this class. After independence, Creoles became the ruling class. Generally conservative, they tended to cooperate with the higher clergy, the army, large landowners, and later foreign investors.

At present the meaning of "creole" varies regionally. In the West Indies, the term is used to denote descendants of any European settlers, and more commonly to refer to all the people, regardless of their class or ancestry, who are part of Caribbean culture. In contrast, in French Guiana the word "creole" refers to those who, whatever the color of their skin, have adopted a European lifestyle. Surinam creoles are the descendants of African slaves. The word may denote any local person of pure Spanish extraction in South America (vs. the Caribbean); referring more strictly to members of old-line families of Spanish descent who have roots in the colonial period; or referring to members of urban Europeanized classes, distinguished from rural Indians. Louisiana creoles are generally denoted as French-speaking descendants of French and Spanish settlers, as well as mulattos who speak creole, or a language combining both French and Spanish. In Peru, as an adjective, it describes a way of life, expressed by the ability to speak wittily and persuasively on a wide range of topics, to turn a situation to one's advantage, to be masculine, or *macho*, to show national pride, and to display a certain gusto at fiestas and other social activities.

creole, languages and cultures

Creole languages arise when there is a radical break in transmission from one generation to the next, typically under conditions of slavery. Although linguists are sharply divided about the primary factors involved in creolization, they usually group them with pidgins.

Most Caribbean cultures either had or still have a creole as home language or, in the words of Edward Kamura Brathwaite, as nation language. Contemporary Jamaican English is the descendant of an autonomous English-related creole now part of a continuum linking "deep" Jamaican, through a gamut of dialects, to standard English. Sierra Leonean *krio*, Cape Verdean *crioulo*, and Maurician *kreol* exemplify creolization under the influence of European languages, but there are a number of purely African-based creoles, such as Kituba and Lingala in western Zaire. In eastern Zaire, Swahili, often said to have resulted from the creolization of Arabic and Bantu, is currently recreolizing.

The complex patchwork of creoles in the Caribbean reflects the history of European jostling for control of this strategic zone. French-related creoles persist in some English environments in the Caribbean (e.g., St. Lucian Patwa); and English-related ones in Dutch settings (e.g., Sranan-Tongo in Suriname). Known to some as Ayisyin, Haitian creole has a particular prominence, since it is now recognized as the mother language of the vast majority of Haitians and has been elevated to official status in recent years. Though still overshadowed by French, Haitian Kréyol shows signs of great vitality and has a long literary tradition. Probably the most firmly established creole in the Caribbean is Papiamento, spoken on Curaçao and related islands of the Netherlands Antilles off the coast of Venezuela. This Spanish-related creole has not only a rich literature in many genres but also radio, TV, and a thriving popular press.

It remains to be seen if creoles will survive into the next century as autonomous languages of print and learning, or be relegated to oral and popular culture. The elites who dominate most creole-speaking countries do not always promote creole literacy, and many creole speakers themselves have distorted, self-deprecating images of their own languages.

Crowther, Bishop Samuel Adjai
(c. 1808–1891)
First black African bishop of the Anglican Church. A member of the Yoruba people in what is now Nigeria, Crowther was captured by slave traders in 1821 but rescued by a British antislavery patrol and taken to Sierra Leone. There he was baptized and educated in missionary schools, and ordained as an Anglican priest in 1843.

Crowther greatly impressed his superiors with his religious devotion and success as a missionary among the African tribes. This period was one of grandiose plans for religious expansion, and when the Anglican Church decided to create a West African diocese, Crowther was appointed bishop in 1864. He held this appointment until his forced resignation in 1890, when the British changed their policy and called for British missionaries to spread British culture in the African colonies. It was an ironic shift: Crowther was initially encouraged as a missionary of the Anglican Church because the British missionaries were dying from diseases contracted on their expeditions.

Besides his missionary work, Crowther was a talented linguist and did much work with the Yoruba, Hausa, and other African languages. He wrote a book of Yoruba grammar and vocabulary, and translated the Bible into Yoruba.

Crusades
Medieval European military expeditions. The Crusades were conducted by the Roman Catholic Church between the eleventh and thirteenth centuries to defend the Christian faith in the face of Islamic expansion in the East. The Crusades were very bloody and cost the lives of many Muslims, Jews, and Christians. While the Church represented the Crusades in spiritual terms—as an individual work of piety, a material avenue to eternal salvation—many participated with a spirit of adventurous opportunism, interested either in looting Islamic cities or in the expansion of Western trade routes to the East.

The First Crusade was organized in 1071 by Pope Urban II after the Turkish invasion of Syria and Asia Minor, the site of the Christian Holy Land. At the Council of Clermont, he urged Christian knights to stop fighting among themselves and to travel to Jerusalem, which at that time was under Muslim control. In return for their hardships, Urban promised full forgiveness of sins. The participants took the name "Crusaders" after the crosses that were distributed at the council. The members of the First Crusade, mostly poor, disorganized, and unarmed, were quickly massacred by the Turks and Hungarians. Later armies, under the control of four barons, pledged allegiance to Emperor Alexis and did successfully reinstate some Byzantine territory. Other recaptured areas, such as Jerusalem, Edessa, and Antioch, were not returned to the emperor, but instead became the "Crusader states" of the East.

In 1144 Edessa was recaptured by the Seluj ruler Zangi, and the call for the Second Crusade was issued by Pope Eugene III. Armies led by Emperor Conrad III of Germany and King Louis VII of France met in Jerusalem in 1148, but were defeated by Zangi's successor, Nureddin. The loss of Jerusalem sparked the Third Crusade (1188–92), which resulted in little territorial gain for the Christians and left the city under Muslim control. Richard I the Lion Heart, King of England, negotiated a treaty with Nureddin's nephew, Saladin, which called for a five-year period of peace and provided for the safe passage of Christian pilgrims to their shrines in Jerusalem.

Pope Innocent III called for the Fourth Crusade in 1198 against Egypt. Short of money and ships, however, the Crusaders joined forces with the Venetians and assisted them in their campaign against the Byzantine empire, capturing the cities of Zara (Hungary) and Constantinople. The Latin empire of Constantinople was then established by the Crusaders, and though it lasted only about sixty years, it created a permanent rift between the Byzantine and Latin churches.

A revival of the crusading fervor produced the pathetic Children's Crusade of 1212. Thousands of children joined the march to the Holy Land, only to be killed or sold into slavery during the journey. Innocent III called for the Fifth Crusade three years after this, in 1215, the last to be organized by the papacy. This attack, too, ended indecisively; stopped by floodwaters of the Nile, the parties negotiated an eight-year truce. Emperor Frederick II of Germany called the Sixth Crusade in 1223, and managed to negotiate a treaty that returned Jerusalem to European control for a period of ten years. This gain was short-lived, however, for in 1244 the Turks, aided by the Egyptians, sacked Jerusalem and regained the city. King Louis IX led both the Seventh (1248–54) and the Eighth (1265–72) Crusades—the Seventh failed in Egypt and the Eighth ended in Louis's demise in Tunis. This last campaign ended the era of the Crusades, though other failing expeditions continued even into the fifteenth century.

Cruz, Sor Juana Inés de la (c. 1651–1695) Mexican poet, playwright, and essayist. Called the tenth muse and phoenix of Mexico by her contemporaries, Sor Juana's literary genius surpassed that of other Mexican writers in the seventeenth and eighteenth centuries. Born

Juana Inés de Asbaje y Ramírez, she is reputed to have composed her first work at the age of eight and to have learned Latin in only twenty lessons. As a child, she was obsessed with learning; she refused to cultivate her "feminine" qualities, and went so far as to not eat cheese because she had heard it made one stupid. Though she begged to be sent to the university in Mexico City, because of her gender she had to resign herself to solitary reading and studying. At sixteen she became a lady of the Marquesa de Mancera at the Viceroy's palace, where she wrote poetry using the name "Laura" and where she soon became a favorite.

When the Viceroy learned of her intelligence, he organized a group of forty scholars from the capital and had them examine her orally, an event that constituted her "graduation" and officially recognized her as an intellectual.

Around 1668, she entered the Order of St. Jerome, where she remained until her death. While there, she amassed a library of over 4,000 volumes, including art and musical pieces. She was often called upon to write *villancicos* (carol sequences) for days of celebration in the church, but did not publish her poetry until 1689, when *Inundación castálida (Muse's Flood)* appeared. *El Primer sueño* (1692), a long baroque poem, and a collection of lyric poetry soon followed. Her secular dramatic works include two plays, *Los Empeños de una casa* (1692; *Household Intrigues*) and *Amor es más labyrinto* (1693; *Love, the Greater Labyrinth*). Among her religious works is her masterpiece, a sacramental play entitled *Divino Narciso* (1690; *Divine Narcissus*).

Sor Juana is perhaps best remembered for her impassioned defense of women's rights, especially the right of women to develop their minds through education. In 1691 she wrote an autobiographical essay, translated as *A Woman of Genius*, in which she declared herself in favor of a Mexican woman's culture, advocated the right of women to learn and to express themselves freely, and affirmed the right to dissent. She became known as "the vindication of her sex," a "feminist" in a world with few feminist traditions, and staunchly defended her own and other women's intellectual rights in her works.

Csezmiczei, János, *see* Pannonius, Janus

Cultural Revolution

Chinese political movement. Also known as the "Great Proletarian Cultural Revolution," the Cultural Revolution resulted in ten years of political turmoil, massive human suffering, and almost total economic collapse. Launched by Chinese Communist Party chairman Mao Zedong in 1966, the Revolution grew out of earlier (failed) attempts to revolutionize Chinese society, most notably the Anti-Rightist Campaign in 1957 and the Great Leap Forward in 1958–59. It represented a new event in the history of Communism: a revolution within a revolution.

By the mid-1960s, the damages inflicted by the Chinese Nationalist Campaign, the Great Leap Forward, had largely healed, and Chinese economy and society were relatively secure. Ultraleftists in the Communist Party, notably Mao's wife, Jiang Qing, convinced Mao that the Chinese revolution was in danger of stagnating. When a controversial play was attacked by Jiang and others based in Shanghai for promoting antisocialist tendencies, a broad array of Communist Party figures met in Beijing and defended the play's existence, if not its content. Mao sided with the Shanghai group, and members of the Beijing faction were ousted.

Then Nie Yuanzi, a young philosophy professor at Beijing University, wrote a large wall poster attacking the corrupt bourgeois attitudes of her university's administration. Attempts by Liu Shaoqi and Deng Xiaoping, members of the top echelon of the Communist Party and rivals of Mao, to send "work teams" onto campuses to quell the disturbances backfired when Mao openly praised Nie's action, writing a poster in her defense and urging students to "bomb the bourgeois headquarters," to root out bourgeois attitudes and agents in the schools and even in the Central Committee. Millions of young people responded, mobilizing as Red Guards and attacking administrators at every level, humiliating old writers and schoolteachers, and demolishing old buildings, temples, and traditional art objects. By 1967 the revolution turned violent, encouraged by the deliberate wording of Jiang Qing's call "to attack with words but defend with weapons." Fearing a full-scale civil war, some top leaders, particularly Mao's trusted ally, Premier Zhou Enlai, urged a quick return to order. Mao agreed, and the People's Liberation Army was called upon to stop violence and disband all militant factional organizations.

Still, the Cultural Revolution continued. The attempt to "abolish the distinction between mental and manual labor" saw students and youths sent to the countryside, to toil with peasants; scholars were sent to "cadre schools" in attempts to "reform" their minds; others were labeled counterrevolutionaries and were imprisoned or killed. The Little Red Book, or *Quotations from Chairman Mao*, was made the basis of all wisdom and acceptable opinion; millions of Red Guard members memorized the book in its entirety.

After an abortive attempt on Mao's life by his defense minister Lin Biao ended with Lin's accidental death, the revolution faltered. By 1973 Mao had been persuaded to revive the educational system and resume trade and other ties with the outside world. Deng Xiaoping was returned to power, and in 1975 was named vice-chairman of the

Communist Central Committee; once in power he swiftly moved to restore pre-1966 practices in all spheres of society. Jiang Qing opposed Deng's return, and with the other members of the Gang of Four, the coterie of Communist Party officials (Zhang Chunqiao, Wang Hongwen, and Yao Wenyuan), she succeeded in persuading Mao to reverse course again. Communist leader Zhou Enlai died in 1976, at the same time that a tremendous earthquake hit. In 1976 Deng was accused of restoring capitalism and ousted, and Mao passed over the Gang of Four, naming Hua Guofeng his successor as chairman of the Communist Party. Mao died later that year, and the ensuing power struggle ended with the arrest of the Gang of Four and the official end of the Cultural Revolution.

Curie, Marie (1867–1934)

Polish-born French physicist. Famous for her work on radioactivity and twice awarded the Nobel Prize, Curie conducted research that has enormously influenced the development of modern nuclear physics and chemistry. Born Manya Sklodowska, Curie was forced by her family's financial difficulties to seek employment as a teacher, then as a governess after the completion of her secondary education at a Russian lycée. Her savings from her governess job enabled Curie to support her sister's medical studies in Paris. Curie joined her sister in Paris and associated herself with a group of well-known physicists at the Sorbonne.

In 1894 she met her husband, Pierre Curie, and their marriage in 1895 marked the beginning of a productive partnership. In 1898 Curie discovered the minerals polonium and radium, and with her husband she devoted herself to isolating pure radium and studying the effects of radiation. For her work in this area she received her doctorate in 1903, and together with Pierre was awarded

the Davy Medal of the Royal Society and the Nobel Prize in Physics the same year. The birth of two daughters, Irène (1897) and Ève (1904), did not infringe on Curie's research, and the sudden death of her husband in 1906 only strengthened Curie's resolve to complete the work she and Pierre had started. Curie was elected to his professorship at the Sorbonne, becoming the first woman to teach there. She was again awarded the Nobel Prize in 1911, this time in chemistry, for her successful isolation of radium. In 1918 the Institut du Radium was completed, and through Curie and her daughter Irène it became a universal center for the study of nuclear physics and chemistry.

In 1922 Curie was appointed to the Academy of Medicine, concentrating her research on the medical applications of radioactive substances. She lectured widely; at one lecture in the United States, President Harding celebrated her accomplishments, presenting her with a gram of radium. Later, Curie founded the Radium Institute in her native Poland. She died of leukemia, caused by her work with radioactivity, but her research paved the way for the discovery of the neutron by Sir James Chadwick and of artificial radioactivity by Irène Curie and her husband, Frédéric Joliot.

Cyril and Methodius, Sts. (d. 869 and 884, respectively)

Missionaries. Though the history and influence of the brothers Cyril and Methodius is muddled by conflicting legends, it is known that they were born in Salonika, the sons of an administrator. Cyril, the younger of the two, was educated at the court in Constantinople and distinguished himself as a scholar. He chose to join the Roman Catholic Church and was appointed librarian at the Hagia Sophia; he later resigned to enter a monastery. Methodius joined the army and was appointed to the government of the Greco-Slavonic province, a position he held for ten years. In 851 both brothers retired to Mt. Olympus to live in seclusion, but their self-imposed withdrawal from the world was brief.

As missionaries, they were sent to convert the Khazars, north of Crimea. There they persuaded the khan of the Khazars to accept Christianity as the true religion, and proceeded to organize a church and vernacular liturgy for the people. After their great success with the Khazars, Cyril and Methodius returned to Constantinople, where they developed the first Slavic alphabet, the Glagolitic. In 863 the brothers journeyed to Moravia at the request of the patriarch Photius. Their success in converting Moravians aroused the hostility of the Germans, who were opposed to the use of the vernacular, Slavonic, in the liturgy. When Photius was excommuni-cated, the brothers traveled to Rome to defend their position. Their petition was successful, and the orthodoxy of vernacular in the liturgy established.

Cyril died in Rome, but Methodius returned to Moravia and assumed the position of archbishop of Sirmium. Despite official sanction, the German authorities contrived to imprison him. Their efforts were halfway successful; though he was released, his influence in the area was greatly diminished. In his later years, Methodius continued translating the Bible and ecclesiastical books into Slavonic, with the Glagolitic alphabet. The Cyrillic alphabet, used in Russia and other Slavic countries, is traditionally ascribed to St. Cyril, though it is probably the accomplishment of a group of his followers, working with Cyril's Glagolitic alphabet.

D

Dada

International visual arts and literary movement. Dada formally began in 1916 at a Zurich cabaret when some young artists randomly struck upon Dada, meaning "hobbyhorse" in French, in a French-German dictionary as the label for their philosophy and practice of art. Artists Jean Arp (1887–1966) and Tristan Tzara (1896–1963) were among the founders and leaders of the movement. The Dadaists were united by antiwar attitudes, a criticism of bourgeois morality, and a nihilistic philosophy of art. French artist Marcel Duchamp's (1887–1968) "ready-made" art was an immediate precursor of the movement.

Best understood as a mood or philosophy that revolted against traditional societal and aesthetic standards, Dada art attacked both traditional canons of art and the more recent avant-garde expressions. Members of the movement expressed these criticisms through works that violated logical patterns or forms. Jean Arp's collages, which were arranged according to chance, exemplify the heady irrationalism and antiart statements that the movement tried to voice. Literary expressions of the mood followed the lead of the visual arts, including the work of such writers as Louis Aragon, André Breton, Paul Éluard, and Philippe Soupalt. These Dada literary artists founded *Littérature* in Paris in 1919, which they published until 1924, when many of the members of the movement left Dada and moved toward Surrealism.

Dada artists shocked the public with their use of junk and trash in modern artworks, as well as their public antics and huge, roaring spectacles intended to rock bourgeois sensibilities. A broad anarchic urge, a zest for revolt, a relish of chance—these were the hallmarks of Dada "theory" and practice in the second decade of the twentieth century.

Though it lasted as a movement only until 1922, Dada had centers in New York, Paris, Zurich, Berlin, and Hanover, Germany. The utopian currents at play in Dada found outlets throughout the century, in the Surrealist, Lettrist, and Situationist movements in France; in the jubilant activities of the unsuccessful revolt in Paris in May 1968; in the negationism of 1977 punk rock; and in Anglo-American conceptual art of the 1970s and 1980s.

Dahomey, kingdom of

African kingdom. Located in what is now southern Benin, Dahomey (also spelled Danhome) was one of the most powerful kingdoms in West Africa in the eighteenth and nineteenth centuries, during the heyday of the African slave trade.

Dahomey has its origins in the seventeenth-century kingdom of Allada. Three princes of Allada quarreled, resulting in the establishment of three distinct kingdoms: Porto Novo, on the coast east of Whydah (now the capital of Togo), Allada, and Abomey. This last, which was founded by Do-Aklin (also known as Dogbari) around 1620, would eventually become the capital city of Dahomey.

Under the rule of Wegbaja (c. 1645–85), Do-Aklin's grandson, Abomey became a large and powerful state. Wegbaja's grandson, Agaja (1708–32),

conquered Allada and Whydah in the 1720s, founding the kingdom of Dahomey, with its capital at Abomey. Its government was an absolute monarchy with a well-established, centralized state and bureaucracy. Dahomey became heavily involved as a supplier to the European slave trade, which had begun in earnest a century earlier with the arrival of the Dutch.

The rule of Gezo (1818–58) marked the pinnacle of Dahomey's power and influence. Military victories enabled the kingdom to end the practice of paying tribute to the Oyo empire of what is now Nigeria. Still, the end of the slave trade in the mid nineteenth century greatly affected the economic fortunes of Dahomey, forcing it to provide primary products for newly important colonial markets. Palm oil, its main export, was never able to generate the same kinds of revenues that the slave trade had yielded. After the French gained control of Porto Novo, commerce declined. Under the leadership of Glele (1858–89), Dahomean troops resisted the French occupation; in 1889 the entire French merchant community was forced to flee into British territory.

Behanzin (1889–94), Glele's successor, was willing to engage in trade with the French, but only if the French agreed to grant Dahomey unconditional independence. In 1892 the French launched a full-scale offensive against Dahomey. Behanzin was forced to surrender in 1894 and was exiled to Martinique, and the kingdom became the French colony of Dahomey.

Dakshina

Region of India. The Sanskrit term *dakshina* (or Deccan) means "south" in English. Originally designating the whole of south or peninsular India, Deccan now refers to the high triangular plateau surrounded by mountain ranges and bounded by the Narmada River in the north and the Krishna River in the

south. It has been the site of bitter contestation for millennia.

In the late sixteenth century, a style of
miniature painting flourished in the sul-
tanates of the Deccan, especially in Bijapur, Ahmadnagar, and Golconda. In
Bijapur some of the finest Deccani portraits were painted for Sultan Ibrahim
Adil Shah (1580–1627,) who was himself
a musician, poet, and connoisseur of the
arts. The Deccani painting style, a blend
of indigenous and foreign art forms, is
marked by elongated figures, enflowered
backgrounds, landscapes, high horizons,
and a rich choice of colors, especially
gold and white. At Badami, Deccan artists Elephanta and Ellora produced dynamic narrative panels. By the mid
eighteenth century, Aurangabad and
the now independent kingdom of Hy-
derabad had become important centers
for the arts. The Deccan plateau is also
famous for its many domed temples
and its Islamic-influenced architecture,
including the Jami Masjid (Friday
Mosque) at Gulbarga and the Gol
Gumbad at Bijapur.

Dalai Lama XIV (1935–)

Spiritual leader of the Tibetans. Born in
the Qinghai province of China but of
Tibetan parentage, the Dalai Lama was
designated the "Buddha to be" of Tibetan Buddhism in 1939. When the People's Republic of China was founded in
1949, the Dalai Lama initially supported
the government, agreeing that Tibet
would become an autonomous region of
China and that the central government
should run its external affairs. But in
1959 a Tibetan uprising broke out and
was quickly curbed. The Dalai Lama
ended his relationship with the Beijing
government, claiming independence for
Tibet, and fled to India. Remaining in
exile, he has continued to advocate Tibetan sovereignty and nonviolent resistance to Chinese control. The Dalai
Lama was awarded the Nobel Peace
Prize in 1989 for his efforts.

Dalton, Roque (1935–1975)

El Salvadoran poet, historian, and revolutionary. Dalton emerged as a leader of
university students in the late 1950s for
his role in organizing strikes and demonstrations against the brutal military
dictatorships in El Salvador; as a result,
he was jailed and exiled many times.
Upon his return to El Salvador in 1973,
he helped found the Ejercito Revolucionario Popular (the ERP, or People's
Revolutionary Army), a guerrilla organization that fought to overthrow the pre-
siding military dictatorship. Dalton was
known above all for his poetry, which
portrayed the harsh conditions of the
daily lives of the peasants in El Salvador
and the people's dedication to fighting
for change. He was greatly interested in
the history of the workers and peasants
who participated in these struggles, and
wrote several books based on lengthy interviews with revolutionary leaders from
the early decades of the twentieth century. The most famous of these is his
history of the life and times of Miguel
Marmol, a leader of a planned uprising
in 1932.

In 1975 a dispute erupted within the
ERP over what form the struggle against
the dictatorship should take. Dalton,
along with several other members of the
organization, was executed by fellow
members of the ERP for "erroneous"
political views.

Damien, Father (1840–1889)

Belgian priest and missionary. Born Joseph de Veuster, Father Damien was
educated at the College of Braine-le-
Comte and joined the Picpus Fathers
(the Society of the Sacred Hearts of Jesus and Mary) in 1858. In 1863 he sailed
for the Sandwich Islands—now Hawaii—
to become a missionary and reached
Honolulu the following year, where he
was ordained a Roman Catholic priest.
Having worked among the islanders for
several years, in 1873 he volunteered to

head the mission on the island of Molokai, where lepers had been deported since 1866. For the next sixteen years Father Damien worked as pastor and physician, often without additional help, on the island. In 1884 he contracted leprosy but refused to leave his mission. He was accused by a rival priest of immorality but was exonerated by a church investigation after his death. Robert Louis Stevenson wrote a famous essay in his defense, *Father Damien: An Open Letter to the Rev. Dr. Hyde* (1890). In 1936 his body was removed from Molokai to Louvain, Belgium, and in 1965 the state of Hawaii nominated him to be honored in the National Statuary Hall of Fame in Washington, D.C.

dan Fodio, Usman (1754–1817)

Fulani leader in the western Sudan. As religious leader of the *jihâd*, or holy war, from 1804 to 1808, Usman helped overthrow the Hausa states and establish a militant Islamic state known as the Fulani empire in what is now northern Nigeria.

Born in the Hausa state of Gobir, Usman studied the Qur'ân with his father, an eminent scholar from the Toronkawa clan, and then moved from place to place to study with other religious scholars. When he was twenty-five he began teaching and preaching, and his reputation as a holy man grew. He appears to have persuaded the anti-Muslim sultan of Gobir to allow him to teach Islam, and he was probably engaged as tutor to the future sultan Yunfa because of his learned reputation. Usman also became widely known for his attempts to reform what he saw as the corrupt practice of Islam. Through these efforts he acquired a wide following in the 1780s and 1790s, and became a political threat to the Gobir sultan, Nafata. By this period Usman had become known as the *shaykh*, and the conflict between the Gobir dynasty and Usman's reformist followers continued after Yunfa suc-

ceeded to the sultanship in 1802, and the repression of Muslims worsened. Following the example of the Prophet Muhammad, Usman went on a *hijrah* (spiritual migration) and was elected *imâm* (leader) of the reformist Muslims, eventually launching the *jihâd* that would bring down Hausa royalty. In the conquered areas, Usman set up emirates whose leaders acknowledged his religious sovereignty, and in October 1808 the Gobir capital, Alkalawa, fell. After 1812 Usman withdrew into private life, writing many works on the proper conduct of the pious Islamic community.

By his death in 1817, most of the area was under Islamic control, and Usman's son Muhammad Bello became first sultan of the Sokoto empire, a flourishing Islamic culture. Usman dan Fodio is remembered as the most important reform leader of the Sudan in the early nineteenth century.

Dante Alighieri (1265–1321)

Italian poet. Dante was born to a noble family in Florence, where he lived until he was exiled from the city in 1301 for his criticism of the papacy. Though his civic and political interests informed much of his prose and poetry, they did not eclipse the sense of spirituality and passion that is prevalent in his verse. Dante taught himself to write poetry at an early age; this passion was further encouraged at the Franciscan schools where he studied. He also possessed a deep knowledge of ancient writers like Cicero and medieval thinkers, including Thomas Aquinas, which is reflected in his works. But perhaps the most formative experience in Dante's life was his meeting Beatrice, a noblewoman of Florence, with whom he was secretly in love throughout his life; his devotion to her plays a central role in his various works.

La vita nuova (1576; *The New Life*), *Convivio* (1490; *The Banquet*), *De monarchia* (1559; *On Monarchy*), and *La divina commedia* (1472; *Divine Comedy*) are among Dante's best-known works. *The New Life* is a collection of prose and poetry in which Dante narrates events of his early life since meeting Beatrice, an event he likens to a conversion experience. *The Banquet* is a more philosophical work, in which Dante brilliantly employs the vernacular as a literary language. This cause, which revolutionized literary culture in the West, would be taken up by many Renaissance figures. In *On Monarchy*, Dante argues for the separation of Church and state, ascribing corruption in the Church to its political ambitions. The *Divine Comedy*, which was completed in the year of Dante's death, is one of the most enduring classics of the late medieval period. Here he again displays his love and devotion for Beatrice and his pursuit of a spiritual life. Written in three sections, *Inferno* (*Hell*), *Purgatorio* (*Purgatory*), and *Paradiso* (*Paradise*), Dante's verse carries the reader on an allegorical journey through hell and purgatory to heaven. In the *Divine Comedy*, Beatrice, who is to be understood as divine, sends Virgil to guide Dante and the reader through this pilgrimage. Overall, the *Divine Comedy* reflects Dante's criticism of the papacy and his command of Western history, religion, and culture, and is the work for which he is best known.

Darío, Rubén (1867–1916)

Nicaraguan poet. Darío was a leader of the Spanish-American literary movement known as modernism, and came to be considered the most important and influential Nicaraguan poet of his day. By the age of fourteen, he had written a ream of poems and prose articles that would not be published until nearly fifty years, after his death. His first printed book appeared when he was eighteen years old, and was an immediate success; by this time he had already changed his name from Félix Rubén García Sarmiento to Rubén Darío. The following year, Darío left Nicaragua to begin the travels that were to last throughout his life. He arrived in Chile in 1886, where he discovered French Parnassian poetry, and applied what he learned from the French in *Azul* (1888; *Blue*), a collection of short stories, descriptive sketches, and verse, which became his first major work and, according to some of his critics, marks the beginning of Spanish Modernism, which is the combination of the European movements Romanticism, Parnassianism, and Symbolism. The book owes most of its historical importance to its stories and poetic prose, rather than to its poems, and was immediately recognized in Europe and Latin America as the herald of a new era in Spanish-American literature.

After two brief marriages—the first ended with his wife's death, the second with separation—Darío left Central America to assume a position in Buenos Aires as consul for Colombia. He found the cosmopolitan atmosphere of Buenos Aires stimulating and wrote nearly thirty short stories of horror in the style of American writer Edgar Allan Poe. Surrounded by young poets and followers of the French Parnassians, he was soon claimed as the leader of the Spanish modernists. When the Colombian consulate was abolished in 1894, Darío worked as a journalist, traveling to Europe as a correspondent for the Buenos Aires newspaper *La Nación* in 1898, and later settled in Paris, where he was named consul by the Nicaraguan government, a position he retained until 1907. Near the end of his life, he became increasingly concerned with the solidarity of all Spanish-speaking people, the revalidation of Hispanic culture, the future of Latin America after the collapse of the Spanish empire in the New World, and the eternal problems of human existence, all of which find expression in his masterwork, *Cantos de vida y esperanza* (1905; *Songs of Life and Hope*). Leaving Europe in 1914 upon the outbreak of World War I, Darío was ill and on the brink of poverty. He began a lecture tour of North America, but he contracted pneumonia in New York and died shortly afterward in Nicaragua. His experiments with forms of verse, his artistic resourcefulness, his technical perfection, and the fact that he probably introduced more metrical innovations than any other Spanish-language poet make him one of the greatest poets ever to write in Spanish.

Darwin, Charles [Robert] (1809–1882)

English scientist and theorist of evolution. Darwin was born and raised in Shrewsbury, England, where he spent much of his time roaming through the countryside hunting and collecting rocks. Following his father's directives, Darwin tried to study medicine at the University of Edinburgh, but he found the lectures boring and became ill while observing an operation. He then went to Oxford to study to become a priest in the Church of England. While at Oxford, he met John Stevens Henslow, a professor of botany. Henslow saw in Darwin the talents and interests that were required of a natural scientist, and arranged for Darwin to fill the post of naturalist on the voyage of the H.M.S. *Beagle* to South America, the Galápagos Islands, and Africa.

In 1831, when Darwin embarked on this voyage, he was not an educated and seasoned scientist. Nor did he question the accepted view of creation, depicted in Genesis, that an immutable number of species were divinely created. By the time of his return voyage in 1836, however, Darwin was an experienced naturalist and carried with him a wealth of data, specimens, and observations, recorded in his first book, *Journal of Researches into the Geology and Natural History of Various Countries Visited by H.M.S. Beagle, 1832–1836* (1839). Moreover, he had begun thinking about the idea of organic evolution. Though Dar-

win was certainly not the first to formulate a theory of evolution, he was one of the first two scientists to collect the data necessary to support such a theory. Darwin was hesitant to publish his work, but was prompted to disclose his ideas after reading a brief work by another naturalist that was nearly identical to his thesis. Darwin was moved to write the book that would dramatically change the scope and function of natural science—*On the Origin of Species by Means of Natural Selection* (1859). After reading Malthus's *Essay on the Principle of Population* in 1838, Darwin developed the concept of natural selection, which maintains that all living species developed from a limited number of simple forms and that the continued existence of a given species depends on its ability to adapt to surrounding environmental conditions. (The age-old idea of the survival of the fittest found a disconcerting echo in Darwin's science.) In the *Descent of Man* (1871), Darwin asserted that natural selection played the central role in the origin and development of humankind.

Darwin's theory of organic evolution by natural selection was highly controversial in the nineteenth century—even into the twentieth century—in large part because it challenged the validity of the biblical account of creation and immediately brought science and theology into conflict. Darwin himself steered clear of these arguments. By the last quarter of the nineteenth century, the theory of evolution had been accepted throughout the natural sciences, and had begun to have an enormous impact on literature and the arts, inspiring Anglo-American naturalism (through writers like Jack London) and French decadence (through the proto-surrealist writings of Isidore Ducasse). Darwin's death, in 1882, was probably due to Chagas' disease, which he had most likely contracted during his expeditions in the 1830s.

Daumier, Honoré (1808–1879)

French painter, lithographer, and caricaturist. Considered the greatest social satirist of his day, Daumier produced almost 4,000 lithographs belittling bourgeois society. He was an impassioned believer in the spirit of 1789, the impatient and scornful anger of the French Revolution; with all the perception and zeal of a muckraking journalist, Daumier turned a cold eye toward the reigning pieties of his day. Early on in his career, Daumier was imprisoned for his grotesque caricature of the "Citizen-King," Emperor Louis-Philippe. This did nothing to deter Daumier, and after *La Caricature*, the journal in which his work appeared, was suppressed in 1835, he joined the staff of the journal *Charivari*. Though *Charivari* adhered to a less satirical line, Daumier continued to publish his scathing lithographs, bitter satires of the hypocrisies of the bourgeoisie, the corrupt practices in government and law, and social injustices. Among his best-known lithographs are *Le Ventre législatif* and *Rue Transnonain, 14 Avril*, both in 1834. Daumier also sculpted small clay busts, which served as models for his drawings, as well as numerous small paintings, which also exhibit the exaggerated characters of his lithographs. Impoverished and nearly blind, Daumier died in 1879, in a house given to him by the painter Jean-Baptiste-Camille Corot.

Davies, [William] Robertson (1913–1995)

Canadian critic, essayist, playwright, and novelist. Raised in Ontario, the young Davies developed an insatiable interest in Freud and later in the works of C. G. Jung, which informed what is considered Davies's most significant contribution to Canadian letters—a trilogy including *Fifth Business* (1970), *The Manticore* (1972), and *World of Wonders* (1975). *Fifth Business*, a Canadian bestseller, explores the commingling of guilt and responsibility in what Davies himself terms "the bizarre and passionate life of the Canadian people." His main characters appear conspicuously individualized and conform in many ways to Jung's archetypal figures. Davies's first sequel to *Fifth Business, The Manticore*, received the Governor-General's Award in 1973. All of Davies's work deals with the oddball offbeat rhythms of Canadian life, the pulse of life in the clean-cut semi-socialist Canadian cities. Davies was very influential as the master of Massey College at the University of Toronto from 1961 to 1981. Other important works include *The Rebel Angels* (1981) and *What's Bred in the Bone* (1985).

da Vinci, Leonardo, *see* Leonardo da Vinci

Davis, Miles [Dewey III] (1926–1991)

African-American jazz trumpeter. A leader in avant-garde jazz, Davis introduced the "cool" playing style that incorporated both the French horn and tuba and contrasted with the "hot" fast bebop sound of the 1940s and 1950s. In 1958 he began experimenting with abstract harmonies far removed from bop, typified by the almost atonal music on numbers like *Nefertiti* and *Sorcerer*. Later, he combined elements from other types of music such as rock and soul, using modal harmonies and melodies as well as electronic instruments, a polyglot musical fusion exemplified in the album *Bitches Brew* (1969).

Growing up in East St. Louis, Illinois, Davis studied music in local public schools and was tutored privately by a local musician. In 1945 he began his studies at the Juilliard School of Music in New York, but left after one semester to play with such famous musicians as Benny Carter, Billy Eckstine, Coleman Hawkins, and Charlie Parker. By 1948 he had his own band, playing in New York nightclubs, and there began changing elements of standard bebop. His wry, relaxed style gave birth to "cool" jazz and contributed to the development of "West Coast" bebop. His recordings, such as *Miles Ahead* (1957), *Kind of Blue* (1958), and *Miles Smiles* (1966), repeatedly established him as an important innovator, one of the most important and compelling figures in jazz, over- or underground.

Davis has been acknowledged as one of the most influential musicians in jazz history, beginning in the bebop era of the 1940s up through the 1970s. Many of his former band members themselves established groups and became leaders in jazz, including such figures as Cannonball Adderly, Ron Carter, John Coltrane, Chick Corea, Bill Evans, Herbie Hancock, Philly Joe Jones, and Jackie McLean.

In keeping with the popular trends in music, Davis performed variations of the work of American music stars Michael Jackson and Cyndi Lauper in his concerts, and even collaborated on a music project with musical performer Prince, in 1986. The year 1981 saw the marriage of Davis to American actress Cicely Tyson, which lasted only until 1988; Davis died in 1991.

Davy, Sir Humphry (1778–1829)

English chemist. Davy was apprenticed to a surgeon and apothecary as a young man, but he was discharged when his chemical experiments ended in explosions. Though he greatly admired the Romantic poets and aspired to write his own verse, a passion for chemistry overwhelmed him after he read the textbook on chemistry by French chemist Antoine Laurent Lavoisier. In 1798 Davy secured a position as the superintendent of a research institute devoted to the study of the therapeutic effects of gases. While there, Davy first acquired his longstanding—and physically debilitating—habit of inhaling and smelling the gases and compounds he tested. He once nearly smothered himself by breathing in four quarts of hydrogen; on another occasion he attempted to inhale pure carbon dioxide. At least once, however, these risky experiments paid off, and in 1800 Davy discovered nitrous oxide, or laughing gas, which had immediate uses as an anesthetic and a recreational drug. The following year, Davy joined the Royal Institute in London, and his chemistry lectures became hugely popular affairs.

However, it was Davy's successful isolation of many of the elements, including potassium and sodium, with the use of electrical currents that would be his lasting accomplishment. His experiments, especially those involving hydrochloric acid, disputed the commonly accepted notion that acidic compounds contained oxygen and advanced the idea that other gases, such as chlorine, behaved in a manner similar to oxygen.

Deadwood Dick (1854–1921)

African-American cowboy. Born Nat Love, a slave in a log cabin in Davidson County, Tennessee, he was the youngest of three children. A lucky raffle ticket brought him enough money to clothe himself and to seek greater opportunities, and so he started on foot for the West in 1869. Upon his arrival in Dodge City, Kansas, he found work as a cowboy. At once he earned admiration for his ability to ride a bucking bronco that his new companions had furnished him for his initiation. Because of this feat, the "tenderfoot" was accepted by the Duval outfit at thirty dollars a month.

At a Fourth of July celebration in 1876, after a cattle drive to Deadwood, South Dakota, Love found himself in competition with the best cowboys in the West. He won the contest to rope, throw, tie, bridle, saddle, and mount an untamed bronco, a feat he accomplished in nine minutes, a record, and won the shooting contests with a rifle at 100 and 250 yards and with the Colt .45 at 150 yards. Entering and finishing these matches with the confidence of a man who declared that "if a man can hit a running buffalo at 200 yards, he can hit pretty much of anything he shoots at," he was given the name "Deadwood Dick" by his admiring fans.

Later that year, Love was captured by American Indians and was unwillingly adopted by the tribe. He escaped after an incredible ride of a hundred miles in twelve hours of darkness, carrying with him two new bullet holes, part of the total of "the marks of fourteen bullet wounds on different parts of my body."

In 1890, with the passing of the great era of the cowboy, he became a Pull-man porter. Despite the slavery-era statutes that outlawed black literacy, Deadwood Dick had learned to read and write at his father's knee, and in 1907 he wrote an autobiography entitled *The Life and Adventures of Nat Love: Better Known in the Cattle Country as "Deadwood Dick."*

Debussy, Claude [Achille] (1862–1918)

French composer. Though Debussy pre-ferred the simple description *musicien français*, his highly original musical style, characterized by free forms, unre-solved discord, and exotic scales, places him squarely within the school of mu-sical impressionism. His most famous compositions are the *Suite Bergamasque* (1890–1905), containing the famous pi-ano piece *Clair de lune*, and the tone poem *Prélude à l'après-midi d'un faune* (1894; *Prelude to the Afternoon of a Faun*), inspired by a work by French poet Stéphane Mallarmé.

The recognition of Debussy's prodi-gious musical talents as a child placed him in rather conflicting circumstances. He commenced his studies at the Paris Conservatoire in 1873, and although he lived with his parents in a poverty-stricken suburb of Paris, he received the patronage of a wealthy Russian woman and spent his vacations traveling throughout Europe with her family. In 1884 Debussy was awarded the Grand Prix de Rome for his composition *L'Enfant prodigue* (*The Prodigal Child*). Much of Debussy's career was spent in Paris and in relative isolation in Eng-land, where he fled to escape the gossip surrounding the birth of his illegitimate daughter and his subsequent marriage to the child's mother. His seminal com-positions, however, dictated many mu-sical developments of the twentieth century. With his use of the destabiliz-ing whole-tone scale, elements from Oriental music, and short, gem-like themes, he declared absolute indepen-dence from German Romanticism, even though he learned much from Wagner. Debussy's career was cut short by can-cer, and his final work, an operatic ad-aptation of American writer Edgar Allan Poe's *Fall of the House of Usher*, was left unfinished.

Dede Korkut

Turkish epic. "The Book of Dede Kor-kut in the Language of the Oghuz," the oldest surviving specimen of the great epic of the Oghuz migration, consists of a cycle of twelve prose stories inter-spersed with verse, written in Turkish. The Oghuz Turks migrated west from their original homelands in Inner Asia during the ninth and tenth centuries, and simultaneously converted to Islam in large numbers. The twelve epic sto-ries record for the most part the struggles of the Oghuz in this time period, though the collection itself dates most probably from the fourteenth or very early fif-teenth century. Dede Korkut, after whom the book is named, is portrayed as the "holy man" of the Oghuz; the title translates as "Father Korkut" or "Grandfather Korkut." Definite histori-cal identification of the figures men-tioned in the narrative is not possible, and the collection is best approached as a repository of nomadic Turkish culture at the onset of Islamization.

Deewali

Hindu holiday. Deewali (also Divali or Diwali) is a major Indian religious fes-tival, lasting five days, beginning on the thirteenth day of the dark half of the

Hindu month of Asvina and ending on the second day of the light half of the month Karttika—roughly coinciding with late October in the Gregorian calendar. Deriving its name from the Sanskrit term *dipavali*, meaning "row of lights," it holds particular significance for the merchant classes. It is held in honor of Laksmi, the goddess of wealth, and in Bengal, in honor of the goddess Kali.

Celebrations involve the lighting of small earthenware lamps which are then placed in streams and rivers or used to line the parapets of temples and houses to commemorate the delayed coronation of the Hindu god Vishnu as king of Ayodhya. Reincarnated in the form of Rama, he is believed to have returned to claim the throne after fourteen years in exile. The fourth day of the festival inaugurates the new year in the Vikrama calendar.

Celebrations involve the exchange of gifts, feasting, gambling, the decoration of houses, and visits. The gambling is particularly encouraged as a means of bringing luck in the coming year, in remembrance of the dice games played between Shiva and Parvati on Mt. Kailasa. Merchants celebrate Deewali by opening new account books and observing religious services.

The festival also holds particular significance for the Jaina community. Deewali is a commemoration of the death of their most recent Jaina Tirthankara, or saint. The passing into nirvana of the revered Mahavira is considered a great loss to the world; the lighting of earthenware lamps constitutes a physical substitution for the holy knowledge that was lost with the death of the great teacher.

Degas, [Hilaire Germain] Edgar
(1834–1917)
French painter and sculptor. Though he was associated with the Impressionists, Degas is renowned for his blending of classical art with Impressionism, and for his bold use of compositional forms, such as off-center subjects and unusual angles, to portray scenes of contemporary life.

As a student at the École des Beaux-Arts, Degas was strongly influenced by the academic orthodoxy of the institution, which was at that time challenged by the work of the French painter Ferdinand Victor Eugène Delacroix (1798–1863). He supplemented his studies of classical form by journeying to Italy, and there carefully studied the works of Italian painter Sandro Botticelli (1445–1510), among others. His highly acclaimed early portraits were gradually replaced with scenes of contemporary Parisian life. Degas subjects included ballet dancers, women at their toilette, laundresses, and racetrack scenes; in all of these, the painter's attention to form and the influence of Japanese graphic art is notable. His famous drawings and paintings include *Le Foyer de la danse* (1872; *Foyer of the Dance*), and *La Repétition de danse* (*The Rehearsal*) and *Les Blanchisseuses* (*Two Laundresses*), both 1882. Later in his career, Degas also worked occasionally as a sculptor, producing small bronze statues of dancers and horses. Even with his failing eyesight, Degas was noted for his ability to reveal the power and beauty in human and animal forms in ordinary movement. Degas's influence can be seen in the work of both French painter Toulouse-Lautrec (1864–1901) and Spanish painter Pablo Picasso (1881–1973).

Delacroix, [Ferdinand Victor] Eugène
(1798–1863)
French painter. The foremost representative of the French Romantics, Delacroix's use of vibrant colors greatly influenced the Impressionist and Post-Impressionist movements. He had a natural taste for the grand manner and for large-scale compositions, and had a particular admiration for the painting styles of Peter Paul Rubens (1577–1640) and

Paolo Veronese (1528–1588). Delacroix was profoundly aware of the appeal of religion to the imagination, drawing heavily on both classical and biblical themes. Although his subject matter was often traditional, his technical style, which relied on the use of contorted forms and deep tones, was thoroughly Romantic.

Born into an artistically gifted family, Delacroix studied the classics until the age of seventeen. Under the influence of the works of an assortment of Romantics, including French writer George Sand (1804–1876), Polish composer Fryderyk Chopin (1810–1849), and French painter Théodore Géricault (1791–1824), the young Delacroix explored a wide variety of subjects, historical and contemporary, in his paintings. *Dante et Virgile aux enfers* (1822; *Dante and Virgil in Hell*) was his first masterpiece, inspired by Dante's *Divine Comedy*. This work was followed by *Scènes des massacres de Chios* (1824; *The Massacre of Chios*), which was influenced by Géricault's *Medusa*, and *Marino Falieri* (1826; *The Execution of Doge Marino Falieri*).

On a trip to Morocco in 1832, Delacroix experimented boldly with color, producing some of his richest, most imaginative paintings—most notably, *Femmes d'Alger dans leur appartement* (1834; *Women of Algiers in Their Apartment*), works that prefigured Expressionist paintings at the turn of the twentieth century. Returning to France, Delacroix immersed himself in building decoration, mostly murals, although these works quite taxed his already fragile health. His apartment in Paris, where he died in 1863, was later turned into a national museum.

Delhi

City and territory in north-central India. In 1912 the British constructed New Delhi, located six miles from Old Delhi. Since that time New Delhi has been the capital of India and site of the government, while Old Delhi has remained the economic and population center.

The dominant trading and commercial center of northern India for centuries, Delhi and its vicinity have been the site of the capital for a succession of emperors and sultans, many of whom constructed their own palaces and town centers within a zone now referred to as the "Delhi triangle." It is the third largest city in India; only Calcutta and Greater Bombay have larger populations.

According to popular lore, the city derived its name from one of its first kings, Raja Dhilu, who reigned in the first century B.C.E., but changed its locality many times. One of the earliest constructions at or around present-day Delhi can be traced back to the eleventh century C.E., when Anangapal, the Tomara king, built a red fort, where the Quṭb Mīnar now stands, three miles south of modern New Delhi.

Delhi sultans were great builders. Working in a hybrid idiom of Indo-Muslim architectural styles, they oversaw the construction of such celebrated edifices as the Quṭb Mīnar, the Quwat-ul-Islam Mosque, and the Dargah of Nizamuddin Auliya with its mosque and tomb of Feroz Shah Tughluq. During the Mughal reign, the Lal Qal'ah (Red Fort) and the Jama Masjid (Principal Mosque) were constructed. The era of the Delhi sultanate also saw the rise of Hindustani music, which reached its zenith under the reign of Mongol emperor Akbar (1556–1605) with the compositions and performances of Tansen, the grandfather of modern-day Hindustani music. Artists during the Delhi sultanate produced illustrated manuscripts in provincial Persian idioms and traditional mural paintings. Under Akbar's reign, book painting or individual miniatures replaced wall painting as the primary art form.

In 1912 the British moved their capital from Calcutta to New Delhi, the construction of which was not completed until 1931. The population of Delhi/New Delhi experienced its greatest growth rate between 1941 and 1951, largely due to the flood of refugees into the city at the time of independence after World War II. The modern city is cosmopolitan in character and reflects the diverse cultural backgrounds of its population. The majority of the population is Hindu; the largest minority profess Islam. Many of India's major cultural institutions are located in Delhi, as are several important universities, including the University of Delhi, established in 1922.

The contrasts between Old and New Delhi, from the street patterns to the neighborhoods to the atmosphere, are striking. In the old city, there is a strong *mohalla* (neighborhood) feeling, while in New Delhi's upper-income, residential Civil Lines, quiet and openness pervade. Delhi and New Delhi are now considered one city, and the boundaries of this ever-expanding capital have, in keeping with its history, been extended and redefined since the independence of India.

DeMille, Cecil B[lount] (1881–1959)

American film director. One of Hollywood's "Golden Age" directors, DeMille is perhaps best remembered as a master director of the historical and religious epic. DeMille relied upon a larger-than-life and elaborate style of storytelling, with a straightforward narrative technique. Despite their popular success, however, DeMille's films were not immune to criticism, and were targeted for his use of grade-school dialogue and overwrought characterizations. Nevertheless, DeMille is credited with making significant contributions to the development and refinement of cinematic technique: his use of the shot/countershot in *The Cheat* (1915) to follow thought rather than action revolutionized film editing.

DeMille began an acting career in 1900. In 1913, along with Samuel Goldfish (Goldwyn), Arthur S. Friend, and Jesse Lasky, he founded the Jesse L. Lasky Feature Play Company and was made director-general; a merger in 1918 created Paramount Pictures Corporation. While at Paramount Pictures, DeMille produced *The Squaw Man* (1914), a success that established DeMille's elaborate style of filmmaking. Many of his early works, especially *Don't Change Your Husband* (1919) and *Why Change Your Wife?* (1920), develop a trademark sexual theme, the dangerous temptations of liberal sexual attitudes.

Beginning with *Carmen* (1915), DeMille turned increasingly to history, high art, the Bible, and English playwright William Shakespeare to find the stuff of epic cinema. With the advent of sound, his productions became more ambitious. DeMille utilized his trademark style of filmmaking throughout the 1940s and 1950s, which saw him produce films such as *North West Mounted Police* (1940), *Samson and Delilah* (1949), *The Ten Commandments* (1956), and *The Greatest Show on Earth* (1952). This last film was named Best Picture by the Motion Picture Academy.

Desai, Anita [Mazumdar] (1937–)

Indian novelist and short-story writer. Considered one of the most eloquent voices in modern India, Desai was born and educated in India, graduating from Delhi University in 1957.

Desai's first two novels, *Cry, the Peacock* and *Voices in the City*, both written in English, were published in Britain in 1963, and identify her as a gifted writer who focuses more on the psychological and spiritual disease of her characters than on the contemporary social issues of their urban Indian settings. Two of her later works, *Bye-Bye, Blackbird* (1968) and *Where Shall We Go This Summer?* (1975), were released only in

India, and her first book to be published in the United States was *Fire on the Mountain* (1977), a character study of a retired woman named Nanda Kaul. *Clear Light of Day* (1980) addresses the complexity of family relationships and the differing ways in which members of a family recall the past. In addition to these numerous literary successes, Desai received a Booker Prize nomination for *Clear Light of Day* in 1980 and for *In Custody* in 1984. More recent titles include *Baumgartner's Bombay* (1989) and *Journey to Ithaca* (1995).

Desaparecidos, Los

Term for victims of political persecution in Latin America. Desaparecidos, or "Disappeared Ones," refers to people who simply disappear, having been kidnapped, most often by government forces. The practice of "disappearances" was refined and has been used systematically for purposes of state repression since the 1950s. Historically, the massive employment of secret police and military units to kidnap and execute political dissidents can be traced to the Guatemalan coup d'état of 1954; in the three decades following the coup, it is estimated that the number of "disappeared" ranged as high as 30,000. The technique was also practiced under the Somoza regime in Nicaragua, and later in the Southern Cone: after the 1964 coup in Brazil; after the 1973 coups in Chile and Uruguay; and since the early 1970s in Argentina, but particularly after the 1976 coup. More than 9,000 people are believed to have disappeared during Argentina's "Dirty War." In most cases, the victims were kidnapped by police or military personnel who wore civilian clothes and drove unmarked cars; they were taken to hidden detention and torture centers known as *pozos* (holes) or "little schools." Military units maintained secret lists with the names of those targeted for abduction, torture, and murder. In the 1970s disappearances

began to take place on a large scale in El Salvador, and were part of the tactics of the state apparatus threatened by Marxist guerrillas. In the 1980s disappearance became a weapon of drug barons in Peru and Colombia. Several human rights groups have been established to trace the disappeared or at least identify the circumstances of their deaths and those responsible for them. The most famous of these are the Mothers of the Plaza de Mayo (Argentina) and the Mutual Support Group (Guatemala). Many writers, including Chilean writer Ariel Dorfman, Uruguayan writer Cristina Peri Rossi, and Argentine writer Marta Traba, treat this theme in their fiction.

Descartes, René (1596–1650)

French philospher. Born in La Haye, France, and educated at the Jesuit college of La Flèche, Descartes graduated from Poitiers in 1616, where he studied law. He left for Holland in 1618, joining the army of Maurice of Nassau. During his military career, he traveled to Germany, deciding while in Ulm to take upon himself the task of rebuilding philosophy and science in conformity with the principles of mathematics, a task that would occupy him for the remainder of his life.

Descartes's early career is marked by two significant events. First, in 1628, in a famous debate with Chandoux, who believed science could only be founded on probability, Descartes asserted that human knowledge must be founded upon absolute certainties. Second, in 1634 he completed his *Le Monde*, which proposed a theory of the solar system that adhered to the Copernican system. He soon suppressed this work, however, upon hearing that Galileo had been attacked by the Church and forced to recant. These two moments are determinative of Descartes's thought: a thought anchored to the axiom that the only true propositions were those that we are absolutely certain of, but also wary of the power of the Church and sensitive to the political constraints on the art of writing.

Descartes's impact on the formation of the modern mind is diverse. In mathematics, his primary contribution was the creation of analytic geometry. In the field of science, Descartes's conception of the universe was eclipsed by Newtonian physics, but Descartes's scientific method—stating a hypothesis, then verifying or rejecting it on the basis of empirically gathered facts—has been a standby of scientific practice since the Enlightenment. His greatest impact has been on the discipline of philosophy.

Writing *Discours de la méthode* (1637; *Discourse on Method*) in French, Descartes directed it at the educated populace and not just at the academy. In this book, he outlines the problem of certainty and skepticism, describing how a rigorous notion of the truth could only arise when a clear mind, engaged in thought, reached the point at which there could be no doubt. As it happened, Descartes could be certain of only one thing: that the existence of consciousness was the only surety, as expressed by *cogito ergo sum*, "I think, therefore I am." In the *Meditationes de Prima Philosophia* (1641; *Meditations on First Philosophy*), Descartes circumspectly added a second truthful clarity, however: that God exists, that the idea of a supreme and perfect being is just as necessary as the concept that the sum of the angles in a triangle equals 180 degrees. Another consequence of Descartes's skepticism was the privileging of mind or self as *cogito* over the body, a gesture (explored in the *Passiones Animae* [1649; *Passions of the Soul*]) that would resonate throughout the Enlightenment.

Both in the areas of epistemology and the philosophy of mind, Descartes formulated problems that later philosophers would have to respond to. In epistemology, he influenced the philosophies of Locke, Berkeley, and Hume. More generally, Descartes's method of doubt has helped to shape Western philosophy since the seventeenth century. The dualism that Descartes asserted in the philosophy of the mind has presented itself forcefully throughout the modern period, expressing itself in the writings of some of the great philosophers of the twentieth century. René Descartes died in Sweden while serving at the court of Queen Christina as her instructor in philosophy.

De Sica, Vittorio (1902–1974)

Italian director. Like other Italian directors of the postwar period, including such noted figures as Visconti and Roberto Rossellini (1906–1977), Vittorio De Sica was a proponent of neorealism in filmmaking. His works generated tremendous controversy, fought over by two of the dominant political factions in postwar Italy, the Communist Party and the Catholic Church. While the Church lauded his works, Communist critics found his neorealist style reminiscent of the so-called calligraphic fascist films of the 1920s and 1930s, movies that took an ahistorical and aestheticized approach to storytelling.

De Sica worked as an actor as early as 1918, achieving great popularity with his role in *La Vecchia Signora* (1931; *The Old Woman*). De Sica continued to work as an actor throughout his directorial career and made over one hundred films in Italy and abroad, gathering funds and connections to finance his own directorial efforts.

De Sica's fourth film, *I bambini ci guardano* (1943; *The Children Are Watching Us*), marked the beginning of a three-decade collaboration with Cesare Zavattini; it is the first of many of his films that focused on the lives of children. His next film, *Sciuscia* (1947), detailed the lives of two street children, and brought De Sica international attention and a special Oscar. *Ladri di biciclette* (*Bicycle Thief*), released in 1948, was the winner of the Oscar for Best Foreign Film in 1949.

In 1953, after much wooing by Hollywood mogul David Selznick, De Sica agreed to make *Stazione termini* (1953; *Indiscretions of an American Wife*), starring actors Jennifer Jones and Montgomery Clift; the film was derided as an empty vehicle for American superstars. With *L'oro di Napoli* (1954; *Gold of Naples*), De Sica and Zavattini returned to comedy, specifically a comedy that utilized satirical and farcical sexual situations. De Sica was a brilliant executor of the sex comedy, a genre that enjoyed enormous popularity in Italy and throughout the world in the 1950s and early 1960s. De Sica continued to make more films into the late 1960s, though he was no longer the center of controversy.

De Valera, Eamon (1882–1975)

Irish prime minister and president. De Valera, or "Dev," was an ardent revolutionary who was elected president of the nationalist Irish political party Sinn Féin in 1918. In 1924 De Valera founded the Fianna Fáil Party and became a leader in the drive to make the Irish Free State a sovereign entity. De Valera also attained recognition as a scholar and the chancellor of the National University of Ireland.

Born in New York City, he was sent to live with his mother's family in County Limerick, Ireland. There he attended the local schools and Dublin's Blackrock College. After graduating from the Royal University, De Valera taught mathematics. In 1913, during the Irish Revival, De Valera joined the Irish Volunteers and organized to oppose Home Rule. He took part in the Easter Uprising of 1916 and was among the last leaders to surrender. The fact that he was American-born saved De Valera from execution, but he was imprisoned

for a year. Following his release in 1917, he was arrested and deported to England. Irish supporters there celebrated him as the most famous survivor of the uprising, and he was elected president of Sinn Féin, the Irish revolutionary party, in December 1918.

In 1919, after his arrest and escape from Lincoln Jail, a disguised De Valera went to the United States to garner support and funds for the cause. De Valera rejected the 1921 treaty that had created the Irish Free State because it excluded Northern Ireland and required an oath of allegiance to the Crown. When the Irish assembly (the Dáil) ratified the treaty, De Valera urged resistance. Following yet another imprisonment and release, he organized an opposition party that refused to sit in the Dáil. In 1927 he argued that signing the oath of allegiance was an "empty political formula." The party he led into the Dáil then demanded abolition of the oath, removal of the governor-general, and abolition of the Irish senate (Seanad).

Fianna Fáil defeated William Cosgrave's Irish Free State ministry in 1932, and Prime Minister De Valera began severing ties with Britain. The Free State declared itself sovereign in 1937, but the new Ireland (Éire) maintained voluntary allegiance to Britain.

De Valera presided over the League of Nations and its assembly in 1932 and 1938. With war threatening, Britain yielded naval bases in Ireland, but De Valera proclaimed Irish neutrality. In 1958 De Valera resigned as leader of the Fianna Fáil Party in order to run for the presidency. He won, and was reelected in 1966. De Valera retired in 1973 and died in a Dublin nursing home in 1975.

Diaghilev, Sergei [Pavlovich] (1872–1929)

Russian promoter of dance and the arts. The child of a general and an aristocrat, Diaghilev trained to study law in the 1890s at St. Petersburg, where he first encountered a group of like-minded people interested in the arts and the social sciences. In 1899 he founded the journal *Miriskusstva* (*World of Art*), which continued to publish until 1904 and featured the works of his Petersburg compatriots, including painters Alexander Benois and Léon Bakst. In 1906 he left Russia for France, where he found a community interested in recent developments in Eastern European art, as well as a culture more tolerant of his homosexuality. In 1909 he organized the Ballets Russes in Paris, a dance company inspired by the underhanded heroic achievements of German composer Richard Wagner (1813–1883) and French poet Charles-Pierre Baudelaire (1821–1867), featuring Russian-born American choreographer Michel Fokine (1880–1942) and Russian dancer Vaslav Nijinsky (1890–1950), among others. Diaghilev worked with numerous composers, collaborating on elaborate productions that consistently broke new creative ground. He produced three works with Russian composer Igor Stravinsky (1882–1971), including *The Firebird* (1910), *Petrushka* (1911), and *The Rite of Spring* (1913), all of which were highly esteemed and controversial pieces. Other collaborators included Russian composer Serge Prokofiev (1891–1953), French composer Claude Debussy (1862–1918), and German composer Richard Strauss (1864–1949). Touring with the Ballets Russes until the late 1920s, Diaghilev succumbed to diabetes in 1929.

Diaspora

Exile of the Jews. The Diaspora (from the Greek, meaning dispersion) is the name for the protracted exile of the Jewish people; however, today it refers to Jews who live outside the state of Israel. The Diaspora (or *galut*, Hebrew for exile) brought Jews into contact with different cultures, philosophies, and ways of life. The rhetoric of the Diaspora has often been linked to Zionism, as the term clearly implies that the homeless or dispersed Jews have a rightful homeland in what was once called Palestine.

The first major Diaspora, the Babylonian exile, occurred after the Babylonians conquered the Kingdom of Judah in 586 B.C.E., sending many Jews into slavery. Later, when the Jews were permitted to return, many of them chose to remain in their new locations throughout the Persian empire. The synagogue became an important institution as Jerusalem and the Temple became an impractical religious center for Jews living in exile.

The most significant Diaspora, which lasted for eighteen centuries and involved over 5 million Jews, began in the first century B.C.E., after the destruction of the Second Temple. Most Jews relocated to Alexandria, where by the first century C.E. forty percent of the population was Jewish. Others settled in Egypt and Syria (which were then parts of the Roman empire), Rome, and Asia Minor, and later Spain, France, and North Africa. Later, the persecutions of the Middle Ages sent many Jews to Eastern Europe, and after the Russian pogroms of the nineteenth century, many Jews fled to America, as well as to Australia and South Africa.

Until modern times, the Diaspora was viewed as a punishment for Israel's past sins. It was believed that the punishment would be lifted through messianic redemption, at the "ingathering of the exiles," when God appeared on earth and brought His people to Him. Discussion of the Diaspora today focuses on the tension between Jewishness and distinct national identities. Mainstream Orthodox Jews support the Zionist movement, which calls for the repatriation of all Jews in Israel. Many also believe in the idea of *shelilat ha-galut* (denial of the exile) and consider the Diaspora a sign of weakness, fearing the loss of Jewish identity through assimilation with other cultures. However, a segment of the Ultraorthodox movement does not recognize the modern state of Israel as legitimate, because it was not brought about by the coming of the Messiah. Reform Judaism maintains a nuanced position: its headquarters are in Jerusalem and its aims entirely in concordance with those of modern political Zionism, even as it acknowledges the validity of the Diaspora and claims no necessary links between Jewish religion, identity, and the land of Israel.

Díaz, Porfirio (1830–1915)

Mexican politican and military leader. Born into poverty in Oaxaca, Díaz was raised by his mother, and later by an uncle who became bishop of Oaxaca. His uncle offered him financial support on the condition that Díaz enter a seminary, which he did at the age of fifteen. But through his contact with Marcos Pérez, the leader of the Oaxacan Liberal faction, Díaz became interested in the new progressive ideas and left the seminary in 1849 to pursue studies in law, scorning his uncle's money. His studies were interrupted by the revolution of Ayutla, however, and Díaz joined the Liberal army, beginning his successful military career. He fought victoriously in the War of the Reform (1857–60) and in the struggle against the French (1861–67), which ended in Díaz's capture of Mexico City and made him a national hero.

Turning to politics, Díaz ran unsuccessfully for president in 1871 and 1875. After his second defeat, he launched the revolution of Tuxtepec, which deposed Sebastián Lerdo de Tejada and gave him the presidency. Díaz served as president from 1876 to 1880, and again from 1884 to 1911, during which time he established a strong, centralized state apparatus. He destroyed local and regional leaders, ensuring that the majority of public employees report directly to him, muffled the press, and controlled the courts. His government had a definite anti-Indian, pro-white racial cast and was more noted for its suppression of revolts than for any public services or improvements. He was, however, a consummate politician, selectively catering to the landed classes, the *mestizos,* and the nobility and playing them against one another; he ignored the Indians, mistreated the peasants, and repressed the labor movement. In 1908, amid growing opposition, Díaz announced that he would not seek reelection in 1910 and welcomed the formation of political parties. He later changed his mind, however, and decided instead to run against Francisco Madero. Madero was defeated, as expected, and resorted to a military takeover. Ciudad Juárez fell to the rebels in 1911 and Díaz went into exile in France, where he spent the last years of his life.

Díaz del Castillo, Bernal (c. 1496–1585)

Spanish soldier and author. Born in Spain to a family of modest means, Díaz sought his fortune in the Indies, spending some time first in Darién and then moving on to Cuba. He enlisted in various expeditions to the New World before joining Cortés's forces in February 1519. After the collapse of the Aztec empire at Tenochtitlán, Díaz participated in a number of punitive or pacifying forces missions, including Cortés's expedition to Honduras. In 1541 he left Mexico and moved to Santiago de los Caballeros de Guatemala, where he became a resident and a *regidor* (councilman) for life in the city's *cabildo* (municipal council). He married Teresa Becerra, the daughter of a *conquistador,* and with the help of her dowry was able to begin enjoying quiet, carefree days as an *encomendero.* It was during this time, when Bernal Díaz was already in his sixties, that he began writing his memoirs, collecting them in *Historia verdadera de la conquista de la Nueva España (The True History of the Conquest of New*

Spain). He had already started his work when he came into contact with Francisco López de Gómara's *Historia general de las Indias* (1552; *History of the Indies and Conquest of Mexico*), a work whose structure he imitated. Díaz made a point, however, of revising Gómara's text, contesting some of his details and emphasizing the role of Cortés's subordinates, including Díaz himself. The chronicle was disregarded, if not ignored, when it was first published more than fifty years after its completion in 1632, and it was not until the nineteenth century that it began to be appreciated. It remains today a priceless source for the study of the history and conquest of Mexico. Díaz's account is not an objective narration, but rather a personal and intuitive reconstruction of a dramatic life experience; it is valued for its description of the conqueror in action and the contradictions informing his life, as well as the expeditions on which he embarked.

Dickens, Charles (1812–1870)

English novelist. Dickens spent his childhood years in Chatham, England. Though his family was middle class, they fell into financial difficulties that propelled the elder Dickens into debtors' prison and caused young Charles to abandon his education for a period, often in order to work in a shoeblacking factory. During this time his family slipped into the ranks of the working class, an experience that would have a decisive impact on his writing. Dickens started his career as a writer in 1833 for magazines and newspapers, and through the course of his literary career, he became more popular than any other author had to that point. By 1836 he was asked to compose a series, which became known as *The Pickwick Papers* (1837). They attracted immediate attention, and he was encouraged to write *Oliver Twist* (1837–39), also published in installments. Both *The Pickwick Papers* and *Oliver Twist* manifest Dickens's concern with social problems and his satirical characterization of inhumane institutions. Dickens's success continued with the popular story *A Christmas Carol* (1843), although his early writing efforts were capped by *Dombey and Son* (1846–48) and the autobiographical *David Copperfield* (1849–50).

Between 1850 and 1870 Dickens produced some of his best-known works. In 1859 he wrote *A Tale of Two Cities*, followed by *Great Expectations* (1860–61), *Bleak House* (1852–53), *Little Dorrit* (1855–57), and *Hard Times* (1854). In these novels, Dickens develops complex characters and paints a critical view of society. He spent the last years of his life giving readings of his works and staging theatrical performances, most notably of the struggle between Sykes and Nancy in *Oliver Twist*. The power of his prose and message of social injustice and reform make Dickens one of the greats of nineteenth-century literature and an influential voice of conscience. The strenuous reading tours that Dickens undertook in England and America were physically exhausting and ultimately contributed to his death in 1870.

Dickinson, Emily (1830–1886)

American poet and letter writer. Considered one of the foremost poets of the American literary tradition, Dickinson was born in Amherst, Massachusetts, and remained there throughout her life, leaving the town on only a few occasions. She was a student at Amherst Academy and attended Mount Holyoke Female Seminary in nearby South Hadley for a year.

While Dickinson's experiences were severely circumscribed, her poetry reveals a woman whose days were marked by a powerful awareness of life and its meaning. A self-conscious individualism characterized her life, as evidenced by her experience with religion: in the midst of the evangelical revivals of the mid nineteenth century, as many of her classmates and family members underwent conversion, she resisted, even making public her doubts about the practices of mainstream Christianity. Her individualism lent itself to a life of increasing solitude, as she never married. Dickinson spent much of her time out-of-doors, taking in the green and flowered vastness of the New England countryside, and nature and its quiet, reflective enjoyment was one of the great themes of her poetry. Love (namely in *Further Poems*, published posthumously in 1929), and especially death, are two others; her musings on the impassioned finality of death are considered some of the most moving and thoughtful in American letters.

Dickinson avoided publishing her poems. During her lifetime, fewer than ten of the approximately 1,800 verses she wrote were published, and these without her consent. In the late 1880s, after her death, her sister, Lavinia, discovered her poems and had them published in three series: *Poems* (1890), (1891), and (1896).

Diddley, Bo (1928–)

African-American rock-and-roll singer and guitarist. Diddley's rumba rhythms, violent guitar playing, and sexy hip gyrations greatly influenced rock-and-roll musicians that followed, including Elvis Presley, Jimi Hendrix, the Rolling Stones, and the Yardbirds. His stage name is taken from the instrument known as a diddley bow.

Born Elias McDaniel, the young Diddley took violin lessons for twelve years, beginning at the age of five, after his move to Chicago from Mississipi. Strongly influenced by Nat "King" Cole, Louis Jordan, and John Lee Hooker, Diddley took up guitar and formed a streetcorner band. By 1955 his first single, "Bo Diddley," reached number two on the rhythm-and-blues chart. An appearance on television's "Ed Sullivan Show" that year brought his strik-ing visuals and infectious music into living rooms across the United States.

Although Diddley recorded only a few pop hits himself, many cover versions of his songs were recorded by American and British groups. He continued to record through 1967; some of his best-known recordings include "I'm a Man" (1955) and "Say Man" (1959). He has toured for over three decades, sporting a charismatic presence and a huge collection of unusually shaped guitars.

Diderot, Denis (1713–1784)

French encyclopedist, philosopher, novelist, dramatist, and art critic. After receiving the degree of master of arts from the University of Paris in 1732, Diderot left the academy to scrape by as a teacher, publisher's hack, and writer of religious sermons for missionaries. During this time he befriended Jean-Jacques Rousseau, beginning a fifteen-year relationship. In order to support his family (he had married Antoinette Champion in 1743), Diderot turned to translation work and in 1745 began work on the twenty-eight-volume *Encyclopédie ou dictionnaire raisonné des sciences, des arts et des métiers*, a massive project that preoccupied him for over twenty years and is considered a major work of the Enlightenment. For this project, originally intended by the publisher as a simple translation of an unambitious English encyclopedia, Diderot assembled some of the greatest minds of the French Enlightenment. The *Encyclopedia*, or "rational dictionary," was to assemble and synthesize the most advanced knowledge known to humankind. The time-consuming and difficult project was also plagued by personal and political struggles, including the covert removal of politically suspect passages by the book's publisher, André Le Breton. Upon completion of this giant work, Diderot once again needed to find a source of income and found a patron in Catherine the Great of Russia. She purchased Diderot's personal library but requested that his books remain in Paris and that he be retained as the librarian of his collection. Diderot continued to publish essays, plays, and novels for the duration of his life. Some of his notable works include *Lettre sur les aveugles* (1749; *An Essay on Blindness*), in which he proposed to teach the blind to read through touch a century before Louis Braille; his correspondence with his friend and mistress Sophie Volland, *Lettres à Sophie Volland*; and philosophical works. Diderot also wrote several plays and novels, including *Le Neveu de Rameau* (1762; *Rameau's Nephew*), *Jacques le Fataliste* (1796; *Jacques the Fatalist*), and the drama *Le Fils naturel* (1757; *Natural Son*).

Disappeared, The, *see* Desaparecidos, Los

Disney, Walt (1901–1966)

American animator, producer, and movie executive. After attending Kansas City Art Institute, Walt Disney began his first film studio, Laugh-o-Gram Films, which went bankrupt. He moved to Hollywood and began work on the *Alice in Cartoonland* series for M. J. Winkler. In 1927, after a salary dispute with Winkler, Disney formed Walt Disney Productions, where in 1928 he produced *Steamboat Willie*, the first synchronized sound cartoon featuring Mickey Mouse. Mickey Mouse was to go on to become one of Disney's most successful and universally recognized animated characters.

Although Walt Disney did not invent film animation, his name has become synonymous with it. Other pioneers in the field, including Emile Cohl (the "first animator," responsible for over 250 films during the early 1900s) and Winsor McCay (the man behind 1914's "Gertie the Dinosaur," the first animated personality), helped set the stage for the modern, full-scale animated movie, but Disney made animation (and Mickey Mouse) a permanent part of the American imagination. Disney was the first to present compelling cartoon characters, figures with distinctive and endearing qualities, readily identifiable and lovable. He was also the first to use sound in an animated film, manipulating sound, text, and image such that the film antics were coordinated with the sound. For example, in a scene featuring an animal concert in *Steamboat Willie*, a cow's body is transformed into a musical instrument, as udders become a bagpipe and teeth become a xylophone. Innovative techniques, combined with a keen business sense, made Disney's studio the nearly unchallenged leader of the animation industry.

In 1932 his studio produced *Flowers and Trees*, the first Technicolor cartoon and the first to win an Academy Award. *Snow White*, the first feature-length cartoon, was released in 1937. In 1954 Disney began hosting the "Disneyland" TV series, which featured Disney Studio productions, including high-quality cartoons, live-action features, and wildlife documentaries. (The show's name was later changed to "The Wonderful World of Disney.") Disneyland, a Disney-themed amusement park featuring many of the famous Disney animated characters, opened in Anaheim, California, in 1955; Walt Disney World opened in 1971 in Orlando, Florida, and EuroDisney in France in the early 1990s.

divine kingship

Ancient sovereign principle. The concept of divine kingship, the belief in the divinity of the king, exists in a number of African cultural traditions scattered across the continent. The origins of the concept are not known, but the famous pharaoh-gods of ancient Egypt provide some of the earliest recorded examples of this type of kingship system.

Divine kingship exists among the Buganda of Uganda, the Asante (or Ashanti) of Ghana, the Nyoro and Nyamwezi of East Africa, the Lunda and

Shona of southern Africa, and many others. There are a number of characteristic beliefs and traits in societies where divine kingship is practiced. Divine kings are usually believed to control the forces of nature, since the main function of a divine king is to supply his subjects' crops with rain for a bountiful harvest. As a god, or as a mortal endowed with the spirit of a divine ancestor, the divine king usually maintains a hierarchical distance from his subjects; in some cultures, the king is always seated behind a curtain, and no one is permitted to gaze on him. Ritual regicide (the killing of the divine king at the end of his reign) was a feature of the ancient Egyptian divine kingship system, and was widespread in many other African cultures. The burial of divine kings was also often accompanied by human sacrifices.

In many societies, a king's life is symbolized by a sacred fire that is kept burning throughout his life, to be extinguished only at his death. Among the ancient Egyptians, divine kings often married their sisters. And in many cultures, divine kings were often identified with the moon and were deified in death, honored with libations and sacrifices.

Dogon

People of Mali, West Africa. The majority of the Dogon live in the Bandigara district of Mali and work in agriculture. Estimated at 250,000, the Dogon have been until recently relatively isolated from outside influences, and for this reason anthropologists have been drawn to study their complex mythology. Believed to be descended from the original inhabitants of the Niger River Valley, many of them live in the caves along the cliffs of the Hombori Mountains. Though there is no centralized government, each large district has a *hogon*, or spiritual leader. *Hogons* are responsible for the highly prized masks used in ceremonies and celebrations. Made of fiber

or wood, the masks portray a wide variety of plants, reptiles, birds, mammals, objects, and people. Some of the more significant ceremonies in which they appear include the great feast of *sigui*, which recurs every sixty years as a celebration of renewal. The *sigui* is orchestrated by the Awa society, which is made up entirely of initiated men. This group also conducts the funerary rites called *bago bundo*, and the *dama* celebration, which closes the period of mourning for deceased men. Both of these rites involve masked dances, and masks are also employed in agricultural rites.

Dome of the Rock

Islamic mosque. Built around a sacred rock in Jerusalem, the Dome of the Rock is the oldest extant Islamic shrine, built in the seventh century, some five hundred years before domes were put to widespread use. Sacred to Jews and Muslims, it is thought to be the site where Abraham was ordered by God to sacrifice his son Isaac. The Temple of Solomon also stood on this ground. Islamic tradition holds that Muhammad was taken from Mecca to Jerusalem by the archangel Gabriel in order to meet Abraham, Moses, and Jesus at this site. Muhammad then ascended from the rock into heaven to receive Allâh's message, which he imparted to the world as the teachings of Islam. The unusual structure was commissioned by 'Abd al-Malik ibn Marwan during his caliphate, as a shelter for pilgrims. At various times during the Crusades, the Dome served as the headquarters for the Knights Templar. Today the mosque is an important destination for Muslim pilgrimages.

Donelaitis, Kristijonas (1714–1780)

Lithuanian poet. The son of peasants living in a mixed Lithuanian-German neighborhood, Donelaitis left home at the age of seventeen to study at the University of Königsberg, graduating in

1740. He became pastor of a Lutheran parish in Tolmingkehmen, East Prussia, in 1743 and remained there until the end of his life. Donelaitis's various poetic works were circulated in manuscript form. Of these, six fables and the epic poem *Metai* (1818; *The Four Seasons*) have survived. Consisting of four parts and written in classical hexameter, *The Four Seasons* depicts the natural setting of the so-called Lithuania Minor, its people, their work, and their customs. The poem gives a realistic portrayal of Lithuanian peasant life in the eighteenth century, as it was affected by German colonization. It also contains many didactic motifs and instructive, moral, and religious precepts. The clarity of its images and the richness of its language place Donelaitis's poem among the classic works of world literature. It was highly esteemed by Goethe and Adam Mickiewicz, and won Donelaitis widespread European recognition, making him the first Lithuanian poet to have an international profile.

Don Juan

Western literary character. Don Juan is one of the more compelling figures in Western literature, a heroic libertine whose refusal to repent for his egregious sins sends him to his doom. Don Juan cannot be traced to a single, originary text; over five hundred versions of the legend tell similar but sometimes conflicting stories. The first fictional appearance of the character occurs in *El burlador de Sevilla* (1630; *The Seducer of Seville*), written by the Spanish dramatist Tirso de Molina. Don Juan is portrayed as a lover of women, using their weaknesses to his advantage by making false promises to peasant girls and by seducing wealthy women. He eventually becomes the victim of his own treachery and is damned to hell.

Most accounts rely to some degree on this version of the legend. Don Juan seduces a young girl and then kills her father, who had dared to disapprove of him. Don Juan visits the man's tomb and casually invites the corpse to dinner. Shockingly, the ghost shows up for dinner, foreshadowing Don Juan's imminent death, though he laughs off this sign. In the end, Don Juan refuses to repent and is therefore eternally damned. The religious and moral undertones of the story are apparent, as is the lesson of punishment for those who sin.

The evolution of the Don Juan character manifested itself in poetry, the novel, and the opera. The most celebrated adaptation of the myth is the opera *Don Giovanni* (1787), by Austrian composer Mozart (1756–1791). Over the centuries, the story became a worldwide phenomenon. Seventeenth-century Italian singers traveled to France with the legend, while German and Flemish versions appeared as well. The eighteenth century brought about more comical readings, in the form of light operas and puppet shows. These renditions, such as *Don Giovanni*, recast Don Juan in a more romantic, almost heroic role. Don Juan's intentions became very idealistic: either he was searching for the perfect woman or he was desiring the company of many to satisfy his insatiable appetite. Other notable versions include French writer Molière's *Le Festin de pierre* (1665; *The Stone Feast*); British poet Lord Byron's epic satire *Don Juan* (1819–24), and English dramatist George Bernard Shaw's *Man and Superman* (1903). *Don Juan Tenorio* (1844), by José Zorrilla y Moral, remains the most treasured version in Spain. Traditionally, on the eve of All Souls' Day (Halloween), this play is performed to enormous crowds. This interpretation is more sympathetic to the main character, as he is spared eternal punishment in the end.

Donne, John (1572–1631)

English poet. Donne was born in London to a well-to-do tradesman father and a mother who came from a high-ranking

Roman Catholic family. Donne was raised in his mother's faith and reared by Jesuits. He and his family often suffered for their unorthodox beliefs; a brother was jailed for concealing a priest, and eventually died in prison. Until he renounced his faith and joined the Church of England, his own career was hindered by his religious affiliation—religious oppression forced him to leave Oxford without a degree. In the 1590s he studied law at the Inns of Court and read widely in theology. It was during this period that he wrote *Songs and Sonnets* (1633), a series of love poems that were mildly bawdy and displayed a coarseness slightly subversive of Elizabethan convention. (He would later renounce these writings.) Looking to improve his position, he took a job as secretary for the powerful Sir Thomas Edgerton. Donne fell in love with Lady Edgerton's niece, a woman named Ann More, and married her secretly. The union was discovered, and Sir Edgerton responded to the socially disastrous marriage by firing Donne and having him imprisoned. Later forgiven, Donne and his new wife had several children and lived in poverty for many years. At the age of forty-three, Donne renounced his Catholicism and took his vows with the Church of England, making possible a career as a member of the clergy. He published several tracts attacking the Jesuits, did much work for the Church, and became dean of Saint Paul's Cathedral in 1621, four years after his wife's death. As dean, he was one of the most powerful religious leaders in England. During these final years, Donne's health declined rapidly and his poetry became obsessively concerned with disease, death, and the idea of communion with God.

Donne's work faded to relative obscurity until the twentieth century, when the first generation of Anglo-American modernists inaugurated a return to Donne. His influence can be seen in the works of such prominent twentieth-century writers as Irish poet W. B. Yeats and American poet T. S. Eliot, among other prominent twentieth-century poets. Some of his most famous verses are the sonnets "Death Be Not Proud" and "Batter My Heart, Three Person'd God," both of which are a part of his "Holy Sonnets," written primarily between 1609 and 1611.

Donoso, José (1924–)

Chilean writer. Born in Santiago to a prominent family, Donoso quit school at age nineteen and traveled in South America, where he worked on sheep farms and as a dockhand. Later, he returned to school in the United States and received a B.A. from Princeton University in 1951. Donoso spent the next decade working as a teacher and journalist in Chile, writing profusely. In 1955 Donoso published his first book, *Veraneo y otros cuentos* (*Summer Vacation and Other Stories*), which received the Municipal Literary Prize; one year later, he published *Dos cuentos* (1956; *Two Short Stories*), and in 1957 his first novel, *Coronación* (*Coronation*), appeared to much critical acclaim. *Coronation* describes the moral collapse of an aristocratic family, a recurrent theme in Donoso's work and the subject of some of his most accomplished writings. Marrying María Pilar Serrano, a Bolivian painter, in 1961, Donoso began writing what is often considered his masterpiece, *El obsceno pájaro de la noche* (1970; *The Obscene Bird of Night*). He also renewed his friendship with Mexican novelist Carlos Fuentes, whom he had met in grade school. While spending some time at Fuentes's home, he completed *El lugar sin límites* (1966; *Hell Has No Limits*) and *Este domingo* (1966; *This Sunday*), grim novels of psychological desolation and anguish.

In the late 1960s Donoso left Chile for Spain, where he completed *The Obscene Bird of Night*. In this disturbing and breathtaking work, the joys and travails of everyday life are set against the degenerate world of the doomed aristocracy, which lives sequestered in a grotesque world of bodily putrefaction. His second great novel, *Casa de campo* (1978; *A House in the Country*), is an allegory of the years preceding the military coup that deposed President Salvador Allende, again inflected with a powerful flair for the grotesque. The surreal existentialism of his early works have become increasingly politicized, as trademark Donoso concerns have been more explicitly set against social and political backgrounds. His most recent work, *Le desesperanza* (1986; *Despair*), is a representation of life under the repressive and often brutal dictatorship of Augusto Pinochet. Donoso's significance as a representative figure of the resurgence of Latin American literature is considered equal to that of Carlos Fuentes and Colombian novelist Gabriel García Márquez.

Dorado, El

A kingdom in a Latin American Indian legend. The legend of the city of El Dorado originated in Latin American Indian stories about a king in the interior of present-day Colombia who had gold dusted over his body and then bathed in Lake Guatavita, offering the gold to the gods. Spanish *conquistadores* who heard the tale as early as 1530 embarked on many expeditions in search of El Dorado, this mythical city full of gold and precious jewels; the legend was so greatly embellished, however, that the Spaniards did not recognize its source in the Chibcha empire when they discovered it. Although El Dorado was never found, belief in this kingdom led to journeys that yielded valuable information about South American geography and particularly the interior of the continent, thereby facilitating its conquest. Numerous expeditions to find El Dorado were attempted, including those led by Gonzalo Pizarro, Francisco de Orellana, and Gonzalo Jiménez de Quesada, but all

failed to find the mythical city. Englishman Sir Walter Raleigh led an expedition in the Orinoco region in 1595, and again in 1617; his plans linked the discovery of El Dorado to an English takeover of Spanish America, but they proved a dismal failure. The legend of El Dorado appears often in Western literature, most notably in English poet John Milton's *Paradise Lost* (1663), Voltaire's *Candide* (1759), and Carpentier's *Los pasos perdidos* (*The Lost Steps*). More recently, the term has come to mean anyplace where wealth can be gained easily and quickly.

Dostoevsky, Fyodor [Mikhailovich] (1821–1881)

Russian novelist. Dostoevsky was born in Moscow, the second of eight children. After his mother's death, he entered the Military Engineering School in St. Petersburg, where he completed the course of study and spent a year in the army before resigning in contempt. He began writing, translating French authors and publishing his first novel, *Bednye liudi* (*Poor Folk*), in 1846. His next novel, *Dvoinik* (1846; *The Double*), and the various short stories he published over the next several years were critical and financial failures. It is believed that the epilepsy that would plague him throughout his life first came to him during these years, although some believe that it began earlier, at about the time that Dostoevsky's father was murdered by his serfs, who killed him by pouring vodka down his throat until he drowned. In 1847 Dostoevsky joined the Petrashevsky circle, a group of democratic-minded St. Petersburg intellectuals, which met often to read and discuss the works of French utopian socialists and other works forbidden to them by the czarist regime. In 1849 members of the group were arrested; Dostoevsky was imprisoned for eight months, then taken to an execution site, blindfolded, and threatened by a shot fired above his head. After this false execution, Dostoevsky and his alleged fellow conspirators were exiled to the labor camps of Siberia.

Four years in a labor camp gave way to six years in the army, a time in which Dostoevsky read extensively in the Bible and came into direct and extended contact with the Russian lower class that he would chronicle so effectively later, combining both influences notably in *Idiot* (1868). During his army service, Dostoevsky met and married the widow Maria Dmitriyevna Isayeva in 1857. He was released from the army in 1859, and returned to St. Petersburg, where he began to write and publish again, producing *Selo Stepanchikovo* (1859; A Friend of the Family), Unizhennye i oskorblënnye (1861; The Insulted and Injured), and Zapiski iz mert vogo doma (1861; Memoirs from the House of the Dead). After a series of trips to Western Europe, in 1864 Dostoevsky assumed the editorship of his brother's new journal, *Epokha* (*Epoch*), in which Zapiski iz podpolia (1864; Notes from the Underground) first appeared. Notes from the Underground is often regarded as his most succinct and brilliant work, a precursor existentialist text that describes the isolation and glib mean-spiritedness of a man on the margins of modernity. Dostoevsky wrote this novel while tending to his dying wife. Pressed for funds after the death of his brother, Dostoevsky tried to make *Epokha* successful, but his conservative political slant hampered sales. Addicted to gambling, he completed a massive text he hoped would pull him out of debt, Prestuplenie i nakazanie (Crime and Punishment), which was serialized in 1866. Igrok (The Gambler) appeared in the same year, but as Dostoevsky was well behind deadline, he was forced to hire a stenographer and dictate his novel to her. This woman, Anna Grigoryevna Snitkina, became his second wife in 1867; though she was not an intellectual, her sober mind and adoration for her husband helped curb his desire to gam-

ble and transformed him into a solid family man for the last quarter of his life. Despite this change of heart, the couple had to flee Russia in 1868 to escape creditors. While abroad, Dostoevsky completed one of his best short novels, Vechnyi muzh (1870; The Eternal Husband), and also began taking notes for his last work, Bratia Karamazovy (The Brothers Karamazov), which was published in 1880; it is often considered to be his greatest work. At times a revision of Crime and Punishment, but also a captivating portrayal of the sources of doubt, faith, and hope, The Brothers Karamazov was a great critical and popular success, the guarantee of his lasting fame.

Douglass, Frederick (1818–1895)

African-American slave and abolitionist. Born Frederick Augustus Washington Bailey, Douglass was an escaped slave who achieved prominence through his work in the abolitionist movement, becoming one of the most important humanitarians of the nineteenth century. Born to a slave, Harriet Bailey, and an unknown white father, Douglass was sent to Baltimore in 1825 to live as a house servant. There he was taught to read by his master's wife, in defiance of state law. This education was soon interrupted by his master, however, and Bailey's further education was gleaned from schoolboys in the street. In 1838 he made his second, successful attempt to escape, settling in New Bedford, Massachusetts, and changing his name to Douglass to avoid capture as a fugitive slave.

In 1841 Douglass was invited to speak to an antislavery convention and so greatly impressed the audience with his oratory that he was catapulted into a new career as an agent for the Anti-Slavery Society. Encountering widespread disbelief that an ex-slave could be capable of such intelligence and eloquent speech, Douglass published his famous autobiography, *The Life and*

Times of Frederick Douglass (1845), in which he revealed his true name and that of his master. To avoid recapture, Douglass traveled to England on a two-year speaking tour, but returned with sufficient funds to purchase his freedom and to start his own antislavery newspaper, *The North Star* (later *Frederick Douglass' Paper*) in Rochester, New York, from 1847 to 1860. During the Civil War, Douglass was a consultant to President Abraham Lincoln, and was instrumental in creating the black regiments of the Union army. Throughout the Reconstruction era, Douglass remained an outspoken advocate for full civil rights for freed slaves. He was assigned to a variety of government posts, but remains best known for his unwavering commitment to social justice and racial equality.

Dovzhenko, Aleksandr [Petrovich] (1894–1956)

Ukrainian film director, writer, and artist. Considered the father of Ukrainian filmmaking, Dovzhenko brought international recognition to the Soviet film industry during the 1930s. Born to a peasant family of Cossack descent, Dovzhenko was one of two surviving children out of fourteen. After graduating from a teachers' seminary, he taught science at a secondary school and participated in the civil war in Ukraine as a member of a left-wing nationalist party. Working at the Ukrainian diplomatic missions in Warsaw and Berlin in 1921–23, he also studied painting. He returned to Ukraine in 1923 and worked as a political cartoonist for a newspaper and as a book illustrator. In 1926 he moved to Odessa and started working at the Odessa film studio, making his directorial debut with a short comedy called *Yagodki lyubvi* (1926; *The Fruits of Love*), followed by a political thriller, *Sumka dypkur iera* (1927; *The Diplomatic Pouch*). Dovzhenko's unique vision was first fully revealed in *Zvenigora* (1928), an extraordinary mixture of leg-

end and history evoking a thousand years of Ukrainian peasant life. The recurrent theme concerns a legendary treasure buried in a magic mountain, Zvenigora. His next film, *Arsenal* (1929), gives a synoptic view of the misery and heroism of the revolution in Ukraine, centering on the struggle for the Kiev munitions factory. In 1930 came Dovzhenko's masterpiece, *Zemlya* (*The Earth*), the first picture he made at the Kiev studio. The story is slight; the film interprets in sensitive visual symbolism the almost mystical closeness of the Ukrainian peasant to his land. In 1958 it was ranked by an international jury at the Brussels film festival among the twelve best films in world cinematography; when it was released in the Soviet Union, however, it was denounced as "counterrevolutionary." Totally shocked by this response and near breakdown, Dovzhenko went to Europe, where he lectured and showed his films. Upon his return, he made his first sound film, *Ivan* (1932), in which he imparted passionate lyricism to the most unlikely subject—the story of a simple young peasant at the construction of the Dnieper dam; it was again severely criticized and led to his dismissal from the Kiev studio. Dovzhenko's later films—*Aerograd* (1935; known as *Frontier*); *Shchors* (1939, which won the first of two Stalin prizes, one in 1941 and the other in 1949); and *Michurin* (1946; *Life in Blossom*)—are marked by his forced submission to the dogmas of Socialist Realism. However, as much as was possible in the Stalinist Soviet Union, he tried to maintain his artistic and philosophic integrity and welcomed the cultural thaw of the 1950s. He also published a few dozen short stories, the autobiographical novel *Zacharovana Desna* (1955; *The En-chanted*), and several film scripts that were made into motion pictures by his widow, Yulia Solntseva.

Dream of the Red Chamber, see Hong Lou Meng

Dreiser, Theodore [Herman Albert] (1871–1945)

American novelist and social realist. Dreiser's literary efforts were greatly influenced by, and associated with, the naturalist movement in the United States, and focused primarily on exposing the adverse social and political effects of the modern industrialized world on the everyday lives of ordinary people.

During Dreiser's childhood, his family experienced severe poverty. His father, a German immigrant millworker, and his Czech mother had ten children, of which Dreiser was the ninth. Dreiser did not receive a formal education, but began working in Chicago and on the East Coast as a newspaper reporter in his early twenties. Reading the works of Herbert Spencer confirmed Dreiser's conviction that people are pushed and controlled by greater, external political and economic events, and that within society itself, people are forced, unfairly, to compete against each other in order to survive.

Dreiser's first novel, *Sister Carrie*, was completed in 1899 but was not widely distributed due to the publisher's reservations concerning the content of the work. Hailed as the first true naturalist novel, *Sister Carrie* tells the story of a small-town girl who runs away to the city to fulfill her ambitions as a Broadway actress. She is used by, and in turn uses, the men in her life. The novel was a commercial failure, and Dreiser fell into a severe depression soon after.

In 1911 Dreiser wrote *Jennie Gerhardt*, his second novel, a tale infused with sexual promiscuity and issues of wealth and power. Next he wrote two volumes of his trilogy on the American financier Charles T. Yerkes, *The Financier* (1912) and *The Titan* (1914). In 1925 Dreiser published a novel based on a famous murder case, *An American Tragedy*, which won him much critical and financial success. The novel's powerful criticism of the American legal system thrust Dreiser into prominence as an advocate for social justice.

Throughout the late 1920s and most of the 1930s, Dreiser's writing took a backseat to his politics, his travels, and his public appearances in support of various social causes. He visited the Soviet Union in 1944. During the 1940s he completed *The Bulwark* and the third volume of the Yerkes trilogy, *The Stoic*, both of which were published posthumously.

Dreyfus Affair

French political controversy. This twelve-year controversy surrounding Captain Alfred Dreyfus (1859–1935), an assimilated Jewish career officer in the French army, revealed the deep roots of anti-Semitism in the French Third Republic. Dreyfus was the son of a wealthy Alsatian textile manufacturer who decided on a military career after attending the École Polytechnique in Paris. In October 1894 he was arrested on charges of selling military secrets to the Germans. The case aroused strong emotions in France, which had never fully recovered from its crushing defeat in the Franco-Prussian War in 1871. Dreyfus was summarily convicted and sentenced to life imprisonment on Devil's Island, despite an almost complete lack of evidence against him.

His family continued to profess Dreyfus's innocence and demand a retrial but were, for years, virtually ignored. The French press, led by Édouard Drumont's virulently anti-Semitic newspaper, *La Libre Parole*, maintained his guilt and stoked popular sentiment against him. As evidence gradually came to light in support of Dreyfus, prominent figures spoke out on his behalf. The acclaimed novelist Émile Zola wrote a famous open letter that was published on the front page of the newspaper *Aurore* under the headline "J'Accuse" ("I Accuse"). Zola's letter, in which he accused the army of covering up the truth, nearly landed him in prison on charges of libel. Zola then fled across the Channel to England.

French opinion was split: the Dreyfusards (his supporters) versus the anti-Dreyfusards (his accusers). In 1898 one of the key witnesses against Dreyfus committed suicide after confessing to perjury. The following year, a second conspirator escaped to England, aware that the truth would soon emerge. A new ministry, headed by René Waldeck-Rousseau, took office in 1899. Dreyfus was brought back to France for a retrial that same year. He was found guilty yet again, but was pardoned by the new government. Finally, in 1906, Dreyfus managed to clear his own name and was reinstated to his position in the army by a special act of parliament.

In retrospect, the Dreyfus Affair was a pivotal event in French history that encouraged a sharper alignment between political and social factions and which prefaced the 1905 separation of church and state and the problematic division between right-wing nationalists and left-wing antimilitarists, affecting French life through the First World War.

Druids

Ancient Celtic priests. In ancient British, Irish, and Gaulish society, these priests or "wise men" were as highly regarded as the chiefs or secular leaders. The earliest mention of the Druids is in the third century B.C.E., although Caesar's *Gallic Wars* is the primary source of reliable information about the Druids and the culture of the Celts. Medieval Irish epics seem to bear out Caesar's account.

The resurgence of interest in the Druids during and after the countercultural revolution of the 1960s emphasized the mystical aspects of the Druids and their society, when in fact their importance to Celtic society made them the equal of secular leaders. As religious and temporal authorities, the Druids made law, judged legal cases, passed sentence, and educated the ruling classes. As society's

advocates before the divine, the Druids performed ritual sacrifices (including occasional human sacrifices, when people and animals were enclosed in enormous wicker baskets and set aflame) and administered grace. The religious and legal spheres overlapped: members of Celtic society who were tried and found guilty of breaking laws were prohibited from participating in religious observance and sacrifice.

Knowledge of the Druids is scant, significantly because the traditions and rituals of the Druids were exclusively oral. However, it is known that the Druids revered the oak tree and believed in the immortality of the soul, thinking that the souls of the dead were transferred to new humans. Following the Roman conquest, after Tiberius (r. 14–37) declared their existence illegal and after the traditions of Roman law displaced Druidic authority, the Druidic class collapsed. Only in Ireland, which did not experience Roman rule, did the Druids survive until 500 C.E., losing their traditional authority as Christianity arrived.

Du Bois, W[illiam] E[dward] B[urghardt] (1868–1963)

African-American teacher, writer, and civil rights activist. Du Bois is one of the most influential figures in the history of the struggle for racial equality in the United States. He was involved in every major African-American movement and organization from 1900 to the 1950s, and he wrote twenty-one books, including novels and poetry collections, edited fifteen volumes, and published well over one hundred major articles on race relations.

Born in Great Barrington, Massachusetts, of mixed African, Dutch, and French heritage, Du Bois was the only black student in his high school. His father left the family when Du Bois was a small child, and his mother died the year of his high school graduation, 1884. With the aid of a scholarship, he graduated from Fisk University in 1888 and entered Harvard, earning a B.A. in 1890 and an M.A. in 1891. After studying at the University of Berlin for two years, he returned to Harvard and in 1895 became the first African-American there to receive a Ph.D. His dissertation, *The Suppression of the African Slave-Trade to the United States of America, 1638–1870*, was published in 1896 as the first of the Harvard Historical Classics. Du Bois taught Latin, Greek, German, and English at Wilberforce College before becoming a professor of economics and history at Atlanta University from 1897 to 1910. During these years he produced some sixteen research monographs on blacks in America, including *The Philadelphia Negro: A Social Study* (1899), the first case study of a black community in the United States, and the partly autobiographical *Souls of Black Folk* (1903). He helped found the Niagara Movement in 1905, a group primarily concerned with countering what Du Bois viewed as the influential accommodationist positions of Booker T. Washington. Though he had originally agreed with the view advocated by Washington that vocational training for unskilled blacks would eventually lead to economic equality, Du Bois came to criticize the gradualist approach and publicly demanded immediate equal economic, civil, and political rights. Moving sharply away from Washington's conservative positions, he cofounded the National Negro Committee in 1909 and then joined its successor, the National Association for the Advancement of Colored People (NAACP) in 1910 as director of research and editor of its journal, *Crisis*.

Du Bois subsequently became the most influential spokesman for equal rights. Due to his outspoken, changing views on the means to that end, including the creation of self-sufficient black communities and his interest in Marxism, Du Bois left the NAACP in 1934. He resumed teaching and research at Atlanta University for ten years, becoming head of its department of sociology; founding *Phylon*, a "review of race and culture"; beginning a projected encyclopedia of black Americans; and publishing *Black Reconstruction: An Essay Toward a History of the Part Which Black Folk Played in the Attempt to Reconstruct Democracy in America, 1860–1880* (1935), a Marxist interpretation of the Reconstruction era, and *Dusk of Dawn: An Essay Toward an Autobiography of a Race Concept* (1940). He returned to the NAACP as director of special research from 1944 to 1948, and headed the Council for African Affairs from 1948 to 1951. During these years Du Bois became convinced of the need for socialism to promulgate world peace and to further the cause of blacks everywhere. He ran for senator from New York in 1950 on the American Labor Party ticket, garnering a quarter of a million votes. He also helped organize and participated in several Pan-African Congresses. Because of his opposition to the Cold War and his membership in the Peace Information Center, he was indicted in 1951 for being an unregistered agent of a foreign power. He was acquitted, but grew increasingly disillusioned about the possibilities of radical change in America. Awarded a Lenin Peace Prize in 1959, he joined the American Communist Party two years later and then emigrated to Ghana, where he transferred his citizenship. He had been invited by President Kwame Nkrumah to supervise the projected *Encyclopedia Africana*. He died in Accra, Ghana, at the age of ninety-five, and was given a state funeral. The year 1993 saw the publication of David Levering Lewis's biography, *W. E. B. DuBois: The Biography of a Race*.

Du Fu (712–770 C.E.)

Chinese poet. Together with Li Bai (701–62), Du is considered to be one of the two greatest poets in Chinese literature—hence the Chinese literary reference "Li Du," which refers to both poets. He spent much of his youth traveling, during which time he met and befriended the older poet, Li Bai. Though born to a conventional Confucian family, he experimented with Taoism during his travels with Li. At this time his verse celebrated the natural world and longed for the unchanging eternal. He returned to settle down and seek his fortune as an official, but repeatedly failed the imperial exams, earning for himself a meager post in Changan. He began writing political tracts couched in poetic and flattering language in an attempt to gain the attention of the court. When the Anlushan rebellion took place in 755, Du was held captive but managed to escape. The emperor Shu Zong then offered him a job as censor, but his style conflicted with that of the emperor and he was soon dismissed from the post. He suffered several years in extreme poverty, lost several children to hunger and malnutrition, and began writing sadly impassioned verse about the travails of humanity caught in the meaningless war. Though he worked briefly for a warlord, recovering some sense of dignity and stability, he spent his last years wandering aimlessly. He was acknowledged as the greatest of Chinese poets, a writer with a grasp of all genres of poetry, accomplished especially in the *Lü Shi*, or "regulated verse." Over 1,400 of Du Fu's poems survive today.

Dunbar, Paul Laurence (1872–1906)

American poet. Dunbar was the first black poet to attain national and international recognition. He was celebrated in his own time for poems written in African-American dialect, and his standard English poems and fiction have recently received attention.

Paul Laurence Dunbar was born in Dayton, Ohio, the son of two former Kentucky slaves. During high school, he became interested in writing, but he lacked the money to attend college and found himself unable to find work as a journalist. While supporting himself as an elevator operator, Dunbar read widely in English poetry and was able to sell a few poems in Standard English to newspapers.

After receiving encouragement from friends to keep writing, Dunbar began experimenting with the dialect poetry that would make him famous. Many of these early poems are collected in his first published work, *Oak and Ivy* (1893). The poems frequently romanticize plantation life and are populated with benevolent, paternalistic masters and happy, simple slaves. Ironically, Dunbar's knowledge of Southern life came entirely from stories he had heard from his relatives; he did not visit the South until 1898.

Dunbar was always ambivalent about his dialect poetry; in his 1895 collection, *Majors and Minors*, he showcased his Standard English poems at the front of the volume and labeled them "majors," while the "minor" dialect efforts were grouped in the back. Despite this emphasis, the novelist and critic William Dean Howells focused on the "happy darky" poems in his glowing review of the book. Howells's praise assured Dunbar's reputation as a major American poet. His *Lyrics of a Lowly Life* (1896) became an instant best-seller in America and abroad. His fame allowed him to travel abroad and eventually brought him a degree of financial security.

In his later career, Dunbar focused increasingly on fiction. His novels, which include *The Fanatics* (1901) and *The Sport of the Gods* (1902), are more directly concerned with race matters. The books explore themes that would become central to later African-American authors, including Southern segregation and black disillusionment with Northern urban life. Dunbar also made significant contributions to American musical theater in his collaborations with composer Will Marion Cook.

Although Dunbar was frequently criticized after his death as an apologist for white racism, much of his work has recently come under closer scrutiny and been acclaimed for its subtle strategies of protesting racial injustice while retaining a broad audience. His poems "We Wear the Mask" and "Sympathy" (with its famous line "I know why the caged bird sings") have become American classics.

Dürer, Albrecht (1471–1528)

German painter and engraver. Trained originally as a goldsmith, Dürer was the first German artist to garner a reputation outside his own country. His travels to Italy introduced him to Renaissance art, which he then adapted into his own work. Dürer was also greatly influenced by the teachings of Martin Luther and sought to reconcile the strict doctrines of the Reformation with the classical beauty and humanist elements of Renaissance art. The result is Dürer's highly rational sense of proportion and perspective, which lends itself both to fantasy and more realistic depictions. Religious themes were central to both Dürer's woodcuts and engravings, in which he displayed an unsurpassed technical mastery, and his portraits. Some of his more famous pieces include the series of woodcuts *Apokalypse* (1498; *Apocalypse*), *Großen Passion* (1504; *Passion of Christ*), and *Marienleben* (1510; *Life of the Virgin*). Dürer also painted numerous self-portraits and religious works, including altarpieces, as well as some delightfully detailed watercolors of landscapes and animal life. In his later years, Dürer also wrote studies of perspective, human anatomy, and geometry.

Durkheim, Émile (1858–1917)

French social scientist. Durkheim established a methodology to combine social theory with rigorous empirical logic and the new discoveries of social anthropology. Working in France during the materialistic revolutions of Marxist thought

and Communist uprisings, Durkheim was a forerunner of French social anthropologist Claude Lévi-Strauss and is considered to be the founder of the French school of sociology.

Durkheim was born in Épinal, France, to a relatively poor Jewish family. The early death of his father and the constant conflict between France and Germany combined to make Durkheim a disciplined young man who preferred hard work to pleasure. He attended the best schools in France, graduating from the École Normale Supérieure in Paris in 1882. In 1887 he became professor of social philosophy at the University of Bordeaux, a position he held until 1902. While there, he began the journal *L'Année Sociologique* in 1896 and wrote some of his most important works, *De la division du travail social* (1893; *The Division of Labor in Society*) and *Le Suicide* (1897; *Suicide*). Becoming a full professor in 1906 at the University of Paris, Durkheim continued his writing, publishing *Les Formes élémentaires de la vie religieuse* (1915; *The Elementary Forms of the Religious Life*).

Very much influenced by contemporary events, including the Paris Commune of 1871 and its bloody repression, the general trend of philosophy to attempt to operate from the real world instead of pure abstraction, and the growing anti-Semitism that he encountered, Durkheim did not believe that strict observation, like historical accounts, could yield knowledge of concrete reality. History could explain how events occurred, but not why they occurred; history could not give causes. Durkheim believed that social groups had an internal unity and social milieu, part of a collective consciousness that determined the norms and goals of individuals and totemic beliefs such as religion. He believed that historical events had to be studied through the collective consciousness.

Through the work of Durkheim, sociology became a recognized discipline that both affected and influenced the study of many other disciplines, including law, economics, and history.

Dürrenmatt, Friedrich (1921–)

Swiss playwright and novelist. Dürrenmatt's writings are characterized by a penetrating irony and a sense of the bizarre. Like German writer Bertolt Brecht, Dürrenmatt also attempts to disrupt the stage illusion of his dramas, to challenge the audience to think about the content of the play in a more detached manner.

Dürrenmatt was the son of a pastor once jailed for writing a satirical political poem. Studying in Bern and Zurich, he left university to pursue a career as a painter. It is at this time that he also began writing, and his first play, *Es Steht Geschrieben* (*It Is Written*), which was loosely based on the fanatic Münster Anabaptist uprising of 1533–36, premiered in 1947, although it was not published until 1959. He acquired international renown for a pair of plays written in the mid-1950s, *Der Besuch der alten Dame* (1956; *The Visit*) and *Die Physiker* (1962; *The Physicists*). Though Dürrenmatt is most noted for *The Visit*, *The Physicists* was almost as successful. Dürrenmatt has written numerous plays, and together with Max Frisch was considered to be a central figure in the post–World War II revival of German-language theater in Switzerland. Dürrenmatt also authored numerous essays, including *Theaterprobleme* (1955; "Problems of the Theatre"), which was originally a lecture he delivered in many European cities, and several detective novels.

Dvořák, Antonín (1841–1904)

Czech composer. Together with Bedřich Smetana (1824–1884) and Leoš Janáček (1854–1928), Dvořák is considered to be one of the greatest Czech composers. As a child, Dvořák had little formal training. He learned to play the violin from the schoolmaster in his home village of Nelahozeves, but was forced to leave school at the age of twelve to train as a butcher. A year later, he sought greater musical opportunities in the town of Zlonice and in 1857 entered the Prague Organ School, where he received an orthodox training as a church musician. After completing his training, Dvořák became the principal violist in the new Provisional Theater Orchestra, which, from 1866, was under Smetana's direction. Dvořák first attracted attention with his patriotic cantata, *Hymnus* (1872; *The Heirs of the White Mountain*; revised in 1880), and with great encouragement by the German composer Johannes Brahms (1833–1897), Dvořák left Prague and performed his compositions for an international audience. It was soon after he produced both *Moravské dvojzpěvy*, Opus 32 (1876; *Moravian Duets*), and the *Slavonic Dances* (1878) for piano duet that he first experienced European acclaim.

Though Dvořák traveled extensively, his first love remained Prague and the Bohemian countryside. After spending three difficult years at the National Conservatory of Music in New York City, Dvořák returned home to Prague in 1895 and resumed his teaching at the Prague Conservatory. An inventive composer, Dvořák sought to incorporate traditional Czech folk music into classical forms. Aside from a prodigious collection of chamber music, orchestral works, and operas, Dvořák is perhaps best known for his *Symphony No. 9* (1893; *From the New World*), written while he was director of the National Conservatory. He focused primarily on opera during his later years, basing many on Czech folk poems and fairy tales. During the first performance of his opera *Armida* (1904), Dvořák became ill; he died five weeks later.

Dyula

West African tribal grouping. Also called Dioula or Jula, the Dyula are a West

African people who speak a Mande language, also called Dyula. The Dyula began to emerge as small trading groups within the ancient kingdom of Ghana (seventh to thirteenth century) and flourished under the Mali empire (thirteenth to sixteenth century). They organized themselves into small groups that were unified by their belief in Islam and were under the leadership of the *Dyulamansa* (company chief). These small groups, or so-called companies, were important as commercial gold traders between the forest lands in the south and the western Sudan and North Africa; they traveled with their own armed escorts and established themselves at relay stations along trade routes, linking one production zone with another. They also traded in kola nuts and were noted as highly skilled craftsmen. Their language came to serve as the commercial lingua franca within their economic sphere of influence. Today the Dyula have settled in areas in the Ivory Coast, parts of Mali, Ghana, and Burkina Faso. Most Dyula communities are still active in commerce in the dry season, although some have become agricultural.

E

Earthdiver

American Indian origin myth. Found among various North American Indian tribes, the earthdiver myth tells the story of the origin of the continents and the formation of the world. According to the legend, before the appearance of land, when all the world was floodwater, a directing voice instructed various animals to dive to the bottom of the waters and bring back sand or dirt. The first animals sent on the mission failed, but eventually one succeeded. The voice revived the animal, took the dirt it retrieved, and cast it out upon the water, whereupon it magically expanded and formed the current world.

Origin myths are somewhat different from creation myths in that in origin myths, the stories always presuppose the existence of some world, some beings or animals, some existing context, rather than the *ex nihilo* of biblical creation. Some scholars believe that American Indian creation myths are syncretic, the result of contact with Christian missionaries. Origin myths vary by tribe and region of the North American continent; the Indian tribes of the Eastern Woodlands had the most richly detailed myths, which accounted for the origins of tribal divisions and clans.

Easter

Christian holiday. Easter is the annual Christian celebration commemorating the Resurrection of Jesus Christ. Although Jesus' disciples did not celebrate Easter—or any other holy days, convinced as they were that each day was holy in the wake of the Resurrection—the festival became important to the religion with the passage of time, as newly Christianized communities began to imbue existing spring feasts with Christian symbolism.

The holiday, termed "a movable feast" because its date of observance changes from year to year, is generally celebrated on the Sunday following the first full moon after the vernal equinox. But a serious and bitter dispute arose over the precise dating of Easter in the first centuries after Jesus' death. Christ's followers of Jewish descent had their Easter-week celebrations coincide with the traditional Jewish feast of Passover, or Pesach, while Gentile Christians adopted what is now the current custom in the West. The Roman emperor Constantine called the Council of Nicaea in 325 in part to resolve the controversy; at Nicaea it was decreed that the "blindness of the Jews" would no longer be followed in the dating of the festival. However, some discrepancy still remains between the Eastern and Western methods of dating Easter.

Besides the Jewish influence, many other pre-Christian traditions have been incorporated into the rituals now associated with Easter. The name may derive from Eastre, the Teutonic goddess of Spring. Easter also draws on the Jewish Pesach and on the classical Greek myth of the goddess Persephone's return from the underworld every spring. Images of renewal and fecundity still figure prominently in celebrations of Easter, from the dyeing of eggs with bright colors to the choice of a rabbit as the holiday's mascot.

Although the commemorations of Easter and the Holy Week that precedes it differ widely according to local custom, a common theme is the contrast between the sobriety of Holy Week and the riotous color of Easter. During Holy Week in Roman Catholic churches in Europe and Latin America, statues of the saints are covered and most decoration is removed from the church, and the week features somber processions of church officials and townspeople robed in black. In Eastern Orthodox practice, the focal point of the holiday is the midnight mass on Holy Saturday, when the priest announces to the congregation that "Christ is risen." The congregation, replying "He is risen indeed," light their individual candles, filling the darkened church with blazing light.

The practice of dyeing eggs has developed a rich symbolism, particularly in the Eastern Orthodox tradition. In Slovenia, a traditional basket filled with food representing Christ on the cross is carried to the church to be blessed. In addition to a smoked ham representing his body and a string of sausages standing in for the ropes that bound him, according to the tradition, five red eggs symbolize the five wounds from which he died. In parts of Greece, an egg is laid beneath a bush during Holy Week in imitation of Christ's burial, and "resurrected"—placed on the mantelpiece—on Easter Sunday.

Eastern Orthodox Church

Christian church. Eastern Orthodox is an unofficial name for the group of churches that make up what is officially designated as the Orthodox Catholic Church. One of the three large branches of Christianity (the others are Roman Catholicism and Protestantism), it is also sometimes called the Greek Orthodox Church.

In its first several centuries, the Christian Church was organized into five united patriarchates, centered at Rome, Constantinople, Alexandria, Antioch, and Jerusalem. Each had a chief bishop and was administered independently. Until about the fifth century, the pope in Rome was recognized as having preeminence in teaching due to his authority as St. Paul's successor, but in the late fifth century, schisms over religious dogma and shifts in political power led to a weakening of the allegiance of the Eastern churches to Rome, as did the spread of Arabic Islam in the seventh century. The patriarch of Constantinople, the capital city of the late Roman empire (the Byzantine empire), became increasingly influential in the East, especially after the spread of Christianity through Russia in the tenth century. The date usually cited for the "Great Schism" is 1054, the year in which Pope Leo IX and the patriarch of Constantinople excommunicated each other. There was, however, no clean official break between the Eastern and Western churches—there were in fact several formal attempts at reconciliation between the thirteenth and sixteenth centuries— and the development of clearly distinct dogmas took hundreds of years.

Today the Eastern Orthodox Church is made up of a number of self-governing churches, each with its own bishop or patriarch. There is no central authority, or pope, though the patriarch of Constantinople is generally given deference by tradition. Only a council of bishops may represent the Church as a whole.

The separate churches differ in their particular dogma and worship, but they agree in following apostolic tradition, the Nicene Creed, the seven ecumenical councils, the seven sacraments (called "mysteries"), and the Byzantine rite. They also agree in opposing the stance of the Roman Catholic Church concerning original sin, papal infallibility, purgatory, marriage for priests, the maintenance of religious orders, and the doctrine of indulgences. In sheer numbers, the Russian Orthodox churches predominate, and Slavonic and Romanian are the two languages in which its rites are most often celebrated. Total membership was estimated at about 90 million in 1986 (though some sources claim as many as 200 million), with half of those living in the then–Soviet Union.

Easter Rising

Irish insurrection. The Easter Rising, also known as the Easter Rebellion, formed the 1916 climax to a long series of revolutionary struggles in Ireland. Taking advantage of the outbreak of World War I in 1914, three local forces combined to foment the Dublin revolt against British rule: the Irish Republican Brotherhood, led by Tom Clarke; its parent organization, the Irish Volunteers, led by Eoin MacNeill and Patrick Pearse; and, more peripherally, the Citizen Army, formed by James Connolly and dominated by participants in the failed anti-British general strike of 1913. The Sinn Féin political party was also peripherally involved. Pearse, the charismatic leader of the revolt, hoped only that world opinion would be swayed in favor of the Irish after the insurrection took place; this hope, however, was not to be realized, as neither troops nor arms supplies were plentiful enough to sustain the fight longer than six days.

The uprising was supposed to be a nationwide demonstration against British rule, but when an informer sent news of the revolt to the British, they promptly arrested Sir Roger Casement, an Irish nationalist, for arms-running. MacNeill attempted to cancel the uprising, but Clarke and Pearse proceeded to mobilize 200 members of the Citizen Army and more than 1,500 members of the Irish Volunteers. On Easter Monday, April 24, 1916, postponed by one day, the insurrection began with the occupation of strategic points in the Dublin city center, most notably the Post Office. Pearse publicly announced the foundation of the Irish republic and formed a provisional government with himself as president and commander in chief. The British responded by attacking rebel outposts in Dublin.

British soldiers and Irish rebels battled in the streets of Dublin for nearly a week, but as the better-equipped British troops continued to shell the city, Pearse and fourteen other leaders of the uprising were forced to surrender. The British tried and executed the republican leaders, and it was this act, regarded as monstrous by apolitical Irish citizens and rebels alike, that ignited the majority of the Irish and virtually elevated the victims to martyrdom. In the next election (1918), the republican Sinn Féin swept the country. The British-backed Irish government collapsed amid the wave of nationalist fervor and violence that swept Dublin, and the British made several failed attempts to govern but were finally forced to accept the establishment of the Irish Free State on December 6, 1921.

East India Company, British

Trading company. Chartered by the British Crown in 1600 to ensure British involvement in the East Indies spice trade, this originally commercial body, ruled by a governor and a committee of twenty-four, dominated the Indian political scene from the beginning of the eighteenth century until the middle of the nineteenth century, during the height of British imperial activities in the region (1708–1873).

The company's rise to power in India took centuries, and resulted from prolonged struggle with the Indians and with competing imperialist powers. After a vicious defeat in Indonesia at the hands of the Dutch, the British withdrew from the lucrative spice trade and concentrated their efforts on exporting textiles from India. They proceeded to develop large areas throughout India: in 1640 the company acquired the modern site of Madras; in 1668 Charles II rented the area surrounding modern Bombay; and in 1690 the company began to lay the foundations of the city of Calcutta in Bengal, from which they traded cloths and silks for silver and copper.

These three harbor cities—Madras, Bombay, and Calcutta—were the sites of British forts and played an important role in the company's establishment of an impressive merchant fleet. During the reign of Charles II (1660–85), the company acquired powers usually reserved for sovereign states, including the right to coin money, the power to make

and change laws, and the authority to make war and peace.

In 1761 the British vanquished their French counterparts at the Battle of Wandiwash. The company also began to exploit internal unrest inside India, forging "subsidiary alliances" with the nominally sovereign sultans of the indigenous Indian states. British troops offered these sultans "protection" in return for loyalty and direct subsidies or taxes. The British Parliament, increasingly alarmed by the extent of the company's power, put it under the control of the British cabinet and appointed Lord Hastings the first governor-general, thereby cementing the ties between the company and the state. Pitt's India Act of 1784 established a board of commissioners as a branch of the English government, charged with the exercise of political, military, and financial control over British territories in India.

As the company grew in political strength, its commercial role diminished. By the time of the Charter Acts of 1813 and 1833, it had been stripped of its monopoly on trade in India and the Far East and increasingly viewed itself as an administrative body. The company met its military and financial needs by imposing extensive taxes on land, a policy that ultimately impoverished many peasant landowners, forcing them to quit the land and migrate to the already overcrowded cities.

British colonial rule, exercised through the East India Company, produced a rich and complicated amalgam of cultures. While company officials were trained in Indian languages and customs, Indians grappled daily with the accoutrements of Empire, including the English language; in 1830 English joined Urdu as an official language of the nation. The selective dispensation of government funding produced a shift in the schools from the study of the classic Indian arts to those of Europe, and the ability to converse in English became a marker of caste distinction, affluence, and power within the English-ruled country. Cultural mores changed, sometimes forcibly; under Lord William Bentinck (1826–36), the company officially abolished the practice of widow-burning.

Throughout the three centuries of company domination in India, native Indians contested its power and influence. While the years 1818–57 marked the apex of company power, India was convulsed by numerous tribal wars and peasant rebellions. In 1851 a constellation of organizations formed by native Indians came together, including the British-Indian Association, the Deccan Association, the Madras Native Association, and the Bombay Association, all of them interested in abolishing or at least radically reforming the company. In 1857 the Sepoy Mutiny rocked British confidence in the stability of company control; the rebellion had been initiated by the last Mughal emperor, Bahadur Shah, whom the company had defeated resoundingly hardly a decade earlier. Although the emperor and the mutinous Bengalese garrisons were defeated and Bahadur Shah sent into exile, the British Crown stripped the company of its powers and assumed full sovereignty over and direct administration of its Indian colonies.

Edo

African tribal grouping. The Edo, also called Bini, live in southern Nigeria west of the Niger River and speak a language belonging to the Kwa branch of the Niger-Congo language group. Most Edo live in small villages, ranging in size from a few dozen people to several thousand, which also serve as the center of political authority. Males dominate Edo society, which is divided into three age grades, and undertake responsibilities ranging from cleaning paths and maintaining public buildings to performing charity, collecting taxes, holding ritual celebrations, and dealing with other villages. The Edo were originally an off-

shoot of the Yoruba, and many Edo religious practices and offices are derivative of Yoruba ones, including the institution of the *oba*, or sacred king, who ruled as the military and religious chieftain of the kingdom of Benin in the great period of Edo culture, which lasted from the fourteenth to the seventeenth century. Though the Edo continue to exist primarily as agricultural workers, since the 1960s many have found work in new industries, such as petroleum; and though the Edo are primarily Christians or Muslims, traditional polytheism continues to be practiced, acknowledging a range of gods and village heroes as well as the spirits of dead ancestors.

Edo

Original name for Tokyo. Used from 1180 to 1868, the name Edo means "river gate." Because of its location on a bay at the lower coast of the main island of Honshū, Edo controlled water and land transport for most of central and northeast Japan. It began as a small coastal settlement, but grew rapidly at the end of the sixteenth century. When the Tokugawa shogunate located in Edo around 1600, the city effectively became the capital of Japan. Tokugawa Ieyasu went to great lengths to increase and fortify the city; he ordered samurai to move to the city, building extensive quarters for them, and began construction on Edo Castle, which would become the largest castle in the world, with a defensive perimeter of ten miles. The mighty fortress was an architectural wonder, though most of its elaborate inner buildings were destroyed in a series of fires in the 1860s. After the Meiji Restoration in 1868, the imperial court came to the city, building the new Imperial Palace on the site of Edo Castle. The city was then officially renamed, henceforth known as the Eastern Capital, or Tokyo.

eight revolutionary operas

Maoist musical theater. After the establishment of the People's Republic of

China in 1949, the traditional Chinese opera was forced to undergo significant revisions. The opera had been the almost exclusive preserve of the upper classes, a form of entertainment with a solidly bourgeois audience. After the revolution, numerous reforms were set in motion to make the opera more accessible. Modifications in staging techniques were supplemented by changed contents, as a whole host of counterrevolutionary sentiments were expunged from the opera. All erotic, mystical, feudal, or elitist themes were banned to bring the genre in line with state ideology. Many plays were banned outright, while others were heavily edited or completely rewritten. During the Cultural Revolution, the high-water mark of proletarian realism, all traditional drama was adjudged "feudalistic propaganda." All traditional opera was banned, and the Chinese stage was dominated by the "eight revolutionary operas." These eight operas were actually five Peking operas, two ballet-dramas, and one symphonic piece. These works were widely criticized as listless and pedantic, largely propagandistic in ambition. After the end of the Cultural Revolution in 1976 and the arrest of the Gang of Four, a coterie of Communist Party officials (including Jiang Qing, Communist leader Mao Zedong's wife, who was partially responsible for the promotion of arts policy during the Cultural Revolution), more traditional works of drama began to reappear on the Chinese stage.

Einstein, Albert (1879–1955)

Physicist. Einstein is widely considered to be the most brilliant and by far the most famous scientist of the twentieth century. Einstein showed no particular promise in childhood, learning to speak so slowly that his parents feared he might be retarded. The son of a Jewish electrochemical manufacturer, he either dropped out or was expelled from his Munich gymnasium in 1894, and re- nounced his German citizenship in order to dodge military service. After completing his secondary education in Switzerland, he passed the entrance exams on his second attempt and entered the Swiss Federal Institute of Technology in Zurich in 1896. Busying himself with independent reading in mathematics and theoretical physics, he once again failed to distinguish himself in his studies. Unable to secure a teaching post, he accepted a position as technical expert third-class at the Swiss Patent Office in Bern.

In 1905 Einstein received his Ph.D. from the Polytechnic Academy of Zurich. He also published several papers in the journal *Annalen der Physik* that established his reputation as an important scientific and mathematical theorist. In one, he applied the earlier quantum theory of Max Planck to the problem of electromagnetic radiation in a way that established the photoelectric effect, setting the stage for the development of quantum mechanics. (For this breakthrough he was awarded the 1921 Nobel Prize in Physics.) Other papers made important contributions to the theory of Brownian motion, the analysis of atoms, and statistical mechanics. Einstein's fame among scientists and with the general public resulted from his special and general theories of relativity, which rejected the Newtonian universe of absolute space and time for the mathematical relativity of the "curved" space-time continuum (symbolized in the popular imagination by the equation $E = MC^2$). Over the next several years Einstein held academic posts in Bern, Zurich, and Prague before settling in Berlin in 1913. A lifelong pacifist, he opposed World War I, continuing to work on the general theory of relativity and publishing his most influential paper in 1916, *Die Grundlagen der allgemeiner der Relativitätstheorie* (*The Foundation of the General Theory of Relativity*). A solar eclipse in 1919 seemed to confirm his theories, and Einstein became a figure of international renown.

Einstein was visiting the United States when Adolf Hitler came to power in 1933, and he took a position at the Institute for Advanced Study in Princeton, New Jersey. He became a U.S. citizen in 1940 and never again left the country. In 1939 he warned President Franklin Roosevelt of the possibility of an atomic bomb, a weapon made possible in large part thanks to his own work. In later years, he campaigned for pacifism and was a strong supporter of Zionism, though he declined an offer to become president of Israel in 1952. He spent his final years searching in vain for a unified field theory and agitating for world peace.

Eisenhower, Dwight D[avid] (1890–1969)

Thirty-fourth U.S. president and supreme commander of Allied forces in Western Europe during World War II. Born into a poor fundamentalist Christian family in Texas, Eisenhower excelled at sports but was an indifferent student. After completing high school in Kansas, he entered the U.S. Military Academy at West Point. There he played football until a knee injury sidelined him in his sophomore year. He graduated in 1915 ranked sixty-first in his class of 164. Commissioned a second lieutenant, he was sent to San Antonio, Texas, where he met and married Mamie Geneva Doud, in July 1916. During World War I, Eisenhower commanded a tank training center, was promoted to captain, and was awarded the Distinguished Service Medal for his achievements in training. In the 1920s he served in the Panama Canal Zone and, returning to the United States in 1924, attended the Army War College, as well as the Army's Command and General Staff School. He served in France and Washington, D.C., from 1929 to 1933 as assistant secretary of war before becoming (in 1933) a senior aide to Army Chief of Staff General Douglas MacArthur, whose political and military views Eisenhower would later oppose. From 1935 to 1939 he was with MacArthur in the Philippines reorganizing that country's army. He returned to the United States shortly after Germany's invasion of Poland and was made a full colonel in 1941.

As U.S. involvement in World War II progressed, Eisenhower began a meteoric rise through the military command structure, being named U.S. commander of the European Theater in June 1942. After successes in North Africa, Sicily, and Italy, he was named the commander of the Supreme Headquarters of the Allied Expeditionary Forces (SHAEF) in December 1943. The Normandy invasion on June 6, 1944, which Eisenhower orchestrated, began the drive that led to Germany's surrender on May 8, 1945. Eisenhower was made a five-star general, and in the following months he headed the U.S. occupation forces in Germany. That November, he became Chief of Staff of the U.S. Army. He resigned in 1948 to become president of Columbia University, but he took a leave of absence in December 1950 in order to help organize the North Atlantic Treaty Organization as the supreme commander of the Allied forces in Europe. He left the army in 1952 to campaign for the Republican presidential nomination, and proceeded to win easily both the nomination and the general election as a much-beloved war hero who pledged to end the Korean War. In the 1956 election, he won the presidency by an even larger margin. Though he was a strong advocate of active military contestation with Communists in the Middle East and Cuba, Eisenhower also warned of the domestic dangers of what he called "the military-industrial complex," a concern that would assume conspiratorial proportions in the rhetoric of the New Left a decade later. Eisenhower's writings include his account of the

Allies in World War II, *Crusade in Europe* (1948), and his presidential memoirs, *Mandate for Change* (1963) and *Waging Peace* (1965).

Eisenstein, Sergei [Mikhailovich] (1898–1948)

Russian film director and theorist. Eisenstein was born in Riga into a family of German-Jewish and Russian origin. In 1920 he went to Moscow and entered the Proletkult Theater as an assistant decorator, quickly advancing to positions as chief decorator and then codirector. In 1923 he produced an avant-garde rendition of an Aleksandr Ostrovskii play. He also published his first important theoretical essay, "Montage of Attractions," which called for the strategic deployment of nonlinear, nonnarrative images that would create abrupt and powerful effects in the psychology of the viewer, communicating ideas by inducing new emotional states. He turned to film in 1924, a medium he found more conducive to his theories. *Stachka* (1924; *Strike*), his first film, was produced as part of a government-sponsored series on the history of Communism, and featured an unparalleled example of Eisenstein's "dialectical" method. In a famous scene at the film's end, scenes of workers being mowed down by machine guns were juxtaposed with shots of cattle being butchered at a slaughterhouse. In 1925 Eisenstein was assigned to make a film to commemorate the twentieth anniversary of the Russian Revolution of 1905. Though the producers expected a carefully researched cinematic history of that fateful year, Eisenstein devoted his film to a series of events that symbolized for him the whole revolution—the mutiny on the battleship *Potemkin*. The film, *Bronenosets Potemkin* (1925; *Battleship Potemkin*), had a momentous impact: it brought the Soviet Union its first victory on the international film market, and it remains among the masterpieces of world cinema.

Oktiabr (1927; *October*, also known as *Ten Days That Shook the World*), Eisenstein's next work, was confused and jarring, a brutal and chaotic work that received harsh reviews in the Soviet Union. His next two works were more subdued: *Generalnaya linya* (1929; *The General Line*, otherwise known as *Staroye i novoye* [*The Old and the New*]) was a lyrical and expansive film about the collectivization of the rural countryside, while *Romance sentimentale* (*The Silver Lining*), filmed in Paris the same year, explored the interplay of image and music. He spent three years in Hollywood at the behest of Paramount Pictures, trying unsuccessfully to develop ideas based on works by American writers Theodore Dreiser and Upton Sinclair. In 1938, in close collaboration with the composer Sergei Prokofiev, Eisenstein then made *Aleksandr Nevsky*, a film celebrating the Russian past and blending music and image in a single rhythmic unity, and in the 1940s Eisenstein began work on his most ambitious project, *Ivan Grozni* (*Ivan the Terrible*), a proposed three-part work about the sixteenth century czar Ivan IV, much admired by Stalin. Though the first part, released in 1945, met with critical acclaim in the Soviet Union, it got mixed reviews abroad, and the second part, released the following year, was banned by the Central Committee of the Communist Party. Eisenstein died in 1948, a few days after his fiftieth birthday, having suffered a heart attack two years previously.

Eisteddfod

Welsh cultural festival. The annual Eisteddfod (the name literally means "a sitting around together") takes place during the first week of August and is the major cultural and social gathering of Wales's Welsh-speaking minority.

Poetry is at the heart of the Eisteddfod. Poets compete for the Crown and the Chair: the Crown (*Y Goron*) goes to the winner of the free-verse competition; the Chair (Y *Gadair*) is awarded for the best metrical poem. The events harken back to the medieval Eisteddfodau, when Welsh bards engaged in poetry competitions to secure the richest patrons. Eighteenth- and nineteenth-century revivals led to the institutionalization of the Eisteddfod as the national cultural festival of Wales.

Today the Eisteddfod includes other literary and artistic competitions, exhibitions, and such "fringe" activities as experimental theater and alternative rock concerts.

Eliade, Mircea (1907–1986)

Romanian philosopher. A religious historian, Eliade was primarily interested in the experience of the sacred. In his studies of the language of religious symbolism, he tried to find a common basis for mythology and mystical experience in the religions of the world by studying "hierophanies," the way societies, past and present, have experienced the sacred. As in the case of Georges Bataille and Michel Leiris, his thinking about the place of the sacred in modern societies was indebted to Friedrich Nietzsche.

Eliade received his education from the University of Bucharest and the University of Calcutta, in India. His dissertation, later published as *Yoga: Essai sur les origines de la mystique indienne* (1933; *Yoga: Essay on the Origins of Indian Mysticism*), introduced his abiding concern with ecstatic experiences. From 1933 to 1939 Eliade served as an assistant professor at the University of Bucharest. He also taught at the Sorbonne in 1945, and in 1956 he became a permanent member of the faculty at the University of Chicago.

Eliade's writings span novels, essays in comparative religion, and philosophy. His nonfiction works include *Traité d'histoire des religions* (*Patterns of Comparative Religion*), *Le Chaminisme et les*

techniques archaiques de l'extase (*Shamanism: Archaic Techniques of Ecstasy*), *Le Mythe de l'éternel retour* (*The Myth of the Eternal Return*), and *Occultism, Witchcraft, and Cultural Fashion: Essays in Comparative Religion*.

Eliot, George (1819–1880)

English novelist. George Eliot was the pen name of Mary Ann (or Marian) Evans, a Victorian pioneer of modern English literature who revolutionized English writing with her use of psychological analysis, an aspect of her work that would become the predominant feature of modern fiction. A master at rendering the social and moral contexts of decisions, Eliot was equally successful at detailing a character's inner reasoning in making specific choices.

After reading Charles Hennell's *An Inquiry Concerning the Origin of Christianity* (1838), Eliot decided she could no longer attend church. In 1843 she took over the translation of D. F. Strauss's *Das Leben Jesu, kritisch bearbeitet* (*The Life of Jesus, Critically Examined*) from Charles Hennell's wife and began an important friendship with the family. From 1843 to 1850, Eliot spent much time with the Hennells, until a minor domestic scandal led to her dismissal.

After her father's death in 1849, Eliot was invited by Hennell's publisher, John Chapman, to work for the *Westminster Review* as an assistant editor. She spent three highly successful years there. Eliot met a number of radicals during these years, among them Herbert Spencer, who was assistant editor of *The Economist* magazine. Through Spencer, Eliot met journalist George Henry Lewes (1817–1878) in 1854, and lived with him as his common-law wife until his death.

In 1857 Eliot assumed her pen name and her first work of fiction appeared. Three short stories were printed in *Blackwood's Magazine*, an English literary journal, and were later published as *Scenes of Clerical Life* (1858). In 1859, Eliot published *Adam Bede*, a country tale marked by realistic detail, humor, and strong moral concerns. In 1860 *The Mill on the Floss* appeared, a work that showcased Eliot's command of English Midlands dialects. Eliot's most famous work, *Silas Marner*, was published in 1861 while she was engaged in research for her only historical novel, *Romola* (1863). Focusing her writing on contemporary Britain, Eliot wrote *Felix Holt, The Radical*, and *Middlemarch*. With its tragic characterizations and political undertones, *Middlemarch* is often regarded as Eliot's masterpiece and one of nineteenth-century England's finest novels. In her last novel, *Daniel Deronda*, Eliot uses her characters to develop her personal moral philosophies.

In 1880 Eliot married J. W. Cross, a banker and clergyman nearly twenty years her junior. She died later that year. After her death, Cross published Eliot's papers, *George Eliot's Life as Related in Her Letters and Journals* (3 vols., 1885–86).

Eliot, T[homas] S[tearns] (1888–1965)

American poet. Born in St. Louis, Eliot attended Harvard University, where he undertook both undergraduate and graduate studies in philosophy. In 1914 Eliot left the United States, settling in London in 1915 and returning to the United States only after 1932, by which time he had become a member of the Church of England and a citizen of Great Britain. While Eliot's education prepared him for an academic post in philosophy, he never pursued this vocation. Rather, he exercised his influence over modern culture as a poet, literary critic, and playwright. Eliot's first acclaimed poem was "The Love Song of J. Alfred Prufrock" (1915), which subtly equated emotional vacancy and sexual frigidity with what Eliot saw as the decline and decay of urban society.

In the teens Eliot apprenticed himself to Ezra Pound, another American expatriate, whose influence on Eliot was pronounced. Pound was the savage editor of "He Do the Police in Different Voices," a poem which eventually became *The Waste Land* (1922), Eliot's most famous work. A profound exploration of social and spiritual isolation— "the white man's ballad of sexual frustration," as one critic put it—*The Waste Land* was immediately heralded as a triumph of the new literary modernism. By the end of the 1920s, however, Eliot had made his confession of faith and been admitted into the Church of England, a step some considered a renunciation of his earlier commitments. In the 1930s he wrote a number of plays for the Church, including *Murder in the Cathedral* (1935), about the life of Thomas à Becket, and *The Family Reunion* (1939). Eliot continued to write plays, poetry, and literary criticism into the 1960s. In 1948 he received the Nobel prize in Literature, as well as the Order of Merit.

Ellington, Edward "Duke" (1899–1974)

African-American jazz musician. Born Edward Kennedy Ellington, he was a pioneer of the "big band" sound in jazz, introducing complex arrangements that required both improvisation and the ability to read scores. Renowned for his extended, abstract compositions, which employ such techniques as irregular phrasing, chromaticism, and unresolved modulations, Ellington is often considered the first jazz composer.

Ellington was born in Washington, D.C., where his father was a White House butler. Both of his parents played piano but were untrained; the young Ellington began piano lessons at the age of six but received most of his musical training from the public schools. He also took informal lessons from Louis Brown, Louis Thomas, and Oliver "Doc" Perry, who influenced his early style.

In 1919 Ellington formed his own

band, which traveled to New York City in 1923 as the Duke's Serenaders, beginning a four-year engagement at the Kentucky Club. The original band from Washington later expanded to a full orchestra. Ellington's band moved to the Cotton Club in 1927, incorporating additional horns and winds. By this time Ellington was recognized, with Louis Armstrong, as the leading force in jazz music. His band made over two hundred recordings in this period, including the internationally successful *Mood Indigo* (1930). Many of these recordings were in the "jungle" style attributed to Ellington; an integration of trumpet and trombone played on a "wa-wa" plunger mute with smoother saxophone sounds. Although Ellington's band saw many changes in membership through the decades, Ellington continued to play and tour with his band until the early 1970s.

Ellington composed an estimated 1,000 to 6,000 works in his lifetime, including film scores (namely, 1959's *Anatomy of a Murder*), liturgical music, and symphonic suites, receiving many honors for his achievements, such as sixteen honorary doctorates from American universities, the President's Gold Medal (1966), the Presidential Medal of Freedom (1969), and the French Legion of Honor.

Ellison, Ralph [Waldo] (1914–1994)

American novelist, short-story writer, and essayist. Ellison's reputation rests largely on his one published novel, *Invisible Man* (1952), considered by many critics to be one of the most important works of the twentieth century.

During his youth in Oklahoma City, Oklahoma, Ralph Waldo Ellison became determined not to be intimidated by American racism; he refused to acknowledge segregationist Jim Crow regulations and resolved to develop his intellect in spite of customs and laws discouraging African-American aspirations.

After three years at Tuskegee Institute, the all-black vocational college founded by Booker T. Washington, financial woes forced him to leave. He traveled to New York City and supported himself with odd jobs through the Depression years. Although he originally hoped to work as a musician, an encounter with the novelist Richard Wright encouraged him to try his hand at writing. He worked for the Federal Writers' Project and wrote frequent reviews and short stories, but he remained relatively unknown until the publication of his masterpiece in 1952.

The protagonist of *Invisible Man* is an unnamed African American whose life story encompasses much of twentieth-century black history. Born in the South, he travels North when he is expelled from a school resembling Tuskegee. On the way, he has a series of picaresque adventures, encountering The Brotherhood, a thinly disguised version of the Communist Party, and Ras the Destroyer, a Marcus Garvey–like black nationalist. The book culminates in the hero's realization of the futility of any efforts to achieve self-definition in a color- and label-obsessed society. This realization, which had much in common with French existentialist thought, made Ellison's book popular among intellectuals such as Jean-Paul Sartre.

With *Invisible Man*, Ellison created what has been called a jazz narrative aesthetic; involving rhythms and "riff" repetitions reminiscent of jazz structure. The novel makes use of black oral traditions, including the church sermon and the insult-trading known as "the dozens." *Invisible Man* is also a meditation on and critique of such American authors as Herman Melville, James Weldon Johnson, Walt Whitman, Richard Wright, Edgar Allan Poe, and Ralph Waldo Emerson, for whom Ellison was named.

Ellison's other works include the essay collections *Shadow and Act* and *Going to the Territory*. Although he began work on a second novel in 1955 and was said to have completed more than a thousand pages, much of the manuscript was destroyed in a catastrophic fire in the late 1960s, and the book remained unpublished at his death in 1994.

Ellora caves

Temple formation. The Ellora caves are a series of temples located outside the village of Ellora in western India. The temples, excavated out of rock cliffs during the Gupta period (sixth to eighth century C.E.), attract thousands of tourists annually. The temple caves commemorate all three indigenous Indian religions: sixteen of the caves are Hindu, twelve are of Buddhist origin, and the remaining five were excavated by Jainists. Many of the temples were decorated with elaborate sculptures and decorative paintings crafted in what has been termed the "medieval" style. Perhaps the most magnificent of the monuments is the Hindu Kailasanatha temple, which stands 165 feet long and 96 feet high and is carved from a single outcropping of rock. It is dedicated to the god of destruction, Shiva, and decorated with intricate and seductively posed sculptures of Hindu divinities and mythological figures.

Emecheta, Buchi (1944–)

Nigerian writer. Born Florence Onye Buchi Emecheta in Yaba, a small village near Lagos, Nigeria, to Igbo parents, Emecheta was orphaned as a young child and placed in a foster home. Educated in a missionary school, she married at the age of sixteen and moved with her husband to London in 1962, and by the age of twenty-two had borne five children. After separating from her husband, she worked as a librarian in the British Museum and as a social worker. She graduated with honors in sociology from the University of London in 1972, the same year her first novel, *In*

the Ditch, was published. Originally appearing as a series of columns in *The New Statesman*, it is in the form of a diary and is a highly autobiographical account of her difficult life in a strange culture. In 1975 her second novel, *Second-Class Citizen*, continued the fictionalized story of her life in London, helping her in 1978 to win the *New Statesman*–Jock Campbell Award, given to new literary talent from Africa or the Caribbean. Her works include *The Bride Price* (1976), *The Slave Girl* (1977), *The Joys of Motherhood* (1979), *Destination Biafra* (1981), *Double Yoke* (1982), *The Rape of Shavi* (1983), *Adah's Story* (1983), and *A Kind of Marriage* (1987). Her work examines the effect on modern African women of the clash of traditional African attitudes and changing Western values. Emecheta has published essays, poetry, children's books, and television screenplays, as well as an authentic autobiography, *Head Above Water* (1984). She has been a visiting professor at universities in the United States, Nigeria, and Britain. Emecheta has been the recipient of numerous literary awards.

Emerald Buddha

Thai statue. That one of Bangkok's many titles is the "City Where the Emerald Buddha Resides" indicates the significance of the Emerald Buddha as a national symbol. Some claim that the statue dates from the first century C.E., although the sitting Buddha was not "discovered" until 1436, in northern Thailand, when lightning reportedly destroyed an outer plaster coating to reveal the green malachite image within. After residing in various temples in Southeast Asia, it was brought back to Thailand in 1779 by General Chao Praya Chakri, the future king Rama I, who installed it in the capital city of Thon Buri. When Rama I ascended the throne, he moved the capital to Bangkok and the statue traveled with him. A popular tourist attraction, it is noted for its three costumes, one each for the winter, the summer, and the rainy season, which are changed regularly by the king himself in a special ceremony. It is surrounded in the Wat Phra Kaeo temple (Temple of the Emerald Buddha) by famous murals depicting Buddhist cosmology, the life of the Buddha, and tales from the Ramakien.

Emerson, Ralph Waldo (1803–1882)

American essayist, poet, and lecturer. As a writer and philosopher, Emerson profoundly affected the course of American and European thought. Educated at Harvard College and Harvard Divinity School, Emerson pursued a vocation as a Unitarian minister. His mind ranged far and free, however, opposed to what he considered the lifeless and spiritless dogmas of the church. In 1832, after the death of his first wife, Ellen Tucker, he left his pulpit at the historic Second Church of Boston and went to Europe. There he met British poets Samuel Taylor Coleridge (1772–1834), William Wordsworth (1770–1850), and Scottish essayist Thomas Carlyle (1795–1881), and came under the influence of German Idealism. When Emerson returned to America, he briefly went back to the ministry, but by 1835 he had settled in Concord, Massachusetts, and focused his attention on writing and lecturing. He became friends with Henry David Thoreau, Nathaniel Hawthorne, Bronson Alcott, and other members of the Transcendentalist movement.

While Emerson's stress upon nature, intuition, and individualism resonated with the themes of Transcendentalism, he did not count himself a member of this movement. In *Nature* (1836), Emerson promoted the Transcendental theme that God was to be found in the reaches of nature. In Emerson's thought, an "over-soul" gave coherence and meaning to the diversity of human experience. In "The American Scholar"

(1837) and the "Divinity School Address" (1838), both delivered at Harvard, Emerson heralded an overarching, aggressively self-creating individualism, as well as superiority of lived experience over taught doctrine. In "Self-Reliance" (1841), he called upon individuals to find the reflection of the divine in their own genius, and to trust their own selves and their own thinking, however capricious.

Emerson's explicit elitism and his passionate depiction of the art of self-creation had an immense influence on subsequent American and continental European thought. Friedrich Nietzsche was a great admirer of Emerson. Through his works, Emerson's thought affected many of the most compelling figures in twentieth-century continental thought, including the phenomenology of Martin Heidegger and the psychoanalytic theory and practice of Jacques Lacan.

Eminescu, Mihail (1850–1889)

Romanian poet. Eminescu's allegorical and patriotic verse drew on Eastern European folk traditions and influenced Romanian writers in the late nineteenth and early twentieth centuries.

Born Eminovici in the Moldavia province of the Ottoman empire, Mihail Eminescu attended school in Czernauti (now Chernovtsy, Ukraine) and studied at the universities of Vienna (1869–72) and Berlin (1872–74). Upon returning to Moldavia, Eminescu worked briefly as a librarian before taking up the editorship of the right-wing paper *Timpul*.

Eminescu's plainspoken and mystical poetry reflected his extremely xenophobic nationalist politics and focused on Romania's medieval past. His poem "Luceafarul" (1883; "The Evening Star"), which appeared in the only volume of his verse to be published in his lifetime, is his best-known work. Also significant is his story "Cezara." In 1883 Eminescu suffered a severe mental breakdown which ended his writing career. He died in an asylum.

Emre, Yunus (c. 1241–c. 1321)

Turkish poet. One of the greatest early Turkish poets; Emre's work was a powerful amalgam of the Islamic mysticism of the Anatolian folk tradition and a sturdy ecumenical humanism. Very little is known about his life; more than a dozen towns and villages in Turkey claim to be his burial place. It has even been speculated that he may have been illiterate for all or part of his life. Nevertheless, his hymns have remained popular for many centuries and are still chanted in rural and urban areas. The lyric poems he composed in a simple, lilting style retain their quintessential appeal and are among the most extensively quoted verses in modern Turkey. Giving voice to the ideals of mysticism, Yunus Emre is regarded as one of the prominent figures of Turkish literature and humanitarianism. Nearly half of his poems have been translated into English and published in the United States. UNESCO proclaimed 1991, the 750th anniversary of his birth, "International Yunus Emre Year."

Engels, Friedrich (1820–1895)

German socialist philosopher. Engels was a scholar, linguist, journalist, soldier, and businessman, but he is famous as the more literal-minded half of the partnership of Marx and Engels, the coauthor of Marxism, and the cofounder of the German Communist Party. He wrote the *Manifest der Kommunistischen Partei* (1848; *Communist Manifesto*) with German social and economic theorist Karl Marx (1818–1883), edited volumes two and three of *Das Kapital* (1885 and 1894) after Marx's death, and was responsible for codifying and systematizing much of Marx's thought in the years after his death.

Born in Bremen, then part of Prussia, Engels followed in his father's footsteps by entering manufacturing, first in Bremen, where he moonlighted as a journalist and became one of the Young Hegelians—leftist intellectuals in the sway of German philosopher Georg Wilhelm Friedrich Hegel's theory of history—and then in Manchester, England, where his father owned part of a cotton mill. While working at the plant, first as a clerk and later as a manager and as part owner, Engels observed the misery of the workers that he would portray in *Die Lage der arbeitenden Klasse in England* (1845; *The Condition of the Working Class in England*). Also in 1844 Engels contributed two articles criticizing current economic doctrine to a journal edited by Marx in Paris. When he visited Marx, whom he had met briefly several years earlier, the two struck up a friendship and intellectual partnership that would alter the course of political thought. Their first joint work, *Die deutsche Ideologie* (1845; *The German Ideology*), was not published until 1938, but the *Communist Manifesto* caused an immediate sensation. After the collapse of the Revolutions of 1848, which helped them to refine their views on historical change, they reunited in London and reorganized the Communist League, a socialist workers' movement. But economic concerns led Engels to return to the family business in Manchester, and he supported himself and the Marx family in the ensuing years. Marx and Engels continued to collaborate by mail on numerous projects, most notably *Das Kapital*. Engels was singularly responsible for *Herrn Eugen Dührings Umwälzung der Wissenschaft* (1878; *Herr Eugen Dühring's Revolution in Science [Anti-Dühring]*), an attack on the reigning scientific positivism exemplified by Berlin professor Karl Eugen Dühring. After Marx's death in 1883, Engels became a tireless promoter of his comrade's thought, formulating Marxism as scientific socialism and lending his own considerable authority to scientific, mechanical readings of Marx's texts. In 1884 he wrote a brilliant and controversial account of the foundations of patriarchy, *Der Ursprung der Familie, des Privateigenthums und des Staats* (*The Origin of the Family, Private Property and the State*). His death in 1895 was the result of cancer.

Enheduanna

Babylonian priestess. Also known as Enkheduanna, Enheduanna was the first of the high priestesses of the moon god in the city of Ur. This religious position was reserved for the sisters and daughters of the reigning monarch, and was one of the most famous and prestigious of all titles through to the end of the Babylonian era (around 2000 B.C.E.–c. 539 B.C.E.). Enheduanna is remembered for an artifact bearing her seal, a text that laments the fate of the city of Ur in the wake of a failed rebellion. In fact, Enheduanna's brother Rimush, the king of Ur, had led a rebellion against the ruling Semites. It stalled, and both he and the city were captured, and the city's protective wall torn down. The priestess's lament bemoans the moon god's ill temper, the anger that moved him to allow the city to fall and his priestess to be driven into exile.

Enlightenment

The Enlightenment, the moment of humanist rationalism that overtook European thought in the eighteenth and nineteenth centuries, was characterized by tolerance, a hope for social progress through the rational structuring of society, and confidence in science and the benevolence of human nature. This growing attitude of toleration was, in part, a reaction against the religious intolerance that was inherited from the Reformation of the sixteenth century. The Enlightenment mood of belief in progress through science and the natural benevolence of humanity had its roots in the scientific achievements of the six-

teenth century and the rejection of the doctrine of original sin. Those who rallied to the cause for these beliefs were the *philosophes*. While some of these thinkers, including German Immanuel Kant, were academic philosophers, most were writers passionate about the application of creative and critical thinking to understand and reorder the world.

The *philosophes* were a sort of loose cosmopolitan community, a group of thinkers committed to free inquiry and the free exchange of critical thought. Their numbers included such figures as Voltaire, Diderot, Beccaria, Hume, Bentham, and Kant.

Voltaire (1694–1778) was one of the primary proponents of Enlightenment thought in France, and his writings were popular throughout Europe. He was a brilliant wit and a vicious polemicist, turning his talents in *Candide* (1759) on what he perceived to be the fanaticism and intolerance of the Christian Church. Denis Diderot (1713–1784), another star of the French Enlightenment, was responsible for the massive seventeen-volume *Encyclopedia*, a comprehensive document that covered the spectrum of Enlightenment thought and that aimed to bring together in one place all of the most current learning on politics, religion, science, and society, which he began in 1745.

The sort of contractual rationalism peculiar to the English Enlightenment is visible in the work of Jeremy Bentham (1748–1832), who maintained that rational laws could be applied to government and society. His utilitarianism sought to organize government, law, and society so that the greatest good could be achieved for the greatest number of people. David Hume (1711–1776), like his countryman Adam Smith (1723–1790), attacked traditional Christianity as part of the Scottish Enlightenment. The philosophical revolt against metaphysics represented by empiricism is powerfully indebted to Hume.

Legalism and the independence of legal authority were the hallmark of the thought of the Italian Cesare Beccaria (1738–1794), whose insistence that criminal punishment be based on a code of law founded in reason rather than the arbitrary will of the government was echoed throughout Europe, and played a major role in the American and French revolutions.

The German Immanuel Kant (1724–1804) was a leading figure of the Enlightenment. His essay "What is Enlightenment?" summoned a vision of humankind maturing, casting aside props and supports like religion and tyranny and ruling over the self, through the exercise of reason. His three critiques, including his most famous, the *Critique of Pure Reason* (1781), attempted to delimit the proper sphere of reason in the formation of knowledge, judgment, and taste.

In the twentieth century, the Enlightenment's ideology of progress and dependence on the technological imagination came under fierce attack, from humanists and Western Marxists as well as fascists. Today the question of the Enlightenment inheritance, and its hidden costs, remains a focal point of political and social theory.

Enuma Elish

Babylonian creation myth. Meaning "when above" or "when on high," the seven-tablet *Enuma Elish*, first published as a text in 1876, is one of the oldest Mesopotamian literary works. It was most likely composed during the reign of Nebuchadnezzar I (c. 1124–1103 B.C.E.), an era of strident Babylonian nationalism.

The myth begins at a time when nothing existed except the primordial waters: the sweet water abyss (Apsu) and the salt seas (Tiamat). The intermingling of these waters set in motion an evolutionary process that produced the gods, including Anu ("born"), and eventually his son, Ea. Disturbed by the activities of Anu and his sons, Apsu wanted to destroy the gods and return to the calm that had reigned before the intermingling of the primordial waters. In the subsequent battle, Apsu was killed by Ea, who established himself as "lord of the Apsu" and produced Marduk, the young super-god who would emerge as the epic's hero.

When Anu later created the wind, further disturbing the waters, the oceanic gods appealed to Tiamat to avenge Apsu's death. Tiamat complied by creating eleven monsters and establishing an army to do battle with the gods. The young Marduk agreed to fight on the gods' behalf, provided that they make him their king and allow his word to determine destinies. In a single battle, Marduk, in the form of a storm, defeated Tiamat by blowing winds into her and then piercing her distended stomach. He divided Tiamat's body in two, separating the halves with the sky. He then created the mountains, the heavenly bodies, and the springs.

On returning from battle, Marduk proposed to build Babylon as a place where the gods could congregate, and he instructed Ea to create man to do the manual labor. He also established a division of labor among the gods, assigning each one a specific function.

In addition to its significance as a creation myth, *Enuma Elish's* portrayal of the cosmos as a political organization provides a mythological foundation for the Babylonian state. Marduk fought Tiamat on behalf of the gods; however, his mission might have ended with Tiamat's victory. Nevertheless, his rule was extended when his plans to construct Babylon and to create mankind to provide manual labor demonstrated that his leadership could provide benefits in peacetime as well as war.

Equiano, Olaudah (1745–1797)

African slave and author. Equiano was born in the Igbo valley of Essaku, then under the influence of Benin, in what is now eastern Nigeria. He was captured at an early age (ten or twelve) by local raiders and sold to British slavers bound for the West Indies. A short time later, he was sold to a British naval officer, Captain Pascal, who gave him the name Gustavus Vassa, which he used for the rest of his life. Equiano served Captain Pascal in the navy and traveled with him during several campaigns, including a voyage to the Mediterranean during the Seven Years' War. He also spent time in England and received some schooling that prepared him for his career as a shipping clerk and for his later literary achievements. After the war, Pascal sold Equiano to Quaker Robert King, a merchant in Philadelphia who was trading in the Leeward Islands. Under this master, Equiano prospered and earned enough money to buy his freedom in 1766, at the age of twenty-one. From this time Equiano traveled widely and made voyages to the Mediterranean, the Arctic, and the Mosquito Shore of Central America, and in 1787 he was appointed commissary of stores on the first expedition to settle freed slaves in Sierra Leone, but was dismissed from this post in the same year, and therefore was able to finish his pinnacle work, his memoirs of his travels and his ascent to freedom, *Interesting Narrative of the Life of Olaudah Equiano, or Gustavus Vassa, the African, Written by Himself* (1789). He also became a staunch supporter of the British abolition movement and wrote on behalf of those who had suffered atrocities at the hands of ruthless slavers. Though he wanted to return to Africa, in 1792 he married Susanna Cullen, an Englishwoman, and died in London in 1797.

Erasmus, Desiderius (c. 1466–1536)

Dutch humanist scholar of the Northern Renaissance. The son of a priest, Erasmus himself was ordained a priest in 1492 and supported the reformation of the Church through learning, rather than through the evangelical fervor of Martin Luther. He studied at several universities in Europe, briefly taught in Cambridge, England, and settled finally in Basel, and later Freiburg, where he produced the writings that established him as one of the great religious thinkers of his time. His most famous works are the satire *Encomium Moriae* (1509; *In Praise of Folly*) and the *Adagia* (1508), a collection of over 3,000 proverbs from classical works, although his writings cover a broad range of topics. Erasmus was a deeply humanist scholar, and thus was highly skeptical of superstitions and excessive religious fervor. Though he was aware, and certainly disapproving, of the widespread clerical corruption that plagued the Church, and initially sympathetic to the efforts of German Reformation leader Martin Luther (1483–1546), the ensuing religious wars and hatreds forced him to emerge as an opponent of Luther's Reformation.

Erhu

Chinese fiddle. The modern Erhu takes its design from the earlier Huqin, a two-stringed instrument with a neck carved in a dragon design, played with a bow made of horse hair, and developed during the Yuan dynasty (1260–1368). The Erhu, very similar to the Huqin, has a stick and drum resonator, as well as pegs all made of wood that come in various shapes—round, hexagonal, and octagonal—with a diameter of eight to nine centimeters. One end-plane of the resonator is covered with boa skin; the other is carved with designs of flowers forming the sound hole.

In the early twentieth century, Liu Tianhua, a famous Erhu and Pipa performer, made great contributions in improving the Erhu's structure and developing its performance techniques. Now the Erhu has become one of the Chinese instruments that can best imitate human voices. In addition to its orchestral role, the Erhu is also a solo instrument. Its performance is characterized by subtle contrasts in bowing strength, powerful vibrato, and glissando. A higher-pitched version with a smaller resonator surface is the gao-hu. In southern China, the gao-hu is often the first bowed-string instrument in orchestras, with the Erhu being the second. Several bass-range versions are also popular

Esarhaddon (r. 681–669 B.C.E.)
Assyrian ruler. Esarhaddon's father, Sennacherib, who ruled Assyria from 705 to 681 B.C.E., was assassinated presumably by one of his sons on the twentieth of Tebet, 681 B.C.E. Though the exact cause of his death still remains shrouded in mystery, it is generally supposed that by naming Esarhaddon his successor, the aging ruler enraged those of his sons in more direct line to the throne. Esarhaddon spent most of his father's reign as the governor of Babylonia, and rebuilt the city of Babylon, which his father had destroyed in 689 because he believed that control of Babylon, plagued by tribal boundary disputes, was impossible. These two rulers, father and son, were quite different from those who had ruled before them. Where Tiglath-pileser III (reigned c. 744–727 B.C.E.) and Sargon II (721–705 B.C.E.) were great military adventurers, Esarhaddon was more circumspect in the exercise of force. His fame as a military leader rests upon two accomplishments: the suppression of the Phoenicians, who had allied themselves with the Egyptians, and the invasion of Egypt itself. In 679 the Assyrian army advanced to the border of Egypt and captured the city of Arza. In 671 the great city of Memphis fell to the Assyrians and Esarhaddon ordered tribute to

be paid to his country and to the god Ashur. After a year fraught with domestic difficulty, another campaign against Egypt was launched in 669. Esarhaddon died en route and this final attempt to secure Egypt was abandoned. Esarhaddon was succeeded by his son Ashurbanipal (668–627 B.C.E.).

Eshu-Elegba
Trickster figure of the Yoruba culture. Eshu, the keeper of the crossroads, is the messenger in the pantheon of Yoruba gods, or orishá, and is the first orishá to be called upon at ceremonies. Because of his strong communicative role, he is a mediator between gods and humans, his power extending throughout the pantheon and even to the High God, called Olofin, Olorun, or Olodumare.

As a trickster, Eshu-Elegba is a mischief-maker, quirky and ominous; sometimes he is very supportive, at other times malicious, and his whimsy is seen as being at the origin of all human troubles and triumphs. He appears variously as a wise old man or an impetuous child, eager to break all the rules. Usually portrayed with a hooked staff and associated with the crossroads and phallic imagery, his colors are red and black, and he is represented by the number three. Within the syncretic Afro-Cuban religion where African and Catholic traditions blend, he is associated with St. Anthony and El Niño de Atocha. Shrines to Eshu-Elegba are placed at gates, doorways, and other points of transition.

The trickster is a predominant character in many of the world's oral literatures, and most often assumes a form common to the surrounding environment. He is usually the centerpiece of a cycle of tales, most of which recount the cunning and deceptive tactics he employs to best his adversaries. The trickster Eshu-Elegba is closely related to other African-derived trickster figures, including Legba of the vodun (voodoo) tradition of the Fon people in Benin,

Papa Legba in Haiti, and Exu in Afro-Brazilian religion. On the Gold Coast of Africa, the trickster is often portrayed as a spider, and among the American Indian tribes in the United States, he most often appears as a coyote, especially in several of the southwestern tribes.

Essenes

Members of a small religious group. The Essenes were a quasi-monastic Jewish sect located in Palestine from the second century B.C.E. to the first century C.E. A relatively small movement, the Essenes, according to the Jewish historian and philosopher Philo Judaeus (13 B.C.E.–45/50 C.E.) of Alexandria, never numbered more than 4,000 and excluded women from membership. Members dedicated themselves to the most austere lifestyle possible in order to purify themselves and avoid the defilement of the outside world. They abhorred private property, slavery, and luxuries of every kind and divided their time between intense study of the Torah and manual labor. The Essenes shared many theological aspects with the Pharisees (another scholarly sect of the Second Temple period) but disapproved of their interaction with the masses, choosing instead self-exile in the wilderness. Nevertheless, personal piety and separation from the impurities of everyday life were stressed by both groups, and they shared a belief in life after death.

New members were admitted only after a three-year initiation phase. They then took an oath not to reveal the sect's secrets and always to abide by its strict rules. The entire community met at dawn for prayers, which were followed by a shared meal and the morning's work in the fields. All meals were eaten together in complete silence. A few communities may have allowed their members to marry, but the Essenes generally led celibate lives.

The early Christian Church probably owes a great deal to the example of the Essene communities, though they are not mentioned in the New Testament. There are obvious similarities between Christian monasticism and its Jewish predecessors. Indeed, John the Baptist lived most of his life within a few miles of an Essene community near the Jordan River. The discovery of the Dead Sea Scrolls in 1947 heightened interest in the Essenes among both Christian and Jewish scholars. It is widely acknowledged that the authors of the Scrolls were members either of an Essene community or of one closely resembling them.

Euripides (c. 485–406 B.C.)

Greek dramatist. The last of the three most renowned Athenian tragic dramatists, after Aeschylus (525–456 B.C.E.) and Sophocles (496–406 B.C.E.), Euripides was pronounced by Greek philosopher Aristotle (384–322 B.C.E.) "the most tragic of poets." He was widely admired and his plays were often revived. He is famous for his portraits of individuals wrestling with chaos and irrational forces, devoid of moral meaning, against which they are helpless. Euripides wrote most of his plays during the critical years of the Peloponnesian War (431–404 B.C.E.), a circumstance reflected in the hard-boiled realism of his portraits of legendary "heroes" and in the questioning of conventional attitudes and practices in his society, including unconditional piety and admiration of the nobility.

Euripides, unlike his rival Sophocles, appears not to have been a prominent public figure, preferring to live and write in isolation. Like Sophocles, however, he was born to a prominent family and received his education from distinguished scholars. He had a reputation for sophism, due in part to his emphasis on rhetoric and the implicit skepticism of his portraits of the gods and heroes; Socrates called him impious. The hostility Euripides encountered, and his middling success at the dramatic competitions, influenced his decision to leave Athens for Macedonia around 408.

Euripides is said to have written ninety-two plays; of those, nineteen survive under his name, including *Suppliant Women* (c. 421 B.C.E.), *Hercules Furens* (c. 420 B.C.E.; *Mad Hercules*), *Trojan Women* (415 B.C.E.), *Electra* (413 B.C.E.), and *Orestes* (408 B.C.E.). Favoring a loose and episodic structure in his plays, and though much of his work is considered melodramatic, his choice of situations and his treatment of them, as well as his clear, natural diction, lend them a realistic element. Addressing this realism, Sophocles said that in his own plays he represented people as they should be, while Euripides represented them as they are. Generally, Euripides creates conflicts of sympathy in his audience through the use of paradox and ambivalence in his characterizations. The irresolution of many of Euripides' plays is highlighted by his use of the *deus ex machina*, the god or goddess who appears at the end to resolve any embarrassing situations or ambiguities in the plot.

Evita, *see* **Perón, Eva**

F

Fanon, Frantz [Omar] (1925–1961)
West Indian psychoanalyst and social philosopher. Born in Martinique, the French Antilles, Fanon attended schools there and in France. After serving in the Free French Army in North Africa and Europe during World War II, he studied medicine and psychiatry at the University of Lyons from 1947 to 1951. In 1953 he was appointed Chief of Service of the psychiatry department of the Blida-Joinville Hospital in Algeria, then part of France. He joined the Algerian liberation movement in 1954 and went to work for its underground newspaper, *El Moudjahid*, two years later. He was a delegate at the First Congress of Black Writers and Artists in Paris in 1956 and at the All African People's Conference in Accra in 1958. After being forced out of the Blida hospital for his political activities, he practiced psychiatry from 1957 to 1959 in Tunisia.

In 1960 he was appointed ambassador to Ghana by the Algerian Provisional Government. Strongly influenced by Jean-Paul Sartre and Aimé Césaire, Fanon is best known as a writer on racism and revolution. He hated colonialism and believed that Third World countries should establish their independence by any means necessary. Unlike Marx, he argued that the revolutionary impetus would not come from intellectuals or the working class but from the peasantry. The poorest people would eventually resort to violence, since they had little to lose, he thought, and in their violence they would find a healing psychological force. His 1952 book, *Peau noire, masques blancs* (*Black Skin, White Masks*), reviews his personal encounters with racism and the colonial system that teaches blacks to hide behind "white masks." *L'An V de la révolution algérienne* (1959; *A Dying Colonialism*) is a further study of the psychology and sociology of colonialism. Published just before his death from leukemia, *Les Damnés de la terre* (1961; *The Wretched of the Earth*) urges a "collective cathar-sis" among oppressed peoples and calls for violent revolution. *Pour la révolution africaine* (*For the African Revolution*) was published posthumously in 1964. His interpretation of the power and re-demptive force of violence influenced many contemporaries in the 1960s gen-eration, including members of the Black Panthers.

al-Fârâbî, Muhammad (c. 870–950)

Arab philosopher. Born in Turkestan, al-Fârâbî was one of the great philosophers of the Islamic world, a thinker who wrote in Arabic and whose passionate love for the classics of Greek philosophy helped make possible the medieval Eu-ropean revival of classical antiquity. Many of the most famous works of Greek philosophy and science made their way into Europe in the form of Ar-abic translations, accompanied by the commentaries of Arab scholars like Ibn Sînâ (Avicenna) and Ibn Rushd (Aver-roës). Best known as a commentator on Aristotle, al-Fârâbî was often referred to as "the Second Teacher"—second, that is, to the teacher Aristotle himself. He is credited with having discerned the exis-tence of an esoteric writing in the mar-gins of Greek philosophy. He wrote a great number of works—over one hun-dred are attributed to him—on an aston-ishing range of topics, from philosophy, metaphysics, logic, and psychology to ethics, music, and politics. His "Perfect City" sketched a plan for an Islamic po-litical utopia, along the lines of Plato's Republic, which would provide for the earthly happiness of its citizens while also spiritually preparing them for the hereafter. Another of his books, *The Enumeration of the Sciences*, constituted the first attempt in the Islamic world to bring together the scientific knowl-edge from Greek, Persian, Indian, and Arab sources in a single, organized presentation.

A gifted musician, al-Fârâbî was also a theoretician of the music of the Is-lamic world. His *Great Book of Music* is an unparalleled encyclopedic treatment of musical instruments, intervals, disso-nance and consonance, rhythms, types of composition, and more. His writings provide the first real analysis of the mi-crotonic musical system that was then emerging and has remained a distinc-tive characteristic of Arab, Persian, and Turkish music to the present day. Un-fortunately, notation systems capable of transcribing the music of his era did not yet exist; we possess al-Fârâbî's musico-logical analysis but none of the music with which he was so engaged.

Farah, Nuruddin (1945–)

Somali poet and novelist. Born in then–Italian Somalia, Farah was educated in both Somalia and Ethiopia. He left for India in 1966 to study literature and phi-losophy, returning to Mogadishu several years later to teach school. In 1974 Farah left for Great Britain, where he studied and continued to write plays, something he had begun to do in India; while in Great Britain, he was commissioned to write several plays for the BBC.

Farah moved to Rome in 1976 to study Italian culture. There he wrote *Sweet and Sour Milk* (1979), a novel concerned with individual choice and compromise; *Sweet and Sour Milk*, the first part of a trilogy, received the 1980 English Speaking Union Literary Award. The second part of the trilogy, *Sardines*, followed in 1981, with the final install-ment, *Close Sesame* (1983), written in Somalia during the military coup of Siad Barre. Bearing witness to the hard-ships imposed on the Somali people by the regime, Farah's novel is critical of the Soviet-backed Siad Barre.

Farah's early novels are set in Soma-lia, and are principally concerned with the difficulties faced by individuals who do not conform to the rigid structure im-posed upon them by traditional Soma-lian culture and society. Many of his works, especially his fiction, are sympa-thetic to the role of women in African and Arab societies, though he has also been criticized for his sometimes harsh depictions of women.

As the leader of his clan, Farah addressed in his poetry the ongoing disputes of his people with the more powerful neighboring Iidegale clan to whom tribute was required. Farah's outspoken role in this conflict is believed to have been instrumental in freeing his people from their bondage and obligation to the Iidegale. His poetry also addressed the European invasion and partitioning of his homeland, and his poem "The Limits of Patience" (in *Somali Poetry*, 1964) addresses British, Italian, and Ethiopian plans to divide Somaliland.

Though Farah's work has been well received in Great Britain, it has been largely ignored in both the United States and Africa. With the exception of *From a Crooked Rib* (1970), none of his other work is available in his homeland.

Farrokhzad, Forugh (1935–1967)

Iranian poet. A unique and talented poet, Farrokhzad is particularly distinguished as a woman who, despite social restraint and taboo, dared to express her innermost feelings about love, sex, society, and self with a frank openness unprecedented in the history of Persian literature.

After a brief and unfortunate marriage, in which she lost custody of her only child, Farrokhzad devoted herself completely to her talents. In the last sixteen years of her life, she published five collections of poetry, as well as a number of translations from French and English. Her early collections, *The Captive* (1955), *The Wall* (1956), and *Rebellion* (1957), consist almost entirely of introspective and confessional poems in traditional lyric style. As the titles suggest, the poet is exploring her identity as a woman entrapped in a society of traditional mores and values. Love—both sexual and romantic—is the primary theme of the first two collections, serv-

ing for Farrokhzad as a means of self-expression and social protest. In the third volume, religion becomes a dominant theme, and her fiery spirit leads her to question conventional religious beliefs.

Farrokhzad broadens her vision of the world in later works: *Another Birth* (1963) and *Let Us Believe in the Beginning of a Cold Season* (1974). She experiences a "rebirth" and becomes concerned not only with her personal conflicts but with the predicaments of the society as a whole. At the peak of her career, Farrokhzad was killed in a car accident.

Fassbinder, Rainer Werner (1946–1982)

German film director. Sometimes compared to the French film director Jean-Luc Godard (1930–), Fassbinder is one of the most important and prolific directors to emerge in postwar Germany. Originally trained as an actor, Fassbinder began making films with members of his "antitheater" group in 1969. Fassbinder took many of his cues from the swelling German avant-garde theater movement of the 1960s, exemplified by Oskar Negt and Alexander Kluge, theoretical compatriots of Jürgen Habermas and other second-generation Frankfurt School theorists. As the name "antitheater" suggests, Fassbinder was greatly influenced by the work of German dramatist Bertolt Brecht (1898–1956), who advocated a theater of estrangement. His work also tended to deal with the problem of fascism and everyday life in postwar German society. In 1969 he made his first film, *Katzel macher*, a depiction of the plight of foreign guestworkers in Germany, a film in which he acted as well. Another film from that year, *Warum läuft Herr R. Amok (Why Does Herr R. Run Amok)*, details the humdrum banality of daily life and one man's increasingly violent attempts to recover a sense of self. Some of his more famous films include *Die Ehe der Maria Braun* (1978; *The Marriage of Maria*

Braun) and the mammoth fifteen-hour film adaptation of Alfred Döblin's expressionist novel, *Berlin Alexanderplatz* (1980; made in thirteen episodes for television). Fassbinder died of a probable cocaine overdose but left in his wake a wealth of probing cinematic visions of German society.

Fatehpur Sikri

Town in northern India. In 1569 the Mughal emperor Akbar (1556–1605) established his capital in Fatehpur Sikri after the Muslim saint Shaikh Salim Chisti, a resident of Sikri, foretold the birth of Akbar's three sons. Construction of the royal city, which began in 1569 and was completed in the space of a few years, included the building of the Jami Masjid, or Great Mosque, in 1571, which contained an ornate tomb for Chisti. The southern entrance of the mosque, the 176-foot-high gateway, Buland Darwāza, or "Victory Gate," is considered one of India's greatest architectural structures.

Renamed Fatehpur (Victory) after Akbar's success in the Gujarat campaign in 1573, the town was henceforth known as Fatehpur Sikri. Although by 1586 Akbar had moved his capital to Delhi because of Fatehpur Sikri's inadequate water supply, his tenure in Fatehpur Sikri nevertheless led to the construction of many impressive and inventive edifices, including a palace for his wife, Jodhā Bāī, as well as the Pānch Mahal, the Diwan-i Khas (House of Private Audience), the House of Birbal, the Elephant Tower, the Khas Mahal, and the Ibadat-Khana (House of Worship). All of these buildings, except the last, still stand, making Fatehpur Sikri the most completely preserved palace city of the Mughals.

Father Divine, *see* Baker, George

Faulkner, William (1897–1962)

American novelist. Faulkner's complex novels made him famous as a chronicler of the American South.

Faulkner was born in New Albany, Mississippi, and grew up in the small city of Oxford. Shy and artistically inclined, he quit high school one year short of graduation. Faulkner was always more interested in his own independent reading of contemporary avant-garde literature than disciplined study, and he dropped out of the University of Mississippi after a year.

He drifted in and out of jobs in Oxford for a number of years before becoming acquainted with litterateurs such as the novelist Sherwood Anderson. Anderson helped Faulkner publish his first novel, *Soldiers' Pay* (1926). Faulkner hit on his distinct style and theme three years later in *Sartoris* (1929), the first of his books set in the mythical Yoknapatawpha County. *Sartoris*'s multiple narrative strands and convoluted family situations would be central aspects of such later major works as *As I Lay Dying* (1930) and *Go Down, Moses* (1942).

Faulkner experimented with modernist techniques in his fiction, scrambling chronological sequences and playing with various states of consciousness in ways reminiscent of James Joyce and Marcel Proust. In *The Sound and the Fury* (1929), he created one of his most famous families, the Compsons. The story of Caddy, Benjy, Quentin, and Jason, with its themes of incest and suicide, is emblematic of Faulkner's dark vision of Southern and human history. His unique treatment of the progression of time in his work suggests the centrality of the past; in Faulkner, history is a living thing, coloring—even somehow coexisting with—present experience.

Other major works are *Light in August* (1932), the story of a man of uncertain racial categorization, and *Absalom, Absalom!* (1936), a tale relating Thomas Sutpen's ambition to create a personal empire in the South.

Much of Faulkner's career was plagued by financial problems and alcoholism. Although he was well known, the difficulty of his work kept it from selling consistently. *Sanctuary* (1931), a sensationalistic novel involving a notoriously gruesome rape, was written as a moneymaker and was his first best-seller. He was forced to spend several years in Hollywood in the 1940s writing movie scripts to support his family. A Nobel Prize in 1950 helped revive his failing reputation, however, and at his death in 1962 he was recognized as one of the greatest American authors.

Faust

Legend of Western literature. Also known as Faustus or Doctor Faustus, the Faust legend has been popular in Western literature since the sixteenth century. The character has its origins in late medieval legends about a German necromancer who made a pact with the devil to gain power and knowledge in return for giving the devil possession of his soul. There was at least one historical Faust, who died around 1540 and left behind references suggesting that he was in league with the devil. The anonymously written *Faustbuch* (1587) is one of the primary sources for the literary works that depict the Faustian character. English dramatist Christopher Marlowe's *Doctor Faustus* (1604) draws extensively on the English version of the *Faustbuch*. In Marlowe's tragedy, Faust meets his fateful end. In the version of German poet and dramatist Johann Wolfgang von Goethe's *Faust*, composed in two parts (1808 and 1832), however, the character's fate is reversed as the divine interferes with the demonic's claim on his soul. Goethe's use of the Faust legend demonstrates the ironic tendencies and possibilities of humankind's thirst for power and knowledge. In the twentieth century, German-born American writer Thomas Mann's novel *Doktor Faustus* (1947) employs the Faust legend to portray the nihilism that occupied the German mind in the first half of the twentieth century. Since the

original *Faustbuch* first appeared, the Faust myth has been employed to provide a commentary on the destructive end that humans face if they pursue knowledge and power at the expense of morality and ethics.

Feast of the Hungry Ghosts, *see* Chung Yüan

Fellini, Federico (1920–1993)

Italian film director. Fellini is considered to be one of the most controversial directors of Italian cinema. His films, especially those made during his middle period beginning in 1959, are highly symbolic in nature and employ extravagant and outrageous imagery. Playing an integral part in the development of neorealist Italian cinema through his collaboration with Italian film director Roberto Rossellini, Fellini later often criticized this body of work for what he considered its overt use of melodrama.

In 1944, after numerous writing and acting jobs, Fellini became involved in the filming of *Roma Citta aperta* (1944; *Rome, Open City*). From 1946 to 1952 Fellini served as screenwriter and assistant director for Roberto Rossellini, Alberto Lattuada, and Pietro Germi. As clearly represented in his first film, *Lo sceicco bianco* (1952; *The White Sheik*), Fellini's films were highly autobiographical in nature, and often drew upon both his journalistic and writing experiences.

Fellini's continuing attraction to autobiography can be seen in *La Strada* (1954; *The Road*), one of his most critically acclaimed neorealist films, where he cast his wife, Giulietta Masina, in the major female role. Interpretive efforts regarding this highly symbolic film have represented it variously as a treatise either on human rights or on women's liberation. Despite the critical success of *La strada*, Fellini was criticized by neorealists for what they perceived as an attempt to justify political oppression.

In *La Dolce vita* (1960; *The Sweet*

Life), continuing in the autobiographical vein, Fellini takes viewers on an exploration of the complexities of the psyche. It was in *La Dolce vita* that Fellini established actor Marcello Mastroianni as his alter ego, using him in many of his following films. In his next film, *8½* (1963), Fellini, again utilizing Mastroianni, explores the source of artistic inspiration. With the exception of *Fellini Satyricon* (1969; *Satyricon*), which made use of imaginative fantasy and represented an altogether different direction, his later films were still more complex explorations of the artist's creative process, interpreted widely as Fellini's exploration of his own creativity. In *Ginger e Fred* (1986; *Ginger and Fred*), Fellini self-consciously explored questions of meaning, impermanence, and joy in the lives of two aging dancers, onetime screen stars "modeled" on Ginger Rogers and Fred Astaire.

Ferré, Rosario (1941–)

Puerto Rican essayist, short-story writer, poet, and novelist. Ferré was born to a wealthy political family in Ponce, Puerto Rico, where she spent the first twenty years of her life. She studied English and North and Latin American literature at various universities in the United States and at the University of Puerto Rico. Married at the age of nineteen, she had three children, and divorced her husband ten years later. Although she had been writing since she was a child, it was only after her divorce that she seriously considered her art as a career. Her first book, *La muñeca menor* (1976; *The Youngest Doll*), consists of fourteen short stories and six poems, which may be read as revisions of the misogynist myth of Pandora. Her literary work has concentrated on the exploration of interior spaces and the condition of women, and on the critique of the bourgeois Puerto Rican family. Her protagonists tend to be women unleashed, setting violently out against the daily abuses of a hypocritical, bourgeois, and sexist world. Other works include a book of essays, *Sitio a Eros* (1980; *Space for Eros*); a book of poems, *Fábulas de la garza desangrada* (1982; *Fables of the Bleeding Heron*); *Cuentos de Juan Bobo* (1981; *Stories of John Bobo*), *El medio pollito* (1976; *The Middle Chick*), and *La mona que le pisaron la cola* (1981; *The Monkey Whose Tail Got Stepped On*), reworkings of Puerto Rican folktales; and *Maldito Amor* (1986; *Sweet Diamond Dust*), a novel. She published a book of criticism on Julio Cortázar, *Cortázar the Romantic*, in 1991. She is also the founder of one of the most important literary magazines in Latin America, *Zona de carga y descarga* (1972–76; *Loading and Unloading Zone*).

Fitzgerald, Ella (1918–1996)

African-American jazz singer. Renowned for her "scat" singing techniques, Fitzgerald rivals jazz instrumentalists in harmonic and melodic improvisation. A wide vocal range and technical virtuosity enhance her interpretive talent, which has received a popular following unusual for a jazz singer.

Although born in Virginia, Fitzgerald grew up in Yonkers, New York, receiving her musical education in the public schools there. In the 1930s she began singing in Harlem nightclubs and was discovered by Chick Webb, a popular Harlem musician, in 1934 after winning an amateur contest at the Apollo Theater. She joined Webb's group and led the band for two years after his death in 1939. Her first recording was made in 1935, but the song that brought her real publicity was "A Tisket, a Tasket" (1938), which she wrote. In the mid-1940s she sang freelance and was established as a leader in jazz singing; thereafter she toured extensively in shows such as Norman Granz's "Jazz at the Philharmonic" (1948–57) and performed with figures such as Duke Ellington at Carnegie Hall in 1958, gaining the title of "First Lady of Jazz."

Fitzgerald won numerous awards in recognition of her musicianship and influence, including several honorary doctorates, the Kennedy Center Honors by the White House for lifetime achievement in the performing arts in 1979, the Golden Needle Award from East Berlin, Germany, and the 1987 National Medal of Arts.

Fitzgerald, F[rancis] Scott [Key] (1896–1940)

American novelist and short-story writer. Fitzgerald became famous for his stories of upper-class American life in the 1920s, the "Jazz Age." Fitzgerald's works subvert the flamboyant and cynical lifestyles of his characters with profound moral doubts. His personal life with his wife, Zelda, was fraught with the same fashionable and aristocratic problems that appear in his novels, including Zelda's mental illness and Fitzgerald's own bouts with alcoholism and eventual breakdown.

Born into an upper-class St. Paul, Minnesota, family, Fitzgerald was named after his ancestor, Francis Scott Key, the author of "The Star-Spangled Banner." He attended Princeton and was an active socialite, although he never received his degree. In 1920 he married Zelda Sayre, whose father served on the Supreme Court of Alabama, and his first novel, *This Side of Paradise*, was published that same year. Fitzgerald received immediate critical and popular acclaim for the novel and followed it with a collection of short stories, *Flappers and Philosophers* (1920), and another novel, *The Beautiful and Damned* (1922). The following years saw the publication of *Tales of the Jazz Age* (1922) and a play, *The Vegetable* (1923). Fitzgerald's next novel, *The Great Gatsby* (1925), is often considered to be his finest work, a spare yet tragic reworking of the American myth of self-invention.

The 1930s were especially emotionally and financially taxing for Fitzgerald. In 1930 and again in 1932, Zelda suffered severe mental breakdowns, a condition that would plague her for the remainder of her life. Fitzgerald relates the strain of Zelda's condition on his life in the posthumously published book *The Crack-up* (1945). Fitzgerald's relationship with Zelda deteriorated after the onset of her illness, and by 1937 he had moved to Hollywood, where he shared a home with gossip columnist Sheilah Graham. Fitzgerald's attempt at a literary comeback with the uncompleted novel *The Last Tycoon* was cut short in 1940 by the heart attack that killed him.

Flaubert, Gustave (1821–1880)

French novelist. Flaubert was born and raised in Rouen, France, the son of a surgeon. Though he recognized in his youth a desire to pursue a literary career, at the age of twenty-one he began legal studies in Paris. However, he did not complete this training; instead, he returned to Rouen and dedicated himself to a rigorous literary career.

In 1851 Flaubert began *Madame Bovary*, which he did not complete until 1856. This novel, in which the unfulfilled wife of a country doctor pursues romantic fulfillment in a series of increasingly bold affairs, was immediately well received. It has remained one of the classics of French literature and is the most commonly known of Flaubert's works. In *Salammbô* (1862), resulting from Flaubert's travels in Tunisia, he explores the harsh side of human nature as he portrays the dilemma of Salammbo, a priestess in Carthage. She is forced to have sexual relations with Matho, the leader of the forces that attacked Carthage in the First Punic War, in order to gain back a holy temple veil. Representative of Flaubert's writing, *Madame Bovary* and *Salammbô* were disciplined efforts in extensive description and historical documentation. Flaubert's intense attention to facts and description caused some to see him as a realist or naturalist, though Flaubert rejected such labels himself. *L'Education sentimentale* (1869; *Sentimental Education*), the third novel for which Flaubert is best known, is a historical novel about Paris during the 1840s. It is an important source for biographical material, especially information about his boyhood infatuation with Madame Schlesinger.

In addition to these three titles, Flaubert produced many more works, although the three mentioned are considered to be his most significant. As a result, Flaubert stands out as one of the most respected French authors of the nineteenth century.

Fleming, Sir Alexander (1881–1955)

Scottish bacteriologist. Fleming is famous for his 1928 discovery of penicillin, a powerful antibiotic that has made an enormous contribution to the treatment of infectious diseases.

After an early education, Fleming began his career as a shipping clerk at the age of sixteen. Only with the assistance of a scholarship and the encouragement of his older brother, a doctor, did Fleming begin his studies at the University of London, where he later became professor of bacteriology. He developed an early interest in bacteriology, particularly the chemotherapy of disease, and in 1922 made his first important discovery, that of lysozyme, which is found in mucus and saliva and has bacteria-killing properties. His later discovery of penicillin occurred accidentally in 1928. Fleming had left a culture of staphylococcus germs uncovered for several days, and when he was about to discard the dish, he noticed that specks of mold had fallen into the dish and killed the bacteria in that area. He tried in vain to isolate the substance from the mold, but it was only with the advent of World War II that interest in antibacterial drugs was revived in the scientific community. Together with the chemists Howard Florey and Ernest Chain, Fleming succeeded in isolating penicillin. For his work, he was knighted in 1944 and awarded the 1945 Nobel Prize in Medicine along with his colleagues.

Flowers in the Mirror, *see* Jing Hua Yuan

Fon

West African ethnic group. The Fon (estimated at 1 million in 1980) are the single largest ethnic group in the Republic of Benin (formerly known as Dahomey). They probably migrated to Dahomey from Oyo, a region in present-day Nigeria, in the thirteenth century during a period of great drought that displaced Adja and Arada as well as Fon peoples. These migrants established a number of small kingdoms, including the Allada kingdom, all of which became subordinate tributaries of the Yoruba Oyo empire in what is now Nigeria.

Political rivalries in the Allada kingdom forced a number of Fon to migrate again; they set off for the interior, overthrowing the city-state of Abomey to establish the Fon kingdom of Dahomey in 1625. The new kingdom based its economy on the slave trade and organized a complex system of state bureaucracy, ensuring political power with religious rites that often involved human sacrifices and expanding the kingdom's influence through wars of conquest that often featured legendary women warriors.

Though initially a subordinate of the Oyo empire to the east, Dahomey rose to challenge Oyo hegemony in the region under a series of militaristic Fon kings, and briefly gained a short-lived independence and a monopoly of the slave trade in the 1720s. With the decline of the slave trade in the 1850s, Dahomey went bankrupt and, after losing a war with France in the 1890s, became a French protectorate.

Today the Fon occupy all strata of Benin society as farmers, civil servants, and administrators, among whom traditional practices such as cosmetic scarification, polygamy, and vodu (ancestor) worship are still common. The glories of the Fon kingdom of Dahomey are preserved in the ancient city of Abomey, where Fon palaces still stand and where Fon art is exhibited.

Fonseca Amador, Carlos (1936–1976)

Nicaraguan political leader. Fonseca was a founding member and leading theoretician of the Frente Sandinista de Liberación Nacional (Sandinista National Liberation Front, or FSLN) of Nicaragua. The Somoza dynasty of father and two sons ruled Nicaragua from 1936 until 1979, when Anastasio Somoza Debayle was overthrown by a mass insurrection led by the FSLN. Brought to power by the U.S. government, the Somozas regarded Washington as their most important constituency and used their command over the army and the National Guard to contain dissent. As a student activist, Fonseca was frequently jailed for his opposition to the Somoza dictatorship. In the 1950s he joined the Socialist Party but became frustrated by the party's reformism. Inspired by the success of the 1959 Cuban revolution, Fonseca and other young Nicaraguan revolutionaries formed the FSLN in 1961. The members of the FSLN, mostly university students, espoused the theory of *focismo* developed by Latin American revolutionary leader Ernesto "Ché" Guevara. Under Fonseca's leadership, they organized clandestine groups of university students that circulated pamphlets condemning the tyranny of the Somoza dynasty and the effect of U.S. imperialism in Nicaragua. Although Fonseca argued that revolutionaries needed to understand the theories of German political theorist Karl Marx (1818–1883) and Russian Communist leader Vladimir Ilyich Lenin (1870–1924), the FSLN gave little importance to political education. In the late 1960s a small number of FSLN militants formed guerrilla columns in the mountains of northern Nicaragua, recalling the struggle of Augusto César Sandino. The Sandinistas, most of whom were from the middle and upper classes, had little or no political or military experience and their activities were detected easily by the National Guard, which killed many of the FSLN's leaders and supporters. Carlos Fonseca died in a clash with the guard in 1976, soon after he joined a guerrilla column in the mountains. Despite these reversals, the FSLN used Fonseca's death as part of a "heroes and martyrs" campaign, underlining the brutality of the Somoza dictatorship and the self-sacrificing spirit of the revolution. The military struggle against the dictatorship proved difficult, however, and the FSLN moved to follow a more broad-based strategy, forming multiclass alliances with other disenfranchised groups. By 1978 virtually the entire population of Nicaragua opposed the dictatorship, and a series of urban insurrections forced Somoza and his associates to flee the country in July 1979. Despite efforts by the United States and the Nicaraguan bourgeoisie to exclude the FSLN from the new government, the Sandinistas controlled the Sandinista People's Army and succeeded in establishing a one-party state in the new Nicaragua.

foot-binding

Chinese custom. Although the precise origins of the practice of foot-binding are unknown, the custom appeared first among the dancing girls of the Tang dynasty in the tenth century. In this ritualistic disfiguration, strips of linen were bound tightly around a young girl's feet to inhibit growth. Since the top toe was bent backwards and the other toes were tucked under the foot, thereby breaking the arch, the process was extremely painful and left the woman in an almost crippled state. Girls who were considered suitably attractive were selected for this nonreversible process between the ages of five and twelve.

In the earliest recorded incidents of its practice, the bound foot had a primarily sexual meaning, and in later centuries it became fetishized as a sexual object in poetry. (The mincing gait of women with the "golden lotus," or bound feet, was considered erotically stimulating.) Foot-binding reached the height of its popularity during the Ming dynasty (1368–1644). Although it originated among upper-class women, it was soon adopted by all social classes; only members of the peasantry too poor to afford the loss of a worker would abstain from the practice. A woman with bound feet became a status symbol for her family, since her condition proclaimed that the family could take on such a burden. By the beginning of the Qing dynasty (1644–1911), no woman with unbound feet could be expected to receive a good offer of marriage. Once married, a woman with bound feet became an object signifying her husband's wealth.

Although the Manchu rulers of the Qing dynasty detested the practice and attempted to eradicate it through a series of edicts, these proved impossible to enforce and useless in ending a custom that was too deeply ingrained in Chinese culture. Foot-binding was banned with the establishment of the Republic of China in 1912, and the practice began to lose its place in Chinese social life. Although it was prohibited once more in 1949 with the establishment of the People's Republic of China, this time the ban was gratuitous: foot-binding had all but disappeared.

Forbidden City

Largest and most complete ancient architectural complex of palaces in China. Situated in the center of the city of Beijing, the Forbidden City (also known as the Imperial Palace) was the palace of the Ming (1368–1644) and Qing (1644–1911) dynasties.

Occupying an area of 101.2 hectares (250 acres), the palace grounds include 150,000 square meters of building area containing more than 9,000 rooms. It is rectangular in shape, surrounded by a 33-foot high (10 meters) wall and a 170-foot wide (52 meters) moat. At each corner of the wall is a resplendent tower. The roofs of the buildings in the palace are all made of bright orange-yellow glazed tiles, except one, which is of dark blue, where the royal family stayed when in mourning. All the walls inside the palace complex are painted vermilion.

The grounds consist of two sections. The main entrance to the Forbidden City, Wumen Gate, at the southern end, leads to the public section. It consists of three gigantic halls where the emperors conducted important state ceremonies, such as royal weddings, the greeting of foreign dignitaries, and the administration of top-level civil service examinations. This section takes up about half of the palace grounds. The other half is composed of three main palaces and several smaller palaces where the royal household resided, and the Imperial Gardens. The royal family, with the emperor and his several wives, several thousand concubines, and very often a large brood of children, all lived inside the wall of the Forbidden City, rarely if ever leaving.

A vast treasure house of invaluable art objects and precious jewels of every dynasty and every description, the Imperial Palace was looted by the Japanese occupation army during the 1930s and the Guomindang forces before their retreat to Taiwan. Today it is a museum, and the halls and palaces with much of the remaining treasures are open to the public.

Forster, E[dward] M[organ] (1879–1970)

English novelist, short-story writer, and essayist. Forster was raised in London by his mother, who was his constant companion until her death in 1945. While at Cambridge, he met G. Lowes Dickinson, a man who accompanied him on his first historic visit to India in 1911. While in Cambridge, Forster became a part of the Bloomsbury group, a clique that included the British literary couple Leonard and Virginia Woolf. The group held in common unconventional beliefs and interests like socialism and homosexuality. Forster was himself an uneasy homosexual; his one gay novel, *Maurice*, was a utopian homosexual coming-of-age story written in 1913. It remained unpublished, at the author's request, until a year after his death.

Forster wrote his first four novels, *Where Angels Fear to Tread* (1905), *The Longest Journey* (1907), *A Room with a View* (1908), and *Howards End* (1910), in a flurry of creative inspiration. He then went on an extended sabbatical, traveling in British India and serving as secretary to the maharajah of Dewas for six months. After this trip, he wrote *A Passage to India* (1924), a progressive study of the abuses of British imperialism. He continued to write and comment upon developments in the arts. *Aspects of the Novel*, a pioneering work of literary criticism, was published in 1928. A collection of essays, interviews, and radio broadcasts, *Two Cheers for Democracy*, was published in 1951. Other works include a biography of his great-aunt, *Marianne Thornton* (1956), and a libretto, written with Eric Crozier, for Benjamin Britten's operatic production of *Billy Budd* (1951).

Fragonard, Jean-Honoré (1732–1806)

French painter. Strongly influenced by the French painter Antoine Watteau (1684–1721) and his teacher Giambattista Tiepolo, Fragonard painted landscapes, mythological love scenes, domestic scenes, and outdoor gatherings in the rococo style—a style that was excessively ornate and characterized by curved spatial forms and elaborate or-namentation. This style severely damaged his popularity after the French Revolution as it was closely associated with the period before the Revolution.

Apprenticed to a lawyer in his youth, Fragonard was encouraged by his employer to pursue studies in the arts. He received a Prix de Rome scholarship and spent much of his time sketching the Roman countryside. He later concentrated on landscapes and sensuous outdoor scenes, such as *Les Hasards heureux de l'escarpolette* (1766; *The Swing*), his best-known work. Fragonard married in 1769, and, after falling in love with his wife's fourteen-year-old sister, turned his talents to domestic scenes, often featuring his son Évariste (born 1780). Fragonard tried to adopt a Neoclassical style and subject matter in the years after the French Revolution, but his artistic reputation was too closely tied to the prerevolutionary period to be considered acceptable. He lost his patrons and spent his final years in relative poverty and obscurity, painting little. His death passed unnoticed, and his paintings remained largely unknown until the late nineteenth century.

Francis of Assisi, St. (c. 1182–1226)

Italian monk, founder of the Franciscan order. Born Giovanni Francesco Bernardone, the son of a prosperous cloth merchant, St. Francis renounced the material world at the age of twenty-six after a serious illness and began a life of asceticism, poverty, and charity, modeled on the life of Jesus Christ. He attracted many followers, and together they ministered to the sick, the poor, and the leprous.

In 1210 St. Francis made a pilgrimage to the pope in Rome, to seek papal recognition of his monastic order. The friars were initially called the Friars Minor, and later became known as the Franciscans. The Franciscans proved more popular than any other order, and by 1220 numbered close to 5,000 brothers. With nothing more than St. Francis's simple rules of life and his personal example to serve as an administrative guide, the orders tended to diverge, and Francis eventually resigned his leadership because of internal administrative disputes.

St. Francis is also known for his love of nature, and is often depicted preaching to the birds, including both human and nonhuman creations in God's family. Two years before his death, he also is said to have received stigmata—open sores resembling Jesus' wounds from the cross—after forty days of fasting on Mt. Alverno. He took care to hide these wounds, and spent his last two years in constant pain and almost completely blind. St. Francis was canonized in 1228, and is, together with St. Catherine of Siena, the patron saint of Italy and of the environment. The letters, sermons, and legends surrounding St. Francis were published a century after his death as *Little Flowers of St. Francis*.

Franklin, Benjamin (1706–1790)

American printer, author, inventor, and statesman. Benjamin Franklin was a crucial participant in the struggle of the American colonies for independence from Great Britain. He was a diplomat and a drafter of the Declaration of Independence and the U.S. Constitution. Franklin's many successful investments provided him with the leisure time to pursue his scientific interests: he invented the lightning rod, bifocal spectacles, and the water-harmonica.

Finished with school by age ten, Franklin soon began an apprenticeship with his brother, James, a newspaper printer, at the age of twelve. Franklin ran away from Boston to Philadelphia in 1723 and eventually set up his own newspaper, *The Pennsylvania Gazette*. He also published an annual report, *Poor Richard's Almanac*, under the pen name Richard Saunders, in which he wrote proverbs stressing the virtues of honesty

and industry. For the next thirty years Franklin vigorously pursued intellectual and social projects, establishing a fire company, a hospital, a philosophical society, and a militia. In 1753 he became deputy postmaster general of the northern colonies and founded the institution that became the University of Pennsylvania. Franklin's invention of the lightning rod led to his induction into the Royal Society in London in 1752, and secured for him the favor of King Louis XV of France.

Franklin was a signer of the Declaration of Independence, and in 1776 he traveled to France on behalf of the colonies for military and financial aid. Hailed in Paris as the living embodiment of all the virtues praised by the *philosophes*, Franklin remained in France until 1778 and the conclusion of the alliance. In 1783 he was one of the diplomats to negotiate the treaty of peace with Great Britain, and in 1787 he attended the Federal Constitutional Convention. His last public service was to urge ratification of the new government under George Washington.

Franko, Ivan Yakovich (1856–1916)

Ukrainian writer, scholar, and public figure. Son of a village blacksmith, Franko graduated from a gymnasium in Drohobych in 1875 and began to study classical philology and Ukrainian language and literature at Lvov University. He began writing poetry at the age of twelve, and became seriously involved in literature and journalism at the university. Franko's political and publishing activities attracted the attention of the police, and in 1877 he was arrested for spreading socialist propaganda, but was released after seven months in prison. In 1880 he was arrested again; though he was released after three months of detention, he was kept under police surveillance and forced to discontinue his university studies. His early works were political poems, such as "Kameniari" (1878; "The

Stonecutters") and "Vichnyi revoliut-
sioner" (1880; "The Eternal Revolutionary"), which became patriotic anthems
and influenced the outlook of a whole
generation; novels, such as *Boryslav
smiiet'sia* (1881; *Boryslav Is Laughing*),
written in a realistic manner; and a historical novella, *Zakhar Berkut* (1883).
His poetry of these years was collected
in *Z vershyn ta nyzyn* (1887; *From the
Heights and Depths*).

In the decade that followed, he
worked extensively in journalism, publishing in Ukrainian, Polish, and
German periodicals. In 1889 he cofounded the Ruthenian-Ukrainian Radical Party, and was its candidate for
parliamentary elections in the 1890s. He
also continued his university studies,
first at Chernovtsy and then at Vienna,
where he defended his doctoral dissertation in 1893. The Symbolist-inspired
volume entitled *Ziv'iale lystia* (1896;
Withered Leaves) collected the best of
his love poetry. Franko also wrote several philosophical narrative poems, of
which "Moisei" (1905; "Moses"), dealing in a biblical setting with the conflict
between the leader and his people, is
considered to be his greatest poetic
achievement.

An extremely prolific writer, Franco
wrote several volumes of poetry, more
than one hundred short stories, dozens
of novels, several dramas, tales for children, and scholarly studies in literature,
linguistics, history, sociology, and economics, as well as a number of translations. Franko was one of the first realists
in Ukrainian literature and is considered
to be the most outstanding Ukrainian
poet after Taras Shevchenko.

French Revolution (1789–99)

Though there is much disagreement
over both the causes and the effects
of the French Revolution, in political terms the Revolution transformed
France from a monarchical state with a
rigid social and political hierarchy into
a modern nation with greater social flex-

ibility and more diffuse political power.
It is conventionally dated from May 1789
to December 1799, ending with the
consolidation of power by Napoleon
Bonaparte.

Since the 1770s, agricultural production had declined, driving up the cost of
food for all segments of the population,
but especially the poor. The political
structure of the *ancien régime* and a disproportionate amount of the nation's
wealth were controlled by the nobility
and the clergy. Philosophically, the
monarchy was operating under the old
feudal patterns of rule (and using taxation to underwrite international war and
court profligacy) in opposition to the
Physiocrats and other Enlightenment
writers who were disseminating ideas
about reform based upon individual
rights.

Regardless of the exact causes, the
Revolution was precipitated by the chaotic state of government finance; participation in the American Revolution
had created a huge debt. Impending
royal bankruptcy led King Louis XVI
(r. 1774–92) to convene the Estates-
General (the legislative body not acti-
vated since 1614 and segmented by the
medieval distinction of the three "estates" of the nobility, the clergy, and
the commoners) at Versailles on May 5,
1789, in order to refinance his depleted
war chest. The nobility, who controlled
the courts, had previously refused to
carry out Louis's money-raising decrees;
on this occasion the "third estate," refusing to play its historically inferior role,
defiantly proclaimed itself a National Assembly, which would require concessions on social and political reforms
by the other two estates. The king
closed their meeting place, but they
moved to an indoor tennis court to continue deliberations, agreeing in 1789 on
what is thus called the "Oath of the
Tennis Court," a vow not to disband until a new constitution had been written.
The king yielded publicly, but at the
same time dismissed his liberal eco-

nomic adviser, Jacques Necker, an advocate of reform, and ordered his troops
to surround Versailles. Emboldened by
the National Assembly's usurpation of
power, on July 14 a Paris mob stormed
the Bastille, a small jail in fact holding
only a handful of prisoners but a symbol
of governmental oppression. To counter
the king's troops, many of them non-
French mercenaries, the National
Guard was organized under the Marquis
de Lafayette; and throughout France,
peasants revolted against their landlords.

Louis relented, recalling Necker and
officially recognizing the National Assembly. The Assembly adopted a "Declaration of the Rights of Man and
Citizen," which outlined a new constitution and a democratic republicanism,
entailing a limited monarchy and a
vastly weaker (and poorer) Church. In
October protesters forced the king and
the queen, Marie Antoinette, to move to
Paris, where they were held as virtual
prisoners.

For the next two years the National
Assembly passed many reforms, altering
radically the social and political structure of the *ancien régime*. After the king,
who had been captured trying to flee the
country, reluctantly agreed to the new
constitution, the National Assembly was
dissolved in the belief that the Revolution was over. On October 1, 1791, a new
Legislative Assembly convened; a variety
of political groups competed—the most
powerful of which were called Jacobins
after the monastery in which they met.
The year 1792 saw the beginning of what
would later be called the Napoleonic
Wars, as France was engaged in fighting
by Austria and Prussia. The wars would
eventually spread throughout Europe
and into Africa and Russia, carried on
by the first national army created by universal conscription. The newly empowered citizenry attributed the early
revolutionary defeats to royalist intrigue,
and in the September Massacres they
killed 1,200 supposed counterrevolutionary prisoners. The National Convention,

headed by Jean-Paul Marat and Georges
Danton, declared France a republic on
September 22, 1792; on January 21, 1793,
King Louis XVI as well as his wife, Marie Antoinette, were beheaded. Soon
France was at war with most of Western
Europe, whose governments feared the
expansion of the Revolution, and the
Convention was racked by dissension
among its many political factions,
including the Girondists, the Monta-
gnards, and the Cordeliers. In an attempt to give focus to the direction of
the Revolution, the Convention established the Committee of Public Safety,
whose first leader, the moderate Danton,
helped forge the constitution of 1793 but
fell out of favor with the more radical
members and was executed in 1794.
From July 1793 its second leader, the
Jacobin Maximilien Robespierre, ruled
France as a virtual dictator through his
influence with the committee, the revolutionary tribunal, and the representatives of the people. The period that
followed is known as the Reign of Terror
because of the violence directed against
the committee's internal and external
enemies, with public guillotining of
those accused of counterrevolution. The
Convention regained power in 1794, and
Robespierre was executed. A popular uprising was averted by the bloody military
suppression of the extreme republican
sans-culottes. In the period of reaction
that encompassed the adoption of a new
constitution in 1795, a directory came to
power that was notable for its corruption and incompetence in directing the
various military campaigns. Napoleon,
hero of the Italian and Egyptian wars,
returned to France and overthrew the directory on 18 Brumaire (November 9–10,
1799), establishing his own consulate, restoring Catholicism, and subsequently ruling as emperor from 1804 until 1814, when
the Bourbon monarchy was installed.

Freud, Sigmund (1856–1939)

Founder of psychoanalysis. Considered
to be the father of modern psychology,

Freud was born in Moravia, now part of the Czech Republic. His family moved to Vienna, where he attended medical school and maintained his primary residence throughout most of his life. Freud's early years in medicine were spent in clinical practice, though he pursued an interest in neurology, experimenting with hypnosis as a treatment for severe neurosis. In 1885 he traveled to Paris, where he first explored the possibility that psychological maladies might have their origins in the mind rather than the brain. His first major work, *Studien über Hysterie* (1895; *Studies in Hysteria*), explored various mental processes that produced physical ailments, and whether these hysterical tendencies could be treated through therapy.

In the early 1880s Freud began working with Dr. Josef Breuer. Together they pioneered a new field in psychology, inspired by the theory and practice of "free association." This was a form of therapy that involved delving into the unconscious of patients in order to release impulses whose repression contributed to neurotic behavior. Freud believed that these impulses were repressed as a result of the conflict in patients' minds between the acceptable and the unacceptable. Therapy could resolve this conflict and allow for the rational rejection or acceptance of these impulses. Freud viewed sexuality as the prime motive for human behavior and believed that central psychological traits could be traced back to early childhood.

The major work of Freud's career began in 1897, when he undertook a thoroughgoing self-analysis. He argued that dreams reveal what people truly desire, though these desires may not be socially acceptable. He elaborates on this theory in *Die Traumdeutung* (1900; *The Interpretation of Dreams*). Dreams are outlets for the energies of the mind, to help fulfill desires not realized in the outside world.

At first, Freud's findings were not accepted by the scientific community, especially those conclusions related to sex. Many of his theories depended on psychological interpretation, and were thus dismissed as insufficiently rigorous or scientific. However, Freud's impact on modern psychology is immeasurable. He defined the terms that still figure prominently today in the language of psychology. His impact on popular culture is even greater. Much of twentieth-century literature and philosophy, from Surrealism to existentialism, found a sort of inspiration in his work, while the spread of psychology and self-help made "Freudian slip," "Oedipus complex," and the "mental structure" comprising the ego, id, and superego part of everyday speech.

Freud was a loyal member of the Jewish community, though not a practicing Jew. While maintaining a large following of Jewish students, Freud encountered anti-Semitism in medical school, as well as from critics of his work. He viewed religion as a construct of the human mind resulting from early conflict within one's self, a type of neurosis. He saw the worship of divinities as the reverence of one's ancestors.

Freud fled Vienna in 1938 following the Nazi invasion and relocated to London, where he died of cancer. His position in history goes much further than the boundaries of science, for he introduced new ways of analyzing the human situation.

Frye, Northrop (1912–1991)

Canadian writer, critic, and teacher. Born Herman Northrop Frye in Sherbrooke, Quebec, he moved with his family at the age of five to New Brunswick and received his early education at home. Entering Victoria College of the University of Toronto, he graduated with honors in philosophy and English in 1933. He studied theology at the university's Emmanuel College, but after a summer as a preacher in Saskatchewan

Frye decided in favor of literature. Ordained in 1936, he studied literature at Merton College, Oxford University, later returning to Victoria to teach.

Frye began to develop his theory of literature as a unified verbal universe while working on his ground-breaking study of the visionary English poet William Blake (1757–1827), *Fearful Symmetry* (1947), in which he argued that Blake's poetry, at the time usually disparaged for incoherence, was in fact a symbolic whole whose materials were also those of earlier mythologists like Spenser and Milton, deriving primarily from the Bible, "the Great Code of Art." His next work, one of the most frequently cited scholarly works of this century, *Anatomy of Criticism* (1957), set out to describe with scientific rigor the mythopoeic structure of all literature as the structure of the human imagination and its fullest expression. This structure can be anatomized into modes that correspond to a spatial and seasonal schematic, all elements of a grand narrative of the quest for salvation. Practically speaking, this means that there can and should be a universally accepted terminology and methodology for literary studies just as there is for biology. The critic's job is to describe how a particular work fits into this schema ("the total order of words") rather than to be preoccupied with making evaluative comments. As Frye went on to elaborate in a series of books, including the widely read *The Educated Imagination* and *The Well-Tempered Critic* (both 1963), the critic retains an ethical role, however, because the description that results is a description of the human psyche as it seeks to imagine the best—and the worst—possible worlds.

In his more than thirty published books and hundreds of articles, speeches, and interviews, Frye touched on a remarkably broad range of subjects; nonetheless, his best work found him turning repeatedly to the writers he found most telling: British writers William Shakespeare (1564–1616), John Milton (1608–1674), William Butler Yeats (1865–1939), and American writer T. S. Eliot (1888–1965). His work from early to late is remarkably consistent, with each publication usually either describing a section of the human-literary mythos or arguing its importance to an understanding of proper social goals.

Fuentes, Carlos (1928–)

Mexican novelist, short-story writer, and critic. Born in Mexico City, Fuentes was the son of a diplomat and traveled extensively during his childhood. In the 1950s he belonged to the Communist Party, an experience that influenced his thinking long after he left the party in 1962. For much of his life Fuentes has worked as a diplomatic functionary. He began his career as a writer in the 1950s, publishing a book of short stories, *Los días enmascarados* (*The Masked Days*), in 1954. That same year, he cofounded the *Mexican Review of Literature*.

His fiction was a stylized blend of history and fantasy, an early take on what would become known as "magical realism" after the "Latin American boom" of the 1960s, when a whole generation of writers, including Julio Cortázar, Gabriel García Márquez, Mario Vargas Llosa, and José Donoso, stormed the Anglo-American literary stage. Although Fuentes has published numerous plays, novellas, and short-story collections—including *Aura* (1962), *Cantar de los ciegos* (1964; *The Song of the Blind*), and *Agua queonada* (1981; *Burnt Water*)—he is best known and lauded as a writer of sensitive, historically-minded novels. *La región más transparente* (1958; *When the Air Is Clear*) describes the fortunes and foibles of the elite class in the aftermath of the Mexican revolution, indicting the new middle class as well as the left-leaning liberal intellectuals. It also featured his trademark jump-start narrative technique, as well as the creative combination of various periods of Mexican national history, from the Aztecs to the revolution. His second full-length novel, *La muerte de Artemio Cruz* (1962; *The Death of Artemio Cruz*), established Fuentes as an international presence. The novel explores the twelve hours before Cruz's death, and with a series of flashbacks introduces the reader to the life of this revolutionary fighter turned opportunist and plutocrat after the revolution. In 1967 Fuentes published *Cambio de piel* (*A Change of Skin*), in which once again he sought to define a collective Mexican consciousness; nearly a decade later, the epic novel *Terra Nostra* (1975), one of Fuentes's most significant literary ventures, appeared. *Terra Nostra* develops stock Fuentian themes—the double; the transmigration of souls; the relationship between individual and national identity; the relationship between Spain and the New World; the portrayal of the Aztec past as a living present, and even the future of Mexico; tyranny and liberation; and experimentation with many narrative styles, tempos, and tones—in its exploration through new and old worlds for signs of Mexico's cultural heritage. Since *Terra Nostra*, for which Fuentes received the National Prize for Literature in Mexico (1984), he has published several works, including *La cabeza de la hidra* (1978; *The Hydra Head*), *Una familia lejana* (1980; *Distant Relations*), *Gringo viejo* (1985; *Old Gringo*), *Cristóbal nonato* (1987; *Christopher Unborn*), and *La campaña* (1990; *Campaign*). His most recent publication was a book of essays written in English entitled *The Buried Mirror: Reflections on Spain and the New World* (1992).

Fulani

Muslim ethnic group living throughout the western Sudanic region of Africa, from Senegal to the Central African Republic. Numbering about 7 million, most Fulani live in Nigeria (4 million), Senegal and Mali (900,000), Cameroon (400,000), and Niger (300,000). In physical appearance they combine Negroid and Caucasoid features. They refer to themselves as the Fulbe and Pullo (as well as Peul, Fula, and Fellata); "Fulani" is the name given to them by the Hausa people, another ethnic group living in northwest Nigeria. Approximately half of the Fulani live among the Hausa as a ruling class, though they have adopted many Hausa customs, as well as the Hausa language.

Having risen from obscure origins, the Fulani are believed to be the descendants of the Tukulor, a group living along the Senegal River in the seventh century. These people were converted to Islam in the eleventh century and later helped spread Islam throughout parts of West Africa. Historians believe that the Fulani migrated eastward sometime around the fourteenth century, and that by the sixteenth century they were established in their present territory. Prior to their conquest by the French at the end of the nineteenth century, they dominated much of the eastern Senegal Valley. Although many Fulani continued to live as pastoralists, others chose to settle in urban communities.

The Fulani trade their dairy products for the various crops cultivated by those groups living around them. In many regions, however, the Fulani have become sedentary agriculturalists, relying heavily on cultivation as a result of depleted cattle herds, or have become permanent settlers, referred to as "town Fulani."

G

Gainsborough, Thomas (1727–1788)

English painter. Known primarily for his portraits and landscapes, Gainsborough was one of the first to depict English scenery, and is considered to be, along with Sir Joshua Reynolds (1723–1792), the most famous English artist of the eighteenth century.

Born in Suffolk, England, Gainsborough moved to London in 1740 to study painting, remaining there until 1746. The French engraver Gravelot (1699–1773) and the traditions of Dutch landscape painting informed his early work, which consisted predominantly of full-length portraits in what is called the "conversation piece" style. In the 1750s and 1760s, influenced by Flemish painters Sir Anthony Van Dyck (1599–1641) and Peter Paul Rubens (1577–1640), Gainsborough painted more intimate portraits with richer colors and greater formal complexity. In 1768 he became a founding member of the Royal Academy of Arts, though his relationship with the group soon became strained, and he ceased to exhibit with them after 1784. Financially secure due to a large number of commissions and increasing fame, Gainsborough continued his work in portraiture, landscape painting, drawings, and the "fancy pictures" (sentimental genre subjects), perfecting an idealizing, highly decorative style. His best-known painting is *Blue Boy* (1770).

Galileo Galilei (1564–1642)

Italian astronomer and physicist. The inventor of the telescope, Galileo was the first person to see the moons of Jupiter, and his subsequent belief in the Copernican view of the solar system almost cost him his life. Galileo's important work set the stage for English mathematician and physicist Sir Isaac Newton's (1642–1727) discoveries a century later.

Born in Pisa, Italy, Galileo was urged by his father, a scholar and musician, to study medicine rather than the sciences. However, failing his courses in medicine at the University of Pisa, Galileo turned to mathematics. In 1589 he was appointed to the chair of mathematics at Pisa, and in 1592 he moved to the chair of mathematics at Padua. By 1610 Galileo had designed and constructed a simple refracting telescope, which he employed to discover the mottled and irregular surface of the moon, as well as four of Jupiter's moons. He published his observations in *Sidereus nuncius* (*Starry Messenger*) the same year.

Galileo's innovative thinking about the sciences began when he was still a teenager studying medicine in Pisa. Watching the chandeliers swinging in the wind during a service in the cathedral, he timed their swing using his pulse and noted that they were all in constant time, though the amplitude of the swings varied. In like manner, he investigated the acceleration of falling bodies by allowing them to roll down an inclined plane; he discovered that the rate of each was equal regardless of weight. Forced to use his imagination without modern scientific appurtenances, Galileo had no accurate way of keeping time, and his mathematics was no more advanced than the geometry of the Greeks. (Dutch scientist Christian Huygens [1629–1695] would develop the metronome out of the pendulum Galileo employed.) His science was simple and elegant, much like the thought experiments that German-born American physicist Albert Einstein (1879–1955) carried out four hundred years later.

Initially, Galileo had been a forceful proponent of the Copernican cosmology, which shifted the galactic center from earth to sun—more forceful, and more public, than Polish astronomer Nicolaus Copernicus (1473–1543) himself. Pope Paul V (1605–21) ordered Galileo to stop supporting Copernicus publicly. When the pope died, however, Galileo used the arrival of a new pope, Urban VIII, to publish *Il saggiatore* (*The Assayer*) in 1623. This work criticized Greek philosopher Aristotle's (384–322 B.C.E.) view of the universe and implicitly endorsed Copernicus. In 1632 he published *Dialogo dei due massimi sistemi* (*Dialogue Concerning the Two Chief World Systems*), in which he attacked the Church-sanctioned view outlined by Alexandrian astronomer Ptolemy (second century C.E.) and Aristotle quite thoroughly. He was summoned to Rome and threatened with torture unless he renounced Copernicus completely. Almost seventy years old, he was sentenced to strict seclusion in his villa in Florence and spent the last eight years of his life in study and experiment. His last published work was *Discorsi . . . a due nuove scienze* (1638; *Discourse on Two New Sciences*).

Gallegos, Rómulo (1884–1969)

Venezuelan novelist, educator, and political leader. Born Rómulo Gallegos

Friere, and raised in Caracas, Venezuela, Gallegos studied law at the Central University of Venezuela. He left school and dedicated himself to a career in education, holding various teaching positions. In 1929 he published *Doña Bárbara*, which established him as one of Latin America's leading novelists. Soon after, he wrote a pair of novels, *Cantaclaro* (1934; *Chanticleer*), about a *llanero* ballad singer, and *Canaima* (1935). All of his novels explore the interaction of civilization and barbarism, idealism and materialism, and document the search for what is firstborn and natural.

Gallegos began his political career in 1931 during the dictatorship of Juan Vicente Gómez (1908–35), when he was elected senator for the state of Apure. He refused to assume this position, however, and went into voluntary exile, first to New York and later to Spain. In 1935, upon Gómez's death, he returned to Venezuela and briefly served as minister of education. He also became an important member of the opposition in Congress. A leader of the Acción Democrática, he was elected president in 1947 with a large majority. His party was unable to work out a successful coalition, however, and he was ousted by a military coup in 1948. Gallegos spent a decade in exile in Mexico and Cuba, returning to Venezuela after the fall of dictator Marcos Pérez Jiménez in 1958, at which time he was awarded the National Prize for Literature for his short story *La doncella y el último patriota* (1957; *The Damsel and the Last Patriot*) and given lifetime membership in the senate. Gallegos's mission as a writer was closely linked to his ambitions as a social actor and a politician: in an era of tentative Latin American nationalism, the struggle to forge a viable national community was linked to the creation of national literatures. Gallegos, then, was primarily responsible for the invention of the Venezuelan novel. Other writings include *Pobre negro* (1937), *El Forastero*

(1942; *The Stranger*), *Sobre la misma tierra* (1943; *Over the Same Ground*), *La brizna de paja en el viento* (1952; *The Strand of Hay in the Wind*), and *Una posición en la vida* (1954; *A Posture in Life*).

gamelan

Indonesian musical ensemble. Native to Indonesia, and particularly to Java and Bali, a gamelan is usually composed of several xylophones, metallophones, tuned gongs, and drums, and may also contain stringed instruments, such as the sitar and the rebab (a two-stringed bowed lute), oboes, flutes, and singers. The word "gamelan" often refers to a particular set of instruments that are always kept and played together, rather than to the performers themselves. Two separate scale systems are employed by gamelan music: slendro, a pentatonic, and pelog, which is heptatonic. "Complete" gamelans have two sets of instruments, one in each tuning, but single-scale gamelans also exist, and some smaller groups of percussion instruments may also be called a gamelan.

Different styles of music are played in different parts of Indonesia, as well as in different settings. In general, gamelan music is highly rhythmic and often quite intricate, with many small-scale variations playing off each other while a voice, reed, or stringed instrument carries a more strident, constant melody. Balinese gamelans are usually more rhythmically based and "brighter" than those of Java. Individual gamelans may be specialized for playing either indoors or out depending on their volume, and may be used uniquely for certain rituals.

The history of the music is not fully known, but it appears to be at least a thousand years old, and some instruments still in use today date back hundreds of years. Gamelans are played primarily at religious ceremonies by tradition, but in recent times they have been employed for a variety of secular events. Western interest in gamelans grew during the 1930s, and many were broken up and sold off before Indonesia made removal of antique instruments from the islands illegal. Gamelan music is used by the Javanese to promote interest in the culture of the country, and the government now attempts to preserve both the music and the instruments themselves.

Gandhi, Indira [Priyadarshini] (1917–1984)

Indian prime minister. The only child of independent India's first prime minister, Jawaharlal Nehru, Gandhi was quite literally born to be a politician. She attended her first session of the Indian National Congress in 1931 at the age of fourteen, and was organizing youth branches of Mohandas Gandhi's Civil Disobedience Movement by the age of twelve. After attending Visva-Bharati University in West Bengal and Oxford University in England, she served as a member of the Congress Party, where she was to meet her husband, Feroze Gandhi (d. 1960), a fellow Congress member (not related to Mahatma Gandhi).

In 1959 Indira Gandhi was elected to the largely honorary position of president of the ruling Congress Party. By 1964 her father's successor, Lal Bahadur Shastri, named her minister of information and broadcasting. After Shastri's sudden death in January 1966, Indira was thrust into the political spotlight. A compromise figure acceptable to both wings of the Congress, Gandhi was promoted to leader of the party and hence prime minister of India. The right wing, however, led by the previous minister of finance, Morarji Desai, contested Gandhi's authority, costing her the majority of votes in the 1967 election and thus necessitating Desai's appointment to deputy minister. By the 1971 elections, Gandhi prevailed, winning a two-thirds majority in the lower house of Parliament over the conservative coalition.

Although she imitated the quasi-socialist policies of her father, Nehru, Gandhi was far more ruthless in centralizing political authority and smothering opposition. She systematically removed ministers who had independent bases, replacing them with her own loyal supporters; extended the power of the government over the states, using central police and intelligence forces to observe and undermine regional competitors, ruining their political operations; and relied increasingly on trusted family members, most notably her son Sanjay. In foreign affairs, Gandhi intervened directly in East Bengal's bid for independence from Pakistan, sending the Indian army to guarantee the sovereignty of what would become the state of Bangladesh. She also succeeded in enlisting the aid of the Soviet Union in India's long-standing dispute with Pakistan.

The 1972 elections resulted in yet another victory for Gandhi's New Congress Party. However, a number of factors, including food shortages and spiraling inflation, bolstered the confidence of her opponents. She was accused of violating election laws, and the High Court of Allahabad found her guilty and disbarred her from her position as prime minister, further prohibiting her from involvement with politics for six years. Gandhi responded by declaring a "state of emergency" on June 26, 1975. The "emergency" lasted for two years, during which time she jailed her opponents, curtailed freedom of expression, forcibly cleared the slums as part of a "beautification" program, and perpetrated the enforced sterilization of India's poor and marginalized as a means of population control. Convinced of the rightness of her actions, Gandhi canceled the state of emergency in 1977 and held national elections. To her surprise and dismay, she and her party were soundly defeated.

Though briefly jailed on charges of official corruption, Gandhi continued to do political work. In 1978 her supporters left the Congress Party and formed the Congress (I)—I for Indira—Party.

Though the ruling Janata Party succeeded in normalizing Indian society, internal conflicts brought the government down in 1979, paving the way for Indira Gandhi's return to power in the elections of 1980. Shortly thereafter, all legal cases against the Gandhi family were dropped.

By the 1980s it was clear that Indira Gandhi had transformed the New Congress Party from a broad-based independent political party into a vehicle for her ambitions and those of her heirs. Sanjay Gandhi, her elder son, was the prime minister's handpicked successor, but his death in an airplane crash in 1980 forced her to turn to her other son, Rajiv. Concerns about the future were disrupted as a long-simmering regional problem came to full boil. In the Punjab, where the Sikhs had long posed a threat to her power base, Gandhi responded violently, attacking the Sikhs in the Golden Temple of Amritsar, their headquarters and one of their most revered shrines. More than 450 were killed. A short time later, the Sikhs exacted revenge: Indira Gandhi was gunned down in her garden, slain by two of her own Sikh bodyguards. Her son Rajiv quickly succeeded his mother as leader of the Congress Party and served as prime minister until 1989. He was assassinated two years later.

Gandhi, Mohandas K[aramchand] (1869–1948)

Indian religious and political leader. As a social reformer and leader of the Indian nationalist movement against British rule, Gandhi was known to his fellow Indians as Mahatma, the Hindi word for "Great Soul," and is perhaps best known for advocating a policy of nonviolent protest or civil disobedience to achieve social and political reform.

Gandhi was born in Porbandar, in western India, the fourth son of his father's fourth wife. His devout mother, an orthodox Hindu, instilled in her young son his pacifism, his vegetarianism, and his respect for all living things. When he was only thirteen, Gandhi married the daughter of a Porbandar merchant named Kasturba (Kasturbai); they had their first child five years later. When his son was only a year old, Gandhi went to England to study law (1888–91). While in England, in the vegetarian restaurants and boardinghouses, Gandhi met English playwright George Bernard Shaw and the Theosophist Annie Besant, who introduced him to both the Bible and the Bhagavadgita, a famous Hindu philosophical poem, which he read first in English, translated by Sir Edwin Arnold, as well as the socialist ideas that would have such a formative influence on Gandhi's dreams for India's future.

In 1893, after a brief and relatively unsuccessful attempt to practice law in India, Gandhi traveled to South Africa, where he encountered racial discrimination firsthand. He was politicized during a train ride from Durban to Pretoria. Although Gandhi had purchased a first-class ticket, a white man who boarded the train had Gandhi ousted from the compartment with the help of local police. Outraged and determined not to run away from injustice, Gandhi undertook to become the spokesperson for Indian nationals in South Africa. He spent twenty-one years there, fighting for Indian civil rights, and was imprisoned many times. During this period he developed an ethics of quiet rebellion. He quit his lucrative legal practice, establishing a communal farm at Phoenix near Durban in 1904, and took a vow of celibacy in 1906. He also developed a correspondence with Russian philosopher and writer Count Leo Tolstoy (1828–1910), whose spiritualism he admired. The seeds of *ahimsa*, or nonviolent resistance, were sown in South Africa; by 1914 the South African government repealed many of the acts Gandhi had worked so long to overturn. Gandhi, satisfied, returned to India.

Swiftly becoming a major force in Indian politics, Gandhi took the helm of the Indian National Congress, fashioning it into a powerful political force, and advocated large-scale *ahimsa*. In 1919 Gandhi began the first of several provocations to protest the passing of the Rowlatt Act, the disbanding of the Khalifat Movement, and the shooting of an unarmed crowd in the Punjab by British soldiers. Though successful at mobilizing large segments of the Indian people, the Non-Cooperation Movement, as it was called, was halted in 1922 after an outbreak of violence. Jailed for a time, Gandhi continued to lead large-scale resistance, including a protest against the British-imposed salt tax in 1930 and the "Quit India" movement in 1942. The avowed aim of these maneuvers was *swaraj*, or moral reformation of the Indian people, which would result, it was hoped, in the conversion of the British or in Indian home rule.

Also during this time Gandhi outlined what he called the "constructive program," which attempted to develop rural India by renovating rural educational systems, promoting cottage industries like spinning, and advocating Hindu-Muslim unity and civil liberties for the "untouchable" castes. The British recognized Gandhi's growing influence, appointing him as the sole representative of the Indian National Congress to attend the second and third Round Table Conferences in London in 1932. Disappointed by negotiations, Gandhi began a series of fasts, and also engaged in numerous acts of civil disobedience; for Gandhi, civil disobedience was a philosophy, one he called *satyagraha* (truth force). Along with most other Congress luminaries, Gandhi was jailed during much of World War II. His wife and lifelong companion was also imprisoned during the war; she died in detention in 1944.

In August 1947, Gandhi successfully completed negotiations with the British, establishing home rule and the independent republic of India. The new state immediately gave way to chaos, however, as religious and political factions struggled to define the new government. While Gandhi envisioned a decentralized, agrarian India based on a socialist economy that avoided the lures of industrialization, many political leaders sought to establish a centralized modern government. The riots in outlying areas and in the capital, Delhi, caused Gandhi to declare a fast "to end only if and when sanity returned." His fast was successful in that it brought an end to the panic and brought the opposing parties to the bargaining table. Tragically, Gandhi only got to experience his longed-for *swaraj* briefly. He was gunned down by a Hindu fanatic, Nathuram Godse, while on his way to an evening prayer session. An estimated 2 million people attended Gandhi's funeral.

Gang of Four

Coterie of Chinese Communist Party officials during the Cultural Revolution. Arrested immediately after the death of Mao Zedong, the founder of the People's Republic of China, in 1976, the Gang of Four were held personally responsible for the widespread political persecution and social turmoil that brought China to the brink of complete economic collapse. The "four" included Jiang Qing, Mao Zedong's widow; Wang Hongwen, once nominated as the future successor to Mao; and Zhang Chunqiao and Yao Wenyuan, both Politburo members of the CCP. All were active during the Cultural Revolution; Jiang Qing had been a strong advocate of revolution in the arts, declaring herself its standard-bearer. The Gang of Four were imprisoned and later tried in 1980–81 for their "atrocities" against the Chinese people during the Cultural Revolution. The attacks on the Gang of Four were complicated by political motives; the new Communist leadership, headed by Deng Xiaoping, could not afford to criticize Mao Zedong directly,

so instead the blame for Mao's terrifying experiment was placed squarely on the heads of four of Mao's confidantes. Jiang Qing and Zhang Chunqiao both received suspended death sentences; Wang Hongwen was sentenced to lifetime imprisonment and Yao Wenyuan to a twenty-year term. Two remain imprisoned; Jiang Qing committed suicide while in prison in 1991, and Yao Wenyuan was released in 1996.

Ganioda'yo (1735–1815)

American Indian chief and prophet. A member of the Seneca tribe, Ganioda'yo (Handsome Lake) was a founder of Gaiwiio (Good Message), more commonly known as the Longhouse religion, which became a revitalizing force among the Iroquois and which still has several thousand followers. Born at the end of a prosperous and peaceful era for the Seneca people, as a youth Handsome Lake witnessed the disintegration of traditional tribal life, largely a result of the influence and strife created by white settlers. As a result, he spent time as a mercenary, fighting against the British in Pontiac's Conspiracy, against the Cherokee and Chocktaw in the French and Indian War (1755–56), and against the Americans in the American Revolution (1775–83). (Handsome Lake himself had voted to remain neutral but had been outvoted.) The Seneca made several unfortunate treaties with the new United States, finally selling off all of their land in the 1797 Treaty of Big Tree.

A few years later, during a serious illness brought on by excessive drinking, Handsome Lake's religious revelations occurred. While near death, he saw three spirits, who revealed to him the will of the Creator. He continued to have visions, and in 1800 became a preacher of the religion he called Gaiwiio. His preaching concentrated on three areas: the definition of sin, the prescription for salvation, and the impending apocalypse. He condemned the practice of witchcraft and the consumption of alcohol and stressed the importance of family and tribal life. This religion, described as a cross between traditional beliefs and Christian ethics, arrived at a crucial time in the history of the Iroquois nation and helped revitalize a threatened and dying culture.

Handsome Lake's popularity and influence, however, suffered from a land dispute with another nationalistic Seneca leader, Red Jacket. Red Jacket favored the sale of a strip of Seneca land along the Niagara River to white settlers, a transaction that Handsome Lake firmly opposed. In the ensuing debate, he accused Red Jacket of witchcraft; this slander, for a time, diminished his reputation as a tribal speaker and prevented his election as tribal *sachem* (chief). After this exchange, Handsome Lake preached a social message, stressing the virtues of temperance in daily life, peace, and the preservation of tribal lands and customs. He died while visiting Onondaga, New York, and was buried in the center of the council house there.

García Lorca, Federico (1898–1936)

Spanish poet and playwright. Considered to be the major Spanish writer of the twentieth century, Lorca revolutionized Spanish literature with his experiments in literary Cubism and Surrealism, and through his interests in traditional Spanish ballad forms.

Lorca spent his early years in Fuente Vaqueros and Asquerosa, two small towns in Andalusia, an arid region in the south of Spain. His father was a wealthy farmer, and in his youth Lorca was surrounded by the bounteous nature he would memorialize in his most famous poems.

His family later moved to the larger Andalusian city of Granada, and there García Lorca became more interested in the arts. Starting in 1919, he took up res-

idence for part of the year in Madrid, becoming acquainted with many of the major writers and visual artists of his day, including the painter Salvador Dalí, the filmmaker Luis Buñuel, and the poet Rafael Alberti. While halfheartedly trying to finish law school, he composed the poems that would be published in *Libro de poemas* (1921; *Book of Poems*) and wrote a play, *El maleficio de la mariposa* (1920; *The Butterfly's Evil Spell*), which flopped.

He achieved widespread fame with his later poetry, especially *Poema del cante jondo* (1933; *Poem of the Deep Song*) and *Romancero gitano* (1929; *Gypsy Ballads*). The books express a deep interest in the landscape and folklore of Andalusia. In much of this poetry, García Lorca combined experimental imagery and popular Andalusian ballad forms. A trip to America and Cuba resulted in his book *Poeta en Nueva York* (1940; *Poet in New York*), which explores García Lorca's alienation from what he perceived as the mechanized, dehumanized modern metropolis. The difficult imagery and obscure organization of these poems make them his most "surrealistic." The poems, especially "Oda a Walt Whitman" ("Ode to Walt Whitman"), also represent García Lorca's first published exploration of his homosexuality.

García Lorca's theatrical endeavors are as highly acclaimed as his poetry. His dramatic trilogy, which includes *Bodas de sangre* (1933; *Blood Wedding*), *Yerma* (1933), and *La casa de Bernarda Alba* (1936; *The House of Bernarda Alba*), is a group of folk plays set in the brooding, vivid landscape of Andalusia. His other work from his late period includes his famous elegy to a gored bullfighter, *Llanto por Ignacio Sánchez Mejías* (1935; *Lament for the Death of a Bullfighter*).

Lorca's prolific career came to an abrupt end during the Spanish Civil War. The protofascist Nationalists who took control of Granada and the surrounding area in July 1936 disapproved of García Lorca's liberal politics, his intellectual status, and his homosexuality. He was killed during mass executions in the small Andalusian town of Viznar and buried in an unidentified grave.

García Márquez, Gabriel (1928–)

Colombian novelist. García Márquez was born into poverty in Colombia, where he was raised by his grandparents. He attended a Jesuit high school and in 1947 enrolled in the law school of the National University of Bogotá. That same year, he published "The Third Resignation," the first of fifteen stories to appear in the daily newspapers *El Espectador* of Bogotá and *El Heraldo* of Barranquilla. García Márquez was in law school when the popular left-wing politician Jorge Eliécer Gaitán was murdered in 1948, inaugurating "La Violencia" in Colombia that was to last into the 1960s. In 1954 he accepted a position with *El Espectador* as a foreign correspondent; the following year he published a short story called "Monólogo de Isabel" ("Monologue of Isabel Watching It Rain in Macondo"), in which the clearly defined geographical setting of Macondo—the fictional location of a majority of his works—appears for the first time. That same year, he also published his first significant novel, *La hojarasca* (1955; *Leaf Storm*), a narrative depicting the social decay of Macondo after a brief period of prosperity initiated by United States exploitation of the banana industry. While he was on assignment in Europe, *El Espectador* was closed down by the government, leaving García Márquez unemployed and penniless. In Paris, he completed the manuscript for *El coronel no tiene quien le escribe* (1961; *No One Writes to the Colonel*). In 1957 García Márquez returned from Europe to work in Venezuela as a journalist, and two years later, after the triumph of Fidel Castro's revolution in Cuba, he joined Prensa Latina, the Cuban government's news agency. He worked for the agency until 1961, in Bogotá, Havana, and New York, then moved with his family to Mexico City. Within a year he had published *No One Writes to the Colonel*, the story collection *Los funerales de la Mamá Grande* (1962; *Big Mama's Funeral*), and *La mala hora* (1962; *In Evil Hour*). In these works, the effects of political repression and a certain breakdown of the frames of reality combine to form a tentative aesthetic, which would come to form the basis of his later works.

While driving to Acapulco with his family, he envisioned a novel that would chronicle the history of Macondo; he spent a year and a half writing furiously, finally producing *Cien años de soledad* (1967; *One Hundred Years of Solitude*), which was immediately hailed as a work of genius, a "literary earthquake." The success of that book brought García Márquez fame and financial security, making possible his move to Spain. It also inaugurated the 1960s boom in Latin American literature that helped make writers like Carlos Fuentes (1928–), José Donoso (1924–), and Isabel Allende (1942–) world players. *One Hundred Years of Solitude* makes use of myth, legend, and popular culture to tell the story of the founding and development of Macondo. Its spiraling, magical, but always human narrative earned the term "magical realism," which came to define the sensibility of the new Latin American novel, indebted to Faulkner and French Surrealism. The following years saw the publication of a wealth of novels, long and short, including *El amor en los tiempos del cólera* (1984; *Love in the Time of Cholera*), and *El general en su laberinto* (1989; *The General in His Labyrinth*). Returning to Colombia, he resumed his journalistic activities, founding a left-wing news magazine, *Alternativa*, in Bogotá. He received the Nobel Prize in Literature in 1982.

Gardel, Carlos (c. 1887–1935)

Argentine singer and stage and film actor. Celebrated throughout Latin America as an interpreter of the tango, Gardel was born either in Uruguay or in Toulouse, France, the illegitimate son of a Frenchwoman. He spent his adolescence on the streets, involved with various underworld figures and honing his craft as a dancer and singer. He became popular as a dancer and singer of the tango song, which was initially closely related to Argentine politics, as the songs were actually political pieces that endorsed the Unión Cívica Radical (Radical Party). His first formal acting role was at the Nacional Corrientes theater in Buenos Aires, where he met Don José Razzano, with whom he later formed a duo and toured for many years both in Latin America and in Spain. Gardel popularized the tango through appearances in nightclubs in the 1920s and films in the 1930s. His first movie, *Luces de Buenos Aires* (1931; *Lights of Buenos Aires*), was filmed in Paris, but later ones were produced by Paramount Pictures for Spanish-speaking audiences. They include *Espérame* (1933; *Wait for Me*), *La casa es seria* (1933; *The House Is Somber*), *Cuesta abajo* (1934; *Downhill*), *El tango en Broadway* (1934; *The Tango on Broadway*), *Tango-Bar* (1935), *El día que me quieras* (1935; *The Day That You Love Me*), and *Cazadores de estrellas* (1935; *Hunters of Stars*). Gardel was killed in a plane crash in Colombia, while on tour. His funeral procession in Buenos Aires was witnessed by tens of thousands of Argentines who mourned him with an intensity rivaling that evoked by Rudolph Valentino's death. Today he is still considered by many to be the father of the tango.

Garvey, Marcus [Moziah, Jr.] (1887–1940)

Jamaican-born African-American leader, founder of the Universal Negro Improvement Association, and champion of the "Back-to-Africa" movement. Garvey is credited with creating the first international mass movement among blacks. Born in St. Ann's Bay, Jamaica, then part of the British West Indies, Garvey was primarily an autodidact, leaving school at fourteen to work as a printer's apprentice. He became a foreman at a printing company in the capital city of Kingston, but he left after participating in a strike for higher wages. He traveled and worked in Central America and lived in London from 1912 until 1914 (attending Birbeck College briefly), where he met many Africans and began studying African history while working as a printer and writer for the periodical *African Times and Orient Review*. In 1914 he returned to Jamaica and with friends founded the Universal Negro Improvement and Conservation Association and African Communities League to promote black unity through education and commerce. Usually called the Universal Negro Improvement Association (UNIA), it had as one of its stated goals the creation of a black-governed state in Africa, but its more immediate goal was to develop an industrial and agricultural school along the lines of African-American educator Booker T. Washington's Tuskegee Institute.

In 1916 Garvey moved UNIA headquarters to New York City's Harlem. He began *The Negro World*, a militant newspaper with several international editions, and established the Black Star Line, a steamship company owned and operated by blacks to link the United States, the Caribbean, and Africa. The UNIA grew rapidly into a genuine mass movement of international scope, reaching its peak around 1920, with some estimates of its membership as high as 8 million. Already advocating racial pride, the unity of those of African heritage, and black separatism, to further the aim of black economic independence, Garvey founded the Negro Factories Corporation to encourage black-owned businesses. He reached the height of his fame at the 1920 UNIA international exhibition in New York, where he was elected president of a provisional African republic by representatives of over twenty-five countries. Garvey began negotiating with the government of Liberia to establish a colony of repatriated blacks there, but was never successful in this pursuit. Known as "Black Moses," he was a better leader than businessman. The Black Star Line suffered drastic losses, and in 1923 Garvey was convicted of mail fraud involving sales of its stock, and began a five-year sentence in the Atlanta Penitentiary in 1925. President Calvin Coolidge commuted his sentence in 1927, and he was deported as an undesirable alien to Jamaica. There he formed the radical Jamaican People's Party and ran for office, but was defeated. His movement continued to decline as the worldwide economic depression advanced, and in 1935 he moved its headquarters to London, where he published the magazine *Black Man*. He held much-reduced UNIA conventions in Canada in 1936, 1937, and 1938. His separatist philosophy brought him many enemies among whites as well as some blacks, including W. E. B. Du Bois, but his advocacy of racial pride and black nationalism were very influential in the later "Black Power" movements. He died in London in 1940 after two strokes.

Gastarbeiter

German term for foreign laborers. The term "guestworker" designates those foreign laborers, working primarily as manual labor or in the service economy, who come from countries as varied as Turkey, Yugoslavia, Italy, and Austria to work in relatively low-paying, temporary jobs in German and Swiss markets, functioning as a sort of "resident alien" class. The *Gastarbeiter* are an integral part of the German economy, contributing to the flexibility of German business. They represent as much as half of the manual laborers in some cities, as well as constituting a significant portion of the population: over 7 percent of the German and over 14 percent of the Swiss, according to the 1980 census. Berlin, for example, has become the city with the fifth-largest Turkish population in the world. From the early 1950s up to the worldwide recession of 1974–76, both countries actively recruited foreign labor to promote their spectacular economic growth, but since the late 1970s there has been strong resistance to further immigration and permanent settlement by foreigners. Due to restrictive labor laws, and even more to the archaic definition of citizenship enshrined in the German constitution, it is virtually impossible for workers not of German descent to become naturalized. In the 1990s Turkish *Gastarbeiter* became targets of some of the most hideous instances of right-wing skinhead violence.

gaucho

Nomadic horseman and cowhand of the Argentine and Uruguayan Pampas and the southernmost state of Brazil. Similar to the cowboy in the United States, the gaucho was a ubiquitous figure in the nineteenth and early twentieth centuries. The term designated, variously, horse thieves, unemployed rural inhabitants, lone ranchers, herdsmen, and mercenaries. The first gauchos were employed to hunt large herds of escaped horses and cattle that roamed free, contrabanding their hides and tallows with the British, Dutch, French, and Portuguese. But later, when private landowners began to fence in the Pampas with their huge *estancias*, the gauchos were forced to become peons, or farmhands. By the mid nineteenth century, the old pastoral economy had disappeared. Gauchos then became active in the armies of the Río de la Plata region, fighting against the Spanish colonial regime, and later taking part in internal struggles between different *caudillos* (provincial military leaders).

In addition to their historical significance, gauchos have had a tremendous cultural influence, particularly in the literature of Argentina and Uruguay. Many of the gauchos that became literary heros were *mestizo*, though some were white or black, and some *mulato*. Distinguished by their costumes, which most often included a *chiripá* (a diaper girding the waist), a poncho, and *bombachas* (long and wide pleated pants that they gathered into high leather boots), they were also equipped with weapons that consisted of a lasso, a knife, and *boleadoras* (a device made from leather cords and three iron balls or stones wrapped in leather that was thrown at the legs of animals to entwine and immobilize them). According to literary legend, gauchos lived in small mud huts topped with grass mats; stereotypically seldom solemnized their marriages; and spent much time gambling, drinking, playing guitar, and singing about their prowess in hunting, fighting, and lovemaking. Gauchos have been immortalized in the literary genre called *literatura gauchesca*, of which perhaps the two best-known representatives are José Hernández's epic poem *Martín Fierro* (1872) and Ricardo Güiraldes's novel *Don Segundo Sombra* (1926). Other works that form part of this tradition include Estanislao del Campo's mock epic, *Fausto* (1866), Domingo Faustino Sarmiento's *Facundo* (1845), and Rómulo Gallegos's *Doña Bárbara* (1929).

Gauguin, [Eugène Henri] Paul (1848–1903) French painter. A leading painter of the Post-Impressionist period, Gauguin experimented with a flattened perspective and a use of color and non-European themes he called "primitive." His novel use of perspective and color had a profound influence on the early moderns, including Henri Matisse (1869–1954) and Pablo Picasso (1881–1973).

Born in Paris, Gauguin was the son of a journalist, who moved his family to Lima, Peru, in 1851, after the coup d'état of Napoleon III. After four years of living in Lima, Gauguin returned to Orléans, France, with his mother. At the age of seventeen, he went to sea, spending six years traveling around the world. In 1871 he returned to Paris and began working as a stockbroker. Only a few years later, in 1873, Gauguin married Mette Sophie Gad, eventually fathering four children.

It was during this period in Paris, while working for a stockbroking firm, that Gauguin was introduced to drawing and painting by a fellow stockbroker, Émile Schuffenecker; in 1876 Gauguin had his first landscape, *Sous-bois à Viroflay (Seine-et-Oise)* (1876; *Landscape at Viroflay*) accepted for the annual exhibition at the Salon. Around the same time that Gauguin was finishing the *Sous-bois à Viroflay*, he became acquainted with the Impressionist painter Camille Pissarro (1830–1903), with whom Gauguin began working on his techniques. By 1880 Gauguin was invited to enter work in the fifth Impressionist exhibit, an invitation that was offered and accepted again in 1881 and 1882. Encouraged by his early success, and in the wake of the Paris stock exchange crash of 1883, Gauguin decided to make his living from art alone. Unfortunately, since he and his wife received no support from his wife's family and were initially strapped for cash, the marriage quickly disintegrated, and by 1885 he was living in poverty and poor health.

Shortly thereafter, Gauguin met Vincent Van Gogh (1853–1890), the Dutch painter, in 1886 and traveled to Panama and Martinique in 1887. Influenced by the passions of Van Gogh and the tropical colors of Martinique, Gauguin turned from what he called "naturalism" to "primitivism." In 1891 he moved to Tahiti and spent most of the rest of his life in the South Pacific. After a suicide attempt in 1897, Gauguin became increasingly ill, and died in the Marquesas Islands. His autobiography, *Noa Noa*

(1901), was written in Tahiti. W. Somerset Maugham wrote an account of Gauguin's life in *The Moon and Sixpence* (1919).

Gèlèdé

Ancient rituals of traditional Yoruba culture centered on women. Gèlèdé masquerades are lavish events featuring carved wooden headpieces, cloth costumes, dances, songs, and drumming found principally among western Yoruba peoples in Nigeria and Benin. According to tradition, Gèlèdé began in the latter part of the eighteenth century among the Ketu Yoruba, spreading rapidly to other Yoruba groups and, as a consequence of the nineteenth-century Atlantic slave trade, to the dispersed Yoruba of Sierra Leone, Cuba, and Brazil. The ceremonies occur annually when the first rains fall; in times of communal distress, such as famine; and as funeral commemorations, occasions when communities entertain and pay homage to the forces operating in the Yoruba cosmos.

The etymology of the word "Gèlèdé" reveals its central concerns and its ultimate significance. *Gè* means "to soothe, to placate, to pet or coddle"; *èlè* refers to a woman's genitals, which symbolize women's secrets and their life-giving powers; and *dé* connotes "to soften with care or gentleness." Together these ideas convey the significance of Gèlèdé, performances carefully conceived and executed to pay homage to women so that the community may partake of their innate power for its benefit.

Consisting of nighttime (Efè) and daytime (Gèlèdé) performances, these masquerades represent a highly visible, artistic expression of a pan-Yoruba belief: that women, primarily elderly women, possess certain extraordinary power equal to or greater than that of the gods and ancestors, a view that is reflected in praises acknowledging them as "our mothers," "the gods of society," and "the owners of the world." With this power, the "mothers" can be either beneficent or destructive. They can bring health, wealth, and fertility to the land and its people, or they can bring disaster—epidemic, drought, pestilence.

With the sanction of the mothers, Gèlèdé has the performative power to marshall the forces in the Yoruba cosmos for society's well-being. Although both an entertaining performance and an efficacious ritual, Gèlèdé is perceived to be more than a mode of persuasion. It is an instrument with which the "gods of society" maintain social control. Gèlèdé comments on male and female roles in society, on traditional and contemporary fashions, and criticizes antisocial individuals and deeds.

Genet, Jean (1910–1986)

French dramatist and novelist, leading figure in the Theater of the Absurd. The work of Genet, who is renowned for his novels and plays, is firmly rooted in his own socially estranged position as an admitted thief and pimp in the Parisian underworld. Abandoned at birth by his mother, Genet was raised by foster parents, and after he was caught stealing at the age of ten, he spent the remainder of his youth in reform institutions and prisons. While in prison, he began to write, producing the novel *Notre-Dame des Fleurs* (1943; *Our Lady of the Flowers*), which vividly portrayed the thugs and criminals of the French underworld and commanded the attention of French intellectuals and writers Jean Cocteau (1889–1963), Jean-Paul Sartre (1905–1980), and Simone de Beauvoir (1908–1986). These authors were instrumental in gaining a state pardon for Genet after he received a life sentence for his tenth burglary conviction. Genet wrote two more novels, *Pompes funèbres* (*Funeral Rites*) and *Querelle of Brest*, both in 1944, before experimenting with drama. His dramas continue to explore underworldly themes, though with *Les Bonnes* (1946; *The Maids*), he also began to unwrap the complexity of human identity, in a style similar to that of English dramatist Samuel Beckett (1906–1989) and Romanian-born French dramatist Eugène Ionesco (1912–1994). His subsequent plays, such as *Le Balcon* (1956; *The Balcony*) and *Les Nègres* (1958; *The Blacks*), are considered to be part of Genet's "Theater of Hatred," works designed to shock and transform audiences by exposing everyday hypocrisies and the complicity of the conventional and the murderous.

Genji Monogatari

Japanese novel. *Genji monogatari (The Tale of Genji)*, written in the eleventh century and attributed to Murasaki Shikibu (c. 980–1015), a court lady, is the most renowned masterpiece of Japanese literature. Preceding the first Western novel by five centuries, its 1,000 pages detail the life and romantic involvements of "the shining Genji," an adventuring prince, and his descendants. Born to the favorite wife of the emperor, Genji is denied royal status and is crushed by his mother's death. The early chapters focus on Genji's efforts to fill the void created by the tragedy, a struggle that leads Genji to fall in love with the wife his father had chosen as the replacement for Genji's mother. His great love Murasaki bears a striking resemblance to his lost mother. Genji makes a political marriage, however, and his life becomes a series of deeply felt affairs. After a tumultuous early adulthood, including at one point a brief exile from the imperial court, Genji finds himself at age forty the father-in-law to the emperor and after him the most powerful man in Japan.

The later part of the book, which includes the death of Genji's beloved Murasaki, introduces a shift in tone toward a somber realism, perhaps the first appearance of such a style in world literature. The closing chapters are alternately tragic and serene. Unable to reconcile himself to this loss, which echoes the searing tragedy of his mother's death, the shattered Genji himself dies soon after. The remaining two hundred pages follow the various emotional and political vicissitudes of the generation after Genji.

The novel's profligate size and brilliant style fall into no neat ordering. It makes its impression more through an immediacy of characterization than through plot intricacies. *The Tale of Genji* strives for psychological realism, providing a profound and gracious delineation of the tragic condition of human mortality.

Genroku era

Japanese imperial era. Genroku is officially used to designate the era from 1688 to 1704, but it also refers to the reign of the shogun Tokugawa Tsunayoshi, the fifth Tokugawa shogun. From the mid seventeenth to the mid eighteenth century, the culture and commerce of Japan's cities blossomed into a rich urban milieu centered in Kyoto, Osaka, and Edo (Tokyo). As the cities grew during the years of Tokugawa peace, samurai gathered in the cities, and the arts were developed to an extraordinary degree.

The durable peace established by the Tokugawa shoguns made possible a shift in the culture of the samurai, as able warriors turned to Confucian philosophy, literature, poetry, music, and other cultural forms. The emergence of a wealthy merchant class reflected new developments in agriculture and commerce, while the relaxation of samurai discipline made the enjoyment of leisure time more plausible for townspeople. During this period the traditional Noh theater was eclipsed by Kabuki and Bunraku (puppet theater), two other forms of Japanese theater. Chikamatsu Monzaemon (1653–1724), the greatest playwright of the Bunraku stage, lived and wrote in the Genroku era.

Advances in printing made classic Japanese literature, philosophical texts, and other writings available to a much wider audience. Small books called *ukiyo-zōshi*, or "booklets of the floating world," sparked new developments in literature. Ihara Saikaku, the most famous author of such works and a poet of short *haikai* verse, perfected these stories, focusing on sexual themes, financial mishaps, and the lives of the samurai. His social commentary highlighted the newly glamorized brothel districts of the burgeoning cities, and the sophisticated dissipation they encouraged.

Famous actors and prostitutes inspired a popular portrait medium called *ukiyo-e*, a spare, simple style of painting and woodblock printing. Other new styles infused more brilliant colors and stronger patterns than the traditionally delicate Japanese effects. In poetry Matsuo Bashō (1644–1694) perfected linked verse (*haikai*) and the seventeen-syllable *haiku* during this era. New and more refined scholarship was also conducted in studies of Confucianism and classical Japanese literature.

Gestapu affair

Indonesian military coup. On September 30, 1965, in Jakarta, six high-ranking generals of the Sukarno government were killed by a revolutionary group of still somewhat mysterious origins. Major General Suharto led the Indonesian military against the Communists (PKI: Communist Party of Indonesia) who were held responsible for the attempted coup. Appropriating President Sukarno's authority, Suharto and his forces initiated a nationwide massacre of Communists and others considered to be dangerous to Suharto's intended regime—the names of which may have been provided by a U.S. embassy group of State Department and Central Intelligence Agency officers. More than half a million people were killed, and hundreds of thousands were imprisoned. Some of those killed or imprisoned were of Chinese extraction, resented for their financial success alongside growing native Indonesian poverty. In his consoli-

dation of power after the crackdown, Suharto formed a centralized New Order alliance with students, technocrats, and Muslims characterized by receptivity to capitalist development and antipathy toward Communism. In 1966 Suharto formally deposed Sukarno. Suharto's mammoth gains as a result of the Gestapu affair have encouraged arguments that he might have helped mastermind the incident, setting up the PKI and securing his own ascendancy. Evidence is solid, however, that the Communists were involved in perpetrating the events of September 30.

Ghalīb, Mirzā Asadullāh Khān (1797–1869)

Indian poet. "Ghalīb" was the pen name of one of the most celebrated poets of his time. He wrote most of his poems in Persian, although he was equally talented in Urdu, as many of his Urdu poems, letters, and prose pieces would attest.

Although Ghalīb was born into a wealthy aristocratic family, he suffered a period of genuine financial hardship shortly after embarking on a career in writing. He married early to Umrao Begam, the daughter of the poet Ilahi Bakhsh Khān. A reprieve from his difficulties came in 1854, when Bahādur Shāh II, the last of the Mughal emperors, appointed him poet laureate to his court in Delhi. The Sepoy Mutiny, which occurred three years later, resulted in Bahādur Shāh's exile from India and put an end to Ghalīb's short-lived financial security.

In his poetry Ghalīb experimented in three traditional forms: the *ghazal* (love lyric), the *māsnavī* (moralistic or mystical parable), and the *qasīda* (panegyric). Ghalīb wrote over 5,000 couplets in Urdu and some 11,000 couplets in Persian. In addition, he wrote several prose works in Persian, including the *Panj-Ahang*, a Persian grammar and vocabulary supplemented with selections from his own writing and poetry; the *Mihr-i-Nimroz*, the first volume of a history of the Mughal dynasty; and *Dastanboo,* an account of the Sepoy mutiny. Ghalîb was one of the literary figures responsible for making possible an Urdu canon to rival the well-entrenched ancient Persian corpus. Many Indians consider Ghalîb to be the greatest Urdu poet.

Ghana, ancient

Great empire of the western Sudan. Ancient Ghana was important in the ninth century C.E. when it controlled the "Wangara" area (between the upper Niger and Senegal rivers), which produced great quantities of gold for trade across the Sahara. Slaves were also traded with the gold, in return for salt from the desert in Teghaza and cloth from North Africa.

In the eleventh century, the Kingdom of Ghana was described by the Islamic historian al-Bakri (c. 1000). Raised in Muslim Spain, al-Bakri wrote historico-geographical surveys of West African kingdoms and empires in Arabic, though from a distance; he never traveled south of the Sahara, but contented himself with the reports of the merchants involved in trans-Saharan trade and well-traveled explorers of the Sudan. Nevertheless, Ghana was at the apex of its power during the years al-Bakri performed most of his investigations, and it was al-Bakri who claimed that Ghana was so rich in gold that dogs there had golden collars, and the ruler of the empire was called "lord of the gold."

Ghana included what is now western Mali and southeastern Mauritania, and its territory was probably as large as modern Nigeria. There was a strong central government at the capital city, which was divided into two parts: a town for the traditional rulers, who were pagans; and a town for the merchants, who were mostly Muslim. Historians believe that the town of Koumbi Saleh (in what is now Mauritania) was the capital of ancient Ghana in its later years.

The power of the empire declined because of competition from other states in the gold trade. In about 1076, the Almoravid rulers of the Maghrib attacked and destroyed Koumbi Saleh, but the invaders were forced to withdraw, and Ghana recovered. In about 1203, however, it was defeated by the army of Sumanguru, the leader of the people from the area of Takrur to the west. Sumanguru captured Koumbi Saleh, but soon after, he, too, succumbed. He was defeated by an army of Mande-speaking peoples, and by the end of the thirteenth century the remains of ancient Ghana became part of the empire of ancient Mali. Kwame Nkrumah, the prime minister (1952–60) and first president of Ghana (1960–66), renamed it the Gold Coast after this illustrious ancient kingdom when it became the first of the British colonies in sub-Saharan Africa to achieve independence in 1957.

Gharbzadegi

Persian term. *Gharbzadegi* is a Persian word coined by Iranian writer Jalâl Âl-e Ahmad in his 1977 book of the same name. Sometimes translated as "Westoxification," "Westruckness," or "Occidentosis," *Gharbzadegi* refers to a phenomenon that dominated Iran during the last two decades of the Pahlavi dynasty (c. 1921–79), when certain strata of Iranian society were obsessed with the imitation of all things European. *Gharbzadegi* conveys Âl-e Ahmad's use of the term in both its meanings: implying the pleasurable aspect of intoxication as well as its deleterious effects.

al-Ghazâlî (1058–1111)

Arab philosopher and mystic. Called the "renewer" of the Islamic faith, al-Ghazâlî was born in 1058 in Tûs in northern Iran. He mastered the Islamic religious sciences, but his relentless skepticism led him to study the Greek disciplines of logic and philosophy. Fearing that absolute truth was unattainable, he suffered a psychological breakdown and left his teaching position in Baghdad to begin a series of journeys both geographical and spiritual. These investigations led him to the conviction that experience, not reason, is the only source of knowledge. The doctrines of Greek philosophy, he claimed, do not lead to certainty. Although his own spiritual journey restored him to Islam, al-Ghazâlî's refutation of philosophy is argued not on doctrinal grounds but on the basis of inconsistencies within philosophy itself. He also attacked the legalistic Islamic scholarship of his day, claiming it had nothing to do with faith. His own newfound religious belief, said al-Ghazâlî, came not from reason but "by a light which God cast into my heart." His teachings were highly influential, and al-Ghazâlî is often considered to be responsible for the reconciliation of Sufi mysticism and orthodox Islam at a crucial point in the development of the Islamic faith.

Ghaznavid

Turkish dynasty that ruled Afghanistan, eastern Iran, and northwestern India from the tenth to the twelfth century. The name derives from the Afghan town of Ghazna, which served as the capital for much of this period. Founded by Sebuktegin, this empire saw its greatest expansion under his son Mahmud. The Ghaznavids were rapidly assimilated into Persian culture and attempted to attract artists and men of letters to their court. The most important among these was Firdawsī, the author of the *Shāh-nāmeh*. The most significant impact of the Ghaznavids came through their conquest of northwestern India and active promotion of Islam in that region. The subsequent emergence of a distinctive Indo-Persian culture eventually resulted in the creation of Pakistan, the first modern republic to be established on the basis of religion.

ghetto

Urban sector, often enclosed by a wall and gate, in which Jews were required to live. Although the term was probably first used in reference to the Jewish quarter in sixteenth-century Venice, the ghetto has been in existence since ancient times. In Europe, segregation was usually (though not always) mandated and enforced by the Gentile community. Middle Eastern Shi'ite Muslim countries quarantined Jews. In contrast, Sunnî Muslim cities rarely contained ghettos, but had Jewish quarters with relatively free access for their inhabitants.

In the twentieth century, the word "ghetto" has taken on several connotations. Under the Nazi regime, Germany's Jewish ghettos became official stopovers on the way to concentration camps and gas chambers. Unaware of their eventual destination, most Jews obeyed orders to relocate to the already crowded ghettos in such cities as Warsaw, Lodz, and Lublin. Living conditions in these ghettos were deplorable, as the Nazis were hoping a large number of the inhabitants would die of "natural" causes such as starvation and disease.

While they were deciding upon the exact terms of the "final solution," the Nazis allowed the ghettos a measure of autonomy. The German authorities coerced Jewish leaders still inside the ghetto, organized into a body called a Judenrat, to maintain discipline and ensure cooperation. Tensions within the Jewish community were exacerbated by this policy of divide and rule, making effective resistance incredibly difficult. The power given to the Judenrats reassured many ghetto residents that they would be left in peace if they kept quiet, but by the time the Nazis began to "liquidate" the ghettos, sending the inhabitants to concentration camps, it was too late.

The Warsaw ghetto was the exception to that rule. Its residents organized a surprisingly successful resistance, though only for a few weeks. With a handful of weapons and a small cache of ammunition bought from the Polish Resistance, the Jewish fighters kept Nazi soldiers at bay until reinforcements arrived and the ghetto was razed. Today a memorial to the Warsaw ghetto uprising marks the place at which the Warsaw ghetto Jews made their stand, and the Ghetto Fighters' House, a memorial in Israel, pays homage to those who died there.

In recent times, "ghetto" has come to signify any urban area settled by a minority or lower-class group, or, more broadly, any narrow enclosure or limitation. The ghetto has become one of the enduring images of urban decay and disarray in the United States. Various efforts to break the cycle of poverty or to attack the problem of the "underclass" involve attempts to reach the urban youths living in these conditions.

Ghost Dance

American Indian revivalist movement. The Ghost Dance, practiced by almost all tribes of the Interior Basin (from the Missouri River to parts of the Rocky Mountains) during the latter part of the nineteenth century, was prevalent during two different historical periods, the first beginning around 1870, followed by the "messiah craze" of 1890–91.

The Ghost Dance was a round dance believed to imitate the dances of the dead. Although American Indian groups disagreed as to the precise meaning of the Ghost Dance, its general purpose was to call back the dead and ensure the renewal of the world. During the Ghost Dance, which generally lasted four or five consecutive nights, women and men danced together with interlaced fingers, moving with shuffling sidesteps. The dancing typically took place without musical accompaniment or fires.

The first Ghost Dance movement began in 1870 on the Walker Lake Reservation in Nevada and was initiated by Wodziwob ("Gray Hair"), a Northern Paiute Indian. While in a trance, Wod-

ziwob was conveyed to the otherworld, where he was taught the round dance. Wodziwob was told that if his people performed this dance, they would be guaranteed, among other things, the restoration of former ways of tribal life, the replenishment of disappearing game animals, and the return of the dead. The Ghost Dance was performed by members of the Paiute, some Oregon Indians, and many of the middle and northern California tribes, although it was discontinued after a few years.

The second Ghost Dance period occurred around 1888, initiated by a medicine man named Wovoka ("The Cutter"), who fell into a delirious trance during an eclipse of the sun. While in this trance, Wovoka was taken by the supreme being in the sky to the land of the dead, where he was promised, as with Wodziwob, both the return of the dead and a restitution of the former ways of tribal life. Wovoka was told that the Ghost Dance was a means of preparing for these events.

During this second period the Ghost Dance became particularly important among the Northern Plains Indians, tribes threatened by the extermination of the buffalo and by the machinations of the federal government. Many of these people, feeling threatened and vulnerable, turned to Wovoka, the prophet or "messiah," to teach them the Ghost Dance and right recent wrongs. Many of the Northern Plains tribes believed that the Ghost Dance would result in the extermination of the white population. The Lakota had Ghost Dancers wear decorated white "ghost" shirts in preparation for confrontations with whites; some believed that the spiritualized shirts would protect them from bullets.

The particularly intense Lakota Ghost Dances during the summer and fall of 1890 caused considerable concern among whites living in South Dakota. Many of the white residents feared that the dances were preparations for attacks on white populations. White authorities acted preemptively to defuse the Lakota "threat," which resulted in the arrest and assassination of Sitting Bull (December 15, 1890) and the indiscriminate massacre of Indian men, women, and children at Wounded Knee (December 29, 1890).

The Ghost Dance has mostly disappeared since then. Some tribes have occasionally practiced the dance, now with drums, though it has lost most of its ritual significance.

Giap, Vo Nguyen (1911–)

Vietnamese military leader. A master of guerrilla warfare, Giap successfully organized the North Vietnamese military forces in both the Second World War and the Vietnam War, finally achieving the reunification of the country in 1976. Giap did not train as a soldier, but rather studied law at the University of Hanoi and later taught history. He became a member of the Communist Party in the early 1930s, and joined Ho Chi Minh in China as a military aide when the party was outlawed in 1939. His wife was captured by the French police and died in prison. Giap organized the Vietnamese resistance, the Viet Minh, which fought to oust the occupying Japanese in World War II and the French armies after the war, successfully ending French colonialism in Asia. As commander in chief, he directed the Viet Minh against U.S. forces, achieving particular success in the Tet offensive of 1968. Giap also held the posts of deputy prime minister and minister of defense until his retirement in 1982.

Gide, André [Paul-Guillaume] (1869–1951)

French writer. André Gide is perhaps most celebrated for his highly autobiographical essays and letters. Raised in a strict Protestant household, he was introduced early on to a world of taboos. Educated for a few years at the École

Alsacienne in Paris, at the age of eleven, after the premature death of his father in 1880, Gide was kept at home and educated by tutors. He returned to the École to study for examinations, receiving his degree in 1889. While in Paris, he met other aspiring writers, including Cuban-born French poet José María de Heredia (1842–1905) and French poet Stéphane Mallarmé (1842–1898). His first publication, *Les Cahiers d'André Walter* (1891; *The Notebooks of André Walter*), reflects Gide's passionate spiritual love for his cousin, Madeleine, and his belief that physical desire should be repressed.

In 1893 Gide traveled to North Africa. He returned there in 1894, and it was on this second trip that Gide met Irish dramatist Oscar Wilde (1854–1900) and wrote *Les Nourritures terrestres* (1897; *The Fruits of the Earth*), a novel in which Gide accepted his homosexuality and even celebrated his search for sexual experience.

Nevertheless, in 1895 Gide married Madeleine and began one of the most fruitful periods of his writing career. *L'Immoraliste* (1902; *The Immoralist*) and *La Porte étroite* (1909; *Strait Is the Gate*), which discuss Gide's attempts to resolve the problems associated with his marriage, reflect Gide's tendency to use personal experience as a portal to philosophical discussions or larger social relationships. Despite his love for his wife, he found it impossible to reconcile marriage with his need for experience and freedom. Estranged for many years, only shortly before her death were Gide and his wife reconciled.

After the First World War, Gide began work on his autobiography, *Si le grain ne meurt* (1924; *If It Die . . .*) and completed his philosophical defense of homosexuality, *Corydon* (1924), which was heavily criticized even by Gide's closest friends. In 1926 Gide returned to Africa and published a scathing critique of French colonial practices in *Voyage au Congo* (1927; *Travels in the Congo*). Upon his return to France, he became a spokesman for the disenfranchised, demanding more humane conditions for criminals and equal rights for women. Following the death of his wife in 1938, Gide's works become more concerned with remembering the past. In *Le Figaro* (a series of imaginary interviews, written in 1941–42), Gide revises his earlier demands for complete individual freedom, and instead declares the necessity of combining freedom with tradition.

In 1947 Gide received an honorary doctorate from Oxford University for his literary contributions. This was followed by the Nobel Prize for Literature, awarded the same year.

Gilgamesh, Epic of

Epic poem written in Akkadian, the language of Babylonia and Syria. Gilgamesh is said to have been the ruler of the city-state of Uruk. His exploits provided the basis both for his deification and for one of mankind's most enduring stories. Sources for parts of the epic circulated independently in Sumerian, probably by 2100–2000 B.C.E. The epic first appears in Akkadian late in the Old Babylonian period (1750–1600 B.C.E.); there are also Middle Bablylonian (c. 1250 B.C.E.) and Neo-Assyrian versions (750–612 B.C.E.).

The text underwent continuous modification and revision, and no single copy survives: the poem that modern readers know in translation is a composite of these various sources. Both the Sumerian and later Babylonian versions of the epic focus on Gilgamesh's unsuccessful quest for immortality and his ultimate appreciation for humanity's limitations. Man's ability to develop values and to accept mortality are the epic's central concerns.

In the Babylonian epic, Gilgamesh is a powerful, part-immortal king of Uruk who rules his subjects harshly. The lord of heaven takes pity on the people and orders the goddess Aruru to mold a wild man out of clay in order to divert the king. This man, Enkidu, challenges Gilgamesh's power, but after Gilgamesh defeats him the two become close friends. Together, the two undertake a series of adventures. They attempt to chop down a cedar tree in a sacred wood guarded by an anthropoid monster named Humbaba. With help from the sun god, they fell the tree and behead its guardian. But their hubris builds, and the heroes eventually antagonize Ishtar by killing the bull of heaven, a crime punished by the death of Enkidu. Tortured by the loss of his friend, Gilgamesh searches for immortality and becomes wise.

While the Babylonian version draws on several Sumerian stories, there are major differences. In the Sumerian sources, Enkidu is a servant to Gilgamesh, not a wild man who becomes his friend. The Babylonian version is probably responsible for the epic's being structured around three periods of six or seven days and nights, each period associated with some important transformation in Gilgamesh.

Gilman, Charlotte [Anna] Perkins (1860–1935)

American writer and feminist theorist. Born Charlotte Anna Perkins, Gilman began her literary career in the 1890s; her poetry, short stories, and social analysis reflected her concern for the economic and social freedoms of women. In *The Yellow Wallpaper* (1892), a work long overlooked, Gilman confronts the sexual politics of marriage. Drawing upon her own experiences, Gilman portrays a woman bullied by her doctor and husband, and creates a chilling depiction of mental illness and its treatment.

Charlotte's father, Frederic Gilman, left her mother soon after Charlotte's birth; as a result, she moved nineteen times in eighteen years as her mother sought work and the charity of relatives.

In 1884 Gilman married artist Charles W. Stetson, but the marriage did not last, and in 1900 she married her cousin, George H. Gilman (d. 1934). From the beginning of her first marriage, Gilman had suffered from depression; her husbands, as well as a number of doctors, failed to recognize the seriousness of her situation, and her illness culminated in a total mental collapse. Separation from her second husband and a move to California improved her condition, but the residual effects of her illness troubled her the rest of her life.

In *Women and Economics* (1898), a satirical analysis of the socioeconomic position of women in American society, Gilman argued that the ineffectual domestic status of women had seriously crippled their development. *Women and Economics* was used as a college text in the 1920s and was translated into several languages. Gilman herself was always unwilling to take on traditional feminine social roles, and for most of her married life Gilman's housekeeping was taken care of by friends.

In 1909 Gilman founded *Forerunner*, a magazine that championed radical social revision. Until 1916, Gilman edited and published the magazine in addition to writing most of the material for it. Suffering from breast cancer, Gilman committed suicide in 1935. Her autobiography, *The Living of Charlotte Perkins Gilman*, was published in 1935, and her other works include *The Home* (1903) and *His Religion and Hers* (1923), in which she argued that as women turned their attention to theology, death and punishment would cease to dominate religious discourse. Gilman's story "Herland," a fantasy describing a utopia inhabited by women who reproduce by parthenogenesis, follows the same line of thought.

Ginsberg, Allen (1926–)

American poet. Although he is still a prolific writer, Ginsberg's best-known work remains *Howl* (1956), the long poem that made him famous. His work revolutionized the form and content of American poetry, making a final break with rigid European verse structures and injecting radical politics, sexual liberation, and Eastern religion into the mainstream of the national poetry.

Ginsberg's parents were leftist Jewish intellectuals, his father, Louis, a published poet, and his mother, Naomi, an ardent member of the Communist Party. Naomi Ginsberg suffered from severe paranoia and was institutionalized when her son was still a child. The incident deeply affected Ginsberg.

Inward and studious, he spent three difficult years at Columbia University producing genteel poetry and agonizing over his homosexuality. He found personal and literary self-confidence only when he left college and befriended Neal Cassady, Jack Kerouac, and William S. Burroughs. With Ginsberg, these writers would become the center of a literary coterie known as the Beats. The Beats expressed a disgust with the complacency and materialism of American life in the 1950s by using hallucinogenic drugs, listening to jazz, exploring Eastern religions like Hinduism and Buddhism, ignoring sexual codes, and eschewing formal, polished poetry.

Howl became the central artistic statement of the group. As its title suggests, it is an angry, biting poem. Opening with the famous line "I saw the best minds of my generation destroyed by madness, starving hysterical naked . . . ," the poem rages on for over seventy lines in a hallucinogenic swirl of images. Whitman is a central inspiration for Ginsberg's long-lined, energetic style, and the poets share an affection for the grit and occasional vulgarity of spoken American language. William Blake's visionary poetics are also a major influence on Ginsberg.

Overnight, Ginsberg became a cultural icon of bohemian resistance to cultural normality. With his friends—a group that came to include the poets Frank O'Hara and Lawrence Ferlinghetti and the musician Bob Dylan—Ginsberg stayed in the public eye during the sixties. He was a vocal political protester, particularly against America's war in Vietnam, and remained notorious for his high-profile antics. Although his later poetry has not received the same critical acclaim or popular renown, Ginsberg remains a symbol of the Beat era and youthful resistance.

His other major works include *Kaddish* (1960), an elegy for his mother named for the Jewish prayer for the dead; *Planet News* (1968); and *Reality Sandwiches* (1981). An edition of his collected poetry was published in 1991.

Glele (d. 1889)

Last great ruler of the Aja kingdom of Dahomey, now Benin. Glele (also spelled Gelele or Glélé) followed Gezo as ruler of Dahomey in 1858 and sustained its renaissance during the nineteenth century as a center of the slave trade and palm oil sales. He harried neighboring kingdoms, notably Ketu and Abeokuta and incorporated Porto Novo into the kingdom, establishing diplomatic relations with the Portuguese, Dutch, French, and British. As the economy prospered, Europeans began to take control of the coastal shipping areas; Glele responded by moving his capital inland to Abomey and making a great show of human sacrifice in front of European visitors. The French ultimately established a customshouse at the Dahomey port of Cotonou and sent an emissary to negotiate with Glele, but the ruler died before his arrival; according to one report, he committed suicide because he refused to bear witness to the decline of his kingdom. The famous English traveler Sir Richard Burton wrote in *A Mission to Gelele, King of Dahome* (1893) that both the power of the Dahomey kingdom and the extent

of human sacrifice had been exaggerated in previous accounts. Glele was succeeded by his son, Behanzin, who tried unsuccessfully to expel the French and was instead banished by them in 1894.

Gnosticism

Philosophical-religious movement that emphasized the redemptive power of esoteric knowledge. Gnosticism (from the Greek *gnosis*, meaning "knowledge") refers to the learning that separates the initiated from the uninitiated. However, Gnosticism is a term applied by modern scholarship and embraces many diverse groups. Generally, the Gnostic movement reached a high point during the Graeco-Roman period in the latter part of the second century C.E. and competed with early Christianity, whose theologians wrote against it. Gnostic groups, though diverse, shared certain characteristic tenets, including a dualistic system of light and darkness, a spiritual world of goodness and a material world of evil, and a supreme God and lower power (the latter sometimes evil) that created the world.

Gnostics typically believed in a complex mystical cosmology. The goddess Sophia ("Wisdom"), or the Great Mother, figured prominently in their theology; she was believed to have descended into the world and to have borne the evil angels. Gnostics also believed in a Primal Man who existed before the world and who came to make war on darkness. The "Soter," or Savior, is this Primal Man set free from the powers of evil that had vanquished him. His salvation is for himself and for the Gnostic initiate. Through knowledge and through separation from the lower world, the Gnostic tries to lift himself toward God and reveal the divine within himself.

Though it influenced many traditional and mystery religions, at times resonating through the Jewish Kabbalah,

Gnosticism was most important in the development of Christianity. Many of the institutions of the Catholic Church were created in direct response to the threat of the Gnostics, including the collection of canonical works that would become the Bible, the various creeds, and the investiture of episcopal authority.

Godard, Jean-Luc (1930–)

French film director. Among the most controversial of postwar directors, Godard began as a film critic in the 1950s. He quickly became a central figure in the French New Wave, a brand of sometimes sly and often grimly humorous cinema that challenged "staid" French filmmaking and admired Hollywood directors. Godard was born in Paris, the son of a doctor. He enrolled at the Sorbonne as an ethnology student but spent more time at Left Bank cinema clubs, eventually contributing articles as a film critic to *Cahiers du Cinéma* as well as *Gazette du Cinéma*, which he helped to found. After traveling in North and South America in 1951, his father cut off his financial support, forcing Godard to take work as a laborer on a dam project in Switzerland. Using his earnings to buy a 35-mm camera, he made his first short film, *Opération Béton* (1954), about the building of the dam. After making four more shorts, Godard completed his first scriptless feature film, *À Bout de Souffle*, in 1960; the film garnered immediate acclaim for what were considered at the time very bold maneuvers: jump cuts, hand-held moving shots, improvisation, and monologues featuring quotes from existentialist writers. (The film is better known by its English title, *Breathless*.) Many of these techniques were employed in his later films, but with an added sociopolitical message, as in *Le Petit Soldat* (1960; *The Little Soldier*), an exposé of the Algerian conflict, and *Alphaville, Une Étrange Aventure de Lemmy Caution* (1965; *Alphaville*), a science-fiction work portraying dehumanization in contemporary Western society.

Godard later lapsed into directing didactic Marxist films that made little use of their visual medium, but his early films had a powerful influence on avant-garde cinema.

Goethe, Johann Wolfgang von (1749–1832)

German poet, playwright, and novelist. Goethe is perhaps the most influential figure in the German literary tradition, and his writings—poetic, dramatic, or scientific—were characterized by an interest in the natural, organic development of living beings.

Goethe began writing lyric poems while in his teens, inspired by various love affairs. He studied in Leipzig, and there developed a friendship with Johann Gottfried Herder, who kindled Goethe's passion for nature, the works of Shakespeare, and German folk songs. While studying law at Strasbourg, Goethe wrote the historical drama *Götz von Berlichingen*, which marks the beginning of his *Sturm und Drang* ("storm and stress") period. Goethe's greatest success came with the publication of *Die Leiden des jungen Werthers* (1744; *The Sorrows of Young Werther*), written after a failed love affair. The book was enormously popular, inspiring a few Werther-style suicides among young German readers disappointed in love.

In 1775 Goethe joined the court at Weimar and there met Frau Charlotte von Stein, whom he worshiped for over a decade. Though Goethe produced little during his Weimar years, his interest in the sciences flourished, as did his involvement with the state theater. Leaving for Italy in 1786, Goethe embarked on a journey that he later recorded in his *Italienische Reise* (1816; *Italian Trip*). While in Italy, he completed his play *Iphigenie auf Tauris* (1787; *Iphigenia in Tauris*), characteristic of the *Sturm und Drang* style, and *Torquato Tasso* (1789), which signaled the beginning of a new style, Weimar classicism, renouncing the emotionalism of *The Sorrows of Young Werther*. After his return to Weimar, Goethe began an affair with Christiane Vulpius; she gave birth to a son in 1789 and they married in 1806. He published several of his scientific writings in this period, including those on plant metamorphosis and optics and his novel *Wilhelm Meister* (1795–96), which is often considered the prototype of the German *Bildungsroman*, or novel of development. Perhaps the most notable event of these years, however, was Goethe's burgeoning friendship with German poet and dramatist Friedrich von Schiller (1759–1805). This was more a literary and intellectual than an emotional kinship, and Schiller proved to be a sympathetic and encouraging critic, especially supportive of Goethe's work on his masterful *Faust* (1809; second part, 1831). The writings of Goethe's later years indicate a return to the more Romantic tendencies of his earlier writings. Goethe died in Weimar and is buried beside the grave of his friend Schiller.

Gogol, Nikolai [Vasilievich] (1809–1852)

Russian short-story writer, novelist, and playwright. Gogol is often considered to be the founder of realism in Russian literature. He was born and educated in Ukraine, the son of a minor nobleman who was also an amateur playwright. As a young man, Gogol moved to St. Petersburg, where he worked as a government clerk and a teacher before turning exclusively to writing. The reviews of his earliest work were negative, but his early stories, collected in *Vechera na khutore bliz Dikan'ki* (1831–32; *Evenings on a Farm Near Dikanka*), explore a wealth of Ukrainian folk motifs and greatly impressed Aleksandr Pushkin, who became a lifelong friend. His next collection of stories, *Arabeski* (1835; *Arabesques*), contains the well-known "Zapiski Sumasshedshego" ("Diary of a Madman"), in which Gogol depicts the lunatic Poprishchin, a civil servant who believes

he is the king of Spain. Gogol continued to publish stories, including a collection of Ukrainian tales and his fantastic tales, such as "Nos" ("The Nose"), in which a nose suddenly takes leave of a man's face and travels about town in a suit of clothes and fancy carriage. *Revizor* (*The Inspector General*), Gogol's satirical comedy, was performed in 1836; its mixed reception by the public and the anger it inspired in the emperor Nicholas I shocked Gogol and sent him on a trip out of the country that lasted twelve years. He lived mostly in Rome, there completing *Myortvye dushi* (1842; *Dead Souls*), which he published with previous work, including the greatly acclaimed story "The Overcoat."

Failing health led Gogol to take an interest in religion; he made a pilgrimage to Palestine. He also published his only overtly political work, *Vybrannye mesta iz perepski s druz'iami* (*Selected Passages from Correspondence with Friends*), in 1846, in which he supported the czarist regime and advised landowners to allow their peasants to read the Bible only, lest any radical material fall into their hands. Russian radicals were outraged, and a famous letter of attack was written in response to this publication by the critic Vissarion Belinsky. *Pis'mo k Gogoliu* (1847; *Letter to Gogol*) was banned in Russia. It was the reading of Belinsky's letter that was used by the government as a pretext to arrest the young Russian writer Fyodor Dostoevsky together with other members of the Petrashevsky circle. Gogol returned to Russia in 1848, where he grew increasingly depressed. Shortly after burning most of his manuscripts, including the nearly completed second part of *Dead Souls*, he took to his bed and died.

Golden Lotus, *see* Jin Ping Mei

Goldman, Emma (1869–1940)

American anarchist and feminist. Nicknamed "Red Emma," Goldman was born in Lithuania but moved to Germany with her family to avoid anti-Jewish persecution. She eventually relocated to the United States in 1885 or 1886 and worked in the dress factories of New York City.

During this period Goldman began to accept her identity as an anarchist, a move precipitated by her outspoken opposition to the execution of a group of anarchists in Chicago for their alleged involvement in the Haymarket bombing. She argued that perpetrators of terrorist acts should not be killed, since their actions were responses to the systemic social injustices perpetrated by the ruling class. She herself was attracted to the terrorist idea; she is suspected to have planned to assassinate steel company executive Henry Clay Frick with a fellow anarchist in 1892, in retaliation for the deaths of ten striking workers during the Homestead Strike in Pennsylvania. Soon thereafter, she abandoned terrorism as a revolutionary tactic, becoming outspoken in her opposition to individual acts of violence.

Due to her political activities, Goldman was persecuted by both the police and mobs. She was jailed repeatedly for her political views, and was even accused of involvement in the 1901 assassination of President William McKinley, although this was never substantiated. From 1906 to 1917 Goldman served as editor of the monthly publication *Mother Earth*, during which time she also published *Anarchism and Other Essays*.

Goldman spoke out against organized religion and the government, lobbying on behalf of individual freedoms, especially the right to birth control and free speech. Her politics were strongly influenced by Peter Kropotkin, a Russian theorist. Like Kropotkin, Goldman considered government oppressive and believed that attempts to undermine capitalism should be economic. She opposed state socialism, since she believed that the state only existed to control and oppress individuals and to protect the interests of private monopolies. For Goldman, anarchy stressed the role of voluntary associations, and the ownership of all property by all citizens of the state.

Goldman's feminist concerns looked beyond suffrage to issues of reproductive freedom and substantive personal autonomy. She saw little use in the right to vote, or for the opportunity to work in what she considered to be underpaid and inferior positions. She opposed compulsory marriage and the institution of obligatory motherhood. She believed that the liberation of the individual was the most important component in any overall systemic change, and that women's freedom was only possible if women could choose their own destiny. As both an outspoken anarchist and a feminist, Goldman continually sought to locate feminist ideology within an anarchist context, as is illustrated in her 1911 publication, *The Traffic in Women*.

During World War I, Goldman organized the No-Conscription League. Convicted for plotting against the draft, she was imprisoned from 1917 to 1919 and was deported with other political radicals to the Soviet Union. Soviet-style socialism proved a disappointment to Goldman, and she became an outspoken critic of the new regime. Goldman eventually became a British citizen, and died in Toronto, Canada, during a visit to raise funds for the antifascists and anarcho-syndicalists in the Spanish Civil War.

Gombrowicz, Witold (1904–1969)

Polish novelist and playwright. Dubbed "the greatest unknown writer of our time," Gombrowicz has attained an international reputation, often compared to Samuel Beckett. Born in Warsaw, Gombrowicz studied law at the University of Warsaw. He published *Pamiętnik okresu dojrzewania* (*Memoirs of an Adolescent*) in 1933 and *Ferdydurke*, his most admired work, in 1937. The latter novel has found widely different interpretations: some critics align Gombrowicz with Existentialism, while others consider his work the precursor to the extravagances of Günter Grass and magical realism. *Ferdydurke*'s satire of the depersonalizing forces of society made it a literary sensation—and a scandal—on publication. The book was suppressed by the Nazis, and in 1939 Gombrowicz immigrated to Buenos Aires, Argentina.

In Argentina, Gombrowicz worked as a bank employee and café regular. His plays—*Iwona, księżniczka Burgunda* (1937; *Ivona: Princess of Burgundia*), *Slub* (1953; *The Marriage*), and *Operetka* (1966; *Operetta*)—are part of the Polish national repertory. In 1962, Gombrowicz returned to Europe, invited by the Ford Foundation to live in West Berlin in 1963–64. He then lived in Paris until his death. His work was suppressed by the Communist regime in Poland, though periodic gestures of liberalization displayed the loyalty of his following: in 1957, when a sympathetic comrade allowed 10,000 copies of *Ferdydurke* to be printed, it sold out in a matter of days. A leading Polish critic, Artur Sandauer, hailed him as "the pride of the nation." Other works include the novels *Trans-Atlantyk* (1953; *Trans-Atlantic*), *Pornografia* (1960; *Pornography*), and *Kosmos* (1965; *Cosmos*). *Pornography* missed winning the Prix International de Littérature in 1965 by one vote, but Gombrowicz won the award in 1967 with *Cosmos*.

González, N[estor] V[icente] M[adali]
(1915–)
Philippine novelist, short-story writer, and poet. A champion of Philippine agrarian folk culture, González was born on Romblon Island, in the Philippines. At an early age, González went with his father as a pioneer to Mindoro Island. The farmers and fishermen he found there would become the subjects of his later writing. Instead of adopting the historical-epic mode characteristic of much Philippine literature, González opted for a form of rural lyricism, a visionary treatment of the cyclical life of the peasantry. The story collections *Seven Hills Away* (1947) and *Children of the Ash-Covered Loam* (1954), as well as the novel *A Season of Grace* (1956), all deal with the hardships and joys of living within a strongly tradition-centered community. In *The Bamboo Dancers* (1959), the aimlessness and spiritual poverty of life cut off from the rural community are exemplified by the central character, Ernie Rama, a rootless intellectual. A similar theme is sounded in the stories that make up *Look, Stranger, on This Island Now* (1963). His explorations of the cultural life of the simple rural people continued in *Mindoro and Beyond: 21 Stories* (1979) and *The Bread of Salt and Other Stories* (1993). In 1990 he published a pair of important nonfiction works, a book of essays entitled *The Father and the Maid: Essays on Filipino Life and Letters* (1990) and an autobiographical work, *Kalutang: a Filipino in the World* (1990). For his defense of traditional Philippine values, González has been the recipient of the Republic Award of Merit in 1954, the Republic Cultural Heritage Award in 1960, and in 1961 the Rizal Pro Patria Award.

Gorée
Island off the coast of Senegal. Settled by southbound Portuguese explorers in the mid fifteenth century, Gorée island was first called Palma and served as a port of call for Portuguese ships sailing along the west coast of Africa. Though small, barren, and lacking fresh water, the island was of strategic importance to the Portuguese because it was sheltered by the tip of the Cape Verde peninsula, was less than four kilometers from the African mainland, had excellent anchorage for large ships, and lay at the

intersection of several major Atlantic shipping routes. Explorers on their way to Asia around the southern tip of Africa, including Vasco da Gama (1460–1524) and Fernando Po, frequently stopped on the island to pick up supplies and conduct repairs; and as contacts with the mainland developed, the island became a key European outpost to Africa. Because of its strategic value, possession of the island was hotly disputed; in 1588 the Dutch seized it from the Portuguese, renamed it Goede Reede (later corrupted to Gorée), and built two defensive military forts on it. In the next three centuries Gorée changed hands seventeen times, fought over by the Portuguese, the Dutch, the French, and briefly the British. The island became increasingly valuable because it offered a monopoly on the trade in hides, gum, ostrich feathers, wax, gold, and, most important, slaves, that began in the mid fifteenth century and grew enormously thereafter.

Through Gorée, Senegambia became one of the most important outlets of the slave trade, supplying at least a third of the captives exported before 1600. By the sixteenth century, Gorée had become a bustling port where slaves from the entire region were assembled, examined, and branded before being sent to the Americas. As one of the principal slave ports of the Atlantic slave trade, Gorée was the site of great cruelty, brutality, and violence for nearly three centuries. After the end of the slave trade in the mid nineteenth century, economic activity shifted to the mainland and Gorée declined steadily. It is now a historical tourist attraction administrated by the Senegalese government.

Gorky, Maksim (1868–1936)

Russian short-story writer, novelist, and playwright. Maksim Gorky was the pen name of Aleksei Maksimovich Peshkov, the first great Russian writer to emerge from the ranks of the proletariat. Aban-

doned by his mother after his father's death, Gorky began living on his own at the age of eleven, working his way in and out of employment as a dishwasher, bakery shop worker, fisherman, docker, railroadman, and clerk, before finally settling down to write. His stories chronicled the hard life and attracted enough attention to get him published in St. Petersburg. In 1898 he published two volumes of short stories, and a novel, *Foma Gordeyev*, in 1899. Proceeds from sales enabled him to set up his own small publishing house. He also joined the Social Democratic Party and contributed much of his earnings to Marxist causes. His radicalization, reflected in the plays *Na Dne* (1902; *The Lower Depths*) and *Meshchane* (1901; *The Petit Bourgeois*), resulted in attempts by the government to keep him out of the Russian Academy, an honorary body of Russian cultural illuminati.

Gorky was arrested in 1905 when his press published material critical of the government, but was released after widespread public protest. Still fearful, he traveled to the United States, where he wrote *Mat'* (1906; *Mother*), a didactic account of the revolutionary movement. He then settled in Italy, where he began his autobiographical trilogy—*Detstvo* (1913; *Childhood*), *Vlindiakh* (1916; *In the World*), and *Moi universitety* (1922; *My Universities*)—often considered to be one of his best works. Gorky returned to Russia in 1913, though he had become suspicious of the cultural politics of the Bolsheviks; his *Nesvoevremennye mysli* (1917; *Untimely Thoughts*) voiced some of these concerns. After the Revolution of 1917, Gorky organized a publishing venture that supported destitute writers, offering them food, shelter, and a place to write. He also used what influence he had with his old friend Russian Communist leader Vladimir Ilyich Lenin (1870–1924) to benefit the Russian intellectual community. He continued to write short stories, novels, and plays during this period, but spent a full eight years abroad, away from the Revolution. Gorky visited Russia in 1928 and 1929 before he returned permanently in 1932, receiving great honors from the government (his hometown, Nizhnii Novgorod, was renamed Gorky, and Moscow's main thoroughfare was renamed Gorky Street). He helped organize the Soviet Writers' Union and was elected its chairman at the Union's first congress in 1934. In this capacity, he was influential in developing the literary doctrine of Socialist Realism, which was soon purged of Gorky's "revolutionary romanticism." Socialist Realism became the stifling cultural policy of state-socialist countries and Communist parties throughout most of the Cold War, a bludgeon that limited the fictional imagination to describing the glories of industry and life in socialist society, denouncing style and formal experimentation as bourgeois, individualistic, and decadent. It is an unfortunate irony that Gorky, never entirely comfortable with state regulation of the arts, should have coauthored one of the most oppressive and far-reaching cultural policies of the twentieth century.

gospel music

Urban religious song of the United States in the late nineteenth and twentieth centuries. Gospel music developed into two different traditions, white gospel and black gospel.

White gospel music, comprised of evangelical hymns, has a text that centers on a biblical theme, usually sung in the first person, and with emphasis added to the thematic message through repetition and a chorus after each stanza. The music resembles American popular song; white gospel itself was popularized by such figures as singer Ira Sankey (1840–1908) and preacher Dwight Moody (1837–1899) in the nineteenth century.

Black gospel music developed in the 1930s during the Great Depression, although it reflects the much older African-American oral traditions of preaching, shouting, and singing that existed in the days of slavery. Though it may be based on traditional hymns, it is related to the spiritual and blues in style of performance and melody. The genre is characterized by a performance style that includes either a soloist or a group, such as a church choir, singing with a variety of vocal effects and embellishing simple melodies using blue notes and glissandos, while adding rhythmic syncopation and improvised text. Influential gospel performers include singer-guitarist Blind Willie Johnson, soloist Mahalia Jackson, and perhaps the best-known gospel composer, Thomas Dorsey.

Goya [y Lucientes], Francisco [José]
(1746–1828)

Spanish painter and etcher. At the peak of his career, Goya occupied the double position of first painter to the king and uncompromising social critic. The royal family portraits that Goya produced were not in any way flattering like the portraits by Spanish painter Diego Rodríguez de Silva y Velázquez (1599–1660) that preceded his. His depictions of both Charles III's and Charles IV's royal families showed the monarchy in a harsh, critical light. It is a testament to the painter's incredible talent that he was able to be the Spanish monarchy's favorite painter while never compromising his own liberal beliefs, convictions that often clashed with those of his benefactors.

It is commonly believed that his early training consisted of instruction from his father, a master gilder, and an apprenticeship to the painter José Luzan. A major turning point in Goya's artistic development was his pilgrimage to Italy (1770–71), where he mastered fresco techniques and won a prize at Parma. The pinnacle of his career, along with his status of first painter (1799), was his appointment as president of the Spanish Royal Academy (1795). His craftsmanship was often matched by his cunning, wicked humor.

A liberal, he was initially supportive of Joseph Bonaparte's (1768–1844; later to become the king of Spain) French occupation until the savagery of the period became apparent to him. His response to this year of upheaval was the series of sketches entitled Los desastres de la guerra (1810–14; The Disasters of War), a chilling collection that documented the nightmarish quality of life in war. With the reinstatement of the Spanish monarchy in 1814, the political climate became harsh for liberals like Goya and he went into voluntary exile in Bordeaux in 1824. His remaining years were spent in France with occasional trips to Madrid to execute commissioned portraits. Goya's techniques were highly influential on later French painters, including Eugène Delacroix (1798–1863), Honoré Daumier (1808–1879), and Édouard Manet (1832–1883). His black humor was later inherited by the Surrealists.

Graham, Martha (1894–1991)

American choreographer, teacher, and dancer. One of the founders of modern dance, Graham began her career with Ruth St. Denis and Ted Shawn, dancing with their company, Denishawn. Attracted by their bold explorations of the world's dances, Graham, influenced by Denishawn, would produce over 180 works during her lifetime. Dancing with Denishawn from 1916 to 1923, she would later become a feature dancer for the Greenwich Village Follies, and would teach and experiment at the Eastman School in Rochester, New York.

Debuting in 1926 in New York City, Graham won the praise of critics and audiences alike. In 1927, however, she abandoned costumes and sets, casting out for a new physical idiom. In avant-garde works like In Revolt (1927) and Lamentation (1930), Graham strove to use the whole body, not pantomime or narrative incident, to express mood. Critics withheld praise, however, as she embarked on what Graham later referred to as the "period of long woolens," in which she wore a plain jersey dress in almost every performance. This "period" provoked the popular vaudeville comedienne Fanny Brice to parody her.

Graham gradually reintroduced sets; with Frontier (1935), she began a collaboration with the sculptor Isamu Noguchi (1904–1988). The ballet symbolized the frontier woman's victory over new domain and replaced the totemic characters of her earlier ballets with more concrete ones, though the gesture remained far less literal than in classical ballet. Graham returned to the theme of the American frontier in the ballet Appalachian Spring (1944), set to Aaron Copland's score, in which she played the bride.

Letter to the World (1940), about Emily Dickinson, and Deaths and Entrances (1943), about the Brontë sisters, were ballets about great historical women. Graham then turned to the myths of Greek antiquity, performing ballets about Greek heroines, including Medea (Cave of the Heart, 1946), Jocasta (Night Journey, 1947), and Clytemnestra (1955). By this time Graham's style was fully developed: jagged, twisting bodies, earthbound dynamics, solos and small groups in between unison choruses, narrative jumps forward and back in time, the portrayal of one character by more than one dancer, and the fully unified use of light, set, and costumes.

Dancing until the age of seventy, Graham continued to teach dance and to choreograph new works until her death. Her training technique remains the most vigorous and disciplined in modern dance, and the older ballets that her company occasionally revives continue to inspire.

Grass, Günter [Wilhelm] (1927–)

German novelist, poet, essayist, dramatist, and artist. Grass is most famous for his first novel, *Die Blechtrommel* (1959; *The Tin Drum*). His writings are socially conscious and focus primarily on Nazi and postwar German society. Grass was born in the free state of Danzig, what is today Gdansk, Poland, and joined the Hitler Youth after Hitler invaded Danzig. He was drafted into the German army, was wounded, and was held prisoner until 1946 in the American sector in Germany. Following his release, Grass studied art in Düsseldorf while working as a farm laborer and a tombstone cutter; in his spare time he was a drummer and washboard accompanist with a local jazz band. Encouraged by members of the Gruppe 47, a German literary group, and disillusioned by what he viewed as the new materialism after the currency reform of 1948, Grass left for Paris in 1956 and there wrote *The Tin Drum*, which immediately identified him as the voice of conscience for his generation. The book chronicles Danzig society as it moves through the Nazi regime and into the postwar *Wirtschaftswunder* (economic miracle), as seen through the eyes of a mad dwarf. Grass's novellas *Katz und Maus* (1961; *Cat and Mouse*) and *Hundejahre* (1963; *Dog Years*) complete the Danzig trilogy, and are similarly politicized. Grass has also written poems and several plays, including the very successful *Hochwasser* (1963; *The Flood*), which reveals the absurdist influence of Romanian-born French dramatist Eugène Ionesco (1912–1994) and English dramatist Samuel Beckett (1906–1989), as well as his play *Die Plebejer proben den Aufstand* (1966; *The Plebeians Rehearse the Uprising*), which utilized the theatrical techniques of his kinsman Bertolt Brecht (1898–1956). He was also politically engaged, both as a citizen in West Berlin politics and as an artist, writing numerous political tracts to support those literary and social projects in which he believed. In 1985 he published a collection of political essays, *On Writing and Politics, 1967–1983*, that reveals a vision of the world even darker and bleaker than that posited in many of his novels. Some of his reflections on the postwar division of Germany appear in *Two States, One Nation* (1990). Grass was an outspoken opponent of unification after the Berlin Wall fell, concerned about the social and political fallout of combining radically unequal economies in one leap. He published *Call of the Toad* in 1992.

Great Leap Forward

Chinese national campaign. Launched between 1958 and 1959 in an attempt to telescope the ambitions of the traditional Soviet Five-Year Plan, the Great Leap Forward (GLF) was a massive mobilization of human resources. Epitomized by the slogan "To build up socialism by producing more, faster, better, and economically," the Great Leap Forward led to a massive squandering of natural and human resources. In order to get more iron and steel for state enterprises, individual families willingly or unwillingly collected and threw anything made of iron and steel into the smelting furnace. Similar acts eroded the bases for future growth in crucial industries. In the countryside, peasants were organized into "communes" to work collectively and share properties. Before long, popular enthusiasm had been exhausted and the dramatic consequences of the event became apparent. Tremendous economic dislocations resulted from the GLF, as well as millions of deaths from famine in the early 1960s.

Great Wall of China

Chinese architectural wonder. The Great Wall of China is the only human artifact that can be seen from space by astronauts. It stretches for nearly 4,000 miles (6,400 kilometers) from Shanhaiguan (the Mountain-and-Sea Pass) on the Yellow Sea westward to Jiayuguan in northern Gansu province and is the longest wall ever erected, built without the help of any machinery.

Around the fourth century B.C.E., northern kingdoms in China began to build walls to protect their borders against the invasions of nomadic tribes. These walls were not connected until Qin Shi Huang (the first emperor of the Qin dynasty, 221–206 B.C.E.) defeated the other rival kingdoms. To strengthen his defenses, Qin Shi Huang had new sections of wall built to join the existing walls into a single long wall. The building of the wall continued through the Han (202 B.C.E.–220 C.E.) and Sui (581–618) dynasties.

Through the centuries, many parts of the wall fell into ruins. During the Ming dynasty (1368–1644) it was rebuilt, and what we see of the Great Wall today is mostly the remains of that wall. It is roughly twenty-five feet in height, twenty feet wide at the base, and fifteen feet across the top. Along the wall there are watchtowers and signal-fire terraces. Sections of the Ming Wall, mainly near Beijing, have been restored since 1949 and have become a tourist attraction.

Greco, El (1541–1614)

Greek-Spanish painter, architect, and sculptor. Known by an extraordinary wealth of names, including Domenikos, Theotokopoulos, Domenico Theotocopuli, and El Griego, El Greco was born in Cardia, Crete, trained in Venice, and is still considered to be one of Spain's most illustrious artists. He lived in a large late-medieval palace, described by the historian Francisco de Pisa as one of the handsomest in the city of Toledo. His importance was not recognized until well after his death, in part due to the eccentricity and individuality of his vision. His paintings contain figures whose physiques are strangely distorted and elongated; they are colored not in the more traditional reds and browns of the period but instead in haunting blues and grays that provide strange flesh coloring and uncommon illuminations. *La adoracion de los pastores* (1567; *Adoration of the Shepherds*) and the unfinished *El vision de San Juan* (*Vision of Saint John*) are two of the most notable.

El Greco's resistance to traditional arrangements of the human frame can be traced to his Byzantine background as well as to his apprenticeship to a painter of religious icons. The influence of his teacher, Italian painter Tiziano Vecellio (Titian; 1488–1576), shines through his work, along with the influence of other Italian masters like sculptor, painter, and architect Michelangelo (1475–1564) and painter Jacopo Robusti (Tintoretto; 1518–1594), all of whom he clearly studied in depth. While he was in some ways aligned with the dramatic Baroque style of the day, his work diverges from this paradigm. Like English writer William Blake (1757–1827), another artistic visionary, El Greco belongs to no school. *El entierro* (1584–86; *The Burial of the Count of Orgaz*) is considered to be El Greco's masterpiece.

Grieg, Edvard [Hagerup] (1843–1907)

Norwegian composer. A renowned nationalist, Grieg was born to an English father who served as the British consul at Bergen and a Norwegian mother who had studied music in Hamburg. From the age of six, Grieg received piano lessons from his mother, then began his formal training at the Leipzig Conservatory. There his work was shaped by the influence of such German composers as Felix Mendelssohn (1809–1847) and Robert Schumann (1810–1856). During a stay in Copenhagen, he met Rikard Nordraak, a young nationalist composer who introduced him to the northern folk tunes of Norway. Later, in 1864–65, he helped found the Copenhagen Concert Society. He met the great Norwegian dramatist Henrik Ibsen (1828–1906) in Rome, this encounter eventually yielding his best known work, *Peer Gynt* (1874–75; the *Peer Gynt Suite*), an incidental accompaniment to Ibsen's play of the same title.

Grieg married his cousin Nina Hagerup, who became a talented interpreter of his songs. Due to a serious bout with pleurisy early in his career, Grieg's health was always delicate, yet he traveled and performed extensively. He toured Scandinavia, England, and much of the rest of Europe, giving music aficionados of more southern climes a chance to hear the lyrical sound of Grieg's beloved Norwegian national music.

Griffith, D[avid] W[ark] (1875–1948)

American film director. Griffith, a prolific director, is perhaps best remembered for the epic *Birth of a Nation*, which at the time of its release in 1915 received intense criticism. Originally an actor, Griffith made the move behind the camera after playing a leading role in *Rescued from an Eagle's Nest* (1907).

Griffith eventually joined Reliance-Majestic Studios as head of production, where he began work on the adaptation of Thomas Dixon's novel *The Klansman*, eventually realized as *Birth of a Nation*. *Birth of a Nation* presents a highly romanticized view of the South during the Civil War and Reconstruction, relating the stories of two families, the Stonemans of the North and the Camerons of the South. The film caused an enormous controversy, as it portrayed blacks as greedy and power-hungry, and whites, notably the Ku Klux Klan, as noble individuals continually besieged by blacks. Many critics, including black groups, called for the banning of the film, while others insisted that Griffith, as a Southerner and the son of a lieutenant colonel who'd fought for the South in the Civil War, was attempting to portray a naïve but honest view of the South and racial prejudices. The film's high production values nonetheless ushered in a new era of a serious medium. Griffith's next film, *Intolerance*, wove four stories—the fall of Babylon, Christ's betrayal and crucifixion, the massacre of the Huguenots in 1572, and a contemporary story of injustice—into what is still considered a masterwork.

Despite critical acclaim, *Intolerance* was a box-office failure, and Griffith joined Adolph Zukor's company, Famous Players–Lasky (later Paramount), where he made several "pastoral romances" with the actress Lillian Gish, including *The Greatest Thing in Life* (1918) and *True Heart Susie* (1919). In 1919 Griffith, along with Mary Pickford, Douglas Fairbanks, and Charlie Chaplin, founded United Artists Corporation, where he continued to make films with Gish. With the production of *Way Down East* (1920) and *Orphans of the Storm* (1922), Griffith achieved a certain critical and commercial success, although he never recovered the luster of his early career. *The Struggle* (1931) was Griffith's last film. In 1936 he was awarded a special honorary Oscar to honor his contributions to the film industry.

Grimm brothers

Jacob Ludwig (1785–1863) and Wilhelm Karl (1786–1859), German philologists and writers. These two brothers contributed to the field of German literature through their philological and literary studies, and by their editorship of *Kinder- und Hausmärchen*, known in English as *Grimm's Fairy Tales*.

Both brothers held professorships at Göttingen but were forced to leave when their political views ran against the grain of Prussian conservatism. In 1841 both Jacob and Wilhelm accepted university posts in Berlin. Their scholarly efforts were shaped by the Romantic movement then current in Germany, an effort to collect and reflect on the heritage of the German people. Jacob produced works on German folklore and grammar; Wilhelm edited medieval texts and produced a work on German legends.

Two of the most significant accomplishments of the Grimm brothers were cooperative efforts. In the early 1850s, under the direction of Jacob, the brothers began to publish the *Deutsches Wörterbuch*, a comprehensive sixteen-volume dictionary of the German language, which was not completed until 1960. *Grimm's Fairy Tales*, also a cooperative effort, is a collection of German stories completed in 1822. It contains such famous tales as "Rapunzel," "Hänsel und Gretel," and "Rumpelstilzchen" ("Rumpelstiltskin").

griot

West African musician. Griot performances usually include tribal and family histories sung to the accompaniment of string music. Griots are in effect professional oral historians who carry on the ancient traditions of praise-singing, storytelling, and genealogy in contemporary African culture; they are often compared to bards from other traditions. Many griots play skin-bellied lutes called *gunbri* or *halam*. In some areas they play alone, while in Senegal they perform in groups. The etymology of the word "griot" is uncertain: it is believed to be derived from the French in the seventeenth century; the first citations appear in a traveler's account from 1820.

grito

Latin American declaration of independence or revolution against established authority. Literally meaning "cry," the *grito* attempts to rally support for the revolution or independence movement, and usually includes a list of grievances as well as revolutionary goals.

When the *grito* serves as a declaration of independence, the day it is uttered is usually celebrated as independence day. There are several famous historical *gritos*: The *Grito de Lares*, which initiated the Puerto Rican revolution on September 23, 1868, was uttered by Ramón Emeterio Betances (1827–1898), Puerto Rico's most important patriot of the nineteenth century. Although the Revolution of Lares was suppressed, from Paris he continued to organize forces against the Spanish, keeping the movement for Puerto Rican independence alive. The *Grito de Ypiranga* was uttered by the Portuguese crown prince and the regent of Brazil, Pedro I, in the province of São Paulo on September 7, 1822, when he was ordered to return to Portugal. His cry of "Independence or death" on the banks of the Ypiranga River sparked the independence movement in Brazil. The *Grito de Dolores* in Mexico was the name given to Father Miguel Hidalgo y Costilla's call for a revolution against Spanish authorities on September 16, 1810. September 16 is now celebrated as Mexico's independence day.

Grotowski, Jerzy (1933–)

Polish theater director. An internationally known leader of experimental theater, Grotowski was born in Rzeszów, Poland, and educated at the National Theatrical Academy in Kraków (1951–59) and at the Faculty of Stage-Directing in Moscow and Kraków. He established the Theater of Thirteen Rows in Opole, also called the Laboratory Theater, and from 1959 until 1964 directed plays that addressed the relationship between plays and the dominant culture, as well as that between the actors and the audience. Grotowski's work with the Laboratory Theater was called "poor theater" because it attempted to produce plays using the simplest available materials, and the use of makeup or other artificial props was kept to a minimum. His work goes beyond the polite conventions of modern society to recover basic human relationships and feelings. His actors understood their craft to be part of that effort, and therefore they worked to understand their own superficiality and repressions and portray their characters by transforming themselves, rather than simply assuming a ready-made persona. Some of his better-known productions include *Faustus* (1963), *Hamlet* (1964), and *The Constant Prince* (1965). In addition, Grotowski's theoretical writings are collected in *Towards a Poor Theater* (1968).

In 1965 Grotowski moved the Laboratory Theater to Wrocław and first traveled to Western Europe in 1966. His guest lectures and directing influenced the avant-garde theaters of England, France, and Scandinavia. In 1969 his troupe made a successful U.S. debut in New York with *Akropolis*, a play based on the 1904 play by Stanisław Wyspiański. His influence in the United States is evident in experimental theater movements such as Living Theater, Open Theater, and the Performance Group. He has lived in the United States since 1982.

Guaraní

South American Indian group. Members of the Guaraní speak a Tupian language and live primarily in eastern Paraguay and adjacent areas in Brazil and Argentina. In the fourteenth and fifteenth centuries, some of these Tupian speakers migrated inland to the Río de la Plata region, becoming the Guaraní of Paraguay. Most of the 1 million peasants who live around Asuncíon speak Guaraní and are descendants of mixed Spanish and Guaraní heritage. The aboriginal Guaraní, like other South American tropical forest cultures, were seminomadic and practiced slash-and-burn agriculture that required them to move their settlements every five to six years. Four to six large thatched houses

made up a village, each house occupied by as many as sixty patrilineally related families. The women cultivated corn, manioc, and sweet potatoes while the men fished and hunted.

Spanish contact with the Guaraní began with Domingo Martínez de Irala in 1536–56, and his search for gold and silver. Founding small ranches around Asunción, the Spanish maintained harems of Guaraní women. These racially mixed descendants became part of the population of modern Paraguay. In 1767 the Jesuit missions established in the previous century among the Guaraní of the Paraná River were destroyed; the expulsion of the Jesuits from over thirty successful mission towns was followed by the scattering of mission Indians, who were often taken into slavery and had their lands confiscated. A few dispersed communities of true Guaraní Indians survive marginally today. They live mostly in the forests of northeastern Paraguay, but they are disappearing. The best known are the Apapocuva. Today Paraguay's cultural nationalism emphasizes the link to continuing Guaraní customs, language, and philosophies.

Guevara, Ernesto "Ché" (1928–1967)

Guerrilla leader in South America and prominent figure in the Cuban revolution (1956–59). The eldest of five children born to a middle-class family of Spanish-Irish descent in Rosario, Argentina, Ernesto Guevara de la Serna, or Ché, the name by which he would become known, completed his medical studies in 1953. His travels through Latin America and his observations of the great poverty of the masses convinced him that the only solution lay in violent revolution. He viewed Latin America not as a collection of separate nations but as a cultural and economic entity whose liberation—particularly from U.S. cultural imperialism—would require an intercontinental strategy. In 1953 he went to Guatemala to help Jacobo Arbenz's progressive regime in its struggle to bring about social revolution. It was at this time that Guevara came to be known as "Ché." Arbenz was overthrown in 1954 with the assistance of the U.S. Central Intelligence Agency, and Guevara moved to Mexico, convinced that the United States would always oppose progressive leftist governments and that the emergence of socialism in Latin America would necessitate worldwide revolution. In Mexico Guevara met Cuban exiles Fidel and Raúl Castro, who were preparing to overthrow Cuban dictator Fulgencio Batista. Guevara joined Castro's struggle and was part of the force that landed in Cuba in late November 1956. Although Castro's group was wiped out almost immediately, Guevara managed to escape to the Sierra Maestra, where he organized a guerrilla army and became one of Castro's right-hand men. The rebels slowly gained strength and in a little over two years succeeded in defeating Batista. Castro's victorious troops marched into Havana on January 2, 1959, and established a Marxist government in which Guevara was given a prominent role, as chief of the Industrial Department of the National Institute of Agrarian Reform, as president of the National Bank of Cuba, and as minister of industry. In the early sixties he became well known for his opposition to imperialism and neocolonialism, including U.S. foreign policy, as exemplified by the "Good Neighbor" policy of the 1930s. During this period Guevara also published accounts of his experiences during the Cuban revolution, including *Ideologia de la revolución cubana* (1963; *Reminiscences of the Cuban Revolutionary War*), *Hombre y el socialismo en Cuba* (1965; *Man and Socialism in Cuba*), and *Guerra de guerrillas* (*Guerrilla Warfare*), a manual on guerrilla strategies. After April 1965 he disappeared from public life and spent the next two years in the Congo with other Cuban guerrilla fighters,

helping to organize the battalion of Patrice Lumumba. In the fall of 1966, Guevara arrived incognito in Bolivia to create and lead a guerrilla group in the region of Santa Cruz. He was wounded and captured by a special detachment of the Bolivian army in 1967, and executed shortly afterward. His image was emblazoned on flags and banners throughout the 1960s and early 1970s; he is considered to be a martyr in the cause of Third World revolution.

Guillén [Batista], Nicolás (1902–1989)

African-Cuban poet. Considered by many to be the greatest poet of Latin America, Guillén was born in Cuba. Of mixed African and European descent, Guillén did not receive an intensive formal education but instead read widely in Spanish and Spanish-American literature. He was later to combine a knowledge of traditional literary form with firsthand experience of Afro-Cuban speech, legends, songs, and *sones* (popular dances) in his poetry. Guillén originated the *son*, a poetic form based on popular Afro-Cuban music that he has used as both a vehicle for lyricism and for social protest. Although Guillén has distanced himself publicly from the radicalism of the Négritude movement that was originated by West Indian poet Aimé Césaire, who was studying in Paris in the 1930s, his poetry has always been dedicated to asserting the influence of African Americans on the formation of New World cultures. In 1921 he moved to Havana to study law, but, lacking the funds to finish more than one year, he left the university to work as a journalist in 1923 for *El Camagüeyano*. Although between 1919 and 1920 he published much poetry, his first book of poetry, *Motivos de Son* (*Motifs of Son*), did not appear until 1930. It was almost immediately hailed as a masterpiece and widely imitated. His next book, *Cantos para soldados y sones para turistas* (1937; *Songs for Soldiers and*

Sones for Tourists), published the same year Guillén attended the Congress in Defense of Culture in Spain and joined the Communist Party, reflected his increasingly outspoken political commitment. He began to campaign for change in the lives of the poor and oppressed and fought with the Republicans in the Spanish Civil War, after which he returned to Cuba. An ardent supporter of both Communism and Cuban revolutionary Fidel Castro (1926–), Guillén was exiled by the Cuban government under President Fulgencio Batista (1952–59), and in 1956 received the Lenin Peace Prize. He was an integral part of the ideological movement that prepared the path for the Cuban revolution in 1959, and in postrevolutionary Cuba held important positions such as the presidency of the National Union of Cuban Writers and Artists from its inception in 1961. Throughout his life, he was a popular hero among revolutionaries in Europe and Latin America and a spokesman for Cubans of African descent. Other collections include *Sóngoro Cosongo* (1931), a collection of lyric poems on subjects from black folklore; *Tengo* (1964; *I Have*); and *El gran zoo* (1967; *The Great Zoo*), to name only a few.

Güiraldes, Ricardo (1886–1927)

Argentinian poet and novelist. Güiraldes is best remembered for his novel *Don Segundo Sombra* (1926; *Don Segundo Sombra: Shadows on the Pampas*), a poetic interpretation of the Argentine gaucho ("cowboy") that has become a classic work of Latin American literature. In this work, he combined objective descriptions of country life with a subtle portrayal of Don Segundo, a member of the vanishing gaucho class, the rural folk-hero of Argentina. Born to a wealthy landowner, Güiraldes grew up on his family's ranch in the province of Buenos Aires. There he received his primary education and became acquainted with the traditions of the gaucho. Never

finishing his university studies in architecture and law, in 1910 he made the first of various trips to Paris, where he was introduced to many avant-garde French writers. In 1913 he married Adelina del Carril, who persuaded him to put together drafts of his early prose and poetry and prepare them for publication. While his first volume of poetry, *El cencerro de cristal* (1915; *The Crystal Bell*), and his first prose work, *Cuentos de muerte y de sangre* (1915; *Tales of Death and Blood*), were harshly criticized, they were influential documents that introduced European modernism to Argentinian literature. After 1915 Güiraldes began concentrating mostly on prose, publishing several novels and short stories in which he combined sophisticated forms with deep and sentimental feelings for his native land and its traditions. His later novels include *Rancho* (1917), *Rosaura* (1922), and *Xamaica* (1923). In 1924 he collaborated with fellow Argentinian writer Jorge Luis Borges (1899–1986) and others in the reviews *Martín Fierro* and *Proa*, and also founded his own publishing house. His greatest success remains *Don Segundo Sombra*, published shortly before his death, in which a young *gauchito* accedes to manhood with the guidance of the elder Don Segundo. Unlike his other works, the novel was almost unanimously well received and brought Güiraldes much fame, as well as the 1926 National Prize for Literature.

gunki monogatari

Japanese narratives. *Gunki monogatari*, or "medieval war tales," dramatized the divisive civil wars that rocked Japan between 1156 and 1221 and resulted in imperial power struggles. Developed during the Kamakura (1185–1333) and Muromachi (1333–1568) periods of Japanese history, these tales institutionalized bravery, courage, and loyalty as a part of the Japanese national character, and formed the basis of many of the plots of the Noh and Kabuki plays of traditional Japanese theater. The most highly regarded of these was the *Heike monogatari*, which dramatized the arrogance of the warring imperial-guard families of the 1180s and their eventual downfall. The medieval war tales contained a strong Buddhist subtext, in that they continually pointed out the ephemeral nature of human life and action.

Gurkha

Nepalese tribe. Originally from India, the Gurkhas (or Gorkha) fled Muslim invasions and resettled in central Nepal. Considered to be the dominant and most warlike ethnic group of Nepal, the Gurkhas achieved preeminence under Prithvinarayan Shah, ruler of the hill state of Gurkha, which conquered the Kathmandu Valley in 1769 and declared their language, Gurkhali—akin to Hindi—the national language of Nepal.

Gurkha religious belief is a blend of Buddhism, Hinduism, and Tantrism. The Tantric cults, which involve rituals and animal sacrifices to appease spirits, are often mixed with Hindu and Buddhist beliefs. Although the Gurkhas are mostly farmers, their diet is extremely limited due to eroded soil conditions in Nepal and the fact that religious practice does not permit them to eat beef; and though generally poor, the Gurkhas celebrate religious festivals elaborately. Polygamy is common, based on the financial position of a man, though wives are independent and may leave their husbands whenever they wish; divorce is widely practiced, as women search for the best situation possible.

British interest in the Gurkhas began with the British campaign against the rajah of Gurkha in 1815. Gurkha soldiers were believed by the British to be so fierce and courageous that the British decided to recruit Gurkha prisoners. In 1816, after defeat by the British army, Nepal became a protectorate of Britain.

By 1825 the British were using Gurkhas as mercenaries in the British Indian army, anticipating and frustrating the Nepalese military endeavor against the Raj. Trained by the British through the nineteenth and twentieth centuries, Gurkha soldiers were used against the Marathas, Sikhs, Afghans, and Burmese in various maneuvers of the British empire, and even fought with Allied forces in each of the world wars. They blocked Japanese expansion into northeast India on the Burma Front in 1944. Upon Indian independence and partition in 1947, treaty terms allowed Britain and India to recruit Gurkha soldiers, and Gurkha regiments were divided between British and Indian armies.

Gutenberg, Johannes [Gensfleisch]

(c. 1400–1468)
German printer and craftsman. Gutenberg invented a printing method that revolutionized bookmaking and thus education. Introducing an efficient movable type to replace woodblock printing, Gutenberg paved the way for the mass production of relatively cheap reading material.

Gutenberg was born the son of a patrician in Mainz in present-day Germany. He moved to Strassburg (now Strasbourg, France) around 1428, and there practiced the craft of gem cutting. Beginning in the late 1430s, he began working in secret on the project that would change the history of the printed word forever. He received considerable financial backing from Johann Fust, a well-off moneylender. Although the two eventually quarreled, Fust's support allowed Gutenberg to build his press and set the type for an edition of the Bible. The now legendary edition of the Bible that Gutenberg printed in 1455 is the first complete book made in the West and the first printed from movable type. Also called the "Forty-two-line Bible," Gutenberg's edition is printed in forty-two-line columns, and features a Gothic typeface. Experts believe its technical expertise was not surpassed until the nineteenth century. Although the number of Bibles Gutenberg produced is not known, about forty are extant (perfect vellum copies are housed in the U.S. Library of Congress, the British Library, and the Bibliothèque Nationale in France).

In 1455 Fust filed a successful lawsuit against Gutenberg and received as settlement the type for both the Bible and a Psalter (a book containing biblical Psalms) that Gutenberg had prepared. Although Fust and his new partner produced an edition of the Psalter in 1457 and inscribed their names on it, experts believe that Gutenberg should be credited with its technical excellence. The lavishly decorated Psalter features two-colored initial letters and intricate scroll borders.

Little is known about Gutenberg's life following the lawsuit, but records show that in 1465 the archbishop of Mainz allotted him a modest annual pension of food and clothing. Although he died in relative obscurity, his invention was one of the signal events during the Renaissance.

Gwilym, Dafydd ap (c. 1320–c. 1370)

Welsh bard. One of the greatest poets of the Welsh language, Dafydd ap Gwilym is also one of the major lyric poets of late medieval Europe. Over 150 of his long poems have survived. He was an early practitioner of the cywydd, a complex, strictly metered poetic form current in the fourteenth century.

While many of his poems explore traditional bardic themes (like the generosity and wisdom of the bard's patron), ap Gwilym is best known for his love lyrics, which have been compared to the love songs of the Provençal troubadours. Although these poems were influenced by Ovid and the European tradition of courtly love, they are unique in their blending of passion and political satire.

He sometimes targets himself for lampoon; in others, the enemies of love and art—often religious—are taken to task.

Gypsies

People thought to have originated in northern India and now living throughout the world. The name "Gypsy" is held to be a corruption of the word "Egyptian," since medieval Europeans believed them to be from that exotic locale; the word first appeared in English in 1537. Many Gypsies refer to themselves as "Romani" or "Rom" ("man" or "husband") and to non-Gypsies as "gadje"; they speak Romani, a language related to those of India, but today made up of many dialects differing among geographical and cultural groups. Though some estimates are as low as 2 million, there may be as many as 7 million Gypsies scattered throughout the world; most of them live in Eastern Europe.

Some scholars distinguish three large ethnic groups: the Vlax-Romani speaking groups (also known as the Kalderash), concentrated in Eastern Europe but spread throughout the world; the Kale (also known as Gitanos), mostly in the Iberian Peninsula, northern Africa, and France; and the Manush, in Western Europe. Though the Gypsies have organized themselves into local political parties (as in Eastern Europe) and are represented in the United Nations with a voting seat, their predominant social structures are often based on the influence of extended families. Some Vlax speakers follow what is known as kris, a body of customary laws and values. Because of their geographical and linguistic diffusion (Romani is not a written language), Gypsies lack cultural representation; since they have little political power, they have often been the targets of official persecution. In Spain during the Inquisition of the fifteenth century, Gypsies caught speaking Romani could have their tongues cut out; during World War II, as many as half a million died in concentration camps (the Nazis did not even record their deaths, because they considered Gypsies to be the "lowest category" in their racial hierarchy).

Much of the popular picture of Gypsy life is the product of stereotype and misinformation. The image of the nomadic Gypsy, living by chicanery and possessing demonic powers, is a staple of literature and art, particularly in Western Europe and Russia. An oft-repeated legend holds that Gypsies are nomadic because their ancestors refused to shelter the Virgin and her child in their flight to Egypt. A countervailing legend claims that the Gypsies are smiled upon by the Christian God because a Gypsy stole one of the nails the Romans were driving into Christ's body, thus sparing the Savior additional pain. In any event, the supposed Gypsy predilection for wandering may be the result of official exile and deportation, most notably after their appearance in Western Europe in the fifteenth century; Gypsy dispersion is often compared to the Jewish Diaspora.

H

hadîth

Words of Islamic prophet Muhammad. In the Islamic tradition, the *hadîth* is a report consisting of the words and/or deeds of the Prophet Muhammad, which serves as a secondary source from whence the customary practice of the Prophet might be ascertained. The primary source, the Qur'ân, was very restricted and obscure, and the problems that faced the early Islamic community required other, more specific kinds of instruction. People turned to oral traditions, which recounted the life and sayings of the Prophet. In its most developed form, this material was transmitted in authenticated reports of pronouncements attributed, for the most part, to Muhammad. The report, or *hadîth*, would consist of a tag identifying the listener or reporter of Muhammad's saying or deed, the circumstances that provoked him, and then the content of the saying or deed, or the *sunnah*. Thus, the *hadîth*, through oral tradition, re-vealed the *sunnah* of the Prophet, his customary practices or sayings.

Medieval Arab scholars attempted to rationalize the complex body of traditions that made up the *hadîth*. In order to ensure the legitimacy of the authority behind it, the report would be traced back through the various reporters, all of whom were adjudged as to reliability and honor, back to the Prophet himself. Thus, a *hadîth* would have to demonstrate its genealogy in order to acquire significance. The necessity to document the personages involved in the chain of reporting of a given *hadîth* resulted in a tertiary literature, an extensive genre of biographical literature. This literature contained such information as was deemed necessary to evaluate the reputation, hence the reliability and integrity, of a given reporter.

By the ninth century, demands for a systematic approach to Islamic law intensified. Those *hadîth* that had passed the various hurdles that authentication required were compiled by topic, collated, and codified in six major collections. The Qur'ân and the nonscriptural guides that made up the *hadîth* formed the basis for the codification of Islamic law.

Hafez (c. 1320–c. 1390)

Persian poet. Though his full name is often spelled Mohammad Shams Od-Din Hafez or Shams-ud-din Muhammad, he is better known as Hafez (or Hafiz), the Persian word for "one who remembers," which designates a scholar who knows the Qu'rân by heart. Born in Shiraz, probably to a family of modest means, he received a classical education evident in the variety of his poetry. Very little is known with certainty about his life, although it is probable that he was a member of the Sufi sect and teacher of the Qur'ân. He addressed many of his poems, as was the custom, to local rulers, and he seems to have been famous throughout the Arab world and India by the time of his death. Though he composed in a variety of forms, his most famous poems are the collection of *ghazals* (also *ghazels*) called the *Divan*. The *ghazal* is a lyric form of interlocking couplets with variable length. Subjects of the *Divan*, said to be edited twenty years before his death, include love, drinking, nature, and spiritual devotion, all of which may stand as allegories of Sufi mysticism. There is no definitive text of this work, and more than one hundred printed editions vary widely as to number, organization, and even wording; the earliest editions contain some five hundred poems. Hafez is usually considered the finest Persian lyric poet. He is buried in an elaborate tomb in Shīrāz.

haiku

Japanese poetic form. As a result of bad translation and usage among students and even poets, *haiku* is also occasionally referred to as *hokku* or *haikai*, and the distinction between the three, if one exists, is difficult to determine. Nevertheless, *haiku*, one of the most important and popular forms of traditional Japanese verse, calls for three lines, the first containing five syllables, the second seven syllables, and the third five syllables. It is best understood by contrasting it with the forms from which it originated: the *haikai renga*, or long linked series of verses, began with a *hokku*, a verse of identical meter as the *haiku* but used only to set the scene for and lead into the linked verses. In 1892 Japanese poet Masaoka Shiki (1867–1902) coined the term *haiku* for the seventeen-syllable poem standing alone. The brief, imagistic flashes of insight available in the best *haiku* call for a subtle, highly refined poetic touch. Swift "cuts" between images ask the reader to form associations between seemingly disparate moments, in order to appreciate the brevity and transitory nature of life. Japanese poet Matsuo Bashō (1644–1694) is the most famous of *haiku* practitioners, writing in the seventeenth century. Following the standardization of the *haiku* at the onset of the twentieth century, it spread across the globe. In the United States it held a special fascination for American Richard Wright, the novelist, who wrote scores of them in the years before his death.

Haile Selassie (1892–1975)

Emperor of Ethiopia. Said to be descended from King Solomon and the queen of Sheba, Haile Selassie (a name he took in 1930, after being named emperor of Ethiopia), was born Tafari Makonnen. Son of Ras Makonnen, a close adviser to the emperor Menelik II (r. 1889–1913), Tafari gained the respect of the emperor, later marrying Menelik's granddaughter, Wayzaro Menen, in 1911. After Tafari's 1916 defeat of Lij Yasu, the grandson of Menelik, whose Islamic sympathies isolated him from the majority of Christian Ethiopians, Menelik's daughter Zauditu was crowned empress and Tafari was named *ras*, one of the highest ranks in Ethiopia, and heir to the throne.

During his reign as king (beginning in 1928) and as emperor (beginning in 1930), Haile Selassie introduced many economic and social reforms, including the abolition of slavery. His visits to Europe convinced him of the need to modernize the country, and he subsequently brought in numerous foreign advisers to achieve this end. In 1935 Ethiopia was invaded by Italy, and Haile Selassie delivered his memorable appeal to the League of Nations, warning the members that "God and history will remember your judgment." His speech went unheard, and Haile Selassie spent the ensuing years working with the British toward the defeat of the Italians. Restored as emperor in 1941, Haile Selassie attempted to consolidate his power and return political stability to his country. His efforts at internal social reforms and international reforms continued, with the establishment of universal suffrage and with the formation of the Organization of African Unity in 1963. These reforms, however, could not quell the widespread social unrest caused by unemployment, inflation, and famine, and in 1974 Haile Selassie was deposed by a coup and placed under house arrest. He died the following year.

The religious cult of Rastafarianism, practiced in Jamaica and in some parts of the United States, is founded on the belief that black Africans will achieve eventual redemption. Named after Ras Tafari, an early title of Haile Selassie, members of the Rastafarian sect believe him to be a god.

Haitian revolution

Eighteenth-century independence struggle. The Haitian revolution of 1792 was a product of gross social inequalities in the French colony then named Saint Domingue. In 1789 Saint Domingue's 40,000 whites lived in luxury, denying

political rights to the country's 30,000 freedmen (who were predominantly mulatto) and denying freedom to the country's 450,000 black slaves.

The French Revolution of 1789, in which French republicans overthrew the nobility, helped to spark the Haitian revolution; freedmen and slaves alike identified with the radical rhetoric of the French revolutionaries and realized that the turmoil in the mother country might make colonial action against insurgents in Saint Domingue difficult.

Two freedmen, Oge and Chavannes, went to Paris in 1791 to demand their political rights; on their return they were ambushed and brutally murdered by whites who quartered their bodies and hung them at a crossroads as a warning to other politically ambitious blacks. These atrocities prompted a bloody revolt; on October 30, 1791, freedmen led by General Louis Beauvais and slaves led by Boukmann, Biassou, and Jean-François rose up against their oppressors, setting fire to thousands of cane fields and slaughtering entire families of whites. The terrified whites enlisted the aid of British slaveholders in Jamaica, who rushed to Saint Domingue and made an alliance with the freedmen's army, forcing the slaves to back down and forcing the slave leaders, including a former slave named Toussaint L'Ouverture, to flee to Santo Domingo, a city in the Spanish part of the island.

While in Santo Domingo, L'Ouverture emerged as the revolution's dominant military leader, and in time he returned to the French part of Saint Domingue to raise his own army against the Spanish and the British. Through excellent military strategies and opportunistic alliances, L'Ouverture drove the British, the Spanish, and the French from Saint Domingue by 1800 and established a government run by Haitian blacks, whites, and mulattoes. He launched a number of important reforms in the fields of education, trade, industry, and agriculture, but he led a life of extravagance and glamour, surrounding himself with former slaveholders and upper-class whites and pledging loyalty to France, to the chagrin of many of his countrymen.

In 1801 L'Ouverture helped his nephew, Moyse, lead a revolt against the new government, killing two hundred whites; shortly after that, a group of mulattoes revolted. L'Ouverture managed to put down both insurrections, but his political strength had already begun to diminish. He declared himself governor for life and attempted to consolidate his power, but this angered the French general Napoleon Bonaparte, who sent an expedition against L'Ouverture in 1802, capturing the general and imprisoning him in the French Alps, where he died in 1803.

Nonetheless, the Haitian revolution against the French continued under Jean-Jacques Dessalines (c. 1758–1806), who allied himself with the British in a hard-fought campaign against the French that finally resulted in victory in 1804, when the independence of Haiti was first officially declared.

hajj

Islamic pilgrimage to Mecca. Practicing Muslims are enjoined by God in the Qur'ân to perform the *hajj* at least once in a lifetime, "if you are able." This is interpreted by most to mean when one can afford the cost and is free from debts and obligations. The *hajj* takes place in the twelfth month of the Islamic (Hijra) lunar calendar.

According to the ritual, the pilgrim must enter *ihram*, or the sacred state of being, before reaching the outskirts of Mecca. For men, this means donning two pieces of unsewn cloth in emulation of the prophet Abraham, one wrapped around the lower half of the body and the other thrown over the shoulders. Women wear a wrap that conceals the entire head, except the face. It is forbidden for women to cover their faces and for men to cover their heads.

Hajj consists of a number of acts performed in emulation of Abraham's movements when in Mecca with his wife, Hajrah, and their son, Isma'il. This includes walking around the Ka'bah (a small, uneven, hollow shrine within the Great Mosque of Mecca) seven times counterclockwise. Usually shrouded in an ornate black covering, the Ka'bah houses the *al-hajar al-aswd*, the sacred Black Stone of Mecca. According to Islamic myth, the stone, originally white, was given to Adam as he fell from paradise. By touching and kissing the stone, pilgrims believe, their sins will be absorbed. Its saturation with sins over the centuries accounts for its black color and its name. (Although it is referred to as the Black Stone, it actually consists of three stones bound together by a silver band.) Destroyed and rebuilt many times, the Ka'bah served as a shrine for pagan idols in pre-Islamic times. Islamic tradition holds that Adam built the first shrine to God where the Ka'bah now stands, and that Abraham built one in the same place.

The pilgrim must also walk between two hills in imitation of Hajrah's troubled search for water for her thirsting baby. Isma'il's discovery of the well of Zamzam is commemorated by pilgrims when they stop there to drink before leaving for the Plain of 'Arafat on the ninth of the month. Here the pilgrim will perform the afternoon prayer and then pray to God for mercy and forgiveness. A sincere prayer is said to result in total absolution. It is here that Adam is said to have prayed for his Lord's forgiveness of his disobedience and asked to be reunited with Hawa (Eve). The believer then leaves shortly before sunset for Muzdalifa, where he or she will gather small pebbles to hurl the next day at the three representations of Satan in the town of Mina.

It is in Mina, on the tenth day of the

month, that certain animals are sacrificed, emulating Abraham's sacrifice of a ram, which the angels miraculously substituted for his son, Isma'il (rather than Isaac as in the biblical tradition). Muslims not on pilgrimage (about 1.5 million Muslims attend each year) celebrate the day as the Feast of Sacrifice, or the "Greater Feast"; many sacrifice animals and distribute the meat among family members and to the needy. The pilgrims return to Mecca for a final circumambulation and have their hair shorn to ritually mark the end of the state of *ihram*. An optional but recommended journey to the Prophet Muhammad's tomb in Medina often follows.

Halakah

Body of laws governing the Jewish people in both religious and day-to-day matters. From the Hebrew, meaning "the way," these laws have evolved since the completion of the Pentateuch, the first five books of the Hebrew Bible. Traditionally, they are ascribed to God's revelations to the Prophet Moses on Mt. Sinai, although some were added later in the spirit of the Sinatic Law. The Halakah deals exclusively with legal matters and embodies history, literature, and ethical teachings.

There are five sources for the Halakah. First are the 613 commandments of Moses that compose what is known as the written law. Second is the Kabbalah, or the traditional statements, which is passed down from one generation to the next. The authority of the Kabbalah is sometimes questioned since its origins are undocumented. Third is the oral law, consisting of interpretations (of the written law) that were either handed down to Moses on Mt. Sinai or the product of subsequent deduction. Fourth is the Advice of the Sages, known as *derabbanan*. The authority of the sages was derived from rulings in the Talmud that allowed them to suspend or alter whichever Halakah they deemed harmful or no longer feasible. Fifth is custom; it is against the law for anyone to impose a restriction that cannot be followed by the majority of the community. Where the Halakah is unclear, custom decides the matter, since it is believed that the community as a whole cannot err.

Since its "closing" at the end of the fifth century, the Halakah has been accepted as the final authority in matters of Jewish law. It became increasingly difficult to follow until Joseph Caro (1488–1575), a Spanish Jew, remedied the problem with a comprehensive guide, the *Beit Yosef*. A shorter version of the *Beit Yosef*, called *Shulhan Arukh* (1565) was disseminated throughout the Jewish world by the newly invented printing press. However, since Caro was from Spain, his work favored Spanish schools of law; therefore, the German Jews added the *Mappah*, a text that listed German-Polish practices whenever they differed from the Spanish. The Halakah continues to evolve today in the form of Response Literature, answering the challenge of maintaining Jewish custom and practice in the modern world.

The Halakah remains respected as the word of God by Jewish people, but opinions differ as to its ultimate authority over their everyday lives. Orthodox Jews obey the Halakah strictly in all matters, while Reform Jews do not accept the Halakah as binding in matters of practical law but do follow its ethical precepts. Conservative Jews fall somewhere in between and attempt to reconcile the traditional Halakah with modern circumstances.

ha-Levi, Judah, *see* Judah ha-Levi

Hals, Frans (c. 1585–1666)

Flemish-born portrait painter. Hals is often referred to as the first great painter of the seventeenth-century Dutch school, despite the fact that his talent has only been recognized since the second half of the nineteenth century. Probably born in Antwerp, Hals was a pupil of Karel van Mander from 1600 to 1603, and entered the Guild of St. Luke in Haarlem in 1610, where he lived the rest of his life.

Particularly well known for his talent as a portrait artist, Hals possessed an exceptional ability to capture an individual's temperament and personality on canvas. Many of Hals's portraits display a characteristic smile, grimace, or laugh, a trademark of his work. His best-known portraits include *La Bohémienne* (c. 1628; *Gypsy Girl*) and *Malle Babbe* (c. 1630–33).

Among Hals's most noteworthy paintings are a series of eight group portraits completed between 1616 and 1666. Commissioned by a wide array of patrons, from musketeers and archers to governors and regents of charities, these portraits include such a fulsome and harmonious display of features, individuals, and costumes that they are often likened to historical paintings. Hals imbued these formal subjects and settings with a celebratory sense of disorder and spontaneity. He had the great talent to portray each subject with equal prominence, capturing each in the middle of some action or emotion; this was an important consideration for Hals, given the fact that each sitter was generally a subscriber. In one of his most famous paintings, *Portret van een officier* (1624; *The Laughing Cavalier*), Hals's brushwork displays a forceful and vibrant exuberance, a style that became much less apparent in his later paintings. Other paintings in this series include *Maaltijd van officieren van den Cluveniers-Doelen* (c. 1627; *Banquet of the Officers of the Company of St. Hadrian*), *Regenten van het oude-mannenhuijs* (1664; *Governors [The Regents]*), and *Regentessen van het oude-mannenhuijs* (1664; *Women Governors [The Regentesses of the Almshouse]*). These later works are often com-

pared to those of Dutch painter Rembrandt (1606–1669).

All of Hals's seven sons were painters, though none were successful. Suffering from financial difficulties, he eventually died in poverty.

Hamer, Fannie Lou (1917–1977)

American civil rights activist and politician. Fannie Lou Hamer was born Fannie Lou Townsend in 1917 to a poor family of sharecroppers in Montgomery County, Mississippi. When she was two, her family moved to Sunflower County in the Delta flatlands, where, at six years of age, Hamer did her first field work, picking cotton with her parents and nineteen older brothers and sisters. In the cotton-picking off-season, Hamer attended school and proved an eager student, reciting poetry and winning spelling bees. She left school after sixth grade to help support her family, but she remained an avid reader.

In 1944 she married Perry "Pap" Hamer, a sharecropper, and moved with him to a plantation near Ruleville owned by the Marlow family, where the couple found work sharecropping and working in the Marlow house. On the Marlow plantation, Hamer was struck by the great disparity between her standard of living and that of her employers. In 1961 Hamer went to the doctor to have a tumor removed from her uterus; instead she was given a hysterectomy, without her knowledge or permission. This type of unsanctioned sterilization of poor black women was common in the South at this time, and it became one of the issues against which Hamer fought as a political activist.

In 1962 Hamer attended a mass meeting of the Student Non-Violent Coordinating Committee (SNCC), a youth civil rights organization that organized voter registration campaigns and championed civil rights across the South. After speaking with the activists, Hamer attempted to register to vote; she failed the voter literacy test and was then evicted by her employer for attempting to register. Thus began her political career; she became a fieldworker for SNCC, successfully registered to vote and began organizing voter registration campaigns. She was jailed and beaten for her efforts but continued her activism.

In 1964 she helped found the Mississippi Freedom Democratic Party (MFDP) as an alternative to the all-white Democratic Party, and helped organize the civil rights youth initiative Freedom Summer. Later that year, she traveled to Guinea, West Africa, with calypso singer and activist Harry Belafonte and a delegation of SNCC members. She ran unsuccessfully for state and federal office as an MFDP candidate on a number of occasions, and she marched through Mississippi with civil rights leader Martin Luther King, Jr., in the Meredith March of 1966.

Embracing a number of different issues in her political career, including the desegregation of public schools, equal rights for women, blacks, and the poor, and the reform of the corrupt voter-registration system, Hamer helped to spearhead a number of short-lived but important initiatives, including food and farming cooperatives like the Pig Bank and the Freedom Farm. Though tireless as a political campaigner, Hamer suffered health problems due to her harrowing schedule and she died in March 1976 of heart failure associated with diabetes, hypertension, and cancer.

hammam

Public establishment for bathing that developed around the fourteenth century in countries under Islamic rule. Often opulently decorated with colorful mosaics, pools, and fountains, these bathhouses provided an area in which people could socialize and relax, in addition to maintaining an uncommonly high level of hygiene for Europeans of this time. The Islamic bath combines primitive Eastern bath tradition with the more elaborate bathing process of Roman origins. Comprising many vaulted rooms, the *hammam* offers a wide range of bathing options, from a chamber with cool running water to one that contains hot water, as well as a room for steaming. These areas correspond roughly to the *frigidarium*, *caldarium*, and *laconicum* of the Roman *thermae*. Some bathhouses save space by eliminating the cold room and instead providing a basin of cool water in the *tepidarium*, or warm room. Adjacent to these central chambers are lavish apartments used for dressing and refreshments after a bath and massage, with separate facilities for men and women.

Some of the most renowned bathhouses still stand today in the Alhambra in Granada, Spain (1358); the Citadel at Aleppo, Syria (1367); and the Haseki Hurrem Hammam in Istanbul (1556).

Hammarskjöld, Dag [Hjalmar Agne Carl] (1905–1961)

Swedish economist, diplomat, and United Nations secretary-general (1953–61). Hammarskjöld is regarded by many as the greatest secretary-general in the United Nations' history. His dynamic and innovative leadership style, negotiation skills, stamina, and views on the role of the U.N. and the secretary-generalship broadened the position's scope, powers, and efficacy.

As the son of Hjalmar Hammarskjöld, a former Swedish prime minister, Dag Hammarskjöld seemed destined for a career in politics. After completing his studies at the universities of Uppsala and Stockholm, Hammarskjöld went directly into government service, assuming chairmanship of the Bank of Sweden in 1930. Exhibiting a flair for diplomacy early on, Hammarskjöld conducted many of the bank's financial negotiations at home and abroad until he joined the Swedish cabinet as a deputy foreign minister in 1951. He was a member of the Swedish delegation to the United Nations for two years, and was then elected to become the U.N.'s second secretary-general in 1953, succeeding the Norwegian statesman Trygve Lie.

Bringing a decisive political style to his new position, Hammarskjöld greatly expanded the U.N.'s international activities, intervening in world crises on several occasions. During the Suez Crisis of 1956, he sent a U.N. peacekeeping force into the Middle East to attempt to defuse a potentially volatile situation; he sent observers to Lebanon in 1958 to calm a brewing crisis there, and did the same in Laos that year. Perhaps most significantly, Hammarskjöld took an aggressive role in containing the violence that erupted in the Congo (now Zaire) in 1961, sending in U.N. forces and attempting to provide constructive mediation, despite the disapproval of the Soviet Union. It was on one such diplomatic mission to the Congo in 1961 that Hammarskjöld's plane crashed in Northern Rhodesia (now Zambia), killing him.

Hammarskjöld viewed the U.N. as the protector and helper of small and new states, and as an institution that should be recognized and respected by all nations. To this end, he sought to reshape the institution's activities and capabilities so that it could meet the needs of member states worldwide. Throughout his U.N. career, Hammarskjöld also sought to redefine the position and functions of the U.N. secretary-general, seeing the role as more than that of an administrator and coordinator. In a 1961 speech delivered at Oxford University in England, he argued that the "secretary-general should be expected to act without guidance from the Council or General Assembly should this appear to him necessary," and he adopted this attitude in his leadership approach, continually seeking to increase the secretary-general's independence throughout his two terms in office. He was posthumously awarded the Nobel Peace Prize in 1961.

Hammurabi's Code

Babylonian legal code. Hammurabi was the sixth and best known of the eleven kings of the Old Babylonian dynasty. His forty-two-year rule (c. 1792–1750 B.C.E.) is best known for a code of 282 case laws that were promulgated and inscribed on a diorite stela in the temple of Marduk.

Discovered at Susa in 1901 by the French archaeologist Jean-Vincent Scheil, Hammurabi's Code covered a broad range of legal issues, including economic matters (prices, tariffs, trade), family law (marriage and divorce), and both civil and criminal affairs. The code aspired to universality: its strictures were meant to apply beyond the borders of Babylon, and they reflected the wisdom of both Semitic and Sumerian traditions. In addition, the code marked a significant advance over tribal custom, as it recognized no blood feuds or marriages by capture, although it did advocate severe punishment for misdeeds and operated under a system of retribution.

Hamsun, Knut (1859–1952)

Pseudonym of Knut Pedersen, Norwegian novelist, dramatist, and poet. Hamsun, although considered to be a naturalistic writer, was an early rebel against what he believed to be the excessive use of naturalism in literature at the turn of the twentieth century. Born in Norway to a peasant family, Hamsun visited the United States during the early 1880s, working in the Nordic enclaves of Wisconsin and Minnesota. He returned to Norway in 1884 to lecture about his experiences, traveling again in the United States from 1886 to 1888, spending time as a lecturer in Minneapolis, as a harvest hand in North Dakota, and as a horse-car conductor in Chicago.

After again returning to Norway in 1889, Hamsun published *Sult* (1890; *Hunger*), a novel, which was immediately successful and which gave him the security he needed to become a professional writer. His next work, *Markens grøde* (1917; *Growth of the Soil*), was his most popular novel, and he was awarded the Nobel Prize for Literature in 1920. In this novel, he illustrated the corrosive influence of urban society on the individual. He was an ardent supporter of the Nazi regime in Germany and of the Nazi occupation of Norway; after the Second World War he was tried and convicted of treason, though he was pardoned, because of his age. His impressionistic style had a strong impact on European letters, inspiring writers from the Russian Maksim Gorky (1868–1936) to the German-born American Thomas Mann (1875–1955).

Handel, George Frideric (1685–1759)

German-born English composer. Handel was the son of a surgeon, and his precocious musical talents were encouraged by his family, although his father wanted him to study law. Nevertheless, Handel was instructed in composition, as well as in keyboard, oboe, and violin performance. While Handel did study law at Halle University in 1702, after becoming an organist for the Calvinist Cathedral, he left school the following year and began his musical career in Hamburg.

While in Hamburg, Handel produced his first opera, *Almira*, which premiered in 1705 and was successful enough to provide him with numerous invitations to write other works for the Italian repertoire. (These works, unfortunately, have been lost.) Traveling to Italy, considered to be the musical capital of Europe, Handel wrote *Rodrigo* (1707) in Florence; for this work he received great praise from some of the major Roman patrons of art. While in Naples, Handel composed the opera *Agrippina*, which was first performed in Venice in 1709 and enjoyed international acclaim.

In 1710, Handel returned to Germany, directing music for the Elector of Hannover. He also made regular visits to London. In 1714, the Elector became King George I of England and Handel followed him, accepting a very generous annual pension. Named a British subject in 1727, Handel was eventually appointed composer of the Chapel Royal. He spent many years composing and staging operas, trying to bring Italian opera form into the musical life of England. Failing in this venture, he established a new dramatic form called the English oratorio, containing solo voices, chorus, and orchestra, but without acting or scenery. The best-known of these is *Messiah*, which premiered in Dublin in 1742 at a benefit for the Foundling Hospital. The English nation adopted Handel and his nobly expressive style. He died in London and was buried in Westminster Abbey.

Handsome Lake, *see* Ganioda'yo

Han-lin Academy

Chinese academic institution. Founded in the eighth century, Han-lin was the highest academy in imperial China, created by Emperor Hsüan Tsung (r. 712–56) of the Tang dynasty (618–906). Although it initially included court favorites, jugglers, and musicians as well as scholars, by the time of the Ming dynasty (1368–1644), only distinguished recipients of the Xueshi degree—then the highest academic degree in China—could gain admission. Those selected served as secretaries and/or advisers to the emperor and other high officials. Their jobs ranged from drafting imperial edicts, compiling histories, and tutoring members of the imperial families, to administering high-level civil service examinations. The academy remained active for more than a thousand years until 1911, when the last emperor of the

Qing dynasty was overthrown. Western-
ers used to call it the National or
Imperial Academy of the Board of
Academicians.

Hanukkah

Jewish holiday. Hanukkah (also spelled
Chanukah) means "dedication" in Hebrew and is one of the most joyous of
Jewish holidays. Commemorating the
Maccabean victories, which eventually
led to Jewish religious freedom and
national independence, Hanukkah, referred to as the "Feast of Dedication" or
more commonly as the "Festival of
Lights," also celebrates the rededication
of the Temple of Jerusalem after its desecration by Hellenized Syrians in 168–
165 B.C.E.

Lasting for eight consecutive days, Hanukkah begins on the twenty-fifth of
Kislev, the third month of the Jewish
year in the ecclesiastical calendar. The
length of the holiday was probably chosen to correspond to the older eight-day
festival of the Tabernacle, but Talmudic
legend holds it to be a celebration of the
miracle whereby one day's worth of holy
oil lasted eight days, until the Temple's
supply could be replenished.

Hillel the Elder (c. first century
B.C.E.–first century C.E.) established the
custom of lighting a single candle of
the menorah, a candelabra with eight
branches, on the first night of Hanukkah, adding another every night until all
are lit. Games and presents for children
accompany the lighting of the menorah,
in addition to the recitation of traditional prayers, including the full Hallel
(Psalms 113–18). Unlike the Jewish Pilgrimage Festivals, Hanukkah places no
restrictions on work and there are no dietary restrictions that must be observed.

Hanuman

Divine monkey chief of Hindu mythology. Literally meaning "having three
jaws," Hanuman plays a central role in
the Hindu epic the *Ramayana* (Romance of Rama). He was born to the
monkey nymph, Anjana, and fathered
by the wind god, Vayu, who endowed
Hanuman with supernatural powers, including the ability to fly and change his
shape.

According to legend, Hanuman, who
is known for his faithful service to Rama,
helped Rama in his quest to rescue his
wife, Sita, from the demon king, Ravana. Sent to spy on the demon in his
kingdom of Lanka, the monkey warrior
was caught and his tail set on fire. However, running around Lanka, Hanuman
set the entire city ablaze with his tail. He
then flew to the Himalayas to obtain medicinal herbs to heal both his tail and
Rama's ailing army. In gratitude, Rama
rewarded him with the gift of perpetual
life and youth. In various stories, Hanuman is portrayed as a buffoon, but he
also appears in literature as the perfect
servant, loyal to his master and wise in
the knowledge of the Vedic hymns.

The hanuman monkey is one of the
most common monkeys in India, and
many regard it as sacred. In his worshiped form, Hanuman stands on hind
legs and has a red face. The god is also
worshiped in Japan, where many town
districts bear his name and a large number of temples are devoted to him.

Haqqi, Yahya (1905–1992)

Egyptian writer, lawyer, diplomat, and
nationalist. Haqqi is considered to be
one of the most versatile Arab authors
and intellectuals. Though raised in traditional Cairo, his family was in many
ways nontraditional. His father had been
educated at al-Azhar, one of the world's
oldest functioning universities, and his
mother was well versed in classical Arabic literature and religious texts. His
brother associated with many of Egypt's
premier writers, and he introduced
Yahya to many of them. After studying
at the prestigious Sultaniya law school
and spending a short period of time in
private practice, Haqqi entered govern-

ment service and spent two years in Manfalut province. During this time he developed the theme that dominated his first short story, "The First Lesson," and later ran consistently through much of his writing: the adjustment of the individual, particularly the oppressed, to a world that was being radically changed by the forces of modernization.

As early as 1954, Haqqi began warning of the dangers of authoritarianism that he saw creeping into the revolution of Egyptian political leader Gamâl 'Abd al-Nâsir (Nasser). One of his best-known works, *Good Morning!*, discusses the alienation brought on by modernization and the danger of the gradual centralization of power in the hands of his character "the professor," a city-trained villager. In order to avoid censorship, Haqqi financed the book's publication out of his own pocket.

In 1955 Haqqi married Jeanne Guihot, a Breton painter, and ended his twenty-four-year career in Egypt's diplomatic corps, moving to the Department of Fine Arts, where he had a powerful impact on the development of Egyptian popular arts. In 1962 he became editor of the literary magazine *al-Majalla*, a post he held until 1970. In 1969 Haqqi was awarded the Egyptian state prize for literature.

harem

The part of a Muslim house set apart for a family's women. Though most frequently associated with Muslim practices, the harem predates Islamic times; the idea of separating the women in the house did not originate with the Prophet Muhammad, as is commonly thought. The Prophet did, however, sponsor the practice, as well as the practice of keeping women under veils. These customs did not become widespread until after the development and success of Islam.

The royal harems contained not only the rulers' wives, who were often exchanged over the course of political alliances, but his concubines, eunuchs, and female servants as well. Because of the competition between wives, as they attempted to maneuver themselves and their sons into positions of power, the harem was often an important political arena; and because these women came from powerful families, the failure to achieve prominence within the court hierarchy could have dramatic repercussions, even causing the downfall of dynasties. The harem was common in most households during the early part of the twentieth century, and even the poorest household provided separate quarters for men and women. But by the latter half of the century, polygamy had been declared illegal in many Islamic countries, and the harem remains in only the most conservative households of Arab society.

Hari-Hara

Khmer divinity. A syncretic divinity combining the Hindu gods Vishnu and Shiva, Hari-Hara (also known as Hari-hara, Vishnu-Siva, and Sankara-Narayana) was especially popular in classical Angkor Khmer culture. Literally meaning "grower-remover" (Vishnu is popularly known as Hari, and Shiva is also known as Hara, or "he who takes away"), this god represents the complementary interplay of life and death, creation and destruction. Hari-Hara first appeared in Indian legend when Vishnu and Shiva were forced to unite themselves into one entity in order to defeat Guha, "he who conceals," a mighty, tyrannical demon whom neither was able to defeat alone. Visually, Hari-Hara is represented by sculptures of a god whose right side is Shiva and whose left is Vishnu, of which many fine examples can be found in the ruins of Angkor.

Harlem Globetrotters

American basketball team. The Harlem Globetrotters are one of the most famous basketball teams of all time. They formed in Chicago in 1926 as the Savoy Big Five, though they renamed themselves the Harlem Globetrotters shortly thereafter, to emphasize their blackness. One of the first all-black basketball teams in America, the Globetrotters had a white manager/coach/substitute player in Abe Saperstein. They began as a serious team of professional athletes: in their first year of regular play, the Globetrotters won 101 out of 117 games.

In 1929 the great Inman Jackson joined the squad, contributing not only his superb skills as player but also a distinctive comic style that would become the Globetrotters' trademark. Their lighthearted approach to basketball arose not only from a desire to alleviate boredom (their habit of trouncing less-skilled local teams took much of the drama out of the game) but also from *realpolitik*: the team needed to please their predominantly white fans so that they, as black athletes, would be invited back to play again. When the first World Basketball Tournament took place in Chicago in 1939, the Globetrotters proved their world-class expertise, advancing to the semifinals, only to lose to the other great all-black team of the era, the New York Renaissance. In 1940 the Globetrotters advanced to the top of the sport, winning the Chicago World Tournament. The Globetrotters were subsequently able to attract the best African-American basketball players in America, including Reece "Goose" Tatum and Marques Haynes.

After the Second World War and the formation of the NBA, the Globetrotters increasingly turned their energy to comic showmanship. They were famous for flashy warm-up routines, the Magic Circle, and razzle-dazzle, performed to their signature song, "Sweet Georgia Brown." Throughout the 1950s the Globetrotters lived up to their name, touring the world as ambassadors of American sport—from the Soviet Union to Vatican City, Berlin to Mexico. The Harlem Globetrotters are largely responsible for the international popularity of basketball today. After Goose Tatum and Marques Haynes left in the mid-1950s to form their own band of basketball wizards, the Globetrotters dedicated themselves exclusively to circus-style basketball, adding the likes of George "Meadowlark" Lemon and Curly Neal. They eventually conquered television as well, with their own Saturday-morning cartoon show, "The Harlem Globetrotters," and a variety show, "The Harlem Globetrotters Popcorn Machine."

Despite the Harlem Globetrotters' enormous successes, since the 1960s some writers have found disturbing overtones in their slapstick antics. These critics suggest that Saperstein realized that Americans were more willing to accept a bunch of African-American clowns than a team of serious black athletes, so he turned his black basketball stars into souped-up versions of plantation-era stereotypes.

The Globetrotters, as a white-owned and -run basketball team, are often compared with the lesser-known, black-owned and -manned team of superstars, the New York Renaissance. From the 1920s through the 1930s the Rens, with the original Celtics, dominated American basketball. By 1933 the Rens were the best team in the land, going on to win the first World Championship in 1939. When they finally disbanded in the late forties, the Rens had an awesome record of 2,588 wins and only 529 losses. The entire Rens team was voted into the Basketball Hall of Fame in 1963.

Harlem Renaissance

American cultural and literary moment. The Harlem Renaissance was a period of renewed cultural awareness among black writers, artists, and musicians and heightened interest in black culture in America and around the world, concurrent with the Jazz Age. Throughout the

1920s, in jazz clubs, literary salons, and publishing ventures, African-American culture was celebrated, popularized, and scrutinized.

Although New York was the focal point of the Renaissance, the artistic and political developments of the twenties were part of a larger phenomenon that was occurring in Chicago, Paris, London, and the Caribbean. The term "New Negro," as popularized by Alain Locke's essay in an edited volume of the same name, referred specifically to the obsolescence of the "Old," rural, Southern Negro. The new, urbanized Negro, as presented by philosophers such as Locke, sociologists such as Charles S. Johnson, and activists such as W. E. B. Du Bois, rejected the social limitations and literary stereotypes of postbellum America. The aesthetic manifesto of the movement was the poet Langston Hughes's 1926 essay entitled "The Negro Writer and the Racial Mountain," which called for a literature that would unapologetically depict black experience and incorporate modern artistic innovations.

The Renaissance also catered to the preconceptions of white Americans hungry for details of the underside of contemporary urban existence, and turned to blacks to interpret it for them. The popularity among blacks and whites of Duke Ellington's shows at the Cotton Club reflected this desire, exemplified, too, by Carl Van Vechten's novel *Nigger Heaven* (1926). Many Renaissance writers were funded by wealthy white patrons who acted separately or formed organizations such as the Harmon Foundation to support and promote black talent. The patronage system was part of a worldwide blossoming of interest in primitivism and Africana in general, which was generated more by curiosity about the workings of the "savage mind" than by an interest in changing the social condition of black Americans.

The efforts of many artists, writers, and musicians in the New Negro movement were directed toward improving the perception of blacks in society. Some of the best-known writers of the period were anthropologist and novelist Zora Neale Hurston, poet Countee Cullen, novelist and songwriter James Weldon Johnson, and novelists Arna Bontemps, Wallace Thurman, and Claude McKay. Perhaps the greatest literary achievement of the period was Jean Toomer's *Cane* (1923), a work that defied conventional literary genres in its presentation of black rural and urban life. In the visual arts, Richmond Barthé achieved notice with his forceful sculpture, and Aaron Douglas gained recognition for his striking, African-influenced woodcuts.

Harvey, William (1578–1657)

English physician. An accomplished surgeon and innovative and insightful researcher, Harvey discovered and proved the circulation of blood and the function of the heart as a pump. Enjoying the best education possible for a student of medicine, Harvey was trained at King's School, Canterbury, Cambridge University, and at the University of Padua. Receiving his doctorate in medicine in 1602, he became a fellow of the Royal College of Physicians in 1607 and a physician at St. Bartholomew's Hospital, London, in 1609. He became physician extraordinary to the court of James I in 1618, and continued as the physician to Charles I after James's death.

In 1628 Harvey published *Exercitatio Anatomica de Motu Cordis et Sanguinis in Animalibus* (*Anatomical Exercises Concerning the Motion of the Heart and Blood in Animals*) and demonstrated the process of blood circulation. Although rejected by other physicians, his simple, elegant arguments prevailed and provided the impetus for a reexamination of the texts of Greek physician and writer

Galen (129–99 B.C.E.) that had dominated the science of physiology since ancient times. Harvey also examined the reproductive process and argued that life arose from the female egg rather than spontaneous generation in the womb. He published *Exercitationes de Generatione Animalium* (*Exercises Concerning the Generation of Animals*) in 1651.

Hašek, Jaroslav (1883–1923)

Czech writer and satirist. Hašek is known for his one unfinished novel; his vision of the first World War and the people caught in the idiocies and absurdities of that conflict endures to this day.

Born in Prague, by age seventeen Hašek was writing satirical articles for newspapers. Though he began working as a bank clerk, he soon quit and became familiar in the Prague literary circles of Franz Werfel (1890–1945), Rainer Maria Rilke (1875–1926), and Franz Kafka (1883–1924). Hašek distinguished himself with practical jokes, erratic behavior, sloppy dress, and the establishment of his own satirical political party, the Party of Moderate Progress Within the Limits of the Law.

He served in the Austrian army in World War I and was captured by the Russians, later becoming a political commissar with the Red Army. He used his experience of war to begin his novel, *Dobrý voják Švejk a jiné podivné historky* (1912; *The Good Soldier Schweik and Other Strange Stories*). The book's hero is an anarchist determined to carry on a struggle against officialdom by means of his considerable gifts of wit and cunning. Hašek died before he could finish the planned six volumes. His friend Karel Vanek completed the work.

Hasidism

Jewish socioreligious movement. Originating in Eastern Europe in the late eighteenth century, Hasidism is noted for its charismatic leadership, mysticism, and close-knit communal life. It was born in the wake of political upheavals, namely the partitioning of Poland-Lithuania, and religious crises (false messianic and kabbalistic movements). The Baal Shem Tov was the spiritual founder of Hasidism and set its basic tone, which stressed the holiness of everyday life and the conviction that mortification of the body and extreme self-denial were not necessary aspects of a devout life. After his death in 1760, however, the movement began to break up into various factions, each headed by local or regional leaders. The vast distances separating the Hasidic communities contributed to the decentralization of the movement; they were scattered across Russia, Poland, the Baltic region, and the Austrian empire. There was even a sizable Hasidic group living in Erez Israel. Consequently, Hasidism grew to encompass diverse strains of thought and styles of living. Community leadership tended to be passed from one generation to the next in a dynastic line. Occasionally, the tensions between the various courts and dynasties of Hasidism sparked open conflict.

Despite Hasidism's great popularity, the sect had to struggle for the right to exist alongside Orthodox Judaism. Among the many attacks on the new faith was the charge that Hasidism's ecstasy, the visions seen and the miracles performed by its leaders, was mere trickery. The Hasidic stress on prayer was seen as a rejection of Talmudic learning and traditionally strong Jewish scholarship. Only after the third generation of leadership in the early nineteenth century did Hasidism win the grudging recognition of the rest of the Jewish world. Even so, the character of Hasidism continued to change, especially after the large-scale migration to Western Europe and the United States in the last decades of the century. The late nineteenth century was a period of routinization for Hasidism; what began as an essentially spiritual movement evolved into an orthodox, increasingly secular societal structure. To halt (or at least slow) the forces of modernization, the Hasidic communities began to isolate themselves. Hasidism rejected the ideas that were changing the face of Judaism, in particular socialism and Zionism. Within an astonishingly short time, Hasidism had been transformed from a dynamic movement into a bastion of conservatism. By the end of the First World War in 1918, Hasidim were practically alone in maintaining their traditional dress, language, and education.

Haskalah

Jewish social and cultural movement of the late eighteenth and nineteenth centuries, parallel to the European Enlightenment. The leaders of the Haskalah were from the educated Jewish elite, the Maskilim, a group whose increased contact with European Christendom moved them to try to break down barriers separating Jews from non-Jews. In the face of seemingly permanent marginalization, where Jews lived in autonomous ghettos, speaking Yiddish and obeying religious authorities, the adherents of Haskalah were prophets of integration.

Although they were sometimes accused of encouraging apostasy, most Maskilim were strongly committed to retaining their Jewish faith. They did, however, encourage Jews to break out of the ghetto and find work in atypical fields: manual labor was especially encouraged, both as part of the Romantic movement and to combat negative stereotypes of "lazy" Jews. The Haskalah was complicated by the status of Jews in various countries; strategies for eliminating the ghetto could only work in countries that had granted Jews full citizenship rights, and many of those countries were ambivalent in their treatment of Jews.

The Maskilim were also responsible for a revolution in Jewish education, in-troducing secular subjects into the traditional religious curriculum and urging the replacement of Yiddish instruction with Hebrew or local languages. The Free School, an exemplary institution, was opened in Berlin in 1778. Originally a school for poor children, the Free School quickly became popular with wealthier Jews anxious to provide their children with worldly knowledge. The Haskalah educational philosophy was evident in the school's curriculum: German and French, arithmetic, geography, history, natural sciences, art, Bible studies, and Hebrew. Schools modeled on the Free School opened across Europe. Women also received extensive schooling: daughters of wealthy German Jews usually received private tutoring at home, while poorer girls could attend one of the newly established schools in Breslau, Königsburg, Dessau, and Hamburg. The move to educate Jewish youth into the secular, Christian mainstream was abetted by the Christian rulers, including Joseph II, the Austrian emperor who supported the establishment of secularized Jewish schools and also opened state schools and universities to Jews.

By the end of the nineteenth century, the grand program of the Maskilim was outflanked by nascent Jewish nationalism, represented by the Zionist movement, and was unable to deal with the wave of virulent anti-Semitism that overtook Europe at the fin de siècle. In Russia, where Haskalah had been a late arrival, the flowering of Jewish schools and a Jewish press did not occur until the 1860s. Though the assimilationist tactics of the Haskalah were briefly successful, the move out of the ghetto and into civil society occasioned massive resentment in the Russian populace. After the assassination of Alexander II in 1881, a series of bloody pogroms shattered the pretensions of the new Jewish middle class. The Dreyfus Affair in France (1894–1906) signaled that even wealthy, patriotic, highly assimilated Jews were likely targets for anti-Semitic hatred. For Zionists like Jewish leader Theodor Herzl, hitherto a proponent of Haskalah, the affair proved that Jews would never be welcome in Europe and that their only hope was the establishment of their own nation-state in Palestine.

The importance of Haskalah in the complicated relationship between Judaism, Jews, and modernity is immense. The assimilationist program resulted in the creation of a secularized Jewish middle class. The modern politics of ethnic identity and its seemingly intractable confusions were first played out for Jews in the fortunes of the Haskalah.

Hausa language

African language. Hausa is the main language of the Niger republic and of the northern parts of Nigeria, and is commonly spoken in other parts of West Africa where groups of Hausa people have traveled for trade. It serves as a localized lingua franca. Like Swahili, Hausa features many words of foreign extraction: many Arabic loanwords appear, as the result of Islamic conquests, as well as many English words.

Hausa has a rich oral tradition, replete with animal stories, fables, proverbs, and mythic explanations. Written literature began about two hundred years ago, with the use of the Arabic script (*ajami*), especially for religious writing. There is much modern writing in Hausa, such as the well-known novels of Alhaji Abubakar Imam, as well as historical and political works. While many modern writings use the Roman alphabet, called *boko* in Hausa, most religious writing is still done in *ajami*. Although written poetry in Hausa has been strongly influenced by Arabic traditions, there is also much modern poetry, in the *boko* script, which is moving away from classical and religious styles.

Oral poetry—often called *waka*—is a very old tradition of the Hausa people. It is performed with music by professional singing poets, or *mawaka*. The subjects of poetry may be great men and rulers who pay the poets and performers, but poems may also be about farming, hunting, politics, and wrestling, and are sometimes specially made up for religious and ceremonial occasions. The most important musical instrument used with oral poetry is the talking drum, or *kalangu*, which can imitate the different tones of the human voice. Stringed instruments such as the *molo* and *garaya* also provide music with the poetry.

Hausa people

Nigerian population who call themselves the Hausawa. One of the three main ethnic groups in Nigeria (Yoruba, Igbo, and Hausa), the Hausa inhabit northwestern Nigeria and southern Niger. The Hausa population is composed of 7 million ethnic Hausa and augmented by 4 million of the Fulani (a people of Nigeria, Mali, Guinea, and Cameroon). These Fulani assimilated Hausa culture and established themselves as a ruling class in the nineteenth century. Intermarriage has since blurred the distinction between the two groups, and they are usually referred to simply as the Hausa. Seven Hausa states were founded in the Middle Ages. The first recorded king of Kano, the principal town, reigned in 999 C.E.

Rigidly stratified, Hausa society is based on class and official rank. Most important official positions are reserved for the aristocracy. Each of the many Hausa states is ruled by an emir, and the political structure is essentially feudal. These relationships were held over during British rule, ensuring a continuity often disrupted elsewhere by colonization. The slow rate of social change among the Hausa contributed to resentment of the more successful Igbo and Yoruba peoples. Clashes between these groups were a factor in the Biafran secession of 1967.

Although many of the Hausa have moved into larger towns and cities (Kano, Sokoto, Zari, Katsina), the majority of the population remains rural, generally living on multifamily farms. Using cattle manure from the herds belonging to the Fulani, the Hausa depend on crops such as sorghum and maize. In addition, Hausa craftsmen work at tanning, weaving, and silversmithing. Trading is an important aspect of Hausa culture, especially in the large towns and cities.

Deeply influenced by the spread of Islam, originating from Mali during the reign of Yaji (1349–1385 C.E.), most of the Hausa profess Islam as their religion, although a small minority of Hausa, most notably the Maguzawa (or Bunjawa), maintain pagan beliefs. Many Hausa words come directly from Arabic; in fact, the Hausa language is written entirely in Arabic characters. Following Muslim law, descent among the Hausa is patrilineal, and intralineal marriages are encouraged and preferred.

Havel, Václav (1936–)

Czech dramatist, poet, and politician. Once imprisioned for his political activity and politically "subversive" writings, Havel was elected president of the Czech Republic after the fall of the Communist government in 1989. He was born and educated in Prague, and though he tried to avoid military service, it was ironically through the army that Havel began his career as a dramatist, with the regimental theater company. Later, he worked with a small Czech theater, Na Zábradlí, and staged the works of other dramatists, as well as his own work. After the Soviet invasion of Prague in 1968, Havel became a leader in the Czech civil rights movement, Charter 77, and suffered constant police harassment, brief imprisonment, confiscation of his passport, and the banning of his writings. Throughout the 1970s and 1980s Havel's farm was a base of op-

erations for avant-garde politics and the arts; several Czech punk records were recorded there. Havel's plays often portray the dehumanizing effect of language on social institutions and human relations, and his work has often been likened to that of English author George Orwell (1903–1950) and Romanian-born French dramatist Eugène Ionescu (1912–1994). In *Vyrozumění* (1965; *The Memorandum*), for example, Havel details the extreme crisis that develops when the bureaucracy develops an artificial language too complex to be functional. Other plays by Havel include *Zahradní slavnost* (1963; *The Garden Party*) and *Ztížena možnost soustředění* (1968; *The Increased Difficulty of Concentration*). Though Havel's plays were neither produced nor published in Czechoslovakia for many years after 1968, his works have enjoyed a revival on numerous stages, including his own Prague, since the revolution of 1989. Books of his nonfiction work, especially his essays, have been phenomenal bestsellers in the West, notably *Dalkovy vyslech* (1990; *Disturbing the Peace*).

Hawthorne, Nathaniel (1804–1864)

American novelist and short-story writer. One of the foremost writers of the American Renaissance, Hawthorne is remembered for his mastery of symbolism and allegory in his novels and short stories. His *The Scarlet Letter* (1850) and *The House of the Seven Gables* (1851) are the novels for which he is best known.

Hawthorne, whose ancestor John Hathorne had been one of the judges at the 1692 Salem, Massachusetts, witch trials, was raised in a family dedicated to a strict Puritan way of life. His father died when Nathaniel was four, and his widowed mother and her family moved in with her brothers in Salem. After attending Bowdoin College, Hawthorne returned to Salem in 1825 and began to refine his skills as a writer. His first attempt, *Fanshawe* (1828), was such a disappointment that Hawthorne attempted to destroy all the copies of the self-published work. By 1835, however, he had published "My Kinsman, Major Molineux," "Roger Malvin's Burial," and "Young Goodman Brown," three of the most respected American short stories of the nineteenth century. All three showed the profound influence of Puritanism on Hawthorne's work and his preoccupation with confronting the Puritan view of man as a "fallen" being.

In 1839, unable to support himself on the income from his writing and unwilling to accept the generosity of his family, Hawthorne took a job at the Boston Custom House. Disillusioned with the life of a "working-man," in 1841 Hawthorne retreated to Brook Farm, an attempt at a utopian agricultural cooperative in West Roxbury, Massachusetts.

Hawthorne married Sophia Peabody in 1842, and the couple moved to Concord, where they met, and were influenced by, resident Transcendentalists such as Ralph Waldo Emerson, Henry D. Thoreau, and Bronson Alcott. In 1846 Hawthorne published *Mosses from an Old Manse*, a collection of short stories that was well received but earned him little money. *The Scarlet Letter* (1850), however, brought Hawthorne a level of acclaim that has lasted to this day. Set in Puritan New England, *The Scarlet Letter* tells the story of a young wife, Hester Prynne, who bears an illegitimate child and is condemned to wear a scarlet letter A. Her husband, Roger Chillingworth, sets out to learn the identity of his wife's lover and discovers that he is the town's young minister, Arthur Dimmesdale. The rest of the story reveals Chillingworth to be vengeful and vindictive, Dimmesdale to be guilt-stricken, and Hester to be strong and self-possessed. Readers have argued endlessly over the meaning of the story and, particularly, of the letter A. Does it stand for "adulterer" or "angel"? Hawthorne's genius was in creating this sense of uncertain meaning within his allegory.

In addition to *The Scarlet Letter, The House of the Seven Gables* (1851), the story of the Pyncheon family and their cursed house, assured Hawthorne's status as one of the greatest American writers. Hawthorne also maintained close contact with other notable American writers, particularly Herman Melville, who had written a glowing review of *Mosses*.

Hawthorne influenced American literature with his insight into the moral dilemmas of American life. His works offer no simple solutions or ideal escapes from moral or social problems, and he has been called America's first psychological writer. Hawthorne's other major works include *The Blithedale Romance* (1852), *The Marble Faun* (1860), and a number of story collections, including *Twice-Told Tales* (1837), *Liberty Tree* (1841), and *A Wonder Book for Boys and Girls* (1851).

Haydn, Franz Joseph (1732–1809)

Austrian composer. Considered to be one of the most influential composers in musical history, Haydn is credited with inventing the string quartet and the symphony.

Haydn's musical gifts were recognized early on by his parents; they sent him to live with a cousin, a school principal and choirmaster. However, Haydn was mistreated by this cousin, and his real musical education did not begin until 1740, when he was invited to serve as a chorister for St. Stephen's Cathedral in Vienna, where he spent nine years. In time, his music made its way into high Austrian circles, and he secured an appointment from the wealthy Esterházy family, to whom he would devote the next thirty years. It was during this period that Haydn befriended Mozart.

Haydn's personal life was marked by considerable disaster. His beloved entered a convent, and the unhappy

Haydn consented to marry her sister instead. Unfortunately, his new wife disliked music, particularly Haydn's, proceeding in one instance to line her pie tins with his manuscripts. He had several mistresses, including a long-standing love affair with a mezzo-soprano in Prince Esterházy's court.

In 1791 Haydn made the first of two very successful journeys to England, where he wrote some of his most treasured musical works, collectively known as "the London Symphonies." On returning to Vienna, Haydn rejoined the Esterházy court and became the teacher of the young Beethoven. During these later years, Haydn composed his two great oratorios: *Die Schöpfung* (1798; *The Creation*), the text of which is based in part on *Paradise Lost*, the epic poem by English poet John Milton (1608–1674); and *Die Jahreszeiten* (1801; *The Seasons*), based on a poem of the same title by Scottish poet James Thomson (1700–1748). At his death, Haydn left a prodigious collection of works, 104 symphonies, numerous concerti, 24 operas, 14 masses, 68 string quartets, 52 piano sonatas, and many songs.

His style is notable for its wit, its liveliness, its thorough unpredictability, and its enormous sophistication. Most major developments in nineteenth-century European music can be traced back to his unfettered invention.

Head, Bessie Emory (1937–1986)

South African author and teacher. Head is considered to be one of the great postwar African novelists. Her writings sound existential themes in unfamiliar terrain, treating such topics as personal and societal alienation, political exile, racial identity, and sexual oppression. She is particularly concerned with describing the institutionalization of evil.

The child of a white woman and a black man, Head was born in the mental institution in which her mother had been placed. She was adopted by a white Afrikaner family when she was very young; however, when her black features revealed themselves, she was sent to live with a black family, where she remained until moving into an orphanage at the age of thirteen. In a few years she acquired a teaching degree and taught school in Durban for two years, later leaving that position to work as a journalist for Drum Publications in Johannesburg.

Head became active in politics in the 1960s, eventually joining the Pan-African Congress (PAC). She married Harold Head in 1961 and had a son. Following several arrests and continual harassment by Afrikaner authorities, Head moved with her son to Botswana, where she lived in the village of Serowe, working both as a schoolteacher and as an unpaid agricultural worker. Her experiences in political exile were extremely traumatic, provoking a nervous breakdown.

When Rain Clouds Gather (1969) is Head's first novel, and is the only work set in and developed from Head's experiences in South Africa. Her second novel, *Maru* (1971), addresses the issue of racism among blacks, focusing on the abuse of the Masarwa or Bushmen, considered to be slaves and outcasts within African society, by Serowe tribal people. As in Head's other novels, the antiracist sentiments expressed in *Maru* are intended not as a condemnation of the village of Serowe, but more as a broader reflection on the racial prejudices found throughout the world in many different societies.

The largely autobiographical *A Question of Power* (1973), Head's third novel, is a portrait of her nervous breakdown, a condition she believes resulted from the ongoing psychological struggles she faced as both a woman and a political exile. This novel is often considered to be a milestone in the development and evolution of African literature, as it is one of the first African novels written from a largely personal and introspective perspective, focusing on the individual as opposed to broader societal issues. Furthermore, as a story written from a woman's perspective, A *Question of Power* gained the attention of feminists and established Head's reputation as a women's author, although she hesitated to embrace the feminist label for herself. Head further established herself among feminists with her short nonfiction piece, *The Collector of Treasures and Other Botswana Village Tales*, a collection of Botswana village stories told from a woman's perspective. These stories are decidedly optimistic and positive in tone, and serve to emphasize the inherent personal and communal strength of women in overcoming male oppressors. Head's major nonfiction work, *Serowe: Village of the Rainwind* (1981), is a history of Serowe, recorded as a series of interviews done by Head herself.

Hegel, Georg Wilhelm Friedrich (1770–1831)

German philosopher. Hegel attempted to detail the structure underlying human history, the natural world, and rational cognition, and his systematic thinking about human history influenced many later social theorists, including Friedrich Wilhelm Nietzsche (1844–1900), Karl Marx (1818–1883), Max Weber (1864–1920), and Claude Lévi-Strauss (1908–); even contemporary figures such as Francis Fukuyama and Leonard Jefferies owe significant debts to Hegel's works.

Hegel believed that the world conformed to a tripartite law called the dialectic. An initial state gives rise to a reaction, which in turn provokes a reconciliation between the two opposites. He named the three stages of this development thesis, antithesis, and synthesis, and believed that dialectical structures could be found in pure logic and natural science, in historical processes, and even in the arts: the pure concepts "existence,"

"nonexistence," and "change" were dialectically related, just as were the physical phenomena of space, time, and the material world. In the human realm, Hegelian dialectics accounted for the "necessary relation" among Greek, medieval, and modern societies. Hegel's chief thought was that similar structures could be found in all of the various spheres of human inquiry. This conviction led to his attempt to outline a systematic compendium of all knowledge, his *Enzyklopadie der Philosophischen Wissenschaften* (1817; *Encyclopedia of the Philosophical Sciences in Outline*).

Taking his dialectical pattern-making to absurd lengths at times, Hegel used it to explain why there must be seven planets, why the Caucasian race is superior to others, and various other early nineteenth-century errors in thought. But despite the essential unsoundness of his methods and much of his argumentation, his work represents an important attempt to grapple with major intellectual problems of his time.

Hegel was born in Stuttgart, and studied philosophy at Tübingen University. As a student, he was friendly with German philosopher Friedrich Wilhem Joseph von Schelling (1775–1854), and spent most of his adult life teaching, serving as rector of the gymnasium of Nuremberg and then professor of philosophy at Heidelberg and Berlin. Hegel died of cholera.

Heidegger, Martin (1889–1976)

German philosopher. Heidegger is generally considered to be one of the leaders of the existentialist movement and the mentor of many European philosophers and thinkers, including Paul Tillich and Jean-Paul Sartre.

Born to a Catholic sexton, Heidegger displayed a keen interest in religion and philosophy at an early age, studying the works of philosopher Franz Brentano in high school. As a student at the University of Freiburg, he concentrated on Catholic and medieval Christian theology. He spent much of his time contemplating the meaning of existence, focusing on pre-Socratic Greek philosophy as a means of understanding the basis of Western thinking. In addition to studying the early Greeks, Heidegger deliberated the ideas of more contemporary philosophers of existentialism and phenomenalism, such as Søren Kierkegaard, Friedrich Nietzsche, Wilhelm Dilthey, and Edmund Husserl (who would later become his mentor).

Heidegger's doctoral thesis probed ways of being by examining particular states of mind. These states included anxiety, awe, forgetfulness, and curiosity; he felt that they could be approached only through disciplines such as psychology, science, or sociology. The work Heidegger produced in these other fields was not meant as psychology or sociology per se, but rather as texts to disclose aspects of being.

In 1927 Heidegger published *Sein und Zeit* (*Being and Time*), a complex essay on the nature of experience. Heidegger was fascinated with the meaning and significance of being in quotidian life. He explored what it means for a human to *be*, while also considering the epistemological import of such a question. In addition, *Sein und Zeit* addresses rampant global technological development, a condition Heidegger felt had been promoted by flaws in Western thinking. He argues that modernity has desensitized people and provides them with artificial ways of being. Heidegger's later works, however, propose that thinking about being is a saving grace in a technological world.

In 1928 Heidegger returned to Freiburg to take Husserl's chair. Husserl had suggested Heidegger as a qualified successor, even as it was becoming clear that Heidegger's philosophical interests diverged from those of his mentor. In 1929 Heidegger published a short work entitled *Was ist Metaphysik?* (*What Is Metaphysics?*), an investigation of the etymologies, meanings, and applications of words and concepts to life and existence. The text deals primarily with the notion of "nothing."

During the 1930s Heidegger experienced what is referred to by scholars as his *Kehre*, or turning point, which is said to have involved a shift from the fundamental questions addressed in *Sein und Zeit*. He participated for a time in promoting the cultural politics of the Third Reich and, under some pressure, joined the Nazi Party. Despite his flirtation with National Socialism, Heidegger was allowed to teach at the University of Freiburg after World War II, and his professional and intellectual status did not seem to be adversely affected by his involvement with the Nazi Party.

Heidelberg School

Australian school of art. Dominating Australian art for some thirty years in the late nineteenth and early twentieth centuries, the group was led by Thomas William Roberts (1856–1931) and included Charles Conder (1868–1909), Sir Arthur Ernest Streeton (1867–1943), and Frederick McCubbin (1855–1917).

Heavily influenced by the Impressionist movement in France, Roberts believed that Impressionism could offer the foundation for an authentically Australian style of art. Meeting in the Australian bush for a series of painting "camps" between 1885 and 1890, the members of the Heidelberg School augmented their incomes by offering painting lessons, often to women.

First gaining recognition at an exhibition in Melbourne in 1889, the Heidelberg School was viewed as a direct challenge to the prevailing trend in Australian art, which was characteristically very polished and dark in color. The work of the Heidelberg artists introduced a new element and direction into Australian art. Some of the best-known work of the period includes Roberts's

The Bullock Team (c. 1893) and *Bailed Up* (1895), Streeton's *The Purple Noon's Transparent Might* (1896), and McCubbin's *Down on His Luck* (1889) and *The Pioneers* (1905).

Heine, Heinrich (1797–1856)

German poet. Considered to be one of the greatest German poets of the nineteenth century, Heinrich Heine is also noted for his prose writings and political commentary. Among the first poets to break away from the Romanticism of German poets Goethe (1749–1832) and Schiller (1759–1805) and turn toward a more realistic style, Heine's literary reputation was sealed with the publication of his first collection of poetry, *Buch der Leider* (1827; *The Book of Songs*). These bittersweet love songs, written in the Romantic style, simultaneously question their own ability to convey the artistic truth at the heart of that movement.

Beset by financial difficulties, Heine's parents were unable to finance his education; however, a wealthy uncle in Hamburg, Salomon Heine, eventually agreed to pay for his nephew's education, but at a high cost in terms of his personal freedom. Heine had no interest in anything other than literature, poetry, and history, but nevertheless, at his uncle's prompting, he received his law degree and even went so far as to convert to Christianity (Jews were not permitted to enter the civil service at that time) in an effort to further his career. (He changed his name from Harry Heine to Christian Johann Heinrich Heine at this time.)

Like many of his contemporaries, Heine was drawn to radical political doctrines and responded enthusiastically to the revolutions sweeping Europe in the 1830s and 1840s. Saint-Simonian socialism appealed to Heine; he believed it might be the solution to older ideologies (mostly religious in nature) that had divided and factionalized mankind. Although he never espoused communism, Heine was on good terms with its young creator, publishing several articles in Karl Marx's newspaper, *Vorwärts*. His biting critiques of reactionary political conditions in his native Germany did not go unnoticed. In 1835 the Federal German Diet voted to ban all his works, making it clear he could never go home.

Though Heine's later years were marred by chronic illness, political scandal, and financial woes, Heine's final poems were among his finest. Published under the titles *Romanzero* (1851) and *Gedichte 1853 und 1854* (*Poems 1853 and 1854*), this darkly powerful poetry reveals the torment suffered by the aging, disillusioned Heine.

Heine's works continued to provoke controversy in the twentieth century. When the Nazis set out to expunge "Jewish" art from Germany's culture, Heine's poems, set to music, were so beloved by the German people that the Nazis were forced to continue publishing his works, though they often changed the byline to read "author unknown."

Hellman, Lillian (1905–1984)

American playwright. Often controversial, Hellman's works are marked by careful craftsmanship, characterization, and denunciation of social injustice. Hellman attended New York University, though she left before earning her degree to work in a publisher's office. Briefly married to playwright Arthur Kober (1925–32), she became involved with author Dashiell Hammett during her marriage, and continued the relationship until Hammett's death in 1961.

Hellman's first play, *The Children's Hour* (1934), shows the devastating effects of a child's lies about a lesbian relationship between two boarding-school teachers. Her subsequent dramas include *The Little Foxes* (1939), *Watch on the Rhine* (1941), *The Searching Wind* (1944), and *Toys in the Attic* (1960). Widely considered to be her best play,

The Little Foxes recounts the story of the Hubbard family's cold-bloodedness and greed, and culminates in the promise of guilt and loneliness as penance for their crimes. Hellman also translated and adapted several European plays, including *The Lark* (1955) and *Candide* (1957). She published three separate memoirs: *An Unfinished Woman* (1969), *Pentimento* (1973), and *Scoundrel Time* (1976), a personal account of the effects of U.S. senator Joseph McCarthy's anti-Communist hearings on her circle of friends. Hellman's *Collected Plays* were published in 1972, and her three autobiographies were published as *Three* in 1979.

Hemingway, Ernest [Miller] (1899–1961)

American fiction writer. A high-profile writer who won the Nobel Prize in Literature in 1954, Hemingway led a notoriously adventurous life, was constantly in the public eye, and wrote his short stories and novels with a characteristically virile and masculine hand.

Hemingway's writing career began as a series of stints as a newspaper reporter for the Kansas City *Star* and the Toronto *Star* while in his late teens. He later entered World War I as an ambulance driver for the American Red Cross after being rejected for military service because of an eye injury, and settled in Paris after the war. Other American writers living in Paris at the time, such as Gertrude Stein and Ezra Pound, encouraged Hemingway to begin writing and printing small pieces of fiction, and in 1925 he published *In Our Time*, his first nonjournalistic work. A year later, he published *The Sun Also Rises*.

During the interwar years, Hemingway traveled extensively to indulge his passions for hunting, bullfighting, and skiing, subjects on which he centered most of his writings. In 1927 he published *Men Without Women*. Later came *A Farewell to Arms* (1929), *Death in the Afternoon* (1932), *Winner Take Nothing* (1933), *Green Hills of Africa*

(1935), *To Have and Have Not* (1937), *The Fifth Column* (1938), *For Whom the Bell Tolls* (1940), *Across the River and into the Trees* (1950), and *The Old Man and the Sea* (1952), for which he won the Pulitzer Prize.

His love affair with war and physical action led him into a number of difficult situations. He became directly involved in the Second World War, and indirectly involved in the Spanish Civil War and the Cuban revolution, after which he settled in Cuba. But despite his glamorous and adventurous lifestyle, Hemingway's later life was troubled. From Cuba he moved to Idaho, where depression and anxieties plagued him; after battling the onset of neurasthenia and undergoing electroshock treatment, he took his own life with a shotgun. After his death, his memoirs and a series of novellas were published in *A Moveable Feast* (1964) and *Islands in the Stream* (1970).

Herbert, Zbigniew (1924–)

Polish poet. Born in Lwów, a city then temporarily under Polish control, Herbert was only fifteen when World War II began but soon became involved in the Polish resistance movement and joined the Polish Home Army. After the war, Herbert studied in Kraków at the Academy of Fine Arts and the Academy of Commerce, from which he received an M.A. in economics. He then moved on to the Nicolaus Copernicus University in Torun, where he received a degree in law and for a time studied philosophy.

Herbert first began to write poetry during the Nazi occupation, and he continued to do so while working at white-collar jobs during the early postwar years. But as a result of the Communist-imposed doctrine of Socialist Realism, the kind of technically innovative poetry Herbert was producing was totally unpublishable. In the wake of the political thaw of 1956, however, he was at last able to publish *Struna światła* (*Chord of Light*), a volume of poems in which he ironically explores the situation of postwar Poland through an intricate veil of classical and historical allusions. A year later he published a second volume in the same vein, *Hermes, pies i gwiazda* (1957; *Hermes, Dog and Star*), which cemented his reputation as a bold and gifted poet. Four years later, in 1961, he put out *Studium przedmiotu* (*Study of the Object*), a volume in which the characteristic irony diminishes somewhat, with Herbert seeming to endorse a highly subjective form of mysticism. A year later, he demonstrated his talent for prose in *Barbarzyńca w ogrodzie* (1962; *Barbarian in the Garden*), a collection of essays based on his experiences in Western Europe.

By the mid-sixties the first wave of de-Stalinization had passed, and unconventional writers again found it difficult to publish in Poland. Herbert increasingly found himself forced to publish his work either outside Poland or in the underground press and began to spend long periods of time teaching or lecturing in Western Europe and the United States. He never allowed himself to be driven into permanent exile, continuing to regard Poland as his home. He played deliberately minor roles in various struggles against censorship, preferring to steer clear of political fashions, although the Communist regime never really accepted his art.

As a poet, Herbert has always combined formal experimentation with an emphasis on classical tradition. He generally takes an ironic attitude toward the present, an attitude perhaps best represented by his whimsical character "Mr. Cogito," who appears in the 1974 volume of the same name, a bewildered innocent adrift in an incomprehensible world. In 1991 he received the Jerusalem Prize.

Herzl, Theodor (1860–1904)

Founder of modern political Zionism. Born into a middle-class Jewish family,

Herzl moved in 1878 from Budapest to Vienna, where he studied law before opting for a career in writing, at which he was moderately successful. In 1889 he married the daughter of a wealthy Viennese Jew, Julie Naschauer. Until 1891, Herzl was a supporter of the Haskalah, the Jewish social and cultural movement of the late eighteenth and nineteenth centuries, believing that assimilation was the best way to overcome anti-Semitism. In that same year, he was assigned by the leading Viennese newspaper, *Neue Freje Presse*, to cover the trial of Alfred Dreyfus, a Jewish officer in the French army accused of espionage. However, the virulent anti-Semitism Herzl witnessed while in France convinced him that Jews would never be welcome in Europe. He came to believe that Zionism offered the only solution. It was by no means an original- idea, but Herzl was the first to organize a world congress of Zionists and formulate a coherent plan for the establishment of a Jewish state.

His first publication on the subject, a pamphlet entitled *The Jewish State* (1896), was well received and established Herzl as a leader of the Zionist movement. Herzl's fund-raising efforts were less successful, which only served to stiffen his resolve. In August 1897 the First Zionist Congress met in Basel, Switzerland, attracting supporters from as far away as the United States. There it was resolved that "Zionism aspires to create a publicly guaranteed homeland for the Jewish people in the land of Israel." Herzl was elected president of the newly created World Zionist Organization. He spent the remaining seven years of his life unsuccessfully negotiating with various world leaders for the Jewish right to settle autonomously in Palestine.

British leaders were sympathetic to the Zionist cause. Backed by the London branch of the powerful Rothschild family, Herzl met on October 22, 1902, with British colonial secretary Joseph Chamberlain to discuss the possibility of settling the Jews in some part of the British empire. Chamberlain rejected a proposed Zionist settlement in Cyprus, but offered Uganda as a viable alternate site. A brutal pogrom in Kishinev in 1903 convinced Herzl that the situation for East European Jews was desperate, and he agreed to consider the British offer. Delegates to the 1903 Zionist Congress overwhelmingly rejected the scheme, which they deemed a betrayal of the original Zionist objective: an autonomous Jewish state in Erez Israel. Herzl was unable to resolve the conflict before his sudden death from heart failure the following year in Vienna. Although he did not live to see the fulfillment of his dream, his remains were moved in 1949 to Jerusalem in accordance with his wishes, and he is honored as one of the founding fathers of the modern Israeli state.

Hesse, Hermann (1877–1962)

German poet and novelist. Hesse's writings, which focus on the individual's path to self-enlightenment and self-realization, have made him a cult figure throughout North America.

Entering the seminary at a young age, Hesse intended to follow in his father's footsteps (the elder Hesse had been a missionary in Asia), but soon left to become a bookseller and then later a freelance writer. An ardent pacifist, Hesse moved to the neutral country of Switzerland during the First World War, becoming a permanent resident in 1919 and establishing Swiss citizenship in 1923; he would remain in Switzerland for the next fifty years.

Overwhelmed by despair and self-doubt, Hesse began psychoanalysis with J. B. Lang, a disciple of Swiss psychologist Carl Gustav Jung (1875–1961); he would eventually befriend both men. Hesse's first major success came with the publication of Demian (1919), a book rich with symbolism and psychoanalytic insights that Hesse had gained from his own experience with analysis. In Demian, Hesse traces the path of self-discovery of a German youth and explores the duality of human existence, a theme that would follow Hesse throughout his career. Perhaps one of the most personal of his books, Siddhartha (1922) is a novel which continues this exploration, based on the early life of the Buddha; it was written in the wake of Hesse's travels in India. A few years after the publication of Siddhartha, Hesse published Der Steppenwolf (1927; Steppenwolf), a book that records the plight of the artist, torn between material and spiritual desires. Das Glasperlenspiel (1943; Magister Ludi) again engages the theme of spiritual self-realization, and is considered by many to be Hesse's finest achievement.

Apart from novels, he also published several stories and volumes of his poetry and essays. Hesse won the Nobel Prize in Literature in 1946, and though he spent the greater part of his life in Switzerland, he is still regarded as an influential German writer.

Hiawatha (c. 1570 C.E.–?)

American Indian leader. Meaning "he who makes rivers," Hiawatha (also spelled Aiowantha) is the name of one of the great chiefs of the Mohawk Indians of eastern New York. Hiawatha was a disciple of Dekanawida, the founder of the League of the Iroquois, a formal confederation of six American Indian tribes, including the Mohawks, Oneida, Onondaga, Cayuga, Seneca, and Tuscarora, which sought to unite neighboring tribes and thereby put an end to infighting and blood feuds. To end the feuds—which involved recurrent, cyclical killings avenging earlier killings—the League assigned a value of ten wampum to a human life, and required a murderer to offer the bereaved family of his victim twenty wampum, ten for the life he had taken and another ten for the murderer's own life, which he had forfeited in the act of murder.

The major obstacle in Hiawatha and Dekanawida's efforts to unite the tribes was the bitter opposition from Chief Watahotarho (also spelled Atotarho) of the Onondaga tribe. After Hiawatha and Dekanawida persuaded other tribes to form a tentative union, the Onondaga eventually joined as well, and it was inferred from this victory that Hiawatha and Dekanawida possessed powers superior to those of Watahotarho, who was believed to be a great sorcerer. In time, with the continual retelling of the feat, Hiawatha achieved almost mythic status, his deeds often becoming confused with those attributed to some of the chief Iroquois gods. The distortion of Hiawatha was made complete by American poet Henry Wadsworth Longfellow (1807–1882) in his poem *The Song of Hiawatha* (1855). Longfellow modeled his famous poem on the Finnish epic *Kalevala* and used the work of American explorer and ethnologist Henry Rowe Schoolcraft (1793–1864) as material for the poem. Unfortunately, Schoolcraft had confused Hiawatha with a Chippewa deity, and Longfellow exacerbated the confusion by identifying Hiawatha with the Algonquin mythic hero Nanabozho. Schoolcraft capitalized on the success of Longfellow's poem and reprinted a number of legends, with a slight modification—the Nanabozho legend was now titled "Hiawatha; or Nanabozho." Thus, the historical figure behind the legends, the Mohawk chief, is misremembered as an Algonquin. Perhaps most problematic was Schoolcraft's 1839 publication of *Algic Researches*, republished in 1856 as *The Myth of Hiawatha*.

Hidalgo y Costilla, Miguel (1753–1811)

Mexican political leader. Often called the father of Mexican independence, Hidalgo y Costilla was born in Corralejo, Mexico. He was ordained a priest in the Catholic Church in 1789, and early in his career worked with the in-habitants of Dolores improving methods of agriculture. When Napoleon invaded Spain in 1808, deposing the Spanish monarch and replacing him with his brother Joseph Bonaparte, secret societies arose in Mexico, some supporting the deposed king, others seeking Mexican independence. Father Hidalgo belonged to one such secret society in San Miguel, a town near Dolores. When Spanish authorities discovered the society's plot to rebel, several members were arrested, and Father Hidalgo was urged to flee. He refused and instead rang the church bell in Dolores on September 16, 1810, calling his parishioners together and proclaiming a revolt against the Spanish authorities. The event is known as the "Grito de Dolores" and September 16 is now celebrated as Mexico's independence day.

However, what began as a movement for independence soon became a class war, in which thousands of Indians and *mestizos* gathered under Father Hidalgo's banner of the Virgin of Guadalupe and took over major cities, including Guanajuato. When Hidalgo came to the gates of Mexico City, however, he hesitated and the battle was lost; the masses that had risen up against the upper classes dispersed and, after the defeat at Calderón on January 17, 1811, Father Hidalgo fled north. He was captured, however, defrocked, and shot as a rebel on July 31, 1811, in Chihuahua, Mexico.

Hikmet, Nazim (1902–1963)

Turkish poet. Thought to be one of the greatest Turkish poets of the twentieth century, Hikmet was born in Turkey and became involved in leftist politics in his early youth. After attending the University of Moscow, where he studied economics and political science, he returned home in 1928 as a Marxist. At the advent of the new Turkish republic, he played an active role in the Communist Party and wrote for a number of journals. His radical and subversive activities landed him in jail, and upon his release in 1950 he left Turkey to live in the Soviet Union and Eastern Europe.

While Hikmet's mastery of language and ability to write on a wide range of poetic themes gained him respect in the literary world, he is most famous for introducing free verse to Turkish poetry. Not bound by previous conventions and influenced by the Russian Futurist Vladimir Mayakovsky and the Russian Imagist Sergei Esenin, he ventured into new territory by indulging in hyperbolized imagery and using unexpected associations. Taking on political overtones, the content of Hikmet's work also broke new ground in its emphasis on Communist visions of equality and economic justice. Although never abandoning his effortless mix of art and politics, his style became more subdued by the time he published *Seyh Bedreddin destani* (1936; *The Epic of Sheikh Bedreddin*) and *Memleketimden İnsan Mazaralari* (1966–67; *Human Landscapes from My Country*), a 20,000-line epic.

Due to the conservative tenor of the time, all of Hikmet's works were censored until 1961. At this time they were released to the public and widely read, and Hikmet became a revolutionary hero of the Turkish left. During the late 1960s and early 1970s many of his pieces were translated into English, and his Marxist-inspired writings entered the international arena.

Hillel the Elder (c. first century B.C.E.– first century C.E.)

Jewish scholar and sage. Active between the second half of the first century B.C.E. and the first quarter of the first century C.E., Hillel the Elder was the leading biblical commentator of the Second Temple period and the founder of the Judaic school of thought that bears his name.

A satisfactory biography of Hillel is not possible because he has been the subject of so many legends and popular tales. It is known that he was born and educated in Babylonia before moving to Palestine for further study with the Pharisees, a powerful and learned Jewish sect. While still a young man, he apparently was appointed *nasi* (spiritual leader of the Jewish community), and it is believed that he founded a dynasty that ruled Jewish life for more than four centuries.

Hillel is best remembered as a proponent (though probably not the author) of seven hermeneutical principles known as the Seven Rules of Hillel, which deal with the practical application of the Halakah, a body of laws governing the Jewish people in both religious and day-to-day matters. These rules introduced a flexibility that had hitherto been missing from the interpretation of traditional Jewish law, enabling Jewish society to adapt to changing times. For instance, as the economy changed, increasing the need for credit and loans, Hillel enacted the *prosbul*, a law that allowed for debts to be extended beyond the sabbatical year. A second important legal decision made it easier to buy or sell a home.

As important as his legal innovations were, Hillel's popularity rests with his image as a great but humble man with infinite patience and an innate love for his fellow man. Most of the stories and proverbs attributed to him reflect these qualities, which made him the very model of the Jewish sage. One such story tells of a nonbeliever who came to Hillel, promising to convert if he could teach him the whole of the Torah while standing on one foot. To which the teacher replied: "What is hateful to you, do not unto your neighbor; this is the entire Torah, all the rest is commentary."

Hinduism

Western term for the religion of the great majority of the population of India. Hinduism is one of the oldest religions on earth, but also a religion without a definitive origin: it has no founder or recorded beginning, but instead has evolved with the religious and cultural movements of the Indian subcontinent. Composed of many different sects, Hinduism has no specific ecclesiastical organization.

When the Aryans invaded India between 1400 and 500 B.C.E., they introduced both their religion, Vedism, and their religious hymns, the Vedas. Although Hinduism consists of numerous and varying religious sects, most Hindus view the Vedas as Hinduism's most sacred scriptures. Primarily interested in the *yajana*, or the fire sacrifice, Vedism influenced Hinduism, which is also concerned with the idea of continual regeneration (reincarnation), which is believed to be linked with fire sacrifice. This sacrifice is performed by the Brahmans (priests), whose position as the representatives of the reality of all things is described in the last of the Vedas, the Upanishads. After the Upanishads, the writings known as the Bhagavadgita (c. 200 B.C.E.–200 C.E.; *Song of the Lord*) introduced Aryan religion to the idea of *karma* (actions), through which the individual is rewarded or punished for good or evil deeds through a series of lifetimes or reincarnations. The ultimate goal of the Hindu is *moksha*, or liberation, an escape from the repetitive cycle of reincarnation by eliminating passions and uniting with God.

With the introduction of Jainism and Buddhism in the sixth century B.C.E., "Hinduism" changed, replacing the Vedic sacrificial cult and incorporating such practices as Yoga, systems of spiritual discipline, as well as the gods and image worship of popular devotional movements. There was also an increased concern with the daily lives of the people, especially in the *Laws of Manu*, a Sanskrit text written sometime between 200 B.C.E. and 200 C.E. The *Laws of Manu* are named for the Hindu lawgiver Manu, who established rules concerning ritual and daily life. These laws included

the ideas of *dharma*, or duty, applied to every aspect of life, based on *varna* (class). According to Hindu law there were four classes, which included Brahmans (priests), Kshatriyas (warriors), Vaishyas (farmers and merchants), and Shudras (laborers). The writings called the *Puranas* specify the duties of people of each class, and the proper stages of life that each individual should attain. In these writings appeared the trinity-God of Brahma, the creator, Vishnu, the preserver, and Shiva, the destroyer. During this period of intense devotional activity, many poet-saints, songs, and epics were introduced into the religion. The popular Vishnu was incarnated in Rama and Krishna; Shiva reappeared as Devi and Kali. All the incarnations of gods were different forms of one Supreme Being.

Regardless of Hindu sect, implicit in Hindu thought is the belief in an eternal, gender-neutral reality referred to as Brahman, which by its most simplistic definition means the self, or *atman*. Linked to the notion of Brahman/*atman* is the idea of *samsara*, or the transmigration of the soul. According to Hindus, the soul (*atman*) is trapped in a series of transmigrations until it reaches a point of spiritual self-realization, at which time the soul is enlightened and is united with God. There are several paths that are believed to lead to this *moksha*, or liberation.

Modern Hinduism has struggled to shift the focus of the religion away from worldly renunciation and asceticism so that the Indian people might concentrate on population pressures and other political problems. Hindu leaders, such as Mohandas Gandhi (1869–1948), worked to unite spiritual life with social concerns.

Hinmaton-Yalaktit (1840–1904)

American Indian leader. Chief of the Nez Percés, Hinmaton-Yalaktit, also known as "Thunder Rolling in the Heights," led members of his tribe in a long and bitter struggle with the U.S. government. He was given the name Joseph by missionaries at a mission school, where his father, a Christian convert, sent him to be educated. Upon his father's death, Joseph assumed the office of chief at age thirty. Very soon after, the Nez Percés were pitted against Americans in a hostile struggle over gold-rich land where the Nez Percés dwelled. In 1868 the U.S. government proposed a treaty to the chiefs designed to uproot the Nez Percés from their lands in the Wallowa Valley of Oregon Territory and resettle them on a small reservation in Idaho. Chief Joseph refused the treaty, but the government managed to obtain the land by fraud. After peacefully resisting countless orders from government agents to relocate, the Nez Percés found themselves in a clash with U.S. Army troops.

Anticipating his defeat by the larger white army, Joseph attempted a dramatic escape to Canada, leading more than 750 men, women, and children some 1,500 miles over the Rocky Mountains and the Missouri River in the space of three months. Joseph very nearly made it. In October 1877, however, the chief and his band were overtaken and forced to surrender in the Bear Paw Mountains of Montana, only forty miles from the Canadian border. Joseph and his Nez Percé followers were forced onto a barren reservation in what is now Oklahoma, where he remained in exile for several years. During the exile, Joseph made two trips to Washington, D.C., to plead with President Theodore Roosevelt for permission to return his people to the Wallowa Valley, but his appeal fell on deaf ears. Eventually, he received permission for what remained of his group to occupy a slightly better space, the Coleville Reservation. Today a white marble monument in Nespelim, Washington, marks the place where Chief Joseph is buried.

Hiroshima

Japanese city. Hiroshima is the capital city of Hiroshima prefecture, on the southwestern island of Honshu. It was a major military center from the late nineteenth century until the arrival of the first atomic bomb, dropped during World War II by the U.S. Air Force on August 6, 1945. Almost the entire city was destroyed by the bomb, and over 200,000 people died (though this figure grows larger as radiation casualties mount through the years). As a result, a large peace movement has grown in and around Hiroshima. On the site of the blast's epicenter now stands Peace Memorial Park, which includes a cenotaph in memory of the victims; the cenotaph is shaped like the clay saddles traditionally left as tokens in ancient Japanese burials. Within this monument, a stone chest holds a scroll listing the names of the dead. Near this memorial is the Atomic Bomb Dome, the only building left standing after the blast, whose half-disintegrated frame bears witness to the bomb's force. Peace Memorial Hall, Peace Memorial Museum, and the World Peace Memorial Cathedral complete this great reminder of the horror of war and the ambivalence of progress.

Hiroshima is again one of the most important industrial and administrative centers in Japan, having been rebuilt by an alliance of government and industry in the 1950s.

Hitchcock, Sir Alfred (1899–1980)

English suspense filmmaker. Alfred Hitchcock was raised and schooled in London, where he majored in engineering at St. Ignatius College and the University of London. His introduction to filmmaking came in 1920 when he started designing title cards for the Famous Players–Lasky Company. Shortly thereafter, he became a scenario writer and an assistant director, and finally directed his first film, *The Pleasure Gar-*

den, in 1925. In 1926 Hitchcock directed *The Lodger*, the first of his many "thrillers," a genre with which he would be identified throughout his career. In the late 1920s and 1930s Hitchcock established himself as a significant English filmmaker, directing the first major British talking picture, *Blackmail*, in 1929, and directing such Hitchcock classics as *The Man Who Knew Too Much* (1934), *The Thirty-nine Steps* (1935), and *The Lady Vanishes* (1938). In 1940 he left England for Hollywood and was welcomed into the American film industry with an Academy Award for the film *Rebecca*.

By now widely acclaimed as a master of the suspense film genre, Hitchcock maintained a prolific directing career from the 1940s through the 1970s. In 1948, after directing *Suspicion* (1941), *Shadow of a Doubt* (1943), *Lifeboat* (1944), *Spellbound* (1945), *Notorious* (1946), and *Rope* (1948), Hitchcock began producing his own movies. The 1950s saw Hitchcock produce and direct a series of big-budget films with famous Hollywood stars, including *Strangers on a Train* (1951), *Dial M for Murder* (1954), *Rear Window* (1954), *To Catch a Thief* (1954), *The Man Who Knew Too Much* (a 1956 remake of the 1934 classic), *Vertigo* (1958), and *North by Northwest* (1959). The next decade witnessed a plethora of original psychological thrillers, including *Psycho* (1960), *The Birds* (1963), and *Marnie* (1964), as well as more traditional spy films such as *Torn Curtain* (1966) and *Topaz* (1969). *Frenzy* (1972) and *Family Plot* (1976) are examples of Hitchcock's return to his earlier fascination with the story of an innocent person trying to make sense of situations he or she does not understand.

Hitchcock crafted his films with a sophisticated degree of wit, humor, and, sometimes, horror. He leads his viewers through a web of intricate narratives, editing skillfully to create unsettling temporal, spatial, and rhythmic effects. His talent for suspense was a direct result of both his technical expertise and his insight into human psychology and drama. Much like Orson Welles, Hitchcock revolutionized filmmaking practices by shooting from creative camera angles, employing surprise editing cuts, and guiding the audience's emotional reactions with original musical scores by acclaimed composers such as Bernard Herrmann. The strength and quirkiness of Hitchcock's own personality is evident in his brief cameo appearances, which, beginning in the 1940s, he included in many of his films, most notably in *Lifeboat* and *The Birds*.

In 1979 Hitchcock was presented with the American Film Institute's Life Achievement Award; he was knighted by Queen Elizabeth II in 1980.

Hitler, Adolf (1889–1945)

Führer and chancellor of the Third German Reich. Born in Branau, Austria-Hungary, Hitler was the son of an Austrian customs official. A poor student, Hitler left school without a certificate in 1905, and in 1907 moved to Vienna to pursue a career as an artist. Twice failing the admissions examination for the Academy of Fine Arts, he eked out a living in a men's hostel on his small inheritance, a government orphan allotment, and sales of copied postcards. In Vienna, he read widely in the literature of liberal crisis, developing ideas about Jews, the "Aryan" race, and bourgeois democracy that he would keep with him throughout his life. Heading to Munich in 1913, he volunteered for the German army and fought in the Great War, which proved to be a humiliating defeat for Germany. Soon after the war, Hitler was given a position as an instructor assigned to indoctrinate the German troops, and in 1919, while an army political agent, he came into contact with the Deutsche Arbeiterpartei (German Workers' Party), a small nationalist, racist group. Hitler left the army in 1920, and, moving through the ranks of the growing club, served on the executive committee, as propaganda officer, and then as president, in the process building its membership dramatically. The group later renamed itself the Nationalsozialistiche Deutsche Arbeiterpartei (National Socialist German Worker's Party, NSDAP, or Nazis), and under Hitler its goals changed to encompass the overthrow of the liberal government of Berlin.

In November 1923 Hitler bungled an attempt to start the German revolution in a beer hall; he was tried and served nine months, although he had been sentenced to five years in prison. While in prison, he wrote the first volume of *Mein Kampf* (*My Struggle*), the definitive statement of the ideals of of the Nazi Party, which sold over 10 million copies and gave Hitler great fame and wealth. By the early 1930s the Nazis had become the largest political party in the country. When Hitler ran for the presidency in 1932, he lost in a runoff to the incumbent, Paul von Hindenburg, but through a deal with former chancellor Franz von Papen he was sworn in as chancellor in 1933. Upon the death of Hindenburg the following year, he merged the offices of chancellor and president (an action approved in a referendum) and took on the title of *Führer* ("leader") of Germany, inaugurating what he called the Third Reich.

Hitler was devoted to promoting what he saw as Germany's natural superiority in world affairs, and the creation of a new order reflecting it. He set about breaking the provisions of the humiliating Treaty of Versailles, culminating in the remilitarization of Germany. In addition, he established the Gestapo as a secret police force, reinstituted military conscription, built up his air force, and began building concentration camps and gas chambers for what he called "subhumans," notably Jews, Gypsies, and homosexuals. Withdrawing Germany from the League of Nations in 1933, he embarked on several wars of expansion, allying himself with fascist leaders Benito Mussolini (1883–1945) in Italy and Francisco Franco (1892–1975) in Spain, annexing Austria after he ordered its chancellor's assassination (1934), and invading Czechoslovakia and Poland (1939), precipitating World War II. By 1941 he had assumed personal control of war decisions and had put in operation a plan for the mass execution of Jews from Germany and German-occupied countries. Much of Northern and Eastern Europe was under German control, but Hitler underestimated the resistance of the British to his massive bombing campaigns and did not anticipate the intervention of forces from the United States and the Soviet Union. By 1944 it was clear that Hitler's war was lost, and he narrowly escaped death from a bomb explosion in an assassination attempt. Nevertheless, he refused to accept defeat and ordered his troops to fight to the death, a decision that resulted in enormous casualties on all sides. On April 29, 1945, he married his longtime mistress Eva Braun, and together they committed suicide the next day in the underground shelter of the chancellery building as the Russian army invaded Berlin.

Hobbes, Thomas (1588–1679)

English philosopher and political theorist. After graduating from Oxford in 1608, Hobbes became the private tutor to William Cavendish, second earl of Devonshire, and his sons, forging a relationship with the Cavendish family that was to last for much of his life. On visits to the Continent with his young pupils, he learned of Italian astronomer and physicist Galileo's (1564–1642) and German astronomer Johannes Kepler's (1571–1630) revolutions in science, and he began a monumental work on the laws of motion based upon geometrical proofs. During the constitutional struggles of the late 1630s, he circulated portions of his manuscript that emphasized his belief that men could live together in peace only if they subjected themselves to an absolute monarchy. His ideas antagonized both parties in the debate, and Hobbes retreated to Paris, where he joined a community of expatriate English. He spent his time socializing, writing against the theories of French philosopher René Descartes (1596–1650), tutoring the young Charles II in mathematics, and developing the ideas that inform his most famous work, the *Leviathan; or, The Matter, Form, and Power of a Commonwealth Ecclesiastical and Civil* (1651).

Leviathan set forth a system based upon the sovereignty of the king and God as a means to "peaceable, social, and comfortable living." This "social contract" relied heavily on Hobbes's belief in empirical proofs from mathematics and the authority of Scripture, though it was criticized at the time for being overly secular. The work begins by deducing the conditions necessary for individual and social peace and security and then describes an ideal state; its fundamental concept is the "natural right" of self-preservation and the idea that the state of nature is barbarism. According to Hobbes, for the sake of peace, natural law must give way to social law. As guarantor of good behavior and arbitrator of all disputes, the monarch is answerable only to God; by definition his power is absolute and always just.

By 1651 Charles I had been deposed, and Hobbes revised the end of his work to account for submission to a new sovereign. Essentially, a subject owed allegiance to the ruler who could protect him. At the end of the year, Hobbes returned to England and enjoyed considerable influence at the court of his former student Charles II, though he was troubled briefly by a charge of atheism submitted to the House of Commons in 1666. For the rest of his life, he attempted to construct a system whereby all phenomena could be explained by mathematical proofs of the motion of bodies. At the age of eighty-four, he produced an autobiography in Latin verse.

Ho Chi Minh (1890–1969)

Vietnamese political leader. The founder and most significant figure of the Vietnamese Communist movement, Ho served as president of the Republic of Vietnam (North Vietnam) from 1945 until his death in 1969. Ho was born Nguyen Sinh Cung; his father was a member of the French imperial bureaucracy in Indochina who resigned in protest of continued French occupation. In like manner, Ho rejected his formal and prestigious schooling at imperially sponsored institutions. In 1911, at the age of twenty-one, Ho left Vietnam as a cook's apprentice on a French steamship and was not to return for thirty years. In a remarkable exodus, stopping for significant periods in many of the world's cities—London, Paris, Moscow, New York, Canton, and Hong Kong— Ho participated in the growing international Communist movement. He also made a moving address at the Versailles Peace Conference, appealing to American president Woodrow Wilson's (1913– 21) ideals of national self-determination. Helping to found the French Communist Party in 1920, Ho articulated a leftist vision that married anticolonial nationalism and socioeconomic revolution. Returning to Vietnam in 1941, Ho established the Vietnamese Independence League (Viet Minh) within the Indochinese Communist Party. The Viet Minh seized control of Vietnam from the Japanese in 1945 and, using the language of the American Declaration of Independence, Ho Chi Minh declared the independence of the democratic republic of Vietnam. In the following year, however, the French began to attempt to reassert control and Ho was forced to lead the Viet Minh to war. By

1954 the French suffered enough military setbacks, including a defeat at Dien Bien Phu, to agree to negotiate. Under the Geneva Accords, Vietnam was split into a Communist North and a non-Communist South. From 1954 to 1960, as president of North Vietnam, Ho attempted to gain control of South Vietnam, whose president, Ngo Dinh Diem, was being sustained by American economic and military assistance. Through the creation of the "Ho Chi Minh Trail," a sort of underground network that ran money and supplies through Cambodia and Laos into South Vietnam, Ho attempted to undermine the stability of South Vietnam and realize his desire for Vietnamese unification and independence. During the 1960s Ho's health declined and he took a much less active role in the ongoing struggles in Laos and Cambodia. However, Ho was recognized for his contribution to Communism in Vietnam by the renaming of the city of Saigon as Ho Chi Minh City in 1975, when the Viet Cong successfully conquered South Vietnam. He is remembered as "the father of his country."

Hogarth, William (1697–1764)

English painter and engraver. Hogarth is generally considered to be the greatest pictorial satirist of England. Trained as an engraver, Hogarth achieved some success with "conversation piece" portraits and book illustration (notably for English poet Samuel Butler's [1612–1680] popular satiric poem *Hudibras*) before turning to engravings, narrative pictures sold as prints, designed to appeal to a mass public. These series, the first of which was *A Harlot's Progress* (1732), typically capture a character's moral decline under the influence of fashionable society, and were inspired by the stage. Hogarth's popular success was continued by *A Rake's Progress* (1735) and *Marriage à la Mode* (1745). The paintings from which the engravings were made reflect the influence of the Continental rococo style, and the subject matter satirizes aristocratic and middle-class manners. In 1753 he published *The Analysis of Beauty*, a volume of his theories about art.

Holiday, Billie (1915–1959)

African-American jazz singer. Born Eleanora Fagan in Baltimore, Maryland, Billie Holiday was an untutored talent who had a keen ear and a unique sense of timing, as well as a coarse vocal texture. Holiday's early life remains obscure. Abandoned by her father, she followed her mother to New York City in 1928, and began singing in a club in Brooklyn sometime after 1930. Soon after, she was playing at Jerry's, a well-known jazz club in Harlem.

In 1933, while singing at Monette's, another Harlem jazz club, she was noticed by talent scout and producer John Hammond, who booked her in clubs throughout the city and arranged for her to record with musician and bandleader Benny Goodman (1909–1986). Between 1935 and 1942 Holiday worked with some of the best jazz musicians of the day. Although most of these recordings were intended for a black jukebox audience, Holiday's rhythmic style, in which she detached the melody line from the ground beat, singing behind the beat and condensing or stretching the figures of the melody, attracted the attention of musicians throughout the country. Holiday sang with several bands, including Count Basie (1904–1994) and Artie Shaw, and was one of the first black singers to be featured with white orchestras. In 1939 she began an engagement at Café Society, a fashionable interracial nightclub in Greenwich Village, that was popular among intellectuals and members of the political left.

It was during this same period that Holiday recorded "Strange Fruit," a song about lynching, which broadened her appeal. She also had popular success with slow and melancholy songs about unrequited love, including "Gloomy Sunday" (1941), a song about suicide, and "Lover Man" (1944).

Plagued by recurring problems with drugs, drinking, and abusive relationships, her health suffered and she lost most of her earnings. Although continuing to tour until the mid-1950s, she suffered from poor health and a deteriorating voice, and her performances became inconsistent. After a concert in Boston, Holiday suffered cardiac arrest and went into a coma, later dying from liver and kidney failure.

Holocaust

Called in Hebrew *Sho'ah* or *Hurban*. The term "Holocaust" refers to the persecution and extermination of European Jewry by the Hitler government in Germany (1933–45). Evolving over a decade from policies of intimidation to genocide, the Holocaust extended to other social and ethnic groups, including the Romani (Gypsies), homosexuals, communists, and antifascist Germans.

Nazi hostility toward Jews (already documented in Hitler's prison notebooks, *Mein Kampf*) was put into practice within months of Hitler's election to the chancellory in 1933, in a series of edicts, confiscatory taxes, and pogroms. The Nuremberg laws of 1935 stripped previously well-assimilated German Jews of their citizenship and forbade intermarriage between Jews and other Germans. Prewar harassment of the Jews crystallized in 1938 on *Kristallnacht*, November 9–10, the "Night of Broken Glass," when anti-Jewish rampages destroyed nearly every synagogue and Jewish-run business throughout the country. New Jewish ghettos and "concentration camps" were created. By 1941 all Jews over six years of age were required to wear the yellow Star of David (just as homosexuals were required to wear pink triangles), and Jews were prohibited from using public transpor-

tation and the telephone. Killings and disappearances of Jews became increasingly common.

The quick victories of the Germans in World War II (over France and Poland, in particular) put the vast majority of European Jewry under Nazi control. In Eastern Europe, special units of the German secret police (the SS) called *Einsatzgruppen* massacred whole villages. Some Jews were placed on trucks or vans and asphyxiated with auto exhaust on the way to mass grave sites. These policies were both inefficient and disquieting to some of the regular army troops stationed in these areas, which led the Nazi leadership at the Wannsee Conference in January 1941 to formulate a plan for the "final solution" to the Jewish question: the creation of death camps in Poland—at Auschwitz, Majdanek, Treblinka, Chełmno, Sobibor, and Belzec, among others—where Jews could be killed and cremated en masse, and in secret.

The death camps were models of bureaucratic efficiency, ruthless in their efficacy as well as their barbarism. Jews were assigned a number for "administrative" purposes, which was indelibly marked on their forearms. Many of the Jews in the camps were unaware of their impending death until the last moment. The Nazis constructed special gas chambers, which they disguised as showers and placed near crematoria. As many as 4 million Jews were killed in the camps alone; an estimated 6 million Jews died in various German offensives throughout the war.

Some Jews did try to resist. Throughout the ghettos of Poland, especially in Warsaw, poorly armed Jews fought German troops and the deportation orders that would send them to the camps. Young Jews joined antifascist brigades in Poland, the Soviet Union, Italy, and Vichy France. Many Jews tried to hide from their persecutors in basements, attics, and neighbors' dwellings; some escaped through Denmark to neutral Switzerland. Beginning in the 1930s, many Jews sought to escape Europe altogether, although few countries were willing to accept them in large numbers.

At the end of the war, as Allied troops liberated the death camps, the full enormity of the Nazi war against the Jews became clear for the first time. The Nuremberg trials were held in part to prosecute the architects of the Holocaust for "crimes against humanity" above and beyond the scope of "normal" war crimes. In 1948 the United Nations approved the Convention on the Prevention and Punishment of the Crime of Genocide, a body created to document the activities of the German government from 1933 to 1945. The memory of the Holocaust was also influential in the decision to create the state of Israel in 1948.

Homer (c. 700 B.C.E.)

Greek epic poet. The likely author of the *Iliad* and the *Odyssey*, Homer is considered to be the greatest writer of the ancient Greek world. The ancients believed that the texts were written by a blind poet named Homer, writing shortly after the Trojan War. There is, however, no solid proof as to the authorship of these founding texts, nor any evidence indicating their date of composition. The mysterious, almost invisible background of Homer and the desire to discover the true source of the *Iliad* and the *Odyssey* provide the setting for a provocative debate among literary academicians. In any case, these texts had a tremendous impact on Greek education and culture; students were required to memorize extensive excerpts. This retention, especially in ancient Greece, helped preserve the poems for future generations, and their simplicity (at the time) heightened their dramatic effect and made their message accessible to broad sectors of the population.

Simplicity was also an aid to repeatability, which was quite important considering the enormous problem of the poems' length. Homer is believed to have been an *aoidos*, or poet, who sang his verses to an audience. Most *aoidoi* in the heroic tradition performed poems that could be heard in a night or two. Homer's epics were extraordinarily long, the *Iliad* alone having upwards of 16,000 verses. The sheer length of these works, which must have taken many nights to relate, testifies to Homer's skill.

What many scholars question is the ability of a single poet to fashion these two enormous works. Some claim that a group of poets must have worked collaboratively on them, citing textual confusions—different moral themes, incongruous scenes, varying views of the gods, changes in vocabulary, the decline of forceful expression in the *Odyssey*—as evidence of multiple authorship. Those who remain convinced of Homer's authorship look to the explanation originally provided by the third century C.E. literary critic Longinus: he presumed that the *Iliad* was written in the style of Homer's youth, while the *Odyssey* was his more mature effort.

To situate the poems chronologically, most scholars rely on the descriptions of specific objects and significant language patterns within the works. Stylistically, they are in the tradition of the Hesiodic poems, from around 700 B.C.E. There are, however, references to objects from the ninth, eighth, and seventh centuries B.C.E. Homer's unique meter is evident in several other poems of the early sixth century B.C.E., and works of sixth-century art depict his epics. Biographies of Homer began appearing sometime in the fifth century B.C.E. However, the only certainty is that the texts were composed after the Trojan War, the subject of the *Iliad*, which occurred in the thirteenth century B.C.E. These factors have helped historians place the *Iliad* around the seventh century. There are archaic elements in both works, implying an early date, but this is usually interpreted as Homer's skill as an *aoidos*. The written versions of both poems were probably undertaken around the ninth or eighth century, when an alphabetic writing system first appeared in Greece. The first complete written text is thought to have existed around the time of the Panathenaic Games in the sixth century B.C.E., though many agree that Homer must have used notes to help him remember such an enormous inventory of poetry.

Hong Kong film industry

One of the largest film industries in the world. In 1978 the Hong Kong Film Culture Center was established to promote archival research and new work by young directors. During the 1970s and 1980s the industry released as many as three hundred feature films a year, boasted Asia's largest studio complex, Movie Town, and initiated the prestigious Hong Kong International Film Festival.

American theater owner Benjamin Polaski is credited with producing the first feature films in Hong Kong in 1909 with *To Steal a Roasted Duck* and *Redressment of Justice by a Porcelain Pot*. In the next decade, Li Min Wei joined with Polaski to establish a film company, eventually breaking off their partnership to work with his family on documentaries in support of the Guomindang political party. Li's *Rouge* (1923) is thought to be the first feature made entirely by a Hong Kong filmmaker. Some studios from mainland China had opened offices on the island by 1930, when Lian-Hau Film Company established its main facilities there. During the 1930s it became a center for Cantonese movies. The Japanese occupation during World War II cast a dark shadow on the industry, imposing censorship, registration of companies, and control over resources like film stock and electricity. After the war, the industry developed fitfully as the battle between the Communists and

the Guomindang on the mainland made for an uncertain market. The quality of the productions varied as well, some produced in less than a week, with much of the financing coming from abroad. By the 1950s and 1960s economic prosperity led to the consolidation of film markets throughout Southeast Asia and marked a growth in the number of film companies; for most of this period, production averaged more than three hundred films per year. The film business was, however, dominated by Run Run Shaw and his three brothers; their organization was the largest entertainment empire in Southeast Asia, modeled on the Hollywood studio system. The Shaws had begun buying theaters and turning out cheap movies for them in the 1920s; having survived Japanese confiscation of their properties and the imprisonment of Run Run in the 1940s, they experienced phenomenal success after 1958. Their Movie Town Studios operated twenty-four hours a day during its heyday, averaging forty features a year. Shaw Brothers produced over 1,000 films from the late 1920s until 1986, when the giant organization stopped producing films of its own to concentrate on film distribution and television production. A former Shaw employee, Raymond Chow, had begun his own Golden Harvest studio and enjoyed international success with his string of kung fu movies, beginning with *Enter the Dragon*, one of the top-grossing films up to that time, starring the former Hollywood bit actor Bruce Lee. Lee died in 1973, but Chow went on to great financial success as the kung fu genre became popular internationally, particularly in the United States. He eventually acquired Cathay Films in 1978 to facilitate worldwide distribution of his product even as half of all Hong Kong studios, unable to break into foreign markets, ceased production by 1981. Multinational conglomerates moved into Hong Kong to fill the filmmaking gap, however, and now the industry is dominated by six companies that produce most of the films for its domestic and international audiences.

Hong Lou Meng

Eighteenth-century Chinese novel. *Hong Lou Meng* (known in English as *Dream of the Red Chamber*) is considered by many scholars to be the most accomplished example of the novel form in Chinese. The bulk of the book was composed in the decade after 1754. The original author, Cao Xueqin, had envisioned a text comprising 120 chapters; at his death in 1764, only the first two-thirds were completed. Another writer, Gao'e, finished the narrative and had it published in 1791.

Hong Lou Meng is structured as a series of episodes, retaining the formal conventions of the Chinese oral tradition. It was innovative, however, as a work of imaginative literature. *Hong Lou Meng* featured a set of new, unique characters, while previous novels focused on the familiar exploits of mythological heroes. The sprawling story, which contains hundreds of characters, focuses on the spiritual and worldly strivings of the hero, Bao Yu ("Precious Jade"), who is believed to be largely an autobiographical portrait of Cao Xueqin himself. Cao Xueqin, the son of well-to-do parents, was expected to follow family tradition and become the inspector of the Jiangsu Imperial Silk Factories, but he turned to writing after failing the necessary imperial examinations.

Composed in a period in which imaginative literature, and novels in particular, were suspected of moral irrelevance, *Hong Lou Meng* dramatizes major Taoist beliefs, especially the necessity of striving to renounce worldly concerns. By the book's end, the hero has become a spirit and entered the Phantom Realm of the Great Void, a name for the Taoist heaven.

Hope, A[lec] D[erwent] (1907–)

Australian poet. Hope, best known for his elegies and satires, was educated in Australia and at Oxford, earning two bachelor's degrees between 1925 and 1931. Having worked throughout New South Wales as a teacher, vocational psychologist, and school counselor, Hope began his literary career as a lecturer in English at Sydney Teachers' College. After holding positions at a number of Australian universities, Hope retired in 1969. He has written poetry most of his life, publishing his work as early as 1930; his poems are noted as modern and revolutionary, though traditional in form. His best-known poems are "Conquistador" (1947) and "Return from the Freudian Iles" (1944). Hope's verse has appeared frequently in literary periodicals; he has won a number of prizes for his writing, including the Robert Frost Award and the Levinson Prize. His first collection of poems, *The Wandering Islands*, was published in 1955. He has also published essays and criticism, including *A Midsummer Eve's Dream* (1970) and *The Cave and the Spring* (1965). Hope was made a member of the Order of the British Empire in 1972.

Hōryūji

Japanese Buddhist temple. Built by Prince Shōtoku in the year 607, north of the Asuka region, Hōryūji was demolished by fire later in that century and rebuilt in 708; this later structure, now the center of the temple complex, contains the oldest wood buildings in the world. The central set of buildings, called the Saiin, or Western Precinct, is flanked by a smaller complex, the Tōin, or Eastern Precinct.

After serving as a Buddhist temple, Hōryūji was eventually converted into a monastery for Buddhist studies. After the Second World War, the temple, which had always been associated with Prince

Shōtoku (who later became the patron saint of Japanese Buddhism), became immensely popular with the newly established Shōtoku sect.

The Hōryūji Treasure House, located on the grounds of the Tokyo National Museum in Ueno Park, Tokyo, currently possesses some of the most ancient Buddhist art once found in Hōryūji, with especially fine representations of the Asuka period (670–710). The treasures of Hōryūji include precious artifacts from the life and posthumous honors of Prince Shōtoku. The Shijū-Hattai Butsu, or "Forty-eight Buddhas," are some of the earliest Japanese Buddhist images; they are cast in gilt bronze, modeled in various styles, and average a foot in height. Other treasures, which include copper reliefs, a magnificent gilt-bronze banner known as Kanchōban, and numerous paintings, lacquerworks, written documents, and miscellany, represent a vast and invaluable collection of Japan's most antique Buddhist art.

Houphouët-Boigny, Félix (1905–)

First president of the Ivory Coast. The son of a Baoulé chief in Yamoussoukro, Houphouët-Boigny received medical training in Dakar before returning to his homeland in 1925 to practice medicine among his tribe for many years, succeeding his father as chief in 1940 as well as becoming a wealthy farmer. In 1944 he cofounded a union of Baoulé coffee farmers to protest French controls, expanding it the following year into the more broadly political Parti Démocratique de la Côte d'Ivoire (PDCI), affiliated with the French Communist Party. In the same year, he was elected his country's representative to the French parliament for the first of many terms. At the Bamako Conference in 1946, organized by French-African leaders to create a coalition party, the Rassemblement Démocratique Africain (RDA), Houphouët-Boigny was elected president. The RDA organized demonstrations calling for greater autonomy throughout French West Africa, but they were severely suppressed by the French. In response, Houphouët-Boigny renounced his links with the Communist Party, rebuilding the RDA in the 1950s as a significant force in African and French politics. In 1956 he became a cabinet minister in the French government, and was instrumental in developing the blueprint for African autonomy, resisting a federation of independent nations since he thought his own relatively wealthy state would be penalized to the benefit of others, instead promoting successfully self-government for individual states under a French protectorate. In 1958 Houphouët-Boigny became the president of the constituent assembly of the self-ruling Ivory Coast (still part of the French Community), in 1959 its prime minister, and in 1960 the first president of the independent Republic of the Ivory Coast. His maintenance of close ties with France and his virtual one-party rule have been criticized often, but he was reelected in 1990 for his seventh consecutive five-year term. Democratic opposition to his rule, and what some see as the increasingly corrupt business practices of Houphouët-Boigny and his PDCI comrades, has increased markedly in recent years. It is uncertain whether his party, and the one-party state, will survive his death.

Hoysala temples

Hindu temples. The famous Hoysala temples were constructed during the reign of the Hoysala dynasty, which ruled in the southern Deccan from 1006 to c. 1346. When the Hindu Hoysala dynasty finally fell to the Vijayanagara dynasty in the middle of the fourteenth century, it left behind a rich architectural legacy in the temples constructed throughout the kingdom. These intricately detailed and exquisitely designed structures are considered by many to be unsurpassed in the history of Indian temple architecture. Some of the most exceptional temples are located in Halebid, Belur, and Somnathpur, and are still standing today. One of the more famous is the Hoysalesvara, dedicated to Shiva, which is located in Dvarasmudra (modern Halebid).

Hrabal, Bohumil (1914–)

Czech author and essayist. Though noted as an author, Hrabal held a myriad of different jobs and occupations as a youth, including office work, a stint as a law student, plate-laying, steelworking, wastepaper-packing, and sceneshifting.

His writing derives much of its style and form from the Czech oral tradition and is infused with vernacular language and profanities. His literary leanings are fundamentally surrealist and convey a sense of musicality, drifting over narratives often devoid of a sense of plot or foundation.

Hrabal's first pieces, *Perlička na dně* (1963; *The Little Pearl at the Bottom*) and *Pabitelé* (1964; *The Blatherers*), are ramblings, seemingly unconnected and formless, replete with personal anecdotes and loose references. The overall effect of his narrative chatter resembles the buzz and commotion of a public hall, in which his off-center characters and autobiographical narrator interact throughout the story, imbuing it with a fantastical element.

His eclectic works were also stylistically ambitious. *Taneční hodiny prostarší a pokročilé* (1964; *Dancing Lessons for Older and Advanced Pupils*) is one ninety-page sentence presenting a conversation between an old man and a presumably younger woman. The man's talk consists of random collections of thoughts and memories, uncontrolled and without order. *Ostře sledované vlaky* (1965; *Closely Watched Trains*) features a more conventional narrative, but its content centers on a young boy's psy-

chological and emotional traumas. The boy discusses his anguish concerning sex, relates his unsuccessful suicide attempt, and describes his failed effort to halt the German train that eventually killed him.

Obsluhoval jsem anglického krále (1977; *I Waited on the King of England*) is a novel depicting the story of a slightly immoral waiter who describes his obsession with wealth and his servile occupation before and during World War II. The story, as told from the waiter's perspective, also refers to more general historical and political themes as the waiter recounts his experiences under both the German occupation and the Soviet Communist order.

Zola is Hrabal's most recent work. Autobiographical at heart and written in prose form, this piece purports to present the differences and similarities of life experiences in a topsy-turvy world.

Hua Mulan

Chinese legendary woman warrior. "Mulan, the maiden chief" first appears in a ballad, which recounts how the maiden Mulan, having no elder brothers, volunteered to serve in the army in her father's place, and how, disguised as a man, she became a general. When the emperor summoned Mulan's father, an army officer, to go to battlefields against the northern states, he was ill. Anxious to avoid the dishonor that would accrue to the family name if her father did not appear, Mulan assumed his identity, arming herself with all the necessary equipment and secretly taking leave of her parents. For twelve years she acted as a man, and fought hundreds of battles with her comrades. When the northern plains were at last seized, she returned as a victorious commander to the emperor's palace in Chang'an. When the Son of Heaven bestowed land and titles on the bravest fighters, Mulan asked for nothing but a camel that could march 1,000 li (310 miles) a day to take her back to her home. After her return, she exchanged her soldier's cloak for her maiden's dress—a surprise to both her parents and the soldiers who had viewed her as a strong male chief for a dozen years.

Huang He

Chinese river. Huang He, the "Yellow River," is considered to be the cradle of Chinese civilization. A Neolithic culture called the Yangshao flourished in the central valley of Huang He from around 10,000 B.C.E. Archaeological findings suggest that people living in this area already knew how to write, make silk, and cast bronze as early as the Shang dynasty (1766–1027 B.C.E.).

Huang He, 3,028 miles (4,873 kilometers) long, cuts through the loess plateau, a massive rock formation composed mainly of silts, which is around two hundred feet deep. The loess plateau loses about 1.6 billion tons of the yellow-brown soil to the river annually, lending it its customary name, the Yellow River. (The Yellow Sea at the end of the river is similarly named for the huge loads of yellow silt that suffuse it.) The dynamics of silt flow have produced disastrous irregularities in the river's depth: where the river enters the vast North China Plain, the riverbed sometimes stands fifteen to forty feet over the surrounding plain. Catastrophic floods have exacted tremendous costs in lives and property, though people have been building dikes and trying otherwise to regulate the river's run for centuries.

The long history of Huang He's devastating floods has earned it the name "China's Sorrow." As the riverbed is elevated, after the dikes burst and the countryside is flooded, the flooding waters cannot return to the river channel and the river is forced to change its course. The changes vary. Five times in recorded history it has shifted radically. One of the worst floods was not, however, the work of nature. In 1938, during the Sino-Japanese War, Chiang Kaishek, the head of the Chinese government, believed that he could halt the southward advance of the Japanese troops by flooding the plain. He ordered his troops to break the dikes in Henan province. About a million peasants lost their lives, and millions more were rendered homeless.

Since the founding of the People's Republic of China in 1949, the government has made controlling the Huang He a major priority. In 1955 the Communist government built a series of large, medium, and small dams to conserve water and retain silt, terracing the loess, and afforestation of surrounding hills and plains to curb soil erosion. Two major dams have already been completed on Huang He, at Liujiaxia and Sanmenxia, providing two huge reservoirs for the retention of silt, as well as two powerful hydroelectric power stations.

Huang Zongxi (1610–1695)

Chinese scholar. Known primarily for his work as a scholar, Huang Zongxi began his career as a minor official in the Ming court. When the dynasty was overthrown in 1644, Huang refused to serve the Qing successors, and instead retired from public life and devoted himself to scholarly pursuits. Although his interests were numerous, he is primarily known for his work as a historian and political theorist. Huang belonged to a school of historians who strove for objectivity in the writing of their histories, attempting to capture the truthful tenor of recent, rather than ancient, events. Many of his own writings on Ming history were used by the editors of the *Mingshi* (*History of the Ming*). He also completed compilations of Neo-Confucian thought from the Song (960–1279), Yuan (1260–1368), and Ming (1368–1644) periods. His most famous work is *Mingyi daifang lu* (*A Plan for the Prince*). In this work, he criticizes the arbitrary authoritarianism of the Chinese dynastic system, and urges systemic change, instead of individual action, as the means of curtailing these abuses of power and justice. In addition, Huang also called for the establishment of universal education and literacy, as well as a medium for the public exchange of ideas. Interest in his work was revived at the beginning of the twentieth century, when reformers looked back upon his critiques of the dynastic system.

Hughes, Langston (1902–1967)

American writer. Hughes is perhaps the best-known black writer of the first half of the twentieth century. His career spanned from the Harlem Renaissance of the 1920s to the Black Arts movement of the 1960s and encompassed poetry, fiction, and drama.

James Mercer Langston Hughes was born in Joplin, Missouri, and spent his childhood in various cities in the Midwest. His parents were divorced when he was young, and Hughes was largely raised by his maternal grandmother. After being encouraged in his poetic efforts during high school, Hughes was able to persuade his father to finance his education at Columbia University in New York City. Hughes soon grew impatient with formal learning, however, and dropped out in 1922. He befriended some of the major black writers and intellectuals of the era, including Claude McKay, Zora Neale Hurston, Countee Cullen, and Arna Bontemps. In this period Hughes worked on his poetry and eagerly attended jazz clubs in Harlem and musical reviews on Broadway.

After a year working as a cabin boy on a freighter, he returned to New York with enough poems to put together a book. With the encouragement of the African-American intellectual Alain Locke and white patron Carl Van Vechten, Hughes published *The Weary Blues* in 1926. The book was immediately acclaimed for its blues-like rhythms and as-

sured poetic voice. He emerged as the major figure of the Harlem Renaissance, and his 1926 essay "The Negro Writer and the Racial Mountain" became a clarion call for the movement. It laid out Hughes's ethic of black pride, and forecast a black literature that would not toe any particular political or aesthetic line.

His persistent concern remained to speak to and about the mass of black people, not just an educated elite. His second book, *Fine Clothes to the Jew* (1927), was criticized by many black intellectuals for its emphasis on the poorer, less seemly aspects of African-American life. *Shakespeare in Harlem* (1942) continued the exploration, and *Montage of a Dream Deferred* (1951) is a lyrical, bitter evocation of life in the black ghetto of New York using free verse and dramatic monologue.

Hughes explored many other areas and genres in his long career. An interest in leftist politics in the 1930s led to a group of protest poems published posthumously in *Good Morning, Revolution* (1973). His "Simple" stories, featuring the everyman figure Jesse B. Semple, became a popular series in the 1950s. Always a devotee of the theater, Hughes set up black drama groups in Harlem and Los Angeles, and his play *Mulatto* (1935) held the record for twenty years as the most financially successful play ever written by a black American. He also penned librettos for several musical projects, including Kurt Weill's opera *Street Scene* (1947). *The Big Sea* (1940) and *I Wonder as I Wander* (1956) are autobiographies.

Hugo, Victor (1802–1885)

French romantic poet, novelist, playwright, and politician. The son of a general in Napoleon's army, young Hugo traveled widely but considered Paris his home. There, at age seventeen, he began his career in letters by publishing in the journal *Le Conservateur Littéraire*. In 1821 he married Adèle Foucher and published his first book of poetry; a year later, his first novel, *Han d'Islande* (1822; *Hans of Iceland*), came out. The books were well received, and Hugo found himself accepted into the literary circle surrounding the journalist and novelist Charles Nodier.

Hugo's poems of the early 1830s idealized Napoleon and defended freedom. Liberty seemed all the more important when Charles X restricted freedom of the press and Hugo's play *Marion Delorme* (1823), about a courtesan purified by love, was censored. Though his political ideas and poetry won him favor with students, it was his novel *Notre-Dame de Paris* (1831; *The Hunchback of Notre Dame*) that brought him widespread fame. It is a medieval story of Quasimodo and the Gypsy Esmeralda, and the unhappiness heaped upon them by Frollo, the archdeacon, and Phoebus, the soldier. As Hugo's fortunes improved, he turned again to plays, in part because *Marion Delorme* was finally staged, and in part to create roles for his young actress-mistress, Juliette Drouet.

In 1841 Hugo was elected to the Académie Française, an achievement that was overshadowed by the death by drowning of his daughter Léopoldine in 1843. For a time he virtually ceased publishing. He did begin to work on the novel *Les Misérables*, distracting himself from his grief by engaging in a rigorous social life at court and by establishing a liaison with the writer Léonie Baird. *Les Misérables* (1862), both a detective story about the underworld of Paris and an epic, restored Hugo's popularity in France and made him famous worldwide. The proclamation of the Third Republic finally brought him back to Paris in 1870, but again he fled after the declaration of the Paris Commune. When he returned, he was elected a senator. During these years Hugo lost his wife and a son, and his daughter Adèle returned to France from a marriage in America mentally unstable. Two years after the death of his loyal Juliette, Hugo died. He was given a national funeral, lay in state under the Arc de Triomphe, and was buried in the Panthéon.

Hurston, Zora Neale (1903–1960)

American novelist, short-story writer, and folklorist. Hurston's work displays the rhythms of spoken language and an uncompromising pride in African-American folk culture.

Hurston was born in Eatonville, Georgia, a black-run, black-populated town. The security and relative prosperity enjoyed by blacks in Eatonville were rare in the Deep South; growing up in Eatonville gave Hurston a passion for African-American culture. Hurston attended all-black Howard University in Washington, D.C., where she met Alain Locke, the philosophy professor who was later known as the "dean" of the Harlem Renaissance, in which Hurston would play a part.

She arrived in New York City in 1925, eager to find work as a writer. While she was at Barnard College on scholarship, working toward an anthropology degree, the anthropologist Franz Boas encouraged her to travel south and collect folkloric material in African-American communities there. The mass of lore, ritual, and history she assembled formed the basis of her 1935 work, *Mules and Men*.

Hurston published four novels during her lifetime. Her most famous, *Their Eyes Were Watching God* (1937), tells the story of Janie Crawford's romantic and spiritual wanderings. Janie's independent spirit and lyrical voice delighted some readers and angered others. Hurston was attacked by many black intellectuals for what they considered to be a romanticized picture of black Southern life. Hurston always claimed she did not "belong to that sobbing school of Negrohood who hold that nature somehow has given them a lowdown dirty deal." This aesthetic and political insistence on affirmation rather than protest gave her fiction a wholly different orientation from the realist writing of other African-American authors, including Richard Wright, with whom she engaged in a spirited polemic.

Other works of the period include *Tell My Horse* (1938), a collection of Caribbean myths and rituals, and the autobiography *Dust Tracks on a Road* (1942). Although this last book sold well, Hurston found it increasingly difficult to sell her manuscripts to publishers. Through the 1950s she supported herself as a maid, a freelance journalist, and a substitute teacher; and when she died in 1960, she was buried in an unmarked grave, her work largely forgotten and out of print. In the 1970s feminists working to recover the tradition of black women writers sparked a Hurston revival and a reconsideration of her work.

Hus, Jan (c. 1372–1415)

Czech religious reformer. Hus (also spelled Huss), a fifteenth-century religious reformer, articulated a severe religious critique of Catholicism one hundred years before the Lutheran Reformation. He was eventually burned at the stake for heresy. The religious and political problems surrounding the Western Schism (a period during which the papal jurisdiction was divided between two popes) occupied most of Hus's efforts and career; during the fourteenth and fifteenth centuries the Roman Catholic Church was in serious danger of dissolution because of internal corruption and divided national or ethnic loyalties, and it was on these tensions that Hus focused his work.

Hus graduated from, and taught at, the University of Prague during the early 1400s, a time rife with struggle against German cultural and intellectual invasion. The German/Czech split within the university was also apparent in the general Czech population, where it was felt that the Germans, as fundamental

nominalists and church-reform oppositionists, were indifferent to the welfare of most Czech people and their notions of nationhood. Due to the burdensome tithes demanded by church clergy, and coupled with the discredit the Schism cost the Church, the Bohemian peasantry were ripe for rebellion. Hus, who was intrigued by the writings of John Wycliffe, a staunch critic of nominalism and an advocate for reform of the Roman Catholic Church, became directly involved in the reform movement. He preached reform at the Bethlehem Chapel, which had been founded by Jan Milic as a reform church, and in so doing gained popularity.

Still teaching at the university, Hus also became adviser to Zbynek Zajíc, who later became archbishop of Prague in 1403. This development should have given the reform movement added strength, but Zbynek soon withdrew his support for the cause. Five years into Zbynek's reign, he charged two of Hus's fellow reformists, Stanislav and Paléč, with heresy and forced them to change their loyalties. Hus, as leader of the reform, was placed in direct opposition to Zbynek. The council deposed both popes (Pope Gregory XII, recognized in Bohemia, and the antipope, Benedict XIII) and replaced them with Alexander V. However, the deposed popes still had some jurisdiction in Western Europe, and thus, all three claimed legitimacy. Zbynek remained faithful to Gregory, while Hus and the reformers recognized Alexander. Zbynek bribed Alexander into prohibiting preaching in private chapels, which included the Bethlehem Chapel. Hus refused to obey the order and Zbynek excommunicated him. Zbynek died soon after, but Hus's heresy was taken up by the Roman Curia because he openly denounced the sale of indulgences initiated by Alexander's successor, John XXIII, and approved by King Wenceslas. Hus was forced to leave Prague and sought refuge in southern

Bohemia, where he took to writing treatises about the Church.

Finally, the trial was resurrected by the new king of Germany, King Sigismund (successor to Wenceslas) who used Hus's heresy trial as an opportunity to unify the Church and end the schism. Sigismund tricked Hus into attending a conference in Konstanz, Germany, assuring him safe passage. However, when Hus arrived in Konstanz, he was confined, tried, and sentenced to death.

Husayn, Taha (1889–1973)

Egyptian writer. Blind since birth, Husayn is best known for his storytelling abilities and his keen sense of the sound of words and the music of language. Husayn did not so much create fiction as create disturbing portraits of individuals and communities through detailed descriptions of their lives and conversations.

Two tensions pervade Husayn's work—his dual Eastern and Western intellectual heritage and his political concerns. Schooled in French writing, Husayn attempted to create a balance between the influences of French Romanticism and the classical Arab canon. The themes of his text cannot be divorced from his political activities: Husayn was a strong advocate of education and social reform, a stance that earned him much rebuke from Egypt's prerevolutionary government. One of his better-known works, *The Tortured Earth*, was a graphic presentation of life among Egypt's poorest peasantry. It was originally printed as individual essays, and its passion and anger so disturbed the ruling elite that the work was not allowed to be published in book form until after the 1952 revolution; it was finally published in 1955. Similarly, *The Call of the Plover* (1934) contains strong ethical and social messages that challenged deeply held traditional values. Husayn wanted to make people aware of the crimes that are often committed in the name of honor, and to indicate that love should assume the place of revenge.

Hu Shi (1891–1962)

Chinese scholar, educator, and diplomat. Born in Shanghai, Hu began his studies as a precocious child who learned 1,000 Chinese characters by the age of four. After winning a scholarship, he studied at Cornell University, where he developed an interest in the ideas of American philosopher and educator John Dewey (1859–1952). Hu went on to get his doctorate under Dewey at Columbia University, and returned to China to become a professor of philosophy at Beijing University. Mainly known as an activist for the adoption of a vernacular Chinese language, Hu was against the ossified and ornate conventions of classical Chinese. Through his involvement with the May 4th movement of 1919, which agitated for the vernacular (or *beifa*), he made a lasting contribution to the deterioration of the old Confucian order, as well as to the spread of literacy. Hu was, throughout his life, a disciple of Deweyan pragmatism, interested in problems and their careful, well-planned, and specific solution. This micropolitical vision did not square with the other main philosophical alternative to Confucianism, Marxism, and Hu opposed revolution as much as he did Communism. He was also against the idea of war with Japan because he felt it would destroy the progress achieved over the last generation.

Serving as Chinese ambassador to the United States from 1938 to 1942, and returning to Beijing University as chancellor in 1946, Hu fled the city when it was surrounded by the Communists in 1948, returning to the United States. In 1958 while in Taiwan, Hu was named president of the Academia Sinica.

Hyksos

Semitic-Asiatic people that first settled in northern Egypt in the eighteenth century B.C.E. From the Egyptian *hikan Khasut*, or *heqakhase*, which means "rulers of foreign land," the Hyksos were warriors of Semitic origin who swept southward from Asia Minor and conquered Egypt during the seventeenth century B.C.E. By around 1630 B.C.E., the Hyksos had seized control and established their capital at Avaris (present-day Telled-Dab'a), ruling as the kings of the fifteenth dynasty (c. 1630–1521 B.C.E.).

Though their advanced weaponry (the composite bow, bronze swords, and horse-drawn chariots) allowed them to collect tribute from all parts of Egypt, the Hyksos were never able to establish a solid governmental base, and eventually the country fragmented into smaller principalities.

After 1600 B.C.E., the Egyptian cities increasingly followed Theban leadership in an effort to drive out the Hyksos. Around 1524 B.C.E., Kamose launched a campaign to retake Avaris. After the city fell, Kamose was named king, and the Hyksos as a people virtually disappeared. In Egyptian art, they are remembered as a barbaric presence, a people who misruled the country and debased its culture; however, the Hyksos were recorded in Egyptian documents as the legitimate kings of Egypt, and it appears that their influence was more pronounced in the political realm than in the cultural.

I

Ibarbourou, Juana de (1895–1979)

Uruguayan poet. Born in Uruguay, Ibarbourou is one of the most famous South American women poets of the twentieth century. She began writing at an early age, gaining recognition as an innovative and talented poet when she published several poems in *La Razón*. Soon thereafter, her first book of poems, *Los lenguas de diamante* (1919; *Tongues of Diamond*), was published in Buenos Aires, followed by the well-received *Ralz salvaje* (1922; *Savage Root*). These initial works pulsated with life, love, and a celebration of youth. Ibarbourou's work makes use of nature and natural settings in the context of a provocative eroticism.

The highlight of her career came in 1929, with a ceremony in her honor in the Legislative Palace of Montevideo, where she was dubbed Juana de Americ. Her work received less acclaim thereafter, as she became more cerebral in depicting the loss of beauty and vitality. Ibarbourou's despair in old age and her melancholy at the approach of death are profoundly expressed in *Perdida (Lost)*, published in 1950, the same year she was named the president of the Sociedad Uruguaya de Escritos (Society of Uruguayan Writers). By the end of her life, she had given up writing poetry altogether, though she remained one of the most popular poets of South America.

Ibn al-Haytham (c. 965–1040)

Arab scientist. Born in southern Iraq, Ibn al-Haytham eventually settled in

Cairo, where the caliph had invited him to try out a plan for controlling the annual flooding of the Nile. He realized that the plan would not work and feigned madness to avoid the anger of the capricious ruler. After the caliph died, Ibn al-Haytham spent his time writing on optics, mathematics, and astronomy until his death.

In *Optics*, his most important work, Ibn al-Haytham formulated an original and rigorously argued theory of perception. He established that light enters the eye from an external source, gave an account of reflection and refraction, and attempted to explain depth perception. The Latin translation of *Optics* was an authoritative source for Western studies of the subject, and one of the problems Ibn al-Haytham solved in *Optics* is still known as "Alhazen's Problem" (based on the Latin version of his name).

In his *Doubts About Ptolemy*, Ibn al-Haytham attacked the long-standing Ptolemaic theory of the universe, which he showed to be fraught with contradictions. Like *Optics*, the work is valuable not only for the individual arguments it contains but also for its exemplification of scientific method. Ibn al-Haytham states in the introduction that since "God did not make scientists immune from error," it is the duty of scholars to correct the work of their predecessors "for the sake of those who will come after." Why practice science at all? "Truth," he said, "is to be sought for its own sake."

Ibn Baṭṭūṭah (1304–1368/9)

Medieval Arab traveler and author of the famous travel book known commonly as *Rihlah (Travels)*. According to his own accounts, Ibn Baṭṭūṭah traveled some 75,000 miles over a period of fifty years, visiting nearly all the Islamic countries as well as Sumatra, Russia, and perhaps China. His work went unnoticed in the West until it was rediscovered in the nineteenth century, during the French occupation of Algeria.

Born Abū 'Abd Allāh Muhammad ibn 'Abd Allāh al-Lawātī aṭ-Ṭanjī ibn Baṭṭūṭah in Tangier, Ibn Baṭṭūṭah received an extensive legal and literary education. His training proved invaluable later, making him an honored guest at many courts and making it possible to finance his journeys. In 1325 he set out on a pilgrimage to Mecca, his first step in pursuing his studies with scholars in the Near East. After several years of study in and around Mecca, he toured the east coast of Africa by ship as far south as present-day Tanzania before heading north to see the Persian Gulf and then returning to Mecca in 1332. There Ibn Baṭṭūṭah decided to seek his fortune at the court of the sultan of Delhi, Muhammad ibn Tughluq (1325–51), well known for his generosity to Muslim scholars. His journey took him through Turkey, Russia, Central Asia, and finally India.

By this time he was a man of some renown, and the Indian ruler rewarded him with the position of grand *gadi* (judge) of Delhi, a post he held for several years. Later, he embarked on a trip to China as the sultan's ambassador, but after several misadventures, including a shipwreck, he wound up in the Maldive Islands for two years. Eventually finding his way to China by way of Ceylon and Sumatra, he claimed to have journeyed all the way to Beijing, though many experts dispute this portion of his account. In 1348 he returned home to Tangier by way of Mecca and northern Africa. In 1353 Ibn Baṭṭūṭah returned to Morocco and at the request of the sultan dictated his memoirs to a royal secretary, who embellished his prose and perhaps his stories. It is believed that he subsequently settled in as a *gadi* in a town in Morocco. Ibn Baṭṭūṭah is often compared to Marco Polo both for the breadth of his travels and the value of his observations of little-known cultures.

Though many of his accounts are questionable, in general his *Rihlah* is considered to be reliable and provides an intimate view of the unusual cohesiveness of the medieval Islamic world.

Ibn Gabirol, Solomon (c. 1021–c. 1058)

Sephardic (Spanish-Jewish) philosopher and poet. Following in the Neoplatonic tradition of Isaac Israeli (the Egyptian-born philosopher often called the first Jewish Neoplatonist), Ibn Gabirol attempted to reconcile Islamic, Greek, and Jewish worldviews. His most important philosophical work, *Fountain of Life*, was carried into Europe in a Latin translation, *Fons vitae* (the original Arabic text has been lost), where it was widely read by medieval Christian intellectuals. As no mention is made of his Judaism, it was only in 1845 that a scholar discovered the true identity of the text's author, who had used the pseudonym "Avicebron."

Ibn Gabirol believed that the Godhead (the transcendent Deity) contained two distinct, yet interrelated entities: divine will and divine essence. Divine will served as the intermediary between God and his creation (matter). Hence, divine will is subordinate to (and emanates from) divine essence. Ibn Gabirol further asserted that matter derives from divine essence while form is a product of divine will—the implication being that matter is somehow superior to form since essence is superior to will. Human intellect, like everything else, is composed of both form and matter; because the intellect encompasses all things, it has the potential to lift man out of the darkness of ignorance and reach "the source of life." The importance of this philosophy lies in its refutation of the Islamic belief that human reason alone is insufficient and that an external intelligence is required for a true understanding of the divine will. Ibn Gabirol asserted that man was fully capable of grasping the immaterial world without

any divine revelation, a view much closer to Jewish theology than Islamic.

Although his philosophical writings (as opposed to his liturgical poetry) were not addressed to a specifically Jewish audience, Ibn Gabirol's concepts of the divine essence and the divine will were influential in terms of the development of Kabbalism, a medieval and modern system of Jewish theosophy and mysticism. Even in the Golden Age of Sephardic arts and letters, Ibn Gabirol stood out as one of the greatest Hebrew poets of all time, writing on subjects both secular and religious. His best-known poem, *Keter Malkhut* (*Royal Crown*), is often recited by worshipers after the evening service on Yom Kippur, and several of his penitential prayers have become standards in Jewish prayer books.

Ibn Khaldûn (1332–1406)

Arab scholar and statesman. Born in Tunis into an aristocratic family, Ibn Khaldûn worked in Granada, Fez, Tlemcen, Cairo, Mecca, and Medina. He lived through turbulent times, and his political ambitions nearly cost him his life on more than one occasion. He is remembered for his masterpiece, a multivolume history of the world, *The Book of Lessons and Archive of Early and Subsequent History, Dealing with the Political Events Concerning the Arabs, Non-Arabs, and Berbers*. Ibn Khaldûn is one of many Muslim historians who wrote detailed histories of the world, attempting to synthesize the knowledge and lore of the ancient civilizations of Persia, Byzantium, and the Near East.

Scornful of other historians' "blind trust in tradition," Ibn Khaldûn took pains to explain the phenomena that he recorded. He paid particular attention to dynasties, which "have a natural lifetime just like individuals." This, he said, is because they draw their strength from a sentiment he called "group solidarity," which is difficult to maintain for more than three forty-year generations. He recognized that a proper understanding of events can be achieved only by comprehending human society in its different manifestations, and attempted to explain the kinds of societies that he knew, nomadic and sedentary, and the effects of geography and climate on them. In short, his book strives for a comprehensive theory of human civilization.

Ibn Khaldûn is unique among his predecessors in the depth of his analysis. His preface to the *History*, the *Mugaddimah* (*Introduction to History*), is a master treatise on his theories of history and society, and was called by English historian Arnold Joseph Toynbee (1889–1975) "the most comprehensive and illuminating analysis of how human affairs work that has been made anywhere." The diverse domains of civilization that Ibn Khaldûn examined are now encompassed by the disciplines of history, sociology, anthropology, folklore, geography, history of science, applied linguistics, economics, and political science.

Ibn Rushd (1126–1194)

Islamic philosopher and scientist known in the West as Averroës. He was born in Cordova, Spain, in 1126 and studied Islamic religion, Greek philosophy, and medicine. Even while employed as a judge and physician, he was able to produce a large number of commentaries and original works in various fields. He enjoyed the patronage of enlightened rulers until 1195, when he was exiled by a caliph (Islamic leader) who considered philosophy dangerous. He was restored to favor shortly before his death.

Ibn Rushd addressed the perennial problem of faith and reason, claiming that truth could be conveyed in three ways: by demonstrative proof, by disputation, and by rhetoric. The first method, according to Ibn Rushd, is the best since it is the most rigorous; but logic, if taught to those who are incapable of understanding it, is dangerous since it can lead to skepticism and unbelief. Therefore, rhetorical representations of the truth, such as those which appear in the Qur'ân, are appropriate for mass consumption. But philosophers are empowered to interpret the Qur'ân figuratively if its literal meaning conflicts with results reached by logical methods. In response to the attack on philosophy launched by Islamic jurist and theologian al-Ghazâlî (1058–1111) in "The Incoherence of the Philosophers," Ibn Rushd launched a devastating counterattack entitled "The Incoherence of 'The Incoherence' " (1079–80).

Ibn Rushd was a great defender of Greek philosopher Aristotle (384–322 B.C.E.) and wrote comprehensive commentaries on his logical, scientific, metaphysical, and literary-critical works. It was through the Latin translations of these commentaries that European scholars rediscovered Aristotle in the thirteenth century. In fact, until the sixteenth century, the texts of Aristotle most commonly used in the West were not those translated directly into Latin, but those translated from Arabic into Latin accompanied by the commentaries of Ibn Rushd.

Ibn Sînâ (980–1037)

Influential Islamic philosopher and physician of the Middle Ages. Born in Bukhâra (then part of Iran), Ibn Sînâ, known in the West by his Latin name, Avicenna, was a child prodigy, teaching his teachers (as he himself tells us) at the age of fourteen. At sixteen, he was a respected physician, and at twenty-two a minister of state. Ibn Sînâ was famed for his vast learning in all the known fields of scholarship, condemned for his sometimes unorthodox views, and feared for his withering contempt of his intellectual inferiors.

As a philosopher, Ibn Sînâ tried to reconcile the Islamic revelation with the rationalism of Greek philosophy. Rationalism is the theory that reason is in itself a source of knowledge superior to and independent of sense perception and hence a basis for the establishment of religious truth. Ibn Sînâ found a place for the conscious apprehension of reality—including revelation—within the Aristotelian conception of the world order by drawing on Plotinus' doctrine of Divine Emanation. According to Ibn Sînâ, God, the necessary Being, produces an Intelligence, which in turn produces another, and so on down to the tenth Intelligence, called the Active Intellect, which governs the terrestrial world. The human soul, if it is both rational and loving, can achieve contact with the Active Intellect, and thus acquire true knowledge. Illuminationism—that is, Ibn Sînâ's belief in direct mystical apprehension of truth—exerted a great influence on subsequent Islamic thought. His metaphysical and logical teachings were eagerly seized upon by European Scholastic philosophers, who were engaged, like their Muslim counterparts, in the reconciliation of faith and reason.

Ibn Sînâ was also an influential figure in the history of medicine, along with other Muslim physicians such as al-Râzî (Latin "Rhazes," d. 925), who diagnosed measles and smallpox, and Ibn al-Nafîs (d. 1288), who gave the first detailed account of pulmonary circulation (an observation not replicated in Europe until 1628). Ibn Sînâ wrote widely on medicine, including a collection of medical information written in verse. His most famous work by far is *Al-gānūn fī al-tibb* (*The Canon of Medicine*), which remained a standard reference, East and West, for at least five hundred years. It includes general principles of health and treatment, medicinal properties of various herbs, pathology of the different systems, and information on the diagnosis of illnesses (including lovesickness), and the treatment of injuries. The *Canon* was translated—completely or in part—no less than eighty-seven times (mostly into Latin), and was taught in European universities until the seventeenth century.

Ibsen, Henrik [Johan] (1828–1906)

Norwegian dramatist. Ibsen is considered by some to be the father of modern drama, and his work changed the face of the theater. He introduced social issues into a genre that was, at the time, basically apolitical; Ibsen's concern with society and its discontents can be clearly seen in the treatment of sexuality in *Gengangere* (1881; *Ghosts*) and his critique of the institution of marriage in *Et dukkehjem* (1879; *A Doll's House*). He was also an early champion of psychological theater, displacing the traditional emphasis on plot with intricate studies of character and emotional conflict.

Born to middle-class parents in the coastal city of Skien, Ibsen was still a boy when the family business failed; as a result, at the age of fifteen, Ibsen was apprenticed to a druggist in the city of Grimstad. Two years after he arrived at this post, a maid at his master's house gave birth to Ibsen's illegitimate child. He took very little interest in the child, but the theme of illegitimacy often surfaced in his work.

At the age of twenty-three, he was appointed manager and official playwright of the new National Theater at Bergen, though he left this post soon after for a more prestigious job managing the Norwegian Theater at Christiana (now Oslo), a position in which he served from 1857 to 1862. After the theater was forced to declare bankruptcy in 1864, Ibsen went into an exile of sorts, spending time in Rome, Munich, and Dresden. He eventually returned to Christiana in 1891, where he spent the remainder of his life.

Although Ibsen wrote many plays, it was not until he wrote *A Doll's House* in 1879 that his voice found the appropriate outlet. The play is about a woman

named Nora who abandons her hypocritical husband. Audiences were scandalized by Ibsen's refusal to write a
"happy ending" and his portrayal of
Nora as an "independent" woman. His
next play, *Ghosts*, dealt with venereal
disease and the power of moral contam-
ination, and did little to restore general
public favor.

Ibsen is particularly remembered for
the extraordinarily strong women in his
writing, a type of "new woman," as exemplified by Nora and the eponymous
heroine of *Hedda Gabler*, supposedly
loosely modeled on his wife, Susannah
Thoresen.

Icaza, Jorge (1906–1978)

Ecuadorian novelist and playwright.
Born in Quito, Icaza is best known for
the brutally realistic portrayals of the exploitation of the Indians in his country.
He produced most of his work, including his most celebrated novel, *Huasipungo* (1934; revised 1951; *The Villagers*),
between the years 1925 and 1944—a period of internal turmoil in Ecuador that
saw more than twenty presidents, as well
as the blossoming of the country's literature. His father died early in Icaza's
youth, and his mother remarried a militant Liberal Party politician; due to political persecution, they were forced to
take refuge with his maternal uncle,
Don Enrique Coronel, on his estate.
There he saw the extraordinary power
wielded by his uncle over the Indians,
who were dying of hunger.

Icaza had hoped to practice medicine
but was forced to abandon the university
upon the death of his mother. He became an actor, married Ecuador's most
gifted actress, Marina Moncayo, and began writing plays. When his comedy *El
dictador* (1933; *The Dictator*) was banned
and he was fired from his job as provincial treasury clerk, Icaza started writing
fiction. He first published a collection of
short stories called *Barro de la sierra*
(1933; *Mountain Clay*), but more significant was *Huasipungo*, his first novel,

which brought him immediate fame
and became the center of much controversy. The title refers to the Indian name
for the piece of land given to the Indians
by landowners in return for their labor,
and the novel describes in fine social
realist form how the Indians were first
deprived of their land and then slaughtered by the landowners when they rebelled. The upper classes were outraged
when the novel appeared, and the
Church silently disapproved; the book,
however, became a tool of radical propaganda and was translated into many
languages, including Russian and
Chinese.

His later novels and plays focus less
on the plight of the Indians and more
on the *mestizos'* rejection of their Indian
heritage; these works are more concerned with depicting the internal life
experiences of the characters and of in-
quiring into Ecuadorian cultural identity. Later works include *En las calles*
(1934; *In the Streets*), *Media vida
deslumbrados* (1942; *Half a Life
Amazed*), *Seis veces la muerte* (1954;
Death Six Times), and *El chulla Romero
y Flores* (1958; *The Loner Romero y Flores*). Over the course of his life, Icaza
was director of the National Library and
served in several government posts, including ambassador to Peru and the Soviet Union.

I Ching, *see* Yi Jing

Id al-Adha

"Feast of the Sacrifice." Also called "the
major feast," Id al-Adha marks the end
of the Muslim pilgrimage, or *hajj*, to
Mecca. Celebrated in the valley of
Mina, outside Mecca, millions of Muslim devotees ritually slaughter cows,
sheep, or larger animals, reenacting the
substitution of a ram for Isma'il, the son
whom Abraham was willing to sacrifice
to God.

Individual Muslims must in turn
slaughter an animal in their own homes,
in imitation of Abraham's sacrifice. The

performance of this ritual devotion is said to aid one in attaining paradise; the slaughtered animal, it is said, will carry its owner over the Sirat Bridge to paradise. In India, where Muslims and Hindus jostle for public space, Id al-Adha is known as Bagar Id, the "Cow Feast." The animal to be slaughtered is always a cow, and this semideliberate provocation often results in rioting by Hindus.

Id al-Fitr

"Feast of the Fast Breaking." Also known as "the lesser feast," Id al-Fitr is the celebration that ends the Muslim holy month of Ramadân. Throughout this month Muslims are required to fast from the moment of sunrise until the sun completely sets. The fast involves the avoidance not only of food during daylight but also of any kind of drink (even water), smoking, and sex. Id al-Fitr heralds the return to normal life, and is an eagerly awaited holiday. In Turkey this feast is called Seker Bayrami, a "sugar feast," a reference to the custom of distributing sweets on this day.

Idrîs, Yûsef (1927–1991)

Egyptian short-story writer. Often considered to be the greatest contemporary short-story writer in Arabic, Idrîs has also made valuable contributions to the development of Egyptian theater. Rejecting European dramatic forms, Idrîs encouraged writers to experiment with drama to explore what might be called "indigenous" cultural forms. In his plays, Idrîs emphasizes popular forms of drama such as mimicry, *aragoz* (puppet show), and dervish dances, which he believes to be specifically Egyptian modes of expression. Imprisoned by both King Farouk and President Nasser, Idrîs has consistently made poverty and social injustice themes central to his writing: his novel *al-Ard* (1954; *The Earth Provides*) offers powerful insight into the lives and personalities of the Egyptian *felaheen* (peasantry), and *al-Haram* (1977; *The*

Sin) describes the moral dilemma of a young girl struggling with the questions she confronts when she goes to work in a corrupt government department. A staunch social realist, Idrîs has sought to narrow the gap between the Egyptian short story and reality by steering his work away from the sentimentality and melodrama that have long dominated the genre.

Ifa oracle

Yoruba religious texts. A form of Yoruba divination, the Ifa sacred texts are a large body of poetry, arranged into 256 collections, or *odu*, and constitute a repository of Yoruba cultural values.

When a member of the Yoruba culture needs some form of assistance, he or she will approach the Ifa priest for help. The priest will then consult the oracle and chant the verses of a particular *odu*, selected by chance, by casting a series of palm nuts, the so-called *opele* chain, which is a chain of dried seed casings. The priest holds sixteen palm nuts in his right hand, then hits his left palm with the hand full of nuts. Generally, one or two nuts fall into the left hand, and the priest makes a mark accordingly. This procedure is repeated for a total of eight casts, and the combination of the marks determines which *odu* is most appropriate in a particular situation. In addition, through such consultation the priest determines the proper action a worshiper should take, in the form of sacrifice, to appeal to his personal orishá, or god.

Igbo

Nigerian ethnic group. One of the three main ethnic groups in Nigeria (Yoruba, Hausa, and Igbo), the Igbo are by far the dominant ethnic group in eastern Nigeria, numbering more than 10 million in the early 1980s.

The Igbo first encountered Christian missionaries in 1857. By 1900 the Igbo had come under British rule. One of the first instances of anticolonial resistance occurred in 1929, when Igbo women organized the Aba Women's War. It was the result of an attempt to extend a "poll tax," which had been in effect for men for some years, to women, children, and animals. The tax was collected by Igbo in the pay of the British, called warrant chiefs. Local market women organized, attacking colonialists and warrant chiefs and sacking shops. In December the uprising was violently crushed by colonial authorities, killing more than fifty women.

Maintaining national unity in Nigeria after gaining independence in 1960 was difficult, given the nation's ethnic diversity. In 1967 the Nigerian Civil War broke out, after Lt. Colonel Odumegwu Ojukwu declared the Eastern Region of Nigeria the independent state of Biafra. His declaration had been motivated by the slaughter of some 10,000–30,000 Igbo in the northern region of Nigeria. The civil war lasted until January 1970, when the independent state of Biafra ceased to exist and federal control was reinstated in the eastern territories. Between 500,000 and several million Igbo died during the war. Igbo authors like Buchi Emecheta (1944–) and Chinua Achebe (1930–) write about the Nigerian national experience.

The Igbo language is classified in the Kwa branch of the Niger-Congo subfamily, which also includes the languages of the Asante and the Yoruba. Numerous dialects are spoken, the two most common being those of the Owerri Igbo and the Onitsha Igbo.

Though most Igbo had adopted Christianity by the mid twentieth century, traditional Igbo religion still flourishes. In this religion, there are three types of supernatural beings: God, spirits, and ancestors. Chukwu, the only God and the creator of the world, is a source of good, bestowing both rain and children upon the earth. Children are named in his honor. Ani, the earth spirit, is one of the most significant and is worshiped throughout the Igbo region. Along with the ancestors, Ani is considered to be a guardian of Igbo morality; the most serious crimes are committed against the earth spirit and require special sacrifices for absolution. Each individual has a personal spirit, or *chi*, which oversees their destiny. The Igbo maintain close and respectful relationships with their deceased ancestors, who are collectively honored in a yearly feast. To attain a new spiritual existence after death, a person must have lived well and have funeral rites performed for them by their survivors. The ancestors are believed to be benevolent forces who protect the family and aid the living in having many children and good harvests.

Īl-Khān

Mongol dynasty (1256–1353) that ruled Iran in the thirteenth and fourteenth centuries. After the division of territory conquered by Chingiz (Genghis) Khan, the task of subjugating Iran, Mesopotamia, Syria, and possibly even Egypt was entrusted to his grandson Hulegu. Invading Iran in the second quarter of the thirteenth century, the Mongol army advanced into Mesopotamia and in 1258 destroyed Baghdad, the seat of the caliphate and the most important city of its day in the Middle East. The armies continued to advance into Syria, but they were finally stopped by Turkish troops from Egypt at 'Ayn Jalut (Goliath's Spring) in 1260. However, the Mongols succeeded in consolidating their hold over Iran, which was ruled until 1355 by a succession of kings known by the title of Īl-Khānid (lesser or deputy khan, acknowledging their subordinate status to the Great Khan, who was the medieval sovereign of China and the ruler of the Turkish, Tartar, and Mongol tribes). The first half of the Īl-Khān period is characterized by a close administrative and cultural relationship with China;

preferential treatment of Nestorian Christians, Shamanists, and Buddhists; and ambivalence toward the Muslim populace of Iran. Following the ascension of Mahmud Ghāzān (a Sunnî Muslim) in 1295, the Īl-Khāns distanced themselves from China and assimilated into the local Turco-Persian culture. However, many Mongol influences remained, manifesting themselves in the art and architecture of the period. In addition to its contribution to Iranian art, the Īl-Khānid period was also significant for its promotion of various branches of science, in particular historiography, astrology, and medicine.

imâm

Spiritual leader of the Shi'ite Muslims. From the Arabic word meaning "leader," the imâm's authority in the Shi'ite Muslim community is derived directly from the Prophet Muhammad (570–632) through his designation of 'Alī (c. 600–661) as the first imâm of Muslims after the Prophet's death in 632. (Those who believed that Abū Bakr [573–634] was the next leader in line for succession after the Prophet's death claim he is the first caliph, or Islamic leader, of Mecca and refer to themselves as Sunnî Muslims). The imâm alone is empowered to interpret Islamic revelation in the age in which he lives. He is regarded as infallible and as possessing the light of God, which attracts people to him. The Shi'ites believe that there is an imâm in every age, but he may be concealed from the public eye in accordance with the divine will, in order to save the imâm, whose safety has been threatened by human design. In Shi'ite theology, divine justice and an ethical world order would be established by the reappearance of the concealed imâm as the mahdi ("divinely guided" deliverer) of the Muslim community. According to the major branch of the Shi'ites—namely, the Twelvers—the twelfth hidden imâm is expected to return as the mahdi and institute an ideal Islamic society.

Both the Sunnî and Shi'ite Muslims use the title "imâm" for the leader of worship in the mosque, who stands in front of the assembled believers to lead them in daily and other forms of congregational worship. The title is also used by Sunnîs for their leading jurists, whose rulings in the matter of Sharî'ah (religious-moral law of Islam) are followed by them. In modern days, the Shi'ites have also adopted the title "imâm" in this latter sense for their leading jurists.

Inanna

Akkadian and Sumerian goddess. Inanna (Ishtar in Akkadian) was the principal goddess in both the Akkadian and the Sumerian pantheons of deities, the goddess of war and sexual love, and perhaps of fertility, earth, and death. The tale of her attempt to steal away control of the underworld from her sister, Ereshkigal, the queen of the underworld, is one of the best-known stories from Sumerian mythology; it also explains the origin of the seasons.

In the story, Inanna, sumptuously dressed, descended to the underworld, where she met one of Ereshkigal's servants. The servant stripped her of her fancy garments and took her, naked and humiliated, to Ereshkigal, who glared death at her, turning her into a corpse and hanging her on a stake. Inanna's servant, Ninshubura, sought help from Enki, the god of wisdom, after her mistress did not return for three days. Enki fashioned two creatures from the dirt under his fingernails and ordered them to go to the underworld to join Ershkigal in her customary mourning for children who die before their time. Moved by these creatures' sorrow, Ershkigal offered to grant them a wish. The creatures requested Inanna's corpse and resuscitated her by tossing the body on the grass and pouring over it the water of life that Enki had given them.

As Inanna was leaving the underworld, its ruling gods stopped her and demanded that she find a substitute for her body. Accompanied by frightening demons, Inanna wandered from city to city in Sumer to find a replacement. All she found, however, were loyal devotees mourning her loss, none of whom she sent to replace her in the underworld.

When Inanna finally returned from the underworld, she found her young husband, Dumuzi, unconcerned about her disappearance. This so angered Inanna that she handed him over to the demons as her replacement. When Dumuzi's sister, Geshtinanna, asked to join her brother in the underworld, Inanna agreed to let Dumuzi serve one half of the year and allow his sister to serve the other half.

Inanna's death and disappearance into the earth was taken to herald the arrival of winter, and her revival to announce the coming of spring.

Inao

Thai literary form. The *inao*, or *inaw*, originated in tales from the Javanese story cycle of the hero Radan Panji, and probably accounts for the presence of numerous Javanese words and phrases in Thai literary language. There are actually two versions, *Inao Yay* (*The Great Inao*), and *Dalang or Inao Lek* (*The Small Inao*), both of which follow the adventures of the same hero, called Inao or Panji. While both of these versions were probably imported into eighteenth-century Thailand by Malay storytellers, they are attributed to the two daughters of King Rama I, Kunthon and Mongkut, who may have heard the stories from their Malay maids. These originals have been lost, but the version by King Rama II, a noted Thai poet, is still highly valued for its refined language and style.

Inca

Pre-encounter South American Indian civilization. At the time of the Spanish conquest, the Incan empire extended along the Pacific coast and Andean highlands and from the northern border of modern Ecuador to central Chile. In the twelfth century, Cuzco became its capital. The great Incan conquests began in the early fifteenth century, and within a century the Inca ruled a population of 12 million, made up of over one hundred ethnic groups, speaking twenty languages. Nonetheless, in 1532 two hundred Spaniards led by *conquistador* Franciso Pizarro (1475–1541) conquered the powerful Incan state. It has been theorized that Don Francisco Cusichaq, lord of the enemy Huanca tribe in central Peru, embraced the Spanish in hopes of destroying the Inca.

The Inca are known for their highways (used by the Spanish) and textiles, and for their extensive knowledge of agriculture and the environment. They regulated their activities according to a thirty-day religious calendar, though little is known about it. The Inca possessed no written language, although judges, commanders, and patriarchs of important families kept detailed records of their dynastic histories with the *quipu*, a distinctively Incan counting tool involving a system of knotted, colored strings.

A person's social position and future occupation were determined at birth. Men and women of the common class began vocational training at age five, while the nobility received an intellectual education and spoke Quechua, the language of the nobility. A child of noble birth learned Quechua in the first year of training; studied religion in the second year; learned to use the *quipu* in the third; and studied history, geography, geometry, and astronomy in the fourth. At the end of this four-year training period, the student was required to pass an exam to become a member of the nobility.

The Inca traced their ancestry to mythical figures who originated from holes in the earth. These holes, or *paqarina*, were regarded as shrines; Paccari Tampu (fifteen miles south of Cuzco) contains the best known. Like the Aztecs, the Incas worshiped the sun. The protector and creator god of the Inca was Viracocha; he was also known as a destroyer and transmogrifier of human beings (he re-created people in stone). Equally important was the sun god, Inti, who nurtured crops, and the god Apu Illapu, the rain-giver and fertility god. Temples were attended by priests and so-called chosen women. Priests practiced divination, heard confessions, and performed sacrifices of humans and animals.

In the fourteenth century, Incan rulers began the expansion of their empire when they recognized that the exhausted soil of the existing land, in combination with insufficient rainfall, would not produce enough food. Expansion began with the fifth emperor, Capac Yupanqui, the first ruler to conquer land outside the Cuzco valley. The Inca repeatedly raided and plundered other ethnic groups whenever necessary, but the culture of empire did not come into being until the early fifteenth century, with Emperor Viracocha Inca. Rapid expansion of the empire was problematic, however, and Incan emperors were hard put to manage the diverse ethnic groups they had conquered.

The real period of Inca expansion occurred, however, under the reign of Pachacuti Inca Yupahqui (r. 1438–71). Son of Emperor Viracocha, Pachacuti (also called Pachacutec) conquered both the Quechua and the Chanca, consolidated power, and then embarked upon a period of social, cultural, and economic reform. The giant Incan fortress of Sacsahuaman, on a hill above Cuzco, is archaeological testimony to this period of

political and military strength. In addition, he enlarged Sacsahuaman when he rebuilt Cuzco. At the same time, he channeled the rivers, leveled the valley floor, built terraces, and increased the productivity of the area. Only after the Spanish conquest in 1532 would the Inca empire experience decline.

Indian

Term used to describe the native peoples of the Americas. The use of the term "Indian" originated with the Italian explorer Christopher Columbus (1451–1506). When Columbus landed on the island he called Hispaniola in 1492 (today the site of the Dominican Republic and Haiti), he declared that he had reached the Orient, the "Indies," and accordingly labeled the inhabitants of the island "Indians." Since that time, the generic term "Indian" has been used to refer to native peoples of the Americas. The term implies a certain illusory unity among the many cultures and ethnic groups in the Americas, but most Indians have appropriated the misnomer as a sign of commonality. Others prefer the words "indigenous" or "Native" American rather than "Indian," terms which serve specific political and pancultural purposes. However, "Native American" is equally misleading as an ethnographic category, in its suggestion of a homogeneous identity.

The distant ancestors of Indians migrated from several geographical regions over many thousands of years. Differences in geographical origins and historical experiences resulted in a great variety of societies. Some three hundred tribes are recognized by the U.S. federal government, and in South America, Central America, and Canada there are hundreds more; in Guatemala, for example, there are more than twenty different tribes, each with a distinct language. Tribal membership is not necessarily based on "blood quantum" (which, when calculated, is generally one-fourth in the United States); some tribes instead require proof of historical lineage to earlier tribal members.

Despite their diversity of culture, customs, and racial composition, Indians share broadly similar interests as deterritorialized or encircled indigenous societies. Because their traditional institutions were intrinsically connected to their relationship to the land, during the long period of colonization the coherence of their way of life was disrupted by policies that alternately aimed at either annihilation or assimilation. Though Indians were affected variously by European expansion, their survival as distinct peoples is evidenced by the fact that of the approximately three hundred languages spoken by their ancestors in the lands that became the United States, nearly half are still in use.

The image of "the Indian" remains central to the national psyche of the United States; as mascot or symbol, the Indian is befeathered, furred, and cast in attitudes of sorrowful nobility or bestial aggression. Most often Indians are depicted in terms that misrepresent and capitalize on the spiritual basis of their systems of belief and practice. The resurgence of interest in Indian spirituality sparked by 1970s New Age philosophy has led to criticisms by many Indian leaders, who feel that backward-looking, romanticized portraits of Indians obscure their contemporary economic and political situation.

Indian film industry

Though its productions are rarely seen in the West, the Indian film industry is by far the largest in the world. In 1985 over nine hundred films produced in sixteen languages were seen on over twelve thousand screens on the Subcontinent. The industry has a major influence on the population of India, and top stars have enormous political clout. Since the 1930s, film has been the dominant form of entertainment in India; it was the country's ninth-largest industry in 1990, with more than 13 million tickets sold daily. Since over a third of India's population of 866 million lives in rural areas, much of the country is served by touring cinemas, temporary structures that travel the countryside.

Harischandra Sakharam Bhatvedekar was the first Indian to film short "actualities" in his homeland, sometime around 1897. In 1907 J. F. Madan opened the first of what would become a chain of theaters in Calcutta; his company grew to be the largest operator of theaters and a major producer of films by the 1920s. The European-trained director Dadasaheb Phalke produced the first feature-length films in India with *Rajah Harischandra* (1913; *Pious King*) and *Bhasmasur Mohini* (1913; *Woman Who Can Seduce Evil*); the latter was the first to employ an actress. The most important figure in the emergent industry, Phalke started the Hindustan Film Company in 1917. The silent *The Light of Asia*, based on the life of Buddha, was produced in 1925 by Himansu Rai as an Indian-German co-venture and was critically acclaimed in England. In 1931 the first Indian talkie, *Alam Ara* (*Beauty of the World*), was done in Hindi. Bombay Talkies, the most important of the sound-film producers in India, was founded in 1934.

French director Jean Renoir went to India in 1950 to film *The River*, and during his stay encouraged the career of Satyajit Ray, who had helped found the Calcutta Film Society in 1947. In 1955 Ray's first feature, *Pather Panchali* (*Father Panchali*), was a hit at the Cannes Film Festival and earned international attention. That film was the first of Ray's "Apu Trilogy," and it helped establish his fame in the West. The last of the large Indian studios, the Prabhat Film Company, closed in 1953 after twenty-five years of production, but its studios in Poona became the home of the Film Institute of India in 1961. The Film Finance Corporation (FFC) was created by the government in 1960 to encourage the funding of films, and in cooperation with the Indian Motion Picture Export Association (IMPEC), a new organization formed, the National Film Development Corporation (NFDC), which assumed many of the earlier responsibilities of the large studios, as well as ensured that film festivals became a major part of Indian culture.

The fact that Indian films are often produced in regional languages and even dialects explains why they are seldom seen internationally and why imports do not play a significant part in the Indian markets. The closest to a countrywide popular product are Hindi-language films, which make up about 20 percent of all Indian productions.

Inuit

Name of the native inhabitants of the Arctic and sub-Arctic regions of the United States, Greenland, Canada, and the former U.S.S.R. "Inuit," which means "real people" in the Inuit language, are perhaps more commonly known as Eskimos, which means "eaters of raw meat." The term was first coined by the Algonquin Indians of eastern Canada to describe the neighboring Inuit people, who were skilled hunters. Appearing in Greenland by the ninth century, the Inuit have retained a rather uniform culture and language despite their wide dispersal over two continents. They are believed to be of Asian origin. Scholars once held that they had migrated north, though physiological differences between northern and southern American Indians suggest that they are unrelated.

The Inuit were the first population of native North Americans to have direct contact with the Europeans. The Norsemen met the Inuit in southeastern Greenland as early as the tenth century, although the Inuit remained largely isolated until the eighteenth century,

when European missionaries arrived in Greenland.

Traditional Inuit culture is conditioned by the brutality of the Arctic region. When summer approaches and the sea is free of ice, the Inuit travel in small, family-sized bands to favorite hunting and fishing sites. As winter approaches, these bands return to a permanent community and begin the difficult work of hunting in the frozen Arctic. The igloo, a structure commonly associated with the Inuit, is used only infrequently by seal hunters. "Igloo" is derived from the Inuit word for "home," and is constructed from packed snow. Seal hunters sometimes built igloo villages on the thick ice covering the sea after they had located the air holes scratched out by seals, and awaited the seals' return.

Animals hunted by the Inuit appeared in their religion and art. Animistic in nature, Inuit religion involved a complex system of taboos and customs to ensure good hunting. Central to this system was the shaman, who divined the causes of ill health or unsuccessful hunting, and reinforced the importance of respecting food or hunting taboos and customs. One widespread custom, for example, was to offer a glass of water to a dead seal when it was brought into an Inuit dwelling, as a sign of hospitality. Much of the art, too, echoes the life of the hunter, both in the materials used (walrus ivory and whalebone, for example) and in the figures depicted. While there have been changes in the traditional practices of the Inuit, change has not been significant enough to consider the Inuit assimilated.

After the Second World War, the Inuit abandoned the traditional nomadic settlement pattern in favor of hunting and fishing villages. Many have settled in industrialized urban areas, especially in and around Alaska. Despite this move to the city, Pan-Eskimo movements, which include the Alaskan, Canadian,

Greenlandic, and even Eurasian communities, are developing and may prove to be an important political and cultural voice. In 1982 the inhabitants of Canada's Northwest Territories gave sanction to a plan designed to divide territories, giving the Inuit greater political control of their regions.

Ionesco, Eugène (1912–1994)

Romanian-born French dramatist. Ionesco pioneered the Theater of the Absurd, a dramatic style that uses comically baffling plot scenarios to emphasize the meaninglessness of existence. Ionesco and other absurdist playwrights incorporated the Surrealist interest in dreams and violent humor into spare theatrical productions.

Raised in France and Romania, Ionesco studied French at the University of Bucharest and then pursued a doctorate in French in Paris. He took up the study of English after he moved to Paris permanently in 1945. For his most famous play, *La Cantatrice chauve* (1950; *The Bald Soprano*), Ionesco used choppy, simplistic sentences similar to those in his English phrase book. The play introduced Ionesco's central theme of modern man's self-alienation. The "plot" focuses on two English middle-class strangers who make cliché-ridden small talk before discovering they are in fact man and wife.

Throughout the 1950s Ionesco continued to explore the one-act form with plays like *L'Avenir est dans les oeufs* (1951; *The Future Is in Eggs*) and *Victimes du devoir* (1953; *Victims of Duty*). In his first three-act play, *Amédée* (1954), a bourgeois couple share the stage with a gigantic corpse representing their dead love. Later plays are somewhat more straightforward in plot and symbolic structure. *Rhinocéros* (1959), which satirizes the Nazi rise to power, features a man who watches in uncomprehending horror as his coworkers and friends metamorphose into a herd of rhinoceri. Although he never matched the success of *The Bald Soprano*, Ionesco's innovations remain of major importance to European and American avant-garde dramatists and audiences. He helped to explode the conventions of naturalistic drama and made the often abstruse achievements of the Surrealists available to a broader audience. His works exerted a profound influence on major playwrights like Samuel Beckett, Jean Genet, Harold Pinter, and Edward Albee. In 1971 he was elected to the Académie Française, and in 1985 received the T. S. Eliot Prize.

Iqbal, Sir Muhammad (1877–1938)

Indian poet and philosopher. Iqbal was born in Sialkot, Punjab, India (now Pakistan), to a pious family of small merchants. After attending Government College, Lahore, Iqbal traveled throughout Europe from 1905 to 1908. During his stay he earned his degree in philosophy at Cambridge University, qualified as a barrister in London, and earned a doctorate from the University of Munich.

On returning to India, Iqbal taught English and philosophy at Government College before opting for law. He became famous for his often quoted Urdu *nazms*, poems that require no formal restrictions except that they be continuous and thematic. Prior to his journey to Europe, Iqbal's poetry had been deeply patriotic, affirming Indian nationalism. After his return from Europe, he became an outspoken critic of nationalism, which he aligned with imperialism and racism. In numerous poems, Iqbal bemoaned Muslim powerlessness in India. His writings called for a Pan-Islamic India and commemorated the past glories of Islam in India, criticizing the decadence of present-day Islamic practices.

With the publication in 1915 and 1918 of two long poems written in Persian— *'Asrār-e khūdī* (1915; Secrets of the Self) and *Rumūz-e bīkhūdī* (1918; Mysteries of Selflessness)—Iqbal sparked heated controversy by criticizing traditional Islamic notions of self-negation and self-surrender. He subsequently published three other volumes in Persian: *Payām-e Mashriq* (1923; *Message of the East*), a response to German poet Johann Wolfgang von Goethe's *West-östlicher Divan* (1819; *Divan of West and East*); *Zabūr-e 'Ajam* (1927; *Persian Psalms*), a collection of *ghazals*, or love poems; and *Jāvīd-nāmeh* (1932; *The Song of Eternity*), which is considered to be his masterpiece. A Persian re-creation of Italian poet Dante's *Divina commedia* (1472; *Divine Comedy*), *The Song of Eternity* narrates the ascent of a poet who is guided through all the realms of thought and experience by the Persian mystic Jalaluddin Rumi.

Considered by many to be the greatest poet of Urdu in the twentieth century, Iqbal did not confine his political and philosophical views to his poetry alone; he lectured extensively for the Pan-Islamic cause throughout his lifetime. The six lectures contained in *The Reconstruction of Religious Thought in Islam* (delivered 1928–29) give voice to his Islamic "modernist" beliefs. Rejecting the static worldview that had dominated Muslim thought since the Mongol invasions, Iqbal envisioned a cultural world in which priesthood and hereditary kingship would be abolished, and the study of history and nature would be emphasized. Through the exercise of *ijtihad*—the principle of legal advancement—and *ijmâ'*—consensus—Iqbal argued, the Islamic code could be altered to meet new circumstances. Although he found similarities between Islam and socialism—both emphasized equality and rejected racism and monarchy—he criticized socialism for its roots in materialism and its lack of moral and spiritual love.

Knighted by the British in 1922, in 1930 Iqbal gave a famous address in which he urged the Muslims of north-western India to demand a separate state. He became an international spokesman for this cause, and although Pakistan was not created until after his death, Iqbal has been acclaimed as the father and spiritual founder of the nation. Every year, Pakistanis celebrate Iqbal Day on June 28 in commemoration of the poet's contribution to the establishment of their country.

Irish heroic narrative

Irish myth cycle. The Irish epic tradition originates with a series of four myth cycles, prose narratives written between 700 and 1300 C.E. The first, the Mythological Cycle, contains the stories of the Tuatha De Danaan—the tribes of the goddess Danaan, the Celtic deity of motherhood and family. The second cycle, the Fenian, chronicles the adventures of the hero Finn mac Cumaill and his son Oisín. The Cycle of the Kings tells of the legendary rulers of Ireland, said to have reigned between the third century B.C.E. and the eighth century C.E.

The last of the four, the Ulster Cycle, deals with the heroes of Ulster, the main province in the northeast. The centerpiece of the Ulster Cycle is the Táin Bó Cuálnge ("The Cattle Raid of Cooley"). The story, which may have been composed in the eighth century—the language suggests such an early date, although the tale only appears in manuscripts from the eleventh and twelfth centuries—concerns a cattle raid launched by the army of Connacht into Ulster. Cú Chulain, Ulster's defender, repels the invading army single-handedly, as the regular Ulster army is incapacitated by imaginary labor pains brought on by an enemy curse.

Iroquois Confederation

Formal confederation of six American Indian tribes: the Mohawk, Oneida, Onondaga, Cayuga, Seneca, and Tuscarora. Referred to by the English as the

Six Nations, the Iroquois Confederation (also referred to as the League of the Iroquois) served as a governing body for all tribes in the confederation and exercised political and military power accorded to it by its individual members. It is relatively uncertain when the confederation was formed. Most evidence suggests that the league was founded between c. 1400 and c. 1600. The Confederation Council, usually numbering fifty representative *sachems*, or civil chiefs, several from each tribe, convened as necessary to arbitrate intertribal feuding (although it was not empowered to arbitrate matters within individual tribes) and to rule on military affairs. In principle, therefore, only the Confederation Council, and not individual tribes, could sanction and declare war. Unanimity governed league decisions and direction. A careful, ritualized electoral process in each tribe eliminated the threat that any single leader would control the league and made for a model democratic political organization.

The Iroquois Confederation is perhaps most famous for its political savvy during conflicts between the French and British in the sixteenth and seventeenth centuries. Principally situated in the region of upper New York State, the Iroquoian tribes occupied a strategic territorial position. The friendship of the tribe was crucial for the French and British, as they sought to control the territory and its lucrative fur trade. Although both courted the Iroquoian tribes, the Iroquois, shrewd middlemen in these conflicts, more often lent military support to the British.

At the outbreak of the American Revolution, the confederation remained neutral, permitting individual tribes to choose positions. Again, individual alliances with the British were strong. However, warfare and disease had already reduced the strength of the Iroquois, and the tribes were a less effective military force than in past conflicts.

Since the time of the formation of the league, three member tribes of the Six Nations have remained in New York State, largely as a consequence of the American Revolution. The Mohawk and Cayuga tribes resettled in Canada, the Oneida in Wisconsin. Today more than 11,000 Iroquois live on 80,000 acres of chiefly reservation land in upstate New York.

Isis

Ancient Egyptian goddess. Isis was the sister and wife of Osiris, the Egyptian god of the underworld. Her worship became the most important of the large number of Near Eastern cults and was eventually absorbed into the religion of the Roman empire. The name Isis comes from the Greek form of the Egyptian hieroglyph for "throne." Isis is often symbolized by a throne; she is also frequently represented with the head of a cow or with cow horns.

The worship of Isis, combined with that of her brother/husband, Osiris, and their son, Horus, was enormously resistant to the influence of early Christian teachings. Her role in Egyptian mythology centers on the story of Osiris' death and its aftermath. According to legend, Isis collects the pieces of the slain body of her husband, which she reassembles; through the power of her mourning she is able to bring Osiris back to life. The myth continues to deal with Isis' relationship with her son, Horus. After reaching an appropriate age, Horus attempts to avenge the death of his father by doing battle with Seth, his father's murderer. It is through the protection of Isis that Horus remained safe throughout his early years of life, and it is because of her role as caretaker that Isis became known as the goddess of protection.

Isis eventually became the prototype of the beneficent mother goddess and the goddess of fertility. Beginning in Lower Egypt, the cult of Isis spread throughout the country, and several temples were dedicated to her.

Isis enjoyed a resurgence of popularity in the United States in the 1960s, when countercultural enthusiasms rekindled interest in ancient or alternative religious traditions. She was the subject of a Hollywood television series on Saturday mornings in the early 1970s and has been appropriated by some members of the New Age goddess movement.

Islam

The youngest of the three major monotheistic religions. In Arabic, Islam literally means "submission" and is so named because of its prerequisite belief in total submission to the will of God, or Allâh. Those who hold this belief are Muslims, literally meaning "ones who submit."

Islam was introduced to the world by the Prophet Muhammad (c. 570–632), who in the year 610 claimed to have received his first revelation from Allâh through the angel Jibril (Gabriel), who encouraged him to utter prophecies in the name of his creator. These revelations comprise the Muslim holy text known as the Qur'ân. Many of Islam's characteristics are shared with the other major monotheistic religions, Judaism and Christianity. In fact, Muslims believe that many major figures from these other religions (such as Adam, Noah, Abraham, Moses, and Jesus) are prophets of Islam, each of them transmitting a message and a warning to humanity. According to Muslim teaching, Allâh has sent numerous prophets to earth, each attempting to show man the proper path to Him; however, people had fallen away from these prophets, and so he sent Muhammad. Islamic belief insists that if man resists the teachings of Muhammad, the last of the prophets to be sent, the world will come to an end.

Muhammad, the Seal of the Prophets and Finalizer of the message of his predecessors, brought to the world a reaffir-

mation of these truths as well as a new religious and social system, which by the early eighth century had traveled out of Arabia through Asia, the Middle East, and Africa—a movement that continues today. Islam accorded special status to Judaism and Christianity, other "People of the Book"; in general, non-Muslims were not forcibly converted, in accordance with the Qur'ânic injunction "There is no compulsion in religion" (2:256).

It is incumbent upon every Muslim (once he or she has attained the age of discernment, at puberty) to perform the five primary obligations of the faith, known as the "Five Pillars": *shahadah*, *salat*, *sawm*, *hajj*, and *zakat*. Shahadah, or "bearing witness," embodies the faith and symbolizes the acceptance of Islam through the uttering of the statement "There is no god but God and Muhammad is His messenger." *Salat*, or "prayer," requires the performance of five daily prayers while in a ritually pure state: shortly before dawn, a little after noon, in the late afternoon, at dusk, and in the evening. *Sawm* is the fast, which takes place during the Muslim holy month of Ramadân, when healthy adult Muslims must forsake all food and drink from just before the first light of day until sundown. *Hajj*, the pilgrimage to the sacred temple Ka'bah, at Mecca, is the duty of every able Muslim once in a lifetime. In addition to visiting the Ka'bah, the *hajj* incorporates many other rituals, which are intended to emulate the actions of Abraham. *Zakat* is the obligation to help the community by contributing a small percentage of one's accumulated wealth to those in need. Ranging from individual acts to communal ones, these obligations define Muslims' lives and connect them with the larger community of Islam.

Since its founding, the religion has spread rapidly. There have been many explanations for this, including the fact that the rules of the faith are relatively simple, and that its promises are definitive. Today Muslims are spread over the entire world, with large populations from China to Africa and a growing presence in Europe and the Americas. Conservative estimates put the world's Muslim population at around 800 million.

Itō Noe (1895–1923)

Japanese feminist, anarchist, and writer. Ito ran the publication of the Seitōsha, or Bluestocking Society, in 1915–16. After rebelling against a forced marriage, she ran away from her home village to Tokyo. She married and divorced a second husband, then moved in with the anarchist Osugi Sakae. Her activism on the part of the anarchist and women's movements included the founding of Sekirankai, a socialist women's group. She had seven children and wrote more than eighty articles, not to mention several autobiographical novels (*Zatsuon* [1916; *Noises*]; *Tenki* [1918; *Turning Point*]), and helped translate major works by anarchists Emma Goldman and Peter Kropotkin. Just after the Tokyo earthquake of 1923, she and Sakae were caught in a government purge of left-wing activists and killed by the military police.

Ivan IV (1530–1584)

Russian ruler. Ivan Vasilievich, called Ivan the Terrible, ruled Russia from 1533 to 1584 and is remembered as a cruel and autocratic leader. He was called *Groznyi* by his contemporaries, a word which has been poorly translated as "terrible," but more accurately means "stern," "formidable," and "feared."

Ivan ascended to the throne in 1547 (he was nominally the ruler of Muscovy since 1533, but the country was actually ruled by his mother and the boyars, or high gentry) and was the first Grand Prince of Muscovy to adopt the title of czar, which meant "caesar." Throughout his reign, Ivan attempted to limit the power of the upper aristocracy (the princes and boyars), which had been a source of trouble during the rule of Elena Ilyinskaya, Ivan's mother. He worked to reorganize and consolidate the administration of the Muscovite state, but was forced to establish his own private state, called the Oprichnina, by the persistent opposition of the boyars. Regions outside the Oprichnina were called Zemshchina, and were ruled over by puppet princes appointed by Ivan.

His conflict with the aristocracy continued, and in addition to external battles—war waged with Poland-Lithuania and invasions by the Crimean Tartars, including one devastating attack on Moscow in which several hundred thousand Russians were killed or sold as slaves—Ivan was troubled by aristocratic dissent and plots to take over his throne. Ivan had numerous "traitors" arrested and executed in a final attempt to squelch his enemies. In his final years, Ivan ceded the title of "czar" to a Tartar prince and attempted a posthumous rehabilitation of his victims, circulating lists of their names to monasteries and requesting prayers for their souls. In 1581 Ivan, in a fit of anger, struck and killed his oldest son and heir to the throne, and soon thereafter became seriously ill. He died while playing chess.

Ivan's stormy life has been a popular theme in many literary and dramatic works, as well as the basis of a proposed three-part film, *Ivan Groznii* (Part I, 1945; Part II, 1946; *Ivan the Terrible*), by Russian film director Sergei Eisenstein (1898–1948). (The third part of the film was never completed.)

Izapa

Site of ancient Izapan civilization in the Mayan lowlands. Located near modern Tapachula, Chiapas, on the Pacific coastal plain, Izapa is the site of eighty earth and clay pyramidal mounds. Chronologically and culturally, Izapa is placed between the Olmec (500 B.C.E.–

1150 C.E.) and classic Mayan (250–900 C.E.) civilizations. Izapa predates Mayan culture with respect to several important features: the stela-altar complex, long-lipped deities, hieroglyphic writing, and relief painting that uses narrative scenes from mythology.

The height of Izapan culture was the city of Kaminaljuyu on the western side of Guatemala City. It was Kaminaljuyu, and not Izapa itself, that was so highly influential for the Maya Indians. Two hundred earth and clay mounds are found here, the tombs of deceased lords who were buried with their riches and sacrificed followers.

When Teotihuacán, an influential civilization (300–900 C.E.), was at its most powerful, around 400 C.E., its people built a miniature replica of the old capital at the ancient site of Kaminaljuyu, in the Guatemalan highlands. The assimilated Teotihuacán culture is called Esperanza. The only architectural difference between the two cities is that the temple platforms were made of clay rather than volcanic stone. The Teotihuacáns in Kaminaljuyu were known as Pocheta, a hereditary guild of armed merchants who would eventually seize the lands and goods of people in the Petén-Yucatán peninsula.

izibongo

Zulu praise-poems. *Izibongo*, which means "praises" or "surname," is a traditional Zulu poetry form that glorifies individuals of high rank and status. These praises are merely listed by the individual's peers in the simple praise-song; but as the individual grows in stature and wealth, he or she often employs a professional praise-singer, or *imbongi*, to weave the praises into verses chanted in couplets, triplets, or stanzas.

Many praise-poems are handed down through generations and repeated to different dignitaries, but innovative praise-singers create their own verses. A qualified *imbongi* must memorize and recite the praises of his employer in addition to the praises of all his employer's ancestors and deliver these at the top of his voice and as fast as possible. Praise-poems are usually also accompanied by vigorous gestures and pacing as the singer acts out his or her words.

Praise-singers act as intermediaries between the community and prominent individuals such as chiefs or wealthy landholders; while the poems usually convey praise, *izibongo* can also serve as vessels for popular criticism of prominent citizens.

J

Jackson, Andrew (1767–1845)

Seventh U.S. president. Andrew Jackson was born in the Waxhaw settlement of what was then South Carolina and is now part of North Carolina. His father, an Irish Presbyterian, died before he was born. Receiving little formal education, he began working as an orderly in the Revolutionary Army at the age of thirteen. After the war, he studied in a law office in Salisbury, North Carolina, and was admitted to the bar in 1787. Barely twenty-one years old, he was sent the following year as prosecuting attorney to the western district of North Carolina, an area that would soon become the state of Tennessee. In Nashville, Jackson established a thriving practice based principally upon debt collection, and while there he met and married Mrs. Rachel Robards (unfortunately, before her divorce was final, leading to charges of adultery throughout his political career). For the next several years he worked his way in and out of public-service jobs, winning election to the U.S. House of Representatives in 1796 and the U.S. Senate in 1797 and eventually securing a position as judge on the state supreme court the following year, in 1798.

By 1802 Jackson had been elected major general of the Tennessee Militia, a position he still held when the War of 1812 was declared. Calling for 50,000 volunteers, Jackson led his troops to victory over the Creek Indians, British allies on the western frontier, at the Battle of Horseshoe Bend in Alabama on March 17, 1814. Following the battle, he went south to Florida (without orders from the U.S. government) to rout the Spanish, allies of the British. Jackson's army took Pensacola, Florida, and marched on New Orleans, culminating in a decisive victory over the British in January 1815. News of the victory reached Washington at about the same time as news that the United States and Britain had signed a peace treaty at Ghent about two weeks before the Battle of New Orleans. Although the War of 1812 had officially ended before Jackson's success at the Battle of New Orleans, he became a national hero and was referred to as "Old Hickory," which became a symbol of America's ability to overcome great odds.

Jackson served as provisional governor of Florida from June to December 1821, and his popularity continued to rise. He was reelected to the Senate in 1823 and nominated for U.S. president in 1824. He narrowly won a plurality of the popular and electoral vote but lost in a run-off in the House of Representatives to John Quincy Adams (served 1825–29). He ran again in 1828, this time defeating Adams and taking office in 1829. His victory was a watershed in American politics: he was the first president from west of the Appalachians, and his success was due to a mass movement rather than an established political party. His maverick tactics and broad-based appeal were the essence of what came to be known as "Jacksonian democracy." He was re-elected in 1832, having weathered crises surrounding the National Bank and local patronage. His protégé and Secretary of State, Martin Van Buren, succeeded him to the presidency in 1837, serving until 1841. Although he continued to take an active interest in politics, Jackson retired to The Hermitage, his family estate in Nashville, in 1837, leaving behind a strong Democratic Party in a two-party system and the myth of his being a powerful, successful political outsider.

Jacobs, Harriet (1813–1897)

American writer. Harriet Jacobs is best known for her *Incidents in the Life of a Slave Girl: Written by Herself,* which was published under the pseudonym Linda Brent and edited by Lydia Maria Child. For more than a century the authorship of the book was in question; most scholars assumed that the book had been written by a white author until a 1987 edition of the text established conclusively that the book was a genuine antebellum slave narrative.

Incidents narrates Jacobs's life as a slave and a fugitive in the South, and culminates in her flight north and emancipation in 1853. After her mother's death, the six-year-old Jacobs and her brother lived at the Horniblow estate, in Edenton, North Carolina, where they were relatively well treated. (Jacobs learned to read and spell, both of which were illegal for slaves at the time.) But when her mistress died, the Jacobs children were willed to the Norcom house, where Dr. James Norcom harassed Jacobs with sexual demands and refused to allow her to marry her free black fiancé. Avoiding the attentions of her owner, Jacobs took a white neighbor as a lover and had two children. When Norcom threatened to enslave her family, Jacobs escaped and hid in a crawl space in her grandmother's house for seven years. Her two children were bought and freed by their father and allowed to live with their grandmother. In 1842 Jacobs went to New York, where she secretly wrote *Incidents* with the encouragement of the Quaker abolitionist Amy Post. A few excerpts appeared in the New York *Tribune*, and the book was finally published in full in 1861.

During the Civil War, Jacobs and her daughter helped the relief effort in Alexandria, Virginia, and established the Jacobs Free School for the children of refugees. They continued to work for better conditions for freed people in the South after the war, but escalating violence led them north to Cambridge, Massachusetts, where they ran a boardinghouse for students and faculty at Harvard University. At the end of her life, Jacobs lived in Washington, D.C., working for the rights of freed people. She is buried in Cambridge's Mt. Auburn Cemetery.

Jainism

Indian religious and philosophical tradition. Jainism was founded in the sixth century B.C.E. by Vardhamana, the "Great Hero" of the Jinas ("Conquerors") in what may have been a protest against early sacrificial practices. Jainism, which espouses no concept of an external creator deity, is based on the doctrine of *ahimsa*, or noninjury to all living creatures, and has as its ultimate goal the perfection of human nature. This goal is to be achieved primarily through the practice of ascetic monasticism.

Central to Jain philosophy is the belief in a system that divides the universe into several components. One category (*jiva*) comprises the soul and all living matter; a second category (*ajiva*) encompasses inanimate matter, as well as nonmaterial concepts like time and space. The other basic concept of Jain philosophy is *karma*, which in Jainism is an invisible, yet material, substance that suffuses the *jiva* and imprisons the soul in endless transmigration. The chain of reincarnations can be broken only by contemplation and good deeds that lead, eventually, to the soul's liberation from terrestrial existence and the attainment of perfection.

Since the ultimate goal of the Jain is the evolution and perfection of the individual soul and those of other living creatures, at the crux of the Jain ethical system is *ahimsa*. Jains believe so strongly in this principle that they keep asylums and hospices for old and diseased animals, feeding and caring for them until they die of natural causes, and sometimes wear breathing masks over their mouths and noses so as to avoid the possibility of inhaling any living microbes.

Jainism has existed throughout the centuries, and tradition holds that its beliefs have been revealed anew in successive ages by perfected and enlightened teachers, called *Tirthankaras*. The first of these, Rsabha, is revered by the Jains as the founder of the tradition. The historical founder of the tradition, however, is thought to be Mahavira (born c. 599 B.C.E.), who was an older contemporary of Siddhartha Gautama (Buddha). Around the age of twenty-eight, Mahavira assumed the life of a monastic and applied himself vigorously to the practices of meditation and work that led to eventual enlightenment. He preached Jainism for thirty years and died in 527 B.C.E.

Jain sacred scripture was preserved

orally until about the fourth century B.C.E., during which time a council was convened to systematize the teachings of Mahavira. In its present configuration, the Svetambara canon consists of some forty-five texts: eleven *Angas* ("Parts"), twelve *Upangas* (subsidiary texts), four *Mula-sutras* (basic texts), six *Cheda-sutras* (on discipline), two *Culika-sutras* (appendices), and ten *Prakirnakas* (mixed, assorted texts). Another strand of Jainism, the Digamaras, accords canonical status to the *Karmaprabhrta* ("Chapters on Karma") and the *Kasaya-prabhrta* ("Chapters on Kasayas").

Like Hindus, Jains believe in a number of lesser gods, known as "gods of the house," "intermediaries," "luminaries," and "astral gods," which are revered but are assigned to positions beneath the *Tirthankaras* and other perfected or liberated souls. For Jains, time is as eternal and formless as the world is infinite and uncreated. Space is pervasive and formless and houses both the universe and the nonuniverse, which has no substance within it. Through the center of the universe is the realm in which humans, gods, animals, and devils dwell, directly above which is the upper world, which consists of two parts. Below the upper world is the lower world, divided into seven parts.

Jainism is a tolerant and noncompetitive religious tradition; it has a policy of noncriticism of other traditions and is not doctrinally interested in conversion on a large scale. The majority of Jains are traders and merchants in the Gujarat and Maharashtra states of India.

James, C[yril] L[ionel] R[obert]
(1901–1989)

West Indian writer and social activist. Born in a small town outside Port of Spain, Trinidad, to a schoolteacher and his well-read wife, James was educated at Queen's Royal College, the government secondary school in Port of Spain, graduating in 1918. While in school, he was a great athlete as well as scholar, acquiring a lifelong love of cricket. He became involved with two short-lived journals important for promoting West Indian literature in the early 1930s, *Trinidad* and *The Beacon*, contributing short stories to both. In 1932 he moved to Lancashire, England, to help write the autobiography of an old sports friend, Learie Constantine, published that year as *Cricket and I*; he also took a job as cricket correspondent for the Manchester *Guardian* and the Glasgow *Herald*.

Becoming interested in Marxism in the early 1930s, by 1936 James had helped found the Revolutionary Socialist League and edited its newspaper, *Fight*. Like many of the best minds of his generation, James spent many years as a Trotskyist, becoming a labor activist and a popular speaker, and was a delegate to the Fourth International in 1938. A prolific writer, between 1936 and 1939 he published a novel, *Minty Alley* (1936); a play in which he also acted, *Toussaint L'Ouverture* (1936); a history of the Third International, *World Revolution* (1937); an account of the Haitian revolution, *The Black Jacobins* (1938); the more general *A History of Negro Revolt* (1938); and a translation from the French, Boris Souvarine's *Stalin* (1939).

In 1938 James traveled to the United States for a lecture tour and remained there until he was expelled by the government in 1953 for his Communist beliefs. Decoupled from the traditional orientation of the proletariat, the "black Marxism" that he developed during this time looked to women, minorities, and students for revolutionary force and leadership. He published his ideas about a black-led revolution in *The Revolutionary Answer to the Negro Problem in the United States* (1948), *Notes on Dialectics* (1948), and *State Capitalism and World Revolution* (1950).

Returning to England, he continued writing about politics for periodicals in the United States and Europe and published his analysis of international labor movements, *Facing Reality*, in 1958. He returned to Trinidad in the same year to become secretary of the Federal Labour Party, but left to protest U.S. involvement in the emerging nation. In 1965 he returned briefly to help found an opposition newspaper and the new Workers' and Farmers' Party before leaving once more for Britain. James published a celebrated book on cricket, *Beyond a Boundary*, in 1963, and worked as a correspondent for *Race Today*. Long involved in the Pan-African movement, in 1977 he published *Nkrumah and the Ghana Revolution*, his history of the first African country to win independence; it focused on the role of his old friend, Ghanian leader Kwame Nkrumah (prime minister 1952–60; first president 1960–66). In his last years, he lived in Brixton, a working-class suburb of London, and published several more books.

James, Henry (1843–1916)
American novelist. James, with William Dean Howells, is considered to be one of the founders of American realism. James is renowned for the subtlety of his psychological portraits, particularly of women. Although frequently labeled one of the most "English" of American writers, his obsessive theme was the American character and its opposition to old-world values.

Henry James was born into a well-to-do and intellectually inclined family; his brother William would become an influential philosopher and psychologist, and his sister Alice was a prolific diarist. The James children grew up in the cultural centers of the old and new worlds, residing in such cities as New York, Geneva, Paris, London, Cambridge, Massachusetts, and Newport, Rhode Island. This cosmopolitan childhood gave James a precise education in the manners of Europe and America that he would later put to use in his fiction.

After an abortive attempt at studying law, James resolved to become a writer. He produced some of his best-known works in his early years, including the story *Daisy Miller* (1878) and the novel *The Portrait of a Lady* (1881). Both are studies of American women abroad that explore the nature of fate and free will.

These themes would continue to dominate his work through the end of the century, from the high-society comedy of *The American* (1877) and *The Europeans* (1878) to tales of the supernatural or eerie suspense like *The Turn of the Screw* (1898) and *The Beast in the Jungle* (1903).

The later James's writing became more abstract and verbose, especially in the three novels of the new century: *The Wings of the Dove* (1902), *The Ambassadors* (1903), and *The Golden Bowl* (1904). Although they were viewed in their day as needlessly difficult, they have subsequently been reevaluated by many critics as his finest achievements. These novels of James's "major phase" anticipate the developments of the twentieth-century Anglophone novel with their experiments in point of view and narrative structure and their ever more refined psychological accounts.

Despite his insight into human interactions, James himself was famous for his diffidence. He remained aloof from intense relationships his entire life. James spent most of his adult years in Europe, becoming an English citizen in 1915 to show support for the British role in World War I.

James, William (1842–1910)
American philosopher and psychologist. William James is famous for his major contributions to the philosophy of pragmatism and the psychological movement of functionalism.

As one of two sons of the eccentric writer and thinker Henry James, and brother of the famous novelist Henry James, William James grew up within an extraordinary, intellectually charged family. Due to his father's penchant for traveling and revelation-seeking, James's formal education was varied and sporadic. He began studying art at age eighteen, then turned to the physical sciences at Harvard University's Lawrence Scientific School and then medicine at Harvard Medical School. He devoted much of his free time to reading the philosophical and psychological works of Charles Renouvier, whose Kantian idealism and relativism greatly influenced James both intellectually and personally. When James was struck ill during an extended visit to Germany in 1868, leaving him housebound on his return to the United States, he went through a period of terrible malaise, a near-suicidal breakdown, and was uplifted by Renouvier's writings on free will. This firm belief in free will, which evolved during his depression, contradicted his academic training in strict scientific, as well as metaphysical, determinism.

In 1890 James completed his ten-year effort, *The Principles of Psychology*, which laid the foundations of psychological functionalism and fused the physiological aspects of medical science with psychology to support the notion of free will. After growing tired of strict psychology, James began to focus almost exclusively on questions of religion, the afterlife, the existence of God, and the place of free will among these entities. *The Will to Believe and Other Essays in Popular Philosophy* (1897) and *The Varieties of Religious Experience* (1902) are both results of James's interest in the psychology of religion, and argue that because such a wide range of different religious beliefs exists, an "energy pool" must also exist at that same level of common consciousness through which we may connect when seeking spiritual comfort.

This subjective approach to religion was extended to include human ideas of any kind. James elaborated these ideas

to conclude that the meanings of whatever truths or falsities our minds can grasp are dependent upon, and specifically related to, our personal experiences. James continued to apply this theory, which he named pragmatism, to the social preoccupations of the day, and his conclusions were published in *Pragmatism: A New Name for Old Ways of Thinking* (1907) and *The Meaning of Truth* (1909). *Some Problems in Philosophy* (1911) and *Essays in Radical Empiricism* (1912) appeared posthumously.

James faced much heated criticism for his belief in subjectivity and causality, especially in the non-Anglophone world. But the value of his ideas, particularly the emphasis on the importance and effect of individual action, was recognized by such pioneers of modern physics as Albert Einstein and Niels Bohr, whose theories in quantum physics emphasized the power of relativity.

Japanese-American internment

Roosevelt administration program during World War II. Shortly after the bombing of Pearl Harbor and the U.S. declaration of war against Japan, 112,000 Japanese-Americans were "relocated" to concentration camps on the West Coast. The process of internment began with President Franklin Delano Roosevelt's (served 1933–45) order of February 19, 1942, which allowed military authorities to designate certain areas "wartime zones," from which any or all people might be excluded. This order was followed by several more that restricted Japanese-American movement on the West Coast. Finally, all Japanese-Americans were ordered to leave their homes and enter one of ten detention centers, or concentration camps. More than 70,000 of those arrested were Nisei, first-generation Japanese-Americans who had been born in the United States and were therefore American citizens.

The outrageousness of the maneuver

was underlined by the fact that the FBI, at the time of the internment, had already arrested those Japanese-Americans it had determined were security risks. Therefore, the action was a fairly straightforward instance of pandering to hysteria and racism. Anti-Japanese sentiment had been fairly high even before the bombing of Pearl Harbor in 1941; afterward, it exploded. The most shocking aspect of the case, some argue, was that the decision to intern a whole segment of the population of the United States was upheld repeatedly when challenged in the courts, the Supreme Court refusing to rescind the order. Those Japanese-Americans held in the camps had few opportunities after their release, and were forced to resettle in new areas. After years of arguing in the courts, some 26,000 claimants were reimbursed in 1982 for about one-third of their material losses.

Japanese imperial family

The present Japanese emperor, Akihito, succeeded his father, Hirohito (emperor 1926–89), upon the latter's death in January 1989. The traditional period of mourning required that Akihito not be officially enthroned until November 22, 1990, at which time a ritual of isolation and meditation representing his spiritual transformation into the acknowledged emperor, 125th of his line, took place.

The emperor is largely irrelevant to the actual governing of Japan, having been stripped of his official powers by the United States after World War II. The constitution written for Japan by the United States at that time makes the emperor "a symbol of the state and of the unity of the people," a figurehead of Japanese cultural identity, representing a certain stability of tradition and culture. In actuality, however, the *tennō,* or "heavenly sovereign," has been a figurehead through most of Japanese history, manipulated by shoguns, or warlords, and other leaders who used his endorse-

ment to legitimate their powers. It was only after the Meiji Restoration in 1868 that the emperor became "sacred and inviolable" as the head of the Japanese state.

In keeping with his identifying role for the Japanese cultural psyche, the emperor is considered the chief priest of Shinto, the national religion, conducting some twenty major ceremonies each year. He lives amid a sprawling retinue termed the Imperial Household Agency, with a staff numbering more than 1,100, all zealous in their attentions to the details of imperial family life, as well as in their defense of the family's privacy.

Akihito is known for his efforts to change the role of the emperor, bringing it out of its sanctified removal from everyday Japan. In his own words, "I find it natural that the imperial family should not exist at a distance from the people."

Jarra, Victor (1934–1973)

Chilean singer of revolutionary songs. During the Popular Unity government of President Salvador Allende in Chile (1970–73), Victor Jarra and his songs became artistic expressions of the class struggle. He wrote and sang about people's fights for land, for socialism, and against exploitation. A member of the Chilean Communist Party, Jarra became famous in Chile and throughout the world for his songs of struggle and for his political commitment to social change. Immediately after the coup of September 11, 1973, when General Augusto Pinochet led the armed forces to overthrow the Allende government, Victor Jarra was captured by Pinochet forces, tortured, and killed by the Chilean military. Throughout Latin America he and his songs remain symbols of the struggle for socialism.

Jātakas

Buddhist story cycle. The *Jātakas,* which date from the fourth century B.C.E., are the most popular text in Pali literature, the sacred literature of Buddhism. A collection of fables describing the past lives of Buddha, the *Jātakas* detail how in his former existences Buddha reached the ten *paramitas*, or perfections, which are prerequisites for Supreme Enlightenment.

The *Jātakas* figure prominently in Pali literary history as well as Buddhist religious tradition. Pali, a vernacular version of classical Sanskrit, was a wholly oral language until shortly after Buddha's death in 483 B.C.E., when his disciples began recording and systematizing Buddha's dialogues, aphorisms, and social thought. The resulting Buddhist canon is divided into three "baskets." The word, which refers to the baskets used by construction workers to transport building materials, serves as a metaphor for the maintenance of Buddhist beliefs and practices.

jazz

American musical idiom. Developed largely from ragtime and blues and characterized by propulsive syncopated rhythms, polyphonic ensemble playing, varying degrees of improvisation, and often deliberate distortions of pitch and timbre, jazz has its roots in New Orleans, Louisiana. Slaves brought African rhythms and folk songs to the Americas, which fused with European melodies and instrumentation to form the blues, then ragtime, and eventually jazz.

Jazz's most immediate ancestor is probably African-American ragtime, a piano-driven musical style that combined the nineteenth-century piano music of Europe (classic minuets, waltzes, polkas, and marches) with an African rhythmic conception. Ragtime was popularized throughout the United States from about 1895 to 1910 by composers like Scott Joplin, one of the era's most successful musical innovators, who published a number of "rags" that were played by traveling musicians in bars and saloons across the country. Joplin's "Maple Leaf Rag" of 1899 is perhaps his most popular work.

Early jazz was born in the 1890s, when innovative musicians like New Orleans cornetist Charles "Buddy" Bolden began to experiment with popular rags by departing from the written score and adding texture and dynamic spontaneity to musical pieces through improvisation. Improvisation is a central aspect of all African-influenced music, and it quickly became the cornerstone of the jazz style.

Often referred to as the only originally American art form, jazz quickly spread beyond New Orleans, propelled to cities like Chicago, New York, and Los Angeles by a number of pioneering performers. Cornetists Joseph "King" Oliver and Louis Armstrong took improvisation to new heights in the 1920s, while Edward "Duke" Ellington explored and perfected the art of jazz composition and arrangement in the famous jazz ballrooms of Harlem. In the 1930s bandleaders like William "Count" Basie and Benny Goodman ushered in the big-band sound of "swing," and the 1940s saw the emergence of the intricate and explosive jazz style called "bebop," stewarded by such innovators as trumpeter John "Dizzy" Gillespie, alto saxophonist Charlie "Bird" Parker, and pianist Thelonious Monk. The 1950s yielded the more mellow tones of "cool jazz" developed by trumpeter Miles Davis, and the 1960s saw both the spiritual, jarring improvisations of tenor saxophonist John Coltrane and the advent of "free" jazz, championed by saxophonist Ornette Coleman, which offered extreme improvisation and a spirit of freewheeling musical anarchy. In the 1970s and 1980s jazz was fused with rock and funk by performers like Miles Davis and pianist Herbie Hancock to yield new hybrids. Gaining tremendous popularity overseas, jazz spawned hundreds of new groups and styles and has remained an enduring and important aspect of American musical culture.

Jefferson, Thomas (1743–1826)

Third U.S. president. Jefferson was born in Shadwell, Virginia; his father was a successful planter and surveyor, and his mother was from a prominent Virginia family. Jefferson's father died when Jefferson was fourteen, leaving him a large farm and many slaves. Educated in small private schools and at the College of William and Mary (though he left after two years to study law), he practiced law thereafter until 1774, when the courts were closed by the war for independence, the American Revolution. By 1772 he had made a "successful" marriage to the wealthy Martha Wayles Skelton, and had begun building his famous home, Monticello. He became a member of the colonial House of Burgesses. His pamphlet A Summary View of the Rights of British America (1774), written for the First Virginia Convention, offered a philosophical argument for the natural rights of American subjects of the British Crown, denying parliamentary authority over the colony while maintaining fealty to the king. Jefferson was appointed to the Second Continental Congress in 1775 and was chosen the following year to draft the Declaration of Independence. Regarded as a classic of literary style as well as a seminal political document, it elaborated a radical democratic philosophy and renounced the sovereignty of the British king over American patriots. It was adopted on July 4, 1776, after only minor revisions. Later that same year, Jefferson moved to the Virginia legislature, where he helped to abolish entail and primogeniture and established the separation of Church and State with his Statute for Religious Freedom. His wife died in 1782, leading to a brief period of withdrawal into private life during which he wrote Notes on the State of Virginia (1785), a "natural history" of the

state and much of North America that established his reputation as an amateur scientist. As a member of the Continental Congress once again in 1783, he advocated decimal coinage and drafted an influential proposal for the annexation of the Northwest Territory.

From 1784 to 1789 Jefferson served in France, first as a negotiator of commercial treaties and then as Benjamin Franklin's successor as U.S. minister. He witnessed the beginnings of the French Revolution with sympathy for the republicans, but as the first Secretary of State under George Washington from 1790 to 1793, he advocated neutrality as the ensuing wars in Europe commenced. After another interlude in private life, Jefferson ran second to the Federalist John Adams in the 1796 presidential election, thereby becoming the vice president according to contemporary law. Opposed to the Federalist attempts to suppress free speech and political opposition with the Alien and Sedition Acts, Jefferson ran against Adams again in 1800, defeating him; but due to the prevailing electoral system, he fell into an unintentional tie with his own running mate, Aaron Burr. Jefferson's victory was announced only after a bitter struggle in the House of Representatives, with many Federalists supporting Burr. After what is sometimes called the "revolution of 1800," his first term was considered to be a success during a period of relative calm, qualified mainly by his rebuke by the Supreme Court for a failed attempt to revoke Adams's lame-duck court appointments. The Louisiana Purchase of 1803, which nearly doubled the size of the United States, is regarded as one of his greatest achievements; he also organized the Lewis and Clark expedition. He was reelected U.S. president in 1804. During his second, less successful term, he attempted to try Aaron Burr for treason, for which Burr was acquitted; Jefferson was accused of politically motivated persecution. Internationally, his attempt to steer clear of British and French hostilities by cutting off exports to both countries proved economically disastrous for the United States, and was not enough to forestall the conflicts that would erupt in the War of 1812.

Succeeded in the presidency by his protégé James Madison (served 1809–17), Jefferson retired to Monticello in 1809 to pursue his interests in science, agriculture, classical literature, and mechanical inventions. His collection of books, which he sold to the government after the burning of Washington in the War of 1812, became the basis for the Library of Congress. He founded the University of Virginia in 1819 and served as its first rector. In his last years, he was reduced to near bankruptcy, and a public lottery was held for his relief. He died on July 4, 1826, the fiftieth anniversary of the Declaration of Independence. His complete writings are projected to fill an edition of sixty volumes.

Jenner, Edward (1749–1823)

English physician. Jenner is credited as the founder of the science of immunology for his discovery of the smallpox vaccine. An epidemic of smallpox broke out during Jenner's lifetime, killing as many as one in three, and leaving survivors pockmarked and disfigured, their skin scarred. It was known that those who suffered a mild case of the disease were immune to the disease after recovery, but there was no way to predict whether the disease would manifest itself in a mild or severe case. Many, including the French scholar Diderot, advocated actively seeking out smallpox from those who had mild cases, in hopes that the disease could be kept at a low level. This method often failed spectacularly.

The idea of inoculation had been introduced to England from Turkey at the beginning of the eighteenth century. In 1775 Jenner became intrigued by the idea, and was inspired by a Gloucestershire old wives' tale which held that those who caught cowpox, a mild cattle disease resembling smallpox, were immune to smallpox. To test this theory, Jenner located a milkmaid, Sarah Nelmes, who had an active case of cowpox. He took fluid from a blister on her hand and injected it into a young boy, James Phipps, who immediately developed cowpox. Upon his recovery, Jenner injected the boy with smallpox, and remarkably, the boy was not affected. It was a risky experiment—had Phipps become ill, Jenner would have been arrested as a criminal, but as he did not, Jenner was celebrated as a hero. Repeating the experiment two years later with the same results, Jenner published his findings, coining the word "vaccination" (from the Latin for cowpox, *vaccina*) in his study, a term and method which would become widespread as a result of the work done by French chemist Louis Pasteur (1822–1895). The practice of vaccination gained acceptance quickly and reduced the deaths attributed to smallpox by two thirds. Many countries were so grateful for this development that in parts of Germany, for example, Jenner's birthday was celebrated as a holiday. Though Jenner was not as warmly honored by the scientific establishment in his own country for his refusal to be tested in the classic theories of the Greek physicians Hippocrates (460–377 B.C.E.) and Galen (129–199), which the English medical world thought essential, he did have the satisfaction of ending the threat of a dreaded disease.

Jesus (c. 4 B.C.E.–28 C.E.)

Founder of Christianity. One of the major religious figures of the world, Jesus' message and works, as transcribed in the New Testament, are the foundation of Christianity. All information regarding Jesus stems from the four Gospels' accounts of his followers, who saw him as the Messiah whose arrival was predicted in the Hebrew Scriptures. As the personification of Christian ideals, Jesus is generally recognized as both a historical person and an object of worship.

Although Jesus was the legal son of Joseph, a Jewish Nazarene carpenter, Gospel tradition states that he was miraculously conceived by his virgin mother, Mary, after a visitation by an angel, and that the newborn was heralded as the son of God. Little is known of the early life of Jesus, although he was apparently born in Bethlehem and later lived in Nazareth, where he took up his father's craft. The bulk of the Gospels focus on Jesus' public ministry, although there are a few, brief depictions of his youth. One account describes the young Jesus preaching on the temple steps to a group of elders, while another recalls his transforming water into wine at a wedding.

Baptized by John the Baptist, Jesus traveled with twelve disciples throughout the countryside, preaching divine love and forgiveness. A mainstay of his message was the power of faith and hope for a better life, and accordingly he was extremely popular with the downtrodden and common people. Besides his use of parables and the message that all had a place in God's kingdom, Jesus purportedly had strong healing powers, and there are many Gospel accounts of the miracles he performed.

Palestine was ruled by the Romans in Jesus' lifetime, and his growing popularity alarmed both Roman and Jewish leaders, who perceived Jesus as a potential political and religious rebel leader. His verbal attacks on hypocrisy and his call for repentance further provoked those who wished to bring his ministry to an end. Upon arriving in Jerusalem for Passover and after celebrating the Last Supper with his disciples, Jesus was betrayed to Roman authorities by one of his apostles, Judas Iscariot. He was crucified as a political rebel by Pontius Pilate and laid in the tomb of Joseph of Arimathea. Christianity holds that Jesus rose from this tomb and continued preaching until his ascension into Heaven.

Jewett, [Theodora] Sarah Orne (1849–1909)

American novelist and short-story writer. One of the more prominent regionalist or "local color" writers, Jewett is known for her depictions of life in small-town Maine.

Jewett was born in South Berwick, Maine, the town she considered home her entire life. In poor health and unable to attend school, she was mostly educated privately, though she did graduate from Berwick Academy in 1865. At an early age, Jewett began to write out of a desire to capture the vanishing customs of rural life; her story "Jenny Garrow's Lovers" was published pseudonymously in 1868, when she was only nineteen. By her twenties, Jewett had already received considerable recognition for such stories as "The Shore House" (1873), which appeared in *Atlantic* magazine. This initial success brought Jewett into contact with the leading lights of Boston literary society; after her father died in 1878, Jewett spent part of each year in Massachusetts or traveling.

In books like *Deephaven* (1877), Jewett demonstrated a remarkable ability to sketch provincial life with empathy while avoiding sentimentality. *The Country Doctor* (1884) is a portrait of Jewett's father, described by her as "the best and wisest man I ever knew." *The Country of the Pointed Firs* (1896), considered her masterpiece, focuses on the elderly residents of Dunnett Landing, a fictional seaside Maine town.

In 1901, Jewett became the first woman to be awarded an honorary degree by Bowdoin College. Thrown from a horse-drawn carriage and immobilized by a spinal injury, she wrote little after 1902.

Jibrân, [Jibrân] Kahlîl (1883–1931)

Lebanese poet. This Romantic poet is often considered the first great Arab Romantic. Jibrân (also spelled Kahlil

Gibran) was born in Lebanon and immigrated to the United States with his family in 1895. He entered college in Beirut at the age of fourteen and later studied art with Rodin, the great sculptor, in Paris. Known for his daring but elegant phraseology and slightly mystical treatment of the world, Jibrân saw himself as a thoroughly Arab writer who could serve as a cultural messenger to the West. Once in America, he was heavily influenced by the writings of the American Transcendentalists, especially Ralph Waldo Emerson (1803–1882), Henry Wadsworth Longfellow (1807–1882), John Greenleaf Whittier (1807–1892), and Walt Whitman (1819–1892).

Jibrân's earliest works were primarily prose poems and plays written in Arabic, and were widely known throughout the Arab world; he also wrote novels. However, Jibrân is probably best known for his prose poems *The Prophet* (1923), which has been translated into thirteen languages, and *The Garden of the Prophet* (1934).

Jing Hua Yuan

Chinese classical novel. *Jing hua yuan*, or *Flowers in the Mirror*, is a great classic of Chinese literature. Li Ruzhen (1763–1830) was a learned scholar based in what is now Beijing. He studied with the great scholar Lin Tingzhan, devoting himself to the classics, linguistics, and phonology, as well as astrology and astronomy, calligraphy and fortune-telling, music and chess playing. *Flowers in the Mirror*, his major work, has been compared to English satirist Jonathan Swift's (1667–1745) *Gulliver's Travels* (1726). Based mainly on ancient Chinese mythology, the book satirizes Chinese society and the "stupidity" of humanity in the course of the character Tang Ao's travels to strange lands.

Though the first part of the novel documents the strange affairs of an upstart empress, the Gulliverian travel to strange lands is considered to be the most intriguing aspect of the novel. Hav-

ing passed the examination to enter the civil service, Tang Ao is nevertheless disappointed when refused a post after a government official slanders him, accusing him of associating with a rebel. He decides to quit the world and its affairs. His wife's younger brother, Lin Zhiyang, offers Tang Ao the use of a seaworthy ship, and the pair embark on an ocean voyage, accompanied by an old sailor named Ninth Uncle Duo. The three of them visit many countries, each governed by a single principle. In the land of gentleness, everyone they encounter displays the most proper conduct. In the country of big men, people walk on clouds whose color indicates whether that person is good or evil. Just as strange is the country without reproduction, where people come back to life 120 years after their death. At the end of the journey, Tang Ao consumes an "eternal grass" and does not return home.

Jinnah, Muhammad Ali (1876–1948)

Founder and first governor-general of Pakistan. Also known as Qa'id-E A'zam, Jinnah was born in Karachi, India (now Pakistan), the first of seven children. He studied law in England, gaining a degree at the age of nineteen, and worked on the successful election campaign of Dadbhai Naoroji, the first Indian ever to sit in the British House of Commons. In 1896 Jinnah returned to India, starting a legal practice in Bombay. After ten years in private practice Jinnah made his entrance into politics in 1906, participating in the Calcutta session of the Indian National Congress. Jinnah's election to the Imperial Legislative Council four years later marked the beginning of his long career in parliamentary politics. He was inspired by the Maratha leader and nationalist Gopal Krishna Gokhale, with whom he worked to forge a lasting Hindu-Muslim unity. During this time Jinnah fought primarily against British rule, still believing that Muslim interests were best served by the cause of Indian nationalism. He kept aloof from the more separatist All-India Muslim League, founded in 1906.

Jinnah was chief organizer and first president of the Bombay branch of the Indian Home Rule League. He soon left the league, however, as it became increasingly aligned with the politics of Mohandas K. Gandhi (1869–1948), whose Non-Cooperation Movement Jinnah opposed. Jinnah turned to the Muslim League, though he clung to the notion that Hindu-Muslim unity and constitutional reform were the appropriate channels for Muslim ambition. As Gandhi's Non-Cooperation Movement led to antagonism between Hindus and Muslims, the Muslim League grew in popularity, and Jinnah sought to promote cooperation between the various Indian organizations to work for the national good. He found himself in an increasingly difficult position: Muslim separatists found him too pro-Hindu and nationalist, while Hindus considered him a crafty Muslim militant. He left the country for London in 1930, to gain a respite from Indian politics, but returned in 1935 at the urging of the Muslim League. Jinnah eventually assumed leadership of the league and dedicated himself to the cause of Muslim independence. The Lahore Resolution of 1940 codified his change of heart, demanding the creation of a separate Muslim nation. The stalemate at the Gandhi-Jinnah talks in 1944 further made evident the move toward a split. Despite opposition from such formidable opponents as Gandhi, Prime Minister Jawaharlal Nehru (served 1947–64), and the British government, Pakistan became a reality in 1947. Jinnah served as president of the league during the entire formative period, from 1937 to 1947.

Jinnah had been suffering from tuberculosis for several years, a fact he kept hidden throughout the negotiations for Pakistan. He served as the first governor-general of Pakistan, though he died soon after assuming power.

Jin Ping Mei

The first realistic Chinese novel. The author of *Jin ping mei*, published in 1610, remains unknown, although most literary historians attribute it to a man called Xiao Xiaosheng.

Although set in the early twelfth century, *Jing ping mei*, or *The Golden Lotus*, depicts Chinese society of the late sixteenth century, when the Ming dynasty (1368–1644) was near collapse. The main character, Ximen Qing, represents the decadent leisure class. He spends his days and nights seeking sexual pleasure and accumulating money. In order to capture Pan Jinlian (Golden Lotus), a beautiful, voluptuous, and shrewd woman, he plots with her to murder her husband. The book describes how with money Ximen manages to buy six wives and escape punishment for his crimes through bribery. Ultimately, Ximen dies an untimely death as a result of his debauchery.

The most striking characteristic of the book is its explicit and rather detailed description of sexuality, particularly in a number of highly erotic passages. It was a highly controversial book upon publication. While its admirers have hailed it as a masterpiece of the Ming novel, an honest and sensitive presentation of aspects of everyday life in imperial China, its critics have attacked its author as sex-obsessed, and the book as corrupt. Nevertheless, it enjoyed popularity for about a century before being officially banned for more than two centuries.

John Paul II, Pope (1920–)

Pope and author. The first non-Italian pope since Adrian VI of Utrecht in 1523, John Paul II (born Karol Wojtyła) is the first Polish pope. His wide knowledge of modern languages (Polish, Italian, English, French, German, Spanish, and Portuguese) have enabled him to represent the Catholic Church in a world grown accustomed to international travel and contact.

Born in Wadowice in 1920 to working-class parents, Wojtyła enrolled in Jagiellon University in Kraków in 1938 to study poetry and drama. During the German occupation of Poland, he worked in a chemical factory, joined the clandestine Rhapsodic Theater, and enrolled in an "underground" seminary in the palace of the archbishop of Kraków. He was ordained in 1946, and sent to study theology at the Angelicum University in Rome. After receiving his doctorate, he returned to Kraków and earned another. In 1954 he joined the faculty at the Catholic University of Lublin, where he taught Christian ethics and moral theology. He was appointed auxiliary bishop of Kraków in 1958 and archbishop in 1964. In 1967 Pope Paul VI made him a cardinal.

After the thirty-four-day reign of John Paul I, Karol Wojtyła was elected on October 21, 1978. He chose the name John Paul II to indicate his intention to continue the programs of his three predecessors. Many of these programs were discussed at the Second Vatican Council (1962–65), where the Church focused on temporal issues such as peace, poverty, human dignity and freedom, and social justice. John Paul II has been a vocal critic, however, of left-wing Catholic activists in the Third World, especially in Latin America. In the face of liberation theologists and Jesuits, John Paul II has made a point of encouraging traditionalist, semiauthoritarian factions within the Church, including Opus Dei. He is the most widely traveled pope; his visits have included extensive trips through Latin America and the Caribbean, the United States and Canada, Europe, Africa, and the Far East.

On May 13, 1981, John Paul II was shot and wounded in St. Peter's Square by Mehmet Ali Agca, a Turkish national. Although three Bulgarians were accused of assisting Agca, they were eventually acquitted, and the reason for the assassination attempt has never been established. The most common belief is that it was a result of John Paul II's outspoken support for the Roman Catholic Church and the Polish trade union Solidarity. Since the fall of the Communist regime in Poland, the Catholic Church has emerged as the major power broker in Polish politics.

Between 1950 and 1966, under the pseudonym Andrzej Jawien, John Paul II published a play, *Przed sklepem jubilers* (1960; *The Jeweler's Shop*), and several volumes of poetry. Other writings include *Milosc i odpowiedzialnosc* (1979; *Love and Responsibility*); *Easter Vigil and Other Poems* (1979); *The Acting Person* (1979); *You Are My Favorites* (1980); and *Crossing the Threshold of Hope* (1994).

Johnson, James Weldon (1871–1938)

American writer, lyricist, and diplomat. The first black attorney in Florida, James Weldon Johnson became a writer and lyricist for music written by his brother, composer J. Rosamond Johnson. One of their collaborative efforts, "Lift Every Voice and Sing" (1900), was so popular that it became known as the "Negro National Anthem."

By 1902 the Johnson brothers had settled in New York City to begin a successful career in songwriting; among their hit songs were "Nobody's Lookin' but the Owl and the Moon" (in the musical *Sleeping Beauty and the Beast*, 1901), "Under the Bamboo Tree" (in *Sally in Our Alley*, 1902), and "The Congo Love Song" (in *Nancy Brown*, 1903). In 1907 their own all-black musical, *The Shoo-fly Regiment*, appeared on Broadway.

In 1906 James Weldon Johnson was appointed as a diplomat to Venezuela, and later served in Nicaragua. Although this marked the end of his career as a lyricist, he continued to write, publishing *The Autobiography of an Ex-Colored Man* anonymously in 1912, which described the ragtime era in New York. In 1915 his English translation of Enrique Granados's opera *Goyescas* was used in the Metropolitan Opera's world premiere performance. Johnson was specifically concerned with the preservation of black American culture. In 1925–26 he issued two volumes of Negro spirituals with his brother, and published a history of black theater and musicals in New York, *Black Manhattan*, in 1930.

Johnson, Samuel (1709–1784)

English critic, translator, and lexicographer. The son of a bookseller, Johnson was educated at home in his father's shop. There he read voraciously, although at school he was known for his tendency to procrastinate. His studies at Oxford were cut short by his family's lack of funds, and after teaching and translating for a few years, Johnson married a widow twice his age, using her dowry to open a school in Litchfield.

At Litchfield, he became friendly with a student who would become important to his later career as a celebrated man of letters. That student, David Garrick, accompanied him to London in 1737. Garrick's career as an actor took off, while Johnson began more modestly, writing regularly for *The Gentleman's Magazine*. In these early years, he finished writing his tragedy *Irene*, and in 1738 published his first important poem, "London." In 1750 he began publishing *The Rambler*, a twice-weekly journal in which he acted on his belief that all writing should be morally instructive. His A *Dictionary of the English Language*, published in two volumes in 1755, was acclaimed for its subtlety and erudition.

Though the *Dictionary* brought Johnson an honorary degree from Oxford and the attention of the king, it did not reward him financially, and in 1756 he proposed a new edition of Shakespeare's plays as a moneymaking venture. He also composed *Rasselas* (1759), a sketch of one man's unsuccessful search for happiness; the book earned him an international following.

In 1763 Johnson began his friendship with James Boswell, a Scottish lawyer who would later produce *The Life of Samuel Johnson* (1791), a book which played the major role in securing Johnson's reputation as a critic and conversationalist. His circle at the time included the painter Joshua Reynolds, the writer Oliver Goldsmith, and the politician and philosopher Edmund Burke, along with Boswell and Garrick. In 1765 Johnson's eight-volume edition of Shakespeare was finally completed; in his commentaries, which accompanied the plays, he argued that Shakespeare's dramas lacked moral purpose, that they were luxurious creations made solely for pleasure. His *The Lives of the Most Eminent English Poets* (1777) included biting criticism of Milton and attacks on the frivolous obscurity of the Metaphysical poets. Johnson's belief in a life with a strong ethical base won him modern supporters both conservative and liberal: while he favored Christian morality and a strong centralized government, he opposed war, censorship, colonialism, poverty, and the campaigns launched against indigenous populations in Africa and North and South America.

Jones, LeRoi, *see* Baraka, Amiri

Joseph, Chief, *see* Hinmaton-Yalaktit

Joyce, James [Augustine Aloysius] (1882–1941)

Irish writer. Born in Dublin, Joyce moved with his family to Bray when he was five years old. Joyce's father was a tax collector pensioned off by the government at an early age and subsequently unable to provide adequately for his family. Educated by Jesuits at Clongowes Wood and Belvedere College, Joyce was admitted to University College, Dublin, in 1898. He continued the passion for writing he developed while at Belvedere, publishing an essay, "Ibsen's New Drama," in the *Fortnightly Review* in 1900.

In 1902 Joyce graduated and moved to

Paris, intending to study medicine and support himself by teaching English. The experience was disastrous, and he had to borrow fare back to Dublin in 1903 when his mother was dying. In 1904 he met Nora Barnacle, who would remain with him and bear their two children; they were finally married in 1931, to protect the rights of their children. He and Nora moved to Trieste in 1904, beginning what would become a lifetime of precarious wandering throughout Europe; Joyce returned to Ireland only twice thereafter.

Ireland never left his writing, however, and his first book of short stories was entitled *Dubliners* (1914). American expatriate poet Ezra Pound (1885–1972) was impressed by the stories and asked to see the autobiographical novel that Joyce had been slowly composing. Pound arranged for it to be published in the *Egoist,* a magazine edited by American poet T. S. Eliot (1888–1965) and Harriet Weaver. *A Portrait of the Artist as a Young Man* appeared in serial form from February 1914 to September 1915, and was published as a book in 1916.

Living in Zurich during the First World War, Joyce wrote *Ulysses*. The *Little Review* in New York accepted the work for serial publication, but publication was stopped in the middle of the fourteenth episode when the editors were prosecuted for publishing obscenity. The complete novel was published in England in 1922 and banned in the United States until 1933. Customs officials in New York had until then burned every copy they seized, which only increased the book's popularity. In 1923 Joyce began work on *Finnegans Wake,* which was published in twelve installments between 1928 and 1937 as *Work in Progress*.

Joyce published two collections of poems: *Chamber Music* (1907) and *Pomes Penyeach* (1927). His widest fame rests on his novel *Ulysses,* which details one day in the life of various characters in Dublin. Joyce was a perfectionist, constantly revising and polishing his work. Like Eliot's and Pound's, his writing is full of references and allusions to everything imaginable. Joyce also experimented with language, not only inventing words but using obscure meanings and references hidden in the etymologies of words. His work employed a technique known as "stream of consciousness," a flowing free-association of words. His last novel, *Finnegans Wake,* is considered to be the most challenging.

Joyce's later years were complicated by heavy drinking and increasing blindness. He died in 1941, after an operation for a duodenal ulcer.

József, Attila (1905–1937)

Hungarian poet, essayist, and translator. József was born on April 11, 1905, and his birthday is celebrated annually as Hungary's national Day of Poetry. One of three children, József came from a working-class family; his father was a factory worker and his mother a domestic worker. When József was three years old, his father abandoned the family, forcing József and his siblings into the care of foster parents in the countryside, where they stayed for four years until their mother could afford to bring them to live with her in Budapest. József's reunion with his mother was short-lived, however: she died soon after. These childhood experiences, especially the loss of his mother, played an important role in József's later writing, especially after he discovered the works of the Viennese intellectual Sigmund Freud and applied some of his ideas about psychoanalysis to his own work.

József's exceptional talent was recognized early and his first volume of verse, *A szépség koldusa* (*The Beggar of Beauty*), was published in 1922, when he was only seventeen years old. In this early phase of his poetic development, József experimented with various verse forms and styles, demonstrating his technical mastery and a mature poetic approach to form and theme with the 1925 publication of *A kozmosz éneke* (*The Song of Kozmos*). As he gained literary fame and became interested in leftist politics, József's poetry brought him censure as well as praise; in 1925 he was expelled from the University of Szeged, where he had enrolled to study French and Hungarian, because a poem, "Tisza szivvel" ("With a Pure Heart"), was deemed scandalous in its anarchistic content. He then studied in Vienna and Paris for one year, and during this time he translated some of his own poetry into German and French.

In the 1930s József tended to focus on meditative poems in which he explored philosophical concerns through the use of poetic images. Poems from this phase of his career include "Külvárosi éj" (1932; "Night in the Outskirts"), "Teji ejzaka" (1933; "Winter Nights"), "Elegia" (1933; "Elegy"), "Oda" (1933; "Ode"), and "Eszmélet" (1934; "Consciousness"). During this period József began to play an even greater role in Hungarian intellectual and political life through his poems and through his cultural journal, *Szép Szó* ("Beautiful Word"), which he founded in 1936 and titled as a testament to his belief in the transforming power of poetic language. By this time he had already severed his connections with the illegal Communist Party but continued his intellectual work in leftist politics and criticism. His political beliefs were often at the forefront of his poetry, which was preoccupied with the social and metaphysical problems of human existence but nonetheless avoided a propagandistic tone. In 1937's "Flora," for example, he used the form of a love poem and images of spring and blooming to express his craving for a better world. And his last poem, "Ime, hat megleltem hazamat" (1937; "At last I have found my homeland"), was a despairing lament of his loss of hope that ominously preceded his suicide in 1937.

Judah ha-Levi (c. 1075–1141)

Jewish poet and philosopher. Ha-Levi was born Yehuda Ben Shemuel ha-Levi into the flourishing medieval Sephardic Jewish culture of Spain, in the days when it was still controlled by the Islamic empire. This was the era of El Cid and the Reconquista (the reconquering of Muslim-held territories by Christian kings), very important events in the history of Spain and in terms of Judah ha-Levi's life and work. While still quite young, he moved to Andalusia in southern Spain, spending several happy years in Grenada with the active Hebrew literary community there. He left Andalusia in 1090, when fundamentalist Muslim Berbers invaded from North Africa, beginning a lifetime of wanderings that would eventually lead him across much of Spain and into the Middle East.

In his travels, ha-Levi found Spanish Jews caught in the crossfire between Islam and Christianity. Residing for a time in Toledo, where he supported himself as a physician, he came to believe that at least in Castille, Jews would be treated tolerably well. When an important Jewish official was murdered by Christian Spaniards on his way back from a state trip, ha-Levi wrote a poetic elegy for the dead man in which he denounced the "Daughter of Edom" (Christianity) for the crime, eventually choosing to return to a part of Spain still under Muslim control. Despite the comfortable life he was able to make in Cordoba, ha-Levi was unfulfilled and dreamed of spiritual renewal. He wrote his most famous poem, the "Zionide" or "Ode to Zion," at this time. In both his poetic and philosophical-religious texts, especially the *Book of the Khazar*, ha-Levi expressed his profound desire to return to the Jewish homeland. With the help of merchant friends who had extensive foreign contacts, he set out from Spain on his pilgrimage in 1140. He died in Egypt in 1141, just short of the Holy Land. In the centuries after his death, a legend built up around ha-Levi and the poet himself became the subject of verse. Heinrich Heine commemorated him in his 1851 masterpiece, the *Romanzero*, while Micah-Joseph Lebensohn published *Rabbi Yehudah ha-Levi* in 1869.

Judaism

The first of the major monotheistic religions of the world. Central to Jewish thought is the belief in one God and the special relation between God and the Jewish people. Jewish tradition holds that God entered into a sacred covenant with Abraham, the progenitor of the Jews, in the mid twentieth century B.C.E. The terms of the agreement were expanded during the thirteenth century B.C.E., when the prophet Moses led the Jews out of enslavement in Egypt and into Canaan.

It was during this exilic period that the official religious texts of Judaism began to be compiled from earlier texts and oral traditions, forming the Pentateuch, "The Five Books of Moses," or the Torah; nineteen more books were eventually added, and the compilation of them all resulted in what became known as the Hebrew Scriptures (Old Testament). Crucial to the covenant is the eventual coming of a messiah, who it is believed will bring peace and justice to the earth. Attributed to the prophet Moses, the Pentateuch, together with the later books, became the foundation for Jewish thought, which over the centuries has divided itself into three main branches: Orthodox, Conservative, and Reform.

Orthodox Judaism is the branch of Judaism that most closely conforms to traditional theology and practice. Orthodox Jews, though they acknowledge adherents of Reform and Conservative as coreligionists, steadfastly renounce the alterations in lifestyle and mode of worship that mark the other two groups. For instance, while Reform Jews have abandoned dietary restrictions as historical anachronisms, Orthodox Jews maintain that the *kashrut* (dietary laws) continue to be legally binding. Orthodox synagogues remain sex-segregated, while Reform and Conservative temples have open seating policies.

Orthodoxy has not been completely inflexible in its resistance to acculturation and modernity. The mid nineteenth century Reform movement forced even the most reactionary Jewish leaders to rethink their positions. Neo-Orthodoxy found its champion in Samson Raphael Hirsch, a rabbi from Frankfurt, who resisted the Reform movement without rejecting its goals entirely. There was, he acknowledged, a need for Jews to integrate more fully with their surrounding societies and to escape the stultifying environment of the ghetto. He advocated the adoption of Western clothes, language, and culture, yet insisted that religious traditions remained unchanged. Orthodoxy, under the successful leadership of Hirsch, retained the support of most Central and Western European Jews. It is the official form of Judaism in the state of Israel, where it also wields considerable power through the chief rabbinate. In the United States, Orthodox Judaism is organized in the Union of Orthodox Jewish Congregations of America, and its intellectual center is Yeshiva University in New York City.

Conservative Judaism was a religious movement that was inspired by the writings of the nineteenth-century Historical School of Judaism. The most influential of its members, Zacharius Frankel, feared the loss of cultural identity and religious faith that might accompany assimilation. Also important in the development of Conservative doctrine was the growth of the Zionist movement toward the end of the nineteenth century, which reinforced the ideas of Conservative Jewish leaders in its spiritual and political objectives. There was, however, some disagreement among the Zionists concerning the relative importance of spiritual and political matters; the founder of political Zionism, Theodor Herzl, emphasized the importance of an internationally recognized Jewish nation-state, while Ahad Ha-Am and his followers considered the real purpose of Israel to be the spiritual and intellectual rebirth of Judaism. The Conservative movement sided squarely with Ahad Ha-Am's group, yet did not discount Herzlian Zionism. Today, however, most Conservative Jews (as well as Orthodox and Reform Jews) strongly support the designation of Israel as a Jewish homeland.

Reform Judaism, a liberal movement that began in Germany, was initiated by eighteenth-century philosopher Moses Mendelssohn. Through what was to become known as "Reform" Judaism, Mendelssohn attempted to align Judaism with broader Enlightenment ideals. However, though the movement first appeared in Europe, it did not always enjoy widespread support there. In fact, it was not until the movement was introduced to the United States through the large influx of German-Jewish immigrants that it gained popularity and came to be considered a credible option to the more conservative forms of Jewish faith.

In 1885 the philosophies of the Reform movement were most clearly defined during the Pittsburgh Platform, a conference attended by Reform rabbis. The conference established the founding principles of Reform Judaism, stressing the need to maintain Jewish historical identity but claiming that Jewish tradition was not a necessary and essential way to do so. In addition, the Talmud was to be regarded as a defining literature, but not absolute law. Policies decided by the conference remained the core of Reform thought until a generation later, when another conference, the Columbus Platform, convened in 1937 and sought to meet growing and changing needs within the Jewish community.

juju music
African music. Juju developed in the 1960s, a blending of Western instruments and indigenous African musical styles. Juju developed from highlife music, a dance music played by bands and very popular in the 1950s in West Africa, particularly Nigeria and Ghana. African music was already influencing musical styles of other cultures in the United States, Latin America, and the Caribbean, and highlife music blended the drum rhythms of the Yoruba people with syncopated guitar melodies and lyrics sung in Yoruba or English. Juju followed this development with the introduction of saxophone, trumpet, clarinet, electric organ, and electric guitar in an attempt to appeal to a more demanding audience. Juju music has found considerable popularity abroad.

Jung, Carl Gustav (1875–1961)
Swiss psychologist. A student and colleague of Sigmund Freud's, Jung broke with Freud's doctrine to found his own school of what he called "analytical psychology," based not upon a theory of sexual motivation but upon the relation of the individual to what he called the "collective unconscious."

Born the son of a clergyman and philologist in Basel, Jung studied at the University at Basel and received an M.D. from the University of Zurich in 1902. He had studied in Paris with the French experimental psychologist Pierre Janet, and in 1900 became an assistant at the Burgholzli Clinic in Zurich under psychologist Eugen Bleuler, and a lecturer in psychiatry from 1905 to 1913. In 1907 Jung met Sigmund Freud (1856–1939), whose work on dreams and neuroses had impressed him deeply, and became his foremost disciple until their bitter split. In 1909 they traveled together to Clark University in Massachusetts to lecture and to receive honorary degrees. The publication in 1912 of Jung's *Wandlungen und Symbole der Libido* (*Psychology of the Unconscious*) signaled his divergence from Freud's views in important ways. He defined libido as more encompassing than Freud's concept of the sexual drive, and he enlarged Freud's notion of the personal unconscious to a universal and timeless collective unconscious.

Influenced by his lifelong interest in archaeology and myth, Jung argued that all humans share an inborn unconscious life that is expressed through archetypal symbols in dreams, fantasies, and myths. Freud refused to accept Jung's broader application of psychological principles, and Jung resigned from the International Psychoanalytic Association. The split led Jung into a long period of self-analysis that is described in his *Erin-nerungen, Traume, Gedanken* (1962; *Memories, Dreams, and Reflections*). Other influential concepts developed by Jung are the "anima" and "animus," the female and male elements of the unconscious; the "shadow," the repressed part of the psyche; and "introvert" and "extrovert" as personality types. His analytical psychology differs from Freudian psychoanalysis also in that it emphasizes the creative potential of the unconscious rather than the analysis of neurotic symptoms. Jung was a professor at the Zurich Federal Polytechnical University from 1933 to 1941 and at the University of Basel in 1943. He wrote many books, including *Collected Papers on Analytical Psychology* (1916), *Psychological Types* (1923), *Modern Man in Search of a Soul* (1933), *Integration of the Personality* (1939), and *Essays on a Science of Mind* (1949).

K

Kabbalah

Esoteric system of Scriptural interpretation, most often associated with Jewish mysticism. Though there is much scholarly dispute, Kabbalah (or Cab(b)ala), from the Hebrew word *qabbalah*, meaning "tradition," appears to have been given its earliest formulation in the eleventh century in France, from whence it spread most notably to Spain. Still, Kabbalistic elements are discernible in Jewish Gnosticism, which has its roots in the early Christian era. Some scholars think that it reflects a strong Neoplatonic influence. A Christian Kabbalah was developed in the late fifteenth and sixteenth centuries. Kabbalah was based on the belief that every word, letter, number, and even accent of the Hebrew Scriptures contained mysteries capable of interpretation by those who possessed secret wisdom. The names for God were believed to contain miraculous power, and each letter of the divine name was considered potent. The two principal sources of the Kabbalah are *Sepher Yezirah* (*The Book of Creation*), probably written in the third century, and the *Zohar* (also known as *Sepher Hazzohar*; *Book of Brightness*), a mystical commentary on the Pentateuch, written by Moses de Leon (d. 1305) but attributed by him to a great scholar of the second century, Simon-ben-Yohai (fl. 70–110). Following the expulsion of the Jews from Spain in 1492, the Kabbalah became more messianic in its emphasis, as developed by the Lurianic school of mystics at Safed, Palestine. In this form it was more widely adopted, and was a major influence in the development of Hasidism. Though interest in the Kabbalah waned in the Age of Enlightenment, in the first half of the twentieth century a resurgent enthusiasm for esoteric mysticisms led several notable thinkers to explore the contemporary relevance of the Kabbalah. Gershom Scholem published several groundbreaking interpretations and collections of Kabbalistic texts, while Walter Benjamin's reflections on history, meaning, and hope reflect the influence of Kabbalistic thought.

Kabir (1440–1518)

Indian mystic, poet and saint. Considered to be a "Sant" poet because of his monistic belief in a transcendental, formless divinity, Kabir worked to unite followers of all religions, including Hindu and Muslim, and preached the essential equality of all individuals. ("Sant" is the name given to those Hindu poets who opposed both Brahmanic orthodoxy and the social stratification of Hindu culture; Kabir is remembered as the best-known of the Sant poets.) His ideas laid the foundation of several cults, including the Kabirpanth, and were also the basis for the Sikh religion, founded by Kabir's disciple Nanak (1469–1539).

Born in confusing circumstances (the sketchy details of his childhood helped fuel rampant speculations about his "immaculate conception"), Kabir spent his early years as a Muslim. He was later introduced to Hinduism by Ramanada, a Hindu ascetic.

Rather than choose between these two religions, Kabir formed his own brand of faith, called *sahaja-yoga* ("simple union"), an amalgamation of the Hindu concept of reincarnation and *karma* and the Muslim belief in one God and the equality of all God's subjects. Kabir thus rejected the Hindu concepts of caste and idolatry, which contradicted the Muslim precepts of equality and monotheism, respectively. He wrote that to him "Hindu and Turk were pots of the same clay: Allah and Rama were but different names." According to Kabir, all could find salvation through an inner search that combined *bhajan* ("devotional worship") with love of one's fellow human beings.

Kabir composed his poetry in Hindi, and the appeal of his couplets (known as *sakhi*, or "witness") to the greater populace may stem from the poet's disregard for rules of grammar or pretensions of elegance, choosing to emphasize communication instead. Examples of his verses can be found in parts of the *Adi Granth*, the Sikhs' sacred book, in the *Bijak* ("account book"), a collection of his poems and observations, and in *The Kabir Book*, a selection of forty-four of Kabir's poems that Robert Bly edited and published in 1977.

Ironically, it is said that when Kabir died, his remains were the subject of a dispute between Hindus and Muslims, both of whom claimed his corpse. Legend has it that in the midst of the wrangling, a voice descended from above, instructing those present to cease fighting, lift the shroud, and divide equally between them what they found there. When the mourners did as instructed, they discovered a heap of flowers, which they divided among themselves.

Kabuki

A form of Japanese theater. Kabuki comes from the sixteenth-century word *kabuku*, which originally meant "inclination" but by the seventeenth century came to mean "unusual." The origin of Kabuki is somewhat obscure. Inspired by the Japanese puppet theater Bunraku, Kabuki made its first appearance onstage during the seventeenth century, when performers presented a series of dances that were perhaps religious in origin. However, regardless of the original intention of the dance, the local brothels soon adopted the form for the entertainment of their clients, a practice that resulted in a 1629 edict forbidding women to appear onstage. Not long after the edict, young boys began performing the dance, and in 1652 a new proclamation banned *them* from stage performances.

But by around 1700 Kabuki had become a well-established and popular form of theater and is still considered to be the most versatile of all Japanese theatrical traditions. Ironically, as a result of its flexibility, Kabuki is often regarded by more conservative theatergoers and critics as a crude and vulgar form, something like the circus in the West.

Individual actors are the real draw to the theater. In Kabuki theater, there are no directors, and the actors themselves determine an appropriate interpretation of the play, which is usually based on a story line familiar to the audience.

Kachin

Southeast Asian ethnic group, most of whom live in Myanmar (Burma). The Kachin are spread throughout the northeast hill country of Myanmar, with about 40 percent of the total population living in China or India. They are divided according to their languages, which are all of the Tibeto-Burmese family, into a number of subgroups. The largest of these is known as the Jingpaw, a word sometimes used as a synonym for Kachin.

The Kachin, who today total only about 250,000, have traditionally lived under a system of local, patrilineal aristocracies known as *gummtsa*. A ruling chief may own all of the land used by his people, who then pay tribute in exchange for protection from evil spirits. The economy is mostly agricultural,

although some Kachins have always exploited their proximity to the Burma-China trade routes, serving as middlemen or raiding trading parties as bandits. The traditional religion is animist and based on a form of ancestor worship, though some Kachins who live in the lowlands closer to the Burmese are Buddhist, and about 10 percent of the population is Christian.

Very little is known about the Kachins prior to the nineteenth century; this lack of knowledge is the result of successful Kachin attempts to deter the ambitions of the surrounding empires, even the Burmese. When the British arrived as overlords of Burma, they sought to bring the Kachins under colonial supervision and to suppress their constant harassment of Shan neighbors. An officer for Kachin affairs was appointed in 1893 to mediate Kachin-Shan relations, but the Kachin lands were still administered as a frontier region, and not as part of Burma proper.

In the tumultuous post–World War II period of nation formation, the Kachins were among the ethnic minorities that distrusted complete unification with the Burmese. Nationalist organizations, including the Kachin Youth League, sought to have an autonomous Kachin state commissioned with only minimal central control, chiefly over matters of foreign relations. Ultimately, however, the Kachin state was incorporated as one of the three subordinate states of the new republic, and the Kachin state remains part of Myanmar. The Kachins are still an independent people, and have rebelled several times since the 1960s. They continue to participate in antigovernment fighting along the eastern and northern borders.

kachina

Pueblo term for the spirit of gods who personify different aspects of nature: clouds, sky, storms, rocks, and trees, among others. There are hundreds of kachinas (also spelled katsinas) recognized at any given time, and the pantheon is constantly changing as old ones are forgotten and new ones recognized. The Hopi Indians have perhaps the largest number of kachinas, and regard them as ancestral or protective spirits, who assist humans if properly petitioned.

Within the tribe, the kachinas are personified, either as a costumed man wearing an elaborate mask or as a doll figure. Both masks and dolls are used to identify the specific spirit, as their names are not ordinarily spoken aloud. The kachinas are believed to reside with the tribe during half the year (January through July) and will allow themselves to be revealed to humans through ceremonial dances; it is believed that the dancer wearing the mask of a specific kachina is actually transformed into the kachina. Kachina dolls are used as children's toys, but also as a catechism, to teach the children how to recognize each kachina and learn the symbolism of their costume.

There are many legends about the origin of the kachinas. A popular legend claims that long ago, the kachinas lived with humans, teaching them hunting and farming, and would bring rain when it was needed by dancing in the fields. Another legend tells how the kachinas, living apart from the humans, kept the sun and the moon in a box. A coyote managed to steal the sun and moon, then accidentally let them escape into the sky, to the benefit of humans.

Kafka, Franz (1883–1924)

Czech-born German author. Kafka was born in Prague to a German-speaking secularized Jewish family. His father, Hermann, whom Kafka identified as the greatest influence on both his life and his writing, was an ambitious, domineering middle-class businessman. His mother was a quiet, subservient woman. Neither parent approved of their son's ambition to be a writer, pushing him instead toward law school and a bureaucratic career. He dutifully followed their instructions, receiving his degree in 1906 from the University of Prague, and found employment at an insurance company. He continued to live at home, and wrote mostly at night, straining his already delicate health.

Though he never married, Kafka was engaged twice to Felice Bauer. In 1917, the year he and Bauer parted ways, he was diagnosed with tuberculosis. For the remainder of his life he would require frequent visits to sanatoria, where he was at last free to pursue his writing full time. He retired in 1922 and a year later moved to Berlin, where he met Dora Dymant, a young Jewish socialist and his companion for the final year of his life.

The disturbing and enigmatic stories of Kafka have come to be seen as fables of the modern age. They combine the everyday with the bizarre, fantastic, and grotesque. One of his most famous stories, Die Verwandlung (1915; The Metamorphosis), chooses for its main character Gregor Samsa, a young man who awakens one morning to find that he has inexplicably become a huge, repulsive insect. His family, horrified at Gregor's disgusting appearance, abuse and neglect him until eventually he dies. The Metamorphosis has been read as narrowly autobiographical, but as with all of Kafka's work, there are many possible interpretations.

Kafka's stories are exemplary modernist texts, defiant of simple or reductive interpretation. His characters are isolated and powerless, adrift in a world that no longer makes any sense. In Der Prozess (1925; The Trial), Kafka's darkest piece, the protagonist is suddenly arrested, tried, imprisoned, and finally executed without ever being charged with a crime. Every attempt to clear his name seems to implicate him further. Another character tells him that his protestations of innocence are themselves a sign of guilt and that the justice he seeks will remain forever beyond his reach. It is a nightmarish vision of cold, impersonal power against which the individual is helpless. In this and similar parables, Kafka sketches a hopeless but compelling denunciation of the malevolent and stultifying structure of everyday life, a poetics of bureaucratic resignation. Other works include *Das Schloss* (1926; *The Castle*) and *Amerika* (1927).

Though most critics find in Kafka's works grim portents and intractable anxiety, a few argue that his parables contain an almost imperceptible optimism, an affirmation of individuals and groups in their struggles against state power. Kafka died of tuberculosis at a clinic near Vienna.

Kahlo, Frida (1907–1954)

Mexican artist. Born Magdalena Carmen Frida Kahlo Calderónin Coyoacán, Kahlo was one of three daughters, the child of a German-Jewish jeweler and photographer who arrived in Mexico in 1891. In 1922 she entered the Escuela Nacional Preparatoria, one among thirty-five women in a student body of 2,000, with the intention of pursuing a career in medicine. Here she first met Mexican painter Diego Rivera (1886–1957), who had been commissioned to paint a mural at the school. A bout with polio at the age of six left her right leg thinner than her left, but the defining moment of her early life was the gruesome accident she suffered at the age of eighteen. In a collision between a bus and a trolley car, part of a handrail shot through her body, traversing her stomach, while bones in her right foot and pelvic bone fractured. Her spinal column fractured in two places. The accident left her immobilized for approximately two years, during which time she had to wear an extremely uncomfortable plaster cast, a type of corset. Her life was completely changed: she suffered complications and much pain throughout the rest of her life, endured numerous operations, and had to have her right leg amputated due to gangrene in 1953. Her physical difficulties also became a focus of her art, as she depicted it in many of her more famous self-portraits.

It was during her period of convalescence that she took up painting, approaching Rivera in 1928 and demanding from him an honest opinion of her talent. The internationally renowned artist, who was forty-three at the time, began to visit her regularly, and they were married in 1929. They immediately moved to Cuernavaca, where Rivera was finishing a mural, and later traveled to San Francisco, Detroit, and New York. Kahlo's painting *Mi vestido cuelga alli* (1933; *My Dress Hangs There*) was completed during their stay in New York. Their marriage seems to have been a stormy one, complicated by Kahlo's frustrated desire to have a child and Rivera's frequent infidelities. Kahlo herself resorted to extramarital affairs, including a famous liaison with Russian intellectual Leon Trotsky (1879–1940), who arrived in Mexico with his wife in 1937.

Kahlo's first personal exhibition took place in New York in 1938. In 1939 she attended the Paris exhibition called "Mexique" organized by French poet André Breton (1896–1966); eighteen of her works were exhibited there, and one (a self-portrait called *Autorretrado con marco integrado y dos pájaros* (1938; *Frame*) was purchased by the Louvre—an honor that had not been bestowed on the great Mexican muralists Rivera, José Clemente Orozco (1883–1949), and David Alfaro Siqueiros (1896–1974). In Paris, she was entertained by the most famous painters of the period, among them Pablo Picasso (1881–1973), Marcel Duchamp (1887–1968), and Wassily Kandinsky (1866–1944), and reaffirmed her ties to Surrealism.

When she returned from Paris, Rivera asked for a divorce; during the separation Kahlo's problem with alcohol grew and she painted *Las Dos Fridas* (1939; *The Two Fridas*). Rivera and Kahlo remarried a year later. Kahlo enjoyed growing popularity, although she did not have a major independent exhibition in her own country until 1953, a year before her death. Her paintings are brilliantly colored and highly stylized, and have been both criticized and admired for their disturbing honesty. Other works include *La columna rota* (1944; *The Broken Column*), *Retrato de Diego Rivera* (1937; *Portrait of Diego*), and *Moisés* (1945; *Birth of Moses*).

Kahlo assisted a protest march against North American intervention in the ousting of Jacobo Arbenz in Guatemala eleven days before her death in 1954. Four years later, and one year after Rivera's death, the Frida Kahlo Museum in Mexico City was inaugurated with funds donated by Rivera.

Kaiiontwa'ko (c. 1732/34–1836)

American Indian leader. Chief of the Seneca, an Iroquois tribe that inhabited what is now western Pennsylvania and New York, Kaiiontwa'ko ("by what one plants") became known as Cornplanter. Son of a white trader and an Indian woman of the Seneca Turtle clan, he developed an early distrust for the white settlers as a result of his father's mistreatment of his mother. Indeed, the marriage itself seems to have been one of convenience, as Cornplanter's father sought allies among the Indians in order to gain an advantage in trade.

With his reputation as a brave warrior and outstanding orator, Cornplanter was unanimously chosen chief of the Seneca. Recognizing that contact with white Europeans was unavoidable, he allied the Iroquois nation with the French in the French and Indian War (1755–59) and sided with the British in the American Revolution (1775–83). After a devastating battle that very few Iroquois survived, he adopted a more conciliatory policy toward the settlers. He became an emissary of George Washington in 1791 and by 1793 had negotiated a peace treaty between the Indians of the North-

west and the U.S. government. Cornplanter continued his attempts to settle disputes between the whites and the Indians, but lost influence over his people due to his conciliatory stance. At one point, Cornplanter even encouraged tribes to relinquish tribal lands to the white government.

Supporting Gaiwiio (Good Message), which was more commonly known as the Longhouse religious movement, begun between 1799 and 1815 by his half-brother, Ganioda'yo (Handsome Lake), another chief of the Seneca tribe, Cornplanter became aggrieved over the dangers of alcohol, becoming an early advocate for temperance and encouraging agriculture, small farms, and religious and moral rejuvenation.

For his work on behalf of the U.S. government, Cornplanter was granted a private parcel of land on the Allegheny River, where he lived until the age of 104; he also allowed other members of area tribes to settle there. By the later years of his life, Cornplanter stressed the need to preserve Iroquois culture; many of the legends of the Iroquois are known through Cornplanter, who late in life dictated them to a white friend.

Kalevala

Finnish national epic. Compiled from old Finnish ballads, lyrical songs, and incantations that were part of the Finnish oral tradition, the *Kalevala* was collected, unified, and published by Elias Lönnrot in thirty-two cantos in 1835 and enlarged to fifty cantos in 1949.

The *Kalevala* begins with the creation of the world and describes the supernatural birth of Väinämöinen, the eternal sage, seer, and minstrel. The adventures of Väinämöinen and four other heroes, Lemminkäinen the warrior, Ilmarinen the blacksmith, Joukahainen the hunter, and Kullervo the serf, tell the story of the historical rivalry between Kalevala (the land of the Finns) and Pohjola (the

Northland, or Lapland) and the magical quest for the *sampo*, the mill that will grind out eternal prosperity. Inserted within these main plots are lyrical tales including the wooing of maidens, Ilmarinen's successful courtship of the Maiden of the North, and the tragedy of Kullervo, who kills himself to make amends for having seduced his sister. The epic ends when the principal hero, Väinämöinen, departs and is superseded by the son of Marjatta, and Christianity seems to follow the decline of paganism.

The poem is in traditional Old Finnish folk poetry meter, an unrhymed octosyllabic trochaic line with abundant alliteration and repetition. Although the *Kalevala* is based on authentic poems and songs, and the number of lines added by Finnish folklorist Elias Lönnrot (1802–1884) are negligible, he did have a Homeric model in mind, and his hand is not invisible. The poem plays a great part in Finnish national feeling, and has influenced Finland's poets, artists, and musicians, including Finnish composer Jean Sibelius (1865–1957). An early German translation influenced the scope and meter of American poet Henry Wadsworth Longfellow's poem *The Song of Hiawatha* (1855).

Kālidāsa (c. fifth century C.E.)

Composer of Sanskrit *kavya* (poetry) and drama. Kālidāsa is considered to be the master of Sanskrit poetry. Though little is known of his personal biography, his name, which translated literally means "servant of Kali," suggests that he was a follower of the destroyer god, Shiva, whose consort was Kali. It is also speculated that he was a high-caste Brahman. Attempts to associate his lifetime with a particular dynasty are also conflicting. Some historians claim that he died during the reign of Kumaradasa, who ruled over Ceylon beginning in 517 C.E. Others claim that Kālidāsa was one of the nine courtiers known collectively as the "gems" of King Vikramaditya of

Ujjain, who was also known as Chandra Gupta II (reigned c. 380–415).

Of the works known to be written by Kālidāsa, the drama *Abhijnanasakuntala* (*Sakuntala and the Token of Recognition*) is perhaps the most famous. It is the story of the seduction of the nymph Sakuntala by King Dusyanta, who misguidedly rejects both the nymph and their child only to be reunited with them in heaven. The drama's historical significance stems from the fact that the child of the union is Bharata, considered the forefather of the Indian nation.

Kālidāsa's other two dramas, if less famous, are still equally fascinating: the *Vikramorvaśī* (*Urvaśī Won by Valor*) tells the age-old story of a mortal's love for a divine maiden, while the *Mālavikāgnimitra* (*Mālavikā and Agnimitra*) diverges from the dyadic love theme of the preceding two dramas and instead centers on a comic harem intrigue.

As for Kālidāsa's epic poems, the *Raghuvaṃśa* (*Dynasty of Raghu*) details the legend and exploits of the Hindu hero Rama and his family, while *Kumārasambhava* (*Birth of the War God*) narrates the seduction of the god Shiva by Rama's consort, Parvati, who is inflamed by Kama, the god of desire. The result of the love match is a son, Kumara, from whom the poem takes its name. The only lyric poem considered to be genuinely written by Kālidāsa, the *Meghadūta* (*Cloud Messenger*), narrates a lover's message to his absent lover, interspersed with various descriptive passages evoking the mountains, rivers, and forests of India and underscoring Kālidāsa's appreciation for the beauty of nature.

Kamasutra

Indian textbook on love and erotic pleasures. The *Kamasutra* is attributed to the sage Vātsyāyana, who lived and wrote between the fourth and sixth centuries C.E. In the thirteenth century an illuminating commentary on the text, the

Jayamangala, was written by Yasodhara, which helped to make it more accessible. The *Kamasutra* has been widely read and respected throughout the ages, up to and including its status as a must-read during the recent Western "sexual revolution."

Kama, satisfaction of desires and appetites, is considered in Indian philosophy to be one of the three primary human goals, along with *artha*, material prosperity and the pursuit of economic and political goals, and *dharma*, the duties of one's station, or righteousness. The *Kamasutra* graphically illustrates how to go about fulfilling the first of these goals. Its story, which ostensibly centers on the exploits of a fashionable dandy, reveals much about the social life of the period. Although primarily an instructional guide on the how-tos of kissing, love-biting, embracing, and so on, the book is guided by Vātsyāyana's philosophical belief that in love, at least, one may do whatever one pleases wherever one pleases.

Kandinsky, Wassily (1866–1944)

Russian artist. Born Vasily Vasilyevich Kandinsky into a cultured Muscovite family, Kandinsky traveled extensively in his childhood. At Odessa, where his parents settled in 1871, he completed his secondary schooling and became an amateur musician. He also became an amateur painter, and already had an impulse toward abstraction, believing that each color had a mysterious life of its own. He graduated from Moscow University in 1893 with a degree in law and economics, having lost much of his enthusiasm for the social sciences. In 1896 he turned down a law professorship and left for Germany to become a painter. He graduated from the Munich Academy in 1900, and spent the next few years painting in the style of Art Nouveau. He exhibited and traveled throughout Europe, Russia, and North Africa.

By 1909 Kandinsky had become the chief animator of the avant-garde movement in Munich. In the years 1909–11 he was already close to abstract painting. In 1911, together with the German artist Franz Marc, Kandinsky founded a Munich artists group, Der Blaue Reiter (The Blue Rider), after the title of one of his works. The group included other important Russian and German artists. In 1912 Kandinsky published "Über die Form Frage" ("On the Question of Form") in *Der Blaue Reiter Almanach*, followed by another programmatic work, *Über das Geistige in der Kunst* (1912; "Concerning the Spiritual in Art").

Kandinsky's works from the years 1912–14, founding documents of Abstract Expressionism, are regarded by many art historians as the peak of the artist's achievement. In 1914, after the outbreak of the First World War, Kandinsky returned to Russia. After the Revolution of 1917, he was initially encouraged by the Soviet government; he became a professor at the Moscow Academy of Fine Arts in 1918 and helped organize many art museums and schools throughout the Soviet Union. He had increasing conflicts, however, with the Constructivists, who proclaimed subordination of art to industrial design and who dominated the country's artistic scene at the time. He left Russia in 1921 to take a teaching position in the already famous Bauhaus, remaining there until it was closed.

His style shifted somewhat to suit his institutional environments. During his Russian years, Kandinsky moved entirely to abstraction, and also shifted from the earlier spontaneous, lyrical style to a more rational, constructional approach, as visible in such works as *Weisser Strich* (1920; *White Line*) and *Blaues Segment* (1921; *Blue Segment*). His pictures became increasingly geometric during the years of the design school known as Bauhaus (1919–33).

In 1924, together with Alexei von Jawlensky, Paul Klee, and other Bauhaus artists, Kandinsky founded the group Blaue Vier (Blue Four), which exhibited in Europe and America. In 1933, when the Nazis closed the Bauhaus, Kandinsky moved to France and settled in one of the suburbs of Paris. His later works, which he called "concrete" rather than "abstract," often look like decipherable messages in pictographs and hieroglyphs, with many of the signs resembling aquatic larvae. In 1937 Kandinsky's paintings were shown by the Nazis in the "Degenerate Art" exhibition, together with the works of other avant-garde artists.

Kang Youwei (1858–1929)

Chinese scholar and leader of the "Hundred Days' Reform" of 1898. After China was defeated by Japan in the Sino-Japanese War of 1894–95, Kang took the risk of appealing directly to the emperor Guangxu for sweeping reforms in the imperial system. Between 1888 and 1898 he wrote to the court seven times, urging the emperor to consider and carry out his plans. He and other reformers advocated streamlining bureaucracy, strengthening military forces, modernizing industry, developing commerce, promoting local self-government, establishing new standards in the civil service examination system, and opening modern schools. The second time Kang submitted his petition to the court, he managed to collect more than 1,300 signatures from his colleagues and students, and mobilized hundreds of provincial graduates in Beijing to protest the humiliating peace treaty imposed by Japan on China.

In June 1898 the reformers prevailed. The emperor Guangxu adopted their plans. Between June and September of that year, he issued an extraordinary series of edicts to put Kang's reform program into practice. Alarmed by this development, a group of powerful conservatives within the court appealed to the Dowager Empress Ci Xi to take action to stop the "radicals." On September 19 she suddenly returned to the Forbidden City, claiming that the emperor had asked her to resume power. The emperor was put under confinement, six of the reform leaders, including Kang's brother, were executed, and scores were arrested. Kang, together with other leading reformers, escaped to Japan. Although the "Hundred Days' Reform" failed, Kang continued his campaign in exile. From 1898 to 1914, in Canada and the United States, he founded the China Reform Association, opened schools and newspapers, and established an international business.

Philosophically, Kang combined Confucianism and Buddhism with a version of Western humanistic, evolutionary theories. His early ideas emphasized change as the universal rule and principle in all matters. But change, or evolution, he argued, should be gradual rather than radical, since more haste means less speed. (This view should be examined when noting Kang's later effort to restore the emperor and resist Sun Yat-sen's revolution.) He was the author of several books, including *A Note on Moderation* and *Memorial to the Wuxu Reform*. In *The Commonwealth*, Kang envisioned a utopian world where the barriers of race, religion, state, class, sex, and family would be removed and where there would be an egalitarian, communal society under a universal government.

Kant, Immanuel (1724–1804)

German metaphysician and philosopher. Kant spent his entire life in Königsberg, Prussia. He entered the university there as a student of theology but was attracted to mathematics and the physics of Newton. He worked as a family tutor while earning his degree and became a lecturer at the university. After fifteen years of increasing fame, he was appointed to the chair of logic and metaphysics in 1770. Though trained in the classical rationalist tradition of Descartes and Leibniz, his thinking as a philosopher was awakened by the skepticism of Scottish philosopher David Hume (1711–1776), whose work he read in middle age. Responding and working through problems in Hume's work, Kant wrote his greatest works: the *Kritik der reinen Vernunft* (1781; *Critique of Pure Reason*), *Kritik der practischen Vernunft* (1788; *Critique of Practical Reason*), and *Kritik der Urteilskraft* (1790; *Critique of Judgment*).

In attempting to defend Newtonian physics, which rested on the existence of necessary connections between causes and effects, Kant argued that a science of nature was possible, contrary to Hume. Such a science was founded upon propositions that were synthetic, wherein the predicate is not logically contained in the subject, and is a priori, independent of experience. The source of certainty about the real world rested no longer in the real world but in the person perceiving it.

Kant also theorized about moral law, essentially the Golden Rule, where each person is an end-in-itself, not a means to an end, and moral duty must be performed for its own sake. The moral law presupposes certain postulates: freedom, immortality, and God. Kant broadened his ethical theory into an idealistic political theory attempting to provide a more scientific basis for the political philosophy of Frenchman Jean-Jacques Rousseau (1712–1778).

Within a generation German philosophers had abandoned the moderate dualism of Kant's morality and knowledge, but late-nineteenth-century scholars began to reconsider his work. He remains one of the most important thinkers of the Western world.

karagöz

Turkish shadow play. Turkish for "Black Eye," *karagöz* is also the name of the central character in the Turkish shadow play, as well as the name of the genre of shadow play itself. The *karagöz* theater is played from behind a lighted muslin screen by the shadow player and his assistant by the use of flat, two-dimensional figures attached to long sticks. Although it probably originated in Southeast Asia, the shadow theater in the Near East dates back to the twelfth century C.E., while the oldest piece of evidence for its appearance in Ottoman lands (including present-day Greece, Tunisia, and Algeria, where varieties of *karagöz* are found) dates back to the sixteenth century. The play itself is always a comedy centered around the uneducated, crude but intelligent, and good-hearted Karagöz and his best friend, Hajivaht, a snob, as well as on cartoon characters from all walks of life.

Karaism

Jewish religious sect. Founded in eighth-century Babylonia by Anan ben David, the distinguishing ideological feature of Karaism was a rejection of Jewish oral law and the Talmud, preferring instead a literal interpretation of the Old Testament; it maintained that the only true religious authority was the Holy Scripture. Originally called Ananites, named for the movement's founder, by the ninth century members of the sect were referred to as Karaites. Karaism spread quite rapidly from its center in Babylonia and Persia to Jewish communities throughout the Middle East (including Erez Israel) and Eastern Europe.

The Karaites were an extremely pious and ascetic group. Sabbath restrictions on activity were so strictly interpreted that believers could not even warm themselves from fires lit on the previous day. Festivals and feast days such as Hanukkah were frowned upon or forbidden completely. In fact, the Karaites often imposed greater hardships on themselves in the name of ritual purity than were called for by the Old Testament. An especially pious group of Karaites were called the Mourners of Zion and lived an ascetic life in mourning for the destruction of the Temple.

Karaism experienced a Golden Age in the eleventh and twelfth centuries, during which time sectarian literature and theoretical writings flourished. However, the movement went into a long period of decline not long thereafter. By the twelfth century, rabbis managed to check its growth by ostracizing its followers completely and forbidding intermarriage with them (reinforced by the Karaites' own strictures on marriage with outsiders). Despite a brief revival in parts of the Russian empire in the nineteenth century, Karaism continued to lose ground. Today all that remains of the sect are a few thousand adherents living outside Tel Aviv, Israel; isolated pockets of Karaites may also still exist in parts of Eastern Europe.

Karamzin, Nikolai [Mikhailovich] (1766–1826)

Russian writer, historian, and journalist. Karamzin introduced the sentimentalism of French philosopher Jean-Jacques Rousseau (1712–1778), British novelist Laurence Sterne (1713–1768), and early German poet Johann Wolfgang von Goethe (1749–1832) into Russian literature. Karamzin was born into an aristocratic family and educated first at home and then at a private school in Moscow. He was briefly associated with the Moscow Freemasons, and during this period translated works by Albrecht von Haller (1708–1777), William Shakespeare (1564–1616), and G. E. Lessing (1729–1781). In 1789 Karamzin left Russia for a year of travel in Germany, Switzerland, France, and England, where he met many important cultural and intellectual figures, including German philosophers Johann Gottfried von Herder (1744–1803) and Immanuel Kant (1724–1804). These encounters and his impressions of the cultural and political forms of these countries were collected in his *Pis'ma russkogo puteshestvennika* (1791–1801; *Letters of a Russian Traveler*). Perhaps inspired by his journey, Karamzin also became the leading sentimental novelist of his day. In these novels, including the very successful *Bednaya Liza* (1792; *Poor Liza*), he introduced many new words into the Russian language, most of them borrowed from the French, to better emulate the European sentimentalists.

His forays into history, too, were fueled by his travel observations, not by any formal training. Critical of the Russian emperors, his twelve-volume *Istoriia gosudarstva rossiiskogo* (1818–26; *History of the Russian State*) was intended primarily to enlighten the emperor. Though his moralizing tone and minor inconsistencies are faulted by critics, Karamzin's *Istoriia* was the most influential and widely read text in nineteenth-century Russia and remains an important text of historical scholarship.

Karen

Collection of several ethnic groups living primarily in the south and eastern parts of Myanmar (Burma). The two largest Karen groups are the Sgaws, who live mostly in the Irrawaddy delta, and the Pwos, a more coastal people. Less populous groups include the Bre, the Padaung, the Yinbaw, and the Zayein. The Karen have a number of distinct languages, varying from tribe to tribe, which are loosely related to the Tibeto-Burman tongues but distinct enough to make their origins obscure. There were no known written forms of any Karen language prior to the mid nineteenth century, when Sgaw and Pwo writing developed with the involvement of American and British missionaries. Very little is known about the Karen prior to the late eighteenth century, although there is evidence of their presence in Myanmar for perhaps 1,500 years. They seem to have always been a rural people, living in small groups and sustaining themselves by rice farming.

Beginning in the 1820s, Baptist missionaries popularized Christianity among the Karen. Over the next few decades as many as 30 percent of the Karen accepted Christianity, influenced by the material benefits of Western sponsorship as well as by a traditional Karen prophecy about the coming of a beneficent white man. Americans and British husbanded the Karen, introducing literacy and encouraging some to go abroad for advanced study. Many became civil servants and professionals under the British, and a pro-British Karen nationalism developed, at odds with the Burmese. In 1881 the Karen National Association was formed as a political body whose express purpose was to promote cooperation with the British and to oppose any attempt at Burmese rule, and in 1886 the Karen were quick to join the British in the suppression of Burmese revolt. Distrust and animosity between Burmese and Karen has been a constant theme of regional politics up to this day.

During World War II, the Burmese undertook mass killing campaigns against the Karen, which were only halted by Japanese intervention. When the state of Burma was organized after the war, the Karen areas were incorporated against the will of the nationalist Karen National Union. In 1948 a Karen revolt broke out, led by the KNU and its military wing, the Karen National Defense Union, and nearly succeeded in taking Rangoon. A truce was eventually called, and the rebels were dispersed. Still, periodic acts of Karen resistance to Burmese rule have continued into the 1980s, and a guerrilla National Democratic Front exists.

Best estimates put the number of Karen in Myanmar today at 3 million, but this is a difficult judgment because their cultural identity is not strictly defined. Along with the Shan, the Karen are one of the largest minorities in Myanmar.

karma

Indian philosophical term. *Karma* (meaning act, action, making, or doing) refers to the influence of an individual's past actions on her or his future lives or reincarnations. The word *karma* actually refers to both action and its "fruit" or effect. The doctrine of *karma* first appears in the Upanishads which accompany the sacred Hindu spiritual text the Vedas. The Chandogya Upanishad states that "those whose deeds in former lives were good get desirable lives such as those of Brahmans [priests], Kshatriyas [warriors] or Vaisyas [agriculturists and merchants]. Those whose lives were bad get such lives as those of Candalas, dogs or swines." The Brhadaranyaka Upanishad proclaims, "A man of good acts will become good, a man of bad acts, bad. He becomes pure by pure deeds, bad by bad deeds."

The *karma* philosophy is, in fact, a bit more complex than these functional statements might lead one to believe. The theory of *karma* is rooted in the Hindu belief in transmigration, the idea that this life is one link in a chain of successive lives and that a person's status in this life is determined by her or his *karma* in a previous life. Used to explain the inequality between individuals in society, *karma* suggests that the moral energy of an act is preserved and carried over into the next life, where it determines one's class, nature, disposition, and character. Certain professions are seen as having appropriate accompanying *karmas*: the Brahman priest's *karma* was sacrifice, a soldier's was fighting, a farmer's was farming, and a serf's was serving.

The theory of *karma* teaches that the *atman* (self), whether a person, animal, or god, has existed without a beginning as the site of experiences and the agent of action. Thus, any action, unless done by a person knowledgeable in the theory of *karma* and hence in a spirit of non-attachment, produces traces which that self must carry along with it. When an *atman* dies, after a brief sojourn in heaven or hell, the karmic traces from the past life become operative and work to determine three features of the coming life: one's birth (as human, animal, or god); the longevity of one's next life; and the experiences one will have in the next life. Although these karmic traces are burned off after this process of determination is complete, they are gradually replaced as the *atman* gains karmic traces through his or her actions in the new life. One cannot improve one's status within a given life but only through reincarnation into a better life; over the course of the chain of lives, individuals can either perfect themselves until they reach the state of the god Brahma himself and achieve liberation from the cycle of birth, death, and rebirth, or degrade themselves to the point where they are reincarnated as an animal.

Both Buddhists and Jainists incorporate doctrines of *karma* into their philosophies, but Buddhists interpret *karma* strictly as a process of cause and effect, while the Jains view *karma* as a substance that also produces the chain of birth and death.

Kashmir

Scenic, mountainous valley located in northwestern India, often referred to as the "happy valley." Considered to be one of the most beautiful areas in the world, Kashmir has been a site of conflict for a millennium. Under Buddhist sway in the pre-Christian era, Kashmir was ruled by a succession of Hindu dynasties and dominated by factional politics until 1346, when the Mughal empire took control of the area and introduced Islam.

The first of the Mughal sultans, who were to rule Kashmir from 1346 to 1526,

proclaimed the valley "Paradise on Earth." Following Mughal rule, the Sikh kingdom of Punjab annexed Kashmir in 1819, but after the First Sikh War in 1846, Kashmir was sold to the rajah Gulab Singh of the Dogra dynasty of Jammu. The Dogra dynasty maintained its sovereignty in Kashmir for a little over one hundred years, until the Partition of India in 1947, at which time Hari Singh, the maharajah of Kashmir, signed an Instrument of Accession to the Indian Union in 1947.

However, the matter of Kashmir's incorporation into India was not so easily resolved. Since Kashmir's population is two-thirds Muslim, Pakistan felt that it would be to its advantage to incorporate Kashmir into the Pakistani state, or at the very least establish Kashmir independence. India, on the other hand, concerned over Kashmir's strategic location at the borders of Pakistan, Afghanistan, and China, felt it necessary to maintain control over the valley. A bitter struggle over the valley erupted between Pakistan and India and it was eventually taken before the United Nations in 1948. A U.N. resolution called for the withdrawal of all Pakistani and Indian troops and the establishment of a Kashmiri plebiscite in which the Kashmiris would decide whether to accede to India or Pakistan. (Kashmiri independence was not considered a viable alternative.) Although Indian prime minister Nehru (served 1947–64) agreed to the proposal of a plebiscite, and even though a cease-fire line was drawn in 1949, to this date both countries have failed to withdraw their troops. The territory and its allegiance remain hotly disputed, and low-level conflicts over the region have broken out several times during the last forty years.

The dispute over Kashmir, however, was not limited to Pakistan and India alone. In the 1950s trouble erupted at yet another of Kashmir's boundaries when the Chinese began performing military maneuvers in the Aksai Chin and Ladakh areas of the region. Fear arose in New Delhi at the possibility of a Sino-Pakistani collaboration in a war against India over Kashmir. The Sino-Indian War of 1962, which sprang from a dispute over the McMahon Line—the boundary established between India and China in 1914—resulted in India losing Ladakh to Pakistan-supported Chinese forces.

India-controlled Kashmir has a special status in India as the only state with its own constitution; its capital is Srinagar in the summer and Jammu in the winter. The Pakistanis refer to their part of the area as Azad Kashmir (Free Kashmir).

kashrut

Jewish dietary laws. Derived from the Hebrew word *kasher*, or kosher (proper), the *kashrut*, or dietary laws, are a set of religious restrictions derived from written and oral law concerning the Jewish diet. These rules are a compilation of rabbinical law and biblical references, and the level of adherence to them is one of the defining characteristics of the different Jewish communities and is often related to the degree of religious devotion. The origin of the rules themselves is obscure; while in keeping with certain biblical strictures, they may also be the result of attempts to eliminate illness-inducing meats (like pork) from the Jewish diet, or a sideways attempt to render contact difficult between Gentile and Jew.

Kosher meats must pass several yardsticks. They must not come from "unclean" animals (as defined biblically) or those not prepared in a ritualistic manner. Permissible meat sources are animals that have cloven hooves and "chew the cud" (cows and sheep). Restricted are fish without fins or scales, birds of prey, and milk from nonkosher animals. Wine prepared by Gentiles is forbidden.

Permissible animals must be slaughtered in a highly ritualized manner. They are killed with a smooth blade under the supervision of a trained *shohet*, who blesses the animal before the slaughter. Before koshering, the vein running along the neck must be slit, to let the blood drain. The meat is either salted (soaked in cold water and then sprinkled with salt) or broiled over an open flame.

The laws of *kashrut* also specify that milk and meat may not be eaten at the same sitting, in accordance with the biblical injunction against "a kid seething in its own mother's milk." One can consume milk after eating kosher meat, but only after a thorough washing of the hands and mouth and after a designated period of time, which can run up to six hours, depending on the strictness of observance.

There are many different views as to the role these laws should play in religious life. At the Pittsburgh Conference of 1885, U.S. Reform rabbis present felt that these laws were construed in an earlier time that was not compatible with modern society. These laws were seen as restrictive and irrelevant to the central aims of Judaism. Orthodox and Conservative Judaism are very strict in their adherence to the *kashrut*. Conservative Judaism, however, is sometimes more lenient, emphasizing the education involved with dietary laws rather than exact adherence to the ancient standards. Reform Judaism, especially in the United States, does not generally follow the *kashrut*, leaving dietary decisions to the individual worshiper.

Kathmandu

Capital of modern Nepal and the largest city in the Kathmandu Valley. Founded in 723 C.E., Kathmandu was historically a separate kingdom during the Malla period (1480–1768), until the conquest of Kathmandu by the Prithvinarayan Shah in 1768. In Kathmandu, ancient culture is strikingly juxtaposed against the modern trappings of Nepalese politics and commerce. An earthquake in 1934 caused extensive damage to the city and required the construction of new buildings. The old town has residential courtyards, Buddhist monasteries, and 336 standing Hindu temples.

Kathmandu is the cultural and religious center of Nepal. The Hindu and Buddhist shrines contain centuries of Newar sculpture, paintings, and artifacts and are testimony to the architectural genius of the Newar people. The Newars consider the entire territory of Kathmandu to be sacred. Every day the narrow streets of this ancient city are filled with pilgrims and local Nepalese celebrating religious festivals. Newar festivals are primarily Hindu and Buddhist, while the Himalayan mountain people tend to practice the Tantric-Shakti cults.

Kaunda, Kenneth (1924–)

First president of Zambia. One of the most prominent political leaders in post-colonial Africa, Kaunda ruled Zambia between 1964 and 1991. Compelled mainly by his resentment of racial discrimination in Central Africa, Kaunda based his political career on the promotion of a philosophy that synthesized Christian socialism and traditional African values.

Born in northern Zambia, Kaunda completed secondary school in the 1940s and became a teacher. His father was a minister and teacher, and his mother was one of Zambia's first women teachers. Kaunda's own teaching career began in Zambia (then Northern Rhodesia), and continued in Tanzania until 1949. After moving to a copper mining area in Rhodesia, where he was a mine welfare officer (1948), he founded a farmers' cooperative.

Kaunda's political career began when Sir Stewart Gore-Browne, a progressive member of the Northern Rhodesian Legislative Council, appointed him as an adviser on African affairs in 1949. In the early 1950s Kaunda was elected secretary-general of the African National Congress (ANC), Zambia's first anticolonial organization, but disagreements within the group led him to create and preside over a new organization, the Zambian African National Congress (ZANC). The organization quickly emerged as an influential group, opposing policies such as a British plan to form a federation composed of Southern Rhodesia, Northern Rhodesia, and Nyassaland, a proposal that was perceived by ZANC as an attempt to solidify the powers and privileges of the white minority. ZANC responded by launching a civil disobedience campaign that Kaunda labeled "positive nonviolent action." Early in his career, Kaunda had committed himself to Gandhian nonviolence, an attitude encouraged by a visit to India in 1957. The colonial administration imprisoned Kaunda for nine months.

As the Zambian independence movement continued, support mounted for emerging militant groups like the United National Independence Party (UNIP), and after his release from prison on January 8, 1960, Kaunda was elected UNIP president. By the end of the year, Kaunda and other UNIP leaders were involved in decolonization negotiations with colonial authorities and the British government. In 1961 Britain approved Zambia's formal independence and scheduled elections for 1962 as the final phase of the process. Though the British election plan favored Northern Rhodesia's European minority by giving it an inflated number of votes, UNIP and the ANC still managed to win.

With Zambia's official independence declared in 1964, Kaunda became the fledgling nation's first president. He was immediately confronted by intricate problems such as tribalism, political violence, and economic instability. Kaunda applied his negotiating skills in an effort to reach compromises on some of these issues, but in the 1970s he became increasingly authoritarian. In 1972 he imposed one-party rule and the following year introduced a constitution that guaranteed UNIP's unchallenged authority over the country. Copper mines and major industries were nationalized, and export industries were accorded the bulk of investments while agriculture and social services were given low priority. Kaunda placed trade sanctions on Rhodesia, further weakening an economy that was already unsteady, since Zambia depended on Rhodesian energy resources and railroads. He also sought aid for a rail line to a Tanzanian port as an alternate route for Zambia's copper exports.

These policies proved ineffective, and deteriorating prices for Zambia's exports, high unemployment levels, and low standards of living eventually eroded Kaunda's popularity. In November 1991 Kaunda was forced to step down as president when his party lost Zambia's first multiparty elections in decades, although he remained the UNIP chairman.

As president, Kaunda was a prominent voice in African politics, particularly in the Organization of African Unity and in the struggle to liberate Southern Rhodesia (Namibia) from South African rule. Of note was his imposition of sanctions against Rhodesia in support of the Zimbabwean independence movement, and his staunch support for anticolonial guerrillas, whom he allowed to train on Zambian soil. Kaunda's provocative speeches at international forums and his eloquence have earned him worldwide recognition and respect despite the domestic problems associated with the later years of his presidency. Kaunda has written several books, among them the autobiographical *Zambia Shall Be Free* (1962), *Letter to My Children* (1973), a statement of his philosophy, and *Humanism in Africa and a Guide to Its Implementation* (1967).

Kawabata Yasunari (1899–1972)

Japanese writer. Kawabata is perhaps the most acclaimed of Japan's modernist writers, having received every major literary award in Japan, several French awards, and the Nobel Prize in Literature in 1968. He began his career in the avant-garde Neo-Sensualist movement, a reaction against the proletarian literature of the 1920s. The Neo-Sensualists were characterized by an impressionistic lyricism, a signature style that Kawabata adopted.

Kawabata was born in Osaka, and his parents died when he was three, followed by his sister and grandmother, then finally his grandfather. He found himself alone in the world at the age of sixteen with a profound awareness of mortality. An early desire to paint also influenced his writing, lending an exquisite sense of detail and a strong sense of color. Kawabata's first book, *Jūrokusai no Nikki* (1925; *The Diary of a Sixteen-Year-Old*), recounts the experience of nursing his grandfather through his last days; the book won him immediate critical recognition. Death, aging, guilt, and isolation were to be persistent themes in his work. In *Nemureru bijo* (1961; *The House of the Sleeping Beauties*), seventy-year old Eguchi goes to a bordello that provides beautiful young girls drugged into death-like sleep; there, in the juxtaposition of youthful beauty and his own decrepitude, Eguchi confronts memory and mortality. *Yama no oto* (1952; *The Sound of the Mountain*) also paints a portrait of aging, as an elderly businessman ruminates on the failures of his life. Other novels include *Izu no odoriko* (1925; *The Izu Dancer*), *Mizuumi* (1961; *The Lake*), and *Utsukushisa to kanashimito* (1965; *Beauty and Sadness*); in *The Old Capital* (1961–62), a novel particularly cited by the Nobel committee in bestowing its award, Kawabata bound together his trademark themes of the anxiety that surrounds sexual difference, the longing for an ideal virginity, and the unity of environment and character.

Kawabata's melancholy novels often treat sexual relationships. For example, *Yukiguni* (1937; revised 1969; *Snow Country*), probably his best-known work in the West, depicts the affair of an aging geisha and an insensitive Tokyo businessman. His works are distinguished by arresting images and poeticized writing, delicately intimating eroticism, nostalgia, and the ephemera of life. Grief and a lingering melancholy hover beneath the texture of the words. The style is extremely difficult to translate, and many Western readers have found it cryptic and inaccessible.

Kawabata once lamented that Japan's defeat in the Second World War left him nothing but elegies to write all the days of his life, and the tone of elegy held true for most of his work. Two years after the spectacular Japanese ritual suicide, *seppuku*, of his protégé Yukio Mishima (1925–1970), Kawabata killed himself by gas in his workroom.

Kazan, Elia (1909–)

Greco-American director. Born Elia Kazanjoglou in Istanbul (then Constantinople), Turkey, Kazan immigrated to New York City with his Greek parents at age four. He made a name for himself with his first feature film, *A Tree Grows in Brooklyn* (1945), and for "crusading" pictures of the 1940s dealing with subjects such as political corruption (*Boomerang*, 1947), anti-Semitism (*Gentleman's Agreement*, 1947, for which Kazan won an Academy Award), and racism (*Pinky*, 1949). In the 1950s Kazan introduced two actors to the screen: Marlon Brando in *A Streetcar Named Desire* (1951), *Viva Zapata!* (1952), and the Oscar-winning *On the Waterfront* (1954); and James Dean in *East of Eden* (1955).

Kazan began as an actor and director of stage plays; after studying drama at Yale in 1932 he acted and worked as assistant stage manager in the Group Theatre. In 1935 he directed his first play, and by the 1940s was an acclaimed Broadway director, having directed *The Skin of Our Teeth* (1942), *One Touch of Venus* (1944), *A Streetcar Named Desire* (1947), *Death of a Salesman* (1949), and others. He worked in film as early as 1937, however, directing a documentary short that year about Tennessee miners, *The People of Cumberland*. His full-length documentary on food rationing for the U.S. Department of Agriculture, *It's Up to You*, was made in 1941. Kazan continued to direct both on film and on the stage until 1963, when he renounced theater, saying, "Movies is where all the action is." In the same year, he made his first semiautobiographical film, *America, America*, based on his own novel, followed in 1969 by a second personal film, *The Arrangement*.

Called a "superficial radical" based on the fact that in 1952 he voluntarily appeared before the House Committee on Un-American Activities, Kazan admitted to membership in the Communist Party from 1934 to 1936, and declared the names of fellow members, including playwright Arthur Miller (1915–). Some see Kazan's 1954 production *On the Waterfront*, which won several awards including an Oscar, as his attempt to defend his testimony; Kazan admitted to similarities between his own predicament and the conflicting loyalties of the main character in the film.

Kazantzakis, Nikos (1885–1957)

Greek novelist, poet, and dramatist. Born in the midst of Crete's revolt against rule by the Ottoman Turks, Kazantzakis considered this centuries-old pattern of the island's fight for freedom important enough for it to constitute the central metaphor of his life and art. However, his struggle for linguistic reform took place away from Crete when he left the island to study law at the University of Athens in 1902 and then went on to study philosophy with Henri Bergson at the Collège de France from 1907 to 1909. The events that followed during his extensive travels through Spain, England, Russia, Egypt, Palestine, and Japan served to greatly influence his later works. His experience working in a lignite mine with Georges Zorbas in the Peloponnesus provided much of the material that went into his renowned piece of fiction *Víos kai politía tou Aléxi Zormpá* (1941–43; *Zorba the Greek*). Traveling through the Soviet Union, Kazantzakis became disillusioned with Communism and developed his own idealistic and spiritual "Meta-Communism." He finally settled in Greece during World War II and embarked on the most prolific period of his life.

His works written during this time include *O Khristós Xanastavrónetai* (1948; *The Greek Passion*); *O Kapetán Mikhális* (1949–50; *Freedom or Death*), a portrayal of Crete's struggle against their Turkish overlords during the nineteenth century; and *O televtaîos pirasmós* (1950–56; *The Last Temptation of Christ*), a work that attempts to enter the mind of Jesus Christ during his final moments on earth. Kazantzakis's international reputation rests upon these and other remarkable pieces, several of which made it onto the movie screen, including *Celui qui doit mourir* (1958; *He Who Must Die*; from *O Khristós Xanastavrónetai* [*The Greek Passion*]), *Zorba the Greek* (1964), and *The Last Temptation of Christ* (1988). Both an autobiography, *Anaforá stón Gréko* (1961; *Report to Greco*), and a biography, *Nikos Kazantzakis* (1968), written by his second wife, were published after his death.

Keaton, Buster (1895–1966)

American comedic actor. Born Joseph Francis Keaton in Kansas to vaudeville performing parents, Keaton joined the family act at the age of three and left after twenty years to perform in a series of silent comedy shorts directed by Fatty Arbuckle. In the 1920s he directed, wrote, and acted in over two dozen of his own silent comedy two-reelers and features.

Keaton was known for his ability to perform dangerous acrobatic feats while maintaining a deadpan expression. His roles often involved the small-framed Buster facing insurmountable odds but ultimately triumphing: in *Seven Chances* (1925) he survives a rockslide, in *Go West* (1925) a herd of cattle, and in *College* (1927) he plays a weakling who emerges as a pentathlon winner. He was not simply a slapstick comedian, however; the films over which Keaton had artistic control reflected his creative use of film to enhance the comedy of his scripts, such as his use of a split screen in *The Playhouse* (1921), his experiments with framing and composition in *The Balloonatic* (1922), and his mobile camera style, which contrasted with the static filming common to silent-era comedies. Keaton also showed a sophisticated use of cinematography in the fantastic dream sequences of *Sherlock Jr.* (1924), which depicts a cinema projectionist who dreams himself into a movie.

Keaton's early film career did not survive the conversion to synchronized sound, however, largely because of his alcoholism. In 1929 Keaton's contract was sold to Metro-Goldwyn-Mayer (MGM), and he was forced to act in a series of dreary situation comedies. Keaton made a comeback in 1952, with a leading role in Charlie Chaplin's *Limelight*; in the 1960s he was "rediscovered" by a new generation of moviegoers. He starred in Samuel Beckett's only film, *Film* (1965), and appeared in Richard Lester's *A Funny Thing Happened on the Way to the Forum* (1966).

Kennedy, John F[itzgerald] (1917–1963)

Thirty-fifth U.S. president. Born in Massachusetts, Kennedy was heir to a family tradition: both his grandfathers were prominent in Boston politics, and Kennedy's father, Joseph Patrick Kennedy, was chairman of the Securities and

Exchange Commission and ambassador to Great Britain in Franklin D. Roosevelt's administration (1933–45), as well as a wealthy businessman. John Kennedy was an average student at Choate and later at Harvard University, receiving his B.S. in 1940. His senior thesis on Great Britain's lack of military preparedness became a best-selling book, *Why England Slept*, that same year. He joined the navy two months before the United States entered World War II and was made commander of a PT boat in the South Pacific in 1943. When his craft was destroyed by a Japanese attack, he swam from island to island for days until he and his crew were rescued. For his heroism he won the Purple Heart and the Navy and Marine Corps Medal; the injuries he suffered troubled him the rest of his life.

Kennedy decided on a career in politics after the death of his older brother, Joseph Jr. In 1946 Kennedy campaigned for the House of Representatives as a Democrat, won by a landslide, and took office at the age of twenty-nine. In 1952 he challenged the incumbent Henry Cabot Lodge, an old family nemesis, for the Senate and won. The following year, he married Jacqueline Lee Bouvier. In 1958 he was reelected by a record margin. As a senator, Kennedy leaned left on domestic issues and right on foreign policy; he supported social welfare programs while vehemently opposing Communism and was considered to be a moderate on civil rights. He also avoided taking a clear stand on Senator Joseph McCarthy's crusade against suspected Communists.

Influential in Congress, Kennedy wrote his Pulitzer Prize–winning *Profiles in Courage* (1956) while recovering from back surgery. He achieved national political prominence at the 1956 Democratic National Convention, where he was a candidate for the vice presidential nomination. The convention chose Estes Kefauver instead, and Kennedy avoided the overwhelming defeat of the Democratic ticket in November. In 1960, however, he was nominated by the convention on the first ballot. He faced his Republican opponent, Vice President Richard Nixon (1913–94), the heir of the popular Eisenhower administration, in the first-ever televised debates. His charisma offset his relative youth and his Catholicism, both uncommon characteristics of previous U.S. presidents, and he won by a narrow margin at age forty-three. His "New Frontier" agenda included a wide range of social programs, including the Peace Corps, a rise in the minimum wage, increased Social Security benefits, housing and job-training bills, and an expanded space program.

The major policy of the Kennedy administration that received the most criticism was the abortive Bay of Pigs invasion of 1961, when U.S.-backed Cuban exiles attempted to overthrow Cuban leader Fidel Castro (1926–). His major triumph, however, was the Cuban Missile Crisis of 1962, when Kennedy persuaded Soviet premier Nikita Khrushchev (1958–64) to withdraw missile installations from Cuba. He also signed a nuclear test ban treaty with the Soviet Union and Great Britain in 1963.

While touring the country in preparation for the following year's election, Kennedy was shot and killed on November 22, 1963, in a motorcade in Dallas, Texas. Lee Harvey Oswald was accused of being the lone sniper, but he was himself murdered two days later while in police custody by a Dallas nightclub owner, Jack Ruby. A commission headed by Supreme Court Justice Earl Warren investigated the assassinations and reported no evidence of conspiracy, though many such theories have been advanced over the years.

Kenyatta, Jomo (c. 1890–1978)

Leader in the African struggle for decolonization and the first president of the independent republic of Kenya. Kenyatta was born at Ngenda in Kenya into a family of Kikuyu farmers and baptized Johnstone Kamau in 1914. He changed his name to Jomo Kenyatta in the 1920s—his first name translates as "Burning Spear." In 1928 he accepted the position of secretary of the Kikuyu Central Association, a political group dedicated to advancing the political rights of the Kikuyu people, especially their right to own land under British colonial rule. In the 1930s Kenyatta studied anthropology at the London School of Economics under Bronislaw Malinowski and wrote *Facing Mount Kenya: The Traditional Life of the Gikuyu* (1938). In this anthropological work, often referred to as a "landmark of cultural nationalism," Kenyatta argues that land tenure has historically existed within Kikuyu society and was essential for the cultural survival of the Kikuyu people. In the 1930s Kenyatta's political interests expanded to include Pan-Africanism, and in 1945, with George Padmore, W. E. B. Du Bois, Kwame Nkrumah, and others, he organized the fifth Pan-African Congress in Manchester, England. In 1947 he was elected to the Kenya African Union (KAU), an inter-ethnic, nationalist political party. In 1953, on sketchy evidence, he was convicted by colonial authorities of leading the anticolonial resistance movement known as the Mau Mau Rebellion. In 1960 he was named president of the newly formed Kenya African National Union (KANU), which won elections in May 1963 based on universal adult suffrage. Kenya achieved independence at midnight, December 11, 1963; Kenyatta became the nation's first prime minister, and in 1964 its first president. As president, Kenyatta steered the country along a conservative course, and

oversaw reasonable economic stability. However, his policies became increasingly autocratic. He banned the major opposition political party in 1969, and in the mid-1970s most of his critics were detained. Upon his death in 1978, he was succeeded in office by Daniel Arap Moi.

Keynes, John Maynard (1883–1946)

English economist. Creator of the so-called New Economics, Keynes was the originator of the economic policies of both Great Britain and the United States during much of the twentieth century. First trained in mathematics, Keynes became a lecturer in economics at King's College, Cambridge, in 1908, a position he held until his death. He served with the British treasury as the principal representative to the Paris Peace Conference of 1919. Keynes first came to public attention with his highly critical *The Economic Consequences of the Peace* (1919), which condemned the severity of reparations extracted from Germany in the Treaty of Versailles. He continued to publish his unorthodox economic theories in such books as *A Tract on Monetary Reform* (1923); *The End of Laissez-Faire* (1926); *A Treatise on Money* (1930); *The General Theory of Employment, Interest and Money* (1936), his most influential text; and *How to Pay for War* (1940). His theories had little impact on British economic policy until after the Second World War, but formed the cornerstone of U.S. president Franklin Roosevelt's policies during the Depression (1930s). It was Keynes who advocated the necessity of government investment in the public sector during a recession, on the assumption that full recovery could occur only if government created a condition of full employment. Though Keynes's doctrines of deficit spending have incurred widespread opposition, his policies were influential and widely adopted in the decades following the Second World War.

Khasas

Nepalese ethnic group. The Khasas comprise one of two ancestral lines of the ancient Pahari tribe mentioned by Roman historians Pliny (23–79) and Herodotus (c. 484–between 430 and 420 B.C.E.). The Pahari people inhabit the Himalayan hill ranges and occupy land from the Indian state of Kashmir in the west through Nepal to Darjeeling in northeast India. Their total population is estimated at 20 million. Primarily Hindu, the Pahari are regarded as unorthodox by Hindus of the plains because of their relatively uncomplicated rituals and caste rules. Accordingly, the Pahari view themselves as culturally distinct from the plains people. They observe an extraordinarily simple caste system that accounts for the two ancestral lines, yet even these two groups have intermingled over time. Khasas are the higher caste and are "clean" or "twice-born," while the Doms constitute the "unclean" or "polluting" caste. The Khasas are agricultural, while Doms are primarily artisans. The Khasas make up three-fifths of the Nepalese population and constitute a majority of the population in Himalayan India.

Significant cultural differences with respect to the treatment of women also distinguish the Pahari from their Hindu neighbors in the plains. For example, widows are allowed to remarry; wives may take two or more husbands (polyandry); and though a woman must be faithful to her husbands while she is living with them, she can behave as though she were single when she leaves their home.

Khmelnytsky, Bohdan (c. 1595–1657)

Leader of the Zaporozhian Cossacks. Khmelnytsky organized a rebellion against Polish rule in Ukraine that ultimately led to the transfer of the eastern part of Ukraine from Polish to Russian control. Son of a petty nobleman, he served in the Cossack registered army, where he held responsible posts. He participated in the Polish-Turkish war of 1620–21; captured by the Turks, he spent two years in prison. In 1648 he was elected *hetman* (leader) of the Zaporozhian Cossacks, at which point he organized a rebellion against Polish rule and marched against the Poles. His victorious advance won him support from the dissatisfied peasants, townsmen, and clergy of Ukraine, who joined him in a mass uprising that enabled him to go as far west as Lwów.

After winning more victories, Khmelnytsky made peace with the Polish king, the terms of which permitted him to establish a virtually independent Cossack principality in Ukraine. However, the treaty did not satisfy either the Polish gentry or Khmelnytsky's followers; he renewed the war in 1651, but was defeated and forced to accept a new, less advantageous treaty. He then sought aid from Moscow and in 1654 directed his Cossacks to take an oath of allegiance to Aleksei (Alexis), the czar of Russia. This event is known as the Pereiaslav Agreement. The Russians subsequently invaded Poland, but Khmelnytsky, not content with his pact with Aleksei, entered into secret negotiations with Sweden, which was also at war with Poland. He was about to conclude a treaty placing the Cossacks under Swedish rule when he died. Although Khmelnytsky sought independence for Ukraine, he succeeded only in devastating the Dnieper lands and in subjecting them to the rule of Moscow, which gradually curtailed Cossack liberties.

Khmer Rouge

Cambodian Communists. The name "Khmer," which was used by the ancient Cambodian people, recalls a glorious Golden Age of Cambodian culture, which lasted from the ninth through the fifteenth century. Originally led by a group of French-educated

Marxists, the Khmer Rouge directed a rebellion against Prince Norodom Sihanouk in the early 1960s, but launched its large-scale insurgency in response to the right-wing military coup of 1970, which established the Khmer Republic. Generals loyal to Sihanouk, Communist-trained Cambodians, and the Muslim minority Chams all joined forces against the Cambodian government. The collapse of military rule was accelerated by the departure of U.S. military advisers who had been working secretly in the region. The Khmer Rouge forces, which had swollen from 3,000 to 30,000, quickly gained control of more than two thirds of Cambodia, primarily in the rural areas, and captured Phnom Penh, the capital city, in 1975.

Under the leadership of Prime Minister Pol Pot, Kampuchea (as the new Khmer Rouge regime was called) undertook one of the most ambitious and horrible cultural revolutions ever envisioned. Fusing millenarian utopianism and rational planning, the Khmer Rouge set about eliminating all traces of heterogeneity in the country. The policy of "urban cleansing" moved all intellectuals and professionals to the countryside; forced to work in the fields, most died of hunger or malaria. Ethnic minorities and anyone with a religious belief were scheduled for death; large populations of Buddhists and Muslims were slaughtered or dispersed. Some 3 million people are estimated to have perished during the four years of Khmer Rouge leadership. Pol Pot was overthrown in 1979, a year after Vietnam undertook a full-scale invasion.

The Khmer Rouge continue to exist, however, and fought a guerrilla war against the Vietnam-backed People's Republic of Kampuchea. Throughout the 1980s they continued to hold the Cambodian seat at the United Nations, which officially still protested the 1978 invasion of Cambodia. (The Chinese Communists had long been quiet pa-

trons of the Khmer Rouge, and opposed the Vietnamese Communists as puppets of Moscow.) Even as Cambodia became a de facto U.N. protectorate before, during, and after the elections of 1993, the Khmer Rouge have continued to fight a guerrilla war against other Cambodian factions.

Khoisan

A group of African languages. Though linguists differ in their classificatory systems, trying to deal with the approximately 1,000 distinct languages and dialects used in Africa, the Khoisan group is generally considered to be one of the four enormous families of African languages, along with the Niger-Kordofanian, the Afro-Asiatic, and the Nilo-Saharan. The Khoisan languages as a whole are often referred to by Western linguists as the "Click languages," due to their distinctive use of click sounds that serve as a subsystem of the consonants. All of them are tonal as well, but they share few grammatical features. The languages that make up the Khoisan are spoken by the Khoikhoin (called Hottentots by white settlers), the San, and other non-Bantu peoples of southern Africa. In addition, some languages of small tribal groups in Tanzania are often included in this classification.

Khoja

Indian Muslim sect. The majority of Khoja, which means "lord" or "master" in Persian, are members of the Nizari Isma'ili sect, whose leader is Aga Khan, and who are known as "Assassins" in Syria, Persia, and Central Asia and as "Khojas" in India and Pakistan. The name Assassin does not arise, as might be expected, from the Assassins' belief that it is their religious duty to murder their enemies, but from the term *hash-shashin* or *hashishiyyin*, which refers to their practice of smoking hashish to induce ecstatic visions before setting out to seek martyrdom. (The Twelver Shi'as and the few orthodox Sunnî Muslims who call themselves Khojas do not follow Aga Khan.)

The Nizari Isma'ili sect was founded in the eleventh century by Hasan Sahab, who was known to his followers as the "Old Man of the Mountain." The sect maintained its power until the thirteenth century, when the Mughal invaders captured their strongholds.

Khoja custom today does not differ greatly from traditional Muslim practices, except in rigid adherence to the strictures of their Indian caste. A relatively well-off people, the Khojas devote a great deal of time to their community, education, and literary works.

Khomeini, Ayatollah Ruholla (1900–1989) Iranian religious leader. From exile Khomeini directed the overthrow of the shah and the Iranian revolution of 1979, and he ruled the new Islamic republic until his death. His family name was Hendi, but he took the name Khomeini from the town of Khomein in central Iran where he was born. He was reared by his elder brother after his father was killed on what Khomeini believed were the orders of Reza Shah Pahlavi, which accounted for his lifelong hatred of the Pahlavi dynasty. He attended religious schools and became a teacher of religion and philosophy. (He was an admirer of Greek philosopher Plato's (c. 428–348/47 B.C.E.) *Republic*, and envisioned an Islamic variation on the idea of a philosopher-king leading the ideal state.)

A popular advocate of Shi'ite Islamic fundamentalism, he received the Islamic honorific title *ayatollah* in the 1950s. He was an outspoken opponent of Muhammad Reza Shah Pahlavi's program of Westernizing the country, especially the shah's adulteration of Islam and his repression of the religious community. Khomeini's public criticisms of the government led to several arrests and then exile to Iraq in 1964. His continued

outbursts there led to his expulsion in 1978, and he and his second wife settled near Paris. Khomeini remained influential with the religious opposition in Iran through taped messages that were smuggled into the country and then broadcast to his supporters. He initiated a general strike for October 1978, which led to an oil field strike in November, culminating in widespread riots and the flight of the shah from the country in January 1979.

In February Khomeini returned from exile to direct the revolution. The shah refused to abdicate, but a referendum in April established an Islamic republic with Khomeini as its de facto head. He accepted no office and retired to the holy city of Qum, but all important issues were referred to him for a final decision as he became known as the *fagih*, or supreme religious guide. Appointing the members of the ruling Revolutionary Council, he ordered the execution of hundreds of the shah's supporters. In November revolutionaries occupied the U.S. embassy in Tehran, declaring that they would release their sixty-six U.S. hostages if the shah were returned to stand trial. The shah sought asylum in Egypt, however, and died there in 1980. Despite a U.S. attempt to rescue the hostages under President Jimmy Carter (served 1977–81), the hostages were not released until January 1981, just as Ronald Reagan was being inaugurated as U.S. president (served 1981–89).

In September 1980 the Iraqi army, under the direction of President Saddam Hussein, had invaded northern Iran in hopes of benefiting from Iran's political turmoil. Iran's army, spearheaded by the Revolutionary Guards, retaliated and continued fighting long after Iraq had asked for a peace settlement in 1982, reportedly because Khomeini wanted to drive Hussein, tacitly supported by the United States, from power. The Iran-Iraq War continued until 1988, when both countries accepted a U.N. cease-fire plan because of their massive loss of soldiers and their depleted economies. Khomeini died a year later.

khön drama

Thai masked performance. The *khön* dance-drama, or "masked play," is part of a tradition of Thai classical dance (*natasin*), shadow-puppet dance-drama (*nang*), female court dance-drama (*lakhon nai*) and male masked-pantomime (*lakhon kawl*). *Khön, nang,* and *lakhon* have had an uninterrupted history since the thirteenth and fourteenth centuries. There is considerable argument over whether the *khön* preceded or followed the development of the *nang*. Yet it is believed that both are Thai appropriations of Hindu ritual dance through the intermediary of Java. All three art forms are related closely to Brahmanic Hinduism, Buddhism—Thailand's national religion—and the ceremonies of popular animist cults.

Khön drama tends to be Hinduistic in theme and emphasizes the military and political elements of Hindu ritual dance-drama. In terms of technique, *khön* dancers utilize leg and trunk movements in a series of martial steps, and *khön* performances tend to be serious and dignified in tone. Typically, *khön* performers wear war costumes. Except for those actors who represented comedic figures or who impersonated women, *khön* performers of the earliest period all wore masks representing Hindu deities like Rama, Shiva, Hanuman, and Ravana, as well as human beings. In the nineteenth century, traditional *khön* spread to other parts of southeastern Asia, in particular Cambodia, through the influence of the Thai rulers. Techniques of staging changed, artists modified the traditional texts more freely, pointed headdresses and crowns began to replace masks for many characters, and the music and dance became more elaborate and stylized.

There are five major types of *khön*:

khön klong plaeng is performed on large open fields; *khön rong nok* and *khön nang rao* are performed on an open stage with a bamboo rod serving as a bench; *khön na cho* is performed in front of a *nang* screen; *khön rong nai* is performed in the style of *lakhon nai*; and *khön chak*, a modernized version of the nineteenth-century style, is now performed in theaters with painted scenery and backdrops. The text of *khön* drama consists of narration, dialogue, lyrics, and verse spoken by a narrator. The actors are silent; at one time it was impossible for the actors to speak because of the masks, but the tradition of mimed performance continued after the masks were discarded. In a performance, the narration, dialogue, and verse describe the movements of the actors while music is played by an orchestra called a *piphät*. Music is an integral part of the *khön*, and the use of voices and instruments is thought to have been taken from *lakhon nai* dance-drama.

A *khön* performance is a quasi-religious event as well as public entertainment. *Khön* masks are revered as sacred objects by the dancers and artists, who attribute supernatural powers to them. There is an annual religious invocation and initiation ceremony for teachers, students, and artists of *khön*. The novice is initiated by a master teacher who wears the masks of Phra Phrot Rusi (Bharata Rishi, the great master of dance) and Phra Phirap (Bhairava, the god of dance, one manifestation of the god Shiva) and the headdress of the *nora chatri* southern dance-drama. Only initiates are permitted to perform the *khön*.

Khun Chang Khun Phaen

Medieval Thai story. This popular medieval Thai tale of love, pathos, and humor is best known as a poem by Sunthon Phu and King Rama II. At its heart is a love triangle: a beautiful middle-class woman who cannot decide between her bald but rich and faithful husband, Khun Chang, and the handsome, gallant but poor warrior, Khun Phaen. Told in common vernacular, it is highly valued for both its portrayal of Thai society and its fine style and diction. A *sebha*-style poem, it is designed to be recited by a solo performer who also provides rhythmic accompaniment and intermittent songs.

kibbutz

Communal settlement developed by early-twentieth-century Zionist pioneers. In an attempt to promote Jewish independence, the idea of a kibbutz, or communal settlement, was envisioned in the land of Erez Israel. This original kibbutz, known as a *kevutzah*, consisted of ten men and two women who established themselves at Um Juni by the Sea of Galilee in 1909. Planning and production, distribution, and consumption were all to be shared equally by the members of the *kevutzah*.

While the first communal settlements were utilitarian, within a few years a consciously socialist ideology began to permeate the movement. By the 1920s Marxist Zionists began to view the kibbutz as the ideal building block with which to construct the new Israel. It was believed that cooperation, equality, mutual aid, and democratic idealism would be fostered within the kibbutz, values that could then permeate the whole country. Moreover, at a time when the numbers of Jewish immigrants to Palestine were still severely limited, the kibbutzim provided far-sighted Zionists with a frontline of Jewish settlement. This strategy proved extremely successful when Israel was granted statehood in 1947, for the borders of the Jewish homeland had to be extended to include even the most remote kibbutzim.

Whereas the early communes were almost exclusively agricultural, today nearly all kibbutzim are involved in some form of industry instead of or in addition to farming. The increased complexity of the kibbutz economy has made it necessary to employ outsiders to manage the community's finances, a development contrary to the original tenet of complete internal control. Nevertheless, most of the decisions important to the future of the kibbutz are still made by the community as a whole, which holds periodic meetings, elects committees, and nominates leaders. The kibbutz is often considered one of the most completely democratic societies in the world.

On kibbutzim private property is practically nonexistent. "To each according to his needs" is the prevailing philosophy. Typically, members eat in the communal dining hall, shop in the commissary (taking only what they need), and send their children to the communal school. One of the most unique features of kibbutz life is the common practice of housing all children together from birth through adolescence, allowing them to stay at their parents' homes only on weekends. However, in recent years more parents have decided to raise their children themselves.

Membership is voluntary, and many young people have opted to leave the kibbutz in favor of a more independent life in one of Israel's cities. Ideological and political tensions have caused serious divisions among those who choose to stay. Only 3.5 percent of the Jewish Israeli population lives on the kibbutzim today. Many communities have experienced serious financial difficulties in the past few decades, and some have even gone bankrupt. Yet Israel's 271 kibbutzim are still important to the country's economy, especially in terms of agricultural produce, the mainstay of its exports.

Kierkegaard, Søren [Aabye] (1813–1855)

Danish religious philosopher. Søren Aabye Kierkegaard was born in Copenhagen, Denmark, the son of Michael Pedersen Kierkegaard, a poor farmer turned successful businessman whose prosperity provided the young Søren with a comfortable upbringing. Søren's father, a Lutheran, was a major influence on his development. As a young farmer, the elder Kierkegaard had cursed God for his then-wretched financial position. Though prosperity had followed, the curse remained an event of symbolic import, particularly after Søren's mother and five of his siblings died during Søren's childhood. As a philosopher, Søren would later explore the questions of faith that the curse had raised.

Kierkegaard first studied philosophy at the University of Copenhagen; however, when his father died in 1838, he took up theology. Kierkegaard also fell in love with Regine Olsen, a girl who comforted him in the wake of his father's death. But troubled by Regine's age and naïveté, Kierkegaard soon decided to break off their engagement. He moved to Berlin, where he began writing the first of many philosophical works in aesthetics and ethics. *Enten-Eller, et live-fragment* (*Either/Or: A Fragment of Life*), published in 1843, is replete with cryptic messages to Regine attempting to explain his behavior to her. Indeed, for the rest of his life Kierkegaard would indulge in melodramatic textual gestures toward Regine, always hoping that she would return to him as a friend, or at least remain unmarried.

Kierkegaard's next writings consider faith and sacrifice. *Frygt og baeven* (1843; *Fear and Trembling*) and *Gjentagelsen* (1843; *Repetition*) assert that faith is inherently paradoxical. In these works, he presents the possibility that in the system of Christian philosophy, free will must be presupposed as a necessary ingredient in the achievement of faith. In his next work, *Begrebet angest* (1844; *The Concept of Dread*), Kierkegaard distinguishes between angst, dread (a formless, detached fear), and objective fear to prove that it is impossible to define freedom logically. Psychology, he contends, lacks the capacity to account fully for freedom, but should at least describe how freedom is possible in the mind. He suggests that the state of mind most conducive to freedom is dread, the precursor to sin: that when one experiences dread, one moves from innocence into sin, and then from sin to redemption. In 1845, Kierkegaard wrote *Stadier paa livets vei* (*Stages on Life's Way*), in which he discusses religion as separate not only from aesthetics but also from ethics.

Kierkegaard's philosophy evolved away from aesthetics toward increased criticism of the theories of Georg Wilhelm Hegel (1770–1831). He argued that truth can only be reached subjectively, which contradicted the Hegelian belief that knowledge can only be objectively realized. Hegel's thesis, Kierkegaard believed, ignored the importance of faith. Through his critiques of Hegelianism, Kierkegaard laid the groundwork for modern existentialism.

While not considering himself an advocate for Christianity, Kierkegaard did feel an obligation to depict a strict view of Christianity. In his last book, *Indøvelse i Christendom* (1850; *Training in Christianity*), Kierkegaard set high ethical standards for anyone claiming to be a Christian, and the book was widely interpreted to be a slap at the leader of the Danish Church.

It was not until after the First World War that Kierkegaard's writings were widely considered. His work was recognized when other seminal existentialist thinkers such as Karl Barth and Martin Heidegger helped push the movement forward. After the Second World War, Kierkegaard's work found a new audience eager for his profound explorations of freedom and suffering.

Kikuyu

Bantu-speaking people, originally of the highlands of south-central Kenya. The Kikuyu (also called Gikuyu) are the largest ethnic group in contemporary Kenya. Jomo Kenyatta, the country's first prime minister and president (c. 1890–1978), was a Kikuyu and wrote a highly influential anthropological account of his people, *Facing Mount Kenya: The Traditional Life of the Gikuyu* (1938). The book served a strategic purpose in the struggles of the Kikuyu people for fair treatment under the British colonial authorities. His book provided a systematic defense of the integrity of the culture of the indigenous people, as well as an implicit attack on the land grab undertaken by colonial authorities.

The Kikuyu were at the forefront of anticolonial resistance in Kenya from the early twentieth century onward. In the late 1920s, the Kikuyu Central Association was formed to advance the political rights of the Kikuyu under British rule. The resistance movement in the 1950s, named the Mau Mau Rebellion by the British, was almost entirely made up of Kikuyu. In response to the uprising, the British declared a state of emergency in 1953, jailing numerous political leaders, including Kenyatta. The rebellion receives a literary representation in Ngugi Wa Thiong'o's *A Grain of Wheat*, which also provides interesting descriptions of Kikuyu culture.

Migrating to their present homeland from the northeast in the seventeenth century, the Kikuyu continued this migration until the mid nineteenth century. Kikuyu social organization is traditionally based on three important factors. The family group, or *mbari*, includes a husband and his wife or wives and their children, grandchildren, and great-grandchildren. Beyond this, there is the *moherega*, or clan, which comprises *mbari* with the same clan name. Finally there is the age-group, or *ruka* system, which cuts across the boundaries of clan and family.

Kim, Ronyoung (1926–1987)

Korean-American artist and author, born Gloria Hahn. As a second-generation immigrant born in Los Angeles, California, Ronyoung Kim devoted her one novel, *Clay Walls* (1986), to the hardships of growing up in America while remaining inextricably linked to a Korean heritage. The book raises issues of identity, racism, and oppression by telling the story of a Korean family that leaves for America in order to escape impending Japanese persecution. Upon arriving, the family soon faces new difficulties in the form of economic distress and American prejudice. Kim's activities in the Korean-American community include contributions to ethnic newspapers and magazines and her involvement in the Society for Asian Art.

Kimbangu, Simon (1889–1951)

African religious leader. The founder of Kimbanguism, one of the largest religious movements of modern Africa, Kimbangu is considered to be both martyr and nationalist symbol by many followers. Kimbangu was born in Zaire and educated at a Baptist mission. He worked briefly as a migrant laborer, but in 1921 began a mission of preaching and healing, which became a mass organization. Though Kimbangu did not preach against Christianity or the colonial governments, his movement became a haven for the anti-European sentiments shared by many in Zaire. Kimbangu's ministry was brief, however; the Belgian government, alarmed by the popularity of the church, banned Kimbanguism and arrested him for sedition. He was sentenced to death, but the sentence was commuted and Kimbangu was imprisoned for life. He died in prison in Elisabethville on October 10, 1951.

Though he was cut off from his followers, Kimbangu was revered as a Christ-like martyr, and remained the symbolic leader of the church. His son became the leader of the underground church, and upon liberation of the Congo from Belgian rule in 1960, Kimbanguism, with a membership of over 3 million, became the first African church to attain full membership in the World Council of Churches.

kimono

Traditional Japanese costume. "Kimono" literally means "clothing," but refers specifically to the traditional Japanese robe-like garment with wide rectangular sleeves, worn by both sexes. The kimono consists of eight vertical cloth panels, all roughly the same size and stitched together in a fairly simple construction, and is bound with a decorative sash called an *obi*. The cloth itself often becomes the canvas for weavers' and dyers' arts, elaborately decorated with hand-painting or brocade. The traditional kimono style for men is black silk decorated with the family crest in white, worn under a jacket (*haori*) and over pleated trousers or a skirt (*hakama*). The women's kimono differs according to the occasion; the wedding version has an elaborately decorated outer robe over two white robes. Other versions are more or less elaborate; the traditional procedures of layering robes and tying the *obi* were once handed down from mother to daughter, and some women take lessons in the exact rites of donning the robes for the proper effect.

Western fashions have been common in Japan since the Meiji period (1868–1912), and nowadays kimonos are worn only on special occasions.

King, Martin Luther, Jr. (1929–1968)

African-American minister, writer, and civil rights activist. Born in Atlanta, Georgia, King was the son of a well-known Baptist minister. At the age of fifteen, he entered Morehouse College, receiving his B.A. in sociology in 1948. Persuaded by his father to enter the ministry, he enrolled at Crozer Theological Seminary, where he began to study Indian leader Mohandas Gandhi's (1869–1948) philosophy of nonviolent protest and contemporary Protestant theology. He graduated first in his class in 1951

and received his Ph.D. in systematic theology from Boston University in 1955. In 1954 King became the pastor of Dexter Avenue Baptist Church in Montgomery, Alabama, where he also headed the Montgomery Improvement Association, which organized the Montgomery bus boycott of 1955.

Recognizing the opportunity to create a mass movement to effect social and political change in the wake of the successful effort to end segregation in public transportation, King and others founded the Southern Christian Leadership Conference (SCLC) as a coordinating body. King traveled and lectured widely in the United States. In 1960 he moved to Atlanta to become copastor with his father at Ebenezer Baptist Church and to devote more time to the SCLC. King participated in many civil rights sit-ins, protest marches, and freedom rides and was often jailed. He wrote his famous "Letter from Birmingham Jail" (1963) as an appeal to clergymen to support the movement actively after he and many demonstrators, including children, were jailed after being attacked with firehoses and dogs.

Upon his release, he began to help organize the historic March on Washington. On August 28, 1963, more than 200,000 people gathered at the Lincoln Memorial to hear King's famous "I Have a Dream" speech, which called for interracial unity based upon Christian principles. (The speech has subsequently been reprinted and rebroadcast throughout the world.) Congress passed the Civil Rights Act, authorizing federal intervention in instances of segregation or discrimination, the following year, in 1964.

In March 1965, King organized the initial protest marches for federal voting rights laws in Selma, Alabama, which Congress passed as the Voting Rights Act the same year. The Watts riots demonstrated the deep resentment of the predominantly black inner cities, and black militancy was increasing, due in part to the visible successes of King and others and in part to the need for far greater substantive change. In 1966 King began a drive to end housing discrimination in Chicago, but an agreement signed by civil rights and civic leaders had little effect.

King's nonviolent approach came under attack from militants; however, he responded by broadening his social goals. In 1966 and 1967 he delivered speeches opposing the Vietnam War and calling for a national coalition of poor people of all races. He planned a Poor People's March to Washington, but plans were interrupted on April 4, 1968, when, on a visit to Memphis to support a city sanitation workers' strike, King was assassinated on a motel balcony. In March of the following year, the accused white gunman, James Earl Ray, pleaded guilty to the murder and was sentenced to ninety-nine years in prison.

King's achievements as a civil rights leader include turning scattered protests into a powerful movement that attracted liberal whites as well as blacks in its appeals to reason, Christian values, and nonviolent methods. For these reasons he was able to exert enormous pressure on the federal government, which under his influence passed landmark legislation guaranteeing the end of systematic, legal racial oppression in the United States. His books include *Stride Toward Freedom: The Montgomery Story* (1958), *Why We Can't Wait* (1964), and *Where Do We Go from Here: Chaos or Community?* (1967). He received the Nobel Peace Prize in 1964, and the U.S. Congress declared January 17 a national holiday in his honor in 1986.

Kingston, Maxine Hong (1940–)

Chinese-American writer. Kingston was born in Stockton, California, and raised in a Chinese immigrant family. Her writing is influenced by the Cantonese peasant talk-story tradition that she was exposed to both within her own family and in the Chinese-American community in Stockton. Credited by critics as having practically invented a new genre of writing, Kingston incorporates myth, legend, and history into her works in such a way that the boundaries between autobiography and fiction are blurred. *The Woman Warrior: Memoirs of a Girlhood Among Ghosts* (1976), her first novel, is an attempt to reconcile the paradox of Chinese and American female identities. The title refers not only to the ghosts of her ancestors that haunted her childhood through stories and tales, but also to the Americans whom her mother referred to as "ghosts" because they were "foreigners." It deals with female powerlessness and empowerment in legend and history, in China and America. Well received by critics, *The Woman Warrior* won the general nonfiction award from the National Book Critics Circle in 1976, and several years later made the list of best nonfiction works of the decade in *Time*. *China Men* (1980), her second best-seller, is a companion piece that elaborates on the masculine side of the Chinese-American experience. Inspired by her father's silence about his own past history and present desires and fears, *China Men* is Kingston's attempt to imagine the various possible untold histories of the men in her family. Here Kingston deals with the cycles of loss and renewal, endurance and change, that coincide with the experience of emigration. Also well received, *China Men* won the American Book Award for general nonfiction in 1981. *Tripmaster Monkey* (1989) was another best-seller. A teacher for many years, Kingston now devotes herself full time to writing.

Kinkakuji

Japanese Buddhist temple. The Kinkakuji, or Temple of the Golden Pavilion, is a three-story temple, covered in gold leaf, which contains a magnificent collection of art treasures, including various images of the Buddha. The temple is set in a splendidly landscaped garden, with a pond at its center. The complex, set in the shade of the Kitayama mountains, was originally built as the luxurious retreat of the fourteenth-century shogun Ashikaga Yoshimitsu. He dedicated it as a temple in his last wishes, and at his death it was named Rokuonji in honor of his posthumous title, *rokuon.*

After burning to the ground in 1565 and being neglected for the greater part of two centuries, the temple was renovated in the Meiji period of the late nineteenth century. In 1950 a disturbed young acolyte, distraught at the commercialization of Buddhism, put the last original building to the torch in an act of protest. This Kinkakuji was rebuilt in 1955, and the dramatic story was retold by Yukio Mishima in his novel *Kinkakuji* (1956; *The Temple of the Golden Pavilion*).

Kipling, [Joseph] Rudyard (1865–1936)

English poet, short-story writer, and novelist. Kipling is remembered primarily as the bard of the British empire. Although frequently dismissed as a vulgar imperialist, Kipling's work has recently received attention for its innovative use of popular forms, its exposure of the grim realities of working-class life, and its critique of Britain's ruling classes.

Joseph Rudyard Kipling was born in Bombay, India. His father was a scholar of architecture and a curator at the Lahore Museum, and the Kipling household was frequented by artists, writers, and intellectuals. At age six, Kipling was sent to England to be educated; he spent five miserable years in a foster home in Southsea, England, before his parents returned to England and enrolled him in the Westward, Ho! school in Devon. While there, Kipling became enamored of the stiff-upper-lip ethos of the British system and penned the poems that would make up his first book, *Schoolboy Lyrics* (1881).

Since his family could not afford an Oxbridge education, Kipling returned to India in 1882, settling into a job as a journalist for an English-language paper in Bombay. During this seven-year period he published six volumes of short stories and several verse collections. His books gained renown almost overnight among British and Anglo-Indian readers, and when he returned to England, Kipling was hailed as a celebrity. The poems in *Departmental Ditties* (1896) exemplify his poetic tendencies, many of which dismayed the modernist sensibilities of British critics. Kipling's verse, written to be read aloud, follows the strict rhythmic patterns of music-hall tunes and ballads. The poems are frequently scornful of the British upper classes and tend to praise working people and soldiers.

After his 1892 marriage to an American woman named Caroline Balestier, Kipling relocated to Vermont. During his American years he published the bulk of his longer fiction, including *The Jungle Books* (1894, 1895), *Captains Courageous* (1897), and *Kim* (1901). The last, which concerns the adventures of a poor Irish orphan in India, is considered to be a modern classic for its evocation of the Indian landscape and social structure. Kipling returned to England in 1902, and during extended travels in South Africa became more firm in his commitment to imperialism—a position that isolated him from increasingly liberal literary and political opinion in Britain. Although he continued to write until his death in 1936, little of the work from the later period met with the acclaim of his earlier production.

Kipling's artistic reputation has suffered because of his jingoistic support of imperialism and his undisguised racism. His imperialism was occasioned by a deep, if condescending, sense of Britain's civilizing mission in the world.

When Kipling urged U.S. president Theodore Roosevelt in 1899 to "take up the white man's burden" and create an empire in the newly acquired Philippine Islands, he revealed an attitude of racial arrogance and a belief in the benefits of empire for the colonized.

Kiš, Danilo (1935–1989)

Serbian writer. Kiš, born to a Jewish father and a Montenegrin mother, survived the persecution of the Jews that claimed the lives of most of his family during World War II, and his personal experiences of loss and subjugation during the conflict are manifested in his work. After the war, Kiš studied literature in Belgrade and also worked as a lecturer in French universities. Kiš first attained recognition during the mid-1960s as one of a group of celebrated and adept young writers, and became a leading figure in Serbian literature. He remained at the forefront of new trends and currents on the literary scene, his progressive nature keeping him in step with new advances, until the end of his life.

Mansarda (1962; *The Attic*) was his first novel, and dealt with the trials and anguish of adolescence. His subsequent novels deal principally with the persecution of the innocent during times of war, with a particular emphasis on the plight of the Jews.

In addition to his novels, his collection of short stories, *Grobnica za Borisa Davidoviča* (1976; *A Tomb for Boris Davidovich*), also deals with the victims of wartime repression and terrorization. Unlike his earlier novels, this one uses a time frame spanning centuries. The collection concentrates on the nature of Communist oppression, a topic of particular relevance to Kiš as a native of Eastern Europe.

Two of his books in particular are tributes to his father, who was killed in a Jewish pogrom. *Bašta, pepeo* (1965; *Garden, Ashes*) and *Peščanik* (1972; *Hour-*glass) reflect the respect and reverence Kiš held for his father, who had a tremendous impact on his son.

kisaeng

Female Korean entertainer. Roughly equivalent to the more familiar Japanese *geisha*, the principal function of the *kisaeng* was to entertain men, which was considered to be a serious job. During the Koryŏ period, a government-sponsored center, the Kyobang, was established to train women (usually lower class) to become courtesans in royal or noble households, as well as "party girls."

Though being a *kisaeng* was never regarded as respectable (a denomination women could earn under Confucian law only in the roles of daughter, wife, and mother), many *kisaeng* women were admired for their skill in composing *sijo* poetry and practicing other literary and musical arts. *Kisaeng* have also been memorialized in legends, most commonly about a courageous and patriotic *kisaeng* woman who, having seduced and intoxicated an enemy general, dances with him to the edge of a cliff from which she leaps, the hapless invader clasped in her arms. This story recurs frequently in Korean folklore and historiography, the identity of the foreign general being suitably altered to represent the current terms of embattlement.

Today, however, the position of the *kisaeng* is the subject of great political controversy. Although they have inherited the name of their more illustrious forebears, the job description of today's *kisaeng* is basically that of a prostitute. Moreover, the suggestion of a culturally sacrosanct tradition of female "entertainers" is often summoned to legitimate what is widely recognized as a highly organized and extremely lucrative system of prostitution. The magnitude of the sex tourism industry in Korea is well documented; travel agencies, primarily (but not exclusively) in Japan, advertise package tours of Seoul, *kisaeng* women included in the price.

Opponents of this practice remark with bitterness on the long history of Japanese exploitation of Koreans in general, and of their past recruitment and commandeering of Korean women as prostitutes in particular. Yet Korea itself promotes the activities of *kisaeng* women. One guidebook published in English by the Tourist Section of the Seoul metropolitan government lists the "Kisaeng House" under the rubric of "Entertainment and Recreation," and lists a number of *kisaeng* houses by name, with phone numbers. A number of women's organizations in Korea and abroad have protested this traffic in women. Students from Seoul's Ewha Women's University, for example, have joined with religious organizations in calling for an end to the Korean government's support of, or tacit consent to, sex tourism.

kiva

Pueblo ceremonial room. The kiva is a room used for ceremonies, social occasions, and weaving, and was considered to be the men's domain. Women are invited into a kiva infrequently and then only on important occasions. A kiva always contains a *sipapu*, which is a hole in the ground through which the ancestors were believed to have entered this world. The walls are decorated with murals depicting sacred figures or everyday scenes from the village, which were frequently plastered over and replaced with new paintings. Some kivas are round in shape and most are built at least partly underground. This is thought to be a cultural holdover from the Anasazi tribe, the pre-Pueblo culture in the North American Southwest that lived in circular pit houses with a *sipapu*. As the building shapes gradually changed to rectangular forms, some tribes maintained a circular pit house as their ceremonial building.

Knopf, Alfred A. (1892–1984)

American publisher. Knopf, with his wife, Blanche, founded their imprint, also known as Borzoi Books, in 1915, and published Willa Cather, H. L. Mencken, and Carl Van Vechten. In 1923 Mencken recommended that Knopf publish Walter White's novel *The Fire in the Flint*, thus becoming one of the first major American publishers to print black fiction. As much as did any other single gesture, Knopf's decision launched the Harlem Renaissance. Two years later, Van Vechten introduced Langston Hughes's *The Weary Blues* to Knopf. Hughes remained with the house for most of his career. Knopf also reprinted key texts about black experiences, including Haldane McFall's novel about Barbados, and James Weldon Johnson's important novel, *The Autobiography of an Ex-Colored Man*. Knopf also published Van Vechten's *Nigger Heaven* in 1926, the most widely read fictional account of Negro life since Harriet Beecher Stowe's *Uncle Tom's Cabin* (1852). He and his wife also published many authors in translation, such as Albert Camus, André Gide, Thomas Mann, and Yasunari Kawabata.

Kobayashi Takiji (1903–1933)

Japanese writer. Kobayashi was a leader and chief writer of the "proletarian literature" movement, which flourished in Japan before World War II. He combined a philosophical concern over social justice with an artistic drive toward careful realism to produce works that finessed the line between propaganda and high literature. He was born into poverty, and suppressed his literary talents to become a bank clerk upon graduating from school in 1924. However, he dabbled in literary politics on the side, founding the magazine *Clarté*, which advocated humanitarian ideals of social justice, pacifism, and intellectual congress with other nations.

Kobayashi read and was greatly affected by the Russian novelists Dostoevsky (1821–1881) and Gorky (1868–1936), and invested his art with the concerns of the lower classes. In 1927 he began to identify himself with the proletarian literary movement and with labor unions, helping to organize strikes. Early the next year, members of the Japanese Communist Party were arrested and tortured, and Kobayashi wrote his first major work, *Senkyūhyakunijūhachinen sangatsu jūgonichi* (1928; *The Fifteenth of March*), describing this atrocity and delineating the underground movement. This work succeeded in attracting literary—and police—attention.

Kobayashi's radical reputation grew with the publication of *Kani kōsen* (1929; *The Factory Ship*). It tells of workers aboard a ship who rebel against their inhumane working conditions when they finally come to understand the collusion of the capitalist system with military force. This powerful story, with its "collective hero," was, like most of his work, banned shortly after publication. In this and similar works, a political coming-to-consciousness brings oppressed groups to act in concert and overthrow the systems that keep them down. His other works include *Bōsetsurin* (*The Snowbreak*), which was finished in 1929 but published posthumously in 1947, and *Fuzai jinushi* (1929; *The Absentee Landlord*).

Kobayashi was eventually fired from his bank post after exposing how the bank cooperated in exploiting farmers. He lived in hiding for several years, but was betrayed by a police spy in 1933. He died under torture in 1933, shortly after his arrest.

Kogawa, Joy (1935–)

Japanese-Canadian poet and novelist. Born in Vancouver, British Columbia, Canada, Kogawa is best known for her novel *Obasan* (1981), a fictionalized account of her traumatic childhood as a Japanese-Canadian in wartime Canada. Strong in its portrayal of Canada's harsh treatment of its Japanese citizens, Kogawa's work echoes the Nazi treatment of the Jews, and, more important, makes an accurate comparison with the Japanese-American internment.

Kogawa's narrator, Naomi Nakane, reconstructs her painful childhood through Kogawa's own memories, the diaries kept by her aunt, and official documents and newspaper clippings. Her story of a splintered family marks the legacy of pain, self-loathing, and alienation that the relocation and internment in prison camps brought to Japanese-Canadians during World War II. She is also the author of a book of poems, *Jericho Road* (1977).

Kojiki

Oldest written record of Japanese history. The *Kojiki* (meaning the Record of Ancient Matters) is a heterogeneous text that chronicles Japanese history from the age of gods to the rule of Empress Suiko (r. 593–628). The text is divided into three sections. The first section of the *Kojiki* is sacred to Japan's official religion, Shintō, and includes the *Jindai no maki* (*The Book of the Age of the Gods*), which explains the founding myths of Japan. The second and third divisions of the *Kojiki* chronicle the early histories of the first emperors and include records of imperial succession. Some historians suggest that the work, attributed to Ō No Yasumaro, was compiled from oral tradition for the empress Gemmei (661–722; r. 707–15), in 712.

As the Japanese had no written language at the time of the composition of the *Kojiki*, its style is an intriguing mix of Chinese characters and Japanese verse forms, with various small linguistic expositions defining terms and describing pronunciations. This classic text of Japanese antiquity is an important source of Shintō thought, and was first translated into English in 1882.

Kokugaku

Philosophical study of classical Japanese literature. Beginning in the seventeenth century, the Kokugaku, or "National Learning Movement," sought to cleanse Japan's cultural identity of foreign ele- ments and articulate a specifically Japanese mentality. These ideological aims came to a head in the "Restoration" school of Shintō, which jettisoned Buddhism and Confucianism in order to ordain Shintō as the national cult of Japan.

Flourishing mostly in the Edo period (1600–1868), orthodox Kokugaku coalesced around the nationalist sentiments of a group of four Shintō scholars: Kada no Azumamaro (1669–1736), Kamo no Mabuchi (1697–1769), Motoori Norinaga (1730–1801), and Hirata Atsutane (1776–1843). However, many modern scholars often attribute this early study of Japanese classics to the scholar Keichū (1640–1701), who stressed that in order to truly appreciate the classics, the modern reader must free his mind from contemporary concepts and rediscover the naïve responses of a simple, ordinary humanity. Keichū's understanding of Kokugaku was distinct from those of the Shintō nationalists; purged of political ideology, Kokugaku represented a humanistic attempt to understand the past with a measure of sensitive objectivity.

The more aggressive Kokugaku provided the intellectual and ideological underpinnings for the imperialist Japanese state before World War II. Its momentum was dispersed after Japan's defeat in that war.

Kollár, Ján (1793–1852)

Slovak poet. Kollár was committed to the literary and cultural unity of the Slavs in the early nineteenth century and expressed these political ideas in his work.

Kollár spent most of his life, from 1819 to 1849, serving as a Lutheran pastor to the Slovak community in Pest. He had a profound reaction to the German nationalism with which he came into contact while at the University of Jena, provoking him to write the epic poem *Slávy dcera* (*The Daughter of Sláva*). In his sermons and other writings, Kollár called for cultural Pan-Slavism as a response to German nationalism. His other works include *Cestopsis druhýa a Paměti z mladších let života* (1841–63; *Travel Diaries*), *Autobiography* (1862), and *Staroitalia slavjanska* (1853; *Ancient Slav Italy*).

Koryŏ dynasty

Korean dynasty. The Koryŏ dynasty (918–1392) was founded by a Sŏn Buddhist adept, Wang Kŏn (King T'aejo), who seized the reins of power from the crumbling Silla dynasty (c. 350–c. 935) by winning and organizing the support of the regional aristocracy, a group that had become alienated from the central Korean government at Kwangju. The new capital of the Koryŏ kingdom was established at Songak (the present-day city of Kaesŏng) on the northwestern border of the old Unified Silla Kingdom. The establishment of the Koryŏ dynasty was further assisted by the cementing of connections between the Songak government and a number of Sŏn Buddhist centers similarly remote from the former geopolitical hub at Kyŏngju.

The Kilsangsa monastery, to the south of Songak, was one of these politically crucial religious sites. Built in the late Silla period by the Sŏn master Hyerin, Kilsangsa was a pile of ruins by the twelfth century, when it was renovated according to the instructions of the great Sŏn priest Chinul, and renamed the Songgwangsa Temple. Chinul (1158–1210) is widely regarded as the most important religious figure of the Koryŏ dynasty. In the tradition of the Hwaŏm Buddhist priest Wŏnhyo, Chinul concerned himself with the resolution of sectarian antagonisms through the advocacy of a syncretic approach to Buddhist thought and practice. Especially remembered for his development of the doctrine of "sudden enlightenment and gradual cultivation," Chinul took a position that incorporated both an invocation of common access to *bodhisattva* (or enlightenment-head) and an acknowledgment of the value of the specialized training endorsed in the tradition of scholasticism. This synthesis has been preserved as one of the central principles of the dominant Chogye sect of Korean Buddhism today.

The ceramic arts also flourished during this period, in particular celadon glazing and inlay. Much of the art produced was later confiscated or stolen by the Japanese during their many occupations of Korea; the fact that such objects remain in Japan today is one of many sources of Korean resentment toward the Japanese. It was during the Koryŏ dynasty that technological innovations such as papermaking, printmaking, and movable type were developed, in many cases before similar advances in Europe.

The establishment of a civil service exam system, known as *kwagŏ*, was one offshoot of the new Confucian spirit of the Koryŏ period. The strict hierarchical prescriptions that are characteristic of Confucianism made a lasting imprint on Korea. Ultimately, the wide distribution of religious and secular power that had first benefited the Koryŏ conquerors of Silla proved to be a fatal impediment to maintaining Koryŏ hegemony. Disputes among local warlords and aristocrats, compounded by the presence and demands of a new class of civil servants, created a state of domestic unrest that made Koryŏ particularly vulnerable to Mongol invasions from the north. In 1392 General Yi Sŏnggye allied his troops with the Mongols long enough to secure their support for his sacking of the Koryŏ dynasty. As Yi T'aejo, the general founded the final dynasty in Korean history.

Kościuszko, Tadeusz [Andrzej Bonawentura] (1746–1817)

Polish statesman and soldier. Born in the Mereczowszczyzna, Kościuszko came from a family of noble origins. He was educated at the Piarist college in Lubieszów and the military academy in Warsaw. King Stanisław II Augustus Poniatowski sent him to Paris to continue his studies in military and civil architecture and painting.

Arriving in North America in 1776, Kościuszko joined the American struggle against the British. In Philadelphia he was given the rank of colonel, and planned the fortifications to defend the Continental Congress. He designed and constructed fortifications at Fort Ticonderoga and West Point and assisted with river crossings and designing the blockade of Charleston in South Carolina. At the end of the war, Kościuszko was given the rank of brigadier general and made a U.S. citizen.

Returning to Poland in 1784, Kościuszko could not secure an appointment in the Polish army because of his associations with the Czartoryski family, opponents of the king. Instead, he lived on a small country estate for five years, where he freed the serfs and lived penuriously as a result. When liberal reforms were instituted in 1789, he rejoined the military with the rank of general major. In 1792, the Russian army invaded Poland, and Kościuszko gained fame commanding the Battle of Dubienka. King Stanisław II promoted him to general lieutenant and the revolutionary government in Paris granted him honorary citizenship, but when the nervous king abandoned the liberal cause and Poland was partitioned, Kościuszko joined the exiles.

In Paris, Kościuszko sought support for Polish independence first from the Girondists and then the Jacobins. In

1794 he arrived in Kraków to command the uprising against the occupying armies of Russia and Poland. Determined to make up for his forces' disadvantage in weaponry and quality with quantity, he instituted conscription and equipped the peasants with pikes and traditional war scythes. But the Russian and Prussian armies were insurmountable, and eventually Kościuszko was forced to retreat to Warsaw, where he was besieged for two months. Although he forced the Prussians to retreat by fomenting a rebellion behind their occupation lines, he was defeated at Maciejowice, where he was wounded and captured.

Imprisoned in St. Petersburg, Kościuszko was freed by Russian emperor Paul I in 1796, and he traveled to the United States. He became a close friend of then–Vice President Thomas Jefferson, but returned secretly to France in 1798 to appeal for Poland's independence. Before leaving the United States, he arranged for his estate to free and educate his slaves. In Paris, he could not find suitable agreement with Napoleon about Polish independence. He died in Switzerland, and in 1819 his remains were carried to Kraków and buried alongside the kings' tombs in the cathedral.

Kossuth, Louis (1802–1894)

Hungarian political reformer. Kossuth, who led the struggle for Hungarian independence from Austria, ruled Hungary from 1848 to 1849, just prior to the Russian invasion. Born to a Slovak father and a German mother, Kossuth was unable to escape his poor Lutheran origins, spending most of his life plagued by financial insecurity.

In 1832 Kossuth was sent by his employer, Countess Etelka Andrássy, to the national Diet, where a group of young Hungarian nationalists opposed to Viennese rule were planning to launch their reformist agenda. Kossuth's radicalism was developed within this fervent

setting, and he later petitioned and labored for Hungarian independence. His political activities began when he published the minutes of the theretofore secret Diet meetings and distributed his embellished accounts to a wide public audience. The Diet ended in 1836, but Kossuth began to write similar reports for the Pest county assembly (for which he did not have parliamentary immunity) and was sentenced to three years' imprisonment for subversion. By the time of his release, Kossuth was a national figure. He briefly edited the biweekly journal *Pesti Hirlap*, but was dismissed under governmental pressure after he declared Magyars superior to Croats.

The county of Pest elected Kossuth to be their Diet representative, and he promised a host of reforms. The French Revolution of 1848 provided a catalyst for the Hungarian revolution, and prompted by the events in Paris, Kossuth successfully demanded independence from Austria. After Prince Metternich's regime collapsed, Kossuth became minister of finance in the new government of Count Lajos Batthyány. Six months later, the Croat army invaded Hungary, and Batthyány resigned, leaving Kossuth in control. For almost a year Kossuth attempted to pursue the original goals of his reform program, and his immense popularity served to protect him from public criticism.

The Russian army invasion of 1849 forced Kossuth to recognize the futility of his situation and the impossibility of his maintaining effective control. He resigned and fled to Turkey, spending a number of years in exile. At the request of the U.S. and British governments, he traveled to America and England to promote Hungary's cause before settling in London.

Napoleon III invited Kossuth to organize a revolt in Hungary with French backing, but despite Kossuth's efforts from abroad to create a "Danubian

Confederation" in 1861, the revolution collapsed, and the country reached a settlement with the Viennese monarchy. In opposition, Kossuth wrote a widely published letter denouncing the agreement. Although the letter appealed powerfully to Hungarian nationalist emotions, the compromise was inevitable. After the establishment of Austria-Hungary in 1867, Kossuth's revolutionary days came to an end. He died in Italy, but his body was brought back to Budapest to be publicly interred and mourned. Regarded by many as a national hero, Kossuth is synonymous with the struggle for Hungarian independence, and his revolutionary legend has grown stronger over time.

Kotliarevsky, Ivan Petrovych (1769–1838)

Ukrainian writer. Considered to be the father of modern Ukrainian literature, Kotliarevsky was the son of a minor official. He was educated at a seminary, then served in the army in 1796–1808, and later held various official posts in his native Poltava. In 1798 a pirate edition of the first three parts of his *Eneïda* (1798–1842), a burlesque-travesty of Vergil's epic, was published in St. Petersburg; the full text of the epic was published in 1842. This work, the first to be written entirely in the Ukrainian of his time, marks the beginning of the new Ukrainian literature.

Kotliarevsky's revision of Virgil transmutes Aeneas and the Trojans into dispossessed Cossacks of the period after the suppression of the Zaporozhian Sich (a Cossack territory) in 1775. The poem's description of the everyday life and customs of all levels of Ukrainian society and the character of the Ukrainian people make it a veritable encyclopedia of Ukrainian life at that time. *Eneïda*, as well as Kotliarevsky's plays, the most famous being *Natalka Poltavka* (*Natalka from Poltava*), first staged in 1819, played a decisive role in shaping Ukrainian as a literary language. His plays still form a part of the classic Ukrainian repertoire.

Kotsiubynsky, Mykhailo [Mykhailovych] (1864–1913)

Ukrainian novelist and short-story writer. A major figure in Ukrainian modernism, Kotsiubynsky was the son of a government official, graduating from a seminary in 1880. He did not begin to publish his works until ten years later, working in the interim as a teacher and statistician. His philosophical and stylistic evolution from populist realism to impressionism was the result of European influences and reflected his concern that Ukrainian writing be integrated into the European literary mainstream.

In 1904 appeared the first and in 1910 the second part of Kotsiubynsky's greatest work, the novel *Fata Morgana*. Here the theme of the social conflicts in the village, traditional in Ukrainian literature, was depicted with brilliant insight, through a studied fragmentation and subjectivity typical of the impressionistic approach. His late works deal primarily with the events of the Russian Revolution of 1905 and its suppression, psychological investigations of men in extremity, possessed of terror, hatred, and the urge to kill. The highly acclaimed lyrical monologue *Intermezzo* (1908) develops the theme of escape from one's fellow beings to nature. His novella *Tini zabutykh predkiv* (1913; *Shadows of Forgotten Ancestors*) recreates the primitive world of the Ukrainian mountaineers, the Hutsuls, in a renewal of the ethnographic-Romantic theme.

Kotsiubynsky had a great influence on later Ukrainian writers, and his works were translated into many languages. A number of his writings were also adapted for film; of these adaptations the most acclaimed is *Shadows of Forgotten Ancestors* (1964), by Sergei Paradzhanov.

Kremlin

Russian government headquarters. From the Russian word *kreml*, Kremlin was first used to designate the walled fortress of a medieval Russian city, within which the city prince, important government officials, and clergy would reside. Today the Kremlin refers more specifically to the walled citadel in Moscow, where the central offices of the Russian government are housed.

Originally, the Kremlin contained the entire population of Moscow, but as the city grew, other walls were constructed to protect the population from attack. As warfare technology advanced, the outer walls became obsolete and were torn down to create streets. Today the Kremlin is still the geographic center of the city, with streets encircling its perimeter. The earliest walls were constructed of wood in 1156 and were gradually replaced with stone as the walls were destroyed or the Kremlin became too small. The stone walls that stand today were built by Italian architects in the fifteenth century. These red-brick walls are twelve to twenty feet thick at the base and fifteen to sixty-two feet tall, with numerous towers, underground passages, and a moat—in short, one of the most impenetrable fortresses constructed in Europe at that time.

The Kremlin served as government headquarters until Peter the Great transferred the capital to St. Petersburg. After the October Revolution of 1917, in which the Bolsheviks seized power, the Kremlin was restored as the administrative center of Russia. The various palaces were transformed into parliament buildings and government reception areas and served during Stalin's rule as his personal residence. Some of the churches and monasteries in the Kremlin (which dated as far back as the fourteenth century) were demolished in the late 1920s. The Kremlin was closed to the public until after Stalin's death in 1953; when it reopened, the Kremlin came to house the Kremlin theater and the Palace of Congresses of the Peoples of the U.S.S.R. (1961), as well as the older palaces and churches constructed by the czars that are now museums. After the fall of Communism, the Kremlin became the center of the new Russian government.

Krishna

Hindu god. Krishna is worshiped as the eighth *avatara* (incarnation) of the supreme god Vishnu. Hindu sects like the Vaisnavas, however, believe that Krishna is not merely an *avatara* but God himself. To many Hindus, Krishna represents *prema* (divine love), *rupa* (divine beauty), and *lila* (playful yet purposeless action associated with the divine).

One famous legend appears in the ancient Hindu epic the *Mahabharata*, which tells of the birth of Krishna to Vasudeva and Devaki, a couple among the Yadavas at Mathura. Devaki's brother, the evil Kamsa, king of Mathura, tried to destroy the baby along with his siblings after hearing a prophecy that one of his sister's children would destroy him. Krishna was saved by being smuggled to Gokula, where he was raised by cowherds. The young Krishna became known and loved not only for his pranks, miracles, and his talent at slaying the demons Kamsa sent to kill him, but also for his prowess in wooing the *gopis* (wives and daughters of the cowherds) with his flute-playing. The idyllic play of Krishna and the *gopis* is regarded in Hinduism as an image of the soul's relationship with God.

Krishna and his brother returned to Mathura and killed their uncle, and later set up court in Dvaraka with many of his Yadava kinfolk. When war erupted between the Kauravas and the Pandavas, two other local races, Krishna offered his personal attendance to one side and his army to the other. The Pandavas opted for Krishna's attendance, and he became the charioteer of Arjuna, a young prince, and taught him about duty and god as captured in the beautiful sacred poem the Bhagavadgita, perhaps the most famous section of the *Mahabharata*.

When Krishna returned to his court, he found the Yadavas feuding among each other, culminating in a brawl in which Krishna's brother and son were murdered. When Krishna retired to the forest to mourn these deaths, a hunter named Jaras mistook him for a deer and killed him, shooting him in the one vulnerable spot on Krishna's body, his heel.

Represented in Indian art and literature more than any other god, Krishna is believed to be the divinity that perfectly represents two forms of love. The first is *vatsalya*, or "calf love," typified by the love a mother feels for her children, and the second is *madhurya*, or "sweet love," a more passionate love that binds adult lovers. Representations of Krishna as a child illustrate the first of these concepts, while those of him during his lusty youth portray Krishna as *nayaka*, the "ideal hero" or "leading man" on which many of the heroes of secular erotic literature were modeled.

In both these portrayals, Krishna is seen as a thief: whether stealing butter as a child or other men's wives as a young adult, Krishna is considered to be a thief of the heart for his ability to win the affections of all who come in contact with him.

Krleža, Miroslav (1893–1981)

Croatian playwright and novelist. Krleža was the leading figure in Croatian literature in the twentieth century. His works reflect his interest in conflicting ideas and the results of clashes between opposing forces.

Although Krleža trained for a career in the military and fought in World War I, he soon applied himself to the promotion of his artistic ideas and founded the literary journal *Danas* ("Today") in 1934. His radical views and his refusal to publish under the fascist Ustasha government that ruled Croatia during World War II often led to the censorship

of his works. After the war, Krleža became director of the Yugoslav Lexicographical Institute, a post he held until his death, as well as editor of the *Encyclopaedia Yugoslovia*.

Of Krleža's poetry, *Balade Petrice Kerempuha* (1936; *The Ballads of Petrica Kerempuha*) is often considered to be his finest work. Written in a native dialect, the ballads give voice to a history of persecution. The trilogy *Glembajevi* (1932; *The Glembaj Family*) is perhaps Krleža's most ambitious work, exploring the powerful themes of hypocrisy, corruption, and the fall of the bourgeoisie. *Hrvatski bog Mars* (1922; *The Croatian God Mars*) and *Novele* (1924; *Short Stories*) were Krleža's two volumes of stories, presenting ideas reminiscent of those in his other works. Krleža's best-known novel is *Povratak Filipa Latinovicza* (1932; *The Return of Philip Latinovicz*), which is a startling account of the essential isolation of the artist.

Kublai Khan (1215–1294)

First emperor of China's Yuan or Mongol dynasty (1271–1368). Transliterated now as Hu Bi Lie. Known as "Great Khan," he conquered the disintegrating Song dynasty in southern China, and subsequently directed military expeditions against Indochina and other countries such as Japan, Malacca, Burma, and Java, glorifying his empire as the center of the world. Within his lavish court in Da-du (the word means "great capital"), what is now Beijing, he received Marco Polo (1254–1324), a Venetian explorer and merchant, who visited and served in the court from 1275 to 1292. After he left China, Marco Polo wrote *Il milione* (*The Travels of Marco Polo*), a document that astounded the West and spurred the imagination of rulers and explorers around the world, including Portuguese explorer Christopher Columbus (1451–1506).

Kublai Khan is commemorated in a famous poem composed by the English

Romantic Samuel Taylor Coleridge (1772–1834), who dreamed, under the influence of opium, of the great emperor and his imperial palace. The unfinished record of that dream, "Kubla Khan," is one of Coleridge's best-known works.

Kūkai (774–835)

Japanese religious leader. One of the great religious leaders of Japan, Kūkai (also known as Kōbō Daishi) founded the Shingon, or "True Word" school of Buddhism. He is known variously as traveling saint, poet, artist, the lexicographer who put together the Japanese dictionary, and "the father of Japanese culture" who invented the Kana syllabary. He is the subject of numerous legends, renowned not least for his severe asceticism. He taught Yogic discipline to intellectuals of the Heian period (794–1185), and is credited with creating the Shikoku pilgrimage circuit of eighty-eight temples.

The writings of Kūkai include *Sangō shiiki* (798), his first work, which promoted Buddhism over Confucianism and Taoism; *Sokushin jōbutsu gi* (*Meanings of Attaining Enlightenment in This Very Existence*); and *Jūjūshin ron* (*Treatise on the Ten Stages of the Development of Mind*).

Kuncewiczowa, Maria (1897–1989)

Polish novelist and short-story writer. Best known for the psychological realism of her novels and short stories, Kuncewiczowa was born Maria Szczepanska in Samara, Russia, to parents who had been exiled from Poland in the wake of the 1863 uprising. After studying literature and music at various Polish universities, she studied opera at both the Warsaw and the Paris conservatories. She made her operatic debut in 1918 and continued to perform as a singer throughout the 1920s; in 1918 she also made her debut as a writer of fiction. In 1921 she married Jerzy Kuncewicz.

By 1927 Kuncewiczowa had written her first collection of short stories, *Przymierze z dzieckiem* (*Alliance with a Child*); in 1928 she published her first novel, *Twarz mężczyzny* (*The Face of the Male*). Both books identified her as a writer willing to depict the female mind with unusual frankness. In 1933 she published *Dwa ksiezyce* (*Two Moons*), an ambitious collection of short stories, all set in the Polish town of Kazmierz. In 1936 her reputation was made with the publication of *Cudzoziemka* (*The Stranger*), a novel depicting, in minute detail, the deathbed turmoil and transformation experienced by an aged female violinist; in 1937 it won the Warsaw Literary Prize.

With the outbreak of World War II, Kuncewiczowa was driven into exile. From 1940 to 1955 she lived in England, where she published *Klucze* (1943; *The Keys*), a diary based on her experience of war. During this same period she also wrote *Zmowa nieobecnych* (1946; *The Conspiracy of the Absent*), a novel that juxtaposes the world of wartime London with the world of occupied Poland, as well as *Leśnik* (1952; *The Forester*), a book dealing with the problem of national identity that afflicts Lithuanian Poles. After moving to the United States in 1956, she found a post as a professor of Polish literature at the University of Chicago, where she remained from 1962 to 1970. In 1962 she published *The Modern Polish Mind*, an anthology of Polish writing.

Later novels included *Gaj oliwny* (1962; *The Olive Grove*), which details a young girl's reactions to murder, and *Tristan 1946* (1967), which weaves a rich web of allegory around the story of the postwar love between a Polish boy and an Irish girl. By the early 1970s Kuncewiczowa had returned to Poland, where she continued to live and write until her death in 1989.

Kundera, Milan (1929–)

Czech short-story writer, playwright, and poet. Kundera's work is noted for its skillful combination of political criticism and erotic comedy. Son of a noted pianist and musicologist, Kundera began studying music but turned to writing and published his first volume of poetry, *Člověk zahrada širá* (1953; *Man: A Broad Garden*), at twenty-four. He published two more collections of poetry, earning the distrust of Communist Party cultural officials. His relationship with the party was always unsteady: he had joined in 1947, was dismissed in 1950, and later was reinstated.

In the 1960s Kundera began writing prose. Three series of short stories, published under the title *Směšné lásky* (1963; *Laughable Loves*), are ironic tales of seduction and politics. The success of these stories and of a one-act play, *Majitelé klíčů* (1962; *The Owners of the Keys*), was followed by the greater success of his first novel, *Žert* (1967; *The Joke*), in which a young Czech intellectual's career is ruined by an ill-timed joke and an even more ill-timed attempt at revenge.

Kundera spoke in 1967 at the Fourth Congress of Czechoslovak writers about the need to preserve the independence of Czech culture through its literature, and participated in the liberalizations of the Prague Spring of 1968. After the Soviet invasion, Kundera's books were banned; he was fired from his teaching positions and expelled, again, from the party. His next novel, *Život je jinde* (1969; *Life Is Elsewhere*), was denied publication in Czechoslovakia, and in 1975 he was allowed to emigrate and stripped of his citizenship.

Settling in France, Kundera wrote *Valčík na rozloučenou* (1976; *The Farewell Party*), a philosophical sexual comedy; *Kniha smíchu a zapomnění* (1979; *The Book of Laughter and Forgetting*), part novel, part short stories, about the systematic loss of memory of Husák, the revanchist Czech Communist leader installed by the Soviets in the wake of 1968; and *Nes nesitelná lehkost byti*

(1984; *The Unbearable Lightness of Being*), one of Kundera's most popular works.

Along with other writers and intellectuals, Kundera restored his Czech citizenship after the fall of the Communist government in 1990. His most recent novel, *Nesmrtelnost* (1989; *Immortality*), includes familiar meditations on sex, identity, and mass society, as well as a brilliant evocation of fame, mortality, meaning, and love.

Kurd

An ethnic and linguistic group that has lived for millennia in the Taurus and Zagros mountains of current-day Turkey, Iraq, and Iran. Most Kurds are Sunnî Muslims, and their language (which contains several dialects) is a West Iranian tongue related to Persian and Pashto. Though the traditional Kurdish lifestyle was based on sheep- and goat-herding, these activities have declined as Kurdish communities become increasingly detribalized, urbanized, and incorporated into the countries in which they live. Kurds have also contributed significantly to the cultures around them, particularly in music, literature, and the arts.

Despite their long-standing occupation of a specific geographic area, the Kurds have never achieved nation-state status. However, this has not prevented the development of strong nationalist feelings. The failure to create a Kurdish state after the fall of the Ottoman empire in the First World War, economic discrimination, and severe reprisals against secessionists by the governments of Iran, Iraq, and Turkey have contributed to the development of a nationalist movement that has worked diligently for increased autonomy. Although there have been Kurdish rebellions in the past and present in Iraq, Iran, and Turkey, these have not yet succeeded. Kurdish demands for political and cultural autonomy also differ from region to region, and opposition groups may represent different political ideologies.

Kurosawa Akira (1910–)

Japanese film director, scriptwriter, and producer. Considered one of Japan's greatest filmmakers, Kurosawa is renowned for introducing his country's cinema to the world. Born in Tokyo and educated at Keika Middle School and Doshusha School of Western Painting, Kurosawa had an avid interest in filmmaking from an early age. He began his career studying in Kajiro Yamamoto's production group around 1936. By that time he already had directing experience from his stay at P.C.C. Studios (Photo-Chemical Laboratory, later Toho Motion Picture Company), but not until 1943 did he direct his first film, *Sugata sanshiro* (1945; *The Legend of Judo*), which explored the master-disciple relationships that frequently appear in Kurosawa's films. He went on to found the Motion Picture Artists Association (1948) with Yamamoto and others and later formed several production agencies, including Kurosawa Productions (1959) and the Yonki no Kai production company (1971).

Kurosawa's work has many different facets, appealing to widely different audiences. His commercial appeal allowed him much creative leeway, so he could experiment with technique and tale alike. His tragic and deeply human film *Yoidore tenshi* (1948; *Drunken Angel*) marks Kurosawa's arrival at artistic maturity by showcasing his characteristic variety of pacing, camera angles, and lighting that he so aptly applied to black-and-white film. Two years later he shocked and pleased the world with *Rashomon*, his 1951 Venice Film Festival Grand Prize Winner. His use of long lenses and multiple cameras in the famous final battle scenes of *Shichinin no samurai* (1954; *The Seven Samurai*) directly influenced the Hollywood western *The Magnificent Seven*, as did the film's plot. He pioneered the use of the widescreen process in Japan with the making of the 1958 samurai entertainment classic *Kakushi toride no san-akunin (Hidden Fortress)*, a film George Lucas drew on when envisioning the *Star Wars* trilogy. His *Yojimbo* (1961; *The Bodyguard*) attracted audience attention with its realistic sword fighting and serious depictions of violence. Finally, his use of Panavision and multitrack Dolby sound with *Kagemusha* (1980; *The Shadow Warrior*) was the first in Japan, which undoubtedly helped the incredibly long film win the Cannes Film Festival's Grand Prize for that year.

Kurosawa was not only an innovator on the technical front, but also the first Japanese filmmaker to adapt Western classical literature to the screen. He made visually arresting versions of Dostoevsky's *Idiot* (1951), Shakespeare's *Macbeth* (1957; *Kumonosu-jo [Throne of Blood]*), and *King Lear* (*Ran*, 1985) in Japan. However, he did not bind himself to any single culture, as can be seen in his use of Japanese Noh theater staging techniques and music in both *Throne of Blood* and *Kagemusha*. In addition, the success of *Ikiru* (1952) and *The Seven Samurai*, two completely original screenplays, show how Kurosawa's natural storytelling ability and universal messages ultimately transcend boundaries of culture, time, and genre.

Kush

Ancient kingdom of the Middle Nile area in what is now Sudan. The area was part of the ancient Egyptian empire until it started to decline in about the eleventh century B.C.E. The city of Napata, an Egyptian colony, began to prosper as a trade and military center. Under the rule of Piankhi (c. 744–710 B.C.E.) and Taharqa (c. 710–633 B.C.E.), the Kush kingdom (also known as ancient Nubia) controlled all of Egypt. Driven out of Egypt around 661 B.C.E. by the Assyrians, the Kush kings ruled the Middle

Nile area for another 150 years, until the leadership shifted to the town of Meroë, farther south on the Nile. Little of its history is known from that point, however. By the fourth century C.E., Meroë was reported to be in ruins. Its remains, including evidence of a written Meroitic language, were discovered by archaeologists in 1909.

Kwangju Incident

Korean political rebellion that took place in the city of Kwangju. Widespread prodemocracy demonstrations by a large cross-section of the Korean population culminated on May 18, 1980, when the U.S. government approved the deployment of four battalions of American-controlled Korean troops to put down the insurrection in Kwangju, a city in southwestern Korea. In the wake of the assassination of right-wing dictator Park Chung Hee in 1979, students, workers, and members of Korea's growing middle classes joined together to demand the reformation of Park's Yushin ("Revitalization" or "Restoration") constitution, which provided for a virtual government-by-presidential-mandate, as well as to demand labor reforms and an end to compulsory military service. While violent confrontation was averted in the capital city of Seoul, due to the intervention of moderate opposition leaders Kim Dae Jung and Kim Young Sam, the citizenry of the economically depressed southwestern Cholla province reacted powerfully to then-military dictator General Chun Doo Hwan's ban on all political activity and his arrest of hundreds of opposition leaders, including Kim Dae Jung.

Violating the prohibition against public assembly, on May 18 approximately five hundred Kwangju students were met with gunfire, clubbing, and bayoneting by a special "Black Beret" detachment of the Korean military. Within days, angry citizens had seized control of government buildings, armories, and vehicles in Kwangju. A new military-backed cabinet administration in Seoul secured American support in the form of troops and a public declaration by the U.S. State Department. An appeal for U.S. mediation issued by the provisional citizen government of Kwangju was declined; within hours thousands of military troops that had encircled Kwangju invaded the city and regained control of its public offices. In the following weeks, demonstrators and suspected members of the opposition were arrested, tortured, and executed.

Official accounts list 193 people killed in the Kwangju Incident, but eyewitness reports range from between 500 and 2,000 dead or missing as a result of the government crackdown. The Kwangju Incident represents a rare moment of political unity among a broad sector of the Korean population; protesters were drawn from the ranks of students, workers, and the middle classes. It also provided a platform for the emergence of a number of individuals who were to become major political figures. Future Korean presidents Chun Doo Hwan and Roh Tae Woo both played crucial roles as generals in suppressing the rebellion; and future opposition leaders Kim Dae Jung and Kim Young Sam (who were to become rival candidates in the 1988 presidential elections) both garnered public support and credibility for their sympathy with leaders of Kwangju.

The Kwangju Incident has proved an enduring wellspring of anti-American sentiment among Koreans, who consider the United States culpable in the affair because of its statements supporting the "restoration of order" and for having provided troops involved in the military strike.

Kyanzittha (c. 1084–1113)

Burmese ruler. As king of the Pagan empire in its early days as a center of Burmese culture and Theravāda Buddhism,

Kyanzittha (or Kalancacsa) is remembered for his success in creating a stable and secure multicultural state. Kyanzittha took power at a crucial period, only a few years after the Pagan empire had come into existence as a result of the conquests of King Anawrahta. The new, expanded empire included the Mons and Shans, foreign peoples who had previously ruled other parts of Burma.

Tradition holds that Kyanzittha was not of royal blood, but rather the child of one of Anawrahta's lords, who had seduced a young bride of the king. As a young man, he fought for Anawrahta, gaining fame as a warrior-hero in many of Anawrahta's wars of conquest. He is credited with saving the city from attack by the Talaings (Mons) in 1084 in a battle that killed King Sawlu. Kyanzittha acceded to the throne of Pagan, uniquely chosen for his extraordinary abilities and proved heroism rather than by divine right or inheritance. After his ascension, he continued to prove his value as a leader in both political and spiritual matters, and set an example for future Burmese kings who ruled not by divine right but by virtue of their own strengths.

An important patron of the arts, Kyanzittha was responsible for much of the beauty of the city of Pagan. In particular, he built the Ananda temple, a great white pagoda decorated with scenes from the life of Buddha, which is today the oldest structure remaining in Pagan. He allowed Mon culture to coexist with the Burmese, such that Mon artisans and scholars enriched the life of the empire. Kyanzittha took on the spiritual role of *bodhisattva*, one whose holiness is so great it may redeem others or guide them to redemption. In this he was also followed by later kings. His reign is remembered as the beginning of what would become the unique culture of Buddhist Burma.

L

Lachish letters

Ancient Hebraic texts. The Lachish letters, written by many different scribes, were the first records ever discovered that depicted the culture of the ancient kingdom of Judah. Written in Phoenician-Hebrew script, the letters suggest to historians that the Phoenician-Hebrew alphabet not only was used for engraving on stone but was, in fact, invented specifically for writing in ink on papyrus (parchment) and potsherds (pottery fragments). Inscribed on eighteen baked-clay potsherds, the letters were found in the ruins of a gate-room (perhaps used in ancient times as a courtroom) in the city of Lachish (now Tell ed-Duweir), which was a stronghold on the western frontier of the Judean kingdom at the time of the second Babylonian invasion (c. 588–587 B.C.E.).

The letters, written in biblical Hebrew of the variety found in the Old Testament books of Kings and Jeremiah, are considered to be among the most intimate corroborations of the Old Testament. They contain the correspondence between Hosha'yahu, the commander of a small outpost (perhaps present-day Qiryat Ye'arim) near the western border of the kingdom, and his superior, Lord Jaush, stationed at the main fort at Lachish.

Collected in what appears to be a dossier used at Hosha'yahu's court-martial, the letters contain various charges against him regarding his possible role in the fall of his outpost to the enemy, as well as his denial of these charges. It is likely that the gate-room where the potsherds were found was also where the case was tried. It was probably one of the last such cases before the fall of Judah to Nebuchadnezzar and the Babylonians in 587 B.C.E.

Lacrosse, *see* baggataway

ladino/ladina

Central American term originally used to describe a person of Spanish descent living in the Americas. *Ladinos* were distinguished from their Indian compatriots mostly by their exclusive use of the Spanish language and a reliance on somewhat more advanced agricultural methods. Like the "creole" distinction used in French colonies, *ladino/ladina* in certain contexts referred to people of mixed Indian and Spanish descent. In these cases it is interchangeable with *mestizo/mestiza*. Today the category is employed more as a description of class or cultural characteristics and less as a mark of lineage. A Central American person who adopts Spanish culture, particularly language and dress, is considered a *ladino/ladina*, regardless of descent.

Lahore

Capital of Punjab province and the second-largest city in Pakistan. According to Hindu legend, Lahore got its name from its founder, Lava or Loh, son of Rama, the hero of the Sanskrit epic the *Ramayana*, probably written around the third century B.C.E.

Although little is known of the city's history prior to Muslim rule, Lahore did serve as the capital of the Ghazni dy-

nasty from 1152 to 1186. Beginning in 1241, when the Mongols sacked Lahore, and continuing throughout the thirteenth and fourteenth centuries, the city suffered repeatedly from numerous, almost annual, Mongol invasions.

In 1524 the Mughal ruler Babur captured Lahore. Mughal occupation marked the beginning of Lahore's "Golden Age," which reached its peak during the reign of Shah Jahan (1628–57) and declined under the reign of Aurangzeb (1658–1707). During the Mughal period, Lahore served as the royal residence of the Mughal emperors Akbar (1556–1605), Jahangir (1605–27), and Shah Jahan.

Following the death of Aurangzeb and until the accession of Ranjit Singh (1798), Sikh insurrections in Lahore were regular, along with invasions by the Afghani leaders Nadir Shah and Ahmad Shah Abdali. Ranjit Singh (1780–1839), himself a Sikh, established a powerful dynasty based in Lahore, but under his successors this power gradually diminished and in 1849 the city passed into British hands.

Lahore was the site of the famous Muslim League conference in 1940, at which a series of demands for the partition of India and creation of an independent Muslim state were made; the charter of Pakistan evolved out of these demands. Following Indian independence in 1947, Lahore was made the capital of West Punjab (later known as Punjab) province and in 1955 became the capital of the newly formed West Pakistan province, which in 1970 was reconstituted as Punjab province.

Modern Lahore is an important industrial, commercial, and educational center. The University of the Punjab (1882), located in Lahore, is the oldest university in Pakistan.

lakhorn

Classical Thai drama form. Based on the *Ramakien*, a Thai literary classic that contains numerous traditional legends, like *khön* drama, *lakhorn* (also called *lakhon* or *lakhornram*) draws heavily on Thai romances, folk tales, and *jatakas* (stories detailing the various lives of Buddha). It is distinguished from *khön* by less vigorous, more graceful action, and acted by unmasked dancers of both genders who sometimes speak. *Lakhorn* is based upon a large vocabulary of conventionalized movements portraying specific actions or emotions, such as "stag walking through the forest." These repertoires are so extensive that, like *khön* players, *lakhorn* players must begin their training as children in order to master them fully.

Lamming, George [William] (1927–)

Barbadian writer. Born on the island of Barbados in the British West Indies, Lamming attended high school there and taught in Trinidad from 1946 to 1950, when he immigrated to England. There he spent time as a factory worker and then as a broadcaster for the BBC Colonial Service.

Lamming's first novel, *In the Castle of My Skin*, was published in 1953, with an introduction by American writer Richard Wright (1908–1960). A quasi-autobiographical account of growing up on a fictional Caribbean island, San Cristobal, the book won wide acclaim and is today regarded as a West Indian classic. *The Emigrants* followed in 1954; closely paralleling Lamming's own experience, it is the story of West Indians who leave their native land to explore their cultural heritage in England. He won a Guggenheim Fellowship in 1955 and the Somerset Maugham Award in 1957. His next two novels, *Of Age and Innocence* (1958) and *Season of Adventure* (1960), follow emigrants on their return to the fictional San Cristobal in search of self-discovery.

In the 1960s Lamming concentrated on poetry and short fiction, much of it collected in anthologies of Caribbean writing. After a long period of revision, in 1972 Lamming published both *Water with Berries*, which uses the framework of Shakespeare's *The Tempest* to explore the effects of colonialism and exile on contemporary West Indians, and *Natives of My Person*, the story of the journey of the ship *Reconnaissance* from Europe to Africa to America in the sixteenth century. Both are set in San Cristobal and both are written in a highly stylized, poetic language. In addition to his many novels, Lamming has published many poems, short stories, and essays, and edited *Cannon Shot and Glass Beads: Modern Black Writing* (1974).

Lang, Fritz (1890–1976)

Austrian-born American film director. The son of an architect, Lang abandoned an early career in architecture to travel the world, supporting himself as a graphic artist. He began writing stories and screenplays for Joe May, a prominent German director, while recovering from wounds he received in combat during the First World War. Lang commenced his film career in 1919 with his self-released film *Halbblut* (*The Half-Breed*).

Lang's early work was melodramatic and expressionist, to the taste of postwar Germany, and always visually impressive. Artistically, his most important work of the silent period was *Metropolis* (1927), a film depicting a future urban labyrinth of an authoritarian society. The most expensive film ever produced in Germany at the time, it exemplifies Lang's visual artistry; the film has been called "pictorially impeccable" due to its elaborate set and cinematography.

M (1931), Lang's first film utilizing sound and his personal favorite, is considered by many to be his masterpiece, blending expressionist and realistic styles to create a chilling depiction of a child-murderer in a city torn by mob violence. It foreshadowed his later interest in social problems, and the fast-paced, terrifying, and fatalistic vision that he would bring to the screen in other thrillers.

Fleeing Germany in 1933 after his

anti-Nazi film *Das Testament des Dr. Mabuse* (*The Testament of Dr. Mabuse*) was banned, Lang left for the United States, leaving behind his wife, Thea von Harbou, a Nazi supporter. Generally, Lang's work for American studios—including the films *Fury* (1936) and *You Only Live Once* (1937), both studies of social injustice; the anti-Nazi films *Man Hunt* (1941) and *Hangmen Also Die!* (1943); and *The Big Heat* (1953), an exposure of violence and corruption, among others—is characterized by concentrated, distilled plots with only the essential imagery and information necessary to create tension in the audience.

In 1957 Lang returned to Germany to direct films based on scripts he and his wife had previously written for Joe May in 1921. Lang stayed in Germany to make his last film, *Die 1,000 Augen des Dr. Mabuse* (1960; *The Thousand Eyes of Dr. Mabuse*).

Lao She (1899–1966)

Manchu novelist. Known for his humor and satire, Lao's novels include *The Life of Niu Tianci* (1934), *The Yellow Storm* (1951), *Luo tuo xiangzi* (1936; *Rickshaw Boy*), and *Gu shu yiren* (1952; *The Drum Singers*). He also wrote numerous plays, of which the best known are *Cha guan* (1957; *The Teahouse*) and *Dragon Beard Ditch* (1951). Born and raised under the name Shu Shiyu in Beijing, he traveled to England in 1924 as a visiting teacher. He helped to translate the great Ming novel *Jin ping mei* (*The Golden Lotus*) into English.

Influenced by Charles Dickens, he began trying his hand as a novelist. His early works, though usually consumed by such serious themes as the role of the individual in reforming Chinese government and society, were already marked by Lao's characteristic humor and satire. After returning to China in 1931, Lao She's writing began to emphasize the importance of the social awareness of the masses. During World War II he was an active patriot, heading the Chinese Anti-Japanese Writers Federation. After the war, in 1946, he traveled to the United States, lecturing and overseeing the translation of several of his novels. He returned to China a year later. The founding of the People's Republic gave his writing new energy. While continuing to produce novels and plays, he participated actively in various cultural and literary movements. In 1966, at the beginning of the Cultural Revolution, Lao She committed suicide.

Lao Tzu (551–479 B.C.E.)

The first sage of Chinese Taoism. Also spelled Lao Zi. The putative author of *Tao-te Ching*, Lao Tzu was, according to a legend, a keeper of the archives at the imperial court. In his eightieth year, he set out for the western border of China, toward what is now Tibet, saddened and disillusioned that men were unwilling to follow the path to natural goodness. At the border, however, the guard Yin Si persuaded him to record his teachings before he left to die in a desert, so he wrote the famous *Tao-te Ching* (*Classic of the Way of Power*). Terse and cryptic in style, the book describes *tao* (the way) as the ultimate source and the inevitable destiny of the human world, of the universe. It particularly advocates the idea of nonaction, *wu-wei*, as described in such experiences as "Take whatever comes" and "Live as naturally as water flows." Lao Tzu observed that water, though softest of all things, in its natural way can wear away the hardest rock; the symbolic meaning is that the universe proceeds smoothly according to its own harmonies. Man's efforts to change or improve nature or himself only destroy these harmonies and produce disorder.

Lapp

Indigenous people of Lapland, the northernmost part of Europe. The majority of Lapland falls within the Arctic Circle in Norway, Sweden, Finland, and Russia. Forty thousand of the 60,000

Lapps live in Norway, and represent 1 percent of Norway's population. While traditionally nomadic, living by hunting, fishing, and herding reindeer, Lapps (or Saami, in their own language) began farming in this century, and those that continue to herd large numbers of reindeer no longer migrate with them year-round. About half of Lapps are coastal fishermen.

Lappish, the language, is part of the Finno-Ugric branch of the Uralic family. Its three dialects are mutually unintelligible and could be considered separate languages. Most Lapps are bilingual, speaking their Lapp dialect and the official language of the country where they live. Christian missionary activity began in the eleventh century and virtually eradicated their shamanistic practices. Today most Lapps are Lutherans, though some belong to a puritanical fundamentalist sect, and those in the East follow the Russian Orthodox Church. The strong kinship bond between brothers and sisters and their spouses remains part of Lapp society, and these relationships are the basis of herding units, though animals are owned individually.

While their origin is obscure, perhaps Asian, Finnish, or Central European, the Lapps have at various times populated most of Norway, Sweden, and Finland, having been pushed farther and farther north. Promises to protect their land have been historically ignored. Lapp political organizations have more recently tried to influence the countries where they live to improve the poor living standards of many Lapps, to protect their traditional herding lands, and to preserve Lapp culture and language. Since 1986, a main concern of Lapps has been to minimize the effects of nuclear fallout from the Chernobyl disaster.

Las Casas, Bartolomé de (1474–1566)

Spanish colonist and priest. Remem-
bered primarily as "the defender of the Indians," Las Casas was born in Spain. His first contact with the New World occurred when, as a young boy, he witnessed the return of the ships of Italian explorer Christopher Columbus, after his first voyage.

In 1502 Las Casas went to Hispaniola (what is now Haiti and the Dominican Republic), where he participated in the military suppression of an Indian uprising; for his service he received a sizable number of Indians and became an *encomendero*. (Under the Spanish *encomienda* system, which began in 1503, an individual colonist was "given" Indians to work for him for a certain number of days a year. In return, the Indians were to be cared for, fed, and introduced to Christianity.) Although Las Casas had initially profited from the Spanish colonization of the New World, his later decision to become a priest made him a fierce defender of Indian rights. Soon after being ordained the first priest in the New World in 1512, Las Casas moved to Cuba as a chaplain of the conquest. He became increasingly disturbed by the treatment of the Indians, nine tenths of whom died. Pondering the extreme poverty and servitude of the Indians, Las Casas gave up his *encomienda* and traveled back to Spain to defend the rights of Indians in court, where he was dubbed the "Protector of the Indians." After failed reform efforts in Hispaniola and Venezuela, Las Casas entered the Dominican order in Santo Domingo (1524), where he remained for eight years, dedicating himself to meditation and self-education.

At the close of this period of reflection, Las Casas resumed an activist role. He preached against the conquest of Indians in Nicaragua and established a successful mission to Tuzulutlán, known as *la tierra de guerra* (the Land of War), in Guatemala. With a few other members of the Dominican order, Las Casas drafted a series of letters to Pope

Paul III (1534–49), who responded by issuing his *Bulla Sublimis Deus* (1537), proclaiming the rationality and full humanity of the Indians.

In the early 1540s Las Casas returned to Spain to argue again for the abolition of the *encomienda*; while there he wrote his most famous work, the *Brevísima relación de la destrucción de las Indias* (1552; *Devastation of the Indies: A Brief Account*). King Charles I (r. 1516–56) issued the New Laws (1542) in response, which called for the suppression of the conquest, the good treatment and care of the Indians, and the phasing out of the *encomienda*.

Las Casas returned to the New World as bishop of Chiapas, but encountered great difficulties in his religious life; he was apparently unable to persuade his congregation to return wealth stolen from the Indians and encountered disagreements with the clergy, royal authorities, and neighboring bishops. Returning yet again to Spain in an attempt to gain royal support, Las Casas debated the justice of the Spanish conquest. He rejected the claim that the Indians were "slaves by nature," arguing instead for the recognition of Indian rationality and claiming that all races are human and consequently equal in their capacity for improvement. Subsequent policies seem to have been drafted according to Las Casas's ideas, namely the Ordinances of Discovery and Settlement (1573), which prohibited the conquest of Indians "by fire and by sword." Las Casas spent the last years of his life recruiting missionaries for work in the New World and revising his writings.

As a result of Las Casas's work, most notably his book *Devastation of the Indies*, a historical legend concerning the Spanish conquest and colonization of the New World arose. Spread and embellished particularly by European rivals of Spain, *la leyenda negra* (the black legend) held that the Spanish *conquistadores* were particularly barbaric in their treatment of the Indians and that Spanish administration in the Americas was oppressive and corrupt. The Black Legend was reinforced by engraver Theodore de Bry's illustrations of sensational episodes in a 1598 Latin edition of Las Casas's *Devastation of the Indies* (and several reprints of the edition), as well as by reports of the Spanish massacre of French settlers at Fort Caroline, Florida, in 1565. Although early Dutch and French translations of Las Casas's account clearly figured as part of a propaganda war against Spain, the Black Legend resonates with the reestimation of the cost of New World colonization in the decades following World War II.

Lawrence, D[avid] H[erbert] (1885–1930)

English writer. D. H. Lawrence was a prolific author, famed for the sexual tension, primitive religion, and sensual mysticism that characterize his work.

Born in Nottinghamshire into an English working-class family, Lawrence was the son of a coal miner. Hypersensitive and fragile in his youth, Lawrence had a complex and difficult childhood. Struggling to become first a teacher, then a writer, Lawrence began his literary career with *The White Peacock*, published in the *English Review* in 1911. However, it was his semiautobiographical novel, *Sons and Lovers* (1913), that eventually secured Lawrence a place within the literary circles of London, though it did little to relieve his financial distress.

A year before the publication of *Sons and Lovers*, Lawrence met Frieda von Richthofen, a German aristocrat, who at the time was married to Lawrence's former college professor. Together Lawrence and von Richthofen left England for Germany; living for a while in Italy, they finally returned to England in 1914. Embarking on a stormy but happy marriage, Lawrence chronicles their relationship in his collection of poems *Look! We Have Come Through* (1917).

The years surrounding the First World War would prove difficult for Lawrence: his novel *The Rainbow* (1915) was considered to be obscene and banned, and he himself was regarded skeptically because he wrote, wore a beard, and was married to a German woman. After the war, Lawrence's financial situation began to improve, as an American publisher agreed to reissue *The Rainbow* and to publish *Women in Love* (1921) in the United States.

After spending several months in Mexico, Lawrence became intrigued with the civilization of the Aztec Indians. This interest spawned the novel *The Plumed Serpent*, which appeared in 1926. That year, he began writing his last and perhaps most famed novel, the controversial *Lady Chatterley's Lover*. First published in limited editions in Florence in 1928 and in Paris in 1929, the complete manuscript of *Lady Chatterley's Lover* was not published until 1959 in New York and in 1960 in London after much-publicized obscenity trials.

Lawrence never relinquished his disdain for Anglo-Saxon puritanism, nor did he cease to challenge social convention in his writing, which made him the object of the most famous censorship cases of his day. One of the most renowned writers of the twentieth century, Lawrence died of tuberculosis in southern France at the age of forty-four.

Lawrence, T[homas] E[dward] (1888–1935) British archaeological scholar, military strategist, and writer. Known more popularly as Lawrence of Arabia, T. E. Lawrence is best known for his role in the Arab revolt against the Turks during World War I and for his account of those events in his work *The Seven Pillars of Wisdom*, published posthumously in 1935.

Lawrence traveled widely in the Middle East as an archaeology student, and his knowledge of the Arabic language and culture made him a useful member of the British administration in Cairo when the First World War erupted in 1914. In October 1916 he traveled with Sir Ronald Storrs to Arabia, where Husayn ibn 'Alī, the *amīr* of Mecca, had declared a revolt against Turkish rule. Seeing a useful opportunity to make trouble for Germany's Ottoman ally, Lawrence persuaded his superiors to support the Arab rebellion with arms and gold. Joining the Arab forces as a political and liaison officer, throughout the war Lawrence helped lead the small but troublesome second front behind the Turkish lines. Most of his group's activities consisted of mining bridges and supply trains, and occupying Turkish forces that otherwise would have been deployed elsewhere.

On one of his campaigns, Lawrence was captured by the Turks and raped before escaping. The episode left emotional wounds from which he never fully recovered.

After the war, Lawrence lobbied in vain for Arab independence and against giving France mandate powers in Syria and Lebanon. He also devoted a great deal of time to the preparation of his account of the war, *The Seven Pillars of Wisdom*. Following a short period of service as an adviser on Arab affairs to Winston Churchill, then the British colonial minister in Cairo, Lawrence made a number of attempts to rejoin the military. He even took assumed names to help him in this endeavor. Lawrence was discharged from the Royal Air Force as an enlisted man in 1935 at the age of forty-six. Retiring, he returned home in great despair over the future course of his life, which he believed would be empty, and died from injuries sustained in a motorcycle accident.

Lawson, Henry (1867–1922) Australian short-story writer and poet. Lawson was known as the "people's poet" for his idiomatic style and his stories of the Australian bush. Deaf since the age of nine and having suffered through a childhood that he described as "a miserable little hell," Lawson was greatly influenced by the poverty of inner-city life in Sydney and by the political meetings that were held in his mother's home.

After having worked for publications in Sydney and Brisbane, Lawson sailed for New Zealand in 1894. While there, his mother published his first collection, *Short Stories in Prose and Verse*. In 1896 his first commercial successes appeared. These two works were entitled *In the Days When the World Was Wide* and *While the Billy Boils*.

Despite his success during this period, Lawson was haunted by melancholia and alcoholism. After deciding to make an attempt at life in England in 1900, Lawson's condition worsened. He returned to Sydney in 1902 and was separated from his wife, Bertha, in April 1903. Though the 1901 publication of *Joe Wilson and His Mates* had placed success within his grasp, Lawson was unable to capitalize on it.

The next twenty years of Lawson's life were spent in penurious circumstances. In 1917 some of his friends banded together and arranged for him to take a government position on the Yanco irrigation project. The time in the dry climate was good for his health, and *The Yanco Book* was the literary result of his sojourn there. In the winter of 1921, Lawson suffered a stroke that left him partially paralyzed. He died alone in his cottage.

Laye, Camara (1928–1980)

West African novelist. Born in Kouroussa, Guinea, Laye was a Muslim by faith. He was educated first at a Qur'ânic school, then at a local French primary school, and afterward at Conakry Technical College, where he graduated in mechanical engineering. He was sent to France for further training in engineer-ing. There he wrote his first book, *L'Enfant noir* (1953; *The African Child*). This enormously influential book, based on his own life, relates his past with great tenderness and sympathy. Like African writer Chinua Achebe's *Things Fall Apart* (1958) in English-speaking Africa, *L'Enfant noir* is widely studied in the schools of French-speaking Africa. Laye's second book, *Le Régard du roi* (1954; *The Radiance of the King*), was beautifully written in classical French. Humor and symbolism—including that of Islam—are combined in the recounting of the attempt by a European, Clarence, to see an African king. The meaning of the novel has provoked much speculation. At the end of the novel, Laye writes, the king's cloak "swept around him and enveloped him for ever." Regardless of its ambiguous ending, many consider *The Radiance of the King* to be Laye's finest work.

Returning from France in 1955, Laye settled in Guinea. His other books include a sequel to *The African Child*, *Dramouss* (1966; *Dream of Africa*). In addition to his novels, Laye also wrote many short stories for the periodicals *Black Orpheus* and *Présence Africaine*.

Layla and Majnun

Islamic epic love story. *Layla and Majnun* occupies a central position in the imagination and mystical literature of Muslims speaking Arabic, Kurdish, Persian, Turkish, Urdu, and other languages. The legend concerns a seventh-century Arab poet, Qays Ibn Mulawwah, of the Banu tribe, who falls in love with a woman named Layla who belongs to another clan of the same tribe. Qays's love is reciprocated, but Layla's father refuses to give his daughter in marriage to Qays. As a result, Qays goes mad, and thereby comes to be known as Majnun, or "the one possessed." Hoping it will cure him, Majnun's family takes him to the Ka'bah, an Islamic holy site, but instead of asking for a cure, Majnun beseeches God to increase his love for Layla so that he may forever be mentioning her name. A local dignitary named Nawfal Ibn Musahiq intercedes on his behalf with Layla's family, but they swear that they would rather die than let Majnun enter their homes. Nawfal decides to abandon Majnun's cause rather than risk war with the Banu *amīr*. Majnun then flees to the desert, living with wild beasts and the remembrance of his beloved Layla. Meanwhile, Layla's family marries her to another man but she remains true to Majnun and refuses her husband. Eventually Layla dies. Immediately following this, depending on the version of the story, Majnun dies either by falling off a precipice or else while pining on his beloved's tomb.

The all-encompassing love of Majnun has been interpreted by mystics as a metaphor for divine love, and Majnun is seen as the epitome of the mystical lover who loses himself for his love of God. Numerous variations on the original narrative emphasize the potential mystical dimension of the poem. At one point, Layla comes to her lover in the desert but he asks her to leave, refusing to look at her. The implication is that Majnun is now obsessed with love itself, and is afraid that the presence of the corporeal Layla will corrupt his perfect love.

The story has been retold in rhymed form with numerous variations; however, it is the epic Persian version by Nizami-yi Ganjavi (d. 1209) that has won lasting fame and has been much imitated. Along with the Turkish version by the Ottoman poet Fizuli (d. 1556), Nizami's *Layla and Majnun* is considered the normative rendition of this tragic legend. From the rendition by the Persian poet Jami (d. 1492), the principal characters have found their way into the popular mystical literature of the Turkic and Indo-Iranian world.

Lean, David (1908–1991)

British film director. Though he was not permitted to watch movies as a child because of his strict Quaker upbringing, as an adult Lean earned recognition as a meticulous film craftsman, giving fastidious attention to production detail. He built his reputation on ambitious projects involving difficult location shooting, such as *Summertime* (1955), *Doctor Zhivago* (1965), and *A Passage to India* (1984). He is also famous for choosing grandiose topics and effects in such films as the Oscar-winning *Lawrence of Arabia* (1962) and *The Bridge on the River Kwai* (1957).

Lean began his career in cinema as a clapper boy at the age of eighteen, and rose through the ranks in the film industry from a cutting-room assistant and assistant director to editor of Movietone News. He first directed in 1942 when he worked with British playwright Noël Coward (1899–1973) on *In Which We Serve* (1942); Coward considered Lean's editing to be the best he had ever seen, and offered to codirect the film with him. Lean's early experience as an editor apparently influenced his style of filmmaking. He revealed in interviews that he preferred cutting-room work to shooting when making a film, and that he tended to fit actors into his preconceived image of the finished film, treating the actors somewhat like "puppets."

Though in no way experimental or avant-garde, Lean's films were careful and ambitious attempts to tell great stories in broad, compelling strokes. The continuing box-office appeal of his works attests to his success.

Le Clézio, Jean-Marie-Gustave (1940–)

French novelist. Le Clézio is considered to be one of France's most important contemporary writers. Born in southern France in the city of Nice, he was educated both in France and in England. With the appearance of his first works,

Le Clézio was associated with the avant-garde movement and the *nouveau roman* (new novel) in France in the 1950s and 1960s, which emphasized sensory experience over conventional structures. His first novel, *Le Procès-verbal* (1963; *The Interrogation*), won the prestigious French literary award the Prix Théophraste-Renaudot, which established him as a promising new French writer. By the 1970s his style became much more individual and his fiction became preoccupied with human alienation from modern culture.

Le Clézio has always been willing to experiment with form and content, and he often probes the relationships among language, sense-making, and the world. The protagonists of his early work are generally victims of a hostile world, while the characters of his later works tend to find their way out of alienation to make peace with the natural world.

Le Clézio's novels include *Le Déluge* (1966; *The Flood*), a novel that begins with a dramatically detailed surrealistic view of the earth. *La Guerre* (1970; *The War*) and *Les Géants* (1973; *The Giants*) both use urban settings and elaborate on man's struggles with impersonal modernity. In addition to his novels, Le Clézio has also published essays, children's books, travel journals, translations, and short stories, many of which are collected in *Mondo et autres histoires* (1978; *Mondo and Other Stories*).

Lenin, V[ladimir] I[lyich] (1870–1924)

Founder and first leader of the Soviet Union. The third of six children, Lenin (born Vladimir Ilyich Ulianov) enjoyed a bourgeois background, though his introduction to radical politics occurred rather early in life: his older brother, Aleksandr, was hanged in 1887 for his participation in a plot to assassinate Czar Alexander III (1845–1894; r. 1881–94).

In 1887 Lenin entered the University of Kazan, only to be expelled within three months for participating in a student revolt. He decided independently to study law and other disciplines, leading to his first intellectual encounters with Marxism. In 1891, after much petitioning, he was allowed to take his law examinations at St. Petersburg University and graduated with a first-class degree. Working as a public defender in St. Petersburg, Lenin made contacts with the city's small but growing cadre of revolutionary Marxists. In 1895 he traveled abroad to bolster ties with radical Russian exiles in Western Europe, and upon his return he helped unify St. Petersburg's Marxist factions into the Union for the Struggle for the Liberation of the Working Class. Through this organization, Lenin and his fellow Marxists attempted to generate class consciousness among the working classes of St. Petersburg by distributing incendiary leaflets, supporting strikes, and offering workers classes on Marxist thought. In December 1895 czarist authorities arrested Lenin and other leaders of the union for their revolutionary activities. After spending a year in prison, Lenin was exiled to Siberia along with his fiancée, Nadezhda Krupskaia, also a union member. The two married in Siberia, and she became Lenin's indispensable secretary and comrade.

Upon completing his term of exile in 1900, Lenin left Russia for Europe, where he achieved great renown and influence through his discussions of post-Marxian socialism printed in newspapers and political pamphlets. In his major work of this period, *Chto delat'?* (1902; *What Is to Be Done?*), Lenin developed his theory of the party as the revolutionary vanguard providing the impetus for the working class to join in socialist revolution. In 1903 he was elected leader of the left-wing faction of the Russian Social Democratic Workers' Party, also known as the Bolsheviks, which had split with the less revolutionary Mensheviks.

Lenin returned to Russia during the

Revolution of 1905 and organized the St. Petersburg Soviet (Council of Workers), but the Revolution's downfall forced him to flee Russia once again in 1907. Continuing his revolutionary writings and agitation from abroad, Lenin vociferously opposed Russian involvement in World War I, a struggle he viewed as an ideologically bankrupt contest between rivaling imperialist forces. He again returned to Russia after the February Revolution of 1917, which replaced Czar Nicholas II (1868–1918; r. 1894–1917) with a parliamentary government led by Russian revolutionary Alexsandr Kerensky (1881–1970), and proceeded to lead the Bolshevik coup d'état known as the October Revolution.

As the new head of the government, Lenin initiated a major land redistribution and nationalized private industry. Though he authorized the signature of a peace treaty with Germany in March 1918, ending Russia's participation in the First World War, civil strife raged in Russia until 1920, as the Bolsheviks fought both internal enemies and the incursions of British, French, and U.S. forces in northern Russia. Realizing that the pressures of civil war undermined his efforts at radical economic reform, Lenin reconsidered his views on the development of the new state and introduced in 1921 his New Economic Policy (NEP), which permitted limited private initiatives as a means of bolstering the nation's feeble economy.

Unlike future Russian leader Josef Stalin (1879–1953), Lenin primarily focused upon economic issues and showed little interest in controlling Russian cultural life—a principal cause of the flourishing of the avant-garde in the first years after the Revolution. Yet Lenin's cultural tolerance did not extend to the political realm: in 1918 he instigated the practice of mass repressions of the Bolsheviks' ideological enemies.

In 1922, although in failing health due to a series of strokes, Lenin contributed significantly to the formation of the Union of Soviet Socialist Republics, the federal system of reorganization he favored against Stalin's unitary scheme. He died after suffering another stroke and was entombed in a massive mausoleum in Moscow's Red Square.

Leonardo da Vinci (1452–1519)

Italian artist. Leonardo is remembered as one of the great Renaissance men, possessed of a wide-ranging genius that went well beyond the confines of his artistic interests. A roving inquisitiveness was the hallmark of his work, whether as a court painter to kings, as an engineer, or as a physicist investigating the laws of motion. In all of his endeavors, he was abetted by his powerful visual imagination, as well as his conviction that the essence of a trained intelligence was knowing how to see, or *saper vedere*.

Leonardo's interest in art was first ignited at the age of fifteen, when he was apprenticed to the artist Andrea del Verrocchio, from whom he learned the basics of painting and sculpture. In these early years, he produced many pen and pencil drawings of mechanical apparatuses and in 1472 was accepted into the painters' guild in Florence.

After a number of years in Florence, Leonardo went to Milan in 1482, where he served under the duke of Milan for seventeen years. As the painter for the royal household, he designed court festivals and oversaw many architectural projects commissioned by the duke. Though best remembered by the general public as a painter, he completed only six works in Milan, including two versions of *The Virgin of the Rocks* (1483–85 and 1494–1508) and *The Last Supper* (1495–97). Another notable project was a monumental bronze equestrian sculpture of Francesco Sforza, founder of the Sforza dynasty. Leonardo worked for twelve years planning the project, producing many sketches of equestrian movement and proportions. A clay version of the horse was put on display in 1492, but the monument was finally scrapped when a mounting threat of war impelled the authorities to reserve all metal stock for cannons.

Leonardo's scientific interest first became apparent in Milan. He began writing down his ideas and experiences concerning the relationship between art and science. Since he believed that a drawing could express more than the written word, his texts are full of drawings accompanied by sparse bits of text. Francesco Malxi, Leonardo's loyal disciple, gathered his many notes and observations into one tome, *Treatise on Painting*, from 1540 to 1550. It contained instructions on the art of painting, as well as the experience of vision as a guiding force in an artist's output. He also addressed the significance of geometry, perspective, and the study of light and its relation to art.

In 1500 Leonardo returned to Florence, where he produced some of his most famous works. In 1503 he was commissioned to paint a mural commemorating the Battle of Anghiari for the Hall of the Five Hundred in the Palazzo Vecchio (1503–06). Leonardo worked for over three years on the project, producing an abundance of preliminary drawings focusing on ideal proportions of figures. The swirling movement of horses in battle allowed him to exhibit his mastery of the science of painting. The work, however, was never completed. During this time he also completed his famous *La Gioconda* (1503–06; *Mona Lisa*).

In 1506 Leonardo was once again summoned to Milan. Tense years of political upheaval induced him to remain there until 1513, and while there he began specializing in anatomical studies, participating in upwards of thirty human dissections to aid his knowledge of the body. He then went to Rome, where he experienced a series of disappointments,

sitting idle while rising talents like Michelangelo and Donato Bramante received numerous commissions. He spent his final years in France, where he was granted the status of *premier peintre* ("first painter") and given the freedom to work as he chose. He devoted himself primarily to technical and mathematical studies.

Lermontov, Mikhail [Yurievich] (1814–1841)

Russian Romantic author. Born into a family of nobility, Lermontov lost his mother at the age of three and was brought up by his domineering grandmother, who forbade the boy's father, a retired army officer of Scottish descent, to visit his son. Beginning to write poetry in 1828 as a teenager, Lermontov first published his books two years later, the same year he entered Moscow University. His early poetry exhibits the strong influence of English poet Lord Byron (1788–1824), whose Romantic innovations would shape Lermontov's writings throughout his brief life.

In 1832, after clashing with a reactionary professor, Lermontov left the university and went to a cadet school in St. Petersburg. Upon graduation in 1834 with a rank of ensign, he was appointed to a Hussar regiment in Tsarskoe Selo near St. Petersburg. His critical observations of the life of the St. Petersburg aristocracy formed the basis of his play *Maskarad* (1835; *Masquerade*) and the novel *Knyaginya Ligovskaya* (1836; *Princess Ligovskaya*).

Greatly shaken by the death of the great Russian poet Aleksandr Pushkin (1799–1837), Lermontov wrote the elegiac "Smert' poeta" (1837; "Death of a Poet"), eulogizing Pushkin while condemning the aristocracy that he perceived as the true culprit in the tragedy. This incendiary poem provoked the wrath of Czar Nicholas I (1796–1855; r. 1825–55), who ordered its author's arrest and transfer to the Caucasus. Receiving a pardon one year later, Lermontov suddenly found himself the darling of the St. Petersburg intelligentsia. His new celebrity enabled him to publish his poetry without difficulty, and in the following years he wrote prolifically, both lyric poetry and prose. His novel *Geroi nashego vremeni* (1840; *A Hero of Our Time*) had a profound influence on later Russian writers, and his idealistic love of freedom, coupled with his bitter, melancholy outlook on Russian society, fueled a brand of lyric poetry that sparked both adulation and outrage among his compatriots.

In 1840 Lermontov's duel with the son of the French ambassador provided a pretext for czarist authorities to send the troublesome poet to his second exile in the Caucasus. The following year, he received a short leave, which he spent in St. Petersburg. He continued writing prolifically, penning among other works the poem "Rodina" (1841; "Motherland"). Returning to the Caucasus, Lermontov was provoked into a duel by a hostile army officer. The challenge ended in tragedy for Lermontov, who is generally recognized as, after Pushkin, the greatest Russian poet of the nineteenth century.

Levi, Primo (1919–1987)

Italian Jewish author. Levi graduated summa cum laude from the University of Turin in 1941 with a degree in chemistry. In 1943, while war ravaged Europe, Levi decided to leave the comparative safety of Turin to join a partisan group in northern Italy. He was soon captured and deported to the concentration camp at Auschwitz. His training as a chemist apparently saved his life, securing him a position in the synthetic-rubber factory of I. G. Farben. When Soviet forces liberated Auschwitz in 1945, only 25 of the 651 Italians imprisoned at the camp had survived.

Levi returned to Turin, where he continued to work as a chemist for the next thirty years. He began writing about his experiences shortly after the end of the war. His first book, *Se questo è un uomo* (1947; *If This Is a Man*), was a critical success and established Levi as an eloquent and gifted writer, able to capture in prose the unspeakable horror of the Holocaust. Levi's two later autobiographical works continued the same themes: *La tregua* (1963; *The Truce*) and *I sommersi e i salvati* (1986; *The Drowned and the Saved*). His 1975 book *Il sistema periodico* (*The Periodic Table*) proved to be his greatest popular and critical success as a writer. Each of the twenty-one stories in this collection bears the name of a chemical element, symbolizing Levi's belief that science and art are not only compatible but interrelated. *Il sistema periodico* won the Viareggio Prize (Italy's top honor for fiction) and garnered Levi worldwide acclaim, placing him on a par with Jewish historian and scholar Elie Wiesel as a literary chronicler of the Holocaust. Yet no amount of literary recognition could erase the scars that Nazi terror had inflicted upon Levi, and he was never able to emerge from the shadow of his Auschwitz memories. Some suggest that Levi's death, which occurred when he fell down a staircase, may have been suicide.

Lévi-Strauss, Claude (1908–)

French social anthropologist. An innovator in the discipline of structural anthropology, Lévi-Strauss analyzed cultural systems of belief in terms of the structural relations among their constituent parts. Lévi-Strauss was born in Brussels, Belgium, to a cultured Jewish family. He studied law and philosophy in Paris from 1927 to 1932; afterward, he became part of the Parisian intelligentsia that revolved around the existentialist philosopher Jean-Paul Sartre.

In 1934 Lévi-Strauss left Paris for a position at the University of São Paulo, Brazil, where he taught as professor of sociology (1935–39) and studied the indigenous peoples of Brazil. He returned to France in 1939 to serve in the army for two years. From 1941 to 1945 he was a visiting professor at the New School for Social Research in New York City, where he met the Russian linguist Roman Jakobson. Jakobson's work in linguistic formalism strongly influenced Lévi-Strauss's thoughts on culture. In 1949 Lévi-Strauss published *Les Structures élémentaires de la parenté* (*The Elementary Structures of Kinship*). He was appointed director of studies at the École Pratique des Hautes Études at the University of Paris in 1950 (serving there until 1974); in 1959 he was appointed chair of social anthropology at the Collège de France. Also during this time he was editor of *Man: Review of French Anthropology*.

Lévi-Strauss first attracted public attention with his *Triste tropiques* (1961; *A World on the Wane*), an autobiography focused on his thought, in addition to being a rigorous, systematic account of four primitive South American tribes. He is perhaps best known for *Anthropologie structurale* (1961; *Structural Anthropology*), *La Pensée sauvage* (1963; *The Savage Mind*), and *Le Totémisme aujourd'hui* (1962; *Totemism*).

With structuralism, Lévi-Strauss attempted a systematic approach to culture that reduced cultural forms to their most basic elements and then examined the relationships among them in order to unravel complex interrelations. He argued that primitive man's conceptual thinking was as richly theoretical as that of advanced man. Postulating that in all humans there exists the concept of the mind (a basic structure for thought), Lévi-Strauss expressed the belief that all humans are intellectual equals. Once the code of the brain's logical structure is discovered, according to Lévi-Strauss, the human sciences can be as tangible and as quantifiable as the natural sciences. All culture, in his view, was a form of communication, and he argued that culture could be interpreted by constructing models based on structural linguistics and other theories of information. Structuralism's influence has been far-reaching in the study of such disciplines as religion, literature, mythology, and ritual. Other notable works by Lévi-Strauss include *La Voie des masques* (1975; *The Way of the Masks*) and *Le Regard éloigné* (1983; *The View from Afar*).

Lewis, Saunders (1893–1985)

Welsh poet, novelist, dramatist, scholar, and political figure. Saunders Lewis is one of the twentieth century's most influential writers and Welsh nationalists, a critic of Wales's colonial status within the British empire.

Lewis's political convictions were informed by his scholarly interest in the ancient literary tradition of Wales. In 1922 he became a lecturer in Welsh at the University of Swansea, where he wrote many important works of Welsh literary history and criticism.

In 1925 Lewis helped found Plaid Cymru, the Welsh Nationalist Party, serving as its president from 1926 to 1939. In his political speeches and writings, he described the Welsh nation in a broader European context, rather than as an adjunct to England. Lewis found a spiritual corollary to this political stand in the internationalism of the Catholic Church, which he joined in 1932.

In the 1930s, when the British government decided to construct a bombing school at Penyberth in North Wales, a predominantly Welsh-speaking region, Lewis led a series of demonstrations against the installation. Their protests ignored by the British authorities, Lewis and two other activists burned down the construction site. They were sentenced to nine months in prison, after which Lewis was fired from his university position.

Decades later, Lewis delivered an oration in defense of Welsh autonomy. The

1962 talk, "Tynged yr Iaith" ("The Fate of the Language") inspired the creation of Cymdeithas yr Iaith Gymraeg (the Welsh Language Society), a civil rights organization devoted to nonviolent resistance to British rule and the promotion of the Welsh language.

Lewis is considered to be Wales's greatest dramatist and one of its major poets. His plays (he published seventeen between 1936 and 1980) draw upon medieval Welsh literature and history; two of his most popular plays, *Siwan* (1956) and *Esther* (1960), give women central roles in their explorations of tension between personal and political responsibilities.

Liang Qichao (1873–1929)

Chinese intellectual and reform leader in the late Qing dynasty (1644–1911). A student of Kang Youwei, a Chinese reformist leader who initiated the famous Hundred Days' Reform in 1898, Liang realized that only through a series of radical reforms of the imperial system could China successfully wash away the humiliation inflicted by foreign military powers since the Opium Wars (1839–1842). He served as editor of *Shiwu Bao*, a newspaper advocating the urgency of reform. Together with Kang Youwei and other leading reformers, he risked his life appealing to the emperor Guangxu for immediate changes, including the establishment of modern schools and the reorganization of the military. Although the emperor was persuaded to enact the proposals, the reform movement lasted just a hundred days when the Dowager Empress Ci Xi (1835–1908), with the support of the army, managed to destroy it. While the emperor was virtually dethroned, orders were given to arrest and execute all the leading reformers. Liang Qichao fled to Japan, where he continued to search for ways to improve the imperial system.

In 1912, when Liang returned to China, the last emperor had already been overthrown and the Republic of China established. Ambivalent about this turn of events, Liang sided with the autocratic president Yuan Shikai against the progressive Sun Yat-sen. He spent his later life lecturing and doing research at Qinghua University, Beijing. His works include *Xian-qin zheng-zhi si-xiang shi* (1930; *History of Chinese Political Thought During the Early Qin Period*) and *Qing-dae xue-shu gai-lun* (1959; *Intellectual Trends in the Qing Period*), both published posthumously.

Li Bai (701–762 C.E.)

Chinese lyric poet. Li Bai was a romantic and witty vagabond, in love with nature, wine, women, friends, and poetry. By the time he reached his teens, he had already traveled widely, and although he spent most of his life in pursuit of public office, difficulties in his life and his growing awareness of the corruption of the human world led him to seek relief in Taoism. Especially in his late life, Li became increasingly absorbed in the study and poetical expression of Taoism. In 756 he became an unofficial poet laureate to Prince Lin, the emperor's sixteenth son, but the prince's execution for allegedly attempting to split the kingdom resulted in Li's brief imprisonment in the capital, Changan. In 758 the charge against him was revived, and he was banished to Ye Lang (in the modern province of Guizhou). Yet before he reached his destination, his sentence was lifted by a general amnesty. The poet immediately resumed his peregrinations and composed many classic poems. Li died in Dangtu (in the province of Anhui); he is said to have drowned when he drunkenly tried to catch the moon's reflection from a boat.

liberation theology

Radical Roman Catholic movement stressing the urgency of social change. Originating in Latin America late in the twentieth century, liberation theology focuses on the poor and seeks to free them from all forms of oppression. The doctrine emphasizes awareness of the socioeconomic structures that breed social inequities and advocates active participation to change these institutions. The movement was made official in Medellín, Colombia, at the Second General Conference of Latin American Bishops in 1968; participants issued a document proclaiming the rights of the poor and stating that industrialized nations unfairly enrich themselves by exploiting Third World countries. The concept gained popularity throughout the 1970s, aided by Peru's leading theologian, Gustavo Gutiérrez, who published the movement's seminal text, *Teología de la liberación* (1971; *A Theology of Liberation*).

Liberation theologists claim that the Bible can only be understood from the perspective of the poor, and with that end in mind have established throughout Latin America *comunidades de base* (base communities), self-sufficient communes similar in structure to Israeli kibbutzim. These groups, composed of ten to thirty members and usually led by laypeople, study the Bible and attempt to meet the basic needs of their community, including food, water, sewage disposal, and electricity.

The influence of liberation theology has spread to include involvement in political and civic affairs; some priests have sought to educate parishioners about political issues affecting their communities and have actively campaigned against political candidates who do not represent the interests of the poor. Although some liberation theologists have used Marxism as a methodological tool, most claim that their enterprise is purely Christian in nature. Nevertheless, they have been criticized from within and without the Roman Catholic Church as naïve expounders of Marxism and supporters of violent social revolution. Brazilian theologian Leonard Boff was even

sentenced by Vatican authorities to a year's silence for his work on behalf of liberation theology. Along with Gutiérrez and Boff, other important leaders of the movement include Archbishop Oscar Arnulfo Romero from El Salvador, who was murdered by army-backed death squads; Jesuit scholar Jon Sobrino; and Enrique Dussel.

Liliuokalani, Queen (1838–1917)

Last ruler of an independent Hawaii. Liliuokalani was the only woman to govern the Hawaiian Islands, which had been unified as a nation in 1810 by King Kamehameha I. European commercial and military interests had supported the first Hawaiian king's ambition to create a single political and administrative bloc out of the various sovereign states and communities that had previously characterized the political map of the region. A united Hawaii, its constitution based on European models, was favorable for the development and expansion of European and American mercantilism, strengthened by the substantial presence in the islands of *haoles* (a Hawaiian term originally signifying foreign businessmen, and later coming to denote all "white" peoples), whose enterprises were greatly facilitated by the modernization and Westernization of Hawaiian life.

The original Kamehameha dynasty ended with the death of Kamehameha V in 1872. By this time the issue of annexation was already paramount in Hawaiian politics, as American business interests clashed with those of native Hawaiians for political control. This delicate political situation was already in place when, in 1891, Liliuokalani succeeded her brother as queen.

Upon the death of her brother the king, Liliuokalani assumed both the Hawaiian throne and the responsibility for mediating the islands' festering economic and political disputes. At first, Liliuokalani proved a popular monarch among both *haoles* and indigenous Hawaiians, acceptable to the former by virtue of her European education and professed Christianity, and embraced by the latter for her strong antiannexation politics. Yet she soon lost her standing among the *haole* population when, immediately upon ascending to the throne, she set about withdrawing and voiding prior treaties and agreements conducive to the expansion of American capital in Hawaii. On the verge of issuing a new constitution that would even more radically reallocate suffrage rights to native Hawaiians, as well as appropriate broad executive powers for the throne, Liliuokalani was faced with an insurrection led by Missionary Party leader Sanford Dole. In the name of the United States, Dole declared the queen deposed and Hawaii subject to U.S. authority. Although President-elect Grover Cleveland (served 1885–89 and 1893–97) supported Liliuokalani's claims to dominion over the kingdom of Hawaii, Dole's own provisional government moved forward with a preemptive strike, backed by proannexation incumbent president Benjamin Harrison (served 1889–1893) and reinforced by the presence of 164 armed U.S. troops. In January 1893 Queen Liliuokalani reluctantly yielded to this military and political intimidation and—after failing to regain her throne in an abortive British-led counteroffensive—formally abdicated the monarchy. In 1898, Hawaii was annexed by the United States by a joint Congressional resolution which made no provision for the participation of the Hawaiian people in the determination of their fate as a nation.

Convicted of treason, Liliuokalani spent nearly two years under house arrest in Hawaii. During this time she composed "Aloha Oe," now Hawaii's state song, originally intended to be a mournful hymn of loss and departure from her country. Liliuokalani spent the remaining years of her life after abdication lecturing and touring in the United States, attempting to raise support for the cause of Hawaiian independence. In 1916 she became a Mormon, citing affinities between the traditional Hawaiian custom of *aloha*—roughly "generosity" or "hospitality"—and the Mormon values of family and community bonds. A year after her conversion, she died in Honolulu.

Lincoln, Abraham (1809–1865)

Sixteenth president of the United States. More than any other figure from the American past, Lincoln is thought to symbolize the romance and pathos of the American dream.

Lincoln spent his boyhood in the pioneer farms of the Kentucky, Indiana, and Illinois frontier. Although he never attended school, he read voraciously, and was known to walk several miles in order to borrow a book. At the age of nineteen, he left his family and later moved to the village of New Salem, Illinois, where at various points he worked in a grocery store, served as village postmaster, and split rails to earn a living. In 1834 the youthful Lincoln began his political career with a successful campaign for the state legislature, where he served for eight years, distinguishing himself as an eloquent and ambitious member of the Whig Party. Lincoln received his law degree in 1836 and developed a thriving law practice when the legislature was not in session. Although he did not run for reelection in 1842, he remained involved in politics and gained election to Congress in 1846. During his term in Congress, he emerged as a vociferous—yet always outvoted—opponent of the Mexican War. He eventually opted to return to his law practice in Illinois instead of running for reelection, yet continued his involvement in partisan politics. As the battle over slavery heated up during the 1850s, Lincoln switched to the new, stridently antislavery Republican Party. As his reputation as an antislavery orator grew, Illinois Republicans nominated him as their senatorial candidate in 1858. He and his opponent, Stephen Douglas, argued slavery policy throughout the state in a series of debates that attracted significant national attention. Although Lincoln lost the election, the publicity his campaign generated eventually propelled him to the Republican presidential nomination in 1860. As the Democrats split four ways, Lincoln easily won election to the White House, albeit with only 41 percent of the total vote and nearly unanimous opposition in the South.

The Southern states swiftly seceded following Lincoln's election, and Confederate troops fired the first shots of the Civil War at Fort Sumter in April 1861. The North was initially slow to respond: Confederate forces threatened Washington, and incompetent generals plagued the Union's early efforts.

As the military tide slowly began to turn, Lincoln felt confident enough to issue the Emancipation Proclamation, which declared that on January 1, 1863, all slaves held in territories in rebellion against the Union would be "henceforth and forever free." While this proclamation freed slaves only in areas over which Lincoln had no practical control, it contained great symbolic importance: it re-energized Northern abolitionists, who had despaired over Lincoln's slow progress on the slavery front, and it gave Southern slaves even more cause to hope for a Union triumph. After the conclusion of the war, the Thirteenth Amendment would abolish slavery throughout the Republic.

As the war dragged on through 1864, Lincoln's prospects for reelection looked doubtful at best. But Union war victories at Atlanta and elsewhere rejuvenated Northern spirits, and Lincoln eked out a victory in November with 54 percent of the vote.

On April 14, 1865, four days after the Confederacy finally surrendered, Lincoln met his death at the hands of the actor John Wilkes Booth. The horrible event shocked a nation still grieving for its war dead. Lincoln's body was placed on a train and slowly transported throughout the North, taking ten days to reach Lincoln's final resting place in Springfield, Illinois. Millions turned out to watch the train wend its way through the nation's cities and farms, all paying their last respects to the assassinated leader. With the exception of presidential elections, more Americans participated in the passage of Lincoln's funeral train than in any other event in the nation's history.

Lincoln's understated eloquence, dramatically displayed in his Gettysburg Address and Second Inaugural Address, both immortalized on the walls of the Lincoln Memorial, have contributed to his vast posthumous renown.

It is thought that more books have been written about Lincoln than any other historical figure with the exception of Jesus Christ.

Lin Yutang (1895–1976)

Chinese scholar and writer. Born in Fujian province, China, he completed his studies at Harvard and Leipzig universities, and then returned to China to teach at Beijing National University, where he helped develop a system of spelling Chinese words using the Roman alphabet. In 1936 he moved to the United States, where he lived until 1966, when he moved to Hong Kong.

Lin, who wrote in both English and Chinese, is best known in the West as a popularizer of Chinese culture. He followed his introduction to China, *My Country and My People* (1935), with *The Importance of Living* (1937) and *The Birth of a New China* (1939). Among his many novels is *Moment in Peking* (1939), and his English translations of Chinese literary and philosophical works (1953) are notable for their accuracy and faithful rendering of the original style when transposed into a foreign tongue. Published in 1952, Lin's *Chinese-English Dictionary of Modern Usage* was the first to be produced by a bilingual Chinese writer.

Lipit-Ishtar (r. 1934–1924 B.C.E.)

Fifth king of Sumerian dynasty of Isin. Lipit-Ishtar is best known for a legal code that was created even before Babylonian king Hammurabi (r. 1792–1750 B.C.E.) established his better-known set of laws, known as Hammurabi's Code. What remain of the code attributed to Lipit-Ishtar are approximately fifty complete clauses covering a rather limited range of topics: matters related to landholding, runaway slaves, inheritance, betrothal and marriage, and injury to hired animals. The clauses pertaining to inheritance are the most extensive.

Lipit-Ishtar's code reveals a number of important elements about Sumerian society at that time. Owning land involved both privileges and responsibilities, the relative rights of free men and slaves were clearly delineated, a man could marry and therefore emancipate a slave woman, and wives possessed definite legal rights—including protection from arbitrary divorce or abandonment. Lipit-Ishtar also proclaimed an annulment of debt, an element that has earned him recognition as a pioneering provider of social justice.

Li Qingzhao (1084–1151)

Poet of the Chinese Song dynasty (960–1279). Born into a literary family in Jinan, Shandong, Li had parents who played significant roles in fostering her interest in literature. At eighteen, she married the noted antiquarian Zhao Mingchen, who later became a source of inspiration in her writing. The couple lived happily until 1128, when the Jin (Jurchen) army attacked Kaifeng and drove the Song emperor south. During their escape from the invaders, Li

Qingzhao's husband died suddenly. The emotional and physical dislocation brought about by these events cast a dark shadow upon her subsequent writings, which diverge markedly from her earlier, more playful prose. It is believed that she produced as many as seven volumes of essays and six volumes of poetry. The best known are *Li Qingzhao Ji* (*Poems of Li Qingzhao*) and *Shuyu Ji* (*A Collection of Jades*).

Lispector, Clarice (1925–1977)

Brazilian short-story writer and novelist. Lispector is one of Brazil's most important twentieth-century writers; her short stories and novels have been adapted for stage and screen, and have been popularized by Brazilian singers and rock-and-roll groups. Much of Lispector's work centers on female protagonists; although not explicitly political, it addresses questions of identity and oppression in universal terms.

Lispector was born in Tchetchelnik, a small village in Ukraine through which her parents were passing as they immigrated to the Americas from the U.S.S.R. They settled in the northeastern part of Brazil, where Lispector lived until she turned twelve. Her mother died when she was nine, and three years later the family moved to Rio de Janeiro, where she finished secondary school and began law school. Lispector met her husband there and married in 1943, graduating the following year. In 1944 she left Brazil with her husband, who worked for the Brazilian diplomatic service, to live abroad and published her first novel, *Perto do coração selvagem* (1944; *Close to the Savage Heart*). The novel won the Fundaçïo Graça Aranha prize and received wide critical acclaim, although its introspective and innovative style confused some of her critics. The novel is a fragmentary, subjective biography of an adolescent and young wife named Joana, and focuses on the quest of this alienated woman for identity and meaning in life. Lispector then wrote two more novels, *O Lustre* (1946; *The Chandelier*) and *A cidade sitiada* (1949; *The Besieged City*), in which she addressed similar themes and manifested the same literary techniques, including the manipulation of time and space and stream of consciousness.

After her divorce in 1959, Lispector lived in isolation, avoided publicity, and dedicated herself to writing. In 1960 she published *Laços de família* (*Family Ties*), a collection of short stories often considered to be her finest prose. In these she focuses on personal moments of revelation in the everyday lives of her protagonists and on the absence of real human communication in urbanized settings and the modern world. Other important works include *A maça no escuro* (1961; *The Apple in the Dark*), *A paixão segundo G.H.* (1964; *The Passion According to G.H.*), and *Água viva* (1973; *White Water*). Her last work, *A hora da Estrela* (1977; *The Hour of the Star*) was awarded a prize from the Fundaçïo Cultural do Distrito Federal and appeared the same year she died. Her fiction has received critical attention from French feminist theorist Hélène Cixous, among others, and has been acclaimed as an example of *écriture féminine*.

Lister, Joseph (1827–1912)

English surgeon. Lister is credited with the development of modern antiseptic surgery, which dramatically reduced deaths from postsurgical infection. The son of Joseph Jackson Lister, who invented an achromatic microscope, the younger Lister specialized in surgery during his medical studies. Inspired by the work of French chemist Louis Pasteur (1822–1895) on bacterial infection, he concentrated his research on the prevention of infection resulting from surgical procedures. After conducting numerous experiments with varying degrees of success, Lister introduced carbolic acid as an antiseptic agent. When combined with the heat sterilization of surgical instruments, this treatment dramatically reduced the number of postoperative fatalities. Lister also developed absorbable ligatures and the drainage tube, both of which have become standard in the treatment of wounds and incisions. During his career, Lister served as a professor of clinical surgery at Edinburgh University and at King's College in London.

Liszt, Franz (1811–1886)

Hungarian composer and virtuoso pianist. The most celebrated pianist of the nineteenth century, and one of its most innovative composers, Liszt had very little formal piano instruction. At the age of ten, he moved with his family from his birthplace of Raiding, Hungary, to Vienna. Recognized at a young age as being immensely gifted, he was given the opportunity to study piano with Carl Czerny and composition with Antonio Salieri, giving his first piano concert when he was nine. Although Liszt continued his private study of composition, he stopped his pianistic training when he moved with his family to Paris at the age of twelve. Denied admission to the conservatory on account of his youth and foreign origins, he nevertheless secured for himself the opportunity to tour as a recitalist, eventually settling in Geneva.

When appointed musical director at the Weimar court in Germany in 1843, Liszt devoted himself wholly to conducting and composition. Many of his best-known compositions were produced during this time, including *Totentanz* (*Dance of Death*), for piano and orchestra, and the *Dante* and *Faust* symphonies. Liszt is known primarily for inventing the symphonic poem, a new form of orchestral composition that followed a literary program, constructed either in loose sonata form or as a one-movement symphony. Eleven of his twelve symphonic poems were written in this first Weimar period. He also won considerable renown for his *Hungarian Rhapsodies*, based on Hungarian urban popular music. Liszt's use of "diablerie," or elusive tempi, and a harmonically unstable idiom were trademarks that first forced the public to recognize his individual voice.

Liszt left Weimar for Rome in 1859 with Princess Carolyne von Sayn-Wittgenstein, with whom he lived until 1863. After they separated, Liszt turned to writing religious music, including two masses and the oratorio *Christus* (1867). In 1865 he received minor orders, and was made an abbé by Pope Pius IX, though he soon abandoned the clergy to remain a musician. In 1875 he was made president of the New Hungarian Academy of Music, dividing his time thereafter among Budapest, Weimar, and Rome. The works from his late years were misunderstood by his contemporaries, who perceived them as collections of random dissonances, structurally loose and careless, but they were actually quite modern in concept, anticipating Debussy's impressionism and the Austrian expressionist school.

Liszt died while attending the annual festival in honor of the composer Richard Wagner in Bayreuth in July 1886. He left behind a formidable body of work, including several books, the best known of which is *Des Bohémiens et de leur musique en Hongrie* (1859; *The Gypsy in Music*). Hailed as one of the great altruists in the history of music, Liszt performed the great piano works of Robert Schumann and Fryderyk Chopin when they were physically unable; he also provided opportunities for Charles-Camille Saint-Saëns, Hector Berlioz, and Wagner to have their work performed. Liszt was also noted for his extensive arrangements; he adapted many of Johann Sebastian Bach's organ works and Wagner's operas for the piano. Universally recognized as the master pianist of his day, Liszt developed an awesome virtuoso technique and composed music to serve it. His piano writing, notoriously difficult, combines Ludwig von Beethoven's orchestral style with the delicacy of Chopin. His pieces' innovative harmony and structure make him one of the most influential composers of the nineteenth century.

Locke, Alain [Leroy] (1889–1954)

American philosopher, writer, and educator. A widely respected scholar and thinker, Locke is perhaps best known for his primary role in conceptualizing, promoting, and interpreting the flowering of African-American creativity known as the Harlem Renaissance.

Born in Philadelphia, Pennsylvania, in 1889, Locke attended local public schools before going on to Harvard University. The first black Rhodes scholar, Locke studied at Oxford University in England from 1907 to 1910 and then at the University of Berlin from 1910 to 1911. Returning to the United States in 1912, Locke began his forty-year tenure at Howard University, the nation's preeminent black college, in Washington, D.C. At Howard, he taught in the English and philosophy departments, becoming head of the philosophy department after receiving his Ph.D. from Harvard University in 1918.

Locke's work sought primarily to identify and celebrate black contributions to American and world culture. He was the editor of the landmark collection *The New Negro: An Interpretation* (1925), a special issue of the journal *Survey Graphic*, which included fiction, poetry, drama, and essays by black writers heralding the arrival of a "Harlem Renaissance" and a "new Negro" who had transcended the twin legacies of slavery and the Jim Crow South. The volume featured poetry by Langston Hughes, Angelina Grimké, and Countee Cullen; visual art by Aaron Douglas and Winold Reiss; stories by Rudolph Fisher, Jean Toomer, and Zora Neale Hurston, and essays by Locke and W. E. B. Du Bois. This new Negro was black, proud, urban, and modern, programmatically aligned with the Euro-American avantgarde and at the forefront of innovations in music, writing, and the visual arts.

Locke continued to serve as an agitator for black art and creativity throughout the first half of the twentieth century. In the 1930s he published an annual review of the state of black writing in *Opportunity*; in 1936 he published *Negro Art: Past and Present* and *The Negro and His Music*. In the 1940s he coedited, with Bernhard Stern, a massive volume entitled *When Peoples Meet: A Study in Race and Culture Contacts* and explored questions of ethnic identity and American nationalism. He was the editor of the Bronze Booklets, a series of studies on black cultural contributions, and reviewed books by and about blacks for the publications *Opportunity* and *Phylon*.

Locke, John (1632–1704)

English philosopher and political theorist. The first of the great empiricists of modern times, Locke more than any other thinker initiated the advent of the Enlightenment in England.

Born into a Puritan family in Wrington, Somerset, Locke became a tutor at Oxford in Greek, rhetoric, and philosophy in 1660. Seven years later, he became secretary to the earl of Shaftesbury and served on the council of the Royal Society. When political difficulties forced Shaftesbury to leave London for the Continent in 1675, Locke joined him in Paris. While there, he studied science and engineering and examined Louis XIV's treatment of Protestants. Locke returned to England four years later only to be accused of radicalism by the government, which led him to flee to Holland, where at age fifty-four he wrote his first famous work, *An Essay Concerning Human Understanding* (1690). This work examines the nature of the human mind and claims that the mind is born a blank slate, or tabula rasa, upon which the world makes its impressions through the five senses. One gathers information through experience and perfects understanding through reflection. Locke distinguishes between the primary quality of things, such as solidity, extension, and number, from the secondary qualities, such as color and sound, which are produced through sensation. Science can exist, he argues, because the primary qualities mechanically influence sense organs, thereby yielding ideas that accurately represent reality.

As a political theorist, Locke became renowned for challenging Thomas Hobbes's belief that human beings in the state of nature must live by individualistic, self-preservationist urges that humans are born with. In his essay *Two Treatises on Government* (1690), Locke argues that the potential for reason and tolerance in human nature takes precedence over any irrational tendencies and that the original state of nature is essentially ordered. That state, characterized by equality and independence, is achieved in society through the social contract, which guarantees that individuals will forgo certain rights in order to preserve the general welfare of all. Property rights are essential in this regard because every man should be guaranteed the fruits of his labor. With this assertion, Locke foreshadowed the labor theory of value; he also developed the system of checks and balances upon which the Constitution of the United States rests, and articulated the notion that at times revolution is not only a right but an obligation. Locke's overarching belief that man's inevitable pursuit of happiness, when conducted rationally, can lead to cooperation and coincide naturally with the common good is the central tenet of modern democracy. His last essay of note, *The Reasonableness of Christianity* (1695), emphasizes his belief that the ethical aspect of Christianity should hold more weight than dogma. In this work and others like it, Locke expounds the notion of religious freedom and a more general belief in man's right to personal liberty. The influence of Locke's philosophy and political theory on modern societies has been incalculable.

Loi Kratong

Thai religious ceremony. In this eighth of the twelve monthly Royal Ceremonies, worshipers cast lotus-shaped floats into the waters of the canals and rivers, which have been decked with candles in preparation for the event. It is believed that the floats will drift upstream to the source of the waters in the Buddha's footprint. Held in the twelfth month of the old Thai calendar—overlapping November and December—this rite of expiation is customarily accompanied by exuberant celebrations and fireworks.

Lomonosov, Mikhail [Vasilievich]

(1711–1765)

Russian poet, scientist, and grammarian. Son of a poor fisherman from northern Russia, he left his native village in 1730 for Moscow, seeking an education. There, pretending to be the son of a priest, he enrolled in the Slavonic-Latin-Greek Academy. Although financial difficulties often threatened to impede his educational path, he received his degree and in 1736 gained admission to the St. Petersburg Academy. Most of his time at the academy was spent in Germany as an exchange student, where he excelled in both philosophy and the sciences.

In 1741 Lomonosov returned to St. Petersburg. Upon his return, he was appointed adjunct to the academy; however, he had constant conflicts with the academy, which at this time was directed by foreigners and incompetent nobles. These conflicts led to his arrest in 1743. Imprisoned for one year, he wrote several treatises on physics and philosophy, as well as two odes dedicated to Empress Elizabeth, which gained him freedom in 1744. While in prison, he also worked out the plan of his future research and wrote several treatises in physics and philosophy. His friend, the celebrated German mathematician Leonhard Euler, recognized the creative originality of Lomonosov's scientific writings, leading to their publication by the Russian Academy. This boost helped Lomonosov become a professor of chemistry at the academy in 1745, and enabled him to finally procure a chemistry laboratory he had been requesting for several years.

For many years he worked on developing a method of producing colored glass, which he used to create mosaics; he did a number of mosaic portraits, including that of Peter the Great and the *Battle of Poltava* (1762–64). Lomonosov's mosaics were highly praised and won him a membership in the Russian Academy of Arts.

Lomonosov's works in the humanities include a short but significant "Foreword on the Utility of Ecclesiastical Books in the Russian Language" and a major study of Russian grammar (1757), commissioned by the empress. Throughout the 1740s and 1750s Lomonosov wrote several poems in the Neoclassical strain, including "Vechernee razmyshlenie o bozh'em velichestve" (1743; "Evening Meditation upon the Greatness of God" and "Pis'mo k I. I. Shuvalovu o pol'ze stekla" (1752; "Epistle to I. I. Shuvalov on the Usefulness of Glass"), as well as two tragedies, *Tamira i Selim* (1750) and *Demofont* (1752). Despite the honors and international recognition that he received, Lomonosov continued to lead a simple and industrious life, surrounded by his family and a few friends. After the death of Elizabeth and the brief reign of Peter III, Empress Catherine cooled to Lomonosov as he declined in both health and fortune. Catherine ensured that the patriotic scholar was buried with great honors, yet she insisted on confiscating all of his papers. Publications of his works were purged of his materialist and humanist ideas, and efforts were made to view him as a court poet and an upholder of monarchy and religion rather than as an enemy of superstition and a champion of public education. The publication of his complete works, an arduous process that began in 1950 and was not completed until 1983, has revealed the full extent of Lomonosov's contributions and confirmed his status as a leading figure in eighteenth-century Russian literature and sciences.

longhouse

Traditional dwelling of the Iroquois tribes in the northeastern United States. The term also describes the church and meeting hall of the Iroquois reservations, although they do not physically resemble the original longhouses. The longhouse frame was made from wooden poles, with a domed roof covered with tree bark. While nearly every longhouse measured 22 or 23 feet wide, its length could vary from 40 to 334 feet. Although families lived together in longhouses, women and men entered through separate doors and opposite ends of the dwelling. The inside was partitioned off by walls built out from the sides of the house about every seven feet, with a long common hall in the middle. While each family had its own room, the arrangement afforded little privacy, since the rooms opened onto a center aisle. The cooking fires were built in this aisle, directly under ventilation holes cut in the roof. The longhouse was abandoned as a residence by 1800.

Long March

Journey of over 6,000 miles undertaken by the Chinese Communist Red Army between 1934 and 1935. Escaping from the attacking Nationalist forces, the Red Army, led by Chinese Communist leader Mao Zedong (1893–1976), marched from the Jinggang mountain toward Yan'an in the Shanxi province. Traveling on foot, the soldiers scaled eighteen major mountain ranges, crossed dozens of deep rivers, and slogged through many forests and swamps—all while fighting off the encroaching Nationalist forces from air, water, and land. When the march ended at Yan'an, of the original force of 90,000 men and women, only about 8,000 survived. Mao later described it as "the first of its kind in the annals of history." The phrase "long march" is now frequently used in China to refer to any difficult task or grand plan in personal as well as national affairs.

Lorca, Federico García, *see* García Lorca, Federico

Louis, Joe (1914–1981)

American boxer. Joe Louis was world heavyweight boxing champion from June 22, 1937, until March 1, 1949, the longest reign in the history of the heavyweight division. He won the title from James J. Braddock in eight rounds and defended it twenty-five times with twenty-one knockouts before retiring undefeated.

Louis was born Joe Louis Barrow in Lexington, Alabama, to a family of sharecroppers. His stepfather relocated the family to Detroit in 1926. By 1933 Louis had won the National Light Heavyweight Amateur Crown of the Golden Gloves, and in 1934 he won the U.S. Amateur Athletic Union's 175-pound tournament. Louis's first professional fight was in July of 1934, and he suffered his first loss to Max Schmeling in 1936. In a 1938 rematch, after Louis had captured the title, Schmeling fell to a first-round knockout in one of the quickest bouts in boxing history. Americans regarded the fight as a symbolic victory of American democracy over the Nazism they saw embodied by the German Schmeling.

Throughout his career, Louis defeated past and future heavyweight champions Primo Carnera, Max Baer, Jack Sharkey, and Jersey Joe Walcott. He earned the nickname "the Brown Bomber" and became, along with contemporary track star Jesse Owens, a symbol of racial pride for millions of American blacks. His service in the U.S. Army during World War II prevented him from defending his title again, though he fought two bouts for Army and Navy Relief.

Louis retired in 1949 but returned to the ring to fight the new champion, Ezzard Charles, in 1950, a bout he lost in a fifteen-round decision. In 1951 Louis was knocked out in eight rounds by Rocky Marciano, thus ending his last significant fight. Poorly managed financial affairs plagued Louis after his second retirement, and he later became employed as a celebrity greeter for Caesar's Palace in Las Vegas.

L'Ouverture, Toussaint, *see* Toussaint L'Ouverture, François

Lowell, Amy (1874–1925)

American poet and critic. Lowell was a leading exponent of the Imagist movement in modern poetry. In addition to her own poetic output, she edited numerous anthologies of Imagist verse, wrote criticism that ranged over the entire Western canon in poetry, and was a tireless lecturer, traversing the country on a campaign to promote her poetic ideals.

Born into a wealthy and socially prominent Boston family, Lowell was educated at home and at private schools in Boston. She did not pursue higher education, but read widely at home, where she had no lack of resources. She had published a few poems of her own by 1913, when she became acquainted with the work of Hilda Doolittle (H.D.), who was then in London. Excited by the poetic kinship she perceived between herself and Doolittle, Lowell journeyed to London, where she became acquainted with Doolittle, Ezra Pound, Ford Madox Ford, and other members of a circle of poets and writers who referred to themselves as "Imagists." During this time Lowell supplanted Pound as the leader of this coterie, as his aesthetic ideas were beginning to diverge from the others'.

After the London visit, Lowell returned to Boston, which became the center of Imagism in America. Imagism, as Lowell conceived it, involved the precise depictions of images and held that poetic force was due to the concentration of language and imagery. The Imagists were attracted to free verse and other innovative techniques, and at the same time were resolved to write poetry that was unmannered and partook of the rhythms of common speech. Her most important collection of poems is *Sword Blades and Poppy Seed* (1914), in which she first began her more daring formal innovations, including the use of "polyphonic prose," her own variant of free verse, which was almost closer to prose than verse. In the decade before her death, she was an indefatigable promoter of Imagism, constantly lecturing and writing articles and reviews in what was virtually a one-woman effort to usher in a new age of poetry and to rehabilitate what she saw as the stagnant state of American letters.

Her other writings include *A Dome of Many-Coloured Glass* (1912); *Six French Poets* (1915); *Tendencies in Modern American Poetry* (1917); *Can Grande's Castle* (1918); *John Keats* (1925); *What's O'Clock* (1925); *East Wind* (1926); and *Ballads for Sale* (1927).

Lumumba, Patrice (1925–1961)

Congolese independence leader and first prime minister of the Republic of Congo. Lumumba, a charismatic statesman, was born in Onalua, a village in the Kasai province of the Belgian Congo (now Zaire). His tribe, the Batetela, was a branch of the Mongo-Nkutshu family of central Congo. After finishing his studies at Protestant and Catholic mission schools, Lumumba found postal work in nearby towns. Writing poetry and essays for local and national journals, Lumumba emerged as a leader of Congolese évolués, or educated Africans.

Settling for a while in Stanleyville (now Kisangani), Lumumba organized a postal workers' union, and in 1955 became regional president of a Congolese trade union of government employees. His ties to the government during this period helped lessen penalties from an embezzlement conviction in 1957. Lumumba served a yearlong prison sentence but returned vigorously to politics after his release in 1958. In October he founded Congo's first national political party, the Mouvement National Congolais (Congolese National Movement, or MNC), dominated by educated, often Catholic Congolese.

In December of that year, Lumumba took an MNC delegation to the All-African People's Conference in Accra, Ghana. He met with Pan-Africanists and African nationalists from all over Africa, and began a long-lasting relationship with Kwame Nkrumah, already the first prime minister of modern Ghana. He was greatly influenced by the militant tide of nationalism and anticolonialism then sweeping the continent, and his rhetoric began to reflect a less compromising posture.

His radicalism disturbed some of the original members of the MNC, and a split occurred in July 1959. Lumumba retained most of the rank and file. Later that year, Lumumba and his nationalist supporters rejected a Belgian government proposal for local elections and a five-year plan for transition to independence, arguing that its purpose was to install Belgian puppets before independence. The threat to boycott the elections was met with repression, and in a confrontation in Stanleyville thirty people were killed. Lumumba was arrested and charged with inciting a riot, but the MNC decided to participate in

the elections and won 90 percent of the votes in Stanleyville. Lumumba was released in time to participate in the Round Table Conference in Brussels on political change in Congo.

In the May 1960 general elections Lumumba and his allies won 41 out of 137 seats, and as the leader of the largest party Lumumba was selected by the Belgians to be prime minister. Joseph Kasavubu, leader of the Bakongo, became president. Soon faced by, in quick succession, a military revolt, a secessionist declaration by rebels in Katanga province supported by Belgian troops, and another separatist threat from southern Kasai, Lumumba appealed to the U.N. for military intervention. Refused aid by the U.N., he turned in desperation to the Soviet Union and to other independent African states. President Kasavubu, who was not completely opposed to local autonomy, dismissed Lumumba in September of 1960.

While Lumumba contested his removal, power was seized by a small faction of the army led by Col. Joseph Mobutu, who eventually cooperated with Kasavubu to establish a new government. Traveling from Léopoldville (now Kinshasa) to Stanleyville, Lumumba was captured by Kasavubu supporters. Flown to Katanga province, he was handed over to his secessionist enemies and killed in January 1961.

His death sent shock waves throughout Africa despite the cover-up attempts of the Katanga government, and the U.N. Security Council resolved to allow the use of force by U.N. troops in Congo if necessary. A civilian regime was eventually restored, and the secessionist movements dissolved. Lumumba, as a champion of the anticolonial struggle, was later seen as a national hero.

Luther, Martin (1483–1546)

German religious reformer and leader of the Protestant Reformation. While studying law at the University of Erfurt, the young Luther was struck by lightning during a violent thunderstorm, catalyzing a spiritual awakening that prompted him to join the Augustinian order of friars. After earning a doctoral degree in theology, Luther became professor of biblical exegesis at the university in Wittenberg. A visit to Rome in 1510 sparked Luther's distress at what he considered to be the spiritual laxity of the Catholic Church, particularly as manifested in the practice of granting indulgences. In 1517, Luther issued his famous Ninety-five Theses, a vitriolic screed against the Catholic Church, which he very dramatically nailed to the door of the Wittenberg Castle church.

Central to Luther's critique of Catholic dogma was his belief that salvation could be earned through faith alone, not through a combination of faith and good works. In addition to opposing indulgences, Luther challenged the very authority of the pope by advocating German control of German churches. Luther was excommunicated in 1521 for his efforts in opposing Catholic doctrine and papal authority. Banned from the Holy Roman Empire by the Diet of Worms, Luther found a safe haven in Wartberg, Germany, where he continued his anti-Catholic writings and agitation, prompting a massive religious upheaval in Germany and beyond.

Luther's theological works include his translation of the Bible into German (New Testament, 1522; Old Testament, 1534); his *Letter on Translation* (1530), in defense of his rendition of the Bible; and forty *Church Songs* (1524). In 1525 Luther married a former nun, Katharina von Bora, with whom he raised six children.

Luther's theological writings formed the foundation for the Augsburg Confession, written by Philip Melanchthon and sanctioned by Luther, which became the foundation of the Lutheran Church. The far-reaching influence of his life and work transcended theological disputes, directly and indirectly affecting the future course of religious, political, and economic arrangements throughout the West. More than any other man of the Renaissance, Luther shaped the ideological and structural underpinnings of the contemporary Western world.

Luxemburg, Rosa (1871–1919)

Polish-born political philosopher, revolutionary, and socialist agitator. Born into a lower-middle-class Jewish family in Zamość, Poland, Luxemburg became thoroughly committed to radical politics while still a teenager. Fleeing Poland for Switzerland to escape the Russian authorities that dominated at the time, Luxemburg studied law and political economy at the University of Zurich, receiving her Ph.D. in 1898. While in Zurich she became involved with an important group of radical Russian émigrés but soon split with them over the issue of national identity. Luxemburg viewed nationalism as one of the principal hurdles to be overcome on the path to socialism, while the leaders of the established Polish Socialist Party sought national self-determination no less fervently than socialist revolution.

In 1898 Luxemburg married Gustav Lubeck to obtain German citizenship and began working with the German socialist movement, then embroiled in the debate between traditional Marxists and advocates of the revisionist theorist Eduard Bernstein. Luxemburg vehemently opposed the ideas of Bernstein, who believed that Marx's emphasis on revolutionary change was outdated and ill-suited to the industrialized nations of Western Europe. He proposed instead a gradualist, evolutionary approach to social and political change, stressing participation in the parliamentary process. Luxemburg pleaded her case in the pamphlet *Sozial reform oder Revolution?* (1889; *Reform or Revolution?*), which caught the attention of German socialist writer Karl Kautsky and helped persuade the leaders of the Second International not to adopt the revisionist line.

After the failed 1905 Revolution in Russia, Luxemburg turned her attention once again to Eastern Europe, where she believed socialism stood the best chance of success. While imprisoned in Warsaw for her activities, she wrote *Massenstreik, Partei und Gewerkschaften* (1906; *The Mass Strike, the Political Party, and the Trade Unions*), in which she advocated the mass strike as the most powerful weapon in the proletariat's arsenal. In contrast to authoritarian leaders like Lenin, she firmly believed that a properly trained and radicalized working class could spontaneously create its own revolution, obviating the need for elaborate planning and a rigid party hierarchy driven by elites. While her working-class supporters admired her dedication to democratic socialism, Luxemburg's antielitist brand of radicalism distanced her from most of her contemporary socialist theorists.

At the outbreak of the First World War, Luxemburg once again found herself at odds with the majority of socialist leaders, who immediately abandoned their pacifist internationalism to take up arms with the rest of Europe. Luxemburg joined forces with other opponents of the war, including German socialist leader Karl Liebknecht, to form the Spartakusbund, or Spartacus League, which advocated an end to the bloodshed through mass desertion and proletarian revolution. Luxemburg was imprisoned through most of the war, however, and the Spartacists wielded little tangible influence within Germany.

The German revolution of November 1918, coming on the heels of military defeat and the Bolshevik victory in Russia, seemed to point to the fulfillment of Luxemburg's hopes and plans. The Spartacists attempted to organize the workers' and soldiers' soviets into a coherent mass movement but were frustrated at every step by the Socialist Party and ultraconservative forces. In December 1918 Luxemburg and others founded the German Communist Party, which she insisted on keeping as free from Bolshevik influence as possible. The following year, Luxemburg and Liebknecht were murdered by extremist right-wing soldiers, with the complicity of the newly established Weimar authorities.

Lu Xun (1881–1936)

Chinese writer. Generally considered to be the most accomplished and influential writer and critic in Chinese literature of the twentieth century, Lu (whose real name was Zhou Shuren) emerged from the May Fourth Movement, appealing for China's self-examination and awakening. His short story "Kuang-ren ri-ji" ("A Madman's Diary") condemned traditional Confucian society through the fantasies of a madman. His *A Q zheng-zhuan* (1921; *The True Story of Ah Q*) manages to mix humor and pathos while satirizing the old order and the self-deceiving passivity lurking within the Chinese character. Although Lu Xun is better known for his fiction, he was also a master of the prose essay, a vehicle he utilized more and more toward the end of his life. His "Outline History of Chinese Fiction" and companion compilations of classical fiction remain standard tomes. Translations, largely from the Russian, also occupy a large place in his complete works.

M

Mabinogion

Medieval Welsh tales. The name *Mabinogion* has been commonly applied to a body of eleven medieval Welsh tales since their translation into English by Lady Charlotte Guest in the nineteenth century. Although they are preserved in manuscripts of the twelfth, thirteenth, and fourteenth centuries, the composition of the tales is thought to predate the actual texts by several centuries. While these tales concern various subjects, the name derives from four legends that form a more or less coherent unit, "The Four Branches of the Mabinogi." These tales focus on legendary rulers of Dyfed (in South Wales) and Gwynedd (in North Wales). The other *Mabinogion* tales include five narratives about King Arthur, including "Culhwch and Olwen," the earliest vernacular Arthurian narrative.

Machiavelli, Niccolò (1469–1527)

Italian statesman and political philosopher. Born in Florence, Machiavelli had by 1498 become a diplomat after the expulsion of the Medici family (in the person of Piero de' Medici [1471–1503]), in 1494, and the eventual fall of the democratic party led by Girolamo Savonarola. As second chancellor and secretary to The Ten, a group of magistrates who were charged with the city's external relations, he carried out a number of missions in Italy, France, and Germany. His abilities brought him to the notice of the head of the Florentine government,

Gonfalonier Piero Soderini, whose assistant he became. When the Medicis returned to power in 1512, however, Machiavelli was arrested and, due to his close relationship with Soderini, forced to leave Florence.

In the works for which he is most famous, *Il principe* (1512; *The Prince*) and *Discorsi sopra la prima deca de Tito Livio* (1513–17; *The Discourses*), he inaugurated a new era by rejecting theology and moral philosophy as the grounds for political thought. These works were also intended to help him regain influence and a position in the Florentine government; each was dedicated to powerful members of the Medici family. Not intended to be systematic political philosophy but to influence with useful advice and to impress with literary style, these writings comment upon military affairs, property rights, ethics, personal behavior, and a host of other topics, illustrated by historical examples rather than proceeding by philosophical assumption. Judging from the changes that he had witnessed at close range, Machiavelli thought that Italy was desperately in need of a strong ruler. *The Prince* especially focuses on the qualities a ruler should possess, rejecting the medieval view that a prince ought to command the loyalty of his subjects by being an exemplar of human virtue; instead the ruler should be willing to do whatever is necessary to achieve success for the state, whether virtuous or vicious. That is, Machiavelli recasts political wisdom not in terms of morals and justice but of efficiency and expansion. As a result, he counseled military strength and the rejection of Christian virtue as a guiding principle in favor of ancient Roman *virtus*, a quality ideally possessed by both the prince and the body politic. Thus, Machiavelli can argue without contradiction in *The Discourses* for a free republican regime, all of whose members share the same goals.

In the 1520s Machiavelli began to gain favor with the Medici family, but the Medicis were driven from power before he could become established; he died in 1527. His other writings include books on the art of war, the government, and the history of Florence; biographies; the plays *La Mandragole* (1518; *The Mandrake*) and *Clizia* (1525); and a novella, *Belfagor*. For several centuries Machiavelli was reviled widely as an atheist and advocate of tyranny; by the nineteenth century he had come to be thought of as the forerunner of the idea of the nation-state.

machismo

Prototype of demeanor in Latin American culture. Also known as the cult of virility, *machismo* stresses male pride and aggressiveness in social and political relations. Its chief characteristics are exaggerated aggressiveness and intransigence in male-to-male relationships and arrogance and sexual aggression in male-to-female relationships. The *macho* man displays strength, courage, self-confidence, daring, sexual prowess, an extremely competitive nature, and pride in his manliness. The appearance of *machismo* as a name for the age-old mode of behavior can be traced to Spanish and Latin American cultures, combining Spanish pride, a sense of personal honor and dignity, the Indian *mestizo*'s fatalistic view of life, and the emotional self-expression encouraged in Latin America. The *macho* man image borrows from the roles of Western literary character Don Juan, the *conquistador*, the solitary hero, the adventurer, and the revolutionary fighter.

Machismo's political significance resides both in its effect on heterosexual relations and on political rule. Some scholars believe that, along with economic change and increasing modernization in the social and political spheres, the rise of the women's movement may alter the manifestation of *machismo*, or do away with it altogether. With regard to government, *macho* behavior has served as the basis for uncooperative and aggressive modes of rule, and as the model for what constitutes authority. Consequently, *machismo* has found expression in feuds, violence, personal dictatorships, unconstitutional modes of political change, aggressive student politics, militarism, and guerrilla warfare.

Machu Picchu

Ancient Inca fortress city in the Peruvian Andes. One of the best-known archaeological sites in South America, Machu Picchu first became known to Western archaeologists in 1911, when the site was discovered by Hiram Bingham of Yale University. Unlike most important preconquest monuments, Machu Picchu escaped detection by the Spaniards, and thus is one of the few Inca sites to remain relatively intact.

Hidden between two sharp peaks about five miles northwest of Cuzco, the five-square-mile site is thought to date from the second half of the fifteenth century, as its style is late imperial Incan. Hints at its existence appear in various sixteenth-century chronicles; it was after reading a newly discovered autobiographical report by the neo-Incan ruler Titu Cusi Yupanqui that Bingham set out in search of this rumored last remote refuge of the Incas. Although clearly a site of religious, economic, and political significance, Machu Picchu is shrouded in mystery, and scholars continue to debate such questions as why it was built in such an inaccessible location, why it was fortified, why it was abandoned, and what purposes it served. It is unclear whether its function was primarily religious, military, or agricultural, and its period of occupancy remains undetermined.

Despite the historical uncertainties surrounding Machu Picchu, it is distinguished by its aesthetic splendor. Much of its fame derives from its impressive location. Set amid lush tropical vegetation and commanding a view of winding rivers below and snowcapped mountains above, the site contains a temple and a citadel that were once surrounded by terraced gardens linked by more than 3,000 steps. Its large main square is flanked by the well-preserved remains of a cemetery, prison buildings, a residential sector, and monuments that are thought to have served an industrial function. Its stonework is impressive, though less refined than that found at other Inca sites.

Macumba

Afro-Brazilian religion. This syncretic mixture of traditional African religions and Roman Catholicism originated with the arrival of African slaves in Brazil in the sixteenth century, though it did not flourish until the mid nineteenth century. Of the many sects of Macumba, perhaps the most prominent are Candomblé and Umbanda.

The Candomblé sect originated in small communities in Salvador, a state in Bahia, and in the northeast, made up of African blacks and their descendants. The language, ceremonial dress, dance, song, and pantheon of the Candomblés vary a great deal. The Candomblé communities are guided by maes de santo and pais de santo (mothers of saints and fathers of saints). Rituals are performed at centers called terreiros, centros, or tendas, and are named after cultic deities of West African origin called orishás or voduns. The pai de santo occupies the highest office in the religious hierarchy,

and has authority over both the filhos and filhas (sons and daughters of the saints, or mediums), who must obey him. Each medium is consecrated to a deity, sometimes more than one, who belongs to the pantheon but takes on a new name and specific identity.

Although the sect is superficially monotheistic, the orishás are organized in an intricate hierarchical system and are identified with Roman Catholic saints. The deities are conceived as natural elements, except Olorun, the high god of the Yoruba (people of the southwest corner of Nigeria), who in Brazil is often identified with the Christian God, and who communicates with human beings through mediums. During the ceremonies, the mediums wear colorful clothes, including voluminous lacy skirts, and the images of the orishás (usually represented by small plaster figures of Roman Catholic saints) are dressed in distinctive garments and adornments. The mediums sing and chant in Yoruba, while the atabaques (drums) beat in different rhythms for each orishá. The filhos de santo dance in a circle to this music and gradually go into a trance; attendants then dress them in ritual vestments. Each orishá is expected to behave in particular ways according to the rules followed in the trance. Animal sacrifices also are commonly performed as part of ritual offerings.

Umbanda is the other of the important Macumba sects. It thrives in the large cities of Brazil, including Rio de Janeiro and São Paulo. Like Candomblé, Umbanda is characterized by Catholic iconography, the worship of saints that have been given African names, animal sacrifices, and mediums who are possessed by spirits, or orishás. Umbanda, moreover, reflects the influence of Buddhist and Hindu religions, and has adopted American Indian gods. The Umbanda sect in Brazil has been officially forbidden and persecuted at various times. Their members generally come from the lower classes, although the sect has a following among the white middle classes.

Madres de la Plaza de Mayo

Argentinian human rights group. The Madres de la Plaza de Mayo (Mothers of the Plaza de Mayo) was formed in Argentina during the Process of National Reorganization military government. This period was otherwise known as the Guerra Sucia (the Dirty War), in which the state, as part of a counterinsurgency campaign, used extrajudicial killings, abductions, and torture to wipe out guerrilla movements in the 1970s and early 1980s. During this period it is estimated that over 30,000 people were killed, including at least 9,000 cases of "disappearances." Repression was particularly intense after the coup of 1976. The Mothers of the Plaza de Mayo carried out their first public demonstration in 1977, when a small group of mothers wearing white headscarves marched around the Plaza de Mayo, which faces the government house, Casa Rosada, in the center of Buenos Aires, demanding information on the fate of their "disappeared" relatives. Thereafter, the group grew, and the demonstrations took place every Thursday. The women, aside from wearing scarves, carried enlarged photographs of their missing children and relatives. The state referred to them as *las locas de la Plaza de Mayo* (the madwomen of the Plaza de Mayo; *locas* can also mean "prostitutes" in Argentine slang), in an effort to ridicule and discredit them. Although for the most part left alone, some members were abducted and others killed. Las Abuelas de la Plaza de Mayo (The Grandmothers of the Plaza de Mayo), a related group, sprang up in 1979, and dedicated their efforts to tracing the children of the "disappeared," many of whom were born in captivity and were secretly given away for adoption. With the advent of civilian rule, the Mothers continued their Thursday demonstrations demanding investigations, and criticized the government of Raúl Alfonsín for being too lenient with military offenders. Similar human rights organizations initiated by women have sprung up elsewhere in Latin America, in response to similar campaigns of terror launched by authoritarian regimes.

Maeterlinck, Maurice (1862–1949)

Belgian poet, playwright, and essayist. Maeterlinck studied at the University of Ghent and then moved to Paris, where he associated with the French writers of the Symbolist movement. Considered to be the major dramatist of this movement, Maeterlinck rejected the predominant naturalism of European theater in favor of otherworldly settings and mysterious moods.

Maeterlinck had early success as a writer in 1889 with the publication of *Douze Chansons (Twelve Songs)* and his play *La Princesse Maleine (The Princess Maleine)*. Although this play was his earliest and perhaps his most fantastic, it was also the play that most directly demonstrates an Elizabethan influence. By 1892 Maeterlinck published his most famous allegorical play, *Pelléas et Mélisande (Pelleas and Melisande)*, which is regarded by many as a literary masterpiece. This play was later adopted by French composer Claude Debussy for his opera of the same name.

In 1894 Maeterlinck dispensed with human actors to write several plays for marionettes, including *La Mort de Tintagiles (The Death of Tintagiles)*. The work of his later years, such as *L'Oiseau bleu* (1909; *The Blue Bird*), explores the occult. In addition to his books of poetry and plays, Maeterlinck wrote philosophical studies, translations, and essays. He was awarded the Nobel Prize in Literature in 1911.

Magna Carta

Charter of English liberties. Known as the Great Charter because of its massive size, the Magna Carta has served as an international model of constitutional law for over seven centuries. The Magna Carta evolved from a document drafted by English landlords to protest a number of highly resented policies enforced by King John I (1167–1216), who was greatly in debt from military campaigns during the Crusades and then against the French. In an unusual sign of unity, the barons rallied together in order to complete a set of demands limiting the power of the monarchy. The king was in a vulnerable position because of his unpopularity with both the people and the papacy, and the English barons recognized an opportunity to reduce his power. Under the guidance of the archbishop of Canterbury, Stephen Langton, the barons produced a document of demands and reforms, known as the Articles of the Barons, which later evolved into the Magna Carta. John refused to sign the document when it was first presented to him, so the unified barons captured London. The king then had no choice but to follow its dictums. On June 15, 1215, the barons met him at Runneymede and the Magna Carta was signed into law.

The Magna Carta reduced the power of the monarchy, establishing a just system of law and order, one that protects the rights of the common man. The king's arbitrary power of taxation was diminished, as was his right to imprison. The right to a trial by a jury of peers in accordance with the laws of the land is an important section of the document. The Magna Carta also contains a clause that would impose a war upon any king infringing upon any part of the document. The document was confirmed by Parliament in 1216–17 and reissued on numerous occasions throughout the thirteenth century. In 1297 Edward I's Parliament confirmed a version that is considered the standard form today.

Mahabharata

Hindu epic. The *Mahabharata*, meaning the "war poems of the Bharata," ex-

ists in a number of versions, and most likely takes place in North India. Containing almost a quarter of a million lines in eighteen books, the *Mahabharata* also comprises the famous Sanskrit religious poem the Bhagavadgita and a much later account of the genealogy and life of the Hindu god Krishna. While portions of the epic were probably composed as early as the fifth century B.C.E., the epic is a compilation to which many legends and folk tales were later added. The text largely consists of dramatic material that is intended to be sung, and forms the base of many popular entertainments in India.

Although there are numerous versions, the *Mahabharata* is the story of dynastic struggle and the civil war that took place in the ancient kingdom of Kurukshetra. The prince Dhritarashtra was initially named the heir to the throne of Kurukshetra; however, since he was blind, it was decided that he should relinquish the throne to his younger brother Pandu, who eventually fled from the throne and lived as a hermit in the Himalayas. As a result, Dhritarashtra was forced to accept the throne once again, but in anger, the five sons of Pandu attempted to dethrone their uncle, claiming to be the rightful heirs. Defending their father, the one hundred sons of Dhritarashtra exiled their cousins from the kingdom, but Dhritarashtra decided that the best way to settle the problem was to divide the kingdom among both his sons and his nephews. Dhritarashtra's sons, unhappy with the agreement, went to war with their cousins, and eventually, although by unfair means, won both the war and the territory. However, the sons of Pandu, with the help of the Hindu god Krishna, returned to the kingdom to claim their rightful place. With the assistance of Krishna, the sons of Pandu won and the eldest son, Yudhisthira, ascended the throne for a long and peaceful reign.

Mahachat Kham Luang

Traditional Thai story. Literally meaning the "great birth," this last and most famous *Jâtaka* story represents the 547th incarnation of the Buddha. In traditional Thai culture, the *Mahachat* has been the focus of an annual village festival, at which it is recited by the local Buddhist monks. The story, also called the *Vessantara Jâtaka*, is divided into thirteen episodes, or *kan*, each of which is sponsored by a different member of the village. Each household arrives in a procession with food and flowers for the festival and important offerings for the monks. This can be an important source of income for the monks, and the village which does not have such a performance loses status. Each *kan* has its own musical theme, and is recited by a different monk in the form of a kind of prose poem in a nonmetrical rhyming pattern.

The recitation allows for much oral embellishment or improvisation, often comic, or even vulgar. The story itself provides opportunity for a variety of different literary modes: comic, tragic, fantastic, moral, pathetic, heroic, spiritual. It concerns a selflessly generous Crown Prince named Vessantara, who is banished by his father, the king, when he gives away the kingdom's magic rain-making elephant to Brahmans (priests) from a famine-stricken country. Before leaving the city, the prince has given away all his valuable property, and soon afterward his chariot and horse, forcing him and his wife to carry their two children on foot. After taking up the life of a forest hermit, the prince then gives away the children to an old man, much to the sorrow of the prince's wife. Vessantara next encounters another old man, who asks for the prince's wife. When the prince freely gives her to him, the old man reveals that he is actually Indra, the king of the gods, and he tells Vessantara to keep his wife. Meanwhile, the prince's children have been restored to their grandfather, the old king, who asks the prince to return to the palace. When Vessantara agrees, he and his wife return amid great celebration.

Mahfouz, Naguib (1911–)

Egyptian short-story writer and novelist. Born in 1911 in Cairo, Mahfouz has said that he began writing by copying European detective stories he had read in translation, substituting his own Egyptian characters. At the time Mahfouz published his first short stories in 1934, fiction was still new to Arabic. Although Arabic had long had its own narrative tradition, both in oral folk tales and in various literary prose forms, the art of storytelling had never enjoyed the high prestige assigned to poetry, for centuries the dominant literary form in Arabic. The novel was considered suspect on two counts: its foreign origin, and the traditional belief that it was merely light entertainment, rather than serious art. Mahfouz and his contemporaries transformed the Arabic novel into a sophisticated and prestigious art form and helped create a new and avid readership for prose narrative.

A prolific author who has experimented with many different techniques, Mahfouz is generally recognized as exemplifying Egyptian realism, with its emphasis on social and political criticism. Among his many works, his famous Cairo trilogy (1956–57)—*Bayna al-quasrayn* (*Palace Walk*), *Qasr al-shawq* (*Palace of Desire*), and *Sukkarîya* (*Sugar Street*)—a three-generation saga of the fate and fortune of a Cairene family from the period just before the First World War to the beginning of World War II, presents a social and political commentary on the development of modern Egypt. Other important novels include *Zuqaq al-Midaqq* (1966; *Midaq Alley*), *Awlad haratina* (1959; *Children of Gebelawi*), and *Mîrâmâr* (1967; *Miramar*). He received the 1988 Nobel Prize in Literature. In 1994 he was the target of an assassination attempt by an Islamic fundamentalist.

Mahler, Gustav (1860–1911)

Austrian composer and conductor. Born in what was then Bohemia, Mahler early in his career wanted to become an operatic composer like his idol German composer Richard Wagner (1813–1883). Failing in that respect, he was nevertheless triumphantly successful in other areas of musical composition. Mahler's works are considered to be Classical-Romantic in style, strongly influenced by such composers as Beethoven (1770–1827), Anton Bruckner (1824–1896), and Wagner. In addition to many songs, he wrote nine symphonies and part of a tenth, all stretching the conventional symphonic form and employing unusual instrumentation. His major innovation was in exploring the radical possibilities of solo instruments in an orchestral setting. In *Das Lied von der Erde* (1908–09; *The Song of the Earth*), he uses the instrument of the human voice to create his most successful song cycle.

Mahler was a conductor in Prague, Leipzig, Budapest, Hamburg, and London before becoming director of the Viennese Imperial Opera in 1897. As a Jew, he had to convert to Catholicism in order to accept such a high post. He was a perfectionist who elevated the status of the company, but his personal manner made him many enemies, and he was forced to resign in 1907. World-famous but still poor at forty-seven, he conducted in the United States for three seasons at the Metropolitan Opera House and at the New York Philharmonic Society before returning to Vienna, where he died of heart failure.

Maimonides (1135–1204)

Jewish rabbi, doctor, and philosopher. Born in Cordoba in Muslim Spain, Maimonides, or Moses ben Maimon, wrote his work entirely within the Muslim world, much of it in Arabic. He was educated in Aristotelianism in Spain by Arab teachers and became one of the greatest of the scholars in the Hebrew tradition. His commentary on the Mishnah (a collection of Jewish traditions translated from Arabic to Hebrew) forms part of the standard version of commentaries on these Jewish texts. Maimonides' most important work was his synthesis of the enormous body of Jewish oral law contained in the Mishnah into a compendium that could be used not only by rabbis and judges but by laypeople. Among Maimonides' many other writings are a number of medical books and the great philosophical work *The Guide for the Perplexed*, which reflects his profound study of Aristotle. Not only has this work been extremely influential in all later Jewish philosophy, it has inspired many Christian thinkers. Maimonides eventually became the physician of Saladin, sultan of Egypt, and died in Cairo.

Makeba, Miriam [Zenzi] (1932–)

South African folk singer. Makeba was born and educated in Johannesburg, South Africa. She began her singing career in the early 1950s in South Africa, including in her repertory contemporary jazz and folk as well as more traditional songs in Xhosa, her mother tongue.

From 1954 to 1957 Makeba toured with the Black Manhattan Brothers, and gained international attention for her performances in the film *Come Back, Africa* (1958) and the jazz opera *King Kong* (1959). She was invited by Emperor Haile Selassie of Ethiopia to sing before the First Annual Conference of the Organization of African Unity (OAU) in 1959 and also sang for President Kwame Nkrumah of Ghana, as well as several other African heads of state during the 1960s. In 1959 Makeba was taken to the United States as the protégée of Harry Belafonte. Makeba has sung and toured with various groups throughout Zimbabwe, South Africa, the United Kingdom, and the United States, and has also appeared on numerous television and radio programs in Europe and the United States. She has made several records for the RCA and Mercury labels.

In 1968 Makeba married African-American activist Stokely Carmichael, a decision that some suggest hurt her popularity in the United States. *Makeba: My Story*, her autobiography, was published in 1988, and in 1990 Makeba was allowed to return to South Africa, from which she had been banned for the previous several years.

Malcolm X (1925–1965)

African-American political and religious leader. Born Malcolm Little in Omaha, Nebraska, Malcolm X was the seventh of eleven children of the Reverend Earl Little, a Baptist minister and organizer for African-American leader Marcus Garvey's Universal Negro Improvement Association. The family left Omaha to escape harassment, and young Malcolm grew up in Lansing, Michigan, where his house was burned by the Ku Klux Klan, his father murdered, and his mother placed in a mental institution. He was kept in a series of detention homes, and he dropped out of school after the eighth grade and drifted between Boston and Harlem, running numbers, selling and using drugs, and organizing a burglary ring. In 1946 he was arrested in Boston and sentenced to eight to ten years for burglary and larceny. While in prison, he converted to the Nation of Islam (NOI), known popularly as the Black Muslims, an organization that adhered to an African-American version of Islam established by Wallace Fard and Elijah Muhammad. He subsequently changed his last name to "X," a Nation of Islam custom signifying that he rejected his former name as a vestige of slavery. In prison, he began his famous reeducation described in his autobiography, starting by copying words from a dictionary from A to Z.

After his release on parole in 1952, he moved to Chicago, where the NOI had their headquarters, and became a minister in the church and an ally of its leader, Elijah Muhammad. Malcolm X became the organization's most popular speaker, establishing new mosques throughout the United States, founding the movement's publication, *Muhammad Speaks*, in 1961, and assuming the leadership of the prominent Mosque Number Seven in Harlem. Drawing upon Elijah Muhammad's religious teachings, he disagreed sharply with civil rights leaders, especially Martin Luther King, Jr., who advocated nonviolence as a means to legal integration. Instead, he argued for black separatism and violence for self-defense, saying that whites were a race of devils created to torment blacks. His increasing popularity as an organizer and the controversy surrounding him as a public figure made him problematic to the NOI leadership, and after he described the assassination of President John F. Kennedy in 1963 as "a case of chickens coming home to roost," a perpetuation of the violence usually directed at blacks, Elijah Muhammad suspended him from the movement; three months later Malcolm X quit the organization.

He formed a rival group, the Muslim Mosque, Inc., in Harlem, and after a pilgrimage to Mecca, where he took the Muslim name El-Hajj Malik El-Shabazz, and travels throughout the Middle East and Africa in 1964 he announced his conversion to Orthodox Islam. His newly founded Organization of Afro-American Unity was intended to be an international body promoting the interests of people of color against white oppression. Due to his outlaw image in the mass media, he was frequently the target of threats by whites and was under surveillance by the Federal Bureau of

Investigation; because of his increasing differences with the Nation of Islam, he believed himself to be under threat of death by Black Muslims. On February 14, 1965, his house was firebombed while he and his family were inside; seven days later he was shot to death while speaking at a rally of his followers in New York City. Three Black Muslims were convicted of the assassination, but there is still controversy surrounding his murder. *The Autobiography of Malcolm X* (1964), which he wrote with Alex Haley, is considered to be a masterpiece of the genre.

Mali, ancient

Sudanese empire. This great empire developed during the thirteenth century in the upper Niger area of the western Sudan region. The word "Mali" comes from a local word meaning "a place of the king," and the empire was not the first state to grow there. Several smaller kingdoms and states, such as that of the Kangaba region, had developed in earlier centuries.

In about 1235 the remaining part of ancient Ghana, led by Sumanguru, was conquered by Sundiata and his army of Mandinka (southern Mande-speaking) people. Sundiata then continued to build up the great empire of Mali. Like ancient Ghana before it, Mali controlled the rich trade of the Sudan region, but it was much larger than Ghana. It was greatest under Emperor Mansa Musa (reigned c. 1307–37) in the early fourteenth century, when it stretched over 1,000 miles from the Atlantic, near the mouth of the Senegal River, to the Middle Niger.

Mansa Musa made a pilgrimage to Mecca in 1324–25. He was said to have taken an army of as many as 100,000 men and so much gold that his power and wealth became famous over Europe and the Middle East. His empire was rich, well administered, and safe for merchants to travel in. Its capital was at Niani, near the present Mali Republic–Guinea frontier, and it included the ancient towns of Jenne, Timbuktu, and Gao.

Mali began to decline after the death of Mansa Musa, when there was no ruler strong enough to hold the empire together. In 1335 Songhai, in the western part of the empire, became independent and later conquered the remaining parts of Mali.

Malinche, La (c. 1505–1529)

Aztec intermediary in Spanish conquest. Born in Painala, Veracruz, to an Aztec chieftain, La Malinche (the Spanish form of her Aztec name, Malintzín) lost her mother when she was very young, and when her father remarried, he sold her as a slave; she was taken to the province of Tabasco where the Spanish *conquistador* Hernán Cortés (1485–1547) found her upon his arrival on March 12, 1519. She was awarded to him as a gift along with nineteen other women, whom Cortés distributed among his captains, giving Malintzín to Alonso Hernández Puertocarrero. When the *conquistadores* discovered that Malintzín spoke Náhuatl and Maya, she became Cortés's interpreter, translating Náhuatl to Maya, which was then translated to Spanish by Jerónimo de Aguilar. Malintzín soon learned Spanish, and when Captain Hernández Puertocarrero returned to Spain, Cortés claimed her as his own, and she became known as La Malinche. (La Malinche is translated as "the bad one.")

She remained by his side through all the most significant moments of the conquest and on the expedition to Honduras, teaching Cortés the customs and ways of life of the different Indian groups he contacted and introducing him to their psychology. In 1522 she had a son by him, whom she named Martín Cortés, later known in Spain as *el Bastardo* (the Bastard). She was baptized and given the name of Marina, and was referred to as Doña Marina by the Spaniards; in the Indians' view, however, La Malinche remained the voice through which Cortés spoke. In their eyes, the union of the two grew to be indivisible: the two figures were conceived of together, always acting as one, and inspiring hate and fear, respect and admiration. The Indians called Cortés "Señor Malinche," or "Malinche's man." In 1524 Cortés married her off to Juan Jaramillo, one of the captains who had participated in the definitive attack on Tenochtitlán in 1521. She lived with her wealthy husband in Mexico City and gave birth to a daughter named María before she died.

Many legends grew around the figure of La Malinche that remain alive today, and volcanoes, mountains, and rivers have been named after her. In the twentieth century the term *malinchismo* was coined, referring to a social phenomenon in which individuals reject their national heritage, preferring that which is foreign. La Malinche has been celebrated as a heroine by some, and rejected by others as a traitor to the native people.

Malthus, Thomas Robert (1766–1834)

English economist. Malthus's father owned a small estate and was one of the executors of French philosopher Jean-Jacques Rousseau's (1712–1778) estate. A graduate of Jesus College, Cambridge, Malthus was a close associate of English poet Samuel Taylor Coleridge (1772–1834) and took orders in the Church of England in 1797. At the same time, from discussions he participated in with his father and his friends, Malthus published *An Essay on the Principle of Population as It Affects the Future Improvement of Society, with Remarks on the Speculation of Mr. Godwin, M. Condorcet, and Other Writers* (1798). Malthus proposed that population, unchecked, increases geometrically, while subsistence increases only arithmeti-

cally. Thus population, regulated by war, famine, pestilence, and by the influence of misery and vice, increases only to the limits of the means of subsistence. Although his views were the subject of controversy, Malthus published an enlarged edition of his theories in 1803, entitled *An Essay on the Principle of Population or a View of Its Past and Present Effects on Human Happiness with an Inquiry into Our Prospects Respecting the Future Removal or Mitigation of the Evils Which It Occasions*, arranging the checks on population into positive or preventative.

Although intended mainly as an argument against utopian visions of society, Malthus's ideas proved very important to English naturalist Charles Darwin (1809–1882), who, in a chance reading, was greatly struck by the idea of the conflict inherent in existence, given limited resources for subsistence. A friend of economist David Ricardo's (1772–1823), Malthus also contributed to economic theory through ideas later developed into the law of diminishing returns as applied to agriculture.

Mammy Wata

West African mythological figure. Mammy Wata (also spelled Mammy Water) is a mythological figure common in many West and Central African cultures. She is a water spirit who inhabits rivers or lakes and often entices young men and children into the depths, where they visit her watery home but are never permitted to leave. She is usually said to possess magical powers and can control and communicate with fish and other marine creatures. Those who beseech her most often seek success in trade and commerce. She is often likened to the Western concept of a siren or mermaid, and she remains a popular folk character in many parts of Africa, where she is immortalized in popular stories, children's books, and popular songs.

Mande

African language group and people. The Mande languages, a group sometimes referred to as Mandingo, make up a branch of the Niger-Congo family of African languages, and are spoken throughout West Africa in Guinea, Mali, Burkina Faso, Sierra Leone, Côte d'Ivoire (Ivory Coast), Senegambia, Ghana, and Nigeria. The most widely spoken of the group are Malinke (also known as Mandingo), Bambara, and Mende. Other major languages of the group are Vai, Toma, and Kpelle. As with most African peoples, the linguistic identity is connected with ethnic identities. Mande languages are tonal — that is, changes in pitch are used to distinguish between words, phrases, and complete utterances that are otherwise identically constructed. Several indigenous writing systems based on the syllable exist for various Mande languages, including Vai, Toma, Mende, and Kpelle. The Mande have a long tradition of oral literature, including histories of the ancient Mali empire. One story tells of a ruler of the old empire who sailed across the Atlantic Ocean toward the Americas in 1312.

The Mande seem to have developed agriculture independently in the fourth millennium B.C.E. They also established some of the earliest civilizations in western Africa, including the states of Soninke in Ghana and the ancient Mali empire of the Malinke people, founded by Sundiata. The Kangaba, a subgroup of the Malinke, maintain one of the world's oldest continuous dynasties, begun in the seventh century C.E. Kangaba, the city from which the Kangaba people took their name, eventually became the capital of the ancient Mali empire.

Mandela, Nelson [Rolihlahla] (1918–)

South Africa's first black president. Mandela was born in Transkei, the son of a royal Tembu family. Although he was groomed to become a chief, his father's death left him in the care of his cousin, who sent him to boarding school. Mandela went on to Fort Hare University College, where he and Oliver Tambo, a future political ally, were both expelled because of their involvement in a student strike.

After leaving the Transkei, Mandela moved to Johannesburg, where he worked as a mine policeman; there he met Walter Sisulu, another future political ally. Mandela completed his B.A. by correspondence in 1941, eventually receiving a law degree and opening a practice with Tambo in the first African legal partnership in South Africa.

Beginning in 1944, Mandela, along with Sisulu and Tambo, became involved in the African National Congress (ANC) Youth League, and he served as national secretary in 1948. Although Mandela initially resisted working with other racial groups opposing the political and economic authority of the white-dominated government, he eventually became involved with the Defiance Campaign of 1952, the purpose of which was to unify resistance efforts, and was appointed the national "volunteer-in-chief." Later that year, Mandela, along with Sisulu and others, was arrested under the Suppression of Communism Act. In addition to serving nine months in prison, he received banning orders that prevented him from attending political meetings for six months; these orders were repeatedly renewed for nine years. Furthermore, Mandela was forced to officially resign from the ANC, of which he was deputy national president, and prevented from leaving Johannesburg. Despite these restrictions, Mandela was instrumental in the establishment of the "M" plan, which divided the ANC into cells that would become operational in the event that it became necessary for the organization to move underground.

In 1956 Mandela and 150 other political leaders were arrested on high-treason charges, but were found not guilty after a four-and-a-half-year trial. Prior to the conclusion of the trial, a campaign organized by the ANC and the PAC (Pan-African Congress) in opposition to the apartheid law requiring nonwhites to carry passes at all times erupted in the 1960 Sharpeville massacre. A bloody conflict in which South African security forces fired on demonstrators, the massacre thrust South Africa into the global spotlight. Following the crisis, the government declared a state of emergency, banned both the ANC and the PAC, and arrested some 1,800 political protesters, including Mandela, without either charging or prosecuting them, though they were eventually released.

In 1961, in response to the tense political environment in South Africa, the All-In Africa Conference was organized. At the conference, Mandela was made honorary secretary of the All-In National Action Council, responsible for organizing a national convention. As secretary, Mandela was also responsible for organizing a stay-at-home strike in May 1961. And although underground, Mandela was instrumental in organizing Umkhonto we Sizwe (the Spear of the Nation), the military branch of the ANC.

Mandela left South Africa in 1962, participating in the Pan-African Freedom Movement meeting, a guerrilla-training program in Algeria, and a meeting with members of the British opposition in London. Upon his return to South Africa, he was arrested and accused of sabotage. Mandela and eight other defendants were found guilty and received life imprisonment. During his imprisonment, his wife, Winnie, a political activist in her own right, became the object of perpetual governmental harassment, including a banishment from Soweto to Brandfort, a distant Free State.

Mandela was released from prison in February 1990, largely through the efforts of National Party president Frederik W. de Klerk, who was responding to a changing political climate in South Africa. As president of the ANC, Mandela continued to campaign against apartheid, winning the Nobel Peace Prize in 1992 and becoming the first black president of South Africa after the country's first democratic elections in April 1994.

Mandelshtam, Osip [Emilievich]
(1891–1938)
Russian poet and literary critic. Mandelshtam was born to a middle-class Jewish family and grew up in the cultural milieu of St. Petersburg at the turn of the century. After graduating from the elite Tenishev School in 1907, he studied at St. Petersburg University, as well as at the Sorbonne and the University of Heidelberg. His first poems appeared in 1910 in the avant-garde literary magazine *Apollon*. Together with Nikolai Gumilyov and Anna Akhmatova, he was one of the founders of the Acmeist school of poetry, which rejected the mysticism and abstraction of Russian Symbolism and demanded clarity, compactness, and perfection of form. Mandelshtam summed up his poetic credo in his manifesto *Utro Akmeizma* (1913; *The Morning of Acmeism*). After his first book of poetry, *Kamen* (1913; *Stone*), Mandelshtam spent the years of civil war and revolution in the Crimea and Georgia. In 1922 he moved to Moscow, where his second volume of poetry, *Tristia*, appeared. Mandelshtam's poetry, apolitical and intellectually demanding, was attacked by party critics and withdrawn from publication. He was able to publish his largely autobiographic prose, collected in *Shum vremeni* (1925; *The Noise of Time*) and *Egipetskaia marka* (1928; *The Egyptian Stamp*). In 1928 he also brought out a volume of his collected poetry and a collection of critical essays, *On Poetry*. An edition of his collected works was prepared in 1933, but

Mandelshtam refused to approve deletions demanded by censors. In 1934 he was arrested for writing an epigram on Stalin and reading it to a small circle of friends. He was exiled to the provincial town of Cherdyn, but after hospitalization and a suicide attempt was permitted to live in the city of Voronezh in central Russia. In 1937, having served his sentence, he returned to Moscow, but was soon arrested again and died at a transit camp near Vladivostok.

Mandelshtam's works of the 1930s were preserved through the efforts of his wife, Nadezhda Iakovlevna. They include prose pieces, such as "Razgovor o dante" (1933; "A Conversation on Dante"), and five notebooks of poetry, two from the Moscow years and three from the Voronezh years. After Stalin's death, Mandelshtam's poetry and prose began to be published again in the Soviet Union. His international fame grew after the publication in the West of the two volumes of his wife's memoirs, *Hope Against Hope* (1970) and *Hope Abandoned* (1974).

Manet, Édouard (1832–1883)

French painter. The son of a magistrate, Manet was born in Paris and inherited considerable wealth when his father died in 1862. He studied at the Collège Rollin from 1844 to 1848, where he met writer Antonin Proust, his future biographer. He then joined the training ship *Guadeloupe* sailing for Rio de Janeiro, and returned to Le Havre in June 1849. He studied with artist Thomas Couture from 1850 to 1856, but he traveled widely, to Fontainebleau in France, and to Italy, Austria, Germany, Belgium, and Holland. His first painting submitted to the Salon in Paris, *Le Buveur d'absinthe* (1859; *The Absinthe Drinker*), was rejected, but he had two paintings accepted in 1861. Then his paintings started provoking sharp controversy.

In 1863 Manet's painting *Déjeuner sur l'herbe* was excoriated for its depiction of a nude woman with two clothed men. His painting *Olympia* caused even worse scandal in 1865, the critics castigating the subject's blatant sexuality. Although writer Émile Zola (1840–1902) and poet Charles Baudelaire (1821–1867) both defended Manet's work, the painter moved to Spain for temporary refuge. He became the focal point of the avant-garde Impressionist painters, including Claude Monet (1840–1926), Pierre-Auguste Renoir (1841–1919), and Alfred Sisley (1839–1899).

Manet never included himself in the society of the Impressionists, preferring to attempt exhibiting in the mainstream Paris salons instead of the Impressionist avant-garde salons organized to exhibit the work spurned by the establishment. Nonetheless, Manet's frequent representation of the nonromanticized, contemporary world and his focus on the painting as an arrangement of paint on canvas greatly influenced the stunning work of the Impressionist painters that subscribed to his radical ideas.

Manila galleons

Philippine cargo ships. Beginning with the conquest of the Philippines by Spain in 1565, the economy of the islands was based almost entirely on these ships. The annual trading voyages carried silks, spices, manufactured goods, and slaves from the Orient to the Spanish port of Acapulco in exchange for silver and gold. The Spanish formed the opinion early on that Manila was ideally placed for orchestrating commerce across the Pacific. The establishment of trade with Chinese merchants and colonial government support of a monopoly helped make the galleon trade lucrative enough to fund the whole colony. Due to the galleon trade that flourished most profitably during the late sixteenth and early seventeenth centuries, Manila was celebrated as one of the most fantastic and luxurious cities in the world.

By the later 1600s, however, increased competition in world trade, combined with the political and military decline of the Spanish empire and the failure to develop the resources of the Philippines themselves, put the colony in decline. Manila continued to rely on the galleon trade into the eighteenth century, but it was no longer able to sustain a growing community. In the last half of the eighteenth century, restrictions were placed on the galleons and other moves were made by the Spanish governors to encourage an open commercial life. International trade was finally allowed when the port of Manila was opened in 1789. While this was the end of the galleon as an economic force, the line continued until it was forbidden by Ferdinand VII in 1813. In 1815 the last ship returned from Acapulco.

Mann, Thomas (1875–1955)

German novelist. Mann was the son of a businessman and senator of the city of Lübeck and a Brazilian-born mother who was half-Portuguese. His early influences included the music of German composer Richard Wagner (1813–1883) and the works of German philosophers Nietzsche (1844–1900) and Schopenhauer (1788–1860), and the German poet and dramatist Friedrich von Schiller (1759–1805). In 1894 Mann finished school in Lübeck and moved to Munich to join his family. While working for a fire insurance company, he began writing. He also began attending classes at the Technische Universität.

His short stories attracted much attention. A short story he finished was sent to the periodical *Neue deutsche Rundschau*, and there was soon a call for all of his previously written works. These were published as the collection *Der kleine Herr Friedemann* in 1898. These stories give the first evidence of a theme Mann was much concerned with, the duality of the inner life of the artist and the outer life of contemporary society.

Mann's first novel, *Buddenbrooks*, published in 1900, used leitmotifs gleaned from music. Through successive generations of the Buddenbrook family, Mann explored the decay of civilization and the change of one generation to the next. His next works included *Tristan* (1903), *Königliche hoheit* (1909; *Royal Highness*), and *Tod in Venedig* (1912; *Death in Venice*). In *Betrachtungen eines unpolitischen* (1918; *Reflections of an Unpolitical Man*), Mann explored his own disinterest in the First World War and Germany's role in it. And in *Der Zauberberg* (1924; *The Magic Mountain*), Mann examined the crumbling foundations of both Europe and Germany.

In 1929 he received the Nobel Prize in Literature, but just four years later the Nazis expelled him from Germany. Mann moved to the United States and became a citizen in 1944. During the 1930s and the Second World War, Mann was very active in his opposition to the fascists, recording radio broadcasts for the German people. His literary production continued with *Vertauschten Kopfe* (1940; *The Transposed Heads*), *Doktor Faustus* (1947; *Doctor Faustus*), and *Bekenntnisse des Hochstaplers Felix Krull* (1954; *Confessions of Felix Krull*), among many others. He settled in Zurich in 1954, and died there a year later.

Mansa Musa I

African Mali king. A nephew of founding emperor Sundiata, Mansa Musa was the king of the Mali empire during the years 1307–37 C.E. He is best known for his legendary pilgrimage to Mecca in 1324–25, and the mythic proportions of his visit to Cairo, where he gave away so much gold that the gold market became depressed. Arab historians say that the emperor's retinue included 60,000 porters and 500 servants dressed in gold, each carrying a gold staff. One source says that the emperor was still in his palace when the head of his caravan reached Timbuktu, two hundred miles away. It was Mansa Musa who inspired a popular European legend of an El Dorado, a city of gold, in Africa, and the legend of Prester John, a medieval mythical emperor thought to rule a magical kingdom in Africa.

Mansa Musa attracted scholars to his kingdom, hired a famous Cairo architect to build his palaces and mosques, exchanged gifts and ambassadors with the merchant cities of the Maghreb, and established Qur'ânic schools. As a patron of the arts and literature, he laid the foundations of the tradition of African-Arabic literature that came to fruition in the great city of Timbuktu in the fourteenth to sixteenth century.

Maori

Indigenous people and language of New Zealand. The name Maori, which literally means "normal," was first used during the nineteenth century by indigenous New Zealanders as a way of differentiating themselves from Europeans.

Maori oral history and legends refer to a period of migrations from a mythical Polynesian homeland called Hawaiki that began in 1100 C.E. and peaked with the "great fleet" of 1350 C.E. This general account is cited by more than sixty tribes throughout New Zealand, although recent archaeological and anthropological evidence suggests that New Zealand was populated, however sparsely, as early as 800 C.E. by preclassical Maori people referred to as Moa hunters. The term Hawaiki itself probably refers not to one specific place but to a number of different Polynesian islands, including Tahiti, Tonga, and the Cook Islands.

Traditional Maori society was based on the recognition of a common ancestry associated with the seven *waka* (canoes) which comprised the "great fleet." These *waka* symbolize the seven major *iwi* (tribes). Iwi are made up of several *hapu* (subtribes), the major landholding

groups, and *whanau* (extended families).

The first European to enter New Zealand waters was the Dutch explorer Abel Tasman, who in 1672 wrote preliminary studies of Maori and New Zealand although he did not set foot on shore. Tasman's observations were continued by Captain James Cook, a British merchant and explorer, over one hundred years later. Cook, who saw New Zealand as a suitable site for colonization, was responsible for introducing musket warfare and profit-oriented trade into Maori traditional life, thus changing it irrevocably. By the early nineteenth century, large numbers of European settlers, traders, and missionaries began to settle in New Zealand permanently, and the demand for land and resources grew immensely.

In 1840 Britain, represented by the colonial governor Sir George Grey, formally annexed New Zealand under the Treaty of Waitangi, although it was not signed by over 60 percent of the Maori chiefs and many more did not grasp the implications of surrendering their chieftainship. Wars between Maori and British soldiers ensued, lasting until 1872, when Britain finally confiscated large tracts of Maori land and sent Maori rebels into exile in the Waikato mountains. As a warrior culture, Maori were particularly adept at fighting a war balanced heavily against them: during the war years, the Maori were outnumbered by British soldiers sixty to one. Nonetheless, Maori tactical acumen, including complex trench-warfare systems and trap-and-lure strategies, coupled with resistance networks such as the Kingitanga movement, the Hauhau warrior cult, and a number of prophet movements, served to maintain Maori resistance to the British for more than twenty-seven years despite the great numerical disadvantage.

As a result of these wars and exposure to European diseases, the Maori population at the turn of the century was decimated. Maori population numbers did recover despite European predictions that they would die out. Miscegenation, urbanization, and British colonial practices and laws, however, have resulted in a Maori underclass, significantly alienated from traditional Maori life and culture, comprising 13 percent of New Zealand's total population today. A Maori cultural, social, and political renaissance, beginning in the 1960s and 1970s with Maori civil rights protests, has focused attention on Maori land and compensation issues to redress grievances against government practices during the nineteenth and twentieth centuries. In the past three years, Maori tribes and groups have petitioned the New Zealand government, with some success, for monetary, legal, and estate compensation.

Mao Zedong (1893–1976)

Founder of the People's Republic of China. Born to a prosperous peasant family in Hunan province, Mao in his youth demonstrated unusual interest and talent in social studies. In 1918, at twenty-five, he went to Beijing, where he became an assistant librarian at the National University. While working there, he avidly read books, newspapers, and magazines, and soon found himself involved in political movements. In 1921 he attended the first meeting of the Chinese Communist Party (CCP), secretly held on a boat in Shanghai, becoming a founding member.

Six years later, when the Guomindang (Nationalist Party) led by Chiang Kai-shek (now written Jiang Jie-shi) launched an attack on Communists in big cities, Mao led the Autumn Harvest Uprisings in Hunan and became a firm advocate of rural revolution. With Zhu De and other Communist fugitives, he founded the Red Army in Jiangxi. However, his ideas did not prevail within the Central Committee of the CCP until 1935, when he led the troops in the 6,000-mile Long March, a trek the CCP made to escape the Guomindang, seeking shelter in the city of Zunyi, where Mao was elected chairman of the party. He then went to Yan'an, which became the base of CCP operations.

During World War II, he negotiated with Chiang Kai-shek to form a united front in the fight against the Japanese invasion. After Japan surrendered in 1945, the uneasy cooperation ended, and a civil war followed between the Nationalists and the Communists in which Mao devised extremely effective rural guerrilla warfare strategies. Despite U.S. aid to the Nationalists, Mao's army emerged victorious, driving Chiang Kai-shek to Taiwan. In 1949 Mao declared a new People's Republic of China.

Paramount leader for the next twenty-seven years, Mao launched a series of political and economic movements redistributing land and wealth and completely revolutionizing Chinese life and society. But some of his policies proved disastrous, including Land Reform (1949–53), the Anti-Rightist Movement (1957), the Great Leap Forward (1958), and the Cultural Revolution (1966–76). Though Mao initially regarded the Soviet Union as a close Communist ally, his ideas drew open attacks from the Soviets, which eventually led to a hostile relationship between the two countries for more than thirty years. China sought allies elsewhere and became very influential in the Third World. In 1972 Mao developed closer ties with the West by meeting U.S. president Richard Nixon in Beijing.

marabout

Muslim religious leader. *Marabouts* were held in high regard by the North African communities in which they lived; today they exist mostly in Algeria. The word *marabout* may be a French corruption of the Arabic *murabit*, or one who lives in a *ribat*, a fortified monastery that is both religious and military. In the eleventh and twelfth centuries, marabouts spread from northwest Africa into Spain and were widely respected as holy men. The Almoravids (from *al-Murabitun*), Muslim rulers of Morocco and parts of Spain in the eleventh and twelfth centuries, descended from them. In the religious wars of nineteenth-century Senegambia, the term was used for any orthodox Muslim. Over the years, the word has lost its military connotations. Marabout also connotes the tomb of a religious leader.

Maran, René (1887–1960)

West Indian writer. Born in Fort-de-France, Martinique, Maran moved to France at an early age and was educated at the Lycée de Talance in Bordeaux, graduating in 1909. Some of his poetry had already been published. He joined the French colonial civil service in Africa the same year and served in various posts for fourteen years. In 1921 he published *Batouala: Veritable Roman nègre* (*Batouala: A True Black Novel*), a story about African tribal life in French Equatorial Africa during World War I. For this highly acclaimed novel Maran became the first black to receive the Goncourt Prize in 1922; it was subsequently translated into more than fifty languages and is considered a masterpiece. Maran moved back to France in 1923, publishing six more novels, three books of poetry, many essays, and several biographies, and winning several writing awards.

Marcos, Ferdinand [Edralin] (1917–1989)

Former president of the Philippines. During World War II Marcos participated in guerrilla fighting against the Japanese. After the war, he served as an assistant to President Manuel Roxas. He was a member of the Philippine House of Representatives from 1949 to 1959 and a senator from 1959 until 1966. He was first elected president as the candidate of the Nacionalista Party in a victory over Liberal Party president Diosdado Macapagal. Marcos solidified his popularity with his powerful talent for oratory and with generous spending on rural roads, electrification, and agricultural improvements. Although he advocated Philippine cultural and economic independence from the West, he was a strong supporter of the United States during the Vietnam War and was a valued U.S. ally for his undying anti-Communism.

In 1969 Marcos was elected to a second term during a period of pressing foreign debts. At the same time, domestic revolutionary agitation was increasing, particularly by the Communist New People's Army and by Muslim separatists in the southern islands. In September 1972, pronouncing the situation unmanageable under the current political system, he declared martial law. The military quickly destroyed virtually all public opposition to Marcos by arresting thousands of critics on both the left and the right and suppressing student demonstrations. In January 1973 a new constitution was introduced that provided a more parliamentary government. Marcos declared himself prime minister and settled in for eight years of rule by decree.

Communist insurgency continued throughout the 1970s, and the economic reforms that Marcos had initiated turned out to support mostly the president's family and rich friends. In 1978, in response to disillusionment with his rule, Marcos finally allowed elections to be held for the constitutional, but never before convened, National Assembly. In a foreshadowing of the 1986 election, the results were altered and almost no anti-Marcos candidates were seated.

In 1981 martial law was suspended and Marcos won a third term as president. In 1983 exiled opposition leader Benigno Aquino was assassinated by the military when he attempted to come back to the Philippines. It was never proven that

Marcos was directly involved in the killing, but the event touched off heightened protest against the administration, already suffering from the country's massive unemployment crisis and multiple corruption scandals. In 1985 Marcos made a surprise announcement that elections would be held in February 1986, fifteen months ahead of schedule. Corazon Aquino, wife of the slain Benigno, eventually emerged as the primary opposition candidate. Accusations of fraud surfaced immediately after the election from both within and outside the Philippines. Both candidates declared victory. On February 21, in a bloodless popular revolution, Aquino was handed the presidency and Marcos was forced to flee to the United States. Only in exile was the extent of his exploitation of power fully discovered. The new government announced that Marcos had appropriated at least $5 billion from the country for his personal use. He and his wife, Imelda, became emblems of ostentation and corruption. In 1988 he was indicted by a U.S. federal grand jury on charges of racketeering and embezzlement, but died in Hawaii of heart and kidney failure before he could face charges.

Marcos, Imelda (1930–)

Filipino politician. Married to Ferdinand Marcos, president of the Philippines from 1965 to 1986, Imelda Marcos served in a variety of governmental positions during her husband's reign, including governor of Metro Manila, member of the Interim Legislative Assembly, and minister of human settlements and ecology. She was a member of her husband's Cabinet Executive Committee and a leader of the Kilusan Bagong Lipunan (New Society Movement). Imelda Marcos also occasionally functioned as a roving ambassador of the Philippine government, going to China in 1976 and in 1977 negotiating with Colonel Moamar Qaddafi of Libya over governance of the southern Philippine islands. In 1984 she was questioned by a Philippine commission investigating the assassination of Filipino politician Benigno Aquino, husband of the future Filipino president Corazon Aquino (serving 1986–). Imelda Marcos denied playing any role in the Aquino killing, and her connection to it remains unproven.

After the fall of Ferdinand Marcos in 1986, Imelda became most notorious for her outrageous luxury as first lady of the Philippines. Reports of over a thousand pairs of shoes and hundreds of evening gowns left behind in the presidential palace were often repeated as evidence of the family's greed and ostentation. Though indicted by a U.S. grand jury in 1988 for embezzlement, she was found not guilty. In 1994 Imelda was elected to the Philippine Congress as a representative from her province of Leyte.

Mardi Gras

Festival before Lent. From the French meaning "fat Tuesday," Mardi Gras refers to the customary use of fats in cooking before Ash Wednesday, the day that begins the Christian period of Lent. In France, this is also referred to as Shrove Tuesday. It is a day of festivities and celebration before the beginning of the penitence associated with Lent. In the United States, Mardi Gras is principally celebrated in New Orleans, where the festival begins ten days before Shrove Tuesday, and is part of a longer carnival season that starts January 6. Rio de Janeiro and Nice are also cities where Mardi Gras is still extravagantly celebrated.

marianismo

Mode of behavior. As widespread as *machismo*, though not as well known, *marianismo* may be understood as its complement. The concept of *marianismo* is prevalent in many cultures, but is thus named in Latin America. It is the cult of feminine spiritual superiority that proclaims women as semidivine, morally superior to and spiritually stronger than men. The ideal woman is characterized by an unassailable purity and a spiritual strength that in turn engenders self-abnegation and an endless potential for self-sacrifice; women are constructed in this ideal as patient and strong, and beneath their submissiveness lies the conviction that men must be humored because they are, after all, like children and cannot help the way they are.

The extent to which this sociocultural phenomenon offers women protection or serves as a positive influence in their lives is arguable. Some critics maintain that women have gained through it a strong sense of identity and historical continuity, as well as a security blanket that protects them from the misdeeds of their men. For example, they argue that this ideal of woman makes divorce highly unlikely, if not impossible; women are not abandoned by their spouses and forced to start a new life in middle age; and if they are mistreated or abandoned, they are likely to have the support of the whole community. Whether these factors constitute privileges is still open to debate; scholars who criticize *marianismo* note the absence of choice in such cultural constructs, women's legal status as dependents in many cases, and the modest participation of women in public/political life.

In any case, this cultural phenomenon also has found expression in literature, and often in the growing corpus of literature by women; one notable example of the celebration of *marianismo* as a female source of strength by a woman writer is Chilean writer Isabel Allende's *La casa de los espiritos* (1982; *The House of the Spirits*).

Mariátegui, José Carlos (c. 1895–1930)

Peruvian revolutionary. After working as a journalist, Mariátegui founded with Victor Raúl Haya de la Torre the Alianza Popular Revolucionaria (Popular Revolutionary Alliance of the Americas; APRA) in the 1920s, a movement that initially was anti-imperialist in character. However, soon after the founding of APRA, Mariátegui left the movement because he considered it too reformist and timid in its politics, and founded the Communist Party of Peru (first called the Socialist Party). Every left-wing group in Peru, legal or extralegal—such as the rural guerrilla group Sendero Luminoso (Shining Path)—has claimed its lineage directly or indirectly from Mariátegui.

Mariátegui wrote on a wide range of issues, with his most important work being *Siete ensayos de interpretación de la realidad peruana* (1928; *Seven Essays of Interpretation of the Peruvian Reality*). He is best known and most influential for his writings on racism and the "indigenous question" in Latin America. He placed great emphasis upon the use of racist myths by the elites for their economic and political advantage. Further, he sought to relate the struggle for socialism in Peru to the cultural and political division between the Europeanized coast of the country and the highland peoples descended from the pre-conquest population. During five centuries of colonial rule and independence, the Europeanized elite ruled Peru in a manner that largely excluded the indigenous population from the political process and the benefits of economic growth. It was Mariátegui's view that the Inca empire of pre-conquest Peru had been essentially communal in nature, in which private property did not exist. This communalism of ancient Peru, whose traditions continued in the indigenous communities of the highlands, could provide the social basis for the modern communalism of socialist society. As a Marxist, he did not consider himself to be a nationalist as such, but concluded that the struggle for socialism required a phase of revolutionary nationalism that would liberate his country from foreign dominance. This first stage would be carried out through an alliance of the working class, peasantry, and middle classes. It was Mariátegui's contribution to recognize that integration of the indigenous population into this struggle for democratic rights would be essential to the modernization of his country.

Mari letters

Ancient Canaanite cuneiform tablets. Excavations of the ancient city of Mari (modern-day Tell el-Hariri) on the Euphrates River near the Syrian-Iraqi border have provided some of the most useful information about the early dynastic period in Mesopotamia and about the period under the reign of Babylonian king Hammurabi (1792–1750 B.C.E.), when the city was destroyed in about 1760 B.C.E. The most enlightening finds were made in the royal diplomatic archives of King Zimri-Lim. Among the nearly 20,000 cuneiform tablets recovered in 1935–38 by Andre Parrot were approximately 5,000 letters, mostly written by the inhabitants of Mari. The letters are written in a Babylonian that is replete with West Semitic vocabulary and grammar, providing evidence of a language ancestral to Hebrew and Aramaic, as well as a wealth of information about Mari's relations with north Syrian kingdoms. Another striking group of Mari texts is a collection of approximately thirty letters describing a form of oracular speaking that bears a resemblance to biblical-style prophecy. It appears that most of this oracular speaking was done by cultic personnel who were transmitting messages from the gods. This suggests that the phenomenon of "prophecy" is a form of divination unique to the western Semites.

The Mari letters are significant for a number of reasons. First, they revealed the extent of Mesopotamian influence in ancient Syria. Combined with other artifacts from Mari, the letters attest to the westward extension of Mesopotamian culture. Second, the letters provided an important source of "objective" information about the Canaanites. Prior to the nineteenth century, the Bible was one of the only sources of information about Canaanite civilization. Discoveries such as the Mari letters, the Amarna letters, and the Ugaritic texts, however, have shown that the ancient Hebrew texts of the Old Testament were a complex mix of legend, myth, polemic, and social history.

marimba

African-originating instrument. A kind of xylophone brought by African slaves to Latin America, the marimba was a favorite instrument among slaves in Cuba around 1690, where it was called *congo* and *angola*, after the places of its origin. The marimba is a keyboard instrument that is supported on the legs or hung by the waist and played with mallets; sometimes the instrument can be played by up to four people. Affixed to the keys are tuned tubular or gourd resonators that distinguish this instrument from other xylophones. Today it remains a popular folk instrument in Central America.

Marlowe, Christopher (1564–1593)

English poet and playwright. Born the son of a shoemaker at Canterbury, Marlowe attended Benet College (now Corpus Christi), Cambridge, and took the B.A. in 1584 and the M.A. in 1587. He almost certainly left Cambridge for London before that date. Little is known of his life during the following years except for his connection as dramatist with the Lord Admiral's and Strange's companies and his acquaintance with many famous people. Though Marlowe may have written a play to be performed by a children's company, *Dido, Queen of Carthage*, in 1586, his first published effort, *Tamburlaine the Great* (in two parts of five acts each), appeared in 1587 and 1588 to wide acclaim; its prologue is credited with changing the use of verse in English drama. It was soon followed by successes with his most celebrated play, *The Tragical History of Dr. Faustus* (1588), and *The Famous Tragedy of the Rich Jew of Malta* (1589). Each of these three is dominated by an almost superhuman protagonist who is driven by a passion that ultimately destroys him. With *Edward II* (1593), Marlowe displayed greater skill with blank verse and more complex characterization. Some scholars think that Marlowe may have cowritten several plays, including Shakespeare's *Titus Andronicus, Henry IV,* and *Richard III.*

Marlowe is also highly regarded for his lyric poetry, which includes a translation of Ovid's *Amores,* the unfinished *Hero and Leander,* a translation of Lucan's *Pharsalia,* and the famous "Come live with me and be my love," all published posthumously. At different times Marlowe was arrested for murder and atheism but was subsequently released. His life has become legendary for its recklessness and unorthodoxy, but this image is based mainly on speculation. Evidence suggests that he was under investigation by the government for unknown offenses when he was stabbed to death by Ingram Frazer in an apparent altercation over payment of a bill for food and ale.

maroon

Fugitive slave. This term was used for fugitive slaves in the West Indies in the seventeenth and eighteenth centuries and later used for their descendants. Called by the French *marron* and the Spanish *cimarrón,* the slaves escaped their colonial masters when the British began their invasion in 1655 to wrest control of the islands from the Spanish. Maroons established their own communities throughout the West Indies and Central and South America, though the word *maroon* is most frequently applied to the groups in the mountains of Jamaica who resisted the British until a treaty of 1739 allowed them to live independently.

Martí, José (1853–1895)

Cuban journalist and poet. José Martí was born in Cuba on January 28, 1853, to Spanish parents. During the first Cuban war against Spain (1868), Martí contributed to the publication of clandestine newspapers and pamphlets, including *El diablo cojuelo* (*The Limping Devil*) and *La patria libre* (*The Free Fatherland*). The following year, he published a dramatic political poem called "Abdala," and in 1869, after co-signing a letter questioning the politics of another student, he was tried and sentenced to six years' hard labor. While serving his sentence, he wrote a political essay, "El presidio político de Cuba" (1871; "The Political Prison in Cuba"). This essay was followed by another called "La republica española ante la revolucíon cubana" (1873; "The Spanish Republic Faced by the Cuban Revolution"), which he wrote from Spain, where he was subsequently exiled by Spanish authorities. In Spain, he earned degrees in law and philosophy from the universities of Zaragoza and Madrid. In Mexico, he met his future wife, Carmen Zayas Bazán, wrote for the *Revista Universal,* helped found the Sociedad Alarcón, and wrote a play called *Amor con amor se paga* (1875; *Love Is Repaid with Love*); in Guatemala he published a short volume entitled *Guatemala* (1878); and in Venezuela he founded an important modernist magazine, *Revista Venezolana.* Martí wrote about life in the United States, where he lived for fifteen years, and in Europe for the New York *Sun* and for Argentina's *La Nación.* His *crónicas* record contemporary events—social, political, and literary—with uncanny perception and vision, showing his Latin American readers both the advantages and disadvantages of modernization. While in New York, Martí also founded the Cuban Revolutionary Party (1892). In New York he published two books of verse, *Ismaelillo* (1882) and *Ver-*

sos sencillos (1891; *Simple Verses*), in the modernist style. Martí wrote his only novel, variously entitled *Amistad funestra* (*Disastrous Friendship*) and *Lucía Jerez*, in 1885. He died while commanding rebel troops in the Cuban revolt of 1895.

Marx, Karl [Heinrich] (1818–1883)

German social and economic theorist. Marx was born of Jewish parents in Treves (now Trier) in Rhenish Prussia. When he was six, his father, a lawyer, had the entire family baptized as Lutherans. During his student years at the universities of Bonn and Berlin, Marx studied law, history, and philosophy and was strongly influenced by the works of German philosopher Georg Wilhelm Friedrich Hegel (1770–1831), whose theories of the dialectic in history and ideas Marx would adapt to his own. In 1841 he received a Ph.D. in Greek philosophy from the University of Jena. Pursuing journalism as a career, he became an editor of the newspaper *Rheinische Zeitung* in Cologne in 1842, and the following year he married Jenny von Westphalen.

Soon after, his newspaper was suppressed and he moved to Paris, where he became acquainted with French socialism and began his lifelong collaboration with philosopher Friedrich Engels (1820–1895), as well as his lifelong exile from Germany. His *Ökonomisch-philosophische Manuskripte aus dem Jahre 1944* (*Economic and Philosophic Manuscripts of 1844*) mapped out many of the ideas he would develop in his later work. Expelled from France in 1845, he moved to Brussels and made his first contact with the workers' movement. There he and Engels wrote the influential *Manifest der Kommunistischen Partei* (1848; *Communist Manifesto*) in support of the workers' movement and as a call to revolutionary action. During the 1848 European revolutions, Marx was expelled from Brussels and moved to Paris and then back to Cologne, where he revived and edited his old newspaper under the title *Neue Rheinische Zeitung* until he was arrested and tried for sedition. He was acquitted but expelled in 1849.

He remained in London for the rest of his life, writing articles for Horace Greeley's New York *Tribune*. He completed two works that are considered to be masterpieces of historiography, *Klassenkampfe in Frankenreich 1848–50* (1850–59; *The Class Struggle in France, 1848–1850*) and *Achtzehnte brumaire des Louis Bonaparte* (1852; *The Eighteenth Brumaire of Louis Napoleon Bonaparte*), but was supported financially for the most part by Engels. Despite chronic poverty, illness, and the death of three children, Marx worked for years in the British Museum researching and writing his monumental analysis of capitalism, *Das Kapital*, only the first volume of which he published during his life (1867); Engels edited the other two volumes after his death, which were published in 1885 and 1894. In 1864 Marx organized the International Working Men's Association (often referred to as the First International), which he disbanded in 1872 after quarreling with the anarchist Mikhail Bakunin over its direction.

His many works were an attempt at a grand synthetic view of human history and culture, and he achieved an elaborate interpretation of philosophy, economics, and society. Marx rejected traditional philosophy as a class-biased ideology that substituted abstractions like reason and justice for an analysis of real human experience. Instead, he began with historical materialism, the view that economic conditions determine all else and that modes of production affect every facet of human life. Under capitalism, human labor is exploited to ensure a profit from the exchange of goods for the investor of money; unlike prior artisans, workers are alienated from their products and are paid just enough from the fruits of their labor to subsist and to reproduce more workers. Dialectically, capitalism is only one stage seen from the long view of historical development, however; eventually, Marx believed, the mass of workers would take control of the means of production and become "a free association of producers under their own conscious and purposive control." This would lead to "communism," a classless, collectivist order in which money as a means of exchange value that could be hoarded by the few would be replaced by the distribution of goods according to need.

Marxism is "scientific" in that it rejects theological, moral, and metaphysical explanations for human suffering and focuses instead upon economic forces. For Marx (and Engels, who contributed much to these theories), the Hegelian dialectic served to elucidate the progress of economic systems, not just ideas: the opposition of forces would result in a new, "synthetic" system. Seeking to understand his own place in this historical continuum, Marx encouraged the dispossessed workers of his time to become aware of their situation and to revolutionize it so that society would be transformed.

Marx's work has had an enormous influence on twentieth-century philosophical and revolutionary thought, and has been the theoretical cornerstone for Communist and socialist revolutionary movements throughout the world.

Masai

East African peoples. The Masai (Maasai) reside in the Great Rift Valley in southern Kenya and northern Tanzania. The lifestyle of the Masai has traditionally been oriented toward the raising of livestock, mostly cattle. Their diet consists primarily of the blood and milk of their cattle; since they consider cattle to be a sacred gift from the deity Enkai, they do not slaughter or sell them. The Masai are pastoral, roaming with their cattle to grazing sites, and they have resisted recent efforts by the Kenyan and Tanzanian governments to force them to settle in villages and raise crops and their cattle on ranches.

Until the early twentieth century, the Masai grazed their cattle on the rich grasslands of the Rift Valley. Expansion of white settlements began to limit their grazing area, and in 1911, through treaties, the British evicted the Masai and relegated them to the semiarid lands of southeastern Kenya, an area one-fifth the size of the Rift Valley. Under Jomo Kenyatta, the first president of the independent republic of Kenya (1964–78), ranches were established for collective cattle grazing. However, with increased population and pressure from the game parks to restrict grazing, the Masai have been restricted from their traditional pasture lands, and encouraged to subdivide and fence the collective ranches.

Another threatened Masai tradition is that of moranism. The moran are a group of Masai warriors and herdsmen whom the Kenyan government has been trying to suppress for years. These men achieve their status after a period of initiation that begins in their mid-teens, when they are circumcised and taken from their community to remote camps called *manyattas*. With other young men of their age group they learn the fundamentals of Masai heritage and develop their strength and skills as herdsmen and warriors. Armed with little more than a knife and spear, they must slay a lion, as final proof of their courage and strength. Opponents of moranism argue that the institution is responsible for low levels of modern education among the Masai. Proponents argue that the institution is important for maintaining Masai cultural heritage and identity.

Masjumi

Indonesian political party. The Madjelis Sjuro Muslimin Indonesia (Masjumi) emerged in 1945 as a political party uniting the many Indonesian Islamic organizations. Shortly thereafter, tensions between various groups within the Masjumi over the aims of Muslim separatism, socialism, and cooperation with non-Muslim parties caused the party to fragment. Despite the departure of historically strong groups like the Saraket Islam—the first large Indonesian nationalist organization—and highly vocal traditionalist groups like the Nahdatul Ulama (the Indonesian council of Islamic scholars and mullahs), the Masjumi remained an effective party, securing more than 20 percent of the National Assembly seats in 1955. During a period of attempted consolidation of power at the center, President Sukarno's government (1945–67) banned the Masjumi Party in 1960 because of the party's refusal to condemn former members who had joined an active revolutionary movement.

maté

South American beverage. Resembling tea, maté is prepared with the dried leaves of an evergreen shrub or tree (*Ilex paraguariensis*), cultivated primarily in Paraguay, but also in Brazil and Argentina. The leaves are placed in a gourd called a *maté* or *culha* that is often decorated, sometimes mounted with silver or made entirely of silver; the leaves are steeped in boiling water and the tea is then sucked from the gourd with the help of a bombilla, a kind of metal straw often made of silver with a strainer at one end to keep the leaves from the mouth. The beverage, less astringent than tea, is greenish in color and contains caffeine and tannin. It was prepared by the Indians long before their encounter with Europeans and was quickly adopted by the Spanish. The wild shrub was first cultivated by Jesuit missionaries, and forms part of the gaucho tradition. Today maté is served plain, and sometimes with sugar, milk, or lemon juice; in Paraguay, the beverage is referred to by its Guaraní name, *tereré*, and is served cold in the summer.

Matisse, Henri [Émile] (1869–1954)

French painter and sculptor. Considered by many to be the most important twentieth-century French painter, Matisse first studied law, but turned to painting while recovering from an illness. Inspired by the Impressionist painters in the person of Camille Pissarro (1830–1903), he exhibited *La Desserte* (*Dinner Painting*), his first, in 1897, after which time he also exhibited work at the Salon des Indépendants and at the notable gallery of Berthe Weill. However, it was not until he completed the portrait of his wife, *Femme au chapeau* (1905; *Woman with a Hat*), that Matisse joined the ranks of the avant-garde artists often referred to as Les Fauves ("the wild beasts"), named for their wild use of color, and established his career.

Matisse's work ranges from the early influence of Neo-Impressionist ideas in his famous *Luxe, calme et volupté* (1904–1905), to the famous *La Danse* and *La Musique* paintings (1909–1910), to the sensuous *Odalisques* (1920–25) of his years on the French Riviera, to the radically simplified color interiors and paintings of women in his later years. Usually bold, abstract forms, Matisse's sculpture exhibits the influence of French sculptor Auguste Rodin and African sculpture.

Although confined to a wheelchair in 1941 after two major operations for cancer, Matisse continued to work until the end of his life, producing one of his most original works, *Chapelles du rosaire à Vence* (1949–50; *The Chapels at Vence*) in appreciation to the nuns who had nursed him through an illness. He also worked with cutouts from colored paper, arranging them in abstract forms.

Matsuo Bashō (1644–1694)

Japanese writer. One of the most important figures of classical Japanese literature, Matsuo Bashō wrote travelogues, essays, and poetry, helping to perfect the poetic form of *haiku*. Called Kinsaku as a child and Matsuo Munefusa after his coming of age, he began writing as a young samurai, but after his lord's death in 1666, Bashō gave up his samurai status and wandered about Kyoto observing fashionable life and continuing to write elegant, humorous short poems. He moved to Edo in 1672; calling himself Tōsei, he soon gathered students and gained a reputation for quick humor and suggestive puns, often poking fun at the classics. In his first book of *haiku* poems, *Kaiōi* (1672; *Covering Shells*), he placed his poems in competition with each other, casting himself as critic and judge, to choose the wittiest commentary on the fashionable city life of his day.

In 1680 he took the name Bashō, which means "banana tree"; shortly thereafter he began studying Zen. Dissatisfaction with material life led him to a spiritual quest, beginning with a long journey in 1684. He traveled to his home village of Ueno, then to Nagoya, where he and a group of other poets composed *Fuyu no hi* (*The Winter Sun*), a five-volume collection of linked verse. Returning to Edo the following summer, he produced the famous travel journal *Nozarashi Kikō* (1688; *Records of a Weather-Exposed Skeleton*). Though it was not considered to be a literary masterpiece, this chronicle reflects a successful resolution of the man and his self-doubts. In other travel sketches, such as *Kashima Kikō* (1687; *A Visit to Kashima Shrine*) and *Oi no kobumi* (1688; *Records of a Travel-Worn Satchel*), Bashō perfected the art of condensing the beauty and wisdom of nature into the strict seventeen-syllable *haiku* pattern. Bashō explored the genre of the travelogue in *Oku no hosomichi* (1694; *The Narrow Road to the Deep North*), which tells of his longest journey, 1,500 miles into Japan's northern wilderness.

This poetic diary exemplified the principle of Sabi, the dialectics of lonely enlightenment between man and nature.

Bashō's style matured in works such as the *haibun Genjūan no ki* (1690; *Prose Poem on the Unreal Dwelling*) and the collection *Sarumino* (1691; *Monkey's Raincoat*). His last major work was *Saga nikki* (1691; *The Saga Diary*). Leading a busy and productive life in Edo for some years after this publication, teaching, writing, and reflecting on the doctrines of Zen, Bashō died, fittingly, on a summer journey in 1694.

Maupassant, Guy de (1850–1893)

French short-story writer and novelist. Maupassant was born wealthy and spent his early life primarily with his mother on her estate in the Norman countryside. French novelist Gustave Flaubert (1821–1880) was a close friend of the family, and the young Maupassant spent many afternoons in the company of Flaubert and his poet friend Louis Bouilhet. Flaubert became Maupassant's mentor and a meticulous editor and critic of Maupassant's writing.

Maupassant served briefly in the Franco-Prussian War, then returned to Paris, where he held a variety of bureaucratic posts and wrote during the evenings. With the guidance of Flaubert, Maupassant worked diligently on his style and published a collection of poems, *Des Vers*, in 1880. He joined the writing circle of novelist Émile Zola (1840–1902), and though he distanced himself somewhat from Zola's school of naturalism, he became renowned as the best young writer within that literary circle. Among Maupassant's major works are the novels *Une Vie* (1883; *One Life*), which details the unhappy existence of a Norman housewife; *Bel-Ami* (1885), the story of a selfish journalist; *Pierre et Jean* (1888; *Pierre and Jean*), the study of the hatred between two brothers; as well as the stories "La Parure" (1884; "The Necklace"), "Boule de suif" (1880; "The

Tallow Ball") and "Le rendezvous" (1889; "The Rendezvous"), among others. In all of these, Maupassant proves himself a master of French psychological realism, with his detached narration and fine use of irony.

Maupassant's life, however, was cut short by the syphilis he had contracted at the age of twenty-six. Toward the end of his life, he became incapacitated for days at a time, and gradually succumbed to syphilitic madness. He attempted to cut his throat in 1892 but was unsuccessful, and spent the last months of his life in a Paris clinic. It has been estimated that in his writing career, Maupassant wrote six pages daily, or about 1,500 pages per year, perhaps taking Flaubert's advice to heart: that he must write above all else.

Maurice, St. (died c. 287 C.E.)

Christian martyr and saint. According to Christian legend, Maurice, the first Christian saint to be explicitly represented as an African, was a *primicerius* (a high-ranking officer) in the Roman army whose legion was massacred by the Romans in the late third century for refusing to participate in a pagan ritual.

Maurice and his legion, who were all baptized Christians, were recruited in Thebaid, an Egyptian province on the upper Nile (near the present-day border between Egypt and Sudan). Thebaid, with its capital at Thebes, was the southernmost region of the Roman empire, then ruled by coemperors Diocletian (284–305) and Maximian.

In 287 Maximian, commander of the Roman army in Gaul, led his troops, including Maurice's legion, in a military campaign against Gaulish insurgents. On the eve of the battle, the army camped at Octodurum (in what is now Martigny, Switzerland) and Maximian ordered his soldiers to participate in a sacrifice to the Roman gods to ensure their success in battle. Maurice, refusing to betray his Christian convictions,

moved his legion to a camp at Agaunum (now Saint-Maurice-en-Valais) to avoid participating in the ritual. Maurice and two other Theban officers, Exuperius and Candidus, refused Maximian's orders to return to Octodurum, and in retaliation, the Roman emperor decimated the Theban legion, killing every tenth soldier in a bloody attempt to force the remaining legionnaires to take part in the sacrifice. When they continued to disobey, the legion, said to number between 3,000 and 6,000 men, was decimated a second time before finally being completely massacred.

From around 380 onward, St. Maurice has been celebrated in cults, cathedrals, monuments, and religious art as the patron saint of the island of Sardinia and numerous cities, and as the protector of infantry soldiers, swordsmiths, weavers, and dyers. His saint's day is September 22.

Though often described as "the first black saint," St. Maurice was not represented as a black man until 1240, when construction began on the Cathedral of Magdeburg, which houses his relics and contains a life-size stone statue of him, clad in chain mail and depicted with dark skin and unambiguously African features. The construction of this figure, which may have indicated a shift in European attitudes toward Africans, was the first explicit representation of a black saint, and through it St. Maurice became a symbol of the Church's conversion mission and of an individual's ability to overcome the stigma of his origins through devotion to God.

mawlid

An Arabic word that literally means the time and place of a birth. More specifically, the word *mawlid* is used to refer to the birth of the Prophet Muhammad (c. 570–632 C.E.)—(*mawlid al-nabī*)—and festival days for other saints (*walīs*) such as 'Alī (600–661) and Fātima (c. 606–633), Muhammad's son-in-law and daughter. While the exact date of Muhammad's birth is unknown, the first recorded celebrations were conducted by the Fatimid elite during their period of rule in Egypt (909–1171). The first popular celebration, however, did not occur until 1207, in the northern Iraqi town of Arbala. It was then that the *mawlid* became an elaborate annual event in which the deeds of the Prophet were celebrated in verse and song. Though the *mawlid* was soon celebrated for other local saints, the Prophet's continued to be the most important.

From Egypt, the *mawlid* spread throughout the Islamic world and has come to be celebrated in many different ways. Despite this diversity, however, the central activity continues to be the recitation of long poems and legends about the life and deeds of Muhammad.

Mawson, Sir Douglas (1882–1958)

Australian scientist and explorer. Mawson was born in England but moved at a young age to Sydney, Australia. He left a lectureship at the University of Adelaide in 1907 to join Ernest Shackleton's expedition to the Antarctic. On this expedition, he was among the first to climb Mt. Erebus, and he was in the party that attempted to locate the South Magnetic Pole. He was concerned, however, that the British were neglecting that part of the Antarctic known as Adelie Land. In the summer of 1911–12, he headed his own expedition to this heretofore unexplored region. It was an ambitious journey deep into the hinterland that cost Mawson his two closest companions. Mawson recorded the trek back from the interior in *The Home of the Blizzard* (1915). In 1914 he was knighted by George V.

During the summers of 1929, 1930, and 1931, Mawson led the British–Australian–New Zealand Antarctic Research Expedition (BANZARE) in its effort to map the Indian-Pacific ocean coastline of Antarctica and to claim territory for the British Crown. Later in his life, Mawson helped to establish the Australian National Antarctic Research Expedition, which continues to maintain bases in Antarctica.

May 4th Movement

Chinese political protest. On May 4, 1919, over 3,000 students from Beijing universities protested the Versailles Peace Conference's decision to grant Japan portions of the Chinese province of Shandong. A protest by the students culminated in a riot in which the Chinese minister to Japan was beaten, and the house belonging to the minister of communications was burned down. Although the government cracked down on the student protests that followed May 4th, the nationalist fervor spread to merchants and labor organizations, who implemented a boycott of all Japanese goods. In the face of this mounting opposition, the government gave in to student demands and the "Unfair Treaty" remained unsigned.

Nevertheless, the May 4th Movement continued as a political, intellectual, and cultural movement between 1916 and 1926 that attempted to fuse a fervent nationalistic spirit with a program that would allow China to become an independent nation in the modern world. Although the movement remained staunchly anti-imperialist, it borrowed heavily from Western culture and ideology for its antitraditionalist impetus. These two contradictory impulses resulted in the movement's opposition to the traditional Chinese hierarchical familial and social relations, and the adoption of Western notions of the sanctity of the individual. This opinion was expressed in the pages of *Xin qing-nian* (New Youth), a magazine founded by Chen Duxiu in Shanghai in 1915, dedicated to the concerns of the new students who were being trained in Western-style universities. They felt that if China was going to adopt military technology and economic institutions from the West, only a corresponding adoption of Western culture would allow China to succeed in the modern world. Another key influence on the character of the May 4th Movement was Cai Yuanpei, the chancellor of Beijing University, who fostered a spirit of eclecticism and liberalism within the university. This liberal program resulted in renewed efforts at mass literacy, the implementation of a written vernacular language and a popular literature around that language, and the first steps toward the emancipation of women in China. The May 4th Movement also stimulated support for the Guomindang, the Nationalists under Chinese leader Chiang Kai-shek (1887–1975), and directly led to the formation of the Chinese Communist Party.

Maya

Ancient Central American Indian civilization. The Mayan empire, which began as early as 1500 B.C.E., stretched across the territory of what is now southern Mexico, Guatemala, and northern Belize. Little is known about the Zapotec, an Early Classic Mayan culture, though it is clear that priests interpreted and kept the ancient calendars that were essential in determining the agricultural cycles. It is also known that calendrics represented the height of religious and intellectual activity. The Zapotec began the enterprise of building large temples such as Mt. Alban and Mitla, where religious rites were practiced by the priestly class. The Yucatec language, a later Mayan dialect, derives from Zapotec.

After its rise to greatness, Classic Mayan civilization (250–900 C.E.) was a theocratic aristocracy ruled by divine right. The priesthood, an inherited position requiring extensive education, was the center of religious and moral life. Under a feudal system, weaving and farming were the basic occupations of

the peasant class. Mayan society was stratified along class lines. In descending order, social structure consisted of the ruling family, administrators, an executive bureaucracy, an intellectual elite (the priesthood, architects, and scribes), artisans, common laborers, and farmers. The nobility was believed to be biologically different from the peasant class. Noble families, who inhabited the center of the cities with the priests, would flatten the foreheads of their newborn in order to create a high, sloping forehead, and teeth were filed to a point and capped with jade, both as signs of intelligence and high birth.

The people of this region continue to make religious pilgrimages to the Mayan ruins, which they regard as sacred sites. At Chichén Itzá, located in the south-central Yucatán state, for example, contemporary Mayans still gather at the great temple at the equinox to witness the pattern of a shadow cast on the temple that forms a snake, a configuration representing Chac-Mool, a rain god associated with fertility. Many descendants of the ancient Maya still worship the rain gods in some form, although many others have embraced Christianity.

The Maya, known for their architecture, particularly their invention of the sturdy corbel vault, and system of writing, were more advanced than the Romans in their knowledge of astronomy and mathematics. They developed the only writing system in pre-Columbian America: hieroglyphs, which evolved in the third century and were developed through the end of the seventeenth century. These inscriptions are found in stone slabs, or stelae. Mexican influence on the Maya, first through the Toltecs and later Aztecs, is in evidence from the *tlachtli* ball courts and in the Mayan adaptation of the Náhuatl language. Uxmal remained mostly Mayan, though Chichén Itzá was influenced by the Toltecs and Aztecs.

The dispersal of the Maya from their

great cities remains a mystery, though the most popular proposition for the decline of Mayan civilization (c. 900–1519) posits soil exhaustion after forest burnings, and lack of the plow or work animals. The Mayans were mostly living in the highlands outside their ancestors' cities when the Spanish conquered the region in the early sixteenth century.

Mayakovsky, Vladimir [Vladimirovich] (1893–1930)

Russian revolutionary poet and political activist. Born in Russian Georgia, Mayakovsky moved to Moscow with his family in 1906 and soon became politically active. Imprisoned several times between 1906 and 1911, he joined the Bolshevik Party in 1908. His first lines of poetry were written in solitary confinement in 1909.

While studying at the Moscow Art School from 1911 to 1914, Mayakovsky joined the Russian Futurist group. Russian Futurism was an avant-garde art movement that advocated an art free from the traditional Russian trappings of — in the eyes of Futurists — extreme aestheticism and mysticism. Mayakovsky's first published piece was the 1912 manifesto "Poshchechina obshchestvennomuvkusu" ("A Slap in the Face of Public Taste"), and he quickly became the dominant voice of the movement. His first book of poetry, *I!*, was published in 1913, and he performed a poetic monodrama, *Vladimir Mayakovsky*, the same year.

Though often driven by political agendas, Mayakovsky's poetry was also profoundly personal; the tension between these two motivations is seen in the poems "Oblako v shtanakh" (1915; "A Cloud in Trousers") and "Fleytapozvonochnik" (1916; "The Backbone Flute"), whose speakers describe their personal failures and disappointments in a style informed both by Futurism's rejection of traditional poetic technique and by Bolshevism's appeal to the masses.

After the Revolution of 1917, Mayakovsky's poetry became more politically charged. His "Oda revoliutsii" (1918; "Ode to Revolution") and "Levyi marsh" (1919; "Left March") were extremely popular, and his epic poem "150,000,000" (1921) was published anonymously as a work for the masses. Mayakovsky also contributed to the Communist Party by creating posters and slogans, writing children's books, and giving lectures throughout Russia. He traveled abroad during the early 1920s and collected some of the stories of his journeys in a compilation entitled *Moye otkrytie Ameriki* (1926; *My Discovery of America*). He was involved in movies and wrote the satirical plays *Klop* (performed in 1929; *The Bedbug*) and *Banya* (performed in 1930; *The Bathhouse*). Later poems such as "Liubliu" (1922; "I Love") and "Pro eto" (1923; "About This") were directly concerned with love.

In keeping with Mayakovsky's lifelong preoccupation with unrequited love and failure, his marriage proposal was refused by Tatyana Yakoleva, a Russian émigrée living in Paris. Perhaps because of his extensive travels, Mayakovsky became estranged from Russian politics, and by the end of the 1920s he was no longer permitted to leave Russia. He committed suicide in April 1930.

McCarthy, Joseph Raymond (1908–1957)

United States senator. McCarthy is remembered almost exclusively for the anti-Communist campaign he waged in the U.S. Senate from 1950 until 1954. His prominence was both evidence of and an impetus to the anti-Communist fervor that characterized American public life for much of the decade, a political paranoia that came to be known as McCarthyism.

McCarthy's early career in public office was marked by stunning electoral victories and undistinguished performance in office. In 1940 he was elected to a Wisconsin circuit judgeship at the record age of twenty-nine. The Wisconsin Supreme Court later reprimanded McCarthy for his conduct on the bench. In 1946 he won the Republican nomination for the Senate in a surprising upset over Senator Robert La-Follette, Jr., and went on to win the election itself. In his first three years in the Senate, his colleagues and the press came to regard him as stubborn and less than knowledgeable about important issues.

His transformation into an anti-Communist crusader reportedly came at the advice of friends who saw this as a way of strengthening his position among his Wisconsin constituency and as a vehicle to political prominence. In a now legendary speech on February 9, 1950, McCarthy brandished a sheet of paper that he claimed was a roster of 205 employees of the U.S. State Department who were "card-carrying Communists." Even at this stage, McCarthy's claims to possess concrete evidence of widespread Communist subversion were clearly false—the number of Communist subversives in the State Department changed daily, and other information he proffered was confusedly drawn from out-of-date documents. However, the political climate favored McCarthy's sensationalism. Members of the Republican Party had for several years been charging that the Democratic Party, which then held the presidency, was paying insufficient attention to the threat of Communist infiltration of government. The Republicans were emboldened by the conviction of alleged Soviet spy Alger Hiss in January 1950 and the arrest of "atomic spy" Klaus Fuchs shortly afterward. These events became linked in the public mind to the Korean War, the Soviets' detonation of an atomic bomb, and the creation of the People's Republic of China; public opinion became marked by an increasingly anti-Communist sentiment.

McCarthy's pronouncements thus electrified the public and were welcomed by his fellow Republicans. He continued to make sensationalistic charges of Democratic complacence in the face of the Communist threat. The press generally supported him, and right-wing business interests contributed generously to his cause. His actual and perceived influence was such that even Republicans who had misgivings about his ill-informed and crude accusations, including the 1952 Republican presidential candidate Dwight Eisenhower, were forced to accept his activities.

McCarthy was reelected in 1952 and appointed chairman of the Government Committee on Operations of the Senate and of its permanent subcommittee on investigations. For the next two years he investigated numerous governmental bodies and subpoenaed government employees to testify before his committee on their alleged Communist sympathies or affiliations. No Communist activity was uncovered as a direct result of McCarthy's efforts, but many of those he questioned were forced to leave their jobs and even those who did not were subjected to public ridicule. His charges became more obviously groundless, and he began, publicly and recklessly, to accuse prominent politicians of actual complicity in Communist activities.

The decline of McCarthy's influence began with his 1954 investigation of Communist activity in the U.S. Army. This thirty-six-day series of hearings was nationally televised, and public support for his mission waned when viewers around the country witnessed his confused, erratic, and arrogantly brutal questioning of army officials. He was further discredited when it was revealed that he had sought special treatment for a member of his staff who had joined the U.S. Army. Later in 1954, the Republican Party lost control of the Senate and McCarthy was removed from his chairmanship. In an extremely rare gesture, he was censured by the full Senate for conduct unbecoming to a senator. His presence was little felt after 1954, and he died in 1957 from complications due to alcoholism.

Despite his failure to discover any Communists in the government, McCarthy's efforts did inspire other investigations that led to the prosecution and conviction of Soviet agents within the government. However, most anti-Communist efforts of this period failed to disclose any real evidence of widespread coordinated Communist activity. The actual result of what was later dubbed McCarthyism was thus the persecution of persons innocent of espionage and an enforced conformity in American political and cultural life.

McCarthy, Mary [Therese] (1912–1989)

American author and critic, best known for her scathing wit and intelligent exploration of sexual politics. After graduating with a B.A. from Vassar College in 1933, McCarthy abandoned her acting hopes and began to write freelance literary criticism for the *Nation* and the *New Republic*. In 1937 she joined the staff of the *Partisan Review*, where she remained an editor and contributor until 1948. It was the critic Edmund Wilson, the second of her four husbands, who suggested that she write fiction.

In 1942 McCarthy published *The Company She Keeps* (1942), a synthesis of several short stories she had written previously. The novel follows a woman through psychoanalysis and divorce. *The Oasis* (1949) presents a group of intellectuals unable to maintain their utopian society. These books, along with *The Groves of Academe* (1952), received considerable attention; some considered McCarthy's work to be both overly preoccupied with the problems of intellectuals and excessively autobiographical,

while others praised her witty treatment of the American class she knew best.

The 1960s brought McCarthy the notice of a wider public with the publication of *The Group* (1963). A best-seller later made into a motion picture, it chronicles the lives of eight Vassar students from graduation as they come to terms with the various intellectual trends of the 1930s and 1940s. In 1967 McCarthy interrupted her writing and traveled to Saigon and Hanoi, after which she wrote a series of essays arguing against American involvement in Vietnam. Her next novel, *Birds of America* (1971), also dealt with the implications and effects of the war. McCarthy's other works include the novel *Cannibals and Missionaries* (1979), her autobiographies (*Memories of a Catholic Girlhood* (1957) and *How I Grew* (1987), and essays collected in *On the Contrary* (1961) and *The Writing on the Wall and Other Essays* (1970).

McCullers, Carson Smith (1917–1967)

American writer. McCullers is generally classified as a writer of Southern grotesque fiction, a genre that goes beyond the depiction of local color in its focus upon moral complexities and the darker and more eccentric facets of life. McCullers's distinctive contribution to this genre, and what separates her work from that of Katherine Anne Porter and Flannery O'Connor, is her deep concern with the sources and consequences of alienation and the breakdown of personal relationships.

Born in Columbus, Georgia, McCullers originally planned to study music, and went to New York City to study at the Juilliard School. Financial problems forced her to work to support herself, and instead of music she began to study creative writing at Columbia and New York universities. She married Reeves McCullers shortly after she completed her studies. Also an aspiring writer, Reeves McCullers had little native talent, and the competition between the two caused much marital friction. Several years into their marriage, both began affairs with members of the same sex. McCullers dedicated her second novel to her occasional lover Annemarie Clarac-Schwarsenbach, while her husband sustained a relationship with the composer David Diamond, to whom both he and Carson were deeply attached. Although Reeves accepted this arrangement equably, McCullers was deeply jealous of Reeves's close relationship with Diamond, and this generated one of the great themes of her fiction—the fear of being excluded from the love of another couple. Her other great subject was the essentially private nature of love, and the tragic ease with which love can go unrequited.

Both these themes find expression in what is regarded as her most accomplished short piece, "The Ballad of the Sad Café" (1951). It is the story of Amelia Evans, proprietress of the café of the title. While her husband, Macy, is in prison, a drifter named Lyman helps her open a café that becomes the social center of the town. When Macy returns, Lyman falls in love with him, and Amelia must confront both the fragility of her and Lyman's love, and the alienation that the men's closeness forces upon her. The story makes use of many traditional devices of the ballad, such as the repetition of phrases for lyrical effect and the construction of parallel series of events in the personal sphere and the wider realms of society and nature.

The two themes are also the subject of McCullers's most perfectly realized novel, *The Member of the Wedding* (1946). Frankie, an awkward and lonely adolescent, tries to partake of the love of her brother Jarvis and his fiancé, Janis. She forces them to let her be a member of the wedding party, changes her name to Jasmine so that it alliterates with theirs, and even attempts to accompany them on their honeymoon, giving up

only when she is forcibly ejected from the newlyweds' car.

McCullers's work has been criticized for its strongly autobiographical character, but it would be untrue to claim that she drew only on her own emotional experience. Her first work, *The Heart Is a Lonely Hunter* (1940), concerns itself with much broader social issues, as does the later *Clock Without Hands* (1961). And although her prose occasionally lapses into vague, abstracted reveries, and her characters at times seem beyond her control, in her more successful works she revealed herself as capable of precise control of both her prose and the psychology of her characters, to emotionally devastating effect.

Her other works include *Reflections in a Golden Eye* (1941); a stage adaptation of *The Member of the Wedding* (1951); *The Square Root of Wonderful* (1958); *Sweet as a Pickle and Clean as a Pig* (1964); *The Ballad of the Sad Café: The Novels and Stories of Carson McCullers* (1951); and *The Mortgaged Heart* (1971).

Meiji Restoration

Japanese political reorganization, 1868. Fundamental to Japan's development as a modern nation-state, the Meiji Restoration reorganized the essentially feudal structure of Japanese government and society. Although the Restoration is often defined as the overthrow of the Tokugawa shogunate by the southwestern domains of Satsuma and Chōshū, and the transfer of power back to the emperor, it also encompasses a series of economic, social, and political reforms that were brought about by the specter of foreign imperialism and control that Commodore Perry's visit to Japan in July 1853 represented. Recognizing the military superiority of the West, the Tokugawa shogunate signed the Harris Treaty in 1858, opening up a number of Japanese ports to foreign trade. This cooperation with Westerners indirectly resulted in the shogunate's loss of power.

Terrorism and political activism increased, as disaffected Japanese thrust aside tradition and disrupted a political system that had allowed foreigners to enter their country. Incidents such as the Chōshū bombardment of foreign ships off the coast, and the murder of an Englishman by Satsuma samurai, were met with quick and decisive reprisals by Western powers. These military defeats inspired both of these domains, as well as the Tokugawa shogunate, to prepare for civil war by importing Western military technology and engaging in trade with foreigners. As the shogunate became weaker, the shogun was forced to resign his office, though he was compensated with the highest position in the new ruling council. When the leaders of Satsuma and Chōshū insisted that the shogun forfeit his lands, he instead amassed an army and moved on the council. The ambush of his forces began the Boshin Civil War, in which the Satsuma, Chōshū, and Tosa armies, representing the imperial army, defeated the Tokugawa shogunate and ended eight centuries of warrior rule in Japan. The restoration of the emperor to power and the issue of the Charter Oath, guaranteeing everyone a place in the new order, marked Japan's return to its ancient form of government but also its move forward into the modern era as a centralized nation-state.

Mei Lanfang (1894–1961)

Chinese theatrical performer. Mei was born in Taizhou, Jiangsu province. The son and grandson of noted opera singers, Mei began studying at the Peking Opera at the age of eight and made his first appearance onstage at twelve, playing two female roles. After *Wang Yaoqin*, in which he acted as the heroine, he specialized in female roles, and over the years developed his own style in music, monologue and dialogue, costume, makeup, and particularly in dancing, establishing the "Mei Lanfang School,"

his unique style of dance that became widely known. At fourteen he joined the Cheng Xilian Theatrical Company and, through performances in Shanghai and around the world, acquired an international reputation. His best works include *The Universal Peak, Drunken Guifei,* and *The King Leaving His Wife.* Mei was largely responsible for preserving the acting traditions of imperial China.

After the outbreak of the Sino-Japanese War, Mei settled in Hong Kong; he later returned to Shanghai. During the years after the People's Republic of China was founded, he served as president of the China Peking Opera Academy and vice chairman of the Chinese Theatrical Association while doing concrete stage and film work. He was active in the Chinese Communist Party.

Meir, Golda (1898–1978)

Prime minister of Israel, 1969–74. Born into a poor Jewish family in Kiev, Ukraine, Golda immigrated to Milwaukee, Wisconsin, in 1906 and later became a leader in the Milwaukee Labor Zionist Party. She married Morris Myerson, a sign painter, in 1917, and the couple immigrated to Palestine in 1921. In the years before and during World War II, she held key posts in the World Zionist Organization and in the Jewish Agency, the highest Jewish authority in British-administered Palestine. By 1934 she had joined the executive committee of Histadrut, the labor federation that served as a shadow government prior to Israel's independence. A leading figure in the establishment of a Jewish state in Palestine, Meir was one of twenty-five signatories of Israel's declaration of independence.

After Israel proclaimed independence in 1948, Meir entered government as a member of the Knesset, the newly formed Israeli parliament, and was appointed ambassador to the then–Soviet Union by Prime Minister David Ben-Gurion. Later, she served as the minister of labor (1949–56) and minister of foreign affairs (1956–66). She was elected Israel's first female prime minister in 1969.

On the eve of the Jewish holiday of Yom Kippur, in October 1973, Egypt and Syria launched a surprise attack on Israel. Although Israeli forces were able to rally and go on the offensive, Meir and her defense minister were publicly criticized for being unprepared. In the spring elections of 1974, the Labor Party suffered a setback and Meir resigned. She remained active in politics until her death.

Menchú, Rigoberta (1959–)

Guatemalan Indian rights activist. A tireless advocate of Indian rights in Central America, Menchú was awarded the Nobel Peace Prize in 1992. Internationally acclaimed as a result of her widely translated book, *Yo, Rigoberta Menchú* (1983; *I, Rigoberta Menchú*), Menchú has been propelled by her personal experiences into the forefront of politics and social justice in Guatemala. A Mayan Indian of the Quiché group, Menchú lost close family members to social injustice: her father died in a fire while protesting human rights abuses by Guatemala's military government, and her younger brother was tortured and burned to death by a military death squad in 1979; the following year, her mother was raped, mutilated, and murdered by soldiers. After fleeing to Mexico in 1981, Menchú joined international efforts to force the Guatemalan government to cease its counterinsurgency attacks against Indian peasants. These efforts resulted in Menchú becoming a leading public speaker and organizer for the achievement of mutual reconciliation in Guatemala.

Mencius (c. 371–289 B.C.E.)

Chinese Confucian philosopher. Born in the Warring States period, Mencius, or Meng-tzu, traveled among the courts of the feudal lords for a period of forty years. A disciple of Zi Si, the grandson of the Chinese philosopher Confucius, Mencius gave advice on ways to end the civil strife that was plaguing the nation, but he was largely ignored. His writings were contained in the *Mencius*. Relatively uninfluential during his own lifetime, Mencius eventually became a central figure in the history of Confucianism. During the Neo-Confucian revival in the Song dynasty (960–1279), the scholar Zhu Xi published the *Mencius* together with *Ssu Shu*, (1190; *Four Books*), both part of the Confucian canon.

Mencius believed that the good of the people would best be served by returning to the political, economic, and social structures of the Zhou dynasty (1027–256 B.C.E.). He believed that only through a strict observation of the hierarchies and distinctions within society would civil harmony result. According to him, a truly moral leader would spontaneously receive the loyalty of the people and a mandate from heaven. When he loses this virtue, he also loses the support of heaven, and his subjects consequently have the right to revolt. Mencius also believed in the innate good nature of man, and in his eventual perfectibility.

Menglong Shi

Chinese literary movement. Menglong Shi ("misty poetry" in English) was a highly controversial phenomenon in the development of Chinese literature after the Cultural Revolution (1966–76). The most prominent poets of this movement—Bei Dao, Gu Chen, Shu Ting, Yang Lian, and Jiang He—were a group of young people who had just survived the "great havoc" of the revolution. Although they never formed a society or issued a manifesto, their works shared some basic characteristics that shocked the reading public. When their poems appeared, a heated debate erupted: some condemned their works as obscure, eccentric, frivolous, bourgeois, decadent, and even antisocialist, while others—particularly young people—hailed them as real and sincere, and thought they represented a breakthrough in the creation of new poetry and the realization of new aesthetic principles. "Menglong" poems were dense, and not confined by conventional rules of rhythm, rhyme, and other poetic patterns. Western scholars sometimes compare the Chinese misty poets with Western Imagists or Symbolists.

Merton, Thomas (1915–1968)

American Roman Catholic monk, writer, and social critic. In his lifetime, his writings and social work made him an international spiritual icon.

Thomas Merton was born in Prades in the south of France to an American mother and New Zealander father. Both his parents died in his childhood, and he spent a lonely youth in various homes in France, Britain, and the United States. Merton attended high school in Scotland and studied at Cambridge University for a few years before returning to New York to enroll at Columbia in 1935. He became involved in the school's humor magazine, edited its yearbook, joined a fraternity, dressed as a dandy, and generally led a dissipated life, which he would later repudiate.

In 1941 he entered the Monastery of Our Lady of Gethsemani in Kentucky. The routine at Gethsemani was harsh, requiring constant hard labor and permitting only infrequent visits to the outside world. Merton responded with joy to the rigorous routine, and Gethsemani remained his home for twenty-seven years. *The Seven Storey Mountain* (1948), Merton's single most famous work, is an account of his early life culminating in his arrival at Gethsemani.

He later grew uneasy with the socially isolated nature of monastic life and became more involved in "worldly" politics. His theological thought eventually formed the basis for a liberal political outlook. When Merton asked that "God prevent us from becoming 'right-thinking' men—that is to say men who agree perfectly with their own police," he uttered sentiments very close in spirit to the radical antiauthoritarian politics of the 1960s.

Merton became an outspoken critic of the Vietnam War, the nuclear arms race, and American racism. In the 1960s he also became intensely interested in Zen Buddhism. His fascination culminated in a trip to Asia in 1968. He died during this journey in a freak accident; during a monastic convention in Bangkok, he was electrocuted by a faulty wire in a fan.

Merton's works include *No Man Is an Island* (1955), *Faith and Violence* (1968), *Zen and the Birds of Appetite* (1968), and *The Asian Journals of Thomas Merton* (1973).

Mesa Verde

American Indian cliff dwellings. Built by Anasazi Indians between the fifth and fourteenth centuries in the southwestern region of Colorado, Mesa Verde, which means "green table," was given its name by eighteenth-century Spanish explorers describing this plateau site atop steep rock walls. The more sophisticated cliff dwellings seem to have developed from single-level, multiroom pueblo dwellings made of stone and adobe into enormous community structures built into the recesses of cliffs, most often two, three, or four stories high, with as many as 1,000 rooms. Made with stone, mud, and even wood, these dwellings, resembling multilevel apartments, were built in a stepped or terrace design, allowing the roofs of lower rooms to serve as porches for those above. Vast storage areas, open courtyards, lookout towers, and farming terraces also characterize the like dwelling, the Cliff Palace. Excavated in 1909, Cliff Palace is perhaps the largest and most famous. It contains over two hundred living rooms and at least twenty-three ceremonial chambers called kivas.

After 1300 C.E., the Anasazi abandoned their Mesa Verde structures but did not disappear altogether. Experts speculate that factional divisions among the tribe, raids by hostile nomads, and prolonged bouts of severe drought between 1276 and 1299 forced the people to migrate to the south and east. For centuries Mesa Verde was left untouched and forgotten, until the nineteenth century, when ranchers rediscovered the ruins of the dwellings. In 1906 the federal government gained control over the area to prevent looting and exploitation of its artifacts, and named Mesa Verde a national park.

mestizo/mestiza

Latin American ethnic category. In the early Spanish colonial period, a *mestizo/ mestiza* was a person in the Americas of mixed Indian and Spanish descent. By the seventeenth century, the category *mestizo/mestiza* came to be socially constructed, rather than strictly a description of lineage. A person of the lower or intermediate classes who adopted Spanish culture was considered a *mestizo/ mestiza*, regardless of his or her descent.

Micheaux, Oscar (1884–1951)

American novelist and filmmaker. Born into a family of thirteen in Illinois, to parents who had been slaves, Micheaux was raised on a farm. Dissatisfied with farm life, he secured work as a Pullman porter. Life on the rails renewed his faith in farm-living, and Micheaux soon purchased a "relinquishment" on a home in South Dakota. As an erudite and successful farmer, he was accepted by his white neighbors. It has been argued that his love of the wide-open spaces of the West and his adherence to Booker T. Washington's agrarian views led Micheaux to disparage urban blacks in his

work. In his first novel, *The Conquest: The Story of a Negro Pioneer* (1913), "Oscar Devereaux," a successful black farmer, falls in love with a white girl but refuses to marry her on principle. His subsequent marriage to the daughter of a Methodist minister ends in despair. This theme, and the accompanying dislike of the black ministry, was associated with Micheaux throughout his career. *Body and Soul* (1924), the film that introduced Paul Robeson, is but one example.

Micheaux enthusiastically promoted his work through tours and talks in the black communities of the South. *The Forged Note: A Romance of the Darker Races* (1915) was based on these experiences and, like most of his early work, is considered to be semiautobiographical. *The Homesteader* (1917) is substantially a retelling of *The Conquest*; the novel was relatively successful, and Micheaux was approached with an offer from the Lincoln Motion Picture Company to turn *The Homesteader* into a film. Micheaux agreed on condition that he have the right to direct. After being refused, he promoted the project on his own and organized the Oscar Micheaux Corporation, which produced *The Homesteader* in 1919.

In the following twenty years, Micheaux produced approximately thirty films in the melodramatic style typical of filmmaking's early period. In times when blacks were often barred from white movie theaters and were relegated to a few stereotypical roles in white films, the "race movies" produced by Micheaux and others provided an important outlet for black talent, opportunities for black moviemakers and theater owners, and a needed escape for black moviegoers. On the strength of his charisma, success, and popularity, Micheaux even managed to persuade white theater owners to hold special screenings of his films for black audiences.

Usually shot in one or two takes on

improvised sets, Micheaux's films were notoriously uneven in quality. As writer, producer, director, editor, and, at times, actor, Micheaux had absolute control over his work. Some of his films, notably *Birthright* (1924), based on a novel by T. S. Stribling, rose above the ordinary to handle Southern race issues in a sophisticated way. In 1925 he married Alice B. Russell, an actress he had met while on tour. The Oscar Micheaux Film Corporation was bankrupt by 1928, but Micheaux continued to produce films and released *The Exile*, his first "talkie," in 1931. His interest in films that dramatized or challenged racial assumptions reached a peak with his production of *God's Stepchildren* (1937), a film that seriously addressed the question of blacks "passing for white." Theaters were picketed after its showing, and Micheaux curtailed his filmmaking until 1948.

In the interim, he wrote and published three novels: *The Wind from Nowhere* (1941), *The Case of Mrs. Wingate* (1944), and *The Masquerade* (1946–47). In 1948 he premiered another film, *The Betrayal*, once again returning to the theme of a successful black South Dakota farmer with marital problems. This ambitious attempt resulted in abysmal failure. The more sophisticated audiences of the 1940s, now accustomed to Hollywood productions, no longer accepted Micheaux's style. He had spent most of his resources on the production of *The Betrayal*, but after its failure, he continued to promote himself and his work. On one of his tours, Micheaux died in Charlotte, N.C. Although often criticized for presenting a fantasy world of bourgeois and light-skinned black people, Micheaux is remembered as a pioneer of independent and black cinema.

Michelangelo (1475–1564)

Italian sculptor, poet, painter, and architect. Michelangelo Buonarroti was born to an impoverished family that took pride in their bloodlines of pure Florentine nobility. However, Michelangelo was disinclined to venerate his roots, for his parents' haughtiness only stood in the way of his desire to become an artist. He began his training with a painter in Florence. His talent for sculpture, however, was noted, and he transferred to the Medici Academy, where he studied under Bertoldo Giovanni, a former student of the great Italian artist Donatello (c. 1386–1466). Here Michelangelo also undertook his study of anatomy, which was to prove most important to his sculpture. After the death of his patron and the deterioration of the political situation in Florence, Michelangelo traveled to Bologna and then to Rome, where he carved the two statues that established his fame: the *Bacco* (1496–1501; *Bacchus*) and the *Pietà* (1498–99). He returned to Florence in 1501, and there carved his major work, the statue *David* (1501–1504), which has since become the symbol of Florentine art. In 1505 Michelangelo was summoned by Pope Julius II to carve his tomb—a project that was finally completed in 1545, and to which Michelangelo contributed only his celebrated statue *Moses* (c. 1515). In the interim, however, Michelangelo's talents were diverted to another project, the frescoes of the Sistine Chapel. Michelangelo decorated the ceiling with scenes from Genesis, from Creation through Noah, as well as with prophets from the Old Testament. The ceiling was unveiled in 1512 and established Michelangelo as the greatest artist of his time, a position as a leading figure in the Italian Renaissance that remained unchallenged throughout his life.

Michelangelo then returned to Florence, where he carved tombs for the Medici family, with the statue *Giorno, notte e crepuscolo* (1520–24; *Day, Night and Dusk*). During the final years of his life, he worked primarily in Rome, and concentrated his talents in architecture, where his achievements rival those in his sculpture. In these years, his major projects include the *Giudizio universale* (1536–41; *Last Judgment*), painted on the wall of the Sistine Chapel, and the construction of the dome of St. Peter's, among other projects. Michelangelo also left behind many letters and poems, many addressed to a young boy, Tommaso Calvino, to whom Michelangelo was devoted. His literary works, first published in a bowdlerized version by his grand-nephew in 1623, and later in their entirety in 1863, chronicle Michelangelo's preoccupation with his art, and his struggle to reconcile a Platonic sense of human beauty with the Catholic doctrines of sin and evil.

Mickiewicz, Adam (1798–1855)

Polish poet. Mickiewicz was born on Christmas Eve in the small town of Nowogródek, Belorussia, on territory that had been Polish until the partition of 1793 divided the country between Russia, Prussia, and Austria. His father, a lawyer, belonged to the middle gentry but was relatively poor. Mickiewicz studied at the University of Wilno, where he participated in clandestine student organizations dedicated to the promotion of Polish nationalism and republicanism, a movement that championed the establishment of a sovereign Polish state—an activity that resulted in his deportation to Russia in 1824. By this time, however, two volumes of his poems had already been published, *Poezja I* (1822) and *Poezja II* (1823), which contained parts of his famous nationalistic narrative, *Dziady* (*Forefathers' Eve*).

During the period of his Russian exile, Mickiewicz formed ties with many Russian writers, including the celebrated poet Aleksandr Pushkin. He published *Sonety Krymskie* (1826; *Sonnets from the Crimea*), and two years later reaffirmed his allegiance to Polish nationalism by publishing his anti-Russian allegory, *Konrad Wallenrod* (1828), a work that found its way past the censors but that nonetheless jeopardized his safety. In 1829, with the help of influential friends, Mickiewicz managed to leave Russia.

After an attempt to return to Poland was frustrated by the Russian army's retaliation against the Warsaw uprising (1830), Mickiewicz settled in Paris. He published, in rapid succession, his two most voluminous and memorable works. The first of these was the third part of *Forefathers' Eve* (1833), in which Mickiewicz allegorizes the sufferings of the Polish nation by means of a heroic romance of redemption. A year later, in 1834, he published *Pan Tadeusz* (*Master Thaddeus*), an epic-length work that has come to be regarded as the national poem of Poland.

In 1833 Mickiewicz married Celina Szymoanowska. After working as a professor in Switzerland for one year, he returned to Paris in 1840 in order to take up the position of professor of Slavonic languages and literatures at the Collège de France, the first person to occupy this position. In 1848, inspired by the nationalist revolutions under way throughout Europe, Mickiewicz traveled to Rome in an abortive attempt to win papal support for the Polish cause. Once back in Paris, he spent March to October 1849 serving as editor of *La Tribune des Peuples* (The Peoples' Tribune), a short-lived radical newspaper. In 1854, during the Crimean War, Mickiewicz traveled to Constantinople with the aim of consolidating the divided Polish factions into a single military force. In the course of his journey, however, he became ill; he died on the day of his arrival in Constantinople.

Milarepa (1040–1123)

Tibetan poet and mystic. Milarepa was the second patriarch of the Kargyupa sect of Tibetan Buddhism. His biography by a holy man called "the madman of Tsang" recounts Milarepa's quest for wisdom. When Milarepa was seven, his father died, leaving Milarepa, his sister, and his mother in the care of an uncle. The greedy uncle seized their property and put them to work, and Milarepa's mother sent him to study sorcery in order to exact revenge. Milarepa regained their wealth through conjuring hailstorms and scorpions, but then renounced black magic and set off on a quest for further knowledge. He suffered many ordeals under the unwilling tutelage of the guru Marpa, but finally earned initiation into the mystical doctrines of Tantra. Milarepa spent the next six years meditating in solitude in a cave, and when he returned home found his family dead. Grief-stricken, he resolved to spend the rest of his life pursuing liberation through hardship. The patron of itinerant actors and comedians, he is usually pictured singing. His "hundred thousand songs" include poems and folk songs that served to popularize Buddhist teachings. He died in isolation, and, according to legend, heaven wept tears of blossoms to mark the event.

Mill, John Stuart (1806–1873)

British philosopher and economist. As a child, Mill was educated exclusively by his father, James Mill, a utilitarian philosopher. In 1823 he assumed a position as a clerk with the British East India Company, where his father was a high official, and advanced through a series of administrative positions until the company dissolved in 1858. His association with the philosopher and legal critic Jeremy Bentham (1748–1832) began early on, with the formation of the Utilitarian Society in 1823. Mill was recognized as a leader of utilitarian thought before the age of twenty, and as his first literary venture, he edited Bentham's *Rationale of Judicial Evidence* (1825). A severe mental crisis in 1826 led Mill to temper the utilitarianism of his father and of Bentham somewhat, and he introduced a more humane and idealistic strain into the system of thought.

In 1831 Mill met and began a relationship with Harriet Taylor, an event that marked a turning point in his life and work. At the time, Taylor was married, and at the request of her husband, she agreed to maintain her residence with him while spending whatever time she could with Mill; they eventually married, two years after the death of her husband. Mill discussed all of his work with Taylor and, because of her influence, developed his influential and, at that time, radical theories on female suffrage. His article "The Enfranchisement of Women," which caused quite a sensation, became the foundation for his larger work, *The Subjection of Women* (1869). The essay makes a convincing case for women's right to suffrage and is considered to be a hallmark work in liberal feminism. Unfortunately, Taylor died prior to the publication of the book that she had so greatly influenced. Following her death, Mill became a member of Parliament (1865–68), an outspoken advocate of women's rights, and a founder of the first women's suffrage society. Other important works by Mill include his *System of Logic* (1843); the essay *On Liberty* (1859) and *Principles of Political Economy* (1848), both of which Mill acknowledged as a joint Mill/Taylor production; *Thoughts on Parliamentary Reform* (1859); and his *Autobiography* (1873).

Miłosz, Czesław (1911–)

Polish poet. Born into a civil engineer's family in Lithuania, Miłosz first began to earn a reputation as a writer while studying law in Wilno, Poland, where he helped to found the avant-garde literary journal *Zagary* (Brushwood). Miłosz himself has written disparagingly of his first volume, *Poemat o czasie zastygłym* (1933; *Poem on Frozen Time*), but with his second volume, *Trzy zimy* (1936; *Three Winters*), he established himself not only as Poland's most prominent and innovative poet but also as the leading practitioner of a genre known as "catastrophism." Throughout his poems of the 1930s there were themes of apocalyptic disaster that were to seem eerily prophetic in the wake of the Nazi invasion. The ensuing period of occupation prompted Miłosz to give his poetry a more specifically historical turn; the poems of this period, collected in *Ocalenie* (1945; *Rescue*), are obsessed with the problem of relating poetic activity to political activity. At the time, he was working actively in the Polish Resistance. After the war, the new Communist government recognized Miłosz's political and poetical achievements by making him a diplomat. But, as Stalinist influence increased, Miłosz defected early in 1951 to Paris.

In 1953 Miłosz achieved his first real fame in the West with the publication in French of *La Prise du pouvoir* and in English of *The Captive Mind*. (It was not published in Polish until 1955 as *Zhiewolony umyst*.) In this collection of essays, Miłosz explored, by means of case studies, the destructive effects of totalitarian thinking on Eastern European intellectuals. The subject matter of these essays had been poetically anticipated in the poems collected in *Swiatto dzienne* (1953; *Daylight*). From this point on, however, Miłosz's poetry would increasingly tend to move away from specifically Polish or East European concerns and would pursue instead a more broadly international perspective. He would also experiment with more innovative verse forms.

In 1960 Miłosz accepted an invitation to teach Polish literature at the University of California at Berkeley, and he became a naturalized American in 1970. In addition to his work as a poet and essayist, Miłosz has published two volumes of his autobiography, as well as a novel, *Dolina Issa* (1955; *The Issa Valley*), based on his Lithuanian boyhood. In 1980 he won the Nobel Prize for Literature.

Milton, John (1608–1674)

English poet. During Milton's childhood in London, his father left the Catholic Church to become a member of the Anglican Church. The young Milton carried on this heritage of dissent and eventually joined the English Puritans. He studied at Christ's College, Cambridge, where he was referred to as "lady of Christ's," a reference most probably to his meticulous behavior and physical beauty. In 1629 he wrote "On the Morning of Christ's Nativity," regarded as one of the first signs of promise in the young poet. He also completed the celebrated works "L'Allegro" and "Il Penseroso," later published in 1645. In 1638 Milton went abroad to tour parts of Europe. The early rumblings of the English Civil War brought him back to England before he could complete his trip, but he was able to spend some time in Italy, where he met the aged Italian astronomer Galileo (1564–1642) and made himself familiar with Italian culture.

His return to England in 1639 began a period of nearly two decades in which Milton participated actively in public life. Written in 1644, *Aeropagitica* was an eloquent argument against censorship. He began to write works that defended the Puritan uprising against Charles I, and in 1649 Milton received the post of Latin secretary in English lord protector Oliver Cromwell's (1653–58) government. His active involvement in the civil war on the side of the antiroyalists gave evidence of his strong Puritan sentiments.

In the late 1650s Milton retired from government. As early as 1639 he had expressed the desire to write an epic poem. In 1658 he began writing *Paradise Lost*, finishing it in 1663. *Paradise Lost* is an allegory of twelve books written in blank verse. It tells the story of the revolt of Satan against God and Satan's subsequent and successful temptation of Adam and Eve, who are responsible for the fall of humanity. Milton dictated *Paradise Lost* because he had lost his sight in the 1650s. In 1671 he published another work entitled *Paradise Re-*

gained. His final long poem was the religious drama *Samson Agonistes* (1671), an autobiographical narrative.

Mishima Yukio (1925–1970)

Japanese novelist. Mishima Yukio, the pen name of Kimitake Hiraoka, was born in Tokyo. He was one of Japan's most prolific writers, with a body of work including novels, essays, short stories, traditional Japanese Noh plays, and film scripts. He first presented his sophisticated fusion of sex and violence in *Kamen no kokuhaku* (1949; *Confessions of a Mask*), a thinly veiled autobiography of his childhood and youth. This first novel addressed the issue of homosexuality, a preoccupation that persisted throughout Mishima's career, with what one critic called "elegant abandon." His second novel, *Ai no kawaki* (1950; *Thirst for Love*), was less well received, as he stepped away from the first-person point of view to tell the story of a young widow who becomes mistress to her father-in-law. *Kinjiki* (1951–53; *Forbidden Colors*) returned to the topic of homosexuality in a more formal tone than *Confessions*. The relationship between death and beauty is at the center of *Kinkakuji* (1956; *The Temple of the Golden Pavilion*), based on the true account of a young Buddhist monk whose sense of his own ugliness creates in him an envy toward the golden temple in which he serves, inspiring him to burn it down. Mishima's work culminated in the tetralogy *Hōjō no umi* (1965–70; *The Sea of Fertility*), a series of four novels in which the spirit of a young woman is reincarnated as a Japanese aristocrat in a doomed love affair (*Haru no yuki* [*Spring Snow*]), a political fanatic (*Homba* [*Runaway Horses*]), a Thai princess (*Akatsuki no tera* [*The Temple of the Dawn*]), and an evil orphan (*Tennin gosui* [*The Decay of the Angel*]). Mishima submitted the final manuscript of this work on the very day of his suicide, and it resembled almost exactly the suicide that the protagonist in *Runaway Horses* had committed.

Among the first modern Japanese writers to attract critical attention in the West, Mishima vividly portrays what he called his "heart's leaning toward death and night and blood." He addresses the tension between Western and Japanese cultures in his many novels, and his own violent nostalgia for the glamour of *bushidō*, the traditional way of the samurai, shaped his work and his life.

Aside from his novels, Mishima was also famous for his modernized Noh plays and for short stories such as "Manatsu no shi" (1953; "Death in Midsummer") and "Yūkoku" (1960; "Patriotism"), which condense his trademark themes into tight, vivid scenes. The latter story is especially haunting in its rehearsal of love and death, as a young army officer and his wife make love before their ritual suicide. Mishima himself starred in a film version of this novella; after his death five years later, his family had the film burned.

In 1968 Mishima founded the Tate no kai (Shield Society), an organization committed to returning Japan to the samurai tradition. In 1970 Mishima and four followers attempted to incite the Japanese army to rebel against the post–World War II constitution that had robbed Japan of her military might. When the soldiers jeered, Mishima shouted, "Tenno Heika Banzai!" ("Long live the Emperor") and committed ritual suicide (*seppuku*) by plunging a ceremonial dagger deep into his stomach.

Mistral, Gabriela (1889–1957)

Chilean writer. Born Lucila Godoy Alcayaga in Vicuña, Mistral was of Basque and Indian ancestry. She was raised by her half-sister after her father abandoned the family when she was three. The family eventually moved to La Serena, where Mistral was inspired to write poetry. She began publishing at the age of fifteen in the Vicuña newspapers, *El Co-*

quimbo and *La Voz de Elqui*. Her tragic love for Romelio Ureta, a railway conductor who committed suicide, formed the inspiration for *Sonetos de la muerte* (1915; *The Sonnets of Death*). It was at this time that she permanently adopted the pen name Gabriela Mistral. Rooted in, but departing from, the elegant and correct verses of modernism, Mistral's poetry is marked by intense passion and lyricism, and explores all forms of love—sexual, maternal, and humanitarian. It also has a dark side in which Mistral focuses on the themes of time, death, and nightly experiences of abandonment and despair. Her poetic language mixes oral qualities of rural speech with learned diction. Traveling throughout Chile as a teacher, she met Pedro Aguirre Cerda, who would later become president of Chile and prove invaluable in the recognition of her talent.

During this time Mistral published in several literary magazines, and also met the young poet Pablo Neruda. In 1922 the president of Mexico, Alvaro Obregón, invited Mistral to collaborate in that country's educational reforms. That same year she published her first book of poetry, *Desolación* (1922; *Desolation*), followed by *Lecturas para mujeres* (1923; *A Reader for Women*) and her second collection, *Tuntura* (1924; *Tenderness*). She served in a number of government posts, including Chilean consul abroad, in the interim also adopting her half-brother's nine-month-old son, whom she raised until his death at the age of twenty-one. The Spanish Civil War and World War II caused her to leave Europe and return to America, where she continued to publish in literary magazines and newspapers. She became the first Spanish-American writer to win the Nobel Prize in Literature, awarded to her in 1945. *Lagar* (1954; *The Wine Press*) was her fourth book of poetry and the last book published during her lifetime. Its more notable poems include the series "Locas mujeres" ("Mad

Women"), "Guerra" ("War"), and "Luto" ("Mourning"), poems dealing with the death of her nephew. Mistral's *Poesías completas* (*Complete Poems*) appeared in 1958, shortly after her death in New York. Her last book of poetry was published posthumously as *Poema de Chile* (1967; *Poem of Chile*), which she did not finish revising. Its novelty and originality emanate from the speaker, an old woman who returns to earth after her death, and her entourage, a ghostly boy and a musk deer.

Modjeska, Helena (1840–1909)

Polish actress. Modjeska, the anglicized version of Modrzejewska, was born in Kraków and attended a convent school. Gustav Sinnmayer (Modrzejewski), a wealthy friend of her mother's with theatrical connections, encouraged Modjeska's growing interest in the stage, and she dropped out of school to begin lessons. In 1861 she gave birth to a son, and she and Sinnmayer left Kraków and settled in Bochnia, possibly married. She made her theatrical debut as Helena Modrzejewska in 1861, touring with the New Sandec Company. After the death of their three-year-old daughter in 1865, Modjeska left Sinnmayer and returned to Kraków with her son.

She obtained a place in a local theatrical company, and soon she appeared in Polish national dramas. In 1866 she appeared at the Comédie Française through the help of Karol Bozenta Chłapowski, a young Polish aristocrat recently released from a Prussian prison. They were married in Kraków in 1868. Next she moved to Warsaw, where she became the leading actress at the Imperial Theater, with a life engagement at the highest salary the theater had ever paid. She was at the center of an intellectual and artistic circle that included the Polish novelist Henryk Sienkiewicz.

In July 1876, Modjeska, her husband, Sienkiewicz, and a few others attempted to establish a colony of Polish immigrants, based loosely on the model of the American Transcendentalists' Brook Farm, in Connecticut. When the experiment failed, Modjeska took up acting parts in the United States, learning English to do so. Throughout the rest of her career, she appeared all over Europe and the United States, fulfilling her dream of acting Shakespeare on a London stage, and premiering Norwegian dramatist Henrik Ibsen's (1828–1906) work in the United States. Modjeska's final appearance was at the Metropolitan Opera House in New York in 1905. Banned from Russian-controlled Poland because of an address at the 1893 World's Columbian Exposition in Chicago, in which she criticized the oppression of Polish women, she retired to California, where she died.

Mogul, *see* Mughal

Molière (1622–1673)

French dramatist. Molière was born Jean-Baptiste Poquelin in Paris, the son of an upholsterer who served in the royal household of Louis XIV. He developed an early interest in drama, and in 1643 he joined the Béjart troupe of actors. After touring the French countryside for thirteen years, the troupe, now headed by Molière, returned to Paris under the patronage of Louis XIV, where it enjoyed great success. At once actor, writer, and director, Molière became famous for his satirical comedies and caricatures, such as *Les Précieuses Ridicules* (1659; *The Affected Misses*), a satire on the affectations and pretensions displayed by members of the Parisian salons. Other masterpieces by Molière include *L'École des maris* (1661; *The School for Husbands*); *L'École des femmes* (1662; *The School for Wives*); *Dom Juan* (1665; *The Stone Guest*), which was removed from the repertory because of continuing attacks; and *Le Misanthrope* (1666; *The Misanthrope*). Molière's gift for satire spared no one from critique—

much to the chagrin of many clergymen, physicians, and rival dramatists. In fact, *Le Tartuffe* (1664; *Tartuffe*), which features a religious hypocrite, was twice banned by the Church. The clergy seemed especially vexed by Molière, and after his sudden death they denied him a holy burial. Molière is considered to be the father of French comedy, rejecting the Italian-influenced farces and comedies of his predecessors and instead using the fabric of seventeenth-century France as his material.

Monet, Claude (1840–1926)

French painter. As a youth, Monet gained a reputation as a caricaturist but was converted to landscape painting by his mentor Eugène Boudin. He studied later in Paris, and with French painters Pierre-Auguste Renoir (1841–1919) and Alfred Sisley (1839–1899), formed the nucleus of the Impressionist group of painters, a name taken from his painting *Impression, soleil levant* (1872; *Impression, Sunrise*). Monet painted almost exclusively outdoors and went to great ends, once even having a trench dug in his garden so that his canvas *Femmes au jardin* (1866–67; *Women in the Garden*) could be painted completely outside. After several years of poverty, Monet began to prosper in 1890, and married his mistress of fourteen years. His paintings of this period, which often detail the same subjects in different light, are some of his most famous and include *Les Meules* (1890–91; *Haystacks*) and *La Cathédrale de Rouen* (1892–94; *Rouen Cathedral*). The water garden he created at his house in Giverny dominates his later paintings, such as the *Nymphéas* (*Water Lilies*) series, begun in 1899. Though troubled by failing eyesight, Monet continued to paint until his death, and was one of the most prolific and celebrated artists of his generation.

Mongkut (1804–1868)

Ruler of Thailand. Mongkut, also called Phrachomklao and, posthumously, Rama IV, did not take the throne until late in life; he ruled from 1851 to 1868 in the country then known as Siam. Before his accession, he spent twenty-seven years as a Buddhist monk. This enabled him to study and travel widely, exposing him to Western ideas and bringing him into closer contact with the people of his country. Thus, after his coronation he was able to accomplish the opening of Thailand to Western influences tactfully and with care, having been sensitized to both the demands of the West and the needs of his people. He made treaties with the United States, Great Britain, and other Western powers beginning in 1855, allowing for commerce that sparked swift economic development in Thailand.

Perhaps Mongkut's most difficult task was to negotiate Thailand's place among world powers and enhance his own reputation among rulers who often thought of Thailand as a backward and barbaric country. His friendly, dignified overtures communicated tolerance and openmindedness, and his insistence on the liberal education of his sons ensured Thailand's further modernization. His character, albeit highly romanticized, has become familiar to modern audiences through the Rodgers and Hammerstein musical *The King and I*, which was adapted from a novel based on the memoirs of Anna Leonowens, an Englishwoman who served briefly as governess to his children.

Mongol

Asian ethnic and linguistic group. The Mongols achieved their greatest power in the thirteenth century under Genghis Khan (c. 1167–1227), who united the often divided nomadic herdsmen of the Central Asian steppes into one military unit. At one point, the Mongols controlled the largest empire in history, comprised of vast territories in modern-day China, Russia, Turkey, and Iran, even if their control over this empire did not last long. Kublai Khan (1215–1294),

the grandson of Genghis, established a Chinese-style dynasty, the Yuan, in 1260, during which Chinese culture flourished. This dynasty fell in 1368, due to internal divisions within the Mongol leadership, wars with the Chinese Ming dynasty, as well as natural disasters and peasant rebellions. Nevertheless, the Mongols continued to harass the powerful Mings and exert an influence within China until their defeat at the hands of the Manchus. The Mongols' absorption into the Manchu resulted in their subordinate status until the Mongolian People's Republic was established in the twentieth century. Mongol culture is more similar to Tibetan than Chinese, not only because of the lifestyle differences between a nomadic and an agricultural people but also because the Mongols never adopted the Chinese character system of writing. Today the majority of Mongols still live in the Inner Mongolian Autonomous Region of China, but there are a substantial number living in the Buryatiya Republic of the former U.S.S.R.

Montesquieu, Charles-Louis de Secondat, baron de La Brède et de (1689–1755)

French political philosopher. Montesquieu was born to wealthy parents in 1689, and when his mother died in 1696 he inherited the family barony. He spent the early years of his life among the villagers of La Brède, years that established in him a deep attachment to the land. In 1700 he left home to receive a progressive education at the Oratorian Collège de Juilly, and then to study law at the University of Bordeaux. In 1715 he married Jeanne de Lartigue. With her dowry and an estate inherited a year later from his uncle (which included the presidency of the Bordeaux Parlement), he diligently exercised his official functions while studying the sciences at the Academy of Bordeaux. The deep interest in the effects of environment on people which Montesquieu developed in his later historical works was in part fueled by his biological investigations at the Academy.

In 1721 Montesquieu published his first book, *Lettres persanes* (1722; *Persian Letters*). Inspired by popular travel literature like *Arabian Nights*, the book was written in the form of letters home from three Persians traveling in Europe. It was a satirical and sharply critical look at European customs and institutions, daring enough to ridicule Louis XIV and the pope. The book was published anonymously, but Montesquieu was soon recognized as the author and acclaimed widely by the public.

Disinterested in local politics and in need of funds, Montesquieu sold his position on the Bordeaux Parlement in 1726. He joined the Académie Française in 1728 and then toured Europe. Especially influential to his later political writings was his stay in England, where he was elected to the Royal Society and was able to observe and study English politics. Montesquieu returned to France in 1731 and in 1734 published *Considérations sur les causes de la grandeur des Romains et de leur décadence* (1734; *Reflections on the Causes of the Grandeur and Declension of the Romans*), in which he argued that the keys to Roman success lay in the virtues of its citizens and the adaptability of its institutions. The book was not as well received as *Lettres persanes*, although it was praised by Voltaire.

Fourteen years later, Montesquieu published what is considered his greatest work, *De l'esprit des lois, ou Du rapport que les lois doivent avoir avec la constitution de chaque gouvernement, les moeurs, le climat, le religion, le commerce, etc.* (1750; *The Spirit of the Laws*). It was not a legal text, but rather an investigation of the social, historical, and environmental factors that lie behind the complex and varied laws which civilizations have adopted. Laws, Montesquieu argued, were "the necessary relationships which derive from the na-

ture of things." Climate, for example, was cited by the author as an important factor influencing the outlook of a society. More than just a deterministic account of human adaptation, the book also recommended attention to environment and circumstance as a political policy; the best legislators, Montesquieu argued, were those who could adjust the laws to fit — and, in some cases, counteract — current conditions.

Montesquieu went on to identify different types of governments and their "animating" principles: virtue in a republic; honor in a monarchy; or fear in despotism. He also argued for the separation of legislative, executive, and judicial powers, citing England as an ideal model. In discussing religion he took a secular approach, treating it as a social phenomenon like any other which could be discussed without regard to its value as truth. The book was widely acclaimed by such figures as philosopher David Hume, but also stirred up controversy and was placed on the Vatican's *Index Librorum Prohibitorum* (*Index of Prohibited Books*) in 1751.

Montesquieu, succumbing to blindness, went into semiretirement at his home in La Brède after the publication of *De l'esprit des lois*. He died in Paris in 1755.

Montezuma (1466–1520)

Ninth Aztec emperor of Mexico. Montezuma took over the Aztec empire, stretching from modern-day Honduras to Nicaragua, from his uncle in 1502. He was commander of the army at the peak of the empire and confronted the forces of the Spanish *conquistador* Hernán Cortés when Cortés entered Tenochtitlán, the capital of the Aztec empire, in 1519. Cortés was aided, however, by subject tribes who feared and resented the Aztec practice of human sacrifice. The *conquistador* was aware of an Aztec prophecy of the return of Quetzalcóatl, the white, bearded god. Cunningly,

Cortés wore a white beard, conscious of the impact of his sudden appearance upon the Aztec imagination. Though Montezuma understood the effect that Cortés would have on the Aztec people, and even tried to buy him off, he was powerless to stop Cortés from making alliances with his enemies. Montezuma prepared an elaborate intrigue in which he welcomed Cortés to the capital city of Tenochtitlán, but the trap failed. With the help of subject nations, Cortés staged a coup and held Montezuma captive in his own city; finally Montezuma was forced to submit. According to Spanish legend, the Aztec emperor was attacked by the stones and arrows of his own people and died three days later. The official story of the Aztecs, however, is that Montezuma was murdered by the Spanish.

Moro

Filipino Muslim sector. Moro refers broadly to the Muslim sector of the population of the Philippines and more narrowly to politically active Muslims in the islands. The term was first used by Spanish invaders in the sixteenth century who associated the Filipino Muslims with the "Moors," the Islamicized North Africans who ruled the Iberian Peninsula from the eighth to the fifteenth century. During the period when the Spanish were attempting to gain control of the Muslim-dominated southern islands of the Philippines, the expression "Moro" took on a pejorative meaning as the Spanish characterized their enemies as ignorant and depraved. In the late 1960s, however, the term was reappropriated by Muslims who formed the Moro National Liberation Front (MNLF). The MNLF sought the independence of the Moros from the regime of President Ferdinand Marcos, who took power in 1966, and demanded the establishment of a separate Moro state on the land that had been supposedly expropriated by Filipino Christians. Af-

ter Marcos's declaration of martial law in September 1972, the Bangsa Moro army of the MNLF began fighting for secession. After several years, a cease-fire was negotiated with the government. In 1985 the Moros renewed their struggle, contributing to the general pressure that resulted in Marcos's ouster in 1986.

Morrison, Toni (1931–)

American writer. Born Chloe Anthony Wofford in Lorain, Ohio, in 1931, Morrison was profoundly influenced by the small Midwestern town in which she grew up, and while none of her books are explicitly autobiographical, elements of her childhood have often appeared in her work.

At an early age, Morrison absorbed the folk tales and legends of the supernatural that were common in the black community in which she lived, and these oral traditions have greatly influenced her work, which often makes reference to African and African-American mythology. Her first book, *The Bluest Eye* (1970), was set in her hometown and chronicled the experiences of a young black girl driven insane with self-hatred caused by her inability to live up to the standards of beauty projected by a white dominant culture. *Sula* (1974), her second novel, was also set in the Midwest and examined the friendship of two black women in a small rural community. Her other works include *Song of Solomon* (1977), *Tar Baby* (1981), *Jazz* (1992), and *Beloved* (1987), which examined the horrors of American slavery and won the Pulitzer Prize for fiction in 1988. Morrison received the Nobel Prize for Literature in 1993.

mosque

Islamic place of worship. From the Arabic *masjid*, literally "place of prostration," the mosque can be any ritually clean area used for a socioreligious center of a Muslim community. The earliest Islamic *masjid* is purported to have been founded by the Prophet Muhammad at Quba near Al-Madînah in 622 C.E. The *masjid jâmi'*, or simply *jâmi'* (congregational mosque), is the site of Friday prayers and is a requirement for any sizable community of Muslims.

Three mosques enjoy special status in Islam. The one in Mecca is considered the site of the first Abrahamic sanctuary to God and is the location of the Ka'bah, a shrine containing a sacred black stone, the relic toward which Muslims face in prayer. The house-mosque and tomb of the Prophet, the *masjid* al-Nabî at Al-Madînah, is Islam's second major sanctuary. The third major shrine is the Holy Sanctuary in Jerusalem, including the al-Agsâ mosque and the Dome of the Rock, Islam's earliest extant building. Of these three, the Al-Madînah mosque was most instrumental in defining the general architectural features of the traditional *masjid*, for it was there that canonical and liturgical changes were first architecturally expressed, prompting changes in other mosques.

The initial and most far-reaching change occurred when a Qur'ânic revelation established Mecca as the new orientation of Islam and the place to which prayer should be directed. This shift was reflected in the construction of mosques facing Mecca rather than Jerusalem. As all mosques follow this orientation, their physical axes converge upon the Ka'bah. A less fundamental change was the addition of the minbar, a raised dais from which the Prophet delivered the Friday sermon. The minbar became a sign of authority, secular and religious, and continues to be a necessity for any congregational mosque. The minaret, a tower appended to the mosque, postdates the Prophet and is often used for sounding the call to prayer.

While changes in the Prophet's mosque at Al-Madînah culminated in a specific and influential type of architectural design (the T-plan mosque), other architectural types also appeared early on and continue to be in use in different regions of the Islamic world. The hypostyle design of the al-Azhar mosque in Cairo or the Great Mosque of Cordova in Spain gives way, in Iran and parts of Iraq, to one that is based on high arched openings arranged around a courtyard. The dome plays an important role in the Ottoman architecture of Turkey, which drew inspiration from Byzantine prototypes, while in India the interaction between local architecture and Islamic requirements has produced a multiplicity of mosque types. Despite the various plans, decorative formulae, and furnishings of mosques, basics such as the minbar, minaret, and mihrâb (a concavity in the wall that faces Mecca) remain constant features.

Mossi

West African peoples. Tradition holds that Mossi ancestors came to the area around Burkina Faso from the east; most scholars trace their origins at least to the thirteenth-century kingdom of Tenkodogo, whose ruler the kings of the other Mossi states claim as a common ancestor. During the fourteenth through seventeenth centuries, they competed for regional power with the kingdoms of Mali in the north and Songhai in the south. They remained independent kingdoms until the French invasions of the nineteenth century. Today the Mossi make up about half the population of Burkina Faso (over 1,750,000) and are organized on the basis of four feudal kingdoms: Tenkodogo, Yatenga, Ouagadougou, and Fada N'Gourma. Their political and religious organization has remained relatively stable for many centuries, preserving their medieval hierarchical class structure and remaining resistant to the Islamic culture surrounding them. Each village is governed by a chief who in turn is subordinate to a divisional chief. The *morho naba* (big lord) of Ouagadougou is the supreme ruler. Most Mossi follow their traditional religion, which emphasizes ancestor worship.

Mozart, Wolfgang Amadeus (1756–1791)

Austrian composer. Mozart was born in Salzburg. A child prodigy, he began composing minuets and playing the harpsichord before he was five years old. Having learned composition, counterpoint, and harmony from his musician father, Leopold, Mozart composed his first symphony at the age of eight. Equally capable on the violin and organ, Mozart played before dignitaries in Vienna, London, Paris, and several other major European cities while still a youth. At age twelve, Mozart composed his first two operas. In 1769 he was appointed concertmaster of the court of the archbishop of Salzburg. After a few years of dutiful service at the court, Mozart set out for Vienna in hopes of securing a more lucrative position, but he was unsuccessful. Not long after his return to Salzburg, Mozart was relieved of his duties there and finally settled in Vienna in 1781. He was married there the next year. It was during Mozart's Vienna years that his three most famous operas were composed: *Le nozze di Figaro* (1786; *The Marriage of Figaro*), *Don Giovanni* (1787), and *Die Zauberflöte* (1790; *The Magic Flute*). At the age of thirty-five, Mozart died deeply in debt and was buried in a common, unmarked pauper's grave somewhere in Vienna. His last work, *Requiem*, was left unfinished; it was completed by his pupil Franz Süssmayr. A monument memorializing Mozart stands over an empty grave in Vienna.

Mo Zi (c. 470–391 B.C.E.)

Ancient Chinese philosopher. According to historians, Mo Zi, a contemporary of Confucius, had been a follower of the other philosopher's teachings before he decided to break away to formulate his own theory. Confronted with the constant warfare among several states that divided China and caused total political and social chaos, Mo Zi ridiculed Confucius's belief that restoration should be achieved mainly through strictly observing fixed rituals and rules. Instead, he advocated the practice of self-sacrifice and universal love. He argued that if the destruction of one's self is for the good of others, one should not hesitate to act, a philosophy he sets forth in *Mo Zi*. His teachings come close to the basic ideas of Christianity. It is important to note that unlike Confucius, who throughout his life actually remained silent about the afterlife, Mo Zi emphasized that there is something immortal after death.

Mo Zi's teachings for a time attracted many followers and became almost as popular as those of Confucius. However, they suffered a fatal blow at the hands of Mencius (c. 370–290 B.C.E.), another contemporary philosopher who greatly enriched and popularized Confucianism. It was not until the twentieth century that Mo Zi was rediscovered and the interest in his ideas revived.

Mphahlele, Ezekiel (1919–)

South African writer. Born in Pretoria, Mphahlele grew up mostly in the black slums of that city. He was educated at St. Peter's Secondary School in Johannesburg, and at Adam's College in Natal, receiving a teacher's certificate. For several years he worked as a clerk in a school for the blind and then for several more teaching English and Afrikaans until he was barred from teaching for protesting the Bantu Education Act in 1952. Thereafter, he served briefly as literary editor of the journal *Drum*, helping organize the Syndicate of Artists and writing short stories. During these years he also attended intermittently the University of South Africa, receiving a B.A. in 1949 and an M.A. in 1956.

In 1957 he moved his family to Nigeria, where he taught at the University of Ibadan. In 1959 he published *Down Second Avenue*, a fictionalized autobiography about growing up black in the slums of South Africa. The following year, he became editor of *Black Orpheus*, a post he held until 1966. *The African Image*, a collection of essays, appeared in 1962 to wide acclaim. In 1963, after moving to Kenya, he worked on *Présence Africaine* and the *Journal of New African Literature and the Arts*. While completing his Ph.D. dissertation in the United States, he wrote a draft of the novel *The Wanderers* (1971). In addition to many articles, poems, and stories published in periodicals (some under the pseudonym Bruno Eseki), his works include short-story collections such as *Man Must Live and Other Stories* (1947) and *In Corner B* (1967), and the cultural critique *Voices in the Whirlwind and Other Essays* (1972). Since his return to South Africa he has published several books under the name Es'kia Mphahlele, including a novel, *Chirundu* (1981).

Mughal

Indian Muslim dynasty. Composed of nineteen sovereigns in total, the Mughal dynasty that ruled large areas of India from 1526 to 1858 was founded by Babur (r. 1526–30), the ruler of Kabul and a descendant of Turkish conqueror Timur (Tamerlane; c. 1336–1404) and the Mongol Genghis Khan (c. 1167–1227). Babur's victory over the sultan Ibrahim Lodi at the first battle of Panipat (1526) gave him control of Delhi and Agra, but he died only four years after founding this dynasty. Babur's son Humayun (r. 1530–56) was driven into exile in Persia by the Suri sultans, who were to control Delhi for fifteen years. Mughal rule was successfully reestablished after the second battle of Panipat (1556), which resulted in the victory of Babur's grandson, Akbar (r. 1556–1605). The young Akbar, who became sultan under the regency of Bairam Khan, was to extend the empire's boundaries from Afghanistan to the Bay of Bengal and southward

to Gujarat and the northern Deccan, and move the capital to Fatehpur Sikri. While the Mughal empire was largely responsible for popularizing Islam throughout India, Akbar's reign was marked by his less-than-orthodox Muslim religious policies and his religious tolerance of Hindus. Akbar was also responsible for the creation of the administrative framework, including the *mansab* and *jagir* system, which sustained the empire for the next 150 years.

Jahangir (r. 1605–27), Akbar's son, and Shah Jahan (r. 1627–58), Akbar's grandson, further extended the empire's sway. Under the reign of the last of the "Great Mughals," Shah Jahan's son Aurangzeb (r. 1658–1707), the empire reached its height of glory and simultaneously sowed the seeds of its decline. The boundaries of the empire were extended to their farthest when Aurangzeb annexed the Muslim Deccan kingdoms of Bijapur and Golconda. However, unrest exploded in the empire's outlying territories, and Aurangzeb became a controversial figure by restoring Sunnî Muslim theologians to power, causing many Hindus in his kingdom to revolt.

After Aurangzeb's death in 1707, the murder of Emperor Farrukhsiyar in 1719 over factional disputes and the revolt of both Hindu landholders and the Marathas in the 1720s and 1730s further weakened the strength of the empire. It received a crushing blow in 1739, under Muhammad's rule (1719–48), when the Persian despot Nadir Shah (r. 1736–47) invaded India and sacked Delhi. The Mughal empire received yet another blow at the third battle of Panipat (1761), when the Mughal emperor Shah 'Alam II (r. 1759–1806) was defeated by Ahmad Shah Abdali (r. 1747–73).

With the growth of the East India Company and the increasing influence of European trade throughout India, the latter part of the eighteenth century saw the Mughal empire's boundaries reduced to the area surrounding Delhi, its capital city. The British company's expanding power throughout India was challenged by the last Mughal emperor, Bahādur Shāh II (r. 1837–57). His support of the Sepoy Mutiny of 1857 led to his deposition and exile in Rangoon by the British in 1858, an event that effectively and finally brought the curtain down on the Mughal empire's long and influential reign.

During the Mughal period, many of India's greatest works of art and architecture were produced. Under the patronage of Mughal sultans, court artisans produced many royal portraits and illustrated literary and historical texts. Domestic metalwork, metal engraving, and jade carving also became prominent art forms during the Mughal period. Akbar established a large school of native artists at his court, who produced works like the *Dastan-e Amir Hamzeh*, a series of about 1,400 miniature cloth paintings. During the sixteenth and seventeenth centuries, Islamic architecture reached its climax under Mughal patronage. The red sandstone and white marble *masjid jâmi'* (friday mosques) at the successive Mughal capitals of Lahore, Delhi, Agra, and Fatehpur Sikri were erected during this period. However, it was the tomb garden, such as the famous Taj Mahal built by Shah Jahan for his deceased wife, that the Mughal emperors developed to perfection.

Muhammad (570–632)

Prophet of Islam. Born in Mecca in western Arabia, the orphaned Muhammad was brought up by an established family of the Quraysh tribe and grew up to become a merchant in the employ of Khadija, an older wealthy woman whom he married and with whom he had four daughters.

In 610 C.E., Muhammad received his first revelation from Allâh (God) through the angel Jibril (Gabriel), who urged him to prophesize in the name of his creator. Encouraged by Khadija,

Muhammad preached submission to the One All-Knowing and Compassionate God as enjoined in the revelations he was to receive throughout his life. These revelations, which he at first shared only with family, friends, and close associates, comprise the Muslim sacred text the Qur'ân.

Muhammad brought Islam to a predominantly animist and cultist pagan Arabia. His teachings posed a threat to the status quo, particularly to the hierarchical tribal and mercantile systems then prevailing in Mecca; his notions of the One Creator and of the equality of all people irrespective of color, caste, gender, or race earned him many prominent enemies. The acceptance of Muhammad by the inhabitants of Yathrib (later Medina) to the north came at a fortuitous time and led to the eventual emigration there of the Prophet and his followers in 622 C.E. This emigration, the *hijrah*, marks the starting point of the Islamic calendar. In Medina, Muhammad was able to consolidate his power base and political authority. Seven years later, in 629, after numerous diplomatic initiatives, offensive and defensive battles, and the conclusion of several treaties, Muhammad was able to return to Mecca in exchange for a guarantee of general amnesty.

Muhammad died at Medina, leaving behind a rapidly expanding polity and faith. According to Islamic teaching, his death marks the end of prophecy for all humanity. Considered a prophet of God like Moses, Abraham, and Jesus before him, he is not worshiped by Muslims but revered and emulated. Besides preaching brotherhood and equality, Muhammad stressed compassion for the needy and the oppressed. He singled out orphans, the destitute, and widows. His concern for the welfare of widows is cited as the reason for his numerous marriages and alliances after Khadija's death. Muhammad's favorite daughter, Fātima (c. 606–633), married his cousin

'Alī (c. 600–661), who would eventually become the fourth caliph of the Muslim faith (656–61), and bore the Prophet's two grandsons, Hasan and Husayn. These personages are accorded special status by Muslims as "the family of the Prophet."

Muhammad I Askia (d. 1538)

West African emperor. Muhammad I Askia, whose full name was Muhammad Ibn Abi Bakr Ture, was the ruler of the Songhai empire, probably the largest of the ancient native kingdoms in West Africa, from 1493 to 1528. Though his origin is unclear, it is now believed that Muhammad was from a Senegalese family that settled in Gao, the Songhai capital. One legend has it that he was the nephew of the Songhai ruler Sonni Ali II, who had expanded the kingdom from 1464 until his death in 1492. His son succeeded him, but Muhammad, one of the father's counselors, challenged him and came to power after victory at the Battle of Anfao in 1493. Muhammad assumed the name Askia, supposedly a title in mockery of his opponents' claim *a si tya* (he will not do).

Muhammad instituted strict Islamic law and established an elaborate administrative system to govern efficiently the vast Songhai holdings, occupying the whole of the Middle Niger Delta. His own efforts at expansion were uneven, but during his reign the empire reached the height of its influence, far outside its boundaries in present-day Mali, Senegal, Guinea, and parts of Niger and Nigeria, especially through the spread of Islam as a religious and political force. But internal dissension plagued the ruling family, and in 1528 Muhammad's eldest son Musa killed Muhammad's brother, who was a chief general in the Songhai army, and banished Muhammad to an island in the Niger River. The self-styled Askia Musa was himself killed by another brother in 1531, who in turn was deposed by a third brother, Askia Is-

mail, in 1537. Askia Ismail returned his aged and blind father to Gao, where Muhammad died the following year. The pyramid-shaped tomb that marks Muhammad's grave has been the site of a revered mosque for centuries.

Mukherjee, Bharati (1940–)

Indian-American novelist. Born into the Brahman caste in Calcutta, India, Mukherjee left the confines of Bengali society to settle first in Canada, then in the United States. Her experience of "Westernization" is the basis of much of her work. *The Tiger's Daughter* (1972), her first novel, is the story of a young Brahman woman who returns to India after a lengthy stay in the West only to find that her memories of an upper-class lifestyle in India no longer correspond to the realities of poverty and hunger that she now sees. In *Wife* (1975) Mukherjee explores the violence lurking beneath the passivity of an Indian wife, brainwashed with notions of female servitude, when she makes the difficult adjustment to life in New York City. *Days and Nights in Calcutta* (1977), coauthored with her husband, Clark Blaise, is a collection of two travel journals, one kept by Mukherjee, the other kept by Blaise, which offer differing accounts of India. While Blaise becomes enthralled by the Bengali love of culture and the magic and myth that seem to surround the society, Mukherjee can see India only through the constrained lives of various women who grew up with her. *Darkness* (1985), a collection of short stories whose composition shows the strong influence of writer Bernard Malamud, deals largely with the lives of various Indians in North America. *The Sorrow and the Terror* (1987), again cowritten with her husband, is a nonfictional account and analysis of the factors leading to the terrorist-caused Air India crash off the shores of Ireland in 1985. Mukherjee's literary works about the precariousness of personal identity within changing cultures continue to gain notice from critics and readers alike.

mulato/mulata

Racial category. The word *mulato* (*mulata* in the feminine) was used in the colonial period and during the nineteenth century to denote a person from North or South America of mixed European and African descent. The population in the Spanish, Portuguese, French, and English colonies in the Americas was differentiated according to socially constructed racial categories that were supposedly based on lineage. These pseudoscientific categories were numerous, purporting to indicate with precision a person's racial origins. The legal rights and obligations of people differed according to each individual's category. This system of categorization reached its most grotesque form in Brazil in the nineteenth century, where there were almost one hundred different categories, supposedly racially determined.

Multan

Punjabi city in east-central Pakistan. Located on the banks of the Chenab River in Punjab province of Pakistan, the city derived its current name from the name of the idol of the sun-god temple located in Multan and erected in the pre-Muslim period. Multan, with its strategic location at the entrance of the southern route into India, has played an important role in Indian commercial and military history. Alexander the Great (356–323 B.C.E.) conquered the area in 326 B.C.E., and it was subsequently invaded by the Muslims in about 712 C.E. The Afghani Ahmad Shah Abdali captured the city in 1779, only to lose it to the Sikh maharajah Ranjit Singh in 1818. In 1848–49 Multan's Sikh governor, Mulraj, rebelled against the encroaching British. The resulting Second Sikh War ended in a British victory and in British rule in Multan. The British maintained their power there until the Partition of India and Pakistan in 1947, when Multan was one of the cities in the Punjab that became a part of Pakistan.

An old textile center, Multan is still famous for its handicrafts and cottage industries. The excellent architectural skills of the Multanis are reflected in the local shrines, including the shrine of Shams-e Tabriz, and in areas outside Multan as well: many of the craftsmen of the world-famous Taj Mahal came from Multan.

Murasaki Shikibu (c. 980–1015)

Japanese novelist and poet. Little of the life of Murasaki is known for certain, as women's histories were rarely recorded in the tenth century. It is believed that Murasaki came from a long line of literary figures. Her great-grandfather Fujiwara no Kanesuke was one of the *sanjūrokkasen*, or "Thirty-six Poetic Geniuses"; her father was noted for his writing in Chinese; and several of her relatives had verses included in the imperial anthologies, *chokusenshū*.

Late in the century, Murasaki married a distant cousin much older than herself, with whom she had a daughter and from whom she was widowed shortly after in the year 1001. Not long afterward, she became a court lady-in-waiting to the daughter of the great shogun Fujiwara no Michinaga. It may well be that her literary reputation preceded her and prompted this invitation to court, where she supposedly began writing her masterwork, *Genji monogatari* (*The Tale of Genji*), an important classic of Japanese literature. Her diary, *Murasaki Shikibu nikki* (*The Diary of Murasaki Shikibu*), is famous as well, and a collection of poems, *Murasaki Shikibu shū*, is also often attributed to her.

Murasaki is often regarded as one of the greatest writers in the history of Japanese literature and is celebrated as such. Some works for the Japanese Noh stage represent her as a patron deity, a goddess among novelists.

Muslim League

Indian political group and Pakistani political party. Originally called the All India Muslim League, it was founded in Dacca, now in East Pakistan, in 1906 as the first continental Muslim political group in British India. Despite its intention to represent and safeguard the rights of all Muslims, the original membership was neither large nor heterogeneous, for the selection process of the hundred or so original all-male representatives stipulated that they must be over twenty-five, educated, and of reasonable income. The league eventually grew both in strength and membership under such leaders as Muhammad Ali Jinnah (1876–1948).

Although the British government supported the league as an effective counter to the largely Hindu Indian National Congress, the Muslims feared that because they constituted only one-fifth of the entire Indian population, their voices would not be adequately represented after the projected independent nation of India was established. Hence, in 1940 the league decided that Muslim rights would best be protected by the establishment of a separate independent Muslim state and declared the formation of Pakistan to be its primary goal. The British government recognized the increasing power of both the Hindu Indian National Congress, led by Mohandas Gandhi (1869–1948) and the league, led by Jinnah, and realized that they had little choice but to give in to these organizations' demands.

After its wish was granted and Pakistan was formed in 1947, the Muslim League became Pakistan's major political party. In the late 1960s it was divided into three smaller groups: the Qayyum Muslim League, the Council Muslim League, and the Convention Muslim League.

Mustang

Final Tibetan kingdom. Located in a mountain principality in the Nepalese-Tibetan borderland, Mustang remains one of the last places in the Himalayas where ancient Tibetan customs are observed. Formerly a part of Tibet, Mustang is now Nepalese, though it has remained a distinctly Tibetan culture since earliest recorded time. The name Mustang is derived from Monthang, Tibetan for "Plain of Aspiration" or "Plain of the Mind's Aspiration." The people of this region are known as Bhotians, the name of Buddhist-Tibetan dialect speakers of the Himalayas. Neither the language (which consists of several dialects) nor the culture has been examined in great detail, and virtually nothing was known to outsiders about Mustang until the 1950s. Mustang has been called the "lost kingdom" and "forbidden kingdom" because only Nepalese and a select group of foreigners have been permitted to enter. Much of Mustang's history is contained in the Mollas, a unique genre of historical and oratorical literature recited at religious gatherings. These tell the history of the princes who ruled Mustang beginning in the fourteenth century and whose power climaxed in the fifteenth century. These local histories originate in Buddhist beliefs and derive from a religious speech-making genre of ancient Tibet.

The contemporary people of Mustang are mainly farmers, livestock breeders, or traders. Once a crucial center for Nepal's entrepôt trade (center of trade and transshipment), Mustang declined because of warfare involving the western Bhotia states and the rise of the Gorkha state. Trade was then directed to the eastern passes.

N

Nabokov, Vladimir [Vladimirovich]
(1899–1977)

Russian-American novelist. Nabokov was born into Russian nobility, the son of an important liberal politician who was the leader of the Russian Constitutional Democratic Party. He started publishing poetry in 1916, producing two collections of poems before leaving Russia. Nabokov's family lost both its land and fortune following the Bolshevik Revolution of 1917. In 1919 they immigrated to Berlin, where Nabokov's father was assassinated three years later by a reactionary rightist. The family stayed on in Berlin, but had to flee the Nazi regime in 1938, traveling first to Paris and then in 1940 to the United States. During his years in exile, Nabokov completed his education at Cambridge University, married another Russian émigré, had a son, and began his prodigious literary output of poems, translations, stories, literary criticism, plays, and novels. His writing until this point was mostly in Russian, and his publications under the pseudonym Vladimir Sirin included the novels *Mashen'ka* (1926; *Mary*), *Korol', dama, valet* (1928; *King, Queen, Knave*), *Dar* (1937; *The Gift*), and *Priglashenie na kazn'* (1938; *Invitation to a Beheading*). *The Gift* is often considered to be Nabokov's best Russian novel, dealing with the problem of the role of art through semiautobiographical description of a young author's development in post–World War I Berlin. Nabokov moved to Switzerland in 1959, and remained there until his death in 1977.

Nabokov began writing in English in 1938, completing *The Real Life of Sebastian Knight* (1941) and *Bend Sinister* (1947). His greatest commercial and artistic success came with the publication of *Lolita* (1955) in France. This brilliant satire, detailing a professor's obsession for a twelve-year-old nymphet (this word, Nabokov's coinage, entered the English language), aroused a strong reaction among the public, and for a time it was banned in the United States. Though his later novels did not achieve the commercial success of *Lolita*, the critically acclaimed novels *Pale Fire* (1962) and *Ada, or Ardor* (1969), and his autobiography, *Conclusive Evidence* (1951; revised and published in 1966 as *Speak, Memory*), attest to both the brilliance of Nabokov's satirical wit and his poetic imagination. He is renowned for his use of obscure literary allusions and clever word games. In the 1960s Nabokov translated several Russian classics, among them Aleksandr Pushkin's (1799–1837) *Eugene Onegin* in 1964, which includes an extensive commentary.

Nahdah

Arabic literary renaissance. From the Arabic meaning "revival" or "renaissance," the Nahdah refers specifically to the literary revival that spread through the Arab provinces of the Ottoman empire in the early nineteenth century. The 1,400-year-old Arabic literary heritage had remained a strong and thriving tradition. However, as a result of European influences in the region, which included ideas of political liberalism, many Arabs began to reevaluate their cultural and historical identity both within and beyond the empire. Revived interest in the cultural importance of language helped Arabs to explore the use of their language in new forms, such as newspapers, short stories, and novels.

The Nahdah began in Syria and Egypt toward the end of the eighteenth century. In Syria, French missionaries had created a network of schools for Eastern Christians that were primarily theological in content but were instrumental in creating a class of literate men who became involved in political affairs. Within a few generations, these students saw a practical need for Arabic. In protest against the dominance of Greeks in the hierarchy of the Greek Orthodox Church, Syrian Christians called for the use of Arabic as the liturgical language and sought out Muslim teachers to tutor them. They came away with a passion for Arabic language and literature. Other Christians studied at Protestant schools in Beirut, where Arabic was also promoted. By the 1820s graduates of these schools had introduced a periodical press to the region.

The French invasion of Egypt in 1798 is often seen as the starting point of the Nahdah there. The French leader Napoleon brought with him scientists, linguists, and writers who enlisted the help of learned Egyptians in governing. Although the French stayed only three years, many of their influences took root. Muhammad 'Ali (c. 1769–1849), the subsequent Ottoman governor of Egypt, used aspects of French civilization as a model to develop the country. He founded military academies and sent delegations of young men to France to study language and military sciences, then commissioned them to translate the material into Arabic. The press that

the French left behind was used to disseminate secular works to an increasingly eager audience.

Other Egyptian students, educated in the Islamic tradition, brought to the Nahdah a more heightened sense of the Islamic world's vulnerability to European colonialism. These students formed the Salafiyya movement, inspired by the teachings of Jamal al-Din al-Afghani, who wrote that not only was Islam compatible with Western science, but many of the tenets of liberalism and the natural sciences had originated in classical Islamic learning. By returning to the ideals of Islamic civilization, Muslims would regain their former strength and be on equal footing with Europe. The Nahdah thus went beyond a literary revival to a redefining of Arabs' sense of identity in a radically changing world. Eventually, this sense of identity emerged in the form of Arab nationalism, which has deeply affected the formation of the modern Middle East.

nang drama

Thai dance drama. The *nang* "shadow-puppet drama" of Thailand is a sister art of the *khön* dance-drama. Both arts have been performed since the Sukhotai period (fourteenth century), but there is considerable debate on the question of which art developed first. The *nang* is intimately associated with the story of Rama, the Hindu hero from whom the *Ramayana* derives its name. It is generally believed that the shadow-puppet play reached Thailand from India by way of Java in the thirteenth century.

The term *nang* may be translated as "hide figures" or "figures of hide," a name that is apparently derived from the cowskin material of which the figures are traditionally made. When the figures were elaborated upon, the *nang* developed into a form known as *nang yai* (big-figure play). When the form includes dancing, it is known as *nang ram omang rabam*. But the term is also applied to modern forms such as motion pictures, because they also employ figures on a screen.

The primary features of traditional *nang* are the cowhide figures, which are cut and colored and manipulated by the *nang* performer, and the screens made of thin white cloth. Figures on the hides can be of individuals or of groups, or they can depict the scenery of earthly or celestial locations. The figures of Hindu deities such as Vishnu or Shiva and the *rishi* are traditionally made from the hide of a virgin cow and elaborate offerings are made to propitiate the gods before the *rang* can be used. For the *rishi* figures, the traditional material of choice was tiger or bear until these animals became endangered. According to tradition, the artist who draws a *rang* figure is required to wear a white ceremonial garment and to complete the work in one day. Each hide figure is supported by two poles in the hands of the performer. As he moves the figure, the actor must bend and sway his torso while executing a series of leg movements in time to the music. In some ways the *nang* practitioner is more a dancer than a puppeteer, the hide figure serving mostly to identify the role that the actor-dancer performs. As in the *khön*, the actor mimes his or her performance to music while the narration, dialogue, and poetry are spoken by other performers.

Nang Loi

Story from the Thai *Ramakien*. The *Nang Loi* is one episode from the *Ramakien*, a Thai literary classic that contains many traditional stories and is considered to be one of the best examples of *khön* recitation, a Thai dramatic technique. Also known as the story of the "Floating Maiden," it tells of the war between the king known as Phra Ram and the Demon King Thotsakan over Phra Ram's wife, Nang Sida. The Demon King abducted Nang Sida and then commanded his niece to take on her form and float past Phra Ram in the river, so that Phra Ram would think her dead and end the war with his grief. The ruse was successful until the white monkey Hanuman, general of Phra Ram's monkey army, suspected deception and had Phra Ram cremate the body, forcing the demoness to expose herself.

Napoleon Bonaparte (1769–1821)

French emperor. Napoleon Bonaparte (also known as Napoleon I, the Little Corporal, or the Corsican) was emperor of France from 1804 to 1815 and earned a reputation for flamboyance, arrogance, and great sophistication as a military leader. Born on the island of Corsica, he received his education at French military schools and became an army officer in 1785. Winning several decisive victories against Austria in northern Italy in 1795, Napoleon became a national hero.

Defeated by the English in Egypt and Syria, Napoleon returned to Paris and led a coup d'état against the failing French government, naming himself First Consul, a position he assumed for life in 1802. Two years later, Napoleon became emperor. During the first few years of his reign, Napoleon instituted various legal, educational, and economic reforms and consolidated his power at home and abroad. Treating most of Europe as his personal empire, Napoleon made his most decisive conquest at the Battle of Austerlitz in 1805, where he defeated Russia and Austria. By 1810 Napoleon was at the peak of his power, controlling much of Europe.

Napoleon's downfall began when the English, under Sir Arthur Wellesley (later the duke of Wellington), aided Spain and Portugal against France in the Peninsular War of 1808. Frustrated in that effort, Napoleon tried instead to spread his empire eastward, invading Russia in 1812. That disastrous campaign ended when his troops found the city of Moscow deserted and in ruins.

In April 1814 Napoleon's defeat at

Leipzig at the hands of a European allied coalition resulted in his forced abdication and exile to Elba. Seeking to regain power, Napoleon escaped and returned to France in March 1815, but his triumphant return was short-lived. His army was badly beaten at the Battle of Waterloo on June 18, 1815, a humiliation that led to Napoleon's second abdication and exile to the island of St. Helena.

Narai the Great (1632–1688)

Thai ruler. Narai was named after the four-armed god Narayana, a fitting namesake for this versatile king whose reign was marked by swift and scattered developments in Thailand's culture, economy, and relations with foreign powers. After Narai seized the throne with foreign help, probably from Persia, his involvement with Western powers, most notably the French, continued as a hallmark of his reign. He took the Greek adventurer Constantine Phaulkon into his trust, conferring on him a title of nobility and a position of chief councillor to the king. Phaulkon and the French later attempted unsuccessfully to convert Narai to Christianity, in order to bring him in line with French and Jesuit interests. Narai resisted these and other efforts to force territorial concessions from him, but xenophobic sentiment gathered during his reign, which ended with an anti-Western coup that virtually closed Thailand to the West for the next 150 years.

Narai's reign is generally considered to be the "First Golden Age" of Thai poetry. He was himself an accomplished poet, composing poetic romances, such as an important revision of *Pra Lo*, a romantic tragedy in verse. New verse forms were created during his reign, and his court made the composition of clever, impromptu verse forms a favorite pastime. He was patron to several of the most influential poets, such as Si Prat, author of *Kamsuang*.

Naram-Sin (2197–2060 B.C.E.)

Babylonian ruler. The grandson of Sargon of Agade, Naram-Sin momentarily restored Babylon to the unity and glory that his grandfather had achieved. In fact, his conquests stretched farther than Sargon's and he took the title "King of the Four Quarters of the Earth." Naram-Sin crushed a widespread rebellion at his accession (a common pattern in Mesopotamian history), and it was probably this that motivated him to strengthen his empire by deifying himself and building an extensive system of provincial control.

Nasrettin Hoja

Turkish and Persian comic figure. Nasrettin Hoja, also called Mulla Nasruddin, is a personage of whom a series of several hundred amusing anecdotes is told among Turkish and Persian speakers in the Near East. Nasrettin Hoja parallels the comic figure of the Arabs known as Juha, and like Juha, his historical origin is wrapped in mystery. The Hoja anecdotes probably came into circulation first among Turkish speakers during or immediately following the thirteenth century, and they continue to be extremely popular in the contemporary Near East.

Nasser, *see* 'Abd al-Nâsir, Gamâl

Nation of Islam

Religious and cultural organization, predominantly of American blacks. Known also as the Lost-Found Nation of Islam, the World Community of Islam in the West, and the American Muslim Mission. The organization was founded in the 1930s by Wallace Fard Muhammad (also Wali Farah, Prophet Fard, The Great Mahdi, or The Savior), an enigmatic figure who immigrated to the U.S. in 1930, said to have been born in Mecca in 1877. Drawing on claims previously made by Prophet Drew Ali, leader of the Moorish Science Temple, Fard maintained that all blacks were members of the ancient Muslim tribe of Shabazz.

Redemption through self-knowledge, Fard taught, would free blacks from their oppression by "white devils" and bring them the favor of Allah. Fard's first ministry was a mosque in Detroit, founded in 1931. His early followers, who regarded him as the earthly incarnation of Allah, were mostly poor African-Americans ghettoized in Northern industrial cities after fleeing the rural South. A disciple, Elijah Poole, became Fard's chosen successor and changed his name to Elijah Muhammad. After Fard's unexplained disappearance in 1934, Muhammad became the leader of the growing organization.

Muhammad founded a second temple in Chicago, and by the end of World War II the Nation of Islam had temples in most major northern U.S. cities. Though some of its basic tenets and ritual practices were borrowed directly from Eastern Orthodox Islam, under Elijah Muhammad the Nation of Islam refined a distinctly black Muslim theology replete with historical and "scientific" theories on the origins of the races. Blacks were the original race, made in the divine image, destined to rule His kingdom; whites were the result of a eugenics experiment gone awry, a devilish race that sought to enslave blacks. The Nation of Islam's mission was to prepare blacks for the coming Battle of Armageddon, in which they would regain control of the world. These radical beliefs attracted a great deal of criticism, and members were accused of being hatemongers, separatists, anti-Semites, and racists.

The Nation of Islam was also responsible for more practical social programs in the tradition of Marcus Garvey's Universal Negro Improvement Association. Black Muslims ran drug rehabilitation programs, educated black convicts, established a paramilitary wing for self-defense called the Fruit of Islam, and spearheaded social service programs in black communities. Under Muhammad's strict leadership, the Nation of Islam became a tight-knit organization with disciplined groups in the ghettos of most major cities. The Nation of Islam also developed a political platform (Muhammad's "ten-point program") that called for the release of black convicts, the establishment of a separate black country within the United States, and black exemption from U.S. federal taxes and military service.

In the 1960s Malcolm X became Muhammad's chief spokesman and propelled the Nation of Islam to great fame and notoriety. A gifted orator and outspoken militant, Malcolm X earned the Nation of Islam extensive media coverage (most memorably on a television special entitled "The Hate That Hate Produced" and in a 1961 book by C. Eric Lincoln entitled *The Black Muslims of America*). He increased the organization's popularity among young blacks while at the same time making it a prime target for federal law enforcement agencies. Disputes between Malcolm X and other members of the Nation of Islam's leadership eventually led to his expulsion, and he was assassinated in 1965.

The 1970s was a radically different period for the Nation of Islam, now under the leadership of Muhammad's son, Warith Deen (or Wallace D.) Muhammad. He rejected the racial teachings of his father and removed all racial restrictions on membership, as well as the rigid code of dress, diet, and personal habits. Members were no longer forbidden to participate in the political process or in the armed services. He renamed the organization the American Muslim Mission but in 1985 declared it defunct, arguing that this move would bring members into a closer relationship with the world Muslim community.

Louis Farrakhan, the leader of the

New York temple and one of Elijah Muhammad's ministers, continued to use the name Nation of Islam. He restored and maintained many of the rigid codes and beliefs abandoned by Warith Deen Muhammad. He also retained the Nation of Islam's confrontational style; the publication of *The Secret Relationship Between Blacks and Jews*, an anti-Semitic text claiming that Jews bear special responsibility for the slave trade, gave Farrakhan and the organization bad publicity. By the 1990s, however, Farrakhan's Nation of Islam had emerged as a powerful alternative to the traditional civil rights establishment. The Million Man March in October 1995, a gathering of mostly male blacks in Washington, D.C., organized by Farrakhan and his peers, embraced the Nation of Islam's traditional goals of community building while tempering its separatism through endorsement of voter registration drives in black communities.

Native American Church

Indian religious body. Situated primarily in the southwestern United States, the Native American Church combines some of the traditional teachings of Christianity and Christian virtue with elements from Indian religious practice, including the observance of the "peyote" sacrament. Peyote is a hallucinogenic drug derived from the cactus plant that, when chewed, induces supernatural visions and is said to put individuals in direct communication with God and the spiritual realm. Adherents of the Native American Church call their religious orientation "the Peyote Road." It is believed that the peyotist movement was begun in the mid-nineteenth century by the Kiowa and Comanche tribes of Oklahoma and quickly developed into a distinct religion that, by 1890, was practiced by over fifty tribes in the United States and Canada.

At the turn of the century, strong efforts by several states and some government agents to curtail the practice of peyotism failed. Generally, the courts have upheld the rights of peyotists to religious freedom. Because the Native American Church is only loosely organized, membership figures are uncertain; in the 1970s it claimed to have 225,000 followers.

Natsume Sōseki (1867–1916)

Japanese novelist. Born Natsume Kinnosuke, as a child Natsume was shuttled back and forth between his blood and foster family, and he developed the insecurity and alienation that would later be expressed in his novels. Natsume graduated from Tokyo University in 1893 with a degree in English literature. Beginning in 1900, he spent two years studying in London. He returned to Tokyo to teach English literature, but he soon grew disillusioned with the academic lifestyle. Natsume quit his post and began working at the newspaper *Asahi Shimbun*, where he also published many of his soon-to-be-written novels in installments. He moved from the pedantic tone and idealized characters of his early novels to the more colloquial style and finer exploration of the suffering human mind of his later books. Early works such as *Wagahai wa neko de aru* (1905; *I Am a Cat*), a satiric attack on human society from the viewpoint of a cat, give way to Natsume's increasing pessimism about life in the modern world. His novel *Sanshirō* (1908) utilizes a "stream of consciousness" technique, one well suited to his investigation of the alienation of the thinking subject from the world outside. Later works such as *Kokoro* (1914), *Michikusa* (1915; *Grass on the Wayside*), and the unfinished *Meian* (1916; *Light and Darkness*) concern the futility of human relationships and the suffering within those relationships. Natsume died of a chronic ulcer in 1916.

Navajo

Indian tribe. By far the largest Indian tribe in the United States, both in terms of population and land, the Navajo, or Navaho, are a composite group. By the sixteenth century, their ancestors had migrated from what is now northwestern Canada to what is now the southwestern United States. This led to conflicts with other tribes of the Southwest, including the Pueblo Indians, as well as with the Spanish. In the eighteenth century, the Navajo lived in bands, under a headman, organized into as many as sixty distinct matrilineal clans. They borrowed significantly from the Pueblo culture, and originally learned the technique for their famous woven rugs from the Pueblo. In the nineteenth century, the Navajo learned the art of silversmithing for which they are still well known. Navajo religion involves numerous deities, songs, chants, and prayers, and such ceremonies as the squaw dance and the night chant. The vast mythology includes a creation myth that states that Esdzanadkhi (who most authorities believe was an earth goddess) created man.

For the first half of the nineteenth century, the Navajo were known as a marauding, warlike tribe, frequently raiding the villages of neighboring tribes and often involved in skirmishes with U.S. troops. Major war defeats in 1864 forced the Navajo to negotiate a treaty with the United States in 1868 that restricted the tribe to a reservation. The reservation now covers over 15 million acres and is home to more than 100,000 Navajo.

Nawruz

Persian New Year's Day. In Achaeminid times (550–330 B.C.E.), this holiday corresponded with the vernal equinox, although earlier it appears to have occurred in midsummer. In addition to symbolizing a time of renewal and rejoicing, Nawruz was also the day of annual tax collection. With the Arab conquest of Iran during the seventh century and the subsequent adoption of Is-

lam by its inhabitants, Nawruz entered the Islamic administrative calendar as tax day. As such, it was tied to the Islamic lunar calendar, and it was not until the eleventh century that the vernal equinox was again proclaimed the start of the new year.

Nawruz came to represent a popular secular festival in many parts of the Islamic world, including Anatolia (Turkey), Central Asia, Afghanistan, northern India (Pakistan), Iraq, and Egypt, although nowhere is its observance as pervasive and symbolically important as in Iran. A central feature of Nawruz celebrations among Iranians is the *sofreh*, a cloth or kerchief that is spread with items imbued with symbolic value. These objects are borrowed from Zoroastrian ritual, both in their nature and in the fact that they number seven (a key number in Persian numerology). It is customary for all members of a household—even the servants—to gather around the *sofreh*, after which they pay a series of visits to other households. This practice of visitation can be selective or communal, depending on the region of Iran and the size of the community.

Nebuchadnezzar II (c. 604–556 B.C.E)

Babylonian king. Nebuchadnezzar was the most celebrated of the kings of the Neo-Babylonian empire. He succeeded his father to the throne in 604 B.C.E. and commanded the Chaldean army that defeated the last of the Assyrians in 605 B.C.E. Soon after his ascension, Nebuchadnezzar occupied all of Syria and the towns on the Philistine coast. In 597 B.C.E., he took Jerusalem and made Zedekiah, the king of Judah, his vassal. When Zedekiah proved himself to be a continuing source of rebellion and anti-Chaldean intrigue, Nebuchadnezzar sacked Jerusalem, burned the Temple, and carried most of the population away into captivity (586 B.C.E.). When Nebuchadnezzar died in 556 B.C.E., the Chaldean empire included Babylon, the southern part of Assyria, and all of Syria and Palestine.

Beyond the military realm, Babylon also prospered during Nebuchadnezzar's rule. The city wall was made wide enough for two four-horse carriages to pass, and Nebuchadnezzar constructed one of the Seven Wonders of the Ancient World—Babylon's famous hanging gardens.

Négritude

Social and political movement. From the French, meaning "blackness," the neologism Négritude was coined by Aimé Césaire (1913–), a poet from Martinique, and Senegalese poet Léopold Senghor (1906–) in Paris in the 1930s, and is used to describe a movement in the arts toward the articulation of the African experience in the world. Because Négritude reaffirms African cultural traditions, and resists the European attitudes, beliefs, and traditions forced upon Africans during periods of colonial rule, it often spilled into African political movements toward national independence.

In its strictest definition, the concept of Négritude advances the idea that black Africans have qualitatively different experiences in the world. They share among themselves a psychological experience of "blackness" denied to other peoples. Not all African artists embrace this movement wholeheartedly, and its assumption of essentialism has been thoroughly critiqued in an ongoing discussion of identity. Nonetheless, the establishment of the Negritude literary school in the 1930s sparked an artistic revolution throughout Africa and among African Americans as well, as writers like Senegalese poet Birago Diop and Cameroonian novelist Mongo Beti produced some of the classics of African literature in this period.

Nehru, [Pandit] Jawaharlal (1889–1964)

First prime minister of independent India. Nehru was born in Allahabad to a Kashmiri Brahman family. His father, Motilal Nehru, was a prominent lawyer who would later act as a lieutenant for the Indian religious and political leader Mohandas Gandhi. The young Nehru was educated at home until he was sixteen, when he was sent to Harrow, a prominent public school in England. Two years later, in 1907, he entered Trinity College, Cambridge, where he took his degree in natural science. Nehru then went on to study law, qualifying as a barrister at the Inner Temple in London.

In 1912 he returned to India, where he initially pursued a career in law but found himself more and more attracted to the growing nationalist movement in India. He began serving as a delegate to the Indian National Congress in 1912 and first met Gandhi in 1916. Nehru admired Gandhi for his commitment to action that was based on the absence of fear, hate, or violence, and although nonviolence would be to Nehru more a policy decision than the faith it was to Gandhi, Gandhi's effect on the future prime minister's life was profound.

In 1919 Nehru joined the surge of nationalism and public outcry throughout India over events like the Amritsar massacre, in which British troops fired on an unarmed crowd, killing 379 and wounding nearly 1,200 people. As a result of these protests, Nehru went to jail with many other members of Congress when the party was outlawed by the British government in his province. This was the first of eight terms Nehru would serve in prison during India's struggle for freedom: all told, he would spend nine years of his life in prison due to his commitment to the nationalist cause, years in which he read the works of Karl Marx in depth (he was to call prison "the best of universities"), later adapting Marxist economic policies to the Indian context.

In 1929 Nehru was elected Congress president and oversaw the Lahore session, at which India's first proclamation of independence was articulated. Gandhi, who had orchestrated Nehru's appointment as president, saw in him the spokesperson for India's youth and for a politics that would mediate and temper the positions of the extreme right and left. Although Gandhi did not appoint Nehru his political heir until 1942, Nehru's apprenticeship under Gandhi, which deepened after the death of Nehru's father in 1931, led many Indians to see the young politician as Gandhi's natural successor.

Under Gandhi and Nehru, the Indian independence movement forged ahead in the 1930s. At the Round Table Conferences in London in 1935, the Indian provinces won a degree of governmental autonomy, and after the outbreak of World War II in 1939, anti-British demonstrations in India intensified in a civil-disobedience protest led by Gandhi. In 1942 the Congress passed the "Quit India" resolution, and as a result the entire Congress was thrown in jail, including Nehru. This last of Nehru's prison terms lasted three years.

As Britain finally prepared to withdraw from India after World War II, Nehru was appointed head of an interim government in 1946. By 1947 India gained its independence after extended negotiations with Lord Mountbatten, the last British viceroy, but at the cost of the partition of its territories into a largely Muslim state, Pakistan, and the predominantly Hindu India. Although Gandhi had worked strenuously for Hindu-Muslim unity throughout his lifetime and had adamantly opposed the partition, Nehru finally acquiesced and on August 15, 1947, the two independent states were established, with Nehru as prime minister of India.

Nehru's reign was marked by his secularism and commitment to modernism. In addition to introducing parliamentary government to India, he was also known for his attention to plural-ism, social reform, industrial development, and the improvement of the lives of the impoverished lower castes and women, particularly widows, who under Nehru's tenure were finally granted inheritance and property rights. He also became an important international spokesman for nonalignment and anticolonialism.

In addition to his autobiography, Nehru published several texts, including *India and the World* (1962); *Soviet Russia* (1949); *Glimpses of World History* (1942); and two collections of his speeches and writings, *The Unity of India* (1941) and *Independence and After* (1949).

Nehru suffered a mild stroke in 1963, and a more crippling one in January 1964. He died shortly after his third and fatal stroke a few months later. He had, however, founded what could be considered a political dynasty, for both his daughter Indira and his grandson Rajiv Gandhi were to follow in his footsteps and serve as subsequent prime ministers.

Nepali sculptural art

Nepali art form. Like most art in Nepal, Nepali sculptural art is concentrated in the Kathmandu Valley and is a product of the Newar people. The art is dedicated to Hindu and Buddhist religious themes. According to the Hindu belief that man can best conceive god in man's own image, the center of Nepalese sculptural art is the human figure. An example is the sculpted figures of the river goddesses Ganga and Yamuna in the Pashupatinath Temple. Stone sculpture is largely medieval; although Nepalese stone sculpture can be traced to the second century B.C.E., it became prominent in the fifth to seventh centuries C.E. (known as the Licchavi period). Newar sculpture used gilt copper extensively from the eighth to eighteenth century C.E., and the art of bronze casting culminated in the thirteenth to fourteenth century. The lost-wax technique and metalworking skills of the Newars were the finest in Asia. The architecture and public spaces of Nepal are adorned with stone sculpture. For example, the many fountains that mark significant watering places, *pranala*, are elaborate sculptures. A typical fountain depicts *makara*, a Hindu water creature with the body of a crocodile and head of an elephant, whose snout is fashioned from gilt copper.

Neruda, Pablo (1904–1973)

Chilean poet, diplomat, and politician. Born Neftalí Ricardo Reyes Basoalto, Neftalí spent most of his youth in Temuco. His father, an engineer, discouraged him from becoming a writer, but in defiance Neftalí abandoned his family name and adopted the surname of Czech writer Jan Neruda, becoming thereafter Pablo Neruda. Attending the University of Chile in Santiago, Neruda published a poetry collection, *Veinte poemas de amor y una canción desesperada* (1924; *Twenty Love Poems and a Song of Despair*), that earned him instant fame in Chile. Though his earliest work is imitative of Latin American modernism, Neruda gradually evolved a highly personal poetic style, which has a consistently dark vision of the human condition. A surrealist, Neruda wrote a free verse that is both obscure and strikingly original. Such evocative poems as those in *España en el corazón* (*Spain in My Heart*), which he wrote in despair as he saw the defeat of the republicans in the Spanish Civil War (1936–39), manage to express the profoundest anguish in a language of startling imagery. Increasingly, after the end of the Spanish Civil War, his poetry evokes the dramatic Chilean landscape to express his aspirations for the common people, raging, for example, against the exploitation of the Indian. In *Canto general* (1950), he created a Latin American epic. Neruda's life as a diplomat and politician gave him a wide experience of the world. He was posted to China, Sri Lanka, and Burma in the late 1920s and to Spain in the mid-1930s. In the late 1940s he was exiled to Mexico as a result of his association with the Chilean Communist Party. His poetry (and his political commitment) have made him the poet with perhaps the greatest influence in contemporary Latin America. Neruda was awarded the 1971 Nobel Prize in Literature.

Newton, Sir Isaac (1642–1727)

English mathematician and scientist. His father having died before Newton was born at Woolsthorpe, Lincolnshire, Newton's remarried mother left him in the care of his grandmother. Widowed for the second time, she brought the fourteen-year-old boy home to run the family farm. With the encouragement of his uncle, Newton entered Trinity College, Cambridge, taking the B.A. in 1665. When the Great Plague caused the school to close, Newton returned to Woolsthorpe, where in a period of about eighteen months he formulated his greatest theories. In 1667 he returned to Cambridge as a fellow at Trinity College, though not until 1669 did he make his discoveries public. In 1684 the astronomer Edmund Halley put to him a question about the mechanics of planetary motion, and Newton's answer formed the basis of his *Mathematical Principles of Natural Philosophy*, published in 1687 to great acclaim. He served the university as its member of Parliament, and later held the position of master of the mint. He was knighted by Queen Anne in 1705. His later years were marked by the controversy over whether Newton or German philosopher and mathematician Gottfried Wilhelm Leibniz (1646–1716) had invented differential calculus (it is now generally agreed that they did so independently); the argument was complicated by the fact that Newton loathed to acknowledge the specific contributions of others, despite his famous statement that he stood "on the shoulders of giants."

In his work on optics, beginning in 1672 and culminating in his *Opticks* of 1704, Newton's experiments with prisms led him to the doctrine of the heterogeneous composition of white light by a spectrum of colors with different refractive indexes. To further his experiments, he built the first reflecting telescope. In the early eighteenth century, the "Newtonian universe" began to supplant the Cartesian worldview, thanks in large part to popularizers like the French writer Voltaire (1694–1778), who believed that his mechanical conception of phenomena and his scientific method could be applied to areas outside science. The story that the discovery of the law of gravity was inspired by the fall of an apple onto Newton's head was first told by Voltaire (who claimed to have been told it by Newton's niece). The eighteenth-century Enlightenment conception of the world as a rationally ordered machine governed by simple mathematical laws was largely an extrapolation from Newton's influential writings.

New York Renaissance, *see* Harlem Globetrotters

Ngo Dinh Diem (1901–1963)
First president of the Republic of Vietnam (South Vietnam). Diem was a member of a prominent Catholic mandarin family. Under Vietnamese emperor Bao Dai (1913–), he was named minister of the interior in 1933 in the French colonial government. He resigned this post in opposition to French restrictions on national self-determination, and held no official post for twenty years. His political views were strongly nationalist and anti-Communist, particularly after the death of his brother and nephew at the hands of the Viet Minh. Despite his absence from formal politics and his strong anti-French stand, the French colonial government, through

the agency of the puppet emperor Bao Dai, named Ngo Dinh Diem prime minister of the "State of Vietnam" while the Geneva Conference was in session in 1954. Rejecting the recommendations for reunification stipulated under the Geneva Accords of 1954, Ngo Dinh Diem staged an election that deposed Emperor Bao Dai and named Diem president of the new republic. Diem consolidated his power by defeating three large-scale independent religiosocial armies, including the Cao Dai. Although he secured U.S. support as a moderate nationalist alternative to the Communist Ho Chi Minh in North Vietnam, Diem was out of touch with the Vietnamese people. He made such unpopular moves as promoting Catholicism in a predominantly Buddhist country and investing his elite family members with exorbitant powers. Many of his policies were repressive, particularly to Buddhists. Invoking "emergency" powers, Diem embarked in 1957 on an extensive purge of Communists and supposed Communists. He quickly lost the good faith of the U.S. government, which in November 1963 tacitly accepted a coup against the Diem regime that resulted in the assassination of Diem and his brother. After the withdrawal of the United States in the 1970s, Diem was invoked as a national hero who had been betrayed by American interests.

Ngugi Wa Thiong'o (1938–)
Kenyan novelist, playwright, and teacher. Ngugi was born in Limuru, where he attended school in his early years. While at Makerere University in Kampala, Uganda, he was the editor of *Penpoint*, a student journal that would launch a number of young East African writers. Ngugi continued his writing career with publications of his short stories in several Kenyan journals and edited the journal *Zuka*, an important English-language review.

A leading East African novelist, Ngugi's often bitter and disillusioned works center on the destructive legacy of colonialism, as well as the betrayal of Kenya by its postindependence leaders. His first novel, *Weep Not, Child*, appeared in 1964, and chronicles the Mau Mau Rebellion and its effect on the lives of one family. Other works by Ngugi include the play *The Black Hermit* (1962) and the novels *A Grain of Wheat* (1967), which outlines the difficult issues facing Kenya during the fight for and after achieving independence, and *Caitaani mūtharaba-inĩ* (1982; *Devil on the Cross*), a bitter indictment of Kenya's postindependence leaders, written in Kikuyu. Ngugi's attacks on the government did not go unnoticed. Imprisoned for nearly a year in 1978, after the production of the play *Ngaahika ndeenda* (1980; *I Will Marry You When I Want*), which criticizes postcolonial Kenya, Ngugi was the first of Kenya's intellectuals to be detained by the postindependence government. That incarceration is chronicled in his book *Detained*, which was published in 1981. He has also written important critical essays and articles on literary, cultural, and political issues, the best known of which appear in *Decolonizing the Mind* (1986).

Nibelungenlied

German epic poem. The *Nibelungenlied* was written around 1200 by an anonymous author believed to be from the Danube region of Germany. Although the poem contains many elements that are consistent with the Arthurian romances, this work provides a more critical or realistic view of the medieval court than the more romanticized view of chivalry and knighthood found in the typical Arthurian romances. In addition, the form of the poem is inconsistent with that of the typical courtly romances, which were written in rhyming couplets with four stresses per line. In contrast, the *Nibelungenlied* is composed of four-line stanzas with seven stresses per line for the first three lines of the stanza, and eight stresses in the last line of the stanza. This meter has come to be known as the Nibelungenstrophe.

The tale is based on Scandinavian legends and refers to actual historical events, such as the overthrow of the Burgundian kingdom by the Huns in 437 B.C.E. The poem is divided into two parts. The first half of the poem begins as the hero, Siegfried, sets out for Worms, despite the warning of his parents, in the hopes of wedding Kriemhild, a Burgundian queen who was known for her exceptional beauty. Siegfried possesses a magic cloak that renders him invisible and is near-invincible due to having bathed in the blood of a slain dragon; he uses his powers to assist Kriemhild's brother, Gunther, to pass a series of physical contests to win the hand of Brunhild, a warrior woman of great beauty and strength. In return, Gunther approves Siegfried's marriage to Kriemhild. Both couples are eventually married, but when Brunhild discovers that Siegfried aided Gunther in his quest for her hand, she plots with the Burgurdian kings to have Siegfried killed. Kriemhild unwittingly reveals to Siegfried's enemies that he is vulnerable in one small spot on his back where a leaf had fallen during his bath in the dragon's blood, and the Burgundian kings murder him.

The second part of the poem deals with Kriemhild's revenge against the murderers of her husband. After mourning the death of Siegfried for some time, Kriemhild agrees to marry Etzel (Attila, king of the Huns) on the condition that he help her carry out her plans for revenge. After their marriage, she persuades him to invite the Burgundian court to his kingdom. When they arrive, Etzel's forces attack and eventually defeat the Burgundians, but Kriemhild dies in the fighting.

Nietzsche, Friedrich Wilhelm (1844–1900) German philosopher and poet. Born the son of a Lutheran minister in the Prussian province of Saxony, Nietzsche was named after the king of Prussia, Friedrich Wilhelm, whose birthday he shared. His father became insane and died in 1849, and Nietzsche moved with his family to Naumburg. He studied at the boarding school at Pforta and at the University of Bonn, but in 1865 he moved to the University of Leipzig, discovering the German philosophers Immanuel Kant (1724–1804), Arthur Schopenhauer (1788–1860), and German composer Richard Wagner (1813–1883). After a year in the military, Nietzsche was appointed an associate professor of classical philology at the University of Basel at the age of twenty-four. Leipzig awarded him a doctorate without thesis or examination in 1869; he moved to Basel and was promoted to full professor. Sometime during these years Nietzsche apparently contracted syphilis, for his later insanity is generally considered to have been the result of tertiary syphilis. There has been much speculation about this issue since Nietzsche was for most of his life celibate.

Published in 1872, Nietzsche's first book, *Die Geburt der Tragödie aus dem Geiste der Musik* (*The Birth of Tragedy from the Spirit of Music*), touched off a controversy over the legacy of "the spirit of Greece" and over scholarly methodology as well. Unsupported by footnotes or Greek quotation, the work argues that Greek tragedy was born out of the music and dance of the frenzied Dionysian cult as a triumph of Appollonian, harmonious form; it ends with a celebration of Wagner's operas as a rebirth of tragedy and a call for a new kind of philosopher, an "artistic Socrates," capable of rational analysis tempered by the visions of art. From 1873 to 1876 Nietzsche published his four "untimely meditations" (*Unzeitgemässe Betrachtungen*), attacking what he saw as the cultural philistinism of the times, the *Zeitgeist*, and beginning his assault on the illusions of Christian morality and his development of a philosophy of self-creation. In 1878 he reached a personal crisis as a result of his public break with Wagner, the most prominent German artist of his time and a close personal friend. From 1878 to 1882 he published five books of mostly aphorisms, including three under the general title *Menschliches, Allzumenschliches* (1878; *Human, All Too Human*) and *Die fröhliche Wissenschaft* (1882; *The Gay Science*). Experimental in form and spirit, they attempt to "give style to one's character" and suggest his later philosophy of the will to power and the contrasts between master and slave moralities. These are developed more fully, as is the concept of the *Übermensch* ("overman"), or the self-creating individual, in his next three books, usually considered to be his best and certainly his most influential: *Also sprach Zarathustra* (1885; *Thus Spoke Zarathustra*), *Jenseits von Gut und Böse* (1886; *Beyond Good and Evil*), and *Zur Genealogie der Moral* (1887; *The Genealogy of Morals*). *Ecce Homo* presents a sarcastic review of his own past writings, but was withheld by his sister until 1908. Insanity disabled him for the rest of his life in 1889. His last book, *Nietzsche contra Wagner* (1888; *The Wagner Case*), was meant to clarify his differences with Wagner. Austrian psychoanalyst Sigmund Freud said of Nietzsche that he had "a more penetrating knowledge of himself than any other man who ever lived or was ever likely to live."

Nijinsky, Vaslav (1890–1950) Russian ballet dancer and choreographer. Born Vatslav Fomich Nijinsky in Kiev to acclaimed Polish dancers Thomas Laurentievich Nijinsky and Eleonora Bereda, Nijinsky studied from 1898 to 1907 at St. Petersburg's Imperial School of Dancing. His phenomenal ability was quickly recognized; after graduation he joined the Mariinsky Theater Imperial Ballet and was immediately given solo roles. He danced all the lead roles at the Mariinsky Theater and at the Bolshoi Theater in Moscow from 1907 until 1911, when he was dismissed from the Imperial Ballet in a controversy over a costume.

Nijinsky then danced primarily with a company directed by Serge Diaghilev, Nijinsky's mentor and, briefly, lover. At this time Nijinsky began to work as a choreographer, starting with *L'Après-midi d'un faune* (1912; *The Afternoon of a Faun*). He also choreographed Stravinsky's *Le Sacre du printemps* (1913; *The Rite of Spring*), though it is unclear if it was his bold style that sparked a riot during the first performance. In 1913 he married Roman de Pulszky, a young Hungarian woman, while on tour in Buenos Aires; Diaghilev fired him soon after out of jealousy. Nijinsky continued dancing until 1919, when he suffered a nervous breakdown and was diagnosed as schizophrenic. He spent most of the rest of his life in treatment and died in London in 1950.

Nilo-Saharan

African language group. Since there are approximately 1,000 distinct languages and dialects used in Africa, linguists accordingly differ in their classification systems, but the Nilo-Saharan group is generally considered to be one of the four enormous families of African languages, the others being the Niger-Kordofanian, the Afro-Asiatic, and the Khoisan. Ranging geographically from Mali to Egypt in the east and north and Tanzania in the south, Nilo-Saharan is comprised of at least six branches: Songhai, Saharan, Maban, Furian, Coman, and Chari-Nile. The Chari-Nile group is the largest of these and includes Nubian, unique in having a surviving written literature that dates from the medieval period.

Nin, Anaïs (1903–1977)

French-American author and diarist. Nin's literary merits remain a subject of dispute. She published several novels and a fair number of short stories in which many find an admirable feminist sensibility and psychological sensitivity, while others deride them as self-indulgent. Her fiction did not gain wide readership until the the publication of the first volume of her diaries which, though factually unreliable, present an occasionally compelling account of Nin's personal trials, as well as details of life among the Paris and New York literati.

Nin was born outside Paris, but taken to New York at age eleven and educated in the United States. She returned to Europe after completing her education, and it was in Paris that she began her celebrated relationship with the American novelist Henry Miller. She was instrumental in the publishing of Miller's *Tropic of Cancer* (1934), and for the next three decades each served the other as muse, confidant, adviser, and lover.

Nin's work challenges the reader in uncomfortable ways, both psychologically and formally. Some of her work betrays a Surrealist influence and a deliberate lack of concern with the construction of an easily comprehensible surface reality. More important, she has a constant interest and faith in the depths of human psychology. Her characters often feel their lives to be inadequate, which lead them to ill-considered affairs, forays into art, and other attempts to acquire a sense of completeness. Often unnerving, these personal quests reflect Nin's interest in psychoanalysis and the pervasive influence of the English novelist and poet D. H. Lawrence.

Her subjects are generally women, and it is as an accomplished archaeologist of the female psyche that she is often admired. Recently, much praise has been lavished on the posthumously published *Delta of Venus* (1977), a collection of short pieces of erotica.

Her other published works include *D. H. Lawrence: An Unprofessional Study* (1932); the novels *Cities of the Interior* (1959), *The House of Incest* (1936), *Seduction of the Minotaur* (1961), and *Collages* (1964); the five-volume series of novels *Ladders to Fire* (1946), *Children of the Albatross* (1947), *The Four-Chambered Heart* (1950), *A Spy in the House of Love* (1954), and *Solar Barque* (1958); a collection of short stories, *Under a Glass Bell* (1944); and a collection of three novelettes, *Winter of Artifice* (1942).

Nizam-ud-din Awliya (1236–1325)

Sufi saint, Chishti leader. Nizam-ud-din Awliya acted as spiritual adviser to Muslims and Hindus alike. Along with his friend Amir Khushrau (1253–1325), he cleared a space in Muslim culture for the acceptance of musical performance in the face of orthodox resistance to music, and championed the development and practice of Indian as opposed to "foreign" Persian, Arabic, and Asian music. He was proclaimed the patron saint of Muslim Delhi, and a great mosque bearing his name was built near his tomb in Delhi.

Nkrumah, Kwame (1909–1972)

First prime minister of modern Ghana. A prominent spokesman for Pan-Africanism and a dedicated anticolonialist, Nkrumah was born in Nkroful in the western province of what was then the Gold Coast colony. Educated as a teacher at Achimota College, he went abroad in 1935 after five years of teaching to study in the United States. In 1945 he settled in London, where he took up anticolonial political activity in earnest. He was an organizer and joint secretary of the fifth Pan-African Congress, held in Manchester, England, in 1945. In 1947 he returned to the Gold Coast to take the position of general secretary of the United Gold Coast Convention (UGCC), a nationalist, anticolonial political movement. In 1949 he broke with the UGCC to form the more radical Convention People's Party (CPP). In the first national elections in 1951, the CPP triumphed and Nkrumah was selected "Leader of Government Business" in the legislative assembly. On March 6, 1957, taking the name of Ghana and with Nkrumah as its first prime minister, the Gold Coast became the first sub-Saharan African nation to gain its independence from colonial rule. In 1960 a plebiscite made Ghana a republic, and another vote elected Nkrumah as its first president. As president, Nkrumah advocated policies of African socialism and Pan-Africanism; however, his term as president was compromised by corruption in the hunger for power, and his leadership oversaw the beginnings of economic decline in Ghana. In 1966 he was ousted in a military coup and forced into exile in Guinea, where he died.

Noh drama

Japanese drama. Noh (or No) drama, an archaic Japanese form based on brief texts usually with very little plot. The Noh form is ascribed to Kan'ami Kiyotsugu (1333–1384), although it was his son Zeami Motokiyo who went on to develop it most fully. Though thousands of Noh plays are thought to have been written, a mere 250 are still performed. Performances of Noh plays are highly stylized and proceed extremely slowly; a play of a few hundred lines can be drawn out into a production of more than an hour. The atmosphere of Noh drama is uniformly tragic. Many devices are used to universalize and objectify what is otherwise a highly emotional and personalized experience. For example, the chorus may speak lines appropriate for the main character as he dances or mimes the action, and it is common for a character to speak lines that seem meant for another character, or to finish up another character's speech. Finally, a character may speak of himself in the third person. Performances integrate singing, speech, instrumental music (three drums and a flute), dancing, and mime into a unity in which no single element dominates. A particularly striking feature of the performances is the use of wood masks by the principal character and female characters (the actual performers are all male).

Nok

Ancient African culture. The name Nok was given to the culture of a group of people who lived in what are now the northern and central parts of Nigeria, in the area north of the confluence of the Niger and Benue rivers, from the fourth century B.C.E. to the second century C.E. Remains of this culture were first discovered in the area of the Jos Plateau, and similar artifacts have been found in the middle valley of the Benue River.

The Nok were also the earliest people yet known in this part of Africa who made iron tools and weapons. They also produced fine sculpture, usually of human forms, in terra-cotta (baked clay). These magnificent pottery heads and figures are the earliest known African sculptures. It is believed that the Nok had a well-organized economy and administrative system, and that their culture influenced later peoples of the region.

Nuer

African ethnic group. The Nuer, who call themselves Nath, principally inhabit the swamps and savannah on either side of the Nile in southern Sudan. The Nuer are a loose federation of tribes and distinguish among themselves between the tribes who live to the east of the Nile (the Eastern Nuer) and those to the west (the Western Nuer). Tribes are headed by chiefs, sacred figures with little political authority, and prophets, religious leaders who communicate with ancestor spirits.

Primarily pastoral herders, the Nuer also grow millet and maize and supplement their diets with fish harpooned from canoes or from dams built in rivers. Cattle play an extremely important role in their culture and society as a measure of wealth and status, as a source of meat and milk, as religious sacrifices, as brideprice, and as the basis of livelihood and prosperity.

Nuer society is highly regimented socially, divided into strict age sets and lineage and gender hierarchies. In recent years, some Nuer have pursued urban lifestyles in Khartoum, the Sudanese capital, but most remain rural herders.

Nyerere, [Kambarage] Julius (1922–)

First president of the United Republic of Tanzania. Nyerere, the son of a Zanaki chief, was born in Butiama in the former Tanganyika. After studying at what was then the nation's only secondary school, he went to Makerere College to study teaching. He taught for two years and then, with a government scholarship, went to Scotland's Edinburgh University as the first Tanganyikan to study at a British university. Nyerere received a master's degree in history and political economy in 1952.

After his return to Tanganyika, which was then a U.N. Trusteeship, Nyerere soon became a leader in the transition to independence. He joined the Tanganyika African Association (TAA), became its president in 1953, and turned it into the Tanganyika African National Union (TANU). In 1955 and 1956 Nyerere obtained hearings at the U.N. to request a set date for independence. The British administration refused to entertain the idea and appointed Nyerere to the Tanganyikan Legislative Council, but he resigned in 1957, impatient at the lack of progress toward independence. In the elections of 1958–59, TANU did exceptionally well, and in 1960 it won seventy out of seventy-one seats on the Legislative Council.

In September 1960 Britain granted Tanganyika self-rule, a move expedited by Nyerere's diplomatic efforts. Nyerere was chosen as prime minister in May 1961. In December Tanganyika gained full independence with Nyerere still at the helm, but in January of 1962 he stepped aside briefly to focus on grassroots political organization for national development. He helped establish the country as a republic and was elected its first president in December 1962.

A year later, in January 1964, a violent coup in Zanzibar set off military mutinies across East Africa. Nyerere went into hiding when the Tanganyika Rifles rebelled, and he had to call upon the British for help. When order was restored, Nyerere persuaded Zanzibar president Abeid Karume to unite with Tanganyika and form the United Republic of Tanzania in April 1964. Nyerere remained president, arguing for and maintaining a one-party system. The ruling party Chama Cha Mapinduzi (CCM; the Revolutionary Party)

was formed in 1977 when TANU merged with Zanzibar's Afro-Shirazi party. Elected to four successive five-year terms starting in 1965, Nyerere resigned the presidency in 1985 but remained chairman of CCM.

While in office, Nyerere promoted a form of socialism based on his idea of *ujamaa*, Swahili for "familyhood." Its philosophy and practice were outlined in his Arusha Declaration of 1967, which called for a self-sufficient, egalitarian society supported by cooperative agriculture. With this goal in mind, he collectivized farmlands and established *ujamaa* villages, to which two thirds of Tanzania's rural population were moved by 1970. His mass literacy campaigns and his establishment of universal public education earned him the nickname Mwalimu, or "Teacher," and at the time of his retirement Tanzania had one of the highest literacy rates in the world. His economic policies were not as successful; Tanzania continues to be one of Africa's poorest countries. Nyerere, however, remained devoted to socialist policies throughout his career, although he openly expressed doubts about the one-party system in 1990, when he resigned as president of CCM.

O

Ocampo, Victoria (1891–1979)

Argentine writer, editor, and publisher. Born Victoria Ocampo de Estradato to an upper-class Argentine family, Ocampo was raised primarily in Paris, and wrote in French until 1940. Her background afforded her the possibility of entering into the until then thoroughly male world of letters, but it also impeded her desire to join the theater in her early twenties.

Ocampo is best known as the founder and publisher of the literary journal *El Sur*. It was the first publication to issue the work of Argentine writer Jorge Luis Borges (1899–1986), and served as a leading journal in the Spanish-speaking world. It published both original works and works in translation of authors such as D. H. Lawrence (1885–1930), William Faulkner (1897–1962), Richard Wright (1908–1960), James Joyce (1882–1941), C. G. Jung (1875–1961), and Virginia Woolf (1882–1941), among others. At the suggestion of her close friend and mentor Spanish philosopher and essayist José Ortega y Gasset (1883–1955), Ocampo founded El Sur in 1931. At the time, many of Argentina's publications were embracing fascism, but El Sur came out strongly against totalitarianism. Throughout her life, Ocampo was thoroughly enmeshed in the international intellectual scene. In 1953 she was imprisoned for her opposition to the government of Juan Domingo Perón (1946–55; 1973–74). Only after her friends Chilean poet and educator Gabriela Mistral (1889–1957) and Indian prime minister Jawaharlal Nehru (1889–1964) interceded on her behalf was Ocampo released.

While primarily known as the publisher of El Sur, Ocampo was also an accomplished writer. Her work, much of which appeared in El Sur, has been collected in her Testimonios (1935; Testimonies) and six volumes of Autobiografía (Autobiography), published posthumously between 1979 and 1984.

O'Casey, Sean (1880–1964)

Irish playwright. Born John Casey, Sean grew up Protestant in a Dublin slum, the last of thirteen children of whom only five survived to adulthood. He worked as an ironmonger and a day laborer, gaining a lifelong sympathy for the worker's point of view. A Marxist, he participated in the Irish Transport and General Workers Union and became the first secretary of the Irish Citizen Army. As a political prisoner of the Easter Rebellion for Irish independence

in Dublin in 1916, O'Casey was nearly executed.

At the same time, he was reading widely and writing journal pieces and essays. His first play accepted by the Abbey Theater, in 1923, was The Shadow of a Gunman. First entitled On the Run, this play is considered to be the first effective representation of Dublin slum life on the Irish stage. In 1923 the Abbey produced Juno and the Paycock and Cathleen Listens, and in 1926 The Plough and the Stars. After this last production, Dublin erupted in a week of rioting because of the unflattering portrayal of the heroes of the Easter Rebellion. Although defended by Irish poet and dramatist W. B. Yeats (1865–1939), who was director of the Abbey Theater, O'Casey left Ireland and settled permanently in England. The Silver Tassie (1928) was rejected by Yeats, and this play marks a change in O'Casey's career from his earlier concern with society to a concern with language and its use as a vehicle to describe contemporary life. Along with many more plays, O'Casey wrote a six-volume autobiography between the years 1939 and 1954.

O'Connor, Flannery (1925–1964)

American short-story writer and novelist. One of the most distinctive of America's twentieth-century writers, O'Connor produced only two novels and about thirty stories in her short life. A devout Roman Catholic, she created grotesque, frequently comic pictures of the American South to illustrate her profound belief in the reality of the fall of man.

Mary Flannery O'Connor was born in Savannah, Georgia. A Roman Catholic in a predominantly Protestant rural South, O'Connor became aware early on of the need to defend and explain her faith. After graduating from the Georgia State College for Women, she studied creative writing at the University of Iowa. Her master's thesis there consisted of six stories, the last of which would become the opening of her first novel, *Wise Blood* (1952).

Her first short-story collection, *A Good Man Is Hard to Find*, was published in 1955 and brought O'Connor recognition as a master of short fiction. The title story is representative of O'Connor's grimly plotted and ironic stories, which concentrate on Southern life and build to violent climaxes. In "A Good Man Is Hard to Find" a crotchety grandmother has a darkly comic exchange with an escaped convict known as "the Misfit" before he murders her and her family. The stories insist on the literal nature of man's fall, God's judgment and the necessity for redemption. They are populated by outcasts through whom O'Connor demonstrates her belief that the most socially, physically, and politically repugnant people may be the most definitively "saved."

Her stories, with their obsession with guilt and judgment and their frequent use of symbolism, descend from Nathaniel Hawthorne's early tales. Parallels can also be drawn with twentieth-century authors, notably with Nathanael West's grotesque fictions and William Faulkner's biblically toned sagas of the Deep South, but O'Connor's eerie combination of blistering comedy and quite serious religious fervor is uniquely hers.

The second novel, *The Violent Bear It Away* (1960), and the second collection of stories, *Everything That Rises Must Converge* (1965), explore similar themes through an even darker lens. Shortly after completing these, O'Connor died of lupus. A collection of her occasional prose was published in *Mystery and Manners* in 1969, and *The Habit of Being* (1979) contains selections from her correspondence.

Oedipus

Legendary king of Thebes in Greek mythology. The figure of Oedipus occurs in many dramas, most notably in Sophocles' tragedy *Oedipus the King*. He has

also been incarnated in many diverse modern works, such as Russian-born American composer Igor Stravinsky's (1882–1971) opera *Oedipus Rex* and in Austrian psychoanalyst Sigmund Freud's (1856–1939) *Traumdeutung* (1900; *Interpretation of Dreams*) as the "Oedipus complex." In Freud's theory, this crucial stage of psychological development involves an obsessive desire for the parent of the opposite sex, and a corresponding rivalry with the parent of the same sex. According to Freud's study, however, this phase is usually resolved by the age of five, and in a much less violent manner than in the original Greek myth.

In the most common version of the myth, King Laius, the father of Oedipus, learns from an oracle that he will be killed by his own son. In desperation, Laius puts a spike through his son's feet and leaves him to die. Oedipus is rescued by an old shepherd and raised by the childless king of Corinth. From another oracle, revealed this time to Oedipus, he learns he will murder his father and marry his mother, and therefore, not knowing that the king and queen of Corinth are not his true parents, he leaves Corinth to avoid this fate. While outside the city, he kills Laius (unaware that Laius is his father) in an argument and journeys to Thebes. When Oedipus enters Thebes, he encounters the Sphinx, a monster-like creature with the body of a winged lion and the breast and face of a woman. After Oedipus solves the riddle of the Sphinx, in despair she kills herself and the city welcomes Oedipus as a savior and hero. In gratitude, Creon, the brother of Queen Jocasta, offers his sister in marriage. Oedipus marries Jocasta, but when the city is ravaged by drought, yet another oracle advises Creon to purge the city of Laius' killer. Since no one suspects that Oedipus is the killer, a search gets under way. However, soon after, it is revealed by the shepherd that Oedipus is the son of Jocasta and Laius.

The oracle's prophecy has been fulfilled. Jocasta kills herself, and Oedipus is horrified. In his anguish, Oedipus blinds himself with Jocasta's brooch, punishing the eyes that "saw" the truth.

Ogun

Yoruba god. Ogun is the god of war and iron in the Yoruba religion of Nigeria, Benin, and Togo. In Haiti he appears under the name of Ogou. Of the hundreds of orishás (deities) in the Yoruba pantheon, Ogun's worship is the most widespread. He is especially patronized by users of metal, such as soldiers and blacksmiths, and his protection is often sought by cyclists, mechanics, and truck drivers. As with the other orishás, Ogun was once human, and, having led a noteworthy life, he became an orishá upon his death. According to one version of his legend, he perished after he had murdered a number of people whose ritual vow of silence he had understood as a personal insult. Thus, Ogun represents the vagaries of violence and death, and the belief that culture cannot exist without the experiences of death and destruction.

Okigbo, Christopher [Ifeanyichukwu] (1932–1967)

Nigerian poet. Born in Ojoto, a small village in eastern Nigeria, Okigbo was the fourth of five children of a Catholic schoolteacher of Igbo heritage. He attended Catholic schools, the Umuahia Government College (secondary school), and the University of Ibadan, receiving a degree in classics in 1956. He worked as a teacher, an editor, a librarian at the University of Nkussa, and as secretary to the Nigerian minister of research and information; he was also the West African editor of the journal *Transition*. He published two volumes of poetry during his lifetime—*Heavensgate* (1962) and *Limits* (1964)—as well as poems in the journals *Horn*, *Black Orpheus*, and *Transition*. Offered the poetry prize at the 1966 Dakar Festival of Negro Arts, Okigbo declined it because he thought it racially exclusive to black writers, a concept he felt was "quite absurd." Deeply committed to political change, he resisted the 1930s neologism Négritude, a concept introduced by Aimé Césaire (1913–) and Léopold Senghor (1906–) that describes a particular mode of black experience and expression in a given culture, in the arts. He had begun planning to establish a publishing house along with Nigerian novelist Chinua Achebe (1930–) when he was killed while fighting on the Biafran side during the Biafran war of independence from Nigeria. His collected poems were published as *Labyrinths with Path of Thunder* (1971). His work shows the influence of Igbo mythology and the American modernists as well as his training in Greek and Latin.

Ophuls, Max (1902–1957)

German film director. Born Max Oppenheimer in Saarbrücken, Germany, to a conservative Jewish family, Ophuls changed his name to avoid embarrassing his parents when he became a stage director at the age of seventeen. In film Ophuls began his career as an actor and stage producer. By 1926 he was invited to direct at the Burgtheater in Vienna, where he met his wife, Hilde Wall, a well-known actress, with whom he had one child. Ophuls worked on films in Germany starting in 1930, after directing about two hundred plays in Germany and Austria. In 1933 he immigrated to France from Germany, and over the next six years directed films in France, Holland, and Italy. After the fall of France during World War II in 1940, Ophuls moved first to Switzerland and then to the United States. There he directed several Hollywood films, including *The Exile* (1947), *Letter from an Unknown Woman* (1948), *Caught* (1949), and *The Reckless Moment* (1949). He finally returned to France in 1950 to complete his last works, *La Ronde* (1950), *Le Plaisir* (1952; *House of Pleasure*), *Madame de . . .* (1953; *The Diamond Earrings*), and *Lola Montès* (1955; *The Sins of Lola Montez*).

Ophuls is renowned for his distinctive cinematography: his films, particularly the later films from the 1950s, all reflect a highly developed style involving ornate decor and a mobile camera technique of tracking and crane shots that often inject objects between the characters and camera. This creates what has been called a visual "baroque texture" that consistently emerges from his films despite the changes in their setting and circumstances of production. Once disparaged by critics for what was seen as an overemphasis on style and neglect of thematic content, Ophuls's films gained admirers in the 1960s after their reevaluation in the context of feminism for the sensitive representation of their female characters.

Opium Wars

Anglo-Chinese conflict. The Opium Wars (1839–42) between China and Britain were a direct result of the illicit opium trade carried out by the British in China, though many other issues underlay the obvious. Opium smoking, which had been introduced from Java to China in the seventeenth century, resulted in severe addictions and an ever-increasing demand for opium. In 1729 only two hundred chests of opium were imported to China; however, the importation of opium increased dramatically after England took over the trade from Portugal and, in 1773, granted the East India Company a monopoly in producing opium in Bengal. Although the Company's monopoly was revoked in 1834, due to Chinese objections, by 1838 the number of imported chests had increased to 40,000. The Chinese government tried to curtail this trade, mainly because it was creating social problems at home while draining the nation's supply of silver currency. In 1839 the government finally confiscated some 20,000 chests from British merchants who had stored them in Cantonese warehouses. A few days later, a Chinese villager was killed by drunken British soldiers. When the British refused to hand over the men who were responsible, ostensibly because they objected to the Chinese legal system, British residents of Macao were ordered to leave, and in December of that year, all trade with Britain was banned. The British sent an expeditionary force that captured various ports and coastal territories between 1840 and 1842. Faced with a superior war machine, the Chinese gave in to British demands and signed the first of the so-called Unequal Treaties. The Treaty of Nanking (now Nanjing) in 1842 provided for a series of ports to be opened to unrestricted British trade, as well as the payments of huge indemnities to Britain, and the cession of Hong Kong, a hitherto sparsely inhabited island. The Opium Wars were one of a series of humiliations for China at the hands of Western powers, and are viewed by some historians as the event that sowed the seeds of a revolutionary nationalist uprising.

orishá

Yoruba god or spirit. Orishá, or *orixá*, is a general term for one of the many secondary gods in the Yoruba pantheon. The orishás may be personal spirits or general deities representing natural forces, and may be communicated with through trances or possession. Belief in many manifestations of the orishás has been transmitted through Yoruba culture to Brazil, Cuba, and the Caribbean. In many cults synthesizing African and Catholic elements, orishás have become associated with Christian saints, with some Brazilian cult churches sporting images both of the saints and their related orishás. For example, Oxossi, the Yoruba hunting god, is identified with St. George, the dragon slayer.

Orozco, José Clemente (1883–1949)

Mexican painter. Born in the state of Jalisco, Orozco studied at the School of Agriculture, the National Preparatory School, and the National School of Fine Arts (1908–14). He lost vision in one eye and the use of his left hand in a chemical accident at school; however, he began his career as a cartoonist and journalist, contributing to several publications. His first mural paintings, done at the National Preparatory School, reflect his interest in the Italian Renaissance, and during this period he also produced the murals *Omnisciencia* (1925; *Omniscience*) and *Revolución social* (1926; *Social Revolution*). First exhibiting his work in Paris in 1925 and in New York in 1930, he further enhanced his international reputation with his painting *Prometeo* (1930; *Prometheus*). The following year, Orozco executed perhaps his most famous murals, with their portraits of political figures such as Russian Communist leader Lenin (1870–1924), and Indian nationalist leader Mohandas Gandhi (1869–1948), at the New School for Social Research in New York City. Following a trip to Europe, he painted the frescoes called *Mundo prehispánico, conquista, civilización occidental* (1932–34; *An Epic of American Civilization*) at Dartmouth College in New Hampshire. These displayed his new style, vibrant color, and form expressing the panorama of American history from the Indian and Spanish past through the violent present.

Upon his return to Mexico, Orozco created a series of works that are considered to be masterpieces, including murals at the Palace of Fine Arts, the University of Guadalajara, the Government Palace, the Hospicio Cabaña, the Gabino Ortiz Library, the Mexican Supreme Court Building, the theater of the National School for Teachers, and the Museum of History at Chapultec. These treat a variety of subjects from Mexican history. He also painted *Bombardero de picada* (1940; *Threat of the Dive Bomber*), six movable panels, for an exhibition called "Twenty Centuries of Mexican Art" at the Museum of Modern Art in New York City, and helped found the National College, where he held six exhibitions from 1943 to 1948. His last finished project was the frescoes in the dome of the Legislative Chamber of the Government Palace in Guadalajara, completed just before his death. Since his work often depicts the horrors of war, he is often called the Mexican Goya. Along with painters Diego Rivera (1886–1957) and David Siqueiros (1896–1974), he is regarded as a founder of the renaissance of mural painting in Mexico in the twentieth century.

Ortega y Gasset, José (1883–1955)

Spanish philosopher and essayist. Born into an aristocratic family, Ortega y Gasset studied first with the Jesuits, then received a Ph.D. in philosophy from the University of Madrid. He studied for five years in German universities in Berlin, Leipzig, and Marburg, and was heavily influenced by the Neo-Kantian philosopher Hermann Cohen. Returning to Spain, he was appointed professor of metaphysics at the University of Madrid in 1910, a position he held until the outbreak of the Spanish Civil War in 1935. While there, in 1923 he founded *Revista de Occidente*, a review and a series of books that introduced Spain to Western, most particularly German, thought.

Along with many volumes of essays and magazine articles of cultural interest, Ortega y Gasset's writings include *La rebelión de las masas* (1930; *The Revolt of the Masses*), *Estudios sobre el amor* (1940; *On Love*), *En torno a Galileo* (1958; *Man and Crisis*), and *Que es Filosofía?* (1956; *What Is Philosophy?*). Ortega's philosophy, which he called the "metaphysics of vital reason," centers on the "radical reality" of human life in which everything is rooted. Later in his life, he was closely associated with the existentialists. Although forced to leave Spain at the outbreak of the Spanish Civil War in 1936, he returned in 1945. In 1948 he and Julián Marías founded the Instituto de Humanidades in Madrid.

Orwell, George (1903–1950)

English novelist. Born Eric Arthur Blair in Motihari, Bengal, Orwell moved with his family back to London when he was four. He attended private preparatory school in Sussex, then Eton. From 1922 to 1927 he served in the Indian imperial police in Burma. While in England on leave, Orwell resigned from the police to pursue a career as a writer. He moved to the East End of London to experience the life of the poor, and then he went to Paris. There he worked as a kitchen porter and dishwasher, contracting pneumonia before returning to England in 1929. His first book, *Down and Out in London and Paris* (1933), described his life living in the slums and working as, among other things, a teacher. While teaching, reviewing, and working in a bookshop, he wrote *Burmese Days* (1934), *A Clergyman's Daughter* (1935), and *Keep the Aspidistra Flying* (1936).

After he married Eileen O'Shaughnessy in 1936, the Left Book Club commissioned him to write about the poor and unemployed. *The Road to Wigan Pier* (1937) was part narrative reporting and part essay on class and socialism. This established Orwell's reputation as a political writer. He traveled to Spain to witness and participate in the Spanish Civil War and was wounded in 1937. After returning to England, he wrote *Homage to Catalonia* (1938), criticizing the orthodox left, though he considered himself to be a revolutionary socialist. Because his health was deteriorating, Orwell was denied entry into the English armed services during World War II, so he worked in various home-front

positions, including two years with the BBC (1941–43). His two antiutopian novels, *Animal Farm* (1944) and *1984* (1949), were written during the next few years and became his most famous works. These were savage criticisms of the power of rulers and authority in society. After recurrent bouts with tuberculosis, Orwell died in London.

Orzeszkowa, Eliza Pawłoska (1841–1910)

Polish novelist. Orzeszkowa spent much of her life in Grodno, a Polish town that had reverted to Russian control in 1795. She was raised by her mother, a staunch Polish nationalist; her father, who died while she was still in her infancy, was a rich landowner. In 1858 she was married to Piotr Orzesko, a man twenty years her senior; the marriage was annulled eleven years later. With the coming of the social unrest precipitated by the emancipation of the serfs, Orzeszkowa played an active role in the national insurrection that began in January 1863 and was finally crushed in April 1864. In the course of the Russian reprisals that followed, her husband was exiled to Siberia and his property was confiscated. Orzeszkowa took up residence on her family's estate, where she undertook a program of self-education and began to pursue a literary career.

In her first novel, *Obrazek z lat głodowych* (1866; *Picture of the Hungry Years*), she focused, with a rather archaic style, on the misery of rural life, a theme to which she would frequently return. Three years later, she achieved her first popular success with *Pan Graba* (1869; *Mr. Graba*), a novel centered on the deficiencies of a traditional aristocratic education. In 1873 she published *Marta*, a work in which she dramatizes the necessity of providing women with a professional education; this novel achieved worldwide notoriety and was widely embraced by the feminist movement. Five years later she wrestled with the question of Jewish identity in *Meir Ezofowicz*

(1878). Still later in *Nad Niemnem* (1888; *On the Banks of the Nieman*), she returned to the period immediately following the insurrection of 1863, uniquely combining Polish nationalist sentiment with sharp social observation and criticism. Orzeszkowa's interest in social problems places her among the Polish "Positivists," with their emphasis on the rationalistic and didactic potentials of literature. Yet there is also a "romantic" vein in her work in those moments when she expresses the traditional values of Polish nationalism and agrarianism.

Orzeszkowa wrote prolifically; as early as the 1880s she was able to publish a forty-seven-volume set of her collected works. In addition to her novels, she published a substantial number of short stories.

Osiris

Ancient Egyptian god of the underworld. Osiris' cult center was in Abydos in Upper (southern) Egypt. He seems originally to have been a local god of Busiris in Lower Egypt. Much of what is now known about the later, widespread myth of Osiris is provided in Plutarch's *Of Isis and Osiris*, which contains the only complete account. Egyptian sources are scarce and less comprehensive, but do support Plutarch's version.

In the most established form of the myth, Osiris is the eldest son of the earth god Geb and the sky goddess Nut. He and his sister-consort Isis rule Egypt as king and queen. Osiris is killed by his brother Seth, who tricks him into entering a coffin and then sets it adrift on the Nile. Isis retrieves the body from Byblos in Lebanon, but Seth dismembers it and scatters the pieces across Egypt (a mythical explanation for Osiris' widespread cult). Isis collects and reassembles the body while Osiris' son, Horus, avenges his father. Horus deposes Seth and becomes ruler of the living; Osiris, restored, rules the dead in the underworld.

Death signified identification with Osiris, a privilege originally reserved for kings but eventually extended to all men. This identification meant not that the dead would be resurrected, but rather that they would enjoy immortality in the underworld. Osiris worship was a central part of funereal rites, and bodies were embalmed and swathed like that of the god. The rites often involved a pilgrimage to Abydos, which was then recorded on the walls of the deceased's tomb.

In addition to his role as king of the dead, Osiris was also a fertility god credited with having introduced agriculture to the Egyptians; the cyclical nature of his death and rebirth is associated with the cycles of growth and destruction prompted by the flooding of the Nile. Osiris is depicted as a mummy by some statues, while in drawings he usually has dark flesh. He has a plaited beard, wears a crown, and holds in his hands the crook and flail of Egyptian kings and the scepter of the gods.

Ottoman

Turco-Islamic empire. The Ottoman empire, which lasted from the years 1300 to 1918, was founded by Osman (1258–1326). According to legend, Osman was born in Söğüt (near present-day Eskisehir, Turkey) in 1258. The rapid Ottoman rise was due to two major factors: proximity to the disintegrating Byzantine empire, and Osman's apparent ability to attract a mercenary military force, both Turk and Byzantine, initially drawn by the promise of booty but subsequently united in dual loyalties to the Ottoman dynasty and to Islam. Osman first aimed at the conquest of Bursa, which succumbed in 1326, and became the first capital. By the mid fourteenth century, the Ottomans had gained a foothold in the Balkans. Murad I (r. 1360–1389), grandson of Osman, succeeded his father, Orkhan (Orhan) I (r. 1326–1360), only after eliminating his rival brothers, setting a precedent to be followed by the succeeding sultans. He was also responsible for establishing the famous standing army, the Janissaries, the terror of Europe until the late seventeenth century.

Byzantine imperial rule, now combined with Central Asian military traditions and Islamic moral mediation, formed the striking amalgam of cultures that made up Ottoman civilization. Mehmed (Mehmet) II (r. 1451–1481) both codified sultanic law as a complement to Islamic religious law (*Shari'ah*) and after capturing Constantinople (Istanbul), the Byzantine crown jewel, in 1453, established the educational and palace institutions characteristic of the empire for the next three hundred years. The reigns of Selim I (r. 1512–1520) and Suleyman I (r. 1520–1566) saw the greatest expansion of the empire, with the incorporation of Egypt by Selim I in 1517, and the annexation of much of Hungary in the west and Baghdad in the east under Suleyman I, whose long rule is considered the zenith of Ottoman glory. At its greatest extent, the Ottoman empire stretched west through North Africa and to the gates of Vienna, south to Yemen, east to Baghdad, and north into the Crimea and Poland.

The Ottoman aristocracy shared a common, carefully nourished culture, the Ottoman Way, a hybrid of the Arabic, Persian, and Turkish civilizations, embodied in the Ottoman language they spoke and the Muslim religion they professed. The magnificent mosque complexes and manuscripts that survive are adequate testimony to the vitality of the Ottoman empire. The non-Muslim groups of the empire, the Christians and the Jews, were organized in their own communities (*millet*) and governed by their own religious leaders, participating only partially in Ottoman affairs.

It was the second unsuccessful attempt to conquer Vienna in 1683 that alerted Europe to the vulnerability of the seemingly indomitable Ottomans. The empire now entered a long period of accommodation to limited and shrinking borders, especially after the Treaty of Karlowitz in 1699, when most of Hungary was returned to Europe. The eighteenth century saw a further reduction of Ottoman territory as a result of numerous wars, and the failure of the Janissaries prompted efforts under Selim III (r. 1789–1807) and Mahmud II (r. 1808–1839) to reorganize the army and the central administration. Reform accelerated during the Tanzimat period, inaugurated by the 1839 Gulhane declaration of the equality of rights and citizenship. By the mid nineteenth century, the political and economic affairs of the now impoverished empire were largely in the hands of Europe, especially Great Britain. At the beginning of the reign of Abdulhamid II (r. 1876–1909), parliamentary government and a constitution were introduced but suspended shortly afterward, when the Ottomans entered war with Russia in 1877.

Nationalism, meanwhile, had prompted rebellions leading to independence from the empire, first in Greece (1821) and subsequently in the Balkans. The Arab and Turkish populations were the last to catch the nationalistic fever, even though Abdulhamid II belatedly strove for legitimization by reviving many of the Islamic aspects of his empire, such as the caliphate. Neither Pan-Islamism nor Pan-Turkism succeeded in stopping the progress toward dissolution. Abdulhamid II's absolutism was cut short by the 1908 revolution of the Committee of Union and Progress, but it had little chance of controlling the nationalistic fervor of the Balkans, whose Bulgarians, Greeks, Serbians, and Montenegrins united briefly to throw out the Ottomans. By 1913 all the European territories of the empire except the area around Edirne (Adrianople) and Istanbul were lost. The Committee of Union and Progress threw its lot in with the Germans during World War I, subjecting the peoples of Anatolia to four years of misery and suppression, as in the forced deportation of the Armenians in 1915. By the 1918 Armistice, the Ottoman empire was effectively dissolved. While the European powers debated the disposition of the occupied territories, however, Mustafa Kemal Atatürk (1881–1938) rallied the Turks and created the republic of Turkey, which was finally accepted by the international community in the Treaty of Lausanne in 1923.

Ovid (43 B.C.E.–17 C.E.)

Roman poet. The major literary figure of the Augustan era, Ovid wrote poetry distinguished by elegance and sensuousness. The *Metamorphoses*, considered his masterpiece, has been a vital source for the stories of classical mythology. His influence was felt by subsequent Roman writers and renewed in the Middle Ages, particularly in the twelfth century, when poets borrowed his style and themes. He was the most influential Latin poet of the Renaissance, and later writers such as Milton and Shakespeare also drew on his work.

Publius Ovidius Naso was born in Sulmo (modern Sulmona), ninety miles east of Rome. His father was a knight and expected Ovid to work in a profession appropriate to his social position. He particularly hoped that his son would become a lawyer and provided Ovid with an excellent education in rhetoric. This training was a significant influence on Ovid's carefully crafted and often didactic poetic style. After serving in several minor judicial offices, Ovid committed himself completely to poetry.

Ovid's first poems were almost all about love, and although he destroyed many of his early works, those he saved were published as the *Amores* (*Loves*) in five books over twenty years (beginning in 20 B.C.E). Most of these poems focused on Ovid's love for a woman named Corinna, thought to be a fictional figure. During this period he also wrote the *Heroides*, which expounds further on the nuances of love. Ovid's own romantic life during this period seems to have thrived: he married three times, the last time to a relative of his patron Paullus Fabius Maximus.

Around 1 B.C.E., Ovid completed his *Ars amatoria* (*The Art of Love*) in three books; the first two books contained advice to men on seduction, while the last book addressed women. The highly successful work ran counter to Emperor Augustus' efforts toward moral reforms and even made thinly veiled references mocking Augustus.

Ovid wrote a version of the *Medea*, now lost, and began the *Fasti* (*Calendar*), which was to be a cycle of poems about the months of the year, though he completed only six before his death. The *Metamorphoses*, written by 8 C.E., is an epic consisting of different stories about characters who change shape. It is structured chronologically and spans the creation of the world to the rule of Julius Caesar; it masterfully brought new life to old stories from Greek mythology and Roman legend. Ovid's retellings are more about human emotion than the physical changes: the metamorphoses are purely physical, while the important personal traits of the characters remain unchanged.

Shortly after the *Metamorphoses* was completed, Ovid was banished by Augustus and his books were removed from public libraries. The full reasons for the exile are unknown; Ovid himself mentions the *Ars amatoria* and a "mistake." It is thought that this might refer to Ovid's knowledge of the libertine behavior of Augustus' daughter Julia and his failure to bring it to the emperor's attention. To protest his sentence, Ovid burned the original manuscript of the *Metamorphoses* (his friends already had copies), but nevertheless was forced to leave at the end of 8 C.E. for Tomis on the Black Sea (in modern Romania). Though the frontier town was periodically attacked by hostile northern tribes and suffered cold winters, Ovid was revered there and exempted from taxes. Still, most of Ovid's writing during the period consisted of complaints and rejected appeals for recall (in his *Sorrows* and *Letters from the Black Sea*).

Oviedo [y Valdes], Gonzalo Fernández de (1478–1557)

Spanish historian, first ethnographer of the American continent. He was born in Madrid, became a page to the Duque de Villahermosa, and later worked for the *infante* Don Juan. He also expanded his education in Italy, where he pursued his military and literary interests, finding the keys in Renaissance humanism to understanding and reconstructing the historic realities he would write about in the New World. He first traveled to the New World at the age of thirty-six, accompanying Pedrarias Dávila's expedition as inspector of mines and general scribe. Pedrarias's expedition was received by Spanish explorer Vasco Núñez de Balboa (1475–1519), whom Pedrarias later deposed, thereby prompting Oviedo's return to Spain in October 1515 to report Pedrarias's misconduct. Upon his return, he published what may have been the first novel written in Spanish in America, *Claribalte* (1515), and confronted Bartolomé de Las Casas, disagreeing with the friar's position on the conversion of the Indians. Although he struggled to record acts of gratuitous cruelty on the part of the *conquistadores* and the *encomenderos*, Oviedo believed that the conquest was God's design, that Spain had sufficient claims to impose its political dominion and appropriate all things, and that the *encomienda* (a grant of land that included the Indians inhabiting it) conformed to the needs of the conquest, which in turn was necessary for the incorporation of this continent into Christendom. Oviedo returned to the New World in 1520, remaining six years and returning to Spain after his wife's death and a quarrel with Pedrarias. In 1526, in response to a special re-quest from Emperor Charles V, Oviedo was able to recount from memory a *Sumario de la natural y general historia de las Indias* (*Summary of the Natural History of the West Indies*), which he published that same year. In 1532 he was appointed official chronicler of the Indies, and worked for at least thirty-five years on what would become the *Historia general y natural de las Indias*, his magnum opus. The work is divided into three parts and made up of fifty books that cover a period of over fifty years and detail every place in America that had been part of the conquest until 1549. He was quite explicit concerning the formal problems he encountered in the presentation of the material and in the task of historical reconstruction, problems that have remained of interest to contemporary critics and analysts who see Oviedo's work as representing many of the problems encountered by Latin American writers struggling with the issue of cultural identity. Oviedo's work is underwritten by a unifying value system typical of a sixteenth-century Spaniard— including militant religiosity, devout allegiance to the monarchy, and to the ideals of chivalry and nobility. Oviedo died in Santo Domingo.

Owen, Robert (1771–1858)

British socialist and reformer. Born in Wales, the son of a shopkeeper, Owen quit school at the age of nine. Nevertheless, by eighteen he was manager of one of Manchester's largest cotton mills. In 1799 he and several partners purchased the mills at New Lanark, Scotland; of the 2,000 people connected with the mills, five hundred were children from the poorhouses of Glasgow and Edinburgh. Addressing himself to their condition, Owen opened a store that sold goods at nearly cost, regulated the sale of liquor, taught habits of cleanliness and thrift, and established a school to educate the children. His original partners worried him about the expense of all these provisions for the workers, so Owen found new partners that included English philosopher Jeremy Bentham (1748–1832). In 1813 he published his system of educational philanthropy as *A New View of Society, or Essays on the Principle of the Formation of the Human Character.*

Owen used his mill as a model on which to base his theories of social reform. In 1825 he bought 30,000 acres of land in Indiana and tried to establish a community he named New Harmony; however, the community failed by 1828, due to differing views over issues of government and religion.

His experiments encouraged young workers to start societies and papers to advocate his views, and when Owen returned to England he found himself the leading exponent of the workers' point of view. Soon he was involved in the Equitable Labour Exchange of 1832 and the formation of the Grand National Consolidated Trades Union in 1833–34. After the government and the courts severely repressed the latter in 1834, British socialism became dormant for a number of years before again influencing unionism. Owen's *Autobiography* (1857–58) is considered one of the great documents of the early socialist movement.

Owens, Jesse (1913–1980)

American athlete. Born in Decatur, Alabama, Owens won athletic fame by setting three world records and tying a fourth all in a single day. On May 25, 1935, he broke world records in the 220-yard dash, 220-yard low hurdles, and the running broad jump. That same day, he tied the 100-yard dash world record. During the XI Olympiad in 1936 in Berlin, Owens, who was called "the Tan Cyclone," was awarded four gold medals—a feat unparalleled by any other athlete in Berlin that Olympiad year. In fact, no athlete besides Owens won more than one gold medal. Owens's accomplishments met with chagrin

from Nazi dictator Adolf Hitler and affronted his theories on Aryan supremacy. Owens's world broad jump record endured for thirty-two years.

Oyo empire

Yoruba empire. The Oyo empire was the most powerful of the Yoruba states during the peak of its power, roughly between 1650 and 1750. Its capital, the town of Oyo, was situated slightly to the north of present-day Oyo in Nigeria. Legend has it that Oyo's first *alafin*, or ruler, was a son of Oduduwa, the mythical ancestor of the Yoruba people. In the sixteenth century, Oyo began its ascent to power under the *alafin* Orompoto, who established a cavalry and maintained a trained army. During the first half of the eighteenth century, Oyo subjugated the neighboring kingdom of Dahomey; in 1818 Dahomey regained its independence from Oyo. Numerous internal disputes, war with Dahomey, and an invasion by the Fulani from the north contributed to the collapse of the empire at this time. In the mid-1830s the old town of Oyo was destroyed by a Fulani invasion, and the capital was subsequently relocated to its present site. In the treaty of 1888, after the Yoruba civil wars of the middle part of the century, Oyo, along with much of Yorubaland, was placed under British rule.

Oyono, Ferdinand Léopold (1929–)

Cameroonian novelist. While he was still a child, Oyono's mother, a devout Catholic, left her traditional, polygamous husband. She worked as a seamstress to support the family, and Oyono, to help out, served for some years as a priest's "boy." Educated in Cameroon and in Paris, Oyono writes novels that often explore Cameroonian life under colonial rule. His first, *Une vie de boy* (1956; *Houseboy*), was written in the form of a diary kept by a houseboy in Cameroon, and was based on Oyono's own experience as a houseboy, which he recounts bitterly. Oyono's other novels, including *Le Vieux Négre et la medaille* (1956; *The Old Man and the Medal*) and *Le Pandemonium* (1971; *The Big Confusion*), have proved enormously popular and have been translated into several languages.

Oz, Amos (1939–)

Israeli author. Born Amos Klausner, Oz was raised in a conservative, scholarly middle-class Jewish family. At fifteen, he left home to join Kibbutz Hulda, an Israeli commune, where he continues to live with his wife and their three children. In addition to his compulsory three years of military service from 1957 to 1960, Oz fought in both the Six-Day War and the Yom Kippur War.

Most of Oz's fiction has been directly inspired by his own experiences on the kibbutz and in the army. *Makom acher* (1966; *Elsewhere, Perhaps*) is considered by many critics to be the best representation of life on a kibbutz, although in his much later book *Menucha nechonah* (1982; *A Perfect Place*), Oz returns to the setting of the modern kibbutz. *Michael sheli* (1968; *My Michael*) was the first book written by Oz to be published in English. Oz's criticism of his homeland has made him a controversial writer in Israel and abroad. Writing a good deal of nonfiction about contemporary Israel, Oz does not hesitate to use his international reputation to influence the political situation at home. His best-known work of nonfiction is a collection of interviews with prominent Israelis entitled *Po ve'sham b'eretz Yisra'el bistav* (1982; *In the Land of Israel*).

Ozu Yasujiro (1903–1963)

Japanese film director. Revered as a film director whose work accurately reflects traditional Japanese family life, Ozu was born in Tokyo in 1903 into a family that would greatly influence and determine the themes and subject matter of his future films. Raised by an overprotective mother, Ozu felt keenly the perpetual absence of his father, who had to live away from the rest of the family in order to work. It is not surprising that one of the major themes in Ozu's films is the disruptive power of work on family life, or that domestic family life became his primary subject matter. Ozu rose quickly in the Japanese film world from an assistant cameraman to a director, and his career spanned the silent film and the color sound film.

Perhaps one of the most distinctive elements of Ozu's films is his simplicity of style. The camera is placed low to the floor, so the perspective is that of a person sitting on a mat in a traditional Japanese room. Ozu used only simple cuts in his films, and in his dialogue he tried to imitate the inconsequential speech of everyday life. Ozu's most highly acclaimed film is *Tokyō monogatari* (1953; *Tokyo Story*), which examines the materialism and bustle of modern life, and its antithetical relationship to the family-oriented values of traditional Japanese life. Some of Ozu's other films that were important in establishing his international reputation include *Banshun* (1949; *Late Spring*), *O-chazuke no aji* (1952; *The Flavor of Green Tea over Rice*), and *Sōshun* (1956; *Early Spring*).

P

Pagan

Classical Burmese city. Pagan was founded in the mid ninth century by the ethnic Burmese. For two hundred years Pagan remained just one of a number of independent cities, but with the reign of King Anawrahta (r. 1044–77), the period of Pagan's greatness began. Anawrahta conquered the Mon people, who until then had ruled much of the south of Burma. The Mons already had a strong artistic and intellectual tradition which Anawrahta and later King Kyanzittha were wise enough to incorporate into the Pagan empire. Anawrahta was converted to the Theravāda form of Buddhism (adopted from Ceylon around 1056) by the monk-evangelist Shin Arahan and spread his religion to his domain. Theravāda became the official religion of the Pagan empire, and thence of all classical Burmese civilization, but it was blended by the people with older animistic ideas and practices to create the uniquely Burmese style of Buddhism.

The city of Pagan was richly decorated with architectural beauty, mostly invested in temples and public buildings, which show the influence of Mon aesthetics as well as a high level of craftsmanship. In its day, Pagan controlled the ports of Burma as well as the inland and was one of the greatest economic powers of the Far East. The Pagan era was relatively peaceful, without hindrance to economic and cultural development.

Pagan prospered for two centuries after the time of Anawrahta before its defeat by the armies of Mongol emperor Kublai Khan in 1287. The Pagans were ultimately unable to hold back the Mongol forces, fortified by many Shan people of the northern hills, who had never been brought under Pagan rule. Although defeated as an empire, the influence of Pagan religion, art, and history persisted, and today Pagan is seen as the foundation of the culture of Burma (now called Myanmar). The old city of Pagan is still standing, and temples dating from the twelfth century are popular pilgrimage sites.

Pahlavi dynasty

Iranian dynasty. The founder of the dynasty, Reza Shah Pahlavi (1878–1944), was from a family of chiefs of the Pahlavan clan. The son of an officer, Rheza Khan (his original name) enlisted in the military, rising rapidly through the ranks of the Persian Cossack Brigade. In 1921 he initiated a coup against the reigning Qajar dynasty, headed by Ahmad Shah, installing a figurehead as prime minister and himself as minister of war and commander of the armies. He used his position to raise money and consolidate power, and he became prime minister in 1923 and shah in 1925, after the Majles (parliament) deposed the absentee Ahmad Shah. Ruling as a virtual dictator, Reza Shah set about revising Iran's foreign policy, once dominated by Great Britain and the Soviet Union, both of whom had maintained occupying forces since World War I. His domestic modernization program included building the Trans-Iranian Railway and the first university, abolishing veils for women, encouraging Western dress, and mitigating the power of the Islamic clergy. In 1935 he changed the name of the country from Persia to the more traditional Iran. During World War II, however, Great Britain and the Soviet Union occupied the country once again to use it as a conduit for supplies, and Reza Shah was forced to abdicate in favor of his eldest son in 1941. The British government sent him to South Africa, where he died in 1944.

Muhammad Reza Shah Pahlavi (1919–1980), Reza Shah Pahlavi's son, was born in Tehran and educated in Switzerland, returning to Tehran in 1935 to attend the military academy there. Upon his father's deposition in 1941, he became the shah and more moderately continued his father's program of Westernizing the country. He survived an assassination attempt in 1949 and was forced to flee the country in 1953 by supporters of Muhammad Mosaddeq, who advocated nationalizing the British-owned oil industry. With the help of the United States, Muhammad Reza was restored only a few days later, as were the foreign oil interests. With further U.S. aid, he instituted the White Revolution, a series of reforms that included redistribution of land, expansion of transportation and communications infrastructure, increased industrialization, improved health care, and literacy programs.

Despite his political coups and the nation's economic success during the oil boom of the 1970s, domestic opposition grew to his dictatorial Westernization, his government's corruption and profligacy, and his suppression of dissent with the notorious secret police, Savak. Riots grew widespread and increasingly violent until in January 1979 the shah left the country, and the popular Shi'ite religious leader, the Ayatollah Ruholla Khomeini, returned from exile in Paris to direct the revolution. The shah refused to abdicate, but a referendum in April established an Islamic republic with Khomeini as its head. In November revolutionaries occupied the U.S. embassy in Tehran, declaring that they would release their more than fifty hostages if the shah were returned to stand trial. The shah moved among several friendly countries, finally being granted asylum in Egypt, where he died of lymphatic cancer in 1980.

Palés Matos, Luis (1898–1959)

Puerto Rican poet. Palés was born in the backwater town of Guayama to Don Vicente Palés Anés and Doña Consuelo Matos Vicil, both poets. Don Vicente died in 1913, having just finished reciting his poem "El cementerio" ("The Cemetery"), a fact that seems to have impressed the young Palés deeply. Palés started writing poetry at thirteen and published his first volume, *Azaleas*, in 1915. After quitting school for financial reasons, Palés became a secretary and a bookkeeper and also worked in journalism. In 1918 he married Natividad Suliveres, who died one year later, leaving him with a son, Edgardo. In 1921 Palés moved to San Juan, where he founded the first avant-garde literary movement in Puerto Rico, calling it Diepalismo. The movement was short-lived and created only one manifesto and a poem collaboratively written. From 1919 to 1925 Palés produced two unpublished manuscripts, *The Darkened Palace* and *Songs at Mid-Life*. In March 1926 his first Afro-Antillean poem, "Pueblo negro" ("Black Town"), was published, followed by several more in the *danza negra* ("black dance") genre. His Negrista poems were collected in a book called *Drumbeats of Kink and Blackness* (1937). These works gave Palés Matos the title, along with African-Cuban poet

Nicolás Guillén (1902–1989), of founder of the literary movement known as Negrismo. The poetry of this genre sought to highlight and exalt the contribution of black tradition and heritage to Latin American history and culture, creating a radically new Caribbean poetry by enriching its vocabulary with words, themes, symbols, images, and rhythms of African-American and African folklore and dance. Matos was criticized both for using a politically suspect theory of race (based on Spengler's *The Decline of the West*) and for writing on behalf of a people whose color he did not share (Matos was white), making his poetry both controversial and influential.

After *Tuntún*, Palés stopped writing Negrista poetry, dedicating himself to "Antillean" verse that did not emphasize African cultural elements. In 1949 he began a cycle of love poems dedicated to a woman he named "Filí-Melé." The first edition of Palés's book *Poesía 1915–1956* appeared in 1957, two years before his death from a heart attack.

Palestine

Eastern Mediterranean coastal region. Since approximately 3500 B.C.E., Palestine has been the home of Semitic peoples. By 100 B.C.E., it had already been conquered and ruled by the Egyptians, Jews, Greeks, Seleucids, and others. In 638 C.E., the Muslims took Jerusalem, offering protection to its inhabitants, and Islamic rule continued for 1,300 years, although Europeans attempted (at times successfully) to seize control of the area between the eleventh and thirteenth centuries during the Crusades.

Jerusalem, long one of Palestine's important cities, is a holy site to Judaism, Christianity, and Islam. During the first year and a half of the Islamic era, Muslims prayed facing Jerusalem. The city is also believed to be the site of the Prophet's night journey, an event recorded in the Qur'ân. Tradition holds that Muhammad met all of God's prophets, from Abraham to Jesus, in the Holy Sanctuary of Jerusalem, and led them in prayer. Thus, Islam inherited the Jewish and Christian traditions concerning Jerusalem, and Muslim rulers quickly erected a Holy Sanctuary containing two major monuments, the al-Aqsâ Mosque and the Dome of the Rock. This Sanctuary is the third holiest sanctuary in Islam, and is an important pilgrimage site.

European intervention in Palestine in the twentieth century proved disastrous. Palestine was dragged into World War I on the side of the Germans by its Ottoman rulers. The British, in the Husain-McMahon Agreement of 1915, gained the support of the Arab leaders in return for the guarantee of independence of Palestine at the end of the war. However, in 1917 British diplomat Lord Balfour pledged to support a homeland for European Jews in Palestine. European Jews immigrated to British-ruled Palestine in increasing numbers. Suppressing the resistance of the majority of the population, the British led the United Nations (U.N.) in partitioning Palestine, and surrendered the territory directly into the hands of Jewish forces in 1948.

In the aftermath of the Israeli occupation of Palestinian territories, the Palestinians have tried for years to bring their situation to the attention of the world community, using both violent and nonviolent methods of resistance. On November 15, 1988, an independent but landless State of Palestine was declared by the governing Palestine National Council, and Yasser Arafat, head of the Palestinian Liberation Organization, was elected head of state. In 1994 the Palestinians were granted self-rule in the Gaza strip and the West Bank. Since then, economic conditions and the opposition to peace—by militant Palestinians and Israelis alike—have undermined recent gains. In 1995 the assassination of Israeli Prime Minister

Yitzhak Rabin and subsequent election of Likud party leader Benjamin Netanyahu, a hardliner unsympathetic to Palestinian concerns, suggest that resolution is still distant.

Pan-Africanism

Ideology of African unification. The concept of Pan-Africanism presupposes the belief that enough common cultural characteristics exist among the myriad of societies in Africa and the diaspora across political and geographic borders to justify the creation of one central African state that will replace all others.

Pan-Africanism evolved during the late nineteenth century when a small, educated, elite group of Americans of African descent, united with freed slaves and their descendants, attempted to establish modern national governments in parts of West Africa. In addition, discontented with predominant notions of white racial superiority and the exclusion of Africans from many social and political positions, many African Christians challenged foreign mission control and established wholly independent "Ethiopian" or "Zionist" churches. These institutions provided the means to mobilize Pan-Africanist sentiment and fight against oppressive colonial rule in several rebellions, including those in Natal (1906) and Nyasaland (1915).

In its most radical form, Pan-Africanism rejects white society entirely. Certain adherents, such as the nineteenth-century intellectual Edward Wilmot Blyden (1832–1912), asserted that blacks could achieve their full potential only in Africa. Subsequent black leaders, most notably Marcus Garvey (1887–1940), advocated this separatist "back-to-Africa" movement, and it was its inherent notion of self-definition through race pride that fueled the "Black Power" movement of the 1960s in the United States. Ironically, most African states gained their independence during the 1960s, thereby decreasing the

likelihood that any one of them would give up their newly acquired sovereignty for a higher ideal that up until that point had not been realized. Nonetheless, certain African leaders were unflagging in their attempts to create a black national state, as seen by the establishment of the Organization of African Unity (OAU) in 1963. This new development left Africans of the diaspora, the originators of the movement, somewhat neglected in its revised continental vision of Pan-Africanism. Alternative assemblies served to transcend international borders, and the sixth Pan-African Congress (1974) served as a complement to the OAU but still rivaled it for the political direction of the Pan-Africanist movement.

Pan-Africanism did not make substantial advances primarily because few of its advocates could agree on how to create a new African state. While some leaders, such as Kwame Nkrumah, former president of Ghana, envisioned a facile merging of African states by accommodating the continent's three major philosophical systems—traditional, Islamic, and Euro-Christian—others believed that the centralization process would take decades, if not centuries, to complete. In addition, Pan-Africanism did not make real progress due to the fact that no one person, or group of people, could organize Africans from such divergent and often conflicting cultures. The trend since the 1970s toward Pan-Arabism also indicates further breakdown of the movement and in fact seems explicitly at odds with the concept of Pan-Africanism. Today the term still resonates in many societies in the notions of black pride, Afro-centrism, and separatism, all of which connote an ideal for many blacks in oppressed circumstances.

Panipat

Indian city. Located in the Haryana state of northwestern India, fifty miles north of Delhi, Panipat is perhaps best known for the three decisive battles that were fought there between Mughal rulers and opposing forces in the sixteenth and eighteenth centuries. The first battle occurred in 1526, between the Mughal chief and ruler of Kabul, Babur, and Sultan Ibrahim Lodi of Delhi. Unable to match the Mughal artillery and cavalry, Ibrahim lost his life and his army was defeated. With this victory, Babur became the first sultan of the powerful Mughal dynasty, which lasted from 1526 to 1857.

In the second battle, in 1556, the young emperor Akbar's regent, Bairum Khan, defeated the Hindu general Hemu, minister of the Afghan king Adil Shah Sur. This battle restored Mughal power in India, which had been lost when Babur's son Humayun was driven into exile by the Afghan despot Sher Khan in 1540.

The third and final battle of Panipat, in 1761, was fought between the Maratha armies under Sadashiva Rao Bha and a large Afghan army under Ahmad Shah Abdali. Encompassing the span of only one day, the battle ended when the Afghans effectively routed the Marathan troops, who, despite their enmity for the Mughals, had fought to protect the rule of the Mughal emperor Shah Alam II. The conflict between the Maratha army and Afghan troops that was engendered at this battle continued for some forty years in the northwest. To the extent that it distracted Indians from the rising power of the British East India Company, it marked the beginning of the end of the Mughal empire.

Pannonius, Janus (1434–1472)

Hungarian bishop and poet. Janus Pannonius, a prominent Hungarian poet, courtier, humanist, and bishop, was born János Csezmiczei in 1434. His father, a low-ranking member of the Hungarian aristocracy, died early in Pannonius's life, and he was raised by his mother under difficult circumstances. When Pannonius was thirteen, he was sent to study in Italy under the sponsorship of János Vitéz, the bishop of Várad, who hoped to groom him for a career in the Church.

Pannonius studied at the famous academic centers of humanism, the universities of Ferrara, Venice, and Padua (where a statue of the poet still commemorates his residence in the city), for fourteen years. The young Csezmiczei was a prolific poet, writing Latin epigrams, elegies, and satires. He always composed in Latin, as was the style among humanists, and eventually took the Latin name Janus Pannonius. (Pannonius derives from a Latin word for a Hungarian region southwest of the Danube.)

Pannonius was named canon of Várad in 1454, and after finishing his studies in Italy, he returned to Hungary in 1458 and received a position in the Royal Chancellery in Buda. He quickly established himself as a powerful member of the court of King Mátyás I, and was named bishop of Pécs in 1459, a position he held until his death. He became an important adviser to the king, counseling him on strategy for military campaigns, accompanying him on foreign expeditions, and supervising the military defense of southern Hungary. Pannonius was appointed the viceroy of Slavonia in 1470, but his relationship with King Mátyás I soured when Mátyás refused to take decisive military action against the Turks. Pannonius became involved in a failed plot against the king in 1472 and was killed attempting to escape when Mátyás caught wind of the conspiracy.

One of the earliest and most important of Hungarian literature's lyric poets, Pannonius had a significant impact on the Hungarian literary tradition, bringing a highly lyrical and personal style to epigrams and elegies about everyday experiences. He also produced Latin translations of Homer, Demosthenes, and Plutarch.

parfleche

American Indian rawhide sack. Originally the name of the rawhide carrying bag of the Plains Indian tribes of North America, parfleche now applies to a variety of rawhide articles. Rawhide was used by the nomadic Plains Indians, who cleaned, dehaired, stretched, and dried the hides in the sun in a process less time-consuming than tanning. The parfleche carrying bag was created by folding the ends of a rectangular piece of rawhide, like an envelope, and tying them together. Two parfleches were used like paniers on both sides of a horse. The bags were usually two feet by three feet, and the broad sides were decorated with colorful abstract geometric designs.

Parker, Charlie (1920–1955)

African-American jazz musician. Charles Parker, Jr., was born in Kansas City, Kansas, but moved to Kansas City, Missouri, in 1927, then a center for black American music. He began playing alto saxophone at thirteen, and by fifteen he had begun his career as a professional musician. By 1937 he was touring with Jay McShann's band, making his first recording in 1941; in 1942 Parker joined Earl Hines's band, which included jazz great Dizzy Gillespie, and in 1944 Parker joined Billy Eckstine's band. In this period Parker would meet other young musicians after hours in the New York clubs Minton's Playhouse and Monroe's Uptown House, where they would play informal jam sessions in small groups, developing a new bebop sound and giving Parker a forum in which to develop his personal style.

In 1945 Parker formed his own group, working with Gillespie in small combos and making well-known recordings such as "Now's the Time" (1945), and "Ornithology" (1946). After confinement in

a California hospital following a nervous breakdown related to narcotic and alcohol addiction, Parker returned to New York to form a quintet that recorded many of his most famous pieces, such as "Scrapple from the Apple" (1947); the group included Miles Davis on trumpet, Max Roach on drums, Tommy Potter on double bass, and Duke Jordan on piano. Although based on chord progressions from other jazz standards and popular songs, many of his compositions from this period themselves became jazz standards. Nicknamed "Bird," "Yardbird," and "Chan," Charlie Parker was idolized by other musicians during his lifetime.

Parker recorded and traveled extensively until 1951, when the narcotics squad revoked his New York cabaret license; the event initiated a period of sporadic employment and failing health for Parker, although the license was reinstated in 1953. His last engagement was in 1955 at Birdland, a New York club named in his honor.

One of the most influential improvising soloists in jazz, Parker was central to the development of bop in the 1940s. Transcriptions of his solos were published for study as early as 1948. Admired for the speed and intense tone of his playing, the complexity of his harmonies, and the asymmetrical phrasing and irregular rhythm of his melodies, Parker was emulated by young musicians on all instruments while he was living and for decades after his death.

Parker, Dorothy [Rothschild] (1893–1967)

American writer. Parker, who is noted for her terse, witty poetry and short stories, was born Dorothy Rothschild in West End, New Jersey. This sharp, perceptive girl grew into a leading figure in the American literary scene of the 1920s and 1930s.

Parker worked for a fashion magazine, springboarding from this job in 1917 to the position of drama critic for *Vanity*

Fair. She married Edwin Pond Parker II that same year; although she later divorced him to marry Alan Campbell, Parker used her first husband's surname professionally for the rest of her life. When her reviews for *Vanity Fair* were deemed too biting by the publisher, she joined the staff of *The New Yorker*, where she was given free rein to produce articles that were often quite scathing. *The New Yorker* also published many of her short stories, which were later collected in *Here Lies* (1939). She is most noted for "A Telephone Call" and "Big Blonde," a fond account of an aging party girl, which won the O. Henry Award in 1929.

After publishing *Enough Rope* (1926), her first book of verse, Parker became a freelance writer. *Enough Rope* contains her celebrated couplet "Men seldom make passes / At girls who wear glasses." Her major poems are collected in *Not So Deep as a Well* (1936).

In addition to writing poems and short stories, Parker collaborated on several plays, including *Close Harmony* (1924), with Elmer Rice, and *Ladies of the Corridor* (1963), with Arnaud d'Usseau. Parker enhanced her legendary status in the twenties and early thirties not only with her sophisticated cynicism but also through her membership in the Algonquin Hotel's celebrated Round Table. Forming the nucleus of the group were Parker; Robert Benchley, the humorist; and Robert Sherwood, the drama critic and playwright. Parker remains respected in both literary and social circles, having left behind countless anecdotes illustrating her dry, calculated wit. When told of the former U.S. president Calvin Coolidge's death, legend has it that Parker responded, "How can they tell?"

Parra, Nicanor (1914–)

Chilean poet and physicist. Born in San Fabian, Parra, along with his sister Violeta Parra, the Chilean singer, used to sing for food at circuses and parties, after the death of their father. Studying physics first at the University of Chile at Santiago and then at Brown University (1943–45) and Oxford (1949–51), Parra became acquainted with Beat poetry that rejected the rarefied, inaccessible verse of the modernist tradition for the language of everyday life. His first book of poetry, which was neither critically well received nor commercially successful, presaged his later experimentation with form and language. With his second book, *Poemas y antipoemas* (1954; *Poems and Antipoems*), Parra mapped out the "school" to which his poetry is meant to belong—the school of antipoetry. Some of the characteristics of the vague grouping of antipoetry poets include the use of stock phrases, clichés, legal parlance, the language of newspaper editorials, funeral announcements, and political jargon. Politically, it can be aligned only with anarchism, comically exalting the insignificance and freedom of the individual. Contrasted with the lyricism of his contemporary Pablo Neruda, Parra's work at times uses theoretical questions about the nature of poetry as its theme, focusing on questions of language and its relation to reality. Since 1986 Parra, who is also a professor of theoretical physics at the University of Chile, has shifted his antipoetry to ecopoetry, writing poetry that concerns itself with nuclear holocaust and humankind's destruction of its own environment. Though not a complete break with his earlier anarchic work, Parra's defense of the environment forces him to place limits on his irony and argue for the continuance of human life.

Parra, Violeta (1917–1967)

Chilean singer. Violeta Parra was born in San Carlos. Her father was a primary school teacher and her mother a peasant; her brother, Nicanor Parra, became one of Chile's outstanding poets. After her father's death, poverty forced her and her brothers to sing at circuses and parties in exchange for food.

Parra began compiling Chilean folklore, recognizing that the "authentic" Chilean music was not sung by folklore groups at feasts celebrating the independence, but was found on the outskirts of the city, and in the country. These songs originated with the troubadors and *romanceros* and had been guarded and sung by the peasants. In 1953 Parra began a popular radio show, introducing local singers she met in her travels around Chile. She was awarded the Caupolicán Prize for her work in compiling and disseminating Chilean folklore. After spending two years in Paris, Parra returned to Chile in 1956 and co-founded the Museo de Arte Popular ("Museum of Popular Art"). She continued to compile songs from rural areas, then returned to Santiago in 1958 and began to compose songs of a more explicitly political nature. In addition, she wrote the music for various movies.

In 1961 she installed herself with her family in Paris, where she created the group Los Parra. During her four-year stay in Paris, Parra composed the majority of her political songs, including "Porque los pobres no tienen" (1960–63; "Because the Poor Have Not"), "Me gustan los estudiantes" (1960–63; "I Like the Students"), "Hasta quando" (1960–63; "Until When"), "Los pueblos americanos" (1964–65; "The American Towns"), and perhaps her most famous, "Gracìas a la vida" (1964–65; "Thanks to Life"). She returned to Chile to sing in La Peña de los Parra, a popular cultural house that her children Angel and Isabel founded in 1964.

Suffering from depression and feeling abandoned by her audience, she killed herself in Comuna de la Reina, a town on the outskirts of Santiago.

Parti Québécois

Quebec nationalist political party. Formed in 1968 by René Levesque, the Parti Québécois espoused quasi-socialist policies and advocated the independence of the Canadian province of Quebec. A few years later, the Parti Québécois gained a political foothold in the local government. In 1980, however, the citizens of Quebec approved a referendum to finally negotiate Quebec's independence. In 1985 Levesque abdicated his position as party leader and the Parti Québécois lost much of its political influence in Quebec. The question of Quebec's sovereignty was temporarily resolved in 1987 by an agreement to constitutionally acknowledge Quebec as a "distinct society" within the Canadian federation, but this solution was later blocked by other provinces and factions, including a strong American Indian lobby, that resented the inequity of the special status.

Pashupatinath temple

Hindu temple. The central Nepal city of Pashupati is situated on the banks of the sacred river Bagmati, three miles east of the Kathmandu Valley. The temple's golden-roofed shrines and silver-crafted doors testify to its cultural and religious importance as one of the most holy temples in the Hindu world. It is dedicated to Shiva, the guardian deity of Nepal, the god of death who destroys so that humans may be reborn.

Pashupatinath (the temple proper) is constructed in the two-tiered pagoda style that is typical of Hindu sacred architecture. The four faces of the shrine correspond to sacred sites and pilgrimage centers in India: Badrinath, Rameshwaram, Dwarka, and Jagannath. The design of the temple symbolizes the medieval concept of the heavenly roof. Like all Hindu temples, Pashupatinath is erected on a holy site. Hindus believe that gods will only come to a site that is *subha* (suitable, beautiful, auspicious, and near water). Such a site is thought to be a "navel" of the world. Important Hindus are cremated on the banks of the Bagmati.

Non-Hindus cannot enter Pashupatinath. Typically, the individual or community that finances the temple, known as the "sacrificer," prays for spiritual rebirth in the "womb room" or "cella," located in the center of the temple and above the "navel," or foundation stone.

Passover

Jewish festival. Passover, or Pesach, commemorates the Exodus of the Jews from slavery in ancient Egypt, when the Angel of Death "passed over" those Jewish households marked with the blood of the sacrificial lamb. It is celebrated for seven days in Israel and by Reform Jews, while Orthodox and Conservative Jews in the Diaspora add another day to the festival. Passover is referred to in the Hebrew Scriptures (the Old Testament) as the feast of unleavened bread, since the Ancient Israelites left Egypt so hurriedly that there was no time for the bread they had baked to rise. During Passover, Jews are forbidden to eat any product containing leaven (se'or) but are instead required to eat the plain matzoh that was consumed by their ancestors as they fled Egypt. So strict are the rabbinical laws governing the Passover diet of practicing Jews that many households purchase special cooking utensils and tableware that they use only during this festival. It is also an old tradition for Jews to sell all products containing leaven to non-Jews just before the first day of Passover and repurchase them at its conclusion.

On the evening of the first day of Passover is the Seder (order of service), the most important at-home ceremony of the liturgical year. The foods of this meal are highly symbolic of the experiences of the Jews; there are bitter herbs to represent slavery as well as wine to symbolize freedom. During and after the meal appropriate passages are recited from the Haggadah (the Telling), a book used only at Passover. Prayers recited at Passover express thanks not only for the release of the Children of Israel from captivity but also for the renewal of spring with its promise of another life-sustaining harvest.

Pasternak, Boris [Leonidovich] (1890–1960)

Russian poet and novelist. Born into the family of well-known painter Leonid Pasternak and his wife, Rozaliya Kaufman, a concert pianist, Pasternak first began publishing his poetry in 1913, after finishing his philosophy studies at Moscow University and at the University of Marburg in Germany. He briefly joined the Futurist literary group led by Russian poet Vladimir Mayakovsky (1893–1930), but soon left to pursue his own course as a writer. Much of his early work, such as the poems collected in *Sestra mo'a zhizn'* (1922; *My Sister—Life*), though written during the years of the Revolution, reflect instead his experience of nature and love. *My Sister—Life*, together with his next volume of poetry, *Temy i variatsii* (1923; *Themes and Variations*), established Pasternak as an outstanding poet of his generation. After publishing two long poems, *Deviat'sot piati god* (1926; *The Year 1905*) and *Leitenant Schmidt* (1927; *Lieutenant Shmidt*), Pasternak produced several other books of poetry, as well as short stories. After 1936, he worked primarily as a translator of works by English dramatist William Shakespeare (1564–1616), German poet Johann Wolfgang von Goethe (1749–1832), and Spanish dramatist Pedro Calderón de la Barca (1600–1681), as well as French and Georgian authors. These won the approval of Russian Communist leader Stalin and probably spared Pasternak from the ongoing cultural purges; indeed he was successfully elected to the Soviet Writers' Union.

During this time, however, Pasternak was also at work on his novel, *Doktor Zhivago* (1957; *Dr. Zhivago*), which, because of its critical appraisal of the

Marxist revolution, had no hope of being published in the Soviet Union. The novel first appeared in Italy and then in the United States, where it became immensely popular. In 1958 Pasternak was awarded the Nobel Prize in Literature, but was forced to decline the award to appease the government. He was expelled from the Writers' Union and spent the remaining two years of his life hounded by the Western press and the state literary factions in his own country, who demanded his exile.

Pasteur, Louis (1822–1895)

French chemist and biologist. Born in the small town of Dôle, the son of a tanner, Pasteur attended primary and secondary schools in Arbois. He attended the Royal College of Besançon, and in 1843 entered the École Normale Supérieure of Paris, earning his degree in 1847.

By 1848, at the age of twenty-six, Pasteur had discovered the phenomenon of optical isomerism in crystals. He was made a member of the Legion of Honor and received the British Royal Society's Copley Medal. In 1852 Pasteur accepted the chair of chemistry at the University of Strasbourg, and two years later he became professor of chemistry and dean of sciences at the new University of Lille. His experiments with fermentation were applied to the local manufacture of alcohol from sugars. During this time he discovered the reaction of yeast in fermentation, and the role of air as a carrier for micro-organisms. From Pasteur's experiments, English surgeon Joseph Lister (1827–1912) in 1865 revolutionized surgery by utilizing carbolic acid to exclude atmospheric germs, and from Pasteur's work on fermentation the pasteurization process for sterilization, now used in the production of milk, was developed.

In 1865 Pasteur was asked to travel to the south of France to examine silkworm diseases that were ruining the silk industry. Although a cerebral hemorrhage in 1868 left part of his left arm and leg permanently paralyzed, he continued to work and eventually isolated the bacilli of two diseases and found methods to detect diseased stock and prevent contagion. He received many honors during this period, among them election to the Académie des Sciences, the French Academy of Medicine, and a life pension from the National Assembly.

In 1880 he was asked to research the chicken cholera that had devastated over 10 percent of French fowls. He isolated the germ and produced a diluted serum that served to inoculate against the disease. Pasteur called his method vaccination (*vacca* meaning "cow" in Latin), in order to show respect to English physician Edward Jenner (1749–1823), who first discovered the vaccine for smallpox based on his research on the cowpox disease. Pasteur also developed vaccines for anthrax and rabies. In 1888 France founded the Pasteur Institute, and Pasteur's seventieth birthday was declared a national holiday with a celebration at the Sorbonne.

Patagonia

South American desert. A semiarid scrub plateau located in southern Argentina, Patagonia is the largest desert of North and South America, extending 260,000 square miles. It borders with the Río Colorado (Colorado River) in the north, the Andes mountains in the west, the Atlantic Ocean in the east, and the Río Coig (Coig River) in the south. The northern zone, primarily open bushland, is characterized by sandy areas where grasses flourish. Irrigated crops, such as peaches, plums, almonds, grapes, vegetables, and alfalfa, are cultivated and large herds of cattle and horses abound. Most of Patagonia's wealth, however, is derived from sheep.

When Portuguese explorer Ferdinand Magellan (c. 1480–1521), the first to visit the area, arrived in 1520, he found "giants" living there, a group of independent and nomadic tribes of Indians he called "Patagones" (their scientific name is *chónecas*) due to their big feet and large stature (many were over six feet tall). The legend of their gigantic size was maintained for many years. Patagonia was the name given to the area they inhabited, and *patagón* is still used to refer to people with big feet.

In the seventeenth century, Spaniards penetrated the area in an attempt to find the mythical city of the Caesars, and Chilean Jesuits continued the search until the end of the following century, establishing missions as they went. Among the more famous explorers of the area were English naturalist Charles Darwin and Robert Fitzroy, who in 1833 discovered and explored the Chubut River. English activities in the region included the founding of Port Madryn, a Welsh settlement, in 1865.

By the nineteenth century, Patagonia became a site of struggle among the Chileans, Argentines, and French. After several attempts to occupy the land, war nearly broke out between Chile and Argentina in 1878. In 1884 Argentina created the national territories of La Pampa, Neuquén, Río Negro, Chubut, Santa Cruz, and Tierra del Fuego, territories that, for the most part, have maintained their designated boundaries to the present day. The dispute with Chile over the western boundary was settled in 1902, at roughly the same time in which Argentine occupation of the area was completed.

Paterson, Andrew Barton (1864–1941)

Australian poet and songwriter. Andrew "Banjo" Paterson is most widely recognized as the composer of "Waltzing Matilda," Australia's unofficial national anthem, but he was also a noted journalist and poet. In his native Australia, Paterson received great popular acclaim with the poetry collections *The Man from Snowy River and Other Verses*

(1895) and *Rio Grande's Last Race and Other Verses* (1902), the former selling more than 100,000 copies before his death.

Paterson practiced law in Sydney before switching to journalism in 1900. His coverage of the Boer War in South Africa led to his becoming editor of the Sydney *Evening News* in 1904, a post he soon left to join the Sydney *Town and Country Journal*. Although Paterson temporarily retired from journalism to become a rancher, he soon interrupted his self-imposed hiatus to go to Europe and cover World War I for the Sydney *Morning Herald*. After the war, Paterson's remaining years were spent primarily as a journalist. His other works include *The Old Bush Songs: Composed and Sung in the Bushranging* (1905); *Digging and Overlanding Days* (1905); *Saltbush Bill, J.P., and Other Verses* (1917), in which "Waltzing Matilda" appeared; and *The Animals Noah Forgot* (1933).

Patrick, St. (fifth century C.E.)

Patron saint of Ireland. Born in Roman-occupied Britain, St. Patrick was captured by Irish marauders as a young man. He spent six years in Ireland as a herdsman; in his suffering he found solace in the Christian religion. After envisioning his escape in a dream, Patrick fled his master and found his way back to England, where he endured further hardship. In another dream, he heard the voices of Irish people pleading for his return.

Returning to Ireland as a missionary, St. Patrick preached Christianity to the pagan Irish. His ministry was extraordinarily popular: he traveled throughout the entire island, baptizing and confirming as he went. He is credited with Christianizing Ireland's Anglo-Saxon and Pict tribes. Many of his earliest converts were slaves.

There are two extant seventh-century Irish accounts of Patrick's life, as well as some of his own writings in Latin. He is the author of one of the earliest recorded slave narratives, the *Confessio*, a spiritual autobiography, and is also known for the *Epistola ad milites coroticus* (*Letters to the Corotican Soldiers*). Addressed to a military group that had committed numerous atrocities against Irish Christian converts, this work deals with the British abuse of the Irish. His life and writings were characterized by a stance of extreme humility. His language, too, is direct and simple, at times awkward.

An enormously popular saint in Ireland and beyond, St. Patrick has inspired numerous legends. One legend tells the story of his driving the snakes out of Ireland with his shillelagh. Another, equally popular, tells of his explaining the Catholic principle of the Holy Trinity (one God who is Father, Son, and Holy Spirit) with a shamrock, or three-leaf clover.

Paubhas

Nepalese style of painting. Paubhas, or Pauva paintings, are a Nepalese form of Thangkas, a trans-Himalayan style of painting. These highly decorative works depict either Hindu or Buddhist iconography, and the most vivid example of Paubhas painting is found in the Kumari temple at Kathmandu, a shrine dedicated to "The Living Goddess."

Historical records of Nepalese Paubhas can be traced to the eleventh century; paintings are found primarily on palm leaves and wooden book-covers of manuscripts. Paubhas painting reached its most fully developed form in the sixteenth century, and continued in this form well into the seventeenth century. The paintings are found on hieratic, or sacred, cotton scrolls dating from the thirteenth century. Although Nepalese paintings of this period lack the depth of Indian art, the lines are smoother and more graceful.

Paubhas scrolls are vertical, vivid in color, and divided into two formats for religious iconography. In one kind, religious imagery surrounds a central deity. The other type features a mandala (Hindu and Buddhist symbol of the universe) wherein a circle surrounds a square that encases the figures of deities. In both types of scroll, narrative panels are found in the margins.

In the late sixteenth and early seventeenth centuries, a narrative style emerged in manuscript illuminations and in horizontal scroll paintings that differed in content and style from the hieratic scrolls. Characters and actions, for example, were depicted more realistically and dynamically. This style gained prominence in the last part of the seventeenth century, when Nepalese painting was influenced by the more realistic Indian Rajasthani painting.

Paul, St. (died c. 65 C.E.)

Apostle and missionary of Christianity. Author of the Pauline Epistles, one of the most important texts of the New Testament, Paul began his life as Saul of Tarsus, a devout Jew and persecutor of Christians. According to legend, while traveling to Damascus to suppress Christianity, Paul was blinded by light, and heard the voice of Jesus asking "Why persecutest thou me?" Upon regaining his sight, St. Paul was baptized, changed his name from the Hebrew Saul to Paul, and spent the next thirteen years preaching and studying Christianity. Accompanied by St. Barnabas and St. Mark, St. Paul made three missionary journeys, bringing Christianity to Jews and Gentiles in Cyprus, Asia Minor, Greece, and Rome. This was seen as a threat to the Roman empire, and on a trip to Jerusalem he was arrested and imprisoned. Finally extradited to Rome in 60 C.E., Paul remained imprisoned but was allowed to conduct his ministry from his cell. The circumstances and date of his death are uncertain, but it is rumored that he was beheaded five or six years later, after converting one of the favorite concubines of the Roman emperor Nero (54–68). The life and teachings of St. Paul were crucial to the spread of Christianity, beginning the movement that would make it the religion of the Roman empire less than three centuries later and ultimately a widespread world religion.

Paz, Octavio (1914–)

Mexican poet, literary critic, essayist, and playwright. Born in Mexico City, Paz comes from a family that has a history of involvement in Mexican intellectual life—his grandfather was a prominent liberal intellectual and his father was a close ally and defender of Mexican revolutionary Emiliano Zapata. Paz published his first book of poetry, *Luna silvestre* (*Silver Moon*), in 1933. While at the university, Paz was involved in avant-garde literary circles, and eventually gave up the study of law to found a progressive school for laborers with some of his classmates in the Yucatán province. His early poems attracted the attention of Chilean poet Pablo Neruda (1904–1973), who in 1937 invited Paz to attend the second Congress of the International Association of Writers.

Like a number of other major Latin American writers, Paz was both a literary figure and a diplomat, serving as his country's ambassador to India in the early 1960s. He resigned in 1968 to protest his home country's actions against student demonstrations.

Paz's books—revealing a depth of insight, elegance, and erudition—place him among the ablest writers of his generation. From the early 1930s he consistently published poetry, but his later works include not only poetry collections—of which *Piedra de sol* (1957; *Sun-Stone*) is perhaps best known—but also volumes of essays, including *El laberinto de la soledad* (1950; *The Labyrinth of Solitude*) and works as diverse as a study of the French social anthropologist Claude Lévi-Strauss, criticism of

French artist Marcel Duchamp, and translation of the Japanese poet Matsuo Bashō. His study of Asian philosophy, which began during his stay in in India, has profoundly influenced his later work. In 1990 Paz won the Nobel Prize in literature.

Pearson, Lester [Bowles] (1897–1972)

Canadian prime minister. Born in Toronto, Pearson was the son of a Methodist minister. At sixteen, he entered the University of Toronto, but left two years later to join the Canadian Army Medical Corps, serving in Greece. He transferred to the Royal Flying Corps in 1917, but was released after he was injured in a traffic accident, and he returned to Canada and the university, graduating in 1919. After study at Oxford University, he taught history at the University of Toronto from 1924 to 1928.

Pearson entered the diplomatic ranks in 1928, serving in a variety of posts in Washington, D.C., and then in London. In 1942 he was transferred back to Washington, where he was the first secretary of the Canadian legation, and where he participated in the founding of the United Nations in 1945. In the same year, he was named ambassador to the United States. He was thought to be the leading candidate for the first secretary-general of the U.N., but he was vetoed by the Soviet Union. In 1946 Pearson returned to Canada to be undersecretary for external affairs under Louis St. Laurent. When St. Laurent succeeded William Lyon Mackenzie King as prime minister in 1948, Pearson joined his Liberal Party cabinet and was elected to Parliament in 1949.

Recognizing Canada's need for a realignment of its foreign relations due to Britain's decline and the rise of the United States and the Soviet Union, Pearson represented his country at the summit creating the North Atlantic Treaty Organization (NATO). He also arranged the compromise of 1955 that expanded the membership of the U.N. and served as the president of the U.N. General Assembly in 1952–53. When Britain invaded Egypt in the Suez Crisis of 1956, Pearson proposed the intervention of a U.N. force, a proposal that met with unanimous approval and defused the potentially explosive situation. For his efforts, he received the Nobel Peace Prize in 1957. When St. Laurent resigned from the government in 1957, Pearson became the Liberal Party leader. Defeated by the conservatives in 1958, Pearson began to rebuild the party and was elected prime minister in 1963. Among his major goals was the attempt to unify a linguistically and geographically divided country. To this end, he brought several French-Canadians, including the future prime minister Pierre Trudeau, into his cabinet. He retired in 1968 to return to teaching and to write his memoirs, entitled *Mike*, his nickname. He completed one volume before his death in 1972.

Pelé (1940–)

Brazilian soccer player. Born Edson Arantes do Nascimento, Pelé began to play the game football, known in the United States as soccer, at age five, and began his professional career at sixteen. As an inside left forward, he led the Brazilian national team to world championships in 1958, 1962, and 1970. Pelé not only holds every Brazilian scoring record, but in 1969 he scored his 1,000th goal, an incredible average of one goal per game. Combining dexterity and control with a mastery of the philosophy of the game, Pelé earned the characterization of his play as "poetry in motion." At the height of his career, he was the world's highest-paid athlete. After an eighteen-year career with the Santos, he retired. Within a few years, Pelé was brought out of retirement to play in the United States, helping to revitalize the game there. He is now retired and lives in Brazil.

Perón, Eva (1919–1952)

Argentine political and social leader. Born Eva Duarte, Evita, an illegitimate child, spent her early youth in Junín, and then moved to Buenos Aires, where she became a radio and motion-picture actress. She met the widowed Colonel Juan D. Perón in June 1943, became his mistress, and dedicated herself fully to his political program. When growing opposition from some sectors of the population forced Perón to resign his governmental posts and become a prisoner on the island of Martín García, Evita rallied the masses of workers in his support. During this time she emerged as a powerful political leader revered by the lower economic classes. It is said that she marched from door to door, gathering the people to pressure the government for Perón's release, an effort that culminated in a massive demonstration in 1945 and Perón's reinstatement. Days later, Juan Perón and Eva Duarte were married in the province of Junín. Evita participated in her husband's political activities, aiding him considerably in his successful 1946 election bid. Evita became a symbol to the *descamisados* (shirtless ones), the working-class people who could identify with her humble beginnings and who found in her a source of hope. During her husband's presidency, Evita acted as de facto minister of health and labor, awarding generous wage increases to the unions that remained loyal to Perón's regime. Cutting off government funds for the traditional Sociedad de Beneficiencia (Aid Society), she replaced it with the Eva Perón Foundation, whose resources were used to establish thousands of schools, hospitals, orphanages, homes for the aged, and similar charitable institutions. Under her leadership, the movement for women's suffrage was born and the Peronista Feminist Party came into being in 1949. In 1951 she was named candidate for the vice presidency, but the army did not allow her to run; nevertheless, Perón was reelected in 1951. Knowing she had cancer, Evita published her autobiography, *La razón de mi vida*, and in 1952 the National Congress proclaimed her the "spiritual leader of the nation." Even after her death, Evita continued to be a stunning presence in Argentine politics and a symbol of the Peronist party. She received full presidential honors upon her death and radio stations continued for a year to transmit five minutes of silence daily in her honor. Efforts were made by working-class people to have her canonized, and although these proved unfruitful, her memory was treated as sacred. When Perón was overthrown in 1955, his political enemies stole her remains in an effort to purge the nation of her influence, returning the body to him sixteen years later in Madrid. Juan Perón died in office in 1974, and his third wife, Isabel Perón, hoping to win the support of the people, had Evita buried with Perón in a crypt in the presidential palace. When Isabel Perón, who had assumed the presidency upon her husband's death, was ousted in 1976, the military junta removed the bodies, and Evita was finally buried in the Duarte family crypt in the Recoleta cemetery.

Persepolis

Ancient Persian capital. Located about thirty-two miles north of modern-day Shīrāz, Iran, Persepolis was an ancient capital of the Achaemenid empire (c. 550–330 B.C.E.). Inscriptions discovered by archaeologists suggest that the city's construction began under Darius I (r. 522–486 B.C.E.) to replace Pasargadae as the capital of Persia. Built in an inconvenient mountainous location, Persepolis was visited mainly in the spring. Most of the actual administration of the empire was done from Susa, Babylon, or Ecbatana. Though Roman conqueror Alexander the Great plundered the city and burned the palace of the king of an-

cient Persia Xerxes the Great (486–465 B.C.E.) in 330 B.C.E., the city continued to serve as the capital of Persia and as a province of the Macedonian empire. In the Seleucid period, the city began a gradual decline from which it never recovered.

Persian

Middle Eastern language. Dating back to the ancient Persian empire in the sixth century B.C.E., Persian is today spoken in Iran and Afghanistan by some 15 million people and is a member of the Indo-Iranian branch of the Indo-European family. Historically, the language is divided into three periods. Old Persian (c. 550–330 B.C.E.) is preserved in some cuneiform inscriptions from the Achaemenid dynasty, which was conquered by Alexander the Great. Middle Persian (c. 226–640 C.E.), also called Pahlavi, is written in a version of Aramaic script and flourished during the Sassanian dynasty from the third to the seventh century. Modern Persian arose in the late tenth century, after the Arab-Islamic conquest of Iran in the seventh century had virtually eliminated it as a written language. Modern Persian was much simpler grammatically than its predecessors, and its vocabulary borrowed heavily from Arabic. Its formal aspects have changed little since that time, and it is still written in Arabic script. Modern Persian was the dominant language of Muslim India from about the fourteenth until the nineteenth century. In Iran, modern Persian is known as Farsi; it is the daily language of over half the population as well as the dominant language of government, commerce, and the educational system.

Persian miniature painting

Middle Eastern painting style. Persian miniature painting developed from Chinese and Mongol influences, primarily as a method of illustrating texts. The most productive period was during the fourteenth through the seventeenth century, in two schools, the Shīrāz and the Safavid.

Persian art is said to be intimate and concerned with the perfection of each small detail, demanding individual, meticulous examination. The majority of Persian miniature paintings are found in manuscripts, and the flowing lines of the paintings complement the flowing lines of the Persian script. This similarity suggests that the style survives from a time when all writing was pictographic. But while painting and illustration were part of the cultures of Egypt, Mesopotamia, Greece, and Rome, Persian art officially began after the destruction of Baghdad in 1258 by Hulagu Khan (1217–1265), the grandson of Mongol conqueror Genghis Khan (c. 1167–1227). With the expulsion of the Arabic rulers of Persia, painting flourished under the Mongolian influence. The Mongols, who ruled China at the time, brought many Chinese artists to Persia, and their representational art with motifs of clouds and realistic landscapes was introduced to the previous mix of subjects and styles.

The Mongols founded the Shīrāz school of painting in the mid fourteenth century. This school developed through the fifteenth century, reflecting the growing synthesis of Chinese influences and Persian art, and changing with the political fortunes of Shīrāz in the fifteenth century. These paintings illustrated texts such as the poet Firdawsī's *Shāh-nāmeh*, tending to feature groups of people with various backgrounds, ranging from the solid-color backgrounds of Chinese art in the beginning, through realistic landscapes during the rule of the Islamic Timurids (early 1400s), to the intensification of colors during the rule of the Turks.

Bihzad, who was born in the middle of the fifteenth century, is considered to be the greatest of the Persian miniature painters. He painted in the Safavid court of Persia, in the new capital of Tabrīz;

his subjects were portraits of rulers and courtiers as album leaves or book illustrations. This style influenced the realistic portraiture of the Ottoman Turks and the decorated miniatures of Mughal India. Bihzad's intense colors, careful composition, and delicate lines are regarded as the hallmarks of the style. The miniature painters Mirak, Sultan-Muhammad, and Riza-i-Abbasi followed the work of Bihzad and are also considered to be great masters. By the eighteenth century, the style is said to have stopped, and though miniatures are still painted, they are no longer viewed as being part of this ancient Persian tradition.

Peshawar

Pakistani city. Peshawar serves as the capital of both the district of Peshawar and of the North-West Frontier Province in Pakistan. Early history of the fertile vale includes its annexation by Eucratides, a Greco-Bactrian king, in the second century B.C.E. In the first century C.E., the city, known both as Purusapura and Parasawara (meaning "town" or "abode" of Purusa), became the capital of the Kushan (Kusana) empire, in the ancient kingdom of Gandhara, under the rule of King Kanisha (c. 120 C.E.).

References to the Peshawar area can be found in early Sanskrit literature as well as in the writings of the ancient Greek geographer Strabo (64/63 B.C.E.– 23 C.E.) and the Alexandrian astronomer Ptolemy (second century C.E.). Peshawar has a historic association with Buddhism, a fact attested to by the presence of the Shahji-ki Dheri mounds, which cover ruins of a second-century C.E. Buddhist *stupa* (dome-shaped mound that serves as a Buddhist shrine), the largest in the Subcontinent. Buddhism remained a powerful force in the area until the time it was captured by the Muslims in 988 C.E. Although the Afghans took possession of Peshawar in the sixteenth century, it remained at least nominally dependent upon Mughal rule until the demise of the Mughal empire in the nineteenth century.

Also known as Begram, Peshawar allegedly received its present name (*pesh awar*: "frontier town") from a Mughal emperor, Akbar (r. 1556–1605). Peshawar became a part of the Sikh kingdom in 1834 and remained so for fifteen years, when it came under British rule. The British maintained their sovereignty in the area until the Partition of India in 1947, when the North-West Frontier in which it is located became one of the four provinces of Pakistan. Between 1971 and 1981 the rate of urban growth in Peshawar increased by 103 percent. The University of Peshawar was founded in 1950, with five constituent and eighteen affiliated colleges.

Peshawar has a long history as the center of caravan trade with Afghanistan and Central Asia; even today, foreign merchants meet at the ancient Qissah (Kissa) Khwani Bazar ("Street of Storytellers") to deal in dried fruits, woolen products, rugs, carpets, *pustins* (sheepskin coats), *karakul* (lambskin) caps, and Chitrali *chughahs* (cloaks).

Petőfi, Sándor (1823–1856)

Hungarian revolutionary and poet. Petőfi is one of the few Hungarian poets who has been widely translated. Born in Kiskörös, Hungary, he led a short but varied life: after entering several schools, he was a journalist, an actor, and then a soldier before being dismissed for poor health. In 1844 he was invited by the preeminent Hungarian poet of the time, Mihály Vörösmarty, to become an assistant editor of the literary journal *Pesti Divatlap*. That same year, Petőfi published his first volume of poetry, *Versek*, which earned him immediate acclaim.

Most of Petőfi's poetry considers patriotism, nature, romantic love, and the Hungarian countryside. His style is similar to that of the Lake Poets (Wordsworth, Coleridge, Southey), whose writing made use of popular idiom and

rejected esoteric, "poetic" language. Much of his best love poetry is addressed to his wife, Julia Szendrey. Often working Hungarian folk songs into his poems, Petőfi wrote verse that marked a departure from conventional Hungarian poetry. The simplicity of his style made his poetry accessible to a broad audience, and he was therefore able to disseminate political and philosophical ideas to the Hungarian public.

His first long narrative work, *A helység kalapácsa* (*The Village Blacksmith*), was a satire on the traditional epic poem. Although he explored many different genres in his writing career, he is best known for his vision of the poet as a deliverer of the oppressed, glorified as a romantic hero. One of the most notable of his beliefs was the concept of *világszabadság* (freedom for all peoples), the principle for which he would give his life.

Prior to the Hungarian revolution of 1848, Petőfi drew attention to the widening gap between the rich and the poor in Hungary. Commenting on the obvious parallels to the situation in France, he denounced the Hungarian aristocracy. Petőfi became editor of the political magazine *Életképek*. He ran for the Hungarian parliament, the Diet, and although he failed to win a seat, his poem "Talpra magyar" ("Rise, Hungarian") was chosen as the anthem of the Hungarian revolution. During the revolution, Petőfi worked as an aide to General Joszef Bem, head of the Transylvanian army. On July 31, 1849, Petőfi disappeared during the Battle of Segesvár. It was at first assumed that he had perished during the fighting, but it was later discovered in Soviet war archives that Petőfi was probably one of nearly two thousand Hungarian prisoners taken to Siberia. Although unverifiable, it is believed that Petőfi died of tuberculosis.

Phoenicians

Ancient Semitic peoples. The Phoenicians were a branch of the Canaanites who lived along a narrow strip of the Levantine coast from Tartus to somewhere south of Mt. Carmel (roughly encompassing present-day Lebanon and parts of Israel and Syria). They were not differentiated from the general Canaanite population until the later half of the second millennium B.C.E.

Given the name "Phoenicians" by the Greeks, these seagoing people were widely known for their skills as explorers, colonizers, merchants, and warriors. However, the most enduring influence came from their alphabet. The Phoenician script, a twenty-two-letter system in use as early as the fifteenth century B.C.E., was the direct ancestor of the writing systems adopted by the Greeks.

The zenith of their power came at the beginning of the first millennium B.C.E. The most important cities were Aradus (Ruad), Byblos (Gebeil), Sidon, Tyre, Marathus (Amrit), Berytus (Beirut), and Ecdippa (Aczib). Beginning in the ninth century B.C.E., Phoenicia's independence came under increasing attack from the Assyrians. The land was eventually taken by Alexander the Great and was incorporated into the Roman province of Syria in 64 B.C.E.

Phra Apahi Mani

Thai novel. This very popular novel in *khön* verse, but using everyday speech, was written by the Thai poet Sunthon Phu (1786–1855). The fantastic story follows the many loves, intrigues, and wild adventures of a young prince as he encounters giants, mermaids, dragons, and flying boats. Especially interesting for Western readers are its portrayals of *farang*, or Westerners. Such characters include an English queen who rules Sri Lanka under the advice of a Roman Catholic priest, and a *farang* pirate with a ship so large it holds a garden of trees.

The *Phra Apahi Mani* is also known under the names *Phra Aphaimani*, *Phra Aphai* and *Phra Abhai Mani*.

Phra Lao

Thai folk tale. This story of romance and adventure depicts a lifelong rivalry between two clans in the north, ending in the tragic death of the hero. Originally ascribed to King Trailok (1448–1488), the mixed verse and poetic prose style of this tale, which is also known as *Phra Law*, has had a great influence on Thai literature, and has grown increasingly embellished through the years.

Picasso, Pablo (1881–1973)

Spanish painter. Known as El Maestro, "the master," of modern art, Pablo Ruiz y Picasso was born in Málaga, Spain. Shortly after the turn of the century, he moved to Paris, a world center of art and literature. He settled on the Left Bank in 1903, and his work was immediately recognized, as his portrayals of day-to-day life of very poor people earned him widespread fame. These portrayals were commonly referred to as products of Picasso's "Blue Period" (1901–1904). The Blue Period was then followed by the lyrical Rose Period (1905–1908), which usually depicted the circus life with which Picasso seemed to be fascinated. Influenced heavily by French Impressionist painter Paul Cézanne (1839–1906) while in Paris, Picasso experimented with geometric form in his painting. In 1907 Picasso's experimentation with geometric forms was conspicuously embodied in his painting *Les Demoiselles d'Avignon* (1907), which signaled the beginning of the Cubist movement for which Picasso and his friend French painter Georges Braque (1882–1963) are perhaps best known. Picasso's *Three Musicians* (1921) was both the climax and finale of Cubism. Unable to be contained within a single artistic mode, Picasso's genius also produced works influenced by Neoclassicism and Surrealism. He and Braque were also among the first to use and therefore validate collage as an art form.

During World War II, because of the Nazi occupation of Paris and the Nazi aversion to modern art, Picasso was forced to hide his paintings in a vault in the Bank of France. In the late 1940s he became a Communist and moved to Vallauris and later Cannes. There his work involved not only painting but also sculpture, printmaking, ceramics, and collage. In 1958 he completed a mural for the United Nations building in Paris.

pidgin languages

Form of language. A pidgin language is a simplified language resulting from repeated contact among peoples with no other common tongue. Often lumped with creoles, pidgin languages are not so abruptly generated as creoles, tending instead to evolve over generations and remain a second language for the majority of their speakers. They range from simple jargon to a more extended language among native speakers, like Tok Pisin ("Talk Pidgin"), for example, the national language of Papua New Guinea.

The paradigmatic trade pidgin was Lingua Franca, which gave its name to trade languages in general. During its heyday in Algiers during the early 1600s, Lingua Franca was a second language to virtually all its inhabitants, whatever their ethnic origin. However, not all pidgins arise from contact between European and non-Western cultures, nor are they solely oral. The Chinook jargon spoken in the U.S. Pacific Northwest during the nineteenth century was initially a lingua franca based in the now extinct Chinook language. This extended pidgin had 100,000 Native and white settler speakers, as well as a print literature and a specially devised stenographic script.

The most dynamic contemporary pidgins are spoken and increasingly written along the west coast of Africa, especially in the Cameroons and Nigeria. In both these countries, the English-related pidgin is acquiring more and more native speakers and offers an alternative and more Africanized lingua franca to official English or French.

Pindar (c. 520–440 B.C.E.)

Greek lyric poet. Pindar produced choral and epinician (victory) odes celebrating victories in the athletic contests of ancient Greece, specifically the Olympian, Pythian, Isthmian, and Nemelan Games. Little is known about his life, though he was thought to be a member of an aristocratic family, the Aegeidae of Thebes. This social standing would have given Pindar a firsthand perspective on the aristocracy, a recurrent theme in his work.

Schooled in Athens, he wrote in a Doric dialect, making his verse accessible to the majority of his countrymen. To date, none of Pindar's early works have been recovered. His first known commission for an epinicia came from the Aleuadaie family, when he was approximately twenty years old. There exist seventeen volumes of Pindar's known work of choral odes, grouped by type. However, only four books of epinicia have survived in complete form, primarily in the form of quotations and transcribed on recently discovered papyrus.

The Persian invasion of Greece put a temporary halt to Pindar's poetic career. Thebes supported Persia, and Pindar remained loyal to the Boeotian aristocracy even as he admired Athenian resistance. When Athens emerged victorious, the power of Thebes was seriously diminished, as was general regard for Theban poetry and art. It was some time until Pindar's artistic efforts were sought for commission. He continued to revere Athens in his work, although this practice was frowned upon by many of his countrymen.

His visit to Sicily in 476 B.C.E. brought

Pindar into contact with the court of Theron of Acragas and Hieron I of Syracuse for two years. His work under these men permitted his reputation to spread even further throughout the Greek world.

Ping-Pong diplomacy

Ping-Pong diplomacy was a term applied to political relations between the United States and China during the early 1970s. The invitation of an American Ping-Pong team in April 1971 to visit and play in the People's Republic of China marked the beginning of a normalization of relations between the two countries. The political motive for the invitation prompted this popular expression for the meetings. Negotiations between the two nations paved the way for U.S. president Richard Nixon's trip to China in February 1972, and the signing of the Shanghai Communiqué.

Piñon, Nélida (1936–)

Brazilian novelist. Piñon is known for her dense and poetic language and for realism in her storytelling despite occasional mysticism, exemplified in her first novel, *Guia-mapa de Gabriel Arcanjo* (1961; *Guide-map of Gabriel Arcanjo*).

Piñon attended the Catholic University of Rio, later working as a journalist. She was a critic of the military dictatorship in Brazil during its reign, which was the topic of many of her short stories, such as those collected in *O calor das coisas* (1980; *The Heat of Things*). Her best-known novels are *A republica dos sonhos* (1984; *The Republic of Dreams*), the story of a Spanish immigrant family in Brazil reflecting Piñon's own Spanish background, and the epic *Fundador* (1969; *Founder*). In 1995 she won the Juan Rulfo Prize in Literature.

pipa

Chinese musical instrument. In the Qing dynasty (1644–1911), a long-necked lute with a round-shaped belly called *xiangu* came to be popular, and gradually evolved into *danxian, qinqin, sanxian, yueqin,* and a few other more or less similar instruments that were generally called *pipa*. These instruments shared a common characteristic: they all had a round body and a short straight neck. During the North-East dynasty, a pear-shaped lute, known as *quxiang pipa*, was introduced into China from the Arab region. In the Tang (618–906 C.E.) and Song dynasty (960–1279 C.E.), these two kinds of lute were combined to produce what we now know as *pipa*.

The modern *pipa* has a shallow, pear-shaped body with a wooden belly and sometimes two crescent-shaped sound holes. It is matched with four *xiang* (phases) on the neck and thirteen *ping* (grades) on the belly. Four silk strings run from a fastener on the belly to conical tuning pegs in the sides of the bent-back pegbox. The performer plays a *pipa* by holding it vertically on the thigh and plucks the strings with the fingers of the right hand. With a long history of development, *pipa* has become a sophisticated instrument capable of subtle inflections in pitch and timbre. It enjoys great popularity both as a solo instrument and in Chinese orchestras.

Pirandello, Luigi (1867–1936)

Italian dramatist and novelist. Celebrated for his radical explorations in the theater as well as for his many fine novels, Pirandello is a major figure of modern theater. After studying in Rome and in Germany, Pirandello taught at a women's teachers' college for several years. He married in 1894, but after the loss of the family's substantial investment in mining, in 1903, which included both his patrimony as well as the substantial dowry belonging to his wife, Pirandello's wife developed a paranoid condition, which worsened over the years. She was eventually admitted to a nursing home in 1919, where she remained until her death.

With the exception of the play *Sei personaggi in cerca d'autore* (1918; *Six Characters in Search of an Author*), Pirandello's plays and novels went largely unnoticed during the early part of the century. Usually his works explored the various "realities" that people constructed for themselves and the problems accompanying these realities. His plays, too, were notable for their departure from standard techniques of drama; often Pirandello would strip the stage of any set, or set the action in the midst of the audience. Notable among his books and plays is the memorable novel *Il fu Mattia Pascal* (1904; *The Late Mattia Pascal*), the short-story collection *Novelle per un anno* (1922–36; *Tales of Suicide*), and the plays *Così è (se vi pare)* (1918; *Right You Are If You Think You Are*) and *Enrico IV* (1922; *Henry IV*).

In 1924 Pirandello left teaching, joined the Fascist Party, and with the support of Mussolini became the director of the state theater in Rome, Teatro d'Arte. Pirandello's plays achieved notable success in this new forum, both in Italy and abroad. He was awarded the Nobel Prize in Literature in 1934.

Pirosmanashvili, Niko (c. 1862–1918)

Georgian painter. Born Nikolai Alsanovich Pirosmanashvili to a peasant family and orphaned at an early age, Pirosmanashvili worked at odd jobs in Tbilisi, finally supporting himself as a self-taught itinerant sign painter. He also painted pictures on themes from the lives of Tbilisi townsmen, as well as landscapes, still-lifes, and animal scenes. Although his work was finally noticed by Georgian professional artists in 1916, his pride would not allow him to accept their assistance, and he died two years later, in obscurity.

Eventually, interest in his work was renewed as part of the growing cult for primitivist, or naïve, painting. His subjects included still-lifes of exotic fruits, fish, and *shashlyks* (shish kebabs), and

scenes from Georgian heroic epics. His predominant use of dark background with colorful highlights was influenced by Georgian folk art. Together with French painter Henri Rousseau (1844–1910), Pirosmanashvili is considered to be one of the world's most important naïve artists. Most of his pictures are in the possession of the Georgian art gallery in Tbilisi, and include such works as *Reebak srehdee skal* (*Fisherman Among the Rocks*), *Kootezh treokh knyaza* (*The Orgy of the Three Princes*), and *Dvornik* (*Janitor*).

Pizarro, Francisco (1475–1541)

Spanish *conquistador*. Pizarro was born in Trujillo in the Extremadura province of Spain, the illegitimate son of a captain in the Royal Infantry and a young girl from an impoverished family. He was raised by his grandparents and is said to have worked as a swineherd. In 1502 he joined a fleet bound for Hispaniola (the site of modern-day Haiti and the Dominican Republic), where he settled.

Pizarro soon became involved with voyages of exploration, and in 1513 he accompanied Vasco Núñez de Balboa on the expedition credited with the European discovery of the Pacific Ocean. His travels brought him fame and prosperity, and in 1519 he was named mayor and magistrate of Panama, where he remained until 1523.

At the age of forty-eight, Pizarro embarked on the journey for which he is remembered, an exploration of the Pacific coast of South America. The first two years proved disappointing, but between 1526 and 1528 he began to detect signs of a more highly developed Indian civilization along the Gulf of Guayaquil. Pizarro asked the governor of Panama for reinforcements to help in his planned conquest of the Incas. When these were denied, Pizarro is said to have drawn a line on the ground with his sword, inviting those in his crew who desired wealth and glory to cross it. With the "famous thirteen" who accepted his challenge, Pizarro continued his voyage, venturing down the coast as far as nine degrees south.

Even with the evidence of the wealth of the Inca empire, Pizarro still encountered opposition from the governor of Panama; he was forced to travel to Spain in 1528 to ask Charles V in person for permission to undertake the conquest. Charles V named Pizarro governor and captain general of the province of New Castile, a region extending six hundred miles south of Panama; he returned to Panama in 1530 with his four brothers, reinforcements, and all the authority and prerogatives of a viceroy.

In January of the following year, he set out with 180 men and 37 horses, and by April he had made contact with Atahualpa, the recently crowned Inca emperor. Pizarro found the Inca empire weakened by years of civil war; though vastly outnumbered, he succeeded in luring Atahualpa into an ambush in the great square of Cajamarca. Atahaulpa arrived at the square on a litter and accompanied by three thousand bodyguards. When he refused to swear allegiance to Charles V or to accept Christianity, Pizarro attacked, astonishing the Incas by capturing their leader.

Pizarro seized Atahualpa and held him hostage, finally executing him on August 29, 1533. Pizarro marched into Cuzco, the Incan capital, and easily occupied it. By 1534 Pizarro and his men had subdued the entire kingdom of the Incas, and that year he founded the new city of Lima, from which the Spanish governed their Peruvian possessions.

Pizarro spent the last years of his life consolidating Spanish control of Peru and defending his share of the spoils during the civil war that raged between Spanish factions for the next twelve years. Pizarro was killed by the son of Diego de Almagro, one of his partners in the original expedition. He is said to have died a slow death in the governor's palace in Lima, drawing a cross with his own blood on the ground, kissing it, and crying "Jesus!" as he fell.

Plato (c. 427–347 B.C.E.)

Ancient Greek philosopher. Plato was born to an aristocratic Athenian family and began his career as a poet, turning to philosophy after his association with Greek philosopher Socrates (c. 469–399 B.C.E.). As Plato was a disciple of Socrates, Socrates is the principal figure in many of Plato's early works, including the *Apology*, *Crito*, and *Charmides*, which are presented as speeches by or dialogues with Socrates.

In the second phase of Plato's work, Socrates is the principal figure but puts forth original Platonic, rather than Socratic, arguments. *Gorgias*, *Protagoras*, and *Phaedo* are works from Plato's middle period, along with the *Republic*, which covers topics spanning justice, poetry, and political evolution, including a description of the philosopher-king, which Plato presents as the ideal ruler. In the last phase of Plato's writing he does not use Socrates as a character as often, but continues to write in dialogue in works like the *Sophist*, *Politicus*, and *The Laws*, which amended the *Republic* and was his last work.

Plato is credited with founding philosophical idealism, the doctrine that reality is fundamentally constituted by abstract universals he called Ideas. He also argued that only the practice of dialectic, or philosophical inquiry, could lead to true knowledge. These views are outlined in many of his works, which are written so artfully that they have established him as one of the greatest writers of Greek prose. Much of Plato's work had an enormous influence on the religious doctrines of Judaism and Christianity, as well as on philosophers of ancient Rome, the European Renaissance, and seventeenth-century England.

Poe, Edgar Allan (1809–1849)

American poet, author, and critic. Poe's parents were itinerant actors; his father died the year after he was born and his mother the year after that. Poe was raised in the home of a Richmond merchant, John Allan, who moved to England in 1815 and there enrolled Edgar in private schools. Although Poe was never officially adopted by the Allan family, in 1824 he took the surname Allan and used it for the remainder of his life. Poe matriculated at the University of Virginia in 1826, but became estranged from his stepfather and was left without financial support. Poe went to Boston in 1827 and published *Tamerlaine and Other Poems* himself, but found no audience. He enlisted in the U.S. Army, and was sent to Sullivan's Island, South Carolina.

The death of John Allan's wife led to some form of reconciliation between Poe and his stepfather, and he secured a place at the military academy in West Point and an allowance to live on. While staying with his father's sister, Mrs. Maria Clemm, in Baltimore, he published *Al Aaraaf* (1829). He attended West Point in 1830 but was expelled for gross neglect of duty, and was thenceforth written out of his stepfather's life and will. He published *Poems by Edgar A. Poe* in 1831 in New York, but lived with Mrs. Clemm in Baltimore until 1835, working as an editor on the *Southern Literary Messenger*.

In 1835, Poe married his cousin Virginia, who was thirteen years old. He moved with his new wife and Mrs. Clemm to Richmond, continuing to work for the *Messenger* until 1837, when he was fired due to excessive drinking. During the course of his career with the magazine, he produced eighty-three reviews, four essays, and three short stories, greatly increasing the magazine's circulation. Poe's drinking and erratic habits kept his terms of employment brief;

however, his employers included *Burton's Gentleman's Magazine* (1839–40), *Graham's Magazine* (1841–42), the New York *Mirror* (1844), and the *Broadway Journal* (1846). In the last two publications listed, he made his celebrated attacks on American poet Henry Wadsworth Longfellow (1807–1882).

Concerned with poetic unity as a completeness of mood or emotion, Poe created macabre, suspenseful tales influenced by the Gothic tradition of literature. Some of his books are *The Narrative of Arthur Gordon Pym of Nantucket* (1838), *Tales of the Grotesque and Arabesque* (1840), *The Prose Romances of Edgar A. Poe, No. I. Containing the Murders in the Rue Morgue and The Man That Was Used Up* (1843), *Tales by Edgar A. Poe* (1845), *The Raven and Other Poems* (1845), and *Eureka: A Prose Poem by Edgar A. Poe* (1848).

After the death of his wife, Virginia, in 1847, Poe's mental condition deteriorated. He suffered severe bouts of depression and he attempted suicide. Determined to marry again, Poe made serious attempts to curb his drinking. Nevertheless, while traveling to Richmond to escort Mrs. Clemm to his wedding, he stopped in Baltimore, and five days later he was discovered in an alcoholic stupor. Since he was found near a saloon used as a polling place, some suggest that he was victimized by political gangs that used drunks as repeat voters. Others claim he died of a rabies infection. He died four days later, and was buried beside Virginia in Baltimore.

Polk, James [Knox] (1795–1849)

Eleventh U.S. president. Born on a farm in Mecklenburg County, North Carolina, Polk was the oldest of ten children. At the age of eleven he moved with his family to what was then the western frontier of the United States and is now Tennessee. Though he received little formal education in his early years, he was admitted to the University of North

Carolina and graduated first in his class in 1818, with special honors in classics and mathematics. Polk returned to Tennessee to study law at a local firm, was admitted to the bar in 1820, and set up a law practice in Columbia (near Nashville). He served as clerk of the state senate until he was elected to the state house of representatives in 1823. He married Sarah Childress the following year, and in 1825 he was elected to the U.S. House of Representatives, where he remained as a powerful advocate for the Democratic Party for the next fourteen years. Polk supported the presidential campaign of his longtime friend Andrew Jackson, and when the latter was elected in 1828, Polk became a prominent spokesman for the administration's policies. (His loyalty to Jackson earned him the nickname "Young Hickory.") Becoming Speaker of the House in 1835, he left Congress to run successfully for governor of Tennessee in 1839, but was defeated in reelection bids in 1841 and 1843. In 1844 Polk was nominated as its presidential candidate by the Democratic convention on the ninth ballot and became the first "dark horse" winner in presidential history. The favorite, Martin Van Buren, had opposed the annexation of Texas because it was a slave state. Polk supported the annexation, and primarily due to this position, he narrowly defeated the Whig candidate, Henry Clay. The youngest man elected up to that time, Polk was extremely successful as president, achieving all four of his major stated goals: reducing federal tariffs, reestablishing the independent treasury system, settling the Oregon boundary dispute, and acquiring the California territory. During the "Oregon crisis," he threatened Great Britain with war until it surrendered its claim. The slogan "54°40' or fight" referred to the boundary the Democrats wanted to establish (though the actual compromise reached was slightly less). Mexico disputed his insistence on the Rio Grande

as the southern border of Texas, and Polk persuaded Congress to declare war. In the ensuing treaty, Polk established claim to Texas as well as the valuable California Territory (much of what is now the American Southwest). When he announced the discovery of gold there in 1848, the "Gold Rush" began that would precipitate the westward expansion of the U.S. population, fulfilling Polk's dream of "manifest destiny." Polk died soon after leaving office.

Polo, Marco (c. 1254–1354)

Venetian explorer. Born into a family of merchants, Polo began his journey to China at the age of seventeen, when he accompanied his father and uncle on their second journey to Beijing. The arduous journey over land and sea took almost three years, and at its completion, they received a warm reception at the court of the Mongol emperor Kublai Khan (c. 1215–1294). Though the khan had requested that the Polos bring with them one hundred Europeans, from whom he could learn, he willingly took the Polos into his court. Especially impressed by young Marco's facility with the Mongol language and abilities as an explorer, the khan kept him in his service for seventeen years. Polo traveled throughout the empire on missions for the khan, and journeyed to Tibet and Burma, and even as far south as India. After some difficulty in leaving the khan's service, Marco Polo returned unrecognized to Venice in 1295. The account of his travels, *Il milione* (c. 1295; *The Travels of Marco Polo*), did much to inspire further journeys to China, and remains an important historical document.

Pope, Alexander (1688–1744)

English poet. The reigning literary figure of his day, Pope is considered to be the best example of Neoclassicism in literature. He was raised a Roman Catholic at a time when virulent anti-Catholic sentiment raged throughout

England. Suffering from a tubercular infection as a child, Pope was left with a severe curvature of the spine, which prevented him from growing taller than four feet six inches. A precocious poet, Pope wrote his *Pastorals* (1709) at the age of sixteen. This was followed by his poem *Essay on Criticism* (1711), considered the definitive work on literary Classicism, which made Pope famous at the age of twenty-three. *Rape of the Lock* (1712) established his reputation as a poet. Pope is renowned for his technical mastery as well as his skilled use of didacticism and wit in verse. Other notable works include "Elegy to the Memory of an Unfortunate Lady" and "Eloisa to Abelard" (both 1717); the satirical *Dunciad* (1728–43), inspired by his friend and occasional collaborator English satirist Jonathan Swift (1667–1745); *An Essay on Man* (1733–34); and his fine translations of Homer's *Iliad* (1715–20) and *Odyssey* (1725–26). Though his satirical verse created some enemies in literary circles—and earned him the nickname "Wicked Wasp of Twickenham"— his literary achievements are enormous, and he is generally considered one of the finest of verse satirists.

Popol Vuh

Mayan sacred document. Aside from its religious intention, the *Popol Vuh* is the most important historical record of the Quiché kingdom in northwestern Guatemala. It was written in the Quiché language, unique to Guatemalan Mayas, and using Latin letters, shortly after the Spanish conquest in 1524. The *Popol Vuh* chronicles the genesis of the earth and the creation of the Quiché Indians, and contains the history of the Quiché kings until 1550. The manuscripts were discovered in the eighteenth century by Francisco Ximenez, a parish priest in highland Guatemala. This account was augmented by Charles Étienne Brasseur's conversations with local Quiché regarding their history and lineage.

Poro

African religious society. The Poro is a traditional secret religious society whose membership is restricted to males. Popular in areas along the northern Gulf of Guinea, members of the secret society control much of the political and social activity of certain groups, including the Mende and Temne in Sierra Leone; the Vali, Kpelle, and Gola in Liberia; and the Senufo on the northern Ivory Coast. One writer has drawn an analogy between the influence of the Poro on society and the role of the Catholic Church in medieval Europe.

Only those men who have undergone special initiation ceremonies are allowed to attend meetings. During initiation and at the society's ritual congregations, members wear masks that are associated with Poro spirits, who are often ancestors. Younger members beat on the ground, enjoining various ancestors to participate in the ceremony. The leaders of the Poro have civil and religious authority, functioning as semijuridical bodies with the power to order, or stay, executions. However, it is believed that the ultimate authority of these societies is spiritual in nature.

Porter, Katherine Anne (1890–1980)

American short-story writer and novelist. Porter is celebrated for her long and vivid stories that explore complex characters. Born in Indian Creek, Texas, she was a descendant of Daniel Boone's brother Jonathan and a cousin of O. Henry (Sidney Porter). Porter's passion for creative writing dates from her childhood, but her early professional career was spent writing for newspapers and, for a brief period, singing Scottish ballads.

Porter traveled through Mexico in the 1920s, writing articles while peripherally involved in the takeover of the Mexican presidency by Álvaro Obregón. She would later claim that during this period she had written numerous manuscripts, only to destroy them. Porter published her first volume of stories, *Flowering Judas*, in 1930. Inspired by her travels, the title story revolves around a relationship between two revolutionaries and tackles the issue of self-betrayal, which Porter claimed was central to her life and work. The book, only moderately successful despite critical acclaim, won her a Guggenheim fellowship on which she traveled to Mexico and Germany.

Her next published work was another collection of stories, called *Hacienda* (1934), followed by a short novel, *Noon Wine* (1937). The latter was also included in the collection of three long short stories *Pale Horse, Pale Rider* (1939), along with the title story and *Old Mortality*. Other works included *The Leaning Tower and Other Stories* (1944), whose title story concerns the Nazi threat, and *The Days Before: Collected Essays and Occasional Writings* (1952; augmented in 1970). Porter's only novel, *Ship of Fools* (1962), examines the dynamics of a group of international travelers and is based on *Das Narrenschiff*, a fifteenth-century work by Sebastian Brant. Her *Collected Stories* (1965) won the National Book Award and the Pulitzer Prize for fiction.

Powhatan Confederation

American Indian tribal organization. This large confederation in eastern Virginia and southern Maryland consisted of over thirty Algonkian-speaking North American tribes and was one of the first known to the white settlers. The confederation is named for Powhatan (Wahunsonacock), who added twenty-five new tribes to the six-tribe union established by his father and brought the confederacy to the height of its power, with 128 named villages and over 9,000 people. The tribes paid taxes, shared food, and provided military support.

The Jesuits first attempted to establish a mission among these tribes in the six-teenth century, but it was only with the Jamestown settlement in 1607 that Europeans managed to initiate contacts with these Indians. Chief Powhatan and his daughter Pocahontas—who married an English settler—attempted to remain on good terms with the whites, but as the settlement expanded and came to occupy more and more of the confederation's best land, this became increasingly difficult. Fighting finally broke out between the settlers and the confederation after Powhatan's death in 1618 and lasted until 1676. The years marked by the most violent conflicts, 1622–44, are known as the Powhatan War. The tribes, led by Powhatan's elderly brother, Opechancanough, waged a violent campaign that destroyed all English settlements except those closest to Jamestown. In 1644, after a final Powhatan uprising in which five hundred English settlers were killed, the British, aided by Christianized Indians, broke the power of the Powhatan Confederation and murdered Opechancanough. Following the peace negotiations, the Powhatan Confederation was dismembered and the tribes moved to reservations. Those who remained on the eastern shore of Virginia mixed with settlers and slaves, and the confederation disappeared. Descendants of the Powhatan include the Chickahominy and other small tribes of the Virginia and Chesapeake area.

powwow

American Indian gathering. This Indian word, which can be roughly translated as "he dreams," describes a wide variety of tribal practices. It is often applied to the conjurings of a medicine man over a patient, and in some tribes even refers to the practice of witchcraft. In New England the powwow referred to a tribal gathering around a fire, usually during a time of food shortage or illness, at which prayers and songs were offered to the spirits. Often these chants were accompanied by drum beating. Perhaps the most widely known form of the pow-wow is the vibrant, celebratory dance festivals of many tribes. These were held in celebration of an event, such as a peace proposal among tribes. As the tribal leaders engaged in peace negotiations, often the deliberations would spark an outbreak of singing and dancing that could last for days. Historically, Europeans misinterpreted the meaning of the powwow celebration and assumed that it served as a "war dance."

Prester John

Mythical medieval character. A mythical priest and emperor of Ethiopia, Prester John was thought to rule over vast domains in India, the Far East, and Africa. A descendant of the African magus who visited the baby Jesus, Prester John purportedly sent a letter in 1165 to Emperor Manuel. The letter, in which Prester John described the wonders of his kingdom, offered the support of the greatest march under heaven in the Christians' attempt to subdue the Muslims.

As legend tells it, the most fantastic beasts and artifacts made up the majority of Prester John's dominions. From the eccentric race of Amazons, to ants that dug gold and fish that created the color purple, his empire bore the fruits of a magical land. Included in his kingdom were also the Fountain of Youth; pebbles that gave light, restored sight, and rendered the possessor invisible; and subterranean streams where the sand was made up of gems. Before his vast armies, thirteen crosses of gold stood in glory to impress the enemies of Christianity, and thousands upon thousands of knights and kings served in their devoted ranks. While he referred to himself as a "presbyter" (a member of an early Christian order of priests), the glory of his reign bespoke the dignity and power which he held.

Much of the impulse of the Portuguese to explore the seas, leading to the discovery of a passageway to India around the horn of Africa and, later, to quests by the Spanish in the New World for El Dorado and the Fountain of Youth, stemmed from the search for this mythical African king.

Prithvinarayan Shah (1723–1775)

Founder of modern Nepal. In 1769 the Prithvinarayan Shah conquered the three Malla kingdoms of the Kathmandu Valley (Kathmandu, Patan, and Bhaktapur) and unified Nepal, moving the capital to Kathmandu. The Shah turned a poor kingdom into a strong nation that was able to contend with the powerful British military in the nineteenth century. Upon his death, the Shah advised his successors to prepare Nepal for British military aggression. His concerns for the nation were collected in a book called the *Divya upadesha*. His successors continued the Shah's policy of expansion into the early nineteenth century; Nepal was involved in a war with China (1792) and with the British in India (1814–16). The death of the Prithvinarayan Shah was followed by a period of political instability that lasted through the early nineteenth century and culminated in the Kot massacre of 1846. Civil and military officials were murdered and Jung Bahadur Rana (1846–1877) came to power. He usurped the traditional power of the king and established a precedent wherein only a descendant of the Rana family could hold the prime ministership. The Rana family controlled Nepal for the next century.

priyayi

Traditional Java aristocracy. The *priyayi* were traditionally landowners and the gentlefolk attached to the royal Javanese courts. As with similar social groups throughout colonized Asia, descendants of this class were the first to be Western-educated and incorporated into the Dutch colonial bureaucracy. In part because of their familiarity with the ideals of Western political philosophies, many *priyayi* at the beginning of the twentieth century began to challenge openly the hypocrisies of colonial rule. Alternatively, other representatives of this elite sector remained loyal to the colonial situation that had privileged them. Sukarno, the Indonesian nationalist and first president of independent Indonesia, was a member of the *priyayi*. In popular usage, the word *priyayi* has come to mean "gentleman" with more or less flattering connotations, depending on the speaker.

Protest Song, *see* Canción de Protesta

Proust, Marcel (1871–1922)

French novelist. Proust was born into a bourgeois household; his father was an eminent doctor in Paris and a member of the faculty of medicine at the University of Paris, and his mother, to whom he was very close, belonged to a respected Jewish family. It is through his education at the Lycée Condorcet (1882–89) that Proust was first introduced to the Parisian elite, through the families of his schoolmates. After a short time in the military at Orléans (1889–90), Proust attended the École des Sciences Politiques, studying both law and literature.

Proust's first published writings were a collection of short stories, *Les Plaisirs et les jours* (*Pleasures and Regrets*). Although published in 1896, they originally appeared in the magazines *Le Banquet* and *La Revue Blanche* between the years 1892 and 1893. These early writings already reveal the delicate and graceful style of his prose, as well as his fascination with drawing-room society. *Jean Santeuil* (1895–99), Proust's autobiographical attempt at a first novel, was in many ways a reaction to the anti-Semitic aspects of the Dreyfus Affair (1894–1906).

At the age of nine, Proust experienced his first serious asthma attack, a condition from which he would suffer for the remainder of his life. As a result, his parents made it a policy to send him off to stay with relatives in the villages of Auteuil and Illiers. His early memories of idyllic summers in the country clearly serve as inspiration for the vivid childhood memories spun in the Combray section that opens his expansive twelve-volume masterpiece, *À la recherche du temps perdu* (1927; *Remembrance of Things Past*), which grew out of a philosophical interest in the nature of memory. In this work, Proust manages to deal with both Judaism and homosexuality in depth by focusing on these issues through various characters throughout the text. Many scholars and writers have suggested that Proust himself was homosexual, although this issue has been widely debated. In 1897 Proust fought an inconclusive duel with Jean Lorrain, a journalist whose crime, according to Proust, was a subtle allusion in print to Proust's homosexuality.

In 1907 Proust moved to an apartment containing a cork-lined bedroom that shielded the artist from any potential distraction or noise. There he commenced the writing of his great masterpiece, which is known, among other things, for the intense beauty of its winding, often page-long sentences. Along with Irish novelist James Joyce's *Ulysses*, *Remembrance of Things Past* is considered by many to be the crowning achievement of modernism. Its publication was delayed due to the First World War, and Proust took advantage of the additional years to make a series of "revisions" that expanded the text to twice the "completed" length.

Puccini, Giacomo (1858–1924)

Italian composer. Puccini came from a family of distinguished musicians and was educated at the Milan Conservatory, where he gained the attention of the publisher of Italian composer Giuseppe

Verdi (1813–1901). Though his first opera, *Edgar* (1889), failed, the second, *Manon Lescaut* (1893), was highly acclaimed. *La Bohème* (1896; *The Bohemians*) was initially not received enthusiastically but now is a mainstay of operatic repertoire. The opera itself was sufficiently dear to Puccini that he engaged in a lifelong quarrel with the Italian composer Ruggiero Leoncavallo (1859–1919), who, having prepared a libretto and music on the same story, never forgave Puccini for stealing his idea. The highly successful *Tosca* (1900) immediately followed and established Puccini as Verdi's successor in Italian opera. With *Madama Butterfly* (1904; *Madame Butterfly*), Puccini again encountered trouble; at the first performance, the opera was practically hissed off the stage. Puccini made minor revisions, and the opera soon emerged as one of the most popular in the world. Later operas include *La Fanciulla del West* (1910; *The Girl of the Golden West*) and the more experimental *Turandot* (1926), which was left unfinished at the time of Puccini's death in 1924.

Pueblo

American Indian tribe. The Pueblo of New Mexico and northern Arizona represent one of the best-preserved American Indian cultures remaining in the United States. The name derives from the Spanish word *pueblo*, meaning "village," and was applied by the *conquistadores* to those people who dwelled in large multistoried apartments of stone or adobe and who shared, if not a common language, at least a common culture based on intensive agriculture and a rich religious ceremonialism, much of which centered on the *kiva*, or underground ritual chamber. The central theme here was that of achieving harmony with the gods of nature to ensure an abundance of crops. The religious hierarchy, composed of native priests, directed all phases of village life, acting through clans, or, in some cases, medicine societies.

Ceramics and weaving were the most advanced arts of Pueblo material culture, and basketry was widespread. Traditionally, the economy was based on agriculture; the principal field crops were maize, beans, squashes, tobacco, and native cotton. An All Pueblo Council, first organized in 1922, now meets periodically at Santo Domingo, New Mexico, to consider matters of general concern.

Pueblo Rebellion

American Indian rebellion. The Pueblo Rebellion was led by Popé against Spanish rule in 1680, and for this reason is often called the Popé Rebellion. When Spain colonized New Mexico in 1598, the indigenous Tewa Pueblo Indians were rendered virtually defenseless against the Spanish colonizers. The tribes were forcibly converted to Catholicism, and their *kivas*, or underground ritual chambers, and ceremonial masks were systematically destroyed. Natives who were suspected of practicing their own religious customs were often consigned to slave status, hanged, whipped, imprisoned, or, most severely, dismembered at the hand or foot.

In 1675 Popé, a Tewa Pueblo medicine man imprisoned for the "crime" of practicing his traditional religion, believed that the *kachinas* (nature gods) had called him to wrest colonial control from the Spanish and restore traditional Pueblo culture and religion. Upon his release from prison, Popé hid in Taos Pueblo, planning and organizing a full-scale revolt against the Spaniards. He persuaded nearly every Pueblo tribe to participate and on August 10, 1680, under Popé's command, the Pueblos besieged the capital of Santa Fe, killing four hundred Spanish, including twenty-one priests. The surviving Spaniards were driven out of Santa Fe and south to the area now called El Paso, Texas.

In celebration of their victory, the Pueblo proceeded to destroy all vestiges of Spanish culture and religion in their territory. Churches were burned, Christian marriages were annulled, and the stains of Christian baptism were symbolically washed away. As a symbol of restored Pueblo custom, Popé traveled throughout the region in ceremonial dress. The natives remained free from colonial domination for twelve years, until drought and internal dissension left them vulnerable. In 1692, two years after Popé's death, the area of present-day New Mexico was reconquered by the Spanish. Spanish rule after the Pueblo Rebellion, however, was never so strong or onerous as the one successfully destroyed by the Pueblo revolt.

Punjab

Pakistani and Indian territory. The name Punjab (or Panjab) is derived from two Persian words, *panj* ("five") and *ab* ("river"), designating the five rivers that originally flowed through the territory. Tradition has it that in 1709–10, the Sikh hermit and military leader Banda Somgj Bajadir laid the foundations of Punjab when he liberated the eastern section of the territory from the Mughal rule of the Delhi sultans. Under such leaders as the maharajah Ranjit Singh (1790–1839), the Sikhs maintained a powerful empire in the Punjab until 1849, when it came under British rule.

Following the Partition of India in 1947, the Punjab was divided between Pakistan and India. Punjabi is spoken by two thirds of the population in Pakistan and by a majority of the population in the Indian states of the Punjab and Haryana. The almost entirely Muslim Pakistani province of Punjab, with its capital, Lahore, is the second-largest province in that country and the most densely populated. In 1955, along with Sindh, the North-West Frontier, and Baluchistan, the Punjab was merged to form the administrative unit of West Pakistan. Indian Punjab was also reorganized in 1966, when the largely Sikh and Hindu Indian territory was further divided on the basis of language into three units: the core Punjabi Suba, the newly formed Hindi-speaking state of Haryana, and Himachal Pradesh.

Although the linguistic reorganization of the state in 1966 was intended to soothe tensions between Hindus and Sikhs, in 1980–84 the "Punjab crisis" erupted. It stemmed in part from the government's failure to complete its reorganization of the state. Beginning in 1980, several extremist parties of the majority Sikh community rose to power and made the Sikh Golden Temple in Amritsar their base of operations. In June 1984 Prime Minister Indira Gandhi sent in the army to clear the temple. The loss of life and desecration of the temple further inflamed the Sikhs, whose anger culminated in the execution of the prime minister by two of her Sikh bodyguards in November 1984. Following her execution, many innocent Sikhs were massacred throughout India, and Punjab was a place of strife. However, in recent years, the armed forces and the police have combined efforts to suppress terrorism and been largely successful.

punk

International musical and cultural movement, 1976–83 (sometimes 1976–present). Inspired by the untutored "garage bands" of the mid-1960s, punks like the Stooges, the Ramones, and the New York Dolls played aggressive, basic guitar rock and sang about teenage frustration. The Sex Pistols, assembled by a London fashion designer–manager, combined the Ramones' simplicity with all-out media shock tactics, advocating anarchy in a hit called "God Save the Queen." Their success—and their lack of training—inspired thousands of other bands; from a local London scene in summer 1976, punk's sound and ethic had spread across Europe and the English-speaking world by the end of 1977.

Punk rockers repudiated technical skill to establish more direct connections between performer and audience. Early on, this meant imitating the Ramones' three-chord tactics, though with a much angrier (often more political) feel, as in early music by the Clash, the Buzzcocks, and Subway Sect in the United Kingdom; the Pagans, the Voidoids, and the Dils in the United States; and Australia's Saints and Radio Birdman. This basic punk rock spawned Oi, a tuneful expression of working-class solidarity later coopted by European right-wingers, and American hard core, whose loud, clipped songs about growing up were perfected by Washington, D.C.'s, Minor Threat, then personalized by Sorry, Rites of Spring, and Squirrel Bait during the mid-1980s.

Equality between artist and audience sometimes meant gender equality; women called the shots in punk bands like the Slits, Kleenex (later Liliput), X-Ray Spex, and Los Angeles's X. Plenty of other men and women made punk an excuse to experiment, applying its stripped-down style to brainy reggae beats (the Slits, Scritti Politti), political white funk (Gang of Four), quiet cabaret (Wales's Young Marble Giants), electronics (France's Metal Urbain), or improvisational atonality (Alternative TV). American art bands, like Cleveland's Pere Ubu, took their dissonant cues from jack-of-all-trades Captain Beefheart. London's Wire and Boston's Mission of Burma combined punk's artier side with its gut-level aggression; few others could.

Punk's urgent and self-reliant ethic was called "Do It Yourself," a far-reaching demand that saw bands sidestepping the big record companies, putting out their own records, communicating via fanzines (homemade photocopied personal magazines, a music-subcultural *samizdat*), and releasing product through independent distributors and small shops, creating the current international network for underground rock and dance music. More delicate pop groups could now form and be heard without wide commercial appeal; London's TV Personalities, Scotland's Orange Juice, Australia's Go-Betweens, and New Zealand's Toy Love and the Clean exemplified this lighter side of punk, musically reliant on 1960s forerunners the Velvet Underground. Later observers saw in punk's theatrics, its democratic economics, and its purified anger an ideology of negation-at-all-costs. But punk's greatest effects have been aesthetic and economic; the sound of pure or early punk continues to influence 1990s rock, and almost every important pop movement since 1977 has adopted its do-it-yourself strategies and tried to reawaken its power.

Purim

Jewish holiday. From the Hebrew, meaning "lots," this holiday commemorates the heroic actions of Queen Esther, who saved the Jews of Persia from extermination during the reign of Xerxes I (485–465 B.C.E.). According to the biblical account told in the Book of Esther, Haman, chief minister of Ahasuerus (Xerxes), had persuaded the king to destroy the Jews. They had drawn lots to determine the day of the massacre, which was to be (in the Hebrew calendar) on Adar 13. But Xerxes' Jewish wife, Esther, at considerable peril to her own life, pleaded for the lives of her people. She managed to convince him that the Jews should be allowed to arm themselves, and in the ensuing battle the Jews proved capable of defending themselves and guaranteeing their own safety. The day after the battle, Adar 14, was set aside for festivities and thanksgiving. Purim is today celebrated by the reading of the *Megillah* (a special parchment scroll containing the Book of Esther) to the men and women of the community on the evening before and the festival day itself. Traditional rattles ("greggers") are shaken at every mention of the name Haman. Sweets and small gifts are given to friends and family members, while donations of food and money are given to the poor. The celebrations culminate in the *seudah*, the traditional Purim banquet, at which wine flows freely and a festive air prevails.

Pushkin, Aleksandr [Sergeevich] (1799–1837)

Russian poet. Pushkin was born in Moscow into a noble family, descended on his mother's side from a member of an Abyssinian princely dynasty who assumed the name of Abram Gannibal and served under Peter the Great. Pushkin's poetry first received attention even before he completed his studies at the Tsarskoe Selo Lyceum in 1817. He then received a sinecure with the government in St. Petersburg and composed his famous poem *Ruslan i Liudmila* (1817–20; *Ruslan and Liudmila*), which drew on a variety of Russian folklore beliefs and established Pushkin as an important presence on the literary scene. In 1820, however, Pushkin was "transferred" to the southern parts of Russia, first to Kishinev and then to Odessa, because of some unfavorable political epigrams he had written and distributed.

During this exile, he traveled widely around the Black Sea coast and the Caucasus and continued his prolific writing. His problems with the government continued, and in 1824 he was banished to his family's estate for spreading atheistic, antigovernment sentiments. Count Vorontsov, Odessa's governor general, with whose wife Pushkin had a lasting love affair and an illegitimate child, was instrumental in having Pushkin banished. At the family estate in Mikhailovskoe, Pushkin continued his work on his great novel *Evgenii Onegin* (1833; *Eugene Onegin*), started in Odessa, and completed his drama *Boris Godunov*, among other works. Released from banishment in 1826, Pushkin returned to St. Petersburg and resumed his active social and literary life. In the fall of 1830, he found himself unexpectedly confined by a cholera epidemic at his family's estate of Boldino in central Russia. There he had an explosion of creativity, known as the Boldino Fall, finishing *Eugene Onegin* and producing some of his finest poems, as well as a cycle of short stories, known as *Povesti Belkina* (1831; *The Tales of Belkin*), and a cycle of short verse dramas, *Malen'kie tragedii* (1830–36; *The Little Tragedies*). In 1831 Pushkin married eighteen-year-old Natalia Goncharova, but it was not entirely a happy match. Goncharova's busy social life and the financial demands of a growing family left Pushkin little time for his creative work. Incensed by his wife's fondness for a guards officer, Baron George d'Anthes, Pushkin challenged him to a duel and was fatally wounded.

As a poet, Pushkin has had a lasting influence on Russian literary tradition. His early work, influenced by French and British Romanticism, gave way to his later experimentation with language and the development of a concise, simple poetic style, as demonstrated in the long poems *Poltava* (1828–29) and *Mednyi vsadnik* (1833; *The Bronze Horseman*). In the 1830s he wrote several important prose works, including the short novel *Pikovaia dama* (1834; *The Queen of Spades*). Pushkin also continued to place politics within the parameters of his writing, in works such as the historical novel *Kapitanskaia dochka* (1836; *The Captain's Daughter*), dealing with the events of the peasant and Cossack uprising of 1773–74 led by Emelian Pugachov.

Pushtun

People of Afghanistan and Pakistan. The Pushtun territory of the North-West Frontier straddles the border between

Afghanistan and Pakistan. The term Pushtun (Pashtun, Pakhtun, Pathan in Indic languages, and Pukhtun in northern dialects) refers specifically to the dominant tribal groups of central and eastern Afghanistan and northwestern Pakistan. The Pushtun were originally known as the Afghan; it was later that the term was applied to all inhabitants of the region. First mention of these Afghans appears in the writings of the Indian astronomer Varaha Mihira in the sixth century. Later works of Islamic historiography describe them as mercenaries and brigands.

Pushtun history claims that all Pushtun are descended from a common Afghani ancestor. Although Afghanistan may be their homeland, there are more Pushtun dwelling in Pakistan than are currently residing in Afghanistan. The Pakistani Pushtun moved to the area now called Pakistan sometime between the thirteenth and sixteenth centuries. A tribal people, the Pushtun consist of approximately sixty tribes altogether, each divided into clans, subclans, and patriarchal families. Kinship is traced through the male bloodline, and tribal genealogies establish not only rights of succession and inheritance but also additional powers like the right to use tribal lands and to speak at tribal councils. Blood feuds among families and even whole clans are not uncommon, usually caused by disputes over property or personal injury.

The Durranis, sometimes known as Abdalis, are the most powerful Pushtun tribe, and it was under a Durrani king, Ahmad Shah, that Afghanistan first emerged as a unified political entity in the eighteenth century. Pushtuns are united by a common culture, and their language is known as Pashto; people with advanced schooling also speak Persian or Urdu. Most Pushtun are sedentary farmers, although some are herdsmen, caravaners, and warriors. With a strong and aggressive military tendency, Pushtun culture has found expression in internecine tribal warfare and repeated incursions into India, occasionally establishing dynasties in northern India. As a result, Pushtun culture has bred a wealth of mystical poets and warrior saints.

The literature of the Pushtun culture reflects their distinct social identity and the influence of Persian culture. The Pushtun folk poetry of the Khatak chieftain Khushhal Khan (1613–1689) illustrates the confluence of Persian-Pushtun themes, for the poet adapts the classic Persian forms of *ghazal* and *rubai* to express Pushtun preoccupations with martial and homoerotic themes. Several other Pushtun poems figure prominently in Pushtun literary history. These include the *divan* of Afghan warlord Ahmad Shah Durrani (d. 1772), the mystical poetry of a Pakistani Pushtun favorite, Rahman Baba (d. 1706), and the contemporary poems of Rehat Zakhili (d. 1963).

Pu Songling (1640–1715)

Chinese poet. Pu Songling was a native of Zichuan in the province of Shandong. He lived at the beginning of the Qing dynasty (1644–1911), during the rule of the foreign Manchu government. A witness to the cruelty and horror of civil war, Pu was deeply conscious of the injustices committed, and his writing exposed, satirized, and attacked the society of his time. As a means of expressing himself under the repression of Qing law, Pu retold popular legends and folklore, namely in his *Liaozhai Zhiyi* (1679; *Strange Stories from a Chinese Studio*), more familiarly known as *Liaozhai*. This Chinese classic is divided into 8 volumes and comprises 431 short stories. Fox-fairies, ghosts, and other spirits abound in *Liaozhai*, meting out rewards and punishment to good or bad mortals.

Pu often used characters and incidents in these tales to express his hatred of the new regime, its corrupt officials, and other injustices, in particular the system of scholarship through examinations. *Liaozhai* was written with a mastery of the classical language, giving Pu an important position in the ranks of Chinese classical writers.

Pu Yi (1906–1967)

Last emperor of China. Pu Yi was the reigning title of Xuan Tong, who was put onto the throne to succeed his uncle, the emperor Guang Xu, when he was only three years old. In 1911 the republican revolution initiated by Sun Yat-sen broke out and put an end to the Qing (Manchu) dynasty (1644–1911), thus also ending the two-thousand-year-old imperial system in China. Pu Yi, overthrown, was nevertheless allowed to remain in the Imperial Palace, the famous "Forbidden City." Here he grew up, married, and taking a Western name, became Henry Pu Yi, a young man aspiring as much to the Western way of life as to the restoration of his imperial power.

In 1931 Japan occupied northeast China and three years later set Pu Yi up as a puppet emperor of the Manchouguo, a position he held from 1934 to 1945. When Japan was defeated at the end of World War II, Pu Yi was already a distressed and lonely man: his wife, the empress, had been suffering from madness, and his concubine had separated from him. He attempted to escape to Japan, but the Soviet Red Army captured him. He was returned to China as a war criminal in 1950. After a nine-year "education" in prison, he was pardoned in 1959. He returned to Beijing, worked as a gardener for a while, remarried, and later became a special representative to the Chinese People's Political Consultative Conference. He wrote his autobiography, *The First Half of My Life*, which was published in serial form between 1964 and 1965. When the Cultural Revolution began in 1966, he was protected by Premier Zhou Enlai.

Pyu

Ancient Burmese civilization. The Pyu were a culturally related group of peoples who formed the earliest known urban civilization in Burma. Little was directly known about the Pyu before the 1960s and 1970s, when many of their cities were discovered by archaeologists. The Pyu civilization seems to have existed from around 200 B.C.E. until the early ninth century C.E. Not a politically unified people, particularly in their early existence, the Pyu lived in a number of more or less autonomous city-states organized on tribal principles. By at least the first century C.E., the Pyu controlled territory from the western coasts into the dry zones and the Irrawaddy basin. The capital of the Pyu dynasty before the sixth century was at Sri Ksetra, on the eastern bank of the Irrawaddy north of the delta. Sometime in that century, the city was abandoned and Pyu society relocated to Hanlan, about three hundred miles to the north. Between 832 and 835 C.E., Hanlan was destroyed by Tibeto-Burmese invaders from the north. This was the end of the Pyu as a political power, although some Pyu cities continued to be inhabited and Pyu writings have been found from as late as the thirteenth century.

Despite their near-total disappearance after 835, the Pyu's legacy to the Pagans and future Burmese culture is great. The Pyu were Sarvastivadin Buddhists, a form similar to the Theravāda Buddhism practiced by the later Pagan empire. Their society at its height was luxurious and gracious, with great value placed on art and education. Their architecture was preserved by the Pagans, who used the Pyu style of vaulted temple. Pagan itself was built according to principles of Pyu design, as were many walled cities into the nineteenth century.

Q

qasîdah

Arab style of poetry. The qasîdah, often translated as "ode" in English, is an ancient and complex Arab mode of poetic expression. It is marked by its strict formal features, comparative length, and polythematic structure. Until the twentieth century, qasîdahs were each composed using a single rhyme and meter that continued throughout the length of the poem.

The qasîdah is usually no less than fifteen lines, although some far exceed a hundred lines, despite the difficulty of the mono-end rhyme and unimetric form. Each line is divided into two hemistichs. The final syllable of the first two hemistichs establishes the rhyme that is thereafter maintained in the final syllable (invariably long) of each line for the duration of the poem. Early classical Arabic qasîdahs were composed in any one of thirteen (and from the eighth century onward, sixteen) recognized meters. Each meter is distinguished by its particular quantitative sequences of long and short syllables, with some capacity for variation.

The qasîdah, at least in its standard form, usually exhibits no less than three discernibly discrete thematic movements. The progression is accomplished through the use of conventional, subtle, tactical shifts wherein the poet, turning upon an image or metaphor, effects a comparison or dramatic segue from one theme to the next. Early themes were the sorrow of lost or unrequited love, descriptions of the poet's traveling beast or battle mount, accounts of raids and skirmishes, tribal panegyrics and lampoons, and descriptions of nature inspired by the mountainous and desert landscapes of the Arabian Peninsula. Among the most celebrated and revered of early Arabic qasîdahs are those of the collection known as the Mu'allaqât (sometimes translated as The Suspended Odes), which, according to legend, were hung in gold calligraphy upon the walls of the Ka'bah, a holy site for Islamic pilgrimage in Mecca; they are believed to date from the fifth to the seventh century C.E.

Although the early themes and form of the qasîdah exerted great influence on Arab poets for centuries, new themes were eventually adopted and developed. In the Middle Ages, themes included descriptions of the hunt, wine drinking, and asceticism. In more recent times, the genre has been deployed for expressions of nationalism, political and social protest, romantic narratives, and other themes. In the latter half of the twentieth century, qasîdah has come to signify merely a poem, without entailing specific formal features. Modern Arabic poetry is most often written in various forms of free verse; the mono-end-rhyme, unimetric qasîdah, however, still exists as a recognized form amid all its younger sibling genres, and is still in use.

Qi Baishi (1863–1957)

Chinese painter. Born to a peasant family in Xiangtan, Hunan province, Qi became a carpenter's apprentice when he was a teenager. Furniture making became the foundation of his desire for beauty and creativity. He learned the art of painting largely by himself. In 1922, after years of independent work, he gave an exhibit in Tokyo representing China's achievements in painting. The exhibit's instant success brought him enormous fame in both China and Japan, and he became the head of the Beijing Institute of Chinese Painting.

An extremely productive artist, Qi painted both the grand and the minute with delicacy and subtlety. He developed the use of Chinese ink in painting, and was especially talented at creating beauty through mixture and contrast of bright colors.

Quetzalcóatl

Ancient deity and legendary ruler of the Mexican Toltec and Aztec civilizations. Quetzalcóatl, whose name means "feathered serpent," represented the forces of good and light pitted against those of evil and darkness, which were championed by Tezcatlipoca. According to one epic legend, Quetzalcóatl, deceived by Tezcatlipoca, was driven from Tula, the Toltec capital, and wandered for many years until he reached his homeland, the east coast of Mexico. There he was consumed by divine fire, his ashes turning into birds and his heart becoming the morning star. Quetzalcóatl was the god of civilization and originator of agriculture, architecture, and the calendar, and was identified with both the planet Venus and the wind. Later, he became an Aztec and a Mayan god as well. Adapting the name, the Aztecs linked it with the worship of the war god Huitzilopochtli and applied it to some of their ranking priests. Another Aztec legend—which probably derives from a confusion between Quetzalcóatl and one of his own high priests who was exiled after trying, and failing, to reform Toltec religion—had him sailing off to a mythical land, leaving behind the promise that he would return in the year *ce*

actal of the Aztec calendar. It is this legend that explains why Montezuma, the last Aztec emperor of Mexico (r. 1502–20) viewed the Spanish invaders, who arrived under Spanish *conquistador* Hernán Cortés (1485–1547) just a year later, as the returning hosts of Quetzalcóatl.

Quezon, Manuel (1878–1944)

First president of the Commonwealth of the Philippines. Quezon began his public career in 1898 as an officer under Filipino leader Emilio Aguinaldo (1869–1964) fighting the Americans for independence. Following the Filipino defeat and a brief imprisonment by the U.S. Army, Quezon completed law school and went to work as a legal bureaucrat in his home province of Tayabas. In 1905 he was elected governor of the province, and quickly rose in the ranks of national power. After serving in the Philippine Assembly as a delegate and floor leader of his Nacionalista Party (1907–1908), in 1909 he was elected resident commissioner to the United States. Remaining in Washington until 1915, he argued for political and economic independence from the United States, including the removal of free trade between the countries, which kept the Philippine economy almost exclusively tied to the United States. He resigned from this position in 1916, after the passage of the Jones Law, which guaranteed Philippine independence as soon as a stable government could be formed. Returning to the Philippines, he was elected president of the Senate, a position he held until 1935.

After World War I, Quezon continued to lead the legal battle for independence with the U.S. Congress, which refused to admit that the Philippines was capable of self-rule. During the fifteen years after the war, Quezon was also involved in an almost constant power struggle with his rival and sometime comrade Sergio Osmeña (1878–1961). In general, Quezon was more insistent than Osmeña on rapid and complete freedom for the nation, but both men remained important to the government, with Osmeña eventually serving as vice president of the Commonwealth under Quezon. In 1934 Quezon led the delegation to the United States and secured the passage of the Tydings-McDuffie Independence Act, which outlined a ten-year Commonwealth period to be followed by full statehood for the Philippines. The next year Quezon was elected president of the Commonwealth, making him the first democratically elected leader of that country. In 1940 he was reelected, but this second term was interrupted by the advent of the Second World War. He was forced to flee the Japanese invasion in 1942, but continued to govern the country from his exile in the United States. Quezon died in Saranac, New York, without ever returning to his country. Among the many places now named for the president are his home province and the capital of the Philippine Republic, Quezon City. After Quezon's presidency (1935–44), Osmeña was elected president of the Philippines and served from 1944 to 1946.

Quiet Revolution

Quebec period of reform. The term Quiet Revolution was coined by an anonymous Quebec newspaper writer to describe the changes that occurred in the Canadian province from 1960 to 1966. In the election of 1960, the Liberal Party won a majority over the conservative Union Nationale party, in power since 1944. During its first two years the Liberal administration, headed by Jean Lesage, carried out many reforms, including revising the electoral system and lowering the voting age to eighteen, and in subsequent years it set about revamping the public education system, nationalizing private electric companies, establishing pension plans, and granting majority legal status to married women. The budget grew rapidly as the govern-

ment expanded its role in society. By 1964 Lesage persuaded the Canadian government to grant Quebec special status as a province, allowing it to withdraw from disadvantageous federal cost-sharing programs. Ottawa balked, however, at proposals that Quebec be allowed to enter into international agreements on its own. By the mid-1960s, inspired in part by these successes, a number of French-Canadian political groups had begun calling for the establishment of Quebec as a separate nation. Some, like the Front de Libération du Québec (Liberation Front of Quebec), resorted to violence to achieve their aims. In reaction some French-Canadians who favored the existing union, including soon-to-be Canadian prime minister Pierre Trudeau (prime minister 1968–79; 1980–84), were elected to Parliament in 1965 to represent the federal Liberal Party's move toward strengthening the Confederation. The largely separatist Quebec Liberal Party suffered a setback in the 1966 elections when they surrendered the majority to the Union Nationale, having lost a great deal of support from the rural population.

Quilombo

Brazilian colony of runaway slaves. One of the most common forms of slave resistance in colonial Brazil, *Quilombos*, also known as *Mocambos*, were settlements organized by runaway slaves, usually in the interior of the country. *Quilombos* were ruled by elected black chiefs and their size varied from fifty huts to several thousand. The first *Quilombo* dates back to the beginning of the slave trade in 1575 and was founded in Bahia. Corn, manioc, sweet potatoes, beans, and other similar crops were cultivated to provide food in addition to that obtained from hunting and fishing. Animal skins and forest edibles were also traded for arms, clothing, and food. Sometimes several *Quilombos* united to form larger, self-sufficient units, as was the case with the Republic of Palmáres.

Palmáres was founded in the province of Pernambuco around 1605 (some sources signal its origin as 1630), mostly by African-born and Bantu-speaking black slaves. Despite a series of attacks from Portuguese authorities, it lasted until 1697. Its population ranged from 6,000 to 30,000, and the republic was ruled by an elected chief called Ganga Zumba (Great Lord), who in turn appointed officeholders in the various confederated settlements. Its prosperity was due both to abundant irrigated agricultural lands and the abduction of slaves from Portuguese plantations. These abducted slaves remained in bondage in Palmáres—only runaway slaves became free citizens. In Palmáres, an African-inspired powerful counterculture to the slavocratic Portuguese coastal zone emerged, and Palmáres is said to have posed as much of a threat to Portuguese America as the Dutch. Resisting six Portuguese expeditions between 1680 and 1686, Palmáres was finally conquered in 1694 by an army of *bandeirantes* (national soldiers) under the command of Domingos Jorge Velha, who was hired by the governor of Pernambuco.

Quiroga, Horacio (1878–1937)

Argentinean/Uruguayan writer of short stories. Quiroga was born in Salto, Uruguay, the son of an Argentine vice-consul, who died when Quiroga was a baby, and a native Uruguayan. In 1897 Quiroga published his first essays in Salto newspapers, under the pseudonym Guillermo Eynhardt, the hero of a nineteenth-century French novel. He founded a literary magazine called *Revista del Salto*, which published works influenced by American author Edgar Allan Poe (1809–1849)—perhaps the strongest literary influence in Quiroga's own life—and the Spanish-American movement called *modernismo* (modernism). In 1900 Quiroga traveled to Paris, where he met the leaders of *modernismo*, including Nicaraguan poet Rubén Darío (1867–1916), but disillusioned with the atmosphere, he returned to Uruguay to found his own group, El Consistorio de Gay Saber. He also published his first book, *De los arrecifes de coral* (1901; *Coral Reefs*), a series of stories and poems written in the modernist style. Two years later, after the accidental shooting of a close friend, Quiroga left Montevideo for an Argentinean post to study the ruins of ancient Jesuit settlements in the jungles of Misiones, a province bordering Brazil.

Enthralled with the tropical forest and pioneer life, Quiroga made the jungle the setting of many of his best stories. His second book of short stories, *El crimen del otro* (*Another's Crime*), appeared in 1904, and one year later he published a long short story called "Los perseguidos" (1905; "The Pursued)." Quiroga returned to Misiones in 1910 with his young wife, Ana María, a former student, with whom he had two children. However, in a moment of despair, his wife took poison and died a slow death in 1915. The ten years that followed constitute Quiroga's most prolific period. He published his most popular story collections, including *De cuentos de amor, de locura, y de muerte* (1917; *Stories of Love, Madness, and Death*), *The Exiles* (1926), and *South American Jungle Tales* (1918). In 1922 he inaugurated the literary magazine *Atlántida*, and soon after returned once again to Misiones, where he fell in love with Ana María Palacio, a frustrated love affair that formed the basis for *Historia de un amor turbio* (1929; *Bygone Love*). In 1927 he married María Elena Bravo, with whom he had his third child. After the Uruguayan consulate closed its offices in Misiones, leaving Quiroga without a salary, his last book, *Más allá* (1935; *The Great Beyond*), appeared. Quiroga's health also declined at this time, and his wife left him, taking their young daughter with her. When his illness was diagnosed as cancer, Quiroga committed suicide by taking cyanide. He died penniless and was buried by friends in Salto.

Qur'ân

Islamic scripture. For Muslims the Qur'ân (or Koran) is the revealed word of God as imparted to the Prophet Muhammad, Messenger of God and Seal of the Prophets. Though eventually encoded in written form, Islamic tradition has continued to emphasize the orality of the revelation. Islamic ritual practice and therefore religious education involves aural memorization of portions of the Qur'ân, and an elaborate system of recitation has evolved to accommodate its formal delivery.

The Qur'ân consists of 114 chapters more or less conventionally arranged in descending order of length. Each chapter is further divided into verses. The Qur'ân is cast in prose, much of which is set to rhyme. More often than not, it is the end rhyme characteristic of its rhymed-prose format that serves to unite sequences of verses within a given chapter. Yet on the whole, the content of the Qur'ân is focused upon a central series of themes that it consistently addresses: the unitary, omnipotent, and omniscient nature of a God at once just and merciful; the status, range, and soteriological implications of the revealed Law; the nature and scope of monotheist prophecy past and present; and the punishments and rewards that await humanity on the Day of Judgment and in the Hereafter.

Internally, the Qur'ân is largely devoid of historical and circumstantial points of reference. As such, the canonical text revelation came to be supplemented by nonscriptural, "traditional" material, the *Hadîth* and the *Sunnah*. During the ninth century, these complementary sources of scripture and tradition came to serve, in one way or another, as the central point of departure for efforts aimed at distilling the essence of the revealed Law. It is through the systematic interpretation of the Law that elements of Islamic orthodoxy and orthopraxis are, at least in theory, derived, instituted, modified, refined, and communally ratified.

Muslims' reverence for the language and text of the Qur'ân per se has meant that only the unchanged (and unchangeable), canonical Arabic version is considered the word of God. There is no Vulgate or ritually acceptable version in another language, although there is a large and influential corpus of exegetical literature in Arabic and other languages. The Qur'ân has been translated into nearly every written language, but these versions are interpretive tools and not substitutes for the Arabic scripture that Islam holds to be inimitable.

Quṭb Mīnar

Indian turret. This *mīnar*, or turret, located in Delhi, was constructed in 1190 C.E. under the direction of Sultan Iltutmish. The tower, which is 288 feet high, stands outside the Qūwat-ul-Islām mosque. Both this mosque, which was built out of the remains of demolished temples, and the Quṭb Mīnar itself number among the earliest examples of Muslim architecture still extant. There are two reputed sources for the turret's name: some claim it came from the saint from Ush who is buried in the turret, while others argue that it was named after the sultan who built its lower level.

Qu Yuan (343–289 B.C.E.)

Ancient Chinese poet. Living in the Warring States period (403–221 B.C.E.), Qu Yuan (Ch'ü Yüan) served as a trusted counselor to the king of Chu state. He advocated resistance to the aggression by Qin, a militarily much stronger state. This stand offended a group of courtiers who preferred the humiliating but safe position of tolerating the enemy, and he was slandered before the king. Banished, Qu wandered south of the Yang-zi River, and in anger and despair over the imminent loss of his country, he wrote many passionate poems. He drowned himself in the Mi-Luo River on the fifth day of May, according to the calendar then in use.

Since then, the Chinese people have honored the poet as a model of patriotism and righteousness. Each year on the fifth day of the fifth month, the Duanwu Festival is celebrated. Dragon Boat races are held and Chinese observe the ritual of eating or throwing *zhongzi* (sticky rice wrapped in bamboo leaves and flavored with beans or pork) into the river in hopes that fish will eat them and not disturb Qu Yuan. His works have been collected in an anthology, *Quci*, with "Lisao" ("Encountering Sorrow") as his most influential and best-known poem.

R

rabab

Arab musical instrument. Once a generic term for a bowed instrument, rabab commonly refers to the Arab fiddle that first appeared in the tenth century. The rabab has a membrane belly, generally has two or three strings, and comes in a variety of body shapes. Unlike the fiddle, there is no fingerboard, and the player stops the strings with the fingers.

The rabab can be found in some form in many areas outside the Middle East, including Africa, northern India, Southeast Asia, and Central Asia. The rabab also traveled to Europe via the Byzantine empire, where it was known as the lira. Arabs brought the instrument to Spain, where it spawned the medieval rebec.

rabbi

Jewish religious leader. Hebrew for "my teacher," rabbi was the original title bestowed upon graduates of the highest academy in Palestine in the era following the catastrophic failure of the second revolt against Rome (132–35 C.E.). The academy, at which students principally studied the Torah and the traditional Jewish learning that would eventually become part of the Talmud, was under the direction of the Nasi, whom both the Roman overlords and the Jewish community acknowledged as the highest secular and religious authority in Jewish Palestine. Thus the rabbis were leaders of the local communities as well as ministers to the religious needs of their congregations. They also served on the Bet Din (the law court) and in other bureaucratic roles.

In the Diaspora, the protracted exile of the Jewish people, the rabbinate was uniquely suited to the task of maintaining ties with tradition in a rootless, often persecuted exile. While many of their civic functions were usurped by non-Jewish authorities, especially after the rise of the nation-state in Europe, rabbis continue to wield ecclesiastical power as the heads of their congregations. In some countries, the rabbinate is more structured and more authoritative than in others. In modern Israel, where rabbis maintain some civil authority, there are two chief rabbis, one for the Ashkenazic community and the other for the Sephardic community. They are a historical holdover from the Turkish empire, when the religious communities (Jewish, Muslim, and Christian) acted as semiautonomous political entities within the larger imperial framework. The United States, despite its substantial Jewish population, has no such central authority, mostly because of the divisions among Conservative, Orthodox, and Reform Jews.

In addition to overseeing the religious needs of the congregation, the modern rabbi's duties, like those of other religious ministers, include philanthropic and social work. The rabbi is also responsible for inspecting food to ensure that it conforms to Jewish law. Because the rabbi does not possess sacerdotal status, many of the duties can be performed by a nonordained layman.

Rabelais, François (c. 1483–1553)

French monk, doctor, novelist. Rabelais is best known for his masterpieces, *Gargantua* and *Pantagruel*, which chronicle the adventures of the giant Gargantua and his son Pantagruel, and which were later combined into one novel.

Only sketchy details are known of Rabelais's life, though it seems certain that he was highly regarded by his peers both as a physician and as a humanist. After a brief study of law, Rabelais joined the Franciscan brotherhood in 1510. In the convent, he was closely associated with the renowned humanist Pierre Amy, and with Amy was briefly imprisoned for studying Greek. Their books were confiscated, as their superiors feared that proficiency in this "heretical" language would allow them to read the original New Testament and therefore further study the Greek origins of the Church. Soon after, Rabelais obtained a papal dispensation to transfer to

the Benedictine order—an order that he later satirized mercilessly in his writing.

By 1530 Rabelais had broken his vows and both adopted secular garb and completed the study of medicine he had begun while in the Benedictine order. He lectured and wrote on the works of Greek physicians, publishing his own translations of Greek physicians Hippocrates' (c. 460–377 B.C.E.) *Aphorisms* and Galen's (129–199 C.E.) *Ars parva (The Art of Raising Children)* in 1532. He also fathered two children during this time, both of whom were given their father's name and "legitimized" by the pope in 1540.

Rabelais's most prolific and important period as a writer also began about this time. While practicing medicine in Lyon, Rabelais published his first novel, *Pantagruel*, under the pseudonym Alcofribas Nasier. Here he displayed his true comic talent: in his parody of the romance, he mocks the Scholastic scholars of the Sorbonne, and extols the humanist ideal of the Christian prince. This novel was followed by another parody, *Pantagrueline Prognostication*, which targeted the astrological almanacs popular at that time. *Gargantua* was published sometime around 1535, and confirms Rabelais's ability as a master of satire.

Rabelais was already unpopular with reigning French scholars, and his next novel, *Tiers Livre* (1546), was condemned by both the Sorbonne and the French Parliament for its mockery of penance and other religious practices. The *Quart Livre*, published in 1552, received a similar reception, this time condemned for its support of a "syncretistic" Christianity, which combined the best of ancient Greek wisdom and Christian scripture. In 1553 Rabelais resigned his position as a physician and was rumored to be imprisoned. He died shortly thereafter, but his works, though included in the "Index of Forbidden Books" by the Council of Trent, continued to be quite influential long after his death.

radif

Persian classical music term. One of the central concepts of the Persian classical musical tradition of Iran, *radif* literally means "order" or "row." *Radif* not only refers to the overall repertory of the classical tradition but can also signify a specific body of composed pieces arranged in a given sequence as passed on from teacher to student.

The modern Persian *radif* appears to have been unified and given its present meaning by the late-nineteenth-century musician Mirza Abdullah, who was transmitting the teachings of his father, Ali Akbar Farahani. All known contemporary versions seem to be related, with some variation, to this authoritative version.

The term *radif* extends to the theoretical basis for the structuring of the pieces. The overall repertory of the *radif* is traditionally broken down into twelve (in some early sources thirteen) modes (*dastgah*), each of which is expressed in a sequence of "melodies" or "pieces" (*gushe*). It is the choice and ordering of the pieces that constitute the key distinction between variant *radifs*. This strict sequence of melodies functions primarily as a teaching tool, an ideal form, acting more or less as the springboard for actual performances in which musicians embellish, improvise upon, allude to, and rearrange the well-known melodic content of the *radif*.

Raffles, Sir Thomas [Stamford]

(1781–1826)
British statesman. Lieutenant-governor of Java and then Sumatra during the British interregnum, Raffles is credited with introducing progressive liberal features to the Dutch colonial style previously implemented in Java. However, although he was one of the first to take steps against slave trading in Southeast Asia, his reforms were limited in their effectiveness, and sometimes detrimental to the colonized people. Raffles promoted an early version of British trusteeship, claiming that the "backward" islanders could improve under enlightened forms of British governance and education. In 1811 Raffles eradicated the forced delivery system of agricultural production in favor of peasant rental of land. But because the government favored rent payment in cash rather than crops, peasants became heavily indebted to moneylenders and to the headmen appointed by the colonial bureaucracy. Raffles also reformed the court system in Java, instituting trial by jury and other measures that were entirely alien to the local styles of law, completely ignoring the customary *adat*, or law, of the region. In 1818 Raffles went to Sumatra as lieutenant-governor and established the British port at Singapore as a trading center and strategic base. The port was extremely successful and firmly established lasting British control in the Malay Peninsula.

Ramadân

Islamic religious observance. The ninth month of the Islamic calendar is the time in which Muslims are enjoined by God to fast from before first light till sunset each day of the lunar month (twenty-nine or thirty days). The Fast of Ramadân is one of the five articles of faith in Islam.

Because the Islamic (*hijrah*) calendar is lunar, Ramadân falls eleven days earlier each year with respect to the fixed solar calendar. The sighting of the new moon, or, increasingly in some countries, reliance on astronomical calendars, signals the end of Ramadân. The following day, the Feast of Breaking Fast (or the "Lesser Feast" in contrast to the "Greater Feast" that commemorates Abraham's sacrifice) is thus the first day of the month of Shawwâl, which comes after Ramadân. On this day, one of the four major holy days of Islam, Muslims celebrate by praying, visiting relatives and friends, exchanging presents, giving gifts to children, and, in some countries, wearing new clothes. It is expressly forbidden to fast on the feast day.

The timing of the fast itself varies from region to region according to the precise hours of sunrise and sunset, but the regulations do not change. The believer must abstain from all food, drink, sexual relations, and lustful thoughts. In some traditions, the abstention may extend to include tobacco and entertainment such as television and movies. In their stead, the believer should engage in acts of worship such as the contemplation of God, prayer, and recitation of the Qur'ân. Young children, pregnant women, travelers, the elderly, and the infirm are all exempt from fasting. Those who are able to fast but do not must make up each missed day of fasting later in the year at any time, but before the next month of Ramadân.

Ramakien

Thai epic poem. As the central work of the Thai literary canon, this version of the Indian *Ramayana* is the exclusive source of both the *khön* and *nang* dramas, and the subject of much Thai painting and sculpture. By the seventeenth century, the *Ramakien* or *Ramakian*, an orally transmitted epic, had developed many exotic episodes and details not found in the Indian original. In the first complete written version, produced in 1797 by King Rama I and his courtiers, the original tales were further transformed in a manner typical of Southeast Asia to reflect the setting, characters, and values of the Thai of Bangkok. This Ramakien is widely known and still frequently quoted, both in Thai literary works and in everyday speech. An allegory of the ultimate triumph of good over evil, it pits a virtuous hero—a Thai king known as Phra Ram—against the ten-headed, twenty-armed demon king Thotsaka of Sri Lanka. After Thotsaka abducts Phra Ram's consort Nang Sida to his island kingdom, he is pursued and defeated by Phra Ram and his allies, including the flying monkey Hanuman. Over 3,000 pages long, it is also valued for its intentional reconstruction, incorporation, and preservation of medieval Thai courtly rites and traditions that were lost during the devastating eighteenth-century wars with Burma.

Ramayana

Indian epic poem. The *Ramayana* is the shorter of two great epics of India, the other known as the *Mahabharata*. The *Ramayana*, Sanskrit for "Romance of Rama," was reputedly written by the poet Valmiki around 300 B.C.E. and comprises 24,000 couplets divided into seven books.

The poem, steeped in court intrigue, romance, and the struggle for good over evil, has a number of versions. It begins with the birth of Rama in the kingdom of the Ayodhya. As a young man, Rama wins the hand of Sita by being the only one to bend the mighty bow of Shiva at the bridegroom tournament. Due to a promise Rama's father made his second wife, Kaikeyi, Rama and Sita are banished to the forest so that Kaikeyi's son will be appointed heir. While in exile, Ravana, the demon king of Lanka, captures Sita, who remains steadfastly faithful to Rama. With the help of Sugriva, king of the monkeys, and Hanuman, the monkey general, Rama conquers Ravana and rescues Sita. In order to prove her fidelity to Rama, Sita undergoes an ordeal by fire that she passes through unscathed. In one version, this proof does not suffice, and Rama banishes Sita to the forest, where she gives birth to his two sons at the hermitage of the author Valmiki. When the two sons come of age, the family is reunited, and Sita, still protesting her innocence, asks to be taken by the earth. In another version, the initial test of fidelity remains valid and Rama and Sita are both welcomed into heaven.

The epic greatly influenced Indian poetry by establishing the Sloka meter (two-line verses, each of sixteen syllables) and many of the characteristics that developed in later Sanskrit poetry. The original epic was reinterpreted by other countries, propagating other national epics. Today the *Ramayana* is celebrated throughout India in dramas and pageants.

Ramkhamhaeng inscription

Thai alphabet. In the year 1283, King Ramkhamhaeng the Great of Sukhothai invented an alphabet for the Thai language, which, because of the difficulty of distinguishing tonal differences in writing, had never been accomplished. Ramkhamhaeng's genius was in large part the invention of marks indicating tone. A scholar of Pali, Sanskrit, and similar languages, he based his script on the Mon and Khmer (Burmese and Cambodian) forms, which derived from the South Indian, and came up with forty-four consonants, thirty-two vowels, and five tonal indications. In 1292 he set this alphabet down for the first time by inscribing on a large block of stone the description of a harmonious kingdom ruled by a benevolent patriarch; the "Ramkhamhaeng inscription" is a prized artifact of Thai culture.

Raphael [Sanzio] (1483–1520)

Italian Renaissance painter. Born Raffaello Sanzio in Urbino, one of the cultural centers of Renaissance Italy, Raphael received his first art lessons from his father, a painter himself. After the death of young Raphael's parents, an uncle arranged for him to receive artistic training with Timoteo Viti and Pietro Perugino, under whom he studied principles of order and proportionality. He also absorbed their humanistic philosophy.

Raphael moved to Florence at the age of twenty-one to study the work of Leonardo da Vinci and Michelangelo. Works like the *Madonna of the Goldfinch* (c. 1505) and *La Belle Jardinière* (1507) show his indebtedness to Leonardo in lighting techniques, composition, and symmetry. Michelangelo's influence is evidenced in the figures and gestures of Raphael's Roman works, especially the frescoes of the Vatican Palace (1508–11). The masterpiece of those frescoes, the *School of Athens*, depicting Plato and Aristotle in a modern Italian palace, moves beyond the tension and darkness of Leonardo and Michelangelo's styles to a new tranquil idealism. In the *Triumph of Galatea* of 1513, his composition is reminiscent of Botticelli's *Birth of Venus*, but Raphael's figure placement and his creation of pictorial space are uniquely his.

His later years were occupied with public appointments in Rome, and with new conceptions of Italian architecture and painting that departed from High Renaissance convention. His early death was publicly mourned, and he was buried in the Pantheon in Rome.

Rastafarianism

Jamaican politico-religious movement. Between 1904 and 1927 several essays, articles, and books were published in Jamaica and the United States focusing attention on Ethiopianism, which identified Jamaican blacks with the Ethiopia of the biblical Psalms. Rastafarians took their name from crowned emperor Haile Selassie of Ethiopia, formerly Ras (prince) Tafari, whom they proclaimed a divine being and the champion of the black race. The movement was also influenced by Jamaican-born African-American leader Marcus Garvey's (1887–1940) Universal Improvement Association.

Original devotees believed in the eventual repatriation of all peoples of African origin back to Africa, specifically

Ethiopia, as a historical inevitability. Through a Rastafarian decoding of the Bible ("reasoning"), the doctrines of Rastafarianism are known, believed to be freed from the distortions created by Christian colonialists. White, Euro-American industrial civilization is allegorically interpreted as "Babylon," the seat of all wickedness. An imminent apocalyptic collapse of Western industrial society will bring about an Eden-like earth led by spiritually powerful Rastafarians.

Living in accordance with the laws of nature and God means adherence to nonviolence, pervasive nonpossessiveness with regard to material wealth, vegetarianism, consuming food uncontaminated by industrial chemicals ("Ital"), dressing in clothes made from natural fibers, and daily Bible consultation to address ethical concerns. Some show their devotion to these laws by letting their hair grow into a lengthy and unprocessed form (dreadlocks), though such a style is optional for believers. Another optional facet of the Rastafarian lifestyle is the smoking of marijuana, recognized as an aid to unlock the allegorical code in which the Bible is masked.

The movement has grown and changed since its beginnings in the 1930s. Focus, for example, has shifted from returning to Africa to "the Africanization of Jamaica"—that is, making Jamaica a place that benefits people of African descent in areas such as employment, education, and the use of the country's resources. Since the 1960s, Rastafarianism has significantly influenced Jamaican popular music through the development of the fast rhythm called *ska*, which was drawn from the rhythm of the Rastafarians' *akete* drums. *Ska* was the most popular indigenous style until the mid-1960s, when it was supplanted by a derivative style called rock steady, which later became reggae.

Ravel, Maurice [Joseph] (1875–1937)

French composer. Ravel was born in the Basque town of Ciboure. As a young man, he studied under the tutelage of Gabriel Fauré at the Paris Conservatory. He began his musical training at a time when Wagnerian music (music by German composer Richard Wagner [1813–1883]) dominated, but he rebelled against Wagnerian excess. His music initially failed to receive critical acclaim, and as a young composer, he was refused the Prix de Rome, an influential musical award, four times. This denial was widely viewed as political, and prompted a change in leadership at the Paris Conservatory. Throughout his career, Ravel was accused of copying French composer Claude Debussy (1862–1918), though their music differed in both inspiration and style. Ravel won widespread popular notice with his hypnotically repetitive orchestral piece *Bolero* (1928). Integrated orchestration and an emphasis upon instrumental virtuosity were major features of such works as the song cycle *Shéhérazade* (1903); the piano compositions *Miroirs* (1904–05; *Mirrors*) and *Le Tombeau de Couperin* (1917; *The Tomb of Couperin*); and the orchestral ballet *Daphnis et Chloé* (1909–12).

Ray, Satyajit (1921–1992)

Indian film director. Ray was raised in a family of artists: his grandfather was a renowned painter and his father a famous Bengali author. The young Ray attended Presidency College in Calcutta, then traveled to Visva-Bharati Santiniketan, where he entered the arts college of the Bengali poet Rabindranath Tagore, a family friend. He returned to Calcutta when Tagore died in 1941, and found work as a layout artist, and eventually as the artistic director at a British advertising firm. In 1945 Ray conceived the idea of translating Bengali writer Bibjuti Bhusan Bandyopadhyay's texts into film. It took Ray seven years to get his proposed project mounted, since producers were wary about backing the work of a beginning filmmaker, especially one who broke with traditional representational techniques. During this seven-year period, Ray married Bijoya Das and traveled to work in London. There he encountered many prominent figures in the film world and was greatly affected by Italian director Vittorio De Sica's (1902–1974) neorealist film *The Bicycle Thief*, which he claimed as an inspiration in his own subsequent work.

Pather Panchali (Father Panchali), the first film of Ray's "Apu Trilogy," was released in 1955 and was an immediate success with both the public and the critics, winning a prize at the Cannes Film Festival in France for "most human document" in 1956. The second film in the trilogy was *Aparajito* (1957; *The Unvanquished*), and the third and final film, *Apu Sansar* (1958; *The World of Apu*), completes the story of the life of a Bengali child, Apu, as he grows into maturity. Ray also found time to make two other films during the creation of the trilogy, one of which was an ultimately tragic comedy of manners called *Jalsaghar* (1958; *The Music Room*). It won a prize at the Moscow Film Festival in 1959.

After making several films dedicated to the memory of Tagore, including a documentary of the poet's life and *Teen Kanya* (1961; *Two Daughters*), Ray produced yet another series of critically acclaimed films, including *Devi* (1960; *The Goddess*) and *Abhijan* (1962; *The Country*). In 1963 he made *Mahanagar* (*The Big City*). In the 1970s Ray directed several films, including *Agani Sanket* (1973; *Distant Thunder*), which departs from his usually subtle and evocative work in its monumental sweep and its polemical focus upon the great Bengali famine of 1943. Ray also filmed *Shatranj Ke Khilari* (1977; *The Chess Players*), his

first non-Bengali film, during this decade. Many Western critics consider *Charulata* (1964; *The Lonely Wife*) to be his masterpiece.

Ream Ker

Cambodian epic poem. Meaning "The Glory of Rama," this poem, most likely first written by a group of seventeenth-century poets, is the Cambodian version of the Indian *Ramayana* epic. However, the behavior, language, and ideals of its characters are those of the local Khmer (people of Cambodia). Indeed, the *Ream Ker*, also called the *Reamker* or *Ram Kerti*, contains only some of the events of the Indian original, many of which it alters in order to reflect a Khmer Theravāda Buddhist philosophy in which good and evil, perpetually at war, balance and define each other. Combining the austerely elegant language and values of the elite with familiar universal themes, the *Ream Ker* was traditionally recited at village festivals to the accompaniment of a mimed performance.

Reed, Sir Carol (1906–1976)

British film director. Reed began his career in the theater, first as an actor and later, by 1927, as a stage manager. In the early 1930s Reed turned to film as an assistant to director/producer Basil Dean, and by 1935 directed his own low-budget features such as *Bank Holiday* (1938), *The Stars Look Down* (1939), and *Night Train to Munich* (1940), treating themes of the life of the working class. During World War II, he was assigned to propaganda films such as *A Letter from Home* (1941), and at the end of the war directed acclaimed war documentaries such as *The Way Ahead* (1944) and *The True Glory* (1945).

Reed's early experience with documentaries may have influenced the films he produced in the late 1940s and early 1950s, during the peak of his career. Award-winning films like *Odd Man Out*

(1947) and *The Third Man* (1949) reflect realism through attention paid to detail and development of atmosphere. Following the acclaim that these films brought Reed, he was knighted in 1952. Reed's popularity declined in the mid-1950s, however, until the box office success of his only musical, *Oliver!* (1968), for which he received a British Academy Award and an Oscar.

Reformation

Sixteenth-century religious revolution. Led primarily by Martin Luther (1483–1546) and John Calvin (1509–1564), the Reformation (also known as the Protestant Reformation) changed the face of the Western Christian Church and created Protestantism, the third branch of Christianity (following the splitting of the Eastern Orthodox Church from the Roman Catholic). The Reformation of the sixteenth century was firmly rooted in the religious reform movements of the fifteenth century. The Czech theologian and reformer Jan Hus had embarked on a campaign to end the Western Schism (a period during which the papal jurisdiction was divided between two popes) and corruption in the Church one hundred years prior to the Reformation, and was burned at the stake as a result of his heresy. Despite his efforts, the abuses of church power continued through the sixteenth century, and reform-minded theologians like John Calvin and Martin Luther sought to end corrupt church practices such as the selling of spiritual privileges, a pursuit that they said exploited the majority of Christians and discredited the spiritual power of the Church.

On October 31, 1517, the eve of All Saints' Day, Martin Luther began his reform crusade by attacking what he considered to be the fundamental problem of the Church—indulgences, the offering of redemption and afterlife security, which are guaranteed freely by God, in exchange for money and labor. In his Ninety-five Theses, Luther denounced the pope's authority to decide who may or may not receive eternal happiness. He announced that the only authority to which all are accountable can be found only in the Scriptures, and that Christians may achieve redemption through faith in the Scriptures, not through working for priests, saints, or the pope. His efforts at reform earned him an excommunication after he was tried by the Imperial Diet of Worms in 1521.

Another group of reformers, known as the Radical Reformers or "Anabaptists," who were originally associated with Huldrych Zwingli although they later separated from him, emerged during this same period. Their radicalism stemmed from their strict adherence to the teachings of the Scriptures and their practice of baptizing adults, not children. The Swiss Anabaptists took the example of Jesus as portrayed in the Gospels literally. They believed in the absolute separation of church and state, which was in direct contradiction to Roman Catholicism.

Calvinism was formally defined when John Calvin published his *Institutes of the Christian Religion* in 1536, a detailed theological treatise explaining the Reformation. While Calvin agreed with Luther's adherence to the absoluteness of faith, he disagreed with other reformers as to the separation of church and state. Rather, Calvin believed that the two authorities could and should be united. He argued that people would live better lives if subjected to both human and scriptural laws.

The rise of the many sects of Protestantism generated by the Reformation divided Europe. For the most part, Lutheranism was welcomed in Northern Europe, especially Germany. Radicalism found a warm reception in much of Eastern Europe, where many varieties of religion already existed. Most of Southern Europe remained strictly Catholic. And in England, a new, self-serving religious reform was initiated by King Henry VIII. Because the pope would not grant him the right to divorce any of his wives, Henry VIII (1491–1547) established his own church, the Anglican Church, which afforded him this right. In addition, Anglicanism adopted the Book of Common Prayer, a conversion of religious writings from Latin into English. In Scotland, the reform movement was furthered by John Knox (1514–1572), who began his own Presbyterian church.

reggae

Jamaican music style. Reggae evolved from Jamaican folk rhythms, rock, gospel, and American rhythm and blues. Originating in Jamaica, reggae passed through the variations *ska*, bluebeat, and rock steady before appearing on the world stage in its final form during the late 1960s and early 1970s. Commonly associated with Bob Marley and the Wailers, reggae gained international recognition due in part to this group's popularity.

Reggae carries a political message about poverty-stricken blacks in Jamaica as well as the oppression of blacks everywhere. The corollary to this message included the back-to-Africa sentiment of the Rastafarian religion, which states that the late ruler of Ethiopia, Haile Selassie (seen as the personification of Jah, or God), will one day return to lead his followers back to Africa. Such themes appear often, especially in early reggae like Bob Marley's 1977 hit, "Exodus: Movement of Jah People," but do not preclude artists from touching on more secular themes such as love, hope, and sorrow.

Many of the more political songs were banned from the airwaves in Jamaica, such as "Mark of the Beast," the response of Peter Tosh (member of the Wailers and solo artist) to an unprovoked beating by Jamaican police in early 1975. Other radical works elicited criticism, such as did Tosh's "Legalize It," which advocates the free use of marijuana, or *ganja*, because Rastafarians believe it allows for enhanced communion with God. Despite these obstacles, reggae moved into the American and British mainstreams and heavily influenced the music of later generations. In the 1990s reggae has taken a backseat to a new Jamaican product called dance hall, or D.J., which blends American rap with heavily synthesized reggae. Political messages have succumbed to a new emphasis on sex and materialism. Adherents of the old school lament the loss of the social, economic, and spiritual message that reggae's originators wanted to impart.

Rembrandt [Harmenszoon] van Rijn
(1606–1669)

Dutch painter and etcher. Rembrandt was trained in Amsterdam in the studio of Pieter Lastman, where he developed his predilection for historical and religious themes. In 1625 he returned to his birthplace, Leiden, where he taught and produced a series of nearly a hundred self-portraits that chronicle his artistic development. He returned to Amsterdam in 1632, and distinguished himself early on as the city's leading portraitist. Of these early paintings, *The Anatomy Lesson of Dr. Nicolaas Tulp* (1632) best illustrates the vitality Rembrandt brought to his portraits. Rembrandt's work is also noted for its dramatic use of light and dark in paintings such as *The Company of Captain Franz Banning Cock* (1642), which is popularly known as *Nachtwacht* (*Night Watch*). After a brief and blissful marriage, Rembrandt was left with a considerable financial fortune, but as his interests turned more to religious themes and landscapes and less to portraiture, his popularity declined, and Rembrandt suffered financial difficulties. He declared bankruptcy in 1656 and was forced to sell his property, including his art collection. Some of his finer paintings of this period include *The Syndics of the Cloth Guild* (1661) and *The Batavians* (1663), of which only a fragment remains.

Rembrandt's prodigious output of more than six hundred paintings, three hundred etchings, and almost two thousand drawings is impressive not only in its originality and technique but also in the breadth of themes it addresses.

Renaissance

The French word *renaissance*, which literally means "rebirth," refers to a period of great cultural and intellectual achievement in Europe during the late fourteenth through the early sixteenth century. The era witnessed a renewed interest in classical Greek scholarship, the exploration of new continents, the acceptance of the Copernican model of the universe, and the introduction of paper, the printing press, the compass, and gunpowder. The achievements of Renaissance art evoke the names of Italian artists like Leonardo da Vinci (1452–1519), Michelangelo (1475–1564), and Raphael (1483–1520).

The origins of the Renaissance can be found in the Humanist school, championed by Dutch scholar Desiderius Erasmus (c. 1466–1536) and French scholar François Rabelais (c. 1483–1553) and preceded by Italian poets Dante (1265–1321) and Petrarch (1304–1374). Humanism, as a school of thought, regarded the creative struggle of humans to control their surroundings as the highest and noblest pursuit. This, in contrast to the Christian Scholasticism that had prevailed in Europe during the Middle Ages, inspired scholars, scientists, and artists to study the world of nature and of knowledge that lay around them. After the Muslim conquest of Constantinople in 1453, many Eastern scholars flocked to Italy, effectively reintroducing the tradition of ancient Greek scholarship.

The Renaissance proper occurred in Italy during the fifteenth and sixteenth centuries. Florence and Rome were especially important sites of artistic genius. In Florence the Medicis and other wealthy merchant families commissioned the statues of Florentine sculptors Donatello (c. 1386–1466) and Ghiberti (c. 1378–1455) and in Rome, Leonardo, Michelangelo, and Raphael dominated the art scene.

In other countries, the Renaissance lasted somewhat beyond the sixteenth century and resulted in different cultural changes. In Germany, for example, the Renaissance is closely linked with the Protestant Reformation. In the Netherlands, the Renaissance saw the work of painter Albrecht Dürer (1471–1528) and in England, the literature of Shakespeare (1564–1616), Sir Thomas More (1478–1535), and Sir Francis Bacon (1561–1626). Spanish writer Miguel de Cervantes created the masterpiece *Don Quixote* (Part I, 1605; Part II, 1615) in Spain. Gradually, the philosophical and artistic traditions of the Renaissance gave way to those of the Enlightenment of the eighteenth and nineteenth centuries.

Renoir, Jean (1894–1979)

French film director. The son of Impressionist painter Pierre-Auguste Renoir (1841–1919), Renoir built his own international reputation as a director whose talents survived the transition from silent to sound films. With some exceptions, Renoir's early work is characterized by realistic cinematography and by an experimental and improvisational quality.

Renoir began as a ceramicist, serving briefly as an officer and a pilot in World War I. After the death of his father, Renoir married Catherine Hessling, one of his father's models. With his inheritance, Renoir formed an independent production company that financed his wife's screen debut in *Une Vie sans joie* (1924; *Catherine*), for which he wrote the script. In the same year, Renoir directed his first film, *La Fille de l'eau* (1924; *The Girl of the Water*), displaying the distinctive style of realism and attention to environment for which he later became known. Renoir made several more silent films, all starring Hessling. Following their separation, Renoir made the sound film *La Chienne* (1931; *Isn't Life a Bitch?*), which foreshadowed a theme that would recur in his later works *La Bête humaine* (1938; *The Human Beast*) and *La Règle du jeu* (1939; *The Rules of the Game*), that of characters whose fate is determined by their social milieu.

By 1941 Renoir had moved to the United States, where he directed several films, of which *The Southerner* (1945) and *The Diary of a Chambermaid* (1946) were his most successful. Returning to Europe in the early 1950s, Renoir continued to direct both on film and on stage, taking a long hiatus in the early to mid-1960s to write two books, one of which was his father's biography. He directed his last film, *La Direction d'acteur par Jean Renoir* (*The Little Theater of Jean Renoir*), in 1969. In 1977 he won an honorary Oscar for his cumulative work, and was inducted as an officer of the French Legion of Honor.

Renoir, Pierre-Auguste (1841–1919)

French painter and sculptor. One of the greatest of Impressionist painters, Renoir is credited with the use of pure, unmixed colors, which became incorporated into the Impressionist style of painting.

After working as a porcelain painter, Renoir met the French artists Claude Monet (1840–1926) and Alfred Sisley (1839–1899), with whom he frequently shared a studio. Renoir contributed to the establishment of the Impressionist school of painting, which concerned itself more with the representation of light and atmosphere than with the physical characteristics of the subject. Typical of his early paintings are charming scenes of women, children, and gardens, such as the famous *L'Enfant à l'arrosoir* (1876). In his later work, Renoir departed from the classic techniques of Impressionism and developed a softer, more supple style. Female nudes became his favorite subject of this period, but he also painted pictures of young girls and mythological subjects. In his later years, Renoir also took up sculpture, but was so crippled by arthritis that much of the work had to be done by assistants under his supervision. Renoir is perhaps best loved of all the Impressionists, celebrated for his wonderful use of color and his delightful scenes. Other notable works of Renoir include *Les Parapluies* (c. 1881–86; *The Umbrellas*) and *Les Grandes Baigneuses* (1884–87; *Bathers*).

Rhodes, Cecil [John] (1853–1902)

British financier. The son of an English vicar, Rhodes was born in England. In 1870 he was sent to his elder brother's plantation in South Africa because of poor health. With the discovery of diamonds in the Kimberly mines, the brothers abandoned cotton farming and made a fortune from the diamond mines. Rhodes then studied at Oxford, where he became convinced of the superiority of the Anglo-Saxon race and thus committed to the policy of British expansion in Africa. Upon his return to Natal, Rhodes continued to expand his financial empire and became active in politics, becoming prime minister and virtual dictator of the Cape Colony in 1890. His attempts to topple the Boer government in the Transvaal backfired, however, and he was forced to resign his position in 1896. He then concentrated on the development of the country Zimbabwe, which was later called Rhodesia in his honor. Rhodes also founded the

Rhodes scholarships, which enable students from the former British empire, the United States, and Germany to study at Oxford University.

Riel, Louis (1844–1885)

Canadian Métis leader. After devoting some years to study for the priesthood in Montreal, Riel returned to his birthplace in the Red River Settlement (now Manitoba) to lead the Métis, a people of French-Indian ancestry, in an armed uprising. In 1869 the Hudson's Bay Company, which owned the title to the region, yielded the land to the Canadian government. The Métis, fearful that their way of life would be disrupted by an onslaught of Canadian settlers in their region, banded together in protest, choosing Riel as their leader. After an abortive attempt to redress their grievances to the Canadian government, the Métis seized Fort Garry (Winnipeg) under Riel's leadership and set up a provisional government of which Riel was chosen president. The Canadian government dispatched a militia to suppress this insurrection. Riel was forced to surrender his provisional government and flee to the United States, but not before he and other Métis representatives successfully negotiated the admission of their province into the Canadian federation as the province of Manitoba. In 1884 Riel was called by Métis and whites to the Saskatchewan region where the Métis, again, had been threatened by Canada's western policies. When peaceful measures proved unsuccessful, Riel established a rebel government and with Indian allies pitted his forces against those of the Canadian government. Upon defeat, Riel was tried and hanged for high treason. His execution generated a bitter public response, as many Canadians viewed Riel's protests as positive efforts to preserve the French-Indian identity.

Rivera, Diego [María] (1886–1957)

Mexican painter and muralist. Rivera was a prominent figure in the Mexican renaissance in art in the twentieth century. His large and simple forms and didactic themes are sometimes criticized as unsophisticated, but Rivera intentionally eschewed technical innovation in favor of creating a popular art suited to the political situation of his time.

Born at Guanajuato, Rivera began studying painting at the San Carlos Academy at the age of ten. After his first exhibition in 1907 in Veracruz, he was given a stipend by the mayor of that city to study in Europe. In 1908–1909 he lived in Spain, and from 1910 to 1921 in Paris, where he studied and was influenced by the Cubist movement and French painter Paul Cézanne (1839–1906). Brief visits to Italy allowed him to see the murals of the Italian Renaissance. Rivera became convinced that art for a new world should be accessible and therefore on the walls of public buildings. In 1919 he met Mexican painter David Siqueiros (1896–1974) in Paris and discussed with him the need for social and artistic revolution in Mexico; they were both interested in the possibilities of the mural as a popular art form. He returned to Mexico in 1921, and the following year executed his first mural at the National Preparatory School and joined the Communist Party. The next few years were spent producing numerous murals, and in 1927 he traveled to the Soviet Union to do a series of drawings at the government's request honoring May Day. The following year, he married Mexican painter Frida Kahlo (1907–1954). In 1930 he went to the United States for an exhibition of his work in California and did a mural for the San Francisco Stock Exchange. Two years later, he painted murals depicting the auto industry for the Detroit Institute of Arts. His perhaps best-known work in the United States was never completed: his commissioned mural for Rockefeller Center in New York was destroyed because Rivera repeatedly refused to delete the visage of Lenin from the composition.

Rivera returned to Mexico City in 1934, and there created a replica of the aborted Rockefeller Center murals entitled *El hombre en el cruce de los caminos* (*Man at the Crossroads*) at the Palace of Fine Arts. In 1937 he published *Portrait of Mexico*, detailing his works in that country. He painted another series in the National Palace depicting pre-Spanish cultures, and in 1948 his *Sueño de una tarde dominical en la Alameda Central* (*Dream of a Sunday Afternoon in the Central Alameda*) for the Hotel del Prado in Mexico City created a scandal because it said "God Does Not Exist." In 1954 Rivera was readmitted to the Communist Party and the following year traveled again to the Soviet Union for an operation. Following the death of Kahlo, he donated both her childhood home and his studio to Mexico City as museums.

Rivera, José [Eustasio] (1888–1928)

Colombian poet and novelist. Born in Neiva, Colombia, to a family of humble origins, Rivera had ten brothers and sisters. After moving with his family to the country, Rivera spent the next twelve years in and out of schools and various jobs. When he was eighteen, he won a scholarship from the government to study at the Escuela Normal de Institutores (Teachers College) of Bogotá headed by the Christian Brothers. Upon the legalization of the separation of Panama in 1909, he led his fellow students from the Escuela Normal through the streets of Bogotá in protest, an act for which he and some of his companions were detained by the police for days. In 1910, during the festivities to commemorate Colombian independence, Rivera won the silver medal for his "Oda a España" ("Ode to Spain") in a public con-

test. By this time he was also publishing in all the major newspapers of the country. Rivera completed the law school of the Universidad Nacional, writing seven unpublished plays during that time. In 1921 he published a collection of fifty-five sonnets called *Tierra de promisión* (*The Promised Land*).

Appointed by the Colombian government as secretary of the Boundary Commission, Rivera settled boundary disputes with Venezuela. He traveled to the jungle, where he remained for the next ten months, journeying as far as Manaus, Brazil, in the heart of the Amazon jungle, living with the Indians and *caucheros* (rubber collectors) and witnessing their struggle to survive. He returned to Bogotá to take possession of a seat in the House of Representatives, but gave it up three months later in frustration with the political machinery. He then completed his masterpiece and only novel, *La Vorágine* (1924; *The Vortex*), portraying the miserable conditions in which the *caucheros* lived. The book incorporates autobiographical material and describes the exploitation by rubber companies. A novel of adventure and social protest, it was to influence countless other Latin American writers. The presence of the Latin American jungle, which rises up to swallow exploitative forces that intrude upon it—what some have referred to as the revenge of Latin America—has become a recurring theme in Latin American fiction. The unexpected success prompted Rivera to start a second novel, to be called *The Oil Spot*, but he died suddenly in 1928 before it was finished and no trace of the manuscript remains.

Rizal, José (1861–1896)

Filipino physician, novelist, poet, and patriot. Rizal is a national hero of his country and is considered to be a founder of Filipino nationalism. He was born in Calamba, on the island of Luzon, and received a Jesuit education in Manila. At the age of seventeen, he began medical studies in Manila, and from 1882 until 1887 lived in Madrid, Paris, and Berlin, where he completed his training as an ophthalmologist and developed his literary career. While in Europe, he wrote political essays critical of the Church-dominated form of Spanish rule in the Philippines, and published his first novel, *Noli me tangere* (1886; *The Social Cancer*), a satire of life under the friars. The book was immediately banned in his homeland, and Rizal was forever after to be treated as an enemy by the Spanish government.

In 1887 he briefly returned to the Philippines but was soon forced out by fearful authorities. For the next five years he lived primarily in Spain and Hong Kong, practicing medicine and writing for the Madrid-based nationalist paper *La Solidaridad*. In 1892, shortly after the publication of his second novel and amid increasing antigovernment sentiment, he returned to Manila to found La Liga Filipina, a short-lived association devoted to reform and Filipino economic and artistic cooperation. Within a month of his arrival, he was captured by the state and exiled to Dapitan, where he built a school and hospital for the local population and lived for the remaining four years of his life. In late 1896, while on his way to Cuba to provide medical assistance to the Spanish army, he was arrested and returned to Manila for the last time. In a hasty trial, he was found guilty of "promoting rebellion" and executed by firing squad.

At his trial, Rizal was depicted as instrumental in promoting the ongoing violent revolt springing up in the country. In fact, Rizal had always been outspokenly opposed to revolution and denounced the Katipunan, a secret Filipino society organized along Masonic lines that served as a spearhead for the liberation of the Philippines from Spain. He criticized the uprisings both publicly and in his correspondence with the revolutionary leaders. Nevertheless, he was adopted as a figurehead by the rebels, and the government clearly felt that his public humiliation and death would aid their cause.

El filibustrismo (1891; *The Reign of Greed*), Rizal's second novel, like his first, is a melodramatic comedy depicting the hardships suffered by Filipinos under the Spanish government. While *The Reign of Greed* is more overtly political, *The Social Cancer* is more widely read and established the author's reputation in his lifetime. His books and poetry, particularly the patriotic "Mi ultimo adios" ("Last Farewell"), written on the eve of his execution, are still widely read by Filipino students and are considered to be classics. Since his death, Rizal has been elevated to the status of national hero and father of Philippine independence.

Robin Hood

Legendary English folk hero. According to legend, Robin Hood was a gentlemanly outlaw who lived in Sherwood Forest in Nottinghamshire. A kindly, carefree band of followers included Maid Marian, Friar Tuck, Little John, and a group of yeomen. Robin Hood protected the common folk from the tyranny of the nobility, robbing the rich and giving the spoils to the poor. He was the nemesis of the despotic Sheriff of Nottingham, the symbol of wealthy nobility.

Scholars are uncertain whether Robin Hood actually existed. Early historians have suggested that he lived in the 1100s. The earliest mention of Robin Hood appears in a 1377 edition of *Piers Plowman*. He appears in Scottish novelist Sir Walter Scott's *Ivanhoe* as well as in English dramatist Alfred, Lord Tennyson's play *The Foresters*. In 1859 Orville Prescott wrote *Robin Hood: The Outlaw of Sherwood Forest*, and Howard Pyle's *The Merry Adventures of Robin Hood* was published in 1883. The story of Robin Hood remains popular in Britain.

Rodin, [François] Auguste (1840–1917)

French sculptor. As a youth, Rodin was rejected three times by the prestigious École des Beaux-Arts and worked for several years as an ornamental mason. He traveled to Italy in 1875, and inspired by the statues of Italian sculptor Michelangelo (1475–1564), he produced his first major work, *L'Age d'airain* (1877; *The Age of Bronze*). Critics were incensed by the naturalistic treatment of the nude figure, and accused him of casting it from a live model, but the controversy gained Rodin the patronage of the government, and he received a studio in Paris in which to work. There he met sculptor Camille Claudel, with whom he maintained a long relationship as a mentor, colleague, and lover. After 1880 he spent much of his time working on the collection of figures in the *Porte de l'enfer* (1880–1917; *Gates of Hell*), which was inspired by the writings of English poet William Blake (1757–1827), Italian poet Dante's (1265–1321) *Divine Comedy*, and Florentine artist Ghiberti's (c. 1378–1455) sculpture *Paradise Gate*. Though this series of 106 figures was never completed, it produced two of Rodin's best-known sculptures, *The Thinker* (1880) and *The Kiss* (1886). Some of Rodin's nontraditional works, such as *The Burghers of Calais* (1885–95) and his monolithic tribute to French novelist Honoré de Balzac (1799–1850), in which, on top of a ten-foot block, the figure's head emerges from the folds of a dressing gown, stirred considerable controversy. However, he achieved the esteem of the contemporary art world, and in 1900 the Paris World's Fair devoted a pavilion to his work.

Roentgen, Wilhelm [Conrad] (1845–1923)

German physicist. Roentgen was born in the town of Lennep, near Cologne. He was a precocious student and received his doctorate from the University of Zurich in 1869. Roentgen experimented with the newly discovered cathode rays and high vacuum tubes and in 1885 discovered a strange new wave phenomenon—the X ray. The first X ray picture, in fact, was of his wife's hand. Though Roentgen failed to recognize the X ray as part of the electromagnetic spectrum, his discovery was of enormous importance to the scientific world and heralded the beginning of the atomic age. He received the first Nobel Prize in Physics in 1901.

Romance of the Western Chamber, *see* Wang Shi-fu

Roosevelt, [Anna] Eleanor (1884–1962)

U.S. First Lady and diplomat. The niece of President Theodore Roosevelt (president 1901–1909) and the wife of President Franklin D. Roosevelt (president 1933–45), Eleanor Roosevelt was educated in England. She married her distant cousin Franklin in 1905 and had six children with him, five of whom survived to adulthood. Eleanor supported her husband during his political campaigns and struggle with polio while she developed a public life of her own, championing the causes of minorities, women, and the poor.

As First Lady, Eleanor greatly expanded the scope and visibility of the role, showing little concern for the criticism her enterprises attracted. She helped place women in important federal government jobs and held press conferences exclusively for women. During the New Deal, Eleanor was credited by many with the creation of such humanitarian programs as the National Youth Administration, child welfare, and slum-clearance projects. In 1939 she publicly resigned from the Daughters of the American Revolution when they refused to let black singer Marian Anderson perform in Constitution Hall. In addition to her own projects and causes, Eleanor traveled across the country to investigate federal programs and public opinion on behalf of her husband.

Eleanor continued her public life after the president's death, most notably as a delegate to the U.N. for the Truman Administration. She served as chair of the U.N. Commission on Human Rights, where she helped draft the Universal Declaration of Human Rights (1948). Eleanor also worked closely with the Democratic Party and, near the end of her life, chaired President Kennedy's Commission on the Status of Women. She wrote three autobiographical works, *This Is My Story* (1937), *This I Remember* (1949), and *On My Own* (1958).

Roosevelt, Franklin Delano (1882–1945)

Thirty-second U.S. president. Born in Hyde Park, New York, to a wealthy family, Roosevelt attended the exclusive Groton School and Harvard University, graduating in 1903 but staying an additional year to edit the college newspaper. After marrying Eleanor Roosevelt, the niece of Theodore Roosevelt (they were distant cousins), in 1905, he entered Columbia University Law School and was admitted to the New York bar in 1907. In 1910 he was elected a New York state senator and was reelected in 1912. In 1913 he was appointed Assistant Secretary of the Navy in Woodrow Wilson's administration (1913–21), a position he held for seven years, including during World War I.

Roosevelt was the Democratic nominee for U.S. vice president in 1920, but after a Republican landslide, he entered business. Stricken with polio in 1921, he was almost completely paralyzed for a time, and though he regained the use of his arms, he used braces and a wheelchair for the rest of his life. His wife helped him remain active in politics, representing him in meetings and becoming an influential speaker in her own right. He was elected governor of New York in 1928 and reelected by a landslide in 1930. As governor he established the first of the state agencies to provide emergency relief to the poor during the Great Depression (1930s). After a campaign in which he outlined his program of federal assistance to provide jobs and speed recovery, he was elected U.S. president over the incumbent Herbert Hoover in 1932.

When Roosevelt took office in 1933, most of the country's banks were closed, industrial production was half that of four years before, and as many as 16 million people were unemployed. Announcing in his inaugural address his complete self-confidence because "the only thing we have to fear is fear itself," he immediately began a program of sweeping economic reform that included the establishment of the Federal Emergency Relief Administration, the Civilian Conservation Corps, the Agricultural Adjustment Administration, and the Public Works Administration. Later programs included the Tennessee Valley Authority, the Securities and Exchange Commission, the Social Security Administration, the Works Progress Administration, and the National Labor Relations Board. A 1935 bill raised taxes on wealthy individuals and large corporations, significantly redistributing income.

Due to his effective policies and his ability to communicate with his constituents with his regular radio "fireside chats," he was reelected overwhelmingly in 1936, carrying every state but two, and he continued to institute his innovative New Deal programs. Determined to avoid the European wars of the late 1930s, he nonetheless supported giving aid to Great Britain and withholding war supplies from Japan. His "Good Neighbor Policy" led to mutual defense agreements in the Americas. Elected president for a historic third term in 1940, he led the United States into World War II after the bombing of Pearl Harbor by the Japanese on December 7, 1941, mobilizing industry in the war effort and playing a key role in the creation of an alliance with Britain and Russia. Roosevelt won a fourth term in 1944, but served only briefly before his death from a massive cerebral hemorrhage.

Roosevelt, Theodore (1858–1919)

Twenty-sixth U.S. president. Born to a well-to-do family of Dutch ancestry, Roosevelt attended private schools and Harvard College and in 1880 entered Columbia University Law School, though he left soon after. The following year, at age twenty-three, he was elected to the New York State Assembly as a Republican. After the death of his first wife and a period as a rancher in the Dakota Territory, he served on the U.S. Civil Service Commission (1889–95) and as president of the New York City Board of Police Commissioners (1895–97). During this period he also published his four-volume history, *The Winning of the West* (1889–96), and several biographies. He became Assistant Secretary of the Navy under President William McKinley in 1897, and when war was declared with Spain in 1898, as he had strongly urged, he resigned this position and organized the First U.S. Volunteer Cavalry. The "Rough Riders," as they came to be known, were very successful in their battles in Cuba, and "Teddy" became a national hero. That same year, he was elected governor of New York, and in 1900 was nominated for vice president at the Republican National Convention to share the ticket with McKinley. When McKinley was assassinated on September 14, 1901, Roosevelt succeeded him as president, the youngest ever. During the remainder of the term, Roosevelt established a reputation as a "trustbuster," intervened in labor disputes, and created a Bureau of Corporations to regulate interstate commerce.

Elected by a record landslide in 1904, he set about establishing more regulatory agencies, thus paving the way for modern governmental bureaucracy. The Interstate Commerce Commission, the Pure Food and Drug and Meat Inspection Acts, a greatly expanded national park system, and a refurbished navy were among his Square Deal initiatives. Quoting an African proverb, Roosevelt said that the best way to conduct foreign policy was to "speak softly and carry a big stick," an approach he carried out with great zeal. His position paper of 1904 that became known as the Roosevelt Corollary to the Monroe Doctrine announced that the United States would police Latin America and intervene in internal affairs to promote its interests. The United States acquired the Panama Canal Zone from Colombia in 1903, encouraged the Panamanian revolution that ensured U.S. control and accelerated construction of the canal, and supported the provisional government in Cuba. Roosevelt involved himself in the peace talks between Russia and Japan to end their war, reaching an informal agreement with Japan in 1905 that effectively gave control of the Philippines to the United States and that of Korea to Japan. For his efforts he won the Nobel Peace Prize in 1906. Roosevelt's arguments with Congress grew increasingly bitter after the financial panic of 1907, and he did not run for reelection in 1908, opting for a hunting safari in Africa and a tour of Europe. Reflecting the split in the Republican Party, he founded his own Progressive Party after losing the Republican nomination, thus virtually assuring victory for the Democrat Woodrow Wilson. He abandoned the Progressive Party in hopes of returning to power as a Republican, but he died suddenly in his sleep not long after the end of World War I.

Rosenzweig, Franz (1886–1929)

German-Jewish theologian. Born into a secularized Jewish family, Rosenzweig converted briefly to Christianity, then renounced his new faith and became a devout Jew. Moving to Berlin, he became close friends with the Neo-Kantian Jewish philosopher Hermann Cohen. He also fought for Germany in the First World War. After the war, Rosenzweig and several other noted German Jews opened the Freies Jüdisches Lehrhaus ("Free Jewish House of Learning") in Berlin, which became a center for Jewish religious revival by the early 1920s.

In 1921 he began showing signs of a serious illness that soon left him almost completely paralyzed. He nevertheless continued his intellectual and religious endeavors. In 1924 he began a new translation of the Bible in collaboration with the noted Jewish philosopher Martin Buber (1878–1965). His position on Zionism was ambivalent; on the one hand he favored Jewish nationalism and the desire to establish a distinctly Jewish culture and homeland, but on the other hand he believed that emphasis on political Judaism was antithetical to his religious interests.

Rosenzweig is best remembered for his 1921 philosophical treatise, *Der Stern der Erlösung* (*The Star of Redemption*), in which he argues that man's natural fear of death is the starting point from which he may begin to question and understand the mysteries of life. The book, which he began writing on postcards while still in the army, is an attempt to develop a coherent religious philosophy capable of embracing both Christianity and Judaism. According to Rosenzweig, the pagan conception of the world as being divided into three distinct spheres (man, the universe, and God) was quite accurate. He rejected the common philosophical assertion that these could be combined into a single entity. Instead, he held that the dialogue between these spheres was the key to knowledge, and that through this relationship with God a person could develop his or her own "truth." Like the existentialist philosophers, Rosenzweig believed that there is no universal "truth" but only that which we construct subjectively. As each human being is (or can be) the conduit

through which God shows himself in the world, and it is incumbent upon us all to remain open to each other.

Finally, Rosenzweig held that Judaism and Christianity were both partial truths, determined by their respective historical circumstances, which developed out of man's inherent longing for permanent community and redemption. Like Buber, Rosenzweig attempted to reopen the dialogue between Jews and Christians by emphasizing common values and principles. At the same time, he was particularly interested in restoring the integrity and authenticity that he feared Judaism had lost due to its overexposure to Christian society and, more recently, modern secularism.

Rosetta stone

Egyptian inscription. A slab of black basalt containing a bilingual inscription in Greek and Egyptian, the stone was discovered near Rosetta, Egypt, in 1799 by a French soldier during Napoleon Bonaparte's expedition to Egypt. The eventual translation of the text provided the essential link to the meaning of ancient Egyptian hieroglyphics, which were not fully decipherable before.

The inscriptions on the slab are divided into three parts: Egyptian hieroglyphics, demotic (regular Egyptian handwriting), and Greek. The Greek text is a translation of the hieroglyphics. In 1802, a Frenchman, Sylvestre de Sacy, and a Swede, Jean David Akerbald, identified the royal names in the demotic text. Later, Thomas Young, an Englishman, discovered that the name "Ptolemy" on the stone was repeated in hieroglyphics, as an enclosure within an oval line, or a *cartouche*. This finding established a link between the written Egyptian word and its actual phonetics. The story of the Rosetta stone takes place in 196 B.C.E. in Memphis, and celebrates the ninth anniversary of the coronation of Ptolemy V. It describes the respect in which Ptolemy V was held by his followers, as well as his noble deeds.

The most important analysis of the Rosetta stone was by the Frenchman Jean François Champollion. He devised a working process for the proper reading of Egyptian and made the important discovery that many hieroglyphics are not actual words, but instead whole ideas.

Rossellini, Roberto (1906–1977)

Italian film director. Born in Rome, Rossellini was the son of an architect. Demonstrating an interest in cinema beginning in childhood, Rossellini made his own amateur shorts before entering the film industry. He began his career in the film industry in 1934, working in dubbing, sound effects, and later in scriptwriting and editing until 1938, while he made his own amateur shorts in a studio inside his home. Initially recruited to work on propaganda films for the Italian Fascist regime in the late 1930s, by 1941 Rossellini directed his own propaganda documentary, *La nave bianca* (*The White Ship*), which developed into a feature. Rossellini's first postwar film, *Roma, città aperta* (1945; *Rome, Open City*) established him as the leader of the neorealist movement; evolving from a documentary about a priest serving as a Communist Resistance leader, the film used a mixed cast of professional and nonprofessional actors. His next two films, *Paisan* (1946) and *Germania, anno zero* (1947; *Germany, Year Zero*), similarly employed neorealist techniques to reveal the war's effects on the psyche of modern Italy and Germany. In the 1950s Rossellini directed a series of films starring his second wife, actress Ingrid Bergman; these include *Stromboli* (1949), *Europa '51* (1952; *The Greatest Love*), *Viaggo in Italia* (1953; *The Strangers*), and *La Paura* (1954; *Fear*). The public scandal surrounding their stormy marriage caused a boycott of his films, and contributed to their box-office failure.

After Rossellini's divorce, he used material from his time in India between 1957 and 1958 to make the documentary feature *India* (1958), which again failed at the box office, but he regained his prestige with *Il Generale della Rovere* (1959; *General della Rovere*), a successful World War II drama. Though Rossellini directed a few feature films afterward, most of his work in the 1960s and 1970s was for television. He is remembered as a director who required the spectator to be active in the cinematic experience, blending fiction and documentary to reveal the internal and subjective feelings of his characters through their external reality.

Roth, Philip (1933–)

Jewish-American novelist. Roth was born in New Jersey and educated at Rutgers, Bucknell, and the University of Chicago. In 1959 he married Margaret Martinson, who died nine years later.

His first major published work, a novella and collection of short stories entitled *Goodbye, Columbus and Five Short Stories* (1959), brought the twenty-six-year-old Roth instant recognition and critical acclaim. Praise for the young writer was not universal, however; many in the Jewish community attacked Roth for his unflattering depiction of the Patimkins, a bourgeois Jewish-American family. Roth deliberately challenged the postwar restrictions Jewish writers had imposed on themselves or felt obliged to accept in the interest of the Jewish community. In 1969 Roth published *Portnoy's Complaint*, which again earned critical acclaim and also charges of pornography for its depiction of the frustrated Alex Portnoy and his sexual life under the onerous care of his mother. Other works written by Roth include *Deception* (1990), *Patrimony* (1991), and *Operation Shylock* (1993).

Rousseau, Jean-Jacques (1712–1778)

Swiss-born French philosopher and political theorist. Rousseau was raised by his father, a watchmaker, but was forced to make his way in the world at the age of sixteen. He was befriended by Madame de Warens, who converted him to Catholicism, and who served as benefactress and protector for Rousseau, as he wandered somewhat aimlessly over the next several years. He traveled to Paris in 1742, hoping to introduce a new method of musical notation. Although this failed, he was introduced to a number of wealthy, influential people, developed a close friendship with French writer Denis Diderot (1713–1784), and was invited to contribute articles to the *Encyclopédie* (begun in 1745). Rousseau began a lifelong affair with a semiliterate servant girl, Thérèse Le Vasseur, in 1745; they produced five children, each of whom Rousseau sent to an orphanage.

With the publication of *Discours sur les sciences et les arts* (1750; *Discourses on the Sciences and Arts*), in which Rousseau contested the widely held view that scientific advancement increased human happiness, he found himself famous overnight. In his second philosophical essay, *Discours sur l'origine de l'inégalité* (1754; *Discourse on the Origin and Bases of Inequality Among Men*), Rousseau cites private property and the political state as the corruption of "natural man." Following this publication, Rousseau traveled to Geneva, reclaimed his Protestant faith, and then in 1756 returned to Paris, where he experienced a productive phase in his writing. In 1762 Rousseau was banished from France, due to the critical passages contained in both *Émile* (1762) and *Du contract social* (1762; *The Social Contract*). At the invitation of his friend Scottish philosopher and historian David Hume (1711–1776), Rousseau traveled to England, and there began his famous autobiographical *Confessions* in 1766. His paranoid tendencies, however, soon emerged, and suspecting Hume of conspiring against him—as he had accused most of his friends—he left England. Over the next few years, Rousseau wandered aimlessly with Thérèse, now his common-law wife, and her mother, eventually returning to Paris.

Protected from the outside world by Thérèse, Rousseau spent his remaining years in poverty and isolation, writing his final works, *Les Rêveries du promeneur solitaire* (*Daydreams of a Solitary Stroller*) and a draft for a constitution of Poland, at the request of a Polish count (1782). Rousseau died in 1784, just a few years short of the Revolution that was so greatly inspired by his ideas. He remains celebrated for his resistance to established political and social orders as well as for his sensitivity and glorification of emotions, which greatly endeared him to the Romantics of the succeeding generation.

Rubaiyat (c. 1100)

Persian collection of poetry. The *Rubaiyat* is a collection of poetry written in quatrains (*murabba'* form, hence called a *ruba'i*, plural *ruba'iyat*) on the rhyme *aaba*. The authorship is commonly attributed to Omar Khayyám ("the tentmaker"), a mathematician and scientist who was born in the Persian city of Nishapur. However, less than twenty of the poems contained in the *Rubaiyat* can be credited to Khayyám with any certainty. One of the oldest known manuscripts of the *Rubaiyat* was written in 1457 and contains only 131 poems, whereas an edition published in 1894 contains 770.

The extraordinary popularity enjoyed by the *Rubaiyat* in the English-speaking world was largely the result of a translation published by Edward FitzGerald in 1859. FitzGerald sacrificed faithfulness to the original in favor of conveying what he felt was the spirit of the poems. The translator adapted the *ruba'i* form to English, trying to relay to the reader the rhyme, rhythm, and mood that exist in the Persian original. These English versions served as the catalyst for the formation of the Omar Khayyám Club in London in 1892. The object of this organization was to engage in group poetry readings and sympathetically study the mystical meaning of the *Rubaiyat*.

Though, like much Persian poetry of this period, the *Rubaiyat* used Sufi religious metaphors, the interpretation of the collection as Sufi mystical poetry was largely incorrect, since it dealt primarily with nihilistic and hedonistic concerns.

Rubens, Peter Paul (1577–1640)

Flemish painter. Born in Westphalia and baptized a Calvinist, Rubens moved with his mother after his father's death to Antwerp and became a Catholic. He was educated in a Latin school and apprenticed for the next few years to local artists. Rubens was named a master in the local painters' guild in 1598, and in 1600 he traveled to Italy. For the next eight years he studied the Italian Renaissance masters, especially the artists Michelangelo (1475–1564), Raphael (1483–1520), and Leonardo da Vinci (1452–1519). Rubens developed his own style while copying their works and creating new designs for his patron, the duke of Mantua. Fluent in at least six languages and well-read (he and his brother Philip published a book on classical studies while living together in Rome in 1607–1608), he also began a diplomatic career that would continue for over twenty years and help to spread his international reputation.

Upon the death of his mother, Rubens returned to Antwerp, never going back to Italy. Almost immediately he achieved great success, establishing himself as the preeminent painter in Northern Europe. In 1609 he was appointed court painter to the Archduke Albert and the Infanta Isabella, the Spanish viceroys in Flanders. At this time he married Isabella Brant, the daughter of a successful lawyer. His two most famous works from this period are the monumental triptychs the *Kruisrechting* (1610; *Raising of the Cross*) and the *Kruisafneming* (1611–14; *Descent from the Cross*). Rubens's studio produced an extraordinary number of works, but it is not known how many assistants or collaborators (among them Flemish painter Sir Anthony van Dyck [1599–1641]) he employed, or to what extent many paintings reflect his personal touch. In addition to paintings, Rubens also designed book illustrations, tapestries, and festival decorations, as well as sculptures, metalworks, and architecture. He undertook commissions for the royal families of France, England, and Spain.

After the death of the archduke in 1621, Infanta Isabella entrusted Rubens with diplomatic missions to Spain (1628–29) and England (1629–30), where he was knighted by Charles I for helping to negotiate a truce between these two countries. His wife died in 1626, and he was married again in 1630 to Helen Fourment, the sixteen-year-old niece of his first wife; she became his frequent model. In his later work, he revealed an increasing interest in landscapes. His enormous influence throughout Europe is often attributed to the grandeur of his paintings as well as the great variety of his subjects.

Rulfo, Juan (1918–1986)

Mexican writer. Born into an age of revolution, Rulfo lived his childhood during civil war. His father and uncle were assassinated when Rulfo was seven years old, during the Cristero revolt of 1926, and his mother died when he was nine, making him an orphan.

Rulfo eventually attended the university in Mexico City, but financial and personal concerns ended his studies of law, and he began a series of jobs. He started publishing short stories in 1945, and his first book, *El llano en llamas y otros cuentos* (*The Burning Plain and Other Stories*), appeared in 1953. With the publication of *Pedro Páramo* (1955; *Pedro Páramo: A Novel of Mexico*), Rulfo guaranteed himself a permanent influence on Mexican and Latin American writing in the twentieth century. *Pedro Páramo* is one of the earliest novels to use the *cacique* as a central character. A *cacique* is a Latin American political boss who runs a town or county; he is now a familiar figure in Latin American fiction. These two works incorporate Rulfo's stylistic trademarks: an obsession with death, the use of innovative narrative technique, and a style that has been described as "magical realism," but could be described more accurately as *lo real maravilloso* ("magical reality"). Rulfo did not publish extensively. His next novel, *La cordillera*, was never finished. During the remainder of his life, Rulfo published several works written for the cinema, including *El gallo de oro* (1980; *The Golden Cock*), and had showings of his critically acclaimed photographs.

Rumi, Jalaluddin (1207–1273)

Muslim mystical poet. Commonly referred to as Mawlana or Mevlevi (our master) as a sign of respect, Rumi was the son of a mystical theologian from Balkh in present-day Afghanistan. Following the Mongol invasion of the 1220s, the family moved westward, eventually settling in Konya, the Anatolian city that served as the Seljuk capital. Rumi's father occupied a chair at a theological school in Konya. Following his death in 1231, Rumi inherited this position.

Rumi continued in the predictable life of a conservative theologian until the arrival in 1244 of a wandering mystic named Shamsuddin (Sun of the Faith), referred to as Shams. Rumi was so taken with this Sufi that he allegedly spent all his time with him, ignoring both his family and disciples. His students secretly murdered Shams, and Rumi's grief at the loss was so immense that he spent the remainder of his life writing poems about his departed friend.

Rumi is remembered primarily for two works of poetry. His largest work is a collection of poems dedicated to Shams, called the *Diwan-e Shams*. These poems, written for the most part in traditional lyric form, convey the depth of his spiritual and mystical feelings and his intense love for Shams, who serves as the metaphor for the absolute pervasiveness of God. Rumi's identity becomes so embroiled in the all-pervasive Shams that he even signs Shams's name to the poems.

The *Masnavi* is a didactic poem that was written at the request of one of Rumi's disciples. In addition to constituting a Sufi instructional work, the *Masnavi* is also an anthology of proverbs and folk stories. Secondary and tertiary narratives are interwoven to create colorful tales and anecdotes. Many of these stories are written in a simple, direct style, devoid of much of the technical terminology of Sufi thought.

Although Rumi was not the most accomplished lyric poet of the Persian language, he has met with the widest acclaim of all Islamic mystical poets. The passion of his poetry is so intense that it is easily apparent even in translation. His work is read, recited, and sung to this day in much of the Islamic world, both in Persian and in numerous translations. Furthermore, he is also the figurative founder of one of the most distinctive Sufi orders, the Mevlevis. A unique whirling dance forms the central component of their prayer exercises, on account of which they have come to be known in the West as the Whirling Dervishes.

Rushdie, [Ahmed] Salman (1947–)

Indian-born British novelist. Rushdie's birth to a Muslim family in Bombay, India, occurred in the same year that an independent India was being formed and that Muslim Pakistan was being created. In 1961, at the age of fourteen and after having attended the Cathedral School in Bombay, Rushdie was sent to England to attend the public school Rugby. There he experienced firsthand prejudice against Indians. In 1964, while Rushdie was still at Rugby, his Muslim parents immigrated to Karachi, Pakistan, and the following year Rushdie reluctantly went on to study at Cambridge University according to his parents' wishes. After graduating in 1968, he traveled to his parents' home in Karachi for a brief stay before returning to settle for good in England. In 1976 he married a publicist, Clarissa Luard; the couple later had a son before divorcing in 1987.

Rushdie's first published novel, *Grimus*, appeared in 1975. This revision of a Persian narrative poem, *Grimus*, which drew also on the genres of science fiction and magical realism, was a commercial failure but did win the young writer some critical attention. As an Indian and an Englishman, Rushdie felt himself to be at an advantage in recounting the intertwining narratives of these two historically linked countries, enabling him to write novels in which whole populations and histories are rewritten, relived, and even at times parodied. In *Midnight's Children* (1981), which won the Booker Prize in 1981, Rushdie traces the history of India both before and after independence. The setting of the political satire *Shame* (1983) is not India but Pakistan, and its insightful depiction of Pakistan led to its being banned in that country.

The Satanic Verses (1988) includes Rushdie's ruminations on his school years in Britain, his attachment to his hometown of Bombay, and his father's death, as well as significant moments in which the author explores his Muslim faith through dream sequences in which the Prophet Muhammad (alias Mahound) appears as a droll character. While the provocative and sardonic text achieved critical acclaim, winning Britain's Whitbread Prize, it was its depiction of the Prophet Muhammad and his words that caused outrage among Muslims worldwide (Muslims believe the Qu'rân to be the word of God revealed; in their eyes, Rushdie's liberties were intolerable). Threats, protests, riots, and deaths in places as far apart geographically as India, South Africa, and Britain caused the book to be banned in countries including India, Pakistan, South Africa, Saudi Arabia, and Egypt. When the Ayatollah Khomeini of Iran announced a death sentence for Rushdie in February 1989, an assurance of martyrdom for the assassin and a reward of over a million dollars sent Rushdie into hiding.

Rushdie and his publisher, as well as bookstores that sold *The Satanic Verses*, received threats. Several U.S. bookstores pulled the book temporarily from their shelves to protect their employees. Rushdie's Italian and Japanese translators were killed. Since the early 1990s, however, Rushdie has made some public appearances and has published a number of books, including *Imaginary Homelands: Essays and Criticism, 1981–1991*, and *East West* (1994). In 1993 Rushdie won the twenty-fifth-year commemorative "Booker of Bookers Prize" for *Midnight's Children*.

Russian Orthodox Church

Branch of Eastern Orthodox Church. Orthodox Christianity appeared as early as 860 C.E. in Russia; it became the country's official religion in 988, and was formally established as an independent patriarchate in 1589. Like other Orthodox churches, it descended from the earlier Church of the Byzantine empire. Though the Church was disempowered in the eighteenth century, during the reigns of Peter the Great (r. 1682–1725) and Catherine the Great (r. 1762–1796), it remained an intellectual center and an important presence among the peasantry, where holidays and fasts were observed and the "pope," or parish priest, figured importantly in community life. In the early twentieth century, the Church became of renewed interest to many members of the Russian intelligentsia, and leading clergy called for the release of the Church from state controls. This religious renaissance was abruptly ended by the Bolshevik Revolution of 1917, when the Church was dismantled and persecuted. Its leaders denounced the Revolution and refused to recognize the new government, and as a result, many clergy were imprisoned and executed. Thousands of churches were closed and many of them were destroyed. The virulent antireligion campaign was abated only when it served government interests, such as during the Second World War when the government needed to rally the people behind the war effort.

Russian Orthodoxy, however, has maintained its following, especially in rural populations, despite state persecution, and is an important cultural, as well as religious, institution for the Russian people. During the changes in the late 1980s, and after the collapse of the Soviet Union, the Church began enjoying increasing rights, and a considerable number of churches, and even monasteries, have been reopened throughout the country.

Russian Revolution of 1905

Russian rebellion. This revolution established a constitutional monarchy and paved the way for the Revolution of 1917. During the czarist regime of Nicholas II (r. 1894–1917), calls for reform increased dramatically, especially after the Russo-Japanese War (1904–1905). The popular unrest culminated in the events of Bloody Sunday (January 22, 1905), when soldiers massacred workers and members of the labor movement participating in a peaceful demonstration. The public was outraged, and a series of strikes and uprisings occurred in other towns and cities. In many industrial centers, the Soviets (councils) of Workers' Deputies were created as the workers' independent organs of self-government. Nicholas was forced to issue the October Manifesto, in which he accepted constitutional rule and promised the creation of a parliament, the Duma. However,

this did not satisfy the masses, and a big workers' uprising followed in December in Moscow. It was suppressed, and although workers' protests continued until 1907, the defeat of the Moscow uprising signified the end of this revolution. The czar's rule was fully overthrown in the Russian Revolution of 1917.

Russian Revolution of 1917

Russian rebellion. This revolution is actually composed of two separate revolutions, the February Revolution, which ended the reign of Czar Nicholas II (r. 1894–1917) and the October Revolution, during which the Bolsheviks, led by Communist leader Vladimir Lenin (1870–1924) seized power. A period of civil war ensued, and it was not until 1920 that the conflicts ended and the first Communist state was established.

The immediate cause of the Revolution lay in the czar's inability to manage the government during the First World War (1914–17). The populace was angered by a lack of food and supplies and 5.5 million casualties in the war, and the unrest that Nicholas had assuaged in 1905 now overwhelmed his divided government. After the czar's abdication in March, a provisional government was established first under Prince Lvov and then under Aleksandr Kerensky. Lenin had returned from exile in April, however, and the Bolsheviks won large majorities in the Petrograd and Moscow Soviets of Workers' and Soldiers' Deputies. Though some Bolsheviks were content with this electoral gain, Lenin prevailed in a coup d'état. The Bolsheviks seized power in November and signed a separate peace treaty with Germany. However, they had to fight a long civil war against the White (counterrevolutionary) armies, which for a time enjoyed support from foreign troops. The insurrection ended finally in a Bolshevik victory in 1920.

Russo-Japanese War (1904–1905)

This war was fought between Russia and Japan over control of Manchuria and Korea. After the Russians rejected the Japanese proposal that the two powers "exchange" rights in the disputed territories—Japan would recognize Russia's rights in Manchuria if Russia recognized Japan's claims on Korea—Japan signed a military alliance with Great Britain in the hopes of deterring Russian aggression. When the Russians repeatedly refused to acknowledge Japan's rights in Korea, the Japanese government succumbed to growing prowar sentiment within the country. The war began when Japan attacked and trapped the Russian fleet at Port Arthur on February 8, 1904, and ended when the two countries signed the Treaty of Portsmouth on September 5, 1905. Though Japan prevailed both on the seas in the Battle of Tsushima and on land in the Battle of Mukden, it was unable to win the war decisively because of high casualties among officers and troops, and a chronic shortage of guns and ammunition. Russia, though possessing superior firepower and manpower, was eager to conclude the fighting because of the threat of an internal rebellion and civil strife within its frontiers.

The resulting treaty, negotiated by U.S. president Theodore Roosevelt, gave the Japanese exclusive rights in Korea and control over the South Manchuria Railway, Japan's first-ever foothold in China. However, Russia was not required to pay any indemnity, a fact that strained relations between the United States and Japan, which had spent more than 1.5 billion yen in the war effort. Nevertheless, the conclusion of the war left Japan a major imperialist power in East Asia.

Ruth, Babe (1895–1948)

American baseball player. Babe Ruth, born George Herman Ruth, Jr., grew up in a poor neighborhood in Baltimore and attended St. Mary's Industrial School, where his interest in baseball began. In 1914 he signed a contract with the minor-league Baltimore Orioles, but was sold to the Boston Red Sox later that year. Even though Ruth is best remembered for his long-ball hitting abilities, he began his career as a successful pitcher and was later switched to the outfield. Setting the major-league record for a single season with twenty-nine home runs, in 1920 Ruth was sold to the New York Yankees, the team with which he is most often associated. During his illustrious career with the Yankees, Ruth led the team to seven American League pennants (1921–23, 1926–28, 1932) and four World Series titles. He broke the major-league home-run record in three consecutive seasons (1919–21) and his lifetime home-run total of 714 stood until Hank Aaron broke the record in 1974. His other records include highest slugging percentage (.690) and most bases on balls (2,056).

The celebrity status that Ruth enjoyed was unmatched at that time, as was the salary (as high as $80,000 per year) and his many lucrative endorsements. Yankee Stadium became "the House That Ruth Built," a tribute to Ruth's impact on the Yankee franchise and on baseball itself. He is still the all-time record holder of the most home runs (60) in a 154-game season (1927). Though he was never given the opportunity to manage a team, Ruth, nicknamed "the Sultan of Swat" and "the Bambino," was among the first set of athletes elected to the National Baseball Hall of Fame in 1936. Ruth died of cancer in New York City.

S

Sabato, Ernesto (1911–)

Argentine writer. Sabato was raised in a rural town, part of a large, prosperous family of Italian origin. He attended the university in Buenos Aires, and found in mathematics and physics an orderliness that he could not find in his new life in the city. There he became involved in political matters, and left to tour Europe as a delegate for the Argentine Communist youth movement. He won a scholarship to study mathematics in Paris and then at the Massachusetts Institute of Technology (MIT) in Boston.

Upon Sabato's return to Argentina in 1940, he took a teaching position at the National University of La Plata. His interest in literary matters, sparked by his exposure to the Surrealist movement in Paris, manifested itself in his writing for the literary section of a Buenos Aires newspaper. In 1945 Sabato was forced to resign his post at the university due to pressure from the Perón government. He published a book of essays that year, *Uno y el universo* (*One and the Universe*), and in 1948 the novel *El túnel* (*The Tunnel*). Both his fiction and his more philosophical essays reflect his readings in existentialism. His problematic relationship with science is revealed by his belief that human reliance on reason and science impedes the ability to acquire self-knowledge, and thus prevents the release of one's true potential.

In 1961 Sabato published his second novel, *Sobre héroes y tumbas* (*On Heroes and Tombs*), which is widely considered to be his best work. Characterized as a psychological novel, it furthers the existential issues raised in *The Outsider*, continuing to question the role of science and technology, as well as critiquing contemporary Argentina with its myriad of political and social problems. Sabato has also published a third novel, *Abaddón, el exterminador* (1974; *The Angel of Darkness*), which won the best foreign book award in France, and numerous essays.

al-Saʿdâwî, Nawâl (1932–)

Egyptian writer, physician, and feminist. As the author of numerous novels, plays, and studies on Arab women, al-SaʿDâwî presents a striking example of the way in which social and economic changes in Egypt during the past forty years have allowed women from various social groups to participate in society and in the feminist movement. Her rural background distinguishes her from previous Egyptian feminists, who were by and large upper-class urban women, often wives of prominent politicians. One such early feminist, Hudâ Shaʿrâwî, founder of the Egyptian women's movement in the 1920s, was born into a wealthy family and educated by private tutors for a life of public service. Unlike Shaʿrâwî, Saʿdâwî overcame the limitations traditionally imposed on women of rural origin to become, by her own description, "a middle-class or lower-middle-class" professional living in

Cairo. Hers was probably the first generation of women for whom such a transition was possible.

Whereas earlier feminists focused on education for girls, personal freedoms for women, and nationalist issues also important to male political activists, Sa'dâwî's feminism calls for more radical reform: she attacks the systematic deformation of women's lives under the current regime, not just abuses of power, and consistently links the workings of the patriarchal system to class and imperialism. Her radical approach, however, is not universally accepted by feminists in Egypt.

Becoming a physician in 1955, Sa'dâwî eventually rose to the position of director of health education, but the publication of her first work of nonfiction, *Women and Sex* (1972), caused such a controversy among the political and religious authorities that the Department of Health was forced to dismiss her. Under similar pressures, she lost jobs as a chief editor of the journal *Health* and as assistant general secretary to the Medical Association of Egypt. In 1981 Sa'dâwî was arrested in a roundup of political dissidents by the Sadat regime and imprisoned briefly.

Sa'dâwî has written many novels and collections of short stories, including *Woman at Point Zero* (1978), which received the Literary Prize for Franco-Arab Friendship in 1982. Other titles include *The Hidden Face of Eve: Women in the Arab World* (1980) and *Mawt al-rajul al-wâhid 'ala al-ard* (1976; *God Dies by the Nile*).

Saladin (1138–1193)

Muslim ruler. To the West, Saladin remains an image of Oriental chivalry; to many Arabs, Salâh al-Dîn al-Ayyûbî is a symbol of strength, unity, and justice. Saladin and other rulers of his time presided over a formative period of Western-Islamic relations: the Crusades. Born in Iraq of Kurdish ethnicity, Saladin began his career as a general in the service of a Turkic dynasty. Sent to conquer Egypt and consolidate Syria, he proclaimed his independence and founded the Ayyûbid dynasty, which ruled Egypt, Syria, Palestine, and parts of western Arabia between 1174 and 1260. He led Muslim armies against European invaders during the Third Crusade (1188–92) and emerged victorious at the dramatic Battle of Hittin in 1187, thus restoring Jerusalem to Muslim rule. Such encounters became the basis for Saladin's image as the exemplar of knightly virtue.

It was in response to the Christian Holy War launched by Europe that Saladin invoked the principle of *jihâd*, or holy war, which in Islamic culture means the exertion against a visible enemy, or the devil.

Saladin died in Damascus after regaining virtually all of the territories that had been seized by the Crusaders and uniting Muslims in a common cause.

samba

Brazilian dance. Of West African origin, the samba borrows from the choreography of certain round dances of Angola and the Congo. Samba is a generic term used to refer to a variety of dances characterized by a vivid rolling and syncopated rhythm, simple forward and backward steps, and tilting and rocking body movements. Another characteristic of the folk samba—and of all Afro-Brazilian dances—is the *umbigada*, a kind of "invitation to dance" in which the couples touch navels. The dancing is always accompanied by singing, usually responsorial, in which the refrain and the stanzas alternate. There are different kinds of sambas, ranging from the ballroom version to that danced in urban centers, during carnival, and that cultivated in the hillside slums of Rio de Janeiro called *batucada*. The *batucada* is a kind of group dance performed either in circles with a soloist or in double lines. The ballroom version was popularized in the United States and Western Europe in the early 1940s, and was accompanied by a large orchestra in which the percussion section was significantly reduced.

Samguk

Korean historical period. The Samguk, or "Three Kingdoms," period denotes a roughly seven-hundred-year political history that prefigured the development of the modern state of Korea. The Three Kingdoms period is generally considered to have ended in 668 C.E. with the final consolidation of the independent kingdoms of Koguryŏ, Paekche, and Silla under the auspices of what is now known as the Unified Silla Kingdom. Dates given for the inception of this era vary depending on which of the constituent kingdoms is credited as prototypical. Though contemporary Chinese records cite the dates of the establishment of the Paekche, Koguryŏ, and Silla kingdoms as 18, 37, and 57 B.C.E. respectively, it is currently thought that the Koguryŏ kingdom was the first to have emerged as a settlement along the Yalu River, which marks the border between the modern states of the Democratic People's Republic of Korea (North Korea) and the People's Republic of China.

The geographic area that was to become known as the Koguryŏ kingdom was in fact contained within the Chinese colony or "commandery" of Lolang. Koguryŏ's nominally independent military government was modeled after Chinese political systems, and it was largely through the adoption and influence of Koguryŏ cultural and military practices that the Sinicization of the southerly kingdoms of Paekche and Silla was accomplished.

If Koguryŏ's chief legacy to the Three Kingdoms was a Chinese-derived political system, Paekche's was the refinement and exportation of Sino-Korean art

and religion. While individuals from the Koguryŏ kingdom traveled to Japan as Buddhist missionaries, the Paekche government made Japanese evangelism a national priority. The Paekche kingdom was also the first to adopt Chinese orthography, making possible both the importation of Chinese literature and subsequently the development of an indigenous Korean literature and literary culture. In addition to Buddhist teachings, Paekche introduced Chinese language and literature to Japan.

Little information exists regarding the third of the Three Kingdoms, Silla, prior to its emergence in the seventh century as the dominant military and political state of the Korean peninsula. It is thought that, ironically, the very political and cultural growth of the Koguryŏ and Paekche kingdoms that led them into increasing involvement in disputes with their Chinese overlords made way for the military buildup of Silla, which defeated and annexed the Paekche and Koguryŏ kingdoms in 660 and 668 C.E., respectively. The consolidation of the Three Kingdoms by Silla marked the beginning of what is sometimes referred to as the Golden Age of Korean history, the Unified Silla period. It is the territorial and cultural integrity of the Unified Silla period to which appeals are often implicitly made even today in debates over the "reunification" of Korea.

Samguk sagi

Korean historical text. The *Samguk sagi* (*History of the Three Kingdoms*) is the earliest and most complete extant account of primarily secular events in Korean history during the Three Kingdoms period. The fifty-volume chronicle was written in 1145 by official Confucian historiographer and military leader Kim Pusik (1075–1151). Reflecting the conservative orientation of its author, it conforms largely to the composition of official Chinese almanacs of the day. While significant as a historical document and account, the *Samguk sagi* reveals little of the political and cultural struggle waged during the Three Kingdoms period among the Three Kingdoms themselves, or against the neighboring and occupying Chinese. The extent of the Chinese influence on Korean culture of the time is perhaps best revealed by the very fidelity of the *Samguk sagi* to Chinese texts in its narrative form and content.

Samguk yusa

Korean historical text. The *Samguk yusa* (*Memorabilia of the Three Kingdoms*), a five-volume collection of Korean legends and stories, was compiled by the Buddhist monk Iryŏn (1206–1289). By focusing on the role and dissemination of Buddhism in Korea during the Three Kingdoms period, the work develops and demonstrates a distinctively Korean literary style. This is especially evident in its biographical treatment of the Son Buddhist patriarch Wonhyo. Using a combination of folk tales, legends, and colorful anecdotes, the *Samguk yusa* depicts this most venerated scholar and prelate as both fallible and fantastical, a lapsed monk whose affair with a widowed princess produced a son (Sŏl Ch'ong, the inventor of the *idu* system of Korean/Chinese orthography), and who subsequently returned to his religious vocation with a populist bent, going among the people to report firsthand his travels and pilgrimages throughout Asia and the undersea world of the Dragon King.

Aside from its value as proof of the interaction and intellectual commerce among the early cultures of the Buddhist world and its insights into the political climate of the Three Kingdoms period, the *Samguk yusa* is also one of the earliest existing Korean texts to transcribe *hyangga*, a form of poetry typically chanted at religious and festival occasions. This recording of *hyangga* is considered noteworthy not only for pre-

serving rare examples of an ancient oral tradition, but also because the very orthographic system used in its transcription represents a radical linguistic and political innovation. While the Korean language belongs to the Ural-Altaic group and is unrelated to the Chinese, Korean scholarship—including all written records and communication—was invariably conducted in Chinese characters. (This preference for Chinese characters in scholarship and business persists in Korea today.) Sŏl Ch'ong, the son of Wŏnhyo, was responsible for the development and implementation of *idu*, a system by which Chinese characters were assigned to spoken Korean, and for the first time it was possible to "write" in the Korean language. *Idu* represented an assertion of political and cultural independence from the Chinese, who had maintained military and cultural hegemony over much of the Korean peninsula during the Three Kingdoms period. Until the mid fifteenth century, when Yi dynasty king Sejong invented *hangŭl*, a twenty-eight-letter phonetic alphabet (known initially as *hunmin chongŭm*, or right sounds for the instruction of the people), *idu* remained the only means of Korean language transcription available. The *hyangga* of the *Samguk yusa* are some of the finest examples of *idu* literature existing today.

Sand, George (1804–1876)

French author. After her father's death when she was four, Amandine Aurore Lucile Dupin, Baroness Dudevant, whose pen name was George Sand, was brought up in Nohant at the country home (near La Châtre in Berry) of her grandmother, a friend of French philosopher Jean-Jacques Rousseau (1712–1778). At thirteen, she was sent to a convent in Paris. In 1822 she married Casimir Dudevant and had two children, but left him in 1831 to pursue a writing career in Paris. She collaborated with Jules Sandeau on articles for *Le Figaro*, using the joint pseudonym of Jules Sand, and took the name George Sand for the 1832 publication of her novel *Indiana*. The story of a woman who leaves an unhappy marriage to seek love was an immediate success, and Sand followed it with *Valentine* (1832) and *Lélia* (1833). These novels attest to Sand's open criticism of the confining position of women dictated by conventional social norms. Instead, she promoted a sense of "romantic feminism" for which she encountered a great deal of opposition. *Mauprat* (1837), *Spiridion* (1839), and *Les sept cordes de la lyre* (1840), among others, were novels advocating social reform and demonstrating the influence of the men whom she knew, namely the philosopher Pierre Leroux, whose beliefs she fully accepted.

Sand was famous for her affairs with prominent artists French writer Prosper Mérimée (1803–1870), French poet Alfred de Musset (1810–1857), and Polish composer Fryderyk Chopin (1810–1849) and her flouting of convention by smoking cigars and wearing men's clothing. Her early enthusiasm for the 1848 Revolution quickly dissipated and she soon returned to Nohant. During the rest of her literary career, Sand wrote many "rustic" novels, celebrating rural life and love that crosses class boundaries, but she is best known for her four-volume *Histoire de ma vie* (1854–55; *Story of My Life*).

Sandino, Augusto [César] (1895–1934)

Nicaraguan political leader. In the 1920s Augusto Sandino left Nicaragua for southeast Mexico, where he worked for U.S. companies in the oil fields. There he was influenced by the political ideologies and the peasant and workers' movements of the Mexican revolution and became ardently opposed to U.S. intervention in Latin America. In 1926, when members of the Liberal Party in Nicaragua took up arms against the Conservative regime installed by the U.S. government, Sandino returned to his country to join the uprising. The next year, after the United States negotiated a cease-fire between the Liberals and Conservatives, Sandino denounced the Liberal Party for selling out to the United States and refused to disarm until troops withdrew from Nicaragua. Sandino and his followers formed the Ejército Defensor de la Soberania Nacional de Nicaragua (EDSN, Army in Defense of Nicaraguan Sovereignty), and waged a guerrilla war in the northwest mountains against the U.S. Marines. Peasants who had struggled for decades against landowners' appropriation of their land and labor supported Sandino's proclamations calling on the government to redistribute land. Using tactics that have become a standard part of guerrilla warfare, Sandino's army inflicted major losses on the U.S. forces. Because the EDSN was supported by, and often indistinguishable from, the local population, the marines bombed villages, burned crops, and tortured and killed civilians in its fight to defeat Sandino's army. These atrocities aroused opposition and gained recognition for Sandino throughout the world. As fighting dragged on in the remote mountains, protest in the United States forced Washington to reformulate its policies. The United States trained a new Nicaraguan army to replace the marines, and the U.S. ambassador in Managua chose Anastasio Somoza García to head the fighting force, which was called the National Guard. The marines withdrew, but the National Guard was unable to defeat the EDSN. In 1933 the United States recommended that the president of Nicaragua sign a cease-fire with Sandino. Exhausted from war, Sandino and his peasant followers agreed to lay down their weapons. Sandino declared that his struggle had been successful; his army had forced the U.S. troops to withdraw. Despite the cease-fire, the guard harassed Sandino and killed many of his supporters. In 1934 he met with the president of Nicaragua to ask for protection for himself and his followers. Upon leaving the presidential palace, Sandino was assassinated by the National Guard, under orders from Somoza and apparently with the acquiescence of the U.S. ambassador. Two years later, with help from the United States, Somoza had himself elected president of Nicaragua. He and his two sons ruled the country for forty-five years, until 1979, when the Frente Sandinista de Liberación Nacional (FSLN, the Sandinista Front for National Liberation) overthrew the Somoza dynasty. The FSLN took the name of Augusto Sandino to honor him and as a symbol of the continuation of the historical struggle against U.S. intervention in Nicaragua.

sand paintings

Ritual in Navajo healing ceremonies. The Navajo Indians share the idea of sand paintings, also known as dry paintings, with the Pueblo Indians, who use the paintings in coming-of-age and agricultural ceremonies rather than for healing, as do the Navajo. Although the sand paintings are forms of artistic expression, the value of these paintings is found in their religious and ritual significance rather than in their aesthetic qualities. The healing ceremonies of the Navajo can last over a week, during which four or more paintings are created. They are stylized, symbolic pictures using the colors white, blue, yellow, red, and black. The pictures are created by pouring dyed sand, charcoal, pollen, or other material onto a sand background and are sometimes as large as ten feet in diameter. The pictures illustrate the chants that are also a part of the healing ritual. Some paintings depict sacred objects, such as the Navajo's sacred mountains (believed to be the houses of the gods), while others show legendary visions. Still others illustrate the dances done during the ritual. Some pictures must be created exactly the same every time, and some allow for artistic variation. Which painting will be used is determined by the healer. After the painting is created, the patient sits in the middle of it and material from the picture is applied to his or her body. The paintings do not last beyond the ritual. Later, the designs are woven into rugs. Originally, exact copies were not allowed to be made, so errors were included in the weaving, but today many of the paintings have been copied correctly in order to preserve both the art and the culture.

Sanguozhi Tongsu yanyi

Chinese classical novel. Luo Guanzhong based his novel *Sanguozhi tongsu yanyi* (*A Tale of the Three Kingdoms*) on *The History of the Three Kingdoms* by Chen Shou of the third century C.E. and on "Sanguo pinghua" and other stories of the Yuan dynasty (1260–1368). The earliest edition, printed in 1494, consists of twenty-four books; the present popular edition has 120 chapters, with two lines of verse providing the title for each chapter.

The story opens with three heroes pledging an oath of brotherhood to one another. The relationship among the three gradually gives way to a panoramic picture of the conflicts among the rulers of the three kingdoms and the social consequences of their constant fighting. From court debates to peasant dialogues, from heroic generals fighting on horseback to tearful women begging in the streets, this panoramic novel offers a vivid description of life during the disunified period following the fall of the Han dynasty in 220 C.E. It contains more than 750,000 characters, although only four hundred are portrayed in detail. Historians value this novel as an important source for the study of the political and military life and strategies during the Three Kingdoms period.

San Martín, José de (1778–1850)

Latin American independence leader. San Martín was born in Yapeyú (now in northeastern Argentina) to Spanish parents. Educated in Buenos Aires and Spain, he served the Spanish monarchy as a soldier until 1811, when he opted to refuse a promotion and return to Lima, the capital of the viceroyalty in Peru.

On his way to Latin America, San Martín stopped in London, where his political alliances began to shift. He joined the Logia Americana, a lodge founded to further the struggle for Latin American independence. Leaving London, San Martín made his way to Buenos Aires, where he immediately joined the revolutionary regime and began organizing against the Spanish in support of liberation. In later life, San Martín claimed that his political loyalties changed due to the "call of his native land." Some historians suspect that Spanish prejudice against people born in the Indies may have forced San Martín to identify with the revolutionaries.

In 1816 San Martín and the other representatives of the Argentine provinces met at the Congress of Tucumán and issued a declaration of independence from Spain. San Martín voiced a preference for a liberal constitutional monarchy, with a prince of the Inca royal family as its head. Beginning a campaign against the Spanish in January 1817, by April 1818 San Martín had managed to rid the country of royalist forces.

Without the backing of the Argentine government, San Martín eventually moved on to Lima, his next military objective. Beginning negotiations with the Spanish, San Martín proposed the creation of an independent monarchy under a Spanish prince. Although these attempts failed, nationalist sentiments were growing and fearful royalists allowed San Martín to take the capital, and the independence of Peru was proclaimed on July 28, 1821. San Martín was made protector of the new, independent nation, but he was unsure of the extent of his popular support: some of his actions, such as the abolition of Indian tribute and forced labor, and the gradual emancipation of black slaves, had been met with suspicion and resistance. In addition, he lacked the arms to defeat the royalist forces in the interior of the country. Matters were further complicated by the fact that Latin American revolutionary Simón Bolívar, who had liberated the northern provinces, had taken Guayaquil, a port and province that San Martín had hoped to incorporate into Peru.

Agreeing to meet in Guayaquil in 1822, the two generals discussed the future of the continent and their role in the struggle for American independence. It is possible that San Martín made a great personal renunciation so that Bolívar and the cause of independence might win, or Bolívar made it clear he would not help in Peru unless San Martín relinquished control, but after the meeting San Martín resigned as protector of Peru and left both Peru and the task of Peruvian independence to Bolívar. San Martín spent the remainder of his life in exile, avoiding all further involvement with the newly independent nations of South America. He died in Boulogne-sur-Mer.

sannyasa

Hindu religious doctrine. From the Sanskrit *sam* and *yam*, which means "to give up completely," sannyasa is the term for institutionalized renunciation. A sannyasi is an ordained monk in Hindu monastic orders who follows an austere and ascetic lifestyle. The term has far wider general significance, however, in the Indian context. Unlike Western traditions, where "renunciation" is not a term of cultural frequency or importance, renunciation has been the cynosure of human achievement and possible perfection within Indian tradition. Priests (Brahmans), who must be married to function as ritualists, have ranked beneath the ascetic renouncer, the sann-yasi, in all literary and oral accounts since the very earliest days of India's recorded traditions.

The main reason for the enormous importance assigned to an ascetic lifestyle, from the Buddha to Indian nationalist leader Mohandas (Mahatma) Gandhi (1869–1948) and onward, seems to lie in the ancient notion that asceticism, particularly celibacy, confers mystical powers on its practitioner, and leads to supreme knowledge and perfection, which is understood as divine status and power.

The devotional, philosophical, and hagiographic literature devolving from sannyasa is as old as it is large. Songs, poems, folk and classical literature, and oral epics all center on the paradigm of renunciation, of sannyasa. Literature by and about holy men and women abounds on the Indian subcontinent; it is as readily available and widely read as pulp writing in America.

Santa Claus

Gift-giver associated with Christmas as celebrated in America. "Santa Claus" is a corruption of "Sinter Klaas," the Dutch name for St. Nicholas. Nicholas was a fifth-century priest in Asia Minor who was said to have performed various altruistic deeds. The most famous involved three young women who were about to be forced into prostitution because of their poverty. Nicholas secretly entered their home through their chimney and left gold in their stockings, which were hung over the embers of the fire to dry. The legends associated with St. Nicholas are believed to have been brought to New Amsterdam and the other Dutch colonies in the New World, where they were combined with Nordic legends involving a Yuletide gift-giving figure who would leave gifts only for children who had been well behaved during the previous year.

The practice of Yuletide celebration and gift-giving itself is of early and non-Christian origin. There are written accounts of at least four different pagan and Roman festivals that Christmas came to replace. Two of these, the pagan festival of the Kalends and the Roman Saturnalia, are characterized by feasting and revelry, while a third is the festival of Libanius, in which the focus is upon gift-giving and largesse generally. The fourth, the Roman cult of Deus Sol Inviticus, took place on December 25, and is often regarded as the source of the date of modern Christmas celebrations. The syncretism in the development of early Christianity thus involved the adoption of various aspects of non-Christian winter celebrations.

As a result of this syncretism, the gift-giving figure is present in various incarnations in different cultures. In some countries, the gift-giver became an avatar of the Christ child, as in Germany, Austria, and Switzerland, where the gift-giver is known as Christkindl or Kris Kringle. Some directly betray a non-Christian origin, as in Scandinavian countries, where gifts are received from a trio of gnomish figures. Poland presents a hybrid of these two models: the Polish gift-giver is known as the Star Man, thought to be so called because of his association with the Star of Bethlehem. Other cultures have a more generic gift-giver, casting either historical figures in the role—as is the case with the Dutch Sinter Klaas and the American Santa Claus—or else an independent character, such as Père Noël in France, Father Christmas in England, and Grandfather Frost in Russia. The last variant of the holiday gift-giver is the direct appropriation of the American custom, including the figure of Santa Claus. An instance of this may be seen in modern-day Japan, where the custom of holiday gift-giving is now widespread and associated with the character of Santa Claus, although some Japanese have adopted the custom of gift-giving while assigning the role of gift-giver to the deity Hoteiosho.

Santería

Cuban religious cult of African origin. Santería developed out of the traditions of the Yoruba people (from modern Nigeria and Benin) who were brought to the island as slaves from the sixteenth to the nineteenth century. Although Santería blends elements of Christianity with West African beliefs, it is essentially an African form of worship that has developed a symbiotic relation with Catholicism. Devotees believe in one Supreme Being, but also in saints or spirits known as orishás. There are many different orishás, and elaborate systems of correspondence have been set up between them and Catholic saints. For example, every worshiper knows that St. Peter is Ogun, the Yoruba patron of miners and workers, and that St. Barbara is the warrior orishá Chango.

Santeros are initiated devotees, believed to have the magical power of the orishás. For ordinary believers, Santería is a means of resolving everyday problems, including those of health, money, and love. The Santeros help individuals understand and grow with their destiny, rather than become its victims. The Santero's success depends on deepening a relationship with a particular orishá, as well as that of the devotees, and this is done largely through food sharing. Rituals involve offers of food and animal sacrifice, divination performed with fetishes made of shells or bones, and ceremonies with drums and dancing in which sometimes the *orishás* "descend" and "seize the head" of an initiate, thereby delivering messages, advice, and admonitions to the devotees. Worshipers also believe that an orishá can penetrate one's being and become part of one's personality, or intervene on one's behalf.

Despite a history of suppression and misunderstanding, and due to the nearly 1 million Cuban exiles who left their country during the Cuban revolution, Santería has survived and currently is also practiced in the United States, Venezuela, Puerto Rico, and other Latin American countries.

Santos, Bienvenido [Nunqui] (1911–)

Filipino-American author. Philippine-born Santos left a ten-year job teaching secondary school in 1942 and began what was to become a lifelong relationship with the United States, serving as a cultural attaché to the Philippine Embassy in Washington, D.C. At the end of the Second World War, Santos returned to the Philippines and resumed his academic career as a professor and administrator at Legazpi College (now Aquinas University). Over the next twenty-five years, Santos taught at various universities in both the Philippines and the United States. He authored over a dozen novels and anthologies of short stories and poetry, including *You Lovely People* (1955), *Brother My Brother* (1960), *Villa Magdalena* (1965), and *Scent of Apples: A Collection of Stories* (1979). His writing dealt primarily with the psychological exile experienced by Filipinos in the United States, often documenting the processes of economic and social marginalization that transformed them from hopeful and idealistic newcomers into cynical and despairing permanent aliens. While Santos was lecturing at the University of Iowa's Writers' Workshop in 1972, martial law was declared in the Philippines. Blacklisted for his left-leaning political sympathies and faced with the state-mandated closing of Philippine universities, Santos effectively became an exile himself.

Since the fall of the regime of President Ferdinand Marcos in 1986, Santos has divided his time between his native and his adopted countries. He has continued to write about the dilemma of the "Pinoys" (Filipinos who have lost contact with their culture because they have lived in the United States for so long), who, like Santos himself, are prohibited by contradictory experiences from ever being fully able to recover or attain a state of belonging in either Philippine society or in American society.

santri

Javanese term for a student of Islam. *Santri* is a committed student of Islam who has adopted the dress and lifestyle of the traditional religious community. The term is popularly used by the self-proclaimed devout to differentiate themselves from the *abangan*, who are identified with a more nominal form of Islam combined with pre-Islamic indigenous elements. In practice, distinctions between the religious styles of the two communities are harder to draw. Historically, the *santri* were more likely to promote local Muslim parties prior to Indonesian independence than were the *abangan*, many of whom were drawn into the Indonesian nationalist and Communist movements. Hostility between the two socioreligious identifications was widespread between 1963 and 1965.

Sappho (c. 600 B.C.E.)

Lyric poet of Greek antiquity. Our knowledge of Sappho's work and life remains fragmentary. She was born and spent most of her life on the island of Lesbos, where she was married to a wealthy man and had a daughter, Cleis. As a wealthy woman, Sappho participated in female salons, in which women gathered to read and compose poetry. Her poetry focuses largely on women, and the loves, hatred, and jealousies between them. Because of the intense, erotic descriptions of women in Sappho's poetry, the word "lesbian" is derived from "Lesbos," to refer to sexual relationships between women. Sappho wrote in several meters, including a graceful ode meter, the Sapphic, named for her. Her influence on later poets— such as Anacreon and Catullus—was considerable, but by the end of the eighth or ninth century C.E., none of her

original work was extant. With the discovery of additional papyrus fragments in the twentieth century, however, the knowledge of Sappho's biography and poetry has been enriched. Sappho remains today one of the most important and influential poets of antiquity and one of the earliest known female poetic voices.

Sarduy, Severo (1936–)

Cuban poet, novelist, critic, and painter. Sarduy is best known for his novel *Cobra* (1972), which won the Prix Medicis literary award in France, and describes the transvestite motorcycle gang, the Gasoline Girls, that Sarduy and art critic Roland Barthes formed, which drove around Paris committing semiterrorist acts. Sarduy was born in Camagüey, a town in eastern Cuba with a long literary tradition. During the fifties Sarduy lived in prerevolutionary Havana, studying medicine, working for an advertising agency, and writing for literary periodicals. When the dictatorship of Cuban president Fulgencio Batista fell to Cuban revolutionary Fidel Castro in 1959, Sarduy began to write for the government, as well as editing the cultural pages of the newspaper *Diario Libre*. In 1960 he received a scholarship from the government to study art criticism at the École du Louvre, in Paris. He became involved in Tel Quel, an important intellectual circle that included the critics Barthes and Jacques Derrida. At the same time, Sarduy was writing and translating for the influential journal *Mundo Nuevo* (New World) that was integral in introducing Latin American writers such as Colombian author Gabriel García Márquez and Argentine author Jorge Luis Borges to European audiences.

In the late 1960s Sarduy became head of the Latin American collection of Éditions du Seuil, the house that published works by members of Tel Quel, as well as works by García Márquez, Borges, Lezama Lima, Cabrera Infante, and

Reinaldo Arenas. Though not as widely known or read as the major figures of the Latin American literary "Boom," Sarduy's work both as an editor and as a novelist and critic has widely influenced the reception of the Latin American novel and the shape the novels themselves have taken and continue to take. His other novels include *Gestos* (1963; *Expressions*), *De donde son los cantanes* (1967; *From Cuba with a Song*), *Maitreya* (1978), and *Colibri* (1984; *Hummingbird*). He has also produced volumes of collected essays and poetry, mixed-media presentations, plays, paintings, and radio broadcasts.

Sargon (2334 B.C.E)

Akkadian ruler. Sargon began to reign in Akkad about 2277 B.C.E. and established the empire of Akkad that would continue for nearly a century and a half. Under him, most of Mesopotamia was united, and he advanced as far west as Syria. Sargon's birth and childhood became the basis for a legend that closely parallels the biblical story of Moses. Sargon was said to have been born to a nomadic father and a woman who was a temple votary. His mother is said to have cast him adrift in a basket of bulrushes that carried him to a gardener who adopted him.

As impressive as his military conquests were, Sargon's rule was not without internal unrest and rebellion. He died at the hands of his own soldiers.

Sargon II (reigned c. 722–705 B.C.E.)

Assyrian ruler. Sargon II was one of Assyria's most feared and honored kings. Under him, the conquest of Israel was completed and an eleven-year campaign brought Babylon under Assyrian control. On other fronts, Sargon II also fought in Urartu, Syria, and Egypt. Impressive though these military campaigns were, they were largely of a defensive character. The country's irrigation system was also allowed to fall into disrepair as revenues were channeled into the construction of Dur-Sharrukin (Sargon's City). Sargon II died while fighting back Cimmerian invaders.

Sarmiento, Domingo [Faustino] (1811–1888)

Argentinean writer and statesman. Sarmiento was born in the provincial city of San Juan. Largely self-taught, he received most of his education in San Juan and began his career as a teacher at the age of fifteen. Education was to remain one of his primary concerns, both as president of Argentina (1868–74) and as a writer.

Sarmiento entered public life early, acting as provincial legislator and fighting on the liberal, centralist side of the civil war raging through the country. In 1831 he fled to Chile, where he worked as a schoolteacher; however, he was granted permission to return to San Juan five years later due to a serious illness. There he started a newspaper that was shut down within six weeks, and in 1840 was sent into exile once again by then-dictator Juan Manuel de Rosas. Focusing his energy on journalism, Sarmiento edited and contributed to various newspapers, including *El Mercurio* and *El Progreso*, and in 1845 he published what has been called the single most important book produced in Spanish America: *Civilización y barbarie: vida de Juan Facundo Quiroga, y aspecto físico, costumbres, y hábitos de la República Argentina* (1845; *Life in the Argentine Republic in the Days of the Tyrants; or, Civilization and Barbarism*). The book—a vicious attack on the dictatorship of Rosas through the biography of his gaucho (roughly, "cowboy") lieutenant, Juan Facundo Quiroga, and a plea for urbanization and industrialization as opposed to the gaucho and *caudillo* (military and/or political dictators) culture of the Argentine Pampas—first appeared in *El Progreso* in serial form.

Not returning to settle in Argentina until 1856, when he was named director of schools in the province of Buenos Aires, Sarmiento later became Bartolomé Mitre's minister of the interior (1860), served as governor of San Juan (1862–64), and was appointed minister plenipotentiary to the United States (1864). When Bartolomé Mitre finished his term as president in 1868, Sarmiento became the first civilian president of Argentina (1868–74). During his presidency, the foundations for national progress were set. Sarmiento immediately implemented his liberal policies, following a plan of action he had laid out in Part III of *Life in the Argentine Republic* and elsewhere.

Affirming his belief in democratic principles and civil liberties, Sarmiento ended the war with Paraguay and concentrated on domestic achievements. Convinced that the key to national welfare was through a system of public education, Sarmiento brought to a largely illiterate population primary, secondary, traditional, and vocational schools, as well as libraries and museums. During his presidency, the number of schools and pupils nearly doubled. He further set out to beautify and modernize Buenos Aires, fostered immigration, increased railroad building, and expanded trade. After his term expired, Sarmiento continued to be active in public life until his death in Paraguay.

Sartre, Jean-Paul (1905–1980)

French philosopher, novelist, dramatist, and critic. Sartre studied at the École Normale Supérieure, where he met two other young "stars" of the university, French intellectuals Simone de Beauvoir (1908–1986) (who would be his companion for more than fifty years) and Albert Camus (1913–1960), thinkers whose careers would eventually intertwine with his own. After graduating, Sartre spent time teaching at various *lycées* in and outside of his native Paris. He left France to travel around the continent, ending up in Germany, where he met and studied alongside two philosophers whose work would be of great importance to his own thinking, Edmund Husserl and Martin Heidegger.

During this time Sartre published his first novel, *La Nausée* (1938; *Nausea*), his first major step toward international prominence. The novel examines the bleak futility of existence as its protagonist, Roquentin, develops a revulsion for both the material world and his own body. Written in a kind of stream of consciousness style, *Nausea* would eventually lay the foundation for Sartre's theories of existentialism. This nascent literary career came to a brief halt in 1939 when Sartre was called to serve in World War II. The following year, he was captured by the Germans. The young philosopher lived in captivity for nine months until he managed to escape and serve in the underground Resistance.

In 1943 Sartre published *L'Être et le néant* (*Being and Nothingness*), his first major philosophical work. The reception to this text was highly positive, and it led to Sartre's crowning as unofficial leader of the existentialist movement. He founded, along with de Beauvoir and Maurice Merleau-Ponty, a left-leaning existentialist journal called *Les Temps Modernes* in 1945.

Sartre's (and existentialism's) relationship to leftist politics was unclear. His relationships with both Camus and Merleau-Ponty ended because of political disagreements. Becoming a Marxist, Sartre maintained an unwavering support of the Soviet system until the 1956 Russian intervention in Hungary. He then renounced his ties and allegiances to Soviet Communism. Sartre's 1960 text *Critique de la raison dialectique* (*Critique of Dialectical Reason*; U.S. title *Search for a Method*) attempted to illustrate the implicit affinities between Marxism and existentialism.

Sartre's career was long and prolific. In addition to novels and philosophical texts, he also wrote plays. Among his most famous are *Huis-clos* (1944; *No Exit*), *Les Mains Sales* (1948; *Dirty Hands*), and *Le Diable et le bon dieu* (1951; *The Devil and the Good Lord*). He was rewarded for a lifetime of cultural and political accomplishment in 1964 with the Nobel Prize in Literature. Sartre declined the award, saying that such prizes falsely magnified an author's accomplishments and undermined political commitment.

Sassanian

Ancient Iranian dynasty. The Sassanian dynasty was developed by Ardashir I (r. 224–41) and lasted from 224 to 651. The dynasty was named for Sassan, one of Ardashir's ancestors, probably his grandfather. Commanded by Ardashir, the Sassanians defeated their Parthinian ruler, Artabarus, and built an empire that would eventually stretch from current-day Georgia in the north to the Mazun region of Arabia in the south. In the east, it would reach the Indus River and, in the west, the upper Tigris and Euphrates river valleys. Aradshir's son Shapur I (r. 241–72) attempted to expand the empire further, defeating the Roman emperor Valerian in 258 or 259.

The Sassanian dynasty spurred a revival of Iranian nationalism. Zoroastrianism became the official religion, and a centralized government was developed to fund agricultural and building projects. Sassanian rule also witnessed a flourishing of art and architecture, as demonstrated by the elaborate palaces at Firuzabad and Ctesiphon, their capital. The Sassanian dynasty was destroyed during the rule of Yazdigird III by Arab campaigns lasting from 637 to 651, though Sassanian institutions survived to influence the 'Abbâsid empire.

Sata Ineko (1904–)

Japanese novelist and critic. Sata was born to young parents before they were formally married, and after an official ceremony, they claimed that Sata was their foster child and that her name was Ine. Growing up in abject poverty and working as a child in knitting mills and restaurants in Tokyo, Sata had the experiences that would form the basis of her career as a novelist and leftist social critic. While working in various jobs, Sata read widely in Western and Japanese literature. After a suicide attempt and the failure of her first marriage, she began to work in a Tokyo café, where she met Marxist critics and novelists. Her first short story, the autobiographical "Kyarameru kōba kara" (1928; "From the Caramel Factory"), was published in the journal *Puroretaria Geijutsu* (*Proletarian Arts*) and made her an instant success. Sata became one of the leading figures of the proletarian literature movement, working both on the political and aesthetic fronts. Her political beliefs resulted in a great deal of personal suffering, since the Japanese Communist Party, of which she was a member, was outlawed by the government. Her second husband, also a member of the party, was arrested in 1932, and she spent two months in prison in 1935 for their "illegal activities." Both of these experiences formed the basis for her novel *Kurenai* (1936; *Scarlet*).

Eventually, Sata became disenchanted with the leftist movement in Japan, and this led to the end of both her involvement with the Communists and her second marriage. Because of her visits to soldiers, Sata was criticized for her collaboration with military authorities during the Second World War. After the war, she rejoined and was expelled from the Communist Party two more times. She wrote about her wartime collaboration and her turbulent experiences in the Communist Party in her novel *Sozō* (1966; *Plastic Sculpture*). Although her relationship with the left was strained, she campaigned for various causes, and in her fiction wrote about the impact of history on people without political allegiances.

sati

Indian cultural practice. *Sati*, a Hindu word meaning "chaste wife," refers to the Indian practice of widow burning, whereby the wife sets fire to herself on her dead husband's funeral pyre. Despite the fact that many widows seemed to submit willingly to the practice, sati's long history in India is filled with numerous instances of coercion, rescue, and escape. A variation on the custom, *jauhar*, refers to the immolation of the wife prior to her husband's expected death in battle, a practice motivated by a desire to save women from the hands of enemy invaders. *Jauhar* was particularly prevalent among the Rajputs during the Muslim era.

Sati stones, memorials to women who have died by immolation, date back as far as 510 C.E. Reputedly, the custom of widow burning arose out of an ancient Indian belief that a man needed as many companions in the afterworld as he did in this one. The earliest references to sati can be found in the ancient Sanskrit text the *Mahabharata*, in which one reads of several queens undergoing sati. Economic hardship experienced by destitute surviving widows during the medieval era may have contributed to the spread of sati.

Between 1680 and 1830 sati was increasingly practiced by the Brahmans of Bengal, largely as a result of their Dayabhaga system of law (c. 1100), which gave inheritances to widows. Greedy relations would thus be inspired to encourage, verbally or physically, the widow's death.

Steps to abolish the practice were first taken by the Mughal emperors Humayun and his son Akbar and were later renewed by reformers like Rajah Ram Moham Roy and Romesh Chander Dutt. The protest against sati ultimately culminated in its outlawing by the Brit-

ish in 1829. However, as recently as 1987 the police officially counted 1,786 incidents of sati (popularly known as "dowry deaths" or "bride burning") in all of India, while the Ahmedabad Women's Action Group estimated that up to 1,000 women may have been burned alive in Gujarat state alone that year. In fact, in both Maharashtra and Bombay, "accidental burns" account for 19 percent of all deaths of women between the ages of fifteen and forty-four.

scar literature

Chinese literary movement. Flourishing shortly after the Cultural Revolution (1966–76), scar literature was a spontaneous expression by individual writers of the pain caused by the disastrous political movement, and an outcry for familial and social love and freedom. The name was derived from Liu Xinghua's short story "Scars" (1978). It was a seemingly simple story: with the revolution over, a girl named Xiaohua hurries back to see her mother after years of separation, only to discover that due to unbearable persecution and suffering, her mother had died a day before her arrival. The story strikes a strong symbolic note as Xiaohua looks at the scars on her mother's forehead. The story led to the designation "scar literature" for hundreds of similar stories that followed.

Schechter, Solomon (1847–1915)

Leader of Conservative Judaism in America. Born in Focsani, Romania, and educated in Vienna, Berlin, and London, Schechter was appointed lecturer in Talmudics at Cambridge University in 1890. He was later named professor of Hebrew at University College, London.

Schechter caused a sensation in 1896 when he discovered a cache of sacred manuscripts in the old synagogue at Cairo. The documents included a fragment of the Hebrew text of Ecclesiastics and a document relating to the Jewish sect the Essenes. Schechter's finds prompted a radical rethinking of Jewish and Mediterranean history. In 1899 he published *The Wisdom of Ben Sira* along with Charles Taylor, the St. John's College master who had enabled Schechter to make the trip to Egypt.

In 1902 Schechter's friend Judge Mayer Sulzberger of Philadelphia invited him to come to the United States as the president of the Jewish Theological Seminary of America. Schechter accepted, bringing with him several distinguished scholars, who made the seminary the most important center for Jewish learning in America. From this point on, much of Schechter's attention was devoted to the strengthening of Conservative Judaism in the United States. Less rigid than Orthodoxy yet less radical than Reform, Conservatism was popular with American Jews. Schechter's reliance on Jewish history and his concept of a "Catholic Israel" (a community of all Jews, past and present) stresses the role of tradition as the means through which the Jewish people remain whole. Schechter acknowledged that change was inevitable but believed that change and reform could not be imposed from above, but had to arise from the Jewish people. Although he remained committed to the Jewish community in America, he nevertheless angered several of his colleagues by supporting the Zionist movement, which he considered to be both "the great bulwark against assimilation" and a natural outgrowth of spiritual and religious renewal. In 1913 he founded the United Synagogue of America, an organization of Conservative Jewish congregations that has grown from twenty-three to more than eight hundred members.

Schiller, Friedrich von (1759–1805)

German dramatist and poet. When Schiller was a young boy, his parents sent him to a Latin school at Ludwigsburg, hoping he would eventually enter the ministry of the Lutheran Church.

The master at Ludwigsburg, Duke Karl Eugen of Würtemberg, who was obsessed with the grandeur of the Bourbons, aroused the young Schiller's disgust at the privileges of that class. He began military school, supervised by the duke, originally studying law (at the duke's insistence) but later switching to the discipline of medicine. His real interest, however, was in literature.

In 1781 he wrote his first play, *Die Räuber* (*The Robbers*), a scathing commentary on the inherent evils of German society. It was first performed at the National Theater at Mannheim, without the approval of the duke. When the duke banned Schiller from writing any more plays, Schiller fled to Mannheim, where the director of the theater granted him a one-year contract as the resident playwright. In 1784 Schiller moved to Leipzig and began the play *Don Carlos* (1787), the story of an idealist and his eventual downfall.

The completion of *Don Carlos* marked the beginning of a ten-year hiatus of dramatic production for Schiller. He left for Weimar in 1787, at the time the literary capital of Germany, and eventually settled in Jena. He began historical writing, such as his *Geschichte des dreissigjährigen kriegs* (1790–92; *History of the Thirty Years' War*). In 1790 he married Charlotte von Lengefeld, with whom he had two sons and two daughters. Two years later, he battled a long illness, and though he fought it, he never fully recovered.

The year 1794 marked the beginning of a lifelong friendship with German poet Johann Wolfgang von Goethe (1749–1832). The two writers met in Jena and supported each other's endeavors. Schiller's themes became more reflective, more concerned with morality. It was around this time that Schiller received a three-year grant from two Danish patrons, so that he could recuperate from his illness at leisure; these years produced many poems and ballads. Schiller and Goethe settled in Weimar in 1799, where Goethe was the director of the regional theater. It was here that Schiller wrote his finest dramas in rapid succession, most notably the Wallenstein trilogy, *Wallenstein, ein dramatisches Gedicht*, comprising *Wallenstein's Camp* (1798), *The Piccolomini* (1799), and *Wallenstein's Death* (1799); *Die Jungfrau von Orleans* (1801; *The Maid of Orleans*), an altered romantic tragedy about Joan of Arc; and his most beloved work, *Wilhelm Tell* (1804; *William Tell*).

Schopenhauer, Arthur (1788–1860)

German philosopher. Born in Danzig to a businessman father and novelist mother, Schopenhauer received a sporadic education as he traveled throughout Europe with his parents until the death of his father (apparently by suicide) in 1805. In 1809 he entered the University of Göttingen as a medical student, but, impressed by the works of philosophers Plato (c. 427–347 B.C.E.) and Immanuel Kant (1724–1804), he left for the University of Berlin in 1811 to pursue a philosophy degree. When the schools were closed due to the uprising of the German states against the French ruler Napoleon, Schopenhauer, who opposed nationalism, moved to Rudolstadt, and in 1813 published his thesis, *Über die vierfache wurzel des Satzes vom Zureichenden Grunde* (*On the Fourfold Root of the Principle of Sufficient Reason*). After writing a short book on the perception of color inspired by German poet Johann Wolfgang von Goethe (1749–1832), whom he had met in his mother's circle in Weimar, he worked for the next four years on his most famous book, *Die Welt als Wille und Vorstellung* (*The World as Will and Idea*), which was published in Leipzig in 1818. Though the work did not receive the acclaim he expected, it helped him obtain the position of lecturer at the University of Berlin, where he scheduled his classes for the same hours as Georg Wilhelm Friedrich Hegel's to underscore his op-

position to the influential philosopher.

Personally arrogant, Schopenhauer grew increasingly pessimistic in his views. For the next several years he traveled throughout Italy and Germany, settling finally in Frankfurt-am-Main and living for the most part on the remnants of the family fortune. He continued to write, publishing *Über den Willen in der Natur* (1836; *On the Will in Nature*) and *Die beiden Grundprobleme der Ethik* (1841; *The Basis of Morality*), a study of ethics. In 1844 he issued a second edition of *The World as Will and Idea*, expanded by fifty supplementary chapters. With the publication of two volumes of collected aphorisms and essays entitled *Parerga und Paralipomena* (*Essays from the Parerga and Paralipomena*) in 1851, Schopenhauer began to receive the attention he had long felt he deserved.

Schopenhauer follows Kant in holding that our perceptions are mediated always by a categorical framework that is a necessary condition of our knowledge of the world as idea and thus cannot be applied to anything outside of sense experience. He differs from Kant in that for him, even the categories of space and time are in this sense subjective. The drives of humankind and the forces of nature are alike manifestations of the will to live. Since this will is expressed by constant striving without satisfaction, life necessarily consists of suffering, reducible in some degree only through the operation of the intellect, which is merely a portion of the will. For Schopenhauer, the world can be viewed as a totality, not of rational or moral order, but of striving, self-conscious "wills," without ultimate purpose, locked in the constant struggle to live. In this respect, Schopenhauer's concept of the will to live is frequently regarded as the forerunner to much of modern psychology.

Schubert, Franz [Peter] (1797–1828)

Austrian composer. Born in a Viennese suburb, Schubert was the son of a schoolteacher. Of his parents' fourteen children, only Schubert and four others lived to adulthood. Despite penury, his father was a fair musician and began Schubert's music training in violin and piano at the age of five. He also learned organ and singing at Lichtenthal Church. In 1808 his voice won him admission to the imperial chapel choir and entrance to the Imperial Konvikt, a Jesuit school Antonio Salieri helped establish as the chief music school of Vienna.

In spite of the privations of the school, Schubert formed friendships that would last him his brief lifetime, and composed pianoforte fantasias, music for string quartets, and a number of songs. At the end of his school days, in 1813, he composed his first symphony. He worked for two years as a teacher in his father's school and studied privately. His first opera, *Des Teufels Lustschloss (The Devil's Pleasure Palace)*, and his first mass, in F major, were written in 1814, along with three string quartets, numerous instrumental pieces, and parts of symphonies. In 1815 he wrote two symphonies, two masses, five operas, a string quartet, four sonatas, smaller compositions for piano, and 146 songs, eight of which are dated October 15, and seven October 19.

Beginning in 1816, Schubert lived with friends, for a while attempting to add to the household finances but finally concentrating on composing. In 1818 he received the only official appointment of his lifetime, the post of music master to the family of Count Johann Esterházy at Zseliz, where he spent the summer. From this period on, Schubert lived in varying degrees of poverty. The years 1821–23 were especially difficult: although he met the German composer Beethoven at this time, his operas were either refused for production or prohibited by the censor. In 1825 he received twenty pounds for his *Sonata in A Minor*, the largest sum he had made for any composition. He continued his tremendous musical production until 1828, when he was attacked by typhus fever and died, at the age of thirty-two.

Schubert's music is usually compared with that of Austrian composers Mozart and Beethoven, two influences he readily credited during his lifetime. His style is not recognized as equal to Mozart's, and his construction not equal to Beethoven's, yet he is characterized as unsurpassed in poetic impulse and suggestion. His most popular works include several symphonies—*B Flat* (1816), *Unvollendete* (1822; *Unfinished*), *C Major* (1828)—as well as the chamber works *Streichquartett in D (Der Tod und das Mädchen* [1824; *Death and the Maiden*]) and *Forellen-Quintett* (1819; *The Trout Quintet*). Many of his songs, Lieder, were set to lyrics of poems by Johann Wolfgang von Goethe, Friedrich von Schiller, Heinrich Heine, and William Shakespeare.

Sealth (1790–1866)

American Indian leader. Sealth (sometimes spelled Seathl) achieved prominence as chief of the Duamish and Suquamish and other tribes of the Puget Sound region of Washington State. Converted to Catholicism by French missionaries, Chief Sealth was friendly to the earliest white settlers in the region, who began calling him Seattle, believing that Sealth was too difficult to pronounce. Negotiating the Port Elliot Treaty with the settlers in 1855, Chief Seattle ceded certain tribal lands and accepted reservation territory for his people. Between 1855 and 1858, skirmishes between the settlers and the Indians from neighboring regions forced Seattle to choose between his friendship with whites and his loyalty to the Indians. Seattle remained loyal to the settlers and in gratitude they named their town after him. However, Seattle was greatly disturbed by the appropriation of his name. He feared, in accordance with tribal superstition, that his eternal sleep in death would be disturbed when a mortal spoke his name, and his body would turn over in his grave. Later, Seattle resigned himself to the honor, and collected a small tax from the settlers as compensation for the use of his name. In 1890, several years after the chief's death, residents of Seattle, Washington, commemorated his life by erecting a monument over his grave.

Seitōsha

First Japanese feminist group. The Seitōsha, or Bluestocking Society, was founded in 1911 with the dowry of one of its original members, Hiratsuka Raichō. Pioneers such as Kishida Toshiko and Fukuda Hideko had advocated women's political rights, but Seitōsha made a much bigger impact as it rode the wave of progressive education that had begun to move women into the public sphere. "New women" entering the professions at the turn of the century and the educated daughters of bourgeois families began to question the intensely patriarchal Japanese order.

The Seitōsha began as a group inspired by the idea of publishing a women's magazine, Seitō. The first issue of Bluestocking came out in September 1911, and the first few runs provided a rare public forum for the works of women writers such as Yosano Akiko, who described the awakening of women's political consciousness in her poem "Sazorogoto" ("Chat"), and Tamura Toshiko, author of the prose poem "Genshi josei wa taiyō de atta" ("In the Beginning Woman Was the Sun"). Other early subjects included the oppression of women in marriage and society and the progress of the feminist movement; Seitōsha also organized lectures on feminism and women in literature.

As with any revolutionary movement, the members of Seitōsha often attracted more attention for their personal conduct than for their political achievement. Scandals associated with members like Otake Kōkichi, a brilliant lesbian painter, garnered the "new women" a reputation for wildness. By 1914 public criticism and the complications of family lives began to turn women away from the society. Raichō herself despaired of continuing to finance the magazine and gave over its publication to the feminist anarchist Itō Noe in January 1915. Noe took a more radical line with Bluestocking, addressing prostitution, abortion, and other issues, but was forced to stop publication in February 1916.

Selassie, Haile, *see* Haile Selassie

Seljuk dynasty

First major Turkish dynasty. The Seljuk dynasty thrived from the late tenth to the thirteenth century in what is now Iran, Syria, Iraq, and Turkey. Members of the Ghuzz (Oghuz) tribe of Central Asian Turks, descendants of the founder Seljuk, established several dynasties of the same name, the two most important based in Baghdad and Konya. The Seljuks probably converted to Islam in the mid tenth century and then migrated west, due to political and population pressures in Central Asia. They first conquered the Ghaznavid dynasty in Persia in 1040; in 1055 they entered Baghdad, the seat of the 'Abbâsid caliph. Tughrul, grandson of Seljuk, thus established the dynasty of the Great Seljuks, who replaced the Persian Buyids (Buwayhids), a Shi'ite dynasty, as the protectors and secular heads of the Islamic community. Muslim rulers previously bound nominally to the 'Abbâsid caliphate now submitted to the Seljuks, who championed Sunnî (orthodox) Islam and retained the caliph as its titular head. The Great Seljuk sultans ruled until the death of Sultan Sanjar in 1157. Sultans such as Malik Shah (r. 1072–92), often themselves ill-educated, entrusted the administration of their empire to viziers of the stature of the famous Nizam al-Mulk, author of a political treatise *Siyasatnamah* (*Book of Government*), which ranks among the great works of Islamic literature.

The Seljuks of Rum rose to power under Suleyman, great-grandson of Seljuk, who came to Anatolia (present-day Turkey) after the famous battle of Malazqirt (Manzikerd) in 1071, when the Seljuks defeated the Byzantines. By 1075 Suleyman was established in Nicaea (modernday İznik) on the doorstep of the Byzantine empire in Constantinople. Nicaea, however, was recaptured in 1097 during the First Crusade and remained in Byzantine hands until the rise of the Ottomans in the late thirteenth century. The Rum Seljuks moved their headquarters thereafter to Konya and Alanya. There, under Suleyman's son Kilic Arslan and his descendants, they flourished until they were defeated in a disastrous confrontation with the Mongols at Kosedag (Kozadagh) in 1243. The dynasty continued nominally until 1302, as Mongol vassals. The first half of the thirteenth century, however, was a glorious period for the Seljuks of Rum, whose strategic position on the southern coast of Turkey gave them access to international trade and led to the construction of massive mosque, school, and caravan complexes that still stand in many parts of Turkey. Under rulers such as Kay-Qubad I (r. 1220–37), the Rum Seljuks were powerful enough to send an expedition to the Crimea. Intellectual life blossomed as the Seljuk sultans invited theologians, poets, and artists to their courts. Their religious tolerance fostered the growth of Sufism as exemplified by the great mystic Jalaluddin Rumi (1207–1273). As a result of the Seljuk custom of dividing kingdoms among their descendants, numerous small Turkish principalities arose in Anatolia. While acknowledging Seljuk sovereignty, they operated independently, ultimately weakening the dynasty's ability to withstand outside opposition. One such principality was that of Osman, the founder of the Ottoman empire.

Sembene, Ousmane (1923–)

Senegalese writer and filmmaker. Born in Senegal, to a family of Wolof fishermen, Sembene attended a technical school for three years and then worked as a manual laborer in Dakar before being drafted into the French colonial army in World War II. He served in Italy and Germany and as a stevedore in Marseilles. After a brief period as a fisherman in Senegal, he returned to Marseilles and his work as a stevedore, eventually becoming a union leader. His first novel, *Le Docker noir* (1956; *The Black Docker*), grew out of these experiences and provided him with a new career after a back ailment removed him from the docks. His second novel, *O Pays, mon beau peuple!* (*Oh My Country, My Beautiful People*), followed in 1957. The story of a Senegalese farmer who returns to his home after eight years accompanied by his white wife was popular throughout Europe and earned Sembene the money and time to travel for the next few years. *Les Bouts de bois de Dieu* (1960; *God's Bits of Wood*) is a fictional account of the strike by African workers on the Dakar-Niger railroad in 1947–48. His collection of short stories and a novella, *Vehi-Ciosane; ou, Blanche-genèse, suivi du mandat* (1965; *The Money Order, With White Genesis*), was a popular and critical success. In order to reach a larger African audience, Sembene turned in the early 1960s to filmmaking, studying briefly at the Gorki Film Studios in the Soviet Union. His first film, *L'Empire Sonhraï* (1963; *The Sonhraï Empire*), was never released, but his second, *Borom Sarret* (*The Cart Driver*), the story of a Dakar donkey-cart driver, appeared in 1964. His short film *La Noire de . . .* (1967; *Black Girl*) was about the humiliations of a young servant girl employed by a French couple. His next film, *Mandabi*, (1968; *The Mandate*), also an adaption of his 1965 publication of *The Money Order*, enhanced his international reputation, and it was followed by *Emitai* (1971), *Xala* (1974; *Impotence*), and *Ceddo* (1977; *Outsiders*), all of which explore the effect of externally imposed values on African traditional culture. He published the novel *Dernier de l'empire* (*The Last of the Empire*) to wide acclaim in 1981.

Sendero Luminoso

Peruvian Maoist insurrectionary organization. El Partido Comunista del Perú–Sendero Luminoso (PCP-SL, the Communist Party of Peru–Shining Path) developed out of a university student movement formed in 1970. It derives its name from José Carlos Mariátegui, the Peruvian revolutionary writer who in the 1920s was a key figure in the formation of the first Peruvian Communist Party. Mariátegui referred to the "shining path of socialism" that would lead to a just and democratic society in Peru.

The major figure in the PCP-SL has been Abimael Guzmán, onetime university lecturer, who interpreted Mariátegui as advocating the establishment of a communal society similar to that of the pre–Spanish conquest Inca epoch, which was seen as a form of primitive communism. In the 1970s the PCP-SL primarily engaged in propaganda and recruitment of members to a revolutionary transformation of Peru, and in 1980 turned to armed struggle. While formally advocating an ideology and strategy of Maoism, in which the overthrow of existing society would be achieved by a protracted peasant war, the PCP-SL has proved to be a uniquely Peruvian phenomenon. In the very few public documents of the PCP-SL, the political analysis closely follows the writings of Chinese communist leader Mao Zedong on the Chinese revolution: that Peru was a semifeudal and semicolonial (rather than predominantly capitalist) country ruled by alliances of large landlords and "bureaucratic capitalists," and the peasantry represented the most op-

pressed and exploited social group. For the PCP-SL, this characterization of Peru implied that the government of the country was antidemocratic, even fascist, and there existed no alternative to armed struggle to achieve the democratic aspirations of the population. Furthermore, this armed struggle would achieve its success through war in the countryside that would isolate the cities and then take possession of them once the old regime collapsed. In actuality, Peru of the 1980s bore little resemblance to the description offered by the PCP-SL. Seventy percent of the population lived in urban areas, and less than a fifth of national production came from agriculture.

The PCP-SL is not significantly linked to revolutionary movements elsewhere, nor has it allied itself with any socialist or Communist government (or received any outside aid). Nevertheless, the PCP-SL has proven extraordinarily successful in waging its armed struggle and has defied attempts by the authorities to crush it. To a great extent, the success of the PCP-SL derived from a manipulation of the historic division of cultures between the elite of Spanish descent and the indigenous highlanders. Guzmán was captured September 12, 1992, by government forces, though the movement remains active.

Senghor, Léopold [Sédar] (1906–)

Senegalese poet, president of the Republic of Senegal. Born in Senegal, Senghor was a brilliant student. He recieved his early education in Dakar and Paris, eventually attending the Sorbonne. While there, Senghor was the first black African to earn the "aggregation." Senghor also taught for a while in French *lycées*, but with the outbreak of the Second World War he became an officer in the French army. Following the war, Senghor returned to France and renewed his artistic and political commitment to his African heritage. In 1947 Senghor, with Alioune Diop, founded the important black cultural journal *Présence Africaine*, and helped organize the political party the Bloc Démocratique Sénégalais to advance the cause of Senegalese liberation from the French.

After a series of political maneuvers, Senghor was elected president of an independent Senegal in 1960, and began the difficult work of consolidating power, reforming the constitution, and negotiating Senegal's position among the various factions of African states. He served as president until 1980.

Together with West Indian poet Aimé Césaire (1913–), Senghor is credited with the introduction of the concept of Négritude, an affirmation of the black African experience, a movement established in Paris in the 1930s. Among Senghor's written works, best known are his important and influential *Anthologie de la nouvelle poésie nègre et malgache* (1948), and his volumes of poetry, *Chants d'ombre* (1945; *Songs of Shadow*), *Ethiopiques* (1956), and *Nocturnes* (1961). Senghor was the first black member ever elected to the French Academy (1984). The year 1990 saw the publication of his collected poems, *Oeuvre poétique* (*Poetical Work*).

Sennacherib (r. 705–681 B.C.E.)

Assyrian king. Sennacherib succeeded his father, Sargon II, as king of Assyria. Though he launched important programs of public works that provided labor to displaced persons, he is better known for his military campaigns against the Babylonians, who tried to throw off Assyrian rule, and the Israelites, who had allied with the Egyptians against Assyria. While Sennacherib succeeded in destroying the city of Babylon, the effort against the Israelites was less successful. Though he captured forty-six cities and villages, his army was unable to take Jerusalem. While the Old Testament says that the Assyrian army was smitten by the Lord, it is more likely that a plague decimated the Assyrian ranks.

Despite this failure to take Jerusalem, Assyrian power so impressed Hezekiah, the king of Judah, that he considered it wise to pay tribute and remain loyal to the Assyrian king.

Sennett, Mack (1884–1960)

Canadian film director. Born Michael Sinnott in Danville, Quebec, Canada, to a working-class Irish immigrant family, Sennett worked his way through the ranks of the entertainment industry, eventually directing and producing silent comedies for his own company, Keystone Studios, which he established in 1912 with Charles Bauman and Adam Kessel. Under Sennett, a new genre of comedy referred to as slapstick was developed at Keystone involving elements of vaudeville, pantomime, the circus, and comic strips; Keystone comedies were largely improvisational and farcical, deriving comic force from visual gags and ridicule of social conventions and institutions through vulgar stereotypes, creating such characters as the Keystone Kops, a burlesque mockery of law and order, and the Bathing Beauties, mocking pornographic sexuality. At Keystone, Sennett also launched the careers of several directors, including Italian-born American film director Frank Capra. The popularity of his films contributed greatly to the American domination of international cinema during and after the First World War.

Keystone grew rapidly in size and produced increasingly longer films, so Sennett recruited other directors to the company and devoted his time to production and editing. In 1915 Keystone was absorbed into the Triangle Film Corporation. The larger budget and more relaxed production schedule that this afforded Sennett made his films more technically polished, and their content moved away from raw slapstick gags toward situation comedy. In 1917 Sennett left Triangle to form a new company, Mack Sennett Comedies, where he continued to produce two-reel comedies and even several feature-length films.

With the advent of sound in 1928, however, Sennett's career began to decline, although in association with Paramount Pictures in 1932 he produced several shorts with performers W. C. Fields and Bing Crosby, as well as several color shorts using an early color process that he called Natural Color. When Sennett retired from filmmaking in the mid-1930s, he was virtually destitute. He was honored for his lifetime achievements at the 1937 Oscar ceremonies with a special Academy Award.

Senufo

Ethnic group of the Ivory Coast. Although the Senufo, who number over 550,000, reside primarily in the northern regions of the Ivory Coast, there are also a significant number of Senufo in Mali and Burkina Faso. The four major languages of the Senufo (Palaka, Dyimini, and Senari, on the Ivory Coast; Suppire in Mali) are grouped within the Gur branch of the Niger-Congo family of languages. The name Senufo is of Mande origin and translates as "those who speak Senari"; it is used by the various groups of Senufo to refer to themselves. The Senufo are traditionally agriculturalists, and raise corn and millet as their primary staples. Their farms are grouped around their villages, which are composed of mud-brick houses with thatched roofs in the south, and flat roofs in the north. The Lo society (also known as Poro), a male secret society that plays an important role in Senufo village life, has an elaborate and lengthy initiation process that lasts almost the first thirty years of a man's life. The process is divided into three stages—childhood, adolescence, and adulthood; between each stage there is a rite of passage. Once a man has been fully initiated, he becomes an elder and is freed from farmwork. Divination is conducted

by the Sandogo society, which is composed entirely of women.

The Senufo are renowned for their music, which is played with marimbas, gongs, drums, horns, and flutes. They also produce a rich variety of sculptures that are primarily associated with the Lo society. These include carved headpieces for initiation ceremonies and several types of masks. Some masks represent human faces. The *kpelie* mask is of a human face ringed with projections and serves to remind initiates of human imperfection. Other masks represent animal faces, often combining the characteristics of several creatures. One animal mask known as the *waniugo* has a receptacle for magic substances on its top and blows sparks through its muzzle during nighttime rituals that protect the village from sorcerers. The women of the Sandogo society use carved figures of male and female twins on horseback in the divination process. These figures represent the spirits who assist in the process. As many African communities do, the Senufo produce large numbers of sculptures for the tourist industry.

Sephardim

Jews of Spanish or Portuguese origin. Those Jews, and their descendants, who were expelled from Spain and Portugal in 1492 are known as Sephardic Jews, distinct from the Ashkenazic Jews, who settled around Germany and make up the vast majority of the Jewish population. Sephardic roots in the Iberian Peninsula were very deep, dating back many centuries. Despite periodic persecutions at the hands of Muslim authorities, Sephardic culture flourished in the Middle Ages. After their reconquest of the peninsula, Christian rulers turned their attention to the Sephardim. In 1391 large numbers of Sephardic Jews converted to Christianity to escape persecution. The discovery that many of them continued to practice their old faith in secret helped fuel the Spanish Inquisition. In

1492 a decree of expulsion offered the Sephardim two choices: convert or leave. Some converted but many more chose exile, launching the Sephardic Diaspora. They settled in North Africa, Europe, Turkey, and Arab lands such as Syria, Iraq, and Egypt, often reestablishing old communities in new locations.

Wherever they went, the Sephardim carried their Judeo-Spanish traditions and culture. Their language, known as Ladino, Judezmo, or Judeo-Spanish, closely resembles medieval Spanish. They have been especially noted for their cultural and intellectual achievements within the Mediterranean and northern European Jewish communities. After their expulsion, the Sephardim tended to settle in areas that allowed them greater freedom than the Ashkenazim enjoyed. Hence, the Sephardim adopted a more relaxed attitude toward the influence of outside culture. In their adherence to the basic tenets of Judaism, however, there is no significant difference between Sephardic and Ashkenazic teachings.

From the eighteenth century on, the strength and influence of the Sephardic Jews has been declining relative to that of the more populous Ashkenazic Jews. After suffering devastating losses in Hitler's attempted genocide, the Sephardim followed their Ashkenazic coreligionists to the United States, Latin America, and above all Palestine. Today the majority of the world's Sephardic population (estimated at 700,000) lives in Israel.

seppuku

Japanese ritual suicide. *Seppuku*, or hara-kiri, as it is more commonly known in the West, is a form of ritual suicide through self-disembowelment that was developed by the Japanese warrior class, or samurai, in the eleventh or twelfth century. The abdomen was chosen as the site of suicide because of the ancient Japanese belief that the soul resided

there. Early incidents of *seppuku* involved plunging a sword into one's abdomen. By the time of the Edo period (1600–1868), however, *seppuku* became much more ritualized. As a result, the cut made into the abdomen was no longer fatal and was instead a form of self-inflicted suffering intended to demonstrate the courage of the samurai. After this cut was made from left to right, the samurai motioned to his assistant. This assistant, or *kaishakunin*, beheaded the samurai with a sword. A *kaishakunin* was especially chosen for his skill in leaving the head attached by a small piece of flesh, so it would not roll away from the body. *Seppuku* became an honored form of capital punishment among the samurai, and was also used to avoid capture by an enemy, to follow a recently deceased lord in death, or to protest the actions of one's superiors. Sporadic incidents of *seppuku* persist into the modern era in Japan. One of the most recent and sensational of these ritual suicides was committed by the noted author Yukio Mishima in 1970.

Sequoyah (c. 1760–1843)

American Indian leader and inventor of the Cherokee alphabet. Sequoyah (also known as Sequoia, Sikwayi, Sogwali, and George Guess [Guest or Gist]) was born in Taskigi, North Carolina colony, the son of Wurteh, a Cherokee woman who was sister to several Cherokee chiefs, and a white man, most likely Nathaniel Gist, friend to first U.S. president George Washington. Sequoyah's childhood years were marked by intense fighting between the Cherokee and the United States, and he later moved from the North Carolina colony to Alabama to escape the white populations. Made lame through illness or injury, Sequoyah's attempts to fight the encroachment of the white man assumed a more intellectual bent. Sequoyah thought that the white man's power lay in his ability to read and write his language, allowing for the easier accumulation of information and passage of ideas. He began work on the Cherokee alphabet in 1809, and continued through 1821. The alphabet he constructed consisted of eighty-six characters, each character representing a different spoken syllable. Although he used English, Greek, and Hebrew letters in his syllabary, he never learned to read or write any language other than the one he invented. His attempts to draw the attention of fellow Cherokees to his work, however, was not easily accomplished. For years he was ridiculed; some even accused him of practicing witchcraft and burned his house and records. Through several demonstrations of his syllabary to Cherokees in the eastern homeland, he gradually convinced the Cherokees of the importance of his invention. Within a few years of the perfection of his alphabet, practically all Cherokee were literate in their own language and could communicate solely through written messages.

Sequoyah was also an active protector of the Cherokees against the policies of the U.S. government. In 1816 he attended a conference in Turkeytown, at which considerable Cherokee lands were ceded to the United States. Two years later, he moved to Arkansas, again to escape the influence of the white settlers. He was a member of the delegation sent to Washington, D.C., in 1828 to discuss the whites' encroachment onto Cherokee land, which resulted in an exchange of land in Arkansas for some in Oklahoma. The following year, Sequoyah moved to what is now called Sequoyah County, Oklahoma, and lived as a farmer. In 1839 he established peace between the western Cherokees and the eastern Cherokee survivors of the Trail of Tears, who had been forced by the U.S. Army to leave Georgia and resettle on reservation land. In 1842 Sequoyah set out to find a legendary tribe of Cherokee said to have moved west in the distant past. He died near San Fernando, Mexico, while conducting his search. The California redwood trees called Sequoias were named in his honor.

Seth, Vikram (1952–)

Indian novelist, poet, and travel writer. Seth was born in Calcutta, India, and studied at Oxford, Nanjing, and Stanford universities. Seth first gained recognition through his travel writing with *From Heaven Lake: Travels Through Sinkiang and Tibet* (1983), chronicling his solitary overland journey from Nanjing University in China to his family's home in Calcutta, India. Through his adventures in various small towns along the way, Seth describes the paradoxes of his own position as an Indian viewing Chinese culture and society. *The Golden Gate* (1986), a series of 593 verse stanzas in sonnet form, was modeled on the Charles Johnston translation of Russian writer Aleksandr Pushkin's *Evgenii Onegin* (1830; *Eugene Onegin*). Praised for its technical brilliance and virtuosity, *The Golden Gate* relates the loves and lives of a group of San Francisco yuppies during the Reagan era. Criticized by some for his superficial rendering of characters, Seth is nevertheless credited with reviving a literary form that had been superseded by the prose novel. Seth's massive *A Suitable Boy* (1993) brought him broader international acclaim.

shah

Persian title for king. The title has been applied to monarchs in all areas where Persian culture has flourished. It is synonymous with Badshah or Padshah. The title Shahanshah is an inversion of Shah-i Shahan, meaning "king of kings" or emperor. The word "shah" has entered the English language in the chess term "checkmate," which derives from the Persian *Shah mat*, roughly translated as "The king is dead."

Shāh-nāmeh

Persian national epic poem. The name means "book of the kings," or "register of the kings." Written by Firdawsī (also spelled Ferdowsī) in the late tenth and early eleventh centuries, through a recasting of traditional legends and tales, the *Shāh-nāmeh* chronicles the history of Persia from its first mythical kings through its Golden Age to its conquest by the Arabs in the seventh century. The poem was composed in New Persian; it consists of between 35,000 and 60,000 rhymed couplets. The poem has been criticized for its lack of historical accuracy, but that criticism ignores its more obvious intent as courtly literature to celebrate the legitimate succession of Persian royalty and the glory of the Persian past through the mythical hero Rostam. It was begun during the Samanid dynasty but dedicated to the succeeding Ghaznavid dynasty and its sultan Mahmud. One story holds that Mahmud rewarded Firdawsī less generously than he had expected for the epic, so he wrote a satire on the king (which is frequently used as a preface) and then fled, returning to his homeland just before his death. Considered to be one of the masterpieces of Persian culture, it has been the inspiration for many Persian miniature paintings since the fourteenth century.

Shaka (c. 1787–1828)

Zulu king. Hailed as the greatest of African military leaders, Shaka created the Zulu empire in southern Africa.

There is disagreement about the details of his life, but Zulu traditions relate the following: Conceived out of wedlock, Shaka was born to a Zulu chieftain, Senzangakhona, and an orphaned princess, Nandi, from a neighboring tribe, who quickly married before Shaka's birth. Nevertheless, both Shaka and his mother were treated with hostility and scorn; Nandi left her new husband and returned to her clan, taking Shaka with her. Even there, however, Shaka was treated as an outcast. Once again, mother and son departed, eventually finding tolerance among the powerful Mtetwa clan. Under the rule of Dingiswayo, the leader of the Mtetwa, Shaka established himself as a great warrior. Dingiswayo believed in diplomatic means for settling disputes, unlike the young Shaka, who felt that military action was most effective.

Around the year 1815, Senzangakhona died, and Shaka, using the Mtetwa armies, went to conquer the Zulu, which at the time was the smallest of the eastern Nguni-Bantu clans. Shaka distinguished himself as a powerful military leader and institutionalized the use of a short stabbing spear. With the conquest of the Zulu, Shaka established a "sub-empire" under Dingiswayo. However, around 1816 Dingiswayo was killed in a confrontation with another clan, and Shaka consolidated both the Mtetwa under Zulu rule.

Much more aggressive than Dingiswayo had been, Shaka led his armies, the *impi*, in their conquest of the area and fought to exterminate neighboring clans, incorporating the surviving members into the Zulu army. One of his first victories was of the Langeni clan of his mother; Shaka sought out the men who had made his childhood difficult and had them impaled on the sharpened stakes of the fences surrounding their village.

By 1823 Shaka had conquered all of present-day Natal, and left the area in ruin. His massive victories disrupted the clan structure of the interior, as clans destroyed each other in their attempts to escape encroaching Zulu. Known as the Mfecane (the Crushing), this period of warfare left 2 million dead and enabled the Great Boer Trek of the 1830s to colonize the area easily, as there were few left to oppose them. Shaka was fascinated by the ways and artifacts of the

Europeans, whom he first encountered in 1824, and though he was convinced of the superiority of his own civilization, he allowed them to stay.

Shaka's mother died in 1826, after which Shaka became distraught. In his grief, he had 7,000 Zulu killed, and for one year no crops were planted and no milk, the staple of the Zulu diet, was consumed. All pregnant women and their husbands were slain, as were milking cows, so that even the calves would share the loss of a mother. After sending his *impi* on two successive raids, Shaka was murdered by three associates, two of whom were his half-brothers.

Shakespeare, William (1564–1616)

English dramatist, poet, and actor. Shakespeare spent his early youth in his birthplace of Stratford-upon-Avon, where, historians believe, he attended the local grammar school and received his introduction to Latin and Greek texts. He married Anne Hathaway at eighteen and became the father of two daughters, Suzanna and Judith, and one son, Hamnet. While it is known that he perfected the art of playwriting while a member of London's leading theater company, the Lord Chamberlain's Company (later known as the King's Men), little has been discovered about his earlier work from 1584 to 1592. It has been estimated that Shakespeare provided, alone or in collaboration, most of the plays for the company's repertory—producing thirty-eight plays between 1590 and 1613.

Shakespeare went through an experimental period in his early writing, and his first histories, *Henry VI* (1589–92) and *Richard III* (1592–93), did not have the sophistication and agility of verse of his later accomplishments, *Richard II* (1595–96), *Henry IV* (1597–98), and *Henry V* (1598–99). His great comedies *Much Ado About Nothing* (1598–99), *As You Like It* (1599–1600), and *Twelfth Night* (1599–1600) also came at this time, and Shakespeare's brilliant use of puns, intricate wordplay, and tales of misguided romantic love make them foremost of their kind. In his tragic tale of love gone awry, Shakespeare makes use of the forces of destiny to render the sad outcome of *Romeo and Juliet* (1594–95).

It was not until after 1599, when his company acquired the Globe Theatre, that he began to introduce the element of human fallibility into his plots in addition to the external and uncontrollable forces that decided his characters' fate. Shakespeare's most renowned tragedies—*Hamlet* (1600–1601), *Othello* (1604–1605), *King Lear* (1605–1606), and *Macbeth* (1605–1606)—use deeply poetic and emotionally expressive language to combine highly developed characterizations with compelling philosophical messages. Coordinating aspects of romance, comedy, and tragedy in his last plays, most notably *The Winter's Tale* (1610–11) and *The Tempest* (1611–12), Shakespeare experimented with lighthearted, fanciful language while maintaining a basically tragic theme. Their emphasis on wonder rather than probability and Shakespeare's expanded use of song and spectacle make these works some of his most fantastic. Nevertheless, certain serious themes run throughout, and the dramatic conflicts are resolved through penitence, forgiveness, and mutual reconciliation.

In addition to writing plays, Shakespeare authored many poems, including two heroic narratives, *Venus and Adonis* (1593) and *The Rape of Lucrece* (1594), based on Ovid's *Metamorphoses* and *Fasti*. He also wrote a sixty-seven-line elegy entitled "The Phoenix and the Turtle," which was published in Robert Chester's *Love Martyr* (1601). Shakespeare was a master of the popular sonnet, and his variation on the firmly established Petrarchan form is now called the Shakespearean sonnet.

Shakespeare retired around 1610 and

returned to his birthplace to live the life of a country gentleman. He died six years later and was buried in the parish church at Stratford. In 1623 the first collected edition of Shakespeare's plays appeared as the First Folio and contained all but one of his extant plays.

shamanism

Religious belief. The term is often applied to a variety of religious practices based on a belief that the world is controlled by spirits, associated with the dead and with forces of nature, that can be propitiated through the intervention of a "shaman."

The word "shaman" is thought to be Slavonic, originating among Siberian tribespeople from "saman," meaning "he who knows." Today shamans are often compared to the American Indian medicine men and the African tribal witch doctors. What these share is an ability to communicate with immaterial spirits that control material forces and events by using supernatural knowledge and power to affect nature. Shamans are thought to be selected not by the tribespeople but by the spirits themselves; distinguishing signs are often physical or psychological abnormalities. In some instances, the position is inherited. Shamans may be expected to perform magic, to heal the sick, or to contact the dead, using song, dance, or sacrifice in performing these rituals, which vary widely by region. Shamans are distinguishable from priests in their lack of training in a formal body of knowledge and in their emphasis on ecstatic states and spiritual possession; they are able to induce autohypnotic trances, and though most are male, they often dress as females or as animals. They enjoy great prestige in their tribes and are consulted on affairs great and small. Shamanism is practiced among Siberian and Ural tribes, and in differing forms among the Inuit and in Southeast Asia and Oceania.

Shan

Burmese ethnic group. Native to eastern and northern Burma (Myanmar), Shans have been variously divided into many smaller states and tribes during their history, and precise distinctions between Shans and non-Shans have often been difficult to make. The Shan language is part of the larger Tai linguistic group, which also includes the tongues of the Tai No, or Northern Tai of Yunnan, China, and the people of Thailand.

Shan people participated in the sacking of the city of Pagan by the armies of Kublai Khan in 1287, and in 1299 Pagan was burned by the "Three Shan Brothers," who assumed control of central Burma. The period of Shan power in central and southern Burma lasted until 1555, when the Shan-built city of Ava was annexed by the kingdom of Burma, but the Shan never controlled a single, unified empire like Pagan. Even under the ethnically Shan rulers, Ava's inscriptions of the era are in Burmese, and the Shan period is remembered for the rise of vernacular Burmese literature. Many of the Shan rulers claimed descent from the Pagan kings in attempts to solidify their authority. After the fall of Ava, the Shan states remained independent, with their own hereditary nobility, but often under the suzerainty of the Burmese. In 1886 the Shan states were annexed by the British, along with the rest of upper Burma. Rebellion against the British continued until the Shan States Act of 1888 clarified somewhat the distribution of power between local Shan leaders and the overlords. Under the act, the governor of Burma had discretion to manipulate the local law, but was to generally leave day-to-day functioning to the locals. In 1922 most of the Shan states were joined into the Federated Shan State and given a greater measure of autonomy in education and local law enforcement.

During World War II, the Shan state

was captured by the Japanese, as was Burma itself. In 1943 the states were ceded to Burma by the Japanese, and they have remained part of the nation of Burma since. Still, the Shan people retain a feeling of difference from the Burmese. In 1960 a Shan federalist movement arose, which culminated in the failed Shan revolution of 1962. Various groups of Shan nationalists have continued to appear from time to time to fight minor battles with the Burmese, but large-scale war has not returned.

The Shans are, for the most part, Theravāda Buddhists like the Burmese, though their traditions have much in common with those of Tai Buddhism as well. As noted, their language is related to Tai, but includes many words taken from Burmese. The alphabet is similar to that used for Burmese. Traditionally, the Shan economy has relied on trade with the Chinese by the northern Shan states, and with the Burmese by those of the south. The lifestyle of the Shan people remains agricultural, based on rice and opium production.

Shang bronzes

Chinese ritual objects. Perhaps one of the greatest innovations of the Shang dynasty (c. 1766 B.C.E.–c. 1122 B.C.E.) was the development of metalworking and the various bronze artifacts that were produced. Shang bronzes, most of which were ritual objects such as cooking pots and wine beakers, were found exclusively at tomb sites, where they played a role in one of the most enduring of Chinese traditions, ancestor worship. These bronzes are known not only for their strength and durability but also for the antinaturalistic use of animal forms as their primary mode of decoration. They also bear the earliest known examples of Chinese writing.

Shanghai Communiqué

United States and Chinese diplomatic agreement. As a result of what was called "Ping-Pong diplomacy," U.S. president Richard Nixon's visit to the People's Republic of China and his meetings with Chinese Premier Zhou Enlai, the Shanghai Communiqué was signed on February 28, 1972. This agreement marked the official beginning of the normalization of relations between the United States and China after more than twenty years of hostility. The contents of the agreement included different policy positions on Japan, Korea, and South and Southeast Asia, but the most important statements refer to Taiwan. The United States agreed that there was only one China, and that Taiwan was a part of this China. In addition, the United States acknowledged that the Taiwan question was a Chinese problem and needed to be solved by the Chinese themselves. The Shanghai Communiqué marked a gradual warming of U.S.-China relations that was made possible with the end of U.S. intervention in Vietnam, and the U.S. belief that China was no longer a chief adversary.

Shango

Yoruba god. Shango is the god of thunder in the Yoruba religion in Nigeria, Benin, and Togo. He is also worshiped in religions derived from Yoruba beliefs in Brazil and Haiti, where he is known as Xango and Chango, respectively. As the god of thunder and lightning, Shango is usually depicted in Yoruba religious art holding a double-edged ax that symbolizes a thunderbolt. Similarly, during Yoruba spirit-possession ceremonies, mediums who are possessed by Shango usually clutch symbolic thunderbolts while they dance in Shango's characteristically energetic fashion.

Like most orishás (gods), Shango lived as a human before dying and becoming a deity. According to Yoruba mythology, Shango's father was Oranmiyan, a great warrior and the founder of the Yoruba Oyo kingdom. His mother was Yemoja, who later became goddess of the Ogun River. As a man, Shango became the king of Oyo and was renowned for his magical powers, including the ability to breathe fire. Legend has it that Shango hanged himself in frustration after losing a magic contest, and now, as a deity, he throws fire and lightning from the sky, intimidating and destroying evildoers and wayward worshipers who violate his taboos or neglect to offer him sacrifices.

Sharî'ah

Islamic law. "The most compelling duty after faith in God is the pursuit of knowledge . . . and knowledge is of two kinds: knowledge of God's unicity, and knowledge of positive law and the elements of the Sharî'ah." Thus does the famous twelfth-century jurist Shams al-dîn al-Sarakhsî begin his lengthy treatise on Islamic law. The word "Sharî'ah" itself derives from one of many Arabic roots meaning "to go"; it signifies the importance of a well-trodden path of correct behavior in the religio-legal sphere. Islamic law governs both the entire range of secular behavior (commercial law, family law, inheritance, trusts, torts, crimes, and so on) and the proper performance of religious rites. In addition, Islamic law, both Sunnî and Shi'-ite, has developed a complex and rich literature of jurisprudence.

Fiqh, whose root meaning is "to understand," is Arabic for "positive law." The first comprehensive book of *fiqh* was written at the end of the eighth century. Such works resemble quite closely the "hornbook," or legal treatise, used in the American legal system, though books of *fiqh* usually treat all areas of law rather than just one. *Usûl al-fiqh*, the "bases" of *fiqh*, signifies jurisprudence. The first comprehensive work on Islamic jurisprudence was authored in the early ninth century. Traditional readings of books on *usûl al-fiqh* have found in them a kind of schematic "master rule of recognition" as formulated by the British legal philosopher H. L. A. Hart. Such readings make of Islamic law's jurisprudence a hierarchy of legal sources that begins with the Qur'ân, followed by the *hadîth* (short narratives of the Prophet Muhammad's exemplary conduct), then by *ijmâ'* (the community's consensus on a particular rule), and finally by *qiyâs* (analogic reasoning based on the first three sources). The general idea would be that legal practitioners search the first three (in that order) for a rule on a point before resorting to the last.

Calls for the application of Islamic law loom large today in the political vocabulary of Muslim societies from North Africa to the Philippines. The wish for a Sharî'ah-based legal system often presupposes that the Sharî'ah qua religious law stands ready to solve the economic and social problems of many poor Muslim nations. In any case, the Sharî'ah does provide a sound fund of legal principles, often strikingly similar to those of common law.

Shari'ati, Ali (1933–1977)

Islamic philosopher. A critical figure in the decade leading up to the Islamic revolution in Iran, Shari'ati was born into a religious family in the northeastern Iranian city of Mashhad and received there his early schooling, combining the public school curriculum with a formal religious education. He then enrolled at a local teachers college and began teaching at a private religious institute. Upon received a scholarship to go to France, Shari'ati spent five years at the University of Paris, where he concentrated on sociology and Islamic studies. After receiving a Ph.D. in social science he returned to Iran in 1964 and was appointed a professor at the University of Mashhad. Arrested because of his revolutionary ideas, Shari'ati was eventually released and allowed to resume his post, but was dismissed again not long after. He then began teaching at a private institution, which was subsequently closed, forcing Shari'ati into hiding. However, he gave himself up when the secret police took his father hostage. Faced with mass protests in his support, the shah's government released Shari'ati and exiled him to France, where he died under mysterious circumstances shortly thereafter.

Central to Shari'ati's thought is the firm belief that Islam is a perfect religion for modern times, since it is the school of thought that was first to recognize the masses as the basis of society and as the fundamental factor in determining the course of events. In fashioning his ideas, he combined the thought of European thinkers like Henry-Louis Bergson (1859–1941), Albert Camus (1913–1960), and Jean-Paul Sartre (1905–1980) with the revolutionary ideology of West Indian psychoanalyst and social philosopher Frantz Fanon (1925–1961). His religious writings suggest that he was heavily influenced by Muhammad Iqbal (1877–1938), the Indian Muslim poet and philosopher who played a critical role in the creation of Pakistan. Despite the fact that Shari'ati died before the realization of the Iranian revolution, he left a strong message in his writings: that it is possible to reconstitute a viable modern society along the lines of religious belief.

Shaw, George Bernard (1856–1950)

Irish playwright and critic. Shaw was born in Dublin in 1856, his father a failing grain merchant. Shaw attended the Wesleyan Connexional School, where he stayed at the bottom of his class; he was considered wild, indulging in idleness when the subjects being taught did not interest him and excelling only in English composition, music, and the graphic arts. At fifteen, he left school to become a clerk in a land agency. His mother's interest in music had attracted a distinguished teacher of music, George John Vandaleur Lee, to their house as a guest, and when Lee moved to London, in 1872, Mrs. Shaw and her daughters followed.

In 1876 Shaw resigned his clerkship and followed his mother and sisters to London. Spending the next nine years in full unemployment, Shaw used a suit of clothes and his ability on the pianoforte to gain access to society. He supplemented his income by ghostwriting musical criticism for Lee in the weekly *The Hornet*. From 1879 to 1883 he wrote five novels, all considered immature for their criticism of Victorian respectability and morality. In 1879 he also joined a discussion club, the Zetetical Society, and learned the art of extemporaneous speaking in front of crowds.

Shaw is known for his plays, the first of which he began writing in 1885 in collaboration with William Archer. Although most of his early plays were banned or refused production due to their political criticism, he published a collection in 1898, *Plays Pleasant and Unpleasant*, which included *Arms and the Man*, *Candida*, and *Mrs. Warren's Profession*. His first collection was followed by a second, entitled *Three Plays for Puritans* (1900). The majority of Shaw's best-known plays come from the period around the First World War; these include *John Bull's Other Island* (1904), *Man and Superman* (1905), *Major Barbara* (1905), *Fanny's First Play* (1912), *Androcles and the Lion* (1912), *Pygmalion* (1913), *Heartbreak House* (1913), *Back to Methuselah* (1921), and *Saint Joan* (1923). Shaw was well known for the prefaces he wrote for his plays, in some cases longer than the play itself. He won the Nobel Prize in Literature in 1925.

In 1882 Shaw had become an advocate of socialism and later joined the Fabian Society. Shaw wrote copiously on social institutions and problems. His longest work in this vein was *The Intelligent Woman's Guide to Socialism and Capitalism* (1928). His writings during the First World War made him unpopular in England, but his worldwide reputation as a playwright protected him. He was working on a comedy when he died at the age of ninety-four in Ayot St. Lawrence, England. His life and thoughts have given rise to the term "Shavian," denoting iconoclasm and boisterous rebellion.

Sherpa

Ethnic group of the Himalaya region. Now physically isolated in the Himalayan highlands in the Solu and Khumbu valleys of Mt. Everest and Darjeeling, India, the Sherpas originally fled from eastern Tibet to escape religious persecution by the Mongols. Sherpas are primarily a Buddhist people who practice a Tibetan form of Lamaism and believe in reincarnation. A Sherpa village is centered on a temple and prayer wheel, though each clan is distinct with regard to the deities it worships.

For matters of the soul, Sherpas rely on the Buddhist divinities, but for mundane problems they appeal to earthly spirits associated with the Tantric cults. Snakes, for example, are regarded as house spirits. Sherpas worship a score of demons and demonesses (often represented in frescoes), which they seek to control through either appeasement or exorcism (routinely practiced by Sherpa Lamas).

Sherpas traditionally make their living as animal herders, farmers, and traders. Relative to other ethnic groups of Nepal, Sherpas have done well economically (though there are many poor Sherpas), and the finest Buddhist monasteries are found in Sherpa villages. At one time, the Sherpas held a trade monopoly in Tibetan salt, iron, wool, and rice, until the British created a trade route from Calcutta to Lhasa in 1904. Despite this setback, many of the Sherpas were able to make a living as guides for climbing expeditions in the Nepalese Himalayas.

Shevchenko, Taras [Hryhorovych] (1814–1861)

Ukrainian poet, artist, and nationalist. Shevchenko was born a serf and was orphaned at an early age. He was bought out of servitude in 1838 by the Russian poet Zhukovsky and the artist Briullov, and became a student at the St. Petersburg Academy of Art. His first collection of poetry, *Kobzar* (1840; *The Bard*), expressed the folkloric interests of the Ukrainian Romantics. However, he soon moved to a more somber portrayal of Ukrainian history in his narrative poem *Haidamaky* (1841; *The Haidamaks*), where he depicted the great popular uprising of 1768 known as the Koliivshchyna. The breadth of Shevchenko's national program, his vision of Ukraine as a completely independent national entity, and his faith in its glorious future made a great impression on his contemporaries. In 1846, while in Kiev, Shevchenko joined the secret Brotherhood of St. Cyril and Methodius. The next year, the Brotherhood was suppressed; Shevchenko was arrested and punished by exile and compulsory service as a soldier in the Urals and Central Asia for writing the poems "Son" (1844; "The Dream"), "Kavkaz" (1845; "The Caucasus"), and "Druzhnieie poslaniie i mertvym i zhyvym i nenarodzhenym zemliakam" (1845; "Friendly Epistle to My Dead, Living, and Yet-Unborn Countrymen"), which satirized the oppression of Ukraine by Russia and prophesied a revolution. Though forbidden to write or paint, he wrote a few lyrical poems in Ukrainian and some prose in Russian. Soon after the death of Czar Nicholas I, Shevchenko was released and had a revival of creativity in 1857. The works of 1857–61 represent the apex of Shevchenko's poetry; in them he treats historical and moral issues, both Ukrainian and universal, many of them imitations of Psalms and biblical motifs. Most of Shevchenko's poetic writings were collected in a new edition of *Kobzar*, which appeared in 1860. Shevchenko also worked in the visual arts, both in painting and engraving.

Shi'ite

Adherent of Islamic sect Shi'ism. Shi'ism is one of the two major divisions of Islam, the other being Sunniism, to which the majority of Muslims belong. The Shi'ite schism originated in the struggles over leadership of the Muslim community following the death of the Prophet Muhammad in 632. Shi'ites hold that the office of leader of the Muslims, termed caliph or imâm, should have been restricted to 'Alī (c. 600–661 C.E.), cousin and son-in-law of the Prophet Muhammad, and his descendants. The Shi'ite derives from a pejorative phrase used to describe 'Alī's supporters: "shī'at 'Alī," meaning 'Alī's "crew" or "gang." Allegiance to a caliph has ceased to define orthodoxy in Sunnî Islam since the early periods of Islam, but the Shi'ites have had limited success in participating as equals in a Muslim world dominated by the Sunnî majority. The martyrdom of Husayn, one of 'Alī's sons, who was killed at the orders of Sunnî tyrants along with a small band of his supporters at Karbalâ' in 680 C.E., has come to symbolize the injustices that the Shi'ite minority has suffered; this martyrdom is reenacted annually by Shi'ites in the month of Muharram of the Islamic calendar (*hijrah*).

Shi'ism represents roughly 20 percent of the Muslims in the world, and has branched into three subsects distinguished by allegiance to different lines of imâms. The majority of modern Shi'ites are Twelvers, so-called because they recognize a succession of twelve imâms, representing ten generations of descent from 'Alī. Twelver Shi'ites represent virtually the entire population of Iran and are a majority in Iraq, Lebanon, and Bahrain. They have significant minority communities in Afghanistan, Pakistan, and India. The Zaydî Shi'ite community, who trace their succession of imâms through Zayd, a great-grandson of 'Alī, are concentrated in North Yemen, where the Zaydî imâms have ruled intermittently for over one thousand years. The Ismâ'îlî succession of imâms goes through ismâ'îl, a fifth-generation descendant of 'Alī. Ismâ'îlîs of two main subgroups, Khojas and Bohras, are now found in small communities in Syria, Pakistan, and India.

Doctrine regarding the nature of the imâms has developed in different ways in the three subsects. Twelvers hold that their imâms were infallible religious authorities by virtue of divine inspiration, but the twelfth imâm went into hiding in 941 C.E., and conscious contact with him is deemed no longer possible. Since then, this hidden imâm has been circulating among the believers incognito, and is expected to reveal himself to inaugurate a thousand-year reign of justice before the Day of Judgment. The Zaydîs have not emphasized the religious or doctrinal authority of their imâms, who are seen primarily as leaders of military opposition to illegitimate governments. In both Zaydî and Twelver Shi'ism, interpretation of the Sacred Law has become the prerogative of a corps of legal scholars. In Ismâ'îlism, however, the doctrinal authority of the imâm has continued to function. The Khojas pledge allegiance to the Agha Khan, whom they regard as the divinely inspired imâm and supreme religious authority. The Bohras look to the Da'i Mutlaq, the representative of their hidden imâm, as their highest religious authority.

Shintō

Ancient Japanese religion. The word *shin-tō* means "the way of the spirits." In Shintō, there are a great number of gods and goddesses—the *kami* (spirits)—that are found throughout the world. Shintō priests pay respect and honor to the *kami* in special shrines, which are usually simple but beautiful. Shintō has no sacred books, no theology, and no philosophical orthodoxy.

There are two forms of modern Shintō: State Shintō and Sect Shintō. The central idea of State Shintō is that the emperor is of divine origin. Beginning in the Meiji Period, all Japanese were required to participate in its religious rites, and the priests who carried them out were supported by the state. At State Shintō shrines, priests made prayers to divinities for such public blessings as good harvests, success in war, and the security of the emperor. State Shintō, which was abolished in Japan by the United States as a condition of the defeat of Japan in the Second World War, was highly nationalistic. Sect Shintō, however, consists of thirteen recognized religious sects, and it is not under government control. Its forms of worship are more private and its prayers are usually more individual. Sect Shintō acquired the same legal basis as Christianity, Buddhism, and Confucianism in the late nineteenth century.

Shiva

Hindu god. One of the greatest gods of Hinduism, Shiva, also called Mahadeva, is supposed to have 1,008 epithets, reflecting, some Hindus hold, the Vedic teaching that there is a single divine power with multiple manifestations. Shiva worship—or Shaivism—is mentioned as early as the Upanishads and the *Mahabharata* (500–200 B.C.E.) Shiva is identified with the fierce Vedic god Rudra and, in his terrible aspect, is the god of destruction and cosmic dissolution. He is commonly worshiped in the form of the lingam, or symbolic phallus. His other main forms are the great yogi, or ascetic, and Nataraja, Lord of the Cosmic Dance. As a yogi, he is depicted as seated deep in meditation in the Himalayas, holding a trident, a snake coiled around his neck, his body smeared with ashes, and his hair long

and matted. As Nataraja, he is shown four-armed bearing various emblems, and dancing on one foot on a prostrate demon. Shiva's mount is the bull Nandi and his consort is the goddess Kālī, who also goes by many other names.

shoin-style architecture

Japanese residential architecture. Originally designed during the Azuchi-Momoyama (1568–1600) and Edo (1600–1868) periods for the Japanese warrior class, shoin-style architecture forms the basis of the contemporary Japanese house. This style of architecture is distinguished from its predecessor, the shinden style, by its division of the interior space through sliding walls and screens. The outside of the structure also utilized a series of sliding doors that were eventually completely constructed of rice paper in order to let in more light. The main room of a shoin-style building typically contained four distinctive elements: a decorative alcove, staggered shelves, a built-in desk, and decorative doors. Although these elements were all initially functional, in time they became simply decorative elements. Shoin-style architecture also made its way into the design of lower-class housing when some buildings in the shoin style incorporated rustic teahouse elements, and created the less formal, more simple, and more diversified sukiya shoin style.

Shui hu zhuan

Chinese Ming novel. The *Shui hu zhuan*, or *Water Margin*, was one of the *si da qi shu* (four masterworks) of the Ming period. Although Luo Guanzhong was the first to publish this book, its authorship remains controversial, and some consider Shi Naian to be its original author or coauthor. The novel tells a detailed story about a peasant rebellion in the Song dynasty (960–1279). The author gives a brilliant description of the 108 rebel heroes on the Liang Mountain, who gathered from different places and across ranks to fight the corrupted officials and help the poor. Loyalty is a dominant theme; the chief of the rebels, Song Jiang, insists on loyalty to the emperor while fighting dishonorable court officials. The book provides historical insight into many of the social conflicts of the late Song dynasty. Because of its lifelike characters and suspenseful tales, the novel remains a popular classic in contemporary China.

Sibelius, Jean [Julian Christian]
(1865–1957)
Finnish composer. The son of a surgeon, Sibelius displayed musical talent from an early age. He entered Helsinki University as a law student, but soon switched to the Conservatory of Music. He later studied in Berlin and Vienna, then returned to Finland, which was then in the throes of a nationalist uprising against Russia. Sibelius's first major statement as a composer featured his musical interpretation of the *Kalevala*, the Finnish national epic. The attempt to capture the Finnish spirit and mythology in music characterizes much of Sibelius's work, including the most popular of his compositions, the tone poem *Finlandia* (1899). In 1897 the Finnish Parliament, then under Russian control, voted Sibelius an annual pension, which he received throughout his life. Though Sibelius did not particularly care for the music of Richard Wagner, his resurrection of Finnish myths in his music is often likened to Wagner's use of ancient German legends in his operas. Sibelius is best known for his symphonic poems and symphonies.

Sienkiewicz, Henryk (1846–1916)
Polish novelist and journalist. Born in Wola Okrzejska, Poland, Sienkiewicz attended the University of Warsaw and studied literature, history, and philology, but left in 1871 without taking a degree. His first publications were critical arti-cles written in 1869; in 1872 he published his first novel *Na Marne* (*In Vain*). Three years later, his first short story, "An Old Retainer," appeared. From 1876 through 1878 he traveled in the United States as a correspondent of the *Gazeta Polska* (Polish Gazette), and lived in the Polish colony founded by the Polish-American actress Helena Modjeska.

After returning to Poland, he published many short stories, and coedited the daily *Słowo* from 1882 until 1887. During this period his novels included his trilogy detailing Poland's struggle for independence in the seventeenth century: *Ogniem i mieczem* (1884; *With Fire and Sword*), *Potop* (1886; *The Deluge*), and *Pan Wołodyjowski* (1887; *Pan Michael*). These are considered to be his best novels, and with these he established a reputation of writing with epic clarity and simplicity. *Bez dogmatu* (1891; *Without Dogma*) and *Children of the Soil* (1895) are considered psychological novels, and his famous *Quo Vadis?* (1896; *Quo Vadis: A Narrative of the Time of Nero*) was also written during this time.

In 1905 he won the Nobel Prize for Literature. He lived in Poland until the First World War, when he started advocating Polish independence and organizing relief for war victims. He died in Vevey, Switzerland.

Sihanouk, Prince Norodom (1922–)
Cambodian political leader. Appointed king of Cambodia by the French governor-general in 1941, Sihanouk began his long and turbulent political career in Cambodia. During his years as king, Sihanouk attempted to liberate Cambodia from the imperialist French government, a goal he finally achieved in 1955, with the founding of the Sangkum Reastr Niyum (People's Socialist Community). Sihanouk managed to achieve a fragile stability in the ensuing years, while much of Southeast Asia was

in a state of upheaval. His policy of neutrality in the Vietnam War ended in 1970, however, when he was deposed by a right-wing coup supported by the United States. Sihanouk fled to Beijing, where he led a government-in-exile that supported the Khmer Rouge. Following the Khmer Rouge takeover of Cambodia in 1975, Sihanouk returned, only to be immediately placed under house arrest. He was released in 1979, as the power of the Khmer Rouge began to falter, and in 1982 became the head of the government-in-exile, an uneasy coalition of the Khmer Rouge, the anti-Communist Khmer People's National Liberation Front, and Sihanouk's neutralist National Liberation Movement of Kampuchea. Sihanouk resigned this position in 1988, but returned in 1991 to negotiate a treaty that attempted to end civil war in Cambodia. He remains a considerable force in national politics and was crowned king of the constitutional monarchy formed after U.N.-sponsored elections in 1993.

Silk Road

Ancient network of caravan trails in China. More than 5,350 miles (7,000 kilometers) long, the Silk Road has a history dating back over 2,000 years. It started in the capital of the Western Han dynasty (206 B.C.E.–25 C.E.), Chang-an (now Xi'an), extending westward across deserts and snowcapped mountains, through Central Asia and the Middle East to the Mediterranean. For more than a thousand years the Silk Road served as the East-West artery carrying silk and other goods to the Roman and Byzantine empires. It was also along this route that Buddhism expanded eastward from India into the heartland of China.

When ancient caravans reached Dunhuang in the west of present-day Gansu province and proceeded farther west, they hit the inhospitable Taklamakan Desert. No caravans could cross the desert and survive, so they skirted it; thus

the route forked, one part following the oasis towns along the northern edge of the desert, the other going south. The two routes joined at Kashgar, in the far west at the foot of the Pamirs, then stretched to the Middle East. Through the Silk Road ancient China kept in contact with the outside world. Among the famous persons who traversed this road are the Buddhist monk Xuanzang of the Tang dynasty (618–906), who went westward on a pilgrimage to India in search of Buddhist scriptures, and the Venetian merchant Marco Polo, who came eastward to serve as an official (1275–91) in the court of Kublai Khan during the Yuan dynasty (1260–1368).

When maritime trade began to develop in the sixteenth century, the Silk Road declined as a commercial artery. Soon it was forgotten and many of the once prosperous way-station towns were buried in the shifting sands until archaeological discoveries in the twentieth century revived interest in this region.

Sinclair, Upton [Beall, Jr.] (1878–1968)

American novelist. Sinclair is perhaps the best known of the American realists, a novelist whose work reflects a constant concern for social justice. His many novels polemicize for socialism and against the injustices of capitalism, typically featuring an idealistic hero who finds in socialism a cure for the evils of society. His most popular and enduring work is *The Jungle* (1906), which exposed the miserable working conditions prevalent in the Chicago meatpacking industry. Conceived, like most of his books, as a specific means to a specific end, *The Jungle* did not have the effect Sinclair intended: its popularity derived from its revelations about the impurities of processed meats, rather than its advocacy in support of the proletariat.

Upton Beall Sinclair, Jr., was born to an alcoholic salesman from Virginia and the daughter of a wealthy Baltimore family. His upbringing, in Baltimore and New York City, combined poverty, respectability, and ambition. This background perhaps accounts for the elitist tendencies in his writings, and for the fact that he led a genteel life, dabbling in spiritualism and vegetarianism while at the same time producing extremely vitriolic fiction. Upon graduating from the City College of New York in 1897, Sinclair began his career as a writer of boys' adventure stories for a pulp-fiction and dime-novel publisher. He attended graduate school at Columbia, where he was drawn to Romantic poetry, but never received his degree.

The Jungle was Sinclair's sixth published book, and his first literary and commercial success. It arose out of the two months he spent in Chicago in the fall of 1904, investigating stockyard conditions for the socialist newspaper Appeal to Reason. With The Jungle, Sinclair established himself as a writer of great social significance, yet despite a prolific output that continued into the 1960s, he never equaled that success. A series of second-rate topical novels followed on the heels of The Jungle; not until the publication of Oil! (1927) did Sinclair recapture the tone and urgency that had earned him his renown. Although Oil!, which was based on the Teapot Dome scandal, is not equal to The Jungle in terms of its historical importance or commercial success, it is considered by some critics to be Sinclair's best work. In 1928 Sinclair published another successful work, Boston, a two-volume exposé of the Sacco and Vanzetti case.

In 1933 Sinclair produced a book entitled I, Governor of California, and How I Ended Poverty, and the following year he became the Democratic candidate for governor of California, propelled by the popularity of his EPIC (End Poverty in California) socialist reform campaign. He was defeated, and later described his experiences in politics in Co-Op (1936).

Sinclair won a Pulitzer Prize in 1942

for Dragon's Teeth, the fourth in an eleven-volume series of historical novels which chronicle the adventures of the antifascist Lanny Budd. In 1960 Sinclair published My Lifetime in Letters, a collection of letters written to him, and in 1962 The Autobiography of Upton Sinclair.

Sindh

Pakistani province. Sindh, located in the Indus River Delta, derives its name from that river, which the locals call the Sindhu. The discovery of the sites of the prehistoric cities of Mohenjo-daro, Amre, and Kot Diji attest to Sindh's long history as the center of ancient civilizations dating as far back as the third millennium B.C.E. Sindh was annexed to the Persian empire under Darius I (r. 522–486 B.C.E.), and came under Alexander the Great's domain after he invaded the region in 326 and 325 B.C.E. After Sindh was annexed by a succession of Indo-Greek, Buddhist, and Brahman empires, Islam was introduced to India as a direct result of the Arab Muhammad bin Qasim's conquest of the province in 711 C.E.

Arab rule in Sindh continued for centuries, up to and ending with Sindh's inclusion in the powerful Mughal empire (1591–1700). After 1700, the independent Sindhian dynasties of the Kalhoras (1700–82) and the Talpur Baluch (1782–1843) ruled the region until 1843, when the British came to power in Sindh. Sindh remained a part of the Bombay Presidency until 1937, when it was established as a separate province. It became part of Pakistan in 1947, and a huge influx of Muslims from India followed. The negotiations (1955–70) subsequent to Pakistani's independence resulted in Sindh's becoming a part of the larger province of West Pakistan. In 1970, with the dissolution of the province of West Pakistan, Sindh once again became a separate province.

Sindh has a long and prominent musical tradition. The Loras, who were Sindh's earliest professional minstrels, brought their lyrics as far as ancient Iran, where they became popularly known and beloved as Luryan music. The famous *Risalo* of Shah Abdul Latif (1689–1752), also known as *Shah jo Rago*, combines Sindhi classical and folk traditions and is considered to be a musical masterpiece. Sachal Sarmast (1739–1826), who composed both in Sindhi and in Siraiki, was also known for his ecstatic lyrics.

Singer, Isaac Bashevis (1904–1991)

Polish-Jewish novelist, essayist, and short-story writer. Born Yitshek Bashyvis Zinger, Singer was the son of a Hasidic rabbi. After beginning a traditional Jewish education in Warsaw, he decided on a career as a writer. From his father Singer learned about cabalistic mysticism; from his mother, nineteenth-century rationalism; and from his brother, Israel Joshua (also a writer), he acquired a taste for bohemianism. After withdrawing from the rabbinical seminary he began working as a translator and proofreader for a newspaper in Warsaw, associating with his brother's literary friends in his spare time. He followed his brother to New York City in 1935 and began working for the *Jewish Daily Forward*, a Yiddish-language newspaper.

Despite his naturalization as a U.S. citizen in 1943, Singer continued to write in Yiddish. Singer's experience as a cultural exile from Poland is a key element in his writing. Many of Singer's short stories and novels are historical fiction, set in Polish *shtetls* (Jewish villages) throughout the past three centuries. His historical novels include his first published work, *Der Sotn in Gorey* (1935; *Satan in Goray*), *Di Familye Mushkat* (1950; *The Family Moskat*), *Der Slave* (1962; *The Slave*), *Der folvark* (1967; *The Manor*), and *Dos farmegn* (1969; *The Estate*). They are heavily influenced by his brother, a gifted social and political ob-

server. I. B. Singer's talents lay in his ability to draw passionate, dynamic characters constrained by the societies to which they belong. In his own words, his protagonist is usually "either a criminal, or he's crazy, or he's an outcast." Typical of such a hero is the title character of *Der kuntsmakher fun Lublin* (1960; *The Magician of Lublin*), a hedonistic, half-assimilated Polish Jew who ultimately renounces his own sensualism in favor of self-deprivation and asceticism.

One of Singer's most powerful novels to date is *Di faind—a roman* (1972; *Enemies, a Love Story*). Set in post–World War II New York, it is the story of Holocaust survivor Herman Broder and his three wives. The Holocaust continues to haunt the characters; its brutality resurfaces in their everyday lives, in their relationships with one another and between man and God.

Singer's individualistic style and subject matter earned him the respect of the world and the 1978 Nobel Prize for Literature, but in Yiddish literary circles he has received a more subdued response. This is because he does not follow the established pattern of most Yiddish writers, who prefer warm, sentimental portrayals of a bygone culture. Singer does not deny or belittle his Old World Jewish heritage, but he attempts to blend it with the modern sensibilities of the New World (including his explicit stress on sexuality), some of which are disturbing to Yiddish readers. His flair for the grotesque, the irrational, and the mystical also set him apart from most contemporary writers. Singer, too, plays on religious themes, and the interplay of good and evil in human existence.

Siqueiros, David Alfaro (1896–1974)

Mexican painter and political activist. Born in Chihuahua, Siqueiros entered the revolutionary army at the age of fifteen and in two years became a staff officer. Sponsored by General Venustiano

Carranza, Siqueiros went to Europe to study art, and later traveled in the Soviet Union, the United States, and throughout Latin America. As the author of the manifesto *Three Appeals of Timely Orientation to Painters and Sculptors of the New American Generation* (1921), Siqueiros became a leading figure in the artistic revival upon his return to Mexico City in 1922. He helped organize the Syndicate of Technical Workers, Painters, and Sculptors, and was one of the founders of the Mexican journal *El Machete*, devoted to promoting revolutionary "people's art." Siqueiros was jailed several times for his political activities. He served in the republican army during the Spanish Civil War, 1936–39. Returning to Mexico City in 1939, he painted the mural *Retrato de la burguesía (Portrait of the Bourgeoisie)* with Luis Arenal, Antonio Pujol, and José Renau. Siqueiros's murals, such as *Nueva Democracia* (1945; *New Democracy*), depict racial, political, and industrial themes. His giant mural *La marcha de la humanidad en la tierra y hacia el cosmos (The March of Humanity)* was painted on the walls of the Audiroio Siqueiros, begun in 1964. Painting in an increasingly simplified style, Siqueiros experimented with modern technological techniques and materials. Many survive in Mexico City, at the headquarters of the Electrical Workers' Syndicate, the Palace of Fine Arts, the Polytechnic Institute, and the National University, among others. In addition to his many murals, Siqueiros also did easel paintings, of which *El eco del llanto* (1937; *Echo of a Cry*) is considered to be his best.

Si-shu Wu-jing

Chinese canonical texts. For over 2,000 years, until the early twentieth century, Si-shu Wu-jing, or the "four books" and "five classics," were the canonical texts officially invoked as norms for Chinese society, law, government, education, lit-

erature, and religion. They are all associated with Confucian ideals. The four books are *The Analects (Lun yu)*, *Mencius (Meng-zi)*, *Great Learning (Da xu)*, and *Doctrine of the Mean (Zhong yong)*. The five classics are the *Classic of Poetry (Shi jing)*, the *Classic of Changes (Yi jing)*, the *Classic of Documents (Shu jing)*, the *Record of Rituals (Li ji)*, and the *Spring and Autumn Annals (Chun qiu)*. In prerevolutionary China, knowledge of these works was considered essential for anyone who aspired to become a "gentleman," a government official, or a successful person in any field.

sitar

Indian musical instrument. A sitar is a fretted string instrument with a gourdlike body and a long neck, similar to the lute. It has from three to seven gut strings, tuned in fourths or fifths (or both), and a lower course of twelve wire strings that vibrate with the first set. It is played alone or in a small ensemble. Indigenous to India, the sitar was popularized in the West in the 1960s by the Indian virtuoso Ravi Shankar.

Sitting Bull, *see* Tatanka Iyotake

Skovoroda, Hryhorii [Savych] (1722–1794)

Ukrainian philosopher, poet. Born into a Cossack family, Skovoroda studied at the Kiev Academy, and later in Vienna, Munich, and Breslau. He taught at Pereyaslav and Kharkov between 1755 and 1765, but was dismissed because of an altercation with his superiors. Using his base among the peasants to produce work critical of clericalism, feudalism, and materialism, he became a "teacher of the people." Skovoroda aspired to be both a moralist and an intellectual. He outlined the idea of a symbolic world that links the macrocosmic world, or universe, and the microcosmic, or human. He believed that these realms were infused with the visible nature of the created world by which one can discover

God. Skovoroda's metaphysics and philosophical anthropology are in the tradition of Platonism, and he was an advocate of Stoic morality. The philosophical works of Skovoroda are written in Ukrainian in the form of dialogues. He also composed a collection of prose fables, a collection of poems entitled *Sad bozhestvennykh pesnei* (1753–85; *The Garden of Divine Songs*), and a number of Latin letters and poems. The democratic spirit of his style and the polyphonic dialogue form he used to express his ideas contributed to the wide popularity of his works and to his renown as a kind of wandering philosopher. Skovoroda's teachings fascinated Leo Tolstoy, among others. He is considered to be a precursor of the Ukrainian national revival that began in the early nineteenth century.

Smetana, Bedřich (1824–1884)

Czech composer. Smetana was a piano prodigy; he practiced intensively as his family moved through various Bohemian towns and was considered to be a virtuoso at the age of eighteen. Settling in Prague in 1843 he eagerly embraced the nationalist revolution of 1848, composing the *Overture in D* (1849), two revolutionary marches (both 1848), and *Písen svobody* (*The Song of Freedom*). After the failed revolution, Smetana established a music school with the encouragement of Hungarian composer Franz Lizst (1811–1886).

Feeling somewhat stymied in the atmosphere of absolutism following the uprising, Smetana left Prague for Sweden in 1856, where he spent five years teaching, conducting, and composing his first symphonic poems, modeled on those by Liszt. Following his return to Prague, Smetana found a culturally renewed city, again stirred by Czech nationalism, at least in the arts. Together with the journalist Karel Sabina, Smetana wrote his first opera, *Braniboři v Čechách* (1863; *The Brandenburgers in Bohemia*). His second collaboration with Sabina, *Prodaná nevěsta* (*The Bartered Bride*), was written while waiting for the production of his first in 1866. A genial portrait of Bohemian folk life, *The Bartered Bride* earned Smetana the directorship of the Czech Provisional Theater. With the onset of deafness at the age of fifty, Smetana was forced to resign his directorship, under which he had composed three more operas. He then concentrated on the composition of a cycle of patriotic symphonic poems called *Ma vlast* (1874–79; *My Country*), the most famous being the second of the series, *Vltava*, a portrait of the river Moldau. These later years were difficult for Smetana, and though encouraged by the success of some of his later works, such as the opera *Hubička* (1876; *The Kiss*), both his mental and physical health deteriorated. In 1884 he was committed to a Prague mental hospital; he died there and was buried alongside other Czech heroes.

Smith, Adam (1723–1790)

Scottish political economist and philosopher. Educated in Glasgow and Oxford, Smith gave a series of public lectures in 1748 in Edinburgh on his theories of economics, which were repeated because they were so successful. In 1751 he was appointed professor at Glasgow University, settling in the department of moral philosophy, and published his *Theory of Moral Sentiments* (1759), which established his reputation. Smith resigned his professorship in 1763 and became a tutor to a young duke. With his pupil, Smith traveled to France, where he met several of the Physiocrats, a group of French thinkers who developed the first system of economics. For the next ten years Smith worked on his magnum opus *The Wealth of Nations*, which argued for a division of labor and proposed that the public welfare could best be served by not restricting business enterprise. This is the fundamental idea of laissez-faire economics.

Through its extensive survey of economic history and its projection of what the economy should look like, *The Wealth of Nations* laid the foundations for making economics a scholarly discipline. As a philosophical work, it emphasizes self-interest as a fundamental part of human nature, which Smith claimed can be used to predict behavioral trends in a developing economy. This notion seems somewhat at odds with his earlier work *The Theory of Moral Sentiments*, which focuses on human capacity for sympathy in determining a moral outcome. However, *The Wealth of Nations* takes precedence over his earlier work in its revolutionary implications and the impact his ideas had on shaping liberal democracy in the Western world.

Smith was one of the first to propound the notion that "every man, as long as he does not violate the laws of justice, is left perfectly free to pursue his own interest his own way, and to bring both his industry and capital into competition with those of any other man, or order of men." His work defined capitalism at its most basic level and became the system of thought against which German social and economic theorist Karl Marx (1818–1883) later formulated his notions of communism. To this day, Adam Smith remains one of the world's most influential thinkers.

Smith, Bessie (1894–1937)

African-American blues and jazz singer. Born to a poor family in Chattanooga, Tennessee, Smith joined her teacher, Ma Rainey, in the Rabbit Foot Minstrels in 1912. Her first recording, *Down Hearted Blues* (1923), sold 800,000 copies and established her fame. She performed slow blues and jazz standards, both in vaudeville and on the almost two hundred recordings that she made in her lifetime, of which the best known

was *Back Water Blues* with James P. Johnson. The most successful black American recording artist of her time, Smith sang blues and jazz with early jazz musicians such as Louis Armstrong and Joe Smith. She was called the "Empress of the Blues," and was known for her emotional intensity and expressive range, as well as her fine intonation, broad phrasing, and blue-note inflections.

Smith, Joseph (1805–1844)

Founder of the Church of Jesus Christ of Latter-Day Saints. Born in Sharon, Vermont, Smith moved with his family to Palmyra, New York, when he was ten. According to Smith's later account, in 1823 an angel called Moroni appeared to him with the message that he should seek the book of golden plates containing the true Gospel that had been lost due to human wickedness. Their location was revealed to him in 1827, and he dictated a translation of the *Book of Mormon* (1830) from what he called "reformed Egyptian" into English with the aid of magic stones he called Urim and Thummim. The book describes American Indians as the descendants of Hebrews who had come to North America centuries earlier. Most non-Mormon scholars have analyzed this book as a mixture of Indian legend, autobiography, and contemporary political and religious writing.

After further revelations, Smith founded the Church of Jesus Christ of Latter-Day Saints, often called the Mormon Church, in Fayette, New York, in 1830. Fearing persecution and seeking greater opportunity, Smith moved his church and its followers to Kirtland, Ohio, in 1831, and several years later to Missouri. In both places, the Mormons lived in self-contained communities, prospering economically, and following the Bible and Smith's revelations, which were rumored to include polygamy. The idea of polygamy especially disturbed the Mormons' neighbors, and it was frequently cited as a pretext for violence against them and frequent arrests of Smith and other Mormon leaders. They were expelled from Missouri in 1837, and most of them moved to Commerce, Illinois, which Smith renamed Nauvoo. There, under the sanction of a state charter, Smith established an autonomous religious community. The group practiced a communal economy, had its own laws and militia, prohibited slaves, and held Smith as its absolute leader.

The community continued to grow and Smith's political influence expanded, but tensions from within and without grew as well. When Smith announced his candidacy for president of the United States in 1844, some dissident Mormons broke away and began publishing the *Expositor*, a newspaper devoted to attacking his power. Smith responded by having its press destroyed, and he and his brother Hyrum were arrested and charged with treason and conspiracy. They were jailed at Carthage, Illinois, and three days later both were shot and killed by an anti-Mormon mob incited by jealousy of the economically prosperous community and outraged at the concept of polygamy. The church split, with Brigham Young leading the majority to Great Salt Lake in Utah, and Smith's eldest son settling with the rest in Independence, Missouri. Among Smith's other publications, still followed by Mormons throughout the world, are *The Pearl of Great Price* (1842) and *Doctrine and Covenants* (1835).

Snake Dance

Religious ceremony of the Hopi Indians. Centuries old, the snake-dance ritual is an elaborate ceremony of regimental processions and dance accompanying fervent prayers. Held in late August, the rainy season in northern Arizona, the snake ceremony consists of eight days of secret rites and prayers performed in underground chambers called *kivas*. On the afternoon of the ninth day, the ceremony becomes a public performance in which dancers boldly handle live rattlesnakes, bull snakes, and garter snakes, placing them in their mouths as part of the ritual. At the conclusion of the ceremony, the snakes, which are considered to be messengers to the gods, are released to carry the prayers of the tribe to the underworld, which the Hopi view as their paradise. They believe that the snakes will inform the Hopi deities of the underworld, namely the Plumed Serpent, that the tribe still lives by the ways of its ancestors, so that the gods will send rain to save the agricultural staples of the tribe.

It is believed that this ritual was perhaps derived centuries ago based on the legend of Tiyo, the Snake Youth who traveled to the underworld and learned the dances and rituals of the snake people, teaching them to his tribe upon his return.

Apparently, the Hopi have no antidote in the event of a snake bite. The dancers, however, knowing that a snake must be coiled or looped in order to strike, never attempt to handle coiled snakes or stand within striking distance. To minimize danger, the handlers always force a snake to uncoil before seizing it.

Socrates (c. 469–399 B.C.E.)

Greek philosopher. Though he wrote nothing, Socrates is the most famous and influential of the Greeks; his philosophy, life, trial, and death were recorded in the writings of his disciple Plato. He also appears in the works of Xenophon, and is brutally parodied in Aristophanes' *The Clouds*, but it is Plato's dialogues that depict him best, at length and in vivid detail.

Socrates was born to well-off Athenians, which allowed him to serve in several military campaigns. His asceticism has been widely remarked upon (Aristophanes, among others, portrayed him dressed in rags, smelly, barefoot, and ugly). Late in life, he was arrested and charged with insulting the gods and corrupting the youth of Athens; despite the protests of his many followers and several wealthy patrons, he was found guilty and chose to drink poison as his sentence required rather than attempt escape. The charges of impiety for which he was executed are considered to be a masked attack on his friendship with the Group of 30, an influential association of antidemocratic Athenians. His teachings, especially his irreverent, constant questioning—the Socratic method—were viewed as immoral.

Socrates believed that the logic or form of an argument was as important as the truth it resulted in: that the quest for truth was itself a form of truth. ("Know thyself" is the famous Socratic injunction.) Socrates' cross-examinations were meant to goad the examinee to self-knowledge by forcing him to argue to an end point of absolute internal self-consistency, even if that knowledge only consisted of the Socratic irony "I know that I don't know." Socrates often claimed that he himself knew nothing, that his relentless questioning was part of his own drive to know himself. Socratic philosophy maintains that attaining perfect self-knowledge is akin to virtue, that there is no distinction between knowledge and ethics.

Solidarność

Polish political party. Solidarność, known as Solidarity, first began to take shape when, on August 14, 1980, 17,000 workers at the Lenin shipyards in Gdańsk, Poland, transformed a spontaneous protest into a strike. Selected as the chief negotiator, Lech Wałesa, in just three days, persuaded management to meet the workers' demands. In the meantime, other groups of Gdansk workers were inspired to go on strike; they successfully urged Wałesa to continue the shipyard strike as a show of solidarity. With the shipyard workers at the core, the entire Gdańsk area became the scene of a general strike that achieved surprisingly rapid results. On August 31, the strikers reached an agreement with the government that provided them not only with wage increases but also with greater religious and political freedom, and the right to establish independent trade unions.

Solidarity was officially founded in September 1980, and was formally registered with the Polish government as a trade union by October.

By the middle of 1981 Solidarity had incorporated approximately 10 million workers. However, the Polish government refused to honor all the terms of the August 1980 agreement, and Solidarity responded by mounting a series of strikes and by calling for free elections and a dissolution of the established government. In December 1981 the military government of General Wojciech Jaruzelski imposed martial law, banned the union, and arrested most of the union's leaders; Wałesa was detained until November 1982. In July 1983 the Polish government eased the restrictions by declaring a formal end to martial law. But the October 1984 kidnapping and murder of Father Jerzy Popieluszko, a pro-Solidarity cleric, made it clear that the policy of intimidation had not yet completely ended.

Despite the hostile political climate within which it was forced to operate, Solidarity continued to provide a visible focus for antigovernment sentiment. The movement's prestige received a significant boost when the pope expressed his support during a visit to Poland in June 1987. In the fall of that year, Solidarity played a key role in defeating a series of austerity measures proposed by Jaruzelski. Then, in the spring and summer of 1988, Solidarity served as a rallying point for a series of protest strikes mounted in the face of intense government repression. Finally forced to seek some sort of compromise, the Polish government underwent a major shakeup, with numerous figures falling from power.

By September 1989 a new coalition government had emerged, dominated by Solidarity rather than by the Communist Party. From its inception, the Solidarity government, led by prime minister and Solidarity member Tadeusz Mazowiecki, was plagued by economic problems and forced to take unpopular measures that served to reduce Solidarity's popularity among the general public. But Mazowiecki's greatest problems were to come from Wałesa, who, by June 1990, was openly using his position as chairman of Solidarity as a means of opposing Mazowiecki's attempts to integrate the union more completely into the structure of the Mazowiecki government. There thus arose within Solidarity a rift between Mazowiecki and Wałesa that grew irreparable. Wałesa eventually defeated Mazowiecki in the presidential election of November 1990. As president, Wałesa has moved along a path sometimes at odds with the revolutionary-minded Solidarity party, which continues to exist as an influential coalition.

From the time of Solidarity's inception, Wałesa's legend has been inextricably linked to its destiny and character. A carpenter's son, Wałesa (1943–) was born in Popowo, Poland. After completing elementary school, he underwent vocational training at the Agricultural Mechanization School in Lipno, from which he graduated in 1961. He spent some time in military service, and then, in 1967, became an electrician at the Lenin shipyards in Gdańsk, where he continued to work, in various positions, until the events of August 1980 changed his situation irrevocably.

Somoza dynasty (1947–79)

Nicaraguan dynasty. The founder of the Somoza dynasty, which ruled Nicaragua for forty-four years, was Anastasio So-

moza García (1896–1956), who was born in San Marcos to a wealthy coffee planter. He was educated at the Instituto Nacional de Oriente in Nicaragua and at Pierce Business School in the United States. When he returned to Nicaragua, he dedicated himself to a military career. Married to the daughter of a prominent Nicaraguan family, his future was secure as he rose quickly through the ranks, becoming chief of the U.S.-trained National Guard in 1933. That same year, U.S. president Herbert Hoover recalled U.S. Marines who had been collaborating with the guard in trying to defeat the nationalist guerrilla forces of Nicaraguan political leader Augusto Sandino (1895–1934). Somoza continued to look after U.S. interests after the marines pulled out. In 1934, after an accord between Sandino and the elected president, Juan Bautista Sacasa, seemed to have been reached, Somoza had Sandino assassinated as he left the presidential palace. Two years later, with the army at his disposal, Somoza ousted the Sacasa government and established himself as Nicaragua's ruler. During his administration—a few years governing as head of the armed forces and then formally elected president in 1951—he fostered reforms that made Nicaragua less dependent on the banana industry; at the same time, however, he amassed an enormous personal fortune, exiled or killed the majority of his political opponents, and claimed ownership of large areas of land and many businesses. Somoza was assassinated in 1956 after announcing that he would seek another presidential term.

His elder son, Luis Somoza Debayle (1922–1967), then took power; he was elected to office in 1957 and ruled until 1963, when he refused a second term. During his single term as president, Luis Somoza Debayle also continued to extend the family's business interests, although he was reportedly a less violent ruler than his father.

His younger brother, Anastasio Somoza Debayle (1925–1980), was elected president in 1967; politicians favoring the Somoza dynasty held the presidency in the interim. Perhaps the most brutal of the three, Anastasio Somoza Debayle ruled aggressively in the manner of his father until 1979. He continued to enrich himself and his family through corruption, and fostered the interests of the National Guard; he referred to Nicaragua simply as "my farm." Systematically, he destroyed opponents by purchase, imprisonment, or murder. During this time Somoza reportedly had the support of the U.S. government, which sought to preserve its influence in the region. In 1972 he relinquished his office, returning to the presidency again in 1974 under a new constitution that allowed him to remain there until 1981. In 1979, however, he was forced to resign in the wake of both violent insurrection against his alleged oppression and foreign accusations of violations of human rights. On July 17, 1979, the Sandinista Front for National Liberation marched triumphantly into Managua, and Somoza fled to Paraguay. In 1980 he was assassinated in that country.

Songhai

North African empire. From as early as the seventh century C.E., Songhai was a kingdom in the area of the great northward bend of the Niger River, and in the thirteenth century it was part of the empire of ancient Mali.

In 1335 the Songhai people broke away from Mali and began to conquer the surrounding area with a well-trained army that included horsemen. Like the empires before it, the wealth of Songhai came largely from the Saharan trade in salt and gold, mostly through the great trading cities of Gao, Jenne, and Timbuktu.

In the late fifteenth century, the empire was led by Sonni Ali (1464–1492), a military commander who defeated armies of the Mossi to the south and the Tuareg to the north. Soon after the death of Sonni Ali, control of the empire was taken by Muhammad I Askia (reigned c. 1493–1528), who was from the Mande-speaking people. The new rulers, whose ancestors had governed ancient Mali, were Muslims who opposed the pagan Songhai rulers. Under Muhammad I Askia, the Songhai empire reached its greatest expanse. It stretched from the borders of Kanembornu and the Hausa states in the east to the upper Senegal River in the west and included the salt-mining area of Teghaza in the desert to the north. The capital was Gao, which is in modern Mali, and which still contains part of the mosque where Askia Muhammad was buried in 1528.

Late in the sixteenth century, the empire began to decline because its area was too large to control effectively. Other states began to compete for the rich Saharan trade. Around 1585 Songhai was attacked by an army from Morocco, which captured the salt-mining areas of Teghaza and Taodeni and defeated the Songhai at the Battle of Tondibi. The Songhai rulers retreated southward to the region of Dendi on the Niger, to the northwest of the present border of Nigeria. There they continued their rule and their traditional life, although their economic and military power in the Sudan was broken. Meanwhile, the Moroccans could not control the many different peoples of the Sudan and the desert, and in the seventeenth century a number of smaller states took the place of the empire. But none of them were powerful enough to bring peace and prosperity to the Sudan region.

Today there are still several hundred thousand Songhai who are descended from the people of the historic empire. They are mainly farmers and fishermen who live along the great north bend of the Niger in Mali.

Song of Roland, *see* Chanson de Roland

Sophiatown

Section of Johannesburg, South Africa, that was the center of a literary and cultural renaissance in the 1950s. "Sophiatown" is now a byword for black urban resistance to apartheid's injustices.

Sophiatown was one of the few urban areas in South Africa in which blacks owned property, and boasted a relatively large black professional class. In the decade after the Nationalist Party's 1948 rise to power, Sophiatown existed precariously as a semi-integrated holdout to apartheid. The area became a symbol of a new, urban Africa, replete with *shebeens* (speakeasies), brutal Chicago-style gangsters known as *tsotsis*, and jazz bands. Sophiatown also became a fashionable destination for white liberals eager to jump the "color bar" and participate in the burgeoning black intellectual scene.

Literary activities centered on the white-owned publication *Drum*, which had a virtually all-black reporting staff. It was at *Drum* that many of South Africa's preeminent black writers learned their trade in the 1950s. Ezekiel Mphahlele, Lewis Nkosi, Can Themba, Bloke Modisane, and Don Mattera all participated in writing a combination of muckraking journalism, short fiction, and opinion pieces heralding a post-tribal, cosmopolitan South Africa. The writing, while frequently vibrant and innovative, has been criticized by some for a lack of coherent political sensibility and a relentless machismo. The scope and political bent of *Drum* was also somewhat hampered by the white owner and editors, who were liberal but anxious to avoid serious conflict with the government.

Theater and music also flourished; 1958's African Theatre Workshop and the jazz opera *King Kong* (1959), which deals with the South African heavyweight champion later found guilty of killing his girlfriend, were both important results of the Sophiatown renaissance.

The ethos of the Sophiatown set was profoundly influenced by American popular and literary culture. The *Drum* writers looked with approval on black American authors and performers like Langston Hughes, James Baldwin, Duke Ellington, and Louis Armstrong, and Sophiatown's gangsters frequently adopted the speech and swaggering attitude of Hollywood's mobster heroes. The music of two Sophiatown legends, singer Miriam Makeba and trumpet player Hugh Masekela, was created through a melding of black American pop and jazz with traditional African music.

The South African government responded to the increasing intellectual and political ferment in the area by initiating deportations in 1955. By 1960 Sophiatown had been virtually drained of its black inhabitants, and in 1962 it was demolished and replaced by a new white neighborhood known as Triomf (Afrikaans for "triumph").

Sophocles (496–406 B.C.E.)

Ancient Greek poet and dramatist. Born in Colonus, near Athens, to a wealthy arms manufacturer, Sophocles received an education comparable to that of the sons of the most distinguished Athenians. As a boy, he excelled in both gymnastics and music, the two most emphasized elements of Greek education; because of his physical beauty, he was chosen at sixteen to lead a chorus celebrating the Athenian victory over the fleet of Xerxes, naked and holding a lyre. At twenty-seven, Sophocles first entered a dramatic competition, winning first place and displacing the Greek dramatist Aeschylus (525–456 B.C.E.), who had held the superior position in dramatic poetry for an entire generation. Sophocles then embarked on a long and prolific career as a dramatist, producing an estimated 123 plays, none of which placed below second in competitions, and writing until his death at the age of ninety. He is credited with several innovations in tragic drama, including the introduction of a third actor when two had been the standard. This made possible the development of more elaborate plots and situations than those created by his predecessor Aeschylus. In addition, Sophocles expanded the chorus from twelve to fifteen members. He abandoned the Aeschylean practice of presenting connected trilogies or tetralogies at dramatic competitions, and made each play a unified work. Sophocles was held in high esteem during his lifetime; in addition to writing poetry, he was twice appointed a general in the Athenian army; was a priest of Amynos, the god of healing; held worship services to the healing deity Asclepius in his own home; and founded a literary and musical society.

Seven of his plays survive today: *Ajax, Antigone, Women of Trachis, Oedipus Tyrannus (Rex), Electra, Philoctetes,* and *Oedipus at Colonus.* Their plots are characterized by a chain of cause and effect that is linked by human motivation, but is later revealed to be the fulfillment of a prophecy or oracle. In this way Sophocles displays religious conviction, portraying the workings of divine will overpowering the efforts of humans, at the same time that he creates human characters admirable for their uncompromising adherence to purpose or duty. Sophocles also employs the "tragic irony" that has come to be associated with his name: the audience recognizes the underlying significance of the characters' words.

The works of Sophocles have been widely read and Austrian psychoanalyst Sigmund Freud (1856–1939) used a psychological analysis of the character of Oedipus to explain his theory of the Oedipus complex, a son's subconscious desire for his mother and jealousy of his father.

Soweto

South African township collective. Soweto is the urban area adjoining the city of Johannesburg, designated by the South African government for residence by blacks. About the same size as Johannesburg, Soweto is a collective of official townships; its name is an acronym derived from South-Western Townships. The townships were established by the government when full apartheid was established in 1948 as a way of regulating the slums and shantytowns peopled by black laborers who migrated to urban centers looking for work; most of the people of Soweto commute to Johannesburg to perform service jobs.

Many ethnic groups make up Soweto's population, and the area has often been the center of antiapartheid protest. The 1976 Soweto Rebellion was a massive uprising against the government's order to use the Afrikaans language in Soweto schools. In 1978 the first community council was elected to administer township affairs from the inside, but many regarded the body as powerless.

Soyinka, Wole (1934–)

Nigerian playwright, poet, and novelist. Soyinka was born in Isara as Akinwande Oluwole to Ayo and Eniola Soyinka. His unique ability to blend Yoruban folk traditions with European dramatic form indicates the high value he places on African culture while tapping into the Western modes of expression introduced to him during his education in the 1950s at the University of Leeds in England. This cultural mingling embodies the tensions within present-day Africa between indigenous traditions and the ever-pressing encroachment of Western civilization.

Before leaving for England to attend college, Soyinka published some poems and short stories in *Black Orpheus,* a prestigious Nigerian literary magazine. While at college, he produced his first play, *The Invention* (1955), which uses comic satire to criticize apartheid policies and the government that upholds them. Upon his return to Africa in 1960, shortly after Nigeria gained its independence from colonial rule, Soyinka began researching Yoruba folklore and drama for his next work, *A Dance of Forests* (1960). Used as a part of independence celebrations, this play warns Africans against glorifying the past by showing how even the most highly revered ancestors were as petty and spiteful as any living people. While Soyinka's subsequent works, most notably *The Lion and the Jewel* (1966) and his novel *The Interpreters* (1965), criticized African society, they offered a sense of optimism in the midst of satire.

After Soyinka's arrest and imprisonment by Nigerian police in 1965 and again in 1967, his works took on a more somber note in their assessment of Africa's future. During his confinement for purportedly supplying jet fighters to Biafrans trying to form their own country, Soyinka wrote many letters and mementos in the margins of books and on scraps of toilet paper. These pieces were later compiled in a diary entitled *The Man Died: Prison Notes of Wole Soyinka* (1972), which essentially bemoans the fate of the country that is rapidly deteriorating outside those prison walls. This sense of loss combined with an almost religious belief in human liberty drove Soyinka to write his second and more brooding novel, *Season of Anomie* (1973).

Soyinka has received many literary awards, including the Nobel Prize for Literature in 1986.

Spengler, Oswald (1880–1936)

German historian and philosopher. Spengler studied mathematics and the natural sciences during his years at the university in Halle, and after a brief stint as a high school teacher, he moved to Munich where he began work on his masterpiece, *Der Untergang des Abendlandes* (1918–22; *Decline of the West*). The book postulates a national life cycle akin to that of a living organism, in which it grows, matures, and decays; the work reflects the pessimism rampant in postwar Germany. Spengler was an ardent nationalist, and though his theories are sometimes cited as conducive to the rise of German fascism, he actually opposed Nazi leader Adolf Hitler's rise to power. His refusal to endorse the Nazi doctrines of genocide led to his ostracism after 1933. Though he was able to remain in Munich, his reputation suffered greatly and he died bitter and resentful of the Nazi rise.

Spinoza, Baruch (1632–1677)

Dutch philosopher. Born to a family of Portuguese Jews who had fled the Inquisition, Baruch Spinoza studied at an Orthodox Jewish school in Amsterdam, where he had a thorough education in both Scholastic theology and philosophy. He was an unlikely philosopher: by trade he was a lens grinder and lived a modest life. Still, he became a leading figure of the seventeenth-century schools of both Rationalism and Pantheism, which denied any separation between humans, God, and nature. His religious views and biblical interpretations were deemed heretical, and Spinoza was excommunicated from the Jewish community in 1656. About this same time, he abandoned the Hebrew name Baruch, meaning "blessed one," and instead adopted the Latin "Benedict." He published only one work in his lifetime, *Tractatus Theologico-politicus* (1670; *A Treatise on Religious and Political Philosophy*). He was offered a professorship at the University of Heidelberg in 1673, but declined the position because he believed it would compromise the independence of his thought. Despite his quiet lifestyle, Spinoza was renowned among his contemporaries and had many correspondents and visitors. He died from tuberculosis, which was aggravated by the glass dust of his trade. Following his death, his major work, *Ethica* (1677; *Ethics*), was published, as were his letters and other philosophical treatises.

spiritual

Religious folk song of the United States. Two related genres of spiritual songs developed out of American revivalist activity in the eighteenth and nineteenth centuries: that of the white community and that of the black community.

In the white community, spiritual referred to the folk hymns, religious ballads, and camp meeting songs used in eighteenth- and nineteenth-century revival meetings, instead of metrical Psalms and traditional hymns. White spirituals were preserved orally and in the shape-note tune books of rural communities, largely unnoticed by the broader American public until they were documented in twentieth-century academic studies.

Black spirituals were first documented in the nineteenth century in the American South and exhibit characteristics both of European hymns, such as their text, and of African music, such as their call-and-response format, their rhythmic embellishment, and their use of a heptonic scale with a flexible seventh degree. Black spirituals became popular nationally after collections were published in the 1860s, and were introduced internationally by tours of the Fisk University Jubilee Singers, who initiated the production of spirituals sung in choral arrangements. Although their publication and arrangement has destroyed the elements of spontaneity and improvisation in some of their performance, black spirituals survive as one of the largest bodies of folk song in the United States.

Spring Festival

Chinese festival. The Spring Festival, or Chinese New Year, starts on the eve of the Lunar New Year and goes on until the third day of the new year. An ancient festive occasion dating back to antiquity, it has been observed with long-established rituals throughout the country, though since the establishment of the People's Republic of China many of the old customs have been reformed to fit the new ideology.

The most important activity of the Spring Festival was originally the worship of gods and ghosts of the ancestors through food offerings and the burning of incense and joss paper. The gods, who range from the God of Heaven to the Kitchen God and the Door God, are thanked for their protection of the household in the past year and asked for good luck and fortune and more protection in the coming year. Today, in Hong Kong, Taiwan, overseas, and on the mainland, people visit each other with the greeting "*Gongxi facai*" ("Congratulations and may you make a fortune"). Spring Festival couplets are pasted on gateposts; generally the contents are wishes for a good year.

Many old customs still persist in rural areas or among older people. For instance, some celebrators do not sweep the floor on New Year's Day, because they believe that if they do, they will sweep out money and good fortune, and money is often given to children as a Lunar New Year gift, called *yasuiqian*, which means "money to keep the time from slipping away." Others believe that if anything is broken it is a sign of bad luck, and one should murmur at once: "*Sui sui ping an*," meaning "Safe and sound for the years to come."

Rural communities often organize Spring Festival performances, mainly folk dances like the dragon dance and local operas, and whole villages turn out to enjoy themselves. In towns and cities, people go to the fair with children. There are special foods for the occasion. In the north, dumplings are served. The whole family will gather to make dumplings together and the meal is called "reunion dumplings." A coin is inserted in one of the dumpling fillings, sometimes a date. The person who bites into such a dumpling will be blessed with money in the coming year. The date dumpling signifies the begetting of a son. In some areas in the south, a fish dish is required, because fish and surplus are both pronounced as *yu*; having a fish dish means having surplus money every year.

Stalin, Josef (1879–1953)

Soviet Communist leader. Stalin was born Iosif Vissarionovich Dzhugashvili into a very poor family in Georgia, which had been under Russian rule since 1800. His father, a shoemaker, died in a brawl when Stalin was a young boy, and his mother struggled to provide him with an education, hoping he would enter the Orthodox priesthood. While attending the seminary, Stalin became deeply involved in the Georgian nationalist movement and interested in political theory, notably Marxist theory. Because of his radical views, he was expelled from the seminary in 1899 and joined the underground social democratic movement. Here Stalin first met Russian Communist leader Vladimir Ilyich Lenin and endorsed his Bolshevik faction, but his involvement was hindered by numerous arrests and imprisonment for his political activities.

After the fall of the czar in 1917, Stalin was released from exile in Siberia and began to work closely with Lenin and other leading Bolsheviks. His role in the party continued to grow, and in 1922 he was promoted to the newly created post of general secretary of the Communist Party, which was initially conceived as a purely administrative position; later this post was held by the party's current leader.

In this same year, however, an irrevocable rift occurred between Lenin and Stalin. They had previously disagreed on the political autonomy of minorities in the Russian state, with Stalin proposing to simply incorporate these ethnic populations within a unitary Soviet state while Lenin favored a confederation. At Lenin's death in 1924, Stalin—through a series of successful moves—emerged victorious in the inner-party struggle for power. By the end of the 1920s he had become the acting head of the party. In this capacity, Stalin became the official interpreter of the Communist ideology and created a party line that he claimed was true to Lenin's doctrines but tolerated no dissent. One key part of this doctrine was the nationalist concept of "socialism in one country" rather than Russian Communist Leon Trotsky's "permanent revolution" on a world scale. (Trotsky was murdered in 1940 in Mexico City, probably on Stalin's orders.)

Without opposition, Stalin began his intensive collectivization of agriculture and industrial construction, called the Five-Year Plan. Though usually touted as one of Stalin's main achievements, the long-term merit of this plan is debatable, and it was not without high personal costs. In fact, it led to a severe famine in the rural parts of Ukraine and southern Russia in 1933, which cost the country several million lives.

In the cultural arena, too, Stalin set the parameters for permitted artistic expression. Those who violated Stalin's conception of "loyalty" to the party often found themselves arrested and sentenced to concentration camps. First this was done through mock trials; however, soon any attempt to keep the appearance of justice was abandoned. Throughout the 1930s and 1940s, millions of intellectuals, as well as anyone who was found "suspected," were murdered or sentenced to hard labor in the numerous concentration camps. The policy of mass repression relaxed somewhat during the Second World War, when Stalin, assuming the position of commander-in-chief, significantly contributed to the Soviet victory. However, his previous erroneous policies, which had considerably weakened the country's defense and almost resulted in an alliance with German leader Adolf Hitler, cost the Soviet Union many millions of dead (of the total number of victims of World War II, estimated at fifty million people, twenty million were Soviets).

Following the Second World War, Stalin's autocratic policies increased. Though he thoroughly defended Soviet interests at the close of the war and made major territorial gains in Eastern Europe, he was seriously concerned with military development and pursued Cold War diplomatic relations with the West. Internally, he suspended party congresses for over a decade, and even Central Committee meetings, and became, with a few associates, the sole governing voice. In 1953 Stalin died of a cerebral hemorrhage and his body was entombed beside Lenin's in Red Square.

Stanislavsky, Konstantin (1863–1938)

Russian theater director, creator of "method acting." Born Konstantin Sergeevich Alekseev to a manufacturer and his wife, who was the daughter of a French actress, Stanislavsky had a rich cultural upbringing, participating in amateur stage performances from the age of fourteen. He subsequently decided to devote his life to theater, adopting the stage name Stanislavsky in 1885, and performed in several theatrical companies, together with Maria Lilina, a celebrated actress whom he married in 1888. That same year, Stanislavsky and others established the Society of Art and Literature with a permanent amateur company.

In 1891 he staged his first independent production, of Russian writer Count Leo Tolstoy's *Plody prosveshcheniia* (1889–90; *Fruits of Enlightenment*). It became a major Moscow theatrical event and impressed a promising playwright

and director, Vladimir Nemirovich-Danchenko, who henceforth followed Stanislavsky's activities closely. In 1897 the two met for the first time and outlined a plan for a people's theater. The Moscow Art Theater, their creation, opened in 1898. The company's second production, of the Russian dramatist Anton Pavlovich Chekhov's *Chaika* (1896; *The Seagull*), which had been a failure in St. Petersburg in 1896, was a triumph for the new theater; the seagull became the company's emblem, and Chekhov became formally associated with the Art Theater, writing specially for the company *Tri sestry* (1901; *The Three Sisters*) and *Vishnevyi sad* (1903; *The Cherry Orchard*).

While staging Chekhov's plays Stanislavsky developed his theory of acting, his "method." Its success was confirmed in the Art Theater's productions of plays by Russian writer Maksim Gorky and Norwegian dramatist Henrik Ibsen. After the Revolution of 1917, Stanislavsky continued his work as the head of the theater, abandoning acting in 1928 and concentrating solely on directing and theoretical work. The sophisticated methodology called "method acting" that he created to guide the actor's performance proved successful and remains influential. Stanislavsky favored a realistic type of acting, in which the actor seeks to actually "live" the character and not merely rely on external theatrics. His theories of acting are detailed in his books *An Actor Prepares* (1936) and *Building a Character* (1950). In 1922–24 he toured with the Art Theater in Europe and the United States, and it was at this time that he wrote his autobiography, *My Life in Art* (1924). Throughout his theatrical career, Stanislavsky adhered to realism, opposing the pompous stereotypical conventions widespread in nineteenth-century theater.

Stanton, Elizabeth Cady (1815–1902)

American women's rights leader. The daughter of a judge, Stanton developed an interest in law at an early age, and, following her graduation from Emma Willard's academy for women, studied law with her father, though she was denied admission to the bar because of her sex. As a young woman, Stanton became active in the temperance and antislavery movements as well, and in 1840 she married the lawyer and abolitionist Henry Brewster Stanton in a ceremony that omitted the word "obey" from the marriage vows. That same year, Stanton traveled with her husband to an antislavery convention in London but was denied admission as a delegate because she was a woman. There she met social reformer Lucretia Mott (1793–1880), another rejected delegate, with whom she organized the ground-breaking Seneca Falls Convention in 1848. There Stanton introduced the *Declaration of Sentiments*—a document fashioned after the Declaration of Independence, but with a few significant modifications, such as a woman's right to control property, more liberal divorce laws, and the first call for female suffrage in the United States. The demand for suffrage received a mixed reception among the convention delegates, but after eloquent defenses by African-American slave and abolitionist Frederick Douglass (1817–1895) and others, it was finally adopted. In 1851 Stanton persuaded Susan B. Anthony to join the suffrage movement, and together they lectured, organized, and edited both a women's rights newspaper, *Revolution* (1868–70) and, with Mathilda Joslyn Gage, *The History of Woman Suffrage* (1881–86).

Though Stanton did not live to see her life's work materialize in the vote, she did achieve notable success in the arena of women's rights, such as the passage of a New York State statute that secured property rights for married women. Stanton also raised seven children and was deeply involved in issues of coeducation and child care. Many of Stanton's concerns about women and family are outlined in her autobiogra-phy, *Eighty Years and More*, published in 1893.

Stein, Gertrude (1874–1946)

American writer. Stein was a leading innovator in modernist writing as well as a famous patron of the arts. Her salon in Paris was the center of the artistic movement known as Cubism.

Gertrude Stein was born in Allegheny, Pennsylvania, and spent most of her adolescence in Oakland, California. As an undergraduate at Radcliffe College, she studied psychology with the philosopher William James. Stein initially planned to become a physician, but after a few years at Johns Hopkins Medical School she moved to Paris to live with her brother, Leo. Together they collected paintings that are now recognized as some of the major pieces of twentieth-century art. The Steins' studio at 27 rue de Fleurus became a gathering place for such artists as Pablo Picasso, Georges Braque, Henri Matisse, and Paul Cézanne.

In 1908 Stein met Alice Babette Toklas, an American woman traveling in Europe. The two remained inseparable until Stein's death thirty-nine years later; they referred to themselves as a married couple, often signing cowritten letters as "Gertrude and Alice Stein." Toklas was the ostensible subject of Stein's most popular and accessible book, *The Autobiography of Alice B. Toklas* (1933).

Stein's interest in Cubism's visual layering of multiple perspectives led her to attempt similar experiments in her prose writing. One of her most respected works is *Three Lives* (1909), the first of her published books. The narrative describes the life histories of three working-class American women, focusing on mundane details and employing frequent repetition and an elementary vocabulary. Among the most famous of her other works are *Tender Buttons* (1914) and *Composition as Explanation* (1926), a lecture on her view of writing.

Although her often abstruse work has

never enjoyed a wide reading audience, Stein is recognized as one of the central theorists and practitioners of literary modernism. Her most famous line, "A rose is a rose is a rose is a rose," is typical of her style: hypnotic, repetitious, recondite, and slightly irreverent in its odd use of one of the central symbols of the Western literary tradition.

Stein remained in Paris through the German occupation during World War II and died there shortly after.

Stendhal (1783–1842)

French soldier, diplomat, and novelist. Stendhal was the pen name of Marie-Henri Beyle, who was born into the upper bourgeoisie of Grenoble; seven years later his mother died, leaving him in the care of a father and an aunt who were lovers and who, as Stendhal wrote in an autobiographical account, "poisoned my childhood." He claimed that the mere mention of Grenoble gave him indigestion throughout his life. Planning on becoming an engineer, at sixteen he moved to Paris to study mathematics, but instead embarked on a peripatetic career as a diplomat, soldier, and writer.

From 1800 to 1802 he served as a second lieutenant in Italy, returning to Paris in hopes of becoming a comic playwright. Unsuccessful in that area, and in the next, the food import business, he obtained a series of governmental posts through the devices of a relative, culminating in the office of state auditor in the War Bureau, and, in 1810, inspector of the crown buildings. In 1812 he traveled with Napoleon's army to Moscow as commissioner of war supplies on that ill-fated campaign, and after the fall of Napoleon and the restoration of the Bourbon monarchy in 1814, he settled in Milan and wrote a series of largely plagiarized books on music and art. In 1821, under suspicion by the Austrian authorities for radical activities, he returned to Paris and became a successful journalist and critic. But after the revolution of July 1830, he was

sent once again to Italy as a consul, a position he held until his death.

Stendhal's work reflects the varied historical and geographical settings of his life, its idealization of Napoleon as the energetic soldier-hero, its interest in the conflict between liberal ideals and bourgeois realities, and its obsession with romantic egoism. Though he often styled himself an intellectual aristocrat who hated bureaucracy, his plots illustrate the clash of class attitudes in a revolutionary period. He frequently described these conflicts as "boredom" versus "energy," often representing them in the same fictional character. His most noted works are the novels *Le Rouge et le noir* (1830; *The Red and the Black*) and *La Chartreuse de Parme* (1839; *The Charterhouse of Parma*); the unfinished *Lucien Leuwen* (1834–35); and the autobiographical pieces *Souvenirs d'égotisme* (1832; *Memoirs of an Egotist*) and *La Vie de Henri Brulard* (1834–35; *The Life of Henri Brulard*). Among his critical works are *Racine et Shakespeare* (1823; *Racine and Shakespeare*) and *De l'amour* (1822; *On Love*). Stendhal is credited with playing a major role in the development of the modern novel, combining elements of the Romantic and realistic movements and pointing the way toward the psychological novel with his complex analyses of character.

Storni, Alfonsina (1892–1938)

Argentinean poet. Storni was born in Switzerland and moved with her parents to San Juan, Argentina, in 1896. In 1907, when she was fourteen, she joined a theater troupe and toured with them for a year. Two years later, she began studies at the Escuela Normal de Coronda, where she was certified as a teacher, and in 1912 she began her teaching career in Rosario. This was the same year in which her son, Alejandro Alfonso, was born as a result of an affair with a married man. Moving to Buenos Aires, Storni was forced to leave the father out of concern for his reputation. There she immersed herself in the literary world, publishing several articles of criticism, at first under the pseudonym of Tao-Lao and then under her own name. Her first collection of poetry, *La inquietud del rosal* (1916; *The Restless Rose Garden*), brought her some recognition in Buenos Aires literary circles. She judged this first work as overcharged with romantic sweetness, but noted that it contained the seeds of her later work, in which she assumed the position of a female critic confronting a patriarchal state. Her major themes concerned women and their lives: their subservient position in a patriarchal society; the difficulty, if not impossibility, of love between men and women when women are subjugated; and the need for more personal freedom and independence. Between 1918 and 1920 she published three books of verse, including *Irremediablemente* (1919; *Without Remedy*). Her later books, described by some of her critics as both tortured intellectual poetry and her best work, include *Ocre* (1925), *Mundo de siete pozos* (1934; *World of Seven Wells*), and *Mascarilla y trébol* (1938; *Mask and Trefoil*). She also wrote several plays, among them *El amo del mundo* (1927; *Master of the World*).

In 1935 Storni had a radical mastectomy that took a heavy psychological toll. For some time she had been suffering periods of depression, and, fearing that the cancer had spread to her lungs, she committed suicide in Mar del Plata by walking into the sea. Storni has been both admired and criticized for the candor with which she discussed and represented her own sexuality and related problems.

Strauss, Richard (1864–1949)

German composer. A greatly underrated force in the history of twentieth-century music, Strauss acquired an equal mastery of orchestral and operatic idioms. He was the son of a virtuoso horn player in the Munich court orchestra and a wealthy brewery heiress. A musical prodigy, Strauss had his first symphony performed in public by the age of eighteen. He left university after only a year to become assistant conductor in Meiningen, under the famous conductor Hans von Bülow. Through von Bülow and the composer Alexander Ritter, he discovered new and more radical influences: Wagner most of all, but also Berlioz and Liszt.

Following the example of Liszt's "symphonic poems," Strauss began composing colorful, vibrant orchestral pieces in the late 1880s and early 1890s, among them *Aus Italien* (1886; *From Italy*); *Don Juan* (1888), *Tod und Verklärung* (1888–89; *Death and Transfiguration*), and *Till Eulenspiegels lustige Streiche* (1894–95; *Till Eulenspiegel's Merry Pranks*). He handled the orchestra with freewheeling brilliance and wit; he searched for fresh combinations of chords, leading to the sharp dissonances of *Also sprach Zarathustra* (1896; *Thus Spake Zarathustra*), inspired by the philosophy of Nietzsche, and *Don Quixote* (1896–97). He also conducted at the Munich Opera and in 1898 took up a demanding post at the Berlin Royal Opera.

Strauss's later orchestral pieces became more uncertain in construction; *Ein Heldenleben* (1897–98; *A Hero's Life*) and *Symphonia Domestica* (1902–1903; *Domestic Symphony*), while never dull, show a diminishment in inspiration. But his adventuresome songs from this period, some with orchestral accompaniment, show an increase of dramatic skill, which blossomed gloriously in his third (but first successful) opera, *Salome* (1905). Strauss responded to the play of the same name by Irish writer Oscar Wilde with cascades of shimmering, shattering sound; single-handedly he ushered in the expressionist style in music, pioneering effects of dissonance and orchestral sonority which were copied by the Austrian composer Arnold

Schoenberg and the Russian composer Igor Stravinsky. *Electra* (1909), based on a play by Austrian playwright Hugo von Hofmannsthal, consolidated his modernist approach.

But Strauss baffled and also delighted his audiences with his next opera, *Der Rosenkavalier* (1911; *The Cavalier of the Rose*), once again from a Hofmannsthal text. This proved to be an exercise in sophisticated nostalgia, imitating Mozart and Johann Strauss (no relation); later Hofmannsthal operas, such as *Ariadne auf Naxos* (1912; *Ariadne on Naxos*) and *Die Frau ohne Schatten* (1919; *The Woman Without a Shadow*), moved in a similar vein, although Strauss's individuality always shone through. Moving to Vienna, Strauss composed operas through the 1920s and 1930s but lapsed into the most inconsistent period of his career.

The tragedy of his life was his collaboration with the Nazi regime after Adolf Hitler came to power in 1933. He accepted a high-profile post but resigned in 1935 when he was criticized for working with the Austrian Jewish writer Stefan Zweig. He suffered neglect during the war years but continued to write music. In his last years, Strauss experienced an astonishing rebirth, closing his career with richly lyrical and Romantic works like *Capriccio* (1942) and the *Vier letz Lieder* (1948; *Four Last Songs*). His strange career still inspires debate, but his music has never lost a large and appreciative audience.

Stravinsky, Igor (1882–1971)

Russian composer. Born near St. Petersburg, Stravinsky would often listen to his father, Fyodor Ignatyevich, a well-known opera singer, rehearse. He took assorted music lessons as a child, but his parents eventually sent him to St. Petersburg University to study law and philosophy.

A chance meeting with the composer Nikolai Rimsky-Korsakov, who eventu-

ally became his musical mentor, proved to be a turning point in his musical career. Stravinsky began studying privately with Rimsky-Korsakov in 1903 and continued for approximately three years. Rimsky-Korsakov had many of Stravinsky's compositions performed in St. Petersburg, and one of Stravinsky's pieces, *Feu d'artifice* (1908; *Fireworks*), was composed for Rimsky-Korsakov's daughter's wedding. After graduating from the university in 1905, Stravinsky married his first cousin, Catherine Nossenko, in 1906. She bore him a son, Fyodor, in 1907 and a daughter, Ludmila, the following year. The 1909 performance of *Scherzo fantastique* (1907–1908) impressed the director of the Ballets Russes, Sergei Diaghilev. They began collaborating soon after on various ballet scores and operas with Russian themes. The partnership produced such works as *Zhar Ptitsa* (1910; *The Firebird*), *Petrushka* (1911), and *Le Sacre du printemps* (1911–13; *The Rite of Spring*), all performed by the Ballets Russes in Paris. The innovative *Rite of Spring* had a very controversial reception, with its explosive score and unconventional rhythms. This work also integrated the piano as a major instrument in Stravinsky's symphonies. Many critics steeped in traditional musical theory could not grasp his message, but progressive musicians heralded *The Rite of Spring* as the beginning of a new musical era.

Stravinsky spent most of his time outside Russia between 1910 and 1914. After living in Switzerland and then France, he composed works that absorbed Neoclassical qualities, an austere and tragic fervor, as heard in *Oedipus Rex* (1927) and *Symphonie de psaumes* (1930; *Symphony of Psalms*). Stravinsky renewed his ties with Diaghilev and wrote an additional ballet score, *Pulcinella* (1920), with him.

In 1939, following the untimely deaths of his wife, mother, and eldest daughter, Stravinsky left Europe and moved to the

United States, becoming an American citizen in 1945. He married the artist Vera de Bosset and settled in Hollywood, where he resided for over twenty-five years. During 1948–51 Stravinsky produced *Die Laufbann des Wüstlings* (*The Rake's Progress*), an opera based on the engravings of Englishman William Hogarth (1697–1764). In the following years, Stravinsky found himself working in a variety of musical genres, ranging from polkas to circus music and even music for a swing band. Notable among his last works were *Variations* (1964) and *The Requiem Canticles* (1966).

Strindberg, [Johan] August (1849–1912)

Swedish dramatist, novelist, and short-story writer. Strindberg was the son of a former waitress and an often bankrupt father, and his childhood was marred by unhappiness and poverty. Working variously as a tutor and a journalist, Strindberg began writing plays for the Stockholm stage in 1870. His creative breakthrough came with *Mäster Olof* (1872; *Master Olof*), which was first written in prose, then for the stage in 1881. Strindberg's satirical novel *Röda rummet* (1879; *The Red Room*) propelled him to fame and is considered to be the first example of Swedish realism. However, with the publication of the story collection *Giftas* (1884; 1886; *Getting Married*), Strindberg's fame turned to notoriety and he was forced to stand trial for its criticism of sexual mores. Though he was acquitted, this experience proved damaging for the artist; not only did it contribute to the demise of his first marriage in 1891, but it instigated feelings of persecution that would increasingly plague Strindberg. His difficulty in getting his plays produced, such as *Fröken Julie* (1888; *Miss Julie*) and *Fordringsagare* (1889; *The Creditors*), only contributed to these feelings, and following a second, disastrous marriage, Strindberg suffered what he called an "Inferno" period, in which he bordered on madness.

During this period he became obsessed with alchemy and the occult, and later recorded this crisis in the autobiographical *Inferno* (1897) and in mystical, allegorical plays such as *Ett drömspel* (1901; *A Dream Play*). The dream-like, surreal dramas written during this recovery phase are often considered to be Strindberg's most brilliant and important contributions to the development of European theater. As Strindberg's emotional health improved, he returned to a more realistic style and wrote a cycle of historical plays, including *Folkungasagan* (1899; *The Saga of the Folkungs*) and *Erik XIV* (1899).

In 1907, together with August Falck, Strindberg established the Intimate Theater in Stockholm, for which he wrote several plays whose success was mixed. Strindberg's collected works—plays, fairy tales, poems, short stories, autobiographical writings, and novels—fill fifty-five volumes and make up a formidable chapter in Scandinavian literature.

Sturges, Preston (1898–1959)

American film director. Preston Sturges was born Edmund P. Biden into a wealthy family and was educated in French, German, and Swiss schools as well as American private schools. Beginning at sixteen, he managed his mother's cosmetics business, progressing to Wall Street and later the air corps; in 1919 he invented kiss-proof lipstick, and until 1927 had varied success as an inventor. During his convalescence following an appendectomy in 1927, Sturges wrote his first few plays. His second play, *Strictly Dishonorable*, launched his career as a playwright, and was the most popular comedy in 1929–30. He achieved success on Broadway with *The Guinea Pig* (1929), and in 1932 he moved to Hollywood to work on screenplays. In 1940 Sturges persuaded Paramount Pictures to allow him to direct his script *The Great McGinty*, the unexpected success of which launched his career as a director. Sturges had a meteoric but brief career as screenwriter and director of several satiric comedies of the early 1940s. *The Lady Eve* (1941), *Sullivan's Travels* (1941), *The Palm Beach Story* (1942), and *The Miracle of Morgan's Creek* (1944) are among his most successful films. He is noted for his mastery of the narrative form, and was among the first to use voice-overs as a narrative device. In 1944 Sturges left Paramount to direct for Howard Hughes, a move that proved disastrous: his standing as a director declined after his next films were unfavorably reviewed, and he made only two more films after *Unfaithfully Yours* in 1948. He then moved to France in self-imposed exile, where he directed his last film, *Les Carnets du Major Thomson* (1957; *The French, They Are a Funny Race*), also unsuccessful. Sturges is remembered for his narrative inventiveness, for his contemporary and sophisticated treatment of sexual relations on screen, and for his development of wide-screen photography.

Su Dongpo (1037–1101)

Chinese poet of the Song dynasty (960–1279). When he was young, Su Dongpo, also called Su Shi, traveled to the capital in search of a government post. When he took the official examinations, his chief examiner, Ouyang Xiu, a famous poet, immediately recognized the young man's talent and potential. Su became an official and eventually a member of the Han-lin Academy (a high-level intellectual institution in imperial China). Though he wrote brilliant poems and carefully observed Confucian rituals, his ambition and literary passion proved to be the downfall of his career. Because of political factionalism in the court, Su was arrested and imprisoned, then banished. He died on his return from exile.

A leader in contemporary literary circles, Su was driven to create new poetry forms and was an early promoter of painting as an art form of the literate.

His epic style was unique and influential. His works include *Dongpo quanji* (*A Complete Collection of Dongpo's Poems*).

Sufism

Islamic mystical movement. The word "Sufism" derives from *suf*, meaning "wool" in Arabic, a reference to the woollen gowns worn by the earliest Muslim ascetics. The roots of Sufism lie in an ascetic movement among certain Muslims who felt the need to go beyond the doctrinal requirements of Islam. Over time, this ascetic movement developed a distinct mystical philosophy. Sufism does not constitute a sect in and of itself, but rather is a movement within the dominant Islamic sects of Sunnism and Twelver Shi'ism.

By the ninth century, Sufi schools of thought had begun to form around charismatic figures. Over time, these schools began to blend with the system of trade guilds, the end result being the emergence of a number of Sufi orders called *tarigas*. These orders traditionally took their names from real or imagined founder figures and were organized in a hierarchy of adherents. These adherents joined the order through a process of initiation in which they formally acknowledged the spiritual authority of the order's leader, who is called a *shaykh* or *pir*. With the disintegration of central authority in the Islamic world in the thirteenth century, the Sufi orders filled the vacuum in religious and social organization.

Sufism can be divided into two forms, the first philosophical and elitist and the second cultic and popular. Intellectual and philosophical Sufism devotes primary attention to the systematic explanation of theological and mystical concepts, whereas popular Sufism emphasizes saint and shrine cults, and the ability of ordinary, poorly educated human beings to experience God directly in their lives. The lack of widespread education in most Islamic lands has caused popular orders to stress the charismatic leadership of individuals at the expense of the unifying tradition and institutions of the order. This division can also be characterized as one between sober and ecstatic mysticism: sober orders stress the philosophical and conceptual dimensions of Sufism, while the ecstatic ones emphasize collective ritual and the religious life associated with local saints and shrines.

Despite their differences, both the popular and elitist forms of Sufism have played a decisive role in the formation of literary expression and social institutions in Islamic civilization. This is particularly true in the Turco-Persian lands, where much of the courtly and folk poetry deals with mystical themes. Schools of music and the fine arts (painting and calligraphy) were also identified with Sufi orders for much of their development.

Although the term specifically refers to the major mystical movement in Islam, it is often applied in a general sense to any Islamic religious belief or practice in the Sunnî world which differs from legalism and orthodoxy. The major surviving Sufi orders include the Naqshbandi, Suhrawardi, Chishti, Shazili, Zahabi, Bektashi, and Mevlevi *tariqas* (road, path, way).

Suharto (1921–)

Indonesian military general and president. Suharto's interest in the military began early in his life. He first served in the Dutch colonial army, then, after the Japanese conquest in 1942, with the Japanese-sponsored defense corps. With the defeat of Japan in the Second World War, Suharto distinguished himself in the anticolonialist uprisings against the Dutch, and steadily progressed through the military ranks after Indonesia became an independent republic in 1950. In 1963 Suharto became major general and head of the Indonesian army. In

1965, after an attempted coup d'état by the Indonesian Communist Party (PKI), Suharto quelled the rebellion and in the following months directed a purge of Communists and leftists. This tactic was followed by the massacres of Communists throughout the country carried out by self-appointed vigilantes throughout the land. As President Sukarno's (1949–67) complicity in the coup attempt became clear, Suharto was elected the second president of Indonesia in 1968, and instituted an economic plan called the New Order, which encouraged Western investment. In 1975 Indonesia invaded East Timor, killing approximately 200,000 of its 700,000 residents.

Despite the conservative and authoritarian nature of his government, Suharto has been reelected five additional times (1971, 1978, 1983, 1988, and 1993).

Sukarno (1901–1970)

First Indonesian president. A member of the *priyayi* class, the Javanese elite who served in the Dutch colonial bureaucracy, Sukarno received his higher education in the Netherlands. With other contemporaries from the same background, he became involved as a young man in an early version of Indonesian nationalism. In the late 1920s the movement had fragmented along religious and ideological lines, and Sukarno assisted in the formation of a secular nationalist organization called the Indonesian Nationalist Party (PNI). Sukarno's political platform from this time forward asserted that the diverse Indonesian communities should submerge their differences and unite in the struggle for Indonesian independence from colonial rule. Seeking a mass base, Sukarno appealed to the "little people" of Indonesia, particularly the Javanese *abangan*, whose Islamic practice incorporated pre-Islamic and precolonial religious and cultural elements. Sukarno claimed that these elements reflected an egalitarian age before colonial discord that could be reclaimed after the expulsion of the Dutch.

In 1945, after the destabilizing effects of the Second World War, Sukarno proclaimed a rudimentary Indonesian state. The next five years were turbulent, with Sukarno at the head of a populist military opposition and the Dutch attempting to regain control of the government. The Dutch finally surrendered sovereignty formally in 1949, and Sukarno accepted the presidential role in the new parliamentary democracy. Consensus under his leadership was short-lived. Conflicts between the military, the Communist Party, and Sukarno's loyalists grew increasingly fractious. The military was able to wrest control in the most intense period of conflict in 1965, and Sukarno was formally deposed in 1967. Versions of the military regime that ousted Sukarno have remained in power since then.

Sukhothai

Ancient Thai state. This ruling state was founded around 1220 in Thailand's Central Plain. Its third ruler, Ramkhamhaeng, left the first example of writing in the Thai language, an inscription on stone describing a prosperous state ruled by a benevolent paternal monarch, a father-king protecting his people and teaching them the benefits of Buddhism. This stands in contrast to the "god-king" of Angkor, Sukhothai's rival power. Sukhothai culture consistently emphasized this humane Buddhist ideal, and Ramkhamhaeng literally shared his throne with Buddhist monks, allowing them to preach from it weekly. The cultural identity and unity of the Sukhothai people drew heavily from this religious basis. Sculpture focused on images of the Buddha, representing him with a distinctively Thai physiognomy in a style marked by the flowing, attenuated grace of its lines. Bronze sculpture and ceramics, influenced by Chinese artisans, were areas of special achievement

for Sukhothai. Indeed, they borrowed widely from others, including Buddhist literatures from India and writing from Cambodia. The Sukhothai period lasted approximately 160 years, falling under the domination of the Ayutthaya state in 1378. It remains a distinguishing classical epoch in Thai history.

Suleyman the Magnificent (1494–1566)

Ruler of the Ottoman empire. Generally considered to be the greatest sultan of the empire, Suleyman ruled from 1520 until his death. Under his aegis, the Ottoman state expanded its frontiers, more than doubling its territories. Spending more than ten years of his life on thirteen major campaigns, Suleyman continued the momentum of the conquests initiated by Mehmed II (sultan 1451–81), who captured Constantinople in 1453. Given further impetus by his father, Selim I (sultan 1512–20), who crushed the Shi'ites in Persia, Suleyman defeated the Mamelukes in Egypt and gained control of Mecca and Medina, Islam's holy cities. When he died in 1566, Suleyman left behind an empire whose lands encompassed what is today all or part of the following countries: Turkey, Iran, Greece, Russia, Iraq, Syria, Kuwait, Jordan, Israel, Lebanon, Libya, Tunisia, Algeria, Morocco, Austria, Romania, Hungary, Yugoslavia, Bulgaria, Egypt, Saudi Arabia, and Albania.

Europeans referred to Suleyman as "the Grand Turk" and often as "the Magnificent." To the Turks, since the sixteenth century he has been known as "Kanuni," meaning "Lawgiver" or "Legislator" in recognition of the codes he promulgated and for his emphasis on justice, which he personally dispensed on innumerable occasions.

Although Ottoman sultans normally did not "officially" marry their women, Suleyman insisted on having wedding rites performed when he decided to take as a bride Hurrem (née Roxelana), a Christian slave, possibly from the Balkans or Russia. He named her "empress" and remained loyal to her for twenty-five years until her death. She wielded a great deal of influence on Suleyman and his government. She was instrumental in the killing of the royal heir Prince Mustafa, Suleyman's son from an earlier marriage, and orchestrated the execution of many palace intrigues. After her death, her own two sons, Bayezid and Selim, engaged in a bloody succession strife while Suleyman was still alive, which weakened the empire. On Suleyman's orders, Bayezid and his four sons were assassinated.

Under Suleyman's lavish patronage, arts and architecture flourished. Suleyman himself was an accomplished goldsmith and wrote close to 3,000 well-crafted poems. His royal chief architect, Sinan, created at least 380 major and small-scale edifices in many parts of the empire during a tenure that lasted half a century. Among his masterpieces, the Süleymaniye (the Mosque of Suleyman) in Istanbul stands out as a sublime and exceptionally functional structure.

At the Topkapi Palace in Istanbul, Suleyman's court maintained an art studio where about thirty artists-in-residence, half of them Turkish and half European, produced miniature paintings as well as oil paintings. The art of calligraphy reached new heights thanks to the virtuosity of Ahmed Karahisari and other masters. The Suleymanic Age was also notable for its exquisite decorative arts, fabric designs, porcelain and tile work, and book illuminations. It was also a Golden Age of classical poetry, boasting lyrics, panegyrics, verse romances, and elegies by such masters as Fuzuli, Baki, and Hayali.

For all its wealth, power, and resplendence, the Age of Suleyman is considered by some Ottoman historians to have sown the seeds of decline, because Suleyman gave some Europeans, especially the French, certain rights and privileges that would harm the empire in later periods.

Sumerians

Ancient Mesopotamian civilization. The Sumerians formed one of the earliest known civilizations, situated in the southernmost part of Mesopotamia between the Tigris and Euphrates rivers. Sumeria would later become known as Babylonia (the southern part of modern-day Iraq). The Sumerians are probably best known for their cuneiform script. Deciphered in the mid nineteenth century, cuneiform writing has provided modern insight into Sumerian mythology, which strongly influenced that of the Assyrians, Babylonians, and other peoples of the Ancient Near East.

By the mid fourth millennium B.C.E., the Sumerians had developed an advanced urban society. In the third millennium B.C.E, ancient songs describe at least twelve separate city-states: Kish, Uruk, Ur, Sippar, Akshak, Larak, Nippur, Adab, Umma, Lagash, Bad-tibira, and Larsa. Each of these comprised a walled city and the immediately surrounding villages and land. Each city also worshiped its own deity.

Struggles among the city-states left the Sumerians vulnerable to attacks from outside, first from the Elamites (c. 2600–2550 B.C.E.), and then from Akkadians under the leadership of Sargon (c. 2334–2279 B.C.E.). After Sargon's reign and a devastating invasion by the Gutians, the various city-states became independent. The third dynasty of Ur was the highest point in the last period of Sumerian civilization; Ur's king, Ur-Nammu, published the earliest known legal code in Mesopotamia. After 1900 B.C.E., the Amorites conquered all of Mesopotamia and the Sumerians gradually lost their separate identity.

sumo wrestling

Japanese sport. Sumo wrestling, 2,000 years old, is the national sport of Japan. It developed into its modern form during the seventeenth century, when it became a professional sport. Wrestlers compete in six tournaments a year, held in four different cities. These tournaments involve matches between two wrestlers at a time, who meet in a ring of packed clay almost fifteen feet in diameter. After an elaborate entrance ceremony and purification rites, the wrestlers charge at each other furiously, in an attempt either to move the opponent outside the ring or to force the opponent to touch the surface of the ring with something other than the soles of his feet. Because the length of a match is often only a few seconds, the careful attention of both the referee in the ring and the judges at floor level is often necessary to determine the winner. The Japanese Sumo Association lists seventy winning techniques, forty-eight of which are "classic," from which each sumo wrestler usually selects between six to eight, making two or three his specialties. Most of the winning techniques involve grasping the opponent's belt, or *mawashi*, and preventing him from grasping one's own belt. The approximately seven hundred sumo wrestlers in Japan are ranked on a graded list, or *banzuke*, based solely on their match performances. Potential wrestlers, who will eventually weigh between 250 and 500 pounds, are traditionally selected from among poor, rural families and brought up in the rigidly hierarchical sumo stable system. In this insular community, they learn the codes and values of the sumo wrestler, as well as the techniques of balance and agility so crucial to a sumo wrestler's success.

Sun Dance

Plains Indian dance ceremony. Performed to solicit supernatural assistance, the Sun Dance reached its peak in popularity as a sacred dance in the mid-1800s.

The legends surrounding the origin of the Sun Dance vary from tribe to tribe. According to the Siksika, a young man journeyed to the sun, where he received great power and the dance. Other tribes claim that the Sun Dance was given to their forefathers through visions. The purpose and ritual of the Sun Dance also vary from group to group. The Shoshone use it for purification and curing, while the Southern Ute emphasize dreaming. The Cheyenne consider it to be a world renewal ceremony, while the Crow ask for personal power. The Sioux use it to gain blessings for hunts.

The dance first appeared in the early part of the eighteenth century among the Arapahoes and Cheyennes. Other sources credit Yellow Hand (Ohamagwaya), a Comanche who learned Christian concepts from the Spaniards, with the introduction of the modified Sun Dance, with Christian undertones, in the early 1800s. Still another version spread in 1941.

The Sun Dance was traditionally held in midsummer, usually when many bands of a tribe met. The ritual lasted four days, during which the participants fasted from food and sometimes water. The dance took place in a ceremonial lodge, with a sacred tree at the center, a small buffalo-skin altar, and stalls along the western walls for dancers to rest. Facing the tree, the dancers took short, shuffling steps from their stall and back again, hour after hour. Often, they played eagle-bone whistles or accompanied the dance with drums and singing. At the end of the fourth day, the dancers sometimes engaged in self-inflicted physical torture, in which skewers were forcibly pulled through the flesh on the chest or the back. The scars from this sacred dance were worn with great pride by the dancers and were considered to be signs of bravery and fortitude. By 1904 this practice was outlawed by the U.S. government. The dance today usually omits this "piercing of the flesh," although some tribes may allow it if the participant has vowed to do it.

Sundiata Keita (d. 1255 C.E.)

African emperor. Known as the "African Alexander," Sundiata was the son of

King Maghan Kon Fatta, who ruled Mali at the beginning of the thirteenth century. Sundiata spent much of his youth crippled, earning for his mother the mockery of the king's other wives. Legend has it, however, that as soon as he learned to walk, he emerged as a leader of his peers. Persecuted by his brother, who succeeded his father on the throne, Sundiata, his mother, and another brother fled to Ghana, where they settled at the court of the king of Mema, Mansa Tun Kapa. When the Malinke people challenged his brother's rule, forcing him to flee the throne, the Malinke sent Mandingo messengers to Ghana to solicit Sundiata's aid. The king of Ghana gave him troops, and Sundiata returned to Mande. Sundiata defeated Sumaguru, king of the Soso, at the historic battle of Kirina in 1235, and founded the Mandingo empire. Sundiata was converted to Islam and became protector of Muslims. He restored relations with other African and Arab traders, and established the constitution of Mali. Between 1230 and 1255 he established civic, legal, and cultural institutions that became the foundation of subsequent civilizations in western Sudan for the next few centuries. Sundiata's fame spread far and wide, through trade with the Arab world, through the heroic saga *Sundiata fassa*, composed by his court griot, Balla Fasseke, and through the chronicles of Ibn Battūtah and Ibn Khaldûn. Several legends describe the great king's untimely death. According to one account he was accidentally drowned, while another story claims that he died from a stray arrow during a ceremony. The *Sundiata fassa* is still recited in West Africa today.

Sunnî

Islamic sect. From the Arabic word *sunnah*, literally "path," which referred in pre-Islamic times to accepted tribal custom, this term came to denote the exemplary behavior of the Prophet Muhammad. Muhammad, beyond being a conveyer of the divine message, is also traditionally accepted in Islam as a model of virtuous living. For many Muslims today, emulating the conduct of the Prophet is an important expression of piety. Six standard collections of reports of the Prophet's words and deeds have come to be the principal references of such information. In the form of these collected reports, the *sunnah* constitutes, next to the Qur'ân, the most revered body of material used in establishing Islamic legal rulings.

"People of the Sunnah," or Sunnîs, is the appellation that came to denote the majority sect of the Muslim community, which had split into two major groups in the early struggles over the leadership of the community following the death of the Prophet in 632. The Sunnîs recognized as legitimate the reign of the first three caliphs, Abû Bakr, 'Umar, and 'Uthman, while Shi'ites recognized an alternate succession of leaders. Since Sunnîs far outnumbered other sect memberships, their claim to represent Islamic orthodoxy has come to be accepted even outside the Islamic world. Shi'ites are their most numerous and influential rivals.

In the early period, allegiance to a line of leaders in the community determined orthodoxy for both groups. Beginning in the ninth century, however, the Sunnî caliphs gradually lost effective religious and political authority, and the office itself was eventually abolished. In Sunnî Islam, religious authority and the interpretation of the Sacred Law became the prerogative of recognized corporations or guilds of legal scholars. Acceptance of the authority of the community of legal scholars is the primary determinant of Sunnî orthodoxy today.

Sun-tzu ting fa

Influential Chinese book of military strategy written by Sunzi (or Sunwu). Born into a family of military officers,

Sunzi became a successful commander and expert in strategy. His book, *Sun-tzu ting fa* (or *Sun-zi Bing fa; The Art of War*), probably written during the Warring States period (403–221 B.C.E.) and originally comprising eighty-two chapters in nine volumes, was eventually condensed into thirteen chapters and covered such topics as strategic assessment, offensive strategy, and the use of spies. Important to generals in China's history, the *Sun-tzu ting fa* has been internationally influential as well, translated into many languages, including English, Japanese, German, French, Czech, and Russian. As a study of the anatomy of organizations in conflict, the *Sun-tzu ting fa* details the factors leading to victory and defeat. Its basic thesis is that it is best to try to defeat the enemy through wisdom rather than through force alone.

Many contemporary students see the successes of postwar Japan as an illustration of Sunzi's dictum, "To win without fighting is best." Instead of trying to overwhelm opponents directly, Sunzi recommends wearing them down by flight, fostering disharmony within their ranks, and manipulating their anger and pride against them. The book stresses the relationship between war and politics, economics, diplomacy, astronomy, and geography. According to Sunzi, a commander is required to judge the hour, assess the situation, and anticipate the enemy's decisions before launching an attack. Also emphasized is the importance of flexibility in troop deployment, based on the position and conditions of your enemy, yourself, and the topography.

Sun Yat-sen (1866–1925)
Chinese revolutionary and leader. Born in Guangdong (Canton) province, Sun Yat-sen (or Sun Zhong-shan) was the son of poor farmers. When he was twelve years old, he followed his brother to Hawaii, where he attended a British missionary school in Honolulu, graduating in 1882, and an American school, Oahu College, for another year. After returning to China for a short time, he moved to Hong Kong, where he studied at the Diocesan Home and then the Government Central School, married the woman chosen by his parents, Lu Mu-chen, and was baptized by a missionary. He entered the Canton Hospital Medical School in 1886 and transferred to the College of Medicine in Hong Kong, graduating as a physician in 1892. In 1894 he returned to Hawaii and founded the Xing Zhong Hai (Revive China Society) among the local Chinese. After China's defeat in the Sino-Japanese War (1894–95), Sun returned to Hong Kong in 1895 and, together with other secret societies, plotted a revolution in Canton that failed. He spent the next sixteen years abroad, seeking support for his revolutionary plans. He became internationally famous when the Chinese government had him arrested briefly in London, an incident that received much press coverage. Thereafter, he spent much of his time in Japan among the expatriate Chinese community. In 1905 he was elected head of the Tong Meng Hui (Revolutionary Alliance) in Tokyo, a position that helped broaden his support among China's educated class. In the same year, he also outlined his Three Principles of the People: nationalism, democracy, and livelihood. As political unrest spread in China, Sun orchestrated at least ten uprisings (all of which failed) before the successful revolution of 1911.

In October 1911, dissidents in Wuchang overthrew the provincial government, provoking similar revolts throughout the country. Learning of the Wuchang revolution from newspaper accounts while traveling in the United States, Sun proceeded to London and Paris to promote diplomatic relations for a new regime. Arriving in China in December, he was elected provisional president of the Republic of China, and assumed office on January 1, 1912, at Nanjing. His power was weak, however, and he made a deal to resign the day after the emperor abdicated (February 12, 1912), turning his new office over on February 13 to the imperial military leader Yuan Shi-kai in order to avert civil war. He was given the title of director general of railway development and the Tong Meng Hui was allowed to become an official political party, now called the Guomindang, or Nationalist Party, with Song Jaio-ren as its titular head. But this arrangement was short-lived, as Song was assassinated in 1913 and Yuan named himself emperor. After a failed attempt at a second revolution, Sun fled to Japan and reorganized his party, renaming it the Zhong-hua Guomindang (Chinese Revolutionary Party).

He returned to the mainland shortly before Yuan's death in 1916 with the intent of establishing his own revolutionary program, but once more had to contend with factional struggles and provincial warlords. Though he set up a rival regime at Canton with himself as head in opposition to the new premier, Duan Qi-rui, in Beijing, he was forced to withdraw to Shanghai for two years after losing the support of local military leaders. Returning to Guangdong, he again lobbied the warlords for backing, and in February 1923 he once more installed himself in an opposition regime with the support of the Soviet Union. Under the direction of the Soviet Mikhail Borodin, the Guomindang was restructured and allied with the Chinese Communist Party. Sun died of cancer in Beijing; he is referred to by the Chinese Communists as the "pioneer of the revolution."

Sunthon Phu (1787–1855)

Thai poet. Considered to be one of the greatest poets of Thai literature, Sunthon Phu was patronized by four kings and held in high esteem by the peasantry, whose concerns and daily lives he attended to more closely than any other poet. During an illustrious but rocky career at court, he was ennobled by Rama II, and later promoted by Mongkut, but was banished because of his tendency to overindulge in wine and women. His colloquial poetry spoke to the needs of the common people, and is still widely read. The romantic epic *Phra Apahi Mani* is often held to be his masterpiece.

Swahili

Bantu language. Swahili is the official language of Tanzania and Kenya, and is spoken as a lingua franca throughout most of East Africa. The language is heavily influenced by Arabic, a result of the long-standing trading relationships in the region. The main dialects of Swahili, or Kiswahili, as it is also called, are Kiunguja, Kimvita, and Kiamu.

Swahili has a long tradition of literary production, and poetry has been written in Swahili since at least the middle of the seventeenth century. It drew on Arabic, Persian, and Urdu literary sources. Though Swahili was originally written in Arabic script, Latin script became more popular in the mid nineteenth century and has since become standard. The oldest surviving epic is the *Hamziya*, which was written by Sayyid Aidarusi in Arabic script in the old Kingozi dialect in 1749. Bwana Muku II, the ruler of the island of Pate, off the east coast of current-day Kenya, commissioned the poem. Mwana Kupona binti Msham was a well-known poet of the nineteenth century who wrote *tenzi*, didactic poems that were traditionally concerned with Islamic religious subjects and public commentary. This form is still used by contemporary poets such as Abdilatif Abdalla. Muyaka bin Haji al-Ghassaniy (1776–1840) wrote poetic commentaries of urban life. Perhaps the most famous contemporary Swahili author is Shaaban Robert, a Tanzanian known for his poetry, children's literature, essays, and novels. Many works of Western authors have been translated into Swahili, such as the well-known renderings of William Shakespeare's plays by Julius Nyerere.

Swift, Jonathan (1667–1745)

English author and satirist. Considered to be one of the greatest satirists of the English language, Swift was born in Ireland during a period of great political instability. He was educated at the finest schools in Ireland, but the revolution of 1688 interrupted Swift's work on his master's degree at Trinity College. He fled to England, where he was ordained in the Anglican Church and began his literary endeavors. Swift's earliest writing, a series of Pindaric odes, was judged harshly by his contemporaries and Swift turned to another form of literary expression, the satire. His first major work, *The Tale of a Tub*, published anonymously in 1704, mocked the religious practice of the period. In 1710 Swift, a Whig by birth and education, was recruited by the satirical poet (and future novelist) Daniel Defoe for the Tory Party in England and became the chief political writer for the party. His reward for political service was the position of dean of St. Patrick's Cathedral in Dublin. With the death of Queen Anne in 1714, the Tory Party was extinguished in England, and with it, Swift's career.

In Dublin, Swift produced a number of pamphlets detailing the bitter reality of the Irish situation under English rule. Swift also began work on his most famous satire, *Gulliver's Travels*, published in 1726. The book, a parody of the travel literature fashionable in this period, chronicles the journey of Gulliver to imaginary, remote societies such as Laputa and Brobdingnag, where his experiences among giants and miniature humans force him to confront the social and moral corruption of his own society.

Gulliver's Travels was an immediate success and remains widely read as both a fantastic children's story and a scathing satire. Swift remained active in church and state affairs throughout the 1730s, but after suffering a debilitating stroke in 1742, he was deemed incapable of caring for himself; he died three years later, in 1745.

synagogue

Jewish house of worship. From the Greek *synagōgē*, meaning "a place of meeting," the origins of the synagogue are unknown. It seems to have already been an integral feature of religious life by the period of the Second Temple, dating from the end of the Babylonian exile to the destruction of the Temple in 70 C.E. This means that even while the Temple and its high priests dominated Judaic life, there was an alternative mode of worship in which believers played a much more active role. In the Diaspora following the destruction of the Temple, the synagogue played a crucial role in preserving the Jewish faith and its traditions.

Synagogue worship is centered on the reading of the Scriptures, which takes place on holy days, festivals, on Monday and Thursday afternoons, and on Sabbath mornings and afternoons. As long as there are at least ten males present, the public service may be celebrated with or without a rabbi or a cantor to officiate. (In Reform and Conservative congregations there need be only ten men and/or women present.) The structural requirements for the synagogue are likewise minimal and ideally suited to the needs of a historically mobile and isolated community of the faithful. A single room, equipped with a cabinet (the holy ark) against the east wall in which the scrolls are kept, a prayer desk from which to recite the service, and a pulpit from which to read the Torah, can constitute a synagogue, although many are far more elaborate. Orthodox

Jewish synagogues are sex-segregated, like the Temple of Jerusalem itself had been, but Reform and Conservative Judaism have abolished this regulation in their congregations. In some places, like the United States, synagogues have become the focus not only of religious worship and instruction but also of social and community activities.

Szilard, Leo (1898–1964)

Hungarian-American physicist and contributor to development of the nuclear bomb. Born in Budapest, the son of a Jewish engineer, Szilard received his doctorate from the University of Berlin in 1922. He remained there on its faculty as physicist Albert Einstein's assistant in physics until 1925. An outspoken opponent of Nazism, Szilard moved to England and began working in nuclear physics at the Clarendon Laboratory at Oxford when German leader Adolf Hitler came to power. He is credited with conceiving of the idea of a nuclear chain reaction in 1934, even applying for a patent for it, but his methods were not practicable. He had also seen the possibility for its use in bombs. Moving to the United States in 1937, he worked in the National Defense Research Division at Columbia University, where he learned of the discovery of uranium fission in 1939. He and other scientists working in America persuaded Albert Einstein to send the famous letter (actually written by Szilard) to U.S. president Franklin Delano Roosevelt that led to the Manhattan Project and the development of the first atomic bomb. With Enrico Fermi, he pioneered the use of graphite in developing the first self-sustained nuclear reactor in Chicago, an innovation that led to the reality of nuclear fission.

In 1943 Szilard became an American citizen; and along with many other nuclear scientists who had worked on the project, he argued that the bomb not be used in warfare, but to no avail. Szilard became a professor of biophysics at the University of Chicago in 1946, and worked to ban nuclear testing and warfare until his death. Organizer of the Council for a Livable World, he received the Atoms for Peace Award in 1959. He published a book of short stories set in the future, *The Voice of the Dolphins*, in 1961.

T

Tabidze, Galaktion (1891–1959)

Georgian poet. The son of a priest, Tabidze entered the Tbilisi Ecclesiastical Seminary, a center of revolutionary ideas, in 1908. He began publishing poetry in periodicals the same year. His first collection, *Leksebi* (1914; *Poems*), received wide acclaim and established his professional reputation. In 1915 Tabidze traveled to Moscow, where he met leading Russian Symbolist poets. Upon his return to Georgia, he contributed to the journal of the nascent Georgian Symbolist movement. In 1916 he again visited Moscow and St. Petersburg and witnessed the twin revolutions of 1917. Tabidze returned to Georgia during its brief period of independence (1918–21) and began to experiment with literary form. In *Crâne aux fleurs artistiques* (*Skull with the Flowers of Art*) and *Artis-tuli leksebi* (*Artistic Poems*), both written in 1919, he developed aesthetics heavily influenced by the French and Russian Symbolists.

The Soviet invasion of Georgia in 1921 put an end to Tabidze's involvement with Symbolism. Not wanting to go into exile, he came to terms with the new regime; in recognition of his literary reputation, he was given editorial control of several literary journals, and in 1924 he cofounded *Mnatobi* (Beacon), which remains to this day Georgia's leading literary journal. During World War II, he wrote numerous obligatory patriotic and antifascist poems; after the war he composed lyrical poetry that evoked historical themes. When Tabidze plummeted from the window of a psychiatric hospital to his death, Georgian authorities declared the event to be an accident. Yet he was known to have been deeply depressed, and his close friends were convinced that he had committed suicide.

Tagore, Rabindranath (1861–1941)

Indian poet and philosopher. Tagore has achieved renown in a variety of fields, through both his creative writings and his theoretical tracts.

Born in Calcutta, Tagore studied law in London, later returning to his native city and marrying in 1883. He began writing for Bengali publications, and founded the Visvabharati, a university at Shantiniketar, in 1901. He received a knighthood from King George V in 1915, only to renounce the honor four years later in protest against British suppression of the Punjabs. His fifteen books of philosophy include *Sadhana, the Realization of Life* (1913), *Personality* (1917), *Creative Unity* (1922), and *Man* (1937). He wrote nearly one hundred books of verse, including *Gitanjali* (1910; *Song Offering*), which contains his most famous poems and has an introduction by Irish poet W. B. Yeats; *The Crescent Moon* (1913); and *Fruit-Gathering* (1916). In addition, he wrote over fifty plays, acting in many of them, and also wrote forty works of fiction, as well as producing several ballets. In 1930 he delivered the Hibbert Lectures at Oxford University, published the following year as *The Religion of Man*. Tagore won the Nobel Prize for Literature in 1913.

Taiping Rebellion

Chinese rebellion. With a death toll of over 20 million, the Taiping Rebellion was one of the bloodiest civil wars in history. Lasting from 1850 until 1864, the rebellion grew out of the economic hardships and natural disasters of the 1840s and 1850s. The rebellious Taipings, a people living in southern China, were led by Hong Xiuquan, a charismatic Protestant who claimed to be the younger brother of Jesus. Through his egalitarian rhetoric, Hong attracted the Chinese peasantry, as well as various other oppressed laboring groups. His attempts at agitation particularly flourished among the partly Christianized Chinese in southern China known as the Hakka. His overt criticism of the Manchu imperial family and his dissatisfaction with traditional Chinese culture increased his popularity among secret society members and outlaws.

In 1851 Hong was crowned the "Celestial King of the Celestial Kingdom of Peace," and he proclaimed Year One of a new imperial dynasty based in Guangxi. The Taipings, gathering strength, embarked on a series of military campaigns in northern and southern China. Their successes in Hunan and the Yangzi Valley culminated in March 1853 with the capture of Nanjing, which became the rebel capital. When the Taipings attempted to capture Beijing and overthrow the imperial regime, they were finally defeated. Their rule continued in the Yangzi Valley for another decade, until Nanjing fell to imperial forces in 1864, finally succumbing to a two-year-long siege. A month before the fall, the increasingly despondent Hong took his own life.

The emergence of efficient, well-trained mercenary armies raised by provincial leaders resulted in the defeat of the Taipings. These armies were primarily local militias that the Chinese government realized would prove more effective at combating the Taipings than would the undisciplined imperial forces.

Internal dissent within the Taiping leadership hastened the end of the rebellion, as did Hong's inability to deliver the various egalitarian reforms that he had promised. Hong and his court adopted extravagant lifestyles that contrasted sharply with the limited means of his followers. The land reforms that should have redistributed land equally among the peasants were thwarted by corrupt officials, many of whom were former landlords themselves. Despite their shortcomings, the Taipings had a lasting impact upon China. Taiping innovations included calendar reform and the abolition of foot-binding, and later nationalist and Communist movements would echo Taiping egalitarian ideals.

Taj Mahal

Indian mausoleum. Built in the seventeenth century by the Mughal emperor Shah Jahan (r. 1627–58), this crowning achievement of Mughal architecture is located outside Agra in India, along the southern bank of the Yamuna (Jumna) River. The name Taj Mahal is a corruption of Mumtaz Mahal (Chosen One of the Palace), the nickname of Shah Jahan's beloved wife, Arjumand Banu Begam, who died during childbirth in 1631. In 1632, after poring over plans drawn by a council of architects from all over the Islamic world, Shah Jahan ordered the construction of his wife's famous domed tomb to begin.

More than 20,000 workmen labored to complete the mausoleum proper by 1643; it was not until 1649 that the mosques, walls, and gardens surrounding the tomb were finally finished. By the time the entire Taj complex was completed in 1654, its cost had reached 40 million rupees.

The mausoleum itself is made of pure white marble, providing a striking chromatic and textural contrast with the red Sikri sandstone of the mosque. The interior of the mausoleum houses the cenotaphs (tombs) of both Arjumand Banu Begam and Shah Jahan, who died in 1658, not long after the completion of the Taj.

Taksin, King (r. 1768–82)

Thai king. In the late eighteenth century, a new Thai nation, the foundation of the modern Thai state, arose from the ruins of the fallen classical kingdom of Ayutthaya, which had been devastated in 1767 by the Burmese. At the center of this rebirth was an intense, charismatic half-Chinese, half-Thai military strategist named Sin, called Taksin because he was governor of the province of Tak. Drawing on both his local military power base and his family connections to the local Teochiu Chinese trading community, Taksin steadily recaptured enough of the old Ayutthaya kingdom to crown himself king in his new capital of Thonburi by late 1768. Throughout the next decade, his armies expanded the Thai state past the old Ayutthayan boundaries.

Taksin was widely recognized as a "man of merit," whose strong *karma* enabled him to be a leader of courage and vision, but by the 1780s his visionary intensity was turning to a madness that threatened the stability of his government. According to contemporary accounts, he began to spend "all his time in prayer, fasting, and meditation, in order by these means to be able to fly through the air." He shocked the Buddhist religious authorities by demanding that all monks bow to him and worship him as a god; those who did not were demoted and often flogged. Taksin was already in many ways an outsider due to his Chinese background, and his increasingly suspicious attitude and paranoid behavior eventually alienated all who might support him. The leader even tortured his own family.

In 1782 an army rebellion easily dethroned Taksin, who was killed according to the fifteenth-century law for regicide: tied up in a velvet sack, he was struck on the back of the neck with a sandalwood club and buried in a secret place. He was succeeded by King Rama I, who began the creation of the modern state of Thailand.

Tale of the Three Kingdoms, *see* Sanguozhi Tongsu yanyi

talking drum

African ritual and communicational object. The sounds of the drums reproduce the tones, stresses, and rhythm of various utterances. Their use is related to African language systems in general, which depend on a phonemic structure that differentiates "words" by tone and inflection rather than the separate and distinct phonemes of most Western languages. As in Chinese, the same sound can have many different meanings, depending on tone and inflection.

In a social context, the drums at a dance provide communication as well as music. The chief drummer calls people out to dance, tells them how to perform, and comments on their dancing, telling them to rejoin the group when they have completed their turn. The drums themselves vary widely, from slit logs to open-ended gourds to hourglass-shaped drums that can play the widest variety of tones. The Hausa and Yoruba people are known for their underarm sling drum, while the Idoma of the Benue-Cross river region use a membrane drum whose tone is varied by striking various regions of the membrane, impeding the membrane's resonance with foot pressure, and striking the side of the drum with the heel.

Talmud

Jewish religious text. From the Hebrew word for "learning," the Talmud is one of the most important texts of the Jewish faith. Two versions exist: the Babylonian and the Palestinian Talmuds, reflecting the dispersal of the Jews following the destruction of the Second Temple in Jerusalem. The Babylonian Talmud is more comprehensive and more frequently used; in fact, the term "Talmud" has come to mean this version unless otherwise indicated. The Talmud is comprised of the Mishna and the Gemara. Written between 30 B.C.E. and 200 C.E. by religious leaders in Roman-ruled Israel, the Mishna is a legal code delineating how to apply all the commandments found in the Torah to everyday life. The Gemara is basically a commentary on the Mishna, edited and completed in the fifth century C.E.

While much of the Talmud is devoted strictly to Jewish law, roughly two thirds of it consists of *aggadah*: parables, sermons, biblical exegesis, theological speculation, and stories. Talmudic scholars throughout the centuries have addressed the same issues, from numerous different perspectives, all turning to their predecessors for guidance while adding their own commentary for the benefit of future generations. In this way, Judaism maintained its traditions without becoming dogmatic or rigid.

Tamar (c. 1165–1213)

Georgian queen. Ruling from 1184 until her death, Tamar is considered to be the greatest of Georgian rulers. During her reign, Georgia achieved many military and political successes. Among her triumphs was the foundation of the empire of Trebizond, which existed from 1204 until 1461 on lands seized from Byzantium. Tamar's troops achieved victories over the Azerbaijani in 1194 and over the sultanate of Konya in 1202. By 1204 almost all of Trans-Caucasia was under Tamar's rule.

Tamar devoted much attention to public works projects, commissioning numerous new roads, bridges, churches, monasteries, and fortresses. She was also a generous patron of the sciences and arts, leading many poets to dedicate works to her, most prominently Shota Rustaveli (c. 1172–1216) in his epic *Vepkhvis' tq'aosani* (*The Knight in the Panther's Skin*). She married Yurii, the son of the Russian prince Andrei Bogoliubsky, in 1185, only to separate two years later. In 1189 she married David Soslan, a representative of the Ossetian branch of the Georgian dynasty of Bagrationi (Bagratids). In death, Queen Tamar swiftly achieved mythic status and became a vivid source of inspiration for Georgian and Russian romantic poets.

Tan, Amy (1952–)

Chinese-American novelist. Tan was born in Oakland, California, the daughter of an electrical engineer from Beijing and a member of the Shanghai upper class. In her highly acclaimed first novel, *The Joy Luck Club* (1989), Tan writes of the alienation and cultural estrangement of the immigrant experience. *The Joy Luck Club* tells the story of four Chinese immigrant mothers and their daughters, all trying to find a happy medium between the competing demands of Chinese and American cultures. The title of the novel refers to the weekly gathering of the mothers to gossip and play mahjongg. Begun as a diversion during the Japanese invasion of China, their club becomes a ritual that attempts to recover a culture that otherwise would recede into the past. Other works by Tan include *The Kitchen God's Wife* (1991); two children's books, *The Moon Lady* (1992) and *The Chinese Siamese Cat* (1994); and *The Hundred Secret Senses* (1995).

tango

Argentine dance form. The tango developed in Buenos Aires in the late nineteenth century. Its sources are numerous; while its major influence was an African dance popular among black slaves in the Río de la Plata region at the beginning of the nineteenth century, the tango's roots also include the Argentine *milonga*, and the Cuban *habañera*. Disreputable at first and confined to the seedier sides of town, probably due to its sensual rhythms and movements, the tango slowly made its way from suburban brothels into the salons of Buenos Aires. The tango became socially acceptable in Argentina by the early 1900s and soon became the craze in fashionable European circles.

Although the first tangos were spirited and gay, by 1920 the music and the lyrics had become extremely melancholy as interpreters of the tango sang about tragic love, betrayal, and death. The dance steps also changed, gradually becoming smoother as they entered the ballroom.

Tang poetry

Golden Age of Chinese poetry. The prosperity of the Tang dynasty (618–906) spawned thousands of talented poets, most prominently Li Bai, Du Fu, Bai Juyi, Wang Wei, and Li Shangyin. Tang poets developed and refined a great variety of forms, producing an extraordinarily personal brand of verse. Many Tang poems stress the role of nature as a medium for communication, a metaphoric and physical mode for sharing emotions. In Li Bai's famous "Drinking Alone with the Moon," the poet views the bright moon as a timely friend who dispels his sense of despair by encouraging him to dance among flowers and hastening the advent of the spring.

Tanizaki Jun'ichiro (1886–1965)

Considered to be one of the greatest Japanese authors of the twentieth century, Tanizaki's writings are remarkable for their blunt sensuality, coupled with a nuanced emphasis upon the workings of the subconscious. Besides the eleventh-century Japanese novelist Lady Murasaki, Tanizaki counted American writer Edgar Allan Poe and Irish dramatist Oscar Wilde among the strongest influences on his work.

The Tokyo-born Tanizaki's long and productive career spanned three modern imperial reigns. While he initially benefited from and reveled in the freedom Western styles brought to Japanese literary conventions, he later regretted what he viewed as the dilution of the Japanese character by Western values and the destruction of his country's beauty by industrialization. The graceful nostalgia of his early treatments of these themes was transformed in later works into a pattern of brutal juxtapositions of the grotesque and the delicate.

Tanizaki consistently explored the darker side of human sexuality, presenting in works such as *Fūten rōjin nikki* (1962; *Diary of a Mad Old Man*) and *Tade kuu mushi* (1929; *Some Prefer Nettles*) visions of erotic despair and bitterness. *Yume no ukihashi* (1959; *The Bridge of Dreams*) describes incestuous longing, while *Kagi* (1957; *The Key*) deals with the corruption of innocence. In "Shisei" (1910; "The Tattooer"), an artist lives out his fantasy of completely covering a beautiful woman's body with painfully intricate tattoos.

His novel *Sasameyuki* (1948; *The Makioka Sisters*) was first suppressed as a threat to the nation's war effort in 1943 because it neither supported nor mentioned the Japanese struggle during the Second World War. However, it won the Imperial Award for Cultural Merit in 1949, four years after Japan's defeat. Tanizaki also wrote drama, literary criticism, essays, and autobiographical pieces, and was one of the first Japanese candidates for the Nobel Prize.

tanka

Japanese poetic style. Literally "short poem," the *tanka* is always composed of five lines and thirty-one syllables. Because the *tanka* dominated classical Japanese poetry, or *waka*, as the only advanced form of vernacular poetry from the seventh century to the early twentieth, the two terms are often synonymous. However, in the twentieth century, the term *waka* was once again used to describe the ultraconservative classical and postclassical poetry, while *tanka* referred to modern Japanese poetry embodying the new realism.

tanna

Jewish scholar. From the Aramaic "teni" (to teach), *tanna* (plural form is *tannaim*) refers to any of several hundred Jewish scholars roughly between the years 135 and 200 C.E., a period often referred to as the "age of the *tannaim*." Following the collapse of Jewish resistance to Roman rule and the subsequent exile of the Jews from Jerusalem, and since both religious and political Judaism had previously centered on the Temple, an alternative leadership and doctrine needed to be established. The ideology of the *tannaim*, which stressed scriptural learning, prayer, and good works, seemed appropriate for an increasingly far-flung Jewish community. Palestine's Roman overlords approved of the *tannaim* and encouraged the adoption of their practices while setting them up as the only legitimate Jewish authorities.

The age of the *tannaim* began under the leadership of the Palestinian scholars Hillel the Elder and Shammai near the end of the first century B.C.E. For the next several hundred years their followers worked to consolidate the scattered literary analyses of the Bible that had accumulated. The Mishnaic and Midrashic literature represented the fruits of this collective labor. The definitive version of the Mishna was produced in the middle of the second century C.E. by Judah ha-Nasi. Texts not included in his edition were later compiled by other scholars in collections called Baraitot (exclusions) and Tosefta (additions).

The *tannaim* were later followed by scholars known as *amoraim*, or interpreters, who were responsible for writing the Gemara, the commentaries on the Mishna.

Tantras

Sacred Indian texts. The Tantras (from the Sanskrit word *tan*, meaning "to span" or "to loom") are sacred texts representing a literary and meditative tradition that usually ran counter to the dominant cultural patterns of Indian life. The Buddhist Tantras, composed between 500 and 800 C.E., and the Hindu Tantras, written between about 900 and 1400 C.E., instruct the devout in physical and mental techniques of concentration designed to enable the individual to escape the otherwise eternal cycle of birth, death, and rebirth. Unlike the conservative asceticism of Yoga, Tantrics (followers of the Tantras) learn to harness and use their sensual powers in the pursuit of supreme freedom and wisdom, rather than eliminating them.

Tantrism

Indian religion. In Tantrism, an offshoot religion based on the Indian sacred texts the Tantras, the supreme being is formless and nameless, manifested only in its primal form, that of the male and female principles. In Hindu Tantrism, the male principle (Siva) is passive and quiescent, and represents perfect knowledge; the female principle (Sakti) is dynamic and active, and represents energy and motion. In Buddhist Tantrism (also called Vajrayana, "the vehicle of the thunderbolt"), the male

Buddha principle (Prajna) represents perfect wisdom.

This duality is often represented through sexual imagery, with the male and female adepts, but without orgasmic termination: the power of retention bestows enormous psychic control on the practitioners, and this control eventually leads them to emancipation. The accompanying rituals also involve activities that contrast sharply with the prevailing norms of the religious, non-Tantric majority: during nightlong rites, Tantrics ingest marijuana and alcohol, in addition to consuming fish, meat, and various aphrodisiacs.

It is for these reasons that Hindu society regards Tantrism and Tantrics with a degree of suspicion. Yet while Tantrism is marginal to Hinduism, it is quite central to Vajrayana Buddhism. Both forms of Tantrism have spawned a prolific quantity of songs and music, as well as numerous types of poetry.

Taoism

Chinese religion and philosophy. The fundamental text of philosophic Taoism is the *Dao-de Jing*, which elaborates the concept of Tao, an intangible force that represents the origin and eventual demise of all things in existence. The concept of Te is also central and closely related to Tao. Te is the embodiment of Tao and describes a state of oneness with nature and its processes. The philosophic aspect of Taoism stresses simplistic living and repudiation of knowledge in keeping with the concepts of Te and Tao.

The aim of religious Taoism, somewhat at odds with philosophical Taoism, is the attainment of eternal life. The *xian*, or immortals, are the people whose lives are held up as a model for others. In the attainment of this goal of eternal life, many breathing techniques, special diets, and magic spells were developed.

Both the religious and philosophical

sects of Taoism were destroyed during the Han dynasty. Since then, two other sects of Taoism have arisen—the Shang Qing Mao Shan and the Ling Bao traditions. These sects, along with the older sects, continue to have a great influence on Chinese society.

Tatanka Iyotake (1831–1890)

Sioux Indian leader. Tatanka Iyotake (or Tattanka Yotanka), commonly known by his English name, Sitting Bull, was a chief of the Hunkpapa Sioux (a branch of the Teton Sioux), who united the numerous Sioux tribes in their struggle to maintain their land on the North American plains. Although Sitting Bull was recognized as a powerful warrior leader early in life, his first skirmish with white soldiers did not occur until 1863, in the Battle of Killdeer Mountain, when the U.S. Army began retaliation against the Santee Sioux for the "Minnesota massacre." Although the Teton Sioux (of whom Sitting Bull was a member) had no part in the original battle, for the next five years Sitting Bull was in constant conflict with the army, as they invaded Sioux lands and destroyed the economy of the Indians. Word of Sitting Bull's courage and wisdom grew, and in 1867 he was appointed chief of the entire Sioux nation.

The discovery of gold in the Black Hills territory in the mid-1870s heightened U.S. hostility toward the Sioux. Though the Sioux had been guaranteed their land in the Second Treaty of Fort Laramie (1868), the prospect of gold changed government policy. In late 1875 all Sioux were ordered to evacuate their land by January 31, 1876, and resettle on reservations, or be declared hostile to the government. Sitting Bull did not leave his camp in the Montana territory; even if he had chosen to cooperate, the bitter cold would have made the 240-mile trek unbearable. The Sioux then moved to Little Bighorn River Valley, where Sitting Bull participated in the ceremonial Sun Dance, to solicit spiritual assistance for his people's plight. When he recovered from a trance induced by self-inflicted torture, he reported a vision in which he saw "soldiers falling into his camp like grasshoppers from the sky." The vision was interpreted as a Sioux victory, and when American Lt. Colonel George Armstrong Custer and his soldiers marched to the camp on June 25, Sitting Bull's prophecy was fulfilled.

This annihilation of Custer's forces caused the U.S. government to demand increased military efforts against the Indians. Though the Sioux were victorious in many of these battles, their survival was also threatened by the depletion of plains buffalo, forcing many Sioux bands to surrender to the U.S. government because of starvation. To avoid this fate, Sitting Bull and his followers left for Canada in May 1877, but were refused a reservation there because they had one in the United States. Suffering from disease and famine, Sitting Bull and his followers surrendered at Fort Buford, North Dakota, in 1881. Sitting Bull was initially detained at Fort Randall as a prisoner of war before being permitted to rejoin his people at the Standing Rock reservation in 1883. Considered to be a threat to government policy by the reservation agent, Major James McLaughlin, in 1885 Sitting Bull was used for exhibition purposes, joining Buffalo Bill's Wild West Show, from which he gained international fame. During his six years at Standing Rock, Sitting Bull worked to protect the 11 million acres of tribal lands guaranteed by government treaties. His efforts met with disaster in 1889, as McLaughlin appointed Indian chiefs who secretly agreed to cede additional lands to the government.

The Ghost Dance movement in 1889, promising the removal of whites and the return of land to the tribes, was embraced by many of the Sioux in Sitting Bull's camp. Although he did not endorse or denounce the craze, he did permit dancing in his camp and was declared an "agitator." Fearing a reprise of Sitting Bull's military leadership, reservation police, including some of his relatives, arrested Sitting Bull in Grand River on December 15, 1890. His followers attempted to stop the police, and in the ensuing melee, Sitting Bull, eight of his followers, including his seventeen-year-old son, and six reservation police were killed. Sitting Bull's body was buried at Fort Yates, North Dakota, but later was moved to Mobridge, South Dakota, where a granite shaft marks his final resting place.

Tchaikovsky, Pyotr Ilich (1840–1893)

Russian composer. Tchaikovsky was a prodigious composer and the writer of many well-received symphonies and symphonic poems.

The second son of a government official in the Ural, he enjoyed the typical, French-accented upbringing of the Russian well-to-do. Young Tchaikovsky's interest in music was not encouraged, however, because his parents felt it would have an unhealthy effect on the child. In 1848 the family moved to Moscow and then to St. Petersburg. In 1854 Tchaikovsky's mother, whom he adored, died of cholera. To alleviate the distress caused both by her death and by what he believed to be his father's easygoing indifference to the tragedy, he started composing short musical pieces. In his school years, he continued his musical self-education, attending the opera quite frequently. In 1859 he took a job as a clerk in the Ministry of Justice but left government service after four years to study at the newly opened St. Petersburg Conservatory. Graduating with honors, he secured a professorship at the Moscow Conservatory, which he held from 1866 until 1878. He published in these years many music reviews, translated several works on music theory, and wrote a textbook, *Rukovodstvo k prak-*

ticheskomu izucheniyu garmoniy (1872; *Guide to the Practical Study of Harmony*). In 1866 Tchaikovsky's *Symphony No. 1* was successfully performed in Moscow. It was followed by the symphonic poem *Romeo and Juliet* (1869) and a comic opera, *Kuznets Vakula* (1872; *Vakula the Smith*), based on a short story by Russian writer Nikolai Gogol (1809–1852). In the mid-1870s he had a nervous breakdown, but recovered sufficiently to write the *Symphony No. 4* (1877) and the opera *Evgeny Onegin* (1877–78; *Eugene Onegin*), based on the verse novel by Russian writer Aleksandr Pushkin (1799–1837). Also in 1877, Tchaikovsky composed his first and greatest ballet score, *Swan Lake*.

In the 1880s Tchaikovsky bought a house in the vicinity of Moscow, where he lived until a year before his death, when he moved to the town of Klin. In his last years, he produced some of his greatest masterpieces, including music for the ballets *Sleeping Beauty* (1890) and *The Nutcracker* (1892); the opera *Pikovaya Dama* (1890; *The Queen of Spades*), based on a short novel by Pushkin; and his dramatic *Symphony No. 6* (1893), known as the "Pathétique" and generally considered to be his greatest symphony.

After a disastrous marriage that lasted only weeks, Tchaikovsky's most stable and nurturing relationship occurred through a long-lasting correspondence with his wealthy patron, Nadezhda Filaretovna von Meck, which began in 1876. She insisted, however, that the two never meet, but continued to support Tchaikovsky financially and emotionally until three years before his death, when she ran out of money. Tchaikovsky's homosexuality, which he could not openly acknowledge in the Russia of his day, proved to be a source of constant anxiety, provoking more than one suicide attempt. There is much speculation surrounding the death of Tchaikovsky: some historians suggest that he died from cholera, while others claim that his death was a suicide.

Tecumseh (1768–1813)

American Indian military leader. Tecumseh was a Shawnee warrior best known for his attempts to create an independent American Indian nation in the Northwest United States. Tecumseh's early life was marred by violence between Indians and white settlers. His father was murdered by white frontiersmen in 1774, and his mother, a Muskogee (part of the Creek Confederacy), left him at the age of seven to accompany part of the tribe to Missouri. Tecumseh was adopted by the Shawnee chief Blackfish and grew up with several white foster brothers captured by Blackfish, most notably American pioneer Daniel Boone (1734–1820), who eventually escaped. In the 1780s Tecumseh organized guerrilla bands and fought the Kentucky and Ohio settlers who encroached upon Shawnee land. In spite of his animosity toward the white man, however, he opposed the torturing of prisoners, and earned great respect for his compassion and integrity.

In November Tecumseh joined the pan-tribal force that destroyed the 2,000-man army led by General Arthur St. Clair, which had been sent to stop the raids. The annihilation of this force temporarily prevented white settlers from entering the Shawnee lands. Tecumseh also fought General Anthony Wayne's forces at the Battle of Fallen Timbers in 1794, but the battle resulted in a decisive defeat for the tribes. The following year, several tribal chiefs signed the Greenville Treaty, effectively giving away large amounts of land in what is now Ohio, Indiana, Illinois, and Michigan. Tecumseh refused to attend this meeting and would not honor the treaty. Creating his own political and philosophical defense to justify the preservation of tribal lands, Tecumseh maintained that collective ownership of tribal land prevented any chief or group of chiefs from ceding any portion without the consent of every tribe.

Tecumseh and his brother Elskwatawa, called "the Prophet," began planning the creation of an autonomous Indian nation. They established Prophet's Town along the Tippecanoe River in Indiana as their headquarters, and tried to unite tribes in a mutual defense pact. They traveled from village to village, preaching the importance of an independent nation and the necessity of abandoning white customs and goods, in particular whiskey, whose effects were enervating many tribes. Tecumseh and Elskwatawa were quite successful in persuading other tribes to join them. On November 6, 1811, while Tecumseh was away on yet another unification mission, U.S. troops led by William Henry Harrison burned the confederation headquarters and scattered Tecumseh's followers. This battle squashed Tecumseh's hope of a tribal nation, and inspired the campaign slogan "Tippecanoe and Tyler too" for Harrison and John Tyler in their successful bid for the White House in 1840.

In the War of 1812, Tecumseh and his followers joined forces with the British, hoping that an American defeat would stem the tide of expansion. Commissioned by the British as a brigadier general, Tecumseh helped capture Detroit and invade Ohio during the war. In October 1813 Tecumseh was killed by Harrison's army at the Battle of the Thames River in Ontario.

Tennyson, Alfred (1809–1892)

English poet; commonly known as Alfred, Lord Tennyson. Appointed Poet Laureate of England in 1850, Tennyson is considered to be the major poet of the Victorian age. Greatly influenced by the Romantics, Tennyson's sentimental style was later denounced by late-nineteenth- and early-twentieth-century poets as shallow and insipid. Yet his poetry is a representative voice of the Victorian era, reflecting the intellectual and moral sensibilities of his social class.

The son of an alcoholic clergyman, Tennyson first published a book of poems with his brother and followed with the prize-winning poem "Timbuctoo" (1829) and the volume *Poems, Chiefly Lyrical* (1830), written while he studied at Cambridge. There he became close friends with Arthur Henry Hallam, whose tragic early death in 1833 inspired one of Tennyson's greatest elegies, "In Memoriam" (1850). This death, soon after the demise of his father, would infuse Tennyson's future poetry with a constant tension between faith and despair.

The publication of his volume *Poems* (1832) established his reputation as a great poet. He received an annual state pension in 1845, and with his financial worries assuaged, he married Emily Sellwood after nine years of courtship. He wrote his famous "Charge of the Light Brigade" (1855), glorifying the exploits of the British army, as part of his duties as Poet Laureate. *Idylls of the King*, Tennyson's chronicle of the Arthurian legend, appeared in 1859.

Tennyson spent his later years in relative comfort, and was highly successful in both literary and critical circles. Though his reputation was diminished somewhat after his death, he has since been recognized as a great poet, celebrated for his masterful technique and sensuous language. At his best, Tennyson could evoke the internal and external struggles of individuals striving for heroism in a world constantly conspiring to deny its possibility.

Tenochtitlán

Aztec capital. Once a metropolis covering more than five square miles, Tenochtitlán was located on two islands in Lake Texcoco and connected to the mainland by causeway dikes. The area now known as Mexico City stands on its ruins. In 1519 the population was 400,000, the largest urban population in Meso-American history. Ancient Tenochtitlán was a nonagricultural society, principally comprising artisans, priests, warriors, and administrators. It had a complex centralized government and a palace housing a library and halls of justice, as well as the home of the Aztec leader Montezuma. The city contained hundreds of temples and three large temples dedicated to Huitzilopochtli, the Aztec war god, and Tlaloc, the Aztec rain god. The great temple contained a ball court where the Aztec ball game *tlachtli* was played, a wooden rack for skulls of sacrificed victims, a sacred pool, and a sacred grove.

Teotihuacán

Ancient Mexican city. Literally meaning "place where the gods were born," Teotihuacán was a sophisticated metropolis covering eight square miles toward the end of the sixth century. At its height, it had a population of 150,000.

In the Early Classic period, Teotihuacán was economically, religiously, and militarily the dominant culture of its day. However, the Mayan culture proved to be more stable. In Late Classic Meso-America, Teotihuacán experienced an economic and military decline, playing an increasingly less important role culturally, while the Mayans dominated intellectually and culturally.

While it is not known whether the inhabitants of Teotihuacán were literate, it was a major manufacturing and trading center and a main source of obsidian mines and artifacts. It was architecturally sophisticated and was organized around two great intersecting avenues that were aligned in a pattern that may have had astrological significance. Near the center of the city was the Citadel, a sunken plaza with temples dedicated to Quetzalcóatl, the ancient deity and legendary ruler of the Toltec; Tlaloc, the rain god; and the Fire Serpent, who carries the sun across the sky; as well as the luxurious residential palace compounds. The builders and workers of the city lived in poor, crowded dwellings on the other side of the center.

Teotihuacán declined primarily due to its arid climate, since the economy relied primarily on irrigation. Though its temples were abandoned and palaces burned, Teotihuacán was never completely abandoned. After 600 C.E., however, Meso-America was politically and culturally fragmented until the Toltec invasions.

terra-cotta warriors

Ancient Chinese sculptures. The discovery in 1974 of over 8,000 figures of men, horses, and chariots in the mausoleum of the first emperor of the Qin dynasty (221–206 B.C.E.) is regarded as one of the century's greatest archaeological discoveries. In 1974 peasants digging in Shanxi province, twenty miles east of the city of Xi'an, accidentally uncovered the tomb when digging a well. The biggest of the three vaults (750 feet long, 200 feet wide, and 16 feet deep) contains 6,000 figures of warriors and horses in battle formation, as well as countless weapons. The terra-cotta warriors are nearly six feet tall, each face bearing a different expression. Originally, the figures were all brightly painted, but the colors have faded over time.

The mausoleum of the emperor Qin Shi Huangdi, of which the vaults for the terra-cotta warriors and horses form only a part, took thirty-six years to be completed. When he assumed the throne in 221 B.C.E., Qin immediately ordered the construction of his tomb. A museum with a hangar-like structure over the vaults was completed in 1979 to enclose the terra-cotta army on its original site and in its original position.

Thai poetic tradition

Thailand's literary tradition was purely oral before Rhamkhamhaeng estab-

lished a standard system of writing in 1283. Thai is a tonal language—that is, words of exactly the same pronunciation vary in meaning according to the level of tone in which they are spoken; this is what gives the language its "singsong" quality to the Western ear. A focus on acoustic effects marks classical Thai literature, which employs strict and complex meters, rhyme schemes, and tonal harmonies. There are no "heavy" and "light" syllable patterns as in Western poetry, but rather a quantitative system, regimenting the numbers of syllables per line and per foot. Often, these patterns necessitate the use of words in Pali or Sanskrit, the "classical" languages of the Thai.

Thematically, classical poetry is mainly religious, drawing on Buddhist and Hindu mythology such as the *Jâtakas*—stories of the former lives of the Buddha—or filtering folk myths through Buddhist doctrine. Nature and death, the immutables of life, are represented as the keys to grace in this pantheistic, profoundly moral literature.

A system of royal patronage shaped the history of Thai literature. Poets and other artisans were traditionally supported by the king rather than by selling their works; these were often attributed to the king under whose reign they were written rather than to the individual poet. However, several kings of the classical period were accomplished poets in their own right, such as Narai (r. 1657–88) and Rama II. Sunthon Phu, Sri Prat, and Khun Phum stand out as representatives of the classical style.

Thant, U (1909–1974)

Burmese diplomat. The third secretary-general of the United Nations, Thant, like many Burmese, used only his given name: the "U" has no direct translation into English, but is similar to "uncle" and used as a title of respect. U Thant spent several years as a high school history teacher and headmaster before receiving a series of civil service posts. He was appointed a delegate to the United Nations in 1952, and in 1957 became Burma's permanent representative. Following the death of U.N. secretary Dag Hammarskjöld in 1961, Thant was chosen as his successor and officially named secretary-general in 1962, a position he held until 1972. During this politically turbulent period, Thant was faced with numerous international conflicts, including the Cuban Missile Crisis, the Vietnam War, civil war in Zaire, and skirmishes between India and Pakistan. Furthermore, Thant needed to assert the power and authority of the United Nations in a geopolitical arena largely dominated by the Soviet Union and the United States.

In addition to his responsibilities as secretary-general, Thant also wrote a number of books, including *Cities and Their Stories* (1930); *Towards a New Education* (1946); and two collections of his public addresses and essays, *Toward World Peace* (1964) and *View from the UN* (1978). When Thant died, his body was returned for burial to Rangoon, where it became the object of a tug-of-war between university students and military forces. The chaos culminated in riots, the imposition of martial law in the city, and several deaths.

Thoreau, Henry David (1817–1862)

American writer. Thoreau called himself "a mystic, a Transcendentalist, and a natural philosopher to boot," and he is considered to be among the greatest American intellectuals of the nineteenth century. Although he published only two books and a few articles during his short life, his thoughts on nonconformity, humanity's relation to nature, and civil disobedience have exerted enormous influence in both America and abroad, more so in the twentieth century than in his own.

Born in Concord, Massachusetts, Thoreau attended Concord Academy and Harvard College, graduating in 1837. Returning to Concord, he taught school for a couple of years and began keeping a series of journals, a project he would continue throughout his life, providing copious amounts of material for his books as well as being a formidable literary achievement in its own right. Deeply influenced by the elder Transcendentalists like American writer Ralph Waldo Emerson and American teacher and philosopher Bronson Alcott, he began writing articles for their journal *The Dial*, later serving as one of its editors.

In 1845 Thoreau decided to build a cabin on Emerson's land next to Walden Pond in Concord. Rejecting the communitarian impulse of the Transcendentalists living at Brook Farm, Thoreau preferred communion with nature to a contrived, artificial "community" that he insisted was doomed to failure. Moving into his cabin on July 4, 1845, he spent much of his first few months writing the account of his 1839 boat trip, published in 1849 as a *A Week on the Concord and Merrimack Rivers*. Thoreau kept detailed notes of his time at the pond, which he would eventually revise for his masterpiece, *Walden*, published in 1854. An ambitious work, *Walden* seamlessly integrates discussions of philosophy, gardening, literature, and science, uniting disparate disciplines through the lens of Thoreau's personal experiences at the pond. Like Emerson an admirer of the *Bhagavadgita*, the Hindu religious text, Thoreau organized *Walden* so that it would contain the same number of chapters.

His retreat ended in 1847 when he was jailed for a day for following the example of a friend and refusing to pay a poll tax during the Mexican War, a tax he felt encouraged the spread of slavery and unwarranted American expansionism. His 1849 essay "Resistance to Civil Government" (retitled "Civil Disobedience" after his death) explains his refusal and his view that personal morality supersedes civil law. He continued his rambles and his journal-keeping, and lectured widely, establishing his credentials as a fierce abolitionist. He refused to rule out the use of violence to combat the evil of slavery, and praised John Brown, who had killed several people in guerrilla raids aimed at freeing slaves, as an "Angel of Light."

Suffering from advanced tuberculosis, Thoreau struggled in his last year to revise his journals for publication. Posthumous collections include *Excursions* (1863), *The Maine Woods* (1864), *Cape Cod* (1865), several volumes of letters and poems, and fourteen volumes from his *Journals* (1906).

Tiananmen Square

Beijing square. Tiananmen Square has been at the center of political movements in China throughout the twentieth century.

The May 4th Movement of 1919 erupted here when 5,000 Beijing students gathered to demonstrate against the reactionary government; though the demonstrators chanted slogans demanding liberty and democracy, the event was also crucial to the early development of the Chinese Communist Party.

Tiananmen was the site of the founding of the People's Republic of China on October 1, 1949. In early April 1976, public mourning in Tiananmen Square at the death of Chinese Communist leader Zhou Enlai doubled as a political event: crowds lamenting Zhou's passing also rallied against the Gang of Four, the coterie of Communist Party officials, and Communist Party chairman Mao Zedong's ongoing Cultural Revolution (1966–76). The mass display against the prevailing policies of the previous ten years was a powerful rebuke to Mao, and signaled the beginning of the end of that revolution.

Beginning in late April 1989 and continuing for about six weeks, Tiananmen Square was the center of the most powerful student movement in Chinese history. Millions of students and their supporters paraded through the square, holding meetings, staging sit-ins and hunger strikes, demanding liberty, democracy, and human rights, and attacking official corruption and profiteering. Blood was shed when tanks and armed personnel carriers charged into the crowds to suppress the nonviolent student demonstrators and their supporters.

The largest public square in the world (40 hectares, or 100 acres), it is flanked by the Great Hall of the People (seat of the National People's Congress) on the west and the Museum of Chinese History and Chinese Revolution on the east. At the head of the square, at its north end, is Tiananmen, the "Gate of Heavenly Peace," which was formerly the main entrance to Beijing, the "Forbidden City." It was built together with the Imperial Palace in the early 1400s and restored in 1651. On top is a rostrum where Chinese leaders review parades on National Day. In the center of the square is the Monument to the People's Heroes, a tribute to all who gave their lives for the liberation of the Chinese nation. It was completed on May 1, 1958.

The most recent addition to the square is the Mao Zedong Memorial Hall, completed in 1977. It sits behind the Monument to the People's Heroes and faces Tiananmen, occupying the most prominent position in the square, and houses the body of Mao.

Tikal

Largest Mayan city and sacred site. It is located in the rain forest jungle of Petén in the southern Mayan lowlands of northwestern Guatemala. Tikal began as a village and became an important ceremonial center with plazas, temples, and palaces. Eventually, it became part of a great trading network with the ancient cities of Teotihuacán and Kaminaljuyu. While Teotihuacán declined,

Tikal flourished and culturally dominated the southern Mayan lowlands in the Late Classic period. Though Tikal was never as spatially consolidated as Teotihuacán, it reached its architectural and artistic peak between 600 and 800 C.E. Tikal declined in 800 C.E. due to depopulation and was abandoned by the tenth century.

At Tikal, Mayan civilization flourished. All the Mayan cultural features are abundantly evident at Tikal: sculpture and vase painting, polychrome pottery, stelae (carved or engraved stone slabs used for ceremonies), evidence of time-counting and calendrics, and temples and palaces for the upper classes. Teotihuacán influence upon the Maya is seen in the wall paintings, which depict scenes of men and gods, though Mayans were more interested in the art of portraiture. The stelae are erect, carved stones, inscribed with Mayan hieroglyph writing (only a few of which have been translated), often involving calendrics. The stelae date from the third to ninth century C.E.; the last Mayan stela is dated 889 C.E. and is found at Tikal. Teotihuacán influence upon Tikal is markedly evident in Stela 31, which depicts a Mayan lord wearing jade ornaments and standing between two warriors from Teotihuacán who carry shields depicting Tlaloc.

Tikal is noted for the Great Plaza with stelae, the Temple of the Great Jaguar, and the Palace of the Nobles. The buildings are constructed with the flat-beam-and-mortar roofs typical of the Maya. The corbel vault, universal to Mayan architecture, was sturdier and more enduring than the Roman arch and consisted of an arched roof extending toward a central meeting point at the top and covered with a flat piece of limestone. Temples and palaces very often were covered in white stucco and opened onto plazas.

Tilaurakot

Archaeological site in the Kapilavastu district, Lumbini Zone of Nepal. Situated on the banks of the River Bana Ganga, Tilaurakot is the site of three famous citadels, constructed in 600, 200, and 150 B.C.E. Tilaurakot is thought by most scholars to be the site of the ancient city of Kapilavastu, capital of a kingdom of the same name during the period of the Skakya rulers. However, the archaeological evidence is only circumstantial, and some experts disagree as to the exact location of Kapilavastu, although all place it near the present Indian-Nepalese border.

Kapilavastu is thought to be the home of Kapila, founder of the Sankhya system of Vedic philosophy (the Vedic period marks Hindu history and culture between 1500 and 500 B.C.E.). Kapilavastu is also believed to be the home of the historical Buddha, Gautama, and the place where he came under the influence of Kapila and the Sankhya system of Vedic Hinduism.

The presence of foundations for ancient Buddhist stupas (dome-shaped mounds or temples that serve as Buddhist shrines) and Hindu temples at Tilaurakot testifies to the mixture of Hindu and Buddhist traditions in Nepal. The ruins are primarily made of brick, rather than the more usual stone. Archaeologists believe that all major stupas of the Kathmandu Valley can be traced to ancient times, although most stupas have been altered in size and decoration through the centuries.

Timbuktu

West African city. Timbuktu, located near the Niger River in the western Sahara in present-day Mali, owes its historical importance to its positioning along major African trade routes, accessible to both land and water traffic.

Around 1000 C.E., Timbuktu was a seasonal camp used by nomadic Tuaregs from North Africa who grazed their herds near the river in the summertime. The area soon became a depot for trans-Saharan travelers, and, according to legends recorded in early Arabic manuscripts that chronicle the history of the region, it took its name from a slave who worked at the growing trading post and rest stop.

As more people established permanent local residences, and as traders from the Ghana empire in the west began to frequent the area, it became a commercial center, a focal point of trade in salt, gold, and textiles. With the rise of the Islamic Mali empire around 1240, Islam was propagated in the entire region by the empire's Mandingo kings, and Timbuktu became a center of Islamic religion, scholarship, and learning in addition to being a center of continental trade.

The Mali emperor Mansa Musa constructed the Great Mosque in Timbuktu on his way home from a pilgrimage to Mecca, and sent needy Islamic scholars from Timbuktu to Fez to further their studies. More mosques were built, and the city's reputation as the intellectual capital of West Africa began to spread as scholars from as far as Muslim Spain began to visit the city. The influence of the Mali empire began to wane in the 1350s, as the Songhai empire rose to prominence and incorporated Timbuktu in 1468.

Timbuktu continued to flourish under Songhai emperors such as Sonni Ali and Muhammad I Askia, who expanded and consolidated the Songhai empire and fostered a climate of stability that protected the trade routes and allowed Timbuktu to prosper. The famous legends of a vigorous and cultured civilization in Africa that found their way to Europe in the fifteenth century described Timbuktu at this stage of its existence. Visitors from Europe and North Africa in the fifteenth and sixteenth centuries spoke with wonder about the city's university, stone palace, bustling markets, ornate mosques, and bountiful, courtly life.

After the death of Muhammad I Askia, fratricidal wars and invasions by Moroccans in the north destroyed the stability and prosperity that had been stewarded by the Songhai emperors. In 1591 Timbuktu fell to Moroccan invaders who ransacked the city's riches, massacred and imprisoned many of the scholars and officials who lived there, and made the city an administrative center for territory that the Moroccans conquered.

Timbuktu declined rapidly as the trade routes became unstable and as wars destabilized the entire region. By 1828, when a European explorer, Frenchman René Caillé, finally visited the famous city that Europeans had heard so much about but never seen, he described it as "a mass of ill-looking houses built of earth." Coming under French control when France became the region's colonial administrator in the late 1800s, the Timbuktu of today is a modest provincial town in the independent republic of Mali.

Timur (Tamerlane) (1336–1404)

Central Asian ruler. One of the most powerful rulers to emerge from Central Asia and the last of the great nomadic conquerors. He was born into the Barlas tribe belonging to the Mongol federation of Genghis (Chingiz) Khan, the son of the governor of a town in Transoxiana. Timur served in the armies of a number of local rulers, proving himself to be a shrewd politician, skillful negotiator, and decisive general. After a series of intrigues, he ascended the throne of Balkh, a major city in Transoxiana, in 1370 and declared himself heir to the Mongol khanate. Following a decade consolidating his hold over Transoxiana, he embarked on a lifetime of campaigns to acquire an empire that, at its prime, extended from Moscovy in the northwest to Delhi in the southeast, and the Tien-Shan mountains of China in the northeast to Anatolia and the Caucasus in the southwest. Timur was both admired and feared for his ability to keep his armies constantly on the march, rapidly moving his troops from one frontier to the other. He led numerous campaigns in Crimea, Georgia, Azerbaijan, Mesopotamia, Persia, and Central Asia; twice occupied Moscow; and sacked Delhi. His most famous conflict was the Battle of Angora (1402), in which he defeated the Ottoman armies and succeeded in capturing Emperor Bayezit. While Timur treated the vanquished Bayezit with great respect, such leniency was not normally displayed toward the defeated. Timur's troops massacred 80,000 people and razed the city in their sack of Delhi in 1398. A similar number were killed after a rebellion in Isfahan, and towers were built of their skulls.

Despite obvious similarities to Genghis Khan and other Mongol rulers, Timur differed from them in several important respects. He considered himself to be a devout Sunnî Muslim and felt charged with the guardianship of the faith. He thus justified campaigns against the Christians of Russia, Crimea, and Georgia, as well as the conquest of the Shi'a areas of Persia, as wars in the service of Islam. Furthermore, unlike his nomadic Mongol forebears, Timur was more interested in the conquest and governance of sedentary populations than those of the steppes. He was actively interested in the furthering of the arts and sciences. His patronage was responsible for the development of what has come to be known as Timurid art, which depended heavily upon the talents of artisans captured in his many campaigns.

Tippu Sultan (1749–1799)

Warrior and sultan of Mysore. Tippu (also spelled Tipu), the Tiger of Mysore, also known as Fateh Ali Tippu, began his military education learning from French officers in the employ of his father, Haidar Ali, the sultan of Mysore. While still in his teens, Tippu commanded a cavalry unit against the Marathas in the Carnatic region of western India, and saw battle with the Marathas on several occasions between 1775 and 1779. His greatest victory came during the Mysore War in 1782, when he defeated British colonel John Brathwaite on the banks of the Coleroon. His father died soon after, and Tippu succeeded him as sultan. He concluded peace negotiations with the British in 1784, though an attack on the raja (prince or nobility) of Travancore a few years later in 1789 provoked a military response from the British, allies of the raja. The fighting went badly, and Tippu was forced to sign the Treaty of Seringapatam in 1792, which demanded that he cede half his dominion to the British, pay a large indemnity, and give the British two of his sons as hostages.

Unable to abide by these humiliating conditions, Tippu began secret negotiations with revolutionary France, though he could not secure aid before British governor-general Lord Wellesley discovered them. A fourth and final Mysore War resulted. When Seringapatam, Tippu's capital, was besieged by the British on May 4, 1799, Tippu died leading his troops against the invaders.

Tippu was a charismatic leader, generous to his Hindu subjects, noted for his literary tastes, and notoriously cruel to his enemies. His hatred for the English was great; unlike many of his fellows, he never allied with the British against any other Indian ruler. British historians portray Tippu as a tyrannical despot, but most non-English people admire Tippu as a fierce and unyielding king, steadfast in the face of foreign aggression.

Titian (c. 1488–1576)

Italian painter. Titian is considered to be the greatest master of the Venetian school and one of the most influential artists in history, providing a stylistic link between the art of the High Renaissance and the Baroque. He revolutionized oil painting with his expressive brushwork, innovations in composition, and complex use of color.

Born Tiziano Vecellio in the Alps, he was sent to Venice at the age of nine to become a painter. He received his early training with Giovanni Bellini and Giorgione. When the latter died in 1510, Titian completed a number of his unfinished paintings. His first great works were three frescoes depicting St. Anthony in Padua. He was recognized as the preeminent artist in Venice when Bellini died in 1516, and was appointed official painter to the republic. The allegorical *Sacred and Profane Love* (1516) marked the beginning of Titian's mature style, in which he produced numerous religious, mythological, historical, and portrait paintings. Best known from this period are three mythological pictures commissioned by Alfonso d'Este—*Offerta a Venere* (*Gli Amore*) (1518–19; *The Worship of Venus*), *Baccanale* (*Gli Andrii*) (1523–25; *Bacchanal*), *Bacco e Arianna* (1523; *Bacchus and Ariadne*)—all notable for their dramatic composition and forceful coloring.

About 1530, the year of his wife's death, Titian's work began to grow more restrained and meditative as his fame spread throughout Europe. In 1533 he did a famous portrait of the emperor Charles V that led the ruler to appoint Titian court painter and to give him the unprecedented rank of Count Palatine and Knight of the Golden Spur. His work of the 1540s reveals the new influence of northern Italian Mannerism, and, after his only trip to Rome in 1546–47, of Italian artist Michelangelo (1475–1564). He received many imperial commissions for portraits of Charles and his son Philip, the future king of Spain and later patron of Titian's career. Works commissioned by Philip II include the poetic and erotic *Danaë* (in several versions), *Venus and Adonis*

(1554), *The Rape of Europa* (1559–60), and *Diana and Actaeon* (1559–60). Titian's studio thrived, while his own late works show an increased subtlety in the use of light and a softening of his once boldly outlined colors. His last and perhaps most famous painting is the *Pietà*, intended for his own tomb and finished after his death by Palma Giovane.

tlachtli

Ancient Mayan game. *Tlachtli*, or "ballgame" was played on long, rectangular courts, with sloping vertical rebound surfaces; the most famous of these ancient courts are found in Tikal, Copán, and Chichén Itzá. For the game, two teams used a large ball of solid rubber that traveled quickly. Players could not hit or touch the ball with open hands or feet—though some tried to strike the ball with their hip, a painful practice. Heavy protective leather padding was worn over hips, knees, and elbows, and sometimes gloves and jousting helmets were used. Despite this protection, the game was violent and injuries often fatal. Bas-reliefs bordering the ball court at Chichén Itzá depict the activities of the game, as well as the more gruesome postgame ceremony: the sacrifice of one of the teams. One of the walls of the court, the *tzompantli*, or skull platform, is covered with hundreds of grinning skulls in bas-relief and is believed to have been used for the display of heads of captured enemies and/or sacrificed victims. The game itself still survives in altered form in northwestern Mexico.

Tocqueville, Count Alexis [Charles Henri Maurice Clérel] de (1805–1859)

French historian. One of the giants of social thought, Tocqueville was born at Verneuil, the only son of an aristocratic family that had narrowly escaped the guillotine during the Reign of Terror (1793–94) during the French Revolution (1792–1802). From 1827 to 1832, Tocqueville was junior magistrate at Versailles. In 1831 he and Gustave de

Beaumont accepted a commission to study the penitentiaries of the United States. They traveled for nine months, resulting in three works: a study of the American penitentiary system, a romantic novel by Beaumont, and Tocqueville's *De la démocratie en Amérique* (vol. I, 1835; vol. II, 1840; *Democracy in America*). This later work was internationally acclaimed, and secured his admission to the Académie Française. He defined democracy as the movement toward equality of conditions, and noted the extent of this process in the United States. He also distinguished between equality and liberty, and noted the prospects for despotism in democratic states. Intermediary institutions, ranging from family and professional organizations to the military and local government, were seen as crucial exercises in citizenship that nourished the foundations of liberty as well as equality.

Tocqueville entered politics, first as deputy for Manche from 1839 until the fall of the July monarchy, then as a member of the Parliament during the Second Republic. In 1849 he was briefly minister for foreign affairs in Odilon Barrot's second ministry. He withdrew from public life after Louis Napoleon's coup d'état. In his remaining years, he wrote *L'Ancien Regime et la Révolution* (vol. 1, 1856; *The Old Regime and the French Revolution*), a brilliant and controversial account of the social development that precipitated the Revolution of 1789. His study of the effects of centralization and the structural evolution of French society pre-1789 led him to deemphasize the significance of the self-understanding of the revolutionaries. Tocqueville refused to succumb to a reductively economic theory, unlike many of his colleagues and successors.

His contributions to the study of political economy and sociology went largely unrecognized in France until late in the twentieth century, when the demise of Soviet Communism and the waning of Marxist historical analysis, as well as the concerted work of a handful of admirers, brought his life and work back into intellectual currency.

Tolkien, J[ohn] R[onald] R[euel] (1892–1973)

English writer. Famous for his books of fantasy, Tolkien was also a professor of medieval literature. Born in South Africa, Tolkien received his degree from Exeter College, Oxford. While still a student, he began to form a language, Elvish, that would turn up in the dialogue of the characters in his first book, *The Hobbit* (1937). Tolkien had an interest in philology and a rigorous intellect that gave his books a cosmological and mythological completeness rarely encountered in fiction. His trilogy, *The Lord of the Rings* (*The Fellowship of the Ring*, 1954; *The Two Towers*, 1955; *The Return of the King*, 1956), sets forth an alternative reality, replete with histories, myths, coherent (but fictitious) languages, religion, and magic. Part of this effect is achieved through Tolkien's invented language, which is vaguely onomatopoetic and readily understandable. After Tolkien's death, his son Christopher published *The Silmarillion* (1977), which contains the cosmology, mythologies, and genealogies from the Middle Earth of the previous books. Since the mid-1980s, Christopher Tolkien has edited *The History of Middle Earth*, a series of lost or unpublished texts and alternate drafts of his father's greatest works.

With all the interest in his fictional works, Tolkien's contributions to his scholarly field have been overlooked. These include *A Middle English Vocabulary* (1922), *Beowulf: The Monster and the Critics* (1937), and *Chaucer as a Philologist* (1943).

Tolstoy, Leo (1828–1910)

Russian novelist and thinker. Born Lev Nikolayevich Tolstoy (or Tolstoi), he is best known for his masterpieces *Voina i mir* (*War and Peace*) and *Anna Karenina*. Tolstoy's happy childhood is recounted in his autobiographical trilogy, *Detstvo* (1852; *Childhood*), *Otrochestvo* (1854; *Boyhood*), and *Iunost'* (1857; *Youth*. Raised by aunts after the death of his father, he briefly studied Asian languages before leaving formal study and retiring to the family estate, where he hoped to work with the peasants living there. This plan, too, was eventually abandoned.

In 1851 Tolstoy served with the Russian army in the Caucasus, transferring to Sevastopol during the Crimean War. He published a series of stories based on the defense of Sevastopol, the *Sevastopolskie rasskazy* (1855–56; *Sevastopol Sketches*), which were incredibly successful and which propelled him into St. Petersburg literary circles. He was not, however, especially popular, as many found him aloof and arrogant.

Traveling in the West for a time before returning to the family estate in 1863, he published *Kazaki* (*The Cossacks*) in 1863, and followed its success with his greatest works, *War and Peace* (1865–69), the grand panoramic description of Russia's war against Napoleon, and *Anna Karenina* (1875–77), the profile of a woman who loves and who fears that her lover will desert her.

While at work on *Anna Karenina*, Tolstoy experienced a religious transformation, finding a religion of love based on a literal interpretation of Jesus' Sermon on the Mount. His writings turned to more philosophical and religious issues, though he continued to write fiction, such as *Smert' Ivana Il'icha* (1886; *The Death of Ivan Ilyich*). The narrative of Tolstoy's last novel, *Voskresenie* (1899; *Resurrection*), is highly irregular, as the authorial voice periodically intrudes to denounce contemporary evils. He condemned capitalism, private property, and the division of labor, extolling a simple life of poverty and physical labor. His fearless criticisms resulted in his excommunication from the Russian Orthodox Church in 1901, but this only increased his popularity. Some followers attempted to create social utopias based on Tolstoy's ideas.

His newfound religious beliefs, however, estranged Tolstoy from his family. His wife was greatly irritated by his ideas about private property, especially by his desire to let his work enter the public domain, since the royalties from his books were the family's only means of support. In 1910 Tolstoy left the family estate with his daughter Aleksandra and set off for a monastery in southern Russia. During the journey, however, he fell ill and died at the railway station in Astapovo. His funeral was a national event.

Toomer, Jean (1894–1967)

American writer. Although he wrote plays, short stories, and religious meditations, Toomer is best remembered for his experimental novel, *Cane* (1922), a central text of American modernism and one of the most important works to come out of the 1920s' flourishing of African-American artistic production known as the Harlem Renaissance.

Eugene Toomer was born and raised in Washington, D.C. He enrolled at the University of Wisconsin, but dropped out after less than a year of studying and began reading intensely while attending classes at various colleges. During this period he started working on what would bécome *Cane*. A stint as a substitute principal at a school in Georgia sparked Toomer's interest in African-American life in the South, and the new culture produced by the massive migration of black Americans to the urban centers of the North in the early part of the century.

Cane combines poetry and avant-garde prose fiction. Divided into three sections, the book opens in a sensuously depicted American South, journeys to the urban sprawl of Washington, D.C., and New York City, and returns south to end with a long piece entitled "Kab-nis" that draws on Toomer's experience in Georgia. The book is elegiac in tone, a celebration of a rural black folk culture that Toomer believed was dying out in the new century. But *Cane*'s view of black life is far from romanticized; Toomer was conscious of the brutalities of American racism north and south, and remained wary of outright celebra-tion of the agrarian past.

In the 1920s Toomer became inter-ested in the mystical philosophy of Georgei Gurdjieff, and would soon ded-icate his life to the understanding of Gurdjieff's religious thought. His new interest coincided with a disavowal of his previous concern with African-American culture. When *Cane* was pub-lished, Toomer, who was extremely light-skinned, had proudly proclaimed himself an African American and pre-dicted that black America would supply the nation with its next important writer. Now, citing his mixed ancestry, he de-clared himself a member of a new "American race" and refused to al-low his work to be published in anthol-ogies specifically dedicated to African-American writers.

Ironically, his subsequent work aroused little interest, and the bulk of his work remained out of print until af-ter his death, when a new interest in African-American literary history em-braced *Cane* as a twentieth-century American classic.

Toomer's other works include the ex-perimental play *Balo: A Sketch of Negro Life* (1924) and *Essentials* (1931), a med-itation on Gurdjieff's philosophy.

Torah

Jewish religious text. Also known as the "Pentateuch" or "The Five Books of Moses," the Torah comprises the first five books of the Bible, from the crea-tion of the universe at the beginning of Genesis to Moses' death at the end of Deuteronomy. In between these events,

the Torah recounts the history of the an-cient Israelites' growth in Canaan and subsequent enslavement in Egypt. In ad-dition, the Torah sets forth, primarily in the book of Leviticus, an elaborate sys-tem of law and custom ranging from the Ten Commandments to dietary injunc-tions against eating certain foods.

In the synagogue, the reading of the Pentateuch is carefully prescribed. The Torah is divided into fifty-four portions, with one read each Sabbath, and occa-sionally on important holidays. Simchat Torah, a joyous holiday, marks the an-nual conclusion of the reading of Deu-teronomy and the beginning, once again, of Genesis. On these joyous hol-idays, worshipers carry the Torah outside the synagogue and dance around with it, celebrating the continuity and renewal of this sacred text.

At the beginning of the services, the Torah is removed from the ark and car-ried around the synagogue for congre-gants to kiss or touch as it passes by. In Orthodox services, the Torah cannot be read unless at least ten adult males—a minyan—are present at the service, though in Reform and Conservative syn-agogues, ten adult Jews of either sex will suffice.

Torres, Camilo (1929–1966)

Colombian priest and revolutionary. Torres was born in Bogotá to an affluent pediatrician and his high-society wife. He was educated at the German School in Bogotá, the National University, and a diocesan seminary, after which he went to study sociology at the University of Louvain, Belgium. Having obtained his master's degree, Torres became vice-rector of the Latin American College Seminary and returned to Colombia in 1958 to research socioeconomic condi-tions in Bogotá for his doctoral thesis.

In the next few years, he became chaplain and lecturer at the Universidad Nacional (1959–62), cofounded its Fac-ulty of Sociology, and was elected rector by the students. The official rector then closed the university and the archbishop of Bogotá ordered Torres to resign both his posts. Later working with the Agrarian Reform Agency, Torres created a rural action unit, an experience which reinforced his beliefs that the only way to secure Catholic social justice would be to alter radically the existing power structures. By combining sociology and Marxism he found the tools for a Christian social and political critique, and in 1965 he called together opposition groups on the left to found the People's United Front, composed mostly of the nonaligned and the popular classes who were disenchanted.

Although his aim was to overthrow the oligarchy through peaceful means, he claimed he was not against the use of violence to counter violent attacks. He soon encountered opposition, once again, from within the Church, which claimed that the United Front platform contained points irreconcilable with church doctrine, and in June 1965, Torres was forced to give up the priesthood. He continued to organize United Front cells all over the country and was jailed at least twice, but despite his efforts, the Front fell apart due to internal dissension. In October Torres joined a group of rural guerrillas, the National Liberation Army, as an ordinary combatant. In January 1966 he issued a declaration from the mountains explaining his decision, and on February 15 was killed in a confrontation with the army in Santander. Although he left no lasting organization, he is seen today, especially by the Latin American left, as a martyr of the "rebel church."

totem pole

American Indian carved pole. Typical of the Northwest Indian culture, these carved and painted vertical poles usually depict symbolic spirits and animals, specific to each family. The carvings utilize a standardized collection of images, familiar to all tribes of the Northwest coast. The totem pole usually contains the equivalent of a family crest, and more rarely, a pictographic version of a family legend, usually complex enough to require an actual family member to interpret properly. At the top of the pole, the ancestor guardian spirit of the family is often carved, and it is from this guardian spirit that the word "totem" is actually derived.

The poles themselves are used in a variety of ways: as grave markers, house poles to support the roof, portal poles through which one walks to enter the house, welcoming poles by bodies of water to identify the owner, mortuary poles that contain human remains, memorial poles erected when a house changes hands to signify the past and present owners, ridicule poles that bear the upside-down image of one who has failed in some way, and debt poles that serve as a marker of debt and are destroyed when the debt is paid in full. The totem pole serves as a measure of wealth, as many artists must be hired to create the elaborate carvings and paintings. The construction of totem poles peaked during the first part of the nineteenth century, a result of the widespread use of metal tools and the increased wealth of Indian chiefs from the European fur trade.

Toulouse-Lautrec, Henri de (1864–1901)

French painter and lithographer. Lautrec's deformed physical appearance is as much a part of the nineteenth-century artist's mythology as are his innovative paintings, lithographs, and posters. Not quite the midget he has been commonly portrayed as being, Lautrec was probably as much as five feet tall. A pair of childhood sporting accidents stopped the growth of his legs after he turned fifteen, leaving him with a disproportionate build: his head appeared enormous atop his stunted body.

Descended from French nobility,

Lautrec was reported to have shown a flair for graphic design early in his childhood. Despite his noble pedigree, he was attracted to the seedier sides of Parisian life. His mature work focused on the theaters, music halls, brothels, cafés, and circuses that he often frequented.

The colors that Lautrec employed were garish and confrontational, and his lines were bold and expressive. Among his influences were Spanish painter Francisco José de Goya (1746–1828), (whose etchings he collected), French artists Edgar Degas (1834–1917) and Paul Gauguin (1848–1903), as well as Japanese color prints. His work was significant in legitimizing the mediums of poster making and lithographs, and his works include his painting *Au bal du Moulin de la Galette* (1889) and his lithograph *La Clownesse assisé* (*Mademoiselle Cha-V-kao*) (1895; *Seated Female Clown*).

Chief among the factors that led to his death at age thirty-six was alcoholism. On exhibit at the Lautrec Museum in his native town of Albi is his walking stick, which concealed a flask of brandy and a tiny drinking glass, testimony to his habit.

Touré, Samory (c. 1830–1900)

Mandingo leader. Touré founded the Muslim kingdom in the Kankan region of Guinea and resisted French colonial expansion in West Africa. Born in Sanankoro, now part of northern Guinea, he became renowned as a warrior and was chieftain of his native town. In 1868 he proclaimed himself an *almami*, or Muslim religious leader, and began to expand his power to the Niger River, where he came against French colonial armies. He did battle with them almost continually from 1883 until his death in exile in Gabon. In 1886 Touré promised the French he would not cross the Niger and moved northeastward instead toward the Black Volta River. He met resistance from the king of Sikasso and

began a slow retreat into present-day Liberia, where he was captured by the French in 1898. At its height in the 1880s, his empire extended throughout what is now Sierra Leone and northern Liberia into Burkina Faso.

Touré was the great-grandfather of the first president of the Republic of Guinea, Sékou Touré (1958–1984), and his career, remembered in many songs and stories, has been an inspiration to African nationalist movements.

Toussaint L'Ouverture, François (c. 1744–1803)

Haitian revolutionary. Toussaint liberated the slaves of the French colony of Saint Domingue (now Haiti) and established the first black-led government in the Western Hemisphere.

Born a slave on the Breda plantation in Saint Domingue, the French portion of the Caribbean island Hispaniola, Toussaint received a limited Jesuit education as a young man. He remained throughout his life a strictly observant Catholic, disdaining voodoo and other non-Christian beliefs. Toussaint became a livestock manager and steward on his master's plantation before being freed in 1777.

In 1791 Toussaint joined a slave revolt that had erupted in the north of the island (after helping his old master to safety), and soon formed his own army, which he trained in the tactics of guerrilla warfare. By 1793 he had appended "L'Ouverture" to his given name. The origin of the epithet, which is French for "The Opening," is uncertain (one report claims that the name was born when the French governor of Saint Domingue said that Toussaint "finds an opening everywhere" to break through enemy lines).

When war broke out in 1792 between the French and the Spanish, Toussaint quickly allied himself with the Spanish forces who possessed the eastern section of Hispaniola. Now a general, Toussaint refused to collaborate with white radicals and won a string of decisive battles in the north. He had almost driven the French out of the area when, in 1794, he abruptly changed sides, and began to fight *with* the French against the Spaniards and their British allies. He claimed that the switch was in recognition of France's recent decision to free all slaves in its territories.

Toussaint and the French quickly drove the Spanish and British forces out, and Toussaint became governor of Saint Domingue, still a French protectorate. Eventually, Toussaint gained control over all Hispaniola and worked to foster reconciliation between blacks, mulattoes, and the remaining whites on the island. Meanwhile, he was justifiably suspicious that Napoleon Bonaparte would attempt to restore slavery on the island. Although Toussaint professed his loyalty to Bonaparte and his revolutionary government in France, the French arrested Toussaint in 1802, allegedly for planning an uprising. Toussaint was taken to Fort-de-Joux in the French Alps, where he died in 1803 after prolonged interrogation.

Trail of Tears

Cherokee name for the forced removal of the Cherokee Indians from their traditional lands in Georgia to "Indian Territory" in what is now Oklahoma. In 1828, when gold was discovered on Cherokee land in Georgia, whites pressured the government to force the Cherokee from the area. In December 1835 the U.S. government drafted the Treaty of New Echota, which purchased all Cherokee land east of the Mississippi for $5 million. When only a small, nonrepresentative minority of Cherokee agreed to the terms of the treaty and signed it, the 14,000 to 16,000 dissenting Cherokee—the overwhelming majority—were forcibly evicted from their land. U.S. president Andrew Jackson proceeded to seize tribal lands in the southeastern portion of the United States and exchange them for lands west of the Mississippi. In 1838 army general Winfield Scott and 7,000 troops quartered American Indians in concentration camps in preparation for the massive relocation, while their homes were pillaged and burned by local white residents.

The Cherokee displacement was undertaken by means of a forced march from Georgia to Oklahoma that came to be called the Trail of Tears. In the fall of 1838, the Cherokee, led by Chief Koowes-Koowe (known as John Ross to the English), traveled in several detachments by foot, horseback, and wagon through Tennessee and parts of Kentucky, Illinois, Missouri, and Arkansas. Insufficient food supplies and a lack of blankets and warm clothing caused widespread illness and suffering, especially after winter set in. Approximately 4,000 Cherokee died from disease and exposure during the six-month-long journey. Roughly 1,000 escaped and lived as fugitives in the Great Smoky Mountains. The main body of those who survived the journey reached eastern Oklahoma in the winter of 1839. Bitter feuds broke out almost immediately between the uprooted Cherokee and those Cherokee who had signed the Treaty of New Echota, voluntarily leaving their Georgia homelands. The uprooted Cherokee were also joined in Oklahoma by the Creek, Chickasaw, Choctaw, and Seminole Indian tribes, all of whom were also deported from their traditional lands, under the Indian Removal Act of 1830. Today much of the acquired territory serves as a federal reservation.

Trollope, Anthony (1815–1882)

English novelist. Born in London to a father who failed in law, then in farming, Trollope encountered difficulties in his early years. His mother supported the family by writing more than forty books.

By 1834 the family was living in Belgium; however, Trollope eventually returned to London to be a clerk in the General Post Office. In 1841 he was made a postal surveyor's clerk and transferred to Ireland, where he saved money, married in 1844, and began his writing career.

Trollope's first novels were not immediately successful, but he persevered, and after traveling extensively for the postal service in Ireland and England, he wrote *The Warden* (1855) and its sequel, *Barchester Towers* (1857), both of which gained him recognition as a major novelist. These were the first two novels of what would become the "Chronicles of Barsetshire," the name of the fictitious county where all the novels are set. Another group of his novels is known as the Palliser novels and includes *Phineas Finn* (1869), *The Eustace Diamonds* (1872), and *The Duke's Children* (1880), to name a few. The earlier series concentrated on the clergy in society, while the later books explored the lives of politicians.

Besides many articles and travel pieces, Trollope produced more than fifty novels and developed an extraordinarily systematic approach to his writing: he would rise every morning at five-thirty and write for three and a half hours before breakfast, writing 250 words every quarter hour, and producing ten pages of a novel per day. He would schedule his days and calculate in advance how long it would require to finish specific projects, recording the number of pages written each day, and exulting in his ability to gauge his output accurately. He was legendary for his industry and punctuality. This is one of the main reasons his works have been accused of being devoid of artistic merit: critics believed they were churned out rather than inspired. In fact, the stories he wrote are complete in their detail and inner consistency, though the subjects tend to be ordinary.

Trudeau, Pierre [Elliott] (1919–)

Prime minister of Canada from 1968 to 1979 and 1980 to 1984. Born Joseph Philippe Pierre Ives Elliotte Trudeau to an affluent family of French and Scottish descent, Trudeau attended an elite Jesuit preparatory school and the University of Montreal, from which he received a law degree in 1943. He did postgraduate study at Harvard, the University of Paris, and the London School of Economics, and returned to Canada in 1949. While in Canada, Trudeau served as consultant to the Privy Council for three years, and in 1950 he helped found the monthly critical journal *Cité Libre* (Free City). Specializing in labor and civil liberties cases, Trudeau practiced law from 1951 to 1961. He founded the Rassemblement movement in 1956 to unite Quebec's leftists, but withdrew when the movement began to support separatism, as he was an ardent anti-separatist.

He served as assistant professor at the University of Montreal from 1961 to 1965, when he ran successfully for a seat in the House of Commons as a "new wave" Liberal. Appointed first as parliamentary secretary (1966) and then minister of justice and attorney general (1967), Trudeau promoted social welfare programs and toured French-speaking Africa on behalf of Prime Minister Lester B. Pearson. When Pearson announced his retirement, Trudeau campaigned for the leadership of the Liberal Party. He became party head on April 6, 1968, and was elected prime minister by a landslide two weeks later. Throughout the 1970s Trudeau endured bitter struggles with the French separatists of Quebec, the weakening of the Liberal Party, and a host of economic and social problems.

In the general elections of 1979, the Progressive Conservative Party gained a majority in the government, though Trudeau retained his seat in Parliament.

The Liberals regained power in the general elections of 1980, and Trudeau began his fourth term as prime minister. After the defeat of the Quebec separatists in a referendum, he began his drive to reform Canada's constitution by seeking independence from the British Parliament. In 1981 the Canadian House of Commons approved his reform resolutions, and in 1982 England formally declared Canada independent. During his final years in office, he focused on promoting greater economic independence for Canada and better trade relations with foreign powers. He resigned as head of the Liberal Party in 1984. His books include *Federalism and the French-Canadians* (1968), *Approaches to Politics* (1970), and *Conversations with Canadians* (1972).

Truffaut, François (1932–1984)

French film director and critic. Truffaut began his film career as a critic of conventional French cinema and as a champion of the Nouvelle Vague (New Wave) of French filmmaking. He helped develop the *auteur* theory, which emphasized spontaneity in film over literary and script-oriented filmmaking. Among the figures of the new French cinema, Truffaut is considered the most gifted and sincere.

Truffaut had a childhood similar to that of the main character in his first major film, *Les Quatre Cent Coups* (1959; *The 400 Blows*). As a child, he was neglected by adults, spent time in a reformatory, and left school to work in a factory by age fifteen. He was drawn to movies early on, however, joining the *ciné* (movie) clubs; his enthusiasm for film brought him to the attention of critic André Bazin, who employed him on the staff of the film magazine *Cahiers du Cinéma*. Following his desertion from military service and subsequent imprisonment, Truffaut rejoined the staff of *Cahiers* and quickly gained a reputation as the most ferocious of the

young critics who formed the French New Wave. Highly regarded even before launching his career as a filmmaker, Truffaut was able to have considerable control over the writing and production of his early work; he eventually formed his own production company, Les Films du Carrosse, which produced films by other directors as well.

Truffaut experimented with many different styles and cinematic structures, blending suspense and humor, using a variety of techniques, in such films as *Jules et Jim* (1961; *Jules and Jim*). He sometimes self-consciously blurred the boundaries around art, life, and fiction, as in *Tirez sur le pianist* (1960; *Shoot the Piano Player*), in which the protagonist tries to become a fictional character. In 1973 he revealed to his audience the craft of filmmaking in a film about making a film, *La Nuit américaine* (*Day for Night*), which won the Oscar for best foreign film that year. Despite their technical innovations, his films always maintained a perpetual youthful enthusiasm, a penchant for intimacy, and a powerful grasp of the comic and tragic dimensions of human beings.

Truth, Sojourner (1797–1883)

Abolitionist, religious leader, and women's rights activist. Sojourner Truth was the adopted name of Isabella Baumfree, later Isabella Van Wagenen. She was born a slave on a Dutchman's estate in Ulster County, New York, and her first language was low Dutch. She was sold several times until reaching the estate of John Dumont in 1810, where she married another slave. She bore five children, some of whom may have been fathered by Dumont.

In 1826 she fled Dumont's house with her infant daughter and was taken in and employed by Maria and Isaac Van Wagenen. That same year, she also fought for her son's freedom when he was sold across state borders in violation of New York law. With the help of Ulster County Quakers, she brought suit successfully against her son's owner. In 1827, after a profound conversion experience, she joined the Methodist Church and the Zion African Church, and began preaching at the camp meetings of the Second Great Awakening.

In 1832 she became involved in a religious society run by the self-proclaimed prophet Matthias. The only black member, she gave her life savings and did domestic work for Matthias's Kingdom, until it dissolved in 1835 after a sex scandal and a suspected murder. She was implicated in the murder but never actually charged. She went on to win a libel suit against those who had maligned her.

She returned to Manhattan and struggled through the economic depression of the 1830s. In June 1843 she felt God had again spoken to her: she took the name Sojourner Truth and began preaching at camp meetings of evangelical Protestants. That winter, she joined the Northampton (Massachusetts) Association, where she met William Lloyd Garrison and Frederick Douglass, and joined the reformers' lecture circuit, speaking on slavery, women's rights, and temperance. She supported herself through charitable contributions and the sale of *The Narrative of Sojourner Truth*, an autobiography she dictated to a white friend, Olive Gilbert, in 1850.

Her reform work was premised on religious faith. Dismayed by Frederick Douglass's suggestion that violence might be of use in the fight against slavery, Sojourner Truth demanded, "Frederick, is God dead?" At a women's rights conference in 1851, in response to men's comments that women were weak and in need of protection, Sojourner Truth reportedly declared, "I have ploughed and planted and gathered into barns, and no man can head me! And ain't I a woman?"—in effect calling for a redefinition of "woman" to include working-class and black females. In 1858, when

a largely male audience said that she was too forceful to be a member of the "gentle sex," she bared her breasts to prove herself and shame her listeners. During the drafting of the Fourteenth Amendment to the Constitution, she also fought for the deletion of the word "male" in the new extension of voting rights.

During the Civil War, she served as a nurse to Union soldiers and collected food and clothing for black volunteer regiments. In 1864 she was invited to the White House to meet President Abraham Lincoln. The next few years were spent in Washington resettling black refugees, initiating protests against illegally segregated streetcars, and lobbying for the establishment of a state for freed slaves in the West. Her skepticism about the prospects for blacks under Reconstruction influenced many ex-slaves to move west to Kansas and Missouri. She herself moved to Battle Creek, Michigan, where she died after several years of ill health.

Tsvetaeva, Marina [Ivanovna] (1892–1941) Russian poet. One of the most important Russian poets, Tsvetaeva had her career cut short by political strife. Born into the family of a famous art critic and the founder of the Pushkin Museum of Fine Arts in Moscow, Tsvetaeva began to write poetry in her childhood and published her first collection of poems, *Vechernii al'bom* (1910; *Evening Album*), at the age of eighteen, followed by several others, such as *Volshebnyi fonar'* (1912; *The Magic Lantern*) and *Versty* (1921; *Mileposts*). Though she was known in literary circles, she avoided the temptation to join an avant-garde movement. Politically, she opposed the October Revolution (1917), and her husband, Sergei Efron, fought with the White Army. Defeated, the couple emigrated in 1922, heading first to Prague and then to Paris. Although her poems were well received in Prague (in 1923, while there, she published *Remeslo* [*Craft*], which many consider to be her best work), her relations with émigré circles became strained in Paris, as reflected in the negative reviews she received for one volume, *Posle Rossii* (1928; *After Russia*), published in Paris.

Her daughter, Ariadne, eventually returned to the U.S.S.R., and her husband became an undercover Soviet agent, participating in a political assassination. Suffering from homesickness and poverty, and estranged from the émigré community, Tsvetaeva went back to the Soviet Union in 1939 to discover that her husband had already been imprisoned and shot before her arrival, and her daughter was imprisoned as well. Though Tsvetaeva fared slightly better under Russian Communist leader Josef Stalin, her life was still quite difficult. Due to her political associations, she was denied an apartment in Moscow and was forced to survive by translation work. Of her poetry, only a single poem from her days in Prague was republished. In the evacuation of Moscow during World War II, Tsvetaeva was relocated to the small, isolated town of Elabuga and, without friends or support, she committed suicide. Through the efforts of many writers and her daughter, Tsvetaeva's work has gradually become reincorporated into Soviet literature.

Tubman, Harriet (c. 1820–1913)

Underground railroad conductor, nurse, and Union spy. Born "Aramenta" to a slave family in Maryland, she took her mother's name later in life. From the age of five, she was hired out by her masters to clean houses. When the thirteen-year-old Harriet tried to protect another slave from a whipping, her overseer threw a rock at her head, resulting in an injury that caused her to suffer seizures for the rest of her life.

In 1844 she married John Tubman, a freedman. In 1849, when she heard rumors that she was to be sold out of the state, she fled north to Philadelphia, though her brothers and husband refused to accompany her. Over the next ten years Tubman made nineteen trips back to the South, rescuing some three hundred slaves on the Underground Railroad. Her methods were strict—she often pointed a gun at slaves who became nervous or panicked—but she never lost one "passenger." On discovering that her husband had remarried, she moved with her parents to Ontario, Canada. She became close to the abolitionist John Brown, missing a chance to participate in his ill-fated 1859 raid on Harper's Ferry due to illness.

During the Civil War, she organized intelligence and scouting missions for the Union, as well as serving as a nurse. After the war, she started the Harriet Tubman Home for Indigent Aged Negroes and fought for freedmen's schools and suffrage rights. In 1869 she married Nelson Davis, a disabled veteran twenty years her junior, who would die in 1888 of tuberculosis. Royalties from two biographies by a local schoolteacher named Sarah Bradford helped pay her living expenses. Although her application for compensation for her wartime services was never accepted, she was buried with military honors.

Tupamaros

Latin American Marxist rebels. The Tupamaros were part of the global Marxist insurgency that erupted throughout the Third World in the 1960s. Founded in 1963 in Montevideo, Uruguay, they took their name from Tupac Amaru, the eighteenth-century Inca descendant who defended the Indians against the Spanish. Raúl Sendic, a young labor organizer, founded the movement, which was initially a sort of "Robin Hood" effort, robbing banks and businesses and distributing money and goods to the poor. The Tupamaros sought to create a socialist state to replace Uruguay's mixed economy.

As economic conditions worsened, Tupamaro activity became more violent: arson, the raiding of arsenals, bombings, assassinations, and kidnappings became commonplace. In an effort to gain public recognition, the Tupamaros kidnapped several prominent figures, including British ambassador Geoffrey Jackson, who remained in captivity for 244 days before being released.

On April 15, 1972, when the Tupamaros were at the height of their power, President Juan María Bordaberry declared an internal war against them, and that same year Raúl Sendic was recaptured (he had escaped from prison in 1971). A military coup in 1973 practically destroyed the movement, using hardline tactics and a well-disciplined army: more than 300 Tupamaros were killed and 3,000 imprisoned. With the return to a democratic government in 1985, most of those jailed were released, including Sendic. Tupamaro membership at this time had decreased to approximately 1,000. The Tupamaros are but one example of similar revolutionary groups who have gone back in history to legitimate themselves with reference to mytho-historic resistance movements. The Monteneros in Argentina and the Sandinistas in Nicaragua represent two such cases.

Turgenev, Ivan [Sergeevich] (1818–1883)
Russian novelist. The first Russian writer to gain fame in Europe, Turgenev was born in Orel to a family of provincial gentry. He was educated at home, then at the Universities of Moscow and St. Petersburg, graduating from the latter in 1837. In 1843 he published *Parasha*, a tale in verse, but his continued idleness inspired his mother to secure him a job with the civil service. By 1845 Turgenev was involved in a love affair with a married woman and had abandoned his job. He lived in France from 1847 to 1850, producing plays and the short-story collection *Zapiski okhotnika* (1852; *A*

Sportsman's Sketches). His mother's death in 1850 left him wealthy. Moving between Europe and his estate in Russia, Turgenev produced a spate of novels in short order, including *Rudin* (1856), *Dvorianskoe gnezdo* (1859; *A Nest of Gentry*), *Nakanune* (1860; *On the Eve*), and *Ottsy i deti* (1862; *Fathers and Sons*).

Turgenev's troubles with his fellow Russians are legendary. *On the Eve* was refused publication in the journal *Sovremennik* (The Contemporary), where most of his previous work had been published, because it had been taken over by radicals, and the protagonist of the novel *Fathers and Sons* sparked such vituperative debate from both sides of the political spectrum in Russia that Turgenev moved back to Europe permanently. Considered to be the most "poetical" of the nineteenth-century Russian writers, Turgenev depends more on "atmosphere" than psychological analysis to create his characters. He spent his last years in the company of the French literary world, where he enjoyed the friendship of writers Gustave Flaubert (1821–1880) and the young Guy de Maupassant (1850–1893).

Turner, Nat (1800–1831)
American slave revolt leader. Nat Turner was born a slave in 1800 on the plantation of John Travis in Southampton County, Virginia. He was a precocious and intelligent child who learned to read early and was a quick and creative student. When Turner was still a youth, his father successfully escaped from the plantation and apparently returned to Africa. The young Turner sought to follow him but was caught and severely beaten. A deeply religious Christian, Turner assumed that his escape attempt had failed because God wanted him to free all the slaves, not just himself; he summarily resolved to plan a slave revolt that would liberate all the slaves in his area.

Turner's convictions were reinforced

when he began having visions and hearing voices suggesting that he rise up against the Virginia slave owners; he fasted and prayed and began spending more and more time by himself, and his visions increased. On May 12, 1828, he believed the Holy Spirit appeared to him and told him he would have to fight against evil and that when the time came he would receive a sign. Three years later, in February 1831, the sign came; there was an eclipse of the sun and Turner heard a voice saying, "Arise and slay the enemies of God with their own weapons."

He was so deeply affected that he trembled as though sick for days, but he told six trusted companions of his plans and assured himself of their support and silence. On August 31, 1831, the seven conspirators strolled into the woods as if for a picnic; instead they planned one of the most significant slave revolts in American history. The seven men decided to launch the revolt that same night, and planned to ride from plantation to plantation slaughtering white families and gathering supporters and weapons, working their way toward Jerusalem, the county seat.

The revolt was proceeding as planned and over fifty whites had been killed when Turner's force, which had swelled to more than fifty men, was intercepted by a group of armed whites and forced to retreat. The rebels were scattered and Turner hid in the woods alone. Meanwhile, at the state government's request, the U.S. government sent two warships carrying eight hundred marines to Virginia and the Virginia state militia was also summoned. These forces participated in indiscriminate reprisals against the slaves, killing over one hundred people on the first day alone and torturing many more. Nat Turner was a fugitive in the woods for eight weeks, hunted by a 1,000-man force, before his whereabouts were revealed by some slaves who stumbled upon him in the woods. He

was tried and hanged on November 11, 1831.

Tutu, Desmond [Mpilo] (1931–)

South African Anglican archbishop. Born in Klerksdorp, Transvaal, South Africa, to parents of Xhosa and Tswana heritage, Tutu attended mission schools where his father taught, Bantu Normal College, and the University of South Africa in Johannesburg, receiving his B.A. in 1954. He taught school for three years before devoting himself to theology, graduating from St. Peter's Theological College in 1960. He was ordained an Anglican priest the following year and ministered to several congregations. He moved to England in 1962 and for the next several years served as a part-time curate while studying at King's College, London, receiving his B.D. in 1965 and his M.Th. in 1966.

Returning to South Africa, Tutu lectured at several universities until he was called back to Britain in 1972 to serve as an assistant director of the World Council of Churches. He returned to South Africa as the dean of Johannesburg Cathedral (the first black to be so named) in 1975, became the bishop of Lesotho from 1976 to 1978, and then general secretary of the South African Council of Churches from 1978 to 1985, during this latter period serving also as the assistant Anglican bishop of Johannesburg.

Under his leadership, the Council of Churches played a prominent role in antiapartheid activity. By this time Tutu had become internationally recognized as a leading advocate of black rights, nonviolent resistance, and abolition of apartheid in South Africa. A collection of his lectures, *The Divine Intention*, was published in 1982, and a collection of sermons, *Hope and Suffering*, in 1983. He traveled throughout the world garnering support for economic sanctions against the white-ruled government in South Africa. In 1984 he was awarded the Nobel Peace Prize as well as the

Martin Luther King, Jr., Humanitarian Award.

In 1986 he became the first black Anglican bishop of Johannesburg, and the following year he was named the first black archbishop of Cape Town, the official head of the South African Church.

Tzevi, Shabbetai (1626–1676)

Jewish leader. A charismatic personality combined with a passion for mystical philosophy led the twenty-two-year-old Shabbetai Tzevi to the conclusion that he was the messiah. Eventually making his way from Smyrna to Constantinople, where the Kabbalistic cult was particularly strong, he received a certificate proclaiming him the savior of the Jewish people. Next he traveled to Cairo and Palestine, making converts along the way. Some of these, like Raphael Halebi, the treasurer to the Turkish governor, were wealthy and influential men who provided generous funding for his mission.

Shabbetai Tzevi found his most avid disciple in a twenty-year-old student from Jerusalem named Nathan of Gaza. Nathan proclaimed the year 1666 to be the apocalypse and Shabbetai Tzevi to be the redeemer. In 1665, with the Jewish leaders of Jerusalem threatening to excommunicate him for heresy, Shabbetai returned to Smyrna, though his movement continued to gain momentum. The following year, he went to Constantinople, where he was imprisoned; in the eyes of his followers this persecution was further proof of his divine mission.

So strong was his appeal that even after his conversion to Islam in September 1666, many of Shabbetai's disciples remained faithful to him. The sultan made him his personal doorkeeper and granted him a sizable allowance. Shabbetai's followers interpreted this apostasy as a step on the path to redemption; it symbolized the relative unimportance of outward professions of faith as long as one remained inwardly Jewish. While his movement continued to gain converts, Shabbetai himself fell out of the sultan's favor and ended his life in exile in Albania.

U

'ūd

Arab instrument. Literally meaning "wood" in Arabic, the 'ūd is a stringed instrument used frequently in Islamic music. It is the parent of the European lute and first appeared in seventh-century Persia as the barbat. The 'ūd takes its name from the aloe wood used in the belly of the instrument, in contrast to the skin bellies of earlier models.

The 'ūd has a deep, pear-shaped body, a fretless fingerboard, and a shorter neck than the lute. It commonly has four pairs of strings that are plucked with a plectrum, and has a pitch range that is similar to that of the lute and the guitar.

Ukrainka, Lesia (1871–1913)

Ukrainian poet, playwright, and literary critic. The daughter of the writer Olena

Pchilka, Lesia Ukrainka, born Larysa Petrivna Kosach-Kvitka, was afflicted with tuberculosis in her childhood and was compelled for many years to live in the southern part of Ukraine. She was educated at home and achieved advanced knowledge of world history and literature, as well as of many foreign languages; she also began writing poetry in her early childhood. Ukrainka's early lyrics, influenced by Ukrainian writers Taras Shevchenko (1814–1861) and Ivan Franko (1856–1916), and by European literary models, were enriched by new "exotic" motifs. Her poetry is marked by an impressionistic subtlety not previously known in Ukrainian literature. Ukrainka was also active in the Ukrainian struggle against czarism; she joined Ukrainian Marxist organizations, translating the *Communist Manifesto* into Ukrainian in 1902. Her greatest achievement is the dramatic poetry she wrote in her last years, which was inspired by various historical milieus—the classical world, early Christian times, the Middle Ages. In one poem, *Kaminnyi hospodar* (1912; *The Stone Host*), she developed her own version of the Don Juan theme. Ukrainka's crowning achievement was the dramatic poem *Lisova pisnya* (1912; *The Forest Song*), derived from folk songs and popular legends. It is a symbolic drama on the universal and timeless conflict between an exalted dream and mean, base reality, and it is characterized by lyricism, melodiousness, and an incomparable richness of language. Ukrainka was a leading figure in the Ukrainian modernist movement.

Umayyad (661–750 C.E.)

First Islamic dynasty. The Umayyads came to power when the shrewd politician Mu'âwiya, then governor of Syria, emerged victorious from a war with 'Alī (c. 600–661), the fourth caliph of Islam. Mu'âwiya succeeded in establishing his son Yazid as heir to the caliphate, thus founding the dynasty that would have a profound impact on the emerging Islamic civilization.

Mu'âwiya moved the capital of the empire from Mecca to Damascus. This brought the Muslims into direct contact with the Hellenistic civilizations in the former Byzantine provinces of Syria and Palestine—civilizations upon which they would draw heavily to forge their own. The skilled and assertive Umayyads were able to subdue internal revolts in Iraq and the Arabian Peninsula and continue outward expansion. By the end of their rule, the Islamic empire had stretched its borders westward to the Pyrenees, and eastward to the Indus River and the Chinese frontier. The building of the Islamic empire and civilization was sparked by the process of assimilating the existing administrations and cultures of the newly acquired Persian and Byzantine territories. Under the sweeping reforms of 'Abd al-Malik (r. 685–705), the financial and political administrations were made Arabic, Islamic currency was issued, and courier service established. Parallel achievements in poetry, art, and architecture exemplify Umayyad mastery. The wealthy court patronized Arabian literary forms, music, and the arts, and built dozens of opulent palaces and monuments, the most famous of which is the Great Umayyad Mosque in Damascus, still standing today.

The Umayyads were overthrown and massacred by the 'Abbâsids in 750. Since most histories of the period were written under 'Abbâsid rule, the Umayyads received biased treatment, and came to be known as impious, tyrannical kings. The sole exception is the caliph 'Umar ibn 'Abd al-'Aziz (r. 717–720), who is ranked with the Rightly Guided Caliphs as a model of piety. 'Abd al-Rahmân managed to escape the massacre and reach North Africa and then Spain, where he established another Umayyad state.

Umm Kulthûm (1910–1975)

Egyptian singer. Umm Kulthûm is considered to be the most famous singer of the Arab world in the twentieth century, and in numerous ways personally influenced the overall development of modern Arab music. Beginning her career in a small village of the Nile Delta of Egypt, she sang religious songs at a time when female vocalists were for the most part considered to be but one step removed from street dancers and prostitutes. Through personal dedication, and more than a touch of stubborn perseverance, she helped create a social niche for female singers and was instrumental in defining a new social role for music in general as the effects of phonograph recordings and radio, followed by musical films and television, began to be felt in the Arab world.

At the height of her career, she regularly commanded song lyrics from the most respected modern Arab poets and had them set to music by the premier composers of the day. She also performed texts from the classical literary tradition (including an Arabic translation of the quatrains of the Persian poet Omar Khayyám), as well as popular lyrics in the colloquial Arabic dialect of Egypt. Her concerts, held on the first Thursday of each month during the winter season, were broadcast live on Cairo radio and attracted millions of listeners. The lyrics were often distributed weeks before the concert, so that thousands of listeners had already memorized the songs before they were even first publicly performed. Umm Kulthûm regularly sang solo concerts of several hours' length, a feat demanding stamina and vocal strength to rival that of any Western opera singer. At her death, millions of mourners crowded the streets of Cairo.

Arab culture has remained particularly rich in musical traditions of diverse types (court, folk, religious, modern popular, and others); however, a special esteem has always been accorded vocal music and the human voice. It is fitting, then, that perhaps more than any other cultural figure in the modern Arab world, a female vocalist, Umm Kulthûm, should have risen to the highest rank of artistic recognition.

Undset, Sigrid (1882–1949)

Norwegian novelist. Undset is best known for her novels of medieval life in Scandinavia, a historical interest she inherited from her father, an archaeologist. As a child, Undset discovered the thirteenth-century Old Norse saga *Brennu-Njáls saga (Njal's Saga)*, and, together with her father, she pored through the text in both Norwegian and Old Norse. When her father died suddenly in 1891, Undset elected not to complete her secondary education and instead enrolled in a secretarial school. Though she had no great talent for this work, and found it very dull, her ten years as a secretary gave her great insight into the lives of her coworkers, which provided much material for her novels. Undset published her first novel in 1907, but only with the novel *Jenny* (1911) and her medieval masterpiece *Kristin Lavransdatter* (1920–22; translated as the trilogy *The Bridal Wreath, The Mistress of Husaby*, and *The Cross*) did she achieve widespread fame. In 1912 Undset married an artist she had met in Rome, with whom she had six children. Persevering as a writer, she published both realistic historical fiction and modern novels, which often chronicled the conflicts women encounter in motherhood and marriage.

Undset became increasingly interested in Catholicism, and her conversion was reflected in her fiction. In 1924 her marriage was annulled by the Church. With the Nazi invasion of Norway in 1940, Undset fled to the United States until the close of the war. There she was an active patriot and published a collaborative effort of refugee authors, *Lykkelige dager* (1947; *Happy Times in Norway*), and an account of her exile, *Tillbake til fremtiden* (1949; *Return to the Future*). After the war, Undset returned to her medieval house in Norway and to her love of medieval lore, often dressing in the gown of a Norse matron of the Middle Ages. Undset died alone, her last project—a biography of the politician Edmund Burke—left unfinished.

Unequal Treaties

Series of Chinese treaties. The Unequal Treaties were a group of concessions that China made following defeat by foreign imperialist powers in the second half of the nineteenth century. The treaties acquired this name from the Chinese because of the unequal nature of the agreements, made in favor of the Western powers under the threat of force. After China's defeat in the first Opium War, the Treaty of Nanking (now written Nanjing) was signed with Britain in 1842. This treaty ceded Hong Kong to Britain and opened five treaty ports to unrestricted foreign trade.

Subsequent treaties with Western powers solidified and increased the commercial advantages that were gained through the Treaty of Nanking. Following defeat in the second Opium War (1856–60), China was forced to accept the Treaty of Tientsin (now written Tianjin) in 1858, which effectively furthered the commercial ventures of foreign powers in China by opening the Yangzi River to foreign trade, thereby creating new potential markets in the interior of China. The Tientsin treaties also provided for foreign diplomatic residency in Beijing, the legalization of the opium trade, unrestricted movement for missionaries, and the establishment of ten new treaty ports. When China failed to ratify these treaties, foreign troops captured Beijing, and the Chinese government was once more forced to capitulate. As a result, the Chinese government signed the Peking Convention (1860), an agreement that simply ratified the particulars of the Tientsin treaties. Another privilege acquired by foreign powers was extraterritoriality, a status that allowed foreigners to set up their own legal, tax, and law enforcement systems, and granted them immunity from Chinese law.

After the fall of the czarist government in the 1917 Russian Revolution, the Soviet government renounced the advantages they had gained through the Unequal Treaties. Chinese Nationalists persuaded foreign powers to return the right to levy their own tariffs by 1931, but it was only in 1946 that the Western powers gave up their extraterritorial privileges, which in many cases had effectively been terminated by the Japanese occupation of much of China.

Unified Silla kingdom

Korean kingdom. The Unified Silla kingdom, which spanned the Korean peninsula from 668 to 918 C.E., is considered to have been the apex of Korean civilization in terms of its developments in the arts, religion, civil service, and government. The Pulkuksa Temple (780 C.E.) and nearby Sokkuram Grotto, which contains a giant granite Buddha and deities carved in relief, was a monument to the achievement of a Unified Silla. Its presence effectively made Kwangju, Silla's capital city, the undisputed center for Hwaom Buddhism. The central doctrine of Hwaom Buddhism, "consummate interfusion," permitted the coarticulation of political and religious authority from their combined seat of power at Kwangju, thereby facilitating the maintenance of centralized government by the Silla rulers.

Just as the ascendance to power of the Silla rulers was rationalized by the doctrinal positions of the prevailing Hwaom school of Buddhism, so was Unified Silla's decline and downfall linked to the internecine struggles between the highly bureaucratic Hwaom and the more populist Son Buddhisms. During the latter part of the Unified Silla period, kings began distributing favors among the aristocracy by establishing provincial capitals and appointing local governors, ostensibly in order to oversee widely dispersed territories. This system of delegating nominal power eventually led to the absolute decay and corruption of the central government itself. The baroque ideological and material investments of the Hwaom priesthood were causing that religious body to be discredited in the eyes of many of the regional nobility, who began to turn increasingly for spiritual and political support to the antischolastic order of Buddhism known as Son. Centers for the teaching and practice of this highly syncretic mélange of Buddhism, Taoism, and Confucianism were established in many parts of the country, further polarizing Kwangju as the stronghold of political and religious tradition. Ultimately, it was a leader in the Son movement, Wang Kon, who took command of the disunified Silla kingdom and thus founded the Koryo dynasty.

Historical memory of the Unified Silla period is critical to present-day claims of a specifically Korean cultural and historical identity, and to the arguments for reunification of North and South Korea. For a country that has been subject for millennia to the incursions and hegemony of its neighbors, particularly China and Japan, the ability to reconstruct a moment in time wherein Korean culture and government flourished relatively unimpeded is singularly important to the vision of the future of an independent Korean state.

United Fruit Company

American multinational corporation. The United Fruit Company was created in 1899 when the Boston Fruit Company merged with Minor Cooper Keith's various Central American enterprises.

Keith had begun, as early as 1872, to acquire banana plantations and to build a railroad in Costa Rica, and twelve years later contracted with the Costa Rican government to fund the national debt and lay about fifty more miles of track, gaining in turn ninety-nine years of full rights to the tracks and 800,000 acres of tax-exempt (for twenty years) virgin land. United Fruit Company quickly rose to the top of this high-risk industry, wiping out competitors and becoming the largest employer in Central America, with holdings in Jamaica, Nicaragua, Costa Rica, Colombia, Cuba, Panama, the Dominican Republic, Honduras, and Guatemala. Aside from building railroads, primarily for private use, the company also operated a large number of vessels—later known as the Great White Fleet—that carried freight to its destinations and inaugurated radio communication between the United States and Central America.

Having assumed the position of land developers and colonizers, United Fruit became the target of much local and popular criticism. In some areas, it was referred to as *el pulpo* (the octopus), and its policies of holding immense reserves of undeveloped lands, discriminating in labor against nationals, repeatedly interfering in the internal affairs of host countries, removing wealth wrung from local resources without adequate return to host countries, importing large populations of English-speaking Caribbean blacks and then abandoning them when banana production shifted, and monopolizing internal banana production as well as railroads, port facilities, internal communications, and ocean transport, have made the United Fruit Company an extremely unpopular presence in Latin America.

However, United Fruit Company has pointed out that it also restored ruins, including those of Zaculeu in Guatemala, and maintained the Pan American School of Agriculture in Zamorano,

Honduras. Some of its early excesses were later mitigated, as the company gradually transferred title of portions of its landholdings to individual growers, providing them with reasonable credit terms, technical assistance, and helping them market their products. In 1970 United Fruit Company merged with the AMK Corporation, a meat-packing and machinery-making conglomerate, to become the United Brands Company, which still owns or leases large banana plantations.

Among Latin American authors who have written about the presence of United Fruit and its consequences in their countries are Guatemalan novelist Miguel Angel Asturias, who described the process of Central American conquest and plunder initiated by Minor Keith in *El Papa verde* (1954; *The Green Pope*); Alvaro Cepeda Samudio, who wrote about it in his novel *La Casa grande* (1967; *The Big House*); and Colombian novelist Gabriel García Márquez, in *Cien años de soledad* (1967; *One Hundred Years of Solitude*).

Upanishads
Hindu scriptures. The Upanishads are speculative and mystical scriptures of Hinduism, regarded as the wellspring of Hindu religious thought. The more general name for the Upanishads is Vedanta (the end of the Vedas), not only because they constitute the final sections of the Vedas (the Indian religious text), but more important because they represent the "end," the consummation of the Vedas.

The Upanishads were composed beginning around 1000 B.C.E., and there are more than one hundred extant. For over 2,000 years all important Hindu religious teachers and reformers wrote commentaries on the Upanishads and on the Bhagavadgita, the Sanskrit Hindu religious poem. Although several schools of thought emerged from these commentaries, the basic tenets of Hinduism remained the same: based on the nature of reality, and following Hindu scripture, the Upanishads support the beliefs that there is one supreme being or truth (Brahman) and that through knowledge a person's self (*atman*) will unite with this supreme truth in order to achieve ultimate enlightenment.

During the nineteenth century, many translations of the Upanishads appeared in Europe and became highly influential with European thinkers, including German philosopher Arthur Schopenhauer. Providing the original impetus to Indian traditions of meditation and mental discipline, the Upanishads are regarded by many Hindus today as the fountainhead of meditational knowledge, leading to perfection.

Urabon
Japanese religious festival. The New Year festival and the Urabon, or Bon festival, are the two major Japanese cultural and religious festivals. Urabon is derived from a Buddhist ceremony and comes from a Sanskrit word meaning "All Saints' Day." During the Urabon, the Japanese celebrate the symbolic return of the spirits of the dead to their places of birth. In midsummer, celebrants build altars, clean and decorate gravesites, and clear paths from the grave to the house in an attempt to facilitate the ancestors' return, hanging lanterns and signal cloths to guide the way home. Symbolic transportation is provided in the form of straw horses or oxen, and the paths are lit by welcoming fires, or *mukaebi*, on July 13. From the thirteenth to the fifteenth, ritually prepared foods are offered on flower-lined altars, and other ceremonies recall the festival's origin in a Buddhist ceremony that honored a faithful son who rescued his mother from purgatory through ritual devotions. On the sixteenth, farewell fires, or *okuribi*, see the spirits away until the next major festival, the celebration of the New Year, welcomes them back.

Urdu

Official language of Pakistan. Urdu is an Indo-Aryan language that originated in the river valley near Delhi. It is the primary language of the Muslims of both Pakistan and India, although it is said that more families in India speak it as a home language than in Pakistan. Its speakers presently number near 50 million.

While the colloquial forms and grammatical structures of Urdu and Hindi are similar, the almost mutually unintelligible literary forms of the two languages are a result of divergent cultural influences: Hindi has been strongly influenced by Sanskrit, while Urdu has felt the influence of Persian and Arabic. Perso-Arabic script is the recognized medium for writing Urdu.

Urdu literature flourished at the courts of Golcanda and Bijapur in South India in the sixteenth and seventeenth centuries, where Muslim sultans, like Muhammad Quli Qutb Shah (1581–1611), himself a poet, patronized the arts. This was an eclectic writing, drawing upon Indian and Persian themes and freely employing a mixture of Prakit, Dravidian, Persian, and Arabic words. While the major works of this dakani period were epic poems and *masnavi* (verse romances), during the classical period of Urdu poetry, which dates from the sixteenth and seventeenth centuries until the final establishment of British rule in 1858, the *ghazal* (lyric) became the dominant form. By the end of the seventeenth century, the center of Urdu poetry had moved farther north to Aurangabad, where poets like Vali Muhammad Vali (1667–c. 1725) and Siraj ud-Din Siraj (1715–1763), composed verses in a Persian mode.

Following the dissolution of the Mughal empire and the establishment of British rule in 1858, Urdu literature became more topical. For the next seventy years Urdu writers and writing were increasingly focused upon the religious and political reform among traditional Indian Muslim elites.

Perhaps the most important Urdu poet in recent times was Muhammad Iqbal (1877–1938), proclaimed the spiritual founder of Pakistan, although he died before he could see his dream realized. Iqbal's poems, the latter ones written exclusively in Urdu, reflect such diverse themes as political activism, mystical rapture, antiorthodoxy, antiimperialism, and Islamic socialism.

In 1936 the influential *taraqqi-pasand tahrik* (the Progressive Movement) was launched. Taking "social realism and progress" as its battle cry, it attracted many of the best Urdu writers of this pivotal time, including Faiz Ahmad Faiz (1911–1984). Its influence dwindled only after India and Pakistan achieved freedom in 1947. At the same time, *jadidiyat* (modernism) came to prominence, with its emphasis on formal experimentation, individual psychology, and moderate social concern. Urdu modernists include N. M. Rashid (1910–1975) and "Miraji" (Muhammad Sanaullah, 1912–1949).

Short stories became a popular genre in the mid twentieth century; its practitioners include Saadat Hasan Manto (1912–1955), Rajinder Singh Bedi (1915–1984), and Ismat Chughtai (b. 1915). Perhaps the finest living Urdu novelist is Qurratulain Haidar (b. 1928), whose *Ag Ka Darya* presents a panorama of Indian history.

Uxmal

Ancient Mayan city. Uxmal is located fifty miles south of Mérida, Yucatán state. The ruin is characterized by Puuc architecture of the Late Classic period. Uxmal is the highest and steepest temple of all Mayan cities and the only elliptically shaped temple in the world. The temple is hollow inside and contains the vast Temple of the Magician. Mayan legend has it that the temple was built by a dwarf, hence its popular name,

Temple of the Dwarf. Four carved human figures flank the entrance of the temple. Stones for the buildings at Uxmal were taken from the limestone wells (cenotes) and were expertly cut and fitted. The Nunnery, consisting of four rectangular buildings and divided into rooms, was probably the priests' quarters. The House of Turtles was the private residence of the ruling Tutul Xius family. Construction of the city ceased when the Toltecs established their capital at Chichén. Uxmal was finally abandoned in 1450.

Uxmal is a monument to the Mayan fertility gods. Masks of the long-nosed fertility rain god Chac protrude from many of the buildings. There are many serpent panels, suggesting phallic imagery. When the Spanish came to Mexico, however, they destroyed much of the phallic symbolism in hopes of destroying paganism and indoctrinating the Indians with Christian dogma. At Uxmal, a large phallic sundial once existed on top of a hill and pointed toward the plains, where crops grew. All that remains is the truncated base, now fallen on its side.

V

Valenzuela, Luisa (1938–)

Argentine writer. Born in Buenos Aires, Argentina, the daughter of a writer and a doctor, Valenzuela was raised in Belgrano and taught by a German governess and an English tutor. Her career as a writer and journalist began at an early age when she published her first stories in *Quince Abriles* (*Fifteen Aprils*) and *Ficción* (*Fiction*) and worked as a journalist for *Esto Es*, *Atlantida*, and *El Hogar*.

Valenzuela has been widely recognized for her talent as a writer who addresses a broad range of issues with a virtuosity in the use of descriptive prose. Focusing on the irrational and tortuous reality of a volatile Argentinean state, Valenzuela combines political themes with more personal messages about male-female relationships. Her ability to play with words and her willingness to experiment with language, in addition to her deft mixture of fantasy and social reality, have led numerous critics to characterize her work as "magical realism." Her works include the novel *Señor de Tacuru* (1983; *The Lizard's Tale*) and the collected works *Clara: Thirteen Short Stories and a Novel* (1976), *Aquí pasan cosas raras* (1979; *Strange Things Happen Here: Twenty-Six Short Stories and a Novel*), and *Open Door* (1988).

Vallejo, César (1892–1938)

Peruvian poet and novelist. Born in the Andean town of Santiago de Chuco, Peru, Vallejo had two Chimu Indian grandmothers, and by a strange coincidence, both his grandfathers were Catholic Spanish priests. Vallejo's socialist impulses were formed by experiences early in his life—at the age of twenty, he worked in the accounts department of a sugar estate. There he witnessed thousands of workers laboring for pennies. This experience was captured in his novel *El Tungsteno* (1931; *Tungsten*).

After completing his education at Trujillo University in Peru, Vallejo began publishing poetry and involving himself in bohemian literary circles. After returning to his hometown in 1920, he became involved in a popular uprising, and when violence erupted, Vallejo was jailed for 105 days for being an "intellectual instigator." He was released after university student associations and several prominent figures in Peruvian culture protested on his behalf. Two years later, he left Peru.

From 1923 to 1931 Vallejo lived in Paris and was involved in the artistic circles of the time. He met French composer Erik-Alfred-Leslie Satie (1886–1925), Spanish painter Pablo Picasso (1881–1973), and French writer Jean Cocteau (1889–1963), and began publishing not only poetry but also narratives and theatrical pieces. His poetry, for which he is best known, has been described as a merging of social issues with Surrealism. During this time he became politicized, helping form the Peruvian Socialist Party. In 1931, due to his leftist political views and connection with Soviet Communism (he had visited the Soviet Union), he was deported from France. He moved to Madrid, where he officially joined the Spanish Communist Party. Penniless and in a political and ethnic minority, Vallejo had trouble getting published. Spanish writer Federico García Lorca (1898–1936) made numerous efforts to find publishers for Vallejo's work, but with little success. From 1933 to 1936 Vallejo was allowed to live again in Paris, but with the stipulation that he refrain from political activity. With the outbreak of the Spanish Civil War in 1936, Vallejo's involvement in the antifascist cause began again.

In the last two years of his life Vallejo wrote prolifically, including the posthumously published works *España, aparta de mí éste cáliz* (1939; *Spain, Take This Cup from Me*) and *Poemas humanos* (1939; *Human Poems*).

Van Dyck, Anthony (1599–1641)

Flemish painter. Born in Antwerp and artistically precocious, Van Dyck began an apprenticeship with Hendrick van Balen at the age of ten and was producing independent work well before his attainment of free master in the painters' guild in 1618. He then worked with Peter Paul Rubens. After visiting England, Van Dyck spent 1621–26 in Italy, studying art and compiling a sketchbook that evidences the attention he gave Titian, Veronese, Guido Reni, Francesco Albani, and Raphael.

After spending some years in Antwerp painting in his mature style, Van Dyck settled in England in 1632 as painter to Charles I (1600–1649), who had him knighted and saw that his name was anglicized to Vandyke. He painted the royal family repeatedly, and his portraits are still the preferred representations of Charles I and his family, displaying a royal nobility and peace isolated from the religious and civil strife that erupted in the English Civil War in 1642. Van Dyck died in Blackfriars, near London. His portraits strongly influenced Gainsborough and all later English portraitists, until the decline of societal portraiture in the early twentieth century.

van Gogh, Vincent (1853–1890)

Dutch painter. One of the most expressive and prolific of painters, van Gogh produced more than 800 paintings and more than 850 drawings during his short life—sadly, he sold only one during his lifetime, and was constantly poor. Prior to becoming an artist, van Gogh worked in a variety of clerical positions, then became a missionary with Belgian miners in Borniage. Though his abundant zeal and extreme asceticism soon caused his dismissal, the intensity with which he embraced God in these years would later become focused on his passionate art. His year with these miners inspired some of his paintings, including the famous *Potato Eaters* (1885). After wandering for a few months, van Gogh returned to his parents' house and decided to become an artist. This decision was not endorsed by his parents, and van Gogh was supported mostly by his brother, Theo, for the rest of his life. He studied briefly at the Antwerp Academy, but had little patience for formal training.

Living among laborers, van Gogh used them as models and inspiration for the approximately 850 drawings he completed. He gradually embraced the more individualistic style of Impressionism and in 1886 left for Paris, where he met French painters Camille Pissarro (1830–1903), Edgar Degas (1834–1917), Paul Gauguin (1848–1903), Georges Seurat (1859–1891), and Henri de Toulouse-Lautrec (1864–1901). Van Gogh's style soon diverged from that of the Impressionists; instead of concerning himself with the reproduction of visual experiences, he used color to convey the true nature of the subject. Van Gogh is known for his characteristically bold, staccato brushwork, a technique perhaps best exhibited in his famous paintings *Sunflowers* (1888) and *Starry Night* (1889). In 1888 van Gogh attempted to establish an artists' colony with his friend Gauguin, but the increasingly strained relationship between the two led van Gogh to cut off part of his left ear. The following year, van Gogh, suffering from inner turmoil and mental anguish, entered an asylum, working intermittently and suffering recurrent attacks of anguish and depression.

Although it has long been believed that van Gogh suffered from both epileptic fits and mental illness—he was hospitalized many times for these reasons—there is some evidence that he suffered instead from Ménière's syndrome, a painful inner-ear disorder. Following his release, van Gogh settled in the French village Auvers-sur-Oise, near Theo. In the last seventy days of his life, van Gogh worked furiously, producing seventy canvases. He died from a self-inflicted bullet wound. The thousands of letters van Gogh wrote to Theo, later published, reveal the complexity of van Gogh's intellect, as well as the discipline and determination it took to become the artist he was.

Vargas Llosa, Mario (1936–)

Peruvian novelist and politician. Raised in the Bolivian lowlands jungle town of Cochabamba by his doting grandparents, Vargas Llosa returned to Peru as a teen and was discovered by his father to be a writer of poetry. Suspicious of this seemingly unmasculine activity, his father sent him to the Leoncio Prado Military Academy. His experience there led him to write his first novel, *La ciudad y los perros* (1963; *The Time of the Hero*). The novel was written while Vargas Llosa was living in Spain ostensibly preparing for his doctoral dissertation. The experimental narrative techniques employed within the novel are characteristic of Vargas Llosa's work, and gained him renown and membership in what has come to be described as the "Boom"—the immense international attention paid to Latin American writers during the 1960s and 1970s. In Peru, the novel's negative depiction of the military led them to burn 1,000 copies of the books on the patio of the Leoncio Prado Military Academy, which assured the book's popular success—sales after the burning immediately skyrocketed. His subsequent literary works, such as the popular *La guerra del fin del mundo* (1987; *War of the End of the World*), are characterized by similarly experimental and innovative forms and politically charged content. Politically, Vargas Llosa has moved to the right. Before 1970 he was a backer of Communist Cuba, but has since withdrawn this support. He describes himself as a centrist—believing that the extreme right and left positions are equally guilty of human rights abuses and political intolerance. His belief in the obligation of the intellectual and artist to involve himself in political life has resulted in his increasing involvement in Peruvian politics. He was a leading presidential candidate in 1990, but was defeated in the election. His controversial free-market economic theories and opposition to nationalizing banks have drawn criticism from the left, while his negative depictions of the military undermined his support from the right.

Vazov, Ivan (1850–1921)

Bulgarian poet, novelist, and playwright. Vazov was born in the village of Sopot to a moderately wealthy merchant family. He was groomed to follow in the family business, but when he was sent to Romania to study international commerce, he became involved with the émigré leaders of Bulgaria's independence movement. He joined the cause as a soldier and journalist. After the successful revolution of 1878, he devoted himself more fully to writing but did not abandon political involvement, serving as a member of the National Assembly, and from 1897 to 1898 as the minister of education. Although Vazov wrote in all genres, he is perhaps most respected for his poetry and work in the Bulgarian theater. Of his many works, Vazov is probably best known for his novel *Pod igoto* (1894; *Under the Yoke*), which recounts the suffering of his countrymen under Turkish rule; the play *Hashove* (1894; *Vagabonds*); and the volumes of poetry *Under Our Heaven* (1900), *Songs of Macedonia* (1914), and *We Will Not Perish* (1920).

Vedas

Indian religious texts. Literally meaning "knowledge" in Vedic Sanskrit, the Vedas are a collection of hymns, incantations, poetic reflections, prayers, and myths compiled by the ancient *rishis*, or seers, whom Hindus regard as the first preceptors and repositories of divine knowledge. There are four Vedas: Rigveda, Yajurveda, Samaveda, and Atharvaveda. To many Hindus, the four Vedas are words of divine origin, as irrefutable as direct perception or correct logical inference. Hindus, like Buddhists, hold that the universe is without beginning and without end and moves in repeating cycles. The Vedas are thought to be revealed at the beginning of each of the four world cycles (*yugas*). The meaning of the texts, the verses, and the words are secondary in importance to their innate power. Vedic pronouncements are mantras (verbal carriers of sacred power). The priests (Brahmans) who knew how to recite the Vedic hymns properly, and to conduct the ritual that uses those hymns, gained power over the universe. It was for this reason that from the earliest days of Indian civilization, kings and powerful chiefs hired Brahmans to perform Vedic rituals for them so that they could conquer and control lands and people.

The age of the Vedas is irrelevant to traditional Hindus. Scholarly research places their actual origin from between 1500 and 700 B.C.E.; assembling this extremely large body of texts took approximately 1,000 years.

The contents of the Vedic hymns are highly varied. There are hymns to various gods, seen by some as personifications of the powers of nature. There are some highly sophisticated, philosophical, even skeptical hymns. There are a large number of chants to prevent disaster and the intrusion of evil forces, and to protect the general welfare of people. There are some highly humorous, and even some bawdy passages. The main thrust seems to be theistic: the many deities can be, and are, worshiped as different entities representing different powers. Others see the Vedas as manipulative-coercive: the proper incantations yield highly pragmatic results, and the divinities must give what the correct Vedic utterance, accompanied by complex Vedic ritual, enjoins upon them. The more abstract and philosophically inclined have seen the Vedas as a means to comprehend the true nature of the universe, and to realize the presence of the absolute spirit in themselves and in everything; they see the many divinities as symbols of this underlying absolute. Modern Hindus often see the Vedas as monotheistic, but this may be due to ideas imported from Islam and Christianity.

Vega, Garcilaso de la (1539–1616)

Peruvian historian. Born Gomez Suarez de Figuaroa in Cuzco, the then-capital of the Incan empire, de la Vega changed his name to El Inca Garcilaso de la Vega to declare his dual heritage. His father was a Spanish soldier who had come to Peru with Spanish explorer Francisco Pizarro, and whose family was of Spanish nobility. His mother (Chimpu Ocllo) was of Incan nobility; she was cousin to Atahualpa, the last Inca king of Peru, and the Inca prince Huascar (Atahualpa's brother). From his mother, de la Vega learned Quechua, the language of the Incans. Before moving to Spain at the age of twenty, de la Vega witnessed firsthand both the destruction of Incan civilization and culture at the hands of the Spanish, and the internal struggles of the Spanish *conquistadores* as they determined the future of sixteenth-century colonial Peru. Using these experiences and the knowledge of Quechua, de la Vega rewrote the histories of the colonizing of Peru and of the New World after moving to Spain. His works, including *Florida del Inca* (1605; *The Florida of the Inca*) and *La historia general de Peru* (1616–17; *The General History of Peru*), retell Peruvian and colonial history, emphasizing the humanity and dignity of the Incan civi-

lization and correcting previous histories written by Europeans. These works are important both for their contribution to the literature of the period and their documentation of what might otherwise have been lost with the civilization they describe. Nationalist revolutionary movements in Latin America in the eighteenth and nineteenth centuries invoked de la Vega's utopic and messianic vision of the reestablishment of an Incan civilization in their quests to be free of Spanish rule. De la Vega's works were banned from Peru after Tupac Amaru II, a person of noble Incan heritage, led a revolt in 1780. In the nineteenth century, Argentine liberator José de San Martín had de la Vega's *Commentarios reales de los Incas* (*Royal Commentaries of the Incas*) published in the hopes of furthering his program of establishing both cultural and political independence from Spain.

Velázquez, Diego Rodríguez de Silva y (1599–1660)

Spanish painter. Born in Seville, Velázquez was apprenticed first to Francisco Herrera the Elder, then in 1611 to his future father-in-law and biographer, Francisco Pacheco. In his early career, he popularized a compositional style called the *bodegón*, paintings of everyday subjects and still-life objects — sometimes with a religious scene in the background.

In 1623, two years after Philip IV became king, the prime minister, Duke Oliváres, called Velázquez to Madrid to paint Philip's portrait. The portrait so impressed the king that Velázquez was appointed court painter with the promise that no one else could portray the monarch. He and the king enjoyed a close relationship; the king even had a chair in Velázquez's workshop where he could sit and watch the artist paint. In 1629 Velázquez traveled to Italy for two years to study. Two paintings, *La Túnica de José* (1630; *Joseph's Coat*) and *La fra-*

gua de Vulcano (1630; *Forge of Vulcan*), indicate the influence of Italian treatment of space, perspective, light, and color in his attempt to render truthful visual appearance. In 1649 Velázquez returned to Italy, where he painted a portrait of Pope Innocent X, considered to be his best work produced outside Spain. In this painting, he combined the forms and traditions already established by Italian artists Raphael (1483–1520) and Titian (c. 1488–1576) with his own fluent, almost imperceptible brush strokes to create what is regarded as a precursor of Impressionism. Returning to Spain in 1651, Velázquez continued painting portraits of the royal family until his death.

Verdi, Giuseppe (1813–1901)

Italian opera composer. When Verdi was a child growing up in a small Italian village, his musical talents drew the attention of his employer, a grocer. He was denied entrance to the musical conservatory in Milan, largely because of his poor training in piano, and so studied privately. He wrote his first major success, *Nabucco* (1842), after the death of his first wife and son. His early operas fully exploit the Italian style, with its emphasis on the set forms of recitative and aria. Among his most famous operas in this style are *Il trovatore* (*The Troubadour*) and *La traviata* (*The Lost One*), both 1853. Verdi's later style, embodied in *Aïda* (1871), the Shakespeare-based *Otello* (1887), and *Falstaff* (1893), is characterized by his unique form of *arioso* (a composition of mixed free recitative and metrical song). Verdi was also an ardent nationalist, and composed his famous *Messa da Requiem* (1874; *Requiem Mass*) for the death of the Italian novelist, poet, and patriot Alissandro Manzoni (1785–1873). Verdi remains one of the grand composers of opera.

Vergil (70 B.C.E.–19 B.C.E.)

Ancient Roman poet. Publius Vergilius Maro was born in Andes, a small village near Mantua, to a prosperous farming family. After his preliminary education at Cremona, his father sent him to Rome to study rhetoric and the physical sciences. His studies in Rome, however, were unsuccessful, and he soon returned to his father's farm, where he studied Greek philosophy on his own.

Around 47–42 B.C.E., a period of great political unrest due to the assassination of Julius Caesar in 44 B.C.E., Vergil wrote ten pastoral poems known as the *Eclogae* (*Eclogues*). At that time, the lands surrounding Mantua and Cremona were being confiscated, and the owners and inhabitants were being forced to leave. Fortunately for Vergil, he was allowed to keep his land thanks to the help of Asinius Pollio. Pollio, impressed by Vergil's poetry, brought the *Eclogae* to the attention of Maecenas, a famous patron of the arts.

Maecenas was pleased with Vergil's work and encouraged him to organize and polish his poems. Vergil worked on the *Eclogae* quite diligently for some time, adding a few poems and organizing the collection into ten idylls, publishing them as *Bucolica* (*Bucolics*). This work deals with nostalgic feelings for a simpler past while at the same time looking toward the future with an almost desperate hope for peace and tranquillity.

Vergil's fame and popularity grew with *Bucolica* and he was invited to stay with Maecenas on his estate in Naples. Vergil accepted the offer and focused on his next poetic work for seven years, producing *Georgica* (*Georgics*) in 30 B.C.E., a didactic poem on agriculture, written in four books and based on Hesiod's *Erga kai Hēmerai* (*Works and Days*). In Book I, Vergil gives advice to farmers and writes at great length about the unrest in the aftermath of Caesar's assassination, expressing his hope that Augustus would save Rome from a civil war. In Book III, Vergil describes a plague that devastates the countryside and kills all living things, but his desperate optimism prevails in Book IV, in which he chronicles a miraculous rejuvenation of humankind. Immediately after *Georgica* was completed, Vergil began working on what was to become one of the best-known epic poems ever written, the *Aeneid*.

The *Aeneid*, though incomplete, is composed of twelve books, and celebrates the legendary Trojan origins of Emperor Augustus' family. The *Aeneid*'s nationalistic glorification of the origins of the Roman people is not surprising, since it was written at the request of the emperor. In the *Aeneid*, Vergil traces the blood lineage from Ascanius, the son of the Trojan hero Aeneas, down to Emperor Octavius Caesar (later Augustus), head of the new Roman regime that Vergil endorsed. The work was received by Vergil's Roman contemporaries with great enthusiasm because of its patriotic sentiments.

Vergil died of a fever in 19 B.C.E. upon his return from Greece, his death interrupting his completion of the *Aeneid*.

Victorianism

Nineteenth-century British political and social climate. Victorianism has its roots in the Protestant movements of the eighteenth century led by such intellectuals as Jean-Jacques Rousseau, Friedrich Schiller, and Immanuel Kant. As its name suggests, the Victorian era refers to the period of British history during the reign of Queen Victoria (1837–1901). Europe enjoyed relative economic prosperity at this time, with the rapid growth of industrialization and the emergence of a large middle class. The rise of the bourgeoisie brought with it an antiaristocratic feeling as well as cosmopolitanism and antiprotectionist fervor. The growing belief in the equality of all people as well as a strong sense of moral responsibility led to critical discussions of the evils of slavery, which was abolished in Britain by an act of Parliament in 1833.

At the core of Victorianism is the desire to keep and maintain order in a postrevolutionary society. Conformity, hard work, religiosity, civic duty, earnestness, and respectable behavior were expected during this era. Individuality and sexuality were often believed to be linked to revolution and were repressed, often replaced with religious fervor. Though repressed in "polite" society, blatant sexuality was displayed in the Victorian underworld, where prostitution flourished. The Victorian era was also characterized by a rise in the support for the police, since legality was a prized Victorian value.

Though celebrated as a period of highly "cultured" and "civilized" behavior, the hypocrisy and conformity of Victorianism did not go unchallenged; contemporary critics such as John Stuart Mill and Charles Dickens wrote scathing critiques and satirical depictions of the Victorian era in essays and novels.

Vieira, Antônio (1608–1697)

Portuguese missionary. Born in Lisbon to a poor family, Vieira moved to Bahia, Brazil, at the age of six and lived there for the next twenty-seven years. He was educated at the Jesuit College of Bahia and was ordained in 1635.

As a missionary in Brazil, Vieira worked with the Amerindians and African slaves and learned both Tupí-Guaraní and Kimbundu in the process. He returned to Portugal after it had regained its independence from Spain and became adviser to King Joïo IV, undertaking several diplomatic missions to Paris and The Hague. During this time he spoke out in defense of the former Jews of Portugal who had been converted to Christianity by force, and also supported the creation of the Brazil Company and a protective fleet system, believing that these were the only ways to stop the harassment and losses of Brazilian shipping and to ensure the survival of Portugal as an independent state.

Vieira returned to Brazil in 1654 to continue his missionary work, but he was finally driven from Brazil six years later by angry colonists who resented his intervention on behalf of the Amerindians. Upon his return to Portugal, he was arrested by the Inquisition and tried for his unpopular support of the new Christians. A change of power allowed his release, and Vieira traveled to Rome, where he continued to preach the cause of the Portuguese Jews and attempted to protect them from the Inquisition, gaining fame as the papal preacher of Pope Clement X. In 1681 he returned to Brazil and remained in Bahia the rest of his life.

Vieira is remembered as a liberal who fought for the rights of the Indians in Brazil and for those of the Jews in Portugal. Fifteen volumes of his sermons, considered to be among the finest literary works in the Portuguese language, were published (1679–1748). His other works include *Esperanças de Portugal* (1863–1864; *Hope for Portugal*).

Viet Minh

Vietnamese political party. The Viet Minh, also known as the Viet Nam Doc Lap Dong Minh Hoi (Vietnamese Independence League), was founded in 1941 by the Indochinese Communist Party (ICP). Under the leadership of Ho Chi Minh (1890–1969), the Viet Minh was established to appeal more broadly to the diverse Vietnamese nationalists, although it remained under party directorship. Both anti-French and anti-Japanese, the Viet Minh was committed to independence before class war. New techniques of rural insurgency, including a dominant strain of guerrilla tactics, enfranchised peasant participants. The Viet Minh took advantage of the power vacuum in 1945 after the surrender of Japan, which had wrested nominal control from France during the war. In August 1945—the "August Revolution"—Ho Chi Minh proclaimed a Declaration of Independence, establishing the Provisional Revolutionary Government of the Democratic Republic of Vietnam. In its brief period of control, the largest practical success of the Viet Minh was the curbing of a pervasive famine in Vietnam. By 1946, however, the French were again on the offensive, driving the Viet Minh back into the hinterland. In 1951 the ICP reestablished itself as the Vietnam Workers' Party, and formed a new anti-French force called the Lien Viet front. The front continued to be popularly referred to as the Viet Minh. In 1954 the Viet Minh secured the surrender of the French garrison at Dien Bien Phu. This victory led to negotiations with the French, resulting in the Geneva Accords of 1954 by which Ho Chi Minh's government in Hanoi was recognized.

Vikings

Bands of Scandinavian sea rovers. Between 700 and 1100 C.E., the Norse Vikings launched several successful raids on England, France, Germany, Ireland, Italy, and Spain. They also explored and settled several small colonies in Greenland as well as in Iceland. Although they made efforts to settle permanent colonies in North America, they were unsuccessful. Also called Northmen, Norsemen, or Danes, the Vikings were the forebears of the Norwegians, the Swedes, and the Danes. Their spoken language was a German dialect that resembled the language of England at that time. Adventurous and highly skilled seamen, the Vikings were proficient shipbuilders whose swift-moving ships carried the raiders throughout the known world. The Viking invasions were often precipitated by political unrest at home or burgeoning population growth. The Vikings adopted Christianity in the 800s, replacing the worship of Norse gods such as the supreme god and creator, Odin, and Thor, the god of thunder, weather, and crops. Some Viking bands gave up their piracy for peaceful trade and commerce after their conversion to Christianity.

Villa, Pancho [Francisco] (1878–1923)

Mexican revolutionary. Pancho Villa, whose real name was Doroteo Arango, was born in San Juan del Río, Durango. Orphaned at an early age, he spent his youth working as a peon (a landless laboring clan in Spanish America) on a hacienda in northern Mexico. He had to flee to the mountains, however, when he defended his sister against the advances of one of the hacienda owners. Spending much of his adolescence in the mountains as a fugitive, he became a bandit leader and a horse trader, changed his name, and joined the political movement the Maderistas, founded by future Mexican president Francisco Madero, in Chihuahua during this time. It is through his association with the Maderistas that Villa received most of his revolutionary training. Lacking any formal education, he also taught himself to read and write. Villa joined forces with revolutionary Abraham González to defeat the dictatorship of Mexican president Porfirio Díaz, who was deposed by the Mexican revolution in 1910. On May 11, 1911, Villa's forces (against Madero's orders) attacked and captured Ciudad Juárez (Juárez City); the victory marked the triumph of Madero's revolution, making him the president of Mexico (1911–13).

After a brief interlude as a civilian businessman, Villa took up arms again—independently at first, later under the leadership of Mexican general Victoriano Huerta—to defend Madero's regime from rebel forces. Huerta imprisoned Villa for insubordination and would have had him executed had Raúl Madero, the president's brother, not intervened. Villa escaped to the United States after this episode, but returned with reinforcements to fight Huerta's usurpation of power after Madero's death in 1913.

In this new struggle against Huerta, Villa formed an uneasy alliance with revolutionaries Venustiano Carranza and Emiliano Zapata; because of a clash in personalities, the three were split after Huerta's defeat. Zapata and Villa joined against Carranza and occupied Mexico City in December 1914, where for five months they took turns occupying the presidential chair. As Alvaro Obregón advanced on the capital with his troops from the southeast, Villa's fortunes began to wane; in the spring of 1915, he retreated northward and finally lost to Carranza, who became president from 1915 to 1920. The legendary power of Villa's troops, La División del Norte, was broken and the myth of his invincibility shattered.

Villa withdrew to Chihuahua, where he is credited with introducing reforms, including land distribution. In March 1916, angered by U.S. support of Carranza, Villa attacked Columbus, New Mexico. American general John J. Pershing was sent out to capture or kill him, but after more than a year, his expedition failed. Villa continued his guerrilla war against the Carranza regime until it was overthrown by rebellion in 1920. Adolfo de la Huerta took over the interim administration, reaching an agreement with Villa whereby Villa laid down his arms in return for receiving the rank of division general and the ranch of Canutillo, Durango. Villa was assassinated three years later, for fear he would oppose the upcoming election of future Mexican president Plutarco Calles (1924–28).

Villa-Lobos, Heitor (1887–1959)

Brazilian composer. Born in Rio de Janeiro, Villa-Lobos received a largely unorthodox music education from his father in music theory, the cello, and the clarinet. He was influenced early on by popular musicians in Rio known as *chô-*

ros, whose type of music included improvisation and variations on simple, sentimental melodies associated with Afro-Brazilian rhythms. He wrote his first compositions between 1900 and 1901 and dedicated them to the *chôros*. Leaving home at eighteen because his widowed mother opposed his musical career, Villa-Lobos for the next eight years became a vagabond, traveling all over Brazil and investigating the rich musical heritage of the rural areas, which he weaved into his own compositions.

In 1913 Villa-Lobos again settled in Rio, having written by this time approximately fifty-five compositions (he was an extremely prolific writer—about 2,000 works are credited to him). He began studying the works of German composers Johann Sebastian Bach (1685–1750) and Richard Wagner (1813–1883), Italian composer Giacomo Puccini (1858–1924) and other major composers in the Western tradition, whose lessons his music began to absorb. Recognition began to come to him in the early 1920s, when the firm Artur Napoleïo started to publish his music and Polish-American pianist Arthur Rubinstein (1887–1982) began including Villa-Lobos's work in his repertoire. The 1920s proved especially productive and he composed some of his best works, including the *Chôros No. 7* (1924), for strings and woodwinds. The *Bachianas Brasileiras* (1930–44) were inspired by the work of Bach. They consist of a set of nine pieces in which Villa-Lobos applied, with extreme liberty, the contrapuntal technique of Bach to Brazilian folk music. Villa-Lobos's twelve symphonies are mostly associated with historic events and places. Other pieces include the symphonic poems *The New York Skyline* (1939) and *Dawn in a Tropical Forest* (1953), a sequence of seventeen string quartets, and *Rudepoema* (piano solo, 1926; orchestra, 1942), which he dedicated to Rubinstein.

Villon, François (1431–1463?)

French lyric poet. Born François de Montcorbier and also called François des Loges, Villon achieved a double fame, partly because of his verse, which combined to a remarkable degree emotional intensity and an almost scholastic concern with form and composition, and partly because of his adventurous criminal activities, which brought him into constant legal difficulties.

Villon was orphaned as a child and raised by a clergyman, from whom he took the name Villon. He attended the University of Paris and received two degrees. His first clash with the law came soon after, and he was banished from Paris for killing a priest during a drunken brawl. He received a pardon a year later and was allowed to return to the city. This pattern was to be repeated throughout his life, as he was convicted again and again for robbery, theft, or brawling. He was exiled from Paris a number of times, but usually received a pardon before the full term of exile expired. In 1462 he was convicted again in Paris, for robbery, and sentenced to death. On appeal, his sentence was commuted to ten years' exile, and he left the city in 1463, after which there is no record of his activities.

Villon's first great work was the poem "Petit Testament" ("Little Testament"), or "Lais" ("Legacy"). It is a satirical poem, leaving ironical bequests to various acquaintances of Villon's. It stands in marked contrast to "Grand Testament" ("Great Testament"), wherein Villon expresses regret that he wasted his youth and talents in his life of excess, and gives voice to a great fear and loathing of all the ills in the world. In addition to these, he wrote numerous ballads and rondeaux (short poems with a complex rhyme scheme).

The perception of Villon as a sort of bohemian artist of the Middle Ages is simplistic. Though undeniably a tragic figure who had a troubled and marginal relationship to society, his work does not support this view. While some of his poems express a delight in coarse pleasures, others describe an almost child-like faith in the Virgin Mary. His sense of form was very strong; not only was he a master of rhyme and traditional verse structure, but he imposed other sorts of order on his poems as well. The sentimental force of his verse is thus tempered by an impressive technical skill. Moreover, the emotional force of his poems often masks deeper philosophical and religious concerns, which often find expression in the structure of the poem itself, rather than in the overt subject.

Violencia, La

Colombian period of civil strife. Between 160,000 and 300,000 people were killed during this period of violence that lasted from approximately 1948 to 1958. La Violencia expressed a historical conflict between Colombia's two major parties, the Conservatives and the Liberals. It was characterized by rural attacks on Liberals by Conservative authorities, especially the police, and by the retaliation of Liberal guerrillas, and was further marked by banditry, criminal lawlessness, and personal feuds (large landowners also took the opportunity to carry out large-scale evictions and killings of peasants).

The beginning of La Violencia is usually tied to the assassination in 1948 of Jorge Eliécer Gaitán, a left-wing candidate for the Liberals. This was followed by two days of rioting in the capital known as El Bogotazo, during which the city was sacked and violence spread to rural areas. When the Liberals refused to take part in the 1949 presidential elections, ultraconservative Lauriano Gómez was elected without opposition and quickly took steps to impose an authoritarian regime. An admirer of German leader Adolf Hitler (1889–1945) and Italian leader Benito Mussolini (1883–1945), Gómez proclaimed a state of siege and began systematically to purge Liberals from the police force, the military, and public office. He was overthrown in June 1953 in a military coup and General Gustavo Rojas Pinilla came to power. This new government offered amnesty to the guerrilla forces, and the violence temporarily abated, but in 1954, as the army was deployed into regions not under government control, more serious fighting broke out and began to spread. When Rojas resigned in 1957, the Conservatives and Liberals agreed on a sixteen-year period of power-sharing that became known as the National Front; it entailed the sharing of government offices equally and alternating the presidency between them, in the interests of peace. Although the politically motivated rural violence for the most part subsided at this time, the criminal banditry and personal vendettas continued to be a problem through the next two decades.

Virgen de Guadalupe

Mexican patron saint. The legend of the Virgin of Guadalupe began in 1531, when an Indian, Juan Diego, claimed he saw the Virgin's image in the area where a basilica erected in her honor now stands in Mexico City. He was not believed until the image reappeared as an impression etched upon his cloak. The Virgin was declared the patron saint of Mexico City in 1737, in a successful effort to stop an epidemic that was rapidly killing the Indian inhabitants of the city.

The patron saint is believed to have been responsible for the conversion of the indigenous population to Roman Catholicism, the religion of over 95 percent of Mexico's present-day population—though, as elsewhere, many Indians maintain traditional religious beliefs in addition to those of Roman Catholicism. The Virgin is also associated with

Mexican Independence Day, September 16, 1810. On this day, Miguel Hidalgo y Costilla, a parish priest from Dolores, demanded an end to Spanish rule; the equality of races; and land redistribution. Initiating a local revolt, Hidalgo encouraged his rebels to fight for the Virgin, a symbol of a country that would allow the practice of religion. At the time, there were fears that Spain would allow Mexico to fall under French rule, which the papacy then viewed as a godless country.

The feast day of the Virgin of Guadalupe is celebrated annually on December 12 in a ceremony at the basilica named for the Virgin in Mexico City. Hundreds of thousands of worshipers attend the annual ceremony, in which some crawl on their knees toward the basilica while performers sing the folk song "Las Mananitas." The original cloak is displayed in the new basilica, which replaced the structurally flawed old basilica.

vision quest

American Indian ritual. Vision quests function as an initiation rite into adulthood, and are usually performed by an adolescent boy (or, less frequently, a girl) of the Great Plains, Eastern Woodlands, or Pacific Northwest tribes. The actual methods employed vary greatly among tribes, but the purpose of the quest is to seek a guardian spirit who will serve as a permanent guide for the child.

As early as ten years of age, the child leaves the village alone and spends several days fasting and praying, searching for a guardian spirit. In some tribal traditions, the youth looks for unusual behavior in an animal as a sign of the spirit's identity. Most often the guardian spirit makes itself known through a vision. Obtaining the vision is often physically stressful and involves sleep deprivation, abstention from food and water, excessive activity such as running, swimming, or diving, exposure to extreme temperatures, and sometimes, in the case of the Pacific Coastal tribes, self-mutilation. These trials are believed to help the youth reach a state of disassociation thought necessary for reception of the vision.

For a seeker, the vision is an encounter with the sacred that grants power to live, understand, and heal. It begins with the gift of self-knowledge and culminates in the sharing of spiritual power, since the personal knowledge acquired is intended for the benefit of the tribe. Although most common as a ritual of initiation, vision quests are also used by older American Indians as a form of communication with the spirit world when they find themselves in need of guidance.

Voltaire (1694–1778)

French poet, playwright, historian, and philosopher. Voltaire (the pen name of François-Marie Arouet) was one of the most prominent French intellectuals of his time and an outspoken critic of the political, social, and economic corruption and injustices of eighteenth-century Europe. He was the son of middle-class parents, though he sometimes claimed to be the illegitimate child of a minor songwriter. However, Voltaire was influenced primarily by his godfather, the Abbé de Châteauneuf, after his mother died when he was seven. He was educated at the Jesuit college of Louis-le-Grand in Paris from 1704 to 1711, where he developed a love of literature and theater along with a skepticism about religious instruction. After leaving college, he rejected the career in law that his father had intended for him and devoted himself to writing. He quickly became a popular figure in Paris, but a verse that mocked the regent caused him first to be briefly exiled and then to be jailed in the Bastille for a year.

His release from prison was followed by the success of his play *Oedipe*, which opened in 1718. The *Henriade*, an epic poem about Henry IV and inspired by Vergil, was published in 1722. A quarrel with a member of a powerful French family resulted in Voltaire's exile to England from 1726 to 1728. There he met prominent intellectuals like Alexander Pope, Jonathan Swift, and George Berkeley and came to admire much of what he learned about British art, politics, and social order. Upon his return to France, Voltaire wrote several unsuccessful plays, though *Zaïre* (1732) was a small triumph. He also wrote histories such as *Charles XII* (1731). In 1734 Voltaire published his *Lettres anglaises* (*English Letters*), which criticized the injustices of the Old Regime and called for social progress. He then fled Paris and lived with Madame du Châtelet, his lover and intellectual companion, in Champagne. There he focused his studies on religion and the sciences.

During these years of study, Voltaire developed his social philosophy of rationalism, which identified four conditions of human society: first, that everything is comprehensible, and that there is always a means or an approach by which we may understand any given event, phenomenon, or experience; second, that relativism is a necessary condition and that tolerance and acceptance of others must exist before we may begin to understand ourselves and others; third, that to be rational is to be opposed to organized religion, especially given the hypocrisy of the Roman Catholic Church, because we should not blindly accept all that we are told; and fourth, that to be rational is to question the legitimacy of absolutism, the notion that there are solid, unbending, external truths. Voltaire sincerely believed that if people were rational, according to his definition of rationality, they could live together harmoniously.

Voltaire's preoccupation with the hypocrisy of organized religion is nowhere more apparent than in his *contes*, or tales. *Micromega* (1752), *Zadig* (1747), and *Candide* (1759) are all works that deal with the philosophical and moral problems of the day. In his *Lettres philosophiques*, Voltaire incites the reader to *écrasez l'infâme* (crush the evils), which refers primarily to the corruption and inadequacy of the Roman Catholic Church.

In 1754 Voltaire settled in Switzerland and spent the rest of his years there, corresponding frequently with his friends in France and journeying occasionally to Paris to support and investigate cases of injustice and religious persecution. He died in Paris in 1778.

voodoo

Religious folk cult of Haiti. Voodoo, also called vudu and voudou, is a syncretic folk religion that combines Roman Catholic ritual elements introduced by French colonizers and African and Islamic theological and magical elements introduced by slaves originally belonging to the Yoruba, Fon, and Kongo tribes. The name "voodoo" comes from the word *vodun*, which in the language of the Fon people means "god" or "spirit." Voodooists believe that God is paramount but not omnipotent, since He is much too busy to take care of daily human affairs. There are *loa*—spirits with attributes similar to those of Christian saints, variously identified with local or African gods, deified ancestors, or Catholic saints—that therefore step in to perform good and evil deeds. Believers say that *loa* were once living persons who now may possess a devotee; through serving *loa*, the possessed may in turn win certain favors. Devotees engage in ritual services devoted to the *loa*, whereby they gather at a temple or other meeting place and are led by a priest or priestess in ceremonies involving song, drumming, dance, prayer, food preparation, and the ritual sacrifice of animals.

The voodoo priest, or *houngan*, and

the priestess, or *mambo*, are central to Haitian rural life. Claiming knowledge through visions and dreams, they act as counselors, healers, and expert protectors against sorcery or witchcraft. Before any major action, believers turn to their priests for counsel; voodoo provides them with supernatural sanction for conduct and contact with ancestors, explains natural events, releases anxiety, and provides people with music, dance, and drama.

The zombi (also spelled zombie) is a peculiar and much sensationalized part of the voodoo religion. Thought to be either a dead person's soul used for magical purposes, or an actual corpse magically raised from the grave and used to perform agricultural tasks in the field as a kind of will-less automaton, zombis are actually simulated by some voodoo priests who administer a particular poison to a victim's skin, causing the victim to enter into a state of deep physical paralysis for several hours.

Voodoo was once revolutionary in its opposition to slavery, but it no longer seems to pose a serious threat to the urban government, nor does it seek to improve the peasants' basic status. The Roman Catholic Church, in turn, having denounced voodoo for decades and advocated the persecution of its devotees, seems to have resigned itself by the late twentieth century to coexisting with the cult. Attempts to wipe out voodoo have failed largely because the cult apparently satisfies peasant needs in a way that urbanized Catholicism has not.

Vynnychenko, Volodymyr [Kyrylovych]
(1880–1951)
Ukrainian writer, thinker, and politician. Born into a poor peasant family, Vynnychenko was constantly harassed, due to his origins, by his teachers and fellow students at the Russian-dominated secondary school he attended. Enrolling at Kiev University in 1901, he founded a radical student organization, and after this, was often arrested by the czarist regime. In 1902 he joined the Revolutionary Ukrainian Party, spreading propaganda among workers, which led to his arrest and banishment from the university. He continued his political activities as one of the leaders of the Ukrainian Social Democratic Labor Party. At this point, he began his literary career, first as a short-story writer, then as a novelist and playwright. His play *Dysharmonia* (1906; *Disharmony*) and the novel *Chesnist z soboyu* (1907; *Honesty with Oneself*) deal with the struggle between the individual and society. The theme of the individual in the time of revolution was explored in the novel *Zapysky kyrpatoho Mefistofelia* (1917; *Notes of the Pug-Nosed Mephistopheles*). After the collapse of the czarist regime in 1917, Vynnychenko became the prime minister of the Ukrainian government, directing negotiations with the Russian provisional government for an autonomous status for Ukraine. When Bolsheviks asserted their control over Ukraine in 1919, he emigrated, writing the three-volume work *Vidrodzennia natsiyi* (1920; *Rebirth of a Nation*), in which he examined events in Ukraine in 1917–19. His late works, such as the novels *Soniashna mashyna* (1928; *The Solar Machine*) and *Nova zapovid* (1949; *The New Commandment*), were a radical deviation for Vynnychenko, in theme and style as well as in their attempt to create a utopian solution to world conflict. His work was banned by the Soviets for its pro-Ukrainian stand and has been shunned by Ukrainian nationalists abroad for its socialist views.

Vytautas the Great (1350–1430)
Lithuanian national leader. Vytautas expanded Lithuanian territory to its maximum breadth and helped drive the Teutonic Knights from the country. He was the eldest son of Kęstitus, who co-ruled Lithuanian principalities with his brother Algirdas. A pupil of Hanno of

Windenheim, Vytautas spoke both German and Latin.

In 1377 Algirdas's son Jogaila attempted to establish himself as the ruler of Lithuania. He captured Vytautas and had Kęstitus murdered in 1382. Vytautas escaped and, two years later, made peace with Jogaila. In 1386 Jogaila, who had married a twelve-year-old Polish princess, was baptized and crowned king of Poland as Władysław II Jagiełło. Vytautas was baptized in Prussia in 1383, and he supported Jogaila's proclamation of universal baptism for the Lithuanian nation in 1387.

Vytautas, at times allied with the Teutons, struggled with his cousin for power. His popularity grew until Jogaila was obliged to offer Vytautas the vice-regency of Lithuania. In 1392 they signed a formal compact making Vytautas ruler of Lithuania. In 1395 Vytautas assumed the title of Grand Prince of Lithuania and asserted that all Russia should belong to Lithuania. The Russian cities of Vilnius and Moscow became rival domains backed by smaller principalities of Eastern Slavs.

Under Vytautas's rule, the Lithuanian lands stretched as far south as the Black Sea and east into central Russia. Vytautas built roads and bridges for the development of trade and traveled widely to make sure that law and order were maintained. He campaigned against the Mongols, though his troops were defeated at the Battle of Vorksla River (1399). In 1407, after taking up the cause of the Samogitians, Vytautas began the campaign to expel the Teutons from the Lithuanian lowlands. In 1409 he signed a treaty with Jogaila, and in 1410 the joint Polish-Lithuanian forces defeated the Teutonic Knights in the Battle of Grunwald (now Tannenberg), Vytautas's crowning achievement.

Vytautas was criticized for sending Lithuanian nobility to distant territories where they were absorbed by foreign ethnic groups, weakening the once-cohesive Lithuanian culture. This redistribution increased Polish influence in Lithuania. Nevertheless, Vytautas remained a strong ruler over a vast kingdom, receiving tribute from as far away as Pskov and Novgorod. Vytautas died soon after his cousin Jogaila agreed to Vytautas's coronation as king, in 1430.

W

Wagner, [Wilhelm] Richard (1813–1883) German composer, conductor, and writer. Wagner pioneered the conception and the production of the "music-drama" as a grand-scale exploration of nationalistic and psychological themes.

His father, a police actuary, died six months after Wagner was born in Leipzig, and Wagner often voiced his suspicion that his mother's second husband, the actor and painter Ludwig Geyer, was his natural father. Wagner was influenced at a young age by classical Greek drama as well as the plays of William Shakespeare (1564–1616), Friedrich von Schiller (1759–1805), Johann Wolfgang von Goethe (1749–1832), and the music of composers Ludwig von Beethoven

(1770–1827) and Carl Maria von Weber (1786–1826). After a brief period at the University of Leipzig, he began to study music with the cantor of the local gymnasium in 1831, and two years later he became the choral director in Würzburg under the supervision of his oldest brother, Albert. During these years he completed his first opera, *Die Hochzeit* (1832–33; *The Wedding*), which he himself destroyed, and his second opera, *Die Feen* (1833–34; *The Fairies*). Wagner conducted his first orchestra in the summer of 1834 at Lauchstädt, where he also met the actress Minna Planer, whom he married in 1836. He moved with her to Magdeburg, where he took a post as musical director of a theater and conducted Italian opera. Resolved to embark on a new career as a composer in Paris, Wagner experienced a notable lack of financial and artistic success there, though he completed two more works, *Rienzi* (1838–40) and *Der fliegende Holländer* (1841; *The Flying Dutchman*). The successful premieres of these operas in Germany in October 1842 and February 1843 enabled him to return in triumph and led to his appointment as the director of music of the Royal Court of Saxony.

In May 1849 Wagner fled Germany after his participation in the revolutionary uprising in Dresden, settling finally in Zurich. There he wrote three books on his philosophy of art, including *Oper und Drama* (1850–51; *Opera and Drama*), in which he elaborated his theory of the *Musikdrama*, a revolutionary kind of stage presentation blending music and drama and having the same social significance as Greek tragedy, the public expression of a national and an individual psyche. As a realization of these ideas, he began the composition of the text and music for *Der Ring des Nibelungen* (1853–74; *The Ring of the Nibelungs*), the monumental work comprising four parts (*Das Rheingold* [1853–54], *Die Walküre* [1854–56; *The*

Valkyrie], *Siegfried* [1856–71]; and *Götterdämmerung* [1869–74; *Twilight of the Gods*]), for which he is most famous. When his old friend Ludwig II succeeded to the throne of Bavaria in 1864, Wagner went to Munich under his patronage. Four years after the death of his wife, Wagner married Cosima von Bülow, who was the daughter of Hungarian composer Franz Liszt (1811–1886) and had already borne Wagner three children.

In 1872 Wagner accepted the offer of the city officials of Bayreuth to move there and develop a theater to be devoted to the production of his works. Only the premiere of the religious drama *Parsifal* (1882) in 1882 allowed the theater to thrive. Wagner died that year of a heart attack in Venice.

Wajda, Andrzej (1926–)

Polish film director. As Poland's leading filmmaker and a pioneer in Eastern European cinema, Wajda brought to the screen the tragedies of his generation in Poland. His films portray the adjustment of the Polish people to communism. In his historical pieces, Wajda revisits crucial moments of World War II to debunk myths surrounding that period. *Kanał* (1957; literally "Sewer," it appeared in English as *They Love Life*), the second film in his war trilogy, which included *Pokolenie* (1954; *A Generation*) and *Popiół i diament* (1958; *Ashes and Diamonds*), challenges the notion of heroic martyrdom. His treatment of contemporary subjects in *Polowanie na muchy* (1970; *Hunting Flies*) reveals a theme common to his work, the individual's attempts to remain faithful to ideals and convictions.

Wajda had a traditional upbringing in a military family, and joined the Home Army at sixteen to fight for the exiled Polish government. After the Second World War, he attended the Kraków Academy of Fine Arts, turning his attention to cinema when he left for the new film school at Lodz. He directed his first feature, A *Generation*, in 1954, using a realistic cinematic style to portray a boy's coming of age while serving in the left-wing Polish Resistance movement. This film, as well as the films that followed, are generally characterized by a romantic concept of history and fate, complemented by an almost baroque style of visual effects and expression. Wajda has come to be recognized internationally as the most prominent of the Polish school of filmmaking, receiving the Palme d'Or at the 1981 Cannes Film Festival for *Czlowiek z zelaza (Man of Iron)*.

Walcott, Derek [Alton] (1930–)

West Indian poet and playwright. Born in St. Lucia, West Indies, Walcott's early life in a racially and culturally mixed community exerted enormous influence on his later plays and poems. The son of European and African parents, Walcott was in many ways a divided or a "culturally schizophrenic" child, as he terms the phenomenon in his essay "What the Twilight Says" (1971). Though English was the language spoken at home and in school, Walcott was surrounded by an island population who spoke a mixture of French and creole French and who engaged in an ongoing struggle to survive, with dignity intact, as a colonized people. This link to both the colonized and the colonizer is important to Walcott's development as a writer and provides him with a distinctive vantage point as an artist.

Walcott's career as a playwright began during his formal studies at the University of West Indies. Inspired by Jacobean drama, his first effort, *Henri Christophe*, was a historical piece written in verse and produced both in St. Lucia (1950) and in London (1951). Walcott later abandoned this historical motif, and concentrated more specifically on the folk culture and cultural synthesis in the West Indies. In 1959, after studying briefly in the United States, Walcott

moved to Trinidad and developed a close association with the Little Carib Theater and its company. There he founded the Trinidad Theater Workshop and together with Little Carib produced five more of his plays. Walcott was also very much involved with the new Trinidad/Tobago nation and wrote both for local art and political journals. Perhaps his best-known play of this period is *Dream on Monkey Mountain*, which, after years in the making, was not staged until 1967 in Toronto. Here he again explores the relations between the colonized and the colonizer, this time through a series of hallucinations of an old charcoal maker.

Walcott continued to produce plays and poems in the 1970s and 1980s. His work has gained a more introspective tone, but is still much attuned to the language and rhythms of West Indian life as well as to the larger issue of colonization. *O Babylon!* (1976), for example, is based on an actual Rastafarian community, its language, and its religious beliefs. Since the mid-1970s, Walcott has also spent much time teaching at various universities in the United States, remaining a prolific poet and playwright. In 1992 he received the Nobel Prize in Literature.

Walker, Alice (1944–)

American novelist and poet. Walker, along with Toni Morrison and Gloria Naylor, helped create the emerging market of black women readers for black books in the 1970s and 1980s. Walker's work is primarily concerned with the interpersonal relations of black women in a racist and sexist society.

Walker found initial acclaim as a poet; her unsentimental works are collected in volumes such as *Once* (1968), *Revolutionary Petunias* (1973), *"Good Night, Willie Lee, I'll See You in the Morning"* (1979), and *Her Blue Body Everything We Know* (1991).

Her early novels explored the themes

and consequences of the civil rights and feminist movements. Her first novel, *The Third Life of Grange Copeland* (1970), describes how the members of a black sharecropping family battle racism. *Meridian* (1976) details the relationship between a black couple involved in a black militant organization. Later short-story collections, *In Love and Trouble* (1973) and *You Can't Keep a Good Woman Down* (1976) highlight multiple facets of racial and sociopolitical elements in the lives of her characters.

The startling success of *The Color Purple* (1982), an epistolary novel in the form of diary entries by a Southern black woman named Celie, changed her career forever. The book won the Pulitzer Prize, and was brought to the screen by Steven Spielberg. (A later novel, 1989's *The Temple of My Familiar*, reintroduces several of *The Color Purple*'s characters.) In 1996 she published *The Same River Twice*, looking back on her most popular story ten years after the release of the hit movie.

In Search of Our Mother's Gardens (1983) is a collection of feminist essays. Walker's nonfiction has been concerned with the question of a black feminist tradition. She has been an admirer and tireless promoter of the works of Zora Neale Hurston (1903–1960), championing the Harlem Renaissance writer when all of her works were out of print. In 1973 Walker identified the likely spot of the unmarked grave where Hurston was buried in Eatonville, Florida.

In 1992 Walker published *Possessing the Secret of Joy*, a novel about the practice of female genital circumcision in some parts of Africa. Just as *The Color Purple* generated controversies over Walker's alleged anti-black-male stance, *Possessing the Secret of Joy* sparked a controversy over human rights and cultural relativism, in which some critics maintained that Walker was a latter-day cultural imperialist, imposing Western values on indigenous African traditions. In 1993 she coauthored, with Pratibha Parmar, an oversize volume entitled *Warrior Marks: Female Genital Mutilation and the Sexual Blinding of Women*, on the same subject.

wampum

American Indian form of currency. The white and violet cylindrical beads fashioned by northeastern American Indians, wampum was variably used as a currency of exchange and as a means of ascribing value to individuals and ceremonies. Produced by natives of Long Island, Rhode Island, and coastal Connecticut, the beads derived from grinding or drilling shells; the white from the whelk (*Buccinum*) and the violet from the quahog (*Mercenaria*).

Wampum production and trade almost certainly existed in pre-Columbian times, although it was not of ancient origin. During the seventeenth and eighteenth centuries, wampum use reached its height as a currency in the fur trade between coastal and inland peoples of the Northeast. Trade dispersed the wampum inland, and it has been found as far north as Nova Scotia.

Although wampum was used as currency, Indians viewed it as having intrinsic as well as exchange value. The Iroquois League established a wampum value for human life—ten strings for a man, twenty strings for a woman. The object was to avoid war in the event that a member of one tribe killed a member of another. The murderer's tribe would pay the injured tribe for the victim and for the criminal.

Europeans quickly comprehended the value of wampum to the Indians, and it came to have a relatively fixed value in both material and monetary exchange. The violet beads generally had double the value of the white ones. Some wampum "factories" were established by Europeans, and by 1640 measures were taken to control the proliferation and value of crude, unfinished beads and wampum made of nontraditional materials.

Politically and culturally significant as well, wampum was also used as a testimonial of authority and sincere intent in speechmaking and the signing of treaties. Used in this way, the beads were woven into belts featuring pictographs representing the particular event. For instance, the Penn Treaty belt shows an Iroquois and a white shaking hands, and the Washington Covenant belt represents the colonies with thirteen human figures and the Iroquois League with two figures touching either side of a longhouse.

Wampum was of particular importance in the Iroquois ritual known as the Requickening Address, which symbolically restored life and alleviated grief after a death. The address begins with a reference to the pain and suffering caused by death and uses a string of wampum to correspond to a particular manifestation of grief, or word. As the grief is named, the speaker passes the wampum to the affected person, removing the hurt.

Wang Shi-fu (1250–c. 1337)

Thirteenth-century Chinese dramatist. Wang Shi-fu, a prominent Chinese playwright and poet of the Yuan dynasty (1260–1368), was born in Da-du (modern Beijing) and wrote between 1295 and 1307.

Although he is believed to have written at least fourteen plays, only three have survived, including Xi xiang ji (The Romance of the Western Chamber), a classic work of Chinese drama. Xi xiang ji is an innovative work that reinterpreted traditional Chinese theater. The play employs the form of the ca-ju, a then-popular theatrical mode, but Wang's play stretched the genre in ways that anticipate chuan qi, a dramatic style that, introduced almost a century later,

would dominate Chinese stages into the twentieth century. In addition to showcasing Wang's talent for well-crafted dialogue, the Xi xiang ji features individualized characters and unprecedented complexity of plot. It also departed from ca-ju convention by giving all of the major characters singing parts, rather than just the lead, and by including five acts instead of one.

Wang Wei (699–759)

Chinese artist and scholar. Due to his excellent work in poetry, painting, and music, Wang Wei, who is also known as Wang Mo-qi and is one of the most famous artist-scholars who lived during a cultural golden era in Chinese history, is generally considered to be a model product of education in humanistic studies. The famous master of artistic critique Dong Qi-chang credited Wang Wei as the founder of an artistic movement involving southern painter-poets, whose work was viewed more as an expression of inner sentiment than as a recreation of a scene. Because of this elevation to near-divine standing as the leader of such literati (wen-ren), the facts of Wang Wei's life have become clouded by mystique—a distortion exacerbated by the fact that none of his paintings have survived.

He lived during the prosperous Tang dynasty (618–906) when the capital city of Chang'an was a thriving cosmopolitan center of trade and culture, and he completed the imperial civil service examinations at the age of twenty-one.

Wang Wei joined the civil service but was demoted soon after attaining a high position. He was sent from the capital to Shantung, where he had little authority and few important duties. In 734 he was recalled to Dong Qi-chang and appointed to the censorate. The capital was occupied in 756 by the insurgent general An Lu-shan, who forced Wang Wei into his rebel administration based at Luo-yang. Imperial forces defeated the rebels in 758, and Wang's name was cleared by some loyalist poems he had written while held captive, as well as by the intervention of his brother Wang Jin, who held a prominent post in the civil service.

Much of Wang's best work was completed later in his life, while he was living at his house at Wang River (Wang quan). He turned to the study of Buddhism in his country retreat, where his solitude and the striking landscape surrounding him had a great impact on his art. No original copies of Wang's work survive, but reconstructions can be devised from surviving replicas and written accounts. He is best known as the founder of the art of landscape painting, having experimented with the genre at his dwelling on the picturesque Wang River.

Aside from his celebrated landscapes, Wang's snowscapes, which also employ the ink monochrome (*shui-mo*) technique, are particularly famous. The snowscapes in particular are associated with Wang because of his characteristic style of "breaking the ink" (*po-mo*), a broad ink-wash technique. His painting is recognized as a marriage between tradition and innovation, but his elevation to near-divinity in Chinese culture is mainly attributable to his reputation as both a master painter and a great poet. His verses can be found in virtually all Chinese poetry anthologies, and he is credited with the perfection of the "lyric poetry" (*shi*) style, along with Tang poets such as Li Bai (701–762) and Du Fu (712–770).

Wang Xizhi (321–379)

Chinese calligrapher. Born in Linyi, Shandong, Wang began studying calligraphy as a child. As a young man, he familiarized himself with all kinds of calligraphic styles, working to appropriate the best of each to produce his own style. Of his works, *Lan-ting xu* (*Preface to the Poems Composed at the Orchid Pavilion*) is his most famous. In it, he recorded the poetry composed by several Chinese literary figures at the Spring Purification Festival in 353 C.E. For centuries Wang Xizhi has been revered as the great master of Chinese *xingshu*, or running script.

Warhol, Andy (1928–1987)

American painter, printmaker, and filmmaker. Warhol was a pioneer and leader of the Pop art movement of the early 1960s that used familiar, mass-produced images and objects to reveal the superficiality of popular culture. Warhol was born Andrew Warhola to Czech immigrants on August 6, 1928, in Pittsburgh, Pennsylvania. He studied design at the Carnegie Institute of Technology in Pittsburgh until 1949, after which he worked as a commercial illustrator in New York. Warhol's early career familiarized him with the styles and techniques of design he would later subvert as an artist.

In 1962 he gained recognition by exhibiting paintings of soup cans and Coca-Cola bottles and a wood sculpture of oversized Brillo soap pad boxes. While these pieces established Warhol's subject matter, subsequent works added the element of mass production. Through photomechanical techniques and silkscreen printing, he began producing a series of variations on famous images—such as Marilyn Monroe's face—often adding vibrant, flashy colors.

Having established himself as a painter and sculptor, Warhol opened a studio, known as the Factory, that became the center for his art and entourage. Surrounded by rock stars, models, celebrities, and assorted misfits, Warhol began to work mostly on making films. His movies are notorious for their excessive length, static tedium, and inventive explorations of sexuality. They include *Eat* (1963), *My Hustler* (1965), *The Chelsea Girls* (1966), *Blue Movie* (1969), and *Trash* (1970).

In 1968, his fame international, Warhol was shot and nearly killed by one of his actresses. During the 1970s he founded *Interview* magazine and published *The Philosophy of Andy Warhol* (1975). in 1979 he published both *Portraits of the Seventies* and *Andy Warhol's Exposures*. He continued to work until his death, producing prints of famous Hollywood and political figures.

Washington, Booker T[aliaferro] (1856–1915)

African-American educator and founder of Tuskegee Institute. Washington was the son of Jane Furguson, a mulatto slave, and an unknown white father. He was born in slave quarters on a plantation outside of Roanoke, Virginia. Washington adopted the surname of his stepfather, a former slave, and moved with his family to Malden, West Virginia, after the Civil War. At the age of nine, he began working in a salt furnace and at ten in a coal mine. At sixteen, he entered Hampton Normal and Agricultural Institute in Virginia, graduating with honors in 1875. Returning to Malden, he taught school for two years before spending a year studying at Wayland Seminary in Washington, D.C., after which he took a job teaching at Hampton. In 1881 he was chosen to head the Tuskegee Normal and Industrial Institute in Alabama, recently established by the Alabama legislature to train black teachers. During his thirty-four years there, Washington built it into an internationally recognized educational and agricultural center with over 1,500 students. A skilled orator and tireless fundraiser, Washington traveled extensively in the United States and Europe, promoting his educational program and garnering financial support. Through these efforts, he came to know many of the business leaders of the day, and he was consulted about government appointments by U.S. presidents Theodore Roosevelt and William Howard Taft.

In his time, Washington's emphasis on vocational rather than academic ed-ucation and on forbearance rather than activism to confront social injustices was extremely influential among blacks and whites. His famous speech at the Cotton States and International Exposition in Atlanta on September 18, 1895, summarized his pragmatic philosophy of economic development. He encouraged blacks to accept segregation as a fact of life, and to work for economic equality before social equality. This speech established him as the most prominent spokesperson for blacks of the time, but angered radical black intellectuals like W. E. B. Du Bois, who called it the "Atlanta Compromise" and decried Washington's approach as ineffectual and quietistic at a time when racial discrimination was being systematically legalized. Later, many black leaders would complain that Washington's acceptance by the white power structure gave him a virtual stranglehold on governmental and philanthropic funding. His influence on black politics was replaced after his death by that of Du Bois and others who championed immediate social change, but he was an important figure in the expansion of black educational opportunities in the United States.

Founding the National Negro Business League in 1900, Washington served as its president until his death, and received honorary degrees from Harvard University and Dartmouth College. He wrote more than a dozen books, including his autobiography, *Up from Slavery* (1901), a best-seller.

Washington, George (1732–1799)

First U.S. president. Born in Westmoreland County, Virginia, to a family of wealthy landowners, Washington had an erratic formal education. His father died when he was eleven, and he went to live with his half-brother Lawrence at the large estate called Mount Vernon inherited from their father. George became a surveyor, working for Lord Fairfax, who owned much of northern Virginia. With Fairfax's help, he was appointed official surveyor of Culpeper County in 1749. Washington became overseer of Mount Vernon in 1752 after the deaths of his brother and niece.

As military adjutant of northern Virginia, Washington was dispatched to the Ohio River Valley to assert British claim to the area. He was sent to engage the French at Fort Duquesne, a captured British fort. Encountering a French detachment he believed was spying, he ambushed them, killing the leader. The French claimed that the group was on a peaceful mission, and the incident touched off the French and Indian War. He accompanied the British army on another mission to Fort Duquesne in 1755, where they also suffered defeat. However, rewarded for his service there, Washington was named commander of the Virginia army. Resigning in 1759, he married the widowed Martha Custis, one of the wealthiest residents of Virginia, and entered the state House of Burgesses, settling into the life of a rich planter. Through the work of his slaves, his plantation produced first tobacco, and then, when tobacco production became too costly under British regulations, a variety of products including fish, cloth, and wheat.

Washington was elected to the first Continental Congress in 1774, and to the second in 1775. Made commander-in-chief of the new Revolutionary Army, which was fighting England for independence, he laid siege to Boston, which the British abandoned after eight months in 1776. The British took over key positions in New York and then Pennsylvania, forcing Washington to retreat across the Delaware River. Washington recrossed the Delaware on December 25–26, 1776, surprising and capturing Hessian mercenaries in Trenton. Further successes were followed by defeats at Philadelphia and Brandywine Creek, and Washington's beleaguered army spent its winter at Valley Forge. An alliance with France in 1778 was the turning point in the war, and the British surrender at Yorktown on October 19, 1781, effectively marked its end. Washington submitted his meticulously detailed bill for expenses (no salary) and returned to Mount Vernon.

One of five Virginia delegates to the Constitutional Convention of 1787, he was chosen as its president, and, after ratification of the new Constitution, he was elected the first president of the United States. His initial term was devoted largely to the creation of the administrative structure of the government. He worked with the Congress to develop the Executive and Judicial branches of government. A series of acts created a national currency and revenue. Strongly opposing viewpoints about centralized control were represented in his own cabinet by Secretary of the Treasury Alexander Hamilton of the Federalist Party (Washington's own) and Secretary of State Thomas Jefferson of the Republican (later Democratic) Party. His second term was dominated by foreign policy: successfully pursuing neutrality in the British-French conflicts and expanding federal influence in the western and southwestern territories. Washington refused a third term as president in order to retire to Mount Vernon. In 1798 the threat of war with France brought him back to nominal service as commander-in-chief for a brief period; he died after a short illness the following year.

wat

Buddhist temple. *Wats*, often referred to as temple compounds or monasteries, are Buddhist religious centers found in villages and neighborhoods in Thailand, Laos, and Cambodia. Staffed by Buddhist monks and sponsored by wealthy patrons, *wats*, also called *vats*, have traditionally functioned as village centers, often providing lodging for travelers, personal counseling, some form of medical and elderly care, a morgue, a library, gathering places for villagers, sites for fairs and festivals, and a general source of both local gossip and news of the outside world. Central to the *wat* is a *bot*, or temple for the monks, many of which are noted for their architectural beauty or for the Buddha images they house. Each *wat* also includes many Buddha images and religious monuments, as well as a separate *wiharn*, or temple for the people, and several *sala*, rooms used for local meetings or to house overnight travelers.

Wat Po

Thai Buddhist temple. The largest and oldest temple complex in Bangkok, Wat Po was built during the reign of Rama I (1782–1809). This *wat* is known for its fifteen-by-forty-five-meter gold leaf and mother-of-pearl statue depicting a reclining Buddha at the moment he is entering nirvana. Having housed various schools and museums, the Wat Po has also functioned as a general center of Thai culture. It is celebrated for the countless singular stone slabs on its walls inscribed with Thai medical, religious, civic, literary, and cultural information from the previous century, called by some a "university in stone." The courtyard contains more than four hundred images of Buddha, as well as a series of large statues meant to demonstrate Buddhist exercises in bodily control. The Wat Po is known by several names, including Wat Poh, Vat Po, Wat Cetuphon, Wat Jetubon, Wat Phrachetuphon, and Temple of the Reclining Buddha.

Welles, Orson (1915–1985)

American actor, film director, and screenwriter. Welles was born to a wealthy investor and his wife, a concert pianist, in Kenosha, Wisconsin. After finishing high school, Welles traveled to Ireland, where he bluffed his way into a leading role with the Gate Theatre in Dublin, claiming to be a stage star from New York. Eventually returning to the United States, he joined Katharine Cornell's road company, and later collaborated with John Houseman, with whom he formed the Mercury Theater in 1937. The Mercury group branched into radio broadcasting, and on Halloween night of 1938 they performed their legendary dramatization of the English novelist H. G. Wells's "War of the Worlds." They broadcast such a realistic description of the invasion of Grovers Mills, New Jersey, by aliens that thousands of listeners panicked, and many evacuated their homes.

Welles is most noted for his film *Citizen Kane* (1941), which he directed and cowrote. The innovative structure of the film, involving flashbacks from the points of view of different characters, as well as Welles's creative use of deep-focus cinematography, low-angle compositions, and the sound track, has influenced the work of many filmmakers. The newspaper magnate William Randolph Hearst, on whose life the film is loosely based, tried to block its release and later launched a systematic critical attack on the film in his newspapers.

Welles directed and wrote several other films after *Citizen Kane*, including *The Magnificent Ambersons* (1942), *The Stranger* (1946), and *The Lady from Shanghai* (1948), although problems with production, editing, and distribution led to the economic failure of these films, as well as his estrangement from Hollywood executives, and finally to his self-imposed exile in Europe. During the almost thirty years of his exile, Welles acted under several other directors to raise money for his own productions: his most popular performances include his role as Rochester in the movie adaptation of English novelist Charlotte Brontë's *Jane Eyre* (1943), and as Harry Lime in Carol Reed's *The Third Man* (1949).

He returned to the United States briefly in 1958, to direct *Touch of Evil* for Universal Studios. He received the American Film Institute's Life Achievement Award in 1975, acquiring the status of the film industry's admired prodigal son.

Wells, H[erbert] G[eorge] (1866–1946)

English novelist, journalist, and historian. The author of over 150 books, Wells was an influential critic of nineteenth-century thought. Wells was born in Kent, the son of a shopkeeper and a maid. After several ill-fated jobs as a young man, he managed to earn a scholarship to study biology at the Normal School of Science in London (now part of London University), where the famous English biologist Thomas Huxley (1825–1895) was one of his teachers. He graduated in 1890, and the next several years were ones of financial and physical hardship. However, in 1895 his first novel, *The Time Machine*, was an immediate success, and he followed it with a string of science fiction works that established him as the successor to French writer Jules Verne (1828–1905). Wells drew upon his lower-middle-class background and scientific training to author such books as *The Island of Doctor Moreau* (1896), *The Invisible Man* (1897), *The War of the Worlds* (1898), *The First Men in the Moon* (1901), and *The Food of the Gods* (1904).

Wells had become a Fabian socialist in 1903, and his turn to political writing and pamphleteering was evident in his realist novels like *Tono-Bungay* (1909), his presentations of his biological and social theory in *A Modern Utopia* (1905), and in the series of works that combined these genres, including *Marriage* (1911). After the war, Wells began to believe in the necessity of human adaptation to a changing environment in a "race between education and catastrophe," ideas that he articulated in *The Outline of History* (1920) and *The Work, Wealth and Happiness of Mankind* (1932). His *Experiment in Autobiography* was pub-

lished in 1934, the year after he had met with both U.S. president Franklin D. Roosevelt and Russian Communist leader Joseph Stalin in an attempt to influence their international outlook. He grew increasingly pessimistic about the future in the late 1930s, and the outbreak of World War II led him to believe that nature had rejected humanity, a view he expresses in *Mind at the End of its Tether* (1945).

Wells, Ida B[arnett] (1862–1931)

African-American civil rights activist, lecturer, and journalist. Born into a slave family in Holly Springs, Mississippi, Wells was orphaned at the age of fourteen when five members of her family died of yellow fever. She assumed responsibility for her remaining four siblings, taking a nearby teaching job while she attended Rust College, an industrial school for blacks in Holly Springs. Wells moved the family to Memphis, Tennessee, for both economic and family reasons in 1884, taking various teaching jobs in and around Memphis.

Wells became the editor and part owner of a local black newspaper, the Memphis *Free Speech and Headlight*, later shortened to the Memphis *Free Speech*. She wrote extensively on race relations, and in 1891 was fired from her teaching job after writing an article under the pen name "Iola" criticizing the school system's decidedly inequitable distribution and allocation of resources for black students. Subsequent editorials speaking out against lynching, and particularly against the lynching of three Memphis blacks, brought threats to her life and the destruction of the building in which the *Free Speech* was housed.

No longer safe in the South, Wells moved to the North and continued to speak out against racial injustice, especially lynching, writing editorials for *New York Age*. She lectured extensively in the United States and abroad against racism. In 1895 Wells published the pamphlet *A Red Record: Tabulated Statistics and Alleged Causes of Lynchings in the United States, 1892–1893–1894.* In 1898 Wells, along with other blacks, met with U.S. president William McKinley to protest lynching.

After marrying Ferdinand L. Barnett in 1895, then assistant state's attorney for Cook County and editor of the first black newspaper in Chicago, the Chicago *Conservator,* Wells became actively involved in local civic activities, organizing a black women's club. This club served as a model for similar women's clubs throughout the country, and led to the eventual incorporation of these clubs into the Federation of Colored Women's Clubs. Wells also traveled throughout Illinois and Arkansas, investigating and reporting on race riots both during and after World War I.

In 1898 Wells was elected secretary to the National Afro-American Council, forerunner of the National Association for the Advancement of Colored People (NAACP); she was active on the council until African-American educator Booker T. Washington, whose policies she felt were accommodationist, assumed control. In this capacity, she spoke out against mob violence and U.S. imperialism, calling on President McKinley to take a more active role in civil rights issues.

Wells was one of the members of the Committee of Forty that organized the NAACP in 1910. However, after 1912, she devoted most of her time to the women's suffrage movement, forming the Alpha Suffrage Club of Chicago, said to be the first Negro female suffrage organization. Although Wells played an increasingly active role in the national women's suffrage movement, she also continued to devote considerable energy to her earlier desegregationist efforts. Active in local Chicago affairs, Wells, along with social activist Jane Addams (1860–1935), successfully deterred the establishment of separate city schools for blacks. She died in Chicago in 1931.

Welty, Eudora [Alice] (1909–)

American writer of short stories and novels. Born in Jackson, Mississippi, Welty attended the Mississippi State College for Women, and then earned a B.A. from the University of Wisconsin in 1929. During the Depression, she traveled through Mississippi as a publicity agent for the Works Progress Administration. A chief outgrowth of this work was a series of her photographs, which were published as a collection in 1971.

Welty's short story "Death of a Traveling Salesman" (1936), and her first collection of stories, *A Curtain of Green* (1941), drew wide acclaim. For one of these early stories, "The Worn Path," Welty won the first of six O. Henry awards. Her second collection of stories, *The Wide Net* (1943), and her first full-length novel, *Delta Wedding* (1946), also contributed to her identification as a formidable presence in the American literary realm, her work noted for its precisely observed details and graceful prose.

Welty has lived virtually her whole life in Jackson, developing an ear for Southern dialect. Her primary motif, the duality of human nature, is frequently expressed through the opposition of essential isolation and the human desire for relationships. Another common theme is a strong focus on the role of family and community bonds.

In 1955 Welty won the William Dean Howells Medal of the American Academy for her novel *The Ponder Heart* (1954). Both it and *The Robber Bridegroom* (1942) were produced as Broadway plays. *The Optimist's Daughter,* published in 1972, earned Welty a Pulitzer Prize. In 1984 she published *One Writer's Beginnings,* an autobiographical sketch based on a series of Harvard lectures.

Wen Xin Diao Long

Chinese book of literary theory. Written by Liu Xie (c. 465–532), *Wen xin diao long (Dragon Carving of the Literary Mind)* is one of the most influential theoretical books on literature produced in ancient China. It explores and crystallizes earlier Chinese literary theories, criticizing the contemporary theoretical bias for formal novelty over content quality, and attempting to bring Chinese literary criticism to a higher level. The book is arranged into fifty chapters in two parts and ten volumes. The first part carefully examines the characteristics and historical evolution of various extant literary forms. The second part focuses on principles and methods of literary creation and criticism, calling special attention to the close relationship between literature and social life. The author believed that any changes in literature largely depend on changes in social conditions, and that the rise or decline of a literary trend is linked to changes in political systems. However, the style is infused by Buddhist philosophy, which gives the overall presentation a transcendental overtone.

West, Nathanael (1903–1940)

American novelist. Born Nathan Weinstein to Russian Jewish immigrants in New York, Nathanael West graduated from Brown in 1924 with a philosophy degree. West's first novel, *The Dream Life of Balso Snell*, was written in college and during a stint in Paris but was not published until 1931. Generally considered his weakest novel, it tells the story of a peculiar cast of characters inside the Trojan horse and attacks Christianity and Judaism. By the time it was published, West had fallen into poverty, after his family suffered severe financial losses. He made a living managing hotels in New York.

West's misfortune continued even with the publication of his next novel, *Miss Lonelyhearts* (1933), which related the downfall of an idealistic advice columnist caught up in the depressing lives of his readers and correspondents. Though critically acclaimed, the first edition sold fewer than 800 copies because the printer refused to deliver most of the edition to West's bankrupt publisher. The novel, regarded as a masterpiece, has sold more than 300,000 copies since West's death. West then worked in Hollywood on a poorly realized film adaptation of the novel. West's other novels were *A Cool Million* (1934), a satire of the Horatio Alger myth of American success, and *The Day of the Locust* (1939), which ruthlessly reveals the emptiness of its characters' lives at the margins of Hollywood.

West died in 1940 in a car crash with his wife, Eileen McKenney, a few days before the opening of *My Sister Eileen*, a hit play written by Mrs. West's older sister, Ruth McKenney. After his death, West's work was lifted from the obscurity it suffered during his life; the publication of *Miss Lonelyhearts* in French translation in 1946 triggered a wave of attention, and his novels have since sold well.

Wharton, Edith (1862–1937)

American novelist and short-story writer. Born Edith Newbold Jones to wealthy New York socialites, Wharton's solitary childhood forced her to invent stories for amusement, and her aristocratic environment later provided the subject matter for some of her best-known works.

Married in 1885 to Edward Wharton, a banker, she began writing stories and poems for *Scribner's Magazine* during the 1890s. Wharton published her first collection, *The Greater Inclination*, in 1899, and then her first novel, *The Valley of Decision* (1902), which was set in eighteenth-century Europe. She first achieved popular success, however, with *The House of Mirth* (1905), a satire of the manners of aristocratic New Yorkers. One of her best-known novels is *Ethan Frome* (1911), a tragic story set on an imaginary New England farm in a town modeled after Lenox, Massachusetts, where Wharton had vacationed. After other novels such as *The Reef* (1912), *The Custom of the Country* (1913), and *Summer* (1917), Wharton published the highly popular *The Age of Innocence* (1920), an exploration of the moral hypocrisy of New York's social world. The novel won a Pulitzer Prize.

Of note in Wharton's life was her close friendship with Henry James during the last twelve years of his life. Reading aloud to him and even helping him (without his knowledge) through financial hardship, she was influenced by his depictions of commonplace tragedies as well as by his attention to form. Wharton died in St.-Brice-sous-Forêt, France, at the age of seventy-five.

Wheatley, Phillis (c. 1753–1784)

American poet. When Phillis Wheatley was approximately eight years old, she arrived in Boston on a slave ship from Gambia and was purchased by John Wheatley as a personal servant for his wife. One of the Wheatley children taught Phillis to read the Bible, and in the preface to her *Poems* (1773), her master John testifies that she learned English in sixteen months before moving on to Latin. She later translated the Niobe episode from Ovid's *Metamorphoses* into English heroic couplets and made her own creative additions to turn it into an epyllion, or short epic. The nephew of Cotton Mather, Mather Byles, took a special interest in Phillis Wheatley and may have lent her books and tutored her.

While John and Susanna Wheatley attended the more loyalist New South Church, Phillis Wheatley went to the largely patriot Old South Church— where town meetings were held after the Boston Massacre, where John Hancock called for the expulsion of the royal governor, and where the Boston Tea Party was organized. Her controversial political positions may have contributed to the disinterest of Boston publishers in her work. But her famous elegy of 1770, "On the Death of the Rev. Mr. George Whitefield," earned her the financial backing of the countess of Huntingdon in England. Her 1772 volume underwent vast revisions to become the *Poems* published in England, losing their overt American patriotism and softened into broadly sentimental appeals: titles like "On the Arrival of the Ships of War and Landings of the Troops" were changed to "On Recollection."

After *Poems* was published in England, there was much indignation abroad that she was still a slave. She was freed by her masters in 1773, she wrote, "at the desire of my friends in England." She regarded her visit to England in 1773 as the high point of her life, but she was forced to return earlier than planned due to the fatal illness of her mistress. On returning, she had largely fallen out with literary circles. In October 1775 she was invited to visit George Washington in his Cambridge headquarters.

In 1778 she married John Peter, a free black man. Her first two children died in early childhood, and her third died with her, unattended, in the winter of 1784. It was not until a distant relation published Wheatley's *Memoir and Poems* in 1834 that she gained widespread recognition for her life and work.

White Lotus Society, *see* Bai-lian Jiao

Whitman, Walt (1819–1892)

American poet and essayist. Whitman's experiments with poetic form and style were overshadowed in his day by his reputation as a scandalous poet. His vivid sensuality and unabashed themes and images of human physicality have since been celebrated for their portrayal of the newness of nineteenth-century America as a nation and a people.

Whitman was born in West Hills, Long Island, the son of a carpenter and builder. In 1823 the family moved to

Brooklyn, where Whitman attended school. Seven years later, he left school, apprenticed to a printer. In 1838, while still working as a printer and an itinerant schoolteacher, he began to write. He edited his own paper, *The Long Islander*, then became editor of the *Aurora* in 1842 and the Brooklyn *Eagle* in 1846. Both papers fired him, however, because he was too politically vociferous. During this period he wrote his only novel, *Franklin Evans* (1842).

In 1848 he traveled with his brother Jeff to New Orleans, and many have credited this journey down the Mississippi with awakening in Whitman the awareness of the vastness of the American continent that lay beyond the confines of the Hudson River. Whitman returned to New York in 1850 and worked in various jobs but was also writing poetry. Borrowing a press from friends, Whitman set thirteen of his poems in type and published them under the name *Leaves of Grass* in 1855. His most famous work, *Leaves of Grass* is a collection of poems written in an unconventional loose form that grew with each edition, and pays tribute to democracy through the song of the individual. The work was startling for the time, both for its style, which made use of catalogues, and its homoerotic images. He published a second edition in 1856 containing more poems. From 1857 to 1859 he edited the Brooklyn *Times*, and in 1860 found a publisher in Boston for a third edition of *Leaves of Grass* with 124 new poems, including "Calamus" and "Children of Adam."

During the Civil War, Whitman worked as a nurse in the field and wrote for *The New York Times*. He nursed both Union and Rebel troops in a hospital in Washington, D.C. In 1865 *Leaves of Grass* enjoyed another printing, this time augmented by his war poems, including "Drum Taps." The 1867 edition included two requiems for U.S. president Abraham Lincoln, "When Lilacs Last in the Dooryard Bloom'd" and "O Captain! My Captain!"

Throughout the rest of his long life, Whitman kept writing poetry, incorporating new poems in new editions of *Leaves of Grass* and supplements published simultaneously. In 1871 he published *Democratic Vistas*, expounding in prose his political ideas of America. He lived the remainder of his life in Camden, New Jersey, and is remembered as one of the greatest American poets.

Wiesel, Elie (1928–)

Romanian-Jewish writer. Born in Romania, Wiesel vigorously studied the Torah and the Talmud in his Hasidic household. In 1944 the Jewish inhabitants of his town were sent to Auschwitz, where his mother and sister were executed. He was later sent to Buchenwald, where his father was killed. After the Second World War, Wiesel moved to Paris to study at the Sorbonne. In Paris he began writing for both French and Israeli newspapers. His first novel, *La Nuit* (*Night*), an account of a young boy's experiences at Auschwitz, was published in 1955. Wiesel's early writings mix nonfiction and myth, creating a mournful, reflective view of the Holocaust. His characters portray Jewish experiences and ways of life. Some of his major works include *Le Mendiant de Jérusalem* (1962; *A Beggar in Jerusalem*), an examination of why men kill; *Célébration hassidique* (1972; *Souls on Fire*), a collection of Hasidic stories; and *Le Testament d'un poète juif assassiné* (1980; *The Testament*). He moved to the United States in 1956 and maintains a permanent residence there.

In 1986 Wiesel received the Nobel Peace Prize for his lifelong efforts to eradicate violence, hatred, and oppression. He was also awarded the Grand Cross of the Order of the Cruzeiro do Sol in 1985, the highest award given by the Brazilian government to a foreigner. As a survivor of the Nazi concentration camps and a devout Orthodox Jew who lost most of his family in the Holocaust, Wiesel has written movingly about the horror of the Holocaust, urging that it be remembered as a constant warning to the world.

Wilder, Billy (1906–)

American film director and screenwriter. A provocative Hollywood screenwriter and director, Wilder is noted for flouting taboos in sexual comedies like *Some Like It Hot* and *The Seven Year Itch* (1959), and satires like *A Foreign Affair* (1950) and *Sunset Boulevard* (1951). He also directed the film noir classic *Double Indemnity* (1944).

Born in Austria, Wilder began his writing career as a sportswriter for a Viennese newspaper, later working as a crime reporter in Berlin. He eventually worked as a scriptwriter on several German films, but fled Germany in 1933, settling in the United States where he eventually became a citizen. In 1938 Wilder began a fruitful collaboration with Charles Brackett, producing Academy Award winners and box-office hits with him until 1950. This association also allowed him to begin directing films starting in 1942.

Wilder's background as a writer is evident in his films; he relies heavily on narration and dialogue, and images often seem incidental to the films. By his own admission, he began directing to protect his scripts, and cinematography was secondary. Nevertheless, Wilder created many memorable images, winning an Oscar in direction for his groundbreaking portrayal of an alcoholic in *The Lost Weekend* (1945).

Wilson, [Thomas] Woodrow (1856–1924)

Twenty-eighth U.S. president. The son of a Presbyterian minister, Wilson was born in Staunton, Virginia, but spent much of his early life in Georgia and South Carolina. He graduated from the College of New Jersey (now Princeton University) in 1879. After a term at the University of Virginia Law School cut short by illness and a brief attempt at a law career in Atlanta, he studied government and history at Johns Hopkins University, where he received his Ph.D. in 1886 with a dissertation on the committee system in Congress. Wilson taught history and political economy at Bryn Mawr College, and then Wesleyan University, before moving on to Princeton, where in 1902 he was selected as president. As the leader of a prominent university, Wilson built a national reputation by speaking and writing often on political issues, and in 1910 he was elected governor of New Jersey. His rapid success continued, and he became the Democratic nominee for president in 1912, winning the election on the strength of his progressive platform. During his first term, he initiated major changes in U.S. politics, including the Underwood Act (1913), which reduced tariffs and created the federal income tax; the Federal Reserve Act (1913), which became the foundation for national financial control; the Clayton Anti-Trust Act (1914), which strengthened labor unions by giving them the legal right to strike and to boycott; and a bill establishing the Federal Trade Commission (FTC).

Wilson sought to keep the United States out of World War I, issuing a formal declaration of neutrality in 1914. He also attempted unsuccessfully to initiate secret peace negotiations. After a German submarine sank the British liner *Lusitania* in 1915, killing more than 1,000 persons, including many Americans, Wilson delivered an ultimatum that eventually led to Germany's agreement to end its submarine campaign against neutrals, and to his reelection in 1916. When Germany announced a renewal of unrestricted naval warfare in 1917, Wilson received overwhelming support from Congress for a declaration of war. In 1918 Wilson made his Fourteen Points address to the nation, which he felt would ensure a lasting peace, and which included the establishment of a League of Nations. The Versailles Treaty, incorporating his Fourteen

Points, was signed on June 28, 1919, and Wilson embarked on a tour of the United States to drum up support. He suffered a stroke, and while he was ill the Republican opposition, led by Senator Henry Cabot Lodge, amended the peace resolution to the point where Wilson himself urged its defeat. Thus, the United States failed to join the League of Nations, but Wilson was awarded the Nobel Peace Prize in 1919 for his efforts. Wilson suffered a series of strokes toward the end of his presidential term, and after leaving office in 1921 he stayed out of the political limelight until his death.

Wise, Isaac Mayer (1819–1900)

Founder of Reform Judaism. The son of a Bohemian teacher who died while he was a young boy, Wise was raised and educated in Prague and Vienna before becoming a rabbi. At the time, the Hapsburg empire held few opportunities for its Jewish citizens, and Wise made the decision to emigrate. In 1847 he arrived in New York and, apparently finding the freedom of his new country to his liking, immediately began instituting reforms in his Albany congregation. While in charge of the Congregation Beth El, he replaced sex-segregated seating with family pews, the first such change in the United States. After moving to Ohio in hopes of finding a more fertile ground for his ideas, he called a rabbinical conference in Cleveland in 1855, an event rendered ineffectual by Orthodox German rabbis who mistrusted Wise, whom they considered too radical. His ultimate goal was the establishment of a union of Jewish congregations in America, to be reinforced by uniform ritual and rabbinical training colleges. After a lifetime spent in pursuit of this goal, Wise had the satisfaction of watching Reform Judaism become a viable and vibrant branch of the Jewish faith.

Wise's most significant contribution as the founder of Reform Judaism was not as a leader or thinker but as an ed-

ucator. In 1875 he was appointed president of Hebrew Union College, the first rabbinical college established by the newly created Union of American Hebrew Congregations. The rest of his life was devoted to building the college and training his pupils, of whom more than sixty were ordained. Although in 1889 Wise became president of the Central Conference of American Rabbis (the fulfillment of his long-held dream), he was not the driving force in the Reform movement, nor did he have much influence over the content of its *Union Prayer Book*. He did, however, allow others the opportunity to develop a blueprint for Reform Judaism.

Witkiewicz, Stanisław [Ignacy] (1885–1939)

Polish dramatist, philosopher, and novelist. A multitalented writer most noted for his innovative dramas, Witkiewicz, who wrote under the pen name Witkacy, was born in Russian-occupied Warsaw, the son of painter and writer Stanisław Witkiewicz. Aside from a year spent at the Kraków Academy of Fine Arts, the chief influences on Witkiewicz's intellectual formation remained almost entirely noninstitutional, a fact that helps to explain the resolutely nonconformist character of both his life and his art.

Under the influence of the Polish formalists, Witkiewicz began to publish essays elaborating his own theory of aesthetics. He was fascinated by the new artistic potentials made available by the avant-garde concept of pure form, and was obsessed with the idea of applying this concept to drama. His major works on aesthetics include *Szkice estetyczne* (1922; *Aesthetic Sketches*) and *Teatr: Wstep doteorii czysteb formy w teatrze* (1923; *Theater: Introduction to the Theory of Pure Form in Theater*).

Dramas such as *Kurka wodna* (performed in 1922; published in 1962; *The Water Hen*) tend to reflect not only his attachment to the doctrine of pure form but also his penchant for catastrophism—his anguished sense of an impending disaster that would result in the annihilation of the human individual. The general tenor of Witkiewicz's dramas is perhaps best summed up by the title of his 1925 publication *Nie me złego, co by na jeszcze gorsze hie wyszło* (1925; *There Is Nothing Bad Which Could Not Turn into Something Worse*).

During his lifetime Witkiewicz published two antiutopian novels, *Pożegnanie jesieni* (1927; *Farewell to Autumn*) and *Nienasycenie* (1930; *Insatiability*), in both of which individuality is depicted as succumbing to totalitarian forces that demand complete conformity. Although both novels are set in a fictional country sometime in the future, they both contain allusions to the interwar period in Poland and reflect Witkiewicz's ominous view of the political developments he saw going on around him. Witkiewicz committed suicide in the woods near the Polish village of Jeziory in 1939.

Witkiewicz did not achieve widespread recognition in his lifetime. However, with the onset of the political thaw of 1956, interest in his work revived, especially among those Polish writers who were seeking a departure from the strict dictates of Socialist Realism. In 1962 his emergence into respectability was solidified with the publication, in Poland, of a two-volume edition of his plays.

Wittgenstein, Ludwig [Joseph Johan]
(1889–1951)
Austrian philosopher. Wittgenstein was born to a well-to-do Austrian family of Jewish descent who had converted to Catholicism. Until the age of fourteen he was educated at home. However, because he showed early mechanical aptitude, his parents sent him to study engineering at Berlin and later Manchester. Discovering the work of English mathematician and philosopher Bertrand Russell (1872–1970), he developed an interest in the philosophical foundations of mathematics. He abandoned engineering, enrolling at Trinity College, Cambridge, for the purpose of studying with Russell. Explaining that he did not feel comfortable among people he felt contempt for, Wittgenstein left Cambridge to live the life of a hermit in Norway. When war broke out, Wittgenstein left Norway and enlisted in the Austrian army. He was captured by the Italians and spent some time as a prisoner of war. During his service and imprisonment, he worked on the project he had started at Cambridge, *Tractatus logico-philosophicus*, the only book he published during his lifetime.

Wittgenstein returned to his native Austria in 1920 and became a village schoolteacher. He resigned his teaching position six years later and went into architecture, building a family mansion for his sister in Vienna. After the completion of this project, his interest in philosophy was rejuvenated and he returned to Cambridge, becoming a research fellow in 1930. Once again interrupted by war, Wittgenstein took on the job of Army hospital nurse. In 1944 he returned to his teaching at Cambridge, but this proved no longer rewarding and Wittgenstein gave up teaching for the final time in 1947. He passed the next few years shut up in a country cabin outside of Dublin, traveling to America, and completing *Philosophical Investigations*, considered by many to be his masterwork.

Central to his philosophical works was the notion that most of philosophy's problems could be better understood by attending to the workings of language outside of philosophy. In *Tractus Logico-philosophicus*, Wittgenstein explained the intimate relationship of language, thought, and the world. He saw thought and language as working alongside each other to construct a reproduction of reality. To understand an utterance, he argued, it was important to comprehend how its components relate to one another and to the real world. *Philosophical Investigations* significantly altered this formula by explaining language as a response to, as well as a depiction of, reality.

Wolf, Christa (1929–)

German writer. An internationally acclaimed writer from the former East Germany, Wolf has been praised for her frank portrayals of East-West relations, her meditations on the heritage of Nazism, and her feminist revisions of history and literary tradition.

Born Christa Ihlenfeld in what is now Poland, Wolf moved with her family to Mecklenburg during the invasion by the Soviet Red Army in 1945. After a stay in a tuberculosis sanatorium, she joined the Socialist Unity Party, and studied at the Universities of Leipzig and Jena, receiving her degree in German literature from the latter in 1953. In 1951 she married the writer Gerhard Wolf; they had two daughters. Over the next years she worked variously in a factory, for the East German Writers' Union, for several publishers, and as the editor of the journal *Neue Deutsche Literatur* ("New German Literature").

Her first novel, *Moskauer Novelle* (1961; *Moscow Novella*), is an allegory of political relations between East Germany and the Soviet Union as well as a love story about an East Berliner and a Muscovite. Published during the building of the Berlin Wall, her second, *Der geteilte Himmel* (1963; *The Divided Heaven*), gained her a wide readership and the Heinrich Mann Prize from the East German government. *Nachdenken über Christa T.* (1968; *The Quest for Christa T.*) received a more mixed reception in both the East and the West, which it has been suggested is the result of her implied criticism of the German Democratic Republic (GDR). Largely autobiographical, *Kindheitsmuster* (1976;

A Model Childhood) is an account of growing up under Nazism. In 1979 she published *Kein Ort, nirgends* (*No Place on Earth*), about the imaginary meeting between the German Romantic writers Heinrich von Kleist and Karoline von Günderode, and received the Georg Büchner Prize the following year. Wolf developed a series of lectures into her best-known work, *Kassandra: Vier Vorlesungen; Eine Erzählung* (1983; *Cassandra: A Novel and Four Essays*), her feminist recasting of Greek myth. The accompanying essays discuss governmental repression and the nuclear threat. These themes are also treated in *Accident: A Day's News* (1987), a fictional re-creation of the accident at the nuclear power plant at Chernobyl in the Soviet Union in 1986. Wolf fell from grace as a celebrated national writer after the collapse of East Germany and the subsequent revelation that she may have been an informant for the East German government.

Wollstonecraft, Mary Godwin (1759–1797)

English author, education reformist, and feminist. Wollstonecraft is best known for her treatise *A Vindication of the Rights of Woman* (1792), which was considered quite scandalous at the time of its publication as much for its reformist ideas about women as for the highly controversial life led by the author herself.

Wollstonecraft was the second of seven children born to a gentleman farmer of declining wealth. Deeply resentful of the favoritism bestowed on the oldest son and the drunken violent outbursts of her father, Wollstonecraft learned early the importance of self-reliance and education for women. Together with her close friend Fanny Blood and her sister Eliza, Wollstonecraft opened a school in 1784 that was greatly influenced by a circle of English intellectuals known as the Rational Dissenters. But following the death of Blood, Wollstonecraft was beset by financial troubles and closed the school. To support herself, Wollstonecraft turned to writing, and in 1787 published her first book, *Thoughts on the Education of Daughters*. The novel *Mary* followed in 1788, and *A Vindication of the Rights of Men* (1790), a heated response to English statesman Edmund Burke's *Reflections on the Revolution in France* (1790). Soon after publishing *A Vindication of the Rights of Woman*, Wollstonecraft traveled to Paris in 1792 to witness the progress of the French Revolution; there she fell in love with an American speculator, Gilbert Imlay. Though Wollstonecraft gave birth to their daughter, Fanny, the relationship with Imlay was short-lived and tumultuous, and in 1795 Wollstonecraft attempted suicide twice.

Determined to renew her life in England and care for her daughter, Wollstonecraft began a new novel, *Maria; or, The Wrongs of Women* (1799), as well as a new relationship—with the radical writer William Godwin. Wollstonecraft again became pregnant and consented to marry Godwin for the sake of the child. The birth of her second daughter, Mary Godwin, proved to be extremely difficult, however, and eleven days later Wollstonecraft died. To assuage his grief, Godwin began work on his *Memoirs* of Wollstonecraft within two weeks of her death, freely disclosing her love affair with Imlay and further scandalizing the English public.

The unconventional life and work of Mary Wollstonecraft was resurrected by feminists in the nineteenth and twentieth centuries. Wollstonecraft's daughter Mary Godwin later married the poet Percy Bysshe Shelley and wrote the horror novel *Frankenstein*.

Wolof

Senegambian people. The predominantly Muslim Wolof people reside in Senegambia, at the western extreme of the African continent, where they are one of the largest ethnolinguistic groups in the area, numbering some three-quarters of a million people. They speak a language of the West-Atlantic branch of the Niger-Congo family. Wolof is spoken as a trade language outside of Senegambia. Though in contemporary Senegambia many Wolof are engaged in urban trade in the cities of Dakar and Banjul, traditionally the Wolof have been agriculturalists, raising groundnuts (peanuts) as their main crop, and most Wolof today remain farmers. Their social organization is markedly hierarchical, with distinct caste and class divisions.

The Wolof empire, founded in the early thirteenth century, dominated the interior of the Senegambia. Ruled by what was called a *burba*, the empire established several satellite states, the most significant being Cayor. With the arrival of the Portuguese in the mid fifteenth century, the Wolof empire engaged in a political and economic alliance with them. In the sixteenth century, the Cayor state achieved independence from the Wolof empire, and cut off its access to the sea, thereby bringing about its economic, and political, decline.

Woolf, [Adeline] Virginia (1882–1941)

English writer. Woolf is widely considered to be one of the most influential twentieth-century prose writers and an important figure in the development of Western feminist movements.

Born Adeline Virginia Stephen in London, Woolf was the daughter of the writer Sir Leslie Stephen. She was educated at home, primarily through self-directed reading in her father's voluminous library, and met many of the literary and political powers of the day there. At the age of thirteen, she suffered a breakdown when her mother died. After her father's death in 1904, she and her siblings moved to another part of London. But after the death of her brother Thoby in 1906 and her sister Vanessa's marriage, Virginia and her brother Adrian moved to the house in Fitzroy Square that would become famous as the meeting place of the Bloomsbury group. Virginia married Leonard Woolf in 1912 and began publishing reviews in several journals. Her first novel, *The Voyage Out*, appeared in 1915. In that year, the Woolfs moved to Hogarth House, bought a hand press, taught themselves typesetting, and published their first book, one short story by each of them, in 1917 under their own imprint, the Hogarth Press. Specializing in avant-garde writers, the press was a success, publishing writers like Katherine Mansfield, E. M. Forster, and H. G. Wells, the first English edition of Austrian psychoanalyst Sigmund Freud's writings, American poet T. S. Eliot's *The Waste Land*, and Woolf's own experimental novels.

Woolf's more critically successful novels include *Jacob's Room* (1922), *Mrs. Dalloway* (1925), and *To the Lighthouse* (1927). In their de-emphasis of material reality in favor of interior reality, Woolf's novels became increasingly innovative in their use of stream of consciousness and their manipulation of time; they are praised for their symbolic richness and psychological complexity. In 1928 her greatest commercial success appeared: *Orlando: A Biography*, dedicated to Woolf's close friend and supposed lover, Vita Sackville-West. A comic view of English literary history and sexual politics, the novel records the adventures of the sex-changing Orlando from the sixteenth until the twentieth century.

In addition to novels, Woolf wrote many short stories and a children's book. Her critical essays are considered to be among the best ever written and are collected in many volumes, including the earliest, *Modern Fiction* (1919), and the two series of *The Common Reader* (1925 and 1932). Her writings on women's issues, the lectures collected as *A Room of*

One's Own (1929) and *Three Guineas* (1938), has had a profound impact on the feminist movement.

Troubled by mental illness for much of her life and often contemplating suicide, Woolf in her last years recorded in her diaries that she feared both her own insanity and the spread of Nazism. In early 1941 she filled her pockets with stones and drowned herself in the River Ouse near her home in Sussex. Her nephew Quentin Bell published a best-selling biography of her in 1972 that revived widespread interest in her work.

Wright, Frank Lloyd (1867–1959)

American architect. Born in Richland Center, Wisconsin, Wright moved with his family to Iowa, Rhode Island, and Massachusetts, before entering the University of Wisconsin at Madison. Remaining at the university for only a few terms, Wright studied engineering, eventually becoming an architect. Leaving Madison in 1887, he moved to Chicago and began working as an architect for the firm of Adler and Sullivan. Six years later, Wright, who had been designing houses on the side, established his own practice in 1893.

Many of Wright's earliest major projects, including the Larkin Building in Buffalo, New York (built 1904; demolished 1950), and the Imperial Hotel in Tokyo, Japan (built 1915–22; dismantled 1967), no longer stand, but his houses, which more clearly demonstrate his philosophy of architecture, remain, mostly in the American Midwest. The plans are cruciform, with the rooms radiating out from the central core of the fireplace and utility areas. The interior spaces flow into each other and are low-ceilinged, and the exterior thrust is horizontal with wide, overhanging roofs. Wright built about fifty homes in this so-called prairie style between the years 1900 and 1910, perhaps the most notable being the Robie House in Chicago (built 1910). In addition, he experimented with steel and concrete, and was one of the first architects to make use of concrete blocks in his designs.

Though known in Europe, Wright was virtually ignored in America in the 1920s, in part because of what was considered to be his unconventional and "scandalous" behavior, namely his estrangement from his wife and his public affair with Mamah Cheney, the wife of one of his former clients. Wright and Cheney lived together at his house, Taliesin, near Green Springs, Wisconsin. However, in 1914, while Wright was on business in Japan, Cheney and her children were murdered at Taliesin and the inside of the house was burned to the ground. Not long after, Wright met and lived with sculptress Miriam Noel, although still married to his first wife; this did not enhance his popularity. Granted a divorce in 1922, Wright began an affair with Olgivanna Hinzenberg. They married in 1928.

In the early thirties, when commissions were scarce due to the Depression, Wright began to theorize about city planning, publishing his first book on urban issues, *The Disappearing City* (1932), as well as *An Autobiography* (1932). In 1936 Wright designed the Kaufmann House, commonly known as Fallingwater, in Bear Run, Pennsylvania. Part prairie style with its dominant horizontals, part international style with its cantilevered terraces and ferro-concrete construction, and built over a waterfall, it is his most famous residence.

Wright continued to experiment with circular structures, the culmination of this exploration being the Guggenheim Museum (1959) in New York City, his last major building. The gallery is a continuous spiral ramp around a skylit atrium that grows wider as it rises.

Remembered as a founder of "organic architecture," Wright died in Phoenix, Arizona, in 1959.

Wright, Richard (1908–1960)

American writer. The first black American writer to sustain himself through his writings alone, Richard Wright was one of the most prominent black voices of the 1940s. With the publication of *Native Son* in 1940, he vaulted to the forefront of black American letters.

An admirer of Hemingway and Zola, schooled in the social realism of the Communist Party (which he joined in 1933) and of the New Deal–era Federal Writers' Project, Wright fused naturalistic description with fierce, sometimes didactic, moralism, dramatizing the plight of the black poor and the slum dweller in the heyday of the Great Migration of rural Southern blacks to the North. *Native Son*, a Book-of-the-Month Club selection, portrayed the career of Bigger Thomas, a young black man who accidentally murders a white girl. *12 Million Black Voices* (1941), a nonfiction essay with photographs by Edward Rosskam, entailed a similar commitment to gritty realism, an exploration of the depth of black nihilism as the necessary precondition for the projection of black hope. *Black Boy* (1945) was an autobiographical account of growing up black in the American South and Midwest.

In 1944 Wright's uneasy relationship with the Communist Party ended with the publication of an essay, "I Tried to Be a Communist," in *The Atlantic Monthly*. In 1947 he left the States for France, where he would remain until his death. In the 1950s he published novels with increasingly overt existential themes, including *The Outsider* (1953) and *Savage Holiday* (1954), the latter about a white businessman who murders his wife. He also published a series of political travelogues, including *Black Power: A Record of Reactions in a Land of Pathos* (1954), an account of black life and strivings on the verge of independence in the Gold Coast (soon to be Ghana), and *Pagan Spain*, an interpretation of Spanish life that suggested that primitivism was as much a European fact as an African one. *White Man, Listen!* collected four European lectures on the contradictions of the black freedom struggle worldwide.

In his last years, he wrote another novel, *The Long Dream* (1958), set in Mississippi. While recovering from amoebic dysentery, he became interested in Japanese *haiku* and wrote several hundred. He died of a heart attack at the age of fifty-two. In the following decades, more of his works appeared, including another story collection, *Eight Men* (1961), and the second, unpublished half of the manuscript for *Black Boy*, finally released in 1977 as *American Hunger*. The definitive, restored editions of *Native Son* and *Black Boy* were published in the 1990s by New American Library.

Wu Zetian (623–704)

Chinese ruler. At fourteen, Wu became a concubine to Emperor Taizong. Upon his death in 649, she was forced to become a nun, but she returned to the palace a year later and soon became the favorite consort of Emperor Gaozong. To secure and promote her position, she influenced the emperor to get rid of the empress, who had remained childless, and other rivals. When Gaozong fell ill for a time, he let her attend to his routine duties. She performed so well that when the emperor recovered he decided to share power with her. She occupied the throne when the emperor was busy elsewhere, attending imperial audiences and giving orders in his name (*shenzhi*). People began to call Wu and the emperor the "Two Holy Ones." When Gaozong also died in 683, she first acted as the regent and then, in 689, appointed herself *huangdi* (the Holy Ruler) and changed the dynastic name from Tang to Zhou. During her reign (682–704), the country, although not becoming more prosperous, remained economically and militarily strong.

X

Xhosa

South African ethnic group. The Xhosa are composed of related groups of Bantu-speaking people who have occupied the territory now known as the South African regions of Ciskei and Transkei for many centuries. These regions were declared independent in 1976 and 1981, respectively. Due to South Africa's migratory labor system, more Xhosa reside outside the homelands than within.

An expanding Xhosa population and encroaching white settlers entered into conflict beginning in the eighteenth century; the struggle lasted nearly a century. The Xhosa were eventually defeated and left with extremely limited political power. The loss, according to legend, was precipitated by the strange prophecy of a Xhosa girl. She claimed that the Europeans would be swept out of Africa if the Xhosa destroyed their own reserves of food and cattle. The mass slaughter of the cattle, in 1856–57, instead resulted in hunger, poverty, and death for the Xhosa themselves. Many historians doubt the accuracy of the story; some suggest that the destruction was encouraged and exploited by white settlers who wanted Xhosa land.

The Xhosa are traditionally governed by a tribal chief and divided into patrilineal clans. The chief rules with the assistance of a council comprised of the heads of various clans. The political system is highly centralized, but there are a series of checks on the chief's power. Religion is deeply rooted in ancestor worship, and medicine, practiced alongside witchcraft, is closely linked to magic. Most Xhosa are farmers, but cattle remain central to the Xhosa economy. Commonly used as *lobola* (bridewealth), cattle serve as a sort of male dowry that a groom offers the family of the bride.

During the 1960s many Xhosa left Transkei and began working as laborers, mostly in Johannesburg. This migration to the cities further eroded the traditional culture of the Xhosa. Numbering 5 million in the late twentieth century, only 40 percent of the Xhosa population remain in Transkei.

Xian Xinghai (1905–1945)

Chinese composer. Born in Fanyu, Guangdong province (Canton), he studied music at a number of schools, including Lingnan University in Guangdong, Beijing Professional School of Arts, Shanghai National Music College, and finally at Paris Music College, under Vincent d'Indy and Paul Dukas. When he returned to China in 1935, Japan had occupied the northeastern part of the country (then known as Manchuria). He immediately took part in patriotic activities, using music as a weapon to protest against the Japanese occupation. He worked in film studios for a time before going to the Communist headquarters at Yan'an in 1938, where he served as director of music in the Lu Xun Academy. (Much of his fame as a composer and a national hero derive from his expressly political activity in the 1930s.) In 1940 he traveled to Moscow for advanced study but died five years later. His last ten years were his most productive. He wrote more than five hundred songs, a number of symphonies, rhapsodies, and solos. His best-known work is the *Yellow River Cantata* in eight parts, for soloists and chorus; collectively adapted as the *Yellow River Concerto*, it has been scored for piano and orchestra by members of the Central Philharmonic Society of Beijing, and has been given pride of place in their repertoire. Most of Xian's work attempts to combine Western and Chinese elements.

Xi You Ji

Chinese epic. Xi you ji, variously translated as *Journey to the West*, *Pilgrimage to the West*, or *The Monkey King*, is regarded as one of the masterpieces of classical Chinese fiction. It was written by Wu Chengen (1505–1580), who drew on the mass of folk stories and plays about Tripitaka's pilgrimage to India.

Tripitaka (602–664), better known as Xuanzang, was a Buddhist monk of the Tang dynasty (618–906). He set off alone across the deserts of Central Asia in 629, aiming to procure a particular set of Buddhist scriptures: a manuscript of the great treatise on metaphysics called *Lands of the Masters of Yoga*. His quest took sixteen years; when he finally returned to the Tang capital of Chang'an in 645, the scriptures in hand, he was greeted by the emperor. A year after his return, one of his disciples used his travel notes to compile a general work on the countries he had visited. The result was the book *Da tang xi yu ji* (*Treatise of the Western Regions in the Days of the Great Tang*). By the Southern Song dynasty (1127–1279), a whole series of fantastic legends about this journey were already widespread. *Xi you ji* derives directly from the wonder tales of the earlier times.

The monk in *Xi you ji* was modeled on Xuanzang, but the three disciples who accompanied him on this journey and the adventures along the way are imaginary. The novel is loved by readers young and old, mostly due to the vivid characterization of Sun Wukong, or Monkey, one of the three disciples. Monkey is possessed of astounding supernatural powers, and always manages to survive the terrible trials that befall them on their westward journey. His weapon is a golden cudgel that can change its size at Monkey's will, hidden in his ear when not in use. He himself can change into seventy-two different forms, and by turning one somersault he can be 18,000 li (9,000 kilometers) away. Episodes from the novel have been brought to the Chinese stage in various traditional operas and have enjoyed enormous popularity. The novel is more than a fairy tale; it has been read as a biting satire of Chinese society and as an allegory of the search for salvation.

Xu Beihong (1895–1953)

Modern Chinese painter. A professor of fine arts whose careful support nurtured many of China's contemporary artists, Xu is known worldwide for his paintings of horses and figures. At thirteen, rudimentarily trained by his father, he encountered Western painting in the form of pictures on cigarette packs imported from abroad; he admired their foreign style, and would recopy the images for himself. His curiosity about Western styles piqued, he chose to become a student of French painting and literature. In 1919 he received a scholarship that enabled him to study in Paris. He returned to China in 1927, and immediately set about incorporating Western methods into Chinese painting. Xu brought Western light shades and oil-painting methods to the traditional Chinese practice of ink painting. At the time of his death, Xu was president of the Central Institute of Fine Arts in Beijing, and chairman of the National Union of Chinese Artists. In theory, he argued that Chinese painting should adopt whatever is good and useful in ancient or Western methods, that delicacy and subtlety are as important as grandeur.

Xu Beihong was respected in China for his progressive views and active struggle against the Japanese invaders and the Guomindang. His revolutionary politics and unique assimilation of Western techniques in traditional Chinese painting make him a fascinating example of China's ambivalent relationship with the West.

Y

Yeats, William Butler (1865–1939)

Irish poet and dramatist. Considered to be one of the greatest poets of the twentieth century, Yeats was the son of the artist John Butler Yeats. He was born in Dublin and claimed kinship with many prominent Anglo-Irish Protestant families. Yeats moved to London soon after his birth but spent much of his youth with his grandparents in County Sligo, where he studied painting before turning to poetry. His early work is highly stylized and melancholy, in the blushing post-Romantic fashion of the time, but at its best, as in *The Wanderings of Oisin* (1889), it suggests what would become the poet's lifelong interest in themes from Irish legend and history. Long interested in magic and the occult, Yeats joined the Order of the Golden Dawn and the Theosophical Society; when he met Madame Blavatsky in London in 1887, he became a devoted disciple of her brand of spiritualism. A number of discrete works on mysticism, written in the 1890s, were later collected as *Per Amica Silentia Lunae* (1917).

A collection of essays, *The Celtic Twilight* (1893), displayed his passion for Irish nationalism, and he was elected the first president of the Irish Literary Society. Returning to Ireland in 1896, he became a central figure in the burgeoning Irish Renaissance, contributing plays and poetry that were intended to speak directly to Irish concerns. At the age of twenty-three, he had met Maud Gonne, a political activist, whom he loved for most of his life and who appears often in his work, namely as the heroine in the play *The Countess Cathleen* (1892). In 1899 Yeats helped found the group that would later be called the Abbey Theatre, the chief symbol of the Irish literary revival. He remained a director of the group to the end of his life, and for many years managed the theater, solicited plays, and wrote many plays for the Abbey, including *The Land of Heart's Desire* (1894), *Cathleen Ni Houlihan* (1902), and *Deirdre* (1907). The poetry of the mature Yeats, the body of work for which he is most respected, was heavily influenced by American poet Ezra Pound, whom he met in 1912. Beginning with *Responsibilities* (1914), the verse is tighter in construction, the symbolism more personal and less extravagant, and the tone more severe. In 1917 he published *The Wild Swans at Coole* and married Georgia Hyde Lees, a spiritualist who recorded "automatic writing" while in trances. He composed *A Vision* (1925) automatically. The hybrid text is part magic system, part theory of history, and part esoteric psychology. He later claimed that a vision was a work in progress, a working through of ideas and symbols he would later make use of in his poetry. Taking the liberty of rewriting many of his earlier works, Yeats prepared his *Collected Poems* in 1933.

Yeats died in the south of France, having completed the *Last Poems* (1939). In keeping with his wishes, his body was returned to Ireland after World War II and buried near Sligo.

Yehoshua, A[braham] B. (1936–)

Israeli novelist and short-story writer. Considered to be the greatest living Israeli writer, A. B. Yehoshua began publishing short stories upon completing military service in 1957. His work is always precisely located in time and space, set against the backdrop of specific moments in Jewish and Israeli history. The powerful story "Mookdam B'Kayib" (1971; "Early in the Summer of 1970") exemplifies this aspect of his writing. His work also captures the unique experiences of the Sephardim as a minority culture in Israel.

Yehoshua's most ambitious work is *Mar Mani* (1990; *Mr. Mani*), the story of five generations of the Mani family, stretching from the revolutions of 1848 to the invasion of Lebanon in 1982. The novel is a record of five conversations, at different places and times, in which the history of the Manis, a Sephardic family, is set against the movement of Jewish life and history, from Lebanon to the Holocaust, the founding of the state of Israel, and the emergence of modern (and predominantly Ashkenazic) political Zionism. The book provides a glimpse of historic alternatives, roads and modes of feeling not undertaken, as with the cosmopolitan Jerusalem at the turn of the century. Both the complicated functioning of time in the novel and the mastery of dialect recall Yehoshua's acknowledged master American novelist William Faulkner.

His other books include the novels *Me Achev* (1977; *The Lover*), *Gerushim Meuharim* (1982; *A Late Divorce*), and *Hamisha Onot* (1987; *Five Seasons*), as well as many acclaimed short stories. A collection of his stories in English translation was published in 1988 under the title *Continuing Silence of a Poet*. A respected teacher and literary figure at Haifa University, Yehoshua was an outspoken critic of Israel's harsh policies toward Palestinians in the occupied territories.

Yellow River, *see* Huang He

Yiddish

Traditional language of Eastern and Central European Jewry written in the Hebrew alphabet. The linguistic roots of Yiddish lay in the Middle East (the Hebrew and Aramaic of the original Semitic settlers in Europe) and in Central Europe (the German dialects of their non-Jewish neighbors). As Jews moved farther east during the Middle Ages, Yiddish was influenced by the Slavic languages as well. Written Yiddish, which flourished after the invention of the printing press, derived from the Western European dialect. After the Haskalah, the Jewish social and cultural movement of the eighteenth and nineteenth centuries, however, German came to replace Yiddish throughout Central Europe, and the oral language all but disappeared there.

Even as Western European Jews were rejecting Yiddish as vulgar and primitive, the language experienced a renaissance in the East. A literary revival began in the early nineteenth century, a movement that assumed international proportions as large numbers of Eastern European Jews began emigrating. Yiddish drama, centered in New York City, also enjoyed a brief efflorescence around the turn of the century.

Today Yiddish is in danger of extinction. Millions of Yiddish-speaking Jews were among those murdered by the Nazis. In the United States and elsewhere, Jewish-Americans have abandoned the Yiddish of their parents and grandparents. In the Soviet Union, and again in post-Soviet Russia, official anti-Semitism imposed restrictions on the use of the Yiddish language, while Israel's single-minded devotion to Hebrew has, until recently, made even the Jewish national homeland inhospitable terrain. Only in the ultra-Orthodox Hasidic communities and in the artificial environment of the university has Yiddish found a community of speakers. Still, international programs like the youth-for-Yiddish movement offer the hope that the language may yet be saved.

Yi dynasty

Korean dynasty (1392–1910). The Yi or Chosŏn dynasty (Chosŏn was the Korean word for the country until the Japanese occupation of 1910) was founded by General Yi Sŏng-gye in a military coup in 1392 C.E. Yi assumed the throne under the name of Yi T'aejo and moved the capital city from Songak (Kaesong) to Hanyang, the site of the present-day capital, Seoul.

The first century of Yi rule was relatively peaceful. The most important cultural achievement of the fifteenth century, and one of the most important in all of Yi history, was the invention of the *hangul* phonetic alphabet by King Sejong in the mid-1400s. This innovation made literacy possible for whole classes of people. While Chinese remained the privileged language of scholarship, and while entry into the civil service (one of the few avenues of potential class mobility available at the time) still depended on knowledge of Chinese characters and literature rather than Korean, a native Korean written literature became possible for the first time in history. The *sijo*, a popular form of narrative poetry from the late Koryo period that had gone out of favor in the early years of Chosŏn, was revived and recorded in *hangul*. The evolution in prestige of the *sijo*, from unvalued ditty-like oral performances in the early Yi dynasty to an eminently respectable written art in the seventeenth and eighteenth centuries, reflects the growing assertion of Korean political and cultural autonomy from neighboring China and Japan during the same period.

The independence and integrity sought by the Yi dynasty was never fully achieved. Although Korea was under virtually constant siege by Japan and China during the sixteenth and seventeenth centuries, the Hideyoshi Invasion of 1592 (also known as the Imjin War, after the year of its initiation) is of singular importance to contemporary Koreans who may cite it as a rare instance of a Korean victory over Japan. Forced at the time into a tributary arrangement with China, Korea refused the Japanese permission to pass through the peninsula en route to invade Chinese territories. The Japanese responded by attacking Korea, whose military resources had dwindled as her cultural capital had increased. After a series of quick defeats, Korea rallied under the leadership of Admiral Yi Sunsin, who commanded a fleet of "turtle boats," the world's first armored vessels to be used in combat. Although the Hideyoshi Invasion itself ended in profound defeat for the Koreans (the Japanese and the Ming government of China negotiated a treaty in which Korea was the Chinese concession to Japan), Admiral Yi remained a heroic figure to generations of Koreans. The Hideyoshi Invasion presaged the Japanese annexation of 1910, which brought down the Yi dynasty and ended Korea's dynastic history.

Yi Jing

Canonical Chinese text. Also called *The Book of Changes*, the Yi Jing (*I Ching*) is a central text of Confucianism and one of the earliest works of Chinese literature. Western interest in the *Yi Jing* exploded in the 1960s and 1970s, when countercultural enthusiasms for Eastern religion and the occult made *The Book of Changes* an underground best-seller.

Chinese scholars have recently made the point that the original Confucian text was different, and much smaller, than commonly thought in the West. The archaic *Yi Jing*, which may have been written as early as the Zhou period (1027–256 B.C.E.), consisted of sixty-four hexagrams, each composed of six divided and undivided lines, which, properly interpreted, contain esoteric meanings about the future and right conduct. In telling fortunes with the *Yi Jing*, one "creates" a hexagram by casting lots. The hexagram is built up from the bottom, line by line, by successive lots. Undivided lines have the number nine, divided lines have the number six. The contrast between divided and undivided lines represents the conflict between *yin* and *yang*, female and male cosmic principles. (Everything exists in a state of flux, changing with the pulsing energies of *yin* and *yang*.)

Later, around the Warring States period (and probably during the Han dynasty), the base text was considerably expanded to include textual exegesis and commentaries by Confucianists. These commentaries, as opposed to the original *Jing*, are known as *Zhuan*. The text familiar to us now has been further modified since those times. The Confucian character of the text is questionable; though the *Yi Jing* has been counted among the Five Classics of Confucian doctrine since the second century B.C.E., many believe that Con-

fucian priests engaged in power struggles with their Taoist contemporaries
claimed the *Yi Jing* for their own canon,
though there was no good evidence to
suggest that Confucius himself had authored any commentaries on the original text.

Yoga

Indian philosophy. One of the few Sanskrit terms completely naturalized in
English, the original means literally a
"tie" or "harness" and is cognate with
the Latin *iugum*, the German *Joch*, and
the English *yoke*. The founder of system-
ized Yoga, Patanjali, who was active in
northern India about 300 B.C.E., defines
Yoga as "the curbing of the mind's out-
ward-going tendencies." The object of
Yoga is to achieve complete control over
the mind by learning to withdraw from
all aspects of external reality, all the trappings of the material world—including
one's own body—and to center the mind
on its own divine essence. This process
of turning away from the world and finding the divine within affords perfect wisdom and an emancipation from rebirth
that is regarded as the supreme achievement by all three indigenous religions
of India: Hinduism, Buddhism, and
Jainism.

A person who practices Yoga is a yogi,
or if it is a woman, a yogini. Highest
honor and total reverence is paid to people who are thought to be perfect yogis;
this explains the phenomenon of guru
worship in India (and, more recently, in
the West). The lifestyle of genuine yogis
is austere, and the preparatory disciplines include the control of sexual and
other passions, absolute truth speaking,
nonviolence, and a number of other
moral exercises. It also involves complete body control through the mastery
of yogic postures (*asanas*). The instruction, discipline, and practice of these is
called the "yoga of control" (Hatha-
Yoga), the one branch of Yoga well
known and received in the West, albeit

mostly with nonreligious connotations.

The philosophy of Yoga is one of the
six classical systems of Hindu thought,
and is based on a radical dualism between the quiescent, inactive, observing
spirit (*purusha*) and active, ever-moving,
ever-changing nature (*prakriti*). Nothing
happens in nature without the presence
of the inactive spirit. Such realization is
total liberation.

Yom Kippur

Jewish holiday. The holiest and most
solemn of Jewish holidays, Yom Kippur
(or Day of Atonement) is a day of fasting
and confession, a time to reflect upon
one's sins and to beg God for forgiveness. Observed on Tshiri 10 according to
the Hebrew calendar, it is linked to the
Days of Judgment celebrated just prior
to it.

In temple times, Yom Kippur was the
one day of the year on which the high
priests were permitted to enter the Holy
of Holies (also called Devir), the most
sacred part of the ancient temple of Jerusalem, which contained the Ark of the
Covenant—the tablets God gave to
Moses on Mt. Sinai. Once inside the sacred area, the priest would make a sacrifice on behalf of the priests and the
people of Israel.

In modern times, the day is spent in
prayer at the synagogue, where the ceremony includes rituals, prayers, and music collected from thousands of years of
Jewish history. It is a day of mortification
and abstention from food, drink, sexual
intercourse, anointing with oil, and for
an Orthodox Jew, the wearing of leather
shoes.

Yoruba

African people. The Yoruba, who number around 30 million, occupy the
southwestern corner of Nigeria along
the border with Benin; a subgrouping of
the Yoruba, the Anago people, actually
live in the Benin Republic. Yoruba live
as far east and north as the Niger River,

though there is evidence that ancestral Yoruba parent cultures once flourished beyond the Niger.

Portuguese explorers came into contact with the cities and kingdoms of the Yoruba in the fifteenth century, but Ife and Benin, among other cities, may have been standing at their present sites four to five hundred years before the arrival of Europeans. Archaeological evidence indicates that a culture sophisticated both artistically and technologically existed north of the Niger river in the first millennium B.C.E. The terracotta art found at Nok, about three hundred miles north of Ife, bears a distinct stylistic resemblance to later Yoruba art. Those works were made around 300 B.C.E., at a time when the Nok people were already working with iron.

Ife is traditionally considered to be the earliest of the Yoruba cities; the kingdoms of Benin and Oyo appeared significantly later. Oyo and Benin were strategically important locations as overland trade became central to the West African economy. The city of Benin was accessible by river from the sea, which lent it added importance as a link in the trade routes. While Ife never developed into a great commercial center or expanded beyond the geographical and political limits of a city-state, it was and is regarded as a sacred city, the origin of the fundamentals of Yoruba religious thought.

Yoruba oral culture centers on the *oriki*, or praise-song, a social and ceremonial art performed to ritualize life experiences. *Oriki* celebrate everything from the quotidian (praise-songs for the hunt, for daily farming) to the festive (weddings, the naming of newborns). Many *oriki* are performed in conjunction with the *dun-dun*, the Yoruba "talking drum," a percussive instrument that, well played, can imitate the complicated tones and rhythms of Yoruba speech. Written culture has been possible since

1853, when Samuel Ajayi Crowther produced the first *Grammar and Vocabulary of Yoruba*.

Manifestations of Yoruba culture can be found throughout the Americas, due to the vicissitudes of the slave trade. Wars between the kingdom of Dahomey and certain of the Yoruba kingdoms, as well as wars among the Yoruba themselves, produced untold thousands of captives and prisoners of war; these captives were often marched to seaports and sold to European slave traders. Yoruba slaves were sent to British, French, Spanish, and Portuguese colonies in the New World. In many of these places, Yoruba traditions were integrated into local cultural and religious practices. In Brazil, Cuba, Haiti, and Trinidad, syncretic religions strongly indebted to Yoruba religious rites, beliefs, music and mythologies survive, even prosper, today. Afro-Haitian religious activities give Yoruba rites and beliefs an honored place, and their pantheon includes numerous deities of Yoruba origin.

Yue Fei (1101–1141 C.E.)

Chinese army general of the Song dynasty (960–1279 C.E.). Born in Tangyin, Henan, Yue joined the Song army as a teenager. According to legend, before he left home, with a needle pen his mother wrote on his back: *"Jinzhong Baoguo,"* meaning "Be purely and forever loyal to your country."

During the war of resistance beginning in 1126 against the Jin (Jurchen) invaders, Yue Fei distinguished himself as a brave and talented soldier, soon becoming an esteemed general. In 1141, when the Song court was divided as to whether to continue actively resisting the Jin, Yue Fei was an ardent proponent of carrying on the war. He criticized, and thereby offended, those at court who were ready to surrender—particularly the chancellor Qin Hui, who later plotted against him and falsely accused him of treason. Although he was a patriot, and victorious on the fields of battle, Yue was killed in a plot perpetrated by corrupt court officials. The Chinese have hailed Yue Fei as a national hero for centuries. His legend is the subject of paintings, plays, stories, and radio broadcasts.

Yu the Great

Mythical Chinese king. Considered to be one of the great sages of Chinese antiquity by no less a figure than Confucius (551–479 B.C.E.), Yu possessed legendary bravery and wisdom. According to myth, Yu and his creator, Gun, were beings of superhuman power and strength and were able to take the form of various animals. Most noted for his strategies against the great floods of the Huang He (Yellow River), Yu successfully moved people and restored floodlands. It is believed that Yu, learning from Gun, built dams and channels through which the flooded water drained to the sea. He is said to be the founder of the first Chinese dynasty, the Hsia (c. 2200 B.C.E.–c. 1766 B.C.E.).

Z

Zangwill, Israel (1864–1926)

Jewish novelist, humorist, and essayist. The son of poor Russian immigrants, Zangwill was raised in Bristol and London, where he attended and later taught at the Jews' Free School. He is best known for the revealing portraits of life in the Jewish East End of London contained in what are commonly referred to as his ghetto novels. Zangwill believed that Judaism was a powerful force, best embodied in the close-knit ghetto community; his novels were some of the first to capture the vagaries of Jewish life in England, and his literary language contained new accents derived from Yiddish.

Zangwill was possessed of a somewhat contradictory but forceful passion for Zionism, the modern Jewish nationalist movement spearheaded by Theodor Herzl. In 1895, after meeting with Herzl, Zangwill organized the English branch of the movement. He split with the Zionists ten years later, after they rejected Great Britain's offer (1903) to establish a Jewish state in Uganda. Greatly disappointed by early attempts to settle in Palestine, as would-be settlers encountered increasingly hostile reactions from native Arabs, Zangwill founded the Jewish Territorial Organization (JTO), a post-Zionist organization that favored the creation of Jewish settlements in locations other than Palestine. Zangwill served as president of the group between the years 1905 and 1925.

His enthusiasm for unconventional arrangements led him to adopt a romantic image of America. In *The Melting Pot* (1909), Zangwill coined the unhappy phrase that has haunted discussions of American culture ever since. Intrigued by the rough-and-tumble dynamism of the New World, he called for the full integration of American Jews into the mainstream of society. He envisioned a future religion that would fuse the best aspects of Western civilization: Hellenism, Judaism, and Christianity.

During his lifetime, Zangwill was well known for his eloquence and wit: some of his aphorisms are still current. Toward the end of his life, he published *The Voice of Jerusalem* (1920), a brilliant collection of essays on "the Jewish question." Politically liberal, he was an ardent supporter of women's rights and an outspoken pacifist during the First World War.

Zapata, Emiliano (1879–1919)

Mexican revolutionary. Born in Anenecuilco, Morelos, Zapata was a tenant farmer who felt the harsh injustices of being an American Indian. Zapata was forced to serve in the army in 1908 as punishment for his attempt to recover land confiscated by a rancher. After his release, he joined in the revolutionary activities organized by the future president of Mexico Francisco Madero (1911–13); however, he later abandoned Madero's cause. By 1911 Zapata had outlined his own agenda, the Plan of Ayala, which demanded the return of land to the Indians.

Gaining the support of the peasant class, Zapata took control of most of Morelos; he joined forces with the Mexican revolutionary Pancho Villa to fight against Venustiano Carranza. Between the years 1914 and 1915 Zapata's forces took control of Mexico City three times, but he eventually returned to Morelos, where he was assassinated by an emissary of Carranza in 1919. As a hero of the Mexican revolution, Zapata was honored at various moments by the governing party, the PRI (Partido Revolucionario Institutional — or Institutional Revolutionary Party). Zapata has been eulogized, also, by rebel movements throughout the Americas, particularly those associated with indigenous peoples; on New Year's Day, 1994, a group of rebels in the Chiapas province declared war on the government, claiming his mantle by calling themselves Zapatistas.

Zeami Motokiyo (1363–1443)

Japanese actor, critic, and playwright. Zeami will forever be synonymous with the classical Japanese Noh theater, which he established. Aided by his father, Kan'ami (1333–1384), with whom he acted as a child, Zeami transformed peasant-based skits and dances into a refined art known as Noh, which had substantial court patronage. Zeami's fortune was made when a performance of the play *Okina* (*Old Man*) in Kyoto in 1374 was noticed by the young shogun Ashikaga Yoshimitsu (1358–1408). Yoshimitsu became Zeami's patron and subsidized his education in the Chinese and Japanese literary classics, upon which Zeami drew for the bulk of his plays. When his father died, Zeami, twenty-one years old, became the head of the troupe.

Zeami's crowning moment occurred in 1408, when he performed before the emperor Gokomatsu. Soon after, Zeami's patron died and the popularity of Noh began to decline. Zeami retired from the company in 1422 and passed on the leadership to his eldest son, Motomasha. When Motomasha died in 1432, an antagonistic shogun attempted to place his own favorite at the head of the troupe. Zeami refused to teach the usurper the secrets of his acting craft, and the shogun banished him to the island of Sado. He remained there until a few years before his death, when he returned to Kyoto.

Zeami is thought to have written about ninety of the 250 surviving Noh plays, although only twenty-one can be definitely ascribed to him. Zeami's ultimate goal as an actor involved something he called *hana*, or flower, which referred to an actor's ability to make an audience feel as though it were seeing an old, familiar role performed for the first time.

Zhang Daqian (1899–1983)

Chinese visual artist. Zhang is considered by many to be the greatest Chinese painter of the last five hundred years. A native of Neijiang, Sichuan province, Zhang first learned to draw under his mother's guidance. As he grew older, his second elder brother taught him how to render human figures and horses, and his elder sister how to paint still-lifes, flowers, and birds. At seventeen, he went to Japan to study industrial dyeing and weaving in Kyoto. Two years later, he returned to Shanghai and became a Buddhist monk. Unsuited to the ascetic monastic life, he left the monastery, got married, and resumed his painting and calligraphy. From the two distinguished masters, Cheng Nongran and Li Mei'an, he learned to draw lotuses in ink monochrome and landscapes with calligraphy techniques. Meanwhile, he traveled widely, from Mount Huang to Kuanming Lake, and from Suzhou through Luoyang to Beijing. Many of his early paintings were produced during those trips.

After the outbreak of the Sino-Japanese War in 1937, Zhang managed to return to his native Sichuan province. Later, he visited the stone caves in Dunhuang, making an extensive study of the frescoes. Determined to revive the technique of human figure painting, which he believed to have been a lost art in China, he devoted his whole energy to copying the murals. Working for two full years he made more than one hundred copies of the murals at Dunhuang, renderings so painstakingly accurate that they were virtually indistinguishable from the originals.

In the winter of 1948, as the likelihood of Communist victory became certain, Zhang decided to travel abroad, first to India, then to Europe, North America, and South America. He lectured and exhibited wherever he went. In 1956 Zhang had a chance encounter with Spanish painter Pablo Picasso, then living in Paris. Picasso, who had been producing ink paintings by imitating Chinese artist Qi Baishi, showed a strong interest in Zhang's work, and the two became friends.

Zhang Daqian incorporated diverse styles from old masters into his own, and was adept not only at ink painting, Chinese painting, scroll painting, and oil painting but also at scripts and calligraphy. In his early years, he painted with extraordinary delicacy and subtlety; later his style became bold and unrestrained; during his last years he applied a splash-ink technique to color painting, producing pictures very similar to Western abstract paintings.

Zhuangzi

Chinese philosophical text. Zhuang Zhou (c. 369–c. 286 B.C.E.), also called Master Zhuang, was the author of the *Zhuangzi*, or *The Book of Master Zhuang*, one of the three texts of classical Taoism. Of the thirty-three chapters of the present edition of the book, Zhuang Zhou is thought to have written only the first seven. The text is an exercise in epistemology and logic, a grand attempt to undermine rationalist ideas about how we know what we know, and how we can prove what we know. Using his mastery of logic to demonstrate the futility of reason, Zhuang espouses intuition as the only means through which the Tao, or "Way," can be apprehended. While Zhuang rejects logic as a means of getting at the truth, he uses poetry, myth, and figurative language to convey his own sense of it. Emphasis on the necessity of rejecting traditional norms and standards, as well as conventional notions of the self, to achieve knowledge of the Tao, set Zhuang squarely against the prevailing Confucian orthodoxy. Only after the dissolution of the Han dynasty, which had promoted Confucianism, did the *Zhuangzi* achieve popular acceptance as well as a permanent place in the canon of Taoism.

Zhu Geliang (181–234)

Chinese historical and fictional figure. Also known as Kong Ming, Zhu appears in the Chinese classic *San-guo yan-yi* (*A Tale of the Three Kingdoms*). The most knowledgeable and wisest of the strategists in the wars of the Three Kingdoms, Zhu was a recluse who had lived in the forest since childhood, reading, observing, and taking notes on society and nature. When wars broke out among Cao Cao, Liu Bei, and Gong Shuenzhan, the respective heads of the Three Kingdoms, only Liu Bei recognized the immeasurable value of Zhu. He went to Zhu three times asking him to serve as his adviser in matters of war. During his third and final visit, Zhu Geliang was impressed by Liu's sincerity, honesty, perseverance, and strong will, and agreed to work for him. With his great intelligence, Zhu helped Liu's army get out of many dangerous situations and win several important battles. He remains a great Chinese cultural hero, a celebrated historical and fictional character.

Zhu Xi (1130–1200)

Chinese philosopher, poet, and prose writer. A government official in the Song dynasty (960–1279), Zhu advocated the doctrine that art has no aesthetic or intrinsic value. The value of art, he believed, was extrinsic or social, and good writing acculturated its readers to the social and ethical norms of Confucian teaching. Zhu Confucianism was both conservative and authoritarian, and he insisted that it was the responsibility of an individual to conform and fulfill his duty within the hierarchy of Chinese society, with the emperor at the head. He emphasized *li*, or the "unifying principle," which he claimed was exemplified in Confucian classics. The Chinese examination system represented the philosophies of Zhu. From 1315 until 1904, when the last examination was administered, Zhu's interpretation of Confucian classics and his brand of Confucianism were considered to be the basis on which the papers of the examination candidates were assessed.

Zhu Xi was a prolific writer. His most famous works are the *Variorum Edition of Chuci* and the *Companion to the Four Classics*, texts that were so influential they became classics themselves.

ziggurat

Babylonian religious center. With the Egyptian pyramids, the Babylonian ziggurats were among the greatest monumental structures of the ancient world. Recognizable by their distinctive architecture, which featured terraces formed of successively tapered layers, the ziggurats were believed to be spiritual staircases connecting human beings with their city's patron deity. Most ziggurats had two temples, one at the top of the structure for the god in his heavenly abode, another at the base to receive him when he came to earth. The lower temple also served as the main temple of the city. The best-known ziggurat is probably the Tower of Babel in the Old Testament.

Zimbabwe, Great

The most famous of a large group of stone-walled enclosures on the Zimbabwean plateau. (In the language of the Shona people of the eastern half of Zimbabwe, the word *zimbabwe* means "stone building"). The highest point of the site is a fortress that has a commanding view of the surrounding grasslands and can only be approached through a series of narrow defiles. Although there is some controversy about its origin, most scholars think that the structure was erected by Shona people over the course of about four hundred years, beginning in the early eleventh century. Great Zimbabwe served as a royal residence until the early fifteenth century, when the king moved elsewhere, perhaps because the adjacent soil was exhausted and thus could no longer support a royal court. It remained an important religious shrine until the nineteenth century. The modern African Zimbabwe nation took its name from this major cultural monument.

Zionism

Jewish nationalist movement. From the outset of the Diaspora at the beginning of the first millennium C.E., some Jews harbored a claim to the land called Eretz Israel in ancient Palestine. As the modern nation-state lurched into existence in the eighteenth and nineteenth centuries, many persecuted minority groups began to conceive of themselves as nations-in-waiting, and started to agitate for land and self-government. In the last decades of the nineteenth century, galvanized by the pogroms in Russia and the resultant waves of West European and American immigration, a political movement for an independent Jewish state became a reality. In 1897 Theodor Herzl organized the first Zionist Congress in Basel, Switzerland, where a platform was adopted that codified the movement's ambitions: "Zionism strives to create for the Jewish people a home in Palestine secured by public law." An offer from the British in 1903 to create a Jewish homeland in Uganda, Africa, was rejected. In 1904 Herzl died, exhausted by years of frustrating international negotiations, and Zionists remained a minority group within the Jewish community. Only in Russia, where Jews suffered severely the political repercussions of the failed 1905 Revolution, did Zionism attract a significant number of adherents. Thousands of young Russian Jews defied international prohibitions, establishing as many as forty-three agricultural settlements in Palestine by the eve of the First World War.

Two Russian Zionists living in England, Chaim Weizmann and Nahum Sokolow, persuaded Britain to support the Zionist cause. On November 2, 1917, the Balfour Declaration formalized that commitment; the League of Nations mandate over Palestine given to Britain in 1922 seemed to assure its ultimate success. As the Jewish population in Palestine inflated throughout the 1920s and 1930s, however, so did the fears of the native Arab majority. The British found their role as mediators between Jews and Arabs increasingly difficult.

In the aftermath of the Second World War and German leader Adolf Hitler's genocidal campaign against European Jewry, Zionism ceased to be a fringe movement. The newly created United Nations voted in 1947 to partition Palestine into Jewish and Arab sectors. The state of Israel was declared on May 14, 1948. The first of many Arab-Israeli wars began soon thereafter.

zodiac

A system of twelve signs that forms the basis of astrological science. Derived from the ancient Greek phrases *zōdiakos kyklos* (circle of animals) and *ta zōdia* (little animals), the word "zodiac" refers to an imaginary trajectory of the sun and planets, divided equally into twelve sections. The names of the twelve signs— Aries (Ram), Taurus (Bull), Gemini (Twins), Cancer (Crab), Leo (Lion), Virgo (Virgin), Libra (Balance), Scorpio (Scorpion), Sagittarius (Archer), Capricorn (Goat), Aquarius (Waterbearer), Pisces (Fish)—are ancient in origin, dating from the early Babylonians and possibly even the Sumerians. The concept of the zodiac, however, appears only later, c. 400 B.C.E., and was developed to provide a frame of reference for planetary movement.

Though the concept of the zodiac spread to a host of different cultures, including Egypt and India, it was not until the Hellenistic period of ancient Greece that the zodiac acquired its prophetic or divinatory function. For the ancient Greeks and their Roman imitators, and even for Christians into the Middle Ages, there was no qualitative difference between astrology and astronomy. After the Copernican revolution of the sixteenth century, the astrological conception of the universe was shattered, replaced by the science of astronomy. Though no longer respected as a natural science, astrology remains a popular interest for many.

Zohar

The Zohar, or Sefer ha-zohar, is a part of the Jewish Kabbalah, the collection of mystical writings designed to interpret the symbolic significance of the words, letters, and numbers that make up the text of the Hebrew Bible. It was probably composed over several decades in thirteenth-century Spain by Moses de León, who claimed to have discovered the text; he named the second-century Jewish scholar Rabbi Simeon bar Yohai as the text's original author.

Sefer ha-zohar is Hebrew for "book of splendor." The Zohar is primarily a mystical commentary on and elaboration of the Pentateuch, or Torah, the first five books of the Bible, thought to have been written by Moses. Following the expulsion of the Jews from Spain in 1492, it was disseminated throughout the Jewish world; the first printed edition appeared in 1588. It is still studied, along with the rest of the Kabbalah, by mystics and occultists as well as by Hasidic Jews.

Zola, Émile (1840–1902)

French novelist and critic. Zola produced numerous works of criticism as well as fiction, and his relentless attention to the material conditions of urban life made him a tremendously popular chronicler of late-nineteenth-century France and the exemplar of French naturalism.

Although born in Paris, Zola lived from 1843 to 1858 in Aix-en-Provence, in southern France. He befriended French painter Paul Cézanne, a fellow schoolmate, and the two roamed the French countryside, settling in Paris in 1858. While in Paris, Zola entered the Lycée Saint-Louis, but flunked out and took a job as a shipping clerk. After publishing his first book, *Contes à Ninon* (1864; *Tales for Ninon*), Zola was encouraged to quit clerking and attempt a living through writing.

His works appeared frequently in newspapers and magazines, and Zola began writing novels. Creating a series of novels, Zola traced with scrupulous detail the story of one family during the Second Empire. The family name was Rougon-Macquart, and the series comprised some twenty novels, beginning with *La Fortune des Rougon* (1871; *The Fortune of Rougon*). Unfortunately, the first few books were not hugely successful. However, with the publication of *L'Assommoir* (1877; *The Dive*), Zola achieved immediate fame. The success of *L'Assommoir* was quickly followed by the equally popular *Nana* (1880), *Germinal* (1885), and *La Débâcle* (1892; *The Debacle*).

Zola gained worldwide attention in 1898 when he published a letter entitled "J'Accuse" ("I Accuse") in the newspaper *Aurore*, offering support for French captain Alfred Dreyfus, who had been arrested and charged with treason in 1894 by the French government. In his letter, Zola accused the French army of being anti-Semitic, and of covering up the truth in the case, an accusation for which Zola was almost imprisoned. Forced to flee to England after being sentenced for libel, Zola eventually returned to Paris in 1899. In September 1902 he was accidentally asphyxiated by fumes from a defective flue in his house. His death occasioned an immense public funeral, attended by Dreyfus (who would be cleared of all charges in 1906), with a graveside oration by the novelist Anatole France.

Zulu

South African ethnic group. Zulu is a name given to Bantu-speaking people who live in specially designated areas in the Natal and Transvaal provinces of South Africa, an area historically referred to as Zululand. The Zulu were originally part of the larger group, the Nguni, with whom they share a common language (also called Zulu) and a highly stratified social structure. The Nguni have lived near the Tugela River since the fifteenth century.

Early in the nineteenth century, during the reign of the Zulu king Shaka, the Zulu empire was at the height of its power and prestige. Under the rule of Shaka, many of the Nguni tribes were consolidated and many nearby regions were conquered with a well-disciplined army and advanced military tactics. Shaka was assassinated by a group of associates led by his half-brother Dingaan, who in turn was deposed in 1840 by another brother, Mpande, with the help of the Boers (Afrikaner farming settlers). Mpande's thirty-year rule saw the deterioration of the Zulu armed forces, as Zululand ceded territory to the Boers and the British.

Mpande's son, Cetshwayo, became king in 1870, promising to restore might and glory to the Zulu. The British, fearful of the Zulu military power, undertook a successful war against the Zulu in 1879, forcing Cetshwayo to surrender in July. Zululand became a British colony in 1887 and was annexed to Natal in 1897 after the Zulu were forced into designated areas and much of their land was confiscated. Uprisings in 1888 and 1906 were squashed by the British.

Zuñi war gods

American Indian statues. Each year, two small wooden statues with sharp features are made by the Zuñi tribes of New Mexico to represent the war gods of the tribe, symbolizing the strength, aggression, and heroism that protect and guide the Zuñi. The statues are placed in cavernous shrines and other secret places, where they are left to decay into dust. Newly carved idols replace old ones that remain in the shrines until they are completely decayed. When the Zuñis visit the shrines of their war gods, offerings are left by those who seek the blessings of the gods. Only members of the Zuñi's Bow Priesthood are allowed to touch the enshrined statues.

Since the late nineteenth century, dozens of Zuñi war gods have been taken from shrines by white scholars intrigued by Indian artifacts; many of these have found their way into the hands of museum curators and private collectors. In 1978 the Tribal Council of the Zuñis began a quietly successful campaign to retrieve what they call their "inalienable communal property." In 1990 the U.S. Congress approved legislation to restrict future sales of such property and require all federally subsidized museums to return these and similar artifacts to their rightful tribes.

zydeco

Hybrid musical style. Zydeco (also known as zodico) is a style of country-dance music descended from Cajun, Afro-Caribbean, and Afro-American traditions; it is played predominantly in southwest Louisiana and east Texas. The music is based on the blues, while the words are sung in creole dialect. The term "zydeco" is credited to Houston folklorist Mack McCormick; it originated in the name of an old step-tune, "L'Haricots sont pas salés" ("The Snap Beans Aren't Salted"), in which the creolization of "les haricots" sounds phonetically like "zydeco."

In the second half of the eighteenth century, the French planters in Louisiana brought many slaves into the area, while at the same time *gens libres de couleur* (free men of color) were arriving from Haiti. Adopting the music, language, and customs of the Cajun people, the African slaves and Haitian free men blended these with elements of their own culture, particularly creole folk songs. Their descendants, called creoles, black French, or black Cajuns, combined the Cajun music with a rhythmic structure based on Afro-Caribbean music, and the result is the fast, syncopated style of zydeco.

Although zydeco is predominantly a regional style of music, mostly performed at rural clubs, church dances, and barbecue picnics, various musicians have gained national recognition as zydeco performers. The most famous of these is probably Clifton Chenier, who toured the United States in 1990 as "the King of Zydeco." The first zydeco recording to gain national attention was Clarence Garlow's "Bon Ton Roula," which made the national rhythm-and-blues charts in the early 1950s. Zydeco is still a thriving musical tradition in Cajun country.